T0297100

Digital Media Processing

DSP Algorithms Using C

Hazarathaiah Malepati

AMSTERDAM • BOSTON • HEIDELBERG • LONDON
NEW YORK • OXFORD • PARIS • SAN DIEGO
SAN FRANCISCO • SINGAPORE • SYDNEY • TOKYO
Newnes is an imprint of Elsevier

Newnes is an imprint of Elsevier
30 Corporate Drive, Suite 400
Burlington, MA 01803, USA

The Boulevard, Langford Lane
Kidlington, Oxford, OX5 1GB, UK

Library of Congress Cataloging-in-Publication Data

Malepati, Hazarathaiah.
Digital media processing : DSP algorithms using C / by Hazarathaiah Malepati.
p. cm.
Includes bibliographical references and index.
ISBN 978-1-85617-678-1 (alk. paper)
1. Multimedia systems. 2. Embedded computer systems—Programming. 3. Signal processing—Digital techniques.
4. C (Computer program language). I. Title.
QA76.575.M3152 2919
006.7–dc22

2009050460

British Library Cataloguing-in-Publication Data

A catalogue record for this book is available from the British Library.

For information on all Newnes publications
visit our website at *www.elsevierdirect.com*

Printed in the United States
10 11 12 13 14 10 9 8 7 6 5 4 3 2 1

This book is dedicated to my late father Mastanaiah Malepati, whose vision and hard work shaped my career a lot.

Contents

On the Website

Part 5 Embedded Systems

Preface

The title of this book could well have been *Digital Media Processing Algorithms: Efficient Implementation Techniques in C*, as it is not only about digital media processing algorithms, but also contains many implementation techniques for most algorithms. The main purpose of it is to fill the gap between theory and techniques taught at universities and that are required by the software industry in the digital processing of data, signal, speech, audio, images, and video on an embedded processor. The book serves as a bridge to transit from the technical institute to the embedded software development industry. Many powerful algorithms in current cutting-edge technologies are analyzed, and simulation and implementation techniques are presented.

Digital media processing demands efficient programming in order to optimize functionality. Data, signal, image, audio, and video processing—some or all of which are present in all electronic devices today—are complex programming environments. Optimized algorithms (step-by-step directions) are difficult to create, but they can make all the difference when developing a new application. This book discusses the most recent algorithms available to maximize your programming, while simultaneously keeping in mind memory and real-time constraints of the architecture with which you are working. General implementation concepts can be integrated into many architectures that you find yourself working with on a specific project.

My interest in writing a book on digital media processing algorithms derives from reading literature in the field and working on those algorithms. This book cannot replace the literature on the background theory related to the algorithms; in fact, what is written here is largely incomplete without it. Although I do not rigorously discuss the theory and derivation of equations and theorems, a brief introduction and basic mathematics are provided for most of the algorithms presented.

Typically, developers of embedded software modules want to know the basic functionality of an algorithm and simulation techniques, in addition to whether any techniques are available to efficiently implement a particular algorithm. Most developers are proficient with equations and algorithms as a result of university training; however, the efficient implementation of such algorithms requires industry experience. But employers, of course, expect developers to immediately begin work. Often they provide training for writing quality software, but not for writing efficient software. Software engineers learn how to do this in time, such as during the course of working on a few efficiently implemented modules or observing a senior engineer's implementation methods. Many such techniques to efficiently simulate and implement digital media processing algorithms are described in this book.

Today many algorithms are available on the Internet, and the software for a number of them is available in the public domain. But the information available on the web is theory oriented, and we may obtain only pieces of the software here and there and not the complete solution. Sometimes, we can obtain the complete software for a particular algorithm that works well, but it may be inefficient for use in a particular project. Consequently, users have to enhance software efficiency by purchasing it from a third-party source. What's here provides the information needed to develop efficient software for many algorithms from scratch.

The book is aimed at graduate and postgraduate students in various engineering subdisciplines and software industry junior-level employees developing embedded systems software. Only college-level knowledge of mathematics is required to understand the equations and calculations. Knowledge of ANSI C is a prerequisite for this book. Knowledge of microcontroller, microprocessor, or digital signal processing (DSP) architectures will provide an added advantage so that you can understand implementation skills a bit faster.

Unlike other DSP algorithm books that concentrate mainly on basic operations, such as the Fourier transforms and digital filters, this book covers many algorithms commonly used in media processing. For most of them, this book provides full details of flow, implementation complexity, and efficient implementation techniques using ANSI C. In addition, simulation results are provided for selected algorithms.

This book uses the Analog Devices, Inc. (ADI) Blackfin processor (BF5xx series) as the reference embedded processor, and it discusses implementation complexity of all algorithms covered with respect to this amazing general-purpose DSP processor. The *Pcode* notation (meaning pseudocode or program code) is used to flag simulation code.

The availability of test vectors is very important for testing the functionality of any algorithm. Test vectors, look-up tables, and simulation results for most of the standalone algorithms described in this book are available on the companion website at *www.elsevier.direct/companions*. In addition, a final part, Embedded Systems, can be found there along with Appendices A and B, References, and Exercises.

Disclaimer

An algorithm can be implemented on an embedded processor in more than one way. Performance metrics vary according to implementation method. Sometimes there may be a flaw in a particular implementation of a given algorithm, even though we get the best performance with it. It may not be possible to test rigorously for all possible flaws in a given time frame. The program code provided in this book is tested for only a few cases, and it provides selected ways of implementing algorithms and corresponding simulation code. The code may contain bugs. In particular, cryptographic systems are very vulnerable to changes in algorithm flow and implementation as well as software and hardware bugs. Neither the author nor the publisher is responsible for system failures due to the use of any of the techniques or program codes presented in this book. In addition, a few techniques provided may be patented by either ADI or another company; check with the patent office before attempting to incorporate any of the implementation methods discussed when developing your own software.

Acknowledgments

I am very thankful to Analog Devices, Inc. (ADI) and its employees for giving me the opportunity to write this book. ADI is a great place to work and to achieve career goals.

In particular, I am very much indebted to Yosi Stein and Rick Gentile, without whom I may not have succeeded in completing this book. The theme for the book originated while working with Yosi at ADI. My dream of writing it came true with the constant support and encouragement I received from Rick Gentile. I am proud to say Rick and Yosi are the heart and soul of this book.

It is with great pleasure that I thank Boris Liberol for reading every page and providing material on loop-filter and motion compensation for the video coding chapter; Chalil Mohammed for providing sections for the audio coding chapter; and Gabby Yi for providing material on motion estimation. David Katz and Rick Gentile generously gave me permission to take a few sections from their book, *Embedded Media Processing*.

I thank Rick Gentile, Pushparaj Domenic, Gabby Yi, and Bijesh Poyil for reviewing selected sections, and external reviewers Seth Benton and Kenton Williston for reviewing some portions of the material and for giving valuable suggestions for improving the book. I thank Goulin Pan, An Wei, and Boris Learner for spending their precious time with me to clarify a few digital media processing concepts.

I am especially grateful to S.V. Narasimhan, V.U. Reddy, and K.V.S. Hari for their guidance. It is with them that I first began my journey into digital media processing.

I thank N. Sridhara, P. Rama Prabhu, Pushparaj Domenic, Yosi Stein, Joshua Kablotsky, Gordon Sterling, and Rick Gentile for giving me a chance to work with them as part of their team.

I offer my heartfelt thanks to *Analog Dialogue* editor Scott Wayne for forwarding this material to Newnes–Elsevier, and to acquisitions editor Rachel Roumeliotis at Newnes for accepting and preparing the contract for this book. I am very thankful to this book's project manager Marilyn E. Rash, copyeditor Barbara A. Kohl, and proofreader Samantha Molineaux-Graham for enhancing the material here by far from my original writing.

Last, but not least, I thank my family for their support and encouragement during this intense period of brainstorming: my mother Mastanamma for her love and sacrifices and the effort she made in shaping my career; my sister Madhavi, brother-in-law Venkateswarulu, father-in-law Guruvaiah, and mother-in-law Swarajyam have been very supportive and taken care of family responsibilities while I was engaged in this endeavor.

Above all, I would like to thank my wife Sunitha Rani for her love, patience, and constant support throughout this project, and my beautiful daughter Akshara Mahalakshmi, who stayed with her grandparents while I was writing this book. I missed her a lot and hope she will forgive me for not being with her during this time.

CHAPTER 1

Introduction

1.1 Digital Media Processing

Digital media processing as it is currently understood and further developed in this book is described in the following subsections.

1.1.1 Digital Media Defined

In this book, *media* comprises data, text, signal, voice, audio, image, or video information, and *digital media* is the digital representation of analog media information. In our daily lives, we typically use many types of media for various purposes, including the following:

- telephoning (voice)
- listening to music (audio)
- watching TV (audio/video)
- camera use (image/video)
- e-mailing (text/images)
- online shopping (text/data/images)
- money transfer (text/data)
- navigating websites (text/image)
- conferencing (voice/video)
- body scanning with ultrasound and/or magnetic resonance imaging (MRI) (signal/image)
- driving vehicles using GPS (signal/audio/video), and so on

Applications that use media are continually increasing.

1.1.2 Why Digital Media Processing Is Required

In all of the previously mentioned applications, media is sent or received. As a sender or receiver, we typically use the media (talking, listening, watching, mailing, etc.) without experiencing difficulties in perceiving (with our eyes, ears, etc.) or delivering (talking, mailing, texting, etc.) the media. In reality, the media that we send or receive passes through many physical channels and each one adds noise (due to interference, interruptions, switching, lightning, topographic obstacles, etc.) to the original media. In addition, users may want to protect the media (from others), enhance it (improve the original), compress it (for storing/transmitting with less bandwidth), or even work with it (for analysis, detection, extraction, classification, etc.). Digital media processing using appropriate algorithms then is required at both the transmitting and receiving ends to prevent and/or eliminate noise and to achieve application-specific objectives mentioned here.

1.1.3 How Digital Media Is Processed

A software-based digital media processing system is comprised of three entities: an algorithm (that which processes), a software language (to implement the processing), and embedded hardware (to execute the processing). Examples of embedded hardware are digital signal processors (DSPs), field-programmable gate arrays (FPGAs), and application-specific integrated circuits (ASICs). In this book, the Analog Devices, Inc. Blackfin

DOI: 10.1016/B978-1-85617-678-1.00001-6

DSP is the reference embedded processor (see Appendix A on the companion website) for executing algorithms. The algorithms are implemented in the C language. Algorithm examples are discussed in the next section.

1.2 Media-Processing Algorithms

In this book, digital media processing algorithms are divided into four categories: data, signal and image, speech and audio, and video. Each category of algorithms are discussed in great detail in various chapters of this book.

1.2.1 Data Processing

Digital systems handle media signals (e.g., data, voice, audio, image, video, text, graphics, and communication signals) by representing them with 1s and 0s, known as binary digits (bits). There are many advantages to digital representation of signals. For example, providing integrity and authenticity to the signal using data security algorithms becomes possible once the signal is digitized. It is also possible to protect data from random and burst errors using data error correction algorithms. In some cases, it is even possible to compress the digital media data using source-coding techniques to minimize the required data transmission or storage bandwidth.

Part 1 of this book covers the most popular algorithms used for data security, error correction, and compression. For all algorithms, a brief introduction, complete details of algorithm flow, C simulation for core algorithm functions, efficient techniques to implement data processing algorithms on the embedded processor, and algorithm computational cost (in terms of clock cycles and memory) for implementing on the reference embedded processor ADI-BF53x (2005) are provided.

Chapter 2 is focused on the most widely used data security algorithms in practice. The algorithms covered include triple data encryption algorithms (TDEA), advanced encryption standard (AES), keyed-hash message authentication code (HMAC), and elliptic curve digital signature algorithm (ECDSA). In addition, cryptography basics and pseudorandom-number generation methods are briefly discussed.

Chapter 3 discusses various data-error detection and correction algorithms. Error detection based on checksum and cyclic redundancy check (CRC) computation is discussed. Both block codes and convolutional codes for error correction and corresponding decoding methods are discussed in detail. The algorithms covered include CRC32, Hamming (N, K), BCH (N, K), Reed-Solomon (RS) (N, K) error correction codes, RS (N, K) erasures correction codes, trellis coded modulation (TCM), turbo codes, low-density parity check (LDPC) codes, Viterbi decoding, maximum *a posteriori* (MAP) decoding, and sum-product (SP) decoding algorithms. Chapter 4 discusses efficient simulation and implementation techniques for all error correction algorithms discussed in Chapter 3.

Widely used data entropy coding methods are discussed in Chapter 5. Variable length codes and arithmetic coding approaches for entropy coding are discussed. The algorithms covered include the MPEG2 VLD, H.264 UVLC and CAVLC, JPEG2000 MQ-coder, and H.264 CABAC.

1.2.2 Digital Signal and Image Processing

We process raw signals using signal processing algorithms to get the desired signal output. Signal processing algorithms have many applications—telecommunications, medical, aerospace, radar, sonar, and weather forecasting, to name the most common. Part 2 of this book is dedicated to signals and systems, time-frequency transformation algorithms, filtering algorithms, multirate signal-processing techniques, adaptive signal processing algorithms, and digital communication algorithms. The later chapters of Part 2 are devoted to image processing tools and advanced image processing algorithms.

In Chapter 6, background theory of digital signal processing algorithms is discussed. We will cover signal representation, types of signals, sampling theorem, signal time-frequency representation (using Fourier series, Fourier transform, Laplace transform, z-transform, and discrete cosine transform [DCT]), linear time invariant (LTI) systems, and convolution operation.

Signal time-frequency representation and signal filtering are discussed thoroughly in most digital signal processing textbooks, including this one. In Chapter 7, we discuss implementation aspects of the fast Fourier transform (FFT), DCT, finite-impulse response (FIR) filters, and infinite impulse response (IIR) filters.

C simulation is provided for all algorithms. Comparative algorithm costs (in terms of clock cycles and memory) for implementation on the reference embedded processor are discussed.

Chapter 8 discusses adaptive signal processing algorithms (minimum mean square error [MMSE] criterion, least mean square [LMS], recursive least squares [RLS], linear prediction [LP], Levinson-Durbin algorithm and lattice filters), multirate signal processing building blocks (e.g., decimation, interpolation, polyphase filter implementation of decimation and interpolation, and filter banks), and wavelet signal processing (multiresolution analysis and discrete wavelet transform). The C fixed-point implementation of the LMS algorithm is also presented.

Chapter 9 discusses the digital communication environment (channel capacity, noise measurement, modulation techniques), single-carrier communication, multicarrier communication system building blocks (discrete multitone [DMT] and orthogonal frequency division multiplexing [OFDM] transceivers), channel estimation algorithms (for both wireline and wireless), channel equalizers (minimum mean square [MMS] equalizer, decision-feedback [DF] equalizer, Viterbi equalizer, and turbo equalizer) and synchronization algorithms (frequency offset estimation, symbol timing recovery, and frame synchronization). As most digital communication algorithms involve basic signal-processing tasks (e.g., DFT, filtering), no exclusive C simulation is provided for these algorithms. However, a few techniques to efficiently implement commonly used basic mathematic operations such as division and square root on fixed-point processors are discussed, and C-simulation code is provided for those basic operations.

Image processing plays an important role in medical imaging, digital photography, computer graphics, multimedia communications, automotive, and video surveillance, to name the most common applications. Image processing tools are basically algorithms used to process the image to achieve aims specific to the application, such as improving image quality, creating special effects, compressing images for storage or fast transmission, and correcting abnormalities in the captured image (sometimes the capturing device itself introduces artifacts in the image due to hardware limitations or lens distortion). Image processing tools are also used in classifying images, detecting objects in the image, and extracting useful information from captured images.

Chapter 10 is focused on discussing and simulating widely used image processing tools such as color conversion, color enhancement, brightness and contrast correction, edge enhancement, noise reduction, edge detection, image scaling, image object corners detection, dilation and erosion morphological operators, and the Hough transform.

Advanced image processing algorithms such as image rotation, image stabilization, object detection (e.g., the human face, vehicle license plates), 2D image filtering, fisheye correction, and image compression techniques (DCT-based JPEG and wavelet-based JPEG2000), are discussed in Chapter 11. The C-simulation code and algorithm costs (in terms of processor clock cycles and memory) are also provided for image rotation and 2D image filtering algorithms.

1.2.3 Speech and Audio Processing

Speech and audio coding are very important topics in the field of multimedia storage and communication systems. Example audio- and speech-coding applications are telecommunications, digital audio broadcasting (DAB), portable media players, military applications, cinema, home entertainment systems, and distance learning. Human speech processing has many other applications, such as voice detection and speech recognition. Part 3 is dedicated to discussion of algorithms related to speech processing, speech coding, audio coding, and audio post-processing, among others.

In Chapter 12, we discuss sound and audio signals, and explore how audio data is presented to the processor from a variety of audio converters. Next, the formats in which audio data is stored and processed are described. Selected software building blocks for embedded audio systems are also discussed. Because efficient data movement is essential for overall system optimization, data buffering as it applies to speech and audio algorithms is examined. There are many speech coding algorithms in the literature and this chapter briefly discusses a few methods. Various speech compression standards are also briefly addressed. Finally, the Voice over Internet Protocol (VoIP) and the purpose of the jitter buffer in VoIP communication systems are discussed.

Audio coding methods are discussed in Chapter 13. While audio requires less processing power in general than video processing, it should be considered equally important. Recent applications such as wireless, Internet, and multimedia communication systems have created a demand for high-quality digital audio delivery at low bit rates. The technologies behind various audio coding techniques are discussed, followed by examination of MPEG-4 AAC codec modules and encoder and decoder architectures. Various commercially available audio codecs and their implementation costs (in terms of cycles and memory) are presented. Finally, we discuss a few audio post-processing techniques for enhancing the listening experience.

1.2.4 Video Processing

Advances in video coding technology and standardization, along with rapid development and improvements of network infrastructures, storage capacity, and computing power, are enabling an increasing number of video applications. Digitized video has played an important role in many consumer electronics applications, including DVD, portable media players, HDTV, video telephony, video conferencing, Internet video streaming, and distance learning, among others. As we move to high-definition video, the computing bandwidth required to process video increases manyfold, and more than 80% of total available embedded processor computing power is allocated for video processing.

Chapter 14 describes video signals, and various redundancies present in video frames are explored. Video coding building blocks (e.g., motion estimation/compensation, block transform, quantization, and variable-length coding) are briefly discussed, followed by a survey of various video coding standards and comparisons with respect to coding efficiency and costs. Computationally complex (high-cost) coding blocks are identified. Efficient ways of implementing video coders are discussed, followed by an examination of the two most widely adopted video coding standards—the MPEG-2 and H.264 decoder modules. Details of H.264-specific decoding modules (e.g., H.264 transform, intraprediction, loop filtering) are provided. Also discussed are a few techniques to efficiently implement the H.264 macroblock layer. A scalable video coding (based on the H.264 scalable extension standard) and its applications are discussed. Video processing, as stated before, when compared to other media processing, is very costly in terms of computation, memory, and data movement bandwidths. Video coding and system issues because of limited MIPS, memory, and system bus bandwidth are presented in Section 16.5 on the companion website, along with the use of proper frameworks to minimize power consumption in low-power video applications.

Video data is often processed after decompression and before sending it to the display for enhancement or rendering it suitable for playing on the screen. This part of the procedure is called "video post-processing." Chapter 15 is focused on video post-processing modules such as video scaling, video filtering, video enhancement, alpha blending, gamma correction, and video transcoding.

1.3 Embedded Systems and Applications

Embedded systems enable numerous digital devices used in daily life, and thus, are literally everywhere. Embedded computing systems have grown tremendously in recent years not only in popularity, but also in computational complexity. In all the applications listed in Table 1.1, digital embedded systems process some form of digital data. Digital media processing algorithms play an important role in all embedded system applications.

This book is focused on digital media and communication processing algorithms—that is, applications involving processing and communication of large data blocks (whether image, video, audio, speech, text blocks, or some combination of these), which often need real-time data processing. For an application, we choose a particular embedded processor along with a peripheral set only after studying its capabilities to run the algorithms of a particular application.

The last part of this book discusses embedded systems, media processing, and their applications. Embedded systems have several common characteristics that distinguish such systems from general-purpose computing systems. Unlike desktops, the embedded systems handle huge amount of data per second with very limited resources (e.g., arithmetic logic units [ALUs], memory, peripherals). In most cases, embedded systems handle very few tasks and usually these tasks must be performed in real time.

In Chapter 16 (see companion website), we discuss the important components of an embedded system (e.g., processor core, memory, and peripherals). Various types of memory and peripheral components are briefly

Table 1.1: Digital media processing applications

Digital Home	Telecommunications	Consumer Electronics
AV receivers	ADSL/VDSL	Digital camera
DVD/Blu-Ray players	Cable modems	Portable media players
TV/desktop audio/video	Wire/wireless smart phones	Portable DVD players
Sound bar	IP phone	Digital video recorder
Digital picture frame	Femto base stations	Personal GPS navigation
Video telephony	Software defined radio	Mobile TV
IP TV, IP phone, IP camera	WLAN, WiFi, WiMAX	Bluetooth
Door phone	Mobile TV	HD/ANC headphones
Smoke detector	Radar/sonar	Video game players
Network video recorder	Power line communication	Digital music instruments
CD clock radio	Video conferencing	
FM/satellite radio		
Automotives	**Industrial**	**Medical**
Advanced driver assistance	Power meter	Ultrasound
Automotive infotainment	Motor control	CT, MRI, PET
Digital audio/satellite radio	Active noise cancellation	Digital x-ray
Vision control	Barcode scanner	Pulse oximetry
Bluetooth hands-free phone	Flow meter	Digital stethoscope
Electronic stability control	Oscilloscope	Blood-pressure monitor
Safety/airbag control	**Security**	Lab diagnostic equipment
Crash detection	Surveillance IP networks	Heart rate monitor
	Fingerprint biometrics	
	Video doorbell	
	Video analytic server	

discussed. The necessity of software–hardware partitioning of embedded systems to handle complex applications is discussed, as well as possible ways to efficiently partition such a system. Finally, we discuss future embedded processor requirements to handle very complex embedded applications.

Chapter 17 (see companion website) briefly discusses various applications. Different embedded applications use different algorithms. The processing power and memory requirements vary from one application to another. We briefly talk about various modules present in a few embedded application sectors. The applications covered in this chapter include automotive, video surveillance, portable entertainment systems, digital communications, digital camera, and immigration and healthcare sectors.

1.4 Algorithm Implementation on DSP Architectures

In Section 1.2, various algorithms that are playing a critical role in diverse applications were mentioned. Although dozens of semiconductor companies are designing embedded processors with a range of architectural features to support different kinds of applications, no single architecture is efficient for processing all types of digital media processing algorithms. This is because processors designed with many pipeline stages (to execute in parallel multiple operations of numeric-intensive algorithms) do not efficiently handle algorithms that contain full-control operations. The architectures developed for executing the control code are not efficient at computing numeric-intensive algorithms. The architectural feature set of the reference embedded processor (see Appendix A on the companion website) is in between, and is good at handling both control and numeric-intensive algorithms.

In the following subsections, DSP architecture and its performance in executing various algorithms are briefly discussed. We also briefly describe a few algorithm implementation techniques.

1.4.1 DSP Architecture

A simplified block diagram of embedded DSP architecture is shown in Figure 1.1. The main architectural blocks of an embedded processor are the processor core (with register sets, ALU, data address generator [DAG], sequencer, etc.), memory (for holding instructions and data, for stack space, etc.), peripherals (e.g., serial peripheral interface [SPI], parallel peripheral interface [PPI], serial ports [SPORT], general-purpose timers, universal asynchronous receiver transmitter [UART], watchdog timer, and general-purpose I/O) and a few others (e.g., JTAG emulator, event controller, direct memory access [DMA] controller). Embedded processor peripherals and memory architectures are discussed in some detail in Chapter 16.

The peripheral features are important when we talk about the overall application. In this book, we assume that the architecture comes with all necessary peripherals to enable a particular application. Also, we assume that the program code and data required for algorithm processing are residing in the faster memory (or level 1, L1) memory, which can be accessed at the speed of the processor core. If we cannot fit data and program in L1 memory, then we store the extra data or program in L2/L3 memory and use DMA to get the data or program from L2/L3 memory without interrupting the processor core. From an algorithm-implementation point of view, the important things are processor core architecture, availability of L1 memory, and internal bus bandwidth.

Even more important than getting data into (or sending it out from) the processor, is the structure of the memory subsystem that handles the data during processing. It is essential that the processor core access data in memory at rates fast enough to meet application demands. L1 memory is often split between instruction and data segments for efficient utilization of memory bus bandwidth. Most DSP architectures support this Harvard-like architecture (in which data and instruction memories are accessed simultaneously, as shown in Figure 1.1) in combination with a hierarchical memory structure that views memory as a single, unified gigabyte address space using 32-bit addresses. All resources, including internal memory, external memory, and I/O control registers, occupy separate sections of this common address space.

The register file contains different register types (e.g., data registers, accumulators, address registers) to hold the information temporarily for ALU processing or for memory load/store purposes. The processor's computational units perform numeric processing for DSP algorithms and general control algorithms. Data moving in and out of the computational units go through the data register file. The processor's assembly language provides access to the data register file. The syntax lets programs move data to and from these registers and specify a computation's data format at the same time.

The DAGs generate addresses for data moving to and from memory. By generating addresses, the DAGs let programs refer to addresses indirectly using a DAG register instead of an absolute address.

The *program sequencer* controls the instruction execution flow, including instruction alignment and decoding. The program sequencer determines the next instruction address by examining both the current instruction being executed and the current state of the processor. Generally, the processor executes instructions from memory in sequential order by incrementing the look-ahead address. However, when encountering one of the following structures, the processor will execute an instruction that is not at the next sequential address: jumps, conditional branches, function calls, interrupts, loops, and so on.

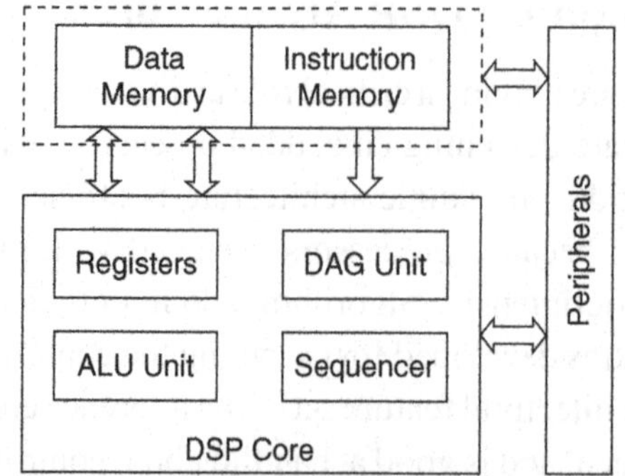

Figure 1.1: Simplified diagram of DSP architecture.

In the next subsection, we consider three algorithms with different processing flow requirements and discuss to what extent the benchmarks provided by processor manufacturers are useful in deciding which processor (from dozens of processors available today in the market) is suitable for a particular application.

1.4.2 Algorithm Complexity and DSP Performance

In this section, we consider three simple algorithms—dot product, RC4 stream cipher, and the H.264 CABAC encode-symbol-normalization process—and discuss embedded processor performance (with a particular architectural feature set) in executing those three algorithms.

Dot Product

Dot product involves accumulation of sample-by-sample multiplication of elements from two sample arrays. The dot product, z, of two N-length sample arrays $x[]$ and $y[]$, can be computed as

$$z = \sum_{n=0}^{N-1} x[n]y[n] \tag{1.1}$$

A simple "for" loop C code that implements the dot product described by Equation (1.1) is shown in Pcode 1.1.

What is the cost (in terms of cycles and memory) of this dot-product algorithm for implementation on the embedded processor, given its processor core architecture? Clearly, we require two buffers of length $2*N$ bytes (assuming the elements are the 16-bit word type), each to hold the two input array buffers in memory.

In terms of computations, it involves N multiplications and N additions. If the embedded processor consumes one cycle for multiplication and one cycle for addition, then we require a total of $2N$ cycles (assuming a single ALU) to execute the corresponding dot-product code given in Pcode 1.1. What about the cycle cost of loading the data from memory to the data registers? Typically, many processors come with separate data load/store units; hence, we assume that the data loads happen parallel to compute operations and therefore they are free.

```
z = 0;
for(i = 0;i < N;i++)
        z += x[i] * y[i];
```

Pcode 1.1: Pseudo code for dot product.

Many embedded processors come with multiply–accumulate (MAC) units, and in this case we require only N cycles, as the dot product contains a total of N MAC operations. For this case, the two memory loads must happen in a single cycle.

Now, you may wonder whether this cycle count can be achieved with the C code ported to the processor assembly using the compiler or with the optimized assembly-level code written manually. Here, when we say that the cycle count is N for executing the dot product, it means that one MAC operation is mapped to a single processor instruction, which consumes exactly one cycle; only then can we describe the cycle count as N cycles for N MAC operations.

Is this the final cycle count for computing the dot product? Not exactly—in the dot-product case, it also depends on the number of MAC units that the processor comes with. For example, if the processor consists of four MAC units, then we require only $N/4$ cycles to complete the dot product. How is this possible? It is possible because we can execute four MAC operations in parallel on a four-MAC processor, as the dot product has no flow dependencies. However, we will have a problem with the data load unless we load 128 bits (four 16-bit words from array $x[]$ and another four 16-bit words from array $y[]$) of data to eight 16-bit registers in a single cycle.

For efficient compilation to run on a four-MAC processor, we unroll the dot-product loop in Pcode 1.1 by four times and reduce the loop count by a factor of 4 as shown in Pcode 1.2. Given that the dot product is a simple algorithm, most compilers can efficiently map the C code to the assembly language so that the difference between cycle estimation and actual cycles measured is negligible.

```
z1 = 0; z2 = 0; z3 = 0; z4 = 0;
for(i = 0;i < N/4;i += 4) {
          z1 += x[i]*y[i];                // MAC unit 1
          z2 += x[i + 1]*y[i + 1];        // MAC unit 2
          z3 += x[i + 2]*y[i + 2];        // MAC unit 3
          z4 += x[i + 3]*y[i + 3];        // MAC unit 4
}
z = z1 + z2 + z3 + z4;
```

Pcode 1.2: Pseudo code for dot product with loop unrolling four times.

Digital media processing algorithms are not just "dot products." Next, we consider another simple algorithm, the RC4 stream cipher.

RC4 Stream Cipher

The RC4 algorithm (see Section 2.1.6, RC4 Algorithm, for more details) is used as a stream cipher in low-security applications and as a pseudorandom number generator in many standard ciphers applications. RC4 is used in many commercial software packages, such as Lotus Notes and Oracle Secure SQL, and in network protocols, such as SSL, IPsec, WEP, and WPA. An RC4 simulation code is given in Pcode 1.3.

```
j = 0;
for (i = 0;i < N;i++) {                  // N: data length in bytes
          k = i & 0xff;                  // i mod 255
          r0 = SBox[k];
          r1 = j + r0;
          j = r1 & 0xff;                 // i mod 255
          r1 = SBox[j];                  // look-up table access with arbitrary offset
          Sbox[j] = r0;                  // swap look-up table elements
          Sbox[k] = r1;
          r1 = r1 + r0;
          r1 = r1 & 0xff;                // i mod 255
          r1 = Sbox[r1];                 // look-up table access with arbitrary offset
          in[i] = in[i] ^ r1;            // encrypt input message bytes
}
```

Pcode 1.3: Simulation code for RC4 stream cipher.

In the iterative procedure of computing RC4 encrypted data using Pcode 1.3, the computation of a new j value requires updated (swapped) S-box values. Thus, computing many j values and swapping them at the same time is not possible due to the dependency of j on updated S-box values. The RC4 algorithm is sequential in nature, although no jumps are present. Even if multiple compute units are available with the processor, we cannot use them in this case for parallel implementation of the algorithm. See Section 2.1.6, RC4 Algorithm, for cycle costs and memory requirements to implement RC4 on the reference embedded processor.

Unlike the dot product, the execution of algorithms, such as RC4 on deep-pipeline processors, may not be efficient in terms of cycles. RC4 can be computed efficiently on microcontrollers with a two-stage pipeline in fewer cycles, compared to DSPs with 10 or more pipeline stages.

In the case of algorithms with frequently occurring conditional branches (e.g., the H.264 CABAC encode symbol normalization process described in Section 5.5), the performance of deep-pipeline DSPs worsens. As shown in Pcode 1.4, the normalization process has many conditional jumps in a "while loop." This process is costly in terms of cycles, as it performs normalization 1 bit at a time with many jumps. Avoiding jumps is the only solution to reduce cycle cost (see Section 5.5 for details).

In summary, DSPs are good at handling FFTs, filters, and matrix operations, and are less effective at handling both control code and sequential algorithms. Simple pipeline processors (e.g., ARM) are good at handling control and sequential algorithms, and less effective at handling signal processing tasks such as transforms, filtering operations, and so on.

In brief, the dot-product benchmark provided by the DSP manufacturer may not provide much useful information because the application at hand rarely contains dot-product kinds of operations. To efficiently run

```
while(pBAC->Range < 256) {// Low, Range, Outstanding bits (or Obits) are CABAC params
        if(pBAC->Low >= 512) {
                pBAC->Low -= 512;
                write_bits(1,1);
                if(pBAC->Obits > 0) {
                        write_bits(0,pBAC->Obits);          // bit-fifo write
                        pBAC->Obits = 0;
                }
        }
        else if(pBAC->Low < 256) {
                write_bits(0,1);
                if(pBAC->Obits > 0){
                        write_bits(1,pBAC->Obits);          // bit-fifo write
                        pBAC->Obits = 0;
                }
        }
        else{
                pBAC->Obits++;
                pBAC->Low -= 256;
        }
        pBAC->Range = pBAC->Range << 1;
        pBAC->Low = pBAC->Low << 1;
}
```

Pcode 1.4: Simulation code for H.264 CABAC encode symbol normalization.

any algorithm on a particular digital signal processor, we need to dedicate some time to understanding the underlying mathematical structure of the algorithm and then tune it to write efficient code for that processor. A few techniques to map algorithms to DSPs are discussed in the next section.

1.4.3 Algorithm Implementation Techniques

Digital data is efficiently processed with an embedded processor by optimizing the corresponding program at both the algorithm flow level and the instruction level. The algorithms are optimized for throughput, memory usage, I/O bandwidth, and power dissipation. In this subsection, we discuss algorithm-level optimization using various techniques for increasing throughput. In most cases, there is a trade-off between throughput and memory.

Algorithm code is optimized at the instruction level to eliminate pipeline stalls due to data dependencies, to minimize the overhead of control code such as jumps and software loop overheads, and to efficiently handle data movement within the system. Instruction-level optimization techniques vary by processor. Compilers also perform some degree of instruction-level optimization. Typically we see a 10 to 20% gain with instruction-level optimization (measured by a decrease in core clock cycles). When optimizing the code at the instruction level, complete knowledge of the algorithm structure may not be necessary.

On the other hand, program-flow optimization at the algorithm level requires knowledge of the algorithm's mathematical structure and properties. Compilers cannot achieve algorithm-level program optimization. Minimizing the number of computations and balancing the CPU and load/store bandwidth are possible with algorithm-level optimization. We can achieve algorithm-level optimization using multiple approaches. A few of these methods considered in this section include changing the algorithm flow, using look-up tables, using algorithm-flow statistics, using symmetry and periodicity, reusing already-computed data, and approximating mathematic functionality. The amount of cycle savings depends on a particular algorithm and its flow. For the algorithms discussed in this book, the amount of cycle savings achieved with algorithm-level optimization ranges from 20 to 80%.

Is Optimizing All the Program Code Worthwhile?

Before we proceed, we ask whether optimizing all the program code is worthwhile. The answer is that it depends on processor capabilities and application demands. Usually, we start optimizing the most critical modules in C, and if the MIPS budget is not met, we continue to optimize other critical modules. If we are still not within the MIPS budget, then we start writing assembly language and optimizing it. For example, consider a video decoder (see Chapter 14 for details); it has many layers and modules (see Figure 14.15). In the slice layer, we decode the slice headers, and this is performed once per slice. We may spend a few hundred cycles decoding the slice headers. Thus, the corresponding code can be in C. Similarly, the next layer is the macroblock layer, which may consume a few thousand cycles since we access it for every macroblock to decode macroblock layer headers. The macroblock layer code can be done in C or in assembly language, and we may optimize the code a little bit depending on performance requirements.

The most critical modules in a video codec are motion compensation, DCT transformation, intraframe prediction, de-block filtering, quantization, zig-zag scanning, and entropy coding. All of these modules work at the pixel level, and therefore consume millions of cycles each second. Thus, optimization of these critical modules comprising a video decoder is important to "play" the video in real time. Apart from these modules, we may be required to perform other critical video post-processing modules (e.g., scaling, filtering, blending, YUV to RGB conversion). Therefore, complicated applications such as video require a lot of optimization at many levels.

Optimization by Changing the Algorithm Flow

A change of algorithm flow sometimes leads to a lower number of computations and may balance the CPU and load/store bandwidth. With a change of algorithm flow, even if the algorithm structure changes, we still output the same data from the program. Consider the data encryption standard (DES) algorithm (see Section 2.2) as an example module for optimization. Without algorithm-level optimization, 4288 cycles are required for implementation on the reference embedded processor, whereas only 896 cycles are required for DES using the algorithm-level optimization techniques discussed in Section 2.2.

In implementing algorithms such as the AES (see Section 2.3), RS decoder (see Section 4.2), Viterbi decoder (see Section 4.4), turbo decoder (see Section 4.5), LDPC decoder (see Section 4.6), and CABAC encoder/decoder (see Section 5.5), program optimization at the algorithm level can save many cycles.

Optimization Based on Algorithm-Flow Statistics

In an algorithm with multiple data paths, all data paths may not occur with equal probability. A few data paths can occur very frequently and a few data paths may occur rarely. If we write the instruction-level optimized code to cover all the data path logic, we may spend too many cycles in parsing all the algorithm paths. Instead, handling the frequently occurring data paths separately and optimizing to the maximum extent saves many cycles. See Section 5.5.4, Normalization Process, for the H.264 CABAC encode symbol normalization process optimization using algorithm-flow statistics.

Optimization Using Symmetry and Periodicity

The number of arithmetic operations in a mathematical transformation algorithm can be reduced if any symmetry or periodicity is present in the transformation matrix coefficients. For example, the symmetry and periodicity properties of the DFT twiddle matrix are used to speed up computation upon implementing FFT algorithms. In Section 7.2, we consider an 8 × 8 DCT computation as an example, and optimize implementation using its symmetry and periodicity.

Optimization by Approximation

Simple approximations to underlying mathematical functions (without substantially compromising performance) sometimes lead to great reductions in computations and cycle counts. In Section 10.6.3, we consider an example of a pixel gradient of magnitude G and quantized angle ϕ as part of the computations in the Canny edge-detector algorithm. We start with the x-gradient G_x and y-gradient G_y of pixels, and compute the pixel gradient magnitude and angle, which involve nonlinear functions of square root and trigonometric functions as follows:

$$G = \sqrt{G_x^2 + G_y^2}, \qquad \phi = \tan^{-1}\left(\frac{G_y}{G_x}\right) \tag{1.2}$$

Usually, we perform the preceding operations on a fixed-point DSP using some kind of approximation.

Optimization by Reuse of Already-Computed Data

In many cases, delay buffers are used to store history or reuse already-computed data. This is especially true in video or image-processing applications, where a huge amount of data is present for processing. If we can reuse some portion of the computed data to process neighboring pixels, we save many computations.

In Section 15.3.1, we consider the example of a 3×3 median image filter, which is commonly used because it preserves the edge information when compared to average 3×3 filters. With the 3×3 median filter, the center pixel is replaced in the 3×3 block of pixels with the median of those $n = 9$ pixels. Computing a median by sorting is very costly, as it involves $3n^2$ operations. The 3×3 median filter can be efficiently computed using the techniques discussed in Section 15.3.1.

Optimization via Precomputing and Using Look-up Tables

The computation of nonlinear functions (e.g., square root, inverse, trigonometric, and exponential) using fixed-point processors can be very costly. Consequently, we precompute the outputs of these functions in advance and store the results in memory to minimize cycle costs. The implementation of bit-processing modules on deep-pipeline DSPs is costly from the MIPS point of view. In such cases, we minimize computations by converting the bit processing to word processing with precomputation of module output for all bit patterns of fixed length and storing the results to a look-up table. A few bit-processing examples that can be implemented efficiently via this optimization technique include DES, CRC error detection (see Section 3.2.3), BCH encoding (see Section 4.1), and turbo encoding (see Section 4.5.1). In addition, the computation of modular arithmetic for arbitrary modules is a costly operation. With precomputing and using look-up tables, we can minimize the cycles required to perform modular arithmetic operations.

1.4.4 C-Level Program Optimization

According to a recent study, most programmers develop embedded algorithms in C rather than in assembly language. There are a number of reasons to use C rather than assembly language: C is much easier to develop and maintain, and it is comparatively portable. However, there is often a poor match between C and the features of embedded processors in vectorization and fractional processing. These hardware features are essential to efficient processing, but they are not natively supported in ANSI C. For this reason, inline assembly code is often used within C programs.

Digital media processing algorithms have specialized characteristics, and compilers usually cannot generate efficient code for them without some level of programmer intervention. Many embedded processors have specialized hardware or instructions to speed up common data-processing algorithms (e.g., FFT butterflies, video processing operations, and Galois field arithmetic). These include, for example, single-cycle MACs with specialized addressing modes, single-cycle quad-byte average and clip operations, and addition and multiplication with Galois field elements. In such cases, C compiler-specific intrinsics are very useful to better utilize the processor-specialized hardware.

Probably the most useful tool for code optimization is a good profiler. In many implementations, 20% of the code accounts for 80% of the processing time. Focusing on these critical sections yields the highest marginal returns. It turns out that loops are prime candidates for optimization in most digital media processing algorithms because intensive numeric processing usually occurs inside those loops.

Compiler-Level Optimization

The global approach to code optimization is to enable compiler optimization options that optimize for either speed or memory conservation. Many other compiler options may exist to support different functionalities. There is a vast difference in performance between compiled optimized and compiled nonoptimized code. In some cases, optimized code can run 2 to 5 times faster.

Intrinsics and Inline Assembly *Intrinsics* are compiler-specific instructions that are embedded within C code and are translated by the compiler into a predefined sequence of assembly-code instructions. Intrinsics give the programmer a way to access specialized processor features without actually having to write assembly code. Many embedded processor compilers support intrinsics.

An example of intrinsic usage is shown in Figure 1.2, a case of fractional dot-product computation. With the code shown in Figure 1.2(a), the compiled code is executed as a multiply, followed by a shift, followed by an accumulation. However, the processor MAC with fractional arithmetic support performs all these tasks in a single cycle. Thus, with the code shown in Figure 1.2(b) using intrinsics for both fractional multiplication and

```
Sum = 0;
for(i = 0; i < 100; i++){
  sum += ((a[i]*b[i]) >> 15);
}
()
```

(a)

```
sum = 0;
for (i = 0; i < 100; i++){
  sum = add_fr32(sum, mult_fr32(a[i],b[i]));
}
()
```

(b)

Figure 1.2: Fractional dot product: (a) without intrinsics and (b) with intrinsics.

addition, the compiler can translate the code of fractional multiply and accumulate into a single MAC instruction supporting the fractional arithmetic mode.

Many compilers also support the use of *inline assembly* code, using the *asm()* construct within a C program. This feature causes the compiler to insert the specified assembly code into the compiler's assembly code output. Inline assembly is a good way to access specialized processor features, and it may execute faster than calling assembly code in a separate function. Using inline assembly, various costs are avoided, such as program flow latencies, function entry and exit instructions, and parameter passing overhead.

Profile-Guided Optimization Profile-guided optimization (PGO) is an excellent way to tune the compiler's optimization strategy for a program's typical runtime behavior. Many program characteristics that cannot be known statistically at compile time can be provided through PGO. The compiler can use this knowledge to bring about benefits, such as accurate branch prediction, improved loop transformations, and reduced code size. The technique is most relevant where behavior of the application over different data sets is expected to be similar.

PGO should always be implemented as the last optimization step. If the application source code is changed after gathering profile data, this profile data becomes invalid. The compiler does not use profile data when it can detect that it is inaccurate. However, it is possible to change source code in a way that is not detectable by the compiler (e.g., by changing constants). The programmer should ensure that the profile data used for optimization remains accurate.

Available C or DSP runtime libraries can also be used for efficient implementation of algorithms. See ADI-VDSP (2006) for more detail on various C-level compiler optimization techniques available for the reference embedded processor.

System-Level Optimization

System optimization starts with proper memory layout. In the best case, all code and data would fit inside the processor's L1 memory. Unfortunately, this is not always possible, especially when large C-based applications are implemented within a networked application.

The real dilemma is that processors are optimized to move data independently of the core via DMA, but microcontroller unit (MCU) programs typically run using a cache model instead. While core fetches are an inescapable reality, using DMA or cache for large transfers is mandatory to preserve performance.

Because internal memory is typically constructed in subbanks, simultaneous access by the DMA controller and the core can be accomplished in a single cycle by placing data in separate banks. For example, the core can be operating on data in one subbank while the DMA is filling a new buffer in a second subbank. Under certain conditions, simultaneous access to the same subbank is also possible.

See Katz and Gentile (2006) for more details on system-level optimization for reference embedded processor applications.

Part 1

Data Processing

CHAPTER 2

Data Security

Data exchange and data storage are common processes that we use every day. The data is usually categorized as unclassified and classified. Unclassified data can be accessed by anyone without restrictions; whereas classified data cannot be accessed by unintended third parties (i.e., other than sender and receiver). Examples of classified data are nations' homeland security- and military-related data, highly innovative and research-related data connected to defense and corporate, and financial transactions.

2.1 Cryptography Basics

Cryptography techniques are used to protect classified data from unintended observers or eavesdroppers (also called adversaries, attackers, interceptors, interlopers, intruders, opponents, or simply the enemy).

2.1.1 Cryptography Terminology

The following is a list of some important cryptography terms:

Plaintext: Message with understandable substance (content).
Encryption: Process of disguising a message in such a way as to hide its substance.
Cipher text: Encrypted message.
Decryption: Process of turning cipher text back into plain text.
Cipher: Mathematical function (algorithm) used for encryption.
Inverse cipher: Mathematical function used for decryption.
Key: Large m-bit number used in the encryption or decryption process. The range of possible values of the key is called *key space*.
Cryptosystem: Algorithm along with all possible plain texts, cipher texts, and keys.
Cryptography: Art and science of keeping messages secure that cryptographers practice.
Cryptanalysis: Art and science of breaking cipher text practiced by cryptanalysts.
Cryptology: Branch of mathematics encompassing both cryptography and cryptanalysis practiced by cryptologists.

2.1.2 Cryptography System

Using cryptographic techniques, we make the information unintelligible to people who do not have a need to know or who should not know. The basic cryptographic module consists of a secret key and a mathematical algorithm as shown in Figure 2.1. The cryptographic process of converting plain text to unintelligent form (termed as cipher text) is called *encryption*. The inverse process of converting cipher text to plain text is called *decryption*.

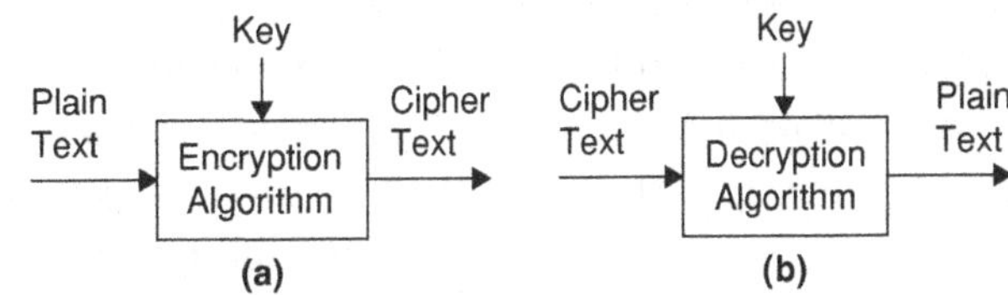

Figure 2.1: Cryptographic modules (a) encryption and (b) decryption.

DOI: 10.1016/B978-1-85617-678-1.00002-8

We can understand the importance of a cryptography system by considering an example of data exchanged between a military commander and his superior as follows:

S	I	R	,		W	E		A	R	E		M	O	V	I	N	G		T	O	W	A	R	D	S		E	N	E	M	Y

We make this classified information unintelligible (to unintended recipients) by encrypting the message before sending it over a communication channel, and we decrypt the message at the receiving side to read the information. To encrypt, we pass the original message (plain text) to the encryption algorithm to generate a cipher text (unintelligent message). An encryption algorithm is a mathematical algorithm along with a secret key. Usually, any cryptographic secret key is a large random number (e.g., a 128-bit number).

To work with the mathematical algorithm, we first use a codeword table (e.g., the 8-bit ASCII table) to generate the numeric equivalent of the plain text. In the previous classified message, we have a total of 32 characters (one comma, five spaces, and 26 letters with few repeats). The equivalent numeric 8-bit ASCII values for the previous message characters are space, 00100000 (0x20); comma, 00101100 (0x2c); A, 01000001 (0x41); D, 01000100 (0x44); E, 01000101 (0x45); G, 01000111 (0x47); I, 01001001 (0x49); M, 01001101 (0x4d); N, 01001110 (0x4e); O, 01001111 (0x4f); R, 01010010 (0x52); S, 01010011 (0x53); T, 01010100 (0x54); V, 01010110 (0x56); W, 01010111 (0x57); and Y, 01011001 (0x59). The binary equivalent form of the previous message follows:

```
01010011 01001001 01010010 00101100 00100000 01010111 01000101 00100000 01000001 01010010 01000101
00100000 01001101 01001111 01010110 01001001 01001110 01000111 00100000 01010100 01001111 01010111
01000001 01010010 01000100 01010011 00100000 01000101 01001110 01000101 01001101 01011001
```

If we represent the previous binary equivalent data in hexadecimal notation, then the plain text becomes

```
53 49 52 2c 20 57 45 20 41 52 45 20 4d 4f 56 49 4e 47 20 54 4f 57 41 52 44 53 20 45 4e 45 4d 59
```

Let us select the following cryptographic key (say, random numbers with 128 bits) in hexadecimal notation:

```
89 fc 23 d5 71 1a 86 22 c1 42 76 dd b3 94 7e a9
```

With a mathematical algorithm along with the previous secret key, we obtain the following cipher data for the previous plain data:

```
da b5 71 f9 50 4d c3 02 80 10 33 fd fe db 28 e0 c7 bb 03 81 3e 4d c7 70 85 11 56 98 fd d1 3e f0
```

Now, if we map the previous hexadecimal cipher data back to cipher text using the ASCII table, we get

```
Ú µ q ù P M Ã STX € DLE 3 ý þ Û ( à Ç » ETX • > M Ç p ... DC1 V ˜ ý Ñ > ð
```

This cipher text is an unintelligent text (as we do not know its substance). The sender transmits this cipher text to the receiver and the recipient decrypts the received cipher text with the same cryptographic key, obtaining the plain text SIR, WE ARE MOVING TOWARDS ENEMY. This example shows the importance of cryptography systems, as it is very difficult for an adversary to obtain message content in the process of communication.

2.1.3 Cryptographic Practices

Cryptographic techniques allow us to transmit or to store the classified data in a secure manner. In the cryptographic process, a cryptographic (or mathematical) algorithm can be in the public domain, but the cryptographic (or secret) key should not be disclosed to the public. Now, the question is, how good is this cryptographic system (i.e., a secret key, an algorithm, plain text, and cipher text)? Will it protect our data from eavesdroppers, or is it possible for eavesdroppers to get the content of message without the cryptographic key? Well, that depends on the properties of the mathematical algorithm and the length and randomness of the key chosen. Here, the cryptographic key should be random enough and eavesdroppers should not have any clue about the key pattern. Eavesdroppers usually know the algorithm that is used in the cryptographic process, but with a well-designed algorithm this knowledge will not help them. In other words, the only way for eavesdroppers to get the content of cipher text is by decrypting the cipher text with each possible key pattern. The possible number of key patterns with a 128-bit number is 2^{128}. We call this set of 2^{128} possibilities the key space for a 128-bit key. Breaking the cipher text with this approach (i.e., breaking cipher text by attempting all possible keys) is called a brute force attack on a cryptographic system.

Brute force attacks are very costly. For example, to break cipher text generated with a 128-bit key, the amount of computational power needed is estimated as follows. Assume that decrypting the cipher text with one key pattern takes about N operations. If the computer performs 1 million (or approximately 2^{20}) such operations per second, or 2^{36} $(24*60*60*2^{20})$ operations per day, or 2^{45} $(365*24*60*60*2^{20})$ operations per year, then with 1 million computers (i.e., 2^{65} operations per year), we would have to work for the next $N*10^{20}$ years. To put this in context, we believe this universe was formed 10^{20} years ago! Even if the cipher text decrypted with one ($N = 1$) operation, breaking the cipher text using the brute force method is impossible with available technology.

Is it only the way to break the cipher text? That's a good question. The answer is *no*. Many types of attacks are used to break the cipher text. We will start by discussing one such attack called the known plain-text attack, and will examine other attacks later. In the known plain-text attack, the eavesdropper knows the content of some portion of plain text and tries to break the cipher text by deducing the key pattern. If the eavesdropper succeeds in this process, then the cryptographic system can be attacked with a simple decryption process and 1 million computers for 2^{20} years need not spend time on breaking the cipher text. Is it possible for the eavesdropper to get the content of plain text and break the present cipher text?

Well, it depends on how the particular organization handles classified information and manages the secret keys. For example, if the secret key of the cryptographic algorithm is not changed for a long time, and the previous plain text messages are obtained by bribing the secretary, then the eavesdropper can succeed in his operation. Most of the time, the eavesdroppers will not succeed in their operation as the secret key patterns are changed periodically. If the cipher is generated with a new key, whatever plain text and cipher text the eavesdropper had are not useful. Thus, secret key management plays an important role in cryptographic applications. Later we present an overview of the key management process. Detailed discussion of the secret key management process is beyond the scope of this book.

Security with Encryption Algorithms

As discussed previously, an algorithm is considered computationally secure if it cannot be broken with available resources, either current or future. We measure the complexity of an attack in different ways:

Data complexity: The amount of data needed as input to perform an attack
Processing complexity: The time required to perform an attack
Storage requirements: The amount of memory needed to perform an attack

The security of a cryptosystem (plain texts, cryptographic algorithm, secret key, and cipher texts) is a function of two things: the strength of the algorithm and the length of the key. If the strength of an algorithm is perfect, then there is no better way to break the cryptosystem other than trying every possible key in a brute-force method. Good cryptosystems are designed to be infeasible to break with the computing power that is expected to evolve for many years in the future.

If we hide the functionality of the encryption algorithm and the security of an algorithm is based on keeping the way that algorithm works a secret, it is a restricted algorithm, and is inadequate by today's standards. A large or changing group of users cannot use them, because every time a user leaves the group, everyone else must switch to a different algorithm. If a user accidentally reveals the secret, everyone must change his or her algorithm. If we do not have a good cryptographer in the group, then we do not know whether we have a secure algorithm. Despite these major drawbacks, restricted algorithms are enormously popular for low-security applications, where users either do not realize or do not care about the security problems inherent in their system.

All of the security in the standardized algorithm is based in the key, compared to none based in the details of the algorithm. Products using these algorithms can be mass produced. It does not matter if an eavesdropper knows our algorithm; if she/he does not know our particular key, she/he cannot read our messages. Cryptosystems that look perfect are often extremely weak. Strong cryptosystems, with a couple of minor changes can become weak. So it is best to trust algorithms that professional cryptologists have scrutinized for years without cracking them.

Attacks

The whole point of cryptography is to keep the plain text (or the key, or both) secret from eavesdroppers. Eavesdroppers are assumed to have complete access to the communications between the sender and receiver. Cryptanalysis is the science of recovering the plain text of a message without access to the key. An attempted cryptanalysis is called an *attack*. There are four general types of cryptanalytic attacks. Of course, each of them assumes that the cryptanalyst has complete knowledge of the encryption algorithm used.

Let P_i, C_i, and E_K denote plain text, cipher text, and encryption algorithm with key K. The four cryptanalytic attacks are described in the following.

1. *Ciphertext-only attack*:
   Given: $C_1 = E_K(P_1), C_2 = E_K(P_2), \ldots, C_i = E_K(P_i)$
   Deduce: Either $P_1, P_2, \ldots, P_i$; K; or an algorithm to infer P_{i+1} from $C_{i+1} = E_K(P_{i+1})$.
2. *Known plain-text attack*:
   Given: $P_1, C_1 = E_K(P_1), P_2, C_2 = E_K(P_2), \ldots, P_i, C_i = E_K(P_i)$
   Deduce: Either K, or an algorithm to infer P_{i+1} from $C_{i+1} = E_K(P_{i+1})$
3. *Chosen plain-text attack*: This is more powerful than a known plain-text attack because the cryptanalyst can choose specific plain text blocks to encrypt that might yield more information about the key.
4. *Adaptive chosen plain-text attack*: This is a special case of a chosen plain-text attack. Not only can the cryptanalyst choose the plain text that is encrypted, but he can also modify his choice based on the results of previous encryption.

Other types of cryptanalytic attacks include chosen cipher text, chosen key, rubber hose cryptanalysis, and purchase key.

Algorithms differ by degrees of security; this depends on how hard they are to break. Categories of breaking an algorithm follow:

Total break: Finding a key
Global deduction: Finding an alternate algorithm that results in plain text without knowledge of key
Instance deduction: Finding plain text of an intercepted cipher text
Information deduction: Gaining knowledge about key or plain text

Key Management

Key management basically deals with the key generation, distribution, storage, key renewal, and updating and key destruction. In the real world, key management is the hardest part of cryptography. Cryptanalysts often attack cryptosystems through the loopholes of key management. Why should we bother going through all the trouble of trying to break the cryptographic algorithm if we can recover the key because of some sloppy key management procedures? Why should we spend $500 million building a cryptanalysis machine if we can spend $500 bribing a clerk?

The security of an algorithm rests in the key. If we are using a cryptographically weak process (reduced key spaces or poor key choices) to generate keys, then our whole system is weak. The eavesdropper need not analyze our encryption algorithm; he/she can analyze our key generation algorithm. Therefore, we should generate the key bits from either reliably random source or a cryptographically secure pseudorandom-bit generator. In Section 2.1.6, we discuss more about pseudorandom number generation for cryptographic applications.

We use encrypted keys in transferring keys from one point to another. The keys of encryption keys have to be distributed manually. No data encryption key should be used for an infinite period. The longer a key is used, the greater the chance that it will be compromised. It is generally easier to do cryptanalysis with more cipher text encrypted with the same key. Given that, the keys must be replaced regularly and old keys must be destroyed securely. The keys of encryption keys do not have to be replaced as frequently. They are used only occasionally for key exchange. However, if a key of the encryption keys is compromised, the potential loss is extreme as the security of the data encryption key rests on the key of encryption keys.

2.1.4 Cryptographic Applications

The cryptographic algorithms are used mainly for three purposes: (1) to keep the classified data confidential, (2) to maintain data integrity, and (3) to have data authenticity.

Data confidentiality: Eavesdroppers try to acquire knowledge of classified data in data communications or data storage systems by tapping the classified data without authorization. By processing the classified data using cryptographic algorithms, we transmit or store the data in a secure manner.

Data integrity: Sometimes we may need to keep the data unchanged. The data may be altered by adding or deleting or substituting with some other data. Data transmission or memory retrieval devices may introduce errors by adding noise. Sometimes unauthorized persons may change the content of data before it reaches to the intended party.

Data authentication: Data authentication basically gives the source of data origin. By generating the authentication code using a secret key, we can have data authenticity after verification. Most of the time the data need not be confidential, but to have confidence in the data, the data should have a trusted source and should not be modified by unauthorized people.

2.1.5 Cryptographic Algorithms

Cryptographic algorithms are broadly divided into three categories: (1) symmetric key algorithms, (2) public-key algorithms, and (3) hash functions based algorithms. In symmetric key algorithms, we use the same secret key for both the encryption and decryption process. In public-key algorithms, we use one key for the encryption process (generation) and a different key for the decryption process (verification). In hash functions, we do not use a secret key to process the data. With these three kinds of algorithms, we achieve data confidentiality, data integrity, and data authentication.

Symmetric Key Algorithms

The examples for symmetric key algorithms are the advanced encryption standard (AES) and the triple data encryption algorithm (TDEA), and are used in most cryptographic applications for data encryption. Sections 2.2 and 2.3 present more details about the TDEA and AES algorithms, simulations, and efficient implementation techniques.

Public Key Algorithms

The example for public-key algorithm is RSA (Rivest, Shamir, and Adelman). Public-key algorithms are used for data authentication. For data authentication, we transmit digital signatures computed using a public key-based digital signature algorithm (DSA). In Section 2.5, the elliptic-curve digital signature algorithm (ECDSA)—that is, elliptic curve-based DSA—is discussed and simulated.

Hash Functions

Examples of hash-based algorithms are SHA functions. Popular and standardized SHA functions include SHA-1, SHA-256, SHA-384, and SHA-512. Hash functions are used in achieving data integrity by computing unique condensed message (or message digest) for data. Hash-based algorithms are also used to generate pseudorandom numbers. In public-key algorithms and in computing message authentication codes, we use SHA functions to condense the messages. In Section 2.4, the keyed hash message-authentication code (HMAC) algorithm is discussed in detail and simulated. In Section 2.5, we use the hash function to generate condensed messages for ECDSA.

2.1.6 Cryptography and Random Numbers

We use random numbers in cryptography for many purposes. For example, all cryptographic keys are random numbers. We also use random numbers as default initial constants or as a seed for some cryptography algorithms. Cryptographic algorithms use random number as input (as a key or as its state) and output random data (as cipher text, as authentication code, or as condensed message). In other words, cryptographic algorithms can also be used for generating random numbers. Typically, we use symmetric key algorithms or hash functions to generate random numbers for public key algorithms.

As discussed previously, given an encryption algorithm that is mathematically proven and has good properties (for randomizing data without having any weak instants for key patterns), the strength and security of the cryptographic system entirely depends on its key management process, as discussed in Section 2.1.3. In particular, the use of good (i.e., random or unpredictable) key patterns for a cryptographic algorithm is very important to improve the strength of the overall cryptosystem. Now, the question is how to generate random numbers? In practice, we have two kinds of random numbers. One kind is truly random; we cannot reproduce them with any deterministic method. Another kind is not truly random, but they look random and they can be reproduced with deterministic methods. We cannot generate true random numbers with software algorithms. Instead, we use a physical phenomenon (e.g., radioactive decay, electronic-parts generated noise, or instant temperature measures) along with hardware for producing true random numbers; the subject of true random number generation is beyond the scope of this book.

Pseudorandom Numbers Generation

A pseudorandom number generator (PRNG) uses a deterministic algorithm to produce the random numbers, and these numbers are not truly random, as we can reproduce them again and again. There is a vast amount of literature on the subject of pseudorandom number generation, and many algorithms have been developed for PRNG by the research community in the last few decades. There are many test procedures in the literature to verify randomness of numbers generated by PRNG. Once again, the subject of PRNG theory and test procedures is beyond the scope of this book. In this section, we discuss PRNGs based on the linear feedback shift register (LFSR) and the RC4 algorithm. We also discuss simulation and implementation techniques for these two algorithms in the next two subsections. Note that these two algorithms may not be practically useful in cryptography and may not pass all PRNG test procedures for reasons discussed later.

Linear Feedback Shift Register

The LFSR contains a small amount of memory to hold its state at any point of time. LFSR is basically used for scrambling (or randomizing) data bits to uniformly distribute energy in the whole bitstream. We can generate a pseudorandom binary sequence (PRBS) by using LFSR. The PRBS sequence is also used for bit interleaving with error correction algorithms such as RS codes and turbo codes. Figure 2.2 shows a signal flow diagram of the LFSR for the following PRBS generator polynomial:

$$p(x) = x^{15} + x^{14} + 1$$

The randomizer is initialized at the very beginning with a seed value of 100101010000000. As this LFSR contains 15 bits of memory, its output bit pattern does not repeat in the cycle of $2^{15} - 1$ bits. In other words, the LFSR shown in Figure 2.2 generates a pseudorandom binary sequence (PRBS) of length less than 2^{15}. Then this PRBS sequence is used for randomizing the input data, interleaving the bit patterns, and generating random numbers. The straightforward simulation code for the LFSR shown in Figure 2.2 is given in Pcode 2.1 and a much more efficient simulation code is given in Pcode 2.2.

LFSR and Pseudorandom Number Generation for Cryptography Applications The LFSR system shown in Figure 2.2 generates random bits without repeating the bit pattern until the loop runs up to $2^{15} - 1$ times. In the interval $[1, 2^{15}]$, the generated bits are random. Now, the question is whether the random numbers generated

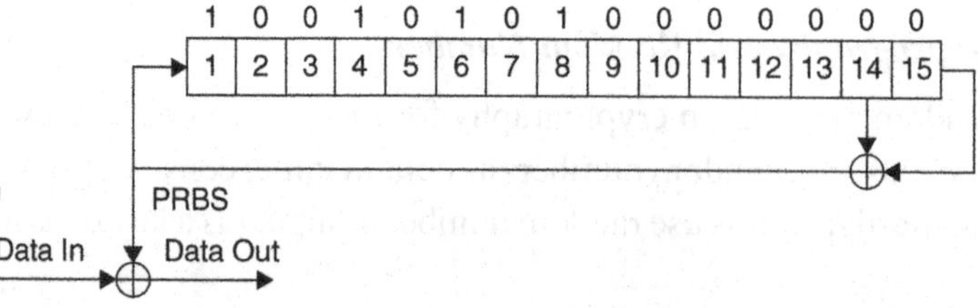

Figure 2.2: Signal flow diagram of data randomizer.

```
S[0] = 1; s[1] = 0; s[2] = 0; s[3] = 1;
S[4] = 0; s[5] = 1; s[6] = 0; s[7] = 0;
S[8] = 0; s[9] = 0; s[10] = 0;
S[11] = 0; s[12] = 0; s[13] = 0; s[14] = 0;
for(i = 0; ; i++){
        tmp = s[14] ^ s[13];
        s[14] = s[13];s[13] = s[12]; s[12] = s[11]; s[11] = s[10];
        s[10] = s[9]; s[9] = s[8];   s[8] = s[7];   s[7] = s[6];
        s[6] = s[5];  s[5] = s[4];   s[4] = s[3];   s[3] = s[2];
        s[2] = s[1];  s[1] = s[0];   s[0] = tmp;
        data_out[i] = data_in[i] ^ tmp;
}
```

Pcode 2.1: Simulation code for LFSR shown in Figure 2.2.

```
A = 0x95000000;       // initial state (15 MSBs)
B = 0xff8000000;      // MASK
for(i = 0; ; i++){
        C = A >> 1;
        A = A ^ C;
        A = A & B;
        A = A << 14;
        if (A) data_out[i] = data_in[i] ^ 1;
        A = C | A;
}
```

Pcode 2.2: Efficient simulation code for LFSR shown in Figure 2.2.

by this LSFR system satisfy the requirement of cryptography standards. The answer is *no*. In cryptographic practices, the algorithm will be in the public domain and for the cryptanalyst, attacking this type of system is very easy even if the cryptanalyst does not have knowledge of the initial seed as the length of seed is only 15 bits. The seed pattern of the LFSR shown in Figure 2.2 can easily be derived from its output sequence with the present day technology by using the brute force method. As per present cryptographic standards, we require a minimum of 160-bit-width polynomial seeds for LFSR. To avoid attacks based on analytical methods, the SHA function (discussed in Section 2.4) is applied on LFSR output and the pseudorandom numbers generated by the LFSR-SHA system may be acceptable for cryptographic applications. For example, the LFSR with output cycle period as $2^{160} - 1$ using primitive polynomial of degree 160 follows:

$$\begin{aligned} p(x) = {} & x^{160}+x^{159}+x^{158}+x^{157}+x^{155}+x^{153}+x^{151}+x^{150}+x^{149}+x^{148}+x^{147}+x^{146}+x^{142}+x^{141} \\ & +x^{137}+x^{134}+x^{133}+x^{132}+x^{130}+x^{128}+x^{126}+x^{125}+x^{121}+x^{120}+x^{118}+x^{117}+x^{116}+x^{114} \\ & +x^{112}+x^{111}+x^{109}+x^{108}+x^{106}+x^{104}+x^{102}+x^{95}+x^{94}+x^{90}+x^{89}+x^{88}+x^{86}+x^{85}+x^{84} \\ & +x^{83}+x^{82}+x^{81}+x^{80}+x^{78}+x^{76}+x^{68}+x^{66}+x^{64}+x^{61}+x^{60}+x^{59}+x^{57}+x^{52}+x^{50}+x^{46} \\ & +x^{45}+x^{41}+x^{40}+x^{39}+x^{38}+x^{37}+x^{36}+x^{35}+x^{31}+x^{29}+x^{27}+x^{26}+x^{25}+x^{23}+x^{20}+x^{18} \\ & +x^{16}+x^{11}+x^{10}+x^{8}+x^{7}+x^{6}+x^{5}+x^{3}+x+1 \end{aligned}$$

The binary coefficients of the previous primitive polynomial $p(x)$ are also represented in hexadecimal vector form as $\boldsymbol{P}$ = [0xf57e313a, 0xb1badaa0, 0x63bfa80a, 0x9d0a31fc, 0x574a86f5, 0x80000000], where the coefficient of highest degree corresponds to the non-zero MSB (most significant bit) of the left-most word. Reproducing the PRBS of this LFSR system without knowing the 160-bit initial seed by using the brute force method is not an easy task. As mentioned earlier, to avoid attacks (or deriving the seeds) for LFSR based on analytical methods, SHA functions are applied on output of LFSR. In the next subsection, we discuss pseudorandom number generation based on the RC4 algorithm.

RC4 Algorithm

In this section, we discuss pseudorandom number generation using the RC4 stream cipher algorithm. The RC4 algorithm involves computation of S-Box (which consists of 256-byte elements, initially assigned with 0 to 255) values using the given key information. RC4 uses a variable length key from 1 to 256 bytes to initialize a 256-byte S-Box table. The S-Box computation is done by iteratively swapping the locations of S-Box elements as given in Pcode 2.3. The S-Box table is used for the subsequent generation of pseudorandom bytes which are then XORed with the input plain text to produce a cipher text. In other words, once we have a computed S-Box, then the input data is encrypted (or randomized) one byte at a time by XORing with an S-Box element, which is accessed through the offset obtained after the manipulation of indices in some particular way as given in Pcode 2.4. The S-Box elements are also continuously swapped in encryption of every input byte and each element in the S-Box table is swapped at least once in this process. Like this, the encryption (or randomization) process will be continued until the input data bytes get over.

The RC4 algorithm is a nonstandardized and yet powerful stream cipher. One of the reasons for not standardizing this RC4 algorithm is because of its simple mathematical structure. However, the RC4 algorithm is used as a stream cipher in low-security-risk applications and used as a pseudorandom number generator in many standard ciphers applications. RC4 is used in many commercial software packages such as Lotus Notes and Oracle Secure SQL, and in network protocols such as SSL, IPsec, WEP, and WPA.

RC4 and Pseudorandom Numbers Generation In this section, we discuss the pseudorandomness of data patterns generated by the RC4 algorithm. As the RC4 state (S-Box) consists of 256 bytes, it is computationally difficult for adversaries to break the RC4-generated random pattern by using the brute force method. However, the RC4 algorithm is vulnerable to analytic attacks of the S-Box table; some weak keys exist for RC4 and some theoretical attacks have been performed on RC4 (Mister and Tavares, 1998).

```
for(i = 0;i < 256;i++)                    // initialize S_Box
      S_Box[i] = i;
j = 0;
for(i = 0;i < 256;i++){                   // update S_Box using 256 bytes key
      r0 = S_Box[i];        r1 = key[i];
      r1 = r0 + r1;
      r1 = r1 + j;
      j = r1 & 0xff;
      r1 = S_Box[j];                      // look-up table access with arbitrary offset
      S_Box[j] = r0;
      S_Box[i] = r1;
}
```

Pcode 2.3: Simulation code for RC4 S-Box computation.

```
j = 0;
for (i = 0;i < N;i++){                    // N: data length in bytes
      k = i & 0xff;                       // i mod 255
      r0 = S_Box[k];                      // can be loaded with circular buffer addressing
      r1 = j + r0;
      j = r1 & 0xff;                      // mod 255
      r1 = S_Box[j];                      // look-up table access with arbitrary offset
      S_Box[j] = r0;
      S_Box[k] = r1;
      r1 = r1 + r0;
      r1 = r1 & 0xff;                     // mod 255
      r1 = S_Box[r1];                     // look-up table access with arbitrary offset
      in[i] = in[i] ^ r1;
}
```

Pcode 2.4: Simulation code for RC4 Cipher.

We can strengthen RC4 security by following a few rules:

1. Drop the first few hundred bytes of output of RC4 to avoid weak key attacks and other key schedule–related attacks.
2. Do not repeat the secret key when generating the S-Box of RC4.
3. Do not use RC4 for generating (or encrypting) lengthy data patterns. For more information on RC4 weaknesses, see Mister and Tavares (1998); Mantin and Shamir (2001); and Fluhrer, et al. (2001).

The other block ciphers such as DES and AES discussed in Sections 2.2 and 2.3, and hash functions discussed in Section 2.4 are also used for generating pseudorandom numbers.

In the following, we discuss the complexity and simulation of RC4 as well as an efficient software implementation method for the RC4 encryption process.

RC4 Simulation and Complexity In the iterative procedure of computing RC4 S-Box or encryption (or randomization) processes given in Pcodes 2.3 and 2.4, the computation of new j value requires updated (swapped) S-Box values. So, computing many j values and swapping them all at one time is not allowed due to dependency of j on updated S-Box values. Every time we access the S-Box element from memory on the reference embedded processor using an arbitrary offset to the S-Box table, we consume extra clock cycles (due to pipeline stalls). This implementation is very inefficient as we cannot interleave the program to avoid the pipeline stalls. We have one such look-up table access in Pcode 2.3 and two in Pcode 2.4.

Next we estimate the complexity of the RC4 algorithm given in Pcodes 2.3 and 2.4 in terms of processor cycles. See Appendix A, Section A.4, on this book's companion website for more information on cycles estimation on the reference embedded processor. With the present program flow, we consume 11 cycles per iteration (assuming three pipeline stalls) in S-Box computation using Pcode 2.3, and we consume 17 cycles per iteration in data byte encryption using Pcode 2.4. With this, we consume $2816 (= 11 * 256)$ cycles for S-Box computation and $17 * N$ cycles for encryption of N data bytes. For $N = 128$, we consume $2176 (= 17 * 128)$ cycles for encryption process.

RC4 Implementation and Optimization The memory access stalls in RC4 can be avoided if we can compute a minimum of two j values (if not more) at a time and interleave the program code. After careful observation, the computation of two j values at a time is possible except for one case, when $j = i + 1$. By conditionally computing the new index value j, we can have two j values and can do two swaps at a time and thereby avoid extra stalls. Computing two random bytes and encrypting two data bytes at a time also achieve similar elimination of the stalls in the data encryption algorithm. This efficient implementation code is given in Pcode 2.5. Here, we have a scope to interleave the program code and to eliminate the memory access stalls. With this approach we

```
j = k = 0; m = 1;
for(i = 0;i < 256;i += 2){
         r0 = S_Box[i]; r1 = key[i];
         r1 = r1 + r0;
         r1 = r1 + k;   r5 = key[m];
         j = r1 & 0xff;                  // mod 255
         r2 = S_Box[j];                  // memory access with arbitrary offset
         if (j == m) r4 = r0;
         else r4 = r3;
         r1 = r4 + r5;
         r1 = r1 + j;
         k = r1 & 0xff;                  // mod 255
         S_Box[i] = r2;
         S_Box[j] = r0;
         r4 = S_Box[k];                  // memory access with arbitrary offset
         r3 = S_Box[m];
         S_Box[k] = r3;
         S_Box[m] = r4; m = m + 2;
}
```

Pcode 2.5: Efficient implementation of RC4 S-Box computation.

can reduce on average two clock cycles per iteration from the simulation code of Pcode 2.3. Now, we consume about 2304 (= 18 * 128) cycles (instead of 2816) in the S-Box computation. The similar approach can be used to eliminate the pipeline stalls in the encryption process due to look-up table accesses with arbitrary offsets.

2.2 Triple Data Encryption Algorithm

The triple data encryption algorithm is based on the data encryption standard, adopted worldwide by most public and private organizations for data communications and data storage. The TDEA algorithm can process data blocks of 64 bits using three different keys, each of 56-bit length. In this section, we discuss the flow description of TDEA-algorithm modules—namely, DES key expansion, DES cipher, and DES inverse cipher. We simulate the TDEA algorithm modules and get the simulation results for given input data and key. Also we discuss the computational complexity of the DES algorithm and efficient techniques to implement the DES cipher and DES inverse cipher.

2.2.1 Introduction to TDEA

As shown in Figure 2.3, the TDEA algorithm consists of three cascaded DES units. Each DES unit uses a separate key to process the data. In the case of the TDEA cipher, we cascade the DES cipher followed by the DES inverse cipher followed by another DES cipher. The TDEA inverse cipher consists of inverse TDEA DES units. In other words, in the case of a TDEA inverse cipher, we cascade the DES inverse cipher followed by the DES cipher followed by another DES inverse cipher. The same set of three keys shall be used for the TDEA cipher and TDEA inverse cipher. Hence we call the TDEA a symmetric cipher.

A few applications of the TDEA include data communications, data storage, Internet, military applications, classified data management, online banking, and memory protection. Similar to TDEA, recently developed AES (advanced encryption standard) is used in all the previous applications. We discuss the AES algorithm in Section 2.3.

The strength of an encryption algorithm depends on its mathematical properties and supported key lengths. The DES is a very old standard with less key space, and analysts have thoroughly understood and attacked the DES cipher text. The T-DES is based on DES with a large key space. AES is the latest standard with very large key space, no known attacks, and no known weak key patterns existed as of this writing.

2.2.2 TDEA Algorithm

The TDEA algorithm uses the DES algorithm as a basic unit as shown in Figure 2.3. TDEA uses a total of three DES units in cascade fashion with a different 56-bit keyword for each DES unit. Effectively, the TDEA algorithm key space is 168 (= 56*3) bits. If we know how DES works, then TDEA is performed by simply cascading three such DES units. From here on, we concentrate on the DES algorithm. The flow diagram of the DES algorithm is shown in Figure 2.4. Input to the DES algorithm is a plain text of 64 bits and a key of 56 bits. (The key starts as a 64-bit encoded key. It is 56 bits after removing the check bits from the 64-bit encoded key.) The input 56-bits of key are then expanded using the DES key scheduler.

DES Key Scheduler

The DES key scheduler consists of three steps as shown in Figure 2.4. In the first step, we obtain the permuted 56-bit key data by applying the permutation choice-1 (PC-1). The second step is basically a loop run 16 times that produces that many 56-bit data words. Before starting the loop, we treat the 56-bit key as two independent

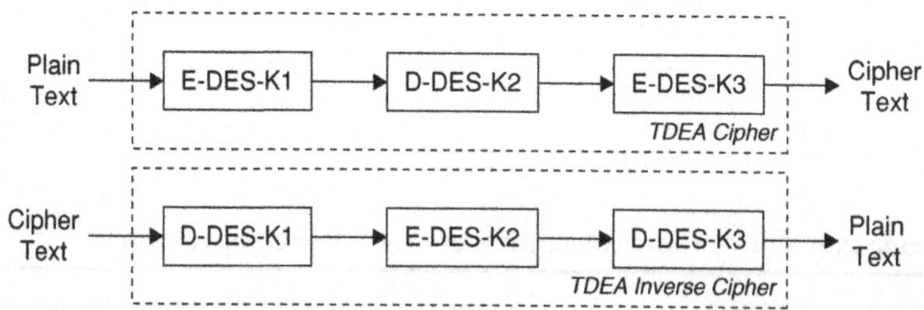

Figure 2.3: Block diagram of the TDEA algorithm.

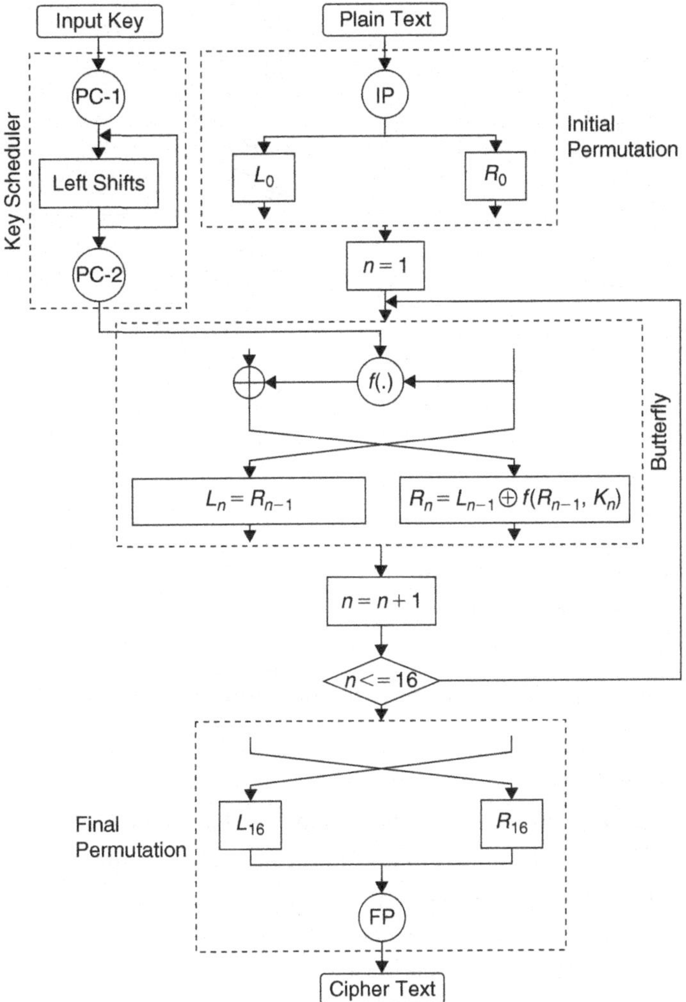

Figure 2.4: Flow diagram of DES algorithm.

28-bit words. In the loop, we rotate the two 28-bit words left by 1 or 2 bits in each iteration. The input to the next iteration of the loop is its previous iteration output. In the third step of key scheduler, we take a 56-bit word (i.e., the result after combing the left shifted two 28-bit words) output from each iteration of the loop and generate a 48-bit word (or eight 6-bit words) by using permutation choice-2 (PC-2). In this way, the key scheduler expands the input 56-bit key to total 128 (= 16*8) 6-bit keywords for performing the DES algorithm (the same key scheduler is used for both cipher/inverse cipher).

DES Cipher

As shown in Figure 2.4, the DES algorithm also consists of three steps, initial permutation, butterfly loop, and final permutation. In the first step, we apply initial permutation on input plain text before entering the butterfly loop. In the second step, the permuted plain text (split into two 32-bit words) passes through a 16-iteration butterfly loop to output the pre-encrypted data using expanded key data. We use eight 6-bit keywords in each iteration of the butterfly loop. As a third step, we apply the inverse of the initial permutation on the butterfly-loop output (i.e., on pre-encrypted data) to get the cipher text. The main module in a DES-algorithm butterfly loop is a nonlinear function $f(.)$. The flow diagram of function $f(.)$ is shown in Figure 2.5.

The nonlinear function $f(.)$ in the DES butterfly loop again consists of three steps. In the first step, we expand (E) the 32-bit data to 48-bit data and then we XOR the expanded 48-bit data with 48 bits of key data (we use eight 6-bit words or 48 bits of key from the key scheduler output in a single iteration of the butterfly loop).

Then in the second step, the XORed 48-bit data is split into eight 6-bit words and passed through 4×16 dimension S-Boxes (6-bit words are used as addresses to the S-Box tables with the first and last bit to specify the row of a table and middle 4 bits to specify the column number, see Section 2.2.3, DES Function Simulation) to get eight 4-bit words (S-Box consists of 4-bit words). Next we merge the eight 4-bit words to a single 32-bit

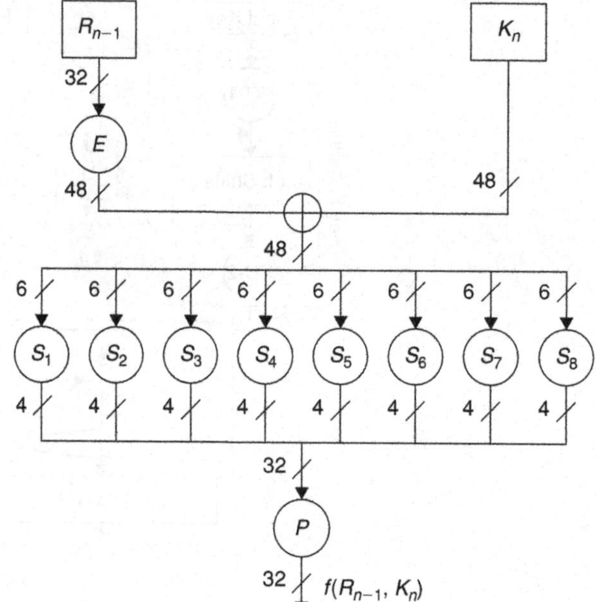

Figure 2.5: Flow diagram of nonlinear function $f(.)$ in DES algorithm.

word and then as a third step we apply permutation (P) on merged 32-bit data to get the nonlinear function $f(.)$ output.

DES Inverse Cipher

The flow of the DES inverse cipher is the same as that of the DES cipher. The only difference between the DES cipher and DES inverse cipher is that the former accesses the keywords from the start of the keyword buffer to~the end of the buffer with its loop iterations (i.e., the first eight 6-bit keywords from 0 to 7 used for first iteration, the next eight 6-bit keywords from 8 to 15 used for second iteration, etc.), whereas the inverse cipher accesses the keywords from the end of buffer (i.e., the last eight 6-bit keywords from 120 to 127 used for first iteration, the next eight 6-bit keywords from 112 to 119 used for second iteration, etc.).

2.2.3 Simulation of DES Algorithm

In the DES algorithm, the permutation or expansion operations are carried out using the mapping tables (specified in the DES standard, Federal Information Processing Standard [FIPS], 1999). For example, the permutation operation in the butterfly function is carried out by using the mapping table given in Table 2.1. By using this bit position mapping table, we get the 1st bit in the permuted word from 16th bit of input word, the 2nd bit in the permuted word from 7th bit of input word and so on. Finally, the last bit of permuted word is coming from 25th bit of input word. In the simulation of all permutation operations, we use the equivalent shift values (precomputed and stored in a memory) instead of standard table values to reduce the cycle cost. For example, we use the derived shift values in Table 2.2 instead of actual bit numbers in Table 2.1 for simulating the DES butterfly

Table 2.1: Bit numbers for permutation

16	7	20	21
29	12	28	17
1	15	23	26
5	18	31	10
2	8	24	14
32	27	3	9
19	13	30	6
22	11	4	25

Table 2.2: Shift values for permutation

16	25	12	11
3	20	4	15
31	17	9	6
27	14	1	22
30	24	8	18
0	5	29	23
13	19	2	26
10	21	28	7

permutation operation. In Table 2.2, the shift values are obtained by subtracting bit position numbers from 32. If we perform the permutation of bits with logical AND, SHIFT, and OR operations as given in Pcode 2.16, then the use of the derived shift value will consume less cycles with C code when compared to the use of bit numbers and bits extract.

DES Key Scheduler Simulation

For simulation purpose, we split the DES key scheduler into four parts: (1) permutation choice-1, (2) permutation choice-2, (3) left shifts, and (4) main key scheduler function. In the left shifts operation, we rotate independently two 28-bit words to the left by 1 bit or 2 bits. As we repeat this left shifts operation many times, we define two macros: DES_KEY_SCH_MACRO_ONE() for 1-bit left shift, and DES_KEY_SCH_MACRO_TWO() for 2-bit left shift to simplify the code. The simulation code for these two macros is given in Pcode 2.6. We call the functions permutation choice-1, permutation choice-2, and the two left-shift macros from the main key scheduler function. The simulation code for the key scheduler function is given in Pcode 2.7.

Permutation Choice-1 FIPS PUB 46-3 standard specifies a look-up table to perform permutation choice-1 (PC-1) operation. According to PC-1 table (shown in Table 2.3), we map 64-bit encoded key bits data to 56-bit permuted bits data as follows. The 1st bit of permuted key is obtained from the 57th bit in the input key, the 2nd bit of the permuted key is obtained from the 49th bit in the input key, and so on, until the 56th bit of the permuted key is obtained from the 4th bit of the input key.

```
DES_KEY_SCH_MACRO_ONE( ) \                                  // rotate left by one bit
        r3 = r1 >> 27;                r1 = r1 << 1; \
        r1 = r1 | (r3 & 0x10);        r3 = r2 >> 27; \
        r2 = r2 << 1; \
        r2 = r2 | (r3 & 0x10);

DES_KEY_SCH_MACRO_TWO( ) \                                  // rotate left by two bits
        r3 = r1 >> 26;                r1 = r1 << 2; \
        r1 = r1 | (r3 & 0x30);        r3 = r2 >> 26; \
        r2 = r2 << 2; \
        r2 = r2 | (r3 & 0x30);
```

Pcode 2.6: Simulation code for DES key scheduler macros.

```
// void DESKeySch( )

PermCh1(pc1);                              // call permutation choice 1
r1 = pc1[0];       r2 = pc1[1];
DES_KEY_SCH_MACRO_ONE( )
PermCh2(r1,r2);                            // call permute choice 2 (--> K1)
DES_KEY_SCH_MACRO_ONE( )
PermCh2(r1,r2);                            // --> K2
for(i = 0;i < 6;i++){
        DES_KEY_SCH_MACRO_TWO( )
        PermCh2(r1,r2);                    // --> K3 to K8
}
DES_KEY_SCH_MACRO_ONE( )
PermCh2(r1,r2);                            // --> K9
for(i = 0;i < 6;i++){
        DES_KEY_SCH_MACRO_TWO( )
        PermCh2(r1,r2);                    // --> K10 to K15
}
DES_KEY_SCH_MACRO_ONE( )
PermCh2(r1,r2);                            // --> K16
```

Pcode 2.7: Simulation code for DES key scheduler function.

Table 2.3: DES key scheduler permutation choice-1 table values

57	49	41	33	25	17	9
1	58	50	42	34	26	18
10	2	59	51	43	35	27
19	11	3	60	52	44	36
63	55	47	39	31	23	15
7	62	54	46	38	30	22
14	6	61	53	45	37	29
21	13	5	28	20	12	4

We do not use Table 2.3 directly in the simulation of PC-1 function; however, we generate the same outputs as what table values say. We simulate PC-1 function using logical AND, SHIFT, and OR operations instead of using a look-up table (since we consume fewer cycles on the reference embedded processor per bit with the analytic method given in Pcode 2.8 when compared to bit-mapping using look-up values). We demultiplex 64-bit key data into seven 8-bit words in a nested loop. In this process, the check bits 8, 16, 24, . . ., 64 present in the 64-bit key are removed by left shifting 2 bits (instead of 1 bit) at the end of each iteration of the inner loop.

After the loop, we obtain two 28-bit permuted words from seven 8-bit words by rearranging the demultiplexed bits. See Section 2.2.3, DES Simulation Results, for PC-1 simulation output results.

```
// void PermCh1(unsigned long *x3)

r1 = r2 = r3 = r4 = r5 = r6 = r7 = 0;
for(j = 0;j < 2;j++){
        tmp1 = des_key[j];
        for(i = 0;i < 4;i++){
                tmp2 = tmp1 & 0x80000000;      r1 = r1 >> 1;
                r1 = r1 | tmp2;                tmp1 = tmp1 << 1;
                tmp2 = tmp1 & 0x80000000;      r2 = r2 >> 1;
                r2 = r2 | tmp2;                tmp1 = tmp1 << 1;
                tmp2 = tmp1 & 0x80000000;      r3 = r3 >> 1;
                r3 = r3 | tmp2;                tmp1 = tmp1 << 1;
                tmp2 = tmp1 & 0x80000000;      r4 = r4 >> 1;
                r4 = r4 | tmp2;                tmp1 = tmp1 << 1;
                tmp2 = tmp1 & 0x80000000;      r5 = r5 >> 1;
                r5 = r5 | tmp2;                tmp1 = tmp1 << 1;
                tmp2 = tmp1 & 0x80000000;      r6 = r6 >> 1;
                r6 = r6 | tmp2;                tmp1 = tmp1 << 1;
                tmp2 = tmp1 & 0x80000000;      r7 = r7 >> 1;
                r7 = r7 | tmp2;                tmp1 = tmp1 << 2; // remove check bit
        }
}
tmp1 = r1;              r2 = r2 >> 8;
tmp1 = tmp1 | r2;       r3 = r3 >> 16;
tmp1 = tmp1 | r3;       r1 = r4 >> 28;
r1 = r1 << 4;
pc1[0] = tmp1 | r1;                                     // store permuted first 28-bits
tmp2 = r7;              r6 = r6 >> 8;
tmp2 = tmp2 | r6;       r5 = r5 >> 16;
tmp2 = tmp2 | r5;       r1 = r4 << 4;
r1 = r1 >> 28;
r1 = r1 << 4;
pc1[1] = tmp2 | r1;                                     // store permuted second 28-bits
```

Pcode 2.8: Simulation code for DES key scheduler PC-1.

Permutation Choice-2 In permutation choice-2 (PC-2), we use the following look-up values (which are derived from the FIPS PUB 46-3 standard PC-2 table) to perform shift operations:

```
pc2[48] = {
18,15,21, 8,31,27,29, 4,17,26,11,22, 9,13,20,28, 6,24,16,25, 5,12,19,30,
19, 8,29,23,13, 5,30,20, 9,15,27,12,16,11,21, 4,26, 7,14,18,10,24,31,28};
```

PC-2 function takes two 28-bit left-shifted inputs and outputs two 24-bit permuted outputs. To perform this process, we get a shift value from the **pc2**[ ] look-up table, and obtain the permuted bit by shifting right a 28-bit input word with that shift value and extracting the first bit by ANDing with 0x01. The output of the PC-2 function (24-bit permuted word) is stored to **ks_key**[ ] buffer. In Pcode 2.7, the PC-2 function is called a total of 16 times, and in each call it produces two 24-bit keywords. We use these expanded keys in both DES cipher and inverse cipher functions. The simulation code for the PC-2 function is given in Pcode 2.9. See Section 2.2.3, DES Simulation Results, for PC-2 simulation output results.

DES Function Simulation

In the DES function, we form a DES state using the given 64-bit input data and we update DES state with DESInitP( ) followed by a 16-iteration butterfly function and then followed by the DESFinalP( ) function. The butterfly loop itself consists of functions ExpandF( ), S-Box( ), and PermL( ). Figures 2.4 and 2.5 show the flow of the DES function. Both the cipher and inverse cipher use the same DES function except that the sequence in which the expanded keys are accessed differs. The simulation code for the DES cipher and DES inverse ciphers are given in Pcodes 2.10 and 2.11, respectively.

DES Initial Permutation The simulation techniques used for DES initial permutation (IP) is the same as the techniques used for simulating PC-1 function. In IP we permute all 64 input bits and output as 64 permuted bits (unlike in PC-1, where we eliminate the redundant bits from input). The simulation code for IP is given in Pcode 2.12. See Section 2.2.3, DES Simulation Results, for IP simulation output results.

DES Final Permutation We perform the DES final permutation (FP) as per the look-up table values of IP^{-1} given in the FIPS PUB 46-3. The function FP takes 64 bits as the input and outputs 64 permuted bits. We can also compute FP using the analytic method. Although we used the analytic method in the simulation code to perform FP, we get the same permuted bits as in the look-up table method. We use logical AND, SHIFT, and OR operations to perform FP with the analytic method. The simulation code for DES FP is given in Pcode 2.13.

```
// void PermCh2(unsigned long x1, unsigned long x2)

k = 0;
for(j = 0;j < 4;j++){
      tmp3 = 0;
      for(i = 0;i < 6;i++){
            tmp1 = pc2[k++];
            tmp2 = x1 >> tmp1;
            tmp2 = tmp2 & 0x01;   tmp3 = tmp3 << 1;
            tmp3 = tmp3 | tmp2;
      }
      ks_key[n++] = tmp3;                    // store permuted first 24-bit word
}
for(j = 0;j < 4;j++){
      tmp3 = 0;
      for(i = 0;i < 6;i++){
            tmp1 = pc2[k++];
            tmp2 = x2 >> tmp1;
            tmp2 = tmp2 & 0x01;   tmp3 = tmp3 << 1;
            tmp3 = tmp3 | tmp2;
      }
      ks_key[n++] = tmp3;                    // store permuted second 24-bit word
}
```

Pcode 2.9: Simulation code for DES key scheduler PC-2.

```
// void DESCipher()

des_state[0] = p_data[0];           des_state[1] = p_data[1];          // DES state
DESInitP();                                                            // initial permutation
j = 0;
for(i = 0;i < 16;i++){                                                 // butterfly loop
    Ln = des_state[0];    Rn = des_state[1];
    des_state[0] = Rn;                                                 // L[n] = R[n-1]
    // R[n] = L[n-1] XOR f(R[n-1],K[n]),f(R[n-1),K[n])-> P(S(E(R[n-1]) XOR K[n])))
    ExpandF(Rn,t);                                                     // E(R[n-1])
    t[0] = ks_key[j++]^t[0]; t[1] = ks_key[j++]^t[1];                  // E(R[n-1]) XOR K[n]
    t[2] = ks_key[j++]^t[2]; t[3] = ks_key[j++]^t[3];
    t[4] = ks_key[j++]^t[4]; t[5] = ks_key[j++]^t[5];
    t[6] = ks_key[j++]^t[6]; t[7] = ks_key[j++]^t[7];
    S_Box(t);                                                          // S(E(R[n-1]) XOR K[n])
    tmp = PermL(t);                                                    // P(S(E([n-1]) XOR K[n]))
    des_state[1] = Ln^tmp;                                             // L[n-1] XOR f(R[n-1],K[n])
}
Ln = des_state[0];                  Rn = des_state[1];
des_state[0] = Rn;
des_state[1] = Ln;
DESFinalP();                                                           // final permutation
```

Pcode 2.10: Simulation code for DES cipher.

```
// void DESInvCipher()

des_state[0] = c_data[0];                des_state[1] = c_data[1];
DESInitP();                                                            // initial permutation
j = 120;                                 // key words accessing index initialization
for(i = 0;i < 16;i++){
     Ln = des_state[0];        Rn = des_state[1];
     des_state[0] = Rn;                                                // L[n] = R[n-1],
     // R[n] = L[n-1] (+) f(R[n-1], K[n]),f(R[n-1),K[n])-> P(S(E(R[n-1]) (+) K[n])))
     ExpandF(Rn,t);                                                    // E(R[n-1])
     t[0] = ks_key[j++]^t[0]; t[1] = ks_key[j++]^t[1];                 // E(R[n-1]) (+) K[n]
     t[2] = ks_key[j++]^t[2]; t[3] = ks_key[j++]^t[3];
     t[4] = ks_key[j++]^t[4]; t[5] = ks_key[j++]^t[5];
     t[6] = ks_key[j++]^t[6]; t[7] = ks_key[j++]^t[7];
     S_Box(t);                                                         // S(E(R[n-1]) (+) K[n])
     tmp = PermL(t);                                                   // P(S(E([n-1]) (+) K[n]))
     des_state[1] = Ln^tmp;                                            // L[n-1] (+) f(R[n-1],K[n])
     j-= 16;
}
Ln = des_state[0];                   Rn = des_state[1];
des_state[0] = Rn;
des_state[1] = Ln;
DESFinalP();                                                           // final permutation
```

Pcode 2.11: Simulation code for DES inverse cipher.

The output of FP gives the cipher text in the case of the DES cipher and gives plain text in the case of the DES inverse cipher.

Expand Function The Expand function (E-function) is part of the butterfly function $f(.)$, which is iterated 16 times in the main DES function. The E-function expands the 32 bit input data to 48 bits by repeating few bits two times. We perform E-function as per the E-BIT SELECTION TABLE given in the FIPS PUB 46-3 standard. In the simulation code given in Pcode 2.14, we used an analytic method to simulate the E-function.

S-Box Mixing In S-Box mixing, we output a 4-bit word from 6-bit input data by using a 2-dimensional S-Box mixing look-up table. As shown in Figure 2.5, we obtain a total of eight 4-bit words (32 bits) from eight 6-bit words (48 bits), by using eight S-Box mixing look-up tables. In the simulation code given in Pcode 2.15, we

```
// void DESInitP( )

r1 = r2 = r3 = r4 = r5 = r6 = r7 = r8 = 0;
for(j = 0;j < 2;j++){
      tmp1 = des_state[j];
      for(i = 0;i < 4;i++){
            tmp2 = tmp1 & 0x80000000;
            r1 = r1 >> 1;   tmp1 = tmp1 << 1;
            r1 = r1 | tmp2; tmp2 = tmp1 & 0x80000000;
            r2 = r2 >> 1;   tmp1 = tmp1 << 1;
            r2 = r2 | tmp2; tmp2 = tmp1 & 0x80000000;
            r3 = r3 >> 1;   tmp1 = tmp1 << 1;
            r3 = r3 | tmp2; tmp2 = tmp1 & 0x80000000;
            r4 = r4 >> 1;   tmp1 = tmp1 << 1;
            r4 = r4 | tmp2; tmp2 = tmp1 & 0x80000000;
            r5 = r5 >> 1;   tmp1 = tmp1 << 1;
            r5 = r5 | tmp2; tmp2 = tmp1 & 0x80000000;
            r6 = r6 >> 1;   tmp1 = tmp1 << 1;
            r6 = r6 | tmp2; tmp2 = tmp1 & 0x80000000;
            r7 = r7 >> 1;   tmp1 = tmp1 << 1;
            r7 = r7 | tmp2; tmp2 = tmp1 & 0x80000000;
            r8 = r8 >> 1;   tmp1 = tmp1 << 1;
            r8 = r8 | tmp2;
      }
}
tmp1 = r2;                        r4 = r4 >> 8;
tmp1 = tmp1 | r4;                 r6 = r6 >> 16;
tmp1 = tmp1 | r6;                 r8 = r8 >> 24;
des_state[0] = tmp1 | r8;                                 // store permuted first 32-bits
tmp2 = r1;                        r3 = r3 >> 8;
tmp2 = tmp2 | r3;                 r5 = r5 >> 16;
tmp2 = tmp2 | r5;                 r7 = r7 >> 24;
des_state[1] = tmp2 | r7;                                 // store permuted second 32-bits
```

Pcode 2.12: Simulation code for initial permutation of DES function.

```
// void DESFinalP( )

r1 = 25;                r2 = 24;
r3 = 25;                r4 = 24;
tmp1 = des_state[0];    tmp2 = des_state[1];
tmp3 = 0;               tmp4 = 0;
for(i = 0;i < 4;i++){
      for(j = 0;j < 4;j++){
            r5 = tmp1 & 0x80000000;     r6 = tmp2 & 0x80000000;
            r5 = r5 >> r1;              r6 = r6 >> r2;
            tmp4 = tmp4 | r5;           tmp1 = tmp1 << 1;
            tmp4 = tmp4 | r6;           tmp2 = tmp2 << 1;
            r1-= 8;                     r2-= 8;
      }
      for(j = 0;j < 4;j++){
            r5 = tmp1 & 0x80000000;     r6 = tmp2 & 0x80000000;
            r5 = r5 >> r3;              r6 = r6 >> r4;
            tmp3 = tmp3 | r5;           tmp1 = tmp1 << 1;
            tmp3 = tmp3 | r6;           tmp2 = tmp2 << 1;
            r3-= 8;                     r4-= 8;
      }
      r1+= 34;  r2+= 34;
      r3+= 34;  r4+= 34;
}
des_state[0] = tmp3;
des_state[1] = tmp4;
```

Pcode 2.13: Simulation code for final permutation of DES function.

perform S-Box mixing by combining eight look-up tables into a single big look-up table **sb**[ ] and accessing the corresponding 4-bit words with appropriate offsets. The look-up table **sb**[ ] values can be found on this book's companion website.

```
// void ExpandF(unsigned long x, unsigned char *y)

r1 = x << 3;      r3 = x << 7;
r2 = r1 >> 26;    r4 = r3 >> 26;
y[1] = r2;        y[2] = r4;
r1 = x << 11;     r3 = x << 15;
r2 = r1 >> 26;    r4 = r3 >> 26;
y[3] = r2;        y[4] = r4;
r1 = x << 19;     r3 = x << 23;
r2 = r1 >> 26;    r4 = r3 >> 26;
y[5] = r2;        y[6] = r4;
r1 = x << 27;     r3 = x << 31;
r2 = r1 >> 26;    r4 = r3 >> 26;
r1 = x >> 31;     r3 = x >> 27;
r2 = r2 | r1;     r4 = r4 | r3;
y[7] = r2;        y[0] = r4;
```

Pcode 2.14: Simulation code for Expand function of DES butterfly function $f(.)$.

```
// void S_Box(unsigned char *y)

for(i = 0;i < 8;i++){
    r1 = y[i];
    r2 = r1 & 1;      r3 = r1 >> 5;
    r1 = r1 >> 1;
    r1 = r1 & 0x0f;   r3 = r3 << 5;
    r2 = r2 << 4;     r3 = r3 | r1;
    r3 = r3 | r2;
    r3 = i*64+r3;
    r2 = sb[r3];
    y[i] = r2;
}
```

Pcode 2.15: Simulation code for S-Box mixing in DES butterfly function $f(.)$.

```
// unsigned long PermL(unsigned char *y)

tmp = 0;                  r2 = 0;
for(i = 0;i < 8;i++){
     tmp = tmp << 4;
     tmp = tmp | y[i];                        // pack 4-bit words to 32-bit word
}
for(i = 0;i < 32;i++){
     r2 = r2 << 1;     r1 = tmp >> PermtL[i];
     r1 = r1 & 1;
     r2 = r2 | r1;
}
return r2;
```

Pcode 2.16: Simulation code for permutation in DES butterfly function $f(.)$.

Permutation The permutation function of the DES butterfly function $f(.)$ takes 32 bits of data as input and outputs 32 bits as permuted data. The simulation code for the permutation operation of the butterfly function is given in Pcode 2.16. We use the following shift values look-up table **PermtL**[ ] (the same as Table 2.2, which is derived from Table 2.1) to perform the permutation operation.

```
PermtL[32] = {
16,25,12,11,3,20, 4,15,31,17,9, 6,27,14, 1,22,
30,24, 8,18,0, 5,29,23,13,19,2,26,10,21,28, 7};
```

DES Simulation Results

Input: **p_data**[ ], 64-bit plain text and **des_key**[ ], 64-bit encoded key

```
p_data[2] = {0x01122334, 0x45566778};
des_key[2] = {0x0f1e2d3c, 0x4b5a6978};
```

Key Scheduler

PC-1 output: **xx**[ ], 56-bit or two 28-bit words (after removing check bits)

```
xx[2]={0x00f0cca0, 0x330fffa0};          // left aligned
```

Left shifts output: **yy**[ ], two 28-bit words (after rotating 1 bit left)

```
yy[2]={0x01e19940, 0x661fff40};          // left aligned
```

PC-2 output: **zz**[ ], eight 6-bit words

```
zz[8]={0x1c, 0x03, 0x03, 0x24, 0x3a, 0x3d, 0x32, 0x38};
```

Key scheduler output: **ks_key**[ ], 128 6-bit words

```
ks_key[128]={
0x1C,0x03,0x03,0x24,0x3A,0x3D,0x32,0x38,0x00,0x09,0x31,0x34,0x22,0x3F,0x3B,0x3A,
0x31,0x06,0x21,0x12,0x2F,0x1D,0x3C,0x31,0x09,0x2E,0x1C,0x20,0x26,0x34,0x39,0x36,
0x32,0x21,0x14,0x03,0x37,0x1E,0x2E,0x14,0x1A,0x18,0x09,0x19,0x2C,0x16,0x1B,0x1D,
0x01,0x1D,0x02,0x0A,0x3E,0x3B,0x0A,0x07,0x0C,0x20,0x27,0x12,0x2D,0x26,0x1E,0x2F,
0x04,0x25,0x28,0x11,0x0D,0x37,0x36,0x07,0x03,0x13,0x25,0x04,0x1B,0x22,0x07,0x37,
0x00,0x26,0x13,0x0D,0x39,0x3F,0x27,0x0F,0x16,0x14,0x14,0x20,0x19,0x29,0x1F,0x1B,
0x30,0x08,0x26,0x29,0x37,0x39,0x15,0x2F,0x24,0x1A,0x08,0x07,0x13,0x2D,0x3F,0x28,
0x08,0x11,0x3A,0x02,0x16,0x0F,0x35,0x3D,0x18,0x03,0x08,0x08,0x3B,0x0D,0x31,0x3D};
```

DES Cipher

DES state: **des_state**[ ], 64-bit data copied from **p_data**[ ]

```
des_state[2]={0x01122334, 0x45566778};
```

Initial permutation output: **des_state**[ ], 64-bit permuted data

```
des_state[2]={0xf0aa7855, 0x00cc8066};
```

DES Butterfly output: **des_state**[ ], 64-bit intermediate data after each iteration

```
des_state[2]={0x00cc8066, 0xc9ed3c55};    // after first iteration
des_state[2]={0xc9ed3c55, 0x8e6d9383};    // after second iteration
des_state[2]={0x8e6d9383, 0xd42d8678};    // after third iteration
des_state[2]={0xd42d8678, 0x67202012};    // after fourth iteration
des_state[2]={0x67202012, 0xa319a3bc};    // after fifth iteration
des_state[2]={0xa319a3bc, 0x80dd257e};    // after sixth iteration
des_state[2]={0x80dd257e, 0x31ead8ed};    // after seventh iteration
des_state[2]={0x31ead8ed, 0x38f0ff66};    // after eighth iteration
des_state[2]={0x38f0ff66, 0xd10d67a6};    // after ninth iteration
des_state[2]={0xd10d67a6, 0xcf0a862c};    // after tenth iteration
des_state[2]={0xcf0a862c, 0x7dd727c4};    // after eleventh iteration
des_state[2]={0x7dd727c4, 0xafceae47};    // after twelfth iteration
des_state[2]={0xafceae47, 0xb9bdad67};    // after thirteenth iteration
des_state[2]={0xb9bdad67, 0xcced41af};    // after fourteenth iteration
des_state[2]={0xcced41af, 0x70cb25bd};    // after fifteenth iteration
des_state[2]={0x70cb25bd, 0x1491f770};    // after sixteenth iteration
```

Pre-encrypted DES output: **des_state**[ ], 64-bit intermediate data

```
des_state[2]={0x1491f770, 0x70cb25bd};
```

Final permutation output: **des_state**[ ], 64-bit output data

```
des_state[2]={0x3e244e22, 0xd78fa536};
```

Output: **c_data**[ ], 64-bit cipher text

```
c_data[2]={0x3e244e22, 0xd78fa536};
```

2.2.4 Computational Complexity of DES Algorithm

Most of the operations involved in the DES key scheduler, DES cipher and DES inverse cipher are bit operations rather than byte or word operations and consume more cycles to run DES on the reference embedded processor as we process all the data in terms of bits. For more details on clock cycle requirements for particular operations, see Appendix A, Section A.4, on this book's companion website.

Complexity of DES Key Scheduler

Permutation Choice-1 In PC-1, we use a permutation table as shown in Table 2.3 to get a permuted key data from input key data. We do not use Table 2.3 directly in the simulation of PC-1; however, using Pcode 2.8, we generate the same outputs as the table values. We estimate the clock cycles requirement for PC-1 operation. With the approach used to simulate PC-1, we have a nested loop in the program. The inner loop runs four times and the outer loop runs two times. In these loops, we basically demultiplex the 64-bit input key into seven 8-bit words. From Pcode 2.8, to demultiplex 1 bit we perform four operations and that takes four cycles. We consume $224(=56*4)$ cycles for 56 input key bits. For rearranging the demultiplexed bits to get the final two 28-bit words, we consume 18 cycles. We consume another 18 cycles in initialization, loading input key and for removing check bits. With this, we consume about 260 cycles to perform the PC-1 operation.

Permutation Choice-2 The next big module in the DES key scheduler is permutation choice (PC) 2. The DES standard, FIPS PUB 46-3, specifies another table for PC-2 functionality. In the simulation of PC-2 operation, we use derived values from a standard table for extracting the permuted bit with a reference embedded processor. The look-up values for PC-2 are generated by subtracting the standard table values from 32. In PC-2 simulation as given in Pcode 2.9, we have two nested loops. For the inner loop, we consume five cycles. The inner loop runs six times, and the outer loop, four times. Therefore, we consume a total of $128(=(6*5+2)*4)$ cycles in a single nested loop. A total $256(=2*128)$ cycles for two nested loops are consumed in performing the PC-2 operation. We perform the PC-2 operation 16 times in the DES key scheduler and we consume a total $4096(=16*256)$ cycles.

Apart from permutations, the DES key scheduler performs left shifts of two 28-bit words and these operations consume about $128(=16*8)$ cycles. With this, to run the DES key scheduler on the reference embedded processor, we spend about $4484(=260+128+4096)$ cycles.

Complexity of DES Cipher

Now we discuss the complexity of the DES cipher module. In the DES cipher, we perform an initial permutation (IP), a butterfly loop with $f(.)$ function and a final permutation (FP). The complex part of the DES cipher is its butterfly loop. The nonlinear butterfly function $f(.)$ consists of three subfunctions, expand, S-Box mixing and permutation.

Initial Permutation The operations IP (Pcode 2.12) for the cipher and PC-1 (Pcode 2.8) for the key scheduler are almost similar and clock cycle consumption of IP is the same as that of PC-1. Therefore, about 260 clock cycles are required to run IP on the reference embedded processor.

Final Permutation The FP operation consists of a nested loop with two inner loops as given in Pcode 2.13. Each inner loop consumes 40 cycles. We consume a total of $346(=[2*40+4]*4+10)$ cycles in performing the FP operation with a reference embedded processor.

Expand Function As given in Pcode 2.14, the simulation code of the expansion subfunction does not have any dependencies and each operation consumes a single cycle. Therefore, the expansion subfunction consumes a total of 28 cycles.

S-Box Mixing We use Pcode 2.15 for S-Box mixing to obtain 4-bit words from 6-bit words. We consume 12 cycles for obtaining a single 4-bit word and we consume about 96 cycles for obtaining eight 4-bit words.

Permutation The third subfunction of the butterfly function $f(.)$ is a permutation operation. This operation is costly in terms of cycle as it involves 32 bits permutation. In butterfly permutation, first we pack eight 4-bit words to a 32-bit word and it takes 16 cycles. Then we use a look-up table to permute the 32-bit word. We consume five cycles in getting 1 permuted bit. Therefore, we consume 160 cycles for permutation of 32 bits. We consume a total of 176 cycles in performing the permutation operation.

With this, the total number of clock cycles required for the butterfly function is $300(=28+96+176)$ cycles. Apart from the butterfly function, we perform adding the key to the expanded input data and storing the temporary data via swapping. These operations take 29 cycles. Therefore, in a single iteration of the DES cipher, we consume $329(=300+29)$ cycles to process the data. Now, for 16 iterations, we consume $5264(=329*16)$ cycles. With this, the total number of cycles required to get a 64-bit cipher text from 64-bit plain text using the DES cipher is 5870(= 260 + 346 + 5264) cycles. As both the DES cipher and inverse cipher have the same flow, the DES inverse cipher also consumes about the same number of cycles.

This clock cycles estimate is meaningful only when we interleave the program code (since many look-up table accesses with immediate usage consume more than one cycle if we do not interleave the program code) in implementation of the DES algorithm. Otherwise (i.e., without interleaving the program code), the cycle estimate for the DES algorithm is much more than the previous estimated numbers. As the DES key scheduler does not work in real time, we not discuss further about its optimization. In the next section, we discuss the optimization techniques for DES cipher modules.

2.2.5 Efficient Implementation of DES Cipher

As discussed in the previous section, the DES cipher module consists of three steps. The first and last steps are permutations and the middle step is the butterfly loop. The costliest step is the butterfly loop, which consumes about 5264 clock cycles to encrypt or decrypt the data using an expanded key. In this section, we discuss the efficient way of implementing the butterfly-loop function.

As discussed, the function $f(.)$ in the butterfly loop consists of three steps: expansion, S-Box mixing and permutation. As shown in Figure 2.5, after expanding 32-bit data ($R[n-1]$) to 48-bit data and XORing with keywords ($K[n]$), we have eight 6-bit words. In the S-Box mixing, we get eight 4-bit output words from eight 6-bit input words. Then, we merge the eight 4-bit words to a single 32-bit word before permutation. The permutation operation maps bits one-to-one from input 32-bit word to output 32-bit permuted word. This one-to-one mapping of bits by the permutation operation gives us the scope for optimizing the butterfly loop. After careful observation, the last two steps of S-Box mixing and permutation operation can be combined as follows. The following equation is valid for S-Box mixing and permutation operations.

$$y = \mathrm{S}_i\text{-Box}[x]$$
$$z = \mathrm{P}(y) = \mathrm{M}_i[x]$$

Here $\mathrm{M}_i[x]$ contains the permuted values of S_i-Box elements. We understand the meaning of the previous equations with an example. Assume $i = 1$ and $x = 48$, then y is obtained from first S-Box and is equal to 15 (as we get second row and eighth column of S-Box from the value 110,000 [= 48] with the first and last bits representing the row index and the middle 4 bits representing the column index). Now the value of z is obtained by permuting the bits of value 15 (= 1111 in binary form). Here we know that $i = 1$ and hence the location of bits in the merged 32-bit word are the first 4 bits (from left). According to the permutation table given in Table 2.1, the 1st bit goes to the 9th position, the 2nd bit goes to the 17th position, the 3rd bit goes to the 23rd position and the 4th bit goes to the 31st position in the permuted word. Therefore the permuted value z is equal to 0x00808202 (0000 0000 1000 0000 1000 0010 0000 0010). If the value of x is the same (equal to 48) but the S-Box number is different (i.e., i is other than one), then the value of z will be different from 0x00808202 as the position of bits of y in the merged word occupy a position different from the first four positions.

We store the look-up table $\mathrm{M}_i[x]$ elements such that the elements are accessed linearly (that means, if $x = 48$, then the corresponding element present in the look-up table $\mathrm{M}_i[x]$ is at the location with offset equal to 48). Therefore, in this case, unpacking and packing of bits (to simulate as specified in the standard, like first and last bit represents row index and middle 4 bits represents column index) is not needed to implement it. The elements in $\mathrm{M}_i[x]$ are comprised of 32-bit words. If we want to permute all eight S-Box values in advance, then we need 2 kB (= 512*4) of on-chip memory. The 512 elements of $\mathrm{M}_i[x]$ can be found on the companion website.

With this, the butterfly-loop flow can be viewed as eight independent parallel flows as shown in Figure 2.6. The simulation code for efficient implementation of the DES butterfly loop is given in Pcode 2.17. In the first step, we get expanded 6-bit words from an input 32-bit word for all eight paths. In the second step we XOR eight expanded 6-bit words with eight 6-bit keywords. In the third step, we get permuted S-Box elements for all eight paths by using eight XORed 6-bit values as offsets to the look-up table $\mathrm{M}_i[x]$. Finally, we OR all eight paths' 32-bit words (which are orthogonal to each other with respect to bit-positions filled by placing four permuted bits) to get one 32-bit word as the butterfly function $f(.)$ output. In this approach, we have more scope to interleave

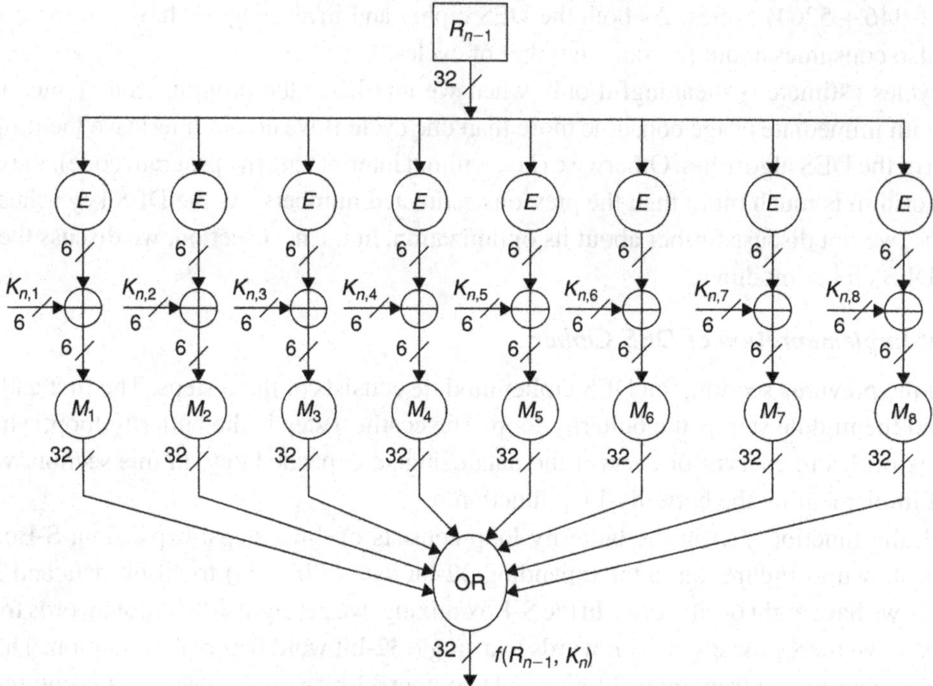

Figure 2.6: Efficient implementation of DES butterfly flow.

```
j = 0;
for(i = 0;i < 16;i++){
     r2 = des_state[1];
     r1 = r2 << 31;     tmp1 = r2 >> 1;
     r1 = tmp1 | r1;
     tmp1 = r1 >> 26;
     tmp1 = tmp1^ks_key[j++];
     tmp2 = M[tmp1];
     for(k=1;k < 7;k++)       {
            r1 = r1 << 4;
            tmp1 = r1 >> 26;                 // get 6-bit words
            tmp1 = tmp1^ks_key[j++];         // XOR with key
            tmp1 = tmp1 + 64*k;              // get offset
            tmp1 = M[tmp1];
            tmp2 = tmp2 | tmp1;
     }
     r1 = r2 >> 31;            tmp1 = r2 << 1;
     r1 = r1 | tmp1;
     tmp1 = r1 & 0x3f;
     tmp1 = tmp1^ks_key[j++];
     tmp1 = tmp1 + 64*7;
     tmp1 = M[tmp1];
     tmp2 = tmp2 | tmp1;  r1 = des_state[0];
     r1 = r1^tmp2;
     des_state[0] = r2;
     des_state[1] = r1;
}
```

Pcode 2.17: Simulation code for efficient implementation of DES loop.

the program code. Also, it is easy to distribute the workload to multiple ALUs of deep pipelined embedded processor.

Now, we discuss the clock cycle consumption of the DES cipher with the suggested implementation of the DES butterfly loop. As seen in Pcode 2.17, in the butterfly loop, we consume six cycles for all three operations—expansion, S-Box mixing and permutation in paths 2 to 6, whereas in 1 and 8, we consume eight cycles. Once we get $f(R[n-1], K[n])$, we update the left and right outputs of the butterfly as $L[n] = R[n-1]$ and $R[n] = L[n-1] \oplus f(R[n-1], K[n])$. These operations consume about four cycles. We consume a total

56 (= 6*6 + 2*8 + 4) cycles for one iteration of the butterfly loop. So, cycles required for the butterfly loop total 896 (= 56*16), whereas the original approach consumes 5624 cycles as discussed in the previous section. As the suggested approach is easily extendable to multiple ALUs, the cycles' consumption for the DES butterfly loop on a four-ALU embedded processor is about 225 cycles. The same look-up table values and suggested butterfly-loop implementation can also be used for DES inverse cipher.

2.3 Advanced Encryption Standard

The advanced encryption standard is the latest data security standard known as FIPS 197 (Federal Information Processing Standard, 2001) adopted worldwide by most public and private sectors, for secure data communications and data storage purposes. The AES is used in a large variety of applications, from mobile consumer products to high-end servers.

2.3.1 Introduction to AES Algorithm

The AES algorithm is a symmetric key algorithm, standardized by the National Institute of Science and Technology (NIST) in 2001. The AES standard (Federal Information Processing Standard, 2001) specifies the Rijndael algorithm that can process data blocks of 128 bits, using keys of 128-, 192-, or 256-bit length (and we call the AES with particular key length AES-128, AES-192, and AES-256). The AES encipher (cipher) converts data (plain text) to an unintelligible form (cipher text) using the cipher key, and the AES decipher (inverse cipher) converts the cipher text back to plain text using the same cipher key. In AES, we use the same key (hence it is a symmetric key algorithm) for both encryption and decryption. AES encryption and decryption are based on four different transformations applied repeatedly in a certain sequence on input data and the flows of encryption and decryption are not same. The AES standard also specifies a key expansion module to supply keys for multiple iterations of the AES algorithm. Depending on input key length, the number of iterations (or complexity) of the AES algorithm (including key expansion, encryption and decryption) will vary.

In this chapter, we discuss the flow of the AES algorithm and simulation of AES-128 key expansion, the AES cipher, and the AES inverse cipher modules. In addition, we discuss the computational complexity of AES and efficient techniques to implement the AES cipher and inverse cipher on the reference embedded processor.

A few applications include data communications, data storage, Internet, military applications, classified data management, and memory protection. Similar to the AES, the TDEA (triple data encryption algorithm) is used in all applications mentioned previously (see Section 2.2). The strength of an encryption algorithm depends on its mathematical properties and supported key lengths. The DES is a very old standard with less key space and analysts thoroughly understood and attacked DES cipher text. Whereas AES was developed recently and its key space is very large. No known attacks and no known weak keys exist for AES as of now.

2.3.2 AES Algorithm Description

The flow diagram of an AES encryption engine is shown in Figure 2.7. The main transformations in the AES Rijndael's cipher are (1) AddRoundKey (AR), (2) SubBytes (SB), (3) ShiftRows (SR), and (4) MixColumns (MC). All these transforms work on a matrix called *state* that is formed using the input data. The AES state is updated in multiple iterations using the previous transformations. The key expansion (KE) module expands the given key for supplying the keys to all iterations of the AES cipher engine. The number of times the state is iterated in a loop of the AES algorithm depends on what key length (N_k) we have chosen. For example, if we choose the key length of 128 bits (i.e., $N_k = 4$ 32-bit words), then we iterate the data ($N_r - 1$) times, where $N_r = N_b + N_k + 2$ and $N_b = 4$. In the AES algorithm, the parameter $N_b (= 4)$ corresponds to the number of rows of state. AR transformation is applied before starting the loop. The transformations present within an AES loop are SB, SR, MC, and AR. In addition, the transformations SB, SR, and AR are applied after the loop before outputting the cipher text. We define each of these transformations in the following. For pictorial illustrations of SB, SR, MC, and AR, please refer to Federal Information Processing Standards (2001).

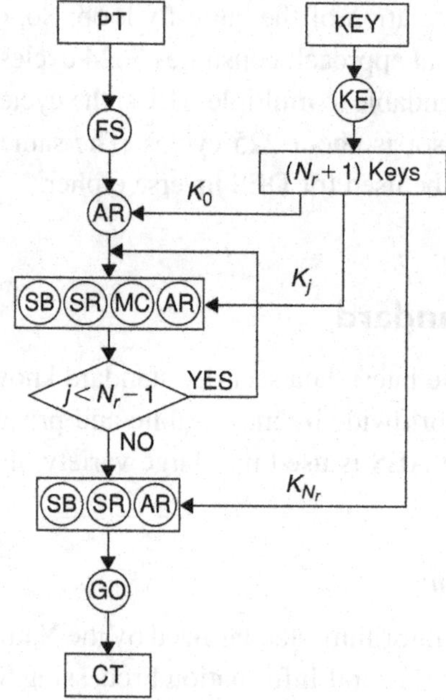

Figure 2.7: AES encryption engine.

The input to the AES algorithm is 128 bits (16-bytes) of plain text and a key of any following three lengths: 128 bits (or 16 bytes), 192 bits (or 24 bytes) or 256 bits (or 32 bytes). An overview of major steps in the AES algorithm follows.

Form State (FS): At the start of the cipher, the input bytes $in_0, in_1, \ldots, in_{15}$ are copied into the state matrix as $S_{r,c} = in_{r+4c}$ for $0 \le r < 4, 0 \le c < 4$. After FormState(), the elements $S_{r,c}$ of AES state are given here.

$$\begin{bmatrix} S_{00} & S_{01} & S_{02} & S_{03} \\ S_{10} & S_{11} & S_{12} & S_{13} \\ S_{20} & S_{21} & S_{22} & S_{23} \\ S_{30} & S_{31} & S_{32} & S_{33} \end{bmatrix} = \begin{bmatrix} in_0 & in_4 & in_8 & in_{12} \\ in_1 & in_5 & in_9 & in_{13} \\ in_2 & in_6 & in_{10} & in_{14} \\ in_3 & in_7 & in_{11} & in_{15} \end{bmatrix}$$

Get Output (GO): Reverse operation of FS.

Key Expansion (KE): The key expansion module generates a total of $N_b(N_r+1)$ keywords, as the AES algorithm requires that many keywords to encrypt the data. As shown in Figure 2.7, we expand the given key with the key expansion module before processing data with the AES algorithm. More details of AES key expansion is given in Section 2.3.3, AES-128 Key Expansion Simulation, and in Section 2.3.4, Complexity of AESKeyExp().

Add Round Key (AR) Transformation: In add round key transformation, $4N_b$ 8-bit keywords are added to the state by a simple bit-wise XOR operation. For $0 \le i \le N_r$, $S_{r,c} = S_{r,c} \oplus K_{16i+4r+c}$ where, $0 \le c < 4$ and $0 \le r < N_b$.

Substitution Bytes (SB) Transformation: The substitution bytes transformation is a nonlinear byte substitution operation that operates independently on each byte of the state using the substitution table. In SB, we simply replace the state elements with the S-Box elements using state element as an offset to S-Box table. The AES algorithm substitution tables for the AES cipher (S-Box) and AES inverse cipher (inverse S-Box) are available on the companion website.

Shift Rows (SR) Transformation: In the shift rows transformation, the byte positions in the last three rows of the state are cyclically shifted (to the left in the case of encryption and to the right in the case of decryption) by different number of offsets. The first row, $r=0$ is not shifted. The shift offset value depends on the row number r as follows:

$$\text{shift}(r=0)=0, \text{shift}(r=1)=1, \text{shift}(r=2)=2 \text{ and } \text{shift}(r=3)=3$$

Mix Columns (MC) Transformation: Mix columns transformation operates on the states column-by-column treating each column as a four element vector: $S'_i = A \cdot S_i$, where

$$S_i = \begin{bmatrix} s_{i,0} \\ s_{i,1} \\ s_{i,2} \\ s_{i,3} \end{bmatrix}, \text{ for encryption } A = \begin{bmatrix} 02 & 03 & 01 & 01 \\ 01 & 02 & 03 & 01 \\ 01 & 01 & 02 & 03 \\ 03 & 01 & 01 & 02 \end{bmatrix} \text{ and for decryption } A = \begin{bmatrix} 0e & 0b & 0d & 09 \\ 09 & 0e & 0b & 0d \\ 0d & 09 & 0e & 0b \\ 0b & 0d & 09 & 0e \end{bmatrix}$$

For details on the computation process of MC transformation, see the following Section 2.3.4, Complexity of MixColumns( ).

2.3.3 AES-128 Simulation

With the AES-128 algorithm, we use 128-bit-length keys. We initialize the parameters for the AES-128 algorithm as $N_k = 4$ (number of 32-bit input keywords), $N_b = 4$ (number of state rows) and $N_r = 10$ $(= N_b + N_k + 2)$, the number of iterations in the AES loop. In the following sections, we simulate the AES-128 key expansion module and the AES-128 cipher and inverse-cipher transformations.

AES-128 Key Expansion Simulation

The AES-128 algorithm uses a total of $176 (= 4 \cdot (N_r + 1) \cdot N_k)$ bytes of key in the encryption or decryption process. We expand the given 16 bytes (or 128 bits) of input key to 176 bytes for the AES algorithm. The simulation code of key expansion module AESKeyExp( ) for AES-128 algorithm is given in Pcode 2.18. We discuss more details on AESKeyExp( ) module in Section 2.3.4, Complexity of AESKeyExp( ).

For a given 128-bit (or 16 bytes) input key, an expanded key of 44 words (or 176 bytes) generated with AESKeyExp( ) module follows:

AES-128 Key Expansion Module Input

```
key[4] = {
0x47f11a71, 0x1d29c589, 0x6fb7620e, 0xaa18be1b};
```

```
i = 0;                          // key expansion array index
while (i < pAes->Nk){
 exp_key[i] = key[i];           // the first Nk words of key expansion is same as input key
 i++;
}
k = pAes->Nb * (pAes->Nr + 1);// loop count
j = 0;
temp = exp_key[i-1];            // at this point, i = Nk,
while (i < k){                  // this while loop code generates 4 key words in one iteration
 Rc = temp << 8;                // substitute bytes + shift rows transformations
 Rc = Rc >> 24;
 w = S_Box[Rc];                 Rc = temp << 16;
 w = w << 8;                    Rc = Rc >> 24;
 w = w | S_Box[Rc];             Rc = temp & 0xff;
 w = w << 8;
 w = w | S_Box[Rc]; Rc = temp >> 24;
 w = w << 8;
 w = w | S_Box[Rc]; Rc = Rcon[j++];
 Rc = Rc << 24;
 temp = w ^ Rc;                 w = exp_key[i-pAes->Nk];
 temp = temp ^ w;               w = exp_key[i-pAes->Nk];
 exp_key[i++] = temp;           temp = temp ^ w;
 exp_key[i++] = temp;           w = exp_key[i-pAes->Nk];
 temp = temp ^  w;              w = exp_key[i-pAes->Nk];
 exp_key[i++] = temp;           temp = temp ^ w;
 exp_key[i++] = temp;
}
```

Pcode 2.18: Simulation code for AESKeyExp( ) module.

AES-128 Key Expansion Module Output

```
exp_key[44] = {
0x47f11a71, 0x1d29c589, 0x6fb7620e, 0xaa18be1b, 0xeb5fb5dd, 0xf6767054,
0x99c1125a, 0x33d9ac41, 0xdcce361e, 0x2ab8464a, 0xb3795410, 0x80a0f851,
0x388fe7d3, 0x1237a199, 0xa14ef589, 0x21ee0dd8, 0x1858862e, 0x0a6f27b7,
0xab21d23e, 0x8acfdfe6, 0x82c60850, 0x88a92fe7, 0x2388fdd9, 0xa947223f,
0x02557d83, 0x8afc5264, 0xa974afbd, 0x00338d82, 0x81086ee0, 0x0bf43c84,
0xa2809339, 0xa2b31ebb, 0x6c7a84da, 0x678eb85e, 0xc50e2b67, 0x67bd35dc,
0x0dec025f, 0x6a62ba01, 0xaf6c9166, 0xc8d1a4ba, 0x05a5f6b7, 0x6fc74cb6,
0xc0abddd0, 0x087a796a};
```

AES Cipher Simulation

As discussed in Section 2.3.2, AES Cipher consists of four transformations, and we use the following function names for each transformation: SubBytes() for substitute bytes transformation, ShiftRows() for shift rows transformation, AddRoundKey() for add round key transformation and MixColumns() for mix column transformation.

AddRoundKey() In add round key transformation, we add 16 key bytes to 16 bytes of AES state. The addition operation is modulo 2 addition and we simulate this operation by XORing key bytes with state bytes as given in Pcode 2.19. As the expanded key **exp_key**[] from AESKeyExp() module is in terms of 32-bit words, we unpack **exp_key**[] words into bytes and add to state.

SubBytes() In simulation of SubBytes() transformation, we replace each AES state byte with S-Box element as given in Pcode 2.20.

ShiftRows() transformation rotates AES state rows to the left by a particular number of bytes depending on the row number. The simulation code for the ShiftRows() transformation is given in Pcode 2.21. As the state elements are represented with bytes, we simulate the shift rows transformation in terms of load and store bytes rather with a logical cyclic shift of 32-bit words.

MixColumns() In the MixColumns() transformation, we multiply each column of state with the matrix A for encryption process as specified in Section 2.3.2. In this process, we multiply each state byte with 0x02 by performing a Galois field multiplication in GF(2^8). More details on the MixColumns() transformation is given in Section 2.3.4, Complexity of MixColumns(). The simulation code for MixColumns() is given in Pcode 2.22.

```
for(j = 0;j < 4;j++){
    tmp1 = exp_key[k++];
    tmp2 = tmp1 >> 24;
    state[0][j] = t[0][j]^tmp2;    tmp2 = (tmp1 & 0x00ff0000) >> 16;
    state[1][j] = t[1][j]^tmp2;    tmp2 = (tmp1 & 0x0000ff00) >> 8;
    state[2][j] = t[2][j]^tmp2;    tmp2 = tmp1 & 0xff;
    state[3][j] = t[3][j]^tmp2;
}
```

Pcode 2.19: Simulation code for AddRoundKey( ) transformation.

```
for(j = 0;j < 4;j++)
        for(i = 0;i < 4;i++)
                state[j][i] = S_Box[state[j][i]];
```

Pcode 2.20: Simulation code for SubBytes( ) transformation.

```
for(j = 1;j < 4;j++)
    for(i = 0;i < j;i++){
        tmp1 = state[j][0];      tmp2 = state[j][1];
        state[j][0] = tmp2;      tmp2 = state[j][2];
        state[j][1] = tmp2;      tmp2 = state[j][3];
        state[j][2] = tmp2;
        state[j][3] = tmp1;
    }
```

Pcode 2.21: Simulation code for ShiftRows( ) transformation.

AESCipher( ) The simulation code for AES cipher algorithm is given in Pcode 2.23. AES cipher uses all the transformations discussed previously along with FormState( ) and GetOutput( ) operations.

```
for(j = 0;j < 4;j++)
    for(i = 0;i < 4;i++){                        // Premultiplication of State bytes with 0x02
        tmp1 = state[j][i];
        tmp2 = tmp1 >> 7;    tmp1 = tmp1 << 1;
        if (tmp2)
        tmp1 = tmp1^0x1b;
        s[j][i] = tmp1;
    }
for(i = 0;i < 4;i++){
    t[0][i] = s[0][i]^(s[1][i]^state[1][i])^state[2][i]^state[3][i];
    t[1][i] = state[0][i]^s[1][i]^(s[2][i]^state[2][i])^state[3][i];
    t[2][i] = state[0][i]^state[1][i]^s[2][i]^(s[3][i]^state[3][i]);
    t[3][i] = (s[0][i]^state[0][i])^state[1][i]^state[2][i]^s[3][i];
}
```

Pcode 2.22: Simulation code for MixColumns( ) transformation.

```
k = 0;                                  // offset to access expanded key
FormState( );
AddRoundKey( );
for (r = 1;  r < 10; r++){
     SubBytes( );
     ShiftRows( );
     MixColumns( );
     AddRoundKey( );
}
SubBytes( );
ShiftRows( );
AddRoundKey( );
GetOutput( );
```

Pcode 2.23: Simulation code for AESCipher( ).

AES-128 Encryption Simulation Results

```
Key:
{0x47, 0xf1, 0x1a, 0x71, 0x1d, 0x29, 0xc5, 0x89, 0x6f, 0xb7, 0x62, 0x0e, 0xaa, 0x18, 0xbe, 0x1b}
Plain text:
{0x9f, 0x5d, 0xbd, 0x6e, 0x43, 0xef, 0xc4, 0xa6, 0x39, 0xa8, 0x31, 0xa4, 0xd3, 0x37, 0xf2, 0x8b}
After FormState( ):
{{0x9f, 0x43, 0x39, 0xd3}, {0x5d, 0xef, 0xa8, 0x37}, {0xbd, 0xc4, 0x31, 0xf2}, {0x6e, 0xa6, 0xa4, 0x8b}}
After AddRoundKey( ):
{{0xd8, 0x5e, 0x56, 0x79}, {0xac, 0xc6, 0x1f, 0x2f}, {0xa7, 0x01, 0x53, 0x4c}, {0x1f, 0x2f, 0xaa, 0x90}}

//Loop Start
r=1 (input):
{{0xd8, 0x5e, 0x56, 0x79}, {0xac, 0xc6, 0x1f, 0x2f}, {0xa7, 0x01, 0x53, 0x4c}, {0x1f, 0x2f, 0xaa, 0x90}}
r=1 (after substitute bytes):
{{0x61, 0x58, 0xb1, 0xb6}, {0x91, 0xb4, 0xc0, 0x15}, 0x5c, 0x7c, 0xed, 0x29}, {0xc0, 0x15, 0xac, 0x60}}
r=1 (after shift rows):
{{0x61, 0x58, 0xb1, 0xb6}, {0xb4, 0xc0, 0x15, 0x91}, {0xed, 0x29, 0x5c, 0x7c}, {0x60, 0xc0, 0x15, 0xac}}
r=1 (after Mix Columns):
{{0x88, 0x02, 0x0f, 0x0f}, {0x5e, 0x78, 0x6a, 0xa7}, {0xb4, 0x91, 0x23, 0x30}, {0x3a, 0x9a, 0xab, 0x6f}}
r=1 (after add round key):
{{0x63, 0xf4, 0x96, 0x3c}, {0x01, 0x0e, 0xab, 0x7e}, {0x01, 0xe1, 0x31, 0x9c}, {0xe7, 0xce, 0xf1, 0x2e}}
r=2 (input):
{{0x63, 0xf4, 0x96, 0x3c}, {0x01, 0x0e, 0xab, 0x7e}, {0x01, 0xe1, 0x31, 0x9c}, {0xe7, 0xce, 0xf1, 0x2e}}
r=3 (input):
{{0x21, 0xa3, 0x71, 0x90}, {0x1b, 0x2e, 0x1b, 0x01}, {0xa0, 0x9b, 0x49, 0x7c}, {0x06, 0x1f, 0x39, 0xaa}}
r=4 (input):
{{0x1d, 0x93, 0x58, 0x0d}, {0xf1, 0x27, 0xee, 0xe5}, {0xb2, 0x95, 0xaa, 0xdc}, {0x86, 0xe6, 0x70, 0xe7}}
r=5 (input):
{{0x3c, 0x13, 0xb6, 0xbc}, {0x04, 0x36, 0x35, 0x6e}, {0x0a, 0x08, 0x86, 0x0e}, {0x8a, 0xee, 0x69, 0xad}}
r=6 (input):
{{0x91, 0x06, 0x4a, 0xa7}, {0x7e, 0x7b, 0x62, 0x74}, {0xca, 0x0b, 0x9a, 0xc5}, {0x06, 0xa1, 0xa3, 0xbb}}
```

```
r=7 (input):
{{0x2a, 0x78, 0xf5, 0x97}, {0xaf, 0x42, 0x33, 0xe5}, {0x93, 0x71, 0x55, 0x6a}, {0x4d, 0x07, 0x5e, 0xaa}}
r=8 (input):
{{0x74, 0xd7, 0x1c, 0xd9}, {0x06, 0x30, 0x75, 0x6f}, {0xab, 0x79, 0x5b, 0x5a}, {0x47, 0x47, 0x9c, 0x52}}
r=9 (input):
{{0x66, 0xd9, 0xc7, 0xd4}, {0xab, 0xd8, 0xdf, 0x49}, {0x60, 0xb7, 0x20, 0x61}, {0x4a, 0x34, 0x49, 0xfd}}
//Loop end
//After Loop
{{0x2b, 0x80, 0xbd, 0x6c}, {0x8b, 0x8c, 0xaf, 0x86}, {0xd9, 0xb5, 0xff, 0x8a}, {0x74, 0x98, 0xec, 0xdf}}
After SubBytes( ):
{{0xf1, 0xcd, 0x7a, 0x50}, {0x3d, 0x64, 0x79, 0x44}, {0x35, 0xd5, 0x16, 0x7e}, {0x92, 0x46, 0xce, 0x9e}}
After ShiftRows( ):
{{0xf1, 0xcd, 0x7a, 0x50}, {0x64, 0x79, 0x44, 0x3d}, {0x16, 0x7e, 0x35, 0xd5}, {0x9e, 0x92, 0x46, 0xce}}
After AddRoundKey( ):
{{0xf4, 0xa2, 0xba, 0x58}, {0xc1, 0xbe, 0xef, 0x47}, {0xe0, 0x32, 0xe8, 0xac}, {0x29, 0x24, 0x96, 0xa4}}
Cipher text after GetOutput( ):
{0xf4, 0xc1, 0xe0, 0x29, 0xa2, 0xbe, 0x32, 0x24, 0xba, 0xef, 0xe8, 0x96, 0x58, 0x47, 0xac, 0xa4}
```

AES Inverse Cipher Simulation

The AES inverse cipher consists of four transformations that are inverse operations of the AES cipher transformation and we use the following function names for each transformation: InvSubBytes( ) for inverse substitute byte transformation, InvShiftRows( ) for inverse shift rows transformation, InvAddRoundKey( ) for inverse add round key transformation and InvMixColumns( ) for inverse mix columns transformation. The functionality of inverse substitute bytes and inverse add round key transformations are the same as cipher substitute bytes and add round key transformations except that the look-up table values and order of accessing keyword values are different in the two cases. Although the same expanded key is used for both cipher and inverse cipher, in the case of cipher the keywords are accessed from the beginning of the expanded array by increasing the array index and in the case of inverse cipher the keywords are accessed from the end of the array by decreasing the array index. Then, both the shift rows and mix columns transformations of cipher and inverse cipher are inversely related.

InvAddRoundKey( ) Same as AddRoundKey( ), but the keywords are accessed from the end of the key expansion array.

InvSubBytes( ) This is the same as SubBytes( ), but it uses **Inv_S_Box**[ ] instead of **S_Box**[ ].

InvShiftRows( ) In the InvShiftRows( ) transformation, we rotate the state rows to the right by a particular number of bytes depending on the row number. The simulation code for InvShiftRows( ) is given in Pcode 2.24. As the state elements are represented with bytes throughout our simulation, we simulate this inverse shift rows transformation in terms of load and stores bytes rather with logical cyclic shift of 32-bit words.

InvMixColumns( ) transformation is the costly transformation in the AES algorithm. It involves multiplication of state bytes with 0x09, 0x0b, 0x0d, and 0x0e element combinations in the Galois field GF(2^8). The simulation code for InvMixColumns( ) is given in Pcode 2.25.

InvAESCipher( ) The simulation code for the AES inverse cipher algorithm is given in Pcode 2.26. The AES inverse cipher uses all the transformations discussed previously along with FormState( ) and GetOutput( ) operations.

```
for(j = 1;j < 4;j++)
    for(i = 0;i < j;i++){
        tmp1 = state[j][3];       tmp2 = state[j][2];
        state[j][3] = tmp2;       tmp2 = state[j][1];
        state[j][2] = tmp2;       tmp2 = state[j][0];
        state[j][1] = tmp2;
        state[j][0] = tmp1;
    }
```

Pcode 2.24: Simulation code for InvShiftRows( ) transformation.

```
for(j = 0;j < 4;j++)
    for(i = 0;i < 4;i++){                          // multiply with 0x02
        tmp1 = t[j][i];
        tmp2 = tmp1 >> 7;      tmp1 = tmp1 << 1;
        if (tmp2)
            tmp1 = tmp1^0x1b;
        s[j][i] = tmp1;
    }
for(j = 0;j < 4;j++)
    for(i = 0;i < 4;i++){                          // multiply with 0x04
        tmp1 = s[j][i];
        tmp2 = tmp1 >> 7;      tmp1 = tmp1 << 1;
        if (tmp2)
            tmp1 = tmp1^0x1b;
        ss[j][i] = tmp1;
    }
for(j = 0;j < 4;j++)
    for(i = 0;i < 4;i++){                          // multiply with 0x08
        tmp1 = ss[j][i];
        tmp2 = tmp1 >> 7;      tmp1 = tmp1 << 1;
        if (tmp2)
            tmp1 = tmp1^0x1b;
        sss[j][i] = tmp1;
    }
for(i = 0;i < 4;i++){
    state[0][i] = (sss[0][i]^ss[0][i]^s[0][i])^(sss[1][i]^s[1][i]^t[1][i])^
                          (sss[2][i]^ss[2][i]^t[2][i])^(sss[3][i]^t[3][i]);
    state[1][i] = (sss[0][i]^t[0][i])^(sss[1][i]^ss[1][i]^s[1][i])^
                          (sss[2][i]^s[2][i]^t[2][i])^(sss[3][i]^ss[3][i]^t[3][i]);
    state[2][i] = (sss[0][i]^ss[0][i]^t[0][i])^(sss[1][i]^t[1][i])^
                          (sss[2][i]^ss[2][i]^s[2][i])^(sss[3][i]^s[3][i]^t[3][i]);
    state[3][i] = (sss[0][i]^s[0][i]^t[0][i])^(sss[1][i]^ss[1][i]^t[1][i])^
                          (sss[2][i]^t[2][i])^(sss[3][i]^ss[3][i]^s[3][i]);
}
```

Pcode 2.25: Simulation code for InvMixColumns( ) transformation.

```
k = 40;                    // offset to access expanded key
FormState( );
k-= 8;
AddRoundKey( );
for (r=1; r < 10; r++){
        InvShiftRows( );
        InvSubBytes( );
        InvAddRoundKey( );
        InvMixColumns( );
        k-= 8;
}
InvShiftRows( );
InvSubBytes( );
InvAddRoundKey( );
GetOutput( );
```

Pcode 2.26: Simulation code for InvAESCipher( ).

AES Inverse-Cipher Simulation Results

As the inverse AES cipher works in the reverse order as AES cipher, the simulation results presented in Section 2.3.3, AES-128 Encryption Simulation Results, can be obtained in reverse order using the inverse AES cipher. Therefore, the same intermediate outputs given in this section can be used to debug the AES inverse cipher.

2.3.4 Computational Complexity of AES

In this section, we analyze AES algorithm complexity for implementing on the reference embedded processor. We discuss the complexity of each transformation in terms of cycles (see Appendix A, Section A.4, on the companion website for cycles' consumption by a particular operation on the reference embedded processor) and data memory usage. Although the transformations AddRoundKey (AR) and ShiftRows (SR) can be computed with fewer cycles by treating the AES state data as 32-bit words (simply XORing word by word for AR transformation and shifting each word cyclically by a particular offset for the SR transform), the other two transformations SubBytes (SB) and MixColumns (MC) work with bytes only, hence we work with bytes in all the transformations.

Complexity of SubBytes( )

In the SB transform, each byte of state is updated with the look-up table value by using the state byte value as the offset for the look-up table. Basically SB transform involves only look-up table access. With a reference embedded processor, though, the look-up table access takes multiple cycles per byte load; as we are not using the output immediately, we can load each byte by consuming two cycles (one cycle for computing the absolute address and one cycle for memory load) with program code interleaving. For updating all 16 bytes of state with the SB transform, we consume a total of 32 cycles.

Complexity of ShiftRows( )

In the SR transform, every row of state is rotated left cyclically except the zeroth row. The amount of rotation for the first row is one byte, for the second row is two bytes and for the third row is three bytes. This is achieved (without cyclic shifts) by loading the first byte to a temporary variable, and then loading the next location byte and storing that to the current byte location as given in Pcode 2.21 of shift rows transformation simulation code. Like in SB, here also we are not using the loaded value immediately. So, we can do this shifting of row left by 1 byte in eight cycles. For the second row, we have to shift 2 bytes left, by applying the previously described procedure twice, which consumes 16 cycles. Finally, in the third row, we have to shift 3 bytes left, by one right shift of the third row. This takes another eight cycles. The SR transform consumes a total of 32 cycles.

Complexity of MixColumns( )

The MC transformation is the costliest operation in the AES algorithm as MC transform involves costly Galois field element multiplications. Now we discuss the MC transformation steps and then we estimate its cycle consumption. First, we understand the process of two Galois field elements' multiplication. If we want to multiply two Galois field elements {0x07} and {0xab}, we use the approach described in AES standard FIPS 197. The field element {0x07} can be written as $\{0x04 \oplus 0x02 \oplus 0x01\}$. Then Galois field multiplication can be expanded as $\{0x07\} \cdot \{0xab\} = \{\{0x04\} \cdot \{0xab\} \oplus \{0x02\} \cdot \{0xab\} \oplus \{0xab\}\}$. If we want to multiply any field element {0x*mm*} with {0x02} and if the MSB of {0x*mm*} is zero, one left shift of {0x*mm*} results in value $\{0xmm\} \cdot \{0x02\}$. If the MSB of {0x*mm*} is not zero, then one left shift of value {0x*mm*} along with XORing of the result with {0x1b} is needed to make the multiplication result belongs to Galois field GF(2^8). This process is equivalent to taking of modulo by dividing the multiplications result with irreducible polynomial specified in the standard. If we want to multiply $\{0x04\} \cdot \{0xmm\}$, we repeat the previous procedure twice.

In the AES cipher MC transform, we multiply the matrix A with a vector to get the transformed output. The Galois field elements present in the matrix are {0x01}, {0x02} and {0x03}. Multiplying any Galois field element by {0x01} results in the same element. Multiplying any Galois field element by {0x02} is done as described previously. Multiplying any Galois field element {0x*mm*} by {0x03} is done by first multiplying the element with {0x02} and then XORing the result with the original value as $(\{0x02\} \cdot \{0xmm\}) \oplus \{0xmm\}$.

With this knowledge, we can simulate the MC transform as follows. First, we multiply all the state elements by {0x02}. Multiplying one state element by {0x02} takes approximately 10 cycles: one load (requires four cycles, including the stall, as we immediately use the loaded value in the next operation), one shift, one condition check, one XOR, one conditional move and one store. So, we spend a total of 160 cycles to multiply all the state elements with {0x02} and store in a temporary buffer. The multiplication of state elements with {0x03} is done by XORing the result of {0x02} multiplication output with the original state elements. Once we have the multiplication of state elements by {0x02}, then computing the MC transform involves only XOR operations as given in Pcode 2.22. To compute one MC transform output element, we calculate a total of four XOR operations (four cycles) and five load operations (five cycles assuming the program can be interleaved; otherwise it takes

20 cycles). For all elements of state we consume 144 cycles (= 16x9). To store all the state elements back to state we consume another 16 cycles. With this, the total number of cycles consumed in applying MC transform on state is 320 cycles.

Complexity of AddRoundKey( )

In the AR transform, we first load the keyword from memory (four cycles) and we unpack the word into bytes (six cycles). We load the four state bytes row-wise (a minimum of eight cycles are needed after interleaving the program code) and XOR with the key bytes (four cycles) and store them back to state (four cycles). So, in applying AR transform for one row of state, we spend approximately 26 cycles, and for complete AR transform on four rows of state we spend 104 cycles.

Overall Complexity of AES Cipher

Total cycles consumed for all the transforms in a single iteration of the AES cipher loop sum up to 488 cycles. For the key length of 128 bits, the AES cipher loop iterates nine times. Thus, the approximate number of cycles for encrypting one block of 128 bits of data using the AES cipher is about 5000 cycles (= 488x9 + cycles consumed by all transforms before and after the loop).

Inverse AES Cipher Computational Complexity

In the case of the AES inverse cipher, except the inverse MC transformation, all other transforms takes the same number of cycles as the cipher transformations. In inverse MC transform, the matrix elements are {0x0d}, {0x0e}, {0x0b}, and {0x09}, and to multiply the state elements with these matrix elements, we need to store multiplication results of {0x08} and {0x04} elements in temporary buffers apart from the {0x02} multiplication result (as we may expand {0x0d} as {0x08 ⊕ 0x04 ⊕ 0x01} to perform multiplication of the state element with {0x0d}). Generation of multiplication outputs for {0x08} and {0x04} elements with each state element take an extra 320 cycles per loop iteration. Also, inverse MC multiplications take an extra 48 cycles per iteration (as the multipliers in this case are large and need more XOR and load operations, as given in Pcode 2.25). With this, the AES inverse cipher loop consumes approximately 856 cycles. So, the approximate total number of cycles for decrypting one block of 128 bits of data using the AES inverse cipher with the reference embedded processor is 8000 cycles (= 856x9 + cycles consumed by the transforms before and after the loop).

Complexity of AESKeyExp( )

Now, we discuss the complexity of AES key expansion module in expanding a 128-bit key. As given in Pcode 2.18, the expanded key first four keywords are copied from the input key and it takes eight cycles for load and store of keywords. The loop of the AES key expansion module is unrolled partially so that each iteration of the "while" loop generates four keywords by avoiding conditional jumps. With this, the loop count for 128-bit key expansion becomes 10 (= Nb • Nr/4 = 4 * 10/4). For generating the first keyword in each iteration of the while loop, from the previous keywords, we perform the transformations, namely, substitute word and rotate word left and then we XOR the result with Rcon. These operations consume 36 cycles (six cycles for unpacking the previous keyword, 16 cycles for loading four S-Box values, four cycles for loading Rcon constant, four cycles for packing the bytes and four cycles for XORing with Rcon and for other operations). The operations substituting word, rotate word, and XORing with Rcon need not be performed in generating the last three keywords in any iteration of the "while" loop. Then, before storing each word as a keyword, we XOR the current word with the already generated keyword. This operation of XORing the current four words with the previously generated four keywords and storing XORed outputs consumes about 24 cycles (16 cycles for loading the previous four keywords, four cycles for XORing and four cycles for storing). With this, total cycles consumed for generation of four keywords in a single iteration of the key expansion loop are 60 (= 36 + 24). For generating all keywords with the key expansion module, we consume approximately 608 (= 60x10 + 8) cycles.

AES Algorithm Memory Requirements

In this section, we analyze the amount of data memory used in the AES algorithm. In key expansion, we used 176 bytes for storing expanded key, and 10 bytes for storing the Rcon constants. Both key expansion and AES cipher use the S-Box values and we need 256 bytes of data memory for storing S-Box values. The AES inverse cipher uses inverse S-Box and it needs another 256 bytes of data memory. We use almost 100 bytes of data memory for input, output, state and for temporary buffers to store Galois field multiplication results. With this, the total amount of data memory used in the AES algorithm is about 0.75 kB.

2.3.5 Efficient Implementation of AES

In the previous section, we discussed the complexity of the AES algorithm in terms of reference embedded processor clock cycles. The key expansion module consumes approximately 600 cycles and the key expansion need not be done in real time as encryption of the data. Moreover, the key expansion module need not be called for every data block. Therefore, we are not going to discuss the optimization techniques for the key expansion module in this section. Next, the transforms used in the AES algorithm before and after the main loop are occurring once per block of data. The costly part of the AES algorithm is the main loop that runs $N_b + N_k + 1$ times. In this section, we discuss the ways to optimize the transformations in the AES main loop.

The main loop of the AES algorithm contains SB, SR, MC, and AR transformations. All of these transformations take input data from the previous transformation's output. On a deep pipelined processor such as a reference embedded processor, implementing this sequential flow of the AES algorithm as it is takes lot of cycles, as discussed in the previous section. If we optimize the algorithm for reduced dependencies in its flow, only then can we utilize full bandwidth and resources of an embedded processor (with multiple arithmetic and logic units) and then the algorithm consumes less cycles. Therefore, in this section, we concentrate on restructuring the AES algorithm for parallel flow to utilize the full bandwidth of the processor.

Now, we discuss how to make the AES algorithm suitable for running on deep pipelined multiple ALU embedded processors. If we can somehow make the process of getting 16 output elements of state at the end of a loop iteration from 16 bytes of state at the beginning of the loop without any dependency between the outputs to the inputs (i.e., having 16 parallel independent flows for a full iteration of the loop), then we can efficiently program such a flow on a deep pipeline embedded processor. The present flow of the AES algorithm is shown in Figure 2.8 with dependencies. If any transformation has cross-inputs or cross-outputs, then there will be a dependency between the transformations as we wait for all the inputs to become available for starting the next transformation. From Figure 2.8, we can clearly see the dependency between SB and SR, SR and MC, and MC and AR. There is no dependency between AR and SB, as the inputs or outputs of these transforms are not crossed.

Efficient Implementation of AES Algorithm

The transformations SB and SR are commutative (Federal Information Processing Standards, 2001), meaning the outputs of both functions SR(SB(state)) and SB(SR(state)) are the same. Out of all transformations, MC transformation is the most costly. We can reduce the cycles for this transformation at the cost of memory. In Daemen and Rijmen (2000), an alternative approach is suggested for fast implementation of AES using 4 kB of data memory. In this approach, instead of computing the intermediate Galois field multiplication values at runtime for performing MC, we precompute the multiplication values for all 255 S-Box elements with all rotated combinations of MC matrix first-row elements and store them in a data memory. In Gladman (2003), with three extra rotate operations, the memory required for fast implementation of AES had been reduced to 1 kB. Here, we precompute the S-Box elements' multiplied values for one row of elements in the MC matrix and store them in memory using 1 kB of data memory. With the precomputed multiplication values, we spend the cycles in MC transformation for loading the multiplication values, for rotations and for XORing them with the input of MC. An efficient flow for the AES-algorithm loop transformations with precomputation look-up tables is possible with the following formula:

$$T = \mathrm{AR}(\mathrm{MC}(\mathrm{SB}(\mathrm{SR}(S)))), \text{ where } S\text{: input state, } T\text{: output state}$$

Figure 2.9 shows the efficient implementation of the previous equation. Let M be the mix column matrix elements, S the input vector, and S' the output of mix columns transformation.

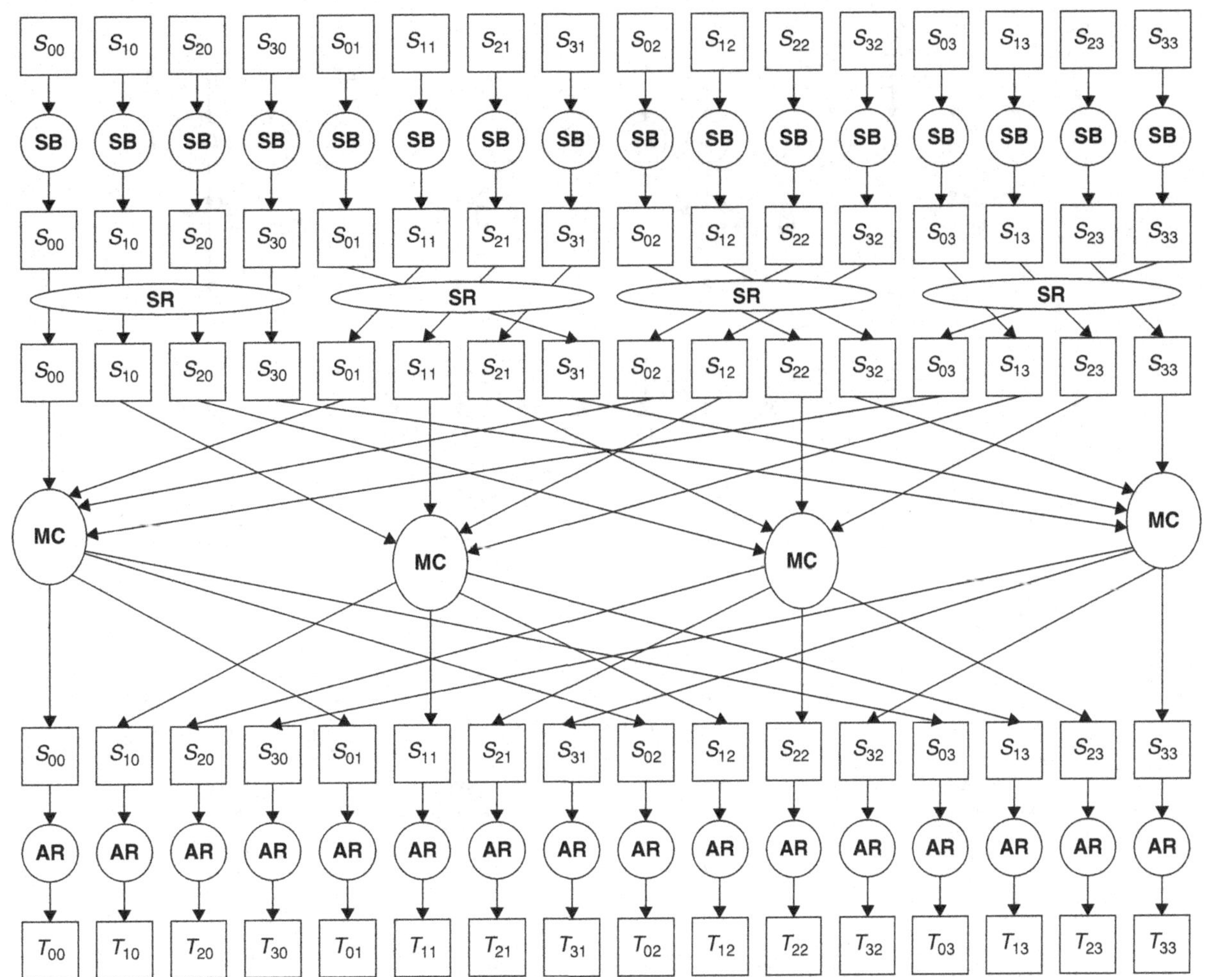

Figure 2.8: Flow of AES cipher algorithm transformations.

$$S' = M \cdot S$$

$$\begin{bmatrix} s'_0 \\ s'_1 \\ s'_2 \\ s'_3 \end{bmatrix} = \begin{bmatrix} m_0 & m_1 & m_2 & m_3 \\ m_3 & m_0 & m_1 & m_2 \\ m_2 & m_3 & m_0 & m_1 \\ m_1 & m_2 & m_3 & m_0 \end{bmatrix} \cdot \begin{bmatrix} s_0 \\ s_1 \\ s_2 \\ s_3 \end{bmatrix} = \begin{bmatrix} m_0 \\ m_3 \\ m_2 \\ m_1 \end{bmatrix} \cdot s_0 \oplus \begin{bmatrix} m_1 \\ m_0 \\ m_3 \\ m_2 \end{bmatrix} \cdot s_1 \oplus \begin{bmatrix} m_2 \\ m_1 \\ m_0 \\ m_3 \end{bmatrix} \cdot s_2 \oplus \begin{bmatrix} m_3 \\ m_2 \\ m_1 \\ m_0 \end{bmatrix}$$

We precompute L_i for $0 \leq i \leq 3$ (Galois field multiplication, $\cdot$, of s_i with first column of M) as follows, and store it in memory.

$$L_i = \{m_0\} \cdot s_i \mid \{m_3\} \cdot s_i \mid \{m_2\} \cdot s_i \mid \{m_1\} \cdot s_i$$

Now, to compute the mix column transformation for one column of state, we load L_i for $0 \leq i \leq 3$ from memory corresponding to s_i. Next, we get L'_i from L_i by rotating L_i to the right by i bytes. Then, we obtain s'_i by XORing all L_is as follows:

$$s'_i = L'_0 \oplus L'_1 \oplus L'_2 \oplus L'_3$$

where

$$L'_0 = \{m_0\} \cdot s_0 | \{m_3\} \cdot s_0 | \{m_2\} \cdot s_0 | \{m_1\} \cdot s_0$$
$$L'_1 = \{m_1\} \cdot s_1 | \{m_0\} \cdot s_1 | \{m_3\} \cdot s_1 | \{m_2\} \cdot s_1$$
$$L'_2 = \{m_2\} \cdot s_2 | \{m_1\} \cdot s_2 | \{m_0\} \cdot s_2 | \{m_3\} \cdot s_2$$
$$L'_3 = \{m_3\} \cdot s_3 | \{m_3\} \cdot s_3 | \{m_2\} \cdot s_3 | \{m_1\} \cdot s_3$$

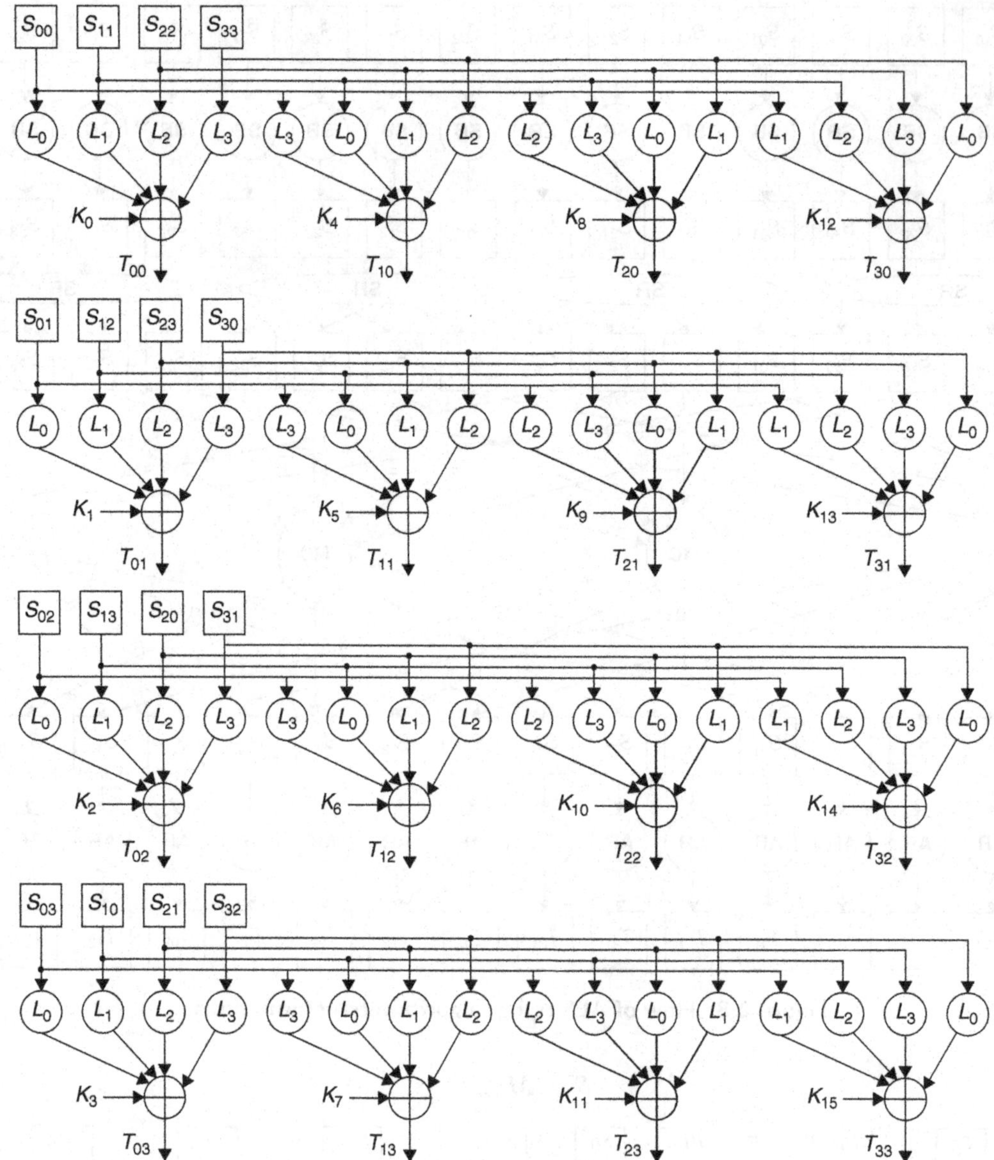

Figure 2.9: Efficient implementation of AES cipher.

Finally, we get the output for one iteration of the AES loop by XORing the mix columns output with round key $T = S' \oplus K$ (here to reduce the number of XORs for AR, we transpose AES round keywords in the key expansion module). Therefore, to compute one column of the state matrix, we require four extracts (to get individual state elements after SR transformation), four loads (SB transformation), three rotations and four XORs (MC and AR). The simulation code for an efficient AES cipher is given in Pcode 2.27. In Figure 2.9, we can see that the outputs T_{00} to T_{33} do not depend on any intermediate results. All 16 outputs can be computed independently if we have sufficient processor compute and data bandwidth. On the deep pipelined embedded processor, by interleaving the program code, we can avoid all the stalls present with the memory (or look-up table) accesses.

In this way, using the approach for AES implementation in Gladman (2003), we can compute AES transformation operations by consuming one cycle for every operation with the program interleaving. In MC, we work on columns; it is convenient if we hold one column of elements in one register. For this, we transpose the state matrix before entering the loop. We again transpose back to the AES state matrix after the loop to work with the last three transformations outside the loop.

Complexity of Optimized AES Algorithm

At this juncture, we estimate the cycles (see Appendix A, Section A.4, on the companion website) for computing output T per iteration from Pcode 2.27 as follows. We have 16 state elements extracts (16 cycles), 16 XOR

```
for(r = 1; r < = pAes->Nr; r++){
    r0 = r4 & 0xff; r1 = (r5 >> 8)&0xff; r2 = (r6>>16) & 0xff; r3 = r7>>24; // SR
    r0 = sbmc[r0]; r1 = sbmc[r1]; r2 = sbmc[r2]; r3 = sbmc[r3];            // SB
    tmp1 = r1 >> 24; r1 = r1 << 8; r1 = r1 | tmp1;                // rotate r1 by one byte
    tmp1 = r2 >> 16; r2 = r2 << 16; r2 = r2 | tmp1;               // rotate r2 by two bytes
    tmp1 = r3 >> 8; r3 = r3 << 24; r3 = r3 | tmp1;                // rotate r3 by three bytes
    r0 = r0 ^ r1; r0 = r0 ^ r2; r0 = r0 ^ r3;                     // MC
    r1 = enc_key_exp[k++]; r2 = r0 ^ r1; temp[0] = r2;            // AR

    r3 = r4 >> 24; r0 = r5 & 0xff; r1 = (r6 >> 8)&0xff; r2 = (r7 >> 16) & 0xff;
    r0 = sbmc[r0]; r1 = sbmc[r1]; r2 = sbmc[r2]; r3 = sbmc[r3];
    tmp1 = r1 >> 24; r1 = r1 << 8; r1 = r1 | tmp1;
    tmp1 = r2 >> 16; r2 = r2 << 16; r2 = r2 | tmp1;
    tmp1 = r3 >> 8; r3 = r3 << 24; r3 = r3 | tmp1;
    r0 = r0 ^ r1; r0 = r0 ^ r2; r0 = r0 ^ r3;
    r1 = enc_key_exp[k++]; r0 = r0 ^ r1; temp[1] = r0;

    r2 = (r4 >> 16)&0xff; r3 = r5 >> 24; r0 = r6 & 0xff; r1 = (r7 >> 8)&0xff;
    r0 = sbmc[r0]; r1 = sbmc[r1]; r2 = sbmc[r2]; r3 = sbmc[r3];
    tmp1 = r1 >> 24; r1 = r1 << 8; r1 = r1 | tmp1;
    tmp1 = r2 >> 16; r2 = r2 << 16; r2 = r2 | tmp1;
    tmp1 = r3 >> 8; r3 = r3 << 24; r3 = r3 | tmp1;
    r0 = r0 ^ r1; r0 = r0 ^ r2; r0 = r0 ^ r3;
    r1 = enc_key_exp[k++]; r0 = r0 ^ r1; temp[2] = r0;

    r1 = (r4 >> 8)&0xff; r2 = (r5 >> 16)&0xff; r3 = r6 >> 24; r0 = r7 & 0xff;
    r0 = sbmc[r0]; r1 = sbmc[r1]; r2 = sbmc[r2]; r3 = sbmc[r3];
    tmp1 = r1 >> 24; r1 = r1 << 8; r1 = r1 | tmp1;
    tmp1 = r2 >> 16; r2 = r2 << 16; r2 = r2 | tmp1;
    tmp1 = r3 >> 8; r3 = r3 << 24; r3 = r3 | tmp1;
    r0 = r0 ^ r1; r0 = r0 ^ r2; r0 = r0 ^ r3;
    r1 = enc_key_exp[k++]; r0 = r0 ^ r1; temp[3] = r0;

    r4 = temp[0]; r5 = temp[1]; r6 = temp[2]; r7 = temp[3];
}
```

Pcode 2.27: Efficient implementation of AES Cipher loop.

operations (16 cycles), 16 look-up table accesses (32 cycles for both address generation and memory load), and 12 rotations ($36 = 3 \times 12$ cycles, as we compute rotate operation in two SHIFTS and one OR, because there is no rotate instruction on the reference processor). Therefore, the total number of cycles per iteration is 100. The total number of cycles consumed for encrypting one block of 128 bits of data with a 128-bit key using the efficient implementation of AES cipher given in Pcode 2.27 is 1050 cycles ($= 100 \times 9 +$ cycles consumed by the transformations before and after the loop). In addition, with the inverse cipher (using the equivalent inverse cipher in Federal Information Processing Standards, 2001), we consume the same number of cycles for decryption of 128 bits of cipher text. We can use the same Pcode 2.27 for the AES inverse-cipher (i.e., for the equivalent inverse cipher) loop as well by simply changing the *SR* code (as ISR and SR are inversely related) and properly accessing the expanded key data (as the inverse cipher uses keys from the end of the expanded key buffer). We use the **sbmc**[ ] and **isbmc**[ ] look-up table in the cipher and inverse cipher, respectively. Look-up values for **sbmc**[ ] and **isbmc**[ ] can be found on this book's companion website.

With the described AES implementation method, we can compute in parallel all 16 output elements of state in a single iteration of the loop. If the embedded processor has more than one compute unit (ALU), then the number of cycles required for processing a block will decline. On the deep-pipelined embedded processor (having similar architectural features as the reference-embedded processor) with four compute units, the suggested method can be implemented within 300 ($= 1050/4 +$ overhead) cycles. The extra overhead may result from uneven compute and data bandwidth issues (meaning that compute slots may be adequate, but load/store slots for executing an algorithm are insufficient) in the processor.

With the previous efficient AES implementation, we require 1.25 kB (1 kB for **sbmc**[ ] and 0.25 kB for **S-Box**[ ]) of L1 data memory for encryption process look-up tables and we require another 1.25 kB of memory for decryption process look-up tables. Now, depending on the processor (with 32- or 8-bit supported registers and on-chip L1 memory sufficiently available or not) used in a particular application, we choose either Pcode 2.23 or 2.27 to implement the AES cipher.

2.4 Keyed-Hash Message Authentication Code

The purpose of the HMAC is preservation of data authenticity and data integrity. Data authentication is intended to prevent the alteration of data (presumed unaltered from sender to receiver) by a third-party. The HMAC uses a cryptographic key in conjunction with secure hash algorithm (SHA) to generate message authentication code (MAC). In this section, we discuss the HMAC using the SHA functions and we simulate the HMAC using the SHA-256 function. Also, we discuss the computational complexity of HMAC using the SHA-256 algorithm.

2.4.1 HMAC Algorithm

The HMAC plays an important role in digital communications and data storage applications to maintain data integrity. With the HMAC, we generate a MAC using a secret key that is shared between two parties, namely sender and receiver. The HMAC uses this secret key for generation and verification of the MAC. The sender sends the message along with the MAC and the receiver receives the message and its MAC (A). Then the receiver also computes a new MAC (B) for the received message. If the transmitted message is unaltered, then A and B will be same, otherwise they will differ. In this way, the HMAC provides data integrity. The HMAC uses one of the four SHA functions—SHA-1, SHA-256, SHA-384, and SHA-512—for computing MAC.

SHA Functions

SHA functions are one-way hash functions used to generate a condensed data representation (called a message digest) for a long data message (the data length for SHA-1 and SHA-256 is $<2^{64}$ bits and for SHA-384 and SHA-512, $<2^{128}$ bits). With one-way functions, we cannot reproduce the original data from the condensed data. Here, one-way function means that the input message cannot be reproduced from the condensed data. With the mathematical structures of existing SHA functions (SHA-1, SHA-256, etc.), it is almost impossible to generate a same message digest value with two different data messages. In other words, a small change in the data will generate an entirely different message digest. Also, it is not computationally feasible to generate an original message from its message digest. This property enables maintaining the integrity of the data in which we are interested. SHA functions are used in digital signature algorithms and HMAC algorithms. The performance (strength) of HMAC depends on the strength of the hash function and key.

2.4.2 HMAC Description

The general block diagram for the HMAC algorithm is shown in Figure 2.10. HMAC algorithm inputs include the message (which supposedly needs authentication) and a key (which is needed in the generation of message authentication). Outputs include the original message and its authentication. The HMAC algorithm has three layers. In the first layer, the HMAC parser prepares the data to the SHA parser, and in the second layer, the SHA

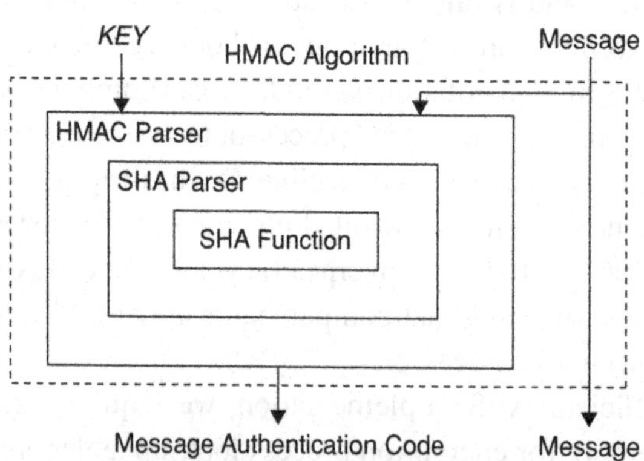

Figure 2.10: Block diagram of keyed-hash message authentication code algorithm.

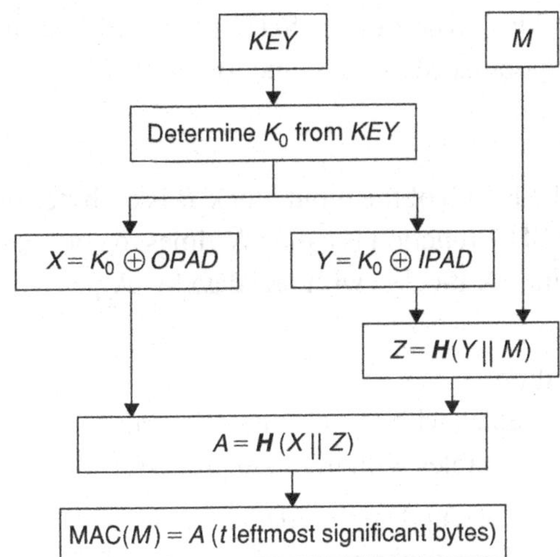

Figure 2.11: Flow diagram of HMAC parser.

parser prepares the data to the SHA function. The core hash algorithm sits in the third layer. In the following sections, we discuss the functionalities of all layers in detail.

HMAC Parser

The HMAC parser consists of many steps and uses the message M, and key KEY to generate the authentication code. The flow diagram of the HMAC parser is shown in Figure 2.11. The first step of the HMAC parser is determining K_0, which is B (where the value of B is the length of the SHA-function input block) bytes of data derived from the given input KEY. The data K_0 is derived as follows. If the length of input KEY is K, then

$$K_0 = KEY, \quad \text{if } B = K$$

$$K_0 = \boldsymbol{H}(KEY), \quad \text{if } B < K \text{ (here } \boldsymbol{H} \text{ is SHA function)}$$

$$K_0 = KEY \,||\, \text{zeros}, \quad \text{if } B > K$$

In the second step, we compute X and Y by XORing the derived K_0 with $IPAD$ and $OPAD$ data (where $IPAD$ is equal to the value of 0×36 repeated B times, and $OPAD$ is equal to the value of $0 \times 5c$ repeated B times). We compute Z in the third step by passing the appended data of Y and input message M to the SHA function through the SHA parser. In the fourth step, A is computed by passing the data from the appended X and Z to the SHA function through the SHA parser. Finally, in the fifth step, we get the input message MAC by extracting the t-left-most significant bytes of A.

SHA Parser

In the SHA parser, basically we prepare B bytes of data blocks to the SHA function. The SHA parser consists of three steps: (1) message padding, (2) dividing the padded message into B-byte length blocks, and (3) initialization of the SHA function state H. We append a bit "1" and a Q-bit value (in the case of SHA-1 or SHA-256, $Q = 64$ and in the case of SHA-384 or SHA-512, $Q = 128$) representing the L (where L is the length of input message in bits) to the message data. Bit 1 is appended immediately after the message, whereas the Q-bit value is appended at the end of the block. To keep the message multiple of $8*B$ bits (or B bytes), we append zeros between bit 1 and the Q-bit value. Zeros (if needed) and the Q-bit value are appended to the message data in step 1 as message padding. In step 2, we divide the message into data blocks of N $8*B$ bits, and pass them to the SHA function one block per iteration for N iterations. The SHA function updates its state $H^{(i)}$ in every iteration. We initialize the SHA state to $H^{(0)}$ in step 3 of the SHA parser before calling the SHA function.

SHA Function

The SHA function is the core module of the HMAC algorithm. The inputs to the SHA function are message data block $M^{(i)}$ of length $8*B$ bits or $B/4$ 32-bit words and SHA state $H^{(i)}$ (for $i = 1, 2, \ldots, N$). All functions—SHA-1, SHA-256, SHA-384, and SHA-512—are quite similar with simple variations (e.g., different input sizes, initial states, and constant values). The flow of SHA-1 is a little bit different from the other three. In the next section, we discuss the most popular SHA-256 function in detail.

2.4.3 SHA-256 Function

For the SHA-256 function, the length of the input block B is 64 bytes or 16 32-bit words, and the length of state H is eight 32-bit words. The SHA function is called N times to compute the hash value or the message digest of the entire message (divided into N blocks) with one data block per iteration as input. In the SHA-256 function, we perform three steps:

1. Prepare data block scheduling.
2. Initialize eight working variables with initial state $H^{(0)}$ values.
3. Updating of eight working variables with iterative process.

At the end of the SHA function, we update the SHA state $H^{(i)}$ by adding eight working variables to $H^{(i-1)}$ in corresponding positions. Full details of the SHA-256 function follow.

In step 1 of the SHA-256 function (i.e., preparing the data block scheduling), we expand the input data block of 16 32-bit words to 64 32-bit words as follows:

$$W_t = \begin{cases} M_t^{(i)} & 0 \le t \le 15 \\ \sigma_1^{\{256\}}(W_{t-2}) + W_{t-7} + \sigma_0^{\{256\}}(W_{t-15}) + W_{t-16} & 16 \le t \le 63 \end{cases}$$

where

$$\sigma_0^{\{256\}}(x) = ROTR^7(x) \oplus ROTR^{18}(x) \oplus SHR^3(x)$$

$$\sigma_1^{\{256\}}(x) = ROTR^{17}(x) \oplus ROTR^{19}(x) \oplus SHR^{10}(x)$$

$$ROTR^n(y) = (y >> n) \,|\, (y << (32-n))$$

$$SHR^n(y) = y >> n$$

In step 2 of the SHA-256 function, we assign eight working variables ($a, b, c, d, e, f, g,$ and h) with the previous iteration's SHA state H values as shown here:

$$a = H_0^{(i-1)},\quad b = H_1^{(i-1)},\quad c = H_2^{(i-1)},\quad d = H_3^{i-1}$$
$$e = H_4^{(i-1)},\quad f = H_5^{(i-1)},\quad g = H_6^{(i-1)},\quad h = H_7^{(i-1)}$$

In step 3, we update eight working variables of SHA-256 through the following iterative process:

Loop: $j = 1{:}64$

$$T_1 = h + \sum\nolimits_1^{\{256\}}(e) + Ch(e, f, g) + K_j^{256} + W_j$$

$$T_2 = \sum\nolimits_0^{\{256\}}(a) + Maj(a, b, c)$$

$$h = g$$

$$g = f$$

$$f = e$$

$$e = d + T_1$$

$$d = c$$

$$c = b$$

$$b = a$$

$$a = T_1 + T_2$$

End Loop

where

$$\Sigma_0^{\{256\}}(x) = ROTR^2(x) \oplus ROTR^{13}(x) \oplus ROTR^{22}(x)$$

$$\Sigma_1^{\{256\}}(x) = ROTR^6(x) \oplus ROTR^{11}(x) \oplus ROTR^{25}(x)$$

$$Ch(x, y, z) = (x \wedge y) \oplus (\tilde{x} \wedge z)$$

$$Maj(x, y, z) = (x \wedge y) \oplus (x \wedge z) \oplus (y \wedge z)$$

$$ROTR^n(y) = (y >> n) \mid ((y << (32 - n))$$

and $K_j^{\{256\}}$ comprises the following 64 constant values array $\boldsymbol{K}[\,]$:

```
K[64] = {
0x428a2f98, 0x71374491, 0xb5c0fbcf, 0xe9b5dba5, 0x3956c25b, 0x59f111f1, 0x923f82a4, 0xab1c5ed5,
0xd807aa98, 0x12835b01, 0x243185be, 0x550c7dc3, 0x72be5d74, 0x80deb1fe, 0x9bdc06a7, 0xc19bf174,
0xe49b69c1, 0xefbe4786, 0x0fc19dc6, 0x240ca1cc, 0x2de92c6f, 0x4a7484aa, 0x5cb0a9dc, 0x76f988da,
0x983e5152, 0xa831c66d, 0xb00327c8, 0xbf597fc7, 0xc6e00bf3, 0xd5a79147, 0x06ca6351, 0x14292967,
0x27b70a85, 0x2e1b2138, 0x4d2c6dfc, 0x53380d13, 0x650a7354, 0x766a0abb, 0x81c2c92e, 0x92722c85,
0xa2bfe8a1, 0xa81a664b, 0xc24b8b70, 0xc76c51a3, 0xd192e819, 0xd6990624, 0xf40e3585, 0x106aa070,
0x19a4c116, 0x1e376c08, 0x2748774c, 0x34b0bcb5, 0x391c0cb3, 0x4ed8aa4a, 0x5b9cca4f, 0x682e6ff3,
0x748f82ee, 0x78a5636f, 0x84c87814, 0x8cc70208, 0x90befffa, 0xa4506ceb, 0xbef9a3f7, 0xc67178f2};
```

After completing three steps of the SHA-256 function, we update the SHA state as follows:

$$H_0^{(i)} = a + H_0^{(i-1)},\quad H_1^{(i)} = b + H_1^{(i-1)},\quad H_2^{(i)} = c + H_2^{(i-1)},\quad H_3^{(i)} = d + H_3^{(i-1)}$$
$$H_4^{(i)} = e + H_4^{(i-1)},\quad H_5^{(i)} = f + H_5^{(i-1)},\quad H_6^{(i)} = g + H_6^{(i-1)},\quad H_7^{(i)} = h + H_7^{(i-1)}$$

Then, we repeat the previous process N times to cover $M^{(i)}$ message blocks. The digest for the entire message is obtained with the last iteration SHA state as

$$H_0^{(N)} || H_1^{(N)} || H_2^{(N)} || H_3^{(N)} || H_4^{(N)} || H_5^{(N)} || H_6^{(N)} || H_7^{(N)}$$

2.4.4 HMAC and SHA-256 Simulation

In this section, we simulate the HMAC with the SHA-256 function. The initial values for the SHA-256 function state H and the defined values for *IPAD* and *OPAD* follow:

```
H[8] = {                    // initial values for SHA-256 state
0x6a09e667, 0xbb67ae85, 0x3c6ef372, 0xa54ff53a,
0x510e527f, 0x9b05688c, 0x1f83d9ab, 0x5be0cd19};

ipad [16]={                 // IPAD for HMAC with SHA-256
0x36363636, 0x36363636,0x36363636, 0x36363636,0x36363636, 0x36363636,0x36363636,
0x36363636, 0x36363636, 0x36363636,0x36363636, 0x36363636,0x36363636, 0x36363636,
0x36363636, 0x36363636};

opad[16] = {                // OPAD for HMAC with SHA-256
0x5c5c5c5c, 0x5c5c5c5c, 0x5c5c5c5c, 0x5c5c5c5c, 0x5c5c5c5c, 0x5c5c5c5c,
0x5c5c5c5c, 0x5c5c5c5c, 0x5c5c5c5c, 0x5c5c5c5c, 0x5c5c5c5c, 0x5c5c5c5c,
0x5c5c5c5c, 0x5c5c5c5c, 0x5c5c5c5c, 0x5c5c5c5c};
```

HMAC Parser

The simulation code for the HMAC parser is given in Pcode 2.28. We define constants and declare variables such that the HMAC parser supports the SHA-256 parser and SHA-256 function. Although the SHA function is computational intensive, it is straightforward with simple operations. The complex part (logically) of the HMAC algorithm is present in the HMAC parser and SHA parser.

Next, we discuss simulating K_0 computation from the given input *KEY*. With the computation of K_0, we basically make the input *KEY* suitable for use with the HMAC + SHA algorithm. Depending on the length of input *KEY* (K in bytes), we have three conditions to check in preparing K_0. If K and B (input block size of the SHA-256 function) are equal, then $K_0 = KEY$. If $K < B$, then K_0 is equal to *KEY* with $(B - K)$ appended zero

```
// prepare K0 of length B (=64) bytes from given key of length K bytes
if (K > 512){
        sha256(key, tmp, K);                     // shorten key to 256 bits
        for(i = 0;i < 8;i++)
                mac_key[i] = tmp[i];
        for(i = 8;i < 16;i++)
                mac_key[i] = 0;                  // append 256 '0' bits
}
else if (K < 512){
        j = K >> 5;
        for(i = 0;i < j;i++)
                mac_key[i] = key[i];
        r0 = key[i];            i = K - (j<<5);
        k =-1;
        k = k << (32-i);
        r0 = r0 & k;
        mac_key[j] = r0;        r0 = 0;
        for(i=j+1;i < 16;i++)
                mac_key[i] = 0;                  // append (B-K) '0x00' bytes
}
else{
        for(i = 0;i < 16;i++)
                mac_key[i] = key[i];
}
for(i = 0;i < 16;i++)                            // K0 XOR ipad and append to in[] as prefix
        in[i] = mac_key[i]^ipad[i];
// apply hash and output to tmp[] array from 16th word to 31st word: H((K0 ^ ipad):text)
sha256(in, &tmp[16], L+512);
for(i = 0;i < 16;i++)                            // K0 XOR opod : H((K0 XOR ipad):text)
        tmp[i] = mac_key[i] ^ opad[i];
sha256(tmp,op,768);                              // H(K0 XOR opad : H((K0 XOR ipad):text))
```

Pcode 2.28: The simulation code for HMAC parser.

bytes from the LSB (least significant bit) side. Simulation of appending $(B-K)$ "0×00" bytes to KEY is not limited to a single instruction code. We have two choices to simulate this: (1) first zeroing the K_0 and adding K bytes from KEY to K_0; and (2) first moving K bytes of KEY to K_0 and zeroing the remaining $(B-K)$ bytes. If $K > B$, then this particular case becomes a bit complex. We first shorten the KEY length to 32 bytes by applying SHA-256 on KEY and then append 32 zero bytes from the LSB side to get K_0.

If we get K_0, then the rest of the HMAC parser is straightforward with operations for XORing, data appending, and computing hash values. Here, we have to take care of the data placement in the buffers properly at the input and output of the SHA function. At the very beginning, the input text is placed in the buffer ***in***[] from the 16th word location and we make sure that the first 16 word positions are empty so that the XORed K_0 and $IPAD$ is placed directly as the prefix in ***in***[] (with this, the simulation of appending K_0 to the input message becomes easy) before calling the SHA function. The SHA function output is also placed after 16 word positions in buffer ***tmp***[] so that the XORed K_0 and $OPAD$ are placed directly as a prefix in the ***tmp***[] buffer. The last SHA function uses ***tmp***[] as its input, and its output (***op***[]) is considered as MAC (message authentication code). Optionally, sometimes we output the left-most t bytes of ***op***[] as MAC.

SHA Parser

The SHA-256 function works on blocks of 512 bits of data at a time. The functionality of the SHA parser prepares those 512-bit blocks for SHA-256 functioning. The SHA parser gets message data along with its length (L) as input. The value of L need not be equal to 512, it can be less than or greater than 512. We insert bit "1" and a 64-bit L value to the message data. If the message data size is not a multiple of 512 bits, then the SHA parser pads "0" bits to message data between the inserted bit 1 and 64-bit value L. Then we divide the message data into N 512-bit data blocks $M^{(i)}$. We compute the hash value for each data block of $M^{(i)}$.

In the SHA parser, first we initialize the SHA state to predefined initial values $H^{(0)}$. Then, if $L > 512$, we compute the hash value with SHA function for each 512-bit message block and add to the SHA state until the length of the message block falls below the 512 mark. If the current length of the remaining message block is 448 bits or more, then we have two more iterations of hash computation, otherwise we compute hash value once. In both cases, we insert a bit "1" at the end of the message and a 64-bit value at the end of the data block along with padded zeros in-between (if needed) to make a 512-bit blocks, and compute its hash values. After each iteration of hash computation, the computed hash values are added to the previous SHA state by the SHA function. The SHA parser outputs SHA state (the final result of all iterations) as a message digest. The simulation code for the SHA parser is given in Pcode 2.29.

SHA-256 Function

The SHA-256 function is a simple algorithm with logical shift and XOR operations. In this SHA function, all additions are performed with module 2^{32}. The SHA-256 function consists of three steps (1) preparation of a 64-word length message from an input 16-word (512 bits) length message, (2) initialization of the eight SHA-256 working variables, and (3) the iterative message digest process. The SHA-256 function gets the previous SHA state and 16 words of message from the SHA parser as an input. In the expanded 64-word message, the first 16 words are the same as the input 16 words. To avoid copying the 16-word input to another buffer in the process of expansion, we pass the input directly into the expand buffer ***W***[ ] by declaring the expand buffer as a global

```
// assign initial values of H
sha_state[0] = H[0]; sha_state[1] = H[1];
sha_state[2] = H[2]; sha_state[3] = H[3];
sha_state[4] = H[4]; sha_state[5] = H[5];
sha_state[6] = H[6]; sha_state[7] = H[7];
// padding zeros
n = L >> 5;      m = n >> 4;
k = 0;
while(m--){
        for(j = 0;j < 16;j++)
                w[j] = in[k++];
        sha256fn(sha_state, w);
}
j = n - k;
if (j >=14){
    i = L - (n << 5);
    tmp1 = 0x80000000;
    tmp1 = tmp1 >> i;                   tmp2 = in[n];
    tmp2 = tmp2 | tmp1;                 w[15] = 0;
    for(i = 0;i < j;i++)
            w[i] = in[k++];
    w[i] = tmp2;
    sha256fn(sha_state, w);
    for(i = 0;i < 15;i++)
            w[i] = 0;
    w[15] = L;
    sha256fn(sha_state, w);
}
else{
    i = L - (n << 5);
    tmp1 = 0x80000000;
    tmp1 = tmp1 >> i;                   tmp2 = in[n];
    tmp2 = tmp2 | tmp1;
    for(i = 0;i < 15;i++)
            w[i] = 0;
    for(i = 0;i < j;i++)
            w[i] = in[k++];
    w[i] = tmp2;                        w[15] = L;
    sha256fn(sha_state, w);
}
out[0] = sha_state[0];  out[1] = sha_state[1];
out[2] = sha_state[2];  out[3] = sha_state[3];
out[4] = sha_state[4];  out[5] = sha_state[5];
out[6] = sha_state[6];  out[7] = sha_state[7];
```

Pcode 2.29: The simulation code for SHA parser.

variable. Now, we expand the message from 16 to 63 words (a total of 48 words) by using the equations given in step 1 of the SHA function (see Section 2.4.3).

In step 2 of the SHA-256 function, we initialize all eight working variables with SHA state values. The iterative process of the SHA-256 in step 3 involves updating of these eight working variables in each iteration (see step 3 of the SHA function in Section 2.4.3). Here, we compute two temporary values. The first temporary value is computed from some of the working variables, expanded message and predefined constants and the second one is computed from only working variables. Then, we update the next iteration eight working variables with the present iteration working variable and with the two temporary values computed. After completion of the iterative process, the updated eight working variables are added to the SHA state. The simulation code for SHA-256 function is given in Pcode 2.30.

```
for(i = 16;i < 64;i++){                                          // prepare 64 word length message
    tmp1 = W[i-7]; tmp2 = W[i-16];
    r0 = W[i-2]; r1 = W[i-15];
    r2 = r0 >> 17; r3 = r1 >> 7;
    r4 = r0 << 15; r5 = r1 << 25;
    r6 = r2 | r4; r7 = r3 | r5;
    r4 = r0 >> 19; r5 = r1 >> 18;
    r2 = r0 << 13; r3 = r1 << 14;
    r2 = r2 | r4; r3 = r3 | r5;
    r6 = r6 ^ r2; r7 = r7 ^ r3;
    r2 = r0 >> 10; r3 = r1 >> 3;
    r6 = r6 ^ r2; r7 = r7 ^ r3;
    r6 = r6 + tmp1; r7 = r7 + tmp2;
    W[i] = r6 + r7;
}
r0 = state[0]; r1 = state[1];                                    // initialize a, b
r2 = state[2]; r3 = state[3];                                    // initialize c, d
r4 = state[4]; r5 = state[5];                                    // initialize e, f
r6 = state[6]; r7 = state[7];                                    // initialize g, h
for(i = 0;i < 64;i++){                                           // start message digest loop
    tmp3 = r4 >> 6; tmp4 = r0 >> 2;
    tmp5 = r4 << 26; tmp6 = r0 << 30;
    tmp1 = tmp3 | tmp5; tmp2 = tmp4 | tmp6;
    tmp3 = r4 >> 11; tmp4 = r0 >> 13;
    tmp5 = r4 << 21; tmp6 = r0 << 19;
    tmp3 = tmp3 | tmp5; tmp4 = tmp4 | tmp6;
    tmp1 = tmp1 ^ tmp3; tmp2 = tmp2 ^ tmp4;
    tmp3 = r4 >> 25; tmp4 = r0 >> 22;
    tmp5 = r4 << 7;  tmp6 = r0 << 10;
    tmp3 = tmp3 | tmp5; tmp4 = tmp4 | tmp6;
    tmp1 = tmp1 ^ tmp3; tmp2 = tmp2 ^ tmp4;
    tmp3 = r4 & r5; tmp4 = r0 & r1;
    tmp5 = ~r4 & r6; tmp6 = r0 & r2;
    tmp3 = tmp3 ^ tmp5; tmp4 = tmp4 ^ tmp6;
    tmp6 = r1 & r2;
    tmp4 = tmp4 ^ tmp6;
    tmp1 = tmp1 + tmp3; tmp2 = tmp2 + tmp4;
    tmp1 = tmp1 + r7;
    tmp1 = tmp1 + K[i];
    tmp1 = tmp1 + W[i];
    r7 = r6; r6 = r5;
    r5 = r4; r4 = r3 + tmp1;
    r3 = r2; r2 = r1;
    r1 = r0; r0 = tmp1 + tmp2;
}
state[0] = state[0] + r0;        state[1] = state[1] + r1;
state[2] = state[2] + r2;        state[3] = state[3] + r3;
state[4] = state[4] + r4;        state[5] = state[5] + r5;
state[6] = state[6] + r6;        state[7] = state[7] + r7;
```

Pcode 2.30: The simulation code for SHA-256 function.

Simulation Results

The simulation results of HMAC using the SHA-256 algorithm follow. Inputs for HMAC are 320 bits of message and 264 bits of key. As the length of key (K) is less than the SHA function input block length (B), we append 248 zero bits (i.e., B-K bytes) to the input KEY to form 512 bits K_0. Intermediate values for main operations are presented along with their output data lengths in bits.

```
Input Message (M): 320 bits
0x00112233, 0x44556677, 0x8899aabb, 0xccddeeff, 0x0f1e2d3c, 0x4b5a6978, 0x8796a5b4, 0xc3d2e1f0, 0x01234567, 0x89abcdef
Input Key: 264 bits //ignore all bits of last word except 8 msbs
0x4a09e669, 0xdb67ae81, 0xec6ef374, 0x554ff539, 0x310e527c, 0x7b056882, 0x7f83d9a1, 0x1be0cd18, 0x20000000
K0: 512 bits
0x4a09e669, 0xdb67ae81, 0xec6ef374, 0x554ff539, 0x310e527c, 0x7b056882, 0x7f83d9a1, 0x1be0cd18, 0x20000000, 0x00000000,
0x00000000, 0x00000000,0x00000000, 0x00000000, 0x00000000, 0x00000000
K0 XOR IPAD: 512 bits
0x7c3fd05f, 0xed5198b7, 0xda58c542, 0x6379c30f, 0x0738644a, 0x4d335eb4, 0x49b5ef97, 0x2dd6fb2e, 0x16363636, 0x36363636,
0x36363636, 0x36363636, 0x36363636, 0x36363636, 0x36363636, 0x36363636
(K0 XOR IPAD)||M: 832 bits
0x7c3fd05f, 0xed5198b7, 0xda58c542, 0x6379c30f, 0x0738644a, 0x4d335eb4, 0x49b5ef97, 0x2dd6fb2e, 0x16363636, 0x36363636,
0x36363636, 0x36363636, 0x36363636, 0x36363636, 0x36363636, 0x36363636, 0x00112233, 0x44556677, 0x8899aabb, 0xccddeeff,
0x0f1e2d3c, 0x4b5a6978, 0x8796a5b4, 0xc3d2e1f0, 0x01234567, 0x89abcdef
H((K0 XOR IPAD)||M): 256 bits
0x4e938d08, 0x322f37e8, 0x8df9483f, 0x1c68c2e1, 0xfe1411e0, 0x85e8b0d0, 0xbc196189, 0x006378d6
K0 XOR OPAD: 512 bits
0x1655ba35, 0x873bf2dd, 0xb032af28, 0x0913a965, 0x6d520e20, 0x275934de, 0x23df85fd, 0x47bc9144, 0x7c5c5c5c,
0x5c5c5c5c, 0x5c5c5c5c, 0x5c5c5c5c, 0x5c5c5c5c, 0x5c5c5c5c, 0x5c5c5c5c, 0x5c5c5c5c
(K0 XOR OPAD)||H((K0 XOR IPAD)||M): 768 bits
0x1655ba35, 0x873bf2dd, 0xb032af28, 0x0913a965, 0x6d520e20, 0x275934de, 0x23df85fd, 0x47bc9144, 0x7c5c5c5c, 0x5c5c5c5c,
0x5c5c5c5c, 0x5c5c5c5c, 0x5c5c5c5c, 0x5c5c5c5c, 0x5c5c5c5c, 0x5c5c5c5c, 0x4e938d08, 0x322f37e8, 0x8df9483f, 0x1c68c2e1,
0xfe1411e0, 0x85e8b0d0, 0xbc196189, 0x006378d6
H((K0 XOR OPAD)||H((K0 XOR IPAD)||M)): 256 bits
0xbaa04656, 0x9880510e, 0x94b6c6c7, 0x58737860, 0xc3ccf3d6, 0xc6100ed5, 0x7566260d, 0x8f8b2f33
Message Authentication Code (MAC): 88 bits (taking t = 11 left-most bytes)
0xbaa04656, 0x9880510e, 0x94b6c600
```

2.4.5 Computational Complexity of HMAC

The SHA function is a complex core module of the HMAC algorithm. First we analyze the complexity of the SHA function in terms of cycles (see Appendix A, Section A.4, on the companion website for more details on the cycle consumption of particular operations on the reference embedded processor). The common operations in the SHA function are ROTR, XOR, ADD mod 2^{32}, SHIFT and OR. The ROTR operation is achieved with two SHIFTs and one OR. In the first step of the SHA-256 function, we iterate the loop 48 times. In a single iteration of the loop, we have five load-store operations and 20 arithmetic and logical operations. We have a total of 25 operations, and a single iteration consumes 25 cycles. Therefore, we consume about 1200 ($= 25*48$) for 48 iterations. We consume eight cycles in assigning eight working variables. In the iterative message digest process, we run the loop 64 times. In a single iteration of the message digest iterative process, we have 41 arithmetic and logical operations and two load operations. Therefore, a single iteration costs 43 cycles. We consume a total of 2752 cycles for the message digest iterative process; at the end we spend another eight to update the SHA state. With this, the SHA-256 function consumes 3968 ($= 1200 + 2752 + 16$) cycles.

In the SHA parser, we spend 16 cycles for initializing the state and for copying the state to the output buffer at the end. We spend 50 to 65 cycles for message padding (includes inserting bit "1", inserting 64-bit value L, padding zeros [if needed] and dividing the padded message into blocks) and for calling SHA-256 function. Here, we consume 50 cycles for only one call of the SHA-256 function. If the length of the message is larger than 448 bits, then we call the SHA-256 function multiple times. In that case, for each extra call, we consume about 28 cycles (for copying 16 words to the working buffer and for the function call).

In HMAC parser, we consume 16 to 24 cycles to prepare K_0 (apart from the SHA-256 function call cycles). We consume 32 cycles for XORing KEY with $IPAD$ and $OPAD$. Another 20 cycles are consumed for two SHA-parser function calls. The overall cycle consumption of the HMAC algorithm depends on message length and key length. Here, we analyze HMAC complexity for message length of 320 bits and key length of 264 bits. The clock cycles distribution is shown in the following:

HMAC Parser:
 K_0 preparation: 24 cycles
 IPAD & *OPAD*: 32 cycles
 Two SHA-parser calls: 24 cycles

SHA Parser: $L = 832, 768$
 Two times 2 SHA-256 calls: 200 ($= 2*(16+28+50+\text{overhead})$) cycles

SHA-256 function:
 Four times called: 15,872 cycles

Total: 16,152

From the previous cycle count information, it is clear that the SHA-256 function consumes more than 98% of cycles and both the HMAC parser and SHA parser consume only less than 2% of total cycles.

2.5 Elliptic-Curve Digital Signature Algorithm

Public key cryptography allows us to have data authentication. Since the invention of public-key cryptography in 1976 by Whitfield Diffie and Martin Hellman, various public-key cryptographic systems have been proposed. Security in all of these systems relies on the difficulty of solving an underlying mathematical problem. In public key cryptographic algorithms (unlike in symmetric key algorithms where we use the same secret key for both encryption and decryption), the key used for encryption is different from the key used for decryption, and hence we also call the public key algorithms as asymmetric key algorithms.

2.5.1 Digital Signature Algorithm

Digital signature algorithm (DSA), based on public key cryptography techniques, is used in conjunction with the hash function SHA to provide data authentication and data integrity. See Section 2.4.3 for more details on how to compute hash value (or message digest) using the SHA function for a given message. In this section more emphasis is given to DSA based on elliptic curve public-key cryptographic systems. We discuss ECDSA (elliptic-curve DSA) algorithms, their simulation techniques and also present a few simulation results at the end.

DSA Algorithm Analogous

Conceptually, today electronic mail (e-mail) system works on the philosophy of public key cryptography. In the e-mail system, the user will have two identifications: (1) e-mail id and (2) password to send or receive e-mail. An e-mail id is in the public domain and the password is with the user (and it's not disclosed to the public). If the user wants to send an e-mail, then that user has to enter into an e-mail system by using his/her password. Once the user is in the electronic mail system, then he or she can send a mail using another end person's e-mail id. If the user wants to receive an e-mail from the other end person, then that person also follows the same procedure to send an e-mail. In other words, the sender uses his/her password to send a message and the receiver views the e-mail with the help of the sender e-mail id.

In the same way, with DSA using the public key cryptographic system, we have a key-pair, namely, public key and private key. If we want to have authenticity and integrity to our communicating message, then we use a DSA scheme to provide authenticity and integrity to the message. Using the DSA scheme, the sender generates a digital signature using his/her private key and send the message along with the signature to the recipient. After receiving the message, the recipient verifies the signature using the sender public key to rule out any third-party involvement in this data communication. In other words, if the received signature is a valid one, then we assume that the message is not altered. Later we briefly discuss three popular DSA approaches to protect data/messages.

The DSA algorithm is intended for use in electronic mail, electronic funds transfer, electronic data interchange, software distribution, data storage, and other applications that require data integrity assurance and data origin authentication. Similar to DSA, the HMAC (keyed-hash message authentication code) algorithm also provides data/message authentication and integrity. The only difference is that the HMAC uses same key for generation and verification of authentication code using SHA, whereas the DSA algorithm uses the public key cryptographic system in conjunction with the SHA function to provide data authenticity and integrity.

2.5.2 DSA Description

Building blocks of digital signature algorithm (DSA) are shown in Figure 2.12. The basic digital signature scheme consists of three blocks and they are (1) the key-pair generation block, (2) the message digest generation block, and (3) the signature generation/verification block. The key-pair generator generates two keys; we call them the private key and public key. Here the private key is a secret key and should not be shared/disclosed. The public key will be in the public domain and anyone can access it. The message digest block computes a unique condensed value (called as message digest) corresponding to the message (that is supposed to be communicated) using an SHA hash function. If party A wants to send a message to party B, and if party B wants to have a message authenticity and integrity, then party A must generate a digital signature for the message using his/her private key and send the message to B along with the signature. Party B checks the validity of the message after receiving it by verifying the signature using sender's public key.

As shown in Figure 2.13, at the source (transmitter side), the sender generates a signature using his/her private key and using the message digest value. At the destination (receiver side), the receiver checks the validity of the message by verifying the received signature using the sender public key and using the message digest value. Note that the receiver also computes the message digest for the received message and that both message digests computed at the transmitter and receiver are the same if the message is unaltered.

The digital signature algorithm uses a mathematical system for its key-pair generation and digital signature generation/verification processes. Any DSA mathematical system consists of a parameter set (field elements,

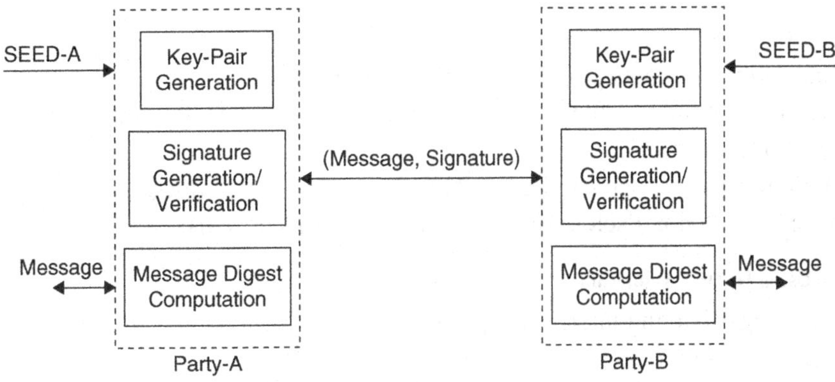

Figure 2.12: Digital signature algorithm building blocks.

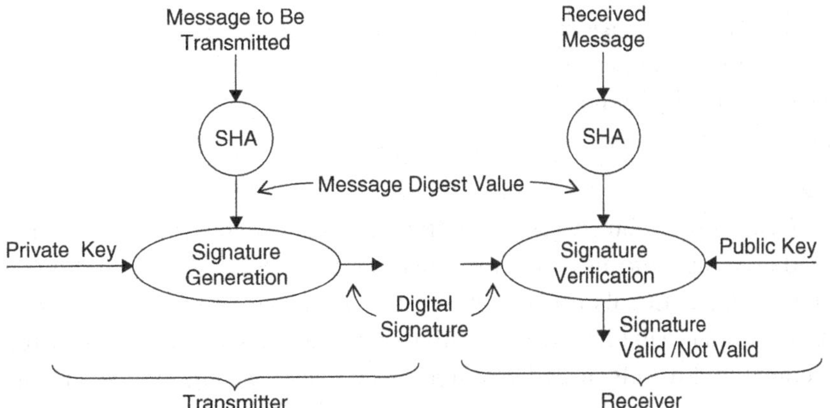

Figure 2.13: DSA algorithm-flow diagram.

order of a field, etc.) and an operation set (modular arithmetic computations and other operations depend on the particular parameter set chosen for DSA). As of today, DSA supports three popular types of parameter sets and they are (1) RSA parameter set, (2) discrete logarithm based parameter set, and (3) elliptic curve-based parameter set. Both sender and receiver must use the same parameter set to communicate with each other. In the following subsections, we discuss and compare three DSA approaches in terms of security (for given key size) and mathematical complexity.

RSA Public Key Cryptography Based DSA

The RSA digital signature algorithm, based on integer factorization problem, is an FIPS approved or NIST recommended cryptographic algorithm for generating and validating digital signatures. The strength of the RSA algorithm depends on the computational difficulty of factoring large numbers. Steps in the RSA algorithm follow.

1. Generate two large prime numbers p and q.
2. Let $n = pq$, and let $m = (p-1)(q-1)$.
3. Choose a small number e, coprime to m.
4. Find d, such that $de(\bmod m) = 1$. Then, publish (e, n) as the *public key* and keep (d, n) as the *secret/private key*. See Appendix B, Section B.2, on the companion website for more details on modulo arithmetic.
5. If T and C denote plain text and cipher text, then encrypted text $C = T^e(\bmod n)$ and decrypted text $T = C^d(\bmod n)$.

Discrete Logarithm-Based DSA

The digital signature algorithm, based on a discrete logarithm problem, is an FIPS-approved or NIST-recommended cryptographic algorithm for generating and validating digital signatures. The strength of DLDSA depends on the computational difficulty of finding a logarithm for large numbers. Key-pair generation, signature generation, and signature verification steps of the DLDSA algorithm follow.

DLDSA Algorithm Key-Pair Generation

1. Choose two large prime numbers p and q such that q divides $p-1$.
2. Choose g, an element of order q in GF(p), see Appendix B, Section B.2, on the companion website for more details on Galois field.
3. Select a random integer x in the range $[1, q-1]$ and compute $y = g^x \bmod p$.
4. Here, x is private key (do not disclose) and y is public key (disclose it).

Signature Generation Using DLDSA Algorithm

1. Select a random integer k in the interval $[1, q-1]$.
2. Compute $r = (g^k \bmod p) \bmod q$.
3. Compute $s = k^{-1}(e + xr) \bmod q$, where $e = \mathrm{SHA}(M)$ is a message digest value.
4. The signature for message M is (r, s).

Signature Verification Using DLDSA Algorithm

1. Compute $e = \mathrm{SHA}(M)$, a message digest value for received message M.
2. Compute $u_1 = es^{-1} \bmod q$ and $u_2 = rs^{-1} \bmod q$, where (r, s) is received signature for M.
3. Compute $v = (g^{u_1} y^{u_2} \bmod p) \bmod q$.
4. If $v = r$, then signature is valid and accept the message.

Elliptic Curve-Based DSA

Elliptic curve DSA (ECDSA) algorithm, based on elliptic curve discrete logarithm problem, is an FIPS-approved or NIST-recommended cryptographic algorithm for generating and validating digital signatures. The strength of ECDSA depends on the computational difficulty of finding a logarithm of an elliptic curve point. The structure and flow of ECDSA are similar to the DLDSA algorithm discussed in Section 2.5.2, Discrete Logarithm-Based DSA. In the later sections, full details of ECDSA along with necessary algorithms and simulation techniques are discussed. In the next subsection, the three approaches of DSA are compared with respect to security level for the given key sizes.

Comparison of Three DSA Approaches

Now, we compare the three DSA approaches, RSA, DLDSA and ECDSA, with respect to key sizes used by a particular approach for a required security. Key sizes of three approaches for a given security level are given in Table 2.4.

If we take care of weak instances of three approaches and if we use a general-purpose algorithm to solve the underlying problem of three approaches, then RSA and DLDSA are solved in subexponential time (solving a problem in subexponential time is still considered as hard) whereas ECDSA can be solved only in exponential time. In simple terms, this means that the elliptic curve discrete logarithm problem is currently considered harder than either the integer factorization problem or the discrete logarithm problem. Table 2.5 compares the time required to break the ECC with the time required to break RSA or DSA for various key sizes using the best-known general algorithm. The values are computed in MIPS years. A MIPS year represents a computing time of 1 year on a machine capable of performing one million instructions per second.

2.5.3 Elliptic Curves Overview

Mathematical systems (with parameter set, operation set) used in DSA forms an algebraic group. A group consists of a set of elements with predefined operations on those elements. In this section, we discuss algebraic groups formed by elliptic curves. For elliptic curve groups, the operation set is defined geometrically. Before going to elliptic curve groups defined over finite fields, we understand elliptic curves with real numbers.

Elliptic Curves

An elliptic curve over real numbers is defined with a set of points $\{(X_i, Y_i)\}$ satisfying an elliptic curve equation $E(x, y)$ of the form $y^2 = x^3 + ax + b$, where a and b are real numbers. With different values of parameters a and b, we have different elliptic curves. One such elliptic curve geometrical view is shown in Figure 2.14.

$P{:}(X_p, Y_p)$, $Q{:}(X_q, Y_q)$, and $R{:}(X_r, Y_r)$ are three points on elliptic curve $E(x, y)$ as shown in Figure 2.14. If $4a^3 + 27b^2$ is not 0, then the elliptic curve $y^2 = x^3 + ax + b$ forms an additive group, meaning that the points on the elliptic curve follows the closure property (i.e., the resulting point after adding two points on elliptic curve also satisfies the elliptic curve), identity property (consists of identity element with respect to addition) and inverse property (consists of inverse element with respect to addition). See the following subsections for rules of addition with the elliptic curve points. An elliptic curve group over real numbers consists of points on the corresponding elliptic curve, together with a special point O called the point at infinity. In elliptic curve operations, O is treated as an identity element and the elliptic curve additive group satisfies the identity property

Table 2.4: Comparison of three approaches with respect to key sizes for a given security level

	Private Key Size	Public Key Size
RSA	2048	1088
DLDSA	160	1024
ECDSA	160	161

Table 2.5: Comparison of security levels of RSA, DLDSA, and ECDSA for given key sizes

	Key Size		
MIPS Years	RSA	DLDSA	ECDSA
4.5×10^5	512	512	128
3×10^{12}	1024	1024	172
3×10^{21}	2048	2048	234
2×10^{33}	4096	4096	314

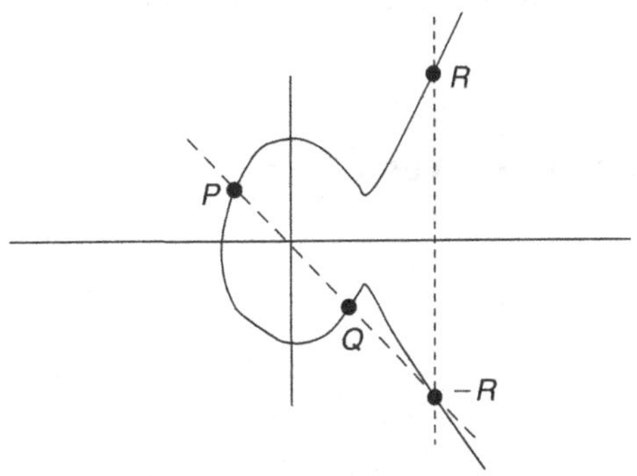

Figure 2.14: Elliptic curve $E(x, y)$.

$P+O=O+P=P$. A reflection of a point R on the elliptic curve with respect to the x-axis is treated as $-R$ and its coordinates are $(X_r, -Y_r)$. If $P=-Q$, then $P+Q=O$, a point at infinity and hence it follows the inverse property over addition.

Addition of Two Points on Elliptic Curve The addition of two points P and Q (where $P \neq Q$) on an elliptic curve is defined as a reflection of point of $-R{:}(X_r, -Y_r)$ which is a point of intersection of the elliptic curve with a line passing through P and Q. Geometric interpretation of the addition of points P and Q on the elliptic curve $E(x, y)$ is shown in Figure 2.14. Algebraically, the coordinates (X_r, Y_r) of the resulting point R after adding points P and Q are obtained as

$$X_r = s^2 - X_p - X_q \quad \text{and} \quad Y_r = -Y_p + s(X_p - X_r)$$

where $s=(Y_p - Y_q)/(X_p - X_q)$, the slope of the line passing through P and Q.

Point Double on Elliptic Curve When P and Q represent the same point on the elliptic curve, then we define another operation called point double instead of points addition. Point double is defined as a reflection of point $-R{:}(X_r, -Y_r)$ which is a point of intersection of an elliptic curve with the tangent line passing through $P{:}(X_p, Y_p)$. The coordinates (X_r, Y_r) of point $R=2P$ are obtained as

$$X_r = s^2 - 2X_p \quad \text{and} \quad Y_r = -Y_p + s(X_p - X_r)$$

where $s=(3X_p^2 + a)/(2Y_p)$, the slope of the tangent passing through point P.

Scalar Point Multiplication Multiplication of point P of an elliptic curve by a constant k is termed as scalar point multiplication. Scalar multiplication of point P with k results in another point S on the elliptic curve. If $k=5$, then $S=5P$ and the point S is obtained from P with point double and point add operations as P, $2P$ after first doubling, $4P$ after second doubling, and $5P$ after adding P to $4P$. As seen in subsequent sections, the scalar point multiplication is a computationally intensive part of ECDSA algorithm.

Elliptic Curves over Finite Fields GF(q)

Elliptic curves over real numbers are of no practical use as they cannot be used in cryptographic applications. Moreover, computationally it is not feasible to work with real number elliptic curves. Therefore, hereafter we consider elliptic curves defined over finite fields. A group over a finite field contains a finite number of elements and the output of the group operation after modulo reduction (either with prime P or an irreducible polynomial depending on the finite field) results in an element that also belongs to the same finite field. The order of the finite field is given by the number of elements in that finite field. Next, we discuss the elliptic curves defined over prime Galois fields GF(P) and binary Galois fields GF(2^m).

Elliptic Curves over Prime Field GF(P)

An elliptic curve $E(p)$ over GF(P) defined by the parameters a and b is the set of solutions $\{(X_i, Y_i)$, for $X_i, Y_i \in \mathrm{GF}(P)\}$, to the equation: $y^2 = x^3 + ax + b$, together with the point O at infinity. The number of points in $E(P)$ is denoted by $\#E(P)$. If $4a^3 + 27b^2 (\bmod P)$ is not zero, then $E(P)$ forms an additive group satisfying closure property, identity property and inverse property. In the prime field GF(P), the equations for elliptic curve points operations are the same as that defined over a real number in the previous section except with the extra computation of modulo reduction on the result of the operation with prime number P to make sure that the result belongs to the prime field GF(P).

Example 2.1: Elliptic Curve over GF(23)

Points that satisfy the elliptic curve $y^2 = x^3 + x + 1$ defined over GF(23) with $a=b=1$ follow: (0, 1) (0, 22) (1, 7) (1, 16) (3, 10) (3, 13) (4, 0) (5, 4) (5, 19) (6, 4) (6, 19) (7, 11) (7, 12) (9, 7) (9, 16) (11, 3) (11, 20)(12, 4)(12, 19)(13, 7)(13, 16)(17, 3)(17, 20)(18, 3)(18, 20)(19, 5)(19, 18). The curve $E(23)$ has 28 points (including the point at infinity O; we can assign $O=(0,0)$ in this example as (0,0) is not on the curve). If $P=(5,4)$, $Q=(7,11)$, then using the points addition rule and point double rule, the points $R = P + Q$ and $W = 2P$ are computed as (see Appendix B, Section B.2.2, on the companion website for more details on computing in GF(P)).

$$P = (X_p, Y_p) = (5, 4),$$
$$Q = (X_q, Y_q) = (7, 11)$$
$$R = (X_r, Y_r) = P + Q$$
$$s = (Y_p - Y_q)/(X_p - X_q) = (4 - 11)/(5 - 7) = -7/-2 = 7/2 = (7 + 23)/2 = 30/2 = 15$$
$$X_r = s^2 - X_p - X_q = 225 - 5 - 7(\text{mod } 23) = 213(\text{mod } 23) = 6$$
$$Y_r = s(X_p - X_r) - Y_p = 15(5 - 6) - 4(\text{mod } 23) = -15 - 4(\text{mod } 23) = -19(\text{mod } 23) = -19 + 23 = 4$$
$$W = (X_w, Y_w) = 2P$$
$$s = (3X_p^2 + a)/(2Y_p) = (75 + 1)/8 = 76(\text{mod } 23)/8 = 7/8 = (7 + 23 \times 7)/8 = 168/8 = 21$$
$$X_w = s^2 - 2X_p = 441 - 2 \times 5 = 431(\text{mod } 23) = 17$$
$$Y_w = s(X_p - X_w) - Y_p = 21(5 - 17) - 4 = -21 \times 12 - 4 = -256(\text{mod } 23) = -3(\text{mod } 23)$$
$$= -3 + 23 = 20$$

Note that the resulting points R and W, after addition and doubling of given points P and Q, also lie on the same elliptic curve.

■

Elliptic Curves over Binary Field GF(2^m)

An elliptic curve $E(2^m)$ over GF(2^m) defined by the parameters $a, b \in \text{GF}(2^m), b \neq 0$, is the set of solutions $\{(X_i, Y_i)$, for $X_i, Y_i \in \text{GF}(2^m)\}$, to the equation $y^2 + xy = x^3 + ax^2 + b$ together with a point O at infinity. The number of points in $E(2^m)$ is denoted by $\#E(2^m)$. The additive inverse of point $R{:}(X_r, Y_r)$ of $E(2^m)$ is defined as $-R{:}(X_r, X_r + Y_r)$. With this, the elliptic curve $E(2^m)$ points form an additive group with satisfying closure, identity, and inverse properties. The operations of the elliptic curve over the GF(2^m) field are defined in the following.

Addition Rule Let $P{:}(X_p, Y_p) \in E(2^m)$ and $Q{:}(X_q, Y_q) \in E(2^m)$ be the two points such that $X_p \neq X_q$. Then the coordinates (X_r, Y_r) of R, the result after the addition of two points P and Q, is given by

$$X_r = s^2 + s + X_p + X_q + a, Y_r = s(X_p + X_r) + Y_p + X_r, \quad \text{where} \quad s = (Y_p + Y_q)/(X_p + X_q)$$

Doubling Rule Let $(X_p, Y_p) \in E(2^m)$ be a point with $X_p \neq 0$. The coordinates (X_r, Y_r) of R, the result after a doubling of P, are given by

$$X_r = s^2 + s + a, Y_r = X_p^2 + (s + 1)X_r, \quad \text{where} \quad s = X_p + \frac{Y_p}{X_p}$$

Example 2.2: Elliptic Curve over GF(2^4)

With the irreducible polynomial $f(x) = x^4 + x + 1$ and primitive element α, the generated elements of GF(2^4) follow (see Appendix B, Section B.2.3, on the companion website for more details on computing in GF(2^m)).

$$\alpha^0 = (0001), \alpha^1 = (0010), \alpha^2 = (0100), \alpha^3 = (1000), \alpha^4 = (0011), \alpha^5 = (0110), \alpha^6 = (1100),$$
$$\alpha^7 = (1011), \alpha^8 = (0101), \alpha^9 = (1010), \alpha^{10} = (0111), \alpha^{11} = (1110), \alpha^{12} = (1111), \alpha^{13} = (1101),$$
$$\alpha^{14} = (1001), \alpha^{15} = \alpha^0(0001)$$

Consider an elliptic curve $E(2^4)$ over GF(2^4), with defining equation $y^2+xy=x^3+\alpha^4x^2+1$ for $a=\alpha^4$ and $b=1$. The solution set of the elliptic curve $E(2^4)$ defined over GF(2^4) is given by:

$$\{(0,\alpha^0),(\alpha^0,\alpha^6),(\alpha^0,\alpha^{13}),(\alpha^3,\alpha^8),(\alpha^3,\alpha^{13}),(\alpha^5,\alpha^3),(\alpha^5,\alpha^{11}),(\alpha^6,\alpha^8),(\alpha^6,\alpha^{14}),(\alpha^9,\alpha^{10}),(\alpha^9,\alpha^{13}),(\alpha^{10},\alpha^1),(\alpha^{10},\alpha^8),(\alpha^{12},\alpha^0),(\alpha^{12},\alpha^{12})\}$$

The solution set has 16 elements (including the point at infinity O, we can assign $O=(0,0)$ in this example as $(0,0)$ is not on the curve). If $P=(\alpha^5,\alpha^3)$ and $Q=(\alpha^6,\alpha^8)$, then, using the points addition rule and the point double rule, the points $R=P+Q$ and $W=2P$ are computed as follows:

$$s=(Y_p+Y_q)/(X_p+X_q)=(\alpha^3+\alpha^8)/(\alpha^5+\alpha^6)=\alpha^{13}/\alpha^9=\alpha^4$$

$$X_r=s^2+s+X_p+X_q+a=a^8+a^4+a^5+a^6+a^4=(a^2+1)(a^2+a)(a^3+a^2)=a^3+a^2+a+1=\alpha^{12}$$

$$Y_r=s(X_p+X_r)+Y_p+X_r=\alpha^4(\alpha^5+\alpha^{12})+\alpha^3+\alpha^{12}=\alpha^4\alpha^{14}+\alpha^{10}=\alpha^3+\alpha^2+\alpha+1=\alpha^{12}$$

$$s=\alpha^5+\alpha^3/\alpha^5=\alpha^2+\alpha+\alpha^{18}/\alpha^5=\alpha^2+\alpha+\alpha^{13}=\alpha^2+\alpha+\alpha^3+\alpha^2+1=\alpha^7$$

$$X_w=s^2+s+a=\alpha^{14}+\alpha^7+\alpha^4=(\alpha^3+1)+(\alpha^3+\alpha+1)+(\alpha+1)=\alpha^0$$

$$Y_w=X_p{}^2+(s+1)X_w=\alpha^{10}+(\alpha^7+1)\alpha^0=(\alpha^2+\alpha+1)+(\alpha^3+\alpha+1)=\alpha^6$$

Note that the resulting points R:$(\alpha^{12},\alpha^{12})$ and W:(α^0,α^6), after addition and doubling of given points P:(α^5,α^3) and Q:(α^6,α^8), also lie on the same elliptic curve.

■

2.5.4 ECDSA

In this section, we discuss the application of elliptic curves defined over finite fields GF(q). Similar to the discrete logarithm problem (DLP), an elliptic curve discrete logarithm problem (ECDLP) is described as, find the integer a given $Q \in E(q)$ and $W=aQ$, where $q=$ prime P or 2^m. As described in Section 2.5.2, Comparison of Three DSA Approaches, solving ECDLP needs exponential computational time. Because of this reason, digital signature algorithms (DSA) over elliptic curve groups are recommended for many applications. Before going into the use of elliptic curves in DSA, we explore some of the standard parameters (also called domain parameters) necessary to work with ECDLP. These domain parameters follow:

- Elliptic curve coefficients: a, b
- Elliptic curve base point: G
- Order of elliptic curve base point G:n (a subset n elements of $E(q)$ are given by rG, $1\le r\le n-1$)
- Cofactor: h (is equal to N/n, where N is the order of the elliptic curve $\#E(q)$)

First we set up the parameter set by selecting coefficients a and b of the elliptic curve defined over GF(q). Then we select a base point G such that the order of the elliptic-curve group base point is the order of n. With this, we can generate a subset of elliptic curve group elements as $\{O, G, 2G, 3G, \ldots, (n-1)G\}$. Here, the choice of the base point G is not a security consideration as long as it has a large prime order as required by the standards. However, sender and receiver must use the same set of elliptic curve domain parameters. One example set of domain parameters follows:

```
a = 00 17858FEB 7A989751 69E171F7 7B4087DE 098AC8A9 11DF7B01
b = 00 FDFB49BF E6C3A89F ACADAA7A 1E5BBC7C C1C2E5D8 31478814
G = (01 F481BC 5F0FF84A 74AD6CDF 6FDEF4BF 61796253 72D8C0C5E1,
     00 25E399F2 903712CC F3EA9E3A 1AD17FB0 B3201B6A F7CE1B05)
n = 01 00000000 00000000 00000000 C7F34A77 8F443ACC 920EBA49
h = 2
```

The previous domain parameters are used with elliptic curve E: $y^2+xy=x^3+ax^2+b$ over GF(2^{193}).

Key-Pair Generation

In the key-pair generation, first we choose a statistically unique random number k in the interval $[1, n-1]$. Usually k is generated using a pseudorandom number generator (block ciphers discussed in Sections 2.2 and 2.3 can be used for pseudorandom number generation) and we assume that k is available for our key-pair generation process. Once we have k, then we compute a point W on $E(2^m)$ as $W = kG$. In other words, we compute point W by multiplying the elliptic curve base point G with a large random number k. The size of random number k can be up to m bits. The flow diagram of key-pair generation is shown in Figure 2.15.

As shown in Figure 2.15, ECDSA key-pair generation process outputs (k, W), where k is a private key and W is a public key. The private key k should not be shared with the public and the sender only uses k for generating the signature of message. Anyone can have access to the public key W, and the recipient verifies the digital signature using W. Techniques to implement key generation process on an embedded processor are presented in Section 2.5.5.

Signature Generation

The ECDSA signature generation process consists of three steps and they are (1) pseudorandom number generation, (2) message digest computation, and (3) signature generation. The flow diagram of the ECDSA signature generation process is shown in Figure 2.16. In the signature-generation process, after generating pseudorandom

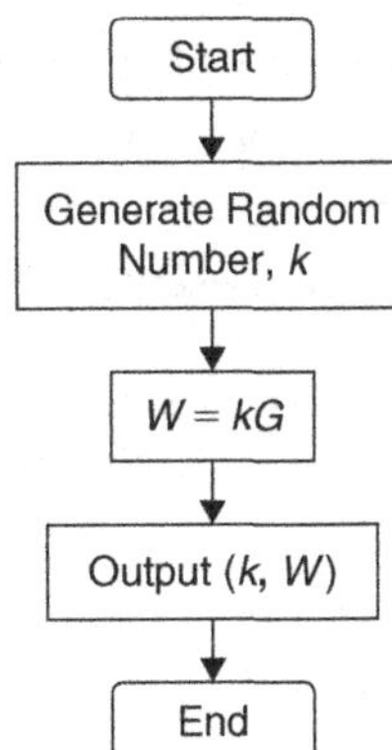

Figure 2.15: Flow diagram of ECDSA key-pair generation process.

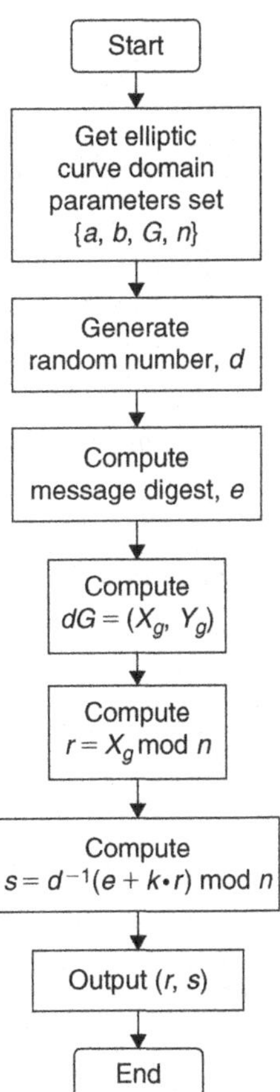

Figure 2.16: Flow diagram of ECDSA signature generation process.

number d, we compute $P{:}(X_P, Y_P) = dG$ by using elliptic curve point scalar multiplication algorithm. We compute the message digest value e using the SHA function (see Section 2.4.3 for more details on message digest generation algorithms). Then we generate $r = X_P \bmod n$ and $s = t \bmod n$, where $t = d^{-1}(e + k \cdot r)$. In scalar point multiplication, the operations involved are over either prime field GF(P) or binary field GF(2^m), whereas the operations involved in generating r and s are over prime field GF(n), where n is the order of the elliptic curve base point G.

In signature generation, we have one inverse, one multiplication and one addition over GF(n). In the later sections, we discuss the algorithms for computing inverse and multiplication over GF(n) in detail. After generating the signature, the sender sends the message 'M' along with the signature (r, s) to the receiver.

Signature Verification

Signature verification is done at the receiving end by the receiver. We get the message M along with signature (r, s) from the sender and we verify the signature by using the sender public key W. The signature verification process also requires message digest, and we compute it by using the same SHA function that the sender used for computing the message digest. The flow diagram of the signature-verification process is shown in Figure 2.17. In the signature-verification process, we have one inverse and two multiplications over GF(n), two scalar point multiplications and one addition of elliptic curve points over GF(q). In Section 2.5.5, signature verification algorithms and their simulation techniques are presented. Next, an example of ECDSA over GF(23) is presented.

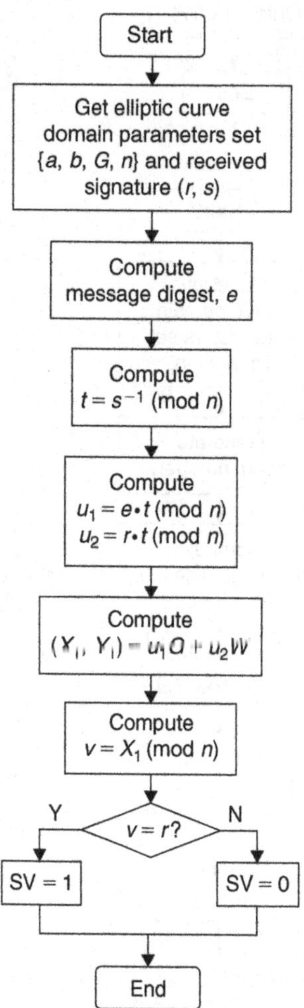

Figure 2.17: Flow diagram of signature-verification process.

Example 2.3: ECDSA over Prime Field GF(23)

In this example, ECDSA algorithm flow for key-pair generation, signature generation, and signature verification are presented. We start the ECDSA by first selecting the domain parameters.

Domain Parameters $(E{:}y^2 = x^3 + ax + b)$
Elliptic curve coefficients: $a = 1, b = 1$
Elliptic curve base point: $G(13, 7)$
Order of elliptic curve base point $G{:}n = 7$(since $7G = O$, a point at infinity)
Cofactor: $h = 4(h = N/n$ [see Section 2.5.4]; curve has a total of $N = 28$ points)

Key-Pair Generation

1. Select random number d in the range $[1, n-1] = [1, 6]$, say $d = 4$.
2. Compute point $W = dG = 4G = 2(2G)$ (i.e., doubling of G two times is required [see Example 2.1 for equation of doubling operation]) $= 4(13, 7) = 2(2(13, 7)) = 2(5, 4) = (17, 20)$.
3. Here $d = 4$ is a private key and point $W = (17, 20)$ is a public key.

Signature Generation

1. Select random number k in the range $[1, n-1] = [1, 6]$, say $k = 3$.
2. Compute point $(X_1, Y_1) = kG = 3G = G + 2G$ (i.e., one point doubling and one point addition are required) $= 3(13, 7) = (13, 7) + 2(13, 7) = (13, 7) + (5, 4) = (17, 3)$; $r = X_1 (\text{mod } n) = 17 (\text{mod } 7) = 3$.
3. Let us assume for now that the message digest value e of given message M is equal to 5. Then, $s = k^{-1}(e + dr)(\text{mod } n) = 3^{-1}(5 + 4 * 3)(\text{mod } 7) = 1$.
4. Signature is $(r, s) = (3, 1)$.
5. We send message M along with its signature (3, 1) to the recipient.

Signature Verification
At the recipient, we have message M along with its signature $(r, s) = (3, 1)$. We compute the message digest value e for message M again for signature verification and $e = 5$ (same as what we computed, or assumed, in signature generation).

$$
\begin{aligned}
t &= s^{-1}(\text{mod } n) = 1^{-1}(\text{mod } 7) = 1 \\
u_1 &= e \cdot t(\text{mod } n) = 5 * 1(\text{mod } 7) = 5 \\
u_2 &= r \cdot t(\text{mod } n) = 3 * 1(\text{mod } 7) = 3 \\
(X_1, Y_1) &= u_1 G + u_2 W = 5(13, 7) + 3(17, 20) \\
&= [(13, 7) + 2(2(13, 7))] + [(17, 20) + 2(17, 20)] \\
&= [(13, 7) + (17, 20)] + [(17, 20) + (13, 7)] \\
&= (5, 19) + (5, 19) = 2(5, 19)
\end{aligned}
$$

(if points P and Q are the same, then $P + Q$ is obtained by $2P$)$= (17, 3)$
$v = X_1 \text{ mod } n = 17 \text{ mod } 7 = 3$
Since $v = r$, the signature is valid and we accept the message, because it was not altered during the transmission.

■

2.5.5 Simulation of ECDSA over Binary Field GF(2^m)

In Section 2.5.4, Examples of ECDSA over Prime Field GF(23), the order of the elliptic curve group used is 7, which we represent with 3 bits as 111. In practice, the order of the elliptic curve generated over binary field GF(2^m) can be up to m bits. At present, most of the applications adapting ECDSA over GF(2^m) use m as greater than or equal to 163 bits. All operations of ECDSA over GF(2^m) involve handling of m-bit integers. This means that the size of elliptic curve coefficients, points and the order of the elliptic curve parameters are all m-bit numbers. The question here is, with 163 or more bit integer numbers, how to compute the elliptic curve operations (e.g., points addition over GF(q), point doubling over GF(q) or scalar point multiplication over GF(q), where q is also of the order of m bits) and modular arithmetic operations (e.g., multiplication modulo n, inverse modulo n, and square modulo n, where $n = 2^m$ or $n =$ prime P) used in ECDSA key-pair generation, signature generation and signature verification processes. Well, we need not worry by seeing that big numbers as we are not manually performing those operations, rather the computer will do it for us. But, we have to program the computer to do it. This section deals with the methods used to program the computer to perform those operations with such big numbers. In ECDSA over GF(2^m), we use modular arithmetic over both prime field and binary field.

Binary Field Arithmetic

In ECDSA, we use binary field GF(2^m) arithmetic in elliptic-curve point operations. The following binary field arithmetic functions, gfb_add() for addition, gfb_mod() for modulo reduction, gfb_sqr() for squaring, gfb_mul() for multiplication, and gfb_inv() for inverse, are used in the implementation of ECDSA over GF(2^m). If $f(x) = x^m + r(x)$ is an irreducible binary (primitive) polynomial of degree m, and if the elements of GF(2^m) are generated using the primitive polynomial $f(x)$, then the elements of GF(2^m) are binary polynomials of degree at most $m - 1$ and we perform modulo $f(x)$ arithmetic operations on the output of GF(2^m) elements arithmetic to make sure the result of the arithmetic operation belongs to GF(2^m). In GF(2^m), a field element is an m-bit number that can be represented in polynomial form as $a(x) = a_{m-1}x^{m-1} + \cdots + a_2x^2 + a_1x + a_0$ or in vector form as $A = [a_{m-1}a_{m-2} \ldots a_2a_1a_0]$.

In arithmetic operations implementation on an embedded processor, we work with either 4-bit, 8-bit, 16-bit or 32-bit words. We do not perform m-bit arithmetic operation bit-by-bit as it is most time-consuming. Because we handle GF(2^m) field elements most of the time as 32-bit words, we represent them with 32-bit words as $X = (x[n-1], \ldots, x[2], x[1], x[0])$, where $n = \lceil m/32 \rceil$ and the right-most bit of $x[0]$ is the LSB bit of the m-bit field element. The left-most $t = (32n - m)$ bits of $x[n-1]$ are not used and are set to zero. For example, if $m = 163$, then we have $n = 6$ words $(x[5], x[4], x[3], x[2], x[1], x[0])$ in a field element of GF(2^{163}) with left-most $t = 29$ bits of $x[5]$ set as zero. Next, we discuss the simulation techniques of arithmetic operations over the binary field GF(2^{163}) and the same simulation techniques can be used for implementation of other binary field elements arithmetic operations.

gfb_add( ): Addition of Two Field Elements $X[\,]$ and $Y[\,]$ of GF(2^{163}) Among all the binary arithmetic operations, gfb_add() is the simplest operation, and $Z[\,]$, the result of adding two elements $X[\,]$ and $Y[\,]$, is computed by XORing the field elements $X[\,]$ and $Y[\,]$, as seen in Pcode 2.31.

gfb_sqr( ): Squaring of Field Element $X[\,]$ of GF(2^{163}) We take a simple example to understand the process of squaring binary field elements. If $b(x) = x^2 + x + 1$, then $b^2(x) = b(x) \cdot b(x) = (x^2 + x + 1) \cdot (x^2 + x + 1) = (x^4 + x^3 + x^2 + x^3 + x^2 + x + x^2 + x + 1) = (x^4 + x^2 + 1)$. If we represent $b(x)$ in vector form $B = [111]$, then $B^2 = [10101]$. So, if we square the binary field element, all the odd exponent terms become zero and only even exponent terms remain. In the vector form, we see alternate zeros and ones in a squared element vector. To achieve this squaring with larger field elements, there are two ways to compute square of field element. In the first approach, we insert the zero bits using shift right, AND, shift left and OR. Each bit takes four cycles on the reference embedded processor (see Appendix A on the companion website) and 163 bits takes 552 cycles. In the second approach, we achieve this squaring in 150 cycles by using a 512-byte look-up table, **gfb_sqr_tbl**[ ]. This look-up table consists of squared values for 8-bit elements. The **gfb_sqr_tbl**[ ] look-up table values can be

```
for(i = 0;i < 6;i++)
    Z[i] = X[i]^Y[i];
```

Pcode 2.31: Simulation code for additions of two field elements in GF(2^{163}).

```
j = 0;
for(i = 0;i < 3;i++) {
        r0 = x[2*i]; r1 = x[2*i+1];
        r2 = r0 & 0xff; r3 = r1 & 0xff;
        r4 = gfb_sqr_tbl[r2]; r5 = gfb_sqr_tbl[r3];
        r2 = r0 >> 8; r3 = r1 >> 8;
        r2 = r2 & 0xff; r3 = r3 & 0xff;
        r2 = gfb_sqr_tbl[r2]; r3 = gfb_sqr_tbl[r3];
        r2 = r2 << 16; r3 = r3 << 16;
        r4 = r4 | r2; r5 = r5 | r3;
        y[0+j] = r4; y[2+j] = r5;
        r2 = r0 >> 16; r3 = r1 >> 16;
        r2 = r2 & 0xff; r3 = r3 & 0xff;
        r4 = gfb_sqr_tbl[r2]; r5 = gfb_sqr_tbl[r3];
        r2 = r0 >> 24; r3 = r1 >> 24;
        r2 = gfb_sqr_tbl[r2]; r3 = gfb_sqr_tbl[r3];
        r2 = r2 << 16; r3 = r3 << 16;
        r4 = r4 | r2; r5 = r5 | r3;
        y[1+j] = r4; y[3+j] = r5;
        j+= 4;
}
```

Pcode 2.32: Simulation code for squaring binary field element in GF(2^{163}).

found on the companion website. First, we unpack the 32-bit words to 8-bit bytes, and then we use the look-up table to get the 16-bit squared equivalent of an 8-bit value. Next, we OR the 16-bit look-up value with 16-bit left-shifted output. The simulation code for the look-up table-based binary-field element squaring is given in Pcode 2.32.

gfb_mod( ): Modulo Reduction with $f(x)$ In binary field arithmetic, if we square or multiply $m-1$ degree polynomials, the degree of output polynomial is $2m-2$. If the arithmetic operation output polynomial $y(x)$ degree is more than the degree of primitive polynomial $f(x)$, then we compute $y(x)$ modulo $f(x)$ to make sure $y(x)$ polynomial degree is less than m. In the binary field, it is true that $x^i = x^{i-m}r(x)(\text{mod } f(x))$ for $i \geq m$. If $m = 163$, then $2m-2$ degree polynomial $y(x)$ can be represented with eleven 32-bit word vectors as $Y = (y[10], y[9], \ldots, y[2], y[1], y[0])$. If $f(x)$ is a trinomial or pentanomial with middle terms close to each other, then reduction of $y(x)$ modulo $f(x)$ can be efficiently performed one 32-bit word at a time. For example, if $f(x) = x^{163}+x^7+x^6+x^3+1$, then we can compute the modulo reduction for $y[9]$ (bits from 288 to 319 of Y) as follows:

$$x^{288} = x^{132}+x^{131}+x^{128}+x^{125}(\text{mod} f(x))$$
$$x^{289} = x^{133}+x^{132}+x^{129}+x^{126}(\text{mod} f(x))$$
$$\ldots$$
$$x^{318} = x^{162}+x^{161}+x^{158}+x^{155}(\text{mod} f(x))$$
$$x^{319} = x^{163}+x^{162}+x^{159}+x^{156}(\text{mod} f(x))$$

By observing the previous congruencies, the reduction of $y[9]$ can be performed by adding $y[9]$ four times to Y, with zeroth LSB of $y[9]$ added to bits 132, 131, 128 and 125 of Y, first LSB of $y[9]$ added to bits 133, 132, 129 and 126 of Y, and so on. Finally, the MSB of $y[9]$ is added to bits 163,162,159 and 156 of Y. Like this, we eliminate $y[10]$, $y[9]$, $y[8]$, $y[7]$, $y[6]$, and $y[5]$ (except three LSBs) of Y. The simulation code for arithmetic modulo reduction over binary field GF(2^{163}) is given in Pcode 2.33.

gfb_mul( ): Multiplication of Two Field Elements of GF(2^{163}) In GF(2^{163}), two binary field elements multiplication is efficiently carried out by using a precompute window method. To better understand this efficient way of implementing multiplication of two field elements A and B of GF(2^{163}) by precomputing, first we work with a simple example. $A = [11010]$ and $B = [10011]$ are vector representations of two mth (= 4) degree polynomials. If we precompute vector B with all first degree polynomial combinations $\boldsymbol{P} = ([11], [10], [01], [00])$, we

```
j = 0;
for(i = 10;i > 5;i--){
        r0 = y[i];
        r1 = r0 << 29; r2 = r0 << 4;
        y[i-6] = y[i-6]^r1; r1 = r0<<3;
        r1 = r1 ^ r2; r2 = r0 >> 3;
        r1 = r1 ^ r2; r2 = r0 >> 28;
        r1 = r1 ^ r0; r3 = r0 >> 29;
        y[i-5] = y[i-5]^r1; r1 = r2^r3;
        y[i-4] = y[i-4]^r1;
}
r4 = 0xfffffff8;      r5 = 0x00000007;
r0 = y[5] & r4;
r2 = r0 << 4; r3 = r0 << 3;
r1 = r2 ^ r3; r2 = r0 >> 3;
r1 = r1 ^ r2; r2 = r0 >> 28;
r1 = r1 ^ r0; r3 = r0 >> 29;
y[0] = y[0] ^ r1; r1 = r2 ^ r3;
y[1] = y[1] ^ r1; y[5] = y[5] & r5;
z[0] = y[0]; z[1] = y[1];
z[2] = y[2]; z[3] = y[3];
z[4] = y[4]; z[5] = y[5];
```

Pcode 2.33: Simulation code for modulo reduction over binary field GF(2^{163}).

have $B' = \mathbf{B.P} = [b_3', b_2', b_1', b_0'] = ([110111], [100110], [010011], [000000])$. Now $C = A \cdot B$ is obtained by dividing A into three 2-bit blocks $[a_2 a_1 a_0] = [01\ 10\ 10]$ (here the last block MSB is appended with zero to make a 2-bit block) and using precomputed B' as

$$C = [000000000], c_2 = a_2 \cdot B = [01] \cdot B = b_1' = [010011]$$

$$C = C + c_2 = [000000000] \oplus [010011] = [000010011]$$

$$C = C \ll 2 = [001001100], c_1 = a_1 \cdot B = [10] \cdot B = b_2' = [100110]$$

$$C = C + c_1 = [001001100] \oplus [100110] = [001101010]$$

$$C = C \ll 2 = [110101000], c_0 = a_0 \cdot B = [10] \cdot B = b_2' = [100110]$$

$$C = C + c_0 = [110101000] \oplus [100110] = [110001110]$$

The previous window method (with window size $w = 2$) involves two left shifts, three loads and three additions. If we increase the window size w to 3, then we will have one left shift, two loads and two additions. From this, we can say that the number of left shifts and number of additions required in multiplying two field elements reduces with the increase of window size w. In this analysis, we did not include the overhead of precomputing and this overhead also increases with the window size w. In GF(2^{163}), two binary field elements A and B multiplication is efficiently carried out by using the precomputed multiplied values of third-degree polynomials (or $w = 4$) of all combinations with one of field element. We use field element B in precompute multiplication with third-degree polynomials and bits of element A for loading the precomputed values. For this, we divide A into 4-bit blocks as (MSB) 4|4|4|... |4|4|4 (LSB) and start the multiplication process from the MSB 4-bit block. Here the field elements are 163 bits in length and we work in terms of 32-bit words.

There are six 32-bit blocks in one field element with some appended MSB zero bits in the last 32-bit block. Multiplication of two field elements is carried out using a nested loop with two loops. The outer loop runs eight times to cover all eight 4-bit blocks of one 32-bit word of A, and the inner loop runs six times to cover all 32-bit words of A. The output C of multiplication contains a total of eleven 32-bit words. Before the start of multiplication we initialize C with zeros. In the inner loop, for six 32-bit words of A, we get multiplication of

```
for(i = 0;i < 12;i++)
    Tmp[i] = 0;                              // C = 0
for(j = 7;j >= 0;j--){
    k = j<<2;      r1 = 0;
    for(i = 0;i < 6;i++){
        r0 = a[i];
        r0 = r0 >> k;
        r2 = r0 & 0xf;
        r2 = r2*6;
        Tmp[r1+0] = Tmp[r1+0]^Bu[r2++]; // modulo 2 additions
        Tmp[r1+1] = Tmp[r1+1]^Bu[r2++];
        Tmp[r1+2] = Tmp[r1+2]^Bu[r2++];
        Tmp[r1+3] = Tmp[r1+3]^Bu[r2++];
        Tmp[r1+4] = Tmp[r1+4]^Bu[r2++];
        Tmp[r1+5] = Tmp[r1+5]^Bu[r2++];
        r1+=1;
    }
    if (j != 0){
        r0 = Tmp[0]; r1 = Tmp[1];           // left shift by w-bits or C = C.x^w
        r6 = r0 >> 28; r7 = r1 >> 28;
        r0 = r0 << 4; r1 = r1 << 4;
        r1 = r1 | r6; Tmp[0] = r0;
        r0 = Tmp[2]; Tmp[1] = r1;
        r6 = r0 >> 28; r0 = r0 << 4;
        r0 = r0 | r7; r1 = Tmp[3];
        r7 = r1 >> 28; r1 = r1 << 4;
        r1 = r1 | r6; Tmp[2] = r0;
        r0 = Tmp[4]; Tmp[3] = r1;
        r6 = r0 >> 28; r0 = r0 << 4;
        r0 = r0 | r7; r1 = Tmp[5];
        r7 = r1 >> 28; r1 = r1 << 4;
        r1 = r1 | r6; Tmp[4] = r0;
        r0 = Tmp[6]; Tmp[5] = r1;
        r6 = r0 >> 28; r0 = r0 << 4;
        r0 = r0 | r7; r1 = Tmp[7];
        r7 = r1 >> 28; r1 = r1 << 4;
        r1 = r1 | r6; Tmp[6] = r0;
        r0 = Tmp[8]; Tmp[7] = r1;
        r6 = r0 >> 28; r0 = r0 << 4;
        r0 = r0 | r7; r1 = Tmp[9];
        r7 = r1 >> 28; r1 = r1 << 4;
        r1 = r1 | r6; Tmp[8] = r0;
        r0 = Tmp[10]; Tmp[9] = r1;
        r6 = r0 >> 28; r0 = r0 << 4;
        r0 = r0 | r7; r1 = Tmp[11];
        r1 = r1 << 4; Tmp[10] = r0;
        r1 = r1 | r6; Tmp[11] = r1;
    }
}
```

Pcode 2.34: Simulation code for window based multiplication of GF(2^{163}) field elements.

a 4-bit block (of A, one 4-bit block per outer loop iteration starting from MSB side) with B and add to C. In each outer loop iteration, we multiply the output after current iteration with x^4 (i.e., shift left C by 4 bits). The simulation code for the window-based multiplication process is given in Pcode 2.34.

gfb_inv( ): inverse of field element GF(2^{163}) modulo $f(x)$ In the binary field GF(2^m), one way of computing the inverse of the field element is by exponentiation of the field element to the power $2^m - 2$ (i.e., $1/\alpha = \alpha^{2^m - 2}$). The following method is used to compute the inverse by exponentiation process. Let $m - 1 = b_r, b_{r-1} \ldots b_1; b_0$ is the binary representation of $m - 1$, where the most significant bit b_r of $m - 1$ is 1.

```
Set β = α and k = 1
For i = r−1:0
    γ = β
    For j = 1:k
        γ = γ^2
    End
```

```
    β = βγ and k=2k
    If b_i=1, then set β = β² α  and k=k+1
End
Output β²
```

The simulation code for computing Y, an inverse of field element $X = (x[5], x[4], x[3], x[2], x[1], x[0])$ in GF(2^{163}) is given in Pcode 2.35.

Prime Field Arithmetic

In ECDSA over GF(2^m), we also use prime field GF(P) (where P is a large prime number and represented with 163 bits) arithmetic in the signature generation and signature verification processes. The following prime field arithmetic functions, gfp_add() for addition, gfp_mod() for modulo reduction, gfp_mul() for multiplication and gfp_inv() for inverse, are used in the implementation of ECDSA key-pair generation, signature generation and verification operations. The prime field arithmetic operations are similar to normal integer arithmetic and the only extra operation present in prime field arithmetic is computing of modulo P for output of arithmetic operation. If the GF(P) field element A is of 163 bits in size, then it is represented with six 32-bit words as $A = (a_5, a_4, a_3, a_2, a_1, a_0)$. In other words, a field element of GF(P) can be represented with a 5th-degree polynomial whose coefficients are of 32-bit words in size. As most of the embedded processor registers precision is limited to 32 bits and multiplication or addition of two 32-bit numbers result in more than 32 bits, we perform field elements arithmetic operations by representing field elements with either 16-bit words or 8-bit bytes. In this section, we simulate the prime field arithmetic by assuming P as a 163-bit number and such GF(P) field elements represented either with six 32-bit coefficient polynomials or with 11 16-bit coefficients or with 21-byte coefficient polynomials.

gfp_add( ): Addition of GF(P) Field Elements The addition of two field elements of GF(P) is carried out by converting field elements' 32-bit coefficients to 16-bit coefficients as given in Pcode 2.36. Here, we perform addition of two 11th-degree polynomials with 16-bit coefficients and the result is also an 11th-degree polynomial with 16-bit coefficients. After addition, the result is converted back to the 5th-degree polynomial by merging the 16-bit coefficients to 32-bit coefficients.

```
r0 = 162;
j = 7;  k = 1;
for (i = 0;i < 6;i++){
   T1[i] = x[i];      T3[i] = x[i];
}
for (j = 6;j > = 0;j--){
    T2[0] = T1[0]; T2[1] = T1[1];
    T2[2] = T1[2]; T2[3] = T1[3];
    T2[4] = T1[4]; T2[5] = T1[5];
    for(i = 0;i < k;i++)
        gfb_sqr(T2,T2);                    // T2² -> T2
    k = k << 1;
    gfb_mul(T1,T2,T1);                     // T1xT2 -> T1
    r1 = r0 >> j,
    r1 = r1 & 1;
    if (r1 == 1){
        gfb_sqr(T1,T1);                    // T1² -> T1
        gfb_mul(T1,T3,T1);                 // T1*x -> T1
        k = k+1;
    }
}
gfb_sqr(T1,T2);                            // T1² -> T2
y[0] = T2[0]; y[1] = T2[1];
y[2] = T2[2]; y[3] = T2[3];
y[4] = T2[4]; y[5] = T2[5];
```

Pcode 2.35: Simulation code for computing inverse of field element in GF(2^{163}).

```
r4 = 0;
 for(i = 0;i < 6;i++){
  r0 = x[i]; r1 = y[i];
  r2 = r0 & 0xffff; r3 = r1 & 0xffff;
  r3 = r2 + r3 + r4;
  r0 = r0 >> 16; r1 = r1 >> 16;
  r2 = r3 & 0xffff; r3 = r3 >> 16;
  r0 = r0 + r1 + r3;
  r1 = r0 & 0xffff; r4 = r0 >> 16;
  r1 = r1 << 16;
  r2 = r2 | r1;
  z[i] = r2;
 }
```

Pcode 2.36: Simulation code for addition of two field elements in GF(*P*).

```
for(i = 0;i < 6;i++){              // convert from 32-bit word coefficient to 8-bit byte coefficient
        r0 = x[i];
        r1 = r0 & 0xff; r2 = r0 >> 8;
        a[j++] = r1; r1 = r2 & 0xff;
        a[j++] = r1; r2 = r0 >> 16;
        r1 = r2 & 0xff; r2 = r0 >> 24;
        a[j++] = r1;  a[j++] = r2; r0 = y[i];
        r1 = r0 & 0xff; r2 = r0 >> 8;
        b[k++] = r1; r1 = r2 & 0xff;
        b[k++] = r1; r2 = r0 >> 16;
        r1 = r2 & 0xff; r2 = r0 >> 24;
        b[k++] = r1;  b[k++] = r2;
}
r0 = 0;
for(i = 0;i < 24;i++){             // compute c0 to c23
        k = i;
        for(j = 0;j < =i;j++)
        r0 = r0 + a[k--]*b[j];
        r1 = r0 & 0xff;
        c[i] = r1; r0 = r0 >> 8;
}
for(i = 24;i < 47;i++){            // compute c24 to c47
        k = 23;
        for(j=i-23;j < 24;j++)
                r0 = r0 + a[k--]*b[j];
        r1 = r0 & 0xff;
        c[i] = r1; r0 = r0 >> 8;
}
c[47] = 0;
for(i = 0;i < 12;i++){             // convert 8-bit byte coefficients to 32-bit word coefficient
        j = i<<2;
        r0 = c[j]; r1 = c[j+1];
        r1 = r1 << 8; r2 = c[j+2];
        r0 = r0 | r1; r2 = r2 << 16;
        r0 = r0 | r2; r1 = c[j+3];
        r1 = r1 << 24;
        r0 = r0 | r1;
        z[i] = r0;
}
```

Pcode 2.37: Simulation code for multiplication of two primary field GF(*P*) elements.

gfp_mul( ): Multiplication of Two Prime Field Elements The multiplication of two field elements of GF(*P*) is carried out by converting their polynomial default, 32-bit coefficients to either 16- or 8-bit coefficients (as multiplication of two 32-bit coefficients needs processor registers of 63 bits of precision to hold the multiplied value, and 32-bit embedded processor registers can only support 32 bits of precision). In the simulation, we represent 163-bit field elements of GF(*P*) with polynomials containing 8-bit coefficients as given in Pcode 2.37 to perform a multiplication operation, and we have 21 such 8-bit coefficients in the 163-bit GF(*P*) field element polynomial. The simulation code supports the following 24 coefficient (or 23rd degree) polynomial multiplication and this can also be used to perform 21 coefficient polynomial multiplication. Let the two polynomials

$$A(x) = a_{23}x^{23} + a_{22}x^{22} + \cdots + a_2x^2 + a_1x + a_0$$

and

$$B(x) = b_{23}x^{23} + b_{22}x^{22} + \cdots + b_2x^2 + b_1x + b_0$$

represent two GF(P) field elements. If $C(x) = A(x).B(x)$, then the coefficients of $C(x)$ is given by

$$\begin{aligned}
c_0 &= a_0b_0 \\
c_1 &= a_0b_1 + a_1b_0 \\
c_2 &= a_0b_2 + a_1b_1 + a_2b_0 \\
&\cdots\cdot \\
c_{23} &= a_0b_{23} + a_1b_{22} + \cdots + a_{21}b_2 + a_{22}b_1 + a_{23}b_0 \\
c_{24} &= a_1b_{23} + a_2b_{22} + \cdots + a_{22}b_2 + a_{23}b_1 \\
&\cdots\cdot \\
c_{45} &= a_{22}b_{23} + a_{23}b_{22} \\
c_{46} &= a_{23}b_{23}
\end{aligned}$$

$C(x)$ is a 46th-degree polynomial with 47 coefficients. We perform the modulo reduction on $C(x)$ to make sure that the result of multiplication of $A(x) \cdot B(x)$ belongs to GF(P). That means we reduce $C(x)$ to a 21-coefficient polynomial by performing modulo reduction.

gfp_mod( ): Modulo Reduction of Polynomials over Prime Field GF(P) There are multiple modulo reduction algorithms in the literature, and we discuss a straightforward simple method (also called classical modular reduction) in this section to perform modulo reduction. In GF(P), we perform modulo reduction for a polynomial $C(x)$ with a degree more than or equal to 20 (since P is of size 163 bits and represented as a 20th-degree polynomial $p(x)$ with 21 byte coefficients) to keep the result of the arithmetic in GF(P). The remainder of the division $C(x)$ by $p(x)$ is treated as a modulo reduction for $C(x)$. In this classical reduction method, we work on bytes (i.e., radix or $b = 2^8$). If $C(x)$ is a polynomial of degree $m - 1$, which is greater than or equal to 20, then we perform modulo reduction of $C(x)$ as follows (we normalize both $C(x)$ and $p(x)$ such that $c_{m-1} \geq b/2$ to speed up the modular operation). Now, we reduce $C(x)$ byte by byte iteratively from the MSB side by first computing a coarse estimate of the quotient, followed by a fine estimation of the quotient. For finding a coarse estimate of the quotient (q) of division of C (dividend) with P (divisor), we divide two leftmost bytes of C with one leftmost byte of P. Then we check whether the estimated quotient is correct or to be adjusted (fine estimation) by subtracting multiplied two leftmost bytes of P with q from three leftmost bytes of C. If the result is positive, then we subtract $q * P$ from C otherwise we reduce the quotient by one and repeat the previous fine estimation process. This modulo reduction process eliminates one leftmost byte of $C(x)$ at a time and it will be continued until the degree of $C(x)$ falls below 20. If the dividend $C(x)$ contains M digits and divisor $p(x)$ contains L digits, then modulo reduction of C with respect to P is done in $M + L - 1$ steps. Simulation code for modular reduction over prime field is given in Pcode 2.38.

gfp_inv( ): Inverse of Element in Prime Field GF(P) If B is an element of prime field GF(P), then C, an inverse of field element B is computed by direct exponentiation as $C = B^{-1} = B^{P-2}$. Finding the inverse of an element in prime fields with straightforward exponentiation is costly because it involves square and multiplication of field elements with modulo reduction. Although there are many algorithms for finding the inverse of the prime field element, we choose the exponentiation method because it can be efficiently implemented on an embedded processor with Montgomery multiplication operation, MonMul(). Montgomery multiplication of a and b is defined as MonMul$(a, b) = a \cdot b \cdot r^{-1}$ (mod P), where a and b are less than P and GCD$(r, P) = 1$. Even though the algorithm works for any r that is relatively prime to P, it is more useful when $r$is taken to be a power of

```
p = k;                  // k = m-n, where m and n are the degrees of A (= C(x)) and B (= P(x))
for(i = 0;i < p;i++){                         // eliminates one MSB byte of A per iteration
        if(a[m] == b[n])
              r0 = 255;                       // q
        else {
              r1 = a[m]; r2 = a[m-1];
              r1 = r1 << 8;
              r1 = r1 | r2;
              r0 = r1/b[n];                   // q: coarse estimate of quotient
        }
        r1 = r1 << 8; r2 = a[m-2];
        r1 = r1 | r2; r2 = b[n];
        r2 = r2 << 8; r3 = b[n-1];
        r2 = r2 | r3;
        while ((r0*r2) > r1)
               r0 = r0 - 1;                   // q: fine estimate of quotient
        r2 = 0;
        for(j = 0;j < = n;j++)  {             // c[n] = q.b[n]
               r1 = b[j];
               r3 = r1 * r0;
               r1 = r3 + r2;
               r3 = r1 & 0xff;
               r2 = r1 >> 8; c[j] = r3;
        }
        c[n + 1] = r2; tmp2 = 0;
        for(j = 0;j < = (n+1);j++){           // x[m:m-n] - c[n+1] -> x[m:m-n]
               tmp1 = a[k+j-1] - c[j] + tmp2;
               a[k+j-1] = tmp1;      tmp2 = tmp1>>8;
        }
        if (tmp2 != 0){                       // if x[m:m-n-1] < 0, then add b[n]
              tmp2 = 0;
              for(j = 0;j < = n;j++){         // x[m:m-n-1] + b[n]
                    tmp1 = a[k+j-1] + b[j] + tmp2;
                    a[k+j-1] = tmp1;     tmp2 = tmp1>>8;
              }
        }
        m = m-1;        k = k-1;
}
```

Pcode 2.38: Simulation code for classical modulo reduction over prime field GF(P).

2. In this case, the Montgomery algorithm performs divisions by a power of 2, which is an intrinsically fast operation on an embedded processor. Let P be a k-bit prime integer in the range $2^{k-1} \leq P < 2^k$ and $r = 2^k$ (here GCD$(P, r) = 1$, as P is a prime number and less than r). To describe the Montgomery multiplication algorithm, we first define P-residue of a (where $a < P$) as $a' = a \cdot r \pmod{P}$. Then c' = MonMul(a', b') $= a' \cdot b' \cdot r^{-1}$ (mod P) which is P-residue of c since $a \cdot r \cdot b \cdot r \cdot r^{-1} \pmod{P} = a \cdot b \cdot r \pmod{P} = c \cdot r \pmod{P}$. To describe the Montgomery modulo reduction we need another element P' such that $r \cdot r^{-1} - P \cdot P' = 1$, where r^{-1} and P' are precomputed using the extended Euclidean algorithm.

Let $Q = P - 2$, then $C = B^Q$ is computed as

```
Q = [q_n q_{n-1} ... q_2 q_1 q_0], binary value of Q with q_n = 1
        B' = B·r (mod P)
        C' = B'
        for i = n-1:0
                C' = MonMul(C', C')
                if(q_i = 1), then C' = MonMul(C', B')
        end
        output MonMul(C', 1) as C
```

The product MonMul(a', b') with Montgomery modulo reduction is computed as

```
g = a'·b'
h = (g + (g·P' mod r)·P)/r.
```

if $h \geq P$, then output $h - P$, else output h. The simulation code for the Montgomery multiplication algorithm is given in Pcode 2.39.

```
gfp_mul(x,y,muly);  // a'.b' -> t1, here both a',b' are in Montgomery domain (i.e., P-residues)
T1[0] = muly[0]; T1[1] = muly[1];                                  // t1 mod r -> t'
T1[2] = muly[2]; T1[3] = muly[3]; T1[4] = muly[4]; T1[5] = muly[5] & 7;
gfp_mul(T1,n_dash,mulx);                                           // t'.n'-> tmp
T2[0] = mulx[0]; T2[1] = mulx[1];                                  // tmp mod r -> t2
T2[2] = mulx[2]; T2[3] = mulx[3];     T2[4] = mulx[4]; T2[5] = mulx[5] & 7;
gfp_mul(T2,modulous,mulx);                                         // t2.n -> t2
r0 = 0;
for (i = 0;i < 12;i++){                                            // t1 + t2 -> t1
       r1 = muly[i]; r2 = mulx[i];
       r3 = r1 & 0xffff; r4 = r2 & 0xffff;
       r3 = r3 + r4 + r0;
       r0 = r3 >> 16; r5 = r3 & 0xffff;
       r3 = r1 >> 16; r4 = r2 >> 16;
       r3 = r3 + r4 + r0;
       r0 = r3 >> 16; r4 = r3 & 0xffff;
       r4 = r4 << 16;
       r5 = r4 + r5;           muly[i] = r5;
}
for (i = 5;i < 11;i++){                                            // t1/r -> u
       r0 = muly[i]; r1 = muly[i+1];
       r2 = r0 >> 3; r3 = r1 << 29;
       r2 = r2 | r3;  z[i-5] = r2;
}
j = 1;
for (i = 5;i > = 0;i--)  {                                         // check whether u > = n or not
       if (z[i] == modulous[i])        continue;
       else if (z[i] < modulous[i]){j = 0;      break;          }
       else      break;
}
if (j){                                                            // if u > = n, then output u - n
      r6 = 0;
      for(i = 0;i < 6;i++){
                r0 = z[i]; r1 = modulous[i];
                tmp0 = r0 & 0xffff; tmp1 = r1 & 0xffff;
                r7 = tmp0 - tmp1 + r6;
                r6 = r7 >> 31;  r2 = r7 & 0xffff;
                r0 = r0 >> 16; r1 = r1 >> 16;
                tmp0 = r0;  tmp1 = r1;
                r7 = tmp0 - tmp1 + r6;
                r6 = r7 >> 31;  r3 = r7 & 0xffff;
                r3 = r3 << 16;
                r2 =r3 | r2;                     z[i] = r2;
      }
}
```

Pcode 2.39: Simulation code for Montgomery multiplication.

Representation of Elliptic Curve Points

In ECDSA signature generation and verification processes (see Section 2.5.4, Signature Generation, and Section 2.5.4, Signature Verification), we need to compute a modulo inverse, which is very costly in terms of computations (one inverse is almost 30 to 50 times more costly compared to multiplication in terms of computational complexity). To avoid these modulo inverse operations, we convert the affine coordinates (X, Y) of elliptic curve points to projective coordinates (X^*, Y^*, Z^*) to take care of the denominator part of the operations with Z^*. At the end, we convert back from projective coordinates (X^*, Y^*, Z^*) to affine coordinates (X, Y) and have more than one kind of projective coordinate. Here are two popular projective coordinate representations.

Standard projective coordinates:

$$\text{Affine to projective conversion: } (X^*, Y^*, Z^*) = (X, Y, 1)$$

$$\text{Projective to affine conversion: } (X, Y) = \left(\frac{X^*}{Z^{*2}}, \frac{Y^*}{Z^{*3}}\right)$$

Modified Jacobian coordinates:

$$\text{Affine to projective conversion: } (X^*, Y^*, Z^*) = (X, Y, 1)$$

$$\text{Projective to affine conversion: } (X, Y) = \left(\frac{X^*}{Z^*}, \frac{Y^*}{Z^{*2}}\right)$$

As conversion from projective to affine coordinates also involves modulo inverse computation, it is not a good idea to use projective coordinates for simple operations such as point double or points addition. But, use of projective coordinates for scalar point multiplication speeds up the process by a lot as it involves many point double and addition operations.

Simulation of Elliptic Curve Operations in GF(2^m)

In the simulation, we use projective coordinates for all three elliptic curve operations, namely, points addition, point double and scalar point multiplication. For point-double and two-points addition, methods using both standard projective coordinates and modified Jacobian coordinates are discussed.

Addition of E(2^m) Curve Points Given two elliptic curve points P: (X_p, Y_p, Z_p) and Q: (X_q, Y_q, Z_q) in projective coordinates, the projective coordinates of point R: (X_r, Y_r, Z_r), which is the result of addition of two points P and Q (i.e., $R = P + Q$), is obtained with **EccPointsAdd**() as follows.

With standard projective coordinates:

$$X_r = a \cdot [Z_p(X_pZ_q^2 + X_qZ_p^2)Z_q]^2 + [Y_pZ_q^3 + Y_qZ_p^3 + Z_p(X_pZ_q^2 + X_qZ_p^2)Z_q][Y_pZ_q^3 + Y_qZ_p^3] + [X_pZ_q^2 + X_qZ_p^2]^3$$

$$Y_r = [Y_pZ_q^3 + Y_qZ_p^3 + Z_p(X_pZ_q^2 + X_qZ_p^2)Z_p]X_r + [(Y_pZ_q^3 + Y_qZ_p^3)X_q + Z_p(X_pZ_q^2 + X_qZ_p^2)Y_q][Z_p(X_pZ_q^2 + X_qZ_p^2]^2$$

$$Z_r = Z_p(X_pZ_q^2 + X_qZ_p^2)Z_q$$

With modified Jacobian coordinates:

$$Z_r = [Z_p(X_qZ_p + X_p)]^2$$

$$X_r = Z_p(X_qZ_p + X_p)(Y_qZ_p^2 + Y_p) + (Y_qZ_p^2 + Y_p)^2 + [(X_qZ_p + X_p)Z_p + aZ_p^2](X_qZ_p + X_p)^2$$

$$Y_r = Z_p(X_qZ_p + X_p)(Y_qZ_p^2 + Y_p) + (Z_rX_q + X_r) + Z_r(Z_rY_q + X_r)$$

The simulation code for two elliptic curve points addition with standard projective coordinates is given in Pcode 2.40 and with modified Jacobian coordinates is given in Pcode 2.41.

Doubling of E(2^m) Curve Points Given an elliptic curve point P: (X_p, Y_p, Z_p) and the projective coordinates of point R: (X_r, Y_r, Z_r), a result of doubling a point P (i.e., $Q = 2P$) is obtained with EccPointDouble() as follows:

With standard projective coordinates:

$$Z_r = X_pZ_p^2$$

$$X_r = (X_p + c \cdot Z_p^2)^4, \quad \text{where} \quad c = b^{2^{m-2}}$$

$$Y_r = X_p^4Z_r + (Z_r + X_p^2 + Y_pZ_p)X_r$$

```
r0 = r2 = 0;
for(i = 0;i < 6;i++){                    // Px -> T1, Py -> T2, Pz -> T3, Qx -> T4, Qy -> T5, Qz ->
T3, a->T9
        T1[i] = x[i];         T2[i] = x[6 + i];
        T3[i] = x[12 + i];    T4[i] = y[i];
        T5[i] = y[6 + i];     T6[i] = y[12 + i];
        T9[i] = a[i];  r2+= y[12 + i];
        r0+= a[i];
}
if (r2 != 1){                           // Qz != 1
        gfb_sqr(T6,T7);                 // T62 -> T7
        gfb_mul(T1,T7,T1);              // T1xT7 -> T1
        gfb_mul(T6,T7,T7);              // T6xT7 -> T7
        gfb_mul(T2,T7,T2);              // T2xT7 -> T7
}
gfb_sqr(T3,T7);                         // T32 -> T7
gfb_mul(T4,T7,T8);                      // T4xT7 -> T8
gfb_add(T1,T8,T1);                      // T1+T8 -> T1
gfb_mul(T3,T7,T7);                      // T3xT7 -> T7
gfb_mul(T5,T7,T8);                      // T5xT7 -> T8
gfb_add(T2,T8,T2);                      // T2+T8 -> T2
gfb_mul(T2,T4,T4);                      // T2xT4 -> T4
gfb_mul(T1,T3,T3);                      // T1xT3 -> T3
gfb_mul(T3,T5,T5);                      // T3xT5 -> T5
gfb_add(T4,T5,T4);                      // T4+T5 -> T4
gfb_sqr(T3,T5);                         // T32 -> T5
gfb_mul(T4,T5,T7);                      // T4xT5 -> T7
if (r2 != 1)
         gfb_mul(T3,T6,T3);             // T3xT6 -> T3
gfb_add(T2,T3,T4);                      // T2+T3 -> T4
gfb_mul(T2,T4,T2);                      // T2xT4 -> T2
gfb_sqr(T1,T5);                         // T12 -> T5
gfb_mul(T1,T5,T1);                      // T1xT5 -> T1
if (r0 != 0){                           // a != 0
         gfb_sqr(T3,T8);                // T32 -> T8
         gfb_mul(T8,T9,T9);             // T8xT9 -> T9
         gfb_add(T1,T9,T1);             // T1+T9 -> T1
}
gfb_add(T1,T2,T1);                      // T1+T2 -> T1
gfb_mul(T1,T4,T4);                      // T1xT4 -> T4
gfb_add(T4,T7,T2);                      // T4+T7 -> T2
for(i = 0;i < 6;i++){                   // T1 -> Rx,  T2 -> Ry, T3 -> Rz
     z[i] = T1[i];    z[6 + i] = T2[i];
     z[12 + i] = T3[i];
}
```

Pcode 2.40: Simulation code for points addition over GF(2^{163}) using standard projective coordinates.

With modified Jacobian coordinates:

$$Z_r = X_p^2 Z_p^2$$

$$X_r = X_p^4 + bZ_p^4$$

$$Y_r = X_r(Y_p^2 + bZ_p^4 + a \cdot Z_r) + bZ_p^4 Z_r$$

For point double using standard projective coordinates, we have to precompute the value $c = b^{2^{m-2}}$. In the case of modified Jacobian coordinates, this precomputation of c is not needed. The simulation codes for point-double using standard projective coordinates and modified Jacobian coordinates are given in Pcodes 2.42 and 2.43, respectively.

Scalar Point Multiplication In this section, we discuss two methods for computing the multiplication of an elliptic curve point P with a constant value k. A scalar multiplication kP of a point P on an elliptic curve is computed with the doubling and add operations defined over elliptic curves. As the doubling and add operations of elliptic curve points are too costly in terms of computations, here we discuss an efficient way of computing

```
r0 = 0;
for(i = 0;i < 6;i++){                    // Xq -> T1, Yq -> T2, Zq -> T3, Xp -> T4, Yp -> T5, a->T9
        T1[i] = x[i];    T2[i] = x[6 + i];
        T3[i] = x[12 + i];  T4[i] = y[i];
        T5[i] = y[6 + i];          T9[i] = pE->coeff_a[i];
        r0 = r0 + pE->coeff_a[i];
}
gfb_sqr(T3,T6);                          // T3^^2 -> T6
gfb_mul(T5,T6,T7);                       // T5xT6 -> T7
gfb_mul(T4,T3,T8);                       // T4xT3 -> T8
gfb_add(T7,T2,T7);                       // T7+T2 -> T7
gfb_add(T8,T1,T8);                       // T8+T1 -> T8
gfb_mul(T8,T3,T1);                       // T8xT3 -> T1
if(r0==0)  {
  T9[0] = T1[0]; T9[1] = T1[1];
  T9[2] = T1[2]; T9[3] = T1[3];
  T9[4] = T1[4]; T9[5] = T1[5];
}
else if (r0==1){
 T9[0] = T6[0]; T9[1] = T6[1];
 T9[2] = T6[2]; T9[3] = T6[3];
 T9[4] = T6[4]; T9[5] = T6[5];
}
else
gfb_mul(T9,T6,T9);                       // axT6 -> T9
gfb_add(T9,T1,T9);                       // T9+T1 -> T9
gfb_sqr(T8,T8);                          // T8^^2 -> T8
gfb_mul(T8,T9,T8);                       // T8xT9 -> T8
gfb_mul(T1,T7,T2);                       // T1xT7 -> T2
gfb_sqr(T1,T1);                          // T1^^2 -> T1
gfb_sqr(T7,T7);                          // T7^^2 -> T7
gfb_add(T7,T8,T7);                       // T7+T8 -> T7
gfb_add(T7,T2,T3);                       // T7+T2 -> T3
gfb_mul(T1,T4,T6);                       // T1xT4 -> T6
gfb_add(T6,T3,T6);                       // T6+T3 -> T6
gfb_mul(T1,T5,T8);                       // T1xT5 -> T8
gfb_add(T8,T3,T8);                       // T8+T3 -> T8
gfb_mul(T2,T6,T2);                       // T2xT6 -> T2
gfb_mul(T8,T1,T8);                       // T8xT1 -> T8
gfb_add(T2,T8,T2);                       // T2+T8 -> T2
for(i = 0;i < 6;i++){
        z[i] = T3[i];  z[6 + i] = T2[i];
        z[12 + i] = T1[i];
}
```

Pcode 2.41: Simulation code for two points addition over GF(2^{163}) using modified Jacobian coordinates.

scalar point multiplication with less points add and double operations. For better understanding of this scalar point multiplication algorithm, two methods of building a 12-bit integer number k (say, $1796_d = 704_h = 011100000100_b$) with very few operations are described in the following.

Comb Method

$$
\begin{aligned}
011100000100 &= 1\cdot 2^{10}+1\cdot 2^{9}+1\cdot 2^{8}+0\cdot 2^{7}+0\cdot 2^{6}+0\cdot 2^{5}+0\cdot 2^{4}+0\cdot 2^{3}+1\cdot 2^{2}+0\cdot 2^{1}+0\cdot 2^{0}\\
&= (1\cdot 2^{1}+1\cdot 2^{0})\cdot 2^{9}+(1\cdot 2^{2}+0\cdot 2^{1}+0\cdot 2^{0})\cdot 2^{6}+(0\cdot 2^{2}+0\cdot 2^{1}+0\cdot 2^{0})\cdot 2^{3}\\
&\quad +(1\cdot 2^{2}+0\cdot 2^{1}+0\cdot 2^{0})\cdot 2^{0}\\
&= (0\cdot 2^{2}+1\cdot 2^{1}+1\cdot 2^{0})\cdot 2^{9}+(1\cdot 2^{2}+0\cdot 2^{1}+0\cdot 2^{0})\cdot 2^{6}+(0\cdot 2^{2}+0\cdot 2^{1}+0\cdot 2^{0})\cdot 2^{3}\\
&\quad +(1\cdot 2^{2}+0\cdot 2^{1}+0\cdot 2^{0})\cdot 2^{0}\\
&= (0\cdot 2^{9}+1\cdot 2^{6}+0\cdot 2^{3}+1\cdot 2^{0})\cdot 2^{2}+(1\cdot 2^{9}+0\cdot 2^{6}+0\cdot 2^{3}+0\cdot 2^{0})\cdot 2^{1}\\
&\quad +(1\cdot 2^{9}+0\cdot 2^{6}+0\cdot 2^{3}+0\cdot 2^{0})\cdot 2^{0}
\end{aligned}
$$

$$= (b_{23} \cdot 2^9 + b_{22} \cdot 2^6 + b_{21} \cdot 2^3 + b_{20} \cdot 2^0) \cdot 2^2 + (b_{13} \cdot 2^9 + b_{12} \cdot 2^6 + b_{11} \cdot 2^3 + b_{10} \cdot 2^0) \cdot 2^1$$
$$+ (b_{03} \cdot 2^9 + b_{02} \cdot 2^6 + b_{01} \cdot 2^3 + b_{00} \cdot 2^0) \cdot 2^0$$
$$= 2(2 \cdot [b_{23}b_{22}b_{21}b_{20}] + [b_{13}b_{12}b_{11}b_{10}]) + [b_{03}b_{02}b_{01}b_{00}]$$
$$= 2 \cdot (2 \cdot (B_2) + B_1) + B_0$$

```
r1 = 0;
for(i = 0;i < 6;i++){                                      // Px -> T1, Py -> T2, Pz -> T3, b^(2^(m-2)) -> T4
        r1 = r1 + x[i + 6];
        T1[i] = x[i];  T2[i] = x[6+i];
        T3[i] = x[12+i];        T4[i] = c_bsqrm_2[i];
}
gfb_mul(T2,T3,T2);                                         // T2xT3 -> T2
gfb_sqr(T3,T3);                                            // T3² -> T3
gfb_mul(T3,T4,T4);                                         // T3xT4 -> T4
gfb_mul(T1,T3,T3);                                         // T1xT3 -> T3
gfb_add(T2,T3,T2);                                         // T2+T3 -> T2
gfb_add(T1,T4,T4);                                         // T1+T4 -> T4
gfb_sqr(T4,T4);                                            // T4^2 -> T4
gfb_sqr(T4,T4);                                            // T4^2 -> T4
gfb_sqr(T1,T1);                                            // T1^2 -> T1
gfb_add(T1,T2,T2);                                         // T1+T2 -> T2
gfb_mul(T2,T4,T2);                                         // T2xT4 -> T2
gfb_sqr(T1,T1);                                            // T1^2 -> T1
gfb_mul(T1,T3,T1);                                         // T1xT3 -> T1
gfb_add(T1,T2,T2);                                         // T1+T2 -> T2
for(i = 0;i < 6;i++){                                      // T4->Qx, T2->Qy, T3->Qz
        x[i] = T4[i];                                      // Xr
        x[i + 6] = T2[i];                                  // Yr
        x[i + 12] = T3[i];                                 // Zr
}
```

Pcode 2.42: Simulation code for point double in GF(2^{163}) using standard projective coordinates.

```
for(i = 0;i < 6;i++){                                 // Xq -> T1, Yq -> T2, Zq -> T3, a -> T6, b -> T7
        T1[i] = x[i];  T2[i] = x[6+i];
        T3[i] = x[12+i];        T6[i] = a[i];
        T7[i] = b[i];
}
gfb_sqr(T1,T1);                                       // T1² -> T1
gfb_sqr(T3,T3);                                       // T3² -> T3
gfb_mul(T1,T3,T4);                                    // T1xT3 -> T4
gfb_sqr(T1,T1);                                       // T1² -> T1
gfb_sqr(T3,T3);                                       // T3² -> T3
gfb_mul(T7,T3,T3);                                    // bxT3 -> T3
gfb_add(T1,T3,T1);                                    // T1+T3 -> T1
gfb_sqr(T2,T2);                                       // T2² -> T2
gfb_add(T2,T3,T2);                                    // T2+T3 -> T2
gfb_mul(T3,T4,T3);                                    // T3xT4 -> T3
gfb_mul(T6,T4,T5);                                    // axT4 -> T5
gfb_add(T2,T5,T2);                                    // T2+T5 -> T2
gfb_mul(T2,T1,T2);                                    // T2xT1 -> T2
gfb_add(T2,T3,T2);                                    // T2+T3 -> T2
for(i = 0;i < 6;i++){
        x[i] = T1[i];                                 // Xr
        x[6+i] = T2[i];                               // Yr
        x[12+i] = T4[i];                              // Zr
}
```

Pcode 2.43: Simulation code for point double in GF(2^{163}) using modified Jacobian coordinates.

where

$$B_j = [b_{j3}b_{j2}b_{j1}b_{j0}] = b_{j3}\cdot 2^9 + b_{j2}\cdot 2^6 + b_{j1}\cdot 2^3 + b_{j0}\cdot 2^0$$

$$\begin{bmatrix} b_{00} & b_{01} & b_{02} & b_{03} \\ b_{10} & b_{11} & b_{12} & b_{13} \\ b_{20} & b_{21} & b_{22} & b_{23} \end{bmatrix} = \begin{bmatrix} 0 & 0 & 0 & 1 \\ 0 & 0 & 0 & 1 \\ 1 & 0 & 1 & 0 \end{bmatrix}$$

In this example, B_j can have 16 possible combinations and they are $[0000] = (0\cdot 2^9 + 0\cdot 2^6 + 0\cdot 2^3 + 0\cdot 2^0)$, $[0001] = (0\cdot 2^9 + 0\cdot 2^6 + 0\cdot 2^3 + 1\cdot 2^0), \ldots, [1111] = (1\cdot 2^9 + 1\cdot 2^6 + 1\cdot 2^3 + 1\cdot 2^0)$. These 16 values are given by 0, 1, 8, 9, 64, 65, 72, 73, 512, 513, 520, 521, 576, 577, 584, and 585. For our example of 1796, the values of B_0, B_1 and B_2 are given by $512 = [1000]$, $512 = [1000]$ and $65 = [0101]$. The number 1796 is obtained from the expression $2\cdot(2\cdot(B_2) + B_1) + B_0$ as $2\cdot(2\cdot 65 + 512) + 512$. This involves two multiplications and two additions, whereas the straightforward method involves 11 multiplications and 10 additions (it also requires 11 precomputed values of power 2). With the precomputation of 16 values, any 12-bit integer value can be computed easily using the previous method with two additions and two multiplications. Preparing offsets B_i for the comb method is illustrated in the following:

	B_2	B_1	B_0	
↑	1	0	0	$\rightarrow b_{i0}$
	0	0	0	$\rightarrow b_{i1}$
	1	0	0	$\rightarrow b_{i2}$
	0	1	1	$\rightarrow b_{i3}$

011 100 000 100

b_{i3} b_{i2} b_{i1} b_{i0}

$B_i = [b_{i3}\, b_{i2}\, b_{i1}\, b_{i0}]$

In the comb method, we basically divide the given binary string into small fixed-length blocks (if the leftmost block does not have sufficient bits, then we add enough zero bits at the MSB side to form a block). We arrange blocks one below another and read from bottom to top column-wise for getting each offset B_i. From this, $B_0 = [1000]$, $B_1 = [1000]$, and $B_2 = [0101]$. The pseudocode for scalar point multiplication kG using the comb method follows:

```
Q = B_{n-1}G;         // assuming n-offsets of B_i
for i = n-2:0
          Q=EccPointDouble(Q);
          Q=EccPointsAdd(Q, B_i G);
end
Output Q;
```

Add-Subtract with Low One Population

In this method, we compute a number h from a given number k by multiplying by 3. Then we compute g by XORing h and k. Let $g = (g_n g_{n-1} g_{n-2} \ldots g_1 g_0)$ and $k = (k_n k_{n-1} k_{n-2} \ldots k_1 k_0)$, where $g_n = 1$. Now, we build the number k from 1 by using the binary strings $(g_n g_{n-1} g_{n-2} \ldots g_1 g_0)$ and $(k_n k_{n-1} k_{n-2} \ldots k_1 k_0)$ in an iterative fashion, as seen in the following:

```
a = b = 1;
for(i = n-1; i > 0; i--){
          a = 2a;
          if (g_i == 0)
                    continue;
          else{
                    if(k_i == 0)
                              a = a+b;
                    else
                              a = a-b;
          }
}
```

Next we use the previous method to compute a 12-bit number k from 1. Let $k = 1796_d = 001110000100_b$, $h = 3*k = 3*1796 = 5388_d = 1010100001100_b$, and $g = k \oplus h = 1001000001000_b = (g_n g_{n-1} g_{n-2} \cdots g_1 g_0)$, where $n = 12$. Then, from the previous iterative method, the updated value at the end of each iteration becomes $a = 2, 4, 7, 14, 28, 56, 112, 224, 449, 898, 1796$. This method requires $n - 1$ multiplications and few additions (in our example case, two additions took place at the non-zero value of g_i). The number of additions depends on the one's population in the binary string of $\boldsymbol{g}$.

For computing scalar point multiplication, in the previous method we replace the multiplication by 2 with **PointDouble**, and addition and subtraction with **FullAdd** and **FullSub** operations. If we have sufficient memory, then use of the comb method reduces computations of scalar multiplication of the elliptic curve point by a lot. As discussed in Section 2.5.2, Elliptic Curve-Based DSA, in ECDSA, we have four scalar point multiplications, one in key-pair generation, one in signature generation, and two in signature verification. Out of four scalar point multiplications, we use base point G in three of them. In some cases, the domain parameters of elliptic curves may not be changed, and precomputation of a few base-point scalar multiplications can speed up signature generation or verification process computation.

The simulation code for scalar point multiplication using the comb method (for computing kG), EccPointMulComb(), and add-subtract method (for computing kP), EccPointMulAddSub(), are given in Pcodes 2.44

```
for(j = m-1;j > = 0;j--){
        EccPointDouble(Q);                          // 2Q->Q
        r0 = 0;
        for(i=5;i > =0;i--){                        // get offset B_i
                r1 = rk[i];
                r1 = r1 >> j; r0 = r0 << 1;
                r1 = r1 & 1;  r0 = r0 | r1;
        }
        if(r0 != 0){                                // get precomputed value
                r0+=-1;  r0 = r0 * 18;
                for(i = 0; i < 18;i++)
                        P[i] = Gu[i+r0];            // Gu[ ] contains precomputed values
                EccPointsAdd(pEC,P,Q,Q);            // Q+[xxxxxx].G -> Q
        }
}
// convert projective to affine coordinates,  (Xq,Yq,Zq) -> (Qx,Qy)
T1[0] = Q[12]; T1[1] = Q[13];
T1[2] = Q[14]; T1[3] = Q[15];
T1[4] = Q[16]; T1[5] = Q[17];
gfb_sqr(T1,T1);                                     // Qz^^2 -> T1
T9[0] = T1[0]; T9[1] = T1[1];                       // T1 -> T9
T9[2] = T1[2]; T9[3] = T1[3];
T9[4] = T1[4]; T9[5] = T1[5];
gfb_inv(T1,T2);                                     // 1/T1 -> T2
T1[0] = Q[0]; T1[1] = Q[1];
T1[2] = Q[2]; T1[3] = Q[3];
T1[4] = Q[4]; T1[5] = Q[5];
gfb_mul(T1,T2,T1);                                  // T1xT2 -> T1
y[0] = T1[0]; y[1] = T1[1];                         // T1 -> Qx
y[2] = T1[2]; y[3] = T1[3];
y[4] = T1[4]; y[5] = T1[5];
T1[0] = Q[12]; T1[1] = Q[13];
T1[2] = Q[14]; T1[3] = Q[15];
T1[4] = Q[16]; T1[5] = Q[17];
gfb_mul(T1,T9,T1);                                  // T1xT9 -> T1
gfb_inv(T1,T2);                                     // 1/T1 -> T2
T1[0] = Q[6]; T1[1] = Q[7];
T1[2] = Q[8]; T1[3] = Q[9];
T1[4] = Q[10]; T1[5] = Q[11];
gfb_mul(T1,T2,T1);                                  // T1xT2 -> T1
y[6] = T1[0]; y[7] = T1[1];                         // T1 -> Qy
y[8] = T1[2]; y[9] = T1[3];
y[10] = T1[4]; y[11] = T1[5];
```

Pcode 2.44: Simulation code for scalar point multiplication in GF(2^{163}) using comb method.

```
r0 = 0; r3 = 3;
for(i = 0;i < 6;i++)  {                          // 3*k -> h
    r1 = k[i];
    r2 = r1 & 0xffff; r1 = r1 >> 16;
    r4 = r2 * r3; r5 = r1 * r3;
    r4 = r4 + r0;
    r1 = r4 & 0xffff; r0 = r4 >> 16;
    r5 = r5 + r0;
    r2 = r5 & 0xffff; r0 = r5 >> 16;
    r2 = r2 << 16;
    r2 = r2 | r1;
    h[i] = r2;
}
for(i = m - 1;i > = 1;i--){
   EccPointDoubleModJac(pEC, Q);                 // 2Q->Q
   r0 = i>>5; r2 = i & 0x1f;
   r1 = k[r0]; r3 = h[r0];
   r1 = r1 >> r2; r3 = r3 >> r2;
   r1 = r1 & 1; r3 = r3 & 1;
   if ((r1 == 0) && (r3 == 0))
    continue;
   if ((r1 == 1) && (r3 == 1))
    continue;
   if((r1 == 0) && (r3 == 1))
    EccFullAddModJac(pEC, Q,P,Q);
   else
    EccFullSubModJac(pEC, Q,P,Q);
}
                                                 // convert from Modified Jacobian to affine coordinates
gfb_inv(&Q[12],T2);                              // 1/Zq -> T2
gfb_mul(Q,T2,y);                                 // XqxT2 -> x
gfb_sqr(&Q[12],T1);                              // Zq^^2 -> T1
gfb_inv(T1,T2);                                  // 1/T1 -> T2
gfb_mul(&Q[6],T2,&y[6]);                         // YqxT2 -> y
```

Pcode 2.45: Simulation code for scalar point multiplication in GF(2^{163}) using add-subtract method.

and 2.45, respectively. In scalar multiplication using the add-subtract method, we have two new functions, namely, EccFullAddModJac( ) and EccFullSubModJac( ). The EccFullSubModJac( ) function first computes the reflection point of the second input, and then calls the function EccFullAddModJac( ). The EccFullAddModJac( ) function is computed as follows.

```
EccAddPointsModJac(X, Y, Z);                  // X+Y-> Z
If (Z=0)
        EccDoublePointModJac(X, Z);           // 2X-> Z
Output Z;
```

Simulation of ECDSA over GF(2^{163})

The ECDSA parameter set over a binary field consists of the following parameters: coefficients a and b, field base-point G, field size s, and field order n. The ECDSA uses the three functions EccKeyPairGen() for key-pair generation, EccSigGen() for signature generation and EccSigVer() for signature verification. The signature generation routine uses a private key to compute the signature, whereas the signature verification process uses a public key to verify the signature. See Section 2.5.4 for more details of ECDSA functionality. Both signature generation and signature verification processes assume that the message digest value is available.

EccKeyPairGen(): Key-Pair Generation Process The key-pair generation process generates two keys, namely, private key and public key by multiplying the base point G with a pseudorandom number k. The simulation code for EccKeyPairGen() is given in Pcode 2.46.

EccSigGen(): Signature Generation Process The signature generation routine uses a private key (k) and a message digest value to compute the signature of a message, as shown in Figure 2.15. The simulation code for EccSigGen() is given in Pcode 2.47.

EccSigVer(): Signature Verification Process The signature verification routine uses the public key (W) and a message digest value to verify the signature of a message as shown in Figure 2.17. The simulation code for EccSigVer() is given in Pcode 2.48.

```
// choose (generate) private key 'k' in the interval [1, n-1], where n = 2^m , m = 163
// we assume the private key K[] (a random number) is available for this simulation
pECC->pvkey_m[0] = K[0]; pECC->pvkey_m[1] = K[1];
pECC->pvkey_m[2] = K[2]; pECC->pvkey_m[3] = K[3];
pECC->pvkey_m[4] = K[4]; pECC->pvkey_m[5] = K[5];
                                                    // compute public key 'W' as W = k.G
EccPointMulComb(pECC, K, pbkey);
for(i = 0;i < 12;i++)
        pECC->pbkey_m[i] = pbkey[i];
```

Pcode 2.46: Simulation code for key-pair generation process.

```
// S = (x,y) = t.G , where 't' is random number in the interval [1,n-1]
EccPointMulComb(pECC, t, randm, X);
// r = Sx mod n, its a m-bit integer modulo reduction
gfp_mod(P,T9,T4);                              // r = Sx mod n -> T4
// check if (sum(z[1:6})==0), then again start signature generation
// h = k.r, m-bit integer multiplication, where k is a private key of signature generator
T1[0] = pECC->pvkey_m[0]; T1[1] = pECC->pvkey_m[1];
T1[2] = pECC->pvkey_m[2]; T1[3] = pECC->pvkey_m[3];
T1[4] = pECC->pvkey_m[4]; T1[5] = pECC->pvkey_m[5];
// k.r, two m-bit numbers integer multiplication
gfp_mul(T1,T4,X);                              // T1 * T4 -> X
gfp_mod(X,T9,T3);                              // k.r mod n -> T3
// generate message digest 'e = msgd[ ]' using SHA-1 function
T1[0] = msgd[0]; T1[1] = msgd[1];
T1[2] = msgd[2]; T1[3] = msgd[3];
T1[4] = msgd[4]; T1[5] = 0;
                                               // e + (k.r mod n)
                                               // two m-bit numbers integer addition
gfp_add(T1,T3,T5);                             // T1+T3 -> T5
                                               // 1/t, inverse for m-bit integer number
gfp_inv(temp_randm,T3);                        // inv(t) -> T3
gfp_mul(T5,T3,X);                              // inv(t)*(e+k.r) -> X
gfp_mod(X,T9,T1);                              // s = inv(t)*(e+k.r) mod n -> T1
                                               // (r,s) -> output as signature
```

Pcode 2.47: Simulation code for EccSigGen( ) process in GF(2^{163}).

2.5.6 Simulation Results of ECDSA over GF(2^{163})

In this section, the simulation results for two recommended elliptic curves in GF(2^{163}) are presented. For each elliptic curve, domain parameters, EccKeyPairGen() output, EccSigGen() output, and EccSigVer() output are presented. For both signature generation and signature verification, we use a temporary message digest value, **msgd[ ]**.

Simulation Results for Koblitz Elliptic Curve over GF(2^{163})

Domain Parameters

```
a = 0x01;                                                       // coefficient 'a'
b = 0x01;                                                       // coefficient 'b'
G:(Xg, Yg) = (02 fe13c053 7bbc11ac aa07d793 de4e6d5e 5c94eee8,
              02 89070fb0 5d38ff58 321f2e80 0536d538 ccdaa3d9); // base point 'G'
N = 04 00000000 00000000 00020108 a2e0cc0d 99f8a5ef;            // order of curve 'n'
h = 02;                                                         // cofactor 'h'
```

Key-Pair Generation

Input:

A "seed" value for random number generator.

```
// assume message digest of message as e = msgd[], compute inverse of 's' of signature (r,s)
for(i = 0;i < 6;i++){
    T1[i] = pECC->outputs[6+i];                              // s
    T5[i] = pECC->outputs[i];                                // r
    T9[i] = pECC->order_g[i];                                // n
}
gfp_inv(T1,T4);                                              // inv(s) -> T4
gfp_mul(msgd,T4,X);                                          // e.inv(s) -> X
gfp_mod(X,T9,X);                                             // e.inv(s) (mod n) -> X
gfp_mul(T5,T4,Y);                                            // r.inv(s) -> Y
gfp_mod(Y,T9,Y);                                             // r.inv(s) (mod n) -> Y
EccPointMulComb(pECC,X,X);                                   // X.G -> X
EccPointMulAddSub(pECC, Y, Y);                               // Y.W -> Y

for(i = 0;i < 6;i++){
  P[i] = X[i];        Q[i] = Y[i];
  P[6+i] = X[6+i];  Q[6+i] = Y[6+i];
  P[12+i] = Zg[i];  Q[12+i] = Zg[i];                         // Zg[] = 1
}
EccFullAddModJacc(pECC, P,Q,Q);                              // X.G + Y.G -> (x,y)
// convert from modified Jacobian to affine coordinates
gfb_inv(&Q[12],T3);                                          // 1/Zq -> T3
gfb_mul(Q,T3,X);                                             // XqxT3 ->  X
gfb_sqr(&Q[12],T2);                                          // Zq² -> T2
gfb_inv(T2,T3);                                              // 1/T2 -> T3
gfb_mul(&Q[6],T3,Y);                                         // YqxT3 -> Y
for(i = 0;i < 6;i++){
    T9[i] = pECC->order_g[i];
    X[6+i] = 0;
}
gfp_mod(X,T9,T2);                                            // x (mod n) -> T2
pECC->valid_s = 1;
for(i = 0;i<6;i++){
   if(T2[i] != pECC->outputs[i]){
           pECC->valid_s = 0;
           break;
   }
}
```

Pcode 2.48: Simulation code for EccSigVer( ) process in GF(2^{163}).

Output:

```
k:03 a41434aa 99c2ef40 c8495b2e d9739cb2 155a1e0d;                      // private key
W:(Xw,Yw) = (03 7d529fa3 7e42195f 10111127 ffb2bb38 644806bc,
             04 47026eee 8b34157f 3eb51be5 185d2be0 249ed776);          // public key
```

Signature Generation

Input:

```
e:00 a9993e36 4706816a ba3e2571 7850c26c 9cd0d89d;           // message digest value
d:00 a40b301c c315c257 d51d4422 34f5aff8 189d2b6c;           // random number ∈ [1,n−1]
k:03 a41434aa 99c2ef40 c8495b2e d9739cb2 155a1e0d;           // private key
```

Output:

```
(r,s):(01 52f95ca1 5da1997a 8c449e00 cd2aa2ac cb988d7f,
       00 994d2c41 aa30e529 52aea846 2370471b 2b0a34ac);     // signature:(r,s)
```

Signature Verification

Input:

```
(r, s):(01 52f95ca1 5da1997a 8c449e00 cd2aa2ac cb988d7f,
        00 994d2c41 aa30e529 52aea846 2370471b 2b0a34ac);          // signature:(r,s)
e:00 a9993e36 4706816a ba3e2571 7850c26c 9cd0d89d;                 // message digest value
W:(Xw, Yw) = (03 7d529fa3 7e42195f 10111127 ffb2bb38 644806bc,
              04 47026eee 8b34157f 3eb51be5 185d2be0 249ed776);    // public key
```

Output:

```
Valid_s: 1                                                         // 1/0:valid/not valid
```

Simulation Results for Random Elliptic Curve Over $GF(2^{163})$

Domain Parameters

```
a=07 b6882caa efa84f95 54ff8428 bd88e246 d2782ae2;                   // coefficient 'a'
b=07 13612dcd dcb40aab 946bda29 ca91f73a f958afd9;                   // coefficient 'b'
G:(Xg,Yg)=(03 69979697 ab438977 89566789 567f787a 7876a654,
              00 435edb42 efafb298 9d51fefc e3c80988 f41ff883);      // base point 'G'
N=03 ffffffff ffffffff ffff48aa b689c29c a710279b;                   // order of curve 'n'
h=02;                                                                // cofactor 'h'
```

Key-Pair Generation

Input:

```
A "seed" value for random number generator.
```

Output:

```
k:03 a41434aa 99c2ef40 c8495b2e d9739cb2 155a1e0d;                   // private key
W:(Xw,Yw)=(05 7f8f4671 cfa2badf 53c57cb5 4e5c48a9 45ff2114,
              07 4da202c5 0a98ec3b badf742d 4c9dcf17 f52dc591);      // public key
```

Signature Generation

Input:

```
e:00 a9993e36 4706816a ba3e2571 7850c26c 9cd0d89d;                   // message digest value
d:00 a40b301c c315c257 d51d4422 34f5aff8 189d2b6c;                   // random number ∈ [1,n−1]
k:03 a41434aa 99c2ef40 c8495b2e d9739cb2 155a1e0d;                   // private key
```

Output:

```
(r,s):(01 40ca54a6 4474606e c63f5dc8 affc2e14 a8acf423,
       00 b653b62f d233247b c3441e64 b57449f2 cc5f1677);             // signature:(r,s)
```

Signature Verification

Input:

```
(r,s):(01 40ca54a6 4474606e c63f5dc8 affc2e14 a8acf423,
       00 b653b62f d233247b c3441e64 b57449f2 cc5f1677);             // signature:(r, s)
e:00 a9993e36 4706816a ba3e2571 7850c26c 9cd0d89d;                   // message digest value
W:(Xw, Yw)=(05 7f8f4671 cfa2badf 53c57cb5 4e5c48a9 45ff2114,
               07 4da202c5 0a98ec3b badf742d 4c9dcf17 f52dc591);     // public key
```

Output:

```
Valid_s:1                                                            // 1/0:valid/not valid
```

CHAPTER 3

Introduction to Data Error Correction

Error-correcting codes, an important part of modern digital communications systems, are used to detect and correct errors introduced during transmission. In many communications applications, as shown in Figure 3.1, a substantial portion of the baseband signal processing is dedicated to keeping a very low bit error rate (BER), usually less than 10^{-10}. As system designers, we can trade coding gain for lower transmit power or higher data throughput, and there is an ongoing effort to incorporate increasingly more powerful channel coding techniques into communications systems. In this chapter, we discuss various channel coding techniques and simulate the most popularly used CRC32 error detection algorithm. The error correction algorithm simulation techniques will be discussed in the next chapter.

3.1 Definitions

Communications channels introduce noise into useful signals during transmission. There are many noise sources that generate noise and add it to the signal. See Section 9.1.2 for more information on noise generation and measurement in communications systems. In his famous paper published in 1948, "Mathematical Theory of Communications," Shannon wrote that reliable communication through a channel is possible only if the rate of data transmission is below the channel capacity. From this paper, it can be understood that the presence of noise and the non-zero response of the channel are the two parameters that determine the channel capacity. It also says that the channel capacity can be achieved through complex channel coding and modulation schemes. See Section 9.1 for more information on channel capacity and modulation schemes. In this chapter, we discuss the channel coding techniques through which we can perform forward error correction (FEC) or the correction of channel errors at the receiver side without requesting retransmission of data. In Figure 3.1, the shaded portion represents the baseband processing related to channel coding.

Depending on the communications system, we may use either an error detection scheme (which may request for retransmission of data from the transmitter) or error-correction schemes, or both error detection and error correction schemes. In two-way communications systems such as telecom or computer data systems, we can use error detection with ARQ (automatic repeat request) schemes to improve communication quality. In Section 3.2,

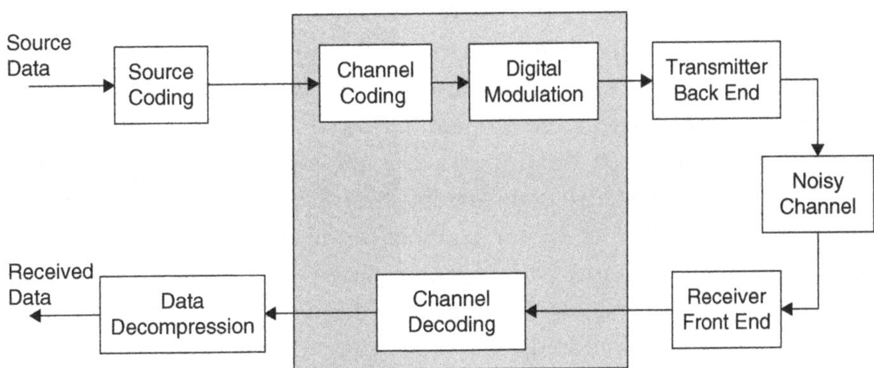

Figure 3.1: Channel coding in digital communications.

DOI: 10.1016/B978-1-85617-678-1.00003-X

we discuss various error detection methods and simulate the popularly used CRC32 error detection algorithm. Communications systems such as broadcast systems are examples of one-way communications systems, where we do not have a backward channel to request for retransmission of error data frames. In such cases, we apply error-correction techniques in the forward direction of the data itself to reduce the number of error frames. An overview of various error-correction schemes based on block coding and convolutional coding methods is provided in Sections 3.3 through 3.11.

3.2 Error Detection Algorithms

Data error detection algorithms with ARQ schemes play an important role in two-way communications systems to minimize the number of error data frames at the user end. The two-way communications systems examples are twisted-pair telephone lines, computer data communication networks, and some satellite communications systems. Error detection is performed by using redundant data added to the original data at the transmitter. We obtain the redundant data using either odd or even parity bit computation or cyclic-redundancy-check (CRC) bit computation. At the receiver, we again compute the check bits from received data bits and compare against the received redundant information. If the transmitted redundant information is the same as the computed check bits at the receiver, then we assume that the received data is error free; otherwise, we treat the current data frame as an error frame and request the transmitter to retransmit the current frame. In this section, we discuss how error detection works with parity or CRC bits, and simulate the widely used CRC32 algorithm.

3.2.1 Error Detection with Parity Bits

Assume that the transmitter and receiver communicate using data frames of n bits. At the receiver, we would like to know whether the current received frame contains any error bits. One way to know if errors are present in the received frame is by adding the parity bit at the transmitter to each transmitted frame. To perform this, we use only $n-1$ data bits and 1 parity bit to make an n-bit frame. At the receiver, we compute the parity bit again from $n-1$ data bits and check whether the computed parity bit matches the received parity bit. If they match, we assume that there are no errors in the received frame; otherwise, an error is detected.

Even or odd parity (i.e., making the number of ones in the n bits frame as even or odd) can be used in computing parity bits. Here we consider even parity. In Example 3.1, we use the data frame length of 8 bits and explain how single-bit errors are detected in the received 8-bit frames with a parity bit. Typically, we use 8 bits for transferring ASCII character data among computer memory, CPU, and peripherals. In these 8 bits, we use 7 bits to transmit actual data and 1 bit for parity.

Example 3.1

Assume that the following 7 bits of data—"1011001"—are to be transmitted. With the even parity, we make the number of 1s present in the 8-bit data even by adding a 0 bit as a parity bit. Then after adding the parity bit, the 8-bit frame becomes "1011001**0**" (where the bit highlighted with a bold letter is a parity bit), and we transmit this 8-bit frame to the receiver through a noisy channel. Assume we received an 8-bit data frame as "10110110" with the 1 bit in error marked with an underscore. If we compute the parity bit with 7 data bits of the received frame, then we get 1 for even parity, whereas the parity bit of the received frame (i.e., 8th bit) is 0. As the parity bits are not matching, the received frame contains errors and we request the transmitter to transmit this frame again. However, we will have a problem if the number of errors occurred are even. For example, if the received frame contains two bit errors, "10100110," then both computed parity bit and received parity bit are the same. So, if an even number of errors occurs in the received frame, we fail to detect the error. In some applications, we use long data frame lengths on the order of hundreds of bits and the probability of an even number of errors to occur is also high. Hence, the error frame detection failure rate is also high with this even-parity bit error detection scheme.

■

With large data frames, to improve the error detection rate, we use more than 1 bit for parity data and compute these parity bits using the data blocks (of length k bits) instead of computing in terms of individual data bits. In this way, we reduce the data length per parity bit by factor k. Also, we overcome the problem of burst error detection as the parity computation module sees the burst errors as distributed across many parity bits. This is explained in Example 3.2.

Example 3.2

Assume that the following 7 data bytes, "B7, CA, 49, 62, AE, DD, 78," are set for transmission. Along with these 7 data bytes, assume that the allowed parity data is 1 byte. Next, we compute a parity byte as 0x5D from the data of 7 bytes and then we transmit an 8-byte or 64-bit frame "B7, CA, 49, 62, AE, DD, 78, **5D**." The first 7 bytes are data and the last byte is a parity byte highlighted with the bold letters. Here, we computed even parity across the data bytes. The parity byte is also obtained by computing the check-sum (or by XORing all 7 data bytes) using the XOR operation. At the receiver, we again compute the check-sum of 7 data bytes. If the check-sum computed at the receiver matches with the parity byte, then we assume that the received 64-bit frame is error free. If the check-sum does not match with the parity byte, then the received 64-bit frame contains errors and we may request retransmission of the entire frame.

1011 0111 (0xB7) -> data bytes
1100 1010 (0xCA)
0100 1001 (0x49)
0110 0010 (0x62)
1010 1110 (0xAE)
1101 1101 (0xDD)
0111 1000 (0x78)
____
0101 1101 (0x5D) -> parity byte

With this scheme, a burst of all lengths, except multiples of 16 bits, can be detected. For example, assume that the received 8-byte data frame is "B7, CA, 49, 62, D1, 22, 78, 5D" with 15 continuous bit errors. If we compute the check-sum again at the receiver as

1011 0111 (0xB7) -> data bytes
1100 1010 (0xCA)
0100 1001 (0x49)
0110 0010 (0x62)
1101 0001 (0xD1)
0010 0010 (0x22)
0111 1000 (0x78)
____
1101 1101 (0xDD) -> parity byte

we get the check-sum 0xDD, which is different from the received parity byte 0x5D. However, if we have a burst of 16 bits, then we may fail to detect that frame as an error frame.

■

To reduce the overall failure rate or to improve the error detection rate significantly, error detection schemes based on CRC bits are widely used. In the next section, we discuss how to compute CRC bits from the given message data for use in error detection schemes.

3.2.2 Error Detection with CRC Bits

Error detection schemes based on a cyclic redundancy check are commonly used in many applications such as digital communications and computer data storage systems for detecting the errors in the presence of noise. Similar to the parity schemes discussed in the previous section, we compute the CRC bits from original (or payload) data at the transmitter and append CRC as overhead to the original data before transmitting through a noisy channel. At the receiver, we again compute the CRC for payload data and compare it with the received CRC bits to verify the integrity of the message. In computing the CRC, we use a division operation instead of addition. While addition is clearly not strong enough to form an effective check-sum, it turns out that division gives better redundant data as long as the divisor is wide enough and satisfies certain criteria to be discussed later. The CRC bits are given by the remainder of the division operation.

The CRC algorithms operate on blocks of data instead of on individual data bits. Usually, a CRC is performed through binary polynomial division with modulo-2 arithmetic. The elements of modulo-2 arithmetic are from Galois field GF(2). In short, GF(2) is a field consisting of the elements 0 and 1, with + and * operations defined as logical XOR and logical AND operations for modulo-2 arithmetic. The modulo-2 addition or XOR (⊕) and modulo-2 multiplication or AND (∩) tables adhere to the following rule.

⊕	0	1
0	0	1
1	1	0

∩	0	1
0	0	0
1	0	1

Polynomial arithmetic with modulo 2 allows an efficient implementation of a form of division that is fast, easy to implement and sufficient for the purpose of CRC computation. In the CRC computation, choosing of the divisor (from now onwards, we call it "generator polynomial") plays an important role to obtain CRC with good characteristics. A well-chosen CRC generator polynomial ensures an evenly distributed mapping of message data to CRC values. A well-constructed CRC value over data blocks of limited size will detect any contiguous burst of errors shorter than the CRC data, any odd number of errors throughout the message, 2-bit errors anywhere in the message, and certain other possible errors anywhere in the message.

Next, we discuss the computation of CRC bits given the message data bits and generator polynomial. We represent all the inputs and outputs of the CRC module, such as message data, the CRC generator, and the CRC value itself, in terms of bits and eventually in terms of polynomials in the computation of CRC bits. For example, a binary vector $\boldsymbol{b}$ = [10010101] is represented in polynomial form as follows:

$$\begin{aligned} b(x) &= 1\cdot x^7+0\cdot x^6+0\cdot x^5+1\cdot x^4+0\cdot x^3+1\cdot x^2+0\cdot x+1 \\ &= x^7+x^4+x^2+1 \end{aligned}$$

For purposes of clarity, in Example 3.3 the division operation is performed separately using binary digits and corresponding polynomials. Here, the division is performed in the same way as long division performed manually on paper.

Example 3.3

Let b = [10010101] be the dividend and g = [101] be the divisor of the division operation. In the polynomial notation, their equivalents are represented as $b(x)=x^7+x^4+x^2+1$ and $g(x)=x^2+1$. The remainder of the division is obtained in the vector form as c = [11] or in the polynomial form as $c(x)=x+1$.

```
        10111
101 |10010101
     101
     ---
      011
      000
      ---
       110
       101
       ---
        111
        101
        ---
         100
         101
         ---
          11
```

$$\begin{array}{r} x^5+x^3+x^2+x \\ x^2+1\;\overline{)\,x^7+x^4+x^2+1} \\ \underline{x^7+x^5} \\ x^5+x^4+x^2 \\ \underline{x^5+x^3} \\ x^4+x^3+x^2+1 \\ \underline{x^4+x^2} \\ x^3+1 \\ \underline{x^3+x} \\ x+1 \end{array}$$

If $b = [10010101]$ is the message vector and $g = [101]$ is a generator vector, then the remainder $c = [11]$ corresponds to CRC value. We append the CRC bits to the message data as $m = b|c$ and transmit to the receiver.

■

Note that the even parity is a particular case of CRC and when the generator vector $g = [11]$ or $g(x) = x + 1$, we get the CRC output the same as even parity output as computed in Example 3.4. For the same 8-bit message vector considered in Example 3.3, if we compute even parity, we get the parity bit as "0" since the number of ones present in the message vector is even. If we perform the division for the same message vector using generator vector $g = [11]$, then the CRC, that is, the remainder of the division, is obtained as "0." Therefore, the even parity and CRC outputs the same redundant bit when CRC uses the generator polynomial $g(x) = x + 1$.

Example 3.4

In this example, we compute CRC with generator polynomial $g(x) = x + 1$, and show that the CRC and even parity outputs the same redundant bit. First, we compute the even parity for a given 8-bit vector 10010101 as 0 since the number of 1s present in the given 8-bit vector are even. We add the 9th bit as "0" to make sure that the parity added 9-bit data vector consists of an even number of 1s. Next, we compute the CRC for the original 8-bit vector using 11 as divisor as follows:

$$
\begin{array}{r|r}
\begin{array}{r}
1110011 \\
11\ \overline{)10010101} \\
\underline{11} \\
10 \\
\underline{11} \\
11 \\
\underline{11} \\
00 \\
\underline{00} \\
01 \\
\underline{00} \\
10 \\
\underline{11} \\
0
\end{array}
&
\begin{array}{r}
x^6+x^5+x^4+x \\
x+1\ \overline{)x^7+x^4+x^2+1} \\
\underline{x^7+x^6} \\
x^6+x^4+x^2 \\
\underline{x^6+x^5} \\
x^5+x^4+x^2+1 \\
\underline{x^5+x^4} \\
x^2+1 \\
\underline{x^2+x} \\
x+1 \\
\underline{x+1} \\
0
\end{array}
\end{array}
$$

With the message vector 10010101 and generator vector 11, the CRC, which is the remainder of division, is obtained as "0" as expected. From this, we can say both CRC and even parity compute the same when the generator polynomial used for CRC is $g(x) = x + 1$.

■

We explore how 1-bit errors and 2-bit errors are detected using CRC. For this, we use Example 3.3 as the transmitter-side CRC generation. Here, we transmit a total of 10 bits (8 bits of message and 2 bits of CRC) as 10010101|11. We consider two cases as in Example 3.5. The first case deals with the received message vector $\boldsymbol{a}$ that contains one error, and the second case deals with the received message vector $\boldsymbol{b}$ that contains two errors. With CRC, we are able to detect both 1-bit and 2-bit errors, as the CRC computed in both cases at the receiver is different from the received CRC.

Example 3.5

Assume that the transmitted message along with CRC bits is 10010101|11 and a noisy channel introduces a 1-bit error in the received sequence, say $a = 10\underline{1}10101|11$. If we then compute CRC again for the received data as follows, we obtain CRC bits 01, which is different from the received CRC bits 11; hence, a single-bit error is detected.

```
        100100
101 | 10110101 => a
      101
       001
       000
        010
        000
         101
         101
          01
```

$$
\begin{array}{r}
x^5+x^2 \\
x^2+1 \,\big)\, x^7+x^5+x^4+x^2+1 \\
\underline{x^7+x^5} \\
x^4+x^2 \\
\underline{x^4+x^2} \\
1
\end{array}
$$

If the noisy channel introduces 2-bit errors in the received sequence, say $b = 10001101|11$, and we then compute CRC again for the received data as follows, we obtain CRC 00, which is different from the received CRC 11; thus, a double-bit error is detected.

```
        101001
101 | 10001101 => b
      101
       010
       000
        101
        101
         001
         000
          101
          101
           00
```

$$
\begin{array}{r}
x^5+x^3+1 \\
x^2+1 \,\big)\, x^7+x^3+x^2+1 \\
\underline{x^7+x^5} \\
x^5+x^3+x^2 \\
\underline{x^5+x^3} \\
x^2+1 \\
\underline{x^2+1} \\
0
\end{array}
$$

■

However, we may fail in some cases with short generator polynomials like $g(x) = x^2 + 1$ in detecting double-bit errors. For example, we receive the message, say $\boldsymbol{d} = 10111101|11$, which corresponds to the transmitted message $\boldsymbol{m} = 10010101|11$. The received message differs from the transmitted message in two bit places as highlighted with underscoring. If we compute the CRC, the computed CRC will be the same as received CRC (i.e., 11), so we fail to detect the received message $\boldsymbol{d}$ that contained a 2-bit error. In practice, we use 16, 24, or 32-bit generator vectors for generating CRC bits to significantly improve the error detection rate. As the message vector lengths are also very long, the overhead added by CRC (i.e., 32 bits) is negligible. Next, we introduce a few notations to simplify and efficiently compute the CRC bits using the LFSR (linear feedback shift register).

Let $m(x)$, $g(x)$, and $c(x)$ represent a message polynomial of degree $k-1$, generator polynomial of degree n, and a CRC polynomial of degree $n-1$, respectively. Then

$$m(x) = m_{k-1}x^{k-1} + m_{k-2}x^{k-2} + \cdots + m_1x + m_0$$

$$g(x) = x^n + g_{n-1}x^{n-1} + \cdots + g_1x + g_0$$

$$c(x) = c_{n-1}x^{n-1} + c_{n-2}x^{n-2} + \cdots + c_1x + c_0$$

If $c(x)$ is the remainder when we divide $m(x)$ with $g(x)$, then $c(x) = m(x) \bmod g(x)$, where "mod" represents a modulo operation that outputs the remainder of the division operation. Since c_{n-1} need not be a non-zero value, we cannot say that the CRC polynomial degree is $n-1$. However, to generate n CRC bits, we have to

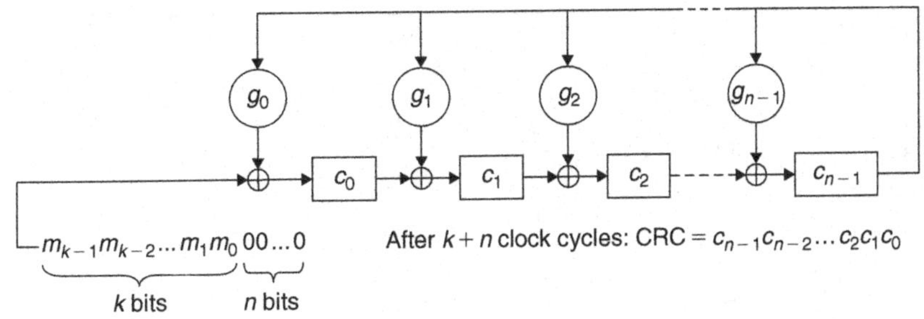

Figure 3.2: CRC computation using LFSR.

use the nth-degree generator polynomial $g(x)$. Then $m(x) = g(x) \cdot q(x) + c(x)$, where $q(x)$ is a quotient of division. As the CRC bits (of length n) are appended at the end of message, we shift the message vector left by n bits (or multiply the message polynomial by x^n) and append n CRC bits. As the division has no effect on the remainder even after multiplying the message polynomial by x^n, we can write $m(x) \cdot x^n = g(x) \cdot Q(x) + c(x)$ or $m(x) \cdot x^n + c(x) = g(x) \cdot Q(x)$, where $Q(x) = q(x) \cdot x^n$. At the receiver, if we compute the CRC for entire $k+n$ bits, that is, by performing division of $m(x) \cdot x^n + c(x)$ by $g(x)$, and if we get zero as remainder, then no errors are present in the received message, as the message is a multiple of the generator polynomial $g(x)$.

LFSR is commonly used to compute the remainder of the division of a message polynomial with a generator polynomial. As shown in Figure 3.2, the LFSR consists of n-shift registers and uses generator polynomial coefficients as its taps. Here, the size of the LFSR is the same as the number of CRC bits. We shift the message left by n bits and pass it through the LFSR 1 bit per clock cycle. After passing all $k+n$ bits through the LFSR, the state of the LFSR gives the CRC bits as shown in Figure 3.2. Then we append the CRC to the message $m_{k-1}\ldots m_1m_0c_{n-1}\ldots c_1c_0$ and transmit it through a noisy channel to the receiver. The LFSR-based CRC computation is explained in Example 3.6.

Example 3.6

We consider the message polynomial used in Example 3.3 to compute CRC using LFSR. The state of shift registers after each clock cycle is tabulated as follows. After $k+n$ cycles (i.e., $8+2=10$), the CRC is given by the shift register values as shown in Figure 3.3.

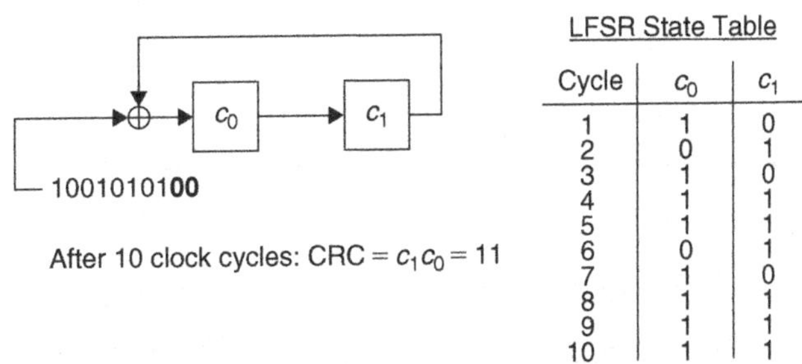

LFSR State Table

Cycle	c_0	c_1
1	1	0
2	0	1
3	1	0
4	1	1
5	1	1
6	0	1
7	1	0
8	1	1
9	1	1
10	1	1

Figure 3.3: Illustration of LFSR-based CRC computation.

The CRC computation using LFSR can be efficiently implemented in hardware. An equivalent software implementation of LFSR-based CRC computation is given in Pcode 3.1. The input message vector is stored in a buffer and loads a 32-bit word at a time from the buffer to pass the data. We pass n 0 bits at the end of the message data to get the final CRC bits from the shift registers.

As Pcode 3.1 computes CRC bits by processing the message data bit by bit, it is not an efficient implementation to compute CRC especially when the input is very long and the LFSR length is in the order of 32 bits. In this

```
k = pCRC->message_length;          // length of input message
n = pCRC->crc_length;              // length of CRC bits
r2 = 0;                            // initialize LFSR
r4 = pCRC->gen_poly;               // generator vector, [101]
r0 = *pCRC->in_data++; mask = pCRC->extract_crc;
m = k >> 5; tb = 1 << (n-1);
if (m != 0) {                      // if k > 32 bits
        for(j = 0;j < m;j++) {
                for(i = 0;i < 32;i++) {
                        r1 = r0 >> 31; r3 = r2 & tb;
                        r2 = r2 << 1; r2 = r2 | r1;
                        if (r3) r2 = r2 ^ r4;
                        r0 = r0 << 1;
                }
                r0 = *pCRC->in_data++;
        }
}
m = k-32*m;
if (m != 0){                       // if n%32 is not zero
        for(i = 0;i < m;i++) {
                r1 = r0 >> 31; r3 = r2 & tb;
                r2 = r2 << 1; r2 = r2 | r1;
                if (r3) r2 = r2 ^ r4;
                r0 = r0 << 1;
        }
}
if (pCRC->enc_flag){               // to compute CRC at transmitter side
        r0 = 0;
        for(i = 0;i < n;i++) {     // passing n zero bits
                r1 = r0 >> 31; r3 = r2 & tb;
                r2 = r2 << 1; r2 = r2 | r1;
                if (r3) r2 = r2^ r4;
                r0 = r0 << 1;
        }
}
else {                             // to verify CRC at receiver side
        for(i = 0;i < n;i++) {
                r1 = r0 >> 31; r3 = r2 & tb;
                r2 = r2 << 1; r2 = r2 | r1;
                if (r3) r2 = r2 ^ r4;
                r0 = r0 << 1; m = m + 1;
                if (m==32) {
                        r0 = *pCRC->in_data++; m = 0;
                }
        }
}
r2 = r2 & mask;
pCRC->crc_bits = r2;
```

Pcode 3.1: CRC implementation using bit-by-bit method.

approach, we consume up to 8 cycles per message bit (see Appendix A, Section A.4, on the companion website for more details on cycle requirements to execute particular operations on the reference embedded processor). In the next section, we discuss efficient block-based software implementation of CRC32 using look-up tables.

3.2.3 CRC32

As discussed earlier, to get CRC bits with good characteristics, we need more CRC bits; hence, longer generator polynomials are used to get wider CRC data. In the industry, the following four CRC generator polynomials are popularly used:

$$\text{CRC-12: } \mathbf{g} = [1100000001111] \text{ or } g(x) = x^{12} + x^{11} + x^3 + x^2 + x + 1$$

$$\text{CRC-16: } \mathbf{g} = [11000000000000101] \text{ or } g(x) = x^{16} + x^{15} + x^2 + 1$$

$$\text{CRC-CCITT: } \mathbf{g} = [10001000000100001] \text{ or } g(x) = x^{16} + x^{12} + x^5 + 1$$

CRC-32: Used in Ethernet, $\boldsymbol{g}$ = [100000100110000010001110110110111] or

$$g(x) = x^{32}+x^{26}+x^{23}+x^{22}+x^{16}+x^{12}+x^{11}+x^{10}+x^{8}+x^{7}+x^{5}+x^{4}+x^{2}+x+1$$

In this section, we concentrate on efficient implementation of CRC32 using look-up tables. To understand the look-up-table–based CRC computation, we consider CRC computation for small size data $\boldsymbol{b}$ = [101100110110] with the generator polynomial $g(x) = x^4 + x + 1$ or $\boldsymbol{g}$ = [10011], as given in Example 3.7. We compute the intermediate CRC value for 4 bits at a time instead of 1 bit.

Example 3.7

In this example, we compute CRC bits on a block basis instead of bit by bit. As shown in the following, we consider the first 4 bits, "1011," of the message vector, and compute the intermediate CRC, and then add this CRC to the next 4 bits of message and shift the message left by 4 bits and continue this process. The length of the intermediate CRC depends on the degree of the generator polynomial. Here, the degree of the generator polynomial is 4; hence, we have intermediate CRC output that contains 4 bits (see Figure 3.4).

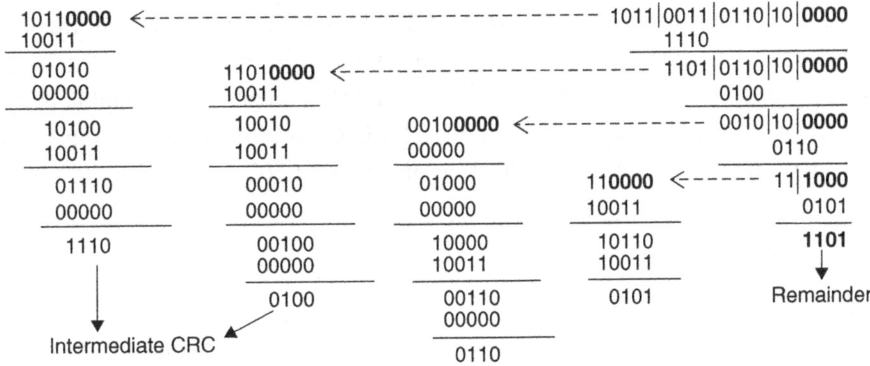

Figure 3.4: Illustration of look-up-table–based CRC computation.

From Example 3.7, it is clear that the intermediate CRC values can be obtained from a precomputed look-up table which contains intermediate CRC values for all possible 4-bit combinations of input values. The intermediate CRC is accessed from the look-up table using the input 4- (= p) bit number as an offset to the look-up table. The look-up-table–based CRC computation scheme works as shown in Figure 3.5.

We generate the values for the look-up table to implement an Ethernet CRC32 scheme. We represent the CRC32 generator polynomial in short by using the hexadecimal notation as G = 0x04c11db7. The program in Pcode 3.2 follows the same approach used in Example 3.7 to generate the look-up table entries, but computes 32-bit intermediate CRC values (as the degree of CRC32 is 32) using 8-bit length bitstream combinations (since

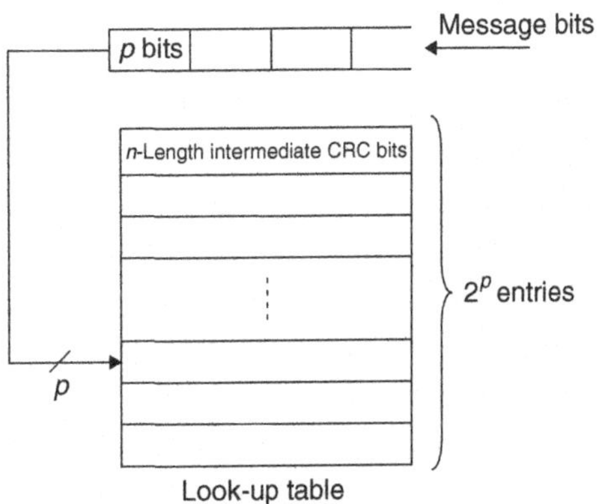

Figure 3.5: Block-based CRC implementation using a look-up table.

8 bits are easily accessed from buffers when compared to 4 bits). As we can represent 256 possible levels with 8 bits, the loop runs 256 times and generates intermediate 32-bit CRC values for all 256 combinations. The CRC32_LUT[] look-up table on the companion website contains the intermediate 32-bit CRC values for an Ethernet CRC generator polynomial with an input of all 8-bit combinations.

```
r2 = pCRC->gen_poly;
for(i = 0;i < 256;i++){
        r0 = (i<<24);
        for(j = 0;j < 8;j++){
                r1 = r0 >> 31;
                r0 = r0 << 1;
                if (r1) r0 = r0 ^ r2;
        }
        CRC_LUT[i] = r0;
}
```

Pcode 3.2: Block-based CRC look-up table generation.

Once the look-up table for intermediate CRC values of all possible combinations of 8-bit data is generated, then computing the CRC of message data is very simple. As given in Pcode 3.3, we extract 8 bits from message, get the 32-bit intermediate CRC value from look-up table **CRC32_LUT**[] and then XOR this value with the next 32 bits of message data, and continue the same process until the end of the message. The look-up-table–based CRC32 computation requires 1 kB of data memory to store a 256-element look-up table and consumes about 4 cycles per byte or 0.5 cycles per bit, whereas the bit-by-bit CRC computation given in Pcode 3.1 consumes about 8 cycles per bit. Example 3.8 describes application of a 32-bit CRC with a small test vector.

```
r0 = 0;
for(i = 0;i < pCRC->message_length_bytes;i++){
        r1 = (r0 >> 24) & 0xff;                       // extract 8-bit or byte of data
        r0 = (r0 << 8) | *pCRC->data_in++;            // append next byte
        r0 = r0 ^ CRC_LUT[r1];                        // XOR with look-up table output
}
if (pCRC->enc_flag){                                  // to generate CRC
        for(i = 0;i < 4;i++){
                r1 = (r0 >> 24) & 0xff; r0 = (r0 << 8);
                r0 = r0 ^ CRC_LUT[r1];
        }
}
else {                                                // to verify CRC
        for(i = 0;i < 4;i++){
                r1 = (r0 >> 24) & 0xff; r0 = (r0 << 8) | *pCRC->data_in++;
                r0 = r0 ^ CRC_LUT[r1];
        }
}
pCRC->crc_bits = r0;
```

Pcode 3.3: Look-up table based CRC32 implementation.

Example 3.8

Let $G = 0x04c117db7$ be the CRC32 generator polynomial represented in hexadecimal notation. Assume that the 2 bytes "0x1c, 0x11" are intended for transmission. The CRC32 is computed using Pcode 3.3 and its 32-bit CRC value is given by "0x97ed3f2f." We append CRC32 to data bytes and transmit as "0x1c, 0x11, 0x97, 0xed, 0x3f, 0x2f." At the receiver, we compute CRC32 again and detect error frames if any. As we compute CRC32 for the entire frame including the transmitted CRC32, we get "0x00000000" as the CRC32 value at the receiver if no errors are present in the received data frame. We verify CRC32 (use the same code given in Pcode 3.3 by setting pCRC->enc_flag to zero) in the following, assuming three cases: received data contains zero errors, received data contains one error, and received data contains two errors.

Case 1: Zero errors

Received data: 0x1c, 0x11, 0x97, 0xed, 0x3f, 0x2f

Computed CRC32 at the receiver: 0x00000000

Result: No errors are present in the received data frame

Case 2: One-bit error

Received data: 0x1d, 0x11, 0x97, 0xed, 0x3f, 0x2f

Computed CRC32 at the receiver: 0xd219c1dc

Result: Errors are present in the received data frame

Case 3: Two-bit errors

Received data: 0x1c, 0x14, 0x97, 0xed, 0x3f, 0x2f

Computed CRC32 at the receiver: 0x17c56b6b

Result: Errors are present in the received data frame

■

In essence, with CRC32, we can ensure the following:

- 100% detection of single-bit errors
- 100% detection of all double-bit errors (except those errors that are separated by $2^{32} - 1$ bits
- 100% detection of any errors spanning up to 32 bits

With one-way communications systems (e.g., broadcast systems), the error detection schemes are not used as the one-way communications systems cannot request for retransmission. In the next section, we discuss error correction algorithms which not only detect errors but also correct them.

3.3 Block Codes

In the previous section we discussed how parity check or cyclic redundancy check bits are used to detect errors in a received data block. With the error detection methods, we request for retransmission of data frames after detecting errors in the received data. In this section, we introduce a few concepts with which we not only detect errors but also correct them. This is called forward error correction (FEC). With FEC, we may not request for retransmission of data frames as those errors are corrected at the receiver with error correction algorithms. All errors can be corrected if the number of errors occurred in the received data is less than or equal to the capability of the particular FEC algorithm used. Before discussing the theory behind the block codes, we consider two examples to get a feel for error correction (see Examples 3.9 and 3.10). Then we introduce linear block codes and discuss encoding and decoding techniques for simple codes. In the later sections, we discuss various types of powerful linear block codes and convolutional codes.

■ Example 3.9

Assume that we want to transmit 4 bits, "1,0,1,1," and we would like to receive them exactly without any errors. In the presence of noise, it is not guaranteed to receive error-free bits. If we receive the bits as "1,0,0,1," we cannot say anything from those bits; we don't know whether they are error free or not since we don't have any extra information about those bits. If we append a few bits to "1,0,1,1" in a specific manner, then it is possible to know whether errors are present or not, and we can correct those errors. For example, we repeat each bit three times like "111, 000, 111, 111," and transmit these 3-bit blocks through a noise channel. That means, for each message bit, we are transmitting 3 bits. At the receiver, we receive those 3-bit blocks as "111, 000, 101, 111" with 1 bit in error in the third block as highlighted with underscoring. If we apply a decoding procedure which simply decodes such that if more zeros are present in a block then decode as a bit "0'and if more ones are present in a block then decode that bit as a bit "1." With this decoding procedure we get decoded bits "1,0,1,1." Although there is a 1 bit in error in the received sequence, we are able to get the transmitted data bits without errors with the repetition of bits three times. We call it a repetition code. With a 3-bit repetition code, we can only correct one error per 3-bit block. The disadvantage with this code is that the bandwidth (i.e., number of bits transmitted per unit time) is increased by three. In a communications system, we want to keep data bandwidth as low as possible. Also, this code treats each bit as an individual block and the channels may not introduce errors in each 3-bit block. Usually, block codes are used in a digital communications system as an outer coder where we will have a bit-error rate (BER) of 10^{-2} or less. The BER is computed as the ratio of total number of error bits to a total number of received bits. So, BER $= 10^{-2}$ or less means that there will be a 1-bit error in 100 or more received bits.

■

■ Example 3.10

We introduce another approach, where we treat a chunk of bits as one block (we call it a "message block") and add redundant bits per message block instead of to each individual bit. For example, we consider the same previous bits for transmission but as one block like "1011" (i.e., input message block length $k = 4$). Let $B = b_0b_1b_2b_3 = 1011$. We add 3 bits, "$p_0p_1p_2$" (we call them "parity bits"), to this block B, and form a new message block (we call it a message codeword) by appending parity bits to data bits as "$p_0p_1b_0p_2b_1b_2b_3$" (i.e., output message codeword length is $n = 7$). The parity bits p_0, p_1, and p_2 are calculated from a matrix arrangement of data and parity bits as shown in the following:

$$\begin{array}{c} \\ 0 \\ 1 \end{array}\begin{array}{c} \begin{array}{cccc} 00 & 01 & 10 & 11 \end{array} \\ \left[\begin{array}{cccc} - & p_0 & p_1 & b_0 \\ p_2 & b_1 & b_2 & b_3 \end{array}\right] \end{array}$$

In this matrix, each bit can be identified with a row index and a column index. For example, p_0: $(0, 01)$, p_1: $(0, 10)$, b_0: $(0, 11)$, and so on. We ignore "," and form one binary string to get the index for message and parity bits as p_0: 001(1), p_1: 010(2), b_0: 011(3), and so on. From the preceding matrix, if we observe carefully, the parity bits are placed such that their corresponding index is a power of 2 (i.e., p_0: 001, p_1: 010, p_2: 100). The parity bit p_0 (note that its index 0th bit = 1) is calculated by XORing the data bits at indexes where the 0th bit of index is 1 (i.e., bits b_0, b_1, and b_3). Similarly, the parity bit p_1 (note that its index 1st bit = 1) is calculated by XORing the data bits at indexes where the 1st bit of index is 1 (i.e., bits b_0, b_2, and b_3). Finally, the parity bit p_2 (note that its index 2nd bit = 1) is calculated by XORing the data bits at indexes where the 2nd bit of index is 1 (i.e., bits b_1, b_2, and b_3). With this, the parity bits p_0, p_1 and p_2 are computed as follows:

$$p_0 = b_0 \oplus b_1 \oplus b_3$$

$$p_1 = b_0 \oplus b_2 \oplus b_3$$

$$p_2 = b_1 \oplus b_2 \oplus b_3$$

From the preceding equations, the parity bits are computed using the message block bits $b_0b_1b_2b_3 = 1011$ as $p_0 = 0$, $p_1 = 1$ and $p_2 = 0$. We transmit the message codeword $p_0p_1b_0p_2b_1b_2b_3 = 0110011$ through a noisy channel to the receiver.

Assume codeword bits $p_0p_1b_0p_2b_1b_2b_3 = 0110\underline{1}11$ are received at the receiver with 1 bit in error as highlighted with an underscore. Next, we discuss a method to correct the bit, which is received with an error. From received data block, we separate data bits and parity bits as $b_0b_1b_2b_3 = 1\underline{1}11$ and $p_0p_1p_2 = 010$. We compute the metrics, called syndromes, $S_0S_1S_2$ (which give an indication of an error if one is present) from the received data bits $b_0b_1b_2b_3$ as $S_0 = (q_0 \oplus p_0)$, $S_1 = (q_1 \oplus p_1)$ and $S_2 = (q_2 \oplus p_2)$. Here, we compute $q_0q_1q_2$ in the same way as parity bits are computed just by replacing ps with qs in the preceding parity equations. With this, $q_0 = 1, q_1 = 1, q_2 = 1$ and $S_0S_1S_2 = 101$. The index $(S_2, S_1S_0) = (1, 01)$ gives the bit position where the error would have occurred. That means from the preceding table, the index (1, 01) says b_1 is in error. As the codeword contains only binary digits (or bits), if we toggle bit b_1 in the received sequence, then we will get the corrected sequence as 0110011, which is the same as the transmitted sequence. If $S_0S_1S_2 = 000$, then no errors are present in the received data block.

■

In the approach discussed in Example 3.10, we added three extra bits to the original message 4-bit block at the transmitter to correct single-bit error in the received block. To compare the two methods discussed above, we define a term called *code rate* (R_c) as the ratio of message block length (k) to the message codeword length (n). In Example 3.9, $k = 1, n = 3$, and $R_c = k/n = 1/3$. In Example 3.10, $k = 4, n = 7$, and $R_c = k/n = 4/7$. Here, if the code rate is more, then we need less transmission bandwidth. Hence, the second method requires less bandwidth to correct the 1 bit per message block transmitted. Therefore, from here onwards, we concentrate and build the framework for block codes based on the second method.

We rearrange the codeword $p_0p_1b_0p_2b_1b_2b_3$ as $B|P = b_0b_1b_2b_3|\,p_0p_1p_2$ to compute the block codes in a systematic way by using the matrix representation. Here, we basically compute the parity data bits and append to the message block to form a codeword. If the input message block length is k and output codeword length is n, then we refer such a code as (n, k) code. If the original message block is present as it is in the output codeword (as in $B|P$), then we call such a code (n, k) *systematic* code. The code that is not systematic is called *nonsystematic* code. Given a message block B, we compute the codeword $C = B|P$ using generator matrix G as:

$$C = B \cdot G \tag{3.1}$$

where $G = [I_k|P]$. One example of generator matrix follows:

$$G = [I_k|P] = \begin{bmatrix} 1 & 0 & 0 & 0 & 1 & 1 & 0 \\ 0 & 1 & 0 & 0 & 1 & 0 & 1 \\ 0 & 0 & 1 & 0 & 0 & 1 & 1 \\ 0 & 0 & 0 & 1 & 1 & 1 & 1 \end{bmatrix} \tag{3.2}$$

In this matrix multiplication, we perform additions using modulo-2 or XOR operation.

In decoding of this (n, k) systematic codeword, we use another matrix called the parity check matrix $H = [P^T|I_{n-k}]$. The H matrix corresponding to G given in Equation (3.2) follows:

$$H = [P^T|I_{n-k}] = \begin{bmatrix} 1 & 1 & 0 & 1 & 1 & 0 & 0 \\ 1 & 0 & 1 & 1 & 0 & 1 & 0 \\ 0 & 1 & 1 & 1 & 0 & 0 & 1 \end{bmatrix} \tag{3.3}$$

This satisfies $G \cdot H^T = 0$, resulting in a $k \times (n-k)$ matrix with all zero elements, and $C \cdot H^T = 0$, resulting in an $n-k$ element row vector.

3.3.1 Linear Block Codes

A block code with input message length k and output codeword length n is referred to as an (n, k) code. With the (n, k) code, we append $(n-k)$-length data as parity to k-length input message to form an n-length codeword. At the receiver, we use this $(n-k)$-length parity data to correct the data errors present in the received sequence. A subclass of block codes, known as *linear block codes*, is commonly used, as they have efficient decoding methods. If k is the input-message-block length, then we can compute a set of 2^k n-length codewords $\{C\}$ using the generator matrix G. A block code is called *linear block code* if the addition of two codewords from $\{C\}$ results in another codeword that belongs to the same block code set $\{C\}$. The performance of such a linear block code depends on the minimum Hamming distance ($d_{\min}$) between the codewords of set $\{C\}$. As we are working with binary digits $\{0, 1\}$, the *Hamming distance* between two binary codewords B and C is defined as the number of positions in which the codewords differ in the bit values. If the *weight* of a codeword is defined as the number of ones present in a codeword, then the Hamming distance between two codewords B and C is also computed as the weight of the codeword D, where D is obtained by adding the two codewords B and C. In the case of linear block codes, as the addition of two codewords results in another codeword, the weight of a particular codeword represents the Hamming distance between some other two codewords. Therefore, the minimum Hamming distance of the code $\{C\}$ is given by the minimum weight of codewords of set $\{C\}$.

Since $C \cdot H^T = 0$, the column vectors of H are linearly dependent if C is a non-zero codeword. If C is a codeword with minimum weight $d_{\min}$, then there are $d_{\min}$ number of columns of H that are linearly dependent.

Alternatively, we may say that no more than $d_{\min}-1$ columns of H are linearly independent. From Equation (3.3), we will have a minimum of $n-k$ linearly independent vectors in H (as H contains I_{n-k}), so $n-k \geq d_{\min}-1$. Therefore, $d_{\min}$ is upper-bounded, as in

$$d_{\min} \leq n-k+1 \tag{3.4}$$

In the case of linear block codes, with minimum distance $d_{\min}$, we can correct at most $(d_{\min}-1)/2$ errors. For example, in Example 3.10, $(d_{\min}-1)/2 = 3/2 = 1$. That means, we can correct at most one error with $(7, 4)$ code as discussed in Example 3.10.

Decoding with Linear Block Codes

At the receiver, the matrix H is used to compute the syndrome vector S as

$$S = R \cdot H^T \tag{3.5}$$

where R is an n-length received noisy codeword corresponding to transmitted codeword C.

Example 3.11

In Example 3.10, we used parity equations to compute the parity bits. We can also use the Equation (3.1) to compute the parity bits and to obtain a systematic codeword $C = [b_0b_1b_2b_3|p_0p_1p_2] = [1011|010]$. If the error occured at bit b_1 in the received sequence, then the received noisy vector R is given by $[b_0b_1b_2b_3|p_0p_1p_2] = [1\underline{1}11|010]$. Then using Equation (3.5), the syndrome vector S is computed as follows:

$$S = R \cdot H^T = [1\underline{1}11010]\begin{bmatrix} 1 & 1 & 0 \\ 1 & 0 & 1 \\ 0 & 1 & 1 \\ 1 & 1 & 1 \\ 1 & 0 & 0 \\ 0 & 1 & 0 \\ 0 & 0 & 1 \end{bmatrix} = [101]$$

If b_0 is in error instead of b_1, then $R = [\underline{0}011|010]$ and we get $S = R \cdot H^T$ as $[110]$. The error location is given by $(0, 11)$ which corresponds to b_0. What will happen if more than one error occurs? Let us assume that the bits p_0 and b_2 are received as an error, then the codeword $R = [10\underline{0}1|\underline{1}10]$. From Equation (3.5), $S = [111]$ or $(1, 11)$, which is the location of b_3. So, we have not corrected the two errors, but we know there are errors in the received sequence as the syndrome vector results in a non-zero vector. So, with $(7, 4)$ code, we can only detect the errors if two errors are present in the received sequence.

■

3.3.2 Popular Linear Block Codes

Depending upon their error correction capabilities and algebraic properties, there are many types of linear block codes that are in use today. The most widely used are Hamming codes, BCH codes, RS codes, and LDPC codes. From Hamming codes to LDPC codes, the error correction capabilities of linear block codes increase and at the same time the decoding complexity and memory requirements to implement these codes also increase by multiple factors.

Hamming Codes

The Example 3.11 that we worked with previously is a $(7, 4)$ Hamming code. There are both binary and non-binary Hamming codes. Here, we consider only binary Hamming codes. The general form of (n, k) Hamming code is as follows:

$$(n, k) = (2^m - 1, 2^m - 1 - m) \tag{3.6}$$

where m is a positive integer. The $(7, 4)$ code is an example for $m = 3$.

The binary (n, k) Hamming code can be extended to $(n+1, k)$ to increase $d_{\min}$ by 1 or can be shortened to $(n-l, k-l)$ by removing l rows from its generator matrix G to yield a code that has same error correction capabilities as (n, k) code. In Section 3.4, we discuss and simulate the popularly used (72, 64) Hamming code, which is a shortened form of (127, 119) Hamming code.

BCH Codes

BCH (Bose-Chaudhuri-Hocquenghem) codes are subsets of linear block codes and comprise a large class of cyclic codes that include both binary and nonbinary codes. An overview of BCH codes with examples are presented in Section 3.5.

RS Codes

RS (Reed-Solomon) codes are nonbinary cyclic linear block codes and these codes are used for FEC in many technologies for their excellent error-correction performance. An overview of RS codes with examples is presented in Section 3.6.

LDPC Codes

LDPC (low-density parity check) codes are the most promising capacity approaching codes; they have been largely forgotten for four decades. Recently, these codes have been reinvented and many standards are adapting these codes in present technologies. An overview of LDPC codes are discussed in Section 3.11.

3.4 Hamming (72, 64) Coder

There are many error-correcting codes (ECC) in the literature for correcting bit errors in the received data. In this section, we discuss the Hamming (72, 64) coder, which is popularly used to correct all single-bit errors and to detect all double-bit errors that could occur during the data transmission or storage and retrieval of data from memory. In this section, we restrict ourselves to memory error-correction application.

The answer to the question of how much improvement we can get in BER (bit-error rate) performance curves using a 1-bit error correction depends on the raw BER (RBER) without error correction and the codeword length used with a single-bit error-correction coder. In Figure 3.6, the BER performance curves improvement (i.e., uncorrectable BER, known as UBER) with zero to six bits error correction is shown for the given raw BER values. Here, the codeword length used to generate BER curves is 2048 bits. For example, with the given BER $= 10^{-7}$, we can achieve an UBER of 10^{-11} with single-bit error correction. For a given RBER, a shorter codeword will provide better error-correcting capability or higher UBER as shown in Figure 3.7.

Given the RBER, P, codeword length, N, and the number of error bits, n, we get the UBER with a 1-bit error correction using the following equation (Mielke, 2008):

$$\text{UBER} = \frac{\sum_{n=2}^{N} \binom{N}{n} P^n (1-P)^{N-n}}{N} = \frac{1 - \binom{N}{n=0}(1-P)^N - \binom{N}{n=1} P(1-P)^{N-1}}{N} \tag{3.7}$$

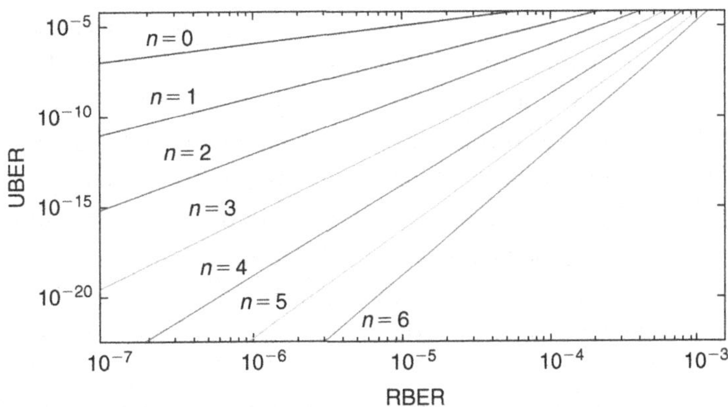

Figure 3.6: RBER versus UBER with various error correction capability coders.

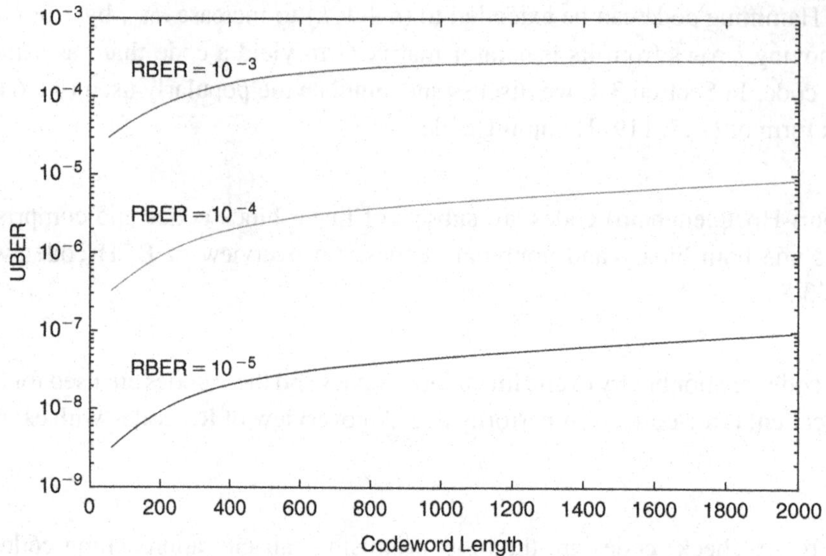

Figure 3.7: Codeword length versus UBER for various RBER.

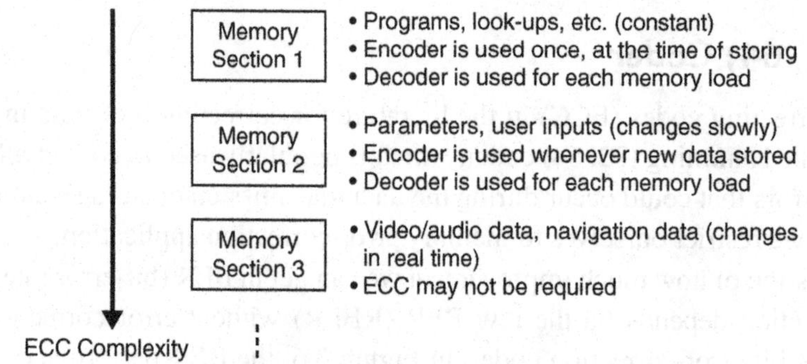

Figure 3.8: Application of ECC in memory error correction.

3.4.1 Memory Error Correction with Hamming Codes

In automotive applications, software integrity level (ASIL) (memory with error correction capabilities) is one of the important issues in choosing embedded processors. Software-based Hamming codes can be used to improve the reliability of the most important sections of memory, thus improving the ASIL metric. Memory is used to store information of various types. Some types of information require strong protection against errors and others do not. For example, application software code, data structures, parameters, and look-up tables are very sensitive and any content alteration may end up with catastrophic errors. On the other hand, information such as data samples and image pixels is not as sensitive and may not require error protection.

A typical automotive application can be broken into different sections of memory consisting of different types of information: (1) constant data such as software code and look-up tables, (2) slowly varying data such as application parameters, and (3) continuously varying data such as audio/video data and navigation data (as shown in Figure 3.8). A software ROM-based error-correction approach that uses Hamming code to correct the single-bit errors in the first two sections of memory can then be implemented using a very small percentage of processor resources. In the first case, as the data is constant, the extra error-correction information is constant and can be generated once. Every time information is retrieved from this memory section an ECC decoder is applied to correct the single-bit errors. In the second case, we call the decoder for each memory load, and the encoder is called to update the error-correction information only when the new data is ready for storing to memory. In these two cases, a software-based single-bit error correction can be implemented using a very small percentage of processor resources.

A schematic diagram of the software-based memory error correction is shown in Figure 3.9. With the Hamming (n, k) coder, we divide the data into k bits long, compute the $n-k$ parity bits, and store the n-bits long block to

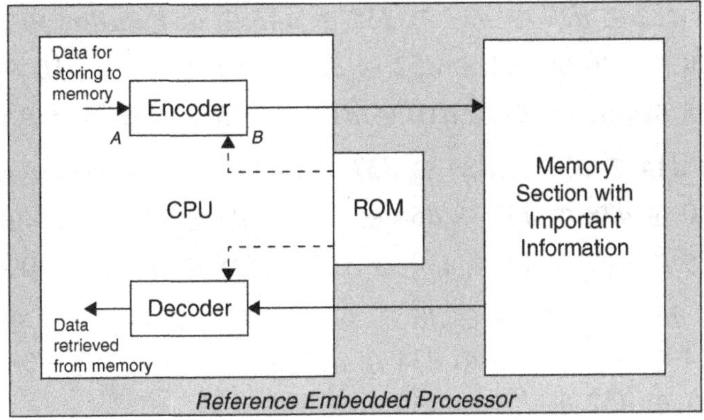

Figure 3.9: Schematic diagram of software-based memory error correction.

000	001	010	011	100	101	110	111	
000	$p1$	$p2$	$d0$	$p3$	$d1$	$d2$	$d3$	0000
$p4$	$d4$	$d5$	$d6$	$d7$	$d8$	$d9$	$d10$	0001
$p5$	$d11$	$d12$	$d13$	$d14$	$d15$	$d16$	$d17$	0010
$d18$	$d19$	$d20$	$d21$	$d22$	$d23$	$d24$	$d25$	0011
$p6$	$d26$	$d27$	$d28$	$d29$	$d30$	$d31$	$d32$	0100
$d33$	$d34$	$d35$	$d36$	$d37$	$d38$	$d39$	$d40$	0101
$d41$	$d42$	$d43$	$d44$	$d45$	$d46$	$d47$	$d48$	0110
$d49$	$d50$	$d51$	$d52$	$d53$	$d54$	$d55$	$d56$	0111
$p7$	$d57$	$d58$	$d59$	$d60$	$d61$	$d62$	$d63$	1000

Figure 3.10: Matrix arrangement of Hamming (72, 64) encoder input–output bits.

the memory area. The parity overhead percentage with respect to data length can be computed as $(n-k)^{*}100/k$. When the data is retrieved, the decoder uses the $n-k$ parity bits to detect and correct errors that corrupted during the time when data was residing in memory. We verify the computed parity with the retrieved parity data. If both parity bits match, then no error bits are present in the received data; otherwise, there will be error bits in the received data. The Hamming decoder can detect and correct all single-bit errors or detect all double-bit errors. Because the error-correction software is permanently stored in the ROM and uses the core resources whenever memory is accessed, we prefer the ECC solution which uses a very small amount memory and the processor cycles.

In the next subsections, we discuss the widely used Hamming (72, 64) coder and also discuss the implementation techniques and the computational complexity for encoding and decoding of Hamming (72, 64) code on the reference embedded processor.

3.4.2 Hamming (72, 64) Encoder

The Hamming (72, 64) encoder generates 8 bits of parity from 64 input data bits. To understand the Hamming (72, 64) encoder parity bits generation, we arrange the data bits (input) and parity bits (output) in a matrix fashion and give binary indexing to each row and column as shown in Figure 3.10. We have eight columns and nine rows. Each bit in the matrix can be uniquely addressed with the row and column index bits. For example, the address of bit $d20$ is 0011 010. Each parity bit $p1$ to $p7$ is placed at a special address that is a power of 2 (i.e., $p1$: 0000 001, $p2$: 0000 010, $p3$: 0000 100, $p4$: 0001 000, $p5$: 0010 000, $p6$: 0100 000, $p7$: 1000 000).

The parity bit $p1$ is generated by XORing the data bits that have "1" at the position "k" in the address field xxxx xxk. Similarly the parity bit $p2$ is generated by XORing the data bits with "1" at the position "k" in the address field xxxx xkx and so on. The equations for generating parity bits $p1$ to $p7$ follow.

$$\begin{aligned} p1 = {} & d4 \oplus d11 \oplus d19 \oplus d26 \oplus d34 \oplus d42 \oplus d50 \oplus d57 \oplus d0 \oplus d6 \oplus d13 \oplus d21 \\ & \oplus d28 \oplus d36 \oplus d44 \oplus d52 \oplus d59 \oplus d1 \oplus d8 \oplus d15 \oplus d23 \oplus d30 \oplus d38 \oplus d46 \\ & \oplus d54 \oplus d61 \oplus d3 \oplus d10 \oplus d17 \oplus d25 \oplus d32 \oplus d40 \oplus d48 \oplus d56 \oplus d63 \end{aligned} \quad (3.8)$$

$$p2 = d5 \oplus d12 \oplus d20 \oplus d27 \oplus d35 \oplus d43 \oplus d51 \oplus d58 \oplus d0 \oplus d6 \oplus d13 \oplus d21 \oplus d28 \oplus d36 \oplus d44 \oplus d52 \oplus d59 \oplus d2 \oplus d9 \oplus d16 \oplus d24 \oplus d31 \oplus d39 \oplus d47 \oplus d55 \oplus d62 \oplus d3 \oplus d10 \oplus d17 \oplus d25 \oplus d32 \oplus d40 \oplus d48 \oplus d56 \oplus d63 \quad (3.9)$$

$$p3 = d7 \oplus d14 \oplus d22 \oplus d29 \oplus d37 \oplus d45 \oplus d53 \oplus d60 \oplus d1 \oplus d8 \oplus d15 \oplus d23 \oplus d30 \oplus d38 \oplus d46 \oplus d54 \oplus d61 \oplus d2 \oplus d9 \oplus d16 \oplus d24 \oplus d31 \oplus d39 \oplus d47 \oplus d55 \oplus d62 \oplus d3 \oplus d10 \oplus d17 \oplus d25 \oplus d32 \oplus d40 \oplus d48 \oplus d56 \oplus d63 \quad (3.10)$$

$$p4 = d4 \oplus d5 \oplus d6 \oplus d7 \oplus d8 \oplus d9 \oplus d10 \oplus d18 \oplus d19 \oplus d20 \oplus d21 \oplus d22 \oplus d23 \oplus d24 \oplus d25 \oplus d33 \oplus d34 \oplus d35 \oplus d36 \oplus d37 \oplus d38 \oplus d39 \oplus d40 \oplus d49 \oplus d50 \oplus d51 \oplus d52 \oplus d53 \oplus d54 \oplus d55 \oplus d56 \quad (3.11)$$

$$p5 = d11 \oplus d12 \oplus d13 \oplus d14 \oplus d15 \oplus d16 \oplus d17 \oplus d18 \oplus d19 \oplus d20 \oplus d21 \oplus d22 \oplus d23 \oplus d24 \oplus d25 \oplus d41 \oplus d42 \oplus d43 \oplus d44 \oplus d45 \oplus d46 \oplus d47 \oplus d48 \oplus d49 \oplus d50 \oplus d51 \oplus d52 \oplus d53 \oplus d54 \oplus d55 \oplus d56 \quad (3.12)$$

$$p6 = d26 \oplus d27 \oplus d28 \oplus d29 \oplus d30 \oplus d31 \oplus d32 \oplus d33 \oplus d34 \oplus d35 \oplus d36 \oplus d37 \oplus d38 \oplus d39 \oplus d40 \oplus d41 \oplus d42 \oplus d43 \oplus d44 \oplus d45 \oplus d46 \oplus d47 \oplus d48 \oplus d49 \oplus d50 \oplus d51 \oplus d52 \oplus d53 \oplus d54 \oplus d55 \oplus d56 \quad (3.13)$$

$$p7 = d57 \oplus d58 \oplus d59 \oplus d60 \oplus d61 \oplus d62 \oplus d63 \quad (3.14)$$

The parity bit 8 is used to detect double-bit errors and is generated by XORing all the data bits as follows:

$$p8 = d0 \oplus d1 \oplus d2 \oplus d3 \oplus d4 \oplus d5 \oplus d6 \oplus d7 \oplus d8 \oplus d9 \oplus d10 \oplus d11 \oplus d12 \oplus d13 \oplus d14 \oplus d15 \oplus d16 \oplus d17 \oplus d18 \oplus d19 \oplus d20 \oplus d21 \oplus d22 \oplus d23 \oplus d24 \oplus d25 \oplus d26 \oplus d27 \oplus d28 \oplus d29 \oplus d30 \oplus d31 \oplus d32 \oplus d33 \oplus d34 \oplus d35 \oplus d36 \oplus d37 \oplus d38 \oplus d39 \oplus d40 \oplus d41 \oplus d42 \oplus d43 \oplus d44 \oplus d45 \oplus d46 \oplus d47 \oplus d48 \oplus d49 \oplus d50 \oplus d51 \oplus d52 \oplus d53 \oplus d54 \oplus d55 \oplus d56 \oplus d57 \oplus d58 \oplus d59 \oplus d60 \oplus d61 \oplus d62 \oplus d63 \quad (3.15)$$

The generated parity bits are concatenated to the original 64 data bits to form 72-bit encoded data. In Figure 3.9, with Hamming (72, 64) coder, 64 bits of data enter into the encoder block at point A and 72 bits of encoded data come out at point B. Then this encoded 72-bit data frame is stored to the memory. This process will be continued for all data blocks.

3.4.3 Hamming (72, 64) Decoder

The Hamming decoder consists of two steps: (1) syndrome computation and (2) error correction. In the syndrome computation step, the Hamming (72, 64) decoder computes eight syndromes using the 72 bits retrieved from memory. The syndromes $s1$ to $s8$ are computed by XORing the encoder parity bits $p1$ to $p8$ (which are retrieved from memory and these parity bits may be different in value due to bit errors) with the decoder parity bits $c1$ to $c8$ (which we compute at decoder) as follows:

$$s1 = c1 \oplus p1, \quad s2 = c2 \oplus p2, \quad s3 = c3 \oplus p3, \quad s4 = c4 \oplus p4$$
$$s5 = c5 \oplus p5, \quad s6 = c6 \oplus p6, \quad s7 = c7 \oplus p7, \quad s8 = c8 \oplus p8$$

In the syndromes computation, to generate the decoder parity bits, we use the same encoder parity bit generator equations from (3.8) to (3.15). For example, if the 64-data bits of 72 bits retrieved from memory are named as $b0$ to $b63$ which corresponds to encoder data bits $d0$ to $d63$, then decoder parity bit $c1$ is generated using the $p1$ parity bit generator equation as follows:

$$c1 = b4 \oplus b11 \oplus b19 \oplus b26 \oplus b34 \oplus b42 \oplus b50 \oplus b57 \oplus b0 \oplus b6 \oplus b13 \oplus b21 \oplus b28 \oplus b36 \oplus b44 \oplus b52 \oplus b59 \oplus b1 \oplus b8 \oplus b15 \oplus b23 \oplus b30 \oplus b38 \oplus b46 \oplus b54 \oplus b61 \oplus b3 \oplus b10 \oplus b17 \oplus b25 \oplus b32 \oplus b40 \oplus b48 \oplus b56 \oplus b63.$$

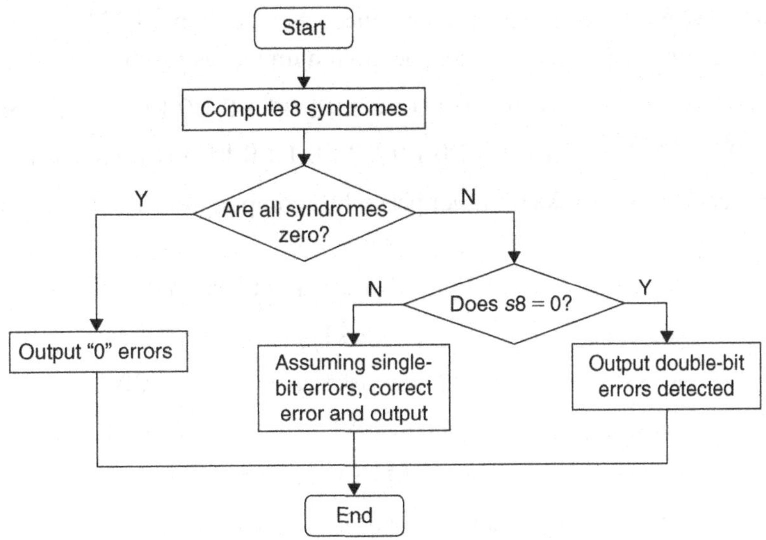

Figure 3.11: Hamming decoder flow chart diagram.

With respect to the retrieved 72 bits from memory, there are four possible cases of bit errors: (1) no occurrence of bit errors, (2) occurrence of 1-bit error, (3) occurrence of 2-bit errors, and (4) occurrence of more than 2-bit errors.

If all the computed eight syndrome values are zero, then there is no bit error in the retrieved 72 bits. The non-zero values of syndromes indicate the presence of errors. The single-bit error is detected and also corrected, if any single-bit error is present in the data bits, using the eight syndromes information in the error-correction step. If any of the syndromes from $s1$ to $s7$ are non-zero and $s8$ is zero, then this indicates presence of two error bits and this cannot be corrected. So, if two bits are in error, Hamming (72, 64) decoder only detects the errors and cannot correct them. Any other result in syndrome values indicates presence of more than two error bits in the retrieved data of 72 bits and they cannot be detected and corrected. The flow chart diagram for Hamming decoder is shown in Figure 3.11.

3.4.4 Hamming (72, 64) Simulation

There are two ways to simulate the Hamming (72, 64) coder. In the first method, we store the bit indices of each parity equation; extract corresponding bits from a 72-bit bitstream using bit indices and then XOR each individual bit to get the parity bit. Although this method is simple to simulate, it is expensive in terms of cycles and memory (as the look-up tables have to be stored in ROM permanently for this software-based memory correction application). In the second approach, we compute the parity bits using the precomputed masks by assuming the input 64 bits are present in two 32-bit registers $r0$ and $r1$.

0 1 2 3 . . . 30 31	32 33 34 . . . 62 63
$r0$	$r1$

The masks for each parity bit are generated using the parity equations given in Equations 3.8 through 3.15. For example, to generate the mask for computing parity bit $p1$, we place "1" if a particular bit is participating in the parity bit $p1$ computation; otherwise, we place bit "0" in that position as shown in the following:

$b0$	$b1$	$b2$	$b3$	$b4$	$b5$	$b6$	$b7$	$b8$	$b9$	$b10$	$b11$	$b12$	$b13$	$b14$	$b15$	$b16$	$b17$	$b18$	$b19$	$b20$	$b21$
1	1	0	1	1	0	1	0	1	0	1	1	0	1	0	1	0	1	0	1	0	1

$b22$	$b23$	$b24$	$b25$	$b26$	$b27$	$b28$	$b29$	$b30$	$b31$	$b32$	$b33$	$b34$	$b35$	$b36$	$b37$	$b38$	$b39$	$b40$	$b41$	$b42$
0	1	0	1	1	0	1	0	1	0	1	0	1	0	1	0	1	0	1	0	1

$b43$	$b44$	$b45$	$b46$	$b47$	$b48$	$b49$	$b50$	$b51$	$b52$	$b53$	$b54$	$b55$	$b56$	$b57$	$b58$	$b59$	$b60$	$b61$	$b62$	$b63$
0	1	0	1	0	1	0	1	0	1	0	1	0	1	1	0	1	0	1	0	1

Since the reference embedded processor is a 32-bit machine, we can only hold 32 bits in a register. So, we split the 64 bits into two 32-bit groups and convert to hexadecimal numbers as follows:

1 1 0 1 1 0 1 0 1 0 1 1 0 1 0 1 0 1 0 1 0 1 0 1 0 1 1 0 1 0 1 0: 0xdab5556a

1 0 1 0 1 0 1 0 1 0 1 0 1 0 1 0 1 0 1 0 1 0 1 0 1 1 0 1 0 1 0 1: 0xaaaaaad5

In the same way, we can generate the masks for other parity bits computation. The mask values for all parity bits computation follow.

$$\text{Mask0}_{p1} = \text{0xdab5556a}, \text{Mask1}_{p1} = \text{0xaaaaaad5},$$

$$\text{Mask0}_{p2} = \text{0xb66cccd9}, \text{Mask1}_{p2} = \text{0x999999b3},$$

$$\text{Mask0}_{p3} = \text{0x01e3c3c7}, \text{Mask1}_{p3} = \text{0x8787878f},$$

$$\text{Mask0}_{p4} = \text{0x0fe03fc0}, \text{Mask1}_{p4} = \text{0x7f807f80}$$

$$\text{Mask0}_{p5} = \text{0x001fffc0}, \text{Mask1}_{p5} = \text{0x007fff80}$$

$$\text{Mask0}_{p6} = \text{0x0000003f}, \text{Mask1}_{p6} = \text{0xffffff80}$$

$$\text{Mask0}_{p7} = \text{0x00000000}, \text{Mask1}_{p7} = \text{0x0000007f}$$

$$\text{Mask0}_{p8} = \text{0xffffffff}, \text{Mask1}_{p8} = \text{0xffffffff}$$

The simulation code for computing the 8 parity bits of Hamming (72, 64) code is given in Pcode 3.4. The preceding precomputed parity bit masks are stored in the look-up table **hm_masks**[ ]. For each parity bit, we get the corresponding masks into $r2$ and $r3$ from the look-up table and AND the masks with the actual data bit words present in $r0$ and $r1$. The ANDed result is stored back into $r2$ and $r3$. Then we XOR $r2$ and $r3$, and get the result to $r2$. If the number of ones present in the $r2$ is even, then the parity bit p_n is set to 1; otherwise, that is, if an odd number of ones present in $r2$, $p_n = 0$. As counting the number of ones present in a 32-bit word requires many operations in C simulation, we achieve it by shift and XOR in a few operations as shown in Pcode 3.4. On the reference embedded processor, we can compute each parity bit in three cycles using a special instruction set.

```
r7 = 0;
for(i = 0;i < 8;i++) {
        r2 = hm_masks[2*i]; r3 = hm_masks[2*i+1];
        r2 = r0 & r2; r3 = r1 & r3;
        r2 = r2 ^ r3;
        r3 = r2 >> 16;
        r2 = r2 ^ r3;
        r3 = r2 >> 8;
        r2 = r2 ^ r3;
        r3 = r2 >> 4;
        r2 = r2 ^ r3;
        r3 = r2 >> 2;
        r2 = r2 ^ r3;
        r3 = r2 >> 1;
        r2 = r2 ^ r3;
        r2 = r2 & 1;
        r2 = r2 << i;
        r7 = r7 | r2;
}
```

Pcode 3.4: Simulation code to generate parity bits of Hamming (72, 64) code.

Single-Bit Error Correction and Double-Bit Error Detection

Once we compute the 8 parity bits at the decoder using the data bits retrieved from memory, then we compute syndromes by XORing both encoder and decoder parity bits. The syndromes provide indications about bit errors. Also, syndromes provide the bit location if a single-bit error occurred and we flip that bit to correct the data. We output a flag value depending on whether the bit errors occurred or not in the retrieved data. For example, we output the decoded data status information by returning the value "0" for no errors occurred or one error occurred and corrected, "1" for two errors occurred and detected, and "2" for multiple errors occurred in the retrieved data. The simulation code for correcting the error bit using Hamming (72, 64) coder is given in Pcode 3.5.

```
r6 = data[2];
r6 = r6 ^ r7;
r6 = r6 >> 24;
r4 = r6 & 0x80;
r6 = r6 & 0x7f;
j = 0;                                  // assume no errors
if (r6 != 0){
        if ((r4 == 0x80) & (r6 != 0)){ // correct single bit errors
                if (r6 < 72){
                        r5 = hm_error_table[r6];
                        if (r5 < 32){
                            r5 = 31 - r5;
                            r4 = 1 << r5;
                            data[0] = data[0] ^ r4;
                        }
                        else if (r5 < 64){
                            r5 = r5 - 32;
                            r5 = 31 - r5;
                            r4 = 1 << r5;
                            data[1] = data[1] ^ r4;
                        }
                }
                else
                    j = 2;              // multiple errors
        }
        else
                j = 1;                  // double bit error detected
        }
}
```

Pcode 3.5: Simulation code for correcting single bit error with Hamming (72, 64) coder.

Computational Complexity

Assuming each operation in Pcode 3.4 consumes one cycle on the reference embedded processor (see Appendix A, Section A.4, on the companion website for more details on cycles estimation), it takes approximately 150 cycles. It takes another 20 to 30 cycles for correcting an error using Pcode 3.5. With this, the Hamming encoder consumes about 2.5 cycles per bit and the decoder consumes about 3 cycles per bit on the reference embedded processor. Using a special instruction set, we can perform Hamming (72, 64) encoding in 0.5 cycles/bit and decoding in 0.75 cycles per bit. We use a total of 136 bytes of data memory for the look-up table.

Simulation Results

Assume the 64 bits that will be stored in a memory are $r0 =$ 0x8f7f6f5f; $r1 =$ 0x4f3f2f1f (0th bit is MSB of $r0$). We compute 8 parity bits using 64 bits as 0xf4000000 (MSB bit is $p8$) and append to data bits to make a 72-bit codeword before storing to memory.

Assume the retrieved 72 bits of data are $r0 =$ 0x8e7f6f5f, $r1 =$ 0x4f3f2f1f, $r2 =$ 0xf4000000 with a 1-bit error in the first 32-bit word. The parity bits $c1$ to $c8$ are computed using the retrieved data as 0x78000000 (MSB bit is $c8$). Then the eight syndromes are computed as 0x8c000000 (MSB bit is $s8$). We use look-up table **hm_error_table**[ ] to get the error location from syndromes. Once we know the error location, we correct the single-bit error (if occurred) using Pcode 3.5. The values of **hm_error_table**[ ] follow.

```
hm_error_table[72] = {
64,64,64, 0,64, 1, 2, 3,64, 4, 5, 6, 7, 8, 9,10,
64,11,12,13,14,15,16,17,18,19,20,21,22,23,24,25,
64,26,27,28,29,30,31,32,33,34,35,36,37,38,39,40,
41,42,43,44,45,46,47,48,49,50,51,52,53,54,55,56,
64,57,58,59,60,61,62,63};
```

3.5 BCH Codes

The framework of BCH codes support a large class of powerful random error-correcting cyclic binary and non-binary linear block codes. With BCH (N, K) codes, we compute $mT(=N-K)$ parity bits from the input block of K bits using generator polynomial $G(x)$ and we correct up to T bit errors in the received block of N bits. At the transmitter side, the BCH(N, K) encoder computes and appends mT parity bits to the block of K data bits and at the receiver side the BCH(N, K) decoder corrects up to T errors by using mT bits of parity information. We work with Galois field GF(2^m) elements for decoding of BCH(N, K) codes. See Appendix B, Section B.2, on the companion website for more details on Galois field arithmetic operations.

3.5.1 BCH Encoder

We represent the data either in polynomial form (like $A(x), B(x), C(x), \ldots$), or in vector form (like $\boldsymbol{A}, \boldsymbol{B}, \boldsymbol{C}, \ldots$). A polynomial over a field GF(q) is a mathematical expression of the form

$$F(x) = f_{n-1}x^{n-1} + f_{n-2}x^{n-2} + \cdots + f_1x + f_0$$

where the symbol x is an intermediate, the coefficients $f_{n-1}, f_{n-2}, \ldots, f_0$ are elements of GF(q) and the indices and exponents are integers. The BCH (N, K) encoder computes $mT(=N-K)$ bits of parity data from K bits of input data by using a generator polynomial $G(x) = g_0 + g_1x + g_2x^2 + \cdots + g_{N-K-1}x^{N-K-1} + x^{N-K}$, where $g_i \in$ GF(2). For BCH (N, K) codes, the generator polynomial $G(x)$ is obtained by computing the multiplication of T minimal polynomials $\phi_{2i-1}(x)$ of field elements α^{2i-1} for $1 \le i \le T$ as follows:

$$G(x) = \phi_1(x)\phi_3(x)\cdots\phi_{2T-1}(x) \tag{3.16}$$

As every even power of α has the same minimal polynomial as some preceding odd power of α, the $G(x)$ is obtained by computing the least common multiple (LCM) of minimum polynomials $\phi_i(x)$ for $1 \le i \le 2T$; hence, $G(x)$ has $\alpha, \alpha^2, \alpha^3 \cdots \alpha^{2T}$ as its roots. In other words, $G(\alpha^i) = 0$ for $1 \le i \le 2T$. See Appendix B, Section B.2, on the companion website for more details on Galois field arithmetic operations (see also Example 3.12).

Suppose that the input message block of K bits to be encoded is $\boldsymbol{D} = [d_0d_1d_2\cdots d_{K-1}]$ and the corresponding message polynomial is $D(x) = d_0 + d_1x + d_2x^2 + \cdots + d_{K-1}x^{K-1}$. Let $\boldsymbol{B} = [b_0b_1b_2\cdots b_{N-K-1}]$ denotes the computed parity data of $N-K(=mT)$ length and its polynomial representation is $B(x) = b_0 + b_1x + b_2x^2 + \cdots + b_{N-K-1}x^{N-K-1}$. This parity polynomial $B(x)$ is given by the remainder when we divide $D(x)\cdot x^{N-K}$ with generator polynomial $G(x)$. The polynomial $B(x)$ is computed as

$$B(x) = D(x)\cdot x^{N-K} \mod G(x) \tag{3.17}$$

After computing parity polynomial $B(x)$, the encoded code polynomial $C(x)$ is constructed as

$$\begin{aligned} C(x) &= D(x)\cdot x^{N-K} + B(x) \\ &= b_0 + b_1x + b_2x^2 + \cdots + b_{N-K-1}x^{N-K-1} + d_0x^{N-K} + d_1x^{N-K+1} + \cdots d_{K-1}x^{N-1} \\ &= c_0 + c_1x + c_2x^2 + \cdots + c_{N-1}x^{N-1} \end{aligned} \tag{3.18}$$

Basically, we append mT bits of parity data to the input block of K bits and form a systematic codeword of length N $(= K + mT)$ bits. The encoded polynomial in the vector form is represented as $\boldsymbol{C} = [c_0c_1c_2\cdots c_{N-1}]$. Equations (3.17) and (3.18) can be realized with an LFSR signal flow diagram as shown in Figure 3.12. To compute parity polynomial $B(x)$ coefficients, we input the data polynomial $D(x)$ coefficients to LFSR with d_{K-1} coefficient as first input. The values present in the delay units (Z) after passing all K coefficients of $D(x)$ gives the coefficients of parity polynomial $B(x)$.

Example 3.12

Let us consider Galois field GF(2^3) with $m = 3$ from Appendix B, Section B.2, on the companion website. With this, we can work with codeword length of $N = 2^3 - 1 = 7$ bits. We choose message length $K = 4$ bits. Then $mT = 7 - 4 = 3$. In this case, we can correct a 1-bit error (since $T = 1$) with BCH(7, 4) code. The generator polynomial for BCH(7, 4) code is $G(x) = x^3 + x + 1$ (Shu Lin, 1983). Let 4-bit message

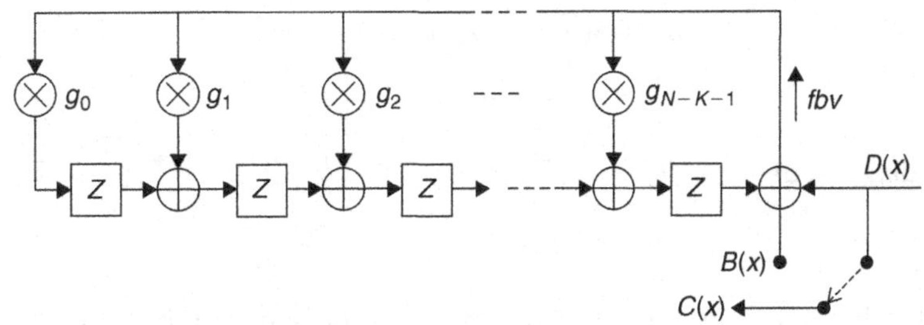

Figure 3.12: Realization of BCH(*N*, *K*) encoder.

data vector $D = [1110]$ or in polynomial notation $D(x) = x^3 + x^2 + x$. Using the generator polynomial $G(x)$ and message polynomial $D(x)$, we compute the parity (or remainder) using the Equation (3.17) or using the shift register realization shown earlier. Here, we compute the parity using shift registers. We initialize the shift registers with zero and then we pass messages through the shift registers one after another. We obtain the parity as $B = [100]$ after passing four message bits through shift registers (Figure 3.13). So, the BCH codeword of 7 bits length is given by $C = [1110100]$ or in polynomial notation $C(x) = x^6 + x^5 + x^4 + x^2$.

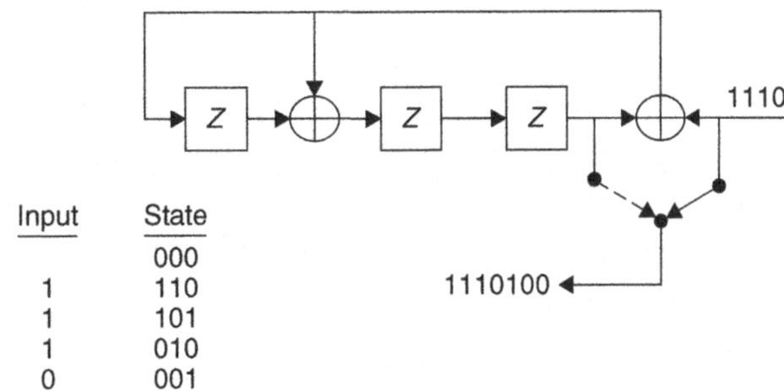

Input	State
	000
1	110
1	101
1	010
0	001

Figure 3.13: LFSR-based parity bits generation for BCH(7,4) encoding. ■

3.5.2 BCH Decoder

At the receiver, we use a BCH (N, K) decoder to detect and correct the bit errors. A BCH decoder consists of the following three steps to decode the received data block $\boldsymbol{R}$.

- Computation of syndromes
- Computation of error-locator polynomial
- Computation of error positions

The received data vector $\boldsymbol{R}$ or its polynomial $R(x) = r_0 + r_1x + r_2x^2 + \cdots + r_{N-1}x^{N-1}$ consists of transmitted data polynomial $C(x)$ along with an added error polynomial $E(x)$.

$$\begin{aligned} R(x) &= C(x) + E(x) \\ &= D(x) \cdot x^{N-K} + B(x) + E(x) \\ &= D(x) \cdot G(x) + E(x) \end{aligned} \tag{3.19}$$

In a BCH decoder (unlike as in a BCH encoder), we have to perform Galois field arithmetic operations in decoding of BCH codes.

Syndromes Computation

To know the presence of errors and the error pattern, we compute $2T$ syndromes using the received data polynomial as follows:

$$\begin{aligned} R(\alpha^i) &= D(\alpha^i) \cdot G(\alpha^i) + E(\alpha^i), \text{ where } 1 \le i \le 2T \\ &= 0 + E(\alpha^i) \\ &= E(\alpha^i) \\ &= S_i \end{aligned} \tag{3.20}$$

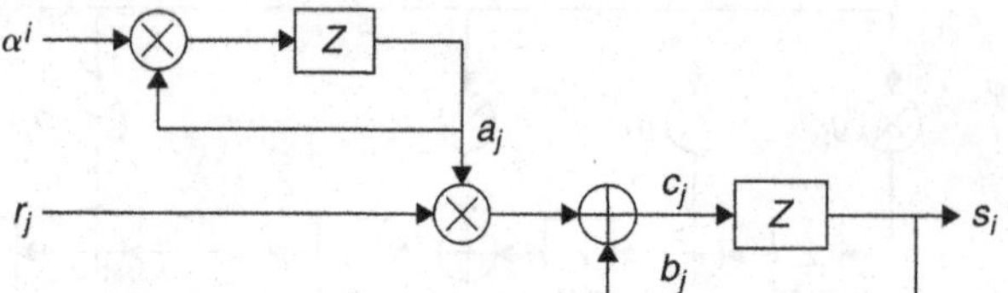

Figure 3.14: Signal flow diagram of syndrome computation.

From the preceding syndromes computation, if no errors are present in the received data vector, we get all computed syndrome values (S_i) as zero. If any one or more syndromes are non-zero, then we assume that the errors are present in the received data vector. The syndromes $S_i = R(\alpha^i)$ are computed with the LFSR signal flow diagram as shown in Figure 3.14 (see also Example 3.13).

Example 3.13

We transmit the codeword $C = [1110100]$ computed in Example 3.12 through a noisy channel. Let the received vector be $R = [11101\underline{1}0]$, which differs from the transmitted codeword by 1 bit, highlighted with an underscore. So, the error vector $E = [0000010]$ or $E(x) = x$ (but we don't know errors in advance). We can find the error vector with the BCH decoder if the number of errors occurred are less than or equal T. In our example, $T = 1$ (i.e., the decoder can correct a 1-bit error) and we can correct one error present in the received data vector. The first step in the BCH decoding is the computation of syndromes. To correct T errors, we have to compute $2T$ syndromes $S_i = R(\alpha^i)$, where $i = 1, 2$. The $R(\alpha^i)$ is obtained after substituting $x = \alpha^i$ in the $R(x)$. We use Galois field GF(2^3) arithmetic (see Appendix B, Section B.2, on the companion website) in computing these two syndromes.

$$R(x) = x^6 + x^5 + x^4 + x^2 + x$$

$$R(\alpha) = \alpha^6 + \alpha^5 + \alpha^4 + \alpha^2 + \alpha = (\alpha^2 + 1) + (\alpha^2 + \alpha + 1) + (\alpha^2 + \alpha) + \alpha^2 + \alpha = \alpha$$

$$R(\alpha^2) = \alpha^{12} + \alpha^{10} + \alpha^8 + \alpha^4 + \alpha^2 = \alpha^7\alpha^5 + \alpha^7\alpha^3 + \alpha^7\alpha + \alpha^4 + \alpha^2$$

$$= \alpha^5 + \alpha^3 + \alpha + \alpha^4 + \alpha^2 = \alpha^2$$

$$\therefore S_1 = \alpha, \quad S_2 = \alpha^2$$

■

Error-Locator Polynomial Computation

An error-locator polynomial computation is the second step in decoding of BCH codes. We use the Berlekamp -Massey recursive algorithm to compute the error-locator polynomial. The flow chart of Berlekamp-Massey recursion is shown in Figure 3.15. If the number of errors present in the received data vector is L (which less than or equal to T), then this algorithm computes the L-degree error-locator polynomial in $2T$ iterations. First, we initialize the error-locator polynomial $\Lambda(x) = 1$ as a minimum-degree polynomial with degree $L = 0$. Then we use syndromes information to build an error-locator polynomial by computing discrepancy delta. If the value of delta is not zero then we update the minimum-degree polynomial with the discrepancy; otherwise, we continue the loop. If the number of errors in the received polynomial $R(x)$ is T or less, then $\Lambda(x)$ produces the true error pattern. At the end of $2T$ iterations of the Berlekamp-Massey recursion, we will have the Lth-degree error-locator polynomial (with $\Lambda_0 = 1$) as follows:

$$\begin{aligned} \Lambda(x) &= \Lambda_0 + \Lambda_1 x + \Lambda_2 x^2 + \cdots + \Lambda_L x^L \\ &= (1 + X_1 x)(1 + X_2 x) \cdots (1 + X_L x) \end{aligned} \tag{3.21}$$

Once we have an error-locator polynomial of degree L, then we can find L error positions by computing the roots of the error-locator polynomial (see Examples 3.14 and 3.15).

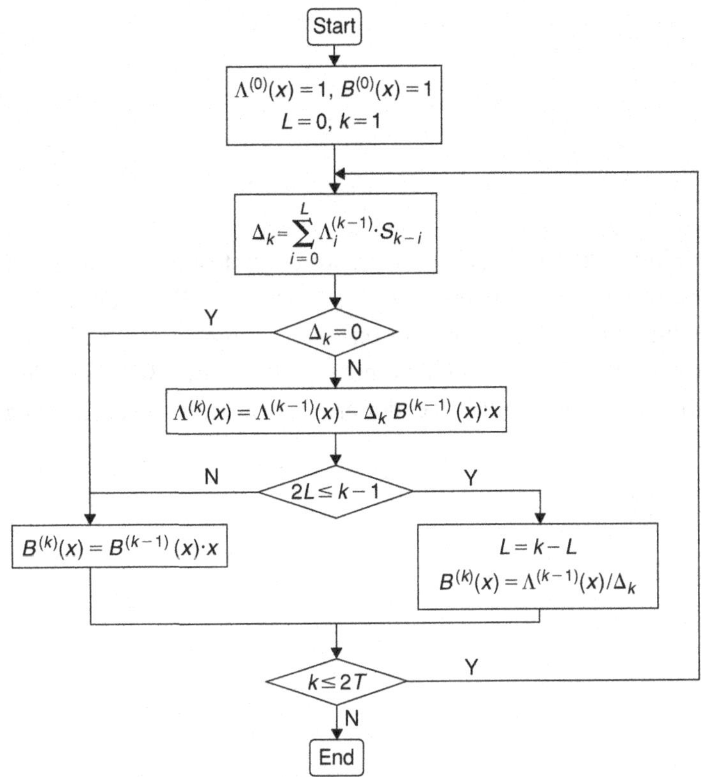

Figure 3.15: Flow chart diagram of Berlekamp-Massey algorithm.

Example 3.14

Using the two syndromes computed in Example 3.13, we build the error-locator polynomial using Berlekamp-Massey recursion as shown in Figure 3.15.

Initialization: $\Lambda^{(0)}(x)=1, B^{(0)}(x)=1, L=0, k=1$

First iteration $(k=1)$: $\Delta_1=S_1=\alpha$

Since $\Delta_1\neq 0$, $\Lambda^{(1)}(x)=1+\alpha x$ (Note: In the Galois field "+" is the same as "−".)

Since $(2L\le k-1)$, $L=k-L=1$ and $B^{(1)}(x)=1/\alpha=\alpha^6$

Second iteration $(k=2)$: $\Delta_2=\Lambda_0^{(1)}S_2+\Lambda_1^{(1)}S_1=\alpha^2+\alpha^2=0$

Since $\Delta_2=0$, $\Lambda^{(2)}(x)=\Lambda^{(1)}(x)$, $B^{(2)}(x)=xB^{(1)}(x)=\alpha^6 x$.

Since $k=2T$ (last iteration reached), stop Berlekamp-Massey algorithm.

The error-locator polynomial $\Lambda(x)=\Lambda^{(2)}(x)=1+\alpha x$.

■

Error Positions Computation

If the number of errors L present in the received data vector is less than or equal to T (i.e., $L\le T$), then the error-locator polynomial can be factored into L first-degree polynomials as in Equation (3.21) and the roots of the error-locator polynomial are $X_1^{-1}, X_2^{-1},\ldots X_L^{-1}$. The error positions are given by the inverse of the roots of the error-locator polynomial. So the L error positions are $X_1, X_2,\ldots X_L$.

As binary BCH codes work on the data bits and if we find the error positions in the received data bits, then correction of data bits is achieved by simply flipping the bit values in those error positions.

Example 3.15

We continue Example 3.14 and find the error locations by finding the roots of the error-locator polynomial. Since the computed error-locator polynomial has degree 1, its root is computed as

$$\Lambda(X_1^{-1})=1+\alpha X_1^{-1}=0 \quad \Rightarrow \alpha X_1^{-1}=1 \Rightarrow X_1^{-1}=1/\alpha=\alpha^6$$

The error position is given by the inverse of roots of the error-locator polynomial. Therefore,

$$X_1 = 1/\alpha^6 = \alpha^1$$

■

Error Correction

As we are working with binary BCH codes, we correct only the bit errors present in the received data (in the next section we discuss how to correct m-bit words with RS codes). The correction of bit errors is achieved by flipping the bit value at the error position (see Example 3.16). If the degree of error-locator polynomial (L) and the number of error positions (P) are not equal then the BCH decoder cannot correct errors as the number of errors occurred is more than the decoder error correction capability. Therefore, we skip error bits correction when $L \neq P$.

■ Example 3.16

We computed the error position in Example 3.15 as $X_1 = \alpha^1$. The exponent of error positions gives the location of errors in the received data vector. In our case, the exponent of error position is 1 and the error is present at position 1 in the received vector $R = [1110110]$. The indexing starts from the LSB side as shown in the following.

1	1	1	0	1	1	0
6	5	4	3	2	1	0

Thus, the corrected data vector is [1110100], which is the same as the transmitted data vector.

■

In Section 4.1, we will further study the BCH codes. Also, we discuss the simulation of BCH codes and the efficient techniques to implement BCH codes.

3.6 RS Codes

Reed-Solomon (RS) codes are block-based linear nonbinary error-correcting codes with a wide range of applications. The RS(N, K) coder works on a block of data and takes a K element block as input and outputs an N element block by adding $N - K$ elements as redundant data, which is used to perform error correction at the receiver side. By adding redundant data before transmission, RS codes can detect and correct errors within blocks of the data frame.

For any positive integer $T \leq 2^m - 1$, there exists a T-symbol error correcting RS code with the following parameters.

$$N = 2^m - 1$$

$$K = N - 2T = 2^m - 1 - 12T$$

$$d_{\min} = 2T + 1 = N - K + 1$$

The RS(N, K) coder works with Galois field elements of m bits width and the data elements of RS(N, K) coder belongs to GF(2^m) Galois field. The RS(N, K) encoder adds $2T = N - K$ elements of redundancy at the transmitter side and the RS(N, K) decoder uses that redundancy to correct up to $T = (N - K)/2$ errors at the receiver side. As RS code consists of m-bit elements, these codes are well suited to correct burst bit errors.

A few applications where RS codes are predominantly used include high-speed modems such as ADSL, xDSL, storage devices (e.g., compact disc [CD], DVD, hard disk), mobile and satellite communications, and digital television and DVB. Like RS codes, BCH codes (see Sections 3.5 and 4.1) are used in some of the previous applications for FEC. Both BCH codes and RS codes are linear block codes. The BCH codes are binary, whereas RS codes are nonbinary.

The error correction capability of BCH codes is inferior when compared to RS codes. In other words, we achieve larger coding gain with RS codes than with BCH codes for given data rates and channel conditions. In burst error cases, RS codes perform better than BCH codes.

In this section, we discuss the RS(N, K) coder to correct T data elements at the receiver side. The block diagram of the RS(N, K) coder is shown in Figure 3.16. The RS(N, K) encoder takes K-element block $\boldsymbol{D}$ as input and outputs N element block $\boldsymbol{M}$. RS(N, K) decoder takes received N element error block $\boldsymbol{R}$ as input and outputs K element block $\boldsymbol{D'}$.

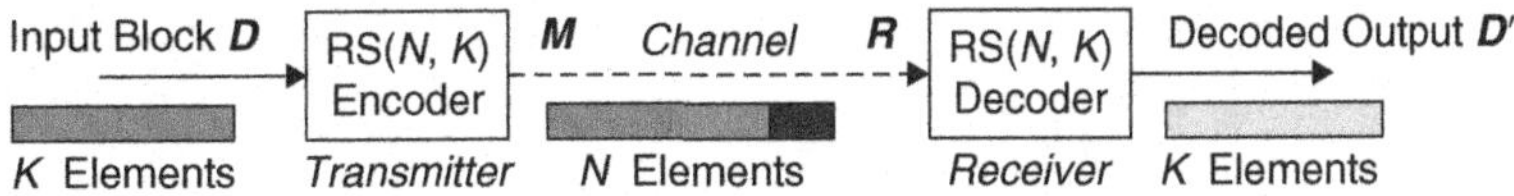

Figure 3.16: Block diagram of RS(*N*, *K*) coder.

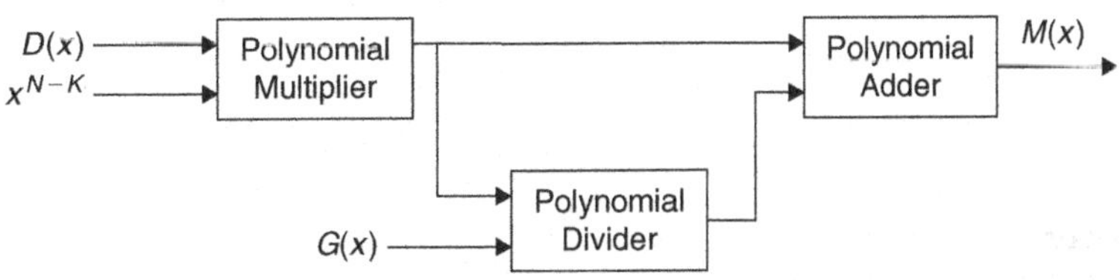

Figure 3.17: Operational blocks of RS(*N*, *K*) encoder.

3.6.1 RS(*N*, *K*) *Encoder*

Using the RS(N, K) encoder, we compute $N-K$ length parity polynomial $B(x)$ from K-length input message $D(x)$ by using the generator polynomial $G(x)$. The encoded message $M(x)$ is obtained as

$$M(x) = D(x) \cdot x^{N-K} + B(x) \tag{3.22}$$

The following generator polynomial is used in the RS(N, K) encoder to compute the parity data:

$$\begin{aligned} G(x) &= (x+\alpha^0)(x+\alpha^1)(x+\alpha^2)\cdots(x+\alpha^{2T-1}) \\ &= g_0 + g_1 x + g_2 x^2 + \cdots + g_{2T-1}x^{2T-1} + x^{2T} \end{aligned} \tag{3.23}$$

where $2T = N-K$. Here, the polynomial $G(x)$ is computed by multiplying $2T$ first-degree polynomials $(x+\alpha^i)$ where $0 \le i < 2T$. The parity polynomial $B(x)$ is computed as

$$B(x) = D(x) \cdot x^{N-K} \bmod G(x) \tag{3.24}$$

The equivalent schematic block diagram of Equations (3.22) and (3.24) is shown in Figure 3.17. In this section, we work with a few examples to better understand RS codes (see Examples 3.17, 3.18, and 3.19).

Example 3.17

Let us consider the data elements with 3-bit width. We work with RS(7, 3) coder and use Galois field GF(2^3) arithmetic (see Appendix B, Section B.2, on the companion website for more details on GF) to encode and decode the data elements. With this, the three parameter values of RS coder are $N = 7$, $K = 3$, $2T = N-K = 4$. Let the K length message vector $\boldsymbol{D} = [3\ 1\ 4]$. In terms of polynomial notation,

$$D(x) = \alpha^3 x^2 + \alpha^1 x + \alpha^4$$

For $T = 2$, the generator polynomial $G(x)$ is given by

$$G(x) = (x+\alpha)(x+\alpha^2)(x+\alpha^3)(x+\alpha^4)$$
$$= x^4 + \alpha^3 x^3 + x^2 + \alpha x + \alpha^3$$

The parity polynomial $B(x)$ is computed using Equation (3.24) as

$$B(x) = x^{N-K} D(x) \bmod G(x)$$
$$= x^4(\alpha^3 x^2 + \alpha x + \alpha^4) \bmod (x^4 + \alpha^3 x^3 + x^2 + \alpha x + \alpha^3)$$
$$= \alpha^3 x^3 + \alpha^5 x^2 + \alpha^5 x + \alpha$$

Then the codeword polynomial $M(x)$ is obtained from Equation (3.22) as

$$M(x) = \alpha^3 x^6 + \alpha x^5 + \alpha^4 x^4 + \alpha^3 x^3 + \alpha^5 x^2 + \alpha^5 x + \alpha$$

■

3.6.2 RS(N, K) Decoder

The RS(N, K) decoder takes data blocks of N elements as input and outputs a K element data block as shown in Figure 3.16. If errors are present in the received data and if they are less than or equal to $(N-K)/2$, then the RS decoder corrects the errors and outputs a corrected data block. Let $R(x) = r_{N-1}x^{N-1} + r_{N-2}x^{N-2} + \cdots + r_1 x + r_0$ be the received polynomial with noise, then $R(x) = M(x) + E(x)$, where $E(x)$ is the error polynomial. If $R(x)$ has v errors at the locations $x^{i_1}, x^{i_2}, \ldots, x^{i_v}$, then $E(x)$ will be represented with corresponding error magnitudes as follows:

$$E(x) = e_{i_1}x^{i_1} + e_{i_2}x^{i_2} + \cdots + e_{i_v}x^{i_v} \tag{3.25}$$

The error correction with the RS decoder is achieved in four steps and the schematic block diagram of the RS decoder is shown in Figure 3.18.

3.6.3 Syndrome Computation

In RS decoding, the first step of the decoder is syndrome computation. Syndromes, which give an indication of presence of errors, are computed using the received data polynomial $R(x)$. The syndromes are nothing but the evaluated values of the received polynomial at $x = \alpha^j$ for $1 \le j \le 2T$.

$$S_j = R(\alpha^j) = M(\alpha^j) + E(\alpha^j).$$
$$\because M(\alpha^j) = D(\alpha^j)G(\alpha^j) = 0, \quad \Rightarrow S_j = R(\alpha^j) = E(\alpha^j)$$

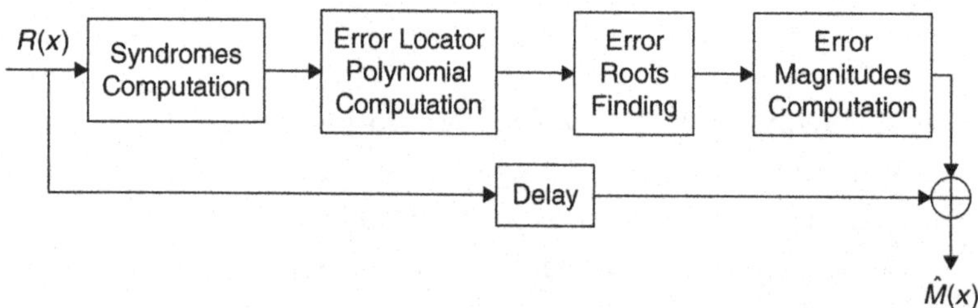

Figure 3.18: Schematic block diagram of RS decoder.

If all the syndromes are zero, then there are no errors in the received data. We compute a total of $2T$ syndromes in the syndrome computation step. An i-th syndrome is computed as follows:

$$S_i = R(\alpha^i) = \sum_{n=0}^{N-1} r_n (\alpha^i)^n \tag{3.26}$$

where addition is modulo-2 and performed using $\oplus$ instead of $+$.

Example 3.18

$R(x)$ is the received noise polynomial corresponding to the transmitted codeword polynomial $M(x)$. The received polynomial with errors in two positions follows:

$$R(x) = \alpha^3 x^6 + \alpha x^5 + \underline{\alpha}^6 x^4 + \alpha^3 x^3 + \underline{\alpha}^3 x^2 + \alpha^5 x + \alpha$$

From Equation (3.26), the $4(=2T)$ syndromes are computed as

$$S_1 = \alpha^5, \quad S_2 = \alpha^3, \quad S_3 = 0, \quad S_4 = \alpha^2$$

■

3.6.4 Error-Locator Polynomial Computation

Let X_i for $i = 1, 2, \ldots, v$, be the error locations and $\Lambda(x)$ be the error-locator polynomial. Then

$$\begin{aligned}\Lambda(x) &= (1 - X_1 x)(1 - X_2 x) \cdots (1 - X_v x) \\ &= \prod_{i=1}^{v} (1 - X_i x) \\ &= 1 + \Lambda_1 x + \Lambda_2 x^2 + \cdots + \Lambda_v x^v\end{aligned}$$

The coefficients $\Lambda_1, \Lambda_2, \cdots \Lambda_v$ of $\Lambda(x)$ are computed using the Berlekamp-Massey recursion (see Figure 3.15) seen in the following.

Initial conditions: $\Lambda^{(0)}(x) = 1, \quad B^{(0)}(x) = 1, \quad L_0 = 0$

***i*-th iteration:** $\Delta_i = \sum_{j=0}^{L_i} \Lambda_j^{(i-1)} S_{i-j}$

$$\delta_i = \begin{cases} 1 & \text{if } \Delta_i \neq 0 \text{ and } 2L_{i-1} \leq i-1 \\ 0 & \text{otherwise} \end{cases}$$

$$\begin{bmatrix} \Lambda^{(i)}(x) \\ B^{(i)}(x) \end{bmatrix} = \begin{bmatrix} 1 & -\Delta_i x \\ \Delta_i^{-1}\delta_i & (1-\delta_i)x \end{bmatrix} \begin{bmatrix} \Lambda^{(i-1)}(x) \\ B^{(i-1)}(x) \end{bmatrix}$$

$$L_i = \delta_i (i - L_{i-1}) + (1 - \delta_i) L_{i-1}$$

We iterate the Berlekamp-Massey algorithm $2T$ times to get an error-locator polynomial $\Lambda(x)$ of degree v that is less than or equal to T. If $v \leq T$, then the roots of the error-locator polynomial $\Lambda(x)$ give the valid error positions in the received data vector.

Example 3.19

We compute the error-locator polynomial by using the syndromes of the received polynomial computed in Example 3.18.

$$\Lambda^{(0)}(x) = 1, \quad B^{(0)}(x) = 1, \quad L_0 = 0$$

For $i = 1$,

$$\Delta_1 = \sum \Lambda_j^{(0)} S_{1-j} = S_1 = \alpha^5$$

$$\delta_1 = 1, \because \Delta_1 \neq 0 \text{ and } 2L_0 \leq 0$$

$$\Lambda^{(1)}(x) = 1 + \alpha^5 x$$

$$B^{(1)}(x) = \alpha^2$$

$$L_1 = 1$$

Like this, continue up to $i = 2T$ (in our case $2T = 4$). The final error-locator polynomial is given by

$$\Lambda(x) = \Lambda^{(4)}(x) = 1 + \alpha x + \alpha^6 x^2 = (1 + \alpha^2 x)(1 + \alpha^4 x)$$

■

3.6.5 Roots of Error-Locator Polynomial

We compute the roots of the error-locator polynomial (ELP) $\Lambda(x)$ with a brute force method (also called Chien's search) by checking all the field elements to know whether any of field elements satisfies $\Lambda(x)$. The Equation (3.27) gives the error roots as $X_i^{-1} = \alpha^k$ where $1 \leq i \leq v$ whenever P_k becomes zero.

$$P_k = \Lambda(\alpha^k) = \sum_{j=0}^{v} \Lambda_j (\alpha^k) \tag{3.27}$$

where $0 \leq k < N$. With ELP from Example 3.19, the error roots are found as $X_1^{-1} = \alpha^5$ and $X_2^{-1} = \alpha^3$. Then the error positions are given by the inverse of error roots. Thus, $X_1 = \alpha^2$ and $X_2 = \alpha^4$.

3.6.6 Error Magnitude Polynomial Computation

The error magnitude polynomial $\Omega(x) = 1 + \omega_1 x^1 + \omega_2 x^2 + \cdots + \omega_{2T} x^{2T}$ is defined as

$$\Omega(x) = \Lambda(x)[1 + S(x)] \bmod x^{2T+1} \tag{3.28}$$

where $S(x) = \sum_{j=1}^{2T} S_j x^j$and $\Lambda(x) = \sum_{i=0}^{v} \Lambda_i x^i$with $\Lambda_0 = 1$ are the syndrome polynomial and error-locator polynomial, respectively. From Equations (3.25) and (3.26),

$$S(x) = \sum_j \left[\sum_{i=1}^{v} Y_i X_i^j \right] x^j = \sum_{i=1}^{v} Y_i \left[\sum_j (X_i x)^j \right]$$

where $Y_k = e_{i_k}$ and $X_k = x^{i_k}$ are error magnitudes and error locations, respectively.

Assuming $|(X_i x)| < 1$ and using infinite geometric series summation result, the $S(x)$ can be approximated as

$$S(x) = \sum_{i=1}^{v} Y_i \left[\frac{X_i x}{1 - X_i x} \right] \tag{3.29}$$

From Equations (3.28) and (3.29),

$$\begin{aligned} \Omega(x) &= \Lambda(x) \left[1 + \sum_{i=1}^{v} Y_i \left(\frac{X_i x}{1 - X_i x} \right) \right] \bmod x^{2T+1} \\ &= \Lambda(x) \bmod x^{2T+1} + \sum_{i=1}^{v} \frac{Y_i X_i x \Lambda(x)}{1 - X_i x} \bmod x^{2T+1} \\ &= \Lambda(x) + \sum_{i=1}^{v} Y_i X_i x \prod_{j \neq i} (1 - X_j x) \end{aligned} \tag{3.30}$$

3.6.7 Error Magnitude Computation

To compute the error magnitudes from the error magnitude polynomial, we use the Forney algorithm. From Equation (3.30),

$$\begin{aligned}\Omega(X_k^{-1}) &= \Lambda(X_k^{-1}) + \sum_{i=1}^{v} Y_i X_i X_k^{-1} \prod_{j\neq i}(1 - X_j X_k^{-1}) \\ &= Y_k \prod_{j\neq k}(1 - X_j X_k^{-1})\end{aligned} \tag{3.31}$$

The error-locator polynomial with its factors follows:

$$\Lambda(x) = \prod_{i=1}^{v}(1 - X_i x) \tag{3.32}$$

Differentiating Equation (3.32) with respect to x on both sides, we have

$$\begin{aligned}\Lambda'(x) &= \frac{\partial}{\partial x}\left[\prod_{i=1}^{v}(1 - X_i x\right] \\ &= -\sum_{j=1}^{v} X_j \prod_{i\neq j}(1 - X_i x) \\ \Lambda'(X_k^{-1}) &= -\sum_{j=1}^{v} X_j \prod_{i\neq j}(1 - X_i X_k^{-1}) \\ &= -X_k \prod_{i\neq k}^{v}(1 - X_i X_k^{-1})\end{aligned} \tag{3.33}$$

From Equations (3.31) and (3.33), the error magnitudes are obtained as

$$Y_k = e_{i_k} = -\frac{X_k \Omega(X_k^{-1})}{\Lambda'(X_k^{-1})} \tag{3.34}$$

3.6.8 Error Correction

Once we know the error locations and error magnitudes, then we can compute the error polynomial $E(x)$ from Equation (3.25). (See Example 3.20.) The corrected data polynomial $\hat{D}(x)$is obtained from the received data vector $R(x)$ as

$$\hat{M}(x) = R(x) + E(x) \tag{3.35}$$

Example 3.20

From Example 3.19, the error positions X_1 and X_2 are obtained as $X_1 = \alpha^2$ and $X_2 = \alpha^4$. From Equation (3.31), the quantities $\Lambda'(X_1^{-1})$ and $\Lambda'(X_2^{-1})$ are computed as

$$\begin{aligned}\Lambda'(x) &= -X_1(1 - X_2 x) - X_2(1 - X_1 x) \\ \Lambda'(X_1^{-1}) &= -X_1(1 - X_2 X_1^{-1}) = \alpha^2(1 + \alpha^4\alpha^5) = \alpha \\ \Lambda'(X_2^{-1}) &= -X_2(1 - X_1 X_2^{-1}) = \alpha^4(1 + \alpha^2\alpha^3) = \alpha\end{aligned}$$

From Equation (3.28), the error magnitude polynomial $\Omega(x)$ from $\Lambda(x)$ and $S(x)$ is obtained as

$$\Omega(x) = 1 + \alpha^6 x + \alpha^3 x^2$$

Then

$$\Omega(X_1^{-1}) = \alpha, \quad \Omega(X_2^{-1}) = 1$$

Using Equation (3.34),

$$Y_1 = \frac{-X_1\Omega(X_1^{-1})}{\Lambda'(X_1^{-1})} = \frac{\alpha^2\alpha}{\alpha} = \alpha^2$$

$$Y_2 = \alpha^3$$

The error polynomial is computed from Equation (3.25) as

$$E(x) = \alpha^2x^2 + \alpha^3x^4$$

The corrected data polynomial from Equation (3.35) is obtained as

$$\hat{M}(x) = \alpha^3x^6 + \alpha x^5 + \alpha^4x^4 + \alpha^3x^3 + \alpha^5x^2 + \alpha^5x + \alpha$$

$$\hat{D}(x) = \alpha^3x^2 + \alpha x + \alpha^4 \text{ or}$$

$$\hat{D} = [3 \quad 1 \quad 4]$$

■

In the Section 4.2, we discuss the simulation techniques for the RS coder. We will consider RS(204, 188) coder for simulation purpose. Also, we discuss efficient implementation techniques for the RS decoder to minimize the cycle cost on the reference embedded processor.

3.7 Convolutional Codes

The difference between block codes and convolutional codes is that the former work on a block-by-block basis without any data dependency between the blocks, whereas in the latter case the output of encoder depends not only on the current input block to encoder but also on the previous $K-1$ input blocks where K is the constraint length of an encoder. A convolutional code is generated by passing the bitstream through a linear finite-state shift register as shown in Figure 3.19. All flip-flop registers are updated for every encoded input data block (so the encoder state changes with the encoding of each input block). The functionality of the convolutional encoder is similar to the convolutional operation (i.e., linear filtering); hence, these codes are called convolutional codes. If we input k bits to the encoder and it outputs n coded bits, then we call it the rate k/n encoder. Usually, convolutional codes perform better than cyclic block codes (e.g., RS codes) for the following reasons: convolutional decoders utilize the dependency among coded bits and are also capable of accepting soft information as input in decoding the bits.

In the following subsections, various representations of convolutional codes are presented, the generation of both systematic and nonsystematic codes is discussed and the decoding of convolutional codes using hard decisions (with Hamming distance criterion) is discussed. The optimal decoding of convolutional codes (with soft data and Euclidean distance criterion) using the Viterbi algorithm is discussed in Section 3.9.

3.7.1 Convolutional Encoder Representation

As we discussed in Section 3.3, the block codes can be represented with a generator matrix. Here we cannot use a generator matrix to represent convolutional codes as these codes are semi-infinite. However, it is possible to represent a generator function for each output bit of a convolutional encoder. In this section, we discuss different ways of representing a convolutional encoder along with individual output bits generator function representation using the rate $1/2$ encoder shown in Figure 3.19.

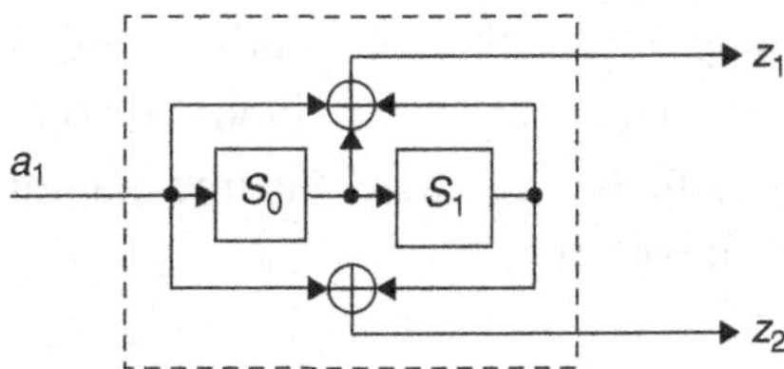

Figure 3.19: Flip-flop register representation of convolutional encoder.

Flip-Flop Register Representation

In the flip-flop representation of the convolutional encoder, we define input and output connections through flip-flop registers. Using the encoder shown in Figure 3.19, with one input bit a_1, we get two output bits z_1 and z_2 (hence, it is rated as a $^1/_2$ coder). The flip-flop registers are updated for every input block (or 1 bit). As per input-output connections shown in Figure 3.19, the state value S_1 of the flip-flop register is updated with S_0 and the state value S_0 of the flip-flop register is updated with the input bit a_1. The constraint length K of this coder is 3, as the output bits depend not only on the current input bit but also on the previous two input bits (which are present in the flip-flop registers S_0 and S_1). The following equations give the relationship between output bits z_1 and z_2 and input bit a_1.

$$z_1 = a_1 \oplus S_0 \oplus S_1 \tag{3.36}$$

$$z_2 = a_1 \oplus S_1 \tag{3.37}$$

Generator/Transfer Function Representation

In transfer function representation, we basically provide the input to output connections by assigning bit "1" if connection to the output is present; otherwise, we assign a bit "0" to say that there is no connection to the output. The number of bits in a generator function depends on the maximum total number of connections to any output bit. For example, in Figure 3.19, there are three connections to output bit z_1 and two connections to output bit z_2. Therefore, in the generator function representation of convolutional coder shown in Figure 3.19, we use three bits for both outputs' generator functions. From Equations (3.36) and (3.37), the generator functions g_1 and g_2 for two output bits z_1 and z_2 are

$$g_1 = [111]$$
$$g_2 = [101]$$

We also can represent the generator functions in the polynomial form as

$$G_1(D) = 1 + D + D^2 \tag{3.38a}$$

$$G_2(D) = 1 + D^2 \tag{3.38b}$$

State Machine Representation

From Figure 3.19, we can see that the output bits of the convolutional coder depend on both input bits and the state values. Using state machine representation of the convolutional coder, we can show the updated states along with output bits for a given input bits. The corresponding state machine representation of the convolutional encoder of Figure 3.19 is shown in Figure 3.20. From Figure 3.20, we can see how the states are updated and what output bits are generated with corresponding input bits. For example, if we input bit "0" when the encoder state is "01," then the output state becomes "10" and the output bits are "01." Similarly, if we input bit "1," then the output state is "11" and the corresponding output bits are "10." The state machine is a compact representation of a convolutional encoder when compared to other representations. With this state machine, we can see all possible states and output bits values for a given input value.

Tree Diagram Representation

In the tree diagram representation, we represent the states as nodes of a tree and the outputs as branches of a tree. We start the encoder at zero state and build the tree for each possible input block bit pattern. The number of branches emerging from any node depends on the number of bits (k) in one input block. For example, in Figure 3.19, each input block contains only 1 bit; hence, there will be two branches (2^k) from each node of the tree diagram. The corresponding tree diagram for the convolutional encoder shown in Figure 3.19 is presented in Figure 3.21. The upward branches from a node are due to input bit "0," whereas the downward branches from a node are due to input bit "1." Starting with the zero state, the tree diagram shows all possible output states and output bits for all possible input block bit patterns.

Trellis Diagram Representation

The trellis diagram is a time-indexed version of a state diagram. With trellis diagram representation, we can see all possible output states and output bits for a given input bit with respect to time scale. In practice, we start trellis from zero state and force zero state at the end of the input bitstream with trellis terminating bits (usually, we use 0 bits to terminate trellis). A trellis diagram is popularly used in decoding of convolutional codes. Figure 3.22 shows the trellis diagram corresponding to the rate ½ encoder shown in Figure 3.19.

Systematic and Nonsystematic Convolutional Codes

As discussed in Section 3.3, the error-correction codes are classified into two types: (1) systematic codes, and (2) nonsystematic codes (NSC). In the case of systematic codes, the original input data block is present as it is

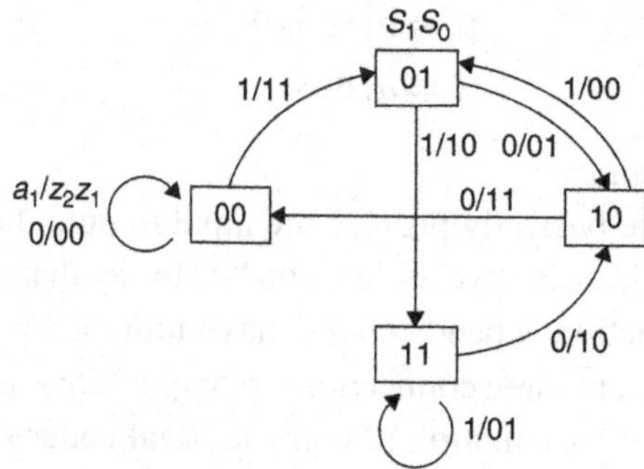

Figure 3.20: State machine representation of convolutional coder.

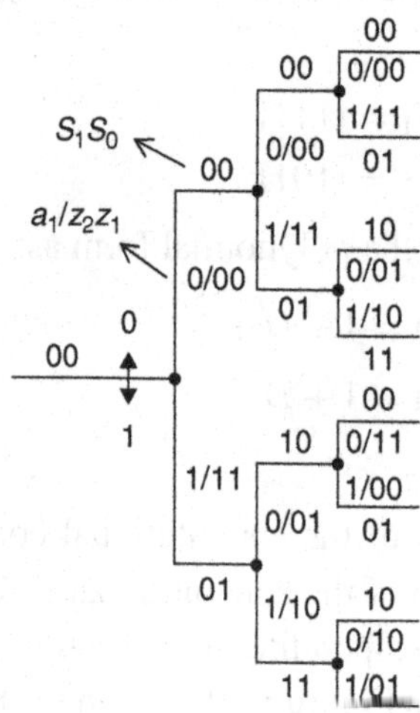

Figure 3.21: Tree diagram representation of convolutional coder.

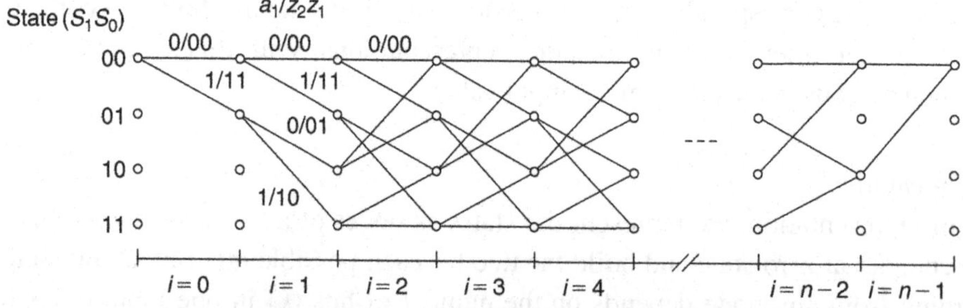

Figure 3.22: Trellis diagram representation of convolutional codes.

along with parity data at the output of encoder, whereas with nonsystematic codes, we do not have a separate input data block in the output data after encoding. The convolutional code generated with the encoder shown in Figure 3.19 is a nonsystematic code as no input data bits are directly present at the output. A class of systematic codes called recursive systematic codes (RSC) is popularly used with turbo coding (see Section 3.10), where we output the input data block along with the parity data block as shown in Figure 3.44.

3.7.2 Decoding Criterion for Convolutional Codes

Usually, in digital communications systems, the convolutional decoding happens after baseband demodulation as shown in Figure 3.23. In the baseband binary phase shift keying (BPSK) demodulation, we have two options to obtain the demodulated data; in the first option, we quantize the data based on the sign of the demodulated output and get bit "0" if the sign is positive and bit "1" if the sign is negative. In this case we used 1 bit to represent the data and these decisions are called hard decisions. In the second option, we quantize the demodulator output with more than one level. In other words, we represent the demodulated data with multiple levels using more than 1 bit (e.g., represented with eight levels as $-4, -3, -2, -1, 0, 1, 2, 3$ using 3 bits) and these decisions are called soft decisions.

Hard Decision versus Soft Decision

At the convolutional decoder output, we will see a considerable performance difference between hard decisions and soft-decision inputs to the decoder. The reason is simple as illustrated in Figure 3.24. Consider a demodulator input sample highlighted with a dashed circle. This sample corresponds to bit "1," which supposedly is downwards with some negative amplitude like other "1" bit input samples to the demodulator. But, because of the presence of more noise at that sample, the noisy sample became a positive sample with value 0.0944. With the hard-decision demodulator, we output bit zero as if it corresponds to a "0" transmitted bit, but actually it corresponds to the transmitted bit "1." With soft decisions, the demodulator outputs the sample with a small positive allowed quantization level.

Now, assume a decoder based on the probability of having the sample close to some constant positive and negative thresholds. In other words, it is more likely to decode a bit as "0" or it is less likely to decode a bit as "1" if the soft decision has more positive value. Similarly, it is more likely to decode a bit as "1" or it is less likely to decode a bit as "0" if the soft decision has more negative value. From a probabilistic point of view, with demodulator hard decision outputs, the highlighted sample (corresponding to bit "1") has the same probability as "0"-bit samples, whereas with soft decisions, when compared to the highlighted sample, the probability of "0"-bit samples is considerably higher. If these kinds of samples occur frequently in a sequence, then the decoders based on the maximum likelihood criterion may make more wrong decisions with hard-decision inputs when compared to soft-decision inputs.

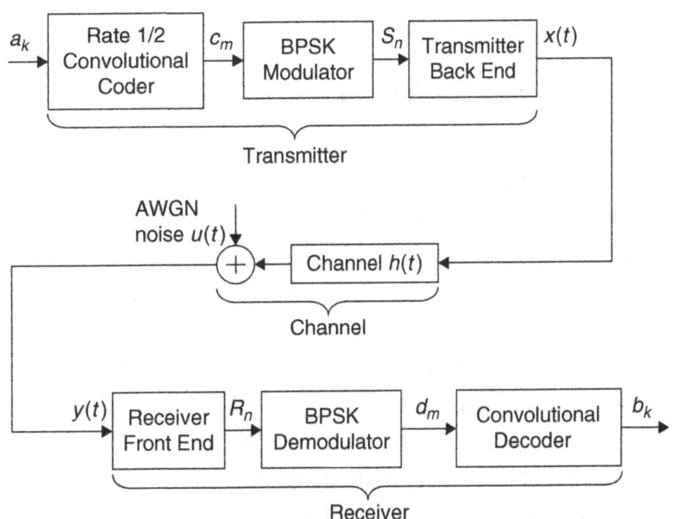

Figure 3.23: Block diagram of baseband digital communications system.

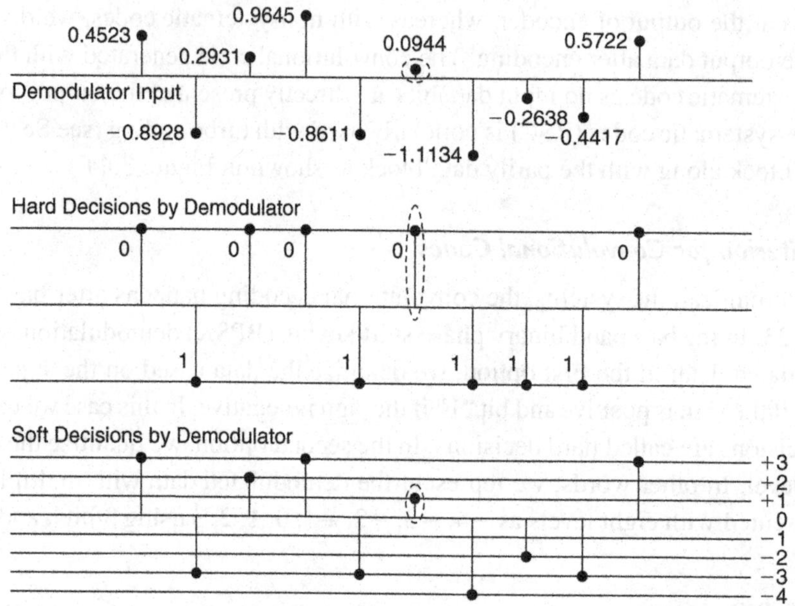

Figure 3.24: Illustration of hard decisions versus soft decisions.

Hamming Distance versus Euclidean Distance

As we discussed in Section 3.3.1, the Hamming distance between two codewords is given by the number of positions in which the bits in those two codewords are different. For example, the Hamming distance between the two codewords, 01011101 and 01001011, is 3, as they differ in three bit positions. We may prefer to use Hamming distance in convolutional decoding if the input to the decoder is hard decisions. In the next subsection, we discuss the decoding of convolutional codes with hard-decision inputs and Hamming distance criterion.

The Euclidean distance is defined as the distance between two vectors or the absolute difference between two scalars. For example, consider two vectors $\overrightarrow{OA}$ and $\overrightarrow{OB}$ with $A = (2.54, -1.98)$ and $B = (1.44, -2.32)$. The Euclidean distance between these two vectors is computed as $\sqrt{(2.54-1.44)^2+(-1.98+2.32)^2} = 1.3256$. The Euclidean distance between two scalars $P = -1.23$ and $Q = 2.45$ is $|-1.23-2.45| = 3.68$. The Euclidean distance is popularly used in convolutional decoding both with soft-decision inputs as well as hard-decision inputs. From a hardware point of view, the Hamming distance can be computed with less complex hardware circuitry and also the computation will be fast, whereas the computation of the Euclidean distance involves floating-point operations so the corresponding hardware is costly and the computations will not be fast due to slow floating point hardware circuitry. However, with soft-decision inputs and Euclidean distance criterion, we will see a considerable performance gain at the convolutional decoder output. In Section 3.9, we discuss the optimal decoding of convolutional codes with the Viterbi algorithm using the Euclidean distance as a criterion.

3.7.3 Convolutional Decoding with Hard Decisions

As we discussed in Section 3.7.1, the convolutional encoder is basically a finite-state machine. The optimum decoding criterion for convolutional codes is maximum likelihood sequence estimation (MLSE). In the decoding using maximum likelihood (ML) criterion, we select the most probable symbols as decoded symbols by minimizing overall symbol errors. This is achieved by processing all the trellis stages corresponding to the encoded symbols. We process the trellis stage-by-stage with the removal of less probable paths of the trellis in each stage and retaining the most probable paths at each node of a trellis stage. For this, we define two metrics, namely branch and state metrics. The branch metrics are obtained by computing the distance between the received symbol and branch symbol values. The state metrics are obtained by selecting the minimum error value obtained after adding the branch metrics to the previous stage state metrics from where these branches are diverged. In this way we obtain the most probable symbol path in the trellis at every stage of trellis processing. The path that includes most probable paths of all trellis stages is called the global most probable path. Then the bits corresponding to

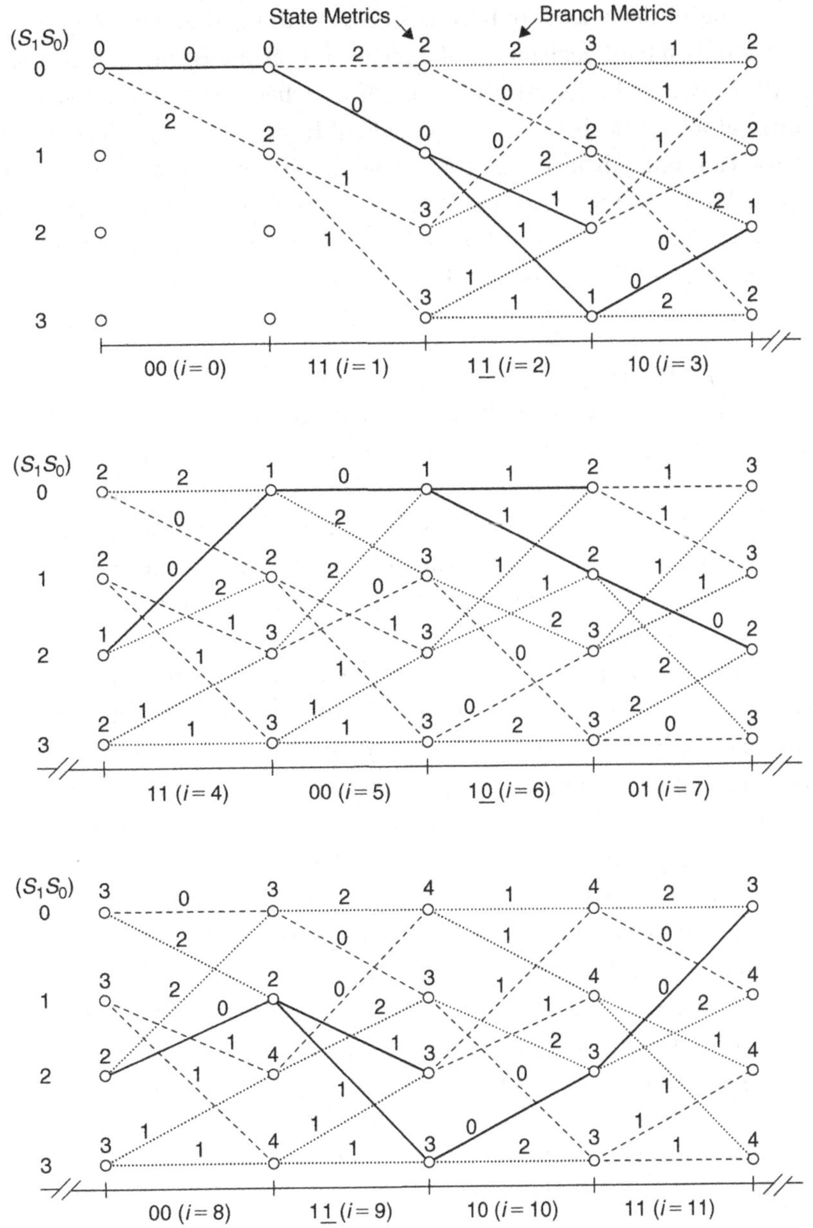

Figure 3.25: Convolutional decoding by trellis processing with Hamming distance.

the trellis global most probable path are output as the decoded bit values. An example of decoding with ML criterion is shown in Figure 3.25.

The two major issues with decoding of convolutional codes using ML criterion are computational complexity and memory usage. The computational complexity of the ML decoder increases exponentially with constraint length K (as the number of trellis states is equal to 2^{K-1}). As we actually start decoding bits after processing all the trellis stages, with large received frames and with large constraint lengths, we need a lot of data memory to store the most probable trellis branches history and all states' metrics information. As shown in Figure 3.25, we needed to store all state metrics as we don't know in advance which state metrics contribute toward the most probable paths. We store the branch connections information for each stage to trace the global most probable path. As an example, we use a rate ½ convolutional coder shown in Figure 3.19 for illustrating decoding of convolutional codes using ML criterion. Assume we want to transmit 10 bits 0110001011**00** (the last 2 bits are used for trellis termination and they are extra bits apart from our 10 bits of information for transmission). We start the encoder at state zero (i.e., $S_1S_0 = 00$). The corresponding encoded codewords for each bit are obtained (updated trellis states are not shown here) as 00, 11, 10, 10, 11, 00, 11, 01, 00, 10, 10, 11. As we used terminating bits, the trellis state at the end of this encoding becomes zero. With the digital communications system shown in Figure 3.23, assume we obtain hard decisions at the receiver after the BPSK demodulator as 00, 11, $1\underline{1}$, 10, 11, 00, $1\underline{0}$, 01, 00, $1\underline{1}$, 10, 11, with 3 bits in error (due to noise), when compared to transmitted bit sequence.

We decode the demodulator hard-decision outputs with the ML decoder by processing the trellis as shown in Figure 3.25. Here, we use Hamming distance for computing the distance between the received codewords and encoder trellis codewords. We know the encoder started from zero state and was forced to zero state at the end of encoding by using two terminating 0 bits and these bits are not part of the information that is intended for communication. At the receiver, we have a total of 12 codewords including two trellis termination codewords. Therefore, to decode 10 transmitted bits, we have to process 12 codewords (or trellis stages) in total.

Convolutional Decoding by Trellis Processing

We use the transmitter encoder trellis shown in Figure 3.25 to decode convolutional codes with the ML decoder. We follow this trellis flow and compute the path (or branch) metrics and state metrics using the received codewords. The received codewords along with the codeword index are shown at the bottom of each trellis stage. At stage $i = 0$, we received a 2-bit codeword of "00." As the encoder started from a zero state, we have only two possible paths at stage $i = 0$. We compute the Hamming distance between the received codeword and the trellis paths codewords of the first stage. For convenience, we use the encoder stabilized trellis stage with output bits for allowed trellis paths as shown in Figure 3.26.

We initialize the state metric to zero value at the start of the encoder trellis, as shown in Figure 3.25. For now we ignore the meaning of branches representation with solid, dashed and dotted lines. At stage $i = 1$, the computed Hamming distance between the received codeword and the trellis path connecting 0<>0 states (here m<>n denotes a branch that connects previous stage state m to current stage state n) is 0 as both codewords have the same bits (i.e., 00). Similarly, the Hamming distance between the received codeword and the trellis path connecting 0<>1 states is 2 as the two codewords differ in both bit positions (since the received codeword is 00 and the trellis branch 0<>1 is 11 as shown in Figure 3.26). We add the branch metrics to the previous (left side to current stage) state metrics and place the accumulated state metrics at the current (right side to current stage) states. At stage $i = 0$, we have two trellis paths; we select the most probable path as the one that connects to the state with minimum state metric (i.e., the path connecting 0<>0 as shown by a solid line). The accumulated state metrics at stage $i = 0$ are 0 and 2. We move to processing the trellis stage $i = 1$. At stage $i = 1$, we have four trellis branches diverging from states at stage $i = 0$ and merging to states at stage $i = 1$. We compute the Hamming distances from those four branches to the received codeword (i.e., 11) at stage $i = 1$. The values of four branch metrics are shown at corresponding branches. Then we add the branch metrics to the previous stage state metrics and place them at the current stage states. Here also (at stage $i = 1$), we have only single branches merging to current states and the most probable path for this stage is given by the trellis branch that merges to the state with the minimum accumulated state metric (i.e., branch 0<>1 at stage $i = 1$).

At stage $i = 2$, the trellis stabilizes and all allowed branches diverge from previous stage states and merge at current stage states. We obtain the branch metrics by computing the Hamming distance between the received codeword (i.e., $1\underline{1}$, the underlined bit is in error) and all trellis stage branch codewords. Then we add branch metrics to previous state metrics. We have more than one branch merging to the same state from this stage onwards. If we have more than one branch merging to the current state, then we choose the probable path as

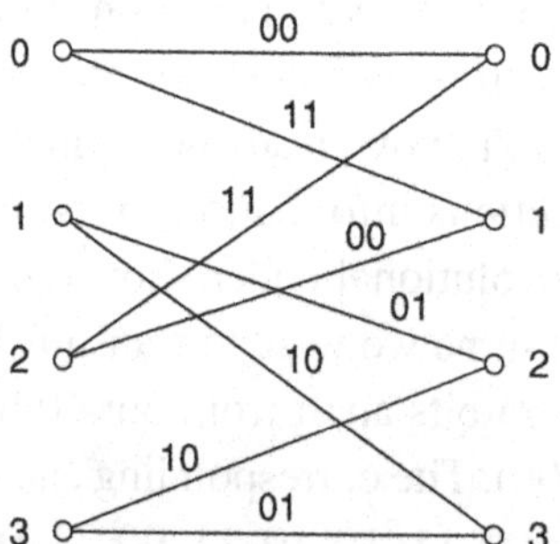

Figure 3.26: Stabilized trellis stage branches with corresponding output bits.

one with which we will have a minimum of accumulated state metric. For example, we consider two branches merging to state "0" (i.e., 0<>0 and 2<>0). With the branch 0<>0, we have an accumulated metric of 4, whereas with branch 2<>0, we have an accumulated metric of 3. Therefore, we choose the branch 2<>0 as a probable path to state "0."

In the same way, we compute the probable paths to all states. Now the most probable path for the current stage is given by the branch that connects to the previous stage's most probable path and converges to the current state with minimum accumulated state metric. We continue in the same manner and compute the most probable paths to all stages of the trellis. Now we understand the meaning of solid, dashed, and dotted lines in the trellis. The dotted line branches are the least probable paths as their metrics after accumulation with previous state metrics end up having relatively big values. The dashed lines represent the probable paths to each current state from previous states and connect to the current state with a smaller accumulated state metric (when compared to the least probable path accumulated state metric). The solid lines represent the most probable paths to a current state from a previous state with minimum state metric (when compared to other state metrics).

Next, we discuss a few specific cases that arise in trellis processing. At stage $i = 2$, we have two state metrics with the same accumulated metric values and those two paths diverge from the same previous state. In this case, as we don't know in advance which path is going to survive, we assume both paths as most probable paths. Because of this, the two paths, 1<>2 and 1<>3, are represented by solid lines. Next, when two branches from different previous states merge to a state with the same accumulated metric value, we choose randomly one path as the probable path. For example, at stage $i = 4$, two paths, 1<>2 and 3<>2, have the same accumulated state metric. We choose randomly one out of those two as a probable path and the other as the less probable path. In this case, we have chosen path 1<>2 as a probable path and path 3<>2 as a less probable path.

As shown in Figure 3.25, the accumulated state metrics grow with errors and we may have more than one most probable path. After processing all the trellis stages, we end up with one path that connects all stages' most probable paths and we consider it the global most probable path. Tracing back the global most probable path and taking the corresponding branch input bits gives the decoded bit sequence. Since we forced the encoder to zero state at the end of the bitstream with terminating 0 bits, the global most probable path starts and ends at the zero state. We know the input bit values for each trellis path that updates the trellis states. Figure 3.27 shows the trellis paths with corresponding input bits. By following the global most probable path, we can retrieve the corresponding stage's most probable path (which is part of global most probable path) bits.

These bits give an estimate of transmitted bits. From Figures 3.25 and 3.27, we retrieve the global most probable path bits as illustrated in Table 3.1, and the retrieved bitstream is 0110001011**00**, where the last 2 bits are trellis termination bits and we ignore them. The remaining 10 bits, 0110001011, are the bits decoded by ML decoder as the estimate of the transmitted information bits. Although we had 3-bit errors at the input of the decoder, we corrected these errors with our convolutional decoder.

As we discussed, the computational cost to perform convolutional decoding depends on constraint length (as the number of states of trellis increases exponentially with the constraint length) of an encoder. For example, decoding the convolutional codes that are encoded using a convolutional coder with constraint length equal to 4 requires processing of an 8 state trellis as shown in Figure 3.28. The memory usage depends on the input data frame length (as an ML decoder works on one frame at a time) and constraint length. We have to store all stages

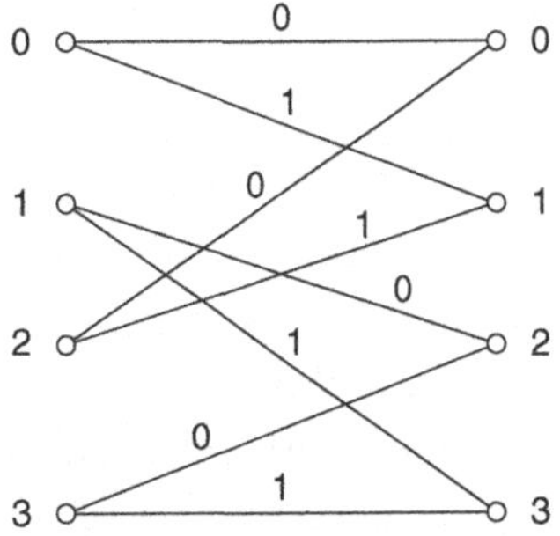

Figure 3.27: Stabilized trellis stage branches with corresponding input bits.

Table 3.1: Global most probable path and corresponding input bits

Stage (i)	Most Probable Global Path	Decoded Bits
0	0<>0	0
1	0<>1	1
2	1<>3	1
3	3<>2	0
4	2<>0	0
5	0<>0	0
6	0<>1	1
7	1<>2	0
8	2<>1	1
9	1<>3	1
10	3<>2	0
11	2<>0	0

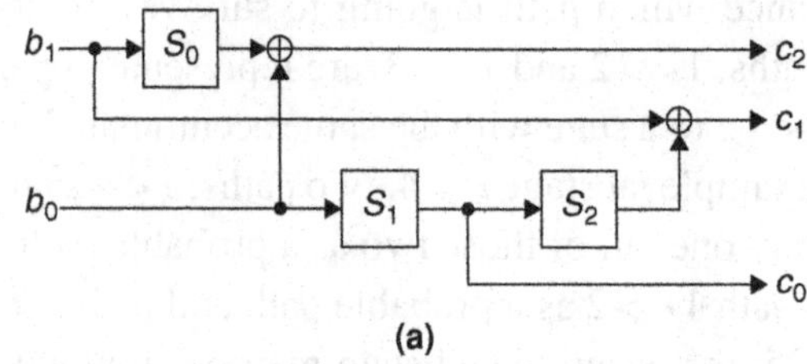

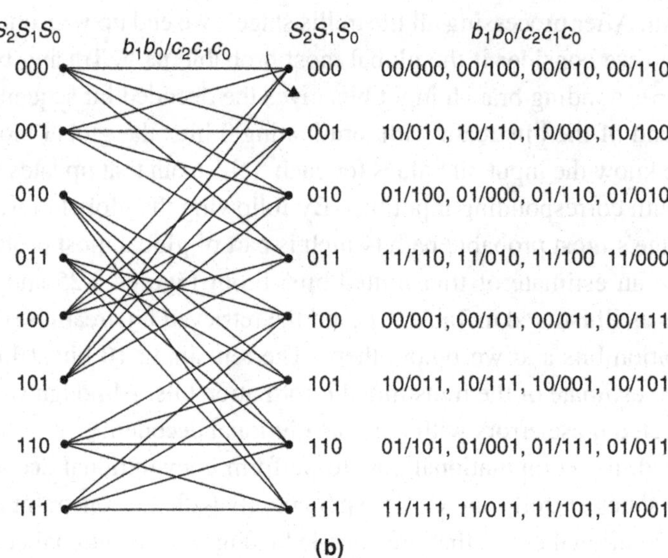

Figure 3.28: (a) Rate 2/3 convolutional coder and (b) Corresponding steady-state trellis.

and all state metrics as well as all most probable paths connections $m<>n$ to trace the global most probable paths to decode the bits. In Section 3.9, we discuss optimal decoding of convolutional codes with the Viterbi algorithm and also we address memory savings by implementing the decoder with the window method.

3.8 Trellis Coded Modulation

Trellis coded modulation (TCM) is a combined coding and modulation technique used for digital transmission over band-limited channels. With TCM, we can achieve significant coding gains over conventional uncoded multilevel modulation without trading bandwidth. In this section, we discuss the coded modulation system and its performance gain over an uncoded system and performance gain over a system where channel coding and modulation is separately performed. We discuss the Viterbi decoder, a decoding technique for TCM symbols, in the next section.

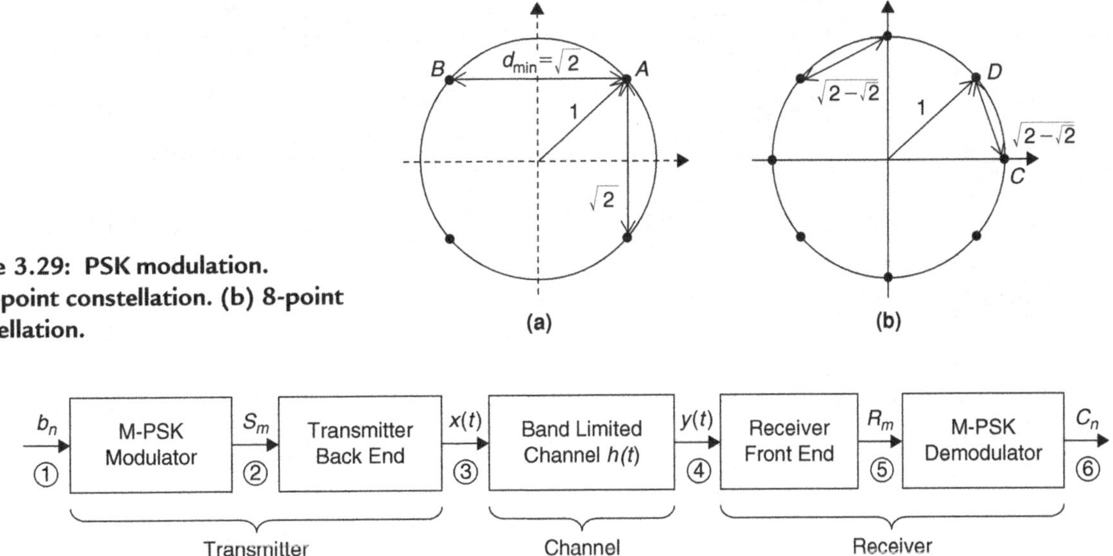

Figure 3.29: PSK modulation. (a) 4-point constellation. (b) 8-point constellation.

Figure 3.30: Uncoded baseband communications system with M-PSK modulation.

We consider bandwidth-constrained channels (e.g., twisted-pair copper telephone lines) to study the TCM systems and to see the performance gain of TCM over other coded and uncoded systems. For such band-limited channels, the digital communications system is designed to use bandwidth-efficient multilevel/multiphase modulation schemes, such as PAM, PSK or QAM. See Section 9.1.3 for more details on baseband modulation schemes (e.g., PSK, QAM). Here, we consider PSK modulation schemes in our performance analysis of TCM systems. For convenience, the 4-PSK and 8-PSK constellations from Section 9.1.3 are redrawn here as shown in Figure 3.29.

Uncoded System

We consider a simple baseband uncoded communications system with a PSK modulation scheme as shown in Figure 3.30. The inputs to the M-PSK modulator are equiprobable binary digits b_n and the outputs are PSK symbols S_m chosen from an M-point PSK constellation array. We assume that the DAC (digital to analog conversion) operation along with low-pass filtering (to filter out-of-band frequency content) is performed in the transmitter back-end module. The output of the transmitter back-end is a continuous time and continuous amplitude signal $x(t)$ that is suitable for transmission over channel $h(t)$. The receiver front-end includes filters (to combat channel distortions such as noise, and ISI), symbol synchronization circuitry (to get accurate sampling time and phase), ADC (analog to digital conversion), and a symbol detector (to get multilevel PSK symbols), among other things. The output R_m of the receiver front-end is the PSK symbol. These PSK symbols are fed to M-PSK demodulator to get back the transmitted binary digits, c_n (which may be different from b_n due to channel impairments). This communications system is an uncoded system since no channel coding is present in the signal chain.

In Figure 3.30, the data rates before the modulator (represented with 1 in a circle) and after the modulator (represented with 2 in a circle) need not be the same. The modulator input data are bits b_n, and its output are PSK symbols S_m. Depending on the constellation used, we map $m\ (= \log_2^M)$ bits to one PSK symbol. If the bit rate at the modulator input is P, then the symbol rate at the output of the modulator is $Q = P/m$. As we discussed in the previous sections and also will discuss later, the channel coding at the transmitter side adds redundancy to the input bitstream and that increases the bit rate P at the input of modulator. However, we can keep the symbol rate the same at the output of modulator by increasing m using multilevel/phase modulation. This important feature of multilevel/phase modulators is very useful in designing a communications system for a band-limited channel. The disadvantage with this type of system is that the constant symbol rate increases the number of bits per symbol when bit rate increases and therefore we have to increase the energy levels of the symbols for transmission to reduce the channel noise effect on the detection of symbols at the demodulator.

This type of communications system design is suitable for wireline communication where we do not have much bandwidth but we can use more energy to transmit data. We use this kind of system design with a small

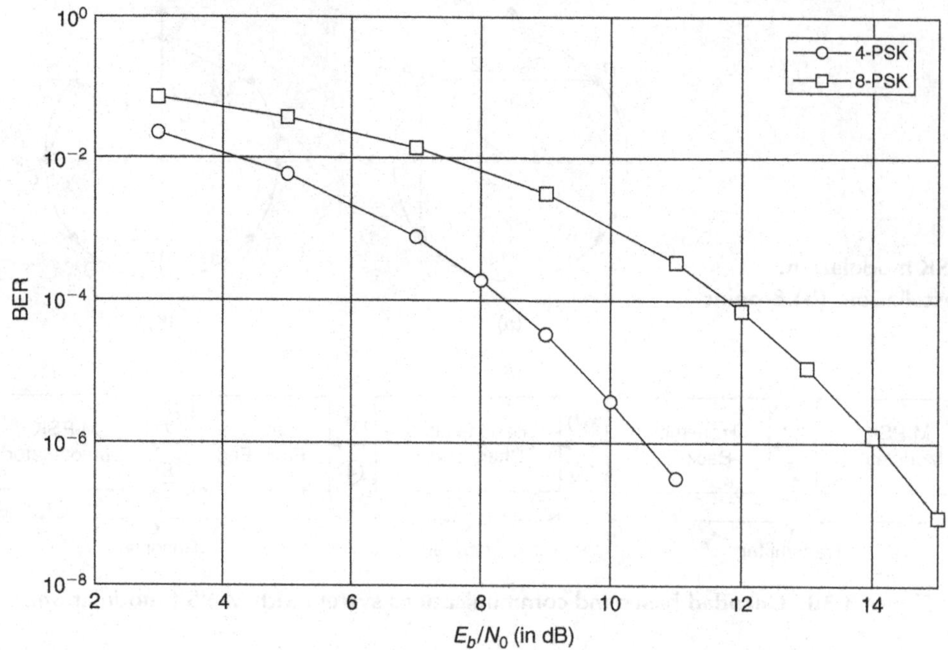

Figure 3.31: Performance curves of uncoded 4-PSK and 8-PSK systems.

value of m for satellite communication too, where we have infinite bandwidth and limited power is available for transmission. Typically, we use 256- or 512-point constellation symbols for wireline communications, whereas we use symbols from 4- or 8-point constellations in the case of satellite communications. The BER (bit error rate) performance curves for this uncoded communication system are shown in Figure 3.31. From the M-PSK performance curves, we can clearly see that the required E_b/N_0 (energy per bit) increases for a given modulator output bandwidth as bit rate (or M, the number of constellation points) increases. At BER $= 10^{-6}$, we need to spend 3.5 dB more energy per bit with 8-PSK symbols when compared to 4-PSK symbols. As no coding is involved in this system, the parameters SNR and E_b/N_0 are related by the following formula (see Section 9.1.2 for more details).

$$E_b/N_0 = (E_s/N_0)/m = \mathrm{SNR}/m \tag{3.39}$$

or

$$E_b/N_0 \text{ (in dB)} = \text{SNR (in dB)} - 10^* \log 10(m) \tag{3.40}$$

Coded System

With channel coding methods, it is possible to trade the bandwidth of the communications system with the transmission power. Here, we discuss the application of channel coding to improve data rates in bandwidth-constrained channels. When coding is applied to such channels, a performance gain is desired without expanding the signal bandwidth. As an example, we consider the system shown in Figure 3.30 using 4-PSK constellation points for modulation. This uncoded 4-PSK modulation achieves 2 bits/sec/Hz (capacity per unit of the channel bandwidth) at an error probability of, say, 10^{-6}. For this error rate, the signal to noise ratio (SNR) per bit (i.e., E_b/N_0) is 10.5 dB (from Figure 3.31). If we want to reduce the SNR per bit using channel coding without expanding the bandwidth, then we have to use symbols from a bigger constellation to accommodate redundant bits (resulted due to channel coding) in the given bandwidth.

Using rate 2/3 coder, we go from 4-PSK (2 bits per symbol) with a minimum distance of $\sqrt{2}$ between the points as shown in Figure 3.29(a) to 8-PSK (3 bits per symbol) with a minimum distance of $\sqrt{2-\sqrt{2}}$ between the points as shown in Figure 3.29(b) to keep the bandwidth constant. With appropriate mapping of the encoded bits to the signal points, the rate 2/3 coder in conjunction with 8-phase PSK yields the same data throughput as the uncoded 4-phase PSK. An increase in the number of signal points from 4 to 8 requires an additional G dB

(3.5 dB in this particular case; see Figure 3.31) approximately in signal power (since the minimum distance CD < AB as shown in Figure 3.29) to maintain the same error rate. Therefore, if coding is used to reduce the SNR per bit, then the rate 2/3 coder must overcome this G dB penalty and yield further gain. If the coding and modulation are performed separately, then the use of very powerful codes (e.g., convolutional codes with large constraint length) is required to offset the loss and provide some significant coding gain.

Coded Modulation System

On the other hand, if we combine the encoding process with the modulation to increase the minimum Euclidean distance between pairs of coded signals, then the loss from the expansion of the signal set is easily overcome and a significant coding gain is achieved with relatively simple codes. The TCM is one such coding scheme that generates modulated codewords. The performance of a TCM system with rate 2/3 convolutional coder of constraint length 3 using an 8-PSK modulation system (that achieves 2 bits/sec/Hz) is shown in Figure 3.32. We use the corresponding Viterbi decoder (see Section 3.9 for more details) to decode this system. From performance curves we can clearly see the performance gain with a TCM system over an uncoded system. At BER of 10^{-6}, with TCM, we see a coding gain of 3 dB with respect to the uncoded 4-PSK system. In the next section, we discuss TCM codeword generation. TCM applications include voiceband modems, DSL modems, cable modems, and satellite communications, among others.

3.8.1 TCM Encoder

In this section, we discuss the generation of TCM encoded symbols. The TCM encoder consists of two operators, a convolutional coder and a modulator, as shown in Figure 3.33. In TCM, we map the coded bits to modulated signal points in a particular way without increasing the data transmission bandwidth.

Convolutional Coder

For convolutional coding, we use a simple rate 1/2 convolutional encoder as shown in Figure 3.34. The dashed lines (in parallel to the solid lines in the trellis diagram) in Figure 3.34 correspond to the uncoded bit paths (or

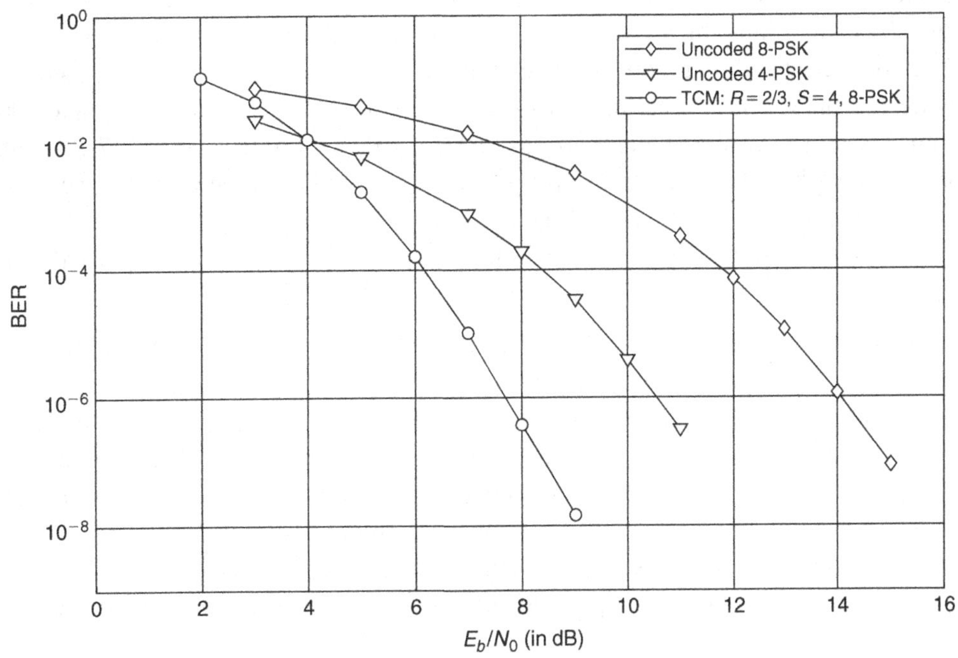

Figure 3.32: TCM system performance.

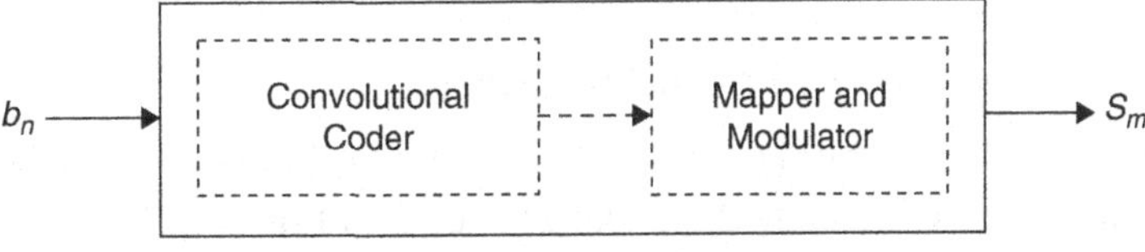

Figure 3.33: Schematic block diagram of a TCM system.

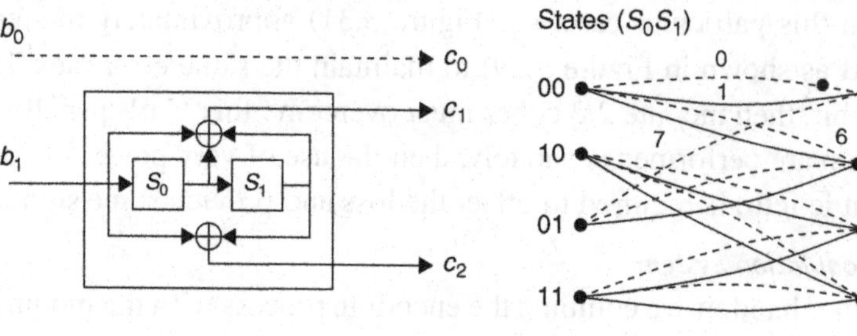

Figure 3.34: A rate 2/3 convolutional coder and its trellis diagram.

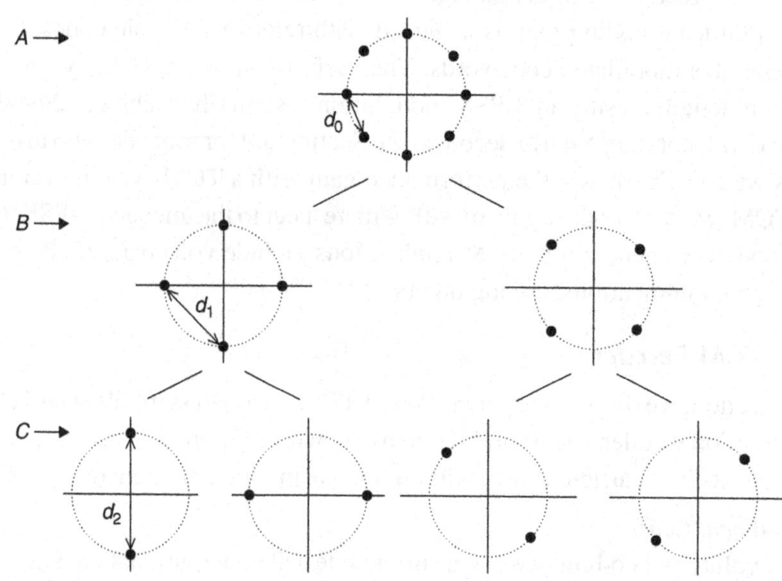

Figure 3.35: 8-PSK symbol constellation and set partitioning.

branches). The encoder consists of two delay units (or shift registers); hence, its constraint length is $K = 3$. Although the encoder takes 1 input bit and outputs 2 bits, due to passing of one uncoded bit, the effective code rate becomes 2/3. For every two inputs, we get three output bits (which we represent with eight levels, 0 to 7). For example, when the encoder is at state (or node) zero (i.e., $S_0S_1 = 00$), if input bits b_1b_0 are 00, 01, 10 and 11 then we obtain corresponding output bits $c_2c_1c_0$ as 000 (0), 001 (1), 110 (6) and 111 (7). As said earlier, the uncoded bits produce parallel paths in the trellis. If we have m uncoded bits then we will have 2^m parallel paths in the trellis. In our case, we have 1 uncoded bit (i.e., $m = 1$) and we have 2 parallel paths diverging from and converging to all states in the trellis. Next, we discuss the mapping of coded bits to modulated signal points.

Mapper and Modulator

The key to this integrated modulation and coding approach is to devise an effective method for mapping the coded bits into signal points such that the minimum Euclidean distance is maximized. For this, we perform partition of constellation points into subpartitions more than once and make sure that the distance between points increases in the subpartitions with each partitioning. The degree to which the signal constellation set is partitioned depends on the characteristics of the code. The constellation set partitioning is shown in Figure 3.35. In Figure 3.35, if d_0 is the minimum distance between points at level A, d_1 is the minimum distance between points at level B and d_2 is the minimum distance between points at level C, then $d_0 < d_1 < d_2$. From Figure 3.34 and Figure 3.35, the assignment of signal points for each coded output is made according to the following Ungerboeck set partitioning rules (Ungerboeck, 1987).

1. Parallel transitions are assigned to signal points separated by the maximum Euclidean distance.
2. The transitions originating from a particular state and merging into any state are assigned to signal points separated by at least the next-largest distance.
3. The signal points should occur with equal frequency.

To satisfy these rules, the coded bits are used to choose a subset of points and the uncoded bits are used to choose the points within a subset. With a rate 2/3 coder as shown in Figure 3.34, we use 2 coded bits to choose one of

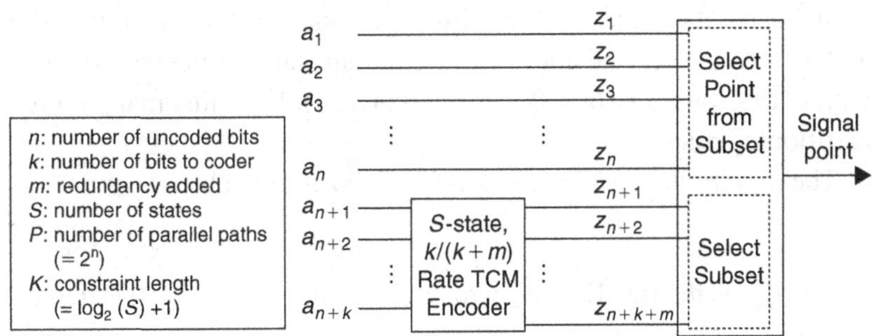

Figure 3.36: General structure of a TCM encoder.

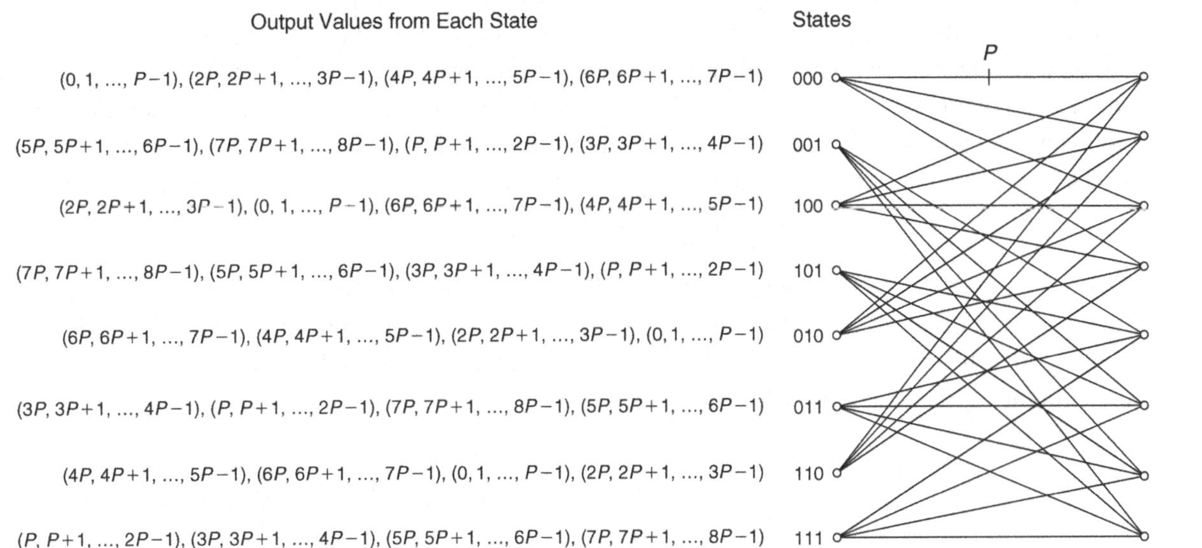

Figure 3.37: Trellis diagram for general TCM rate 2/3 encoder with $K = 4$.

four subsets at level C in Figure 3.35, and the uncoded bit is used to choose one of two points from the selected subset.

The general block diagram of a TCM encoder is shown in Figure 3.36. This general encoder consists of S-state nonsystematic convolutional rate $k/(k+m)$ encoder with constraint length K and outputs $n+k+m$ bits by taking $n+k$ bits as input. Out of $n+k$ input bits, first n bits are uncoded and the rest of k bits are coded to output $k+m$ coded bits. We map the output $n+k+m$ bits of encoder to signal constellation points with the help of the mapper. For particular realization of the encoder with $k = 2, m = 1, S = 8$ and $K = 4$, the steady-state trellis diagram is shown in Figure 3.37. The "n" uncoded bits results in $P = 2^n$ parallel transitions in each branch of trellis. The output values from each state of the trellis are also shown in Figure 3.37.

3.8.2 Coding Gains with TCM

To observe the coding gain (C_{gain}) with TCM, we consider the TCM encoder shown in Figure 3.34 and for a comparison we consider an uncoded system shown in Figure 3.30 with which we transmit 2 bits per symbol by using a 4-PSK modulation scheme. The symbol constellations, considered in this section, are scaled so that the average symbol energy is unity. From the signal constellation of Figure 3.29(a), if the radius of the circle is unity, then the coordinates of points A and B are given by $A{:}(1/\sqrt{2},\ 1/\sqrt{2})$ and $B{:}(-1/\sqrt{2},\ 1/\sqrt{2})$. The minimum Euclidean distance of the constellation is $d^{uc}_{\min}$ (uncoded) $= \sqrt{2}$. Now, consider the TCM scheme shown in Figure 3.36 with $k = m = n = 1$ and $S = 3$. The output bits of the encoder are mapped to symbols in different subsets of the constellation according to the Ungerboeck set partitioning rules. Using set partitioning as shown in Figure 3.35, we assign a set of points (which have the largest minimum distance) at level C to the trellis *parallel paths* (that diverge from a particular state at the current stage and converge to the same state at the next stage, for example the paths of the trellis in Figure 3.34 with output values 0, 1 or 6, 7). We assign a set of points (which have the next largest minimum distance) at level B to the trellis paths that diverge from the same state at the current stage and converge to different states at the next stage (e.g., the paths of the trellis in Figure 3.34 with output values 0, 6 or 0, 7, or 1, 6 or 1, 7). With this mapping procedure, we can satisfy Ungerboeck's set partitioning rules.

The *asymptotic coding gain* for this TCM is given by

$$C_{\text{gain}} = 10\log((d^c_{\text{free}})^2/(d^{un}_{\text{min}})^2)$$

where d^c_{free} is the free Euclidean distance of the trellis, which is defined as the minimum distance between those transition paths which diverge from a state at the current stage and converge to the same state at later stages. This is illustrated in Figure 3.38 with two paths A and B. The two paths A and B diverge from the state zero at one stage and converge to the same zero state again at some other stage. The Euclidean distance with path A is d_2 (as we assigned parallel paths with points that are separated by maximum possible distance), whereas the squared Euclidean distance with path B is $d_1{}^2 + d_0{}^2 + d_1{}^2 = d_0{}^2 + 2d_1{}^2 = d_0{}^2 + d_2{}^2$. Hence, in this case the minimum Euclidean distance separation between paths that diverge from any state and converge to the same state is d_2.

For the TCM scheme considered, the value of d^c_{free} is equal to 2. Therefore, the coding gain is obtained as

$$C_{\text{gain}} = 10\log((d^c_{\text{free}})^2/(d^{un}_{\text{min}})^2) = 10\log(4/2) = 3.01\text{dB}$$

With TCM, we can achieve coding gains of about 2 dB to 6 dB depending on the type of coder used (i.e., the number of states, the amount of redundancy added and the dimensionality of constellations considered) used. An example of 8-state and 16-state rate 2/3 convolutional encoders with corresponding steady-state trellis diagrams are shown in Figure 3.39 and Figure 3.40, respectively.

Figure 3.38: Trellis-free Euclidean distance illustration.

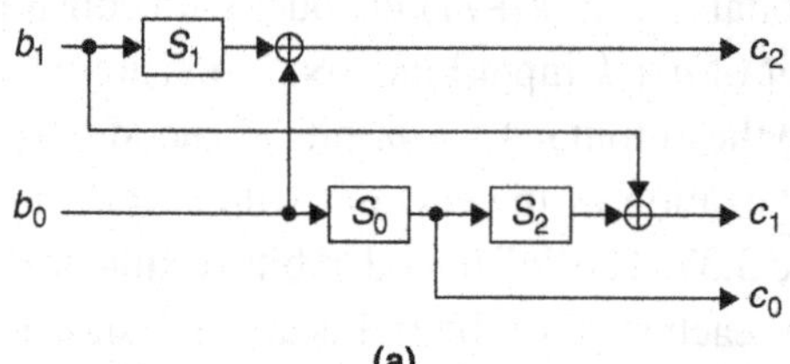

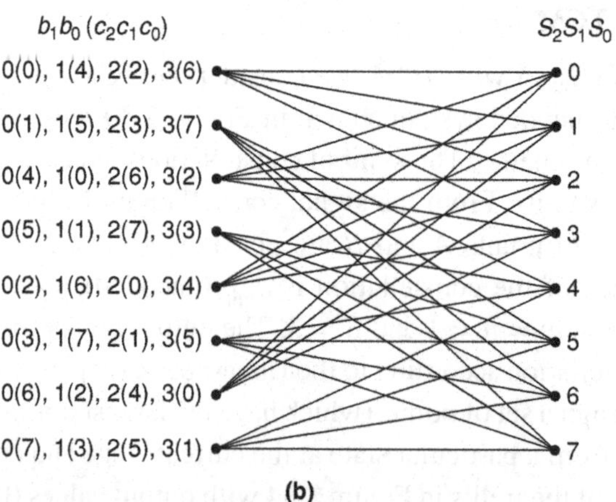

Figure 3.39: 8-state rate 2/3 convolutional coder.

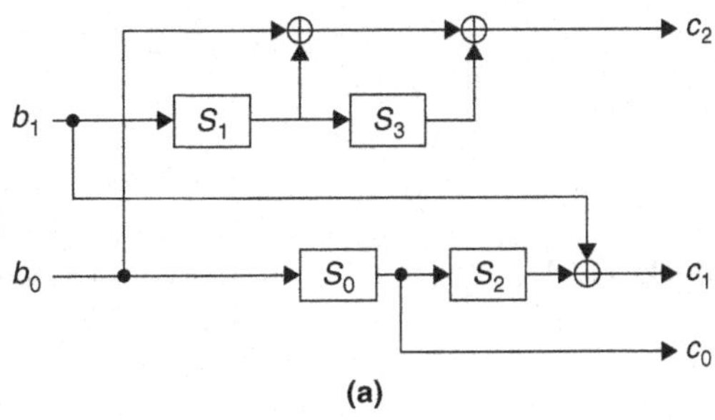

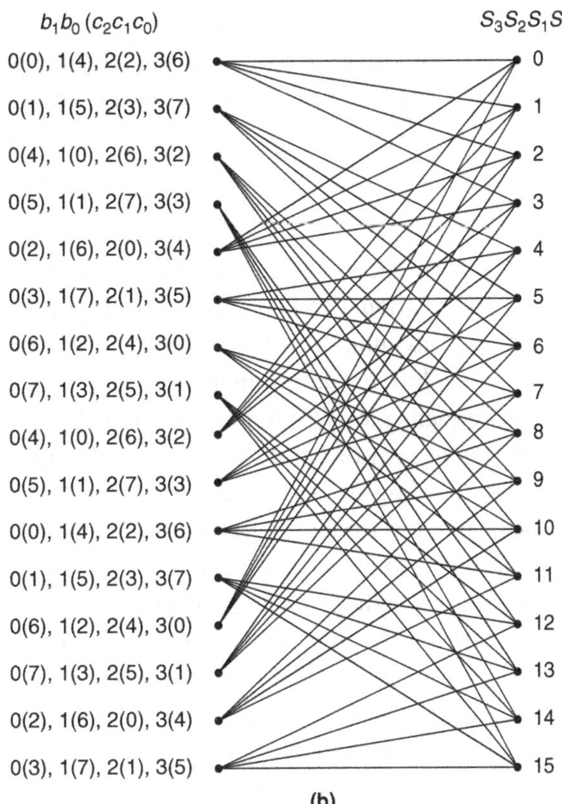

Figure 3.40: 16-state rate 2/3 convolutional coder.

3.8.3 TCM for DMT systems

One application of TCM is an ADSL modem which is based on a DMT (Discrete Multi Tone) system. See Section 9.2.3 for more details on DMT transceiver. Consider a DMT system with N subchannels. Let the number of information bits per symbol in the i-th subchannel be b_i. TCM for DMT can be implemented in two ways—coding separately in each subchannel and coding across the subchannels. In the former case, we perform coding and decoding separately and need $(N/2)+1$ encoders and an equal number of decoders. This means a large amount of hardware when N is large. Also, if the DMT symbol interval is T, then the decoding delay in this case is approximately $5KT$ to $8KT$ where $K = \max(K_i)$ with K_i denoting the constraint length of the i-th subchannel encoder.

Usually, TCM coders used in DMT applications works across the subchannels with a code rate of $b_{\min}/(b_{\min}+1)$, where $b_{\min}$ is the minimum number of bits carried by a subchannel in a DMT block. The remaining $b_i - b_{\min}$ bits, where b_i is the number of bits carried by the i-th subchannel, are uncoded. The TCM across the subchannels encoder for a DMT system is shown in Figure 3.41.

First, $b_{\min}$ bits of b_0 input bits, corresponding to the $0th$ subchannel, are coded into $b_{\min}+1$ bits and the remaining $b_0 - b_{\min}$ bits are passed to the output uncoded. Next the encoder will work on input bits corresponding to the first subchannel, while the input state of the encoder is the output state determined by the input bits of the previous subchannel, that is, $0th$ subchannel. Thus, in general, the state of the encoder, attained after the input

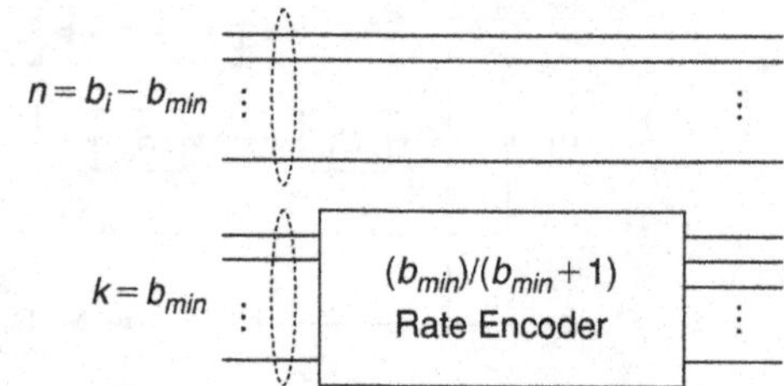

Figure 3.41: Across subchannels TCM encoder for a DMT system.

bits of the i-th subchannel is encoded, becomes the initial state of the encoder for the $(i+1)th$ subchannel. The decoding is performed accordingly. Note that the channel SNR is different from subchannel to subchannel because of the nonflat response of the channel. This may also be due to different noise variances in the subchannels. In such a situation, we have to take the noise variance into consideration at each stage of the trellis while implementing the Viterbi algorithm.

3.9 Viterbi Algorithm

The Viterbi algorithm is an optimum decoding algorithm used for decoding of convolutional codes (see Section 3.7 for more details on convolutional codes) and it has often been served as a standard technique in digital communications systems for maximum likelihood sequence estimation (MLSE). The Viterbi algorithm application area is not limited to convolutional decoding in communications where the algorithm was originally developed. It is used for channel equalization (Viterbi equalizer) in modern communications systems. It also covers diverse applications such as pattern recognition, data storage, and target tracking. In this section, we discuss the Viterbi algorithm and decoding of TCM (see Section 3.8 for more details on TCM) symbols. The simulation and implementation techniques for the Viterbi algorithm are discussed in Chapter 4.

The Viterbi algorithm is commonly expressed in terms of a trellis diagram (which is a time-indexed version of a state diagram). In the convolutional coding, a Viterbi decoder at the receiver follows the trellis used by the transmitter and attempts to estimate the transmitted sequence through the trellis whose distance is closest to the received noisy sequence. In other words, the Viterbi algorithm finds the sequence at a minimum Euclidean distance from the received signal using a transmitter trellis. The sequence computed by the Viterbi algorithm is the global most likely sequence. To compute the global most likely sequence, the Viterbi algorithm first recursively computes the survivor path entering each state. After computing the survivor paths for all states, we select the survivor path with a minimum path metric as the most likely path. We compute in this manner the global most likely path for all symbols of a received sequence. We take this global most likely path and trace back to get the bits of survivor branches. This decoded bits sequence corresponds to an estimate of the transmitted bits sequence.

3.9.1 Maximum Likelihood Sequence Estimation

Assume that an N-length symbol sequence $\boldsymbol{X} = \{x_0, x_1, \ldots, x_{N-1}\}$ is transmitted, where x_j is a symbol from a signal constellation that consists of a finite number of points S with unit average energy. The corresponding N-length received sequence is $\boldsymbol{Y} = \{y_0, y_1, \ldots, y_{N-1}\}$. With an AWGN (additive white Gaussian channel) channel, $y_j = x_j + u_j$, where u_j is a noise sample and it is a zero mean white Gaussian random variable. Let $\boldsymbol{X}^i$ denote an N-length symbol sequence corresponding to the i-th path of the trellis diagram as shown in Figure 3.42 (which corresponds to the TCM encoder shown in Figure 3.34). Then the maximum likelihood (ML) sequence estimate $\boldsymbol{X}^d$ (representing the global most likely sequence) of $\boldsymbol{X}$ is given by

$$\boldsymbol{X}^d = \arg\max\{p(\boldsymbol{Y}/\boldsymbol{X}^i)\} \tag{3.41}$$

where $p(\boldsymbol{Y}/\boldsymbol{X}^i)$ denotes a conditional density function of $\boldsymbol{Y}$ given $\boldsymbol{X}^i$.

Since $y_j = x_j + u_j, \boldsymbol{X}^d$ can be expressed as

$$\boldsymbol{X}^d = \arg\max\{p(\boldsymbol{u} = \boldsymbol{Y} - \boldsymbol{X}^i)\} \tag{3.42}$$

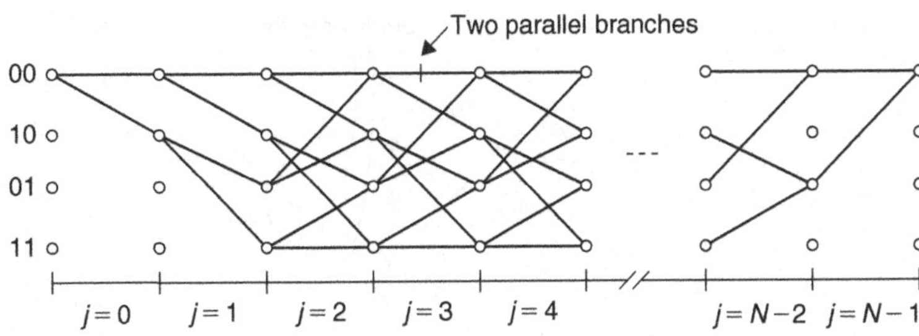

Figure 3.42: Trellis (of encoder shown in Figure 3.34) with *N* stages.

where $\boldsymbol{u}$ is an N-length vector and is a multivariate Gaussian with mutually uncorrelated components which have zero mean and variance $\sigma^2 = E(|u_j|^2)$. The $p(\boldsymbol{u})$ forms a Gaussian probability density function (pdf) as follows:

$$X^d = \arg\max_i \left\{ \prod_j \frac{1}{\sqrt{2\pi}\sigma} \exp\left(-\frac{\left|y_j - x_j^i\right|^2}{2\sigma^2} \right) \right\} \tag{3.43}$$

After observing the Gaussian pdf given in Equation (3.43), the expression for $\boldsymbol{X}^d$ can be simplified by keeping only factors that affect the maximization criterion as

$$X^d = \arg\max_i \left\{ \exp\left(-\frac{1}{2\sigma^2} \sum_j \left|y_j - x_j^i\right|^2 \right) \right\} \tag{3.44}$$

or

$$X^d = \min_i \left\{ \sum_{j=0}^{N-1} \left|y_j - x_j^i\right|^2 \right\} \tag{3.45}$$

3.9.2 Viterbi Algorithm

Using the Viterbi algorithm, we obtain the global most likely sequence $\boldsymbol{X}^d$ as derived in Equation (3.45). In Figure 3.42, each path consists of N stages. Let the branch metric (BM) at the j-th stage for the i-th path be defined as $\text{BM}_{j,i} = |y_j - x_j^i|^2$ where y_j and x_j^i denote the received signal and the transmitted symbol on the i-th path corresponding to the j-th stage of the trellis, respectively. Then the state metric for the i-th path can be defined as $\text{SM}_i = \sum_j |y_j - x_j^i|^2$. The estimate X^d of the transmitted symbol sequence is given by the path with the minimum state metric. The following steps describe the computations present in obtaining the global most likely sequence using the Viterbi algorithm.

1. At stage $j = 0$, set SM to zero for all states.
2. At a node in a stage of $j > 0$, compute BM for all branches entering the node.
3. Add the BM to the present SM for the path ending at the source node of the branch to get a candidate SM for the path ending at the destination node of it. After the candidate SM has been obtained for all branches entering the node, compare them and select only one with the minimum value. Let this corresponding branch survive and delete all other branches to that node from the trellis current stage. This process is shown in Figure 3.43.
4. Return to step 2 for dealing with the next node. If all nodes in the present stage have been processed, go to step 5.
5. If $j < N$, increment j and return to step 2, else go to step 6.
6. Take the path with minimum SM (as the global most likely path) and follow the survivor branches backward through the trellis up to the beginning of the trellis. Now collect the bits corresponding to the survivor branch at all stages of the trellis to form the estimate of the transmitted information bits.

Figure 3.43 corresponds to the encoder shown in the Figure 3.34. Each branch contains two parallel transitions before processing. For the most likely path sequence, the parallel transitions are resolved by selecting the signal

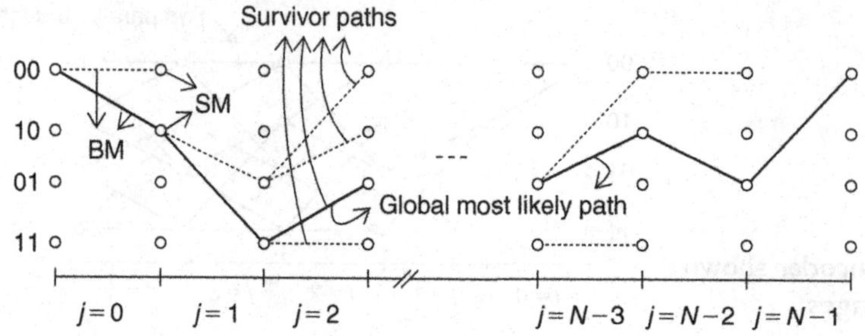

Figure 3.43: Processing of trellis stages in Viterbi decoding.

points closest to the received sequence. The performance of the Viterbi decoder depends on the free distance d^c_{free} of the trellis. $d^c_{\text{free}} = \min(d^c_{\text{parallel}}, d^c_{\text{non-parallel}})$, is the minimum distance between paths, which diverge from a particular node at the present stage and converge to the same node later at some stage. Note that the processing of the trellis results in the solution of the Equation (3.45).

3.10 Turbo Codes

Turbo codes have attracted the research community as well as the industry greatly since their introduction in 1993 because of their remarkable performance. The turbo codes operate near (with SNR gap of 0.7 dB or less) the ultimate limits of capacity of a communication channel (i.e., Shannon channel-capacity limit). Turbo codes were first proposed in Berrou et al. (1993). Turbo codes are constructed using concatenated constituent convolutional coders. In the turbo coding scheme, we generate two or more component codes on different interleaved versions of the same information sequence. On the decoder side, we use SOVA (soft-output Viterbi algorithm) or MAP (maximum a posterior) algorithms to decode the decisions in an iterative manner. The decoding algorithm uses the received data symbols, parity symbols (which correspond to parity bits computed from actual and interleaved versions of data bits) and other decoder soft output information to produce more reliable decisions. In this section, we discuss turbo codes generation and MAP decoding algorithm. We discuss the simulation and implementation techniques for turbo codes in Section 4.5.

Turbo codes gave rebirth to concatenated coding and iterative decoding schemes. In turbo decoding with two component codes, we pass soft decisions from the output of one decoder to the input of a second decoder and iterate this process several times to produce more reliable decisions. The decision-making concept by iterative decoding allows one to explore applications of turbo coding beyond coding theory. One such application is channel equalization. The turbo equalizers overcome the limitations of zero-forcing and decision-feedback equalizers.

The turbo decoding algorithms (e.g., MAP) use both forward and reverse state metrics information and also support iterative decoding using an interleaved priori information generated from the other decoder output's soft information to produce more reliable decisions. With turbo codes, we approach Shannon channel capacity and can achieve an SNR gap below 0.7 dB. Turbo codes perform very well at low SNRs, however these codes suffers from error floor characteristics at high SNRs. Use of a good random interleaver in turbo coding improves the turbo codes' performance to a great extent. Sometimes an RS coder is used as the outer coder along with the turbo coder to overcome the error floor of turbo codes at high SNRs.

Sample Turbo Code Applications

- Mobile radio
- DVB-RCS
- Deep space exploration
- W-CDMA, UMTS (3GPP), CDMA2000 (3GPP2)
- Satellite communication
- DSL

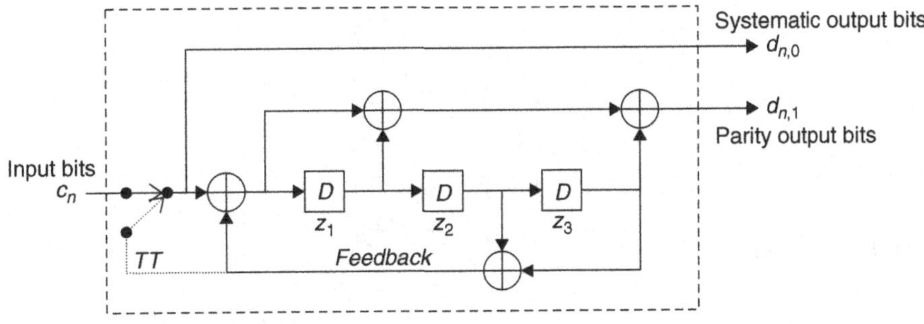

Figure 3.44: Recursive systematic convolutional encoder.

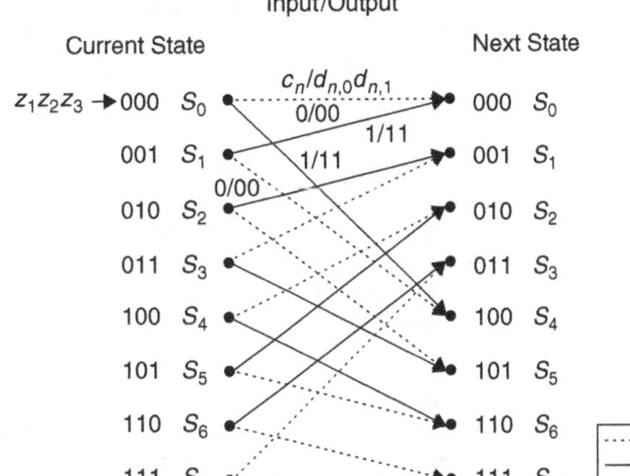

Figure 3.45: Trellis data flow for RSC encoder (of Figure 3.44).

3.10.1 Turbo RSC Encoder

Turbo codes are produced by parallel concatenation of constituent convolutional coders. The encoder can be visualized either as an FIR (finite impulse response) system that produces nonsystematic convolutional (NSC) codes or as an IIR (infinite impulse response) system that produces recursive systematic convolutional (RSC) codes. At any given SNR (signal to noise ratio), for high code rates, RSC codes give better error performance when compared to NSC codes. In this section, we discuss the RSC encoder.

In the RSC encoder shown in Figure 3.44, we continually feed back the intermediate outputs to the encoder's input. The corresponding trellis is shown in Figure 3.45. At any time, we input 1 bit ($c_n = 0$ or 1) and output 2 bits ($d_{n,0}d_{n,1} = 00, 01, 10$ or 11). The code rate (the ratio of the number of input bits to the number of output bits) for this encoder is $^1/_2$. With each input bit, the state of the encoder is updated and the allowed input state (current state) and output state (next state) combinations by the RSC encoder shown in Figure 3.44 are given by the trellis as shown in Figure 3.45. For example, if the encoder is at state "001" and if we input a 0 bit to the RSC encoder, then the output bit (parity bit) and output state of the RSC encoder are "0" and "100," respectively. Due to feedback, the encoder shown in Figure 3.44 produces an infinite bit sequence and we enable a dotted line (TT) at the end of input bit sequence c_n to terminate the trellis by forcing the encoder state to zero.

In turbo coding, we concatenate two such RSC encoders in parallel with an interleaved bit sequence as input to the second encoder as shown in Figure 3.46. From the second encoder, we take only parity information bits ($d_{n,2}$). Therefore, the effective code rate is 1/3 for the turbo encoder shown in Figure 3.46. We transmit the triplet ($d_{n,0}d_{n,1}d_{n,2}$) for each input c_n after multiplexing the output bits of two RSC encoders. The code rate of the encoder may be increased by puncturing the 2-parity bitstreams. For example, 1 parity bit produced from 2 parity bits by puncturing increases the code rate from 1/3 to 1/2. (See Section 4.5 for efficient implementation techniques of the turbo encoder.)

3.10.2 Turbo Decoder

The triplet ($d_{n,0}d_{n,1}d_{n,2}$) obtained from the turbo encoder is passed through a mapper (i.e., a baseband modulator) before transmitting through the channel. With BPSK modulation, we map "0" to "+1" and "1" to "−1." Here, we

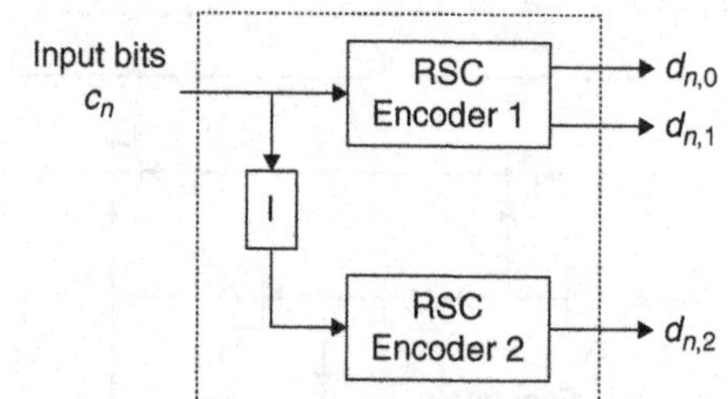

Figure 3.46: Turbo encoder.

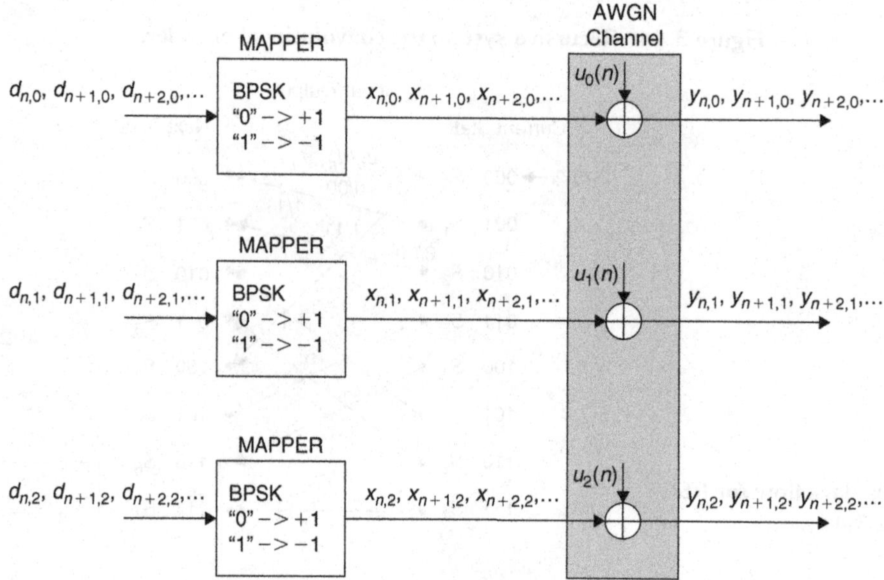

Figure 3.47: Modulator and channel model for transmission.

use the AWGN channel model to mitigate the impairments in a real communication channel because the AWGN model approximates the effect of accumulation of noise components from many sources. Figure 3.47 shows the BPSK modulator along with the AWGN channel. The noise sequences $u_i(n)$ are from i.i.d. (independent and identically distributed) random process with zero mean and variance σ^2.

At the receiver side, we receive a noisy sequence $\ldots, y_{n-1,0}, y_{n-1,1}, y_{n-1,2}, y_{n,0}, y_{n,1}, y_{n,2}, y_{n+1,0}, y_{n+1,1}, y_{n+1,2}, \ldots$ and pass the received noisy symbols to the turbo decoder to get reliable transmitted data symbols as shown in Figure 3.48. Here, we assume that proper synchronization of data symbols (i.e., the boundaries of triplets in the received sequence corresponding to transmitted triplets) are identified properly. After data symbols synchronization, we identify received triplets as $\ldots(y_{n-1,0}, y_{n-1,1}, y_{n-1,2}), (y_{n,0}, y_{n,1}, y_{n,2}), (y_{n+1,0}, y_{n+1,1}, y_{n+1,2})\ldots$. Then we pass *intrinsic information* (systematic bits $[y_{i,0}]$ and first encoder parity bits $[y_{i,1}]$ of the received sequence) to the first decoder along with *extrinsic information*, *Ext*.2 (soft information) from the second decoder. For the first iteration, we use zeros for *Ext*.2 by assuming equiprobability for intrinsic information symbols. After completing decoding with the first decoder, we start a second decoder with *intrinsic information* (interleaved systematic bits, I$[y_{i,0}]$ and second encoder parity bits, $y_{i,2}$) and *extrinsic information*, *Ext*.1 (soft information) from the first decoder as input. This process is repeated many times until we get reliable decisions from the second decoder output. At the end of the iterative decoding, we deinterleave the output of the second decoder (LLRs) to get a transmitted symbol sequence. Then we obtain hard bits by using sign information of output symbols. At the heart of turbo decoding we use a MAP decoder to get the likelihood ratio of received symbols. In the next section we discuss the turbo decoding using the MAP algorithm.

3.10.3 MAP Decoding

In turbo decoding, we use the *maximum a posteriori* (MAP) algorithm to determine the most likely information bit that has been transmitted. In the MAP algorithm, we first obtain *a posteriori probabilities* (APPs) for each

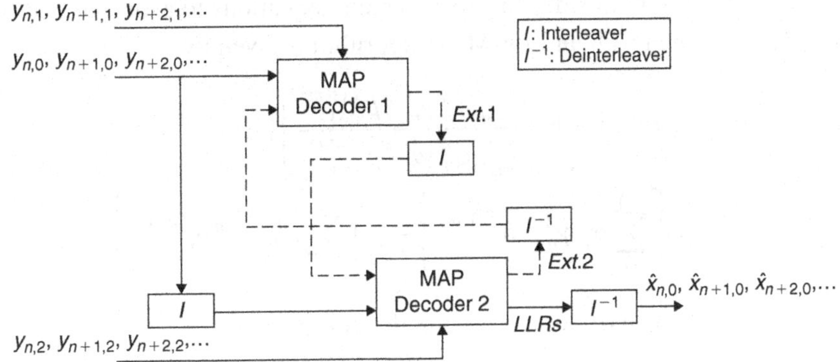

Figure 3.48: Turbo decoder.

transmitted data bit and then to decode a data bit, we assign to the data bit a decision value that corresponds to the maximum a posteriori probability. The MAP algorithm using APPs minimizes the bit error probability (BER) by calculating the likelihood ratio (LR) for every transmitted bit $d_{n,0}(= c_n)$ as follows:

$$\delta_n = LR(c_n) = \frac{P(c_n = 1|Y_1^N)}{P(c_n = 0|Y_1^N)} \tag{3.46}$$

where Y_1^N is the received corrupted data symbol sequence from time $n = 1$ through some time N. If $\delta_n > 1$ then the decoded bit $c_n = 1$ else if $\delta_n < 1$ then the decoded bit $c_n = 0$.

For the RSC (recursive systematic coder) codes with the AWGN channel model, the APP of a transmitted coded bit c_n is equal to the sum of all encoder states joint probabilities.

$$P(c_n = i|Y_1^N) = \sum_m \lambda_n^{i,m}, \quad i = 0, 1 \tag{3.47}$$

where $\lambda_n^{i,m} = P(c_n = i, S_n = m|Y_1^N)$ and S_n is the encoder state at the time n. Therefore,

$$\delta_n = LR(c_n) = \frac{\sum_m \lambda_n^{1,m}}{\sum_m \lambda_n^{0,m}} \tag{3.48}$$

For $1 < n < N$, the sequence Y_1^N can be represented as $Y_1^N = \{Y_1^{n-1}, Y_n, Y_{n+1}^N\}$ and therefore

$$\lambda_n^{i,m} = P(c_n = i, S_n = m|\{Y_1^n, Y_n, Y_{n+1}^N\}) \tag{3.49}$$

Using Bayes' theorem, the Equation (3.49) can be simplified and can be factored into three metrics as follows:

$$\lambda_n^{i,m} = \frac{\alpha_n^m \gamma_n^{i,m} \beta_{n+1}^{f(i,m)}}{P(Y_1^N)} \tag{3.50}$$

where

$\alpha_n^m \cong P(Y_1^{n-1}|S_n = m)$, a forward state metric at time n and state m

$\gamma_n^{i,m} \cong P(c_n = i, S_n = m, Y_n)$, a branch metric at time n and state m

$\beta_{n+1}^{f(i,m)} = P(Y_{n+1}^N|S_{n+1} = f(i,m)$, a reverse state metric at time $n+1$ and state $f(i,m)$, is the next state for a given input bit i and state m.

Then the MAP algorithm is translated to

$$\delta_n = LR(c_n) = \frac{\sum_m \alpha_n^m \gamma_n^{1,m} \beta_{n+1}^{f(1,m)}}{\sum_m \alpha_n^m \gamma_n^{0,m} \beta_{n+1}^{f(0,m)}} \tag{3.51}$$

We take the natural logarithm on both sides for the preceding equations to avoid the multiplications present in computing likelihood ratios. The resultant Log-MAP algorithm is given by

$$\begin{aligned}\bar{\delta}_n = LLR(c_n) &= \ln\left[\frac{\sum_m \alpha_n^m \gamma_n^{1,m} \beta_{n+1}^{f(1,m)}}{\sum_m \alpha_n^m \gamma_n^{0,m} \beta_{n+1}^{f(0,m)}}\right] \\ &= \ln\left[\sum_m \alpha_n^m \gamma_n^{1,m} \beta_{n+1}^{f(1,m)}\right] - \ln\left[\sum_m \alpha_n^m \gamma_n^{0,m} \beta_{n+1}^{f(0,m)}\right]\end{aligned} \tag{3.52}$$

If $\ln(ab) = \ln(a) + \ln(b) = \bar{a} + \bar{b}$, then $ab = e^{\bar{a}+\bar{b}}$. Using this transformation,

$$\bar{\delta}_n = \ln\left(\sum_m e^{\left(\bar{\alpha}_n^m + \bar{\gamma}_n^{1,m} + \bar{\beta}_{n+1}^{f(1,m)}\right)}\right) - \ln\left(\sum_m e^{\left(\bar{\alpha}_n^m + \bar{\gamma}_n^{0,m} + \bar{\beta}_{n+1}^{f(0,m)}\right)}\right) \tag{3.53}$$

where $\bar{\alpha}_n^m$, $\bar{\beta}_{n+1}^{f(1,m)}$, $\bar{\gamma}_n^{1,m}$ and $\bar{\delta}_n$ are logarithms of α_n^m, $\beta_{n+1}^{f(1,m)}$, $\gamma_n^{1,m}$ and δ_n, respectively.

Forward Metric Computation

The forward state metrics $\bar{\alpha}_n^m$ are recursively computed (or updated by accumulation) with the trellis representation of encoder states (at each time instance n) from time $n = 0$ assuming initial values for $\bar{\alpha}_0^m$ as $\bar{\alpha}_0^0 = 0$ and $\bar{\alpha}_0^k = -\infty$, where $1 \le k \le 2^M - 1$ and M is the number of memory units present in one RSC encoder. The forward state metrics $\bar{\alpha}_n^m$ at time n are computed from forward state metrics $\bar{\alpha}_{n-1}^{b(j,m)}$ at time $n-1$ according to

$$e^{\bar{\alpha}_n^m} = e^{\bar{\alpha}_{n-1}^{b(0,m)} + \bar{\gamma}_{n-1}^{0,b(0,m)}} + e^{\bar{\alpha}_{n-1}^{b(1,m)} + \bar{\gamma}_{n-1}^{1,b(1,m)}} \tag{3.54}$$

where $b(j,m)$ corresponds to the previous state (at time $n-1$) connecting to the present state m (at time n) for $j = 0$ and 1.

Reverse Metric Computation

The reverse state metrics $\bar{\beta}_n^m$ are recursively computed (or updated by accumulation) from $n = N+1$ assuming initial values for $\bar{\beta}_{N+1}^m$ as $\bar{\beta}_{N+1}^0 = 0$ and $\bar{\beta}_{N+1}^k = -\infty$, where $1 \le k \le 2^M - 1$. The reverse state metrics $\bar{\beta}_n^m$ at time n are computed from reverse state metrics $\bar{\beta}_{n+1}^{f(j,m)}$ at time $n+1$ using the encoder state trellis as

$$e^{\bar{\beta}_n^m} = e^{\bar{\beta}_{n+1}^{f(0,m)} + \bar{\gamma}_n^{0,m}} + e^{\bar{\beta}_{n+1}^{f(1,m)} + \bar{\gamma}_n^{1,m}} \tag{3.55}$$

Branch Metric Computation

The branch metric $\bar{\gamma}_n^{i,m}$ is computed from its definition as follows:

$$\begin{aligned}\gamma_n^{i,m} &= P(c_n = i, S_n = m, Y_n) \\ &= P(Y_n | c_n = i, S_n = m)\, P(S_n = m | c_n = i)\, P(c_n = i) \\ &= P(Y_n | c_n = i, S_n = m)\, P^a(i), \quad \text{where} \quad P^a(i) = P(S_n = m | c_n = i)\, P(c_n = i) = \frac{1}{2^M} P(c_n = i)\end{aligned}$$

We provide *intrinsic information* (both systematic symbols and parity symbols) to the first decoder as $\{y_{n,0}, y_{n,1}\}$ and for the second decoder as $\{I[y_{n,0}], y_{n,2}\}$. We derive the branch metric for first decoder and the same approach can be used to obtain the branch metric for the second decoder. For the first decoder, $Y_n = \{y_{n,0}, y_{n,1}\}$. Assuming an AWGN channel with noise of zero mean and variance σ^2 and replacing the joint probability with the pdf (probability density function), the metric $\gamma_n^{i,m}$ is computed as

$$\gamma_n^{i,m} = P^a(i) e^{-\frac{(y_{n,0} - x_{n,0}^i)^2 + (y_{n,1} - x_{n,1}^i)^2}{2\sigma^2}} \tag{3.56}$$

Although the right-hand side of Equation (3.56) appears to be independent of state m, actually it is not true—the parity symbols $x_{n,1}^i$ are state dependent.

Extrinsic Information Computation

From log-MAP Equation (3.52),

$$\bar{\delta}_n = LLR(c_n) = \ln\left[\frac{\sum_m \alpha_n^m \gamma_n^{1,m} \beta_{n+1}^{f(1,m)}}{\sum_m \alpha_n^m \gamma_n^{0,m} \beta_{n+1}^{f(0,m)}}\right]$$

$$= \ln\left[\frac{\sum_m \alpha_n^m P^a(1) e^{-\frac{(y_{n,0}-x_{n,0}^1)^2+(y_{n,1}-x_{n,1}^1)^2}{2\sigma^2}} \beta_{n+1}^{f(1,m)}}{\sum_m \alpha_n^m P^a(0) e^{-\frac{(y_{n,0}-x_{n,0}^0)^2+(y_{n,1}-x_{n,1}^0)^2}{2\sigma^2}} \beta_{n+1}^{f(0,m)}}\right]$$

$$= \ln\left[\frac{P^a(1)}{P^a(0)} \frac{e^{-\frac{(y_{n,0}-x_{n,0}^1)^2}{2\sigma^2}}}{e^{-\frac{(y_{n,0}-x_{n,0}^0)^2}{2\sigma^2}}} \frac{\sum_m \alpha_n^m e^{-\frac{(y_{n,1}-x_{n,1}^1)^2}{2\sigma^2}} \beta_{n+1}^{f(1,m)}}{\sum_m \alpha_n^m e^{-\frac{(y_{n,1}-x_{n,1}^0)^2}{2\sigma^2}} \beta_{n+1}^{f(0,m)}}\right]$$

$$= \ln\left[\frac{P^a(1)}{P^a(0)}\right] + \ln\left[e^{\frac{4y_{n,0}}{2\sigma^2}}\right] + \ln\left[\frac{\sum_m \alpha_n^m e^{-\frac{(y_{n,1}-x_{n,1}^1)^2}{2\sigma^2}} \beta_{n+1}^{f(1,m)}}{\sum_m \alpha_n^m e^{-\frac{(y_{n,1}-x_{n,1}^0)^2}{2\sigma^2}} \beta_{n+1}^{f(0,m)}}\right]$$

$$LLR(c_n) = L_{1e} + 2\frac{y_{n,0}}{\sigma^2} + L_{2e}$$

where $L_{1e} = \frac{P^a(1)}{P^a(0)}$ is the input *a priori* probability ratio, L_{2e} is the output extrinsic information (or *a priori* information for the second decoder to minimize the probability of decoding error within an iterative decoding framework). This extrinsic information is computed from the likelihood ratio as

$$L_{2e} = LLR(c_n) - L_{1e} - 2\frac{y_{n,0}}{\sigma^2} \tag{3.57}$$

See Section 4.5 for simulation and implementation techniques of turbo codes.

3.10.4 Interleaver

In general, the purpose of the interleaver is to spread burst errors (which occur due to lightning or switching interference) across the entire received data sequence. First, we understand the importance of the interleaver in the case of block codes' (e.g., RS codes) performance. RS codes, discussed in Section 3.6, can correct up to T errors in a block of N data elements. If we assume that the received k-th block has zero errors and $(k+1)$th block has $L(>T)$ errors, then the RS decoder does nothing in the k-th block and cannot correct errors of $(k+1)$th block as it has more than T errors. In Figure 3.49, we considered two RS codewords for $N = 15$, $K = 7$ and $T = 4$ to illustrate the purpose of the interleaver. We can see in Figure 3.49 how we overcome this problem by interleaving the codewords at the transmitter and by spreading (or by deinterleaving) the errors at the receiver. In both X (without interleaver) and Y (with interleaver) schemes, we assume that the errors have occurred at the same positions in a data frame after the transmission. The interleaver shown in Figure 3.49 is a simple two-element-depth matrix interleaver. In practice, the data is handled in terms of data frames with hundreds of elements. We have to interleave total data frame elements at one time and that is why the matrix dimension is usually very large. In a simple interleaver, we fill the matrix of size $P \times Q$ in row-wise and read in column-wise. In the case of the deinterleaver, we fill the matrix column-wise and read the elements row-wise as shown in Figure 3.50.

If we do not have sufficient elements to fill the matrix of $P \times Q$, we fill the rest of the matrix with zeros as shown in Figure 3.50. In general, after filling the matrix row-wise and before reading the matrix column-wise, we randomize the matrix row and column elements to get random data elements. The concept of interleaving reflects

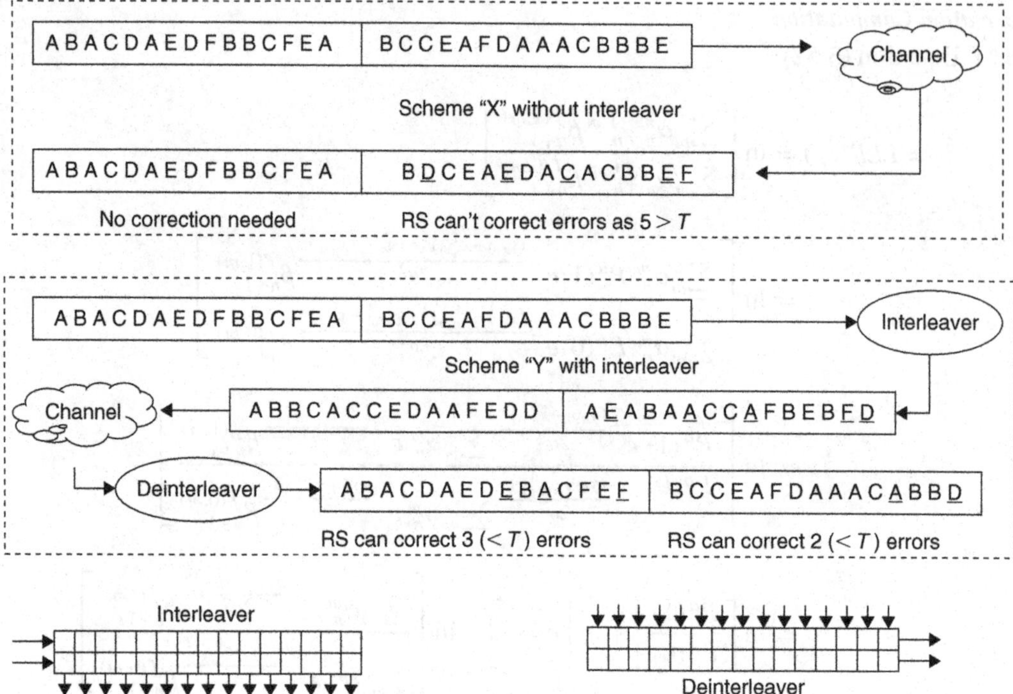

Figure 3.49: Interleaver purpose illustration.

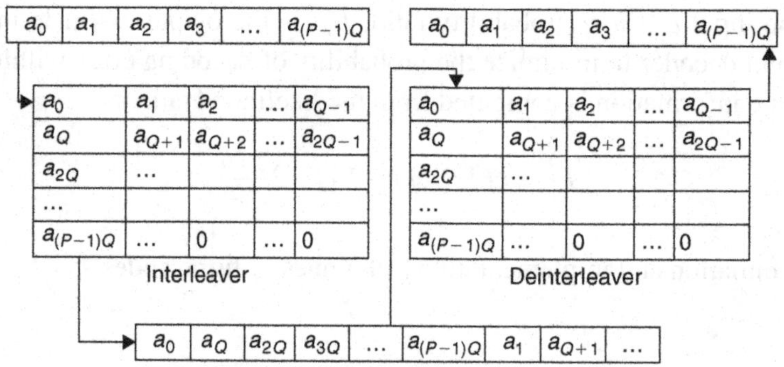

Figure 3.50: Interleaver and de-interleaver.

the Shannon view of random and very long complex codes which can approach channel capacity. Shannon (1948) showed that as the length of code approaches infinity, the random codes achieve channel capacity. Although we work (i.e., encoding or decoding) on a small block of data elements at a time within a data frame, because of interleaving, the dimension of codes increases to the size of the data frame. By permuting the elements in rows and columns of the matrix, we obtain random codes. The interleaver requires a large amount of data memory and introduces delay in the communications system.

In Figure 3.49, we see the effect of the interleaver on the block codes' (e.g., RS codes) performance. We see how the interleaver improves the performance of convolutional codes (e.g., turbo codes). With simple convolutional decoding (e.g., using trellis codes with Viterbi decoding), we know that the decoding converges after 6K stages (where K is a constraint length of coder). If a burst of errors (of order of 6K length) occurs in a particular coded data block, then we never converge in that particular region at the time of decoding of the coded sequence. With turbo codes using an iterative MAP decoder, by performing interleaving and deinterleaving of data, the decoding process converges after a few iterations (as we spread burst errors across the entire data frame). We output more reliable decisions with increased number of iterations. In practice, we iterate between 6 to 18 times. See Section 4.5, for simulation of the turbo RSC encoder and the MAP decoder.

3.11 LDPC Codes

Low-density parity check (LDPC) codes, introduced by Gallager (1963), are linear block codes defined by sparse parity check matrices. These efficient error control codes have attracted a lot of attention due to (1) their remarkable bit error rate (BER) versus signal-to-noise ratio (SNR) performance, and (2) availability of elegant decoding schemes. LDPC codes with larger frame lengths can perform within 0.0045 dB of the Shannon limit. Like turbo codes, LDPC codes are also decoded iteratively. The following table summarizes coding differences between turbo codes and LDPC codes.

Turbo Codes	LDPC Codes
Generated with convolutional codes	Generated with block codes
Use trellis representation for decoding	Use graphical representation for decoding
Use MAP algorithm for decoding	Use sum-product algorithm for decoding
On average require 8 iterations	On average require 30 iterations
Decoding complexity per iteration is high	Decoding complexity per iteration is low

3.11.1 Graphical Representation of Parity Check Matrix

As we discussed in Section 3.3, linear block codes are defined by parity-check matrix H. An $M \times N$ parity-check matrix H defines a linear block code of length N, where each codeword $C = [c_0 c_1 c_2 \ldots c_{N-1}]$ satisfies M parity check equations. The parity-check matrix can also be represented using a Tanner graph (which is a bipartite graph with two types of nodes). One set of nodes called parity (or check) nodes represents the parity check constraints and the other set of nodes called bit (or variable) nodes represents the codeword bits as shown in Figure 3.51. The edge connections between bit nodes and parity nodes are defined based on H matrix elements, $h_{ji} \in \{0, 1\}$. If $h_{ji} = 1$, then a bit node b_i (corresponding to column i in H) is connected to the parity node p_j (corresponding to row j in H). Thus, each edge in the Tanner graph represents an entry of H that is equal to 1. With the bipartite graph, the nodes of the same type cannot be connected (i.e., a bit node cannot be connected to another bit node). All bit nodes connected to a particular parity node must sum (modulo-2) to zero.

A cycle of length L in a Tanner graph is a path of L distant edges, which closes on itself. One such cycle of length $L = 4$ is shown **with dark edges** in Figure 3.51. The shortest possible cycle in a Tanner graph has length 4. The presence of short cycles in a Tanner graph limits the decoding performance of graph codes such as the LDPC code. We avoid the presence of short cycles (especially of length $L = 4$) in designing of parity check matrices for Tanner graph codes.

We consider a parity check matrix $H_{4\times 7}$ as given in Equation (3.58) to work with an example graph code. The corresponding Tanner graph is shown in Figure 3.52. The number of parity nodes in a Tanner graph is equal to the number of rows of a parity check matrix and the number of bit nodes is equal to the number of columns of parity check matrix.

$$H_{4\times 7} = \begin{bmatrix} 1 & 0 & 1 & 0 & 0 & 1 & 1 \\ 0 & 0 & 1 & 1 & 1 & 0 & 0 \\ 1 & 1 & 0 & 0 & 0 & 1 & 0 \\ 0 & 1 & 0 & 1 & 1 & 0 & 1 \end{bmatrix} \tag{3.58}$$

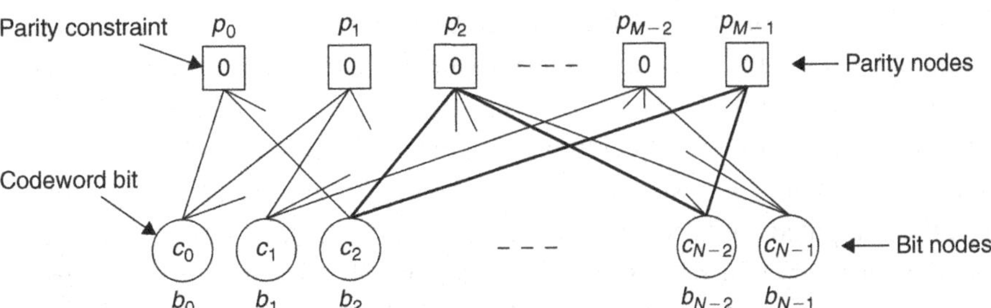

Figure 3.51: Graphical representation of parity-check matrix *H*.

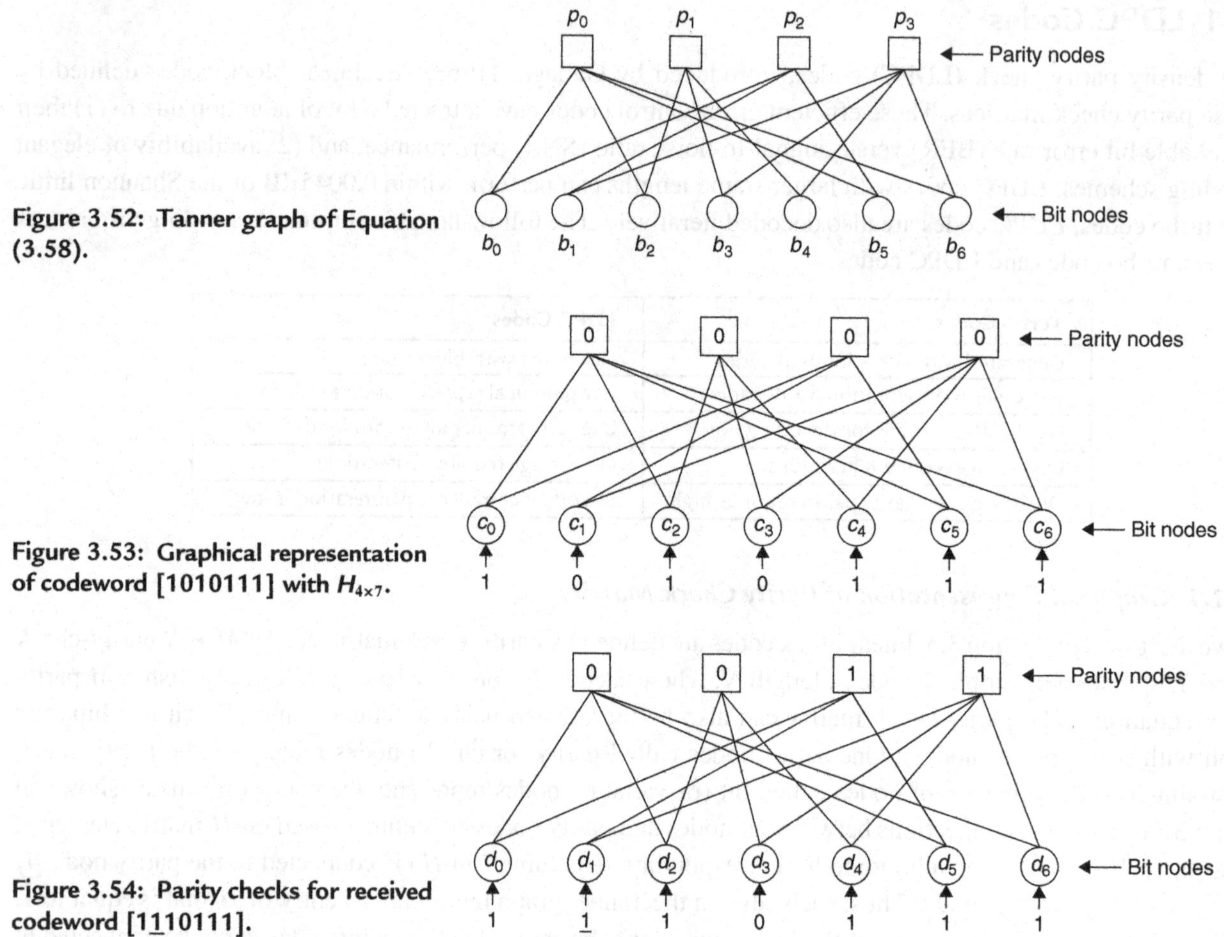

Figure 3.52: Tanner graph of Equation (3.58).

Figure 3.53: Graphical representation of codeword [1010111] with $H_{4\times7}$.

Figure 3.54: Parity checks for received codeword [1$\underline{1}$10111].

Decoding Hard-Decision Channel Output: Bit-Flip Algorithm

Before discussing the practically used graph codes, we work with a simple hard-decision decoding example to understand the graph codes a bit more. With the parity check matrix H given in Equation (3.58), the encoded codeword C for the input message vector $M = [101]$ is computed as $C = [c_0c_1c_2 \ldots c_6] = [1010111]$. Usually, to get an encoded codeword, we multiply the message vector M with a generator matrix G, which is obtained from the parity check matrix H. We can verify that the parity check constraint of H is satisfied (i.e., the modulo-2 sum of all bit nodes connected to any particular parity node is zero) for the codeword [1010111] as shown in Figure 3.53.

Assume that the received data (hard-decision channel output) after transmitting through a noise channel is $D = [d_0d_1d_2 \ldots d_6] = [1\underline{1}10111]$. There is a 1-bit error (highlighted with an underscore) in the received data. With this, we will have some parity nodes that do not satisfy the parity constraint as shown in Figure 3.54. We use the bit-flip algorithm to correct the error bit in the received codeword by passing the message bits between bit nodes and parity nodes.

With the bit-flip algorithm, we flip the bit values passing from a parity node (p_i) to bit nodes (b_i) whenever the parity constraint (i.e., modulo-2 sum of inputs is equal to zero) at that parity node is not satisfied. To better understand the bit-flip algorithm for the decoding of a codeword using Figure 3.54, we tabulate the values of message bits passed from bit nodes (b_i) to parity nodes (p_i) and parity nodes (p_i) to bit nodes (b_i) as in Tables 3.2 and 3.3. In Table 3.2, we use the received hard-decision bits to pass from bit nodes to parity nodes. The computed parity for the received bits is given in the right column of Table 3.2. If all received bits are error free, then we get the computed parity as zero. In our case, we get some non-zero parity bits as the received bits contain one error. In the last two rows, the computed parity bits are not zero and it means that the error bit is present in those two rows. As we do not know in reality which bit is in error, we tentatively pass the flipped bits from the parity nodes, at which the parity constraint is not satisfied, to the bits nodes by assuming the message bit from the current bit node is in error and the bits from the other bit nodes are error free. In Table 3.3, the bits that are flipped at

Table 3.2: Message bits passing from bit nodes to parity nodes

Message passing from bit nodes to parity nodes				Parity constraint
$b_0 \rightarrow p_0$ 1	$b_2 \rightarrow p_0$ 1	$b_5 \rightarrow p_0$ 1	$b_6 \rightarrow p_0$ 1	0
$b_2 \rightarrow p_1$ 1	$b_3 \rightarrow p_1$ 0	$b_4 \rightarrow p_1$ 1		0
$b_0 \rightarrow p_2$ 1	$b_1 \rightarrow p_2$ 1	$b_5 \rightarrow p_2$ 1		1
$b_1 \rightarrow p_3$ 1	$b_3 \rightarrow p_3$ 0	$b_4 \rightarrow p_3$ 1	$b_6 \rightarrow p_3$ 1	1

Table 3.3: Message bits passing from parity nodes to bit nodes

Message passing from parity nodes to bit nodes		Received bit	Decoded bit
$p_0 \rightarrow b_0$ 1	$p_2 \rightarrow b_0$ **0**	1	1
$p_2 \rightarrow b_1$ **0**	$p_3 \rightarrow b_1$ 0	1	0 ← Corrected
$p_0 \rightarrow b_2$ 1	$p_1 \rightarrow b_2$ 1	1	1
$p_1 \rightarrow b_3$ 0	$p_3 \rightarrow b_3$ **1**	0	0
$p_1 \rightarrow b_4$ 1	$p_3 \rightarrow b_4$ **0**	1	1
$p_0 \rightarrow b_5$ 1	$p_2 \rightarrow b_5$ **0**	1	1
$p_0 \rightarrow b_6$ 1	$p_3 \rightarrow b_6$ **0**	1	1

the time of passing from parity nodes to bit nodes are highlighted with bold letters. Then we decode the bits at bit nodes with the majority vote criterion using bits from parity nodes and the received bit for that bit node. The decoded bits are shown in the right-most column of Table 3.3 and the error bit is corrected with the bit-flip algorithm.

With hard decisions as the input to the graph code as shown in Figure 3.54, it is difficult to correct more than one error per codeword with the given parity check matrix $H_{4\times7}$. In the later sections, we introduce a sum-product algorithm (which can take soft decisions as input) to decode graph codes and with that we correct more than a 1-bit error per codeword using the same $H_{4\times7}$ parity check matrix.

3.11.2 LDPC Encoder

Since the LDPC codes are block codes defined by parity check matrix $H_{M\times N}$ like any other block codes, we can compute the LDPC encoder codeword vector for the given message vector by simply multiplying the message vector with the generator matrix G, which is derived from the parity check matrix H. However, to achieve bit-error rate performance with LDPC codes close to the channel capacity, we require a codeword of a size in the order of thousands of bits. The matrix multiplication for that big codeword size demands huge memory and computational requirements. Also, generating the parity check matrices of that order is not a simple task. Due to this reason and due to the lack of linear time decoding algorithms in earlier times, the LDPC codes were forgotten for decades.

With the recent developments in semiconductor technology, deterministic ways of computing the large parity check matrices, and the introduction of polynomial time decoding algorithms for LDPC codes (e.g., the sum-product algorithm), LDPC codes were rediscovered in the late 1990s. Since then LDPC codes have gained momentum, and these codes were also recently embedded in a few standards such as WiMax, 802.16e, and DVB. In the WiMax standard, the parity check matrices are compactly represented with a few elements for storing. Since the parity check matrix H of LDPC code is a sparse (or low in density) binary matrix, it can be represented with small size zero matrices and permutations of an identity matrix as in 802.16e. The WiMax standard describes the way to uncompress the compact base parity check matrix to get actual parity matrix and also describes how to encode the lengthy codewords using small message blocks without computing the generator matrix G from the parity check matrix H. Refer to the 802.16e standard for more details on implementing the LDPC encoder for practical applications.

The number of 1s participating in any parity bit generation of the LDPC code is very small due to the low density of ones present in the parity check matrix H. Let w_r be the weight of j-th row, then the number of 1s participating in j-th parity bit generation is w_r (here the weight of a binary vector is defined as the number of 1s present in it). Similarly, the i-th column weight w_c gives the number of parity constraints which depends on the i-th message bit. The LDPC codes are of two types: *regular* and *irregular*. If the row weights w_r and the column weights w_c are uniform (or are almost uniform), then we call such code regular LDPC code; otherwise, we call the irregular LDPC. Usually, irregular LDPC codes perform better than regular LDPC codes. In this chapter, we concentrate on the regular LDPC codes. To generate a regular LDPC code, a small ($\geq$3) column weight w_c is selected first and values for N (the block length) and M (the redundancy length) are selected. Then an $M \times N$ matrix H is generated, which has weight w_c in each column and weight w_r in each row. To get a uniform row of weight w_r, we have to satisfy $w_c N = w_r M$. One more important characteristic of regular LDPC code is that the minimum distance of the code increases linearly with N provided that $w_c > 3$.

3.11.3 LDPC Decoder

In this section, we discuss the sum-product algorithm, a practically usable soft-decision decoding algorithm for LDPC codes. Like the bit-flip algorithm discussed in Section 3.11.1, the sum-product algorithm uses the concept of message passing or belief propagation between bit nodes and parity nodes in an iterative manner. The advantage of the sum-product algorithm is that it can accept soft values and thus we do not pass the message hard-decision bits between nodes in the sum-product algorithm, instead we pass the message reliability information between bit nodes and parity nodes. As we iterate the sum-product algorithm more and more using the Tanner graph, the reliability of soft information (called *a posteriori* probability) will improve with the iteration count.

Suppose that an encoded LDPC codeword $C = [c_0 c_1 c_2 \ldots c_{N-1}]$ is modulated using the binary phase shift keying (BPSK) modulation and let $X = [x_0 x_1 x_2 \ldots x_{N-1}]$ be the resultant message symbol vector after BPSK modulation. With BPSK, we map codeword bit "0" to symbol "1" and codeword bit "1" to symbol "−1." Then this BPSK symbol vector X is transmitted through an AWGN channel, and $Y = [y_0 y_1 y_2 \ldots y_{N-1}]$ is the corresponding received symbols. Assume that the codewords (Y_j) and symbols (y_i) are properly synchronized before passing to the LDPC decoder.

3.11.4 Sum-Product Algorithm

At the receiver, we use the sum-product algorithm to decode the LDPC codeword. The ultimate goal of the sum-product algorithm is to find the LLR of the encoded bit c_i, which is defined as

$$LLR_i = \text{Log}\left[\frac{P(c_i = 1)/Y_0^{N-1}}{P(c_i = 0)/Y_0^{N-1}}\right], \quad Y_0^{N-1} = [y_0, y_1, y_2, \ldots y_{N-1}] \tag{3.59}$$

Then we make the hard decision to get the decoded bit $\hat{c}_i$ as follows:

$$\hat{c}_i = \begin{cases} 1 & \text{if } LLR_i < 0 \\ 0 & \text{otherwise} \end{cases} \tag{3.60}$$

Here, we do not provide complete derivations for the sum-product algorithm; instead we will use the final metrics computation equations to work with the sum-product algorithm. For full derivations of LDPC decoding equations and sum-product algorithms, Gallager (1963) and MacKay (1999) are recommended. We use the following notations for the sum-product algorithm:

Q_{ij} = Extrinsic information to be passed from bit node i to parity node j
R_{ji} = Extrinsic information to be passed from parity node j to bit node i
$U_i = \{j$ such that $h_{ji} = 1\}$, the set of row locations of the 1s in the i-th column

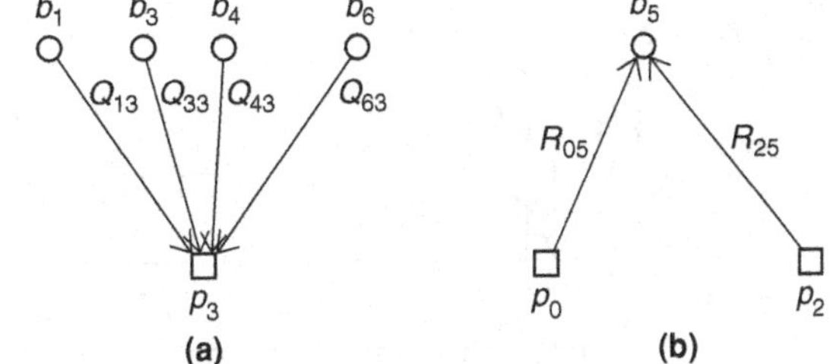

**Figure 3.55: (a) Connections to third parity node from 4-bit nodes.
(b) Connections to 5th-bit node from two parity nodes.**

$U_{i\backslash a} = U_i - \{a\}$, the set of row locations of the 1s in the i-th column excluding the a-th row
$V_j = \{i$ such that $h_{ji} = 1\}$, the set of column locations of 1s in the j-th row
$V_{j\backslash b} = V_j - \{b\}$, the set of column locations of the 1s in the j-th row excluding b-th column
$\alpha_{ij} = \text{sign}(Q_{ij})$, sign of Q_{ij}
$\beta_{ij} = |Q_{ij}|$, magnitude of Q_{ij}
$\phi(x) = -\log[\tanh(x/2)] = \log\left[\frac{e^x+1}{e^x-1}\right] = \phi^{-1}(x)$
$\lambda_i = 2y_i/\sigma^2$, the channel *a posteriori* probabilities (APPs)

From Figure 3.55 and Example 3.21, we understand the previous notations with illustrations and examples. For this, we use the parity check matrix in Equation (3.58), and we consider the 5th-bit node connecting to two parity nodes and the third parity node connecting to 4-bit nodes as shown in Figure 3.55.

Example 3.21

The set of row locations with 1s in the 5th column of H is $U_5 = \{0, 2\}$ and the set of columns with 1s in the 3rd row of H is $V_3 = \{1, 3, 4, 6\}$ as highlighted in Figure 3.56.

$$\begin{array}{c} \longrightarrow i \\ \begin{array}{ccccccc} 0 & 1 & 2 & 3 & 4 & 5 & 6 \end{array} \end{array}$$

$$H = \begin{bmatrix} 1 & 0 & 1 & 0 & 0 & 1 & 1 \\ 0 & 0 & 1 & 1 & 1 & 0 & 0 \\ 1 & 1 & 0 & 0 & 0 & 1 & 0 \\ 0 & 1 & 0 & 1 & 1 & 0 & 1 \end{bmatrix} \begin{array}{c} 0 \\ 1 \\ 2 \\ 3 \end{array} \downarrow j$$

Figure 3.56: Parity check matrix illustrating the node connections of Figure 3.55.

■

Then

$$U_{5\backslash 0} = U_5 - \{0\} = \{2\}, U_{5\backslash 2} = U_5 - \{2\} = \{0\}$$

$$V_{3\backslash 1} = V_3 - \{1\} = \{3, 4, 6\}, V_{3\backslash 3} = V_3 - \{3\} = \{1, 4, 6\}, \text{ and so on.}$$

We initialize $Q_{ij} = \lambda_i$ at the start of the sum-product algorithm. After some manipulations, the Equation (3.59) using the Tanner graph is computed as

$$LLR_i = \lambda_i + \sum_{j \in U_i} R_{ji} \tag{3.61}$$

The extrinsic information R_{ji} is computed as

$$R_{ji} = \left(\prod_{i' \in V_{j\backslash i}} \alpha_{i'j} \right) \phi \left(\sum_{i' \in V_{j\backslash i}} \phi\left(\beta_{i'j}\right) \right) \tag{3.62}$$

The sum-product algorithm is iterated many times to converge the LLR_i values to true APPs, and the single iteration involves computation of Q_{ij} at bit nodes, R_{ji} at parity nodes and LLR_i at end of each iteration. The

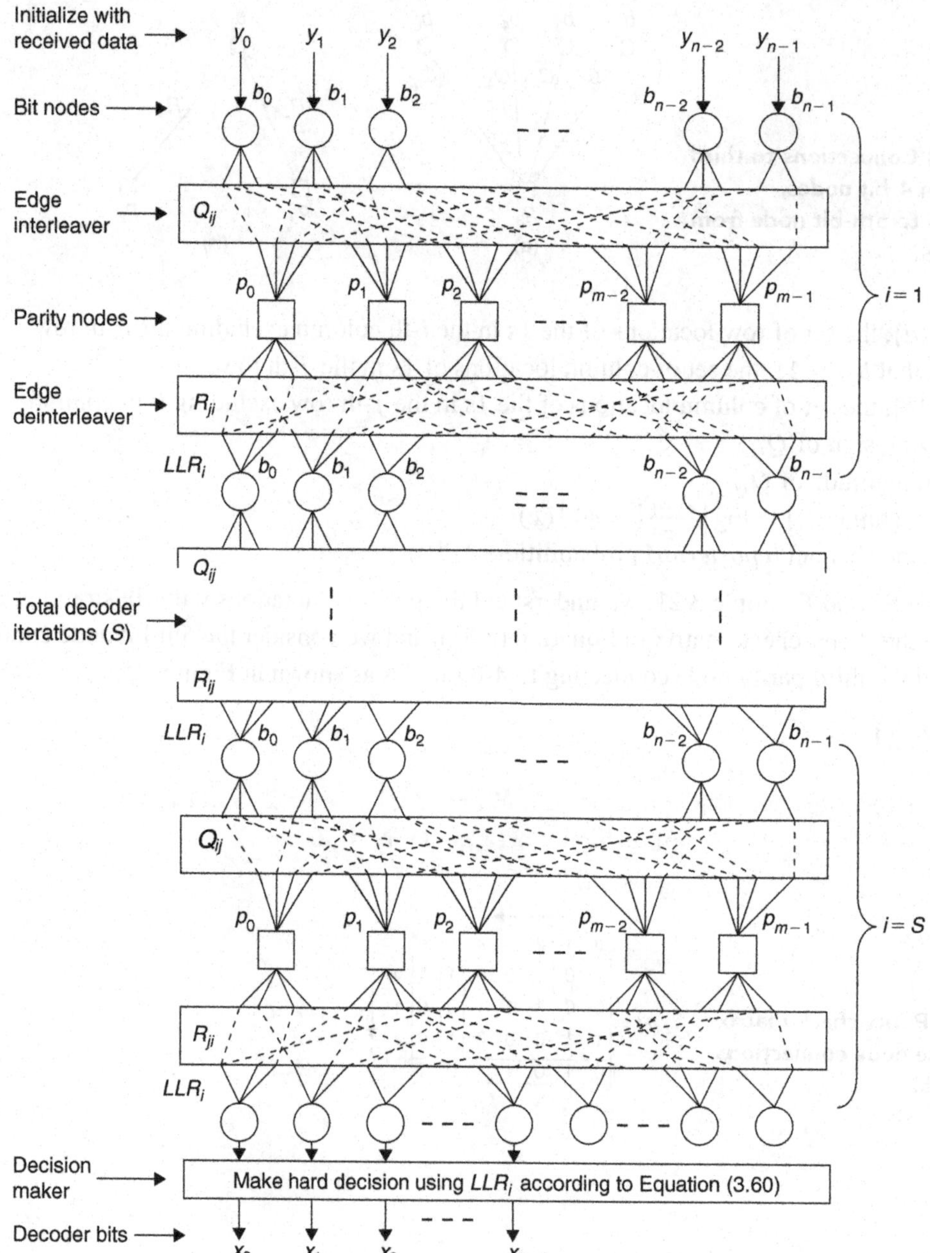

Figure 3.57: Data flow diagram of multi-iteration LDPC decoder.

extrinsic information Q_{ij} to be passed from bit nodes to parity nodes is updated in subsequent iterations as follows:

$$Q_{ij} = LLR_i - R_{ji} \tag{3.63}$$

An S-iteration LDPC decoding with the sum-product algorithm using an unrolled Tanner graph is illustrated in Figure 3.57. All bit nodes are initialized with received data symbols y_i. The channel APPs λ_i are computed from y_i. At the start of iterative decoding, the Q_{ij} values are initialized with λ_i for all j wherever $h_{ji} = 1$. Then we compute R_{ji}s using Equation (3.62) and LLR_is using Equation (3.61). These steps account for the first iteration.

In the subsequent iterations, we use Equations (3.63), (3.62), and (3.61) to compute Q_{ij}, R_{ji} and LLR_i. In any iteration, we compute Q_{ij} at the bit nodes and pass it to the connected parity nodes; then we compute R_{ij} at the parity nodes and pass it to the connected bit nodes; next we update LLR_i at every bit node and this completes a single iteration of the sum-product algorithm. If the Tanner graph contains zero cycles, then LLR_is converges to true APPs as the number of iterations tends to infinity. However, in practice we halt the sum-product algorithm if any one of the following conditions is satisfied:

Halt if $\hat{c}H^T = 0$ (this requires computation of $\hat{c}$ at the end of each iteration), or
Halt if the maximum number of iterations (S) is reached

Unlike the turbo coder, the LDPC coder does not have an external interleaver for randomization of messages. However, the edge connections from bit nodes to parity nodes act as interleaving of extrinsic information (i.e., Q_{ij}'s) passed from bit nodes to parity nodes and the edge connections from parity nodes to bit nodes act as deinterleaving of extrinsic information (i.e., R_{ji}'s) passed from parity nodes to bit nodes and vice versa.

3.11.5 Min-Sum Algorithm

The sum-product algorithm is computationally expensive as it involves of the processing of nonlinear function $\phi(.)$. For this reason, we use the min-sum algorithm (which is an approximation of the sum-product algorithm) in practical LDPC decoders. As the nonlinear function $\phi(.)$ is a hyperbolic self-inverse function, we can approximate the sum-product algorithm as follows:

$$\phi\left(\sum_{i'} \phi\left(\beta_{i'j}\right)\right) \approx \phi\left(\phi\left(\min_{i'} \beta_{i'j}\right)\right) = \min_{i'} \beta_{i'j} \tag{3.64}$$

Using the approximation in Equation (3.64), we can approximate the computationally expensive metric R_{ji} computation as

$$R_{ji} = \left(\prod_{i' \in V_{j} \backslash i} \alpha_{i'j}\right) \min_{i' \in V_{j} \backslash i} \beta_{i'j} \tag{3.65}$$

To avoid the biased estimate of R_{ji} in Equation (3.65), we multiply the Equation (3.65) with a constant k, where $k < 1$.

$$R_{ji} = k\left(\prod_{i' \in V_{j} \backslash i} \alpha_{i'j}\right) \min_{i' \in V_{j} \backslash i} \beta_{i'j} \tag{3.66}$$

The computation of R_{ji} using Equation (3.66) involves the computation of a minimum of magnitudes and the XOR of sign information. This greatly reduces the complexity of the sum-product algorithm. The performance loss due to the approximation is about 0.2 dB, which is acceptable for practical applications. The c-simulation of the min-sum algorithm is presented in Section 4.6.

3.11.6 Simulation Results

We use the same parity check matrix H given in Equation (3.58) to work with the min-sum algorithm for decoding the LDPC codeword. We consider the same codeword used with the bit-flip algorithm, that is, $C = [1010111]$. The BPSK modulated symbols of codeword C are $X = [-1, 1, -1, 1, -1, -1, -1]$. We pass the BPSK modulated symbols through an AWGN channel with noise variance $\sigma^2 = 1$. At the receiver we decode the message bits with the min-sum algorithm using received noisy symbols for four test cases with corresponding hard decisions containing 1-, 2-, 3-, and 4-bit errors. If we look at the soft values of the corresponding hard-decision bits that are in error, those soft values are nearer to zero with a flip of sign in all four cases. In terms of probability, their probability is around 0.5 indicating that they have equal chances to become 0 or 1. The value for constant k in Equation (3.60) is chosen as 0.8 (for better performance results k is chosen between 0.8 and 0.9). In all four cases, we present the first few iterations and the last iteration outputs. We stop the decoding if the hard decisions contain no errors at the end of any particular iteration or if the maximum iteration counts of $S = 10$ is reached.

Case 1: One-bit error in hard decisions of channel output—Let the received noisy vector $Y = [-0.85, -0.05, -0.91, +0.88, -0.79, -0.90, -0.81]$ and the corresponding hard-decision vector $D = [1\underline{1}10111]$. The error bit is highlighted with underscoring.

Initialization and First Iteration

Channel APPs:

$$\lambda_i = [-1.70, -0.1, -1.82, 1.76, -1.58, -1.80, -1.62]$$

Extrinsic information passed from bit nodes to parity nodes:

$$Q_{ij} = \begin{bmatrix} -1.70 & 0 & -1.82 & 0 & 0 & -1.80 & -1.62 \\ 0 & 0 & -1.82 & 1.76 & -1.58 & 0 & 0 \\ -1.70 & -0.10 & 0 & 0 & 0 & -1.80 & 0 \\ 0 & -0.1 & 0 & 1.76 & -1.58 & 0 & -1.62 \end{bmatrix}$$

Extrinsic information passed from parity nodes to bit nodes:

$$R_{ji} = \begin{bmatrix} -1.30 & 0 & -1.30 & 0 & 0 & -1.30 & -1.36 \\ 0 & 0 & -1.26 & 1.26 & -1.41 & 0 & 0 \\ 0.08 & 1.36 & 0 & 0 & 0 & 0.08 & 0 \\ 0 & 1.26 & 0 & -0.08 & 0.08 & 0 & 0.08 \end{bmatrix}$$

Updated LLRs for transmitted message bits:

$$LLR_i = [-2.91, 2.52, -4.38, 2.94, -2.908, -3.02, -2.9]$$

Hard-decision output:

$$\hat{C} = [1010111]$$

At the end of the first iteration we got the right outputs after making hard decisions, and we stop decoding for Case 1 with the min-sum algorithm.

Case 2: Two-bit errors in hard decisions of channel output—Let the received noisy vector $Y = [-0.85, -0.05, -0.91, +0.88, -0.79, 0.10, -0.81]$ and the corresponding hard-decision vector $D = [1\underline{1}1010\underline{1}]$. The error bits are highlighted with underscoring.

Initialization and First Iteration

Channel APPs:

$$\lambda_i = [-1.70, -0.10, -1.82, 1.76, -1.58, 0.20, -1.62]$$

Extrinsic information passed from bit nodes to parity nodes:

$$Q_{ij} = \begin{bmatrix} -1.70 & 0 & -1.82 & 0 & 0 & 0.20 & -1.62 \\ 0 & 0 & -1.82 & 1.76 & -1.58 & 0 & 0 \\ -1.70 & -0.10 & 0 & 0 & 0 & 0.20 & 0 \\ 0 & -0.10 & 0 & 1.76 & -1.58 & 0 & -1.62 \end{bmatrix}$$

Extrinsic information passed from parity nodes to bit nodes:

$$R_{ji} = \begin{bmatrix} 0.16 & 0 & 0.16 & 0 & 0 & -1.29 & 0.16 \\ 0 & 0 & -1.26 & 1.26 & -1.41 & 0 & 0 \\ -0.08 & -0.16 & 0 & 0 & 0 & 0.08 & 0 \\ 0 & 1.26 & 0 & -0.08 & 0.08 & 0 & 0.08 \end{bmatrix}$$

Updated LLRs for transmitted message bits:

$$LLR_i = [-1.62, 1.00, -2.92, 2.94, -2.91, -1.02, -1.38]$$

Hard-decision output:

$$\hat{C} = [1010111]$$

At the end of the first iteration we got the right outputs after making hard decisions and we stop decoding for Case 2 with the min-sum algorithm.

Case 3: Three-bit errors in hard decisions of channel output—Let the received noisy vector $Y = [-0.85, -0.05, -0.91, -0.08, -0.79, 0.10, -0.81]$ and the corresponding hard-decision vector $D = [1\underline{1}1\underline{1}1\underline{0}1]$. The error bits are highlighted with underscoring.

Initialization and First Iteration

Channel APPs:

$$\lambda_i = [-1.70, -0.10, -1.82, -0.16, -1.58, 0.20, -1.62]$$

Extrinsic information passed from bit nodes to parity nodes:

$$Q_{ij} = \begin{bmatrix} -1.70 & 0 & -1.82 & 0 & 0 & 0.20 & -1.62 \\ 0 & 0 & -1.82 & -0.16 & -1.58 & 0 & 0 \\ -1.70 & -0.10 & 0 & 0 & 0 & 0.20 & 0 \\ 0 & -0.10 & 0 & -0.16 & -1.58 & 0 & -1.62 \end{bmatrix}$$

Extrinsic information passed from parity nodes to bit nodes:

$$R_{ji} = \begin{bmatrix} 0.16 & 0 & 0.16 & 0 & 0 & -1.29 & 0.16 \\ 0 & 0 & 0.128 & 1.26 & 0.127 & 0 & 0 \\ -0.08 & -0.16 & 0 & 0 & 0 & 0.08 & 0 \\ 0 & -0.128 & 0 & -0.08 & -0.08 & 0 & -0.08 \end{bmatrix}$$

Updated LLRs for transmitted message bits:

$$LLR_i = [-1.62, -0.387, -1.53, 1.024, -1.53, -1.016, -1.54]$$

Hard-decision output:

$$\hat{C} = [1\underline{1}10111]$$

At the end of the first iteration, we have a 1-bit error in the outputs after making hard decisions and we continue decoding with the min-sum algorithm.

Second Iteration

Extrinsic information passed from bit nodes to parity nodes:

$$Q_{ij} = \begin{bmatrix} -1.78 & 0 & -1.69 & 0 & 0 & 0.28 & -1.70 \\ 0 & 0 & -1.66 & -0.24 & -1.66 & 0 & 0 \\ -1.54 & -0.227 & 0 & 0 & 0 & -1.095 & 0 \\ 0 & -0.26 & 0 & 1.104 & -1.452 & 0 & -1.459 \end{bmatrix}$$

Extrinsic information passed from parity nodes to bit nodes:

$$R_{ji} = \begin{bmatrix} 0.224 & 0 & 0.224 & 0 & 0 & -1.354 & 0.224 \\ 0 & 0 & 0.192 & 1.328 & 0.192 & 0 & 0 \\ 0.182 & 0.876 & 0 & 0 & 0 & 0.182 & 0 \\ 0 & 0.883 & 0 & -0.207 & 0.207 & 0 & 0.207 \end{bmatrix}$$

Updated LLRs for transmitted message bits:

$$LLR_i = [-1.29, 1.659, -1.404, 0.96, -1.18, -0.97, -1.188]$$

Hard-decision output:

$$\hat{C} = [1010111]$$

We got the right outputs at the end of the second iteration after making hard decisions and we stop decoding for Case 3 with the min-sum algorithm.

Case 4: Four bit errors in hard decisions of channel output—Let the received noisy vector $Y = [0.14, -0.05, -0.91, -0.08, -0.79, 0.10, -0.81]$ and the corresponding hard-decision vector $D = [\underline{1}\underline{1}1\underline{1}1\underline{0}1]$. The error bits are highlighted with underscoring.

Initialization and First Iteration

Channel APPs:

$$\lambda_i = [0.28, -0.10, -1.82, -0.16, -1.58, 0.20, -1.62]$$

Extrinsic information passed from bit nodes to parity nodes:

$$Q_{ij} = \begin{bmatrix} 0.28 & 0 & -1.82 & 0 & 0 & 0.20 & -1.62 \\ 0 & 0 & -1.82 & -0.16 & -1.58 & 0 & 0 \\ 0.28 & -0.10 & 0 & 0 & 0 & 0.20 & 0 \\ 0 & -0.10 & 0 & -0.16 & -1.58 & 0 & -1.62 \end{bmatrix}$$

Extrinsic information passed from parity nodes to bit nodes:

$$R_{ji} = \begin{bmatrix} 0.16 & 0 & -0.16 & 0 & 0 & 0.224 & -0.16 \\ 0 & 0 & 0.128 & 1.264 & 0.128 & 0 & 0 \\ -0.08 & 0.16 & 0 & 0 & 0 & -0.08 & 0 \\ 0 & -0.128 & 0 & -0.08 & -0.08 & 0 & -0.08 \end{bmatrix}$$

Updated LLRs for transmitted message bits:

$$LLR_i = [0.36, -0.068, -1.852, 1.024, -1.53, 0.344, -1.86]$$

Hard-decision output:

$$\hat{C} = [\underline{0}\underline{1}1010\underline{0}1]$$

At the end of the first iteration, we have 3-bit errors in the outputs after making hard decisions and we continue decoding with min-sum algorithm. Here, we skip a few iterations and give the outputs for the fifth iteration.

Fifth Iteration

Extrinsic information passed from bit nodes to parity nodes:

$$Q_{ij} = \begin{bmatrix} 0.502 & 0 & -1.845 & 0 & 0 & 0.435 & -1.77 \\ 0 & 0 & -2.22 & 0.009 & -1.73 & 0 & 0 \\ 0.68 & 0.81 & 0 & 0 & 0 & 0.65 & 0 \\ 0 & 0.122 & 0 & 1.257 & -1.605 & 0 & -2.02 \end{bmatrix}$$

Extrinsic information passed from parity nodes to bit nodes:

$$R_{ji} = \begin{bmatrix} 0.348 & 0 & -0.348 & 0 & 0 & 0.402 & -0.348 \\ 0 & 0 & 0.008 & 1.384 & 0.008 & 0 & 0 \\ 0.524 & 0.524 & 0 & 0 & 0 & 0.545 & 0 \\ 0 & 1.006 & 0 & 0.098 & -0.098 & 0 & -0.098 \end{bmatrix}$$

Updated LLRs for transmitted message bits:

$$LLR_i = [1.15, 1.429, -2.16, 1.32, -1.67, 1.146, -2.06]$$

Hard-decision output:

$$\hat{C} = [\underline{0}01010\underline{0}1]$$

At the end of the fifth iteration, we have 2-bit errors in the outputs after making hard decisions and we continue decoding with min-sum algorithm. Again, we skip a few more iterations and give the outputs for 11th iteration.

Eleventh Iteration

Extrinsic information passed from bit nodes to parity nodes:

$$Q_{ij} = \begin{bmatrix} 1.033 & 0 & -2.04 & 0 & 0 & 0.983 & -2.16 \\ 0 & 0 & -2.62 & 0.376 & -2.116 & 0 & 0 \\ 1.08 & 1.077 & 0 & 0 & 0 & 1.04 & 0 \\ 0 & 0.65 & 0 & 1.454 & -1.802 & 0 & -2.42 \end{bmatrix}$$

Extrinsic information passed from parity nodes to bit nodes:

$$R_{ji} = \begin{bmatrix} 0.786 & 0 & -0.786 & 0 & 0 & 0.827 & -0.786 \\ 0 & 0 & -0.301 & 1.693 & -0.301 & 0 & 0 \\ 0.832 & 0.832 & 0 & 0 & 0 & 0.862 & 0 \\ 0 & 1.163 & 0 & 0.523 & -0.523 & 0 & -0.523 \end{bmatrix}$$

Updated LLRs for transmitted message bits:

$$LLR_i = [1.898, 1.895, -2.907, 2.056, -2.404, 1.88, -2.929]$$

Hard-decision output:

$$\hat{C} = [\underline{0}0101\underline{0}1]$$

At the end of the 11th iteration, we still have 2-bit errors in the outputs after making hard decisions, and we passed the maximum iteration count of 10. So, we stop decoding with the min-sum algorithm, although all errors are not corrected.

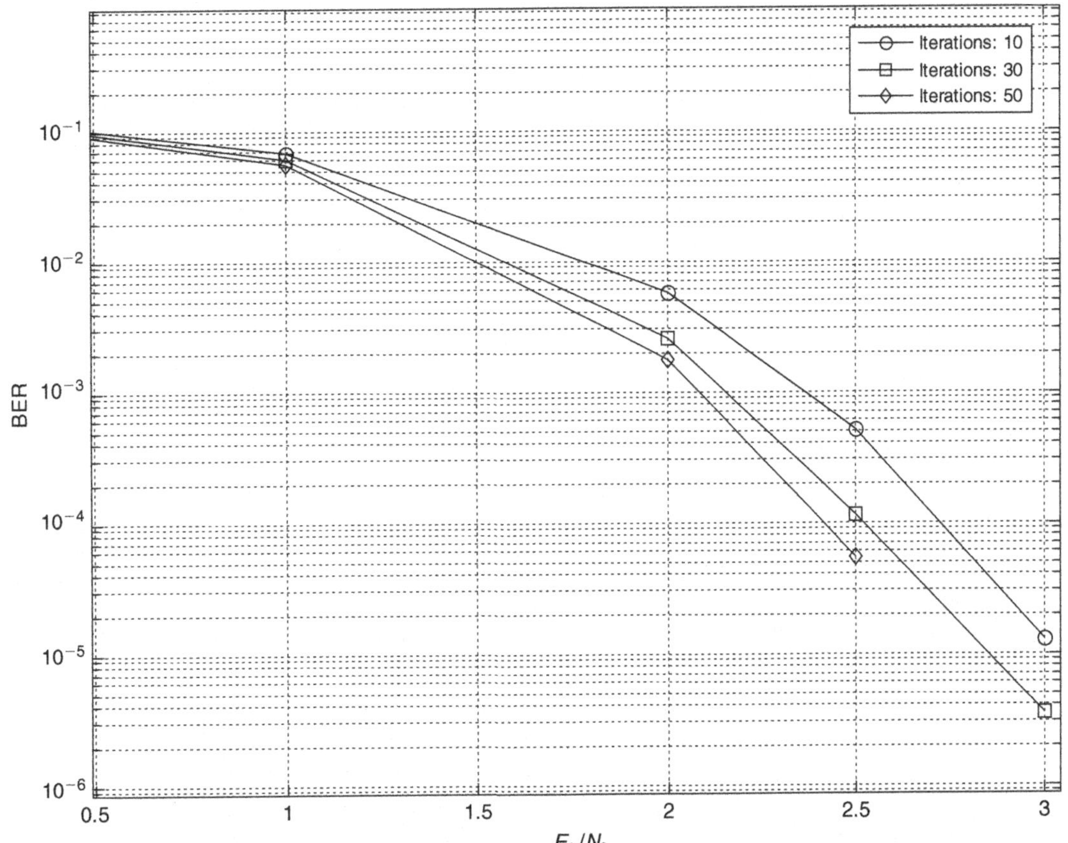

Figure 3.58: LDPC BER versus E_b/N_0 curves for cod eword length of 576 bits.

Usually the decoder fails to correct errors if the number of errors occurred are greater than the error correction capability of the decoder irrespective of the number of iterations. The error correction capability of the LDPC coder depends on the length of the codeword and the characteristic of the parity check matrix. With good parity-check matrices, the decoder gives a better performance with larger codewords. In practice, the length of the LDPC codeword used is in the order of thousands of bits. In Figure 3.58 on the previous page, the BER performance versus E_b/N_0 curves are shown using codeword length of 576 bits for different iteration counts. In Figure 3.58, we can see the improved BER performance with the number of iterations for a given codeword length. The encoder used is a rate ½ coder defined by parity check matrix $H_{288\times576}$, which is obtained from the WiMax standard base matrices. The LDPC decoder uses the min-sum algorithm. The value for constant k is chosen as 0.8.

CHAPTER 4

Implementation of Error Correction Algorithms

In Chapter 3, we briefly discussed various error correction algorithms and their related theory with a few examples. In this chapter, we discuss efficient implementation techniques for widely used error correction algorithms. Section 4.1 covers Bose-Chaudhuri-Hocquenghem (BCH) code simulation and implementation techniques. The BCH codes are popularly used in correcting the bit errors in the header information included in data frame communications. A subset of BCH codes called Reed-Solomon (RS) codes is discussed in Section 4.2. The RS coder is widely used in cutting-edge communications systems as an outer coder. In Section 4.3, we discuss RS erasure codes that are commonly used for further error correction in forward error correction (FEC) systems. Section 4.4 covers simulation of the Viterbi algorithm used for decoding convolutional codes. The Viterbi algorithm is a popular decoding algorithm used in many applications (apart from digital communications). Next, we discuss turbo codes in Section 4.5. The most promising at present, turbo codes operate at near channel capacity with an SNR gap of about 0.7 dB. Finally, in Section 4.6, we discuss the oldest and newest codes, namely low-density parity-check (LDPC) codes. The LDPC codes were discovered in the 1960s, mostly forgotten for almost four decades, and then reinvented in 1999. Like turbo codes, LDPC codes also operate at near channel capacity. In this chapter, we simulate most of the algorithms that are popularly used in the industry.

4.1 BCH Codes

The BCH code framework supports a large class of powerful, random-error-correcting cyclic binary and non-binary linear block codes. With the BCH(N, K) codes, we compute $mT(= N - K)$ parity bits from an input block of K bits using the generator polynomial $G(x)$, and we correct up to T bit errors in the received block of N bits. At the transmitter side, the BCH(N, K) encoder computes and appends mT parity bits to the block of K data bits, and at the receiver side the BCH(N, K) decoder corrects up to T errors by using mT bits of parity information. We work with the Galois field GF(2^m) elements for decoding the BCH(N, K) codes. See Section 3.5 for more details on theory and examples of the BCH(N, K) codes. In this section, we discuss the simulation and implementation details of the BCH(N, K) binary codes. Also we discuss the optimization techniques to efficiently implement the BCH(N, K) coder on embedded processors. We consider the BCH(67, 53) coder as an example to discuss the implementation complexity and deriving efficient implementation techniques. The BCH(67, 53) coder is used in the DVB-H standard for correcting bit errors in the received TPS data. The BCH(67, 53) codes are a short form of the BCH(127, 113) systematic codes, which are decoded using the Galois field GF(2^7). The field elements of GF(2^7) are generated using primitive polynomial $P(x) = 1 + x^3 + x^7$. As $mT = N - K = 67 - 53 = 14 = 7 \times 2$, this BCH(67, 53) coder is capable of correcting up to $2(= T)$ random bit errors using $14(= mT)$ redundancy (or parity) bits.

4.1.1 BCH Encoder

The BCH(N, K) encoder computes $mT(= N - K)$ bits of parity data from K bits of input data by using a generator polynomial $G(x) = g_0 + g_1x + g_2x^2 + \cdots + g_{N-K-1}x^{N-K-1} + x^{N-K}$. For the BCH($N$, K) codes, the generator polynomial $G(x)$ is obtained by computing the multiplication of T minimal polynomials $\phi_{2i-1}(x)$ of field elements α^{2i-1} for $1 \le i \le T$ as follows:

$$G(x) = \phi_1(x)\phi_3(x)\cdots\phi_{2T-1}(x) \tag{4.1}$$

DOI: 10.1016/B978-1-85617-678-1.00004-1

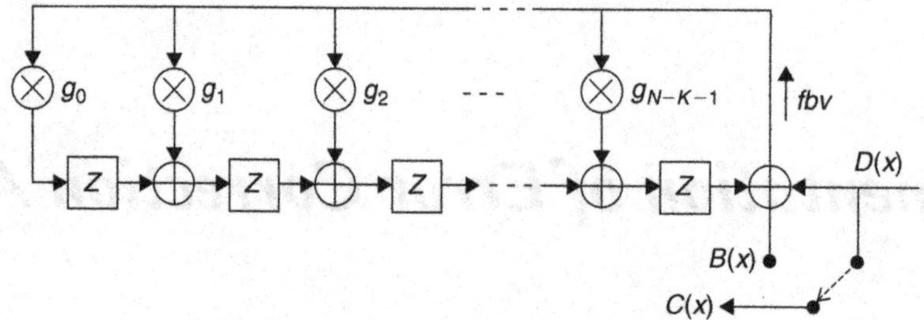

Figure 4.1: Realization of BCH(N, K) encoder.

As every even power of α has the same minimal polynomial as some preceding odd power of α, the $G(x)$ is obtained by computing the LCM (least common multiple) of minimum polynomials $\phi_i(x)$ for $1 \le i \le 2T$, and hence $G(x)$ has $\alpha, \alpha^2, \alpha^3, \ldots, \alpha^{2T}$ as its roots. In other words, $G(\alpha^i) = 0$ for $1 \le i \le 2T$.

Suppose that the input message block of K bits to be encoded is $D = \left[d_0 d_1 d_2 \cdots d_{K-1}\right]$ and the corresponding message polynomial is $D(x) = d_0 + d_1 x + d_2 x^2 + \cdots + d_{K-1} x^{K-1}$. Let $B = \left[b_0 b_1 b_2 \cdots b_{N-K-1}\right]$ denotes the computed parity data of $N - K (= mT)$ length and its polynomial representation is $B(x) = b_0 + b_1 x + b_2 x^2 + \cdots + b_{N-K-1} x^{N-K-1}$. This parity polynomial $B(x)$ is given by the remainder when we divide $D(x).x^{N-K}$ with the generator polynomial $G(x)$. The polynomial $B(x)$ is computed as

$$B(x) = D(x) \cdot x^{N-K} \bmod G(x) \tag{4.2}$$

After computing the parity polynomial $B(x)$, the encoded code polynomial $C(x)$ is constructed as

$$\begin{aligned} C(x) &= D(x) \cdot x^{N-K} + B(x) \\ &= b_0 + b_1 x + b_2 x^2 + \cdots + b_{N-K-1} x^{N-K-1} + d_0 x^{N-K} + d_1 x^{N-K+1} + \cdots + d_{K-1} x^{N-1} \\ &= c_0 + c_1 x + c_2 x^2 + \cdots + c_{N-1} x^{N-1} \end{aligned} \tag{4.3}$$

Basically, we append mT bits of parity data to the input block of K bits and form a systematic codeword of $N (= K + mT)$ bits. The encoded polynomial in the vector form is represented as $C = \left[c_0 c_1 c_2 \ldots c_{N-1}\right]$. Equations (4.2) and (4.3) can be realized with linear feedback shift register (LFSR) signal flow diagram as shown in Figure 4.1. To compute parity polynomial $B(x)$ coefficients, we input the data polynomial $D(x)$ coefficients to LFSR with the d_{K-1} coefficient as the first input. The values present in the delay units (Z) after passing all K coefficients of the data polynomial $D(x)$ represents the coefficients of the parity polynomial $B(x)$.

Next, we discuss the simulation of the BCH(N, K) encoder. We use the LFSR signal flow diagram as shown in Figure 4.1 for simulation of the BCH(N, K) encoder. We initialize all delay units with zero values. We start with the data polynomial coefficient d_{K-1} and compute the feedback value (fbv). If the value of fbv is not zero, then we update all delay units using fbv along with generator polynomial coefficients and using the present values of the delay units. Otherwise, if the value of fbv is zero, then we update all delay units with the present values of delay units. The simulation code for the BCH(N, K) encoder is given in Pcode 4.1.

4.1.2 BCH Decoder

At the receiver, we use the BCH(N, K) decoder to detect and correct the bit errors. The BCH decoder consists of the following steps to decode the received data block R.

1. Computation of syndromes
2. Computation of error locator polynomial
3. Computation of error positions

```
for (i = 0; i < N - K; i++)
        delay_unit[i] = 0;
for (i = K - 1; i >=0; i--) {
        fbv = data_in[i] ^ delay_unit[N - K - 1];
        if (fbv != 0) {
                for (j = N - K - 1; j > 0; j--)
                        if (bch_gp[j] != 0)
                                delay_unit[j] = delay_unit[j - 1] ^ fbv;
                        else
                                delay_unit[j] = delay_unit[j - 1];
                delay_unit[0] = bch_gp[0] & fbv;
        }
        else {
                for (j = N - K - 1; j > 0; j--)
                        delay_unit[j] = delay_unit[j - 1];
                delay_unit[0] = 0;
        };
        data_out[N - 1 - i] = data_in[K - 1 - i];
};
for (i = N - K - 1; i >=0; i--)
        data_out[i] = delay_unit[i];
```

Pcode 4.1: The simulation code for BCH(N, K) encoder.

The received data vector R or its polynomial $R(x) = r_0 + r_1x + r_2x^2 + \cdots + r_{N-1}x^{N-1}$ consists of the transmitted data polynomial $C(x)$ along with the added error polynomial $E(x)$:

$$\begin{aligned} R(x) &= C(x) + E(x) \\ &= D(x) \cdot x^{N-K} + B(x) + E(x) \\ &= D(x) \cdot G(x) + E(x) \end{aligned} \tag{4.4}$$

In the BCH decoder (unlike as in the BCH encoder), we have to perform the Galois field arithmetic operations in decoding of the BCH codes. See Appendix B, Section B.2, on the companion website for more details on the Galois field arithmetic operations and their computational complexity analysis. In the simulation of the BCH(67, 53) decoder, we use the Galois field GF(2^7) element look-up tables from the companion website; use **Galois_Log**[ ] for performing the logarithm and **Galois_aLog**[ ] for performing the anti-logarithm.

Syndrome Computation

To determine the presence of errors and the error pattern, we compute $2T$ syndromes for the received data polynomial as follows:

$$\begin{aligned} R(\alpha^i) &= D(\alpha^i) \cdot G(\alpha^i) + E(\alpha^i), \text{ where } 1 \le i \le 2T \\ &= 0 + E(\alpha^i) \\ &= E(\alpha^i) \\ &= S_i \end{aligned} \tag{4.5}$$

Considering the previous syndrome computation, if no errors are present in the received data vector, all computed syndrome values (S_i) are zero. If any one or more syndromes are non-zero, then we assume that the errors are present in the received data vector. The syndromes $S_i = R(\alpha^i)$ are computed with the LFSR signal flow diagram as shown in Figure 4.2.

We simulate the signal flow diagram shown in Figure 4.2 for computing syndromes. The simulation code for computing syndromes is given in Pcode 4.2. The Galois field element value a_j, the j-th power of the Galois field element α^i, is computed by taking the Galois anti-logarithm for $i \cdot j$ mod$N$. As the received vector consists of binary coefficient values (r_j), we do not really perform the Galois field multiplication r_ja_j in computing $c_j = b_j + r_ja_j$, instead we conditionally add a_j to b_j.

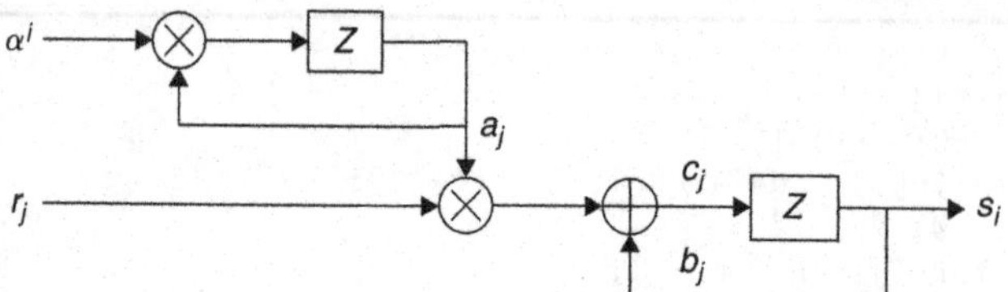

Figure 4.2: Signal flow diagram of syndrome computation.

```
for (i = 0; i < 2*T; i++) {
          Syndromes[i] = 0;
          for (j = n - 1; j >=0; j--)
                   if (r[j] != 0) {
                              a = (i + 1)*(n-1-j)%N;
                              Syndromes[i] = Syndromes[i] ^Galois_aLog[a];
                   }
}
```

Pcode 4.2: Simulation code for syndrome computation.

Error Locator Polynomial Computation

Computing an error locator polynomial is the second step in decoding of the BCH codes. We use the Berlekamp-Massey recursive algorithm to compute the error locator polynomial.

If the number of errors present in the received data vector is L (which is less than or equal to T), then this algorithm computes the L-th degree error locator polynomial in $2T$ iterations. As discussed in Section 3.5, first we initialize the error locator polynomial $\Lambda(x) = 1$ as minimum-degree polynomial with degree $L = 0$. Then, we use syndromes information to build the error locator polynomial by computing discrepancy delta. If the value of delta is not zero, then we update the minimum degree polynomial with the discrepancy, otherwise we continue the loop. If the number of errors in the received polynomial $R(x)$ is T or less, then $\Lambda(x)$ produces the true error pattern. At the end of $2T$ iterations of the Berlekamp-Massey recursion, we have an L-th degree error-locator polynomial (with $\Lambda_0 = 1$) as follows:

$$\begin{aligned}\Lambda(x) &= \Lambda_0 + \Lambda_1 x + \Lambda_2 x^2 + \cdots + \Lambda_L x^L \\ &= (1 + X_1 x)(1 + X_2 x) \cdots (1 + X_L x)\end{aligned} \tag{4.6}$$

The simulation code for computing the error-locator polynomial is given in Pcode 4.3. Once we have the error locator polynomial of degree L, then we can find L error positions by computing the roots of the error locator polynomial.

Error Position Computation

If the number of errors L present in the received data vector is less than or equal to T (i.e., $L \leq T$), then the error locator polynomial can be factored into L first-degree polynomials as in Equation (4.6) and the roots of the error locator polynomial are $X_1^{-1}, X_2^{-1}, \ldots, X_L^{-1}$. As described in Section 3.5, the error positions are given by the inverse of roots of error locator polynomial. So the L error positions are $X_1, X_2, \ldots, X_L$. The simulation code for finding the error positions is given in Pcode 4.4.

Because binary BCH codes work on the data bits, when we find the error positions in the received data bits, correction of data bits is achieved by simply flipping the bit values in those error positions.

Error Correction

When working with BCH binary codes, we correct only bit-errors present in the received data. The correction of bit errors is achieved by flipping the bit value at the error position. If the degree of the error locator polynomial (L) computed using Pcode 4.3 and the number of error positions (k) computed using Pcode 4.4 are not the same, then the BCH decoder cannot correct errors as the number of errors that occurred is greater than the decoder's error-correction capability. Therefore, we skip error bit correction when $L \neq k$. The simulation code for correcting bit errors with the BCH decoder is given in Pcode 4.5.

```
L = 0;                                                  // initialization
Elp[0] = 1; Tx[0] = 1;
for(i = 1;i < 2*T; i++){
          Elp[i] = 0; Tx[i] = 0;
}
r0 = Syndromes[0];                                      // starting delta
for(k = 0;k < 2*T;k++){
          for(i = 0;i < T+1;i++)
          Conn_poly[i] = Elp[i];                        // Conn_poly = Elp
          if (r0 != 0) {                                // Elp = Conn_poly - Delta*Tx
                    r2 = Galois_Log[r0];                // log (delta)
                    for(i = 0;i < T+1;i++){
                              r1 = Conn_poly[i]; r3 = Tx[i];
                              r3 = Galois_Log[r3];      // log (delta), log(Tx[i])
                              r3 = r2 + r3;
                              r3 = Galois_aLog[r3];
                              r1 = r3 ^ r1;             // Conn_poly[i]^Delta*Tx[i]
                              Elp[i] = r1;
                    }
                    if (2*L < (k+1)){
                            L = k+1 - L;
                            for(i = 0;i < T+1;i++) {    // Tx = Conn_poly/Delta
                                      r1 = Conn_poly[i];
                                      r1 = Galois_Log[r1];
                                      m = r1 - r2;
                                      if (m < 0) m+= 127;
                                      r1 = Galois_aLog[m];
                                      Tx[i] = r1;
                            }
                    }
          }
          for(i = T+1;i > 0;i--)                        // Tx = [0 Tx]
                        Tx[i] = Tx[i-1];
          Tx[0] = 0; r0 = Syndromes[k+1];
          if(L > 0) {
                        for(i = 0;i < L;i++) {
                            // compute delta by convolution of Syndrome poly and Elp
                            r1 = log_Syndromes[k-i+1]; r2 = Elp[i+1];
                            r2 = Galois_Log[r2];
                            r1 = r1 + r2;
                            r2 = Galois_aLog[r1];
                            r0 = r0 ^ r2;
                        }
          }
}
```

Pcode 4.3: Simulation code for error-locator polynomial computation.

4.1.3 BCH Codes: Computational Complexity

In this section, we discuss the computational complexity of the BCH encoder and decoder, and we estimate cycles from the simulations presented in Sections 4.1.1 and 4.1.2. See Appendix A, Section A.4, on the companion website for more details on cycle requirements to execute specific operations on the reference embedded processor.

BCH Encoder

In the BCH encoder simulation (as given in Pcode 4.1), we initialize $N-K$ delay units with zeros at the beginning, and we move the parity data from $N-K$ delay units to the data buffer at the end. For this, we consume about $2*(N-K)$ cycles. We use all bits of the message block to compute the parity for that message block. We compute the parity with K input data bits using the BCH(N, K) encoder. For K input data bits, we have to compute the feedback value and it consumes about K cycles. Depending on feedback value, **fbv**, we have two paths to proceed. If **fbv** is zero, then we update $N-K$ delay unit values with the current delay unit values by consuming $N-K$ cycles. If **fbv** is not zero, then depending on generator polynomial coefficients,

```
k = 0;
for(i = 127;i>=1;i--) {
          r0 = Elp[0];
          for(j = 1;j < L+1;j++) {
                  r1 = i*j;
                  r2 = r1 >> 7; r1 = r1 & 0x7f;
                  r3 = log_Elp[j]; r1 = r1 + r2;
                  r2 = r1 >> 7; r1 = r1 & 0x7f;
                  r1 = r1 + r2;
                  r1 = r1 + r3;
                  r2 = Galois_aLog[r1];
                  r0 = r0 ^ r2;
          }
          if (r0 == 0){
                    Error_positions[k] = 127-i;
                    k++;
          }
}
```

Pcode 4.4: Simulation code for finding error positions.

```
p = 1;
for(i = 0; i < L; i++) {
          m = Error_position[i];
          k = n-1-m;
          data[k] = data[k]^p;
}
```

Pcode 4.5: Simulation code for bit errors correction.

we conditionally update $N-K$ delay unit values. To update one delay unit, we consume 3 cycles (1 cycle for generator polynomial coefficient checking, 1 cycle for computing value to update delay unit, and 1 cycle for conditional update of delay unit), and we consume $3*(N-K)$ cycles to update $N-K$ delay units. Assuming equal probability for **fbv** to become zero or one, on average we consume $2*(N-K)+X$ cycles to update delay units for 1 bit of the message block. Here, X cycles are overhead cycles consumed for conditional check and conditional jump depending on **fbv**. Therefore, we consume $[2*(N-K)+X]*K$ cycles to compute parity for a K-bit input message block. With this, we consume about $2*(N-K)+[2*(N-K)+X]*K$ cycles to execute the BCH(N, K) encoder on the reference embedded processor.

As an example, we estimate the computational complexity of the BCH(67, 53) encoder. We consume a total of $28(=14+14)$ cycles to initialize parity bits (before the main loop) and to move the computed parity bits (after the main loop) to the output buffer. We assume the jump taken (9 cycles) when feedback value is zero. If the feedback value is not zero, then a single iteration of the main loop consumes 42 cycles. If the feedback value is zero, then a single iteration consumes 24 cycles (including conditional check and conditional jump). Assuming equal probability for feedback value to become one or zero, single iterations of the main loop require an average of 33 cycles. The main loop runs 53 times for the BCH(67, 53) encoder. With this, implementation of the BCH(67, 53) encoder using the method given in Pcode 4.1 takes about $1777(=28+53*33)$ cycles.

BCH Decoder

Syndrome Computation Based on Pcode 4.2, in syndrome computation, we have to compute the Galois field element powers and that involves a costly modulo operation. In addition, look-up table access requires addition of an arbitrary offset to the base address and we have stalls to load values from the **Galois_aLog**[ ] table due to arbitrary offsets. We estimate the cycles for syndrome computation by assuming the interleaving of the program to avoid stalls and circular buffer usage to mimic modulo operation (see Appendix A.4 on the companion website). We consume 1 cycle to get a power of the Galois field element value from the **Galois_aLog**[ ] look-up table using circular buffer registers. We conditionally update the accumulation value for syndrome by checking the received bit (whether zero or not) and consume 4 cycles. We consume a total of 5 cycles to update a syndrome for one received bit. We do not jump on checking the received bit as it takes about 10 cycles for a conditional check and conditional jump. Next, to compute one syndrome, we use all N received bits and consume about $5*N$ cycles.

With this, to compute 2* T syndromes, we consume about $2 * T * 5 * N$ cycles. For computing syndromes of the BCH(67, 53) decoder, we require about $1380(= 2*2*5*67+\text{overhead})$ cycles.

Error Locator Polynomial Computation Based on Pcode 4.3, in the i-th iteration, we use $L_i - 1$ Galois field additions and multiplication in convolving syndromes with $\Lambda(x)$ to compute discrepancy delta Δ_i. We use the Galois logarithm and anti-logarithm look-up tables for the Galois field multiplication. As we know all syndromes in advance, we get logarithm values for all syndromes before entering the loop of $\Lambda(x)$ computation. We have to get the logarithm values for $\Lambda(x)$ coefficients in all iterations as they change from iteration to iteration. With this, we can compute the i-th iteration delta Δ_i in $6 * (L_i - 1)$ cycles. Depending on current iteration discrepancy Δ_i, we update $\Lambda(x)$ (if $\Delta_i \neq 0$) as

$$\Lambda^i(x) = \Lambda^{i-1}(x) - x \cdot \Delta_i \cdot T^{i-1}(x) \tag{4.7}$$

where $T^{i-1}(x)$ is computed in the previous iteration as

$$T^{i-1}(x) = \begin{cases} \Lambda^{i-2}(x)/\Delta_{i-1} & \text{if } \Delta_{i-1} \neq 0,\ 2L_{i-1} \leq i-1 \\ x \cdot T^{i-2}(x) & \text{otherwise} \end{cases} \tag{4.8}$$

If $\Delta_i \neq 0$, we spend a total of $7 * (T+1)$ cycles for computing $\Lambda^i(x)$ and another $7 * (T+1)$ cycles for computing $T^i(x)$ if $2L_i \leq i$. We spend an overhead of another 20 cycles for moving the data to and from buffers and for conditional checks. With this, we consume about $2T * [6 * (L_i - 1) + 14 * (T+1) + 20]$ cycles for computing the error locator polynomial using the simulation code given in Pcode 4.3. Assuming $L_i = 2$, we consume about $272(= 4 * 68)$ cycles to compute the error locator polynomial.

Error Position Computation The error locator polynomial roots inverse $\{X_i,\ 0 \leq i \leq L\}$ give the error positions in the received data vector (if at all errors are present and the number of errors are less than or equal to T).We find roots of the error locator polynomial $\Lambda(x)$ by substituting every possible error position (Chien's search) in $\Lambda(x)$ and checking for whether the particular error position satisfies $\Lambda(x)$. In the error locator polynomial roots finding, we need to find the powers of the Galois field elements and we compute the powers here with the analytic method (instead of using circular buffer registers as in syndrome computation). Here, we consume 7 cycles (which can be achieved with one cycle on an embedded processor with circular buffer registers) to find the power of the Galois field element. To find a particular data element that is in error (if that element position satisfies the $\Lambda(x)$) or not, we spend $11 * L$ cycles. We search for all the data element positions to find the roots of $\Lambda(x)$. Therefore, to find the roots of the error locator polynomial $\Lambda(x)$ with an analytic method (without using the circular registers of an embedded processor), we consume about $N * (11 * L + 4)$ cycles. Assuming $L = T = 2$, we consume about $1742(= 67 * (11 * 2 + 4))$ cycles to find the roots of the error locator polynomial of the BCH(67, 53) decoder.

4.1.4 BCH Coder Optimization

In this section, we discuss efficient implementation of the BCH(N, K) coder for particular values of N and K. As an example, we consider the BCH(67, 53) coder.

BCH(67, 53) Encoder

It is clear from Pcode 4.1 that the conditional update of delay units in the loop is costly and it is very inefficient. Given that we know the generator polynomial coefficients in advance for the BCH(67, 53) encoder, we can avoid the conditional flow of the encoder by coding for this particular configuration. The LFSR flow diagram of the BCH(67, 53) encoder is shown in Figure 4.3. The BCH(67, 53) encoder computes $14(= mT)$ parity bits from $53(= K)$ input bits by using the following generator polynomial:

$$G(x) = 1 + x + x^2 + x^4 + x^5 + x^6 + x^8 + x^9 + x^{14} \tag{4.9}$$

As $m = 7$ and $T = 2$ for the BCH(67, 53) codes, the generator polynomial $G(x)$ of the BCH(67, 53) coder is obtained from Equation (4.1) as

$$G(x) = \phi_1(x)\phi_3(x)$$

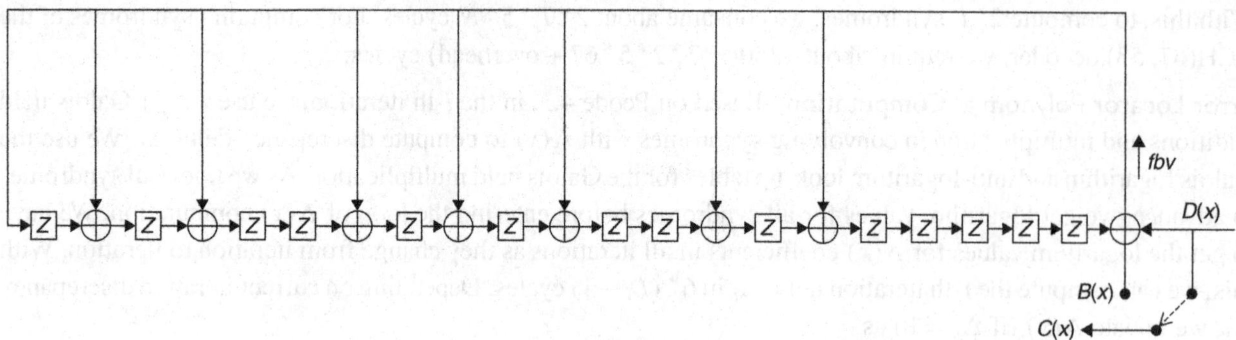

Figure 4.3: Realization of BCH(67, 53) encoder.

where $\phi_1(x) = 1 + x^3 + x^7$ and $\phi_3(x) = 1 + x + x^2 + x^3 + x^7$. For more details on minimal polynomials working with other BCH(N, K) encoders for different values of m and T, see Shu Lin (1983).

In Figure 4.3, as the $G(x)$ has binary coefficients, we avoid multiplication of feedback values with $g_i s$. The feedback connections to the delay units are shown only to the non-zero coefficients of the generator polynomial given in Equation (4.9). The simulation code for the BCH(67, 53) encoder is given in Pcode 4.6. As the BCH codes contain only binary elements and we know in advance the generator polynomial non-zero coefficient positions, we further simplify the simulation code by working with packed delay unit elements instead of array of individual delay unit elements. The simulation code for the efficient BCH(67, 53) encoder method is given in Pcode 4.7.

```
for (i = 0; i < 14; i++)
          delay_unit[i] = 0;
for (i = 52; i >= 0; i--) {
          fbv = data_in[i] ^ delay_unit[13];
          delay_unit[13] = delay_unit[12];
          delay_unit[12] = delay_unit[11];
          delay_unit[11] = delay_unit[10];
          delay_unit[10] = delay_unit[9];
          delay_unit[9] = delay_unit[8] ^ fbv;
          delay_unit[8] = delay_unit[7] ^ fbv;
          delay_unit[7] = delay_unit[6];
          delay_unit[6] = delay_unit[5] ^ fbv;
          delay_unit[5] = delay_unit[4] ^ fbv;
          delay_unit[4] = delay_unit[3] ^ fbv;
          delay_unit[3] = delay_unit[2] ;
          delay_unit[2] = delay_unit[1] ^ fbv;
          delay_unit[1] = delay_unit[0] ^ fbv;
          delay_unit[0] = fbv;
          data_out[i+14] = data_in[i];
}
for (i = 13; i>=0; i--)
          data_out[i] = delay_unit[i];
```

Pcode 4.6: The simulation code for BCH(67, 53) encoder.

Next, we estimate the cycle consumption of the simulation code given in Pcode 4.7 for the BCH(67, 53) encoder. We consume about 7 cycles outside the main loop, about 6 cycles in a single iteration of the loop, and about 318($= 53 \times 6$) cycles for 53 iterations. With this efficient method, we consume a total of about 325 cycles (instead of 1777 cycles using the general method) for the implementation of the BCH(67, 53) encoder.

BCH(67, 53) Decoder

Syndrome Computation The syndrome computation block is one of the costliest blocks in the BCH(N, K) decoder. Instead of computing the Galois field elements' powers on the fly, we use precomputed Galois field element powers and avoid performing modulo operations in computing powers. The simulation code for efficient syndrome computation is given in Pcode 4.8. The **BchSynTbl**[ ] look-up table values for computing syndromes of the BCH(67, 53) decoder can be found on the companion website.

```
delay_units = 0;                          // 14 MSB bits represents bit values in delay units
gpc = 0x0ddc0000;                         // generator polynomial coefficient positions
for (i = 52; i >= 0; i--) {
        fbv = delay_units >> 31;
        temp = 0;
        if (fbv != data[i]) temp = gpc;   // data[] consists of unpacked bits of data_in[]
        delay_units = delay_units << 1;
        delay_units = delay_units ^ temp;
}
data_out[0] = data_in[0];                 // first 32-bits of data
temp = delay_units >> 21;                 // 11 MSB bits of parity
data_out[1] = data_in[1] | temp;          // remaining 21 data bits | 11 parity bits
temp = delay_units << 11;                 // 3 LSB bits of parity
data_out[2] = temp;                       // remaining 3 bits of parity, total data_out is 67 bits
```

Pcode 4.7: Efficient implementation of BCH(67, 53) encoder.

```
for(i = 0;i < 4;i++) {
     Syndromes[i] = 0;
     for(j = n-1;j>=0;j--) {
          temp = BchSynTbl[67*i+n-1-j];
          temp = temp ^ Syndromes[i];
          if(data[j] != 0)
                 Syndromes[i] = temp;
     }
}
```

Pcode 4.8: Efficient implementation of syndrome computation.

In Pcode 4.8, we consume 4 cycles to update conditionally the accumulation of the Galois field elements powers. With $N = 67$ and $K = 53$ of the BCH decoder, we consume about $1080(=4*67*4+\text{overhead})$ cycles to compute $2T$ syndromes. In this method, we do not use any circular buffer registers to access look-up table **BchSynTbl**[ ].

Error Correction

As we know that the BCH(67, 53) decoder can correct up to two errors, we take a few shortcuts in computing the error locator polynomial. Most of the time errors may not present in the received data. We can find the absence of errors by checking the values of syndromes. If all syndromes are zero, then no errors are present in the received data and we stop the BCH from further decoding. We handle one-error and two-errors cases separately. The correction of single errors does not require computation of an error locator polynomial and roots finding. This avoids 50% of computations of the BCH decoder.

Single-Bit Error Correction After computing $2T$ syndromes $\{S_1, S_2, S_3, S_4\}$ with the BCH(67, 53) decoder, if $S_1 \neq 0$ and $S_3 = S_1^3$, then a single error is present in the received data vector. The error position is given by S_1^{-1}. The simulation code for correcting single-bit errors after computing syndromes is given in Pcode 4.9.

```
r0 = Syndromes[0];
r0 = Galois_Log[r0];
m = n-1 - r0;     p = 1; // n = 67
rec_msg[m] = rec_msg[m]^p;
```

Pcode 4.9: Simulation code for correcting single bit errors.

Double-Bit Error Correction After computing syndromes, if $S_1 \neq 0$ and $S_3 \neq S_1^3$, then two-bit errors are present in the received data vector. If two-bit errors are present, then the maximum degree of the error locator polynomial is two and the coefficients Λ_1 and Λ_2 of the error locator polynomial $\Lambda(x) = 1 + \Lambda_1 x + \Lambda_2 x^2$ are given by

$$\Lambda_1 = S_1, \quad \Lambda_2 = \frac{S_3 + S_1^3}{S_1} \tag{4.10}$$

Once we know the error locator polynomial coefficients, we find the error positions by using Chien's search algorithm. As discussed in Section 4.1.2, Error Correction, and Section 4.1.3, BCH Codes: Computational Complexity, the computation of roots for $\Lambda(x)$ using Chien's search is a costly process and we consume 1742 cycles to compute roots of the second-degree error locator polynomial. Instead, we rearrange the second-degree polynomial as seen in the following to reduce the number of computations with Chien's search algorithm. If z is a root of $\Lambda(x)$, then

$$\begin{aligned}
\Lambda(z) &= \Lambda_2 z^2 + \Lambda_1 z + 1 = 0 \\
&\Rightarrow z^2 + \tfrac{\Lambda_1}{\Lambda_2} z + \tfrac{1}{\Lambda_2} = 0 \\
&\Rightarrow z\left(z + \tfrac{\Lambda_1}{\Lambda_2}\right) + \tfrac{1}{\Lambda_2} = 0 \\
&\Rightarrow z(z+a) + b = 0
\end{aligned} \tag{4.11}$$

where $a = \frac{\Lambda_1}{\Lambda_2}$ and $b = \frac{1}{\Lambda_2}$.

We precompute a and b from Λ_1 and Λ_2 before starting Chien's search algorithm. With the previous rearrangement, we compute the Galois field element substitution value with two additions and one multiplication. The simulation code for the efficient error locator polynomial computation, error locator polynomial roots finding and error correction is given in Pcode 4.10. Next, we estimate the cycles for the error locator polynomial and error position computation. We consume approximately 30 cycles (here most look-up table access operations consume 4 cycles as we do not have much scope to interleave the program code) to compute the error locator polynomial $\Lambda(x) = x(x+a) + b$. In error position computation, we have scope to interleave the program by computing more than one substitution value per iteration of the loop. Therefore, we consume 8 cycles (6 cycles for computing substitution value and 2 cycles for checking and continuing the loop) to know whether the bit at the i-th position is in error or not. We consume a total of $536 (= 67 * 8)$ cycles for finding the error position.

```
//Compute error locator polynomial: Delta(x) = x(x+a) + b
r0 = Syndromes[0];      r1 = Syndromes[2];
r0 = Galois_Log[r0];
k = r0 * 3;             m = r0*2;
if (k>=127) k-=127;     if (m>=127) m-=127;
if (k>=127) k-=127;
r2 = Galois_aLog[k];
r2 = r2 ^ r1;
r2 = Galois_Log[r2];
k = m - r2;             m = r0 - r2;
if (k < 0) k+= 127;     if (m < 0) m+= 127;
r1 = Galois_aLog[k];    r2 = Galois_aLog[m];    // a, b
for (i = 127; i>=60; i--) {                            // roots finding
        r0 = Galois_aLog[i];                           // z
        r0 = r0 ^ r1;                                  // z + a
        r0 = Galois_Log[r0];
        r0 = r0 + i;
        r0 = Galois_aLog[r0];                          // z(z + a)
        r0 = r0 ^ r2;                                  // z(z + a) + b
        if (r0 == 0)
                data[i-127+n-1] ^= r3;                 // bit error correction, n = 67
}
```

Pcode 4.10: Simulation code for efficient BCH(67, 53) decoder error correction.

With the previous suggested techniques, we consume about $1646 (= 1080 + 30 + 536)$ cycles to correct two-bit errors using the BCH(67, 53) decoder. Without this algorithm level optimization, we consume (as estimated in Section 4.1.3, BCH Codes: Computational Complexity) about $3394 (= 1380 + 272 + 1742)$ cycles to correct two-bit errors using the BCH(67, 53) decoder. The cycle saving with the optimized BCH(67, 53) decoder is about 51%. The cycle cost may vary if we implement the BCH decoder on a particular embedded processor by taking advantage of its architectural and instruction set features.

BCH Decoder: Further Optimization for $T=2$

In the case of $T=2$, we know that the BCH decoder can correct up to two errors. Based on Equation (4.10), to compute the error locator polynomial $\Lambda(x)$, we use only two syndromes S_1 and S_3 out of $2T(=4)$ computed syndromes. The value of S_1 only dictates whether errors are present (if $S_1 \neq 0$) or not (if $S_1 = 0$). In addition, if errors are present, then how many (whether one or two) errors are present is also decided by using the relation between S_1 and S_3. Because syndrome computation is very costly in terms cycles, we do not have to compute S_2 and S_4 to correct up to two errors (when $T=2$) with the binary BCH decoder because we can calculate them using S_1 and S_3. This saves 50% of syndrome computation cycles.

The other costly routine is Chien's search method, used to find error positions when two or more errors are present in the received data. As we can correct up to two errors for $T=2$, the resultant second-degree error locator polynomial consists of two parameters as given in Equation (4.11). We can find the two roots of the second-degree polynomial using the precomputed look-up table method if we have a second-degree polynomial with only one parameter. In this case, we do not have to use Chien's search and therefore we save a lot of cycles. In the look-up table method, discussed by Okano and Imai (1987), we precompute two roots (if they exist) of the second-degree single parameter polynomial for all its possible values. We convert the second-degree polynomial with two parameters (a and b) given in Equation (4.11) to one parameter of the second-degree polynomial by substituting $z = a \cdot y$ as follows:

$$\begin{aligned} \Lambda(z) &= z(z+a)+b=0 \\ \Lambda(ay) &= ay(ay+a)+b=0 \\ &\Rightarrow a^2y^2+a^2y+b=0 \\ &\Rightarrow y^2+y+c=0 \end{aligned} \tag{4.12}$$

where $c = \frac{b}{a^2}$.

If $m=7$, then $c \in \mathrm{GF}(2^7)$ and we have 128 possible values for c. Next, we precompute all existing roots of the polynomial in Equation (4.12) for all 128 possible values of c. The precomputed look-up table **elp_roots[ ]** for the roots of the second-degree polynomials with a single parameter that belong to $\mathrm{GF}(2^7)$ follows. The roots y_1 and y_2 of the polynomial in Equation (4.12) are obtained by using c as the index (or offset) to the look-up table **elp_roots[ ]** that can be found on the companion website. If roots do not exist for particular values of c, then the table is filled with zeros at those offset values of c. The actual roots z_1 and z_2 for Equation (4.11) are obtained by back substitution as $z_1 = a.y_1$ and $z_2 = a \cdot y_2$. The simulation code for efficient implementation of the BCH(67, 53) without Chien's search method is given in Pcode 4.11. If we get the two roots z_1 and z_2 as zeros, then there are no roots for Equation (4.11) and this indicates that more than two errors occurred and we have to exit from the decoder without any bit errors correction.

An example of the previously described method of finding roots of the second-degree polynomial follows. Let $a, b \in \mathrm{GF}(2^{127})$, $a = \alpha^{122}$, and $b = \alpha^{77}$. The computed roots for the polynomial given in Equation (4.11) using the Chien search method given in Pcode 4.10 are $z_1 = \alpha^0$ and $z_2 = \alpha^{77}$. Next, $c = \frac{b}{a^2} = \alpha^{87}$. Given that the look-up table values start from $c=0$ (its logarithm value is not defined), and if we access the look-up table with logarithm values of c, then we should access the look-up table with offset $88(=87+1)$ to get the correct roots. The roots of Equation (4.12) are obtained from the look-up table **elp_roots[ ]** as $y_1 = \alpha^5$ and $y_2 = \alpha^{82}$. Then, the roots of Equation (4.11) are computed as follows:

$$z_1' = a \cdot y_1 = \alpha^{122} \cdot \alpha^5 = \alpha^{127} = \alpha^0 = z_1$$

$$z_2' = a \cdot y_2 = \alpha^{122} \cdot \alpha^{82} = \alpha^{204} = \alpha^{77} = z_2$$

Next, we estimate the cycle cost of this efficient method. As we need only two syndromes, we consume $536(=2*67*4)$ cycles to compute syndromes S_1 and S_3 using Pcode 4.8. Then we consume approximately 30 to 70 cycles to find error positions and to correct one and two-bit-errors with the simulation code given in Pcode 4.11. With this, the BCH(67, 53) decoder can be implemented on the reference embedded processor with in 600 cycles to correct up to two-bit errors in the received 67 data bits. The suggested techniques for the BCH decoding simulation is also valid for other values of N and K as long as $T = 2$.

```
r4 = Syndromes[0];
r0 = Galois_Log[r4];              r1 = Syndromes[2];
k = r0 * 3;                       m = r0*2;
if (k>=127) k-=127;               if (m>=127) m-=127;
if(k>=127) k-=127;
r2 = Galois_aLog[k];
if (r4 != 0){
        if (r2 == r1)
                data[n-1-r0] ^= 1;                           // single error correction
        else {
                r2 = r2 ^ r1;
                r2 = Galois_Log[r2];
                k = m - r2;                  m = r0 - r2;
                if (k < 0) k+= 127;          if (m < 0) m+= 127;     // a, b
                m = m - 2*k;
                if (m < 0) m+= 127;
                if (m < 0) m+= 127;
                r0 = elp_roots[2*(m+1)];              r1 = elp_roots[2*(m+1)+1];
                if ((r0!=0) && (r1 != 0)) {                  // double error correction
                        r0 = r0 + k;                  r1 = r1 + k;
                        if (r0 > 127) r0-=127;        if (r1 > 127) r1-=127;
                        data[r0-127+n-1]^=1;          data[r1-127+n-1]^=1;
                }
        }
}
```

Pcode 4.11: Simulation code for efficient BCH decoding (for $T = 2$).

4.2 Reed-Solomon Error-Correction Codes

RS codes are widely used in digital communications and digital storage and retrieval systems for forward error correction (FEC). See Section 3.6 for more information on theory and example of RS codes. In this section, we discuss the simulation of RS(N, K) block codes. In particular we discuss the simulation techniques for the RS(204, 188) coder, which is used in DVB-H standard for FEC. We also discuss the computational complexity of the RS coder in terms of cycles and memory to implement on the reference embedded processor.

4.2.1 RS(N, K) Encoder

Using the RS(N, K) encoder, we compute $N - K$ length parity data $B(x)$ from K length input message $D(x)$ by using the generator polynomial $G(x)$. The encoded message $M(x)$ is obtained as

$$M(x) = D(x) \cdot x^{N-K} + B(x) \tag{4.13}$$

The following generator polynomial is used in the RS(N, K) encoder (see Section 3.6) to compute the parity data:

$$\begin{aligned} G(x) &= (x+\alpha^0)(x+\alpha^1)(x+\alpha^2)\cdots(x+\alpha^{2T-1}) \\ &= g_0 + g_1 x + g_2 x^2 + \cdots + g_{2T-1}x^{2T-1} + x^{2T} \end{aligned} \tag{4.14}$$

where $2T = N - K$. Here, the polynomial $G(x)$ is computed by multiplying $2T$ first-degree polynomials $(x + \alpha^i)$ where $0 \le i < 2T$. The parity data $B(x)$ is computed as

$$B(x) = D(x) \cdot x^{N-K} \bmod G(x) \tag{4.15}$$

Equations (4.13) and (4.15) can be realized with a feedback system as shown in Figure 4.4.

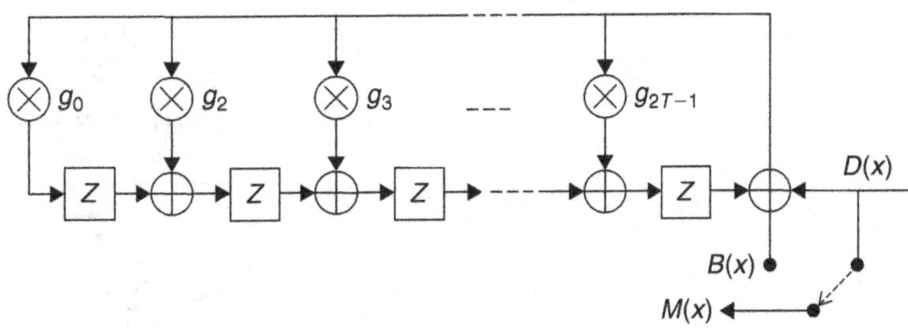

Figure 4.4: Realization of RS(*N*, *K*) encoder.

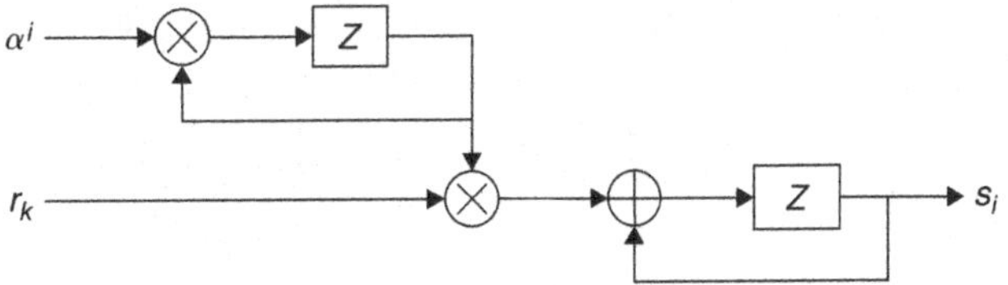

Figure 4.5: Syndrome computation signal flow diagram.

4.2.2 RS(N, K) Decoder

As discussed, the RS(N, K) decoder takes data blocks of N elements as input and outputs K elements as a decoded data block. If errors are present in the received data and if they are less than or equal to $(N-K)/2$, then the RS decoder corrects the errors and outputs a corrected data block.

The error correction with the RS decoder is achieved with the following four steps:

1. Syndrome computation
2. Error locator polynomial computation
3. Error locator polynomial roots computation
4. Error magnitude polynomial computation

Syndrome Computation

In the RS decoder, the first step of decoding is a syndrome computation. Syndromes, which give an indication of presence of errors, are computed using the received data polynomial $R(x)$. If all the syndromes are zero, then there are no errors in the received data. We compute $2T$ syndromes in the syndrome computation step. An i-th syndrome is computed (see Section 3.6) as follows:

$$S_i = R(\alpha^i) = \sum_{n=0}^{N-1} r_k(\alpha^i)^n \tag{4.16}$$

where addition is modulo-2 addition and performed using $\oplus$ instead of $+$. Equation (4.16) can be realized with a feedback system as shown in Figure 4.5.

Computation of Error Locator Polynomial

The error locator polynomial is computed using the Berlekamp-Massey (BM) recursive algorithm as shown in Figure 4.6. We iterate the BM algorithm $2T$ times to get an error locator polynomial $\Lambda(x)$ of degree v which is less than or equal to T. If $v \leq T$, then the roots of the error locator polynomial $\Lambda(x)$ give the correct error positions in the received data vector. The error locator polynomial $\Lambda(x)$ of degree v is represented as

$$\Lambda(x) = 1 + \Lambda_1 x + \Lambda_2 x^2 + \cdots + \Lambda_{v-1} x^{v-1} \tag{4.17}$$

Computation of Error Locator Polynomial Roots

We compute the roots of the error locator polynomial (ELP), $\Lambda(x)$, with a brute-force method (also called Chien's search) by checking all of the field elements to know whether any of the field elements satisfy the Equation (4.17). The following equation (with $\Lambda_0 = 1$) gives the error location as i whenever P_i become zero:

$$P_i = \Lambda(\alpha^i) = \sum_{j=0}^{v} \Lambda_j(\alpha^i) \tag{4.18}$$

where $0 \leq i < N$. Equation (4.18) can be realized with the signal flow diagram as shown in Figure 4.7.

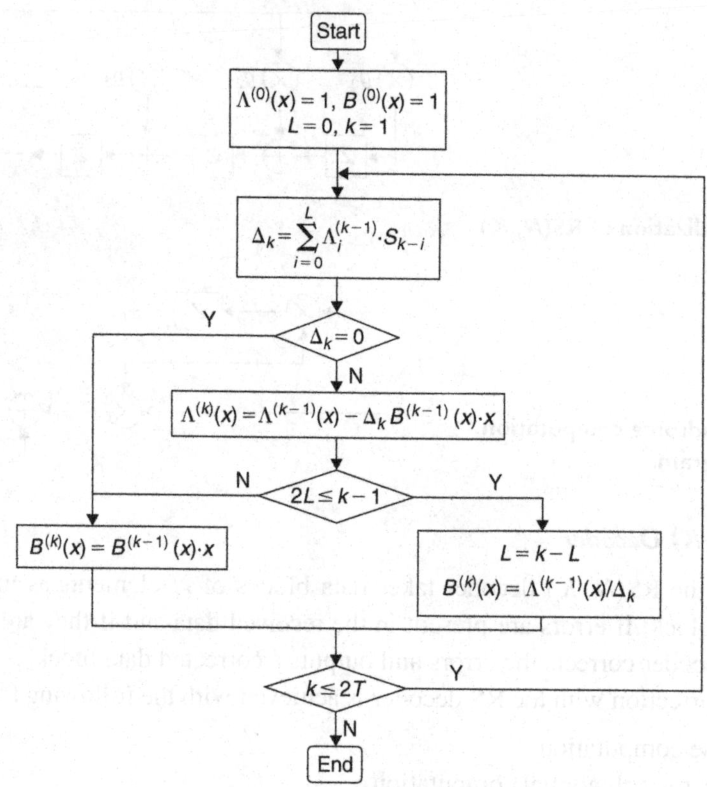

Figure 4.6: Flow chart diagram of Berlekamp-Massey algorithm.

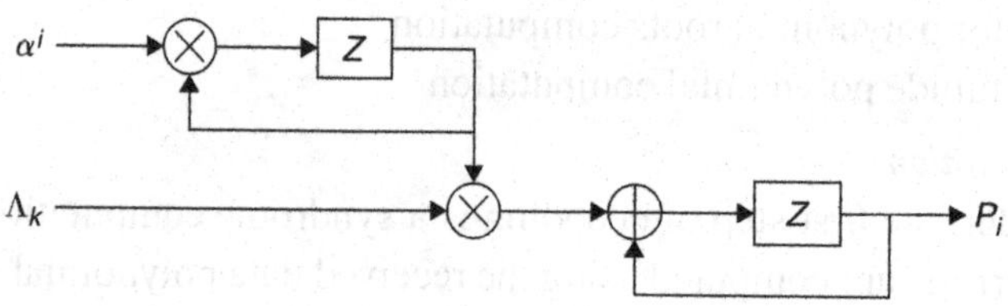

Figure 4.7: Chien's brute-force search method for finding error locations.

Computation of Error Magnitude Polynomial

The error magnitude polynomial $\Omega(x) = 1 + \omega_1 x^1 + \omega_2 x^2 + \cdots + \omega_{2T} x^{2T}$ is computed as

$$\Omega(x) = \Lambda(x)\,[1 + S(x)] \bmod x^{2T+1} \tag{4.19}$$

where $S(x) = \sum_{j=1}^{2T} S_j x^j$ and $\Lambda(x) = \sum_{i=0}^{v} \Lambda_i x^i$ with $\Lambda_0 = 1$

Error Correction

If $\Lambda'(x)$ represents the derivative of the error locator polynomial $\Lambda(x)$ and i_k represents error positions, then error magnitudes $Y_j = e_{i_k}$, where $i_k \in [0, N)$, are computed using error positions information $X_j = (\alpha^j)^{i_k}$, $0 \leq j < v$, $i_k \in [0, N)$ as follows:

$$Y_j = -\frac{X_j \Omega\left(X_j^{-1}\right)}{\Lambda'\left(X_j^{-1}\right)} \tag{4.20}$$

Once we know error positions i_k and error magnitudes e_{i_k}, then we can obtain the error polynomial as

$$E(x) = e_{i_1} x^{i_1} + e_{i_2} x^{i_2} + \cdots + e_{i_v} x^{i_v} \tag{4.21}$$

The corrected data polynomial $\hat{M}(x)$ is obtained from the received data vector $R(x)$ as follows:

$$\hat{M}(x) = R(x) + E(x) \tag{4.22}$$

4.2.3 RS(204, 188) Coder

The RS(204, 188) coder, used in the DVB-H standard (see Section 17.4), is derived from the RS(255, 239) coder, whose field elements belong to GF(2^8) and the Galois field elements for RS(255, 239) coder are generated using the primitive polynomial $p(x) = x^8 + x^4 + x^3 + x^2 + 1$. The generator polynomial used to compute parity data is obtained as $G(x) = (x + \alpha^0)(x + \alpha^1) \cdots + (x + \alpha^{15})$. The RS(204, 188) (shortened version of RS(255, 239)) coder uses the Galois field GF(2^8). See Appendix B, Section B.2, on the companion website for more information on the Galois field GF(2^n) arithmetic operations and respective simulation techniques.

RS(204, 188) Coder Data Representation

The polynomial and the corresponding vector representation of RS(204, 188) coder inputs, outputs, parity data, generator polynomial, and error polynomial follow.

Generator polynomial (17 coefficients):

$$G(x) = x^{16} + g_{15}x^{15} + \cdots + g_2x^2 + g_1x + g_0$$

$$\boldsymbol{G} = [1, g_{15}, \ldots, g_2, g_1, g_0]$$

Encoder input (188-coefficient polynomial):

$$D(x) = d_{187}x^{187} + d_{186}x^{186} + \cdots + d_2x^2 + d_1x + d_0$$

$$\boldsymbol{D} = [d_{187}, d_{186}, \ldots, d_2, d_1, d_0]$$

Parity data (16-coefficient polynomial):

$$B(x) = b_{15}x^{15} + b_{14}x^{14} + \cdots + b_2x^2 + b_1x + b_0$$

$$\boldsymbol{B} = [b_{15}, b_{14}, \ldots, b_2, b_1, b_0]$$

Encoder output (204 coefficients):

$$M(x) = m_{203}x^{203} + m_{202}x^{202} + \cdots + m_2x^2 + m_1x + m_0$$

$$\boldsymbol{M} = [m_{203}, m_{202}, \ldots, m_2, m_1, m_0]$$

$$\boldsymbol{M} = \boldsymbol{D}|\boldsymbol{B}$$

Error polynomial (maximum T coefficients) with ν errors:

$$E(x) = e_{i_1}x^{i_1} + e_{i_2}x^{i_2} + \cdots + e_{i_\nu}x^{i_\nu}$$

$$\boldsymbol{E} = \left[0, 0, \ldots, e_{i_1}, 0, 0, 0, \ldots, e_{i_2}, 0, 0, 0, \ldots, 0, 0, 0, \ldots, 0, e_{i_\nu}, 0, 0, 0, \ldots, 0\right]$$

Decoder input (204-coefficient polynomial):

$$R(x) = r_{203}x^{203} + r_{202}x^{202} + \cdots + r_2x^2 + r_1x + r_0$$

$$R = [r_{203}, r_{202}, \ldots, r_2, r_1, r_0]$$

$$\boldsymbol{R} = \boldsymbol{M} + \boldsymbol{E}$$

Decoder output (188 coefficients):

$$D'(x) = d'_{187}x^{187} + d'_{186}x^{186} + \cdots + d'_2x^2 + d'_1x + d'_0$$

$$\boldsymbol{D}' = \left[d'_{187}, d'_{186}, \ldots, d'_2, d'_1, d'_0\right]$$

In RS decoding, if $v \leq T$, then $D = D'$. In other words, if the number of errors v present in the received data vector $\boldsymbol{R}$ is less than or equal to T, then we can correct v errors using the RS decoder and the decoded output $\boldsymbol{D}'$ and actual transmitted data $\boldsymbol{D}$ will be the same; otherwise, $\boldsymbol{D}$ and $\boldsymbol{D}'$ will be different.

RS(204, 188) Coder Generator Polynomial

Coefficients of the RS(204, 188) coder generator polynomial $G(x) = (x+\alpha^0)(x+\alpha^1)\cdots+(x+\alpha^{15})$ are obtained with the simulation code given in Pcode 4.12. We compute $G(x)$ from first-degree polynomials iteratively in $2T$ iterations. As we do not compute generator polynomials in runtime, we will not discuss its computational complexity and optimization. The simulation results of Pcode 4.12 (i.e., the coefficients of polynomial $G(x)$ of the RS(204, 188) coder) are provided in Section 4.2.6. In later sections, we discuss the simulation of RS(204, 188) encoder and RS(204, 188) decoder modules.

```
Gx[0] = 1 ;                Gx[1] = 1 ;                 // [1 1] = (x+alpha^^0), initialization
for(i = 2;i<=2*T;i++) {                                // multiplying with (x+alpha^^i)
          Gx[i] = 1 ;                                  // coefficient x^^i = 1
          for (j = i-1; j > 0; j--)
          if (Gx[j]!= 0) {
                    r0 = Gx[j-1]; r1 = Gx[j];
                    r1 = Galois_Log[r1];
                    r1 = r1 + i-1;
                    r2 = r1 >> 8; r1 = r1 & 0xff;
                    r1 = r2 + r1;                      // mod 255
                    r2 = Galois_aLog[r1];
                    r0 = r0 ^ r2;
                    Gx[j] = r0;                        // coefficients from x^^(i-1) to x^^1
          }
          else
                    Gx[j] = Gx[j-1];
          r1 = Gx[0];
          r1 = Galois_Log[r1];
          r1 = r1 + i-1;
          r2 = r1 >> 8; r1 = r1 & 0xff;
          r1 = r2 + r1;                                // mod 255
          r0 = Galois_aLog[r1];
          Gx[0] = r0;                                  // coefficient x^^0
}
```

Pcode 4.12: Simulation code for computing a generator polynomial.

4.2.4 RS(204,188) Encoder Simulation

We simulate the RS(204, 188) encoder using the signal flow diagram shown in Figure 4.4. We generate $16(= 2T = N - K = 204 - 188)$ parity data elements with the RS(204, 188) encoder using input message of 188 data elements. The simulation code for computing parity data vector $\boldsymbol{B}$ from input message vector $\boldsymbol{D}$ is given in Pcode 4.13. We obtain the encoded message $\boldsymbol{M}$ by appending data bytes to parity bytes as $\boldsymbol{M} = \boldsymbol{data\ bytes}|\boldsymbol{parity\ bytes}$. The computation of the parity data vector involves multiplication and addition of the Galois field elements. We obtain the parity data vector from shift registers of the feedback loop by passing all data elements of the message vector one at a time to the feedback loop. The complexity of the RS(204, 188) encoder is estimated (see Appendix A.4 on the companion website for cycles estimation on the reference embedded processor) as follows. To update the feedback loop with one message data element, we spend $6+2*T*9$ cycles by interleaving the program code. Thus, we consume $K*(2*T*9+6)$ cycles for updating the feedback loop with K input message elements.

4.2.5 RS(204,188) Decoder Simulation

With the RS(204,188) decoder, we process a data block of 204 elements at a time. In the receiver, before coming to the RS decoder, the data had been processed by other physical layer modules such as demodulation, equalization,

```
for(i = K-1;i>=0;i--) {
        r0 = Dx[K-1-i];            r1 = Bx[2*T-1];
        r0 = r0 ^ r1;                                   // addition of Galois field elements
        r7 = Galois_Log[r0];                            // feedback
        if (r7 != log0) {
                for (j = 2*T-1;j > 0;j--)
                        if (log_Gx[j] != log0) {
                                r1 = log_Gx[j];         r0 = Bx[j-1];
                                r1 = r1 + r7;           // multiplication of Galois field elements
                                r2 = r1 >> 8; r1 = r1 & 0xff;
                                r1 = r1 + r2;           // modulo 255
                                r2 = Galois_aLog[r1];
                                r2 = r2 ^ r0;
                                Bx[j] = r2;
                        }
                        else
                                Bx[j] = Bx[j-1];
                r1 = log_Gx[0];
                r1 = r1 + r7;
                r2 = r1 >> 8;  r1 = r1 & 0xff;
                r1 = r1 + r2;                           // modulo 255
                r2 = Galois_aLog[r1];
                Bx[0] = r2;
        }
        else {
                for (j = 2*T-1;j > 0;j--)
                        Bx[j] = Bx[j-1];
                Bx[0] = 0;
        }
}
for(i = 0;i < 2*T;i++)                  // multiply input msg with x^^(N-K) and add parity data
        Dx[K+i] = Bx[2*T-1-i];
```

Pcode 4.13: Simulation code for RS(204, 188) encoder.

and so on (see Section 17.4). We assume that the proper data block (i.e., a block corresponding to the encoder output block) with 204 elements is available to the RS decoder as an input after data symbols synchronization. Due to channel impairments, the received data vector $\boldsymbol{R}$ may not be same as the transmitted data vector $\boldsymbol{M}$ (see Figure 3.16). Some of the byte elements in the received vector $\boldsymbol{R}$ may be in error and we can correct all the error data bytes using the RS decoder if the number of errors are less than or equal to T, where $T = (N-K)/2 = 8$. As discussed in Section 4.2.2, the RS decoder consists of four steps as follows:

1. Syndrome computation
2. Error locator polynomial computation
3. Finding roots for error locator polynomial
4. Error magnitude polynomial computation

Simulation of these four steps follows.

Syndrome Computation

Computation of one syndrome (see Figure 4.5) involves computation of the Galois field N (= 204) element powers $((\alpha^i)^k)$, N multiplications $(r_k\alpha^{i\cdot k})$, and $N-1$ additions $(\oplus)$. We compute the Galois field two-element multiplication using logarithm and anti-logarithm look-up tables of the Galois field elements (see Appendix B, Section B.2.4, on the companion website). The x and y multiplication, $z = x \cdot y$, using logarithm and anti-logarithm look-up tables involves four steps:

1. Get a, the logarithm of x using the **Galois_Log[ ]**
2. Get b, the logarithm of y using the **Galois_Log[ ]**
3. Compute $c = a + b$
4. Get z, the anti-logarithm of c using the **Galois_aLog[ ]**)

Given the Galois field element $\beta = \alpha^i$, implementation of the Galois field element power ($\gamma = \beta^k$) also involves four steps:

1. Get i, an exponent of α or logarithm value of β
2. Compute $i * k$
3. Compute $j = i * k$ modulo 255
4. Get $\gamma =$ anti-logarithm of j

These steps consume approximately 7 cycles on the reference embedded processor. Instead, we use the look-up table with precomputed Galois field element powers. We perform the Galois field addition using the XOR operator. The simulation code for syndrome computation is given in Pcode 4.14. The 0-th syndrome ($S_0 = R(\alpha^0) = R(1)$) is computed by adding all received message polynomial coefficients. We handle computation of 0th syndrome separately as it involves only XOR operations. Syndromes from S_1 to S_{15} are computed in a loop using a look-up table for the Galois field element powers, **sGalois_elem_pow**[ ]. For each syndrome, we need to compute 204 Galois field element powers, and hence the **sGalois_elem_pow**[ ] look-up table consists of 3060 (= 204 * 15) elements. In the inner loop, we perform syndrome computation for two data elements at a time with 12 instructions per iteration. If we interleave the program code, then the inner loop consumes 12 cycles per iteration. Therefore, the syndrome computation block consumes $(12 * (2T - 1) * N/2 + N)$ cycles. With this, for $T = 8$, we require about 18,600 (= 12 * 102 * 15 + 204 + etc.) cycles to implement the syndrome computation module on the reference embedded processor.

```
r0 = 0;
for(i = 0;i < N;i++)
        r0 = r0 ^ rec_msg[i];
Syndromes[0] = r0;
for(j = 1; j < 2*T; j++) {
        r0 = 0;
        r7 = j*N;
        for(i = 0; i < N; i+=2) {
                r1 = rec_msg[N-i-1]; r2 = rec_msg[N-i-2];
                r3 = Galois_Log[r1]; r4 = Galois_Log[r2];
                r5 = sGalois_elem_pow[r7+i]; r6 = sGalois_elem_pow[r7+i+1];
                r3 = r3 + r5; r4 = r4 + r6;
                r3 = Galois_aLog[r3]; r4 = Galois_aLog[r4];
                r4 = r4 ^ r3;
                r0 = r0 ^ r4;
        }
        Syndromes[j] = r0;
}
```

Pcode 4.14: Simulation code for syndrome computation.

If all computed syndromes are zero, then no errors are present in the received data and we skip the next steps of RS decoding. The received data is not in error most of the time. Even if data is in error, only a few elements (one or two with high probability) of data will be in error. With the RS(204, 188) decoder, we can correct up to 8 (= T) error data elements. If errors are present in the received data block, then not all syndromes are zero and the degree of the error locator polynomial gives the indication of the number of errors present in the data. Next, we discuss the simulation of the error location polynomial generation process.

Error Locator Polynomial Computation

We use the Berlekamp-Massey recursion to compute the error locator polynomial $\Lambda(x)$. With Berlekamp-Massey recursion, error locator polynomial $\Lambda(x)$ is generated using $2T$ syndromes in $2T$ iterations. Before entering the loop, we initialize L, the degree of $\Lambda(x)$ polynomial, as zero (i.e., $\Lambda(x) = 1$, assuming zero errors). We compute the discrepancy Δ at the beginning of every iteration, and if the discrepancy is not zero, then we update $\Lambda(x)$ with the discrepancy. For the first iteration, Δ (discrepancy) is a 0th syndrome. For convenient simulation, we get the first discrepancy Δ before entering the loop and we compute discrepancy for the next iteration always at the end of the current iteration.

The discrepancy Δ is computed by convolving syndromes with the current error locator polynomial, $\Lambda(x) = 1 + \Lambda_1 x + \Lambda_2 x^2 + \cdots + \Lambda_{L-1} x^{L-1}$ of degree $L-1$. For the i-th iteration, discrepancy Δ_i is computed as follows:

$$\Delta_i = \sum_{j=0}^{L_i-1} \Lambda_j S_{i-j}$$
$$= \Lambda_0 S_i \oplus \Lambda_1 S_{i-1} \oplus \cdots \oplus \Lambda_{L_i-1} S_{i-(L_i-1)}$$
$$= S_i \oplus \Lambda_1 S_{i-1} \oplus \cdots \oplus \Lambda_{L_i-1} S_{i-(L_i-1)}$$

In the i-th iteration, we use $L_i - 1$ Galois field additions and multiplications in convoluting syndromes with current $\Lambda(x)$ to compute discrepancy Δ_i. We use the Galois logarithm and anti-logarithm look-up tables for the Galois field elements multiplication. Because we know all syndromes in advance, we get logarithm values for the syndromes before entering the loop of $\Lambda(x)$ computation. We have to compute the logarithm values for $\Lambda(x)$ coefficients in every iteration as they change from iteration to iteration. With this, we can compute the i-th iteration discrepancy Δ_i in $6^*(L_i - 1)$ cycles.

Depending on the current iteration discrepancy Δ_i computed at the end of the previous iteration, we update $\Lambda(x)$ (if $\Delta_i \neq 0$) as $\Lambda^i(x) = \Lambda^{i-1}(x) - x \cdot \Delta_i \cdot T^{i-1}(x)$, where $T^{(i-1)}(x)$ is computed in the previous iteration as

$$T^{(i-1)}(x) = \begin{cases} \Lambda^{i-2}(x)/\Delta_{i-1} & \text{if } \Delta_{i-1} \neq 0 \text{ and } 2L_i - 1 \leq i - 1 \\ x \cdot T^{i-2}(x) & \text{otherwise} \end{cases}$$

If $\Delta_i \neq 0$, we spend a total of $(T+1)^*7$ cycles for computing $\Lambda^i(x)$ and another $(T+1)^*7$ cycles for computing $T^i(x)$ if $2L_i - 1 \leq i - 1$. We spend an overhead of another 20 cycles for moving the data to and from buffers and for conditional checks. Thus, for $T = 8$ we consume about $16^*[6^*(L_i - 1) + 14^*9 + 20]$ cycles for computing error locator polynomial. The simulation code for computing the error locator polynomial $\Lambda(x)$ using the Berlekamp-Massey recursion routine is given in Pcode 4.15.

Once we compute the error locator polynomial $\Lambda(x)$, depending on the degree of $\Lambda(x)$, we get an idea about the number of errors present in the received data. However, we cannot come to a conclusion about the number of errors present by seeing the degree of $\Lambda(x)$ as it gives wrong information when the number of errors present in the received data vector is more than T. By finding the roots of the error locator polynomial $\Lambda(x)$, we can get exact information about the number of errors (if the errors are less than or equal to T) present and about the error positions in the received data vector.

Roots Computation for Error Locator Polynomial

The roots $\{X_i, 0 \leq i < L\}$ of the error locator polynomial gives the error positions in the received data vector (if at all present and if they are less than or equal to T). We find the roots of the error locator polynomial $\Lambda(x)$ by substituting every possible error position (Chien's search) in $\Lambda(x)$ and checking for whether the particular error position satisfies the $\Lambda(x)$. In error locator polynomial roots finding, we need to find the powers of the Galois field elements and we compute the powers here with an analytic method (instead of using look-up tables as in syndrome computation). Here, we consume 7 cycles (and this can be achieved with one cycle on an embedded processor with circular buffer registers; see Appendix A, Section A.4, on the companion website) to find the power of a Galois field element. To find whether a particular data element is in error (if that element position satisfies the $\Lambda(x)$) or not, we spend $(7+4)^*L$ cycles. We search all data element positions to find the roots of the $\Lambda(x)$. Therefore, to find the roots of error locator polynomial $\Lambda(x)$ with an analytic method (without using the modular arithmetic registers of an embedded processor), we consume about 204^*11^*L cycles. The simulation code of Chien's search algorithm for finding the roots of an error locator polynomial is given in Pcode 4.16.

Computation of Error Magnitude Polynomial

We need to know error magnitudes (since the data elements are nonbinary) to correct the errors present in the received data. The error magnitudes are computed with the help of an error magnitude polynomial. We compute

```
L = 0;
r0 = Syndromes[0];                                    // starting delta
for(k = 0;k < 2*T;k++) {
     for(i = 0;i < T+1;i++)
           Conn_poly[i] = Elp[i];                     // Conn_poly = Elp
     if (r0 != 0) {                                   // Elp = Conn_poly - Delta*Tx
          r2 = Galois_Log[r0];                        // log (delta)
          for(i = 0;i < T+1;i++) {
               r1 = Conn_poly[i]; r3 = Tx[i];
               r3 = Galois_Log[r3];                   // log (delta), log(Tx[i])
               r3 = r2 + r3;
               r3 = Galois_aLog[r3];
               r1 = r3 ^ r1;                          // Conn_poly[i]^Delta*Tx[i]
               Elp[i] = r1;
          }
          if (2*L < (k + 1)) {
               L = k + 1 - L;
               for(i = 0;i < T+1;i++) {               // Tx = Conn_poly/Delta
                    r1 = Conn_poly[i];
                    r1 = Galois_Log[r1];
                    m = r1 - r2;
                    if (m < 0)
                         m+= 255;
                    r1= Galois_aLog[m];
                    Tx[i] = r1;
               }
          }
     }
     for(i = T+1;i > 0;i--)                           // Tx = [0 Tx], increment degree by 1
           Tx[i] = Tx[i-1];
     Tx[0] = 0;
     r0 = Syndromes[k+1];
     if(L > 0) {
           for(i = 0;i < L;i++) {                // compute delta by convolution of Syndromes and Elp
                r1 = log_Syndromes[k-i+1]; r2 = Elp[i+1];
                r2 = Galois_Log[r2];
                r1 = r1 + r2;
                r2 = Galois_aLog[r1];
                r0 = r0 ^ r2;
           }
     }
}
```

Pcode 4.15: Simulation code for Berlekamp-Massey recursion.

the error magnitude polynomial $\Omega(x)$, as described in Section 3.6, using the following equation:

$$\Omega(x) = \Lambda(x)[1 + S(x)] \bmod x^{2T+1}$$

$$\text{where } S(x) = \sum_{j=1}^{2T} S_j x^j \text{ and } \Lambda(x) = \sum_{i=0}^{v} \Lambda_i x^i \text{ with } \Lambda_0 = 1$$

Computation of the error magnitude polynomial $\Omega(x)$ involves multiplication of two polynomials, $\Lambda(x)$ and $S(x)$. If $\Omega(x) = 1 + \omega_1 x^1 + \omega_2 x^2 + \cdots$, then the coefficients of $\Omega(x)$ are obtained as follows:

$$\omega_1 = \Lambda_1 + S_1$$

$$\omega_2 = \Lambda_2 + \Lambda_1 S_1 + S_2$$

$$\ldots$$

As we know both the error locator polynomial and syndromes in advance, we precompute logarithm values for syndromes and error locator polynomial coefficients to efficiently perform the Galois field multiplication

```
k = 0;
for(i = 203;i>=0;i--)  {
        r0 = Elp[0];
        for(j = 1;j < L+1;j++) {
                 r1 = i*j;                           // power of Galois field
                 r2 = r1 >> 8; r1 = r1 & 0xff;       // take modulo 255
                 r3 = log_Elp[j];  r1 = r1 + r2;
                 r2 = r1 >> 8; r1 = r1 & 0xff;
                      r1 = r1 + r2;
                 r1 = r1 + r3;             // addition of powers (same as multiplication of log values)
                 r2 = Galois_aLog[r1];
                 r0 = r0 ^ r2;
        }
        if (r0 == 0) {
                Error_position[k] = 255-i;
                k++;
        }
}
```

Pcode 4.16: Simulation code for finding roots of error locator polynomial.

```
Emp[0] = 0;                    // error magnitude polynomial first coefficient logarithm
value
for(j = 1;j<=T;j++) {
        r0 = 0;
        for(i = 0;i<=j;i++) {
                 r1 = log_Elp[i];     r2 = log_Syndromes[j-i];
                 r1 = r1 + r2;
                 r2 = Galois_aLog[r1];
                 r0 = r0 ^ r2;
        }
        r0 = Galois_Log[r0];
        Emp[j] = r0;        // logarithm of error magnitude polynomial i-th coefficicent
}
```

Pcode 4.17: Simulation code for computing error magnitude polynomial.

in computing $\Omega(x)$. As we can only correct T data element errors, we compute $\Omega(x)$ up to degree T. The simulation code for computing the error magnitude polynomial is given in Pcode 4.17. For $T = 8$, we consume about $4*T + (5+10+15+\cdots+40)$ cycles to compute the error magnitude polynomial.

Data Error Correction

To correct data errors, we have to know both the error positions and error magnitudes. We know error positions from the roots of the error locator polynomial. We find error magnitudes with the help of the error magnitude polynomial, differentiated error locator polynomial, and error roots $\{X_i, 0 \le i < L\}$ by using the following equation:

$$e_i = -\frac{X_i \Omega(X_i^{-1})}{\Lambda'(X_i^{-1})}$$

where $\Lambda'(x)$ is the differentiated error locator polynomial of $\Lambda(x)$, and is achieved by simply zeroing alternate coefficients of $\Lambda(x)$. Therefore, $\Lambda'(x) = \Lambda_1 + \Lambda_3 x^2 + \cdots$. We compute error magnitudes (Y_i) for all error positions (X_i) by substituting the inverse of error position (X_i^{-1}) in $\Omega(x)$ and $\Lambda'(x)$ and then computing the Galois field arithmetic expression $X_i\Omega(X_i^{-1})/\Lambda'(X_i^{-1})$. The simulation code for computing error magnitudes and for correcting data errors is given in Pcode 4.18. By interleaving the program code, we consume about $144 (= T*18)$ cycles to compute $\Omega(X_i^{-1})$ and $\Lambda'(X_i^{-1})$, 7 more cycles to perform division and multiplication for computing error magnitude (e_i) and about 3 cycles for getting the error data element and correcting with error magnitude. Therefore, we consume a total of 154 cycles for correcting one data element. If we have data with L errors, then we spend $L*154$ cycles to correct all the error data elements.

```
for(j = 0;j<=T;j+=2)  {                        // logarithm of derivative of error locator polynomial
        log_Derv_Elp[j] = log_Conn_poly[j+1];
        log_Derv_Elp[j + 1] = log0;            // log0 = a value not in the Galois field GF(2^8)
}
for(i = 0;i < L;i++)  { // Find error magnitudes using Forney algorithm, and correct data errors
        r0 = 0;    r5 = 0;
        r2 = Error_position[i];
        for(j = 0;j<=T;j++) {
                 r1 = Omega_gf[j]; r6 = log_Derv_Elp[j];
                 r3 = r2 * j;
                 r4 = r3 >> 8; r3 = r3 & 0xff;
                 r3 = r4 + r3;
                 r4 = r3 >> 8; r3 = r3 & 0xff;
                 k = r4 + r3;
                 k = 255 - k;
                 if (k < 0)
                        k+= 255;
                 r1 = r1 + k; r6 = r6 + k;
                 r1 = Galois_aLog[r1]; r6 = Galois_aLog[r6];
                 r0 = r0 ^ r1; r5 = r5 ^ r6;
        }
        r0 = Galois_Log[r0]; r5 = Galois_Log[r5];
        k = r0 + 2*r2 - r5;
        if (k < 0)
                k+= 255;
        r0 = Galois_aLog[k];
        m = N-1 - r2;
        rec_msg[m] = rec_msg[m]^r0;
}
```

Pcode 4.18: Simulation code for computing error magnitudes and data correction.

4.2.6 RS(204, 188) Simulation Results

In this section, we present the simulation results of the RS(204, 188) coder. We get input data of 188 bytes and compute parity data of 16 bytes from the input data using the RS(204, 188) encoder. To frame 204 elements of encoded data, we left shift the input data vector by 16 bytes and append parity data on the right side. Then we add eight random errors (as RS(204, 188) can correct up to eight errors) to the encoded data, and we input to the RS(204, 188) decoder. The simulation results for the RS(204, 188) coder with encoder input, decoder output and intermediate results follow.

Generator polynomial coefficients vector:

G=[0x3b, 0x24, 0x32, 0x62, 0xe5, 0x29, 0x41, 0xa3, 0x8, 0x1e, 0xd1, 0x44, 0xbd, 0x68, 0xd, 0x3b, 0x1]

RS(204, 188) encoder simulation results:

Input data vector

D=[0x70, 0x18, 0x00, 0x36, 0xc9, 0xd1, 0x25, 0xa2, 0x95, 0x34, 0xb4, 0xff, 0xd2, 0xc4, 0x03, 0x01,
0x6d, 0x53, 0xc0, 0x6f, 0xb5, 0xf3, 0xb5, 0x23, 0x52, 0xc9, 0x49, 0xcc, 0x36, 0x62, 0xee, 0xfb,
0xc0, 0x9e, 0x0e, 0x56, 0x3d, 0x88, 0xad, 0x38, 0xa9, 0x1e, 0xda, 0x2a, 0x9d, 0xa2, 0xc4, 0x8b,
0x68, 0x36, 0xa0, 0xd4, 0xc3, 0xc3, 0xb3, 0xd1, 0x30, 0x32, 0x36, 0xc4, 0xe9, 0x3b, 0x58, 0xb2,
0x04, 0x8e, 0x9b, 0x73, 0x07, 0xfd, 0x0a, 0x0c, 0x1d, 0x4f, 0xb5, 0x1f, 0x83, 0x18, 0xb1, 0x46,
0x76, 0xa4, 0x09, 0xe5, 0xf7, 0x31, 0x27, 0x37, 0x8e, 0xe3, 0x51, 0x73, 0x73, 0x96, 0xb6, 0xb6,
0x41, 0x1d, 0x1b, 0x1d, 0x59, 0xba, 0x61, 0xb4, 0x5b, 0x03, 0x2a, 0xdd, 0x8e, 0x08, 0x2a, 0x2b,
0x18, 0xc1, 0x3e, 0xc3, 0x89, 0xf2, 0xfd, 0x0b, 0xfb, 0x51, 0x74, 0xb7, 0xee, 0x8c, 0x1e, 0x86,
0x90, 0x30, 0x4f, 0xf5, 0xf0, 0x37, 0xce, 0x44, 0xcf, 0x69, 0x9f, 0x8c, 0x83, 0x05, 0x6d, 0x05,
0x06, 0x79, 0x86, 0xf4, 0xc6, 0x29, 0x9f, 0xbf, 0x27, 0x95, 0xee, 0x78, 0xc8, 0x9f, 0x0b, 0x14,
0x78, 0x6d, 0xfd, 0x8b, 0xf1, 0x1b, 0x2a, 0x5e, 0xaf, 0xfa, 0x0d, 0x17, 0x14, 0xad, 0xea, 0x12,
0x97, 0x3a, 0xf9, 0x66, 0x83, 0x82, 0x97, 0x5e, 0x1c, 0x9b, 0x87, 0x81]

Parity vector generated by RS(204, 188) encoder

B=[0xd4, 0x02, 0x65, 0xb2, 0x97, 0x1b, 0xa2, 0x06, 0x3b, 0xbf, 0xd5, 0xe7, 0x5c, 0xa4, 0x3b, 0x99]

Encoder output (parity bytes are bolded): D | B

M = [0x70, 0x18, 0x00, 0x36, 0xc9, 0xd1, 0x25, 0xa2, 0x95, 0x34, 0xb4, 0xff, 0xd2, 0xc4, 0x63, 0x01,
0x6d, 0x53, 0xc9, 0x6f, 0xb5, 0xf3, 0xb5, 0x23, 0x52, 0xc9, 0x49, 0xcc, 0x36, 0x62, 0xee, 0xfb,
0xc0, 0x9e, 0x0e, 0x56, 0x3d, 0x88, 0xad, 0x38, 0xa9, 0x1e, 0xda, 0x2a, 0x9d, 0xa2, 0xc4, 0x8b,
0x68, 0x36, 0xa0, 0xd4, 0xc3, 0xc3, 0xb3, 0xd1, 0x30, 0x32, 0x36, 0xc4, 0xe9, 0x3b, 0x58, 0xb2,
0x04, 0x8e, 0x9b, 0x73, 0x07, 0xfd, 0x0a, 0x0c, 0x1d, 0x4f, 0xb5, 0x1f, 0x83, 0x18, 0xb1, 0x46,
0x76, 0xa4, 0x09, 0xe5, 0xf7, 0x31, 0x27, 0x37, 0x8e, 0xe3, 0x51, 0x73, 0x73, 0x96, 0xb6, 0xb6,
0x41, 0x1d, 0x1b, 0x1d, 0x59, 0xba, 0x61, 0xb4, 0x5b, 0x03, 0x2a, 0xdd, 0x8e, 0x08, 0x2a, 0x2b,
0x18, 0xc1, 0x3e, 0xc3, 0x89, 0xf2, 0xfd, 0x0b, 0xfb, 0x51, 0x74, 0xb7, 0xee, 0x8c, 0x1e, 0x86,
0x90, 0x30, 0x4f, 0xf5, 0xf0, 0x37, 0xce, 0x44, 0xcf, 0x69, 0x9f, 0x8c, 0x83, 0x05, 0x6d, 0x05,
0x06, 0x79, 0x86, 0xf4, 0xc6, 0x29, 0x9f, 0xbf, 0x27, 0x95, 0xee, 0x78, 0xc8, 0x9f, 0x0b, 0x14,
0x78, 0x6d, 0xfd, 0x8b, 0xf1, 0x1b, 0x2a, 0x5e, 0xaf, 0xfa, 0x0d, 0x17, 0x14, 0xad, 0xea, 0x12,
0x97, 0x3a, 0xf9, 0x66, 0x83, 0x82, 0x97, 0x5e, 0x1c, 0x9b, 0x87, 0x81, **0xd4, 0x02, 0x65, 0xb2,**
0x97, 0x1b, 0xa2, 0x06, 0x3b, 0xbf, 0xd5, 0xe7, 0x5c, 0xa4, 0x3b, 0x99]

RS(204, 188) decoder results:

Received data (error data elements are underlined)

R=[0x70, 0x18, 0x00, 0x36, 0xc9, 0xd1, 0x25, 0xa2, 0x95, 0x34, 0xb4, 0xff, 0xd2, 0xc4, 0x63, 0x01,
0x6d, 0x53, 0xc9, 0x6f, 0xb5, 0xf3, 0xb5, 0x23, 0x52, 0xc9, 0x49, 0xcc, 0x36, 0x62, 0xee, 0xfb,
0xc0, 0x9e, 0x0e, 0x56, 0x3d, 0x88, 0xad, 0x38, 0xa9, 0x1e, 0xda, 0x2a, 0x67, 0x38, 0xc4, 0x8b,
0x68, 0x36, 0xa0, 0xd4, 0xc3, 0xc3, 0xb3, 0xd1, 0x30, 0x32, 0x36, 0x10, 0xe9, 0x3b, 0x58, 0xb2,
0x04, 0x8e, 0x9b, 0xa5, 0x07, 0xfd, 0x0a, 0x0c, 0x1d, 0x4f, 0xb5, 0x1f, 0x83, 0x18, 0xb1, 0x46,
0x76, 0xa4, 0x09, 0xe5, 0xf7, 0x71, 0x27, 0x37, 0x8e, 0xe3, 0x51, 0x73, 0x73, 0x96, 0xb6, 0xb6,
0x41, 0x1d, 0x1b, 0x1d, 0x59, 0xba, 0x61, 0xb4, 0x5b, 0x03, 0x2a, 0x48, 0x8e, 0x08, 0x2a, 0x2b,
0x18, 0xc1, 0x3e, 0xc3, 0x89, 0xf2, 0xfd, 0x0b, 0xfb, 0x51, 0x74, 0xb7, 0xee, 0x8c, 0x1e, 0x5c,
0x90, 0x30, 0x4f, 0xf5, 0xf0, 0x37, 0xce, 0x44, 0xcf, 0x69, 0x9f, 0x8c, 0x83, 0x05, 0x6d, 0xb1,
0x06, 0x79, 0x86, 0xf4, 0xc6, 0x29, 0x9f, 0xbf, 0x27, 0x95, 0xee, 0x78, 0xc8, 0x9f, 0x0b, 0x14,
0x78, 0x6d, 0xfd, 0x8b, 0xf1, 0x1b, 0x2a, 0x5e, 0xaf, 0xfa, 0x0d, 0x17, 0x14, 0xad, 0xea, 0x12,
0x97, 0x3a, 0xf9, 0x66, 0x83, 0x82, 0x97, 0x5e, 0x1c, 0x9b, 0x87, 0x81, 0xd4, 0x02, 0x65, 0xb2,
0x97, 0x1b, 0xa2, 0x06, 0x3b, 0xbf, 0xd5, 0xe7, 0x5c, 0xa4, 0x3b, 0x99]

Syndrome vector

S=[0xd9, 0x9c, 0xfd, 0x0, 0x84, 0x16, 0x96, 0x3e, 0x60, 0x3a, 0x18, 0xd3, 0xfb, 0xcf, 0x90, 0xf0]

Error locator polynomial vector

Λ=[0x1, 0x9a, 0x3f, 0xe1, 0xc1, 0x34, 0x13, 0x7b, 0x62]

Error position vector

X=[0x3c, 0x4c, 0x60, 0x76, 0x88, 0x90, 0x9e, 0x9f]

Error magnitude polynomial vector

Ω=[0x1, 0x43, 0x13, 0xad, 0x86, 0xfd, 0xad, 0x88, 0xaa]

Error magnitudes

e=[0xb4, 0xda, 0x95, 0x40, 0xd6, 0xd4, 0x9a, 0xfa]

Decoder output (corrected data elements are italicized and underlined)

D=[0x70, 0x18, 0x0, 0x36, 0xc9, 0xd1, 0x25, 0xa2, 0x95, 0x34, 0xb4, 0xff, 0xd2, 0xc4, 0x63, 0x1,
0x6d, 0x53, 0xc9, 0x6f, 0xb5, 0xf3, 0xb5, 0x23, 0x52, 0xc9, 0x49, 0xcc, 0x36, 0x62, 0xee, 0xfb,
0xc0, 0x9e, 0xe, 0x56, 0x3d, 0x88, 0xad, 0x38, 0xa9, 0x1e, 0xda, 0x2a, *0x9d*, *0xa2*, 0xc4, 0x8b,
0x68, 0x36, 0xa0, 0xd4, 0xc3, 0xc3, 0xb3, 0xd1, 0x30, 0x32, 0x36, *0xc4*, 0xe9, 0x3b, 0x58, 0xb2,
0x4, 0x8e, 0x9b, *0x73*, 0x7, 0xfd, 0xa, 0xc, 0x1d, 0x4f, 0xb5, 0x1f, 0x83, 0x18, 0xb1, 0x46,
0x76, 0xa4, 0x9, 0xe5, 0xf7, *0x31*, 0x27, 0x37, 0x8e, 0xe3, 0x51, 0x73, 0x73, 0x96, 0xb6, 0xb6,
0x41, 0x1d, 0x1b, 0x1d, 0x59, 0xba, 0x61, 0xb4, 0x5b, 0x3, 0x2a, *0xdd*, 0x8e, 0x8, 0x2a, 0x2b,
0x18, 0xc1, 0x3e, 0xc3, 0x89, 0xf2, 0xfd, 0xb, 0xfb, 0x51, 0x74, 0xb7, 0xee, 0x8c, 0x1e, *0x86*,
0x90, 0x30, 0x4f, 0xf5, 0xf0, 0x37, 0xce, 0x44, 0xcf, 0x69, 0x9f, 0x8c, 0x83, 0x5, 0x6d, *0x5*,
0x6, 0x79, 0x86, 0xf4, 0xc6, 0x29, 0x9f, 0xbf, 0x27, 0x95, 0xee, 0x78, 0xc8, 0x9f, 0xb, 0x14,
0x78, 0x6d, 0xfd, 0x8b, 0xf1, 0x1b, 0x2a, 0x5e, 0xaf, 0xfa, 0xd, 0x17, 0x14, 0xad, 0xea, 0x12,
0x97, 0x3a, 0xf9, 0x66, 0x83, 0x82, 0x97, 0x5e, 0x1c, 0x9b, 0x87, 0x81, 0xd4, 0x2, 0x65, 0xb2,
0x97, 0x1b, 0xa2, 0x6, 0x3b, 0xbf, 0xd5, 0xe7, 0x5c, 0xa4, 0x3b, 0x99]

4.2.7 RS(N, K) Coder Computational Complexity

The cycle consumption estimates of the RS encoder and decoder discussed in Sections 4.2.4 and 4.2.5 are meaningful only with the particular approach followed in the simulation of the RS encoder and decoder. In this implementation, we assumed sufficient on-chip memory (1.5 kB for the **Galois_aLog[ ]**, 0.5 kB for the

Galois_Log[ ] and for temporary working buffers, and 3.2 kB for precomputed look-up tables in syndrome computation) is available to store the look-up table values. Whatever approach we use in the implementation of RS codes, the overall cycle cost of RS coding depends on its error-correction capability (i.e., T). If we want to correct more errors with RS coding by adding more redundancy to the original data, then the computational cost of RS coding also increases. Next, we discuss the computational complexity of the RS coder for two different values of T with the same implementation techniques used in this chapter to perform RS encoding and decoding. The expressions used for cycles estimate is valid only with the assumption of one cycle per operation (including data loads) after interleaving the program code to eliminate pipeline stalls of the reference embedded processor. If we do not interleave the program code, then the cycle consumption increases by a lot as the approach for implementation of RS codes involves many data load/store memory accesses. In addition, we did not include the overhead of initialization of variables, jumps and other pipeline stalls in obtaining cycle consumption expressions.

RS Encoder Computational Complexity

Based on Section 4.2.4, the cycles estimate for the RS(N, K) encoder in terms of T follows:

$$\text{encoder cycles} = K^*(2^*T^*9+6)$$

For the RS(204, 188) coder with $T = 8$ error correction capability, we consume about 28,200 (= 188 * (2 * 8 * 9 + 6)) cycles to compute 16 parity elements using the RS(204, 188) encoder. For $T = 16$, we consume about 55,272 (= 188 * (2 * 16 * 9 + 6)) cycles to compute 32 parity elements using the RS(220, 188) encoder.

RS Decoder Computational Complexity

To correct up to T data errors using the RS(N, K) decoder, the total cycles we consume in all four steps of decoding as seen in Section 4.2.5 follows:

$$\text{Decoder cycles} = [12^*(2^*T-1)^*N/2+N]+2^*T^*[6^*(L_i-1)+14^*(T+1)+20]+N^*11^*L$$
$$+[W+L^*(T^*18+10)]$$

where L_i is the length/degree of the error locator polynomial in the i-th iteration of the Berlekamp-Massey recursive algorithm, L is actual number of data errors occurred in the received data and W is the number of cycles consumed by the error magnitude polynomial computation. The decoder cycles expression depends on many parameters and we assume some values for L_i and L parameters in obtaining cycles. For $T = 8$ (or 16), we obtain the RS decoder cycles by assuming the actual errors occurred as $L = 6$ (or 12) and the average iteration count used for computing discrepancy ($L_i - 1$) as 4 (or 8). The value of W is 212 (or 744). The computational complexity of the individual steps of the RS(204, 188) (or RS(220, 188)) decoder in terms of cycles follows:

- Syndrome computation: 18,600 (or 41,030)
- Error locator polynomial computation: 2720 (or 9792)
- Roots finding: 13,464 (or 29,040)
- Error magnitudes and correction: 1136 (or 4320)

Total cycle consumption for RS(204, 188) is obtained by summing individual step cycles and is equal to 35,920 (or 84,182). Of the four steps comprising the RS decoder, the syndrome computation and roots-finding steps consume 80 to 90% of total cycles. As we see from the previous estimated figures, the cycle consumption of the RS(N, K) decoder increases with T (i.e., cycles consumption increases with the error-correction capability of the RS decoder).

4.2.8 RS Decoder: Efficient Implementation

As discussed in Section 4.2.7, the RS decoder is too costly in terms of cycle consumption. For example, if we are working with a 1 Mbps bit rate application, and we want to correct the errors present in the received data using RS (204,188) decoder, then we consume about 191 (= 35920 * 5319) processor MIPS to handle 5319 (= 1000000/188) output data blocks per second. In general, embedded processors will have 500 to 1000 MPIS budget. If the RS decoder only consumes 20 to 40% of the MIPS, then running all other (physical layer) modules on a single embedded processor will not be possible. Typically, we consider average MIPS as a criterion to determine the MIPS budget for a particular application.

We may not find errors in the received data all the time and even if present, most of the time one or two errors will be present. If no errors are present in the current block of received data frame, then the RS decoder cycle cost for that particular block can be reduced to 50% of the RS decoder total cycles. For this, we check the syndrome values after syndrome computation and stop further decoding if all syndromes are zero. If all syndromes are not zero and we obtain the error locator polynomial degree as one after the error locator polynomial computation, then we have one error in the received data block. If one error is present in the received data block, then computing error roots and error magnitude polynomial can be avoided. In this case, the error correction of the received data block is performed using the syndrome values and first-degree error locator polynomial coefficient. The simulation code for correcting single errors in the received data is given in Pcode 4.19.

```
r2 = log_Conn_poly[1]; r0 = Syndromes[0];
m = N-1 - r2;
rec_msg[m] = rec_msg[m]^r0;
```

Pcode 4.19: Simulation code for correcting single data errors.

If two errors are present in the received data block (i.e., $v = L = 2$), then we use the efficient method (for finding two roots of the error locator polynomial) as described in Section 4.1.4, BCH Decoder: Further Optimization for $T = 2$. After finding two roots of the error locator polynomial, we use direct error correction for correcting two data elements (in this case we can avoid error magnitude polynomial computation and also avoid Forney algorithm for error magnitude computation). The simulation code for correcting double errors with the RS(204, 188) decoder is given in Pcode 4.20. With this, although the full the RS decoder needs 191 MIPS, we consume on average 100 MIPS for RS(204, 188) decoding at a 1-Mbps data rate on the reference embedded processor.

```
r4 = Error_position[0];  r5 = Error_position[1];      // i1, i2
r2 = Galois_aLog[r4]; r3 = Galois_aLog[r5];           // X1, X2
r0 = r4 + log_Syndromes[0];  r1 = Syndromes[1];
r0 = Galois_aLog[r0]; m = N-1-r4;
r0 = r0 ^ r1;  r2 = r2^r3;                            // S1+S0·X1, X1+X2
r0 = Galois_Log[r0]; r2 = Galois_Log[r2];
r2 = 255-r2;  r4 = rec_msg[m];                        // 1/(X1+X2)
r0 = r0 + r2; r2 = Syndromes[0];                      // (S1+S0·X1)/(X1+X2)
r0 = Galois_aLog[r0];  k = N-1-r5;
r2 = r2 ^ r0; r5 = rec_msg[k];                        // S0 + (S1+S0·X1)/(X1+X2)
r4 = r4 ^ r2; r5 = r5 ^ r0;
rec_msg[m] = r4;
rec_msg[k] = r5;
```

Pcode 4.20: Simulation code for correcting double data errors.

4.3 RS Erasure Codes

In Section 3.6, we discussed the RS(N, K) coder that corrects $T = (N - K)/2$ errors. With the RS(N, K) coder, we compute $2T$ parity symbols at the transmitter side from K message symbols to form N symbols' length codeword. At the receiver, using these $2T$ parity symbols, we correct up to T errors in the received N length codeword. In this section, we discuss a different kind of RS(N, K) coder, called the RS *erasure coder*, that can correct up to $2T$ errors given the error locations present in the received data. We discuss the encoder structure and decoding procedure for RS erasure codes, as well as simulation and optimization techniques for efficient implementation of RS erasure codes.

4.3.1 Erasure Codes

RS codes with known error locations are called erasure codes. In Section 4.2, we computed the error locator polynomial from the syndromes, and then computed it roots to find the error locations. At these error locations,

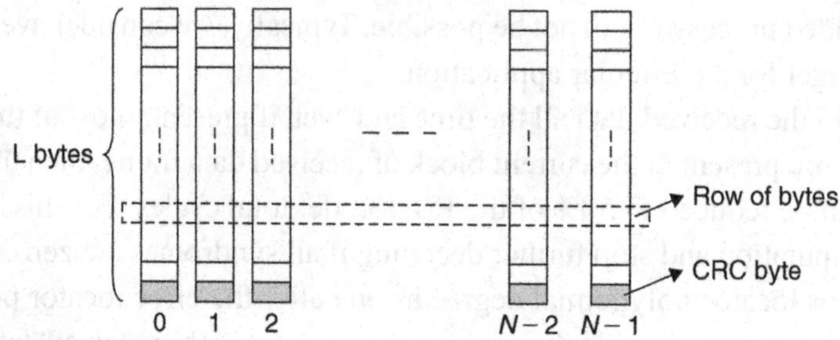

Figure 4.8: Illustration of erasure information.

we could correct the received codeword symbols using error magnitudes which are computed from the syndrome polynomial and error locator polynomial. We could build the error locator polynomial using the Berlekamp-Massey algorithm until degree T and not more than that due to incomplete information from the convolution of the syndrome polynomial and connection polynomial. We can get only T error locations from the roots of the error locator polynomial of degree T. Actually, the RS decoder has the capability to correct up to $2T$ errors if we know $2T$ error locations in advance. How come we know error locations at the receiver in advance? Well, in some receivers using upper layer error check on received data, we can know the error locations. For example, in the DVB-H receivers, the MPE-FEC module (see Section 17.4) design provides the erasure information and allows us to correct up to $2T$ errors using the RS decoder.

We discuss a simple system that generates erasure information for us. Assume that the data is divided into N blocks (or packets) of length L bytes each and arranged as shown in Figure 4.8. Out of L bytes, $L-1$ bytes are payload (or message) and 1 byte (the last one) is CRC data (see Section 3.2 for more details on CRC computation). Next, we transmit all NxL bytes as one frame to the receiver. At the receiver, assume that the received frame contains a few error bytes. If we arrange the received frame as in Figure 4.8 and compute the CRC for each payload block (with $L-1$ bytes), then we know whether any particular block was received with error bytes. We tag those data blocks whose computed CRCs do not match their received CRC and treat them as error blocks. Next, if we obtain the codeword from a row of data bytes as shown in Figure 4.8, then we know the error locations of that codeword in advance from the tag information.

4.3.2 RS Erasure Encoder

Given the data frame, we discuss how to compute the parity symbols to work with erasure codes. For this, we consider a DVB-H MPE-FEC module that supports erasure decoding. The MPE-FEC frame is arranged as a matrix with 255 columns and a flexible number of rows. As we discussed, the RS coder is a block code that takes K data symbols as input and output N symbol codeword by adding computed $2T$ parity symbols to K data symbols. Here, $N = 255 = 2^m - 1$ and hence $m = 8$ (i.e., symbol = byte, represented with a field element that belongs to the Galois field GF(2^8)). Next, we choose K depending on how much error-correction capability we are targeting. In the case of the DVB-H MPE-FEC module, K is chosen as 191. The size of columns (i.e., L) can be a variable and we specify its value from the length of payload data that we want to pack in a single frame. If Q is the length of data bytes and if $L*191 < Q$, then we pad $Q - L*191$ zero bytes to the data frame before computing parity, as shown in Figure 4.9. The payload data section may not occupy a full column of matrix, in which case we continue the next data section immediately after the current data section. The data of S sections are stored to the matrix in columns one after another and zeros are padded at the end to make the payload data length $L*191$.

Next, we work row-wise to compute the RS parity bytes. We compute 64 ($= 2T$) parity bytes from 191 ($= K$) data bytes using the RS encoder given in Section 3.6.1. The generator polynomial $G(x)$ used in computing 64 parity bytes follows:

$$G(x) = (x+\alpha^0)(x+\alpha^1)(x+\alpha^2)\cdots(x+\alpha^{63}) \tag{4.23}$$

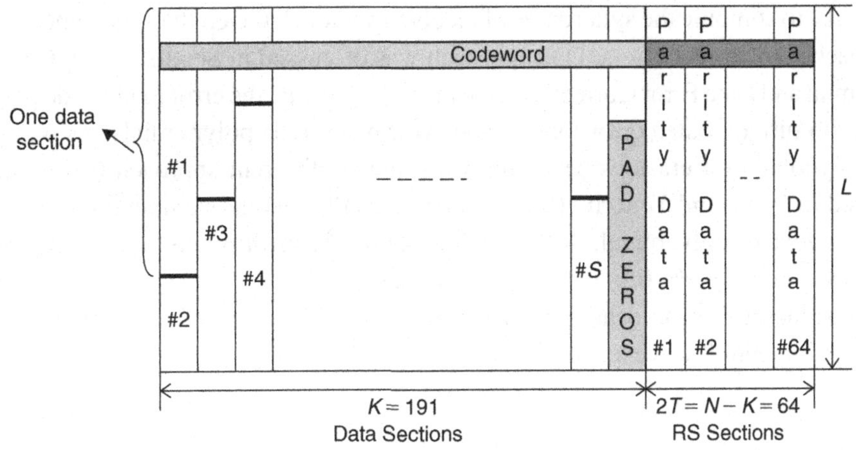

Figure 4.9: Structure of RS erasure encoder.

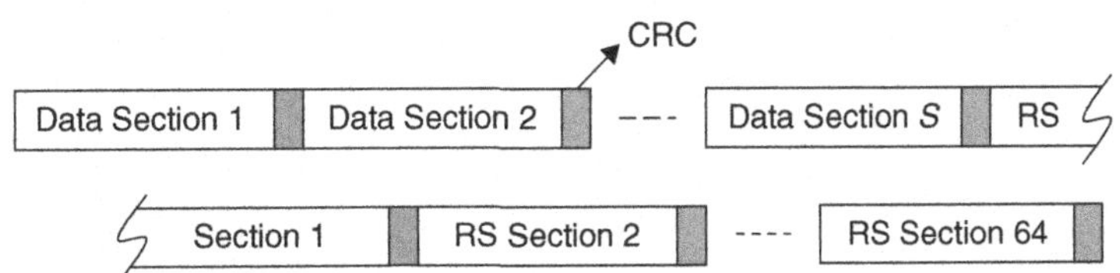

Figure 4.10: One MPE-FEC frame with CRC appended to data and RS sections.

We append 64 parity symbols to 191 data symbols to form a 255 (= N) length systematic RS codeword. Let $M(x)$ be the encoder output message (or codeword polynomial), represented with an $N-1$ degree polynomial as

$$M(x) = m_{254}x^{254} + m_{253}x^{253} + m_{252}x^{252} + \cdots + m_2x^2 + m_1x + m_0 \tag{4.24}$$

where m_i are field elements belongs to GF(2^8). In Figure 4.9, one row of matrix can be represented with vector $\boldsymbol{M} = [m_{254}, m_{253}, m_{252}, \ldots, m_2, m_1, m_0]$, which consists of $N = 255$ bytes.

With the computation of parity data, the matrix is completely filled with data bytes and parity bytes and contains a total of $N * L$ bytes as shown in Figure 4.9. Next, we compute the CRC for each data section (except for the zero padded portion) and for each RS parity data columns and append it to corresponding sections, and then transmit to the receiver as a single frame, as shown in Figure 4.10.

At the receiver, we again compute the CRC for each section and compare it with the received CRC of that section and we classify those sections as unreliable or error sections if the CRCs of those sections do not match. After classification of each section as reliable or unreliable, we arrange them again in matrix form as shown in Figure 4.9. Next, we have the information about which columns contain the error data. Let $\boldsymbol{R} = [r_{254}, r_{253}, r_{252}, \ldots, r_2, r_1, r_0]$ be the vector representing one row of matrix; we come to know the error locations in that vector from the sections' CRC check tagged information. Note that the CRC tagged information may say current byte as an error byte, but actually this byte need not be in error (since the tagged information only conveys that there is a error data somewhere in the column to which the current byte belongs). We treat the current byte as an error byte if the CRC tagged information says so. In the next section, we discuss the RS decoder that corrects up to $2T$ errors given the erasure (or error locations) information.

4.3.3 RS Erasure Decoder

As discussed in Section 3.6, given the received codeword $\boldsymbol{R} = [r_{N-1}, r_{N-2}, \ldots, r_2, r_1, r_0]$ of length N symbols, RS decoding consists of four steps: (1) syndrome computation, (2) error locator polynomial computation, (3) error root computation to find error locations, and (4) error magnitude computation to correct the errors. Of these four steps, we don't need to compute Steps 2 and 3 for erasures correction as erasure gives the error locations.

We can use Pcode 4.14 to compute the syndromes of received vector $\boldsymbol{R}$. Given the syndromes and error locations, we have two approaches to correct errors. One approach was discussed in Section 4.2.2, Computation of Error Magnitude Polynomial and Data Error Correction, in which we compute the error magnitude polynomial and then error magnitudes from differentiated error-locator and error magnitude polynomials. As we are not computing the error-locator polynomial for erasures decoding, we follow a different approach (using the Bjorck-Pereyra algorithm) discussed in Hong and Vetterli (1995), which doesn't need the computation of an error magnitude polynomial and error locator polynomial. We recursively build the error magnitudes using the syndromes and error location values. Let $S_i = \alpha^{a_i}, 0 \le i \le 2T-1$, and $E_j = \alpha^{b_i}, 0 \le j \le L-1$, where $\alpha^{a_i}, \alpha^{b_j} \in \mathrm{GF}(2^8)$ represent syndrome values and error location values. Given $L(\le 2T)$, the number of error locations, a recursive algorithm to get error magnitudes, is executed as follows:

```
for i = 0:L-1
        for j = L:-1:i+1
                S_j = S_j - E_i^* S_{j-1}
        end
end
for i = L-2:-1:0
        for j = i+1:L-1
            S_j = S_j/(E_j - E_{j-i})
            S_{j-1} = S_{j-1} - S_j
        end
end
for i = 0:L-1
        e_i = S_i/E_i
end
```

The values $e_i, 0 \le i \le L-1$ give the error magnitudes at the error locations E_i. Using error magnitudes e_i, we correct the errors present in the received codeword at locations E_i. The simulation code for the Bjorck-Pereyra algorithm to compute error magnitudes is given in Pcode 4.21.

Next, we discuss the computational complexity of RS erasure decoding presented in this section to execute on the reference embedded processor. As discussed in Section 4.2.7, RS Decoder Computational Complexity, we consume approximately 97,000 cycles to compute syndromes using Pcode 4.14 when $N = 255$ and $2T = 64$. To compute error magnitudes using Pcode 4.21, we consume approximately $(10+15)^*L^*(L+1)/2$ cycles (i.e., 52,000 cycles when $L = 64$). Thus, we require about 150,000 cycles (or approximately 100 cycles per bit or 100 MIPS at 1-Mbps bit rate) to perform the erasure decoding algorithm. This figure increases when we want to correct errors other than erasures. Once errors (for which we don't know locations) are present in the received sequence, we then have to compute the error locator polynomial and error roots. As discussed in the previous subsection, roots finding using Chien's search is as complex as finding syndromes. We will discuss a few optimization techniques in Section 4.3.5 with which the cycle consumption for decoding errors and erasures declines significantly.

4.3.4 Decoding Errors and Erasures

We may come across a received sequence containing errors along with the erasures information, and in such cases we have to perform RS decoding to correct both errors and erasures. To compute errors, we have to know the ELP. To build the ELP, we use syndromes, which contain information about erasures. In other words, the computed ELP also has information about erasures. But, with syndromes we can build an ELP only up to degree T, which is not useful as we already know of more than T error locations with erasures. Since we know the error locations in advance for erasures, we can also compute the erasure locator polynomial $Er(x)$. Then we build the ELP on that using the Berlekamp-Massey algorithm. For this, we modify the Berlekamp-Massey algorithm a little bit to accommodate erasures in the ELP.

Computation of Erasure Locator Polynomial

Given the L error locations $a_0, a_1, \ldots, a_{L-1}$, we compute the erasure locator polynomial as $Er(x) = (x+\alpha^{a_0})(x+\alpha^{a_1})\cdots(x+\alpha^{a_{L-1}}) = u_{L-1}x^{L-1} + u_{L-2}x^{L-2} + \cdots + u_2x^2 + u_1x + u_0$, where $u_i \in \mathrm{GF}(2^8)$. The coefficients u_i of $Er(x)$ are obtained using the Pcode 4.22. The polynomial $Er(x)$ is computed iteratively by multiplying the factors one after another.

```
// correct errors

for(i = 0;i < L;i++){
          r0 = Error_position[i];
          sxr[i] = Galois_aLog[r0];
}
for(i = 0;i < L-1;i++){
          for(j = L-1; j > i; j--){
                    r0 = Error_position[i]; r1 = log_Syndromes[j];
                    r0 = r0 + r1;
                    r0 = Galois_aLog[r0]; r1 = Syndromes[j];
                    r0 = r0 ^ r1; r1 = Galois_Log[r0];
                    Syndromes[j] = r0; log_Syndromes[j+1] = r1;
          }
}
for(i = L-2;i>=0;i--){
            for(j = i + 1;j < L;j++){
                    r0 = sxr[j]; r1 = sxr[j-i-1];
                    r0 = r0^r1;
                    r0 = Galois_Log[r0];
                    r1 = log_Syndromes[j+1];
                    m = r1 - r0;
                    if (m < 255) m+= 255;
                    r0 = Galois_aLog[m]; r1 = Syndromes[j-1];
                    Syndromes[j] = r0; log_Syndromes[j+1] = m;
                    r0 = r0 ^ r1; r1 = Galois_Log[r0];
                    Syndromes[j-1] = r0; log_Syndromes[j] = r1;
          }
}
for(i = 0;i < L;i++){
          m = Error_position[i];
          r0 = rec_msg[N-m-1]; r1 = Syndromes[i];
          r0 = r0 ^ r1;
          rec_msg[N-m-1] = r0;
}
```

Pcode 4.21: Error magnitudes computation and errors correction.

```
erasure_poly[0] = erasure_loc[0];
for(i = 1;i < p;i++) {
         r0 = erasure_poly[0]; r3 = erasure_loc[i];
         r0 = Galois_aLog[r0]; r1 = Galois_aLog[r3];
         r0 = r0 ^ r1;
         r6 = Galois_Log[r0]; r2 = erasure_poly[i-1];
         r4 = 0;
         for(j = i;j > 1;j--){
                  r0 = r2; r2 = r2 + r3;
                  r1 = Galois_aLog[r2]; r2 = erasure_poly[j-2];
                  r1 = r1 ^ r4;
                  r5 = Galois_Log[r1];
                  erasure_poly[j] = r5; r4 = Galois_aLog[r0];
         }
         r2 = r2 + r3;
         r1 = Galois_aLog[r2];
         r1 = r1 ^ r4;
         r5 = Galois_Log[r1];
         erasure_poly[1] = r5;
         erasure_poly[0] = r6;
}
```

Pcode 4.22: Erasure polynomial computation.

Modified Berlekamp-Massey Algorithm With the modified Berlekamp-Massey algorithm, we compute the ELP, $\Lambda(x)$, using $Er(x)$ as the initial polynomial. The connection polynomial $T(x)$ is also initialized with $Er(x)$. The value of L gives the degree of the initial ELP. The simulation code for the modified Berlekamp-Massey algorithm is given in Pcode 4.23. With this ELP, we can get $(2T - L)/2$ extra error locations information.

For example, if parity length $2T = 64$ and erasures numbers $L = 60$, then we can get two more extra error location information by building the ELP from $Er(x)$.

```
for(k = q; k < 2*T; k++){
        for(i = 0;i < k;i++)
                 Conn_poly1[i] = Conn_poly0[i];        // Conn_poly_temp = Conn_poly
// compute discrepancy delta by convolution of Syndrome poly and Conn_poly
       r0 = Syndromes[k];
       for(i = 0;i < L;i++){
                 r1 = log_Syndromes[k-i]; r2 = Conn_poly0[i];
                 r2 = Galois_Log[r2];
                 r1 = r1 + r2; r2 = Galois_aLog[r1];
                 r0 = r0 ^ r2;
       }
       if (r0 != 0) {                                 // Conn_poly = Conn_poly_temp - Delta*Tx
                r2 = Galois_Log[r0];                   // log (delta)
                for(i = 0;i < 2*T + 1;i++) {
                         r1 = Conn_poly1[i]; r3 = Tx[i+1];
                         r3 = r2 + r3; r3 = Galois_aLog[r3];
                         r1 = r3 ^ r1;                 // Conn_poly_temp[i]^Delta*Tx[i]
                         Conn_poly0[i] = r1;
                }
                if (2*L < (q + k + 1)){
                          L = q + k + 1 - L; m = 255 - r2;
                          Tx[0] = m;
                          for(i = 0;i < 2*T;i++){      // Tx = Conn_poly_temp/Delta
                                    r1 = Conn_poly1[i];
                                    r1 = Galois_Log[r1];
                                    m = r1 - r2;
                                    if (m < 0) m+= 255;
                                    Tx[i+1] = m;
                          }
                }
       }
       for(i = 2*T + 1;i > 0;i--)                     // Tx = [0 Tx]
           Tx[i] = Tx[i-1];
       Tx[0] = log0;
}
```

Pcode 4.23: Berlekamp-Massey recursion to compute ELP with erasures.

Errors and Erasures Correction Given the ELP that contains both errors and erasures information, we can use the simulation codes from Pcode 4.16 to 4.18 to perform Chien's search (which finds error locator polynomial roots), to find an error magnitude polynomial and to perform a Forney algorithm (which gives error magnitudes).

Computational Complexity with Errors Correction

To correct both errors and erasures, we have to compute the erasure locator polynomial, error locator polynomial, error roots and error magnitude polynomial. These extra computations are not required if only erasures are present in the received data. We estimate the complexity for this portion of modules as follows. If we have L number of erasures and $(2T - L)/2$ number of errors, then to compute the erasure locator polynomial we consume $L * 14 + 8 * L * (L+1)/2$ cycles. For example, if $L = 60$, then we consume 15,480 cycles to compute the erasure locator polynomial. Based on Section 4.2.7, RS Decoder Computational Complexity, we can get the cycle counts for computing the error locator polynomial from the erasure locator polynomial by assuming $L_i = 61$ as 3368; we consume 1,73,910 cycles for finding error roots, approximately 2000 cycles for computing error magnitude polynomial and 36,332 cycles for finding error magnitudes. With this we consume about 328,090 (97,000 (to find syndromes) + 15,480 (to compute the erasure locator polynomial) + 3368 (to compute the remaining error locator polynomial) + 173,910 (to find the roots) + 2000 (to find the error magnitude polynomial) + 36,332 (to find the error magnitudes)) cycles to run the RS erasure decoder on the reference embedded processor for correcting 60 erasures and 2 errors.

4.3.5 Erasure Decoder Optimization

As we saw in the previous section, the two most cycle consuming modules in RS decoding are syndrome computation and error locator polynomial roots finding. The reason for this is that the complexity of these two modules depends on block length N and on the error-correction capability T of the RS code. By contrast, the complexity of determining the error locator polynomial and the error values is a function of only T. Usually the value of N is very big when compared to T. The modules, syndrome computation and error roots finding of RS decoding, are similar in that both entail the evaluation of polynomials at particular elements of extension field. The technique most often employed to carry out these two modules is Horner's method of polynomial evaluation for finding syndromes and error locations. The high cost of syndrome computation and error roots finding can be traced to the iterative nature of their computation procedure. The set of computations carried out for finding a particular syndrome or an error root is repeated in finding other syndromes or error roots too. Moreover, for the erasure code RS(255,191) with the value of $T = 32$, we evaluate 64 syndromes and up to 63 (i.e., 62 erasures + 1 error) error roots. This is like computing the DFT (discrete Fourier transform; see Section 7.1) without using FFT. In DFT computation, we evaluate each frequency component at a time. Whereas with the FFT method, using periodicity and symmetric properties of DFT twiddle factors, we evaluate all frequency components together. Here, in RS decoding, if all the syndromes or all the error roots can be computed together, then a reduction in complexity is perhaps possible. In the following subsections, we examine the syndromes and error roots computation from the spectral point of view.

FFT-Based Computation

Consider the syndrome computation:

$$S_i = R(\alpha^i) = \sum_{j=0}^{N-1} r_j (\alpha^i)^j, \quad i = 0, 1, 2, \ldots, 2T-1 \tag{4.25}$$

Since α is an element of order N, these equations may be interpreted as a DFT with the syndromes representing $2T$ contiguous components of the spectrum of received polynomial $R(x)$. Thus, an alternative way to compute the syndromes is to perform FFT on $R(x)$ and discard the unwanted spectral components. Similarly, roots finding can be performed in a spectral domain. Given the error locator polynomial $\Lambda(x)$, the roots of $\Lambda(x)$ are those powers of α that satisfy

$$\Lambda(\alpha^i) = \sum_{j=0}^{L-1} \Lambda_j (\alpha^i)^j = 0 \tag{4.26}$$

or

$$\sigma_i \cong \Lambda(\alpha^i) = \sum_{j=0}^{N-1} \Lambda_j (\alpha^i)^j, \quad \text{with } \Lambda_L = \Lambda_{L+1} = \Lambda_{L+2} \cdots = \Lambda_{N-2} = \Lambda_{N-1} = 0 \tag{4.27}$$

In Equation (4.27), the error locations are given by the indices of i for which $\sigma_i = 0$. If the spectrum is zero at index i, then $\Lambda(x)$ has a root at i. This provides another way to compute the roots of the error locator polynomial. If we observe carefully, the syndrome computation uses a few outputs of FFT and the error roots finding contains a few inputs of FFT. To reduce the cost of the FFT method, we use FFT output pruning for syndrome computation and FFT input pruning for error roots finding. See Sections 7.2.5 and 7.2.6 for more detail on input and output pruning. However, we may not benefit much from this FFT method when T is a small quantity. As the RS (255, 191) erasure decoder requires the computation of sizable syndromes and error roots, we benefit more from the FFT method.

FFT-Based Implementation Since $255 = 15 \times 17$ and 15 and 17 are relatively prime, we can map the one-dimensional FFT into a twiddle-factor-free two-dimensional FFT via the Good-Thomas mapping. To compute the two-dimensional transform, we compute the row/column DFT transform followed by the column/row DFT transform. In the case of syndrome computation, as we want to perform output pruning with FFT, the way to compute the transform is to perform the 17 15-point column transforms followed by point-wise evaluation of the 64 points along the rows. Similarly, in the case of error roots finding, we perform the first 17-point row transforms by straightforward multiplications, and then perform 17 15-point column transforms.

In addition, $15 = 3 \times 5$, and 3 and 5 are relatively prime; we further simplify the 15-point row transform by mapping the one-dimensional 15-point FFT into a twiddle-factor-free two-dimensional FFT via Good-Thomas mapping as described in the following.

The Good-Thomas FFT is given by

$$X[n_1, n_2] = \sum_{k_1=0}^{N_1-1} W_{N_1}^{n_1 k_1} \sum_{k_2=0}^{N_2-1} x[k_1, k_2] W_{N_2}^{n_2 k_2} \tag{4.28}$$

If $N = N_1 N_2$, where N_1 and N_2 are relatively prime, then at the input of FFT, the two-dimensional vertical and horizontal indices k_1 and k_2 and one-dimensional index k are related by

$$k = (N_2 k_1 + N_1 k_2) \bmod N, \quad \text{where } k_i = (k) \bmod N_i \tag{4.29}$$

At the output side of FFT, we use m_i, which is defined as $m_i = N/N_i$ and satisfies $m_i m_i^{-1} \equiv 1 \bmod N_i$, to get the relationship between one-dimensional and two-dimensional frequency indices:

$$n = (m_1((m_1^{-1} n_1) \bmod N_1) + m_2((m_2^{-1} n_2) \bmod N_2)) \bmod N, \text{ where } n_i = (n) \bmod N_i \tag{4.30}$$

Example 4.1

For $N = 15$, $N_1 = 3$, and $N_2 = 5$, it follows that:

$$m_1 = N/N_1 = 5; \quad m_1^{-1} = 2 \quad \because (2*5) \bmod 3 = 1$$

$$m_2 = N/N_2 = 3; \quad m_2^{-1} = 2 \quad \because (2*3) \bmod 5 = 1$$

Table 4.1 contains the time-domain (i.e., input to FFT) and frequency-domain (i.e., output of FFT) one-dimensional and two-dimensional indice relationships using Equations (4.29) and (4.30).

Using Equation (4.28), we can perform two-dimensional FFT computed using N_1 DFTs of length N_2 and N_2 DFTs of length N_1 without using an intermediate twiddle factor correction. In the implementation, we use look-up tables for getting indices for input pruning, output pruning, obtaining one-dimensional and two-dimensional FFT mapping indices, and for storing twiddle factors. The simulation code for computing 15-point FFT using two-dimensional 3x5 FFT is given in Pcode 4.24.

■

Look-up tables **tp_w[]** and **fp_w[]** on this book's companion website were used to compute 3-point and 5-point FFTs. The look-up tables for input and output indexing to compute the 17 3x5 FFT are also on the website.

Table 4.1: FFT input and output side of Good-Thomas mapping

Input					
$k_1 \backslash k_2$	0	1	2	3	4
0	x[0]	x[3]	x[6]	x[9]	x[12]
1	x[5]	x[8]	x[11]	x[14]	x[2]
2	x[10]	x[13]	x[1]	x[4]	x[7]
output					
$n_1 \backslash n_2$	0	1	2	3	4
0	X[0]	X[6]	X[12]	X[3]	X[9]
1	X[10]	X[1]	X[7]	X[13]	X[4]
2	X[5]	X[11]	X[2]	X[8]	X[14]

```
for(p = 0;p < 17;p++){
        r7 = p*m; r6 = 0;
        for(k = 0;k < 3;k++){  // compute three horizontal 5-point FFTs
                for(i = 0;i < 5;i++){
                        r5 = 0;
                        for(j = 0;j < 5;j++){
                                r4 = input_ index_fp[r7+k*5+j]; r2 = 5*i+j;
                                r3 = rec_msg[N-r4-1]; r2 = fp_w[r2];
                                r3 = Galois_Log[r3]; r0 = r2 + r3;
                                r0 = Galois_aLog[r0];
                                r5 = r5^r0;
                        }
                        sxc[r7+r6] = r5; r6 = r6 + 1;
                }
        }
        r6 = 0;
        for(k = 0;k < 5;k++){  // compute five vertical 3-point FFTs
                for(i = 0;i < 3;i++){
                        r5 = 0;
                        for(j = 0;j < 3;j++){
                                r4 = sxc[r7+k+j*5]; r2 = 3*i+j;
                                r4 = Galois_Log[r4]; r2 = tp_w[r2];
                                r0 = r2 + r4; r0 = Galois_aLog[r0];
                                r5 = r5 ^ r0;
                        }
                        r2 = output_index_fp[r6];
                        sxr[r7+r2] = r5; r6 = r6 + 1;
                }
        }
}
```

Pcode 4.24: Simulation code for 15-point two dimensional FFT computations.

```
j = 0;
for(k = 0;k < 2*T;k++){
        r3 = sxn1[k]; r4 = sxn2[k];
        r5 = 0;
        for(i = 0;i < n;i++){
                r1 = sxr[m*i+r4]; r2 = sp_w[r3*n+i];
                r1 = Galois_Log[r1];
                r0 = r1 + r2; r0 = Galois_aLog[r0];
                r5 = r5 ^ r0;
        }
        Syndromes[j] = r5;
        j = j + 1;
}
```

Pcode 4.25: Syndromes computation with output pruning.

Output Pruning and Syndrome Computation

With Pcode 4.24, we could perform 17 15-point column FFT transforms. Next, using column FFT outputs, we perform 17-point row FFTs only for required spectral outputs. The simulation code to perform 17-point FFT with output pruning is given in Pcode 4.25. We use look-up tables **sxn1**[ ] and **sxn2**[ ] to choose the corresponding input points. We use the look-up table **sp_w**[ ] for storing 17-point FFT twiddle factors. (See the companion website for all three of the look-up tables.)

Input Pruning and Error Location Computation

In the FFT-based error locations computation, first we perform 17-point row DFT with input pruning followed by 17 15-point column transforms. We use the look-up tables **sxn1**[ ] and **sxn2**[ ] for input pruning, and look-up tables **ern0**[ ] and **ern1**[ ] on the website for computing 17-point FFT at points of interest. Once we have a 17-point FFT row transform output, we use Pcode 4.24 to compute 15-point FFT with 3x5 two-dimensional FFTs. Next, we search for spectral nulls in FFT output and the indices of those spectral nulls give the error locations.

```
m = 15;
sxe[0] = 1;
for(i = 1;i < L + 1;i++){
          r2 = sxn1[i]; r3 = sxn2[i];
          r4 = Conn_poly0[i-1];
          sxe[r2*m+r3] = r4;
}
// seventeen point DFT with input pruning
for(k = 0;k < 6;k++){
          for(i = 0;i < n;i++){
                    r5 = 0;
                    for(j = 0;j < 5;j++){
                              r4 = ern0[k*5+j]; r2 = r4*n+i;
                              r3 = sxe[r4*m+k]; r2 = sp_w[r2];
                              r3 = Galois_Log[r3];
                              r0 = r2 + r3; r0 = Galois_aLog[r0];
                              r5 = r5^r0;
                    }
                    sxc[i*m+k] = r5;
          }
}
for(k = 6;k < m;k++){
          for(i = 0;i < n;i++){
                    r5 = 0;
                    for(j = 0;j < 4;j++){
                              r4 = ern1[(k-6)*4+j]; r2 = r4*n+i;
                              r3 = sxe[r4*m+k]; r2 = sp_w[r2];
                              r3 = Galois_Log[r3];
                              r0 = r2 + r3; r0 = Galois_aLog[r0];
                              r5 = r5^r0;
                    }
                    sxc[i*m+k] = r5;
          }
}
```

Pcode 4.26: 17-point DFT with input pruning to compute error locations.

FFT-Based Polynomial Evaluation and Computational Complexity

To compute 15-point DFT, we use the two-dimensional 3x5 FFT as given in Pcode 4.24. To compute three 5-point FFTs we consume approximately 630 cycles and to compute five 3-point FFTs we consume another 450 cycles. With this, to compute the 15-point FFT, we need 1080 cycles and we require 18,360 (= 1080 * 17) cycles to compute 17 15-point FFTs on the reference embedded processor. To compute one syndrome using a 17-point FFT, we consume about 110 cycles using Pcode 4.26. Like this, we consume 7040 (= 110 * 64) cycles to compute 64 syndromes. Thus, total cycles required for syndrome computation are about 25,400 cycles which is far less when compared to Horner's method of syndrome evaluation, which consumes about 97,000 cycles. With the FFT method, for error locations finding also we consume about the same number of cycles as syndrome computation. Based on this, total RS erasure and errors decoding with FFT implementation consumes about 107,980 (= 2 * 25,400 + 15,480 + 3368 + 2000 + 36,332) which is about 1/3 of cycles when compared to non-FFT-based implementation that consumes about 328,090 cycles.

4.3.6 RS Erasure Decoding Simulation Results

As part of the simulations, we consider a codeword ***M*** from the matrix in Figure 4.9, and this codeword is one complete row belonging to that matrix. Let its 255 values be as follows:

M =

```
0x1C, 0x11, 0xC2, 0x4F, 0xD1, 0x27, 0x6E, 0x3D, 0xC6, 0x01, 0x8D, 0x3F, 0x66, 0x5A, 0x40, 0x1A,
0x68, 0x80, 0x07, 0x4B, 0xF0, 0x0A, 0x4A, 0x63, 0x57, 0x82, 0xE6, 0x03, 0x3A, 0xAA, 0xBD, 0xCF,
0x7A, 0xC3, 0x72, 0xBE, 0x53, 0xF1, 0x52, 0xC4, 0x9A, 0x22, 0xDF, 0x6B, 0xA9, 0xAF, 0x06, 0xA1,
0x4C, 0x20, 0xC2, 0x2F, 0x53, 0x91, 0x76, 0x39, 0x29, 0x19, 0x7B, 0x6C, 0x95, 0xEF, 0x70, 0xB4,
0xE7, 0x7A, 0xF7, 0x68, 0xD6, 0xD0, 0xC5, 0x82, 0xA6, 0xD7, 0x7E, 0xEC, 0x49, 0x79, 0xBB, 0x09,
0x70, 0x19, 0xB6, 0x6E, 0xC1, 0xD1, 0xF5, 0x04, 0x78, 0x00, 0xB3, 0xAE, 0x04, 0x24, 0x65, 0xC6,
0x34, 0xBF, 0x57, 0x2F, 0x8D, 0xF1, 0x7D, 0x3D, 0xC1, 0x40, 0x6E, 0x75, 0x04, 0xDE, 0xBF, 0x69,
0x88, 0xCD, 0x42, 0x98, 0xAB, 0xAC, 0xD3, 0x7E, 0x98, 0x63, 0x78, 0x22, 0x77, 0x4F, 0x36, 0x7D,
```

```
0x19, 0x71, 0xAD, 0xAC, 0x70, 0x1C, 0x00, 0x29, 0x81, 0xC9, 0x8C, 0x57, 0x62, 0x01, 0xB8, 0xA7
0xB3, 0x32, 0xBE, 0x57, 0x2C, 0x69, 0xC1, 0xB1, 0x07, 0xFD, 0xDC, 0xCA, 0xDA, 0xC3, 0x3B, 0xE1,
0x13, 0x21, 0x55, 0x51, 0x67, 0x38, 0x65, 0x7F, 0xDE, 0xF6, 0x5E, 0x09, 0xDC, 0xD5, 0xE4, 0x32,
0x35, 0xD0, 0x66, 0x5C, 0xF2, 0x1A, 0xFD, 0x62, 0x4B, 0x5B, 0x0E, 0x05, 0xE5, 0x43, 0x1E, 0x1B,
0xE5, 0x7B, 0x2B, 0x47, 0x15, 0x62, 0xA1, 0x57, 0x07, 0xC6, 0x34, 0x0A, 0xC9, 0x16, 0x96, 0xDC,
0x95, 0xE5, 0xEE, 0x69, 0x66, 0xC6, 0xA4, 0x2A, 0x1F, 0x93, 0x4F, 0xE7, 0xA1, 0x89, 0x9B, 0xB8,
0x7B, 0x01, 0xBA, 0x2E, 0x6A, 0x88, 0x83, 0xD9, 0x77, 0x87, 0xBE, 0x9C, 0x92, 0xD3, 0x13, 0x09,
0x9B, 0x92, 0x15, 0xD7, 0x98, 0x61, 0xBA, 0x03, 0xEE, 0xF7, 0xC3, 0xEA, 0xF9, 0xDD, 0x1D
```

Out of 255 bytes, the first 191 bytes belong to payload (or data section) and the next 64 bytes belongs to parity (or RS section). The parity bytes are bolded, italicized hexadecimal numbers. Next, at the receiver, this codeword is received (after arranging the total frame into matrix form, checking parity check, tagging the error columns and extracting that particular row from matrix) as ***R***. The codeword ***R*** contains a total of 60 erasures (meaning that the locations are known for these 60 errors) and two errors (for these two errors we don't have error location information). The total incorrect bytes present in the ***R*** is 62 and this is also the RS(255, 191) erasure coder maximum correction capability (since erasure coder correction capability $= L + (64 - L)/2 = 60 + (64 - 60)/2 = 62$). All 60 erasure bytes are highlighted with underscores and the two-error bytes are highlighted with underscored bold numbers.

R =

```
0x1c, 0x11, 0xc2, 0x4f, 0xd1, 0x27, 0x6e, 0x3d, 0xc6, 0x01, 0x8d, 0x3f, 0x66, 0x5a, 0x40, 0x1a,
0x68, 0x80, 0x00, 0xba, 0xf0, 0x0a, 0x00, 0x63, 0x57, 0x82, 0x00, 0x03, 0x3a, 0xaa, 0x00, 0xcf,
0x7a, 0xc3, 0x00, 0xbe, 0x53, 0xf1, 0x00, 0xc4, 0x9a, 0x22, 0x00, 0x6b, 0xa9, 0xaf, 0x00, 0xa1,
0x4c, 0x20, 0x00, 0x2f, 0x53, 0x91, 0x00, 0x39, 0x29, 0x19, 0x00, 0x6c, 0x95, 0xef, 0x00, 0xb4,
0xe7, 0x7a, 0x00, 0x68, 0xd6, 0xd0, 0x00, 0x82, 0xa6, 0xd7, 0x00, 0xec, 0x49, 0x79, 0x00, 0x09,
0x70, 0x19, 0x00, 0x6e, 0xc1, 0xd1, 0x00, 0x04, 0x78, 0x00, 0x00, 0xae, 0x04, 0x24, 0x00, 0xc6,
0x34, 0xbf, 0x00, 0x2f, 0x8d, 0xf1, 0x00, 0x3d, 0xc1, 0x40, 0x00, 0x75, 0x04, 0xde, 0x00, 0x69,
0x88, 0xcd, 0x00, 0x98, 0xab, 0xac, 0x00, 0x7e, 0x98, 0x63, 0x00, 0x22, 0x77, 0x4f, 0x00, 0x7d,
0x19, 0x71, 0x00, 0xac, 0x70, 0x1c, 0x00, 0x29, 0x81, 0xc9, 0x00, 0x57, 0x62, 0x01, 0x00, 0xa7,
0xb3, 0x32, 0x00, 0x57, 0x2c, 0x69, 0x00, 0xb1, 0x07, 0xfd, 0x00, 0xca, 0xda, 0xc3, 0x00, 0xe1,
0x13, 0x21, 0x00, 0x51, 0x67, 0x38, 0x00, 0x7f, 0xde, 0xf6, 0x00, 0xad, 0xdc, 0xd5, 0x00, 0x32,
0x35, 0xd0, 0x00, 0x5c, 0xf2, 0x1a, 0x00, 0x62, 0x4b, 0x5b, 0x00, 0x05, 0xe5, 0x43, 0x00, 0x1b,
0xe5, 0x7b, 0x00, 0x47, 0x15, 0x62, 0x00, 0x57, 0x07, 0xc6, 0x00, 0x0a, 0xc9, 0x16, 0x00, 0xdc,
0x95, 0xe5, 0x00, 0x69, 0x66, 0xc6, 0x00, 0x2a, 0x1f, 0x93, 0x00, 0xe7, 0xa1, 0x89, 0x00, 0xb8,
0x7b, 0x01, 0x00, 0x2e, 0x6a, 0x88, 0x00, 0xd9, 0x77, 0x87, 0x00, 0x9c, 0x92, 0xd3, 0x00, 0x09,
0x9b, 0x92, 0x00, 0xd7, 0x98, 0x61, 0x00, 0x03, 0xee, 0xf7, 0x00, 0xea, 0xf9, 0xdd, 0x00,
```

The erasure locations ***Er*** follow: Note that the location indexing starts from the end of vector ***R*** since its corresponding polynomial $R(x) = r_{254}x^{254} + r_{253}x^{253} + \cdots + r_1 x + r_0$ in vector form is represented as $\boldsymbol{R} = [r_{254}, r_{253}, \ldots, r_1, r_0]$.

Er =

```
0, 4, 8, 12, 16, 20, 24, 28, 32, 36, 40, 44, 48, 52, 56, 60, 64, 68, 72, 76, 80, 84, 88, 92, 96, 100, 104, 108,
112, 116, 120, 124, 128, 132, 136, 140, 144, 148, 152, 156, 160, 164, 168, 172, 176, 180, 184, 188, 192,
196, 200, 204, 208, 212, 216, 220, 224, 228, 232, 236
```

The coefficients $\{Er_{60}, Er_{59}, \ldots, Er_2, Er_1, Er_0\}$ of 60th degree erasure locator polynomial $Er[x]$ (corresponding to erasure vector ***Er***) computed using Pcode 4.22 follow:

```
0x01, 0xf6, 0x5,  0xd,  0x46, 0x25, 0x50, 0xa6, 0xc9, 0x42, 0xc9, 0xce, 0x96, 0xf0, 0xa4, 0xce,
0x24, 0x81, 0xf9, 0x47, 0x8f, 0x4d, 0x9,  0x1d, 0xa0, 0xc,  0x3d, 0xa7, 0xce, 0xa4, 0x31, 0x2e,
0xca, 0x52, 0x49, 0xdc, 0xc8, 0x2e, 0xbc, 0x7a, 0xe1, 0xee, 0x58, 0x3b, 0xf9, 0xe7, 0x11, 0xe8,
0xb6, 0x20, 0x92, 0x6c, 0x7c, 0x3,  0xd0, 0xbc, 0x5f, 0x22, 0x18, 0xb8, 0x64
```

The syndrome values S_i for received codeword ***R*** computed with the FFT-based method using Pcode 4.24 and 4.25 follow:

S =

```
0x10, 0x45, 0xa8, 0x9a, 0x7c, 0xb0, 0x5d, 0x2f, 0xc8, 0xd8, 0xad, 0xc9, 0xc6, 0x19, 0x70, 0x36,
0xbb, 0xfb, 0x6e, 0x1c, 0x00, 0x25, 0xda, 0x9d, 0x00, 0xe9, 0x5d, 0x39, 0x98, 0xb7, 0x28, 0xff,
0xad, 0x84, 0x74, 0xe4, 0xf5, 0x35, 0xdc, 0x8a, 0x7c, 0x87, 0x18, 0xcf, 0x7d, 0xc6, 0x9,  0xd3,
0xe0, 0x8f, 0xe8, 0x13, 0x1d, 0x4,  0xd2, 0x9c, 0xf6, 0x53, 0x70, 0xa9, 0x4d, 0x46, 0x89, 0x64
```

As the errors are present along with erasures in the received codeword ***R***, we have to compute the effective error-erasure locator polynomial. The coefficients E_i of the error-erasure locator polynomial computed using the modified Berlekamp-Massey algorithm using Pcode 4.23 follow:

$E_i =$
```
0x01, 0xa6, 0x34, 0xcb, 0xee, 0x1f, 0x41, 0xf0, 0x64, 0x58, 0x61, 0x82, 0xb6, 0xfa, 0xb4, 0x4,
0xcc, 0xff, 0xe1, 0x3f, 0x71, 0x5a, 0x78, 0xa6, 0xbe, 0xd,  0x1d, 0x74, 0xfb, 0xb2, 0x20, 0xbc,
0xa5, 0x87, 0x76, 0x3d, 0x7f, 0x2e, 0x39, 0x50, 0x23, 0xf0, 0x52, 0x39, 0x84, 0xa4, 0x52, 0x79,
0x6b, 0x80, 0xa4, 0x53, 0x33, 0x8f, 0x8b, 0xfd, 0xdf, 0x3f, 0xa6, 0xad, 0xa9, 0x52, 0x8
```

Once we know the error-erasure locator polynomial, we compute the 62-error position vector (this is not necessary when only erasures are present) with the FFT-based method using Pcode 4.26. The error positions vector ***Ep*** follows:

Ep
```
0, 204, 136, 68, 172, 104, 36, 208, 140, 72, 4, 176, 108, 40, 144, 76,
8, 212, 180, 112, 44, 148, 80, 12, 216, 116, 48, 235, 184, 84, 16, 220,
152, 120, 52, 188, 88, 20, 224, 156, 56, 192, 124, 24, 228, 160, 92,60,
196, 128, 28, 232, 164, 96, 200, 132, 64, 236, 168, 100, 83, 32
```

Note that the error positions output by the FFT method are not in order.

Using the syndromes and error positions, we compute the error magnitudes Em_i using Pcode 4.21. The error magnitude vector ***Em*** follows. The error magnitudes are also not in order, however they do correspond to the error positions.

Em
```
0x1d, 0xc2, 0xd3, 0xe,  0xb6, 0xc1, 0x4f, 0x6,  0x42, 0xfd, 0xc3, 0xbb, 0xbe, 0xa4, 0xbf, 0x66, 0xba, 0xdf,
0x7e, 0xb8, 0xee, 0x6e, 0xe4, 0x15, 0x52, 0x8c, 0x96, 0xf1, 0xc5, 0x5e, 0x13, 0x72, 0x7d, 0x0,  0x34, 0xf7,
0x65, 0xbe, 0xbd, 0x57, 0xa1, 0x70, 0xad, 0x83, 0xe6, 0x65, 0x55, 0x2b,
0x7b, 0x36, 0xba, 0x4a, 0xb3, 0x3b, 0x76, 0x78, 0x1e, 0x7,  0xf5, 0xdc, 0xa4, 0x9b
```

The RS(255, 191) erasure-decoder corrected output follows. All corrected bytes are highlighted with bold hexadecimal numbers.

$M' =$

0x1C, 0x11, 0xC2, 0x4F, 0xD1, 0x27, 0x6E, 0x3D, 0xC6, 0x01, 0x8D, 0x3F, 0x66, 0x5A, 0x40, 0x1A,
0x68, 0x80, **0x07**, **0x4B**, 0xF0, 0x0A, **0x4A**, 0x63, 0x57, 0x82, **0xE6**, 0x03, 0x3A, 0xAA, **0xBD**, 0xCF,
0x7A, 0xC3, **0x72**, 0xBE, 0x53, 0xF1, **0x52**, 0xC4, 0x9A, 0x22, **0xDF**, 0x6B, 0xA9, 0xAF, **0x06**, 0xA1,
0x4C, 0x20, **0xC2**, 0x2F, 0x53, 0x91, **0x76**, 0x39, 0x29, 0x19, **0x7B**, 0x6C, 0x95, 0xEF, **0x70**, 0xB4,
0xE7, 0x7A, **0xF7**, 0x68, 0xD6, 0xD0, **0xC5**, 0x82, 0xA6, 0xD7, **0x7E**, 0xEC, 0x49, 0x79, **0xBB**, 0x09,
0x70, 0x19, **0xB6**, 0x6E, 0xC1, 0xD1, **0xF5**, 0x04, 0x78, 0x00, **0xB3**, 0xAE, 0x04, 0x24, **0x65**, 0xC6,
0x34, 0xBF, **0x57**, 0x2F, 0x8D, 0xF1, **0x7D**, 0x3D, 0xC1, 0x40, **0x6E**, 0x75, 0x04, 0xDE, **0xBF**, 0x69,
0x88, 0xCD, **0x42**, 0x98, 0xAB, 0xAC, **0xD3**, 0x7E, 0x98, 0x63, **0x78**, 0x22, 0x77, 0x4F, **0x36**, 0x7D,
0x19, 0x71, **0xAD**, 0xAC, 0x70, 0x1C, **0x00**, 0x29, 0x81, 0xC9, **0x8C**, 0x57, 0x62, 0x01, **0xB8**, 0xA7,
0xB3, 0x32, **0xBE**, 0x57, 0x2C, 0x69, **0xC1**, 0xB1, 0x07, 0xFD, **0xDC**, 0xCA, 0xDA, 0xC3, **0x3B**, 0xE1,
0x13, 0x21, **0x55**, 0x51, 0x67, 0x38, **0x65**, 0x7F, 0xDE, 0xF6, **0x5E**, **0x09**, 0xDC, 0xD5, **0xE4**, 0x32,
0x35, 0xD0, **0x66**, 0x5C, 0xF2, 0x1A, **0xFD**, 0x62, 0x4B, 0x5B, **0x0E**, 0x05, 0xE5, 0x43, **0x1E**, 0x1B,
0xE5, 0x7B, **0x2B**, 0x47, 0x15, 0x62, **0xA1**, 0x57, 0x07, 0xC6, **0x34**, 0x0A, 0xC9, 0x16, **0x96**, 0xDC,
0x95, 0xE5, **0xEE**, 0x69, 0x66, 0xC6, **0xA4**, 0x2A, 0x1F, 0x93, **0x4F**, 0xE7, 0xA1, 0x89, **0x9B**, 0xB8,
0x7B, 0x01, **0xBA**, 0x2E, 0x6A, 0x88, **0x83**, 0xD9, 0x77, 0x87, **0xBE**, 0x9C, 0x92, 0xD3, **0x13**, 0x09,
0x9B, 0x92, **0x15**, 0xD7, 0x98, 0x61, **0xBA**, 0x03, 0xEE, 0xF7, **0xC3**, 0xEA, 0xF9, 0xDD, **0x1D**

4.4 Viterbi Decoder

In this section, we discuss the simulation and implementation techniques for decoding convolutional codes by using the Viterbi algorithm. In particular, we implement the Viterbi decoder that decodes trellis-coded modulation data. Refer to Sections 3.7 through 3.9 for more details on convolutional codes, TCM, and the Viterbi algorithm. As we discuss later, the Viterbi algorithm is costly both in terms of computations and memory usage. We discuss the window-based method to avoid huge memory requirements in implementation of the Viterbi decoder. At the end, we provide simulation results for the 1/2-rate, four-state convolutional coder with 8-PSK modulation and for the corresponding Viterbi decoder.

4.4.1 TCM Convolutional Encoder

In this section, we simulate the TCM encoder. In particular, we simulate the TCM coder shown in Figure 3.34 by using the set partitioning as shown in Figure 3.35. This coder takes 1 bit as input and outputs 2 bits (hence, rate $R = 1/2$). However, the overall rate of the code is 2/3 as we are passing 1 bit as uncoded. At each time instance, we get 3 bits (2 bits from the convolutional coder and one uncoded bit) and we use 8-PSK to modulate them.

The look-up table, **psk_8_tbl_tcm**[ ], is used to map 3 bits to 8-PSK constellation points. We take care of the Ungerboeck set-partitioning of constellation points at the time of filling **psk_8_tbl_tcm**[ ] as follows:

```
psk_8_tbl_tcm[8][2] = {{1,0}, {-1,0}, {1/sqrt(2),1/sqrt(2)}, {-1/sqrt(2),-1/sqrt(2)},
{-1/sqrt(2), 1/sqrt(2)}, {1/sqrt(2),-1/sqrt(2)}, {0,1}, {0,-1}}
```

```
Subset 0: {(1,0), (-1,0)}
Subset 1: {(1/sqrt(2),1/sqrt(2)), (-1/sqrt(2),-1/sqrt(2))}
Subset 2: {(-1/sqrt(2),1/sqrt(2)), (1/sqrt(2),-1/sqrt(2))}
Subset 3: {(0,1), (0,-1)}
```

```
S0 = S1 = 0;
for(m = 0;m < N;m++){
        x = (float) rand() / RAND_MAX;
        b0 = (int) (x+0.5);                     // b0: 0/1
        x = (float) rand() / RAND_MAX;
        b1 = (int) (x+0.5);                     // b1: 0/1
        in_buf[2*m] = b0; in_buf[2*m+1] = b1;
        c0 = b0; c1 = S0^S1^b1; c2 = S1^b1;     // inputs b0, b1 and outputs c0,c1, c2
        S1 = S0; S0 = b1;                       // update encoder states
        j = 4*c2 + 2*c1 + c0;                   // compute offset for 8-PSK look-up table
        tx_seq[2*m] = psk_8_tbl_tcm[j][0];
        tx_seq[2*m+1] = psk_8_tbl_tcm[j][1];    // store transmitted sequence
}
```

Pcode 4.27: Simulation code for TCM encoder.

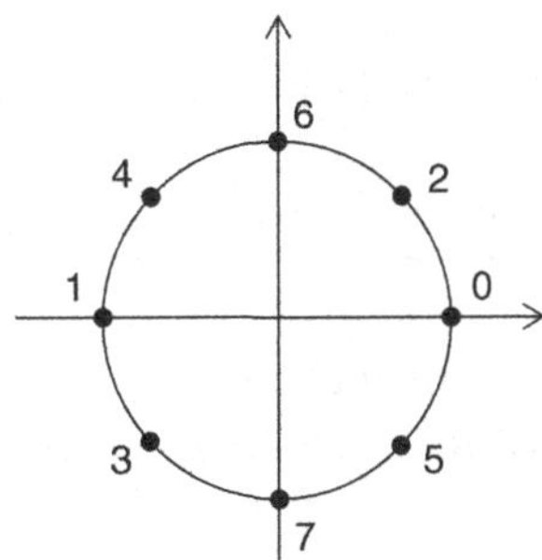

Figure 4.11: 8-PSK constellation point numbering with TCM set partitioning.

The simulation code for the TCM coder is given in Pcode 4.27. The output of encoder "$c_2c_1c_0$" forms offsets ranging from 0 to 7. Bits "c_2c_1" decide which subset to choose and bit "c_0" decides which point to choose from a subset. For example, $c_2c_1c_0 = 110$, then $c_2c_1 = 11$, and $c_0 = 0$. We choose Subset 3 and 0-th point (i.e., (0,1) or the point numbered with 6 in Figure 4.11). The constellation points are numbered as shown in Figure 4.11.

4.4.2 Viterbi Decoder Simulation

The Viterbi decoder, as we discussed in Section 3.9.2, basically involves the computation of Equation (3.45) or the processing of trellis as shown in Figure 3.43. The input to the Viterbi decoder is the received sequence **rx_seq**[ ], which is a corrupted (by AWGN noise; see Section 9.1.2 for more details on noise generation and measurement) version of transmitted sequence **tx_seq**[ ] (generated by the encoder given in Pcode 4.27).

We encode the bits with the TCM encoder that usually starts at zero state and is forced to the zero state at the end of the encoding. Hence, we know the starting and ending states of the TCM encoder. Therefore, the corresponding trellis diagram also starts and ends at zero state as shown in Figure 3.42. We simulate the Viterbi decoder by following the six steps given in Section 3.9.2. The corresponding simulation code of the Viterbi decoder is given in Pcode 4.28 through Pcode 4.30.

Computational Complexity and Memory Requirements

Using the simulation code in Pcodes 4.28 through 4.30, we decode the whole frame of length N samples. In other words, the corresponding trellis consists of N stages. We obtain the survivor paths by computing all states'

```
r0 = rx_seq[0]; r1 = rx_seq[1];                          // received sequence
r2 = psk_8_tbl_tcm[0]; r3 = psk_8_tbl_tcm[1];
r4 = r0 - r2; r5 = r1 - r3;                              // stage: 0
r2 = psk_8_tbl_tcm[2]; r3 = psk_8_tbl_tcm[3];
r6 = r0 - r2; r7 = r1 - r3;
r4 = r4*r4 + r5*r5; r6 = r6*r6 + r7*r7;
if (r6 > r4) {r2 = r4; r3 = 0;}
else {r2 = r6; r3 = 1;}
vm[1][0] = r2; vn[1][0][0] = 0; vn[1][0][1] = r3;
r2 = psk_8_tbl_tcm[12]; r3 = psk_8_tbl_tcm[13];
r4 = r0 - r2; r5 = r1 - r3;
r2 = psk_8_tbl_tcm[14]; r3 = psk_8_tbl_tcm[15];
r6 = r0 - r2; r7 = r1 - r3;
r4 = r4*r4 + r5*r5; r6 = r6*r6 + r7*r7;
if (r6 > r4) {r2 = r4; r3 = 0;}
else {r2 = r6; r3 = 1;}
vm[1][1] = r2; vn[1][1][0] = 0; vn[1][1][1] = r3; // store survivor branches and state metric
r0 = rx_seq[2]; r1 = rx_seq[3];
for(i = 0;i < 4;i++){                                    // stage: 1
            a = vt_st_out0[2*i]; b = vt_st_out0[2*i+1];
            r2 = psk_8_tbl_tcm[2*a]; r3 = psk_8_tbl_tcm[2*a+1];
            r4 = r0 - r2; r5 = r1 - r3;
            r2 = psk_8_tbl_tcm[2*b]; r3 = psk_8_tbl_tcm[2*b+1];
            r6 = r0 - r2; r7 = r1 - r3;
            r4 = r4*r4 + r5*r5; r6 = r6*r6 + r7*r7;
            a = vt_st_in0[2*i]; b = vt_st_in0[2*i+1];
            r5 = vm[1][a]; r7 = vm[1][b];
            r4 = r4 + r5; r6 = r6 + r7;
            if (r6 > r4) {r2 = r4; r3 = 0;}
            else {r2 = r6; r3 = 1; a = b;}
            vm[2][i] = r2; vn[2][i][0] = a; vn[2][i][1] = r3; // store survivor branches and metrics
}
```

Pcode 4.28: Viterbi decoder initial two stages processing.

(i.e., $S = 2^{K-1}$ states, where K is a constraint length of encoder) state metrics (SM) for all N stages. If we have n uncoded bits at each stage, then each path of the trellis consists of 2^n parallel branches. The state metrics are computed using the current stage branch metrics and previous stage state metrics. Thus, the number of computations in decoding performed at each stage increases exponentially with n and K.

We determine the global most likely sequence by taking the survivor branch (i.e., a branch with minimum state metric) at zero state of $(N-1)$th stage and tracing back to the beginning of the trellis. To perform this, we have to store all state metrics and the survivor branches information. If one trellis stage contains S states and if we use 4 bytes per state to store one SM and if we use 1-byte per state to store the survivor branch information (i.e., the index of the previous stage state which connects to the current stage state through the survivor branch), then we need $(4+2^n)*S*N$ bytes of on-chip memory to store the processed trellis data. For example, if the frame length N is 2000 samples and if we use a 4-state encoder with 1-bit uncoded, then we require 48 kB ($= (4+2)*4*2000$) of data memory to store only trellis data. However, we can reduce this memory requirement by using window-based trellis processing (which is suboptimal when compared to the original Viterbi algorithm). Based on computer simulations, it has been found that the decision taken at the current stage for a bit of stage back in time of L stages (where L is greater than or equal to $6K$) results in a correct decoded bit with a very high probability. This convergence property of trellis allows us to implement Viterbi decoder with less memory.

In Pcode 4.28 and 4.29, we use the look-up tables **vt_st_in0**[ ] and **vt_st_int1**[ ] to access the trellis branches connected to appropriate states and we use look-up tables **vt_st_out0** and **vt_st_out1** to access the corresponding branches' outputs. These look-up table values follow:

vt_st_in0[8] = {0,0,0,0,1,1,1,1}
vt_st_in1[16] = {0,0,2,2,0,0,2,2,1,1,3,3,1,1,3,3}
vt_st_out0[8] = {0,1,6,7,2,3,4,5}
vt_st_out1[16] = {0,1,6,7,6,7,0,1,2,3,4,5,4,5,2,3}

```
j = 2;
while(j < N){
        r0 = rx_seq[2*j]; r1 = rx_seq[2*j+1];
        for(i = 0;i < 4;i++){
                a = vt_st_out1[4*i]; b = vt_st_out1[4*i+1];
                r2 = psk_8_tbl_tcm[2*a]; r3 = psk_8_tbl_tcm[2*a+1];
                r4 = r0 - r2; r5 = r1 - r3;
                r2 = psk_8_tbl_tcm[2*b]; r3 = psk_8_tbl_tcm[2*b+1];
                r6 = r0 - r2; r7 = r1 - r3;
                r4 = r4*r4 + r5*r5; r6 = r6*r6 + r7*r7;
                a = vt_st_in1[4*i]; b = vt_st_in1[4*i+1];
                r5 = vm[j][a]; r7 = vm[j][b];
                r4 = r4 + r5; r6 = r6 + r7;                          // add
                if (r6 > r4) {r2 = r4; r3 = 0;}                      // compare and select
                else {r2 = r6; r3 = 1; a = b;}
                vm[j+1][i] = r2; vn[j+1][i][0] = a; vn[j+1][i][1] = r3; // store temporarily

                a = vt_st_out1[4*i+2]; b = vt_st_out1[4*i+3];
                r2 = psk_8_tbl_tcm[2*a]; r3 = psk_8_tbl_tcm[2*a+1];
                r4 = r0 - r2; r5 = r1 - r3;
                r2 = psk_8_tbl_tcm[2*b]; r3 = psk_8_tbl_tcm[2*b+1];
                r6 = r0 - r2; r7 = r1 - r3;
                r4 = r4*r4 + r5*r5; r6 = r6*r6 + r7*r7;
                a = vt_st_in1[4*i+2]; b = vt_st_in1[4*i+3];
                r5 = vm[j][a]; r7 = vm[j][b];
                r4 = r4 + r5; r6 = r6 + r7; r5 = vm[j+1][i];         // add
                if (r6 > r4) {r2 = r4; r3 = 0;}                      // compare and select
                else {r2 = r6; r3 = 1; a = b;}
                if (r5 > r2){ // state metrics and survivor branches
                        vm[j+1][i] = r2; vn[j+1][i][0] = a; vn[j+1][i][1] = r3;
                }
        }
}
```

Pcode 4.29: Viterbi decoder total frame trellis processing.

```
// trace back and decode bits (baseband demodulation done automatically with Viterbi)
k = 0;
for(i = N;i > 0;i--){
        b = (i-1) << 1;;
        j = vn[i][k][0];                    // get previous stage state index
        a = vn[i][k][1];                    // get branch (out of two parallel branches)
        dec_bits[b] = vb[j][k][a][1];       // get first decoded bit
        dec_bits[b+1] = vb[j][k][a][0];     // get second decoded bit
        k = j;
}
```

Pcode 4.30: Simulation code for decoding bits by trace back.

We use the following look-up table, **vb**[ ][ ][ ][ ], for obtaining the associated input bits of the survivor branches belonging to the most global likely sequence in the trace back.

```
vb[4][4][2][2] = {
{{{0,0},{0,1}},{{1,0},{1,1}},{{0,0},{0,0}},{{0,0},{0,0}}},
{{{0,0},{0,0}},{{0,0},{0,0}},{{0,0},{0,1}},{{1,0},{1,1}}},
{{{0,0},{0,1}},{{1,0},{1,1}},{{0,0},{0,0}},{{0,0},{0,0}}},
{{{0,0},{0,0}},{{0,0},{0,0}},{{0,0},{0,1}},{{1,0},{1,1}}}}
```

4.4.3 Viterbi Decoder Implementation

The simulation codes presented in the previous section to decode the TCM codes using Viterbi not only consume a huge amount of memory but also use floating-point computations. In this section, we discuss a fixed-point Viterbi decoder to decode fast and use a window-based method to reduce the overall memory requirement in TCM decoding. We perform fixed-point arithmetic for the Viterbi decoder by converting the input data to

8.8 fixed-point Q-format (which is achieved by multiplying the fractions by 2^8) and by using the 8.8 Q-format look-up table **psk_8_fix_tcm**[] for 8-PSK constellation points as follows:

psk_8_fix_tcm[16] =
{255,0,-255,0,181,181,-181,-181,-181,181,181,-181,0,255,0,-255}

rx_fix_seq[i] = 256***rx_seq**[i], $0 \leq i \leq N-1$

The algorithm for window-based Viterbi decoding follows:

1. At stage $j = 0$, set SM to zero for all states.
2. At a node in a stage of $j > 0$, compute BM for all branches entering the node.
3. Add the BM to the present SM for the path ending at the source node of the branch, to get a candidate SM for the path ending at the destination node of it. After the candidate SM has been obtained for all branches entering the node, compare them and select only that with the minimum value. Let this corresponding branch survive and delete all the other branches to that node from the trellis. This process is shown in Figure 4.12.
4. Return to step 2 for dealing with the next node. If all nodes in the present stage have been processed, go to step 5.
5. If $j < L$ (where $L > 6K$, the window length), increment n and return to step 2, else go to step 6.
6. Take the path with minimum SM (as the global most likely path) and follow the survivor branches backward through the trellis up to the beginning of the window considered. Now collect the bits that correspond to the survivor branch of the global most likely path at the start of the window to form the estimate of the original information bit sequence.
7. If $j < n-1$, move the window one stage forward and go to step 2.

To process the first two stages of the window-based Viterbi in a fixed-point format, we can use the same code presented in Pcode 4.28 by replacing **rx_seq**[] with **rx_fix_seq**[] and **psk_8_tbl_tcm**[] with **psk_8_fix_tcm**[]. In window-based Viterbi decoding, we process the trellis up to L-samples (or a window length) and perform decoding of a bit by tracing back. Then we move the window by one sample and compute the state metrics for the new sample entered into the window and decode the next bit by performing the traceback again. In this process, we perform the traceback for each decoded bit and it is too costly. Instead, we perform window-based Viterbi decoding in a different way in which we perform the traceback once per L-sample. For this, we process the trellis for the first two windows before starting the trace back. In other words, we process the next window trellis in advance. At the end of the trellis processing of the second window, we perform the traceback and decode at once all bits of the first window. The simulation code for this window-based Viterbi decoder is given in Pcodes 4.31 and 4.32. With the program in Pcode 4.31, we only process the trellis for the first window without any trace back. In Pcode 4.32, we always perform trellis processing of the next window and decode all the bits of the previous window by performing the traceback.

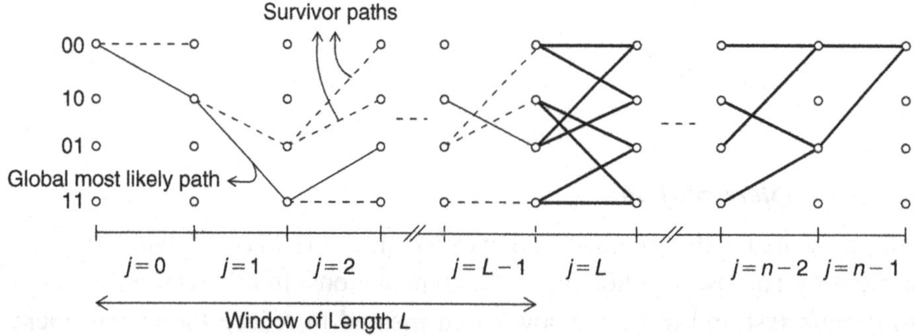

Figure 4.12: Processing of trellis stages in window-based Viterbi decoding.

```
// stages: 2 to 23
m = 2;
for(j = m;j < m + 22;j++){
        r0 = rx_fix_seq[2*j]; r1 = rx_fix_seq[2*j+1];
        for(i = 0;i < 4;i++){
                a = vt_st_out1[4*i]; b = vt_st_out1[4*i+1];
                r2 = psk_8_fix_tcm[2*a];  r3 = psk_8_fix_tcm[2*a+1];
                r4 = r0 - r2;  r5 = r1 - r3;
                r2 = psk_8_fix_tcm[2*b];  r3 = psk_8_fix_tcm[2*b+1];
                r6 = r0 - r2;  r7 = r1 - r3;
                r4 = (r4*r4 + r5*r5)>>8; r6 = (r6*r6 + r7*r7)>>8;
                a = vt_st_in1[4*i]; b = vt_st_in1[4*i+1];
                r5 = vm[j][a];  r7 = vm[j][b];
                r4 = r4 + r5; r6 = r6 + r7;
                if (r6 > r4) {r2 = r4; r3 = 0;}
                else {r2 = r6; r3 = 1; a = b;}
                vm[j+1][i] = r2;
                vn[j+1][i][0] = a; vn[j+1][i][1] = r3;

                a = vt_st_out1[4*i+2]; b = vt_st_out1[4*i+3];
                r2 = psk_8_fix_tcm[2*a];  r3 = psk_8_fix_tcm[2*a+1];
                r4 = r0 - r2;  r5 = r1 - r3;
                r2 = psk_8_fix_tcm[2*b];  r3 = psk_8_fix_tcm[2*b+1];
                r6 = r0 - r2;  r7 = r1 - r3;
                r4 = (r4*r4 + r5*r5)>>8; r6 = (r6*r6 + r7*r7)>>8;
                a = vt_st_in1[4*i+2]; b = vt_st_in1[4*i+3];
                r5 = vm[j][a];  r7 = vm[j][b];
                r4 = r4 + r5; r6 = r6 + r7; r5 = vm[j+1][i];
                if (r6 > r4) r2 = r4; r3 = 0;
                else r2 = r6; r3 = 1; a = b;
                if (r5 > r2){
                        vm[j+1][i] = r2;
                        vn[j+1][i][0] = a; vn[j+1][i][1] = r3;
                }
        }
}
m+= 22;
```

Pcode 4.31: Simulation code for first window trellis processing.

4.4.4 Simulation Results

This section presents the simulation results for a four-state, 8-PSK, 1/2-rate convolutional coder (effective rate is 2/3 as 1 bit is uncoded) as shown in Figure 3.34. We consider 128 random bits for transmission as follows:

Input

Input bits (b_n): 128 bits

```
1, 1, 0, 0, 1, 0, 1, 0, 1, 0, 0, 1, 1, 0, 1, 0, 0, 1, 1, 0, 0, 0, 0, 1, 0, 1, 0, 1, 1, 0, 1, 0,
1, 0, 0, 0, 0, 0, 1, 0, 0, 1, 1, 0, 0, 1, 1, 0, 0, 1, 1, 0, 0, 1, 1, 0, 0, 1, 1, 0, 1, 1, 1, 0,
1, 0, 0, 1, 0, 1, 1, 1, 0, 1, 0, 0, 1, 0, 1, 1, 0, 1, 1, 1, 0, 1, 1, 1, 0, 0, 1, 0, 1, 0, 0, 1,
1, 1, 0, 1, 1, 1, 1, 0, 1, 0, 0, 1, 1, 0, 0, 0, 0, 1, 1, 0, 1, 1, 0, 1, 0, 1, 1, 1, 1, 1, 0, 0
```

Convolutional Encoding

We encode the bits b_n using a rate 1/2 convolutional encoder as shown in Figure 3.34. With a rate 1/2 coder, we output 2 bits for every 1 input bit. We pass 1 more bit as uncoded (so, the effective code rate is 2/3). Hence, we have three output bits for every two input bits. At the start, the encoder state "S_1S_0" is initialized to zero. The encoded bits (192 output bits correspond to 128 input bits) follow:

Encoded bits (c_k): 192 bits

```
1, 1, 0, 1, 1, 1, 1, 0, 1, 0, 0, 1, 1, 1, 1, 1, 0, 1, 1, 1, 0, 1, 0, 1, 0, 0, 0, 1, 1, 0, 1, 1,
1, 0, 0, 0, 0, 0, 1, 0, 0, 1, 1, 1, 0, 0, 1, 1, 0, 0, 1, 1, 0, 0, 1, 1, 0, 0, 1, 1, 1, 0, 1, 1,
1, 1, 0, 1, 0, 0, 1, 1, 0, 1, 0, 0, 1, 1, 1, 1, 0, 0, 1, 1, 0, 1, 1, 1, 0, 0, 1, 1, 1, 0, 0, 1,
1, 0, 0, 1, 1, 1, 1, 0, 1, 1, 0, 1, 1, 1, 0, 1, 0, 1, 1, 1, 1, 0, 0, 0, 0, 1, 1, 1, 1, 1, 0, 0,
1, 0, 1, 1, 1, 0, 1, 1, 1, 0, 1, 1, 1, 1, 0, 0, 0, 0, 0, 0, 0, 0, 0, 0, 0, 1, 1, 1, 0, 0, 1, 1,
1, 1, 0, 1, 0, 1, 1, 0, 1, 1, 0, 1, 1, 0, 1, 0, 0, 1, 1, 0, 1, 0, 0, 1, 0, 1, 1, 0, 0, 1,  1, 1
```

```
while(m < 1001){
        for(j = m;j < m + 24;j++){ // compute metrics for next 6K stages
                p = j&0x3f; q = (j+1)&0x3f;
                r0 = rx_fix_seq[2*j]; r1 = rx_fix_seq[2*j+1];
                for(i = 0;i < 4;i++){
                        a = vt_st_out1[4*i]; b = vt_st_out1[4*i+1];
                        r2 = psk_8_fix_tcm[2*a]; r3 = psk_8_fix_tcm[2*a+1];
                        r4 = r0 - r2;  r5 = r1 - r3;
                        r2 = psk_8_fix_tcm[2*b]; r3 = psk_8_fix_tcm[2*b+1];
                        r6 = r0 - r2;  r7 = r1 - r3;
                        r4 = (r4*r4 + r5*r5)>>8; r6 = (r6*r6 + r7*r7)>>8;
                        a = vt_st_in1[4*i]; b = vt_st_in1[4*i+1];
                        r5 = vm[p][a];  r7 = vm[p][b];
                        r4 = r4 + r5; r6 = r6 + r7;            // add
                        if (r6 > r4) {r2 = r4; r3 = 0;}        // compare and select
                        else {r2 = r6; r3 = 1; a = b;}
                        vm[q][i] = r2; vn[q][i][0] = a; vn[q][i][1] = r3;
                        a = vt_st_out1[4*i+2]; b = vt_st_out1[4*i+3];
                        r2 = psk_8_fix_tcm[2*a];  r3 = psk_8_fix_tcm[2*a+1];
                        r4 = r0 - r2;  r5 = r1 - r3;
                        r2 = psk_8_fix_tcm[2*b];  r3 = psk_8_fix_tcm[2*b+1];
                        r6 = r0 - r2;  r7 = r1 - r3;
                        r4 = (r4*r4 + r5*r5)>>8; r6 = (r6*r6 + r7*r7)>>8;
                        a = vt_st_in1[4*i+2]; b = vt_st_in1[4*i+3];
                        r5 = vm[p][a];  r7 = vm[p][b];
                        r4 = r4 + r5; r6 = r6 + r7; r5 = vm[q][i];
                        if (r6 > r4) {r2 = r4; r3 = 0;}
                        else {r2 = r6; r3 = 1; a = b;}
                        if (r5 > r2){vm[q][i] = r2; vn[q][i][0] = a; vn[q][i][1] = r3;}
                }
        }
        k = 0; a = vm[q][0];                   // trace back and get decoded bits
        if (a > vm[q][1]) {k = 1; a = vm[q][1];}
        if (a > vm[q][2]) {k = 2; a = vm[q][2];}
        if (a > vm[q][3]) {k = 3; a = vm[q][3];}
        for(i = m + 24-1; i > m; i--){
                p = i&0x3f; k = vn[p][k][0];
        }
        for(i = m;i > m-24;i--){
                b = (i-1)<<1; p = i&0x3f;
                j = vn[p][k][0]; a = vn[p][k][1];
                dec_bits[b] = vb[j][k][a][1]; dec_bits[b+1] = vb[j][k][a][0];
                k = j;
        }
        m+= 24;
}
```

Pcode 4.32: Subsequent window trellis processing and decoding by trace back.

PSK Modulation

At the time of encoding, the output of the encoder is mapped to 8-PSK symbols by using each 3-bit encoder output as an offset to the 8-PSK look-up table **psk_8_fix_tcm**[ ] (which is constructed based on Ungerboeck's set-partitioning rules and makes sure that the distance between trellis parallel transitions is maximum). This 8-PSK modulated data follows:

8-PSK normalized constellation points to transmit (S_m): 64 constellation points

```
0,-1, 0.707106769, 0.707106769, 0,-1,-1, 0,-1, 0, 0, 1,-0.707106769,-0.707106769, 0,-1,
0, 1,-0.707106769,-0.707106769, 0, 1, 0, 1,-0.707106769, 0.707106769,
0.707106769, 0.707106769, 0.707106769,-0.707106769, 0,-1,
-1, 0, 1, 0, 1, 0, -1, 0, 0, 1, -0.707106769, -0.707106769, 1, 0,-0.707106769,-0.707106769,
1, 0,-0.707106769,-0.707106769, 1, 0,-0.707106769,-0.707106769, 1, 0,
-0.707106769,-0.707106769,-1, 0,
-0.707106769,-0.707106769, 0,-1, 0, 1,-0.707106769, 0.707106769,
-0.707106769,-0.707106769, 0.707106769, 0.707106769,-0.707106769, 0.707106769, 0,-1,
```

```
0,-1,-0.707106769, 0.707106769,-0.707106769,-0.707106769, 0.707106769, 0.707106769,
-0.707106769,-0.707106769,-0.707106769, 0.707106769, 0,-1,-1, 0, 0, 1,
0.707106769,-0.707106769, 0.707106769, 0.707106769,-0.707106769, -0.707106769,
0.707106769,-0.707106769, 0,-1, 0, 1,-0.707106769,-0.707106769, 0, 1,
0, 1,-0.707106769,-0.707106769,-1, 0,-0.707106769, 0.707106769, 0.707106769, 0.707106769, -0.707106769,
-0.707106769,-0.707106769,-0.707106769,-0.707106769, 0.707106769
```

Passing through AWGN Channel

We transmit the PSK points S_m (after converting them to analog signals) over a noisy channel. For the simulation purpose we add AWGN noise to constellation points. At the receiver, we get noisy PSK constellation points (at the output of the receiver front end) as follows:

Received noisy PSK constellation points (r_m): 64 points

```
0.157108262, -0.876191974, 0.777749598, 0.572184622, -0.0493549667, -0.779661775,
-1.04820085, 0.129765883,-0.754512846, 0.0238341205, 0.113822095, 1.08242452,
-0.830362678,-0.480324298,-0.00643539662,-1.09403169, 0.139023885, 0.993276477,
-0.764336884,-0.95889169, 0.0967011526, 1.0580529, 0.0155533217, 0.864503026,
-0.576663733, 0.72110486, 0.439940155, 0.867248893, 0.187527895, 0.900946856,
0.269263357,-1.00332797,-0.965083599, 0.127240837, 0.969807982, 0.1253566,
1.0114671, 0.0736974776,-1.10441804, 0.208328649, 0.025401894, 1.40040243,
-0.696813524,-0.711368084, 1.2361176, 0.201338947,-0.751767278,-0.69719702,
0.685953498,-0.0994339064,-0.590031147,-0.872876346, 1.08380294, 0.272845447,
-0.854398847,-0.510077894, 0.770515382,-0.0814026967,-0.841046274,-0.553521454,
-0.767543256,-0.11693459,-0.900310397,-0.909833312, 0.364312947,-1.22945499,
-0.17605862, 0.983639538,-0.774587214, 0.775650978,-0.858343899,-1.18007827,
0.615384161, 0.283505648,-0.393607974, 0.756205738, 0.0724883378,-0.78575933,
0.185971975, -1.3460393,-1.04868209, 0.653228343,-0.779842257,-0.512806058,
0.724324882, 0.492230177,-0.558885276,-0.866437376,-0.738605142, 0.714647472,
0.401384085,-0.90096128,-1.04960263, 0.140945986, 0.12148124, 1.07132232,
0.84473902,-0.770106435, 0.83484894, 0.708259106,-0.634552479,-0.87108928,
0.501765013,-0.930042982,-0.214983284,-1.13528705, 0.107488595, 0.880786121,
-0.718424797,-0.988860965, 0.431062669, 1.19838154, 0.0879992619, 1.43463016,
-0.625213265,-0.663498342,-0.936734319, 0.0526892953,-0.609834671, 0.482433826,
1.04271317, 0.66147238,-0.550259411,-0.517056823,-0.646719575, -0.730190217,
-0.631949961, 0.655985713,
```

Preparing Soft Decisions

To work with fixed-point code, we convert (by quantizing) the received noisy PSK points to soft-decisions (multilevel) using 8.8 Q-format (i.e., 256 levels) as follows:

Quantized received soft data (R_m): 64 points (in 8.8 format)

```
40, -223, 199, 146, -12, -199, -267, 33, -192, 6, 29, 277, -212, -122, -1, -279,
36, 254, -195, -244, 25, 271, 4, 221, -147, 185, 113, 222, 48, -230, 69, -256,
-246, 33, 248, 32, 259, 19,-282, 53, 7, 359, -177, -181, 316, 52, -191, -177,
176, -24, -150, -222, 277, 70, -218, -130, 197, -20, -214, -141, -195, -29, -229, -232,
93, -314, -44, 252, -197, 199, -219, -301, 158, 73, -100, 194, 19, -200, 48, -344,
-267, 167, -199, -130, 185, 126, -142, -221, -188, 183, 103, -230, -268, 36, 31, 274,
216, -196, 214, 181, -161, -222, 128, -237, -54, -290, 28, 225, -183, -252, 110, 307,
23, 367, -159, -169, -239, 13, -155, 124, 267, 169, -140, -131, -165, -186, -161, 168
```

Viterbi Decoding

Next, we are ready with the data to feed the Viterbi decoder. The Viterbi decoder copies the transmitter side encoder trellis and processes it. The trellis starts from a zero state (as we assumed at the start of the encoder on the transmitter side) with zero-state metrics. Then we follow the Viterbi algorithm presented in Section 4.4.3 for each received data point. For purposes of clarity, we tabulated the processed trellis that follows on the next page. The first column in the table gives the data points index, the second column gives the state metrics, the third column gives the traceback information, and finally, the fourth column gives the decoded bits (an estimate of transmitted bits) obtained from the global most likely sequence.

Stages	State Metrics				Traceback Information				Decoded Bits
0	0	0	0	0	----	----	----	----	1, 1
1	438	72	0	0	0<>0	0<>1	0<>0	0<>0	0, 0
2	640	746	125	417	0<>0	0<>0	1<>0	1<>1	1, 0
3	193	567	628	604	2<>1	2<>1	3<>1	3<>1	1, 0
4	238	673	838	801	0<>1	2<>1	3<>0	1<>0	1, 0
5	307	679	871	859	0<>1	0<>0	1<>1	1<>0	0, 1
6	810	358	927	985	0<>0	0<>0	1<>0	1<>0	1, 0
7	975	1092	448	692	0<>1	2<>1	1<>1	1<>0	1, 0
8	473	981	972	970	2<>1	2<>1	3<>1	3<>1	0, 1
9	946	510	1199	1188	0<>0	0<>0	1<>0	3<>0	1, 0
10	1250	1152	587	949	0<>1	0<>1	1<>1	1<>1	0, 0
11	628	1088	1245	1195	2<>0	2<>0	3<>0	3<>0	0, 1
12	1100	666	1305	1313	0<>0	0<>0	1<>0	1<>0	0, 1
13	1393	1317	998	704	0<>1	0<>0	1<>0	1<>0	0, 1
14	1144	1362	1039	813	2<>0	2<>0	3<>0	3<>0	1, 0
15	1112	1217	995	1091	2<>1	0<>1	3<>1	3<>1	1, 0
16	1065	1182	1278	1404	2<>1	0<>1	3<>1	1<>1	1, 0
17	1107	1320	1461	1395	0<>1	2<>1	1<>1	1<>0	0, 0
18	1146	1500	1536	1600	0<>0	2<>0	1<>0	1<>1	0, 0
19	1169	1559	1740	1778	0<>0	2<>0	1<>0	1<>1	1, 0
20	1249	1653	1894	1788	0<>1	0<>0	1<>1	1<>0	0, 1
21	1856	1360	2005	2019	0<>0	0<>0	1<>0	1<>0	1, 0
22	2115	2107	1364	1718	0<>1	0<>1	1<>1	1<>1	0, 1
23	1883	1477	2086	1982	2<>0	2<>0	3<>1	3<>0	1, 0
24	2124	2152	1491	1845	0<>1	0<>1	1<>1	1<>0	0, 1
25	1898	1594	2007	2055	2<>1	2<>0	3<>1	3<>0	1, 0
26	2190	2081	1666	1966	2<>1	0<>1	1<>1	1<>1	0, 1
27	2128	1758	2288	2173	2<>0	2<>0	1<>0	3<>0	1, 0
28	2295	2455	1846	2106	0<>1	2<>1	1<>1	1<>0	0, 1
29	2278	1924	2283	2323	2<>1	2<>0	3<>1	3<>0	1, 0
30	2460	2465	1997	2279	0<>1	2<>1	1<>1	1<>0	1, 1
31	2418	2086	2503	2445	2<>1	2<>1	3<>0	3<>1	1, 0
32	2676	2670	2185	2544	0<>1	0<>1	1<>1	3<>1	1, 0
33	2337	2661	2765	2891	2<>1	2<>0	3<>1	1<>1	0, 1
34	2800	2384	2957	2869	0<>1	0<>0	1<>0	1<>0	0, 1
35	3057	3053	2780	2418	0<>1	0<>0	1<>1	1<>0	1, 1
36	3045	3117	2938	2576	2<>1	2<>1	3<>1	3<>1	0, 1
37	3215	3108	2853	2707	0<>0	2<>0	3<>1	3<>0	0, 0
38	3014	3202	2801	3001	2<>0	2<>1	3<>0	3<>0	1, 0
39	2875	3088	3182	3220	2<>1	0<>1	3<>1	3<>1	1, 1
40	3319	3012	3480	3384	2<>1	0<>1	1<>1	1<>1	0, 1
41	3498	3659	3446	3112	0<>1	2<>1	1<>1	1<>0	1, 1
42	3684	3632	3441	3181	0<>1	2<>1	3<>0	3<>1	0, 1
43	3755	3637	3492	3240	2<>0	2<>0	3<>1	3<>0	1, 1
44	3668	3826	3603	3319	2<>1	2<>1	3<>1	3<>1	0, 0
45	3863	3853	3328	3690	2<>0	2<>1	3<>0	3<>1	1, 0
46	3456	3710	3817	3980	2<>1	2<>0	3<>1	1<>1	1, 0
47	3505	3866	4014	3942	0<>1	2<>1	1<>1	1<>0	0, 1

Stages	State Metrics				Traceback Information				Decoded Bits
48	4003	3555	4109	4171	0<>0	0<>0	1<>0	1<>0	1, 1
49	4238	4278	3967	3605	0<>0	0<>1	1<>1	1<>1	0, 1
50	4255	4189	4000	3638	2<>0	2<>0	3<>1	3<>0	1, 1
51	4194	4316	4021	3699	2<>1	2<>1	3<>1	3<>1	1, 0
52	4167	4340	3808	4064	2<>1	0<>1	3<>1	3<>1	1, 0
53	3897	4256	4408	4300	2<>1	0<>1	3<>1	3<>1	0, 1
54	4349	3955	4453	4497	0<>0	0<>0	1<>0	3<>0	1, 0
55	4639	4535	4028	4390	2<>1	0<>1	1<>1	1<>1	0, 0
56	4190	4480	4732	4587	2<>0	2<>0	1<>0	3<>0	0, 1
57	4789	4325	4824	4870	0<>0	0<>0	1<>0	1<>0	1, 0
58	5054	5034	4359	4677	0<>1	0<>1	1<>1	1<>1	1, 1
59	4840	4388	4903	4929	2<>0	2<>1	3<>0	3<>1	0, 1
60	5064	5126	4719	4471	0<>1	0<>0	1<>1	1<>0	0, 1
61	5072	4900	4907	4569	2<>0	2<>0	3<>1	3<>0	1, 1
62	5171	5153	4922	4660	2<>1	2<>1	3<>0	3<>1	1, 1
63	5156	5198	5011	4681	2<>1	2<>1	3<>1	3<>1	0, 0

4.4.5 TCM-Viterbi Performance

The previous table provides only 128 decoded bits. With 128 bits, we cannot say whether the decoder works correctly or not. To see the performance of the TCM-Viterbi coder, we test the decoder with millions of bits (that means we have to encode and transmit that many bits). For example, to test the bit-error-rate (BER) of 10^{-8}, we have to process at least 10^9 bits. In the following, BER versus E_b/N_0 data for the TCM-Viterbi coder shown in Figure 3.34 are provided. The corresponding BER plot for this data is shown in Figure 3.32.

BER versus E_b/N_0 Data:

```
EbNo = 9.000000   error_count = 3    BER = 1.500000e-08
EbNo = 8.000000   error_count = 76    BER = 3.800000e-07
EbNo = 7.000000   error_count = 2104    BER = 1.052000e-05
EbNo = 6.000000   error_count = 32888    BER = 1.644400e-04
EbNo = 5.000000   error_count = 345240    BER = 1.726200e-03
EbNo = 4.000000   error_count = 2254097    BER = 1.127049e-02
EbNo = 3.000000   error_count = 8798461    BER = 4.399231e-02
EbNo = 2.000000   error_count = 21351731    BER = 1.067587e-01
```

4.5 Turbo Codes

In this section, we simulate a turbo encoder and decoder. There are more than one encoder configurations to generate turbo codes and we use the RSC encoder configuration from the 3GPP standard (3rd Generation Partnership Project, 2007) in the simulations. We use the maximum *a posteriori* (MAP) decoding algorithm to decode turbo codes and for this we use derived equations from Section 3.10 to compute corresponding metrics in the simulation of the MAP algorithm. We estimate the computational complexity of the turbo decoder in terms of the number of computations and the amount of memory needed to decode turbo codes by using the MAP algorithm.

4.5.1 RSC Encoder Simulation

For achieving better error-correction performance, we use RSC encoder to generate turbo codes. The 3GPP standard specifies parallel concatenation of two RSC encoders for turbo codes generation as shown in Figure 4.13. These RSC encoders consists of 3 ($= M$) delay units each and hence the constraint length of each RSC encoder is 4 (i.e., $M+1$). The two RSC encoders are separated by an interleaver and the interleaver input and output sequence index relations are specified in the 3GGP standard. The first encoder works on a direct input bit sequence and outputs a systematic output bit sequence and a parity bit sequence whereas the second decoder

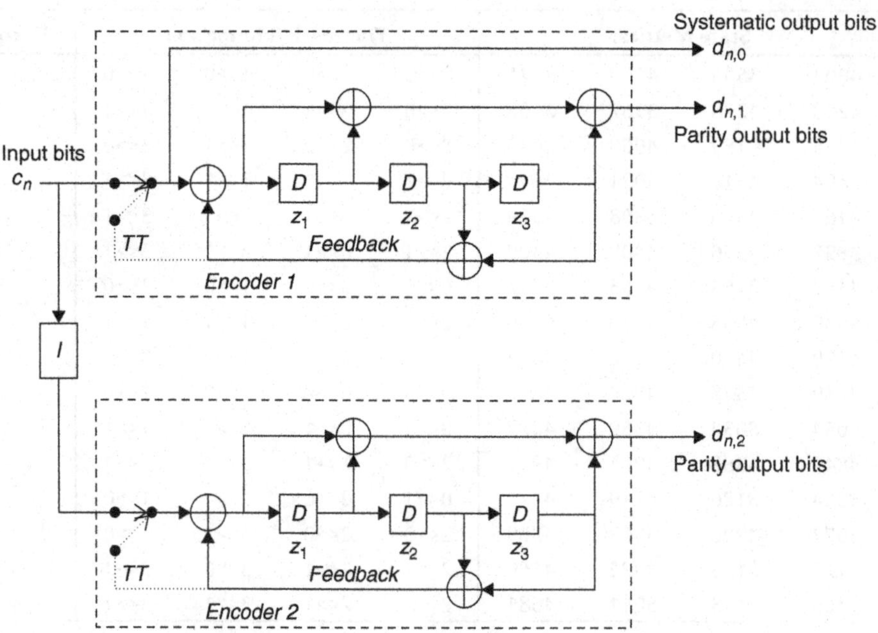

Figure 4.13: Parallel concatenation of two RSC encoders with interleaver.

works on the interleaved bit sequence and outputs another parity bit sequence. In other words, we generate three output bit sequences from one input bit sequence and hence the encoder shown in Figure 4.13 is a rate 1/3 coder.

At the beginning we initialize two RSC encoder states with zeros, and then the state of each encoder is updated based on their input sequence bit and feedback bit. Typically, tracking of the RSC encoder state for each input bit (and feedback bit) is carried out with the help of a trellis diagram as shown in Figure 4.14(a). The trellis has three phases and they are (1) initialization phase, (2) steady-state phase, and (3) termination phase. After the start of encoding, we needed three stages to get into steady-state. Similarly, the termination phase also involves three stages. For trellis termination (TT), we use bits from a feedback loop instead of from input bits by switching, as shown in Figure 4.13.

A zoomed version of the steady-state trellis in Figure 4.14(a) is shown in Figure 4.14(b). We rearrange the output states of the trellis to get the simple flow of the steady-state trellis, and we use this rearranged flow throughout the simulation as it has certain advantages in the implementation of the MAP algorithm on the reference embedded processor. In Figure 4.14(b), a solid line represents the RSC encoder state update from the current state to the next state when the input bit is "1," and similarly the dotted line represents the state update when the input bit is "0." The state diagram shown in Figure 4.14(b) corresponds to the first RSC encoder as we output two bits (one systematic bit and one parity bit) from one input bit. The trellis for the second RSC encoder is also the same as the first RSC encoder; the only difference is that the number of output bits in this case is one (i.e., a second parity bit). The simulation code of the 3GPP RSC encoder and the BPSK modulator is given in Pcode 4.33. This simulation code assumes an interleaved input bit sequence is available to the second RSC encoder; the study and simulation of the 3GPP interleaver is not in the scope of this book.

Typically, the input data bits are accessed in terms of 8-bit bytes from memory as the minimum size of the data that the processor can access from memory is a byte (or an 8-bit quantity). Once we get a byte of data, then to encode bit-by-bit, we have to unpack the bits which takes about 1.125 cycle per bit (or a total of 9 cycles with the first bit unpack requiring 2 cycles and rest of the bits requiring 1 cycle per bit) on the reference embedded processor. Then, an additional 7 cycles are required to code this bit as coding involves only sequential operations. After coding, we have to pack the coded bits and store them in memory for other processing and transmission. Packing of data takes the same number of cycles as unpacking 1.125 cycles per bit. Thus, a total of 10 cycles are required for encoding 1 bit of data and outputting one parity bit (including overhead).

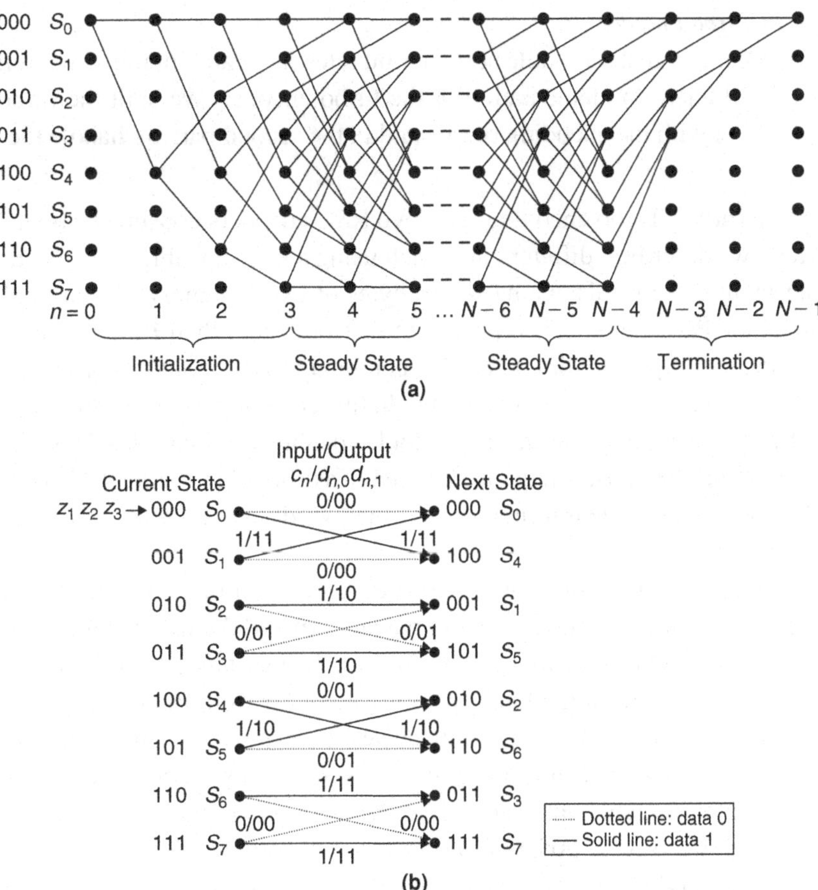

Figure 4.14: (a) Trellis diagram flow for RSC encoder. (b) Steady-state trellis data flow of RSC encoder.

```
S1[0] = 0; S1[1] = 0; S1[2] = 0;
S2[0] = 0; S2[1] = 0; S2[2] = 0;
for(i = 0;i < N;i++) {
        // first RSC encoder
        feedback = S1[1] ^ S1[2]; tmp1 = c[i];      // c[] contains input bit sequence
        tmp1 = feedback ^ tmp1; *x++ = 1 - 2*c[i]; // x[] contains output symbols
        tmp2 = tmp1 ^ S1[2]; S1[2] = S1[1];
        tmp2 = tmp2 ^ S1[0]; S1[1] = S1[0];
        S1[0] = tmp1; *x++ = 1-2*tmp2;             // modulate parity bit one and store
        // second RSC encoder
        feedback = S2[1] ^ S2[2]; tmp1 = c_in[i];  // c_in[] contains interleaved input bits
        tmp1 = feedback ^ tmp1;
        tmp2 = tmp1 ^ S2[2]; S2[2] = S2[1];
        tmp2 = tmp2 ^ S2[0]; S2[1] = S2[0];
        S2[0] = tmp1; *x++ = 1-2*tmp2;             // modulate parity bit two and store
}
```

Pcode 4.33: Simulation code for 3GPP RSC encoder and BPSK modulator.

Turbo Encoder Complexity

Since we use the look-up table for interleaver addresses instead of computing on the fly, we only spend cycles for look-up table accesses (which may come for free with compute operations). To interleave one data bit, it takes about three cycles (one cycle for loading offset, two cycles for computing absolute address). Since turbo encoding involves two RSC encoders and one interleave operation, in total we consume 25 cycles (including overhead) for encoding one data bit. In other words, for applications with 14.4 Mbps bit rate (e.g., femtocell base station), we require about 360 MIPS and this is about 60% of the total available 600 MIPS of the reference embedded processor.

Efficient Implementation of Turbo Encoder

As discussed, a turbo encoder is a costly module at higher bit rates if we are not implementing it properly. Next, we discuss techniques for efficient implementation of the turbo encoder. We split the turbo encoder into two parts. In the first part, we deal with the encoding of bits and in the second part we handle the interleaving of the data bits.

Encoding Using Look-up Table Turbo encoding with two RSC encoders consumes about 20 cycles per input bit as we discussed. Here, we describe a different approach using a look-up table that consumes only 2.5 cycles (for both encoders) per input bit. For this, we need 256 bytes of extra memory for storing look-up table data. Given the present *state* of the RSC encoder, it is possible to encode more than 1 bit at a time using this look-up table. By precomputing the look-up table for all possible combinations of input bits of length L and for all three combinations of state bits, we can encode L bits at a time. In this encoding, we use a look-up table that has 2^{L+3} entries. As the value of L increases, then the size of the look-up table also increases. With $L = 4$ (i.e., encoding 4 bits at a time), we have 2^7 or 128 entries in the look-up table as shown in Figure 4.15(a). Each entry contains 4 encoded bits and 3 bits of updated state information. In other words, a byte (or 8 bits) is sufficient to represent each entry of the look-up table.

Exploring closely the details of the 8-bit look-up table design, it can be seen that to compute a 7-bit offset to the 128-entry look-up table from 4 input bits (say in register $r0$) and 3 current-state bits (say in register $r1$), we have to extract (1-cycle) 4 data bits (say to register $r2$) from the input byte (or from $r0$); extract (1-cycle) of the current state (say to register $r3$) from the look-up table output (or from $r1$) of the previous encoding; shift (1-cycle) 3 state bits by $4(r3 = r3 << 4)$; and OR (1-cycle) the extracted 4 input data bits to state bits (i.e., $r4 = r2|r3$). We can avoid the extract and shift operations for state bits by properly designing the look-up table. If we use 2 bytes for each look-up table entry and place the state bits in the shifted position as shown in the Figure 4.15(b), we can avoid two (saving 50%) of the offset calculation cycles.

Next, after computing the encoded bits, we have to pack the encoded bits. As we are encoding 4 bits at a time and simultaneously outputting an encoded 4-bit nibble, packing nibbles into bytes is easy. We pack 2 nibbles into a byte in 2 cycles (with one left shift and one OR or ADD operation). For packing two encoder outputs, we spend 4 cycles on the reference embedded processor. By using the multiply-accumulate (MAC) unit, we can do this packing in 2 cycles for two encoders since we have two MAC units on the reference embedded processor. It is clear from this that the turbo encoding of 1 byte consumes 20 cycles or 2.5 cycles per bit.

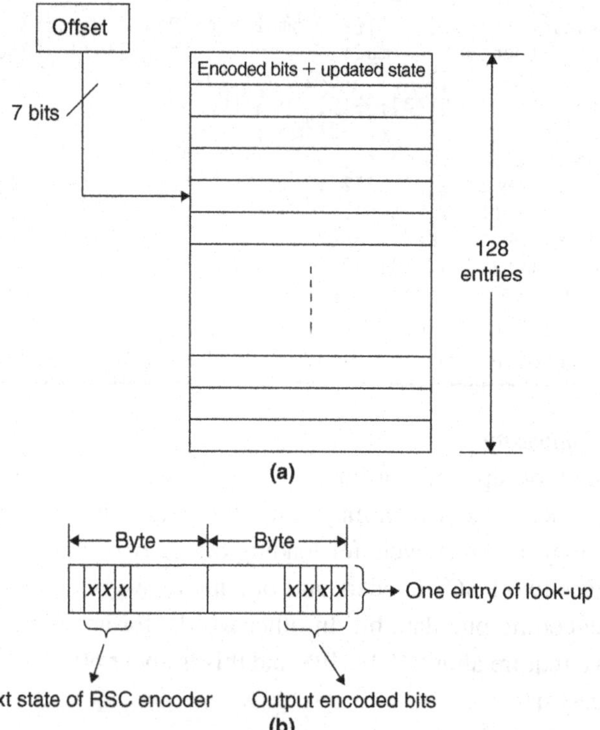

Figure 4.15: (a) Look-up table-based turbo encoding. (b) Look-up table design for efficient turbo encoding.

In the previous discussion, we encoded 4 bits at a time for two encoders. But, in reality the second encoder doesn't get the data directly from the input bitstream bytes. We have to interleave the input bitstream before passing it to the second encoder. In the previous section, we assumed that the interleaving bits are available for the second encoder. The stored interleaved bits are accessed directly from the buffer for encoding by storing the interleaved bits in an addressable boundary (i.e., a minimum of a byte has to be used for storing 1 bit).

Here, since we are encoding in terms of nibbles using the look-up table approach, we have to pack the interleaved bits back to bytes before storing them to the interleaver buffer. Therefore, to feed the bits to the second encoder in the right order, we have to perform the following three steps: unpack, interleave and pack. As we represent the data in terms of bytes, packing and unpacking involves demultiplexing and multiplexing of bytes into bits and bits into bytes, respectively. Packing of bits to bytes needs all interleaved bits, so we have to first perform interleaving completely. We perform unpacking and interleaving together to avoid the stalls. The two operations, unpacking and interleaving, consumes about 3 cycles per bit. Then we pack the bits back to bytes and this packing operation consumes one cycle per bit on the reference embedded processor.

Based on the previous discussion, the cycles consumed per bit for unpacking, interleaving and packing of interleaved data arc 4. In encoding of data, we spend 2.5 cycles per bit. With this, the turbo encoder total cycle cost is 6.5 cycles per bit. Assuming an overhead of 1 cycle per bit, we consume about 7.5 cycles per bit for performing turbo encoding. With this efficient implementation, we use 108 MIPS of the reference embedded processor or approximately 18% of processor MIPS at a bit rate of 14.4 Mbps. In comparison, we used 60% of processor MIPS with simple implementation of turbo encoding discussed previously.

With the look-up table method described in this section for turbo encoding, we need 256 bytes of data memory to store precomputed encoding information. With this efficient method, we need less data memory (by a factor 8) for storing the interleaved data as we pack the bits to bytes. Both methods require the same data memory for storing interleaver addresses as it is costly to compute interleaver addresses on the fly.

Modulation and Transmission of Bits

The output of the turbo encoder is passed through a mapper to obtain a modulated encoded bit sequence $x_{n,0}, x_{n,1}, x_{n,2}, x_{n+1,0}, x_{n+1,1}, x_{n+1,2}, \ldots$ before transmitting through a channel as shown in Figure 3.47. With BPSK modulation, we map "0" to "+1" and "1" to "−1." Here, we use the AWGN channel model to mitigate the real communication channel because the AWGN model approximates the effect of accumulation of noise components from many sources. The noise sequences $u_i(n)$ from i.i.d. (independent and identically distributed) random process with zero mean and variance σ^2 are added to $x_{n,i}$ to obtain $y_{n,i}$. At the receiver side, we receive noisy sequence $y_{n,0}, y_{n,1}, y_{n,2}, y_{n+1,0}, y_{n+1,1}, y_{n+1,2}, \ldots$ and pass the received noisy symbols to the turbo decoder to get reliable transmitted data symbols as shown in Figure 3.48. Here, we assume proper synchronization of data symbols (i.e., the boundaries of triplets in the received sequence corresponding to transmitted triplets should be identified). After data symbols synchronization, we identify received triplets as $(y_{n,0}, y_{n,1}, y_{n,2}), (y_{n+1,0}, y_{n+1,1}, y_{n+1,2})$, and so on.

Next, we pass *intrinsic information* (systematic bits $(y_{n,0})$ and the first encoder parity bits $(y_{n,1})$ of the received sequence) to the first decoder along with *extrinsic information*, *Ext*.2 (soft information) from the second decoder. For the first iteration, we use zeros for *Ext*.2 by assuming equiprobability for intrinsic information symbols. After completing decoding with the first decoder, we start the second decoder with *intrinsic information* (interleaved systematic bits, $\mathrm{I}[y_{n,0}]$ and the second encoder parity bits, $y_{n,2}$) and *extrinsic information*, *Ext*.1 (soft information) from the first decoder as input. This process is repeated many times until we get reliable decisions from the second decoder output. At end of the iterative decoding, we deinterleave the output of the second decoder (LLRs) to get back the transmitted symbol sequence. Then, we obtain hard bits by using sign information of output symbols. In the next section, we discuss the computation of metrics to simulate the turbo decoder.

4.5.2 MAP Decoder Metrics Computation

Turbo codes are decoded by using more than one approach or algorithm type (e.g., SOVA, MAP). In this section, we discuss a few techniques to simulate the MAP algorithm presented in Section 3.10.3 for decoding turbo codes. In the MAP algorithm, we need to compute alphas (forward-state metric using Equation 3.54), betas (reverse-state metric using Equation 3.55), gammas (branch metric using Equation 3.56), LLRs (using alphas, betas and gammas) and Extrinsic information (using Equation 3.57). In computing alphas, betas, and LLRs, we have to compute an equation of the following form:

$$e^z = e^x + e^y \tag{4.31}$$

Equation (4.31) can be simplified using a correction factor as follows:

$$e^z = e^{\max(x,y)}(1 + e^{-|x-y|}) \tag{4.32}$$

Taking the natural logarithm on both sides of Equation (4.32) results in

$$\begin{aligned} z &= \max(x, y) + \ln(1 + e^{-|x-y|}) \\ &= \max{}^*(x, y) \end{aligned} \tag{4.33}$$

The operator in Equation (4.33) is called a log-MAP operator. Sometimes we approximate the expression $\ln(1 + e^{-|x-y|})$ using a constant, and then we call it a constant-log-MAP operator:

$$\ln(1 + e^{-|x-y|}) = \begin{cases} 0 & \text{if}|x - y| > 1.2 \\ 0.5 & \text{if}|x - y| \le 1.2 \end{cases}$$

If we completely ignore the value of $\ln(1 + e^{-|x-y|})$ in Equation (4.33), then we call that particular operator a max-log-MAP:

$$z = \max(x, y) \tag{4.34}$$

If the absolute difference between x and y is greater than 3, then the difference between the evaluated values of Equations (4.33) and (4.34) is negligible. For example, if $x = 4$ and $y = 7$, the computed values of z from Equations (4.33) and (4.34) is going to be 7.04 and 7, respectively. Depending on embedded processor capabilities, we use one of the previous operators in computing state metrics alpha and beta and the value of LLRs.

We use the flow of RSC encoder steady-state trellis data (after BPSK modulation) to compute alphas, betas, gammas, and LLRs. The rearranged steady-state trellis is shown in Figure 4.16. After mapping (with BPSK modulator), the output binary digits $d_{n,a}$:{0, 1} in Figure 4.13 are changed to $x_{n,a}$:{+1, −1}. The forward and backward state metrics computation flow (with Equations (3.54) and (3.55)) is realized in Figure 4.17(a) and (b). In computing state metrics (i.e., $\bar{\alpha}_n^m$ and $\bar{\beta}_n^m$), we use $\bar{\gamma}_n^{i,m}$.

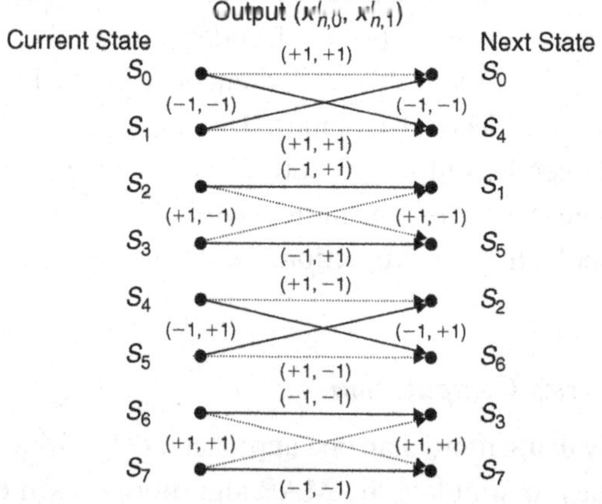

Figure 4.16: Rearranged steady-state trellis data flow diagram (after modulation).

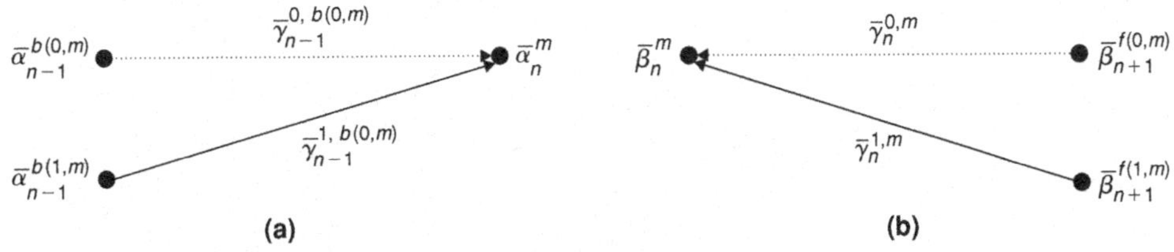

Figure 4.17: State metrics computation realization. (a) Forward-state metric computation. (b) Reverse-state metric computation.

We compute gammas using the Equation (3.56). For $m=0$, based on Figures 4.16 and 4.17(b), $\left(x_{n,0}^{0}, x_{n,1}^{0}\right)=(+1,+1)$ and $\left(x_{n,0}^{1}, x_{n,1}^{1}\right)=(-1,-1)$. Thus,

$$\gamma_n^{0,0} = P^a(0)e^{-\frac{\left(y_{n,0}-x_{n,0}^0\right)^2+\left(y_{n,1}-x_{n,1}^0\right)^2}{2\sigma^2}} = P^{(a)}(0)e^{-\frac{y_{n,0}^2+y_{n,1}^2+2}{2\sigma^2}}e^{\frac{y_{n,0}+y_{n,1}}{\sigma^2}}$$

$$= \sqrt{P^{(a)}(0)P^{(a)}(1)}\sqrt{\frac{P^{(a)}(0)}{P^{(a)}(1)}}\,e^{-\frac{y_{n,0}^2+y_{n,1}^2+2}{2\sigma^2}}e^{\frac{y_{n,0}+y_{n,1}}{\sigma^2}}$$

$$\bar{\gamma}_n^{0,0} = \ln\left(\sqrt{P^{(a)}(0)P^{(a)}(1)}\right)+\ln\left(\sqrt{\frac{P^{(a)}(0)}{P^{(a)}(1)}}\right)-\frac{y_{n,0}^2+y_{n,1}^2+2}{2\sigma^2}+\frac{y_{n,0}+y_{n,1}}{\sigma^2}$$

$$= \ln\left(\sqrt{P^{(a)}(0)P^{(a)}(1)}\right)-\frac{y_{n,0}^2+y_{n,1}^2+2}{2\sigma^2}-\ln\left(\sqrt{\frac{P^{(a)}(1)}{P^{(a)}(0)}}\right)+\frac{y_{n,0}+y_{n,1}}{\sigma^2} \tag{4.35}$$

$$\bar{\gamma}_n^{0,0} = C_0+\bar{\gamma}_n^h \tag{4.36}$$

where $C_0=\ln\left(\sqrt{P^{(a)}(0)P^{(a)}(1)}\right)-\frac{y_{n,0}^2+y_{n,1}^2+2}{2\sigma^2}$ contains terms which always result in positive values and $\bar{\gamma}_n^h = -\ln\left(\sqrt{\frac{P^{(a)}(1)}{P^{(a)}(0)}}\right)+\frac{y_{n,0}+y_{n,1}}{\sigma^2}$ contains terms which affect the maximum *a posteriori* probability. In a similar manner, we can compute $\bar{\gamma}_n^{1,0}$ as

$$\bar{\gamma}_n^{1,0} = C_0-\bar{\gamma}_n^h \tag{4.37}$$

Then, after ignoring constant terms,

$$e^{\bar{\beta}_n^0} = e^{\bar{\beta}_{n+1}^{f(0,0)}+\bar{\gamma}_n^{0,0}} + e^{\bar{\beta}_{n+1}^{f(1,0)}+\bar{\gamma}_n^{1,0}}$$

$$= e^{\bar{\beta}_{n+1}^0+\bar{\gamma}_n^h}+e^{\bar{\beta}_{n+1}^4-\bar{\gamma}_n^h}$$

Using Equations (4.31) to (4.33),

$$\bar{\beta}_n^0 = \max{}^*\left(\bar{\beta}_{n+1}^0+\bar{\gamma}_n^h,\ \ \bar{\beta}_{n+1}^4-\bar{\gamma}_n^h\right) \tag{4.38}$$

Similarly, for $m=2$, from Figures 4.16 and 4.17(b), $\left(x_{n,0}^{0}, x_{n,1}^{0}\right)=(+1,-1)$ and $\left(x_{n,0}^{1}, x_{n,1}^{1}\right)=(-1,+1)$. Then,

$$e^{\bar{\beta}_n^2} = e^{\bar{\beta}_{n+1}^{f(0,2)}+\bar{\gamma}_n^{0,2}}+e^{\bar{\beta}_{n+1}^{f(1,2)}+\bar{\gamma}_n^{1,2}}$$

where $\bar{\gamma}_n^{0,2}=C_2-\bar{\gamma}_n^g, \bar{\gamma}_n^{1,2}=C_2+\bar{\gamma}_n^g$, $C_2=C_0$, $\bar{\gamma}_n^g=-\ln\left(\sqrt{\frac{P^{(a)}(1)}{P^{(a)}(0)}}\right)+\frac{y_{n,0}-y_{n,1}}{\sigma^2}$ and then

$$e^{\bar{\beta}_n^2} = e^{\bar{\beta}_{n+1}^1-\bar{\gamma}_n^g}+e^{\bar{\beta}_{n+1}^5+\bar{\gamma}_n^g}$$

Using Equations (4.31) to (4.33),

$$\bar{\beta}_n^2 = \max{}^*\left(\bar{\beta}_{n+1}^1-\bar{\gamma}_n^g,\ \ \bar{\beta}_{n+1}^5+\bar{\gamma}_n^g\right) \tag{4.39}$$

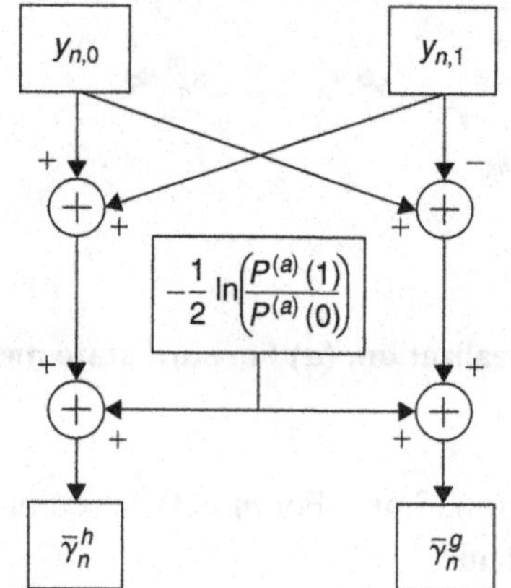

Figure 4.18: Branch metric (gamma) computation.

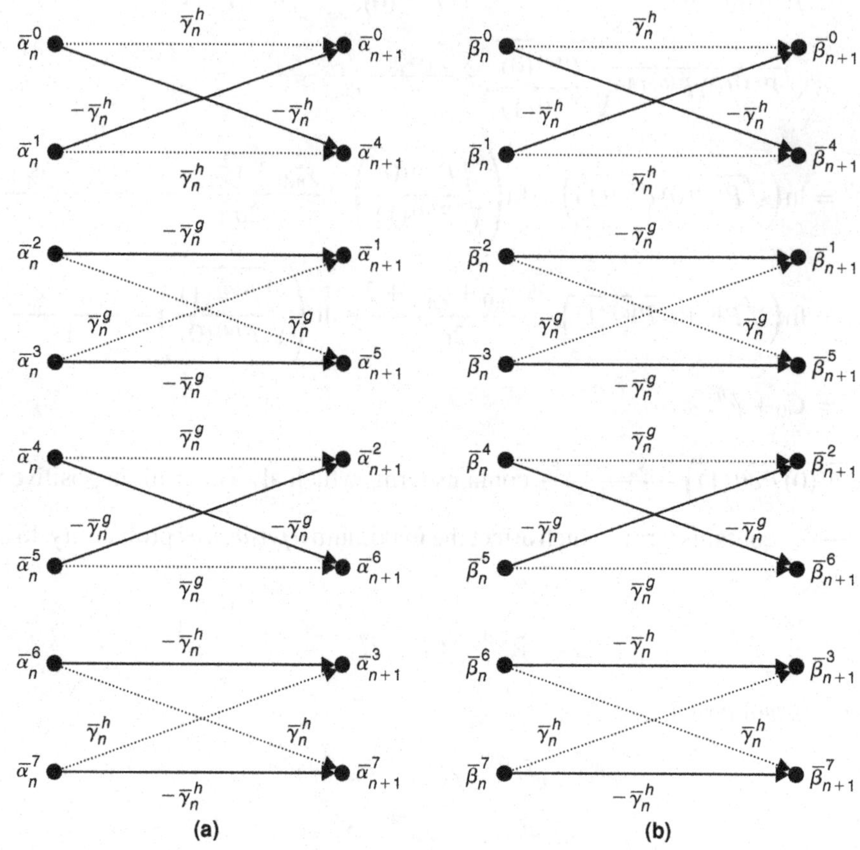

Figure 4.19: State metric butterflies computation.

In the same fashion we can derive $\gamma_n^{i,m}$ for other values of m (or branches). With BPSK modulation, we have only two branch metrics $\{\bar{\gamma}_n^h, \bar{\gamma}_n^g\}$ per stage; the realization of branch metrics (gammas) computation is shown in Figure 4.18. For a particular stage (at time n), state metrics alphas and betas are computed using the same branch metric gammas as shown in Figure 4.19.

We calculate LLR using Equation (3.52) as follows:

$$\begin{aligned} LLR &= \ln\left[\sum_m \alpha_n^m \gamma_n^{1,m} \beta_{n+1}^{f(1,m)}\right] - \ln\left[\sum_m \alpha_n^m \gamma_n^{0,m} \beta_{n+1}^{f(0,m)}\right] \\ &= \ln\left[\sum_m e^{\bar{\alpha}_n^m + \bar{\gamma}_n^{1,m} + \bar{\beta}_{n+1}^{f(1,m)}}\right] - \ln\left[\sum_m e^{\bar{\alpha}_n^m + \bar{\gamma}_n^{0,m} + \bar{\beta}_{n+1}^{f(0,m)}}\right] \end{aligned} \tag{4.40}$$

Equation (4.40) for $M = 3$ (i.e., for $0 \leq m \leq 2^M - 1$) can be interpreted using the data flow in Figures 4.18 and 4.19. The first term in Equation (4.40) explains the connection from alpha to beta through gamma for bit "1" as shown in Figure 4.20(a) and the second term in Equation (4.40) explains the connection from alpha to beta through gamma for bit "0" as shown in Figure 4.20(b).

We obtain *a posteriori probabilities* (APPs) in Equation (3.46) from Figure 4.20(a) and (b) for bit "1" and bit "0" at time n given received sequence Y_N as follows:

$$\begin{aligned}\ln(\Pr(c_n = 1/Y_N)) = \ln\Big(& e^{-\bar{\gamma}_n^h}\left(e^{\bar{\alpha}_n^0+\bar{\beta}_{n+1}^4} + e^{\bar{\alpha}_n^1+\bar{\beta}_{n+1}^0} + e^{\bar{\alpha}_n^6+\bar{\beta}_{n+1}^3} + e^{\bar{\alpha}_n^7+\bar{\beta}_{n+1}^7}\right) \\ &+ e^{-\bar{\gamma}_n^g}\left(e^{\bar{\alpha}_n^2+\bar{\beta}_{n+1}^1} + e^{\bar{\alpha}_n^3+\bar{\beta}_{n+1}^5} + e^{\bar{\alpha}_n^4+\bar{\beta}_{n+1}^6} + e^{\bar{\alpha}_n^5+\bar{\beta}_{n+1}^2}\right)\Big)\end{aligned} \tag{4.41}$$

$$\begin{aligned}\ln(\Pr(c_n = 0/Y_N)) = \ln\Big(& e^{\bar{\gamma}_n^h}\left(e^{\bar{\alpha}_n^0+\bar{\beta}_{n+1}^0} + e^{\bar{\alpha}_n^1+\bar{\beta}_{n+1}^4} + e^{\bar{\alpha}_n^6+\bar{\beta}_{n+1}^7} + e^{\bar{\alpha}_n^7+\bar{\beta}_{n+1}^3}\right) \\ &+ e^{\bar{\gamma}_n^g}\left(e^{\bar{\alpha}_n^2+\bar{\beta}_{n+1}^5} + e^{\bar{\alpha}_n^3+\bar{\beta}_{n+1}^1} + e^{\bar{\alpha}_n^4+\bar{\beta}_{n+1}^2} + e^{\bar{\alpha}_n^5+\bar{\beta}_{n+1}^6}\right)\Big)\end{aligned} \tag{4.42}$$

Based on Equations (3.46), (4.41), and (4.42), the LLR for the n-th trellis stage is computed as

$$LLR\,(c_n) = \ln(\Pr\,(c_n = 1/Y_N)) - \ln(\Pr\,(c_n = 0/Y_N)) \tag{4.43}$$

4.5.3 MAP Decoder Computational Complexity

The LLR value in Equation (4.43) is computed from APPs which are obtained using Equations (4.41) and (4.42). In computing APPs, we use the n-th stage trellis all-states alphas (forward-state metrics), betas (reverse-state metrics), and gammas (branch metrics). At the n-th stage, gammas are computed using the received information and extrinsic information of the n-th stage, alphas are computed using $(n-1)$-th stage alphas and gammas, and betas are computed using $(n+1)$-th stage betas and gammas. In other words, to compute the LLR value at the n-th stage, we use information from alphas computed from previous n stages and betas computed from future $(N-n)$ stages of the trellis as shown in Figure 4.21.

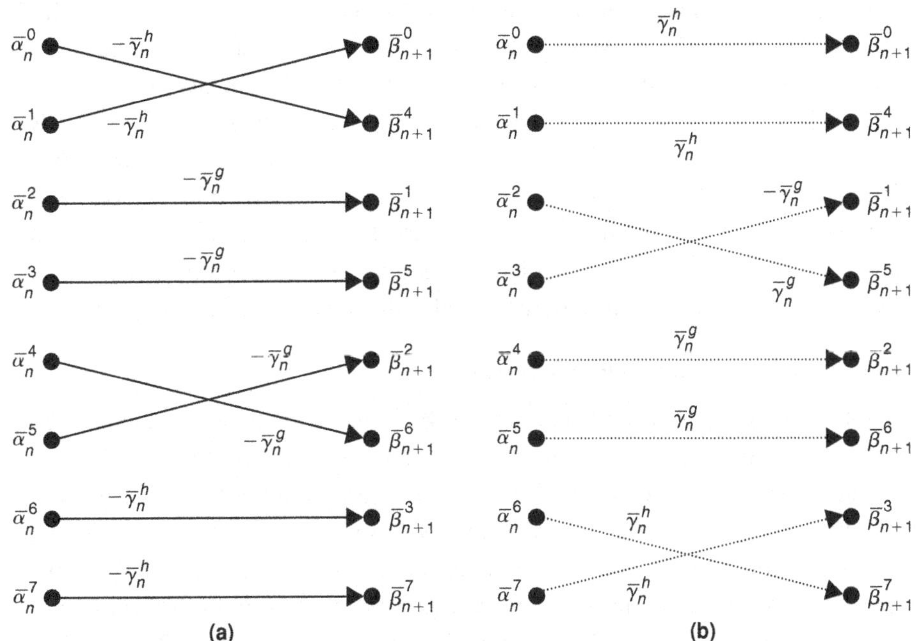

Figure 4.20: (a) Bit "1" MAP connections. (b) Bit "0" MAP connections.

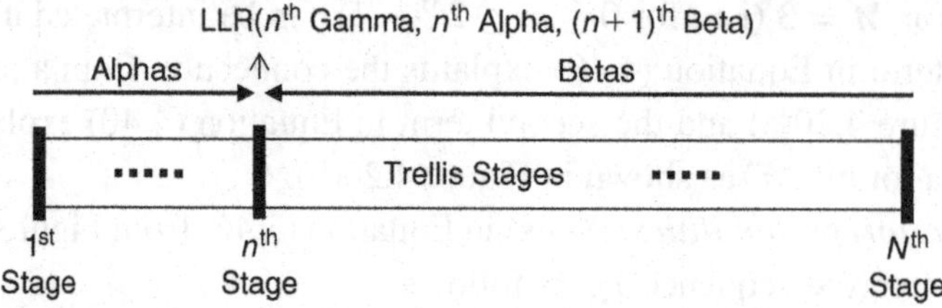

Figure 4.21: Illustration of LLR computation at *n*-th stage.

In Figure 4.21, to compute the LLR at the n-th stage we need the alpha and gamma of the n-th stage and the beta of $(n+1)$-th stage. To compute alpha, we need previous alpha values, and to compute beta, we need future beta values. To compute alphas, betas, and LLRs at a particular stage, we need gammas of that particular stage. In other words, we have to keep all the stages alphas, betas, and gammas in the buffer alive for calculating LLRs.

The turbo decoder shown in Figure 3.48 works on a sequence or frame of length N symbols at a time. The value of N ranges from a few tens of symbols to many thousands of symbols. For example, the range of N specified by the 3G standard is 40 to 5044. If we are using turbo codes in a particular application, we have to support all the data lengths used by that particular application or standard. The number of states (2^M) present in the trellis stage depends on the number of delay units present in the encoder. If $M = 3$ delay units are present in an RSC encoder (as in UMTS 3G), then we have eight states in a trellis stage. Here, we consider $N = 5044$ and $M = 3$ for estimation of turbo coder computational complexity in terms of the number of operations and memory requirements.

Decoding Complexity and Number of Operations

In decoding of turbo codes using the MAP algorithm, we use two MAP decoders per iteration and repeat for many iterations. In the maximum *a posteriori* algorithm, we compute all metrics in the logarithm domain to avoid multiplications and to avoid frequent normalization of alpha and beta as they grow with errors. In the logarithm domain, we predominantly use additions and subtractions and the log-MAP operator in computing the LLR metrics. Table 4.2 shows the number of operations required (per trellis stage per decoder per iteration) to compute gamma, alpha, beta, LLRs, and extrinsic information.

Memory Requirements

For $M = 3$, we have 2 gammas, 8 alphas and 8 betas in every stage of the trellis. We use 16 bits (or 2 bytes) to represent each value (to avoid saturation before normalization). If $N = 5044$, then we need approximately 20 kB (= 5044 x 2 x 2) for gammas, 80 kB (= 5044 x 2 x 8) for alphas, 80 kB for betas, and another 40 kB for storing LLRs, extrinsic information of both decoders and intrinsic information for both decoders. The MAP algorithm involves computation of betas from the last stage of the data frame to the first stage of the data frame and alphas from the first stage of the data frame to the last stage of the data frame. We can avoid storing one of either alpha or beta. For example, we store computed gamma and alpha for full frame, then we compute LLRs (in a backward direction) using betas computed on the fly without storing them. The other way is storing computed gamma and beta for full frame, then compute LLRs (in a forward direction) using alphas computed on the fly. In either case, we need approximately 140 kB of data memory on an embedded processor (see Appendix A on the companion website for more information on reference embedded processor resources) to implement the turbo decoder for $N = 5044$ and $M = 3$. Consequently, we can say turbo codes demand a lot of memory in their decoding.

4.5.4 Window-Based Turbo Decoder Implementation

The huge requirement on memory in turbo decoding can be reduced by using a *window-based method*. This method involves dividing the entire data frame into smaller data blocks and performing the decoding on smaller windows. In this window-based method, we needed to store gamma and either one of alpha or beta. In the implementation, we always compute alphas for full window and store them whereas we compute betas on the fly and use them. As we compute LLRs using the gammas, alphas and betas of data within the present window and if we divide the total frame into Q blocks, then the memory required with the window method is $1/Q$ of straight forward implementation. The turbo decoding using the window-based method is shown in Figure 4.22. By dividing the whole data frame into smaller windows, betas can be computed from the last stage of each

Table 4.2: Number of operations involved in computing MAP algorithm metrics per trellis stage per decoder per iteration

Metric Number of Operations	Additions, Subtractions, Others	Log-MAP Operations
Alpha	16	8
Beta	16	8
Gamma	8	0
LLR	21	14
Extrinsic information	6	0

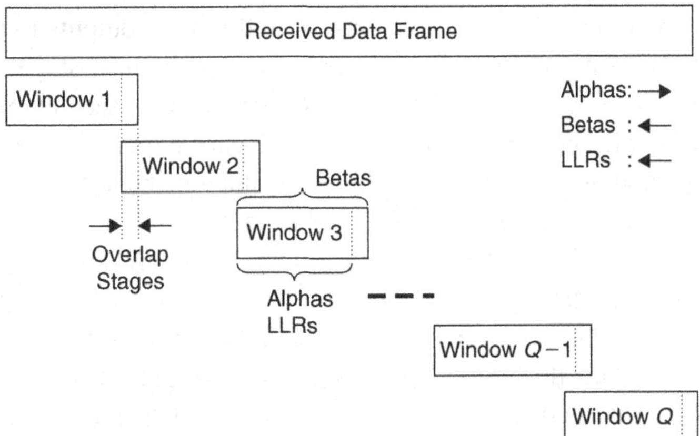

Figure 4.22: Turbo decoder window-based implementation.

data window instead of the last stage of the data frame. In the case of the full data frame, we use the trellis termination sequence for betas to converge before the start of computing of LLRs from the last stage. But with the window-based method, we do not know the state of the transmitted trellis at the last stage of the window and hence we require a few overlap stages for betas to converge. Therefore, the window-based method requires extra (of overlap length) beta computation in its implementation. Since we do not decode any information bits during these overlap stages, this adds to the overall cost of MAP decoding.

The disadvantage with the window-based method is the computational overhead, estimated as follows. Typically, the length of overlap stages needed is about $6K$ stages, where K is the constraint length of the RSC encoder. If we need "B" cycles to compute betas per stage, then we spend $6^* K^* B$ extra cycles for computing betas in the window-based method. This overhead depends on the number of windows that are used in decoding the full frame. If the number of windows is less, then the overhead is also less (but requires more memory) and if the number of windows is more, then the overhead is also more (but requires less memory).

Turbo decoding demands huge computations as well as huge memory requirements. Implementation of turbo decoding on deep pipelined embedded processors needs a lot of optimization at both algorithm level and instruction level. The optimization at algorithm level includes rearranging the algorithm flow to suit the processor architecture and taking a few shortcuts (if possible) to avoid some of the computations. The optimization at the instruction level includes gathering many operations and feeding them to all compute units of the processor, balancing bandwidth of ALU and DAG units, avoiding pipeline stalls, and so on. Typically, we interleave the program code to avoid pipeline stalls in running the program on deep pipelined embedded processors. To interleave the program code, we have to gather as many operations that are independent from one another (i.e., their input does not depend on the output of other operations) as possible. In MAP decoding, the three major operations (which consume almost 90% of cycles) are computation of alphas, betas, and LLRs. Here, we have two options to implement the MAP decoder: (1) computation of all stages of alphas at once, all stages of betas at once, and all stages of LLRs at once; and (2) simultaneously computing the alpha, beta, and LLR for one stage.

Next, we discuss the advantages and disadvantages with the previous two approaches. An advantage of the first method is that the coding becomes simple, but there are many disadvantages. Based on Figures 4.19 through 4.21,

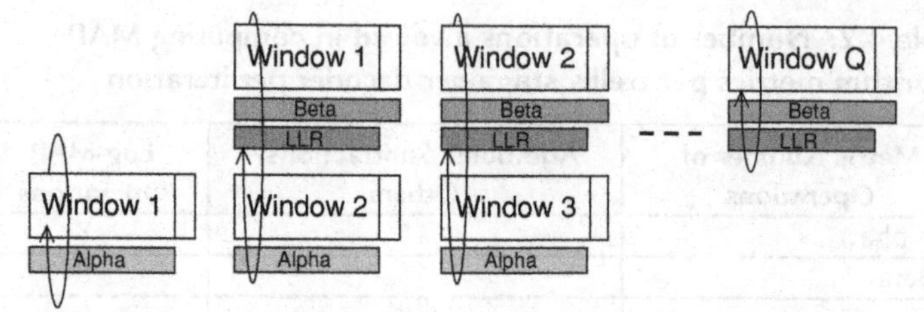

Figure 4.23: Efficient implementation of window-based MAP decoder.

disadvantages of using the first method include (1) more memory is needed to store all metrics, (2) computation of alphas and betas of the next trellis stage requires current trellis stage outputs (whose trellis states are not the same as the inputs, and accessing them in the right order delays the next stage metric computation), and (3) reduced scope to interleave the program code. Next, a disadvantage of the second method is that simultaneous computation of all three terms (alpha, beta, and LLR) is not possible for the same stage (as shown in Figure 4.21). Advantages of the second method are (1) sufficient storage of alpha or beta, (2) no delay in data access, and (3) good scope to interleave the program code to avoid pipeline stalls.

As the MAP decoder implementation with the second method has many advantages, we concentrate on the realization of this approach for simulation of the MAP decoder. We can overcome the disadvantage with the second method in the window-based implementation as shown in Figure 4.23. Here, we compute only the alpha of the first window before entering into the loop (as given later in Pcode 4.44), then in every iteration, we compute beta and LLR for the current window and alpha for the next window, and the process continues. In this approach, as we are computing at times alpha, beta, and LLR per iteration, we have sufficient time to arrange the data to compute units and also have a good scope to interleave the program code.

4.5.5 Turbo Decoder Simulation

In this section, we simulate the window-based turbo decoder shown in Figure 4.23. We choose the length of the input data frame to the turbo decoder as 5088. Based on this input data frame size, we define other parameter sizes in the simulation of the window-based turbo decoder as given in Pcode 4.34. We divide the input data frame into eight small data windows. We use $24 (= 6 * K = 6 * 4)$ overlap stages for each window. We iterate five times to get reliable decisions using the MAP decoder. The other parameters such as window length, maximum window length and number of stages are defined based on parameters chosen previously. In this turbo decoder simulation, we use the max-log-MAP operator (i.e., taking a simple maximum of two inputs). In addition, we use a Ping-Pong buffer concept to reduce the L1 data memory size. We use approximately 45 kB of data memory to store intermediate data, as given in Pcode 4.35. We store the whole received input data sequence (one systematic sequence, one interleaved systematic sequence and two parity sequences) in L3 memory. We precalculate offsets in advance for mitigating interleaver and deinterleaver functionality and store in L3 memory.

```
#define DATA_SIZE               5088
#define NUM_ITERATIONS          5
#define OVERLAP_LENGTH          24
#define NUM_WINDOWS             8
#define WINDOW_LENGTH           DATA_SIZE/NUM_WINDOWS
#define MAX_WINDOW_LENGTH       WINDOW_LENGTH + OVERLAP_LENGTH
#define NUM_STAGES              DATA_SIZE + OVERLAP_LENGTH
```

Pcode 4.34: Window-based turbo decoder implementation parameters.

Data Handling and Transfer between L3 and L1

In the turbo decoder, we handle a huge amount of data in MAP decoding by storing the input data in slow L3 memory. We store three inputs, interleaver input and interleaver matrix in L3. As we compute beta and LLR for the current window and alpha for the next window, we need branch metrics for both windows. To reduce the data transfers,

```
// Memory bank-1: approx. 22.5 kB for N = 5088
signed char Extrinsic1[NUM_STAGES];                  // extrinsic info from MAP-1, 5kB
signed char Extrinsic2[NUM_STAGES];                  // extrinsic info from MAP-2, 5kB
signed char inputX1[MAX_WINDOW_LENGTH];              // X in 5.3 format, 0.7 kB
signed char inputX2[MAX_WINDOW_LENGTH];              // 0.7 kB
signed short Alpha0[WINDOW_LENGTH*8+8];              // Alpha0, 10 kB
signed short interM1[WINDOW_LENGTH];                 // interleaver look-up,1.3 kB
unsigned long Turbo_Struct[16];

// Memory bank-2: approx. 22.5 kB for N = 5088
signed short Alpha2[WINDOW_LENGTH*8+8];              // Alpha2, 10 kB
signed short interM2[WINDOW_LENGTH];                 // 1.3 kB
signed short Gamma0[2*MAX_WINDOW_LENGTH+2];          // Gamma0, 2.7 kB
signed short Gamma1[2*MAX_WINDOW_LENGTH+2];          // Gamma1, 2.7 kB
signed short LLR01[WINDOW_LENGTH];                   // 1.3 kB
signed short inputX3[MAX_WINDOW_LENGTH+4];           // 1.4 kB
signed short inputX4[MAX_WINDOW_LENGTH+4];           // 1.4 kB
signed char inputY1[MAX_WINDOW_LENGTH];              // Y in 5.3 format, 0.7 kB
signed char inputY2[MAX_WINDOW_LENGTH];              // 0.7 kB
signed short Beta[8];
```

Pcode 4.35: Data buffers used in turbo decoder simulation.

we bring the input data (intrinsic information + interleaver matrix for interleaving the output) for one window and store the needed information for computing gamma for the next window temporally in L1 memory. As data transfer (using DMA) introduces some latency, we always bring the data for the next window to avoid the data transfer latency. We use the Ping-Pong buffer concept in this data transfer process.

MAP Decoder Metrics Simulation

As the MAP decoder involves the computation of many metrics, we define macros for each metric simulation. We simulate the MAP decoder from bottom to top, meaning that we simulate the turbo decoder in the following order: (1) simulate individual metrics, (2) simulate one window, (3) simulate one MAP decoder, (4) simulate a single iteration, and (5) repeat this simulated code for many iterations. We use the data structure given in Pcode 4.36 to handle all data and addresses.

Branch Metric: Gamma Based on Figure 4.18, the computation of the branch metric gamma requires intrinsic information (systematic input and parity input) and extrinsic information (a priori information). In addition, we multiply the intrinsic information with the channel noise variance (which is estimated at the receiver). A macro definition for gamma computation is shown in Pcode 4.37. In the current window, we always compute gamma for the next window and we store systematic input data temporally in L1 memory for future use (to compute extrinsic information of next window). We compute two gammas per trellis stage as we require two gammas per trellis stage to compute state metrics alphas and betas and to compute APPs for LLRs.

```
typedef struct TurboDec_tag {
        signed char *xx;             // holds systematic input array address
        signed char *yy;             // holds parity input array address
        signed char *Ext1;           // holds first decoder extrinsic information array
        signed char *Ext2;           // holds second decoder extrinsic information array
        signed short *AlphaC;        // holds current window Alpha metrics array
        signed short *AlphaN;        // holds next window Alpha metrics array address
        signed short *GammaC;        // holds current window Gamma metrics array
        signed short *GammaN;        // holds next window Gamma metrics array
        signed short *mm;            // holds interleave offsets array
        signed short *xC;            // holds current window systematic input
        signed short *xN;            // holds next window systematic input
        signed long Sigma;           // assign estimated channel noise variance
 } TurboDec_t;
```

Pcode 4.36: Data structure to handle turbo decoder parameters.

```
#define COMP_GAMMA_N()\
j = i<<1;\
r2 = pT->Ext2[i+n];    r1 = pT->yy[i];    r0 = pT->xx[i];\
r4 = r2 + (r0 + r1) * pT->Sigma;    r5 = r2 + (r0 - r1) * pT->Sigma; pT->xN[i] = r0;\
*(pT->GammaN+j) = r4; *(pT->GammaN+j+1) = r5;
```

Pcode 4.37: Macro for gamma computation.

```
#define ALPHA()\
r0 = pT->AlphaN[m+0];    r1 = pT->AlphaN[m+1]; r2 = pT->GammaN[n+0];\
tmp0 = r0 + r2; tmp1 = r1 - r2;    tmp2 = r0 - r2;    tmp3 = r1 + r2;\
tmp0 = max(tmp0, tmp1); tmp2 = max(tmp2, tmp3);\
pT->AlphaN[k+0] = tmp0; pT->AlphaN[k+4] = tmp2;\
r0 = pT->AlphaN[m+2]; r1 = pT->AlphaN[m+3];    r2 = pT->GammaN[n+1];\
tmp0 = r0 - r2; tmp1 = r1 + r2; tmp2 = r0 + r2;    tmp3 = r1 - r2;\
tmp0 = max(tmp0, tmp1); tmp2 = max(tmp2, tmp3);\
pT->AlphaN[k+1] = tmp0; pT->AlphaN[k+5] = tmp2;\
r0 = pT->AlphaN[m+4];    r1 = pT->AlphaN[m+5];    r2 = pT->GammaN[n+1];\
tmp0 = r0 + r2; tmp1 = r1 - r2;    tmp2 = r0 - r2;    tmp3 = r1 + r2;\
tmp0 = max(tmp0, tmp1); tmp2 = max(tmp2, tmp3);\
pT->AlphaN[k+2] = tmp0; pT->AlphaN[k+6] = tmp2;\
r0 = pT->AlphaN[m+6];    r1 = pT->AlphaN[m+7];    r2 = pT->GammaN[n+0];\
tmp0 = r0 - r2; tmp1 = r1 + r2;    tmp2 = r0 + r2;    tmp3 = r1 - r2;\
tmp0 = max(tmp0, tmp1); tmp2 = max(tmp2, tmp3);\
pT->AlphaN[k+3] = tmp0; pT->AlphaN[k+7] = tmp2;
```

Pcode 4.38: Macro for alpha computation.

State Metric: Alpha We simulate alpha computation based on the data flow shown in Figure 4.19(a). To compute forward-state metrics (alpha, indexed with k), we use the previous stage state metrics (alpha, indexed with m) and current stage branch metrics (gamma, indexed with n). The simulation code for alpha computation macro definition is given in Pcode 4.38.

State Metric: Beta We simulate beta computation based on the data flow shown in Figure 4.19(b). We compute reverse-state metrics (beta) from the last stage to the first stage. To compute current trellis state beta metrics, we use next stage state beta metrics and next stage branch metrics (gamma, indexed with n). The simulation code for beta computation macro definition is given in Pcode 4.39.

```
#define BETA()\
r0 = Beta[0]; r1 = Beta[4]; r2 = Beta[1]; r3 = Beta[5];\
r4 = Beta[2]; r5 = Beta[6]; r6 = Beta[3]; r7 = Beta[7];\
tmp2 = pT->GammaC[n]; tmp3 = pT->GammaC[n+1];\
tmp0 = r0 + tmp2; tmp1 = r1 - tmp2; r0 = r0 - tmp2; r1 = r1 + tmp2;\
tmp0 = max(tmp0, tmp1); r0 = max(r0, r1);\
Beta[0] = tmp0; Beta[1] = r0;\
tmp0 = r2 - tmp3; tmp1 = r3 + tmp3; r0 = r2 + tmp3; r1 = r3 - tmp3;\
tmp0 = max(tmp0, tmp1); r0 = max(r0, r1);\
Beta[2] = tmp0; Beta[3] = r0;\
tmp0 = r4 + tmp3; tmp1 = r5 - tmp3; r0 = r4 - tmp3; r1 = r5 + tmp3;\
tmp0 = max(tmp0, tmp1); r0 = max(r0, r1);\
Beta[4] = tmp0; Beta[5] = r0;\
tmp0 = r6 - tmp2; tmp1 = r7 + tmp2; r0 = r6 + tmp2; r1 = r7 - tmp2;\
tmp0 = max(tmp0, tmp1); r0 = max(r0, r1);\
Beta[6] = tmp0; Beta[7] = r0;
```

Pcode 4.39: Macro for beta computation.

LLRs Computation We compute LLRs based on bit "0" and "1" MAP connections shown in Figure 4.20(a) and (b). We use current stage alphas, gammas and next stage betas for computing LLRs. The macro definition for LLR computation is given in Pcode 4.40. In Pcode 4.38, we used array names **alphaN**[] and **gammaN**[] to represent the metrics of the next window. In Pcode 4.40, we used array names **alphaC**[] and **gammaC**[] to represent the metrics of the current window. Assuming limited data registers on an embedded processor, we use

```
#define LLRS()\
r0 = pT->AlphaC[m+0]; r2 = Beta[0]; r1 = pT->AlphaC[m+1]; r3 = Beta[4];\
tmp0 = r0 + r2; tmp1 = r1 + r3; tmp2 = r0 + r3; tmp3 = r1 + r2;\
tmp0 = max(tmp0, tmp1); tmp2 = max(tmp2, tmp3);\
Turbo_Stack[0] = tmp0; Turbo_Stack[1] = tmp2;\
r0 = pT->AlphaC[m+6]; r2 = Beta[7]; r1 = pT->AlphaC[m+7]; r3 = Beta[3];\
tmp0 = r0 + r2; tmp1 = r1 + r3; tmp2 = r0 + r3; tmp3 = r1 + r2;\
tmp0 = max(tmp0, tmp1); tmp2 = max(tmp2, tmp3);\
Turbo_Stack[2] = tmp0; Turbo_Stack[3] = tmp2;\
r0 = pT->AlphaC[m+2]; r2 = Beta[5]; r1 = pT->AlphaC[m+3]; r3 = Beta[1];\
tmp0 = r0 + r2; tmp1 = r1 + r3; tmp2 = r0 + r3; tmp3 = r1 + r2;\
tmp0 = max(tmp0, tmp1); tmp2 = max(tmp2, tmp3);\
Turbo_Stack[4] = tmp0; Turbo_Stack[5] = tmp2;\
r0 = pT->AlphaC[m+4]; r2 = Beta[2]; r1 = pT->AlphaC[m+5]; r3 = Beta[6];\
tmp0 = r0 + r2; tmp1 = r1 + r3; tmp2 = r0 + r3; tmp3 = r1 + r2;\
tmp0 = max(tmp0, tmp1); tmp2 = max(tmp2, tmp3);\
Turbo_Stack[6] = tmp0; Turbo_Stack[7] = tmp2;\
r0 = Turbo_Stack[0]; r1 = Turbo_Stack[1]; r2 = Turbo_Stack[2]; r3 = Turbo_Stack[3];\
tmp0 = max(r0, r2); tmp1 = max(r1, r3);\
r0 = Turbo_Stack[4]; r1 = Turbo_Stack[5]; r2 = Turbo_Stack[6]; r3 = Turbo_Stack[7];\
tmp2 = max(r0, r2); tmp3 = max(r1, r3);\
r0 = pT->GammaC[n]; r1 = pT->GammaC[n+1];\
r2 = tmp0 + r0; r3 = tmp1 - r0; r0 = tmp2 + r1; r1 = tmp3 - r1;\
tmp0 = max(r0, r2); tmp1 = max(r1, r3);\
r0 = tmp1 - tmp0; LLR01[p--] = r0;
```

Pcode 4.40: Macro definition for LLR computation.

array **Turbo_stack**[ ] as a stack to store intermediate results in computation of LLRs. After computing the LLR of the current stage, we store it in array **LLR01**[ ].

State Metrics Initialization As discussed in Section 3.10.3, we initialize state metrics alpha and beta before we start computing the initial alphas (i.e., for the first stage) and betas (i.e., the last stage). We initialize the first state with zero and all other states with a large negative value (that can be represented within the allowed precision for state metrics) and usually we assign with a negative value that is equal to half of the extreme end value (to avoid saturation due to the initial fluctuations). The macro definition for state metrics initialization is given in Pcode 4.41.

State Metrics Normalization The values of the state metrics (alpha and beta) grow with errors. If we do not control the range of the state metrics, then we see a saturation of alpha and beta values after some stages of computation. To avoid saturation, we normalize state metrics for every L stages. The interval L depends on the number of bits or precision (i.e., 8, 16, 24, or 32 bits) used to represent state metrics. In the simulations, we used 16 bits precision to represent state metrics alpha and beta and we use $L = 64$. We perform normalization using either one of the following. Normalization of alphas is done by subtracting the maximum of all states metric value or the first state metric value from all state metrics of current stage alphas. We also perform normalization of betas in the same way. The macro definition for alpha and beta normalization is given in Pcode 4.42.

```
#define ALPHA_INIT()\
tmp0 = -4096*4;\
pT->AlphaC[0] = 0; pT->AlphaC[1] = tmp0;\
pT->AlphaC[2] = tmp0;  pT->AlphaC[3] = tmp0;\
pT->AlphaC[4] = tmp0;     pT->AlphaC[5] = tmp0;\
pT->AlphaC[6] = tmp0;  pT->AlphaC[7] = tmp0;

#define BETA_INIT()\
tmp0 = -4096*4;\
Beta[0] = 0;  Beta[1] = tmp0; Beta[2] = tmp0; Beta[3] = tmp0;\
Beta[4] = tmp0;       Beta[5] = tmp0; Beta[6] = tmp0; Beta[7] = tmp0;
```

Pcode 4.41: Macro for initialization of state metrics.

```
#define ALPHA_NORM()\
tmp0 = pT->AlphaN[m];\
pT->AlphaN[m+0] = pT->AlphaN[m+0] - tmp0;\
pT->AlphaN[m+1] = pT->AlphaN[m+1] - tmp0;\
pT->AlphaN[m+2] = pT->AlphaN[m+2] - tmp0;\
pT->AlphaN[m+3] = pT->AlphaN[m+3] - tmp0;\
pT->AlphaN[m+4] = pT->AlphaN[m+4] - tmp0;\
pT->AlphaN[m+5] = pT->AlphaN[m+5] - tmp0;\
pT->AlphaN[m+6] = pT->AlphaN[m+6] - tmp0;\
pT->AlphaN[m+7] = pT->AlphaN[m+7] - tmp0;

#define BETA_NORM()\
tmp0 = Beta[0];\
Beta[0] = Beta[0] - tmp0; Beta[1] = Beta[1] - tmp0;\
Beta[2] = Beta[2] - tmp0; Beta[3] = Beta[3] - tmp0;\
Beta[4] = Beta[4] - tmp0; Beta[5] = Beta[5] - tmp0;\
Beta[6] = Beta[6] - tmp0; Beta[7] = Beta[7] - tmp0;
```

Pcode 4.42: Macro for normalization of Alpha and Beta.

Extrinsic Information Computation and Interleaving

Once we compute LLRs, the next step in MAP decoding is the computation of present decoder extrinsic information from present decoder systematic input and LLRs and from other decoder extrinsic information. Then, we clip the computed extrinsic information between some thresholds to keep it within the same precision used to represent the received input data. We interleave the extrinsic information before storing it (as we pass this to another decoder in a future iteration) to be compliant with the other decoder inputs. The macro definition for extrinsic information computation and interleaving is given in Pcode 4.43. We interleave the data using the precalculated interleaving offsets and it is costly to compute these interleave offsets on the fly.

```
#define COMP_EXT()\
r3 = 127; r2 = -127;\
r0 = pT->Ext2[j]; r1 = pT->xC[j];\
r0 = (r0 + r1)*2; r1 = LLR01[j];\
r0 = (r0 - r1)/2; n = pT->mm[j];\
r0 = min(r0, r3); r0 = max(r0, r2);\
pT->Ext1[n] = r0;
```

Pcode 4.43: Macro for extrinsic information computation and interleaving.

To reduce L1 memory usage, we do not store betas of trellis stages in an array; instead we use betas immediately after their computation in obtaining LLRs. As we split the entire data frame into small windows, we simulate alphas, betas and LLRs based on Figures 4.22 and 4.23. We bring one window of received data at a time to L1 memory from L3 memory. We consider current window last stage alphas as the initial alpha values for the next window. But, in the case of betas, we do not have future window betas, and we have to compute them for every window. How many betas we need to compute to converge (or to get the initial valid beta values) for the current window depend on the constraint length (K) of the encoder. For betas to converge we have to compute betas for $6K$ stages of the future window, and therefore we have to bring that much extra data from L3 to L1 as overlap data, as shown in Figure 4.22.

We compute LLRs for one window at a time and for this we should have alphas, betas and gammas of that window to compute LLRs. To efficiently implement the turbo decoder by interleaving the program code, we compute alphas for the first window outside the loop and we always compute betas, LLRs and extrinsic information for the current window and alphas for the next window in the loop. In addition, we compute gammas for the next window before entering the loop as the alphas computation for the next window needs those gammas. To compute LLRs of a current window in a loop, we first compute betas for overlap data (that belongs to next window) to get converged betas, then we start computing LLRs from the last stage of current window by computing beta on the fly without storing in L1 data memory (as given in Pcode 4.39). In the window-based decoding, to reduce pipeline stalls and to utilize the system's full bandwidth (i.e., ALU operations and

```
// CompBetaLLRsAlpha(pTD)
m = WINDOW_LENGTH*8;
ALPHA_NORM_TX()                                 // normalize Alpha for next window
n = WINDOW_LENGTH;          N = MAX_WINDOW_LENGTH;
for(i = 0;i < N; i++){
          COMP_GAMMA_N()                        // Compute Gamma for Next window
}
BETA_INIT()                                     // Initialize Beta
n = (MAX_WINDOW_LENGTH<<1)-2; M = OVERLAP_LENGTH;
for(i = 0;i < M;i++){                           // Compute overlap Beta
          BETA()
          n = n - 2;
}
k = 8; m = 0; p = 0; Turbo_Struct[9] = m; Turbo_Struct[10] = p; //push to stack
N = WINDOW_LENGTH >> 6; L = 63;
m = (WINDOW_LENGTH<<3)-8; p = WINDOW_LENGTH-1;
Turbo_Struct[11] = m; Turbo_Struct[12] = n;     //push to stack
for(j = 0;j < N;j++){ // Compute current window LLR's, current Beta and next window Alpha
          for(i = 0;i < L;i++){
                    m = Turbo_Struct[11]; n = Turbo_Struct[12];
                    LLRS()                      // Compute LLR's for current stage
                    BETA()                      // compute Beta for current window stage
                    m = m - 8; n = n - 2; Turbo_Struct[11] = m; Turbo_Struct[12] = n;
                    m = Turbo_Struct[9]; n = Turbo_Struct[10];
                    ALPHA()                     // compute Alpha for next window stages
                    m+=8; k+=8; n+=2; Turbo_Struct[9] = m; Turbo_Struct[10] = n;
          }
          ALPHA_NORM()                          // normalize Alpha
          BETA_NORM()                           // normalize Beta
          L = 64;  // next Alpha and Beta normalization occur after 64 iterations
}
M = WINDOW_LENGTH - ((WINDOW_LENGTH)>>6)*64+1;
for(i = 0;i < M;i++){                           //last sub window without normalization
          m = Turbo_Struct[11]; n = Turbo_Struct[12];
          LLRS()                                // Compute LLR's for current stage
          BETA()                                // compute Beta for current window stage
          m = m - 8; n = n - 2; Turbo_Struct[11] = m; Turbo_Struct[12] = n;
          m = Turbo_Struct[9]; n = Turbo_Struct[10];
          ALPHA()                               // compute Alpha for next window stages
          m+=8; k+=8; n+=2; Turbo_Struct[9] = m; Turbo_Struct[10] = n;
}
N = WINDOW_LENGTH; r3 = 127; r2 = -127;
for(j = 0;j < N;j++) {
          COMP_EXT()                            // compute extrinsic information for current window
}
```

Pcode 4.44: Simulation code for turbo decoding in a given window.

load–store operations), we compute current window LLRs and betas, and then next window alphas as given in Pcode 4.44. We normalize alphas and betas once for every L stages. To avoid stages counting, conditional checks and jumps in performing normalization of alpha and beta after L stages, we use a hardware loop setup and compute L stages in a loop, and then we perform normalization. For the last M stages (where M is less than L), we compute alphas and betas in a separate loop at the end. Once we have LLRs, we compute extrinsic information of the current decoder by using current decoder LLRs, systematic input and other decoder extrinsic information.

As shown in Figure 4.23, we compute alphas for the first window before entering the loop, we compute betas and LLRs for the current window and alpha for next window inside the loop and we compute LLRs and betas for last window after the loop. These three functions for two MAP decoders are handled with the following macros MAP_ONE_A, MAP_ONE_B, MAP_ONE_C, MAP_TWO_A, MAP_TWO_B, and MAP_TWO_C.

The simulation code for the MAP decoder 1 is given in Pcode 4.45 and the simulation code for the MAP decoder 2 is given in Pcode 4.46. We use different input and output buffers for MAP decoders 1 and 2. The main function that calls all six macros for MAP decoders 1 and 2 is given in Pcode 4.47 (see page 218).

```
#define MAP_ONE_A()\
Get_X(inputX1,0);\
Get_Y(inputY1,0);\
pTD->xx = inputX1; pTD->yy = inputY1;\
pTD->Ext2 = &Extrinsic2[0]; pTD->GammaC = Gamma0; pTD->AlphaC = Alpha0;\
CompGamma(pTD);\
CompAlpha(pTD);

#define MAP_ONE_B()\
Get_M(interM1,j);\
Get_X(inputX2,j+1);\
Get_Y(inputY2,j+1);\
pTD->xx = inputX2; pTD->yy = inputY2; pTD->xC = inputX3; pTD->xN = inputX4;\
pTD->Ext1 = Extrinsic1; pTD->Ext2 = &Extrinsic2[j*WINDOW_LENGTH];\
pTD->mm = interM1; pTD->AlphaC = Alpha0; pTD->AlphaN = Alpha2;\
pTD->GammaC = Gamma0; pTD->GammaN = Gamma1;\
CompBetaLLRsAlpha(pTD);\
Get_M(interM2,j+1);\
Get_X(inputX1,j+2);\
Get_Y(inputY1,j+2);\
pTD->xx = inputX1; pTD->yy = inputY1; pTD->xC = inputX4; pTD->xN = inputX3;\
pTD->Ext1 = Extrinsic1; pTD->Ext2 = &Extrinsic2[(j+1)*WINDOW_LENGTH];\
pTD->mm = interM2; pTD->AlphaC = Alpha2; pTD->AlphaN = Alpha0;\
pTD->GammaC = Gamma1; pTD->GammaN = Gamma0;\
CompBetaLLRsAlpha(pTD);

#define MAP_ONE_C()\
Get_M(interM1,6);\
Get_X(inputX2,7);\
Get_Y(inputY2,7);\
pTD->xx = inputX2; pTD->yy = inputY2; pTD->xC = inputX3; pTD->xN = inputX4;\
pTD->Ext1 = Extrinsic1; pTD->Ext2 = &Extrinsic2[6*WINDOW_LENGTH];\
pTD->mm = interM1; pTD->AlphaC = Alpha0; pTD->AlphaN = Alpha2;\
pTD->GammaC = Gamma0; pTD->GammaN = Gamma1;\
CompBetaLLRsAlpha(pTD);\
Get_M(interM2,7);\
pTD->Ext1 = Extrinsic1; pTD->Ext2 = &Extrinsic2[7*WINDOW_LENGTH];\
pTD->mm = interM2; pTD->AlphaC = Alpha2; pTD->AlphaN = Alpha0; \
pTD->xC = inputX4; pTD->GammaC = Gamma1; pTD->GammaN = Gamma0;\
CompBetaLLRs(pTD);
```

Pcode 4.45: Simulation code for window-based MAP decoder-1.

4.6 LDPC Codes

In Section 3.11, we discussed LDPC codes generation and their decoding algorithms. Before reading this section, refer back to Section 3.11 for an introduction to LDPC codes. In this section, we simulate the min-sum algorithm to decode LDPC codes. We also discuss the efficient way of implementing an LDPC decoder with larger parity check matrices. As discussed, the LDPC codes are defined by the low-density parity check matrix H. At the transmitter side, we generate the LDPC code by multiplying the message vector with the corresponding generator matrix G derived from H (see IEEE, "802.16E Standard," 2005, for other efficient encoding methods to compute the LDPC codeword). Then we modulate the codeword bits using the BPSK modulator and transmit over a noisy channel. At the receiver, we receive the corresponding noisy symbols (here we assume that the symbols and frames are properly in sync). We convert the floating-point values of noisy symbols to fixed-point symbols. We use the 5.3 format in the simulation to convert floating-point values to fixed-point values. For example, if we receive the noisy symbol as -0.81, then its fixed-point format is obtained by multiplying it by 2^3. The 5.3 fixed-point equivalent of -0.81 is -6 (after truncation).

4.6.1 Decoding of LDPC Codes on Tanner Graph

The parity check matrix H of LDPC codes can be represented using a Tanner graph which is a bipartite graph with two type of nodes, bit nodes and parity nodes. We decode the LDPC code symbols iteratively processing the Tanner graph by using the sum-product algorithm. We use less complex min-sum algorithms in the simulations

```
#define MAP_TWO_A()\
Get_iX(inputX1,0);\
Get_Z(inputY1,0);\
pTD->xx = inputX1; pTD->yy = inputY1;\
pTD->Ext2 = &Extrinsic1[0]; pTD->GammaC = Gamma0; pTD->AlphaC = Alpha0;\
CompGamma(pTD);\
CompAlpha(pTD);

#define MAP_TWO_B()\
Get_iM(interM1,j);\
Get_iX(inputX2,j+1);\
Get_Z(inputY2,j+1);\
pTD->xx = inputX2; pTD->yy = inputY2; pTD->xC = inputX3; pTD->xN = inputX4;\
pTD->Ext1 = Extrinsic2; pTD->Ext2 = &Extrinsic1[j*WINDOW_LENGTH];\
pTD->mm = interM1; pTD->AlphaC = Alpha0; pTD->AlphaN = Alpha2;\
pTD->GammaC = Gamma0; pTD->GammaN = Gamma1;\
CompBetaLLRsAlpha(pTD);\
Put_LLR(LLR01,j);\
Get_iM(interM2,j+1);\
Get_iX(inputX1,j+2);\
Get_Z(inputY1,j+2);\
pTD->xx = inputX1; pTD->yy = inputY1; pTD->xC = inputX4; pTD->xN = inputX3;\
pTD->Ext1 = Extrinsic2; pTD->Ext2 = &Extrinsic1[(j+1)*WINDOW_LENGTH];\
pTD->mm = interM2; pTD->AlphaC = Alpha2; pTD->AlphaN = Alpha0;\
pTD->GammaC = Gamma1; pTD->GammaN = Gamma0;\
CompBetaLLRsAlpha(pTD);\
Put_LLR(LLR01,j+1);

#define MAP_TWO_C()\
Get_iM(interM1,6);\
Get_iX(inputX2,7);\
Get_Z(inputY2,7);\
pTD->xx = inputX2; pTD->yy = inputY2; pTD->xC = inputX3; pTD->xN = inputX4;\
pTD->Ext1 = Extrinsic2; pTD->Ext2 = &Extrinsic1[6*WINDOW_LENGTH];\
pTD->mm = interM1; pTD->AlphaC = Alpha0; pTD->AlphaN = Alpha2;\
pTD->GammaC = Gamma0; pTD->GammaN = Gamma1;\
CompBetaLLRsAlpha(pTD);\
Put_LLR(LLR01, 6);\
Get_iM(interM2,7);\
pTD->Ext1 = Extrinsic2; pTD->Ext2 = &Extrinsic1[7*WINDOW_LENGTH];\
pTD->mm = interM2; pTD->AlphaC = Alpha2; pTD->AlphaN = Alpha0;\
pTD->xC = inputX4; pTD->GammaC = Gamma1; pTD->GammaN = Gamma0;\
CompBetaLLRs(pTD);\
Put_LLR(LLR01, 7);\
```

Pcode 4.46: Simulation code for window based MAP decoder-2.

to decode LDPC codes on the Tanner graph. We pass the extrinsic information computed at one type of nodes to another type of nodes through the Tanner graph edges back and forth; this mechanism of passing information is known as *message passing* or *belief propagation*. The edge connections, which are defined by parity check matrix elements, act as interleavers when passing extrinsic information through them.

Processing at Bit Nodes

We compute the LLR_i at the i-th bit node using the extrinsic information R_{ji} passed from parity nodes that are connected to the i-th bit node and using the channel APP λ_i at the i-th bit node. Then, we compute the extrinsic information Q_{ij} at the i-th bit node using the LLR_i of the i-th bit node and using the extrinsic information R_{ji} passed to the i-th bit node from all connected parity nodes except from the j-th parity node. At the beginning, we initialize the Q_{ij} s with λ_i. The computed Q_{ij} is passed from the i-th bit node to all parity nodes which are connected to the i-th bit node.

Processing at Parity Nodes

We compute the extrinsic information R_{ji} (to pass to the i-th bit node) at the j-th parity node using the extrinsic information Q_{ij} passed to the j-th parity node from all connected bit nodes except the i-th bit node. The magnitude value of R_{ji} is obtained as the minimum of absolute values of participated Q_{ij} and the sign of R_{ji} is

```
//GenerateInterleaverMatrix(DATA_SIZE);
//InterleaveInputX();
pTD->Sigma = 1;                  // one_by_sigma_square: 1
for(i = 0;i < NUM_ITERATIONS;i++){
      // ----- first MAP decoder --------
      // pre-compute Gamma and Alpha for first window of first MAP decoder
      MAP_ONE_A()
      for(j = 0;j < NUM_WINDOWS-2;j+=2){
                  // compute LLRS, Beta for current window and Alpha for next window
                  MAP_ONE_B()
      }
      // compute LLRS and Beta and compute Extrinsic info for second MAP
      MAP_ONE_C()

      // ------ second MAP decoder --------
      // pre-compute Gamma and Alpha for first window of second MAP decoder
      MAP_TWO_A()
      for(j = 0;j < NUM_WINDOWS-2;j+=2){
                  // compute LLRS, Beta for current window and Alpha for next window
                  MAP_TWO_B()
      }
      // compute LLRS and Beta and compute Extrinsic info for first MAP
      MAP_TWO_C()
}
```

Pcode 4.47: Simulation code for window-based turbo decoder.

obtained by multiplication of signs of participated Q_{ij}. Here participated Q_{ij} nodes mean those Q_{ij} nodes that are involved in the computation of R_{ji}.

4.6.2 Min-Sum Algorithm

The min-sum algorithm discussed in Section 3.11 is summarized in the following.

Initialization:

$$\lambda_i = 2y_i/\sigma^2 \tag{4.44}$$

First iteration:

$$Q_{ij} = \lambda_i$$
$$R_{ji} = k\left(\prod_{i' \in V_{j\backslash i}} \alpha_{i'j}\right) \min_{i' \in V_{j\backslash i}} \beta_{i'j} \tag{4.45}$$

where $\alpha_{ij} = sign\left(Q_{ij}\right)$, $\beta_{ij} = abs\left(Q_{ij}\right)$, $V_{j\backslash i}$ is the set of column locations of the 1s in the j-th row excluding the i-th column in parity check matrix H, and k is a constant less than 1.

$$LLR_i = \lambda_i + \sum_{j \in U_i} R_{ji} \tag{4.46}$$

where U_i is the set of row locations of 1s in the i-th column of parity check matrix H.

Second iteration onwards:

$$Q_{ij} = LLR_i - R_{ji} \tag{4.47}$$

$$R_{ji} = k\left(\prod_{i' \in V_{j\backslash i}} \alpha_{i'j}\right) \min_{i' \in V_{j\backslash i}} \beta_{i'j} \tag{4.48}$$

$$LLR_i = \lambda_i + \sum_{j \in U_i} R_{ji} \tag{4.49}$$

Repeat the computations using Equations (4.47) through (4.49) for the remaining iterations. Here, we are not checking for the decoder halting at the end of the iteration. We run the decoder for all L iterations. After L iterations, we make hard decisions using the soft values of LLR_i s. The values of LLR_i grow fast once they start converging and we have to perform normalization of LLR_i to avoid the saturation of metric values.

Hard decision making:

$$\hat{c}_i = \begin{cases} 1 & \text{if } LLR_i < 0 \\ 0 & \text{Otherwise} \end{cases} \tag{4.50}$$

4.6.3 LDPC Decoder Simulation

In this section, we simulate the min-sum algorithm described in the previous section for decoding LDPC codes. We assume the noise variance $\sigma^2 = 1$ throughout the simulations and the received noisy floating-point symbols are converted to 5.3 fixed-point format. The simulation code for initialization of the min-sum algorithm is given in Pcode 4.48. We use Equation (4.44) for initialization. Since the noise variance is assumed as 1, we simply multiply the received sequence y_i by 2 to get λ_i. Then, we initialize Q_{ij} with λ_i wherever $h_{ji} = 1$. The matrix Q_{ij} contains zeros in places where $h_{ji} = 0$.

```
for(i = 0;i < ldpc->n;i++){
        Lambda[i] = 2*y[i];
}

for(j = 0;j < ldpc->m;j++){
        for(i = 0;i < ldpc->n;i++){
                   if (H[j][i] == 1)
                              Qij[j][i] = Lambda[i];
                   else
                              Qij[j][i] = 0;
        }
}
```

Pcode 4.48: Simulation code for initialization of min-sum algorithm.

The extrinsic information R_{ji} passed from parity nodes to bit nodes is computed using the Equation (4.47). The simulation code for computing R_{ji} is given in Pcode 4.49. If h_{ji} is equal to 1 (i.e., an edge connection is present from the i-th bit node to the j-th parity node), then the magnitude of R_{ji} is equal to the minimum of all the j-th row Q_{ij} elements excluding the i-th column Q_{ij} element. If the minus sign is represented with bit 1 and the plus sign is represented with bit 0, then the sign of R_{ji} is computed as XOR of all the j-th row Q_{ij} elements' sign bits excluding the i-th column Q_{ij} element sign bit. Then, we multiply the R_{ji} by 0.8 (or 6 in 5.3 format) to get unbiased extrinsic information.

Once the extrinsic information R_{ji} is available at bit nodes, then we can compute LLR_is of the transmitted bits using λ_i and R_{ji}. The simulation code for computing LLR_is using Equation (4.48) is given in Pcode 4.50. At the end of all iterations we make hard decisions from LLR_is using Equation (4.49). The simulation code for making hard decisions from soft LLR_i values is given in Pcode 4.51.

We compute the Q_{ij} using LLR_i and R_{ji} from the second iteration onwards. The simulation code for computing Q_{ij} is given in Pcode 4.52.

4.6.4 Complexity of Min-Sum Algorithm

We estimate the complexity of the min-sum algorithm in terms of the number of compute operations (or clock cycles) and in terms of memory requirements. As discussed, a single iteration of the min-sum algorithm involves the computation of Q_{ij} from LLR_i and R_{ji}, computation of R_{ji} from Q_{ij} and computation of LLR_i from λ_i and R_{ji}. The total computations involved in the min-sum algorithm depends on the complexity of previous three metrics times the number of iterations the decoder runs before stop decoding.

```
for(j = 0;j < ldpc->m;j++)
        for(i = 0;i < ldpc->n;i++){
                if (H[j][i] == 1){
                        sign = 0; mag = 32768;
                        for(k = 0;k < ldpc->n;k++){
                                if(i!=k){
                                        if (H[j][k] == 1){
                                                x = Qij[j][k];
                                                b = x < 0 ? 1: 0;
                                                a = abs(x);
                                                sign = sign ^ b;
                                                if (mag > a) mag = a;
                                        }
                                }
                        }
                        mag = (mag * 6) >> 3;
                        Rji[j][i] = (sign==1) ? -mag : mag;
                }
        }
```

Pcode 4.49: Simulation code for computing R_{ji}.

```
for(i = 0;i < ldpc->n;i++){
        mag = 0;
        for(j = 0;j < ldpc->m;j++){
                if (H[j][i] == 1)
                                mag = mag + Rji[j][i];
        }
        LLRi[i] = Lambda[i] + mag;
}
```

Pcode 4.50: Simulation code to compute LLR_i.

```
for(i = 0;i < ldpc->m;i++){
        if (LLRi[i] < 0)
                        ch[i] = 1;
        else
                        ch[i] = 0;
}
```

Pcode 4.51: Simulation code for making hard decisions from LLR_is.

```
for(j = 0;j < ldpc->m;j++)
        for(i = 0;i < ldpc->n;i++)
                if (H[j][i] == 1)
                        Qij[j][i] = LLRi[i] - Rji[j][i];
```

Pcode 4.52: Simulation code for computing Q_{ij}.

Q_{ij} Computational Complexity

The computation of Q_{ij} involves one conditional arithmetic operation as shown in Pcode 4.52. A conditional arithmetic operation consumes 3 cycles on the reference embedded processor (see Appendix A.4 on the companion website for more details on cycles estimate on the reference embedded processor). As the loop of Q_{ij} computation runs for $M * N$ times, we require $3 * M * N$ cycles to compute Q_{ij}.

R_{ji} Computational Complexity

The costliest module in the min-sum algorithm is an R_{ji} computation. Based on Pcode 4.49, the innermost loop of the R_{ji} computation consumes 7 cycles per loop iteration. As the computation of magnitude is performed conditionally, we consume two more cycles to assign the computed value conditionally. This means, whether the condition is true (for computation) or not (for jump), we spend 9 cycles, and so to run the innermost loop N

times we require $9 * N$ cycles. However, the innermost loop itself runs conditionally depending on the presence of element 1s in the parity check matrix. If $h_{ji} = 0$, then we spend about 10 cycles (for conditional jump + overhead); otherwise, we spend $9 * N$ cycles. Therefore, the total cycles cost of R_{ji} computation is estimated as $10 * (M * N - S) + 9 * N * S + 7 * S$ (overhead to initialize parameters in the loop and to compute the final R_{ji}) cycles, where S is the total number of 1s present in the parity check matrix.

LLR_i Computational Complexity

Based on Pcode 4.50, LLR_i computation involves one conditional arithmetic operation and is computed $M * N$ times. We have one more addition operation outside the inner loop and for that we consume N cycles as it runs for N times. Thus, we spend a total of $(M * N * 2 + N)$ cycles to compute LLR_i.

Next, if $M = 288$, $N = 576$, $S = 2000$, and $L = 10$ (number of iterations that the Tanner graph iterated), then we require approximately 120 million cycles for decoding 288 bits or 0.42 million cycles per bit. At this complexity, we cannot decode 2 kbps bit rate sequence on 600 MIPS of the reference embedded processor because it requires 840 MIPS. With the efficient implementation techniques discussed in the next section, we can reduce the computational cycles by far.

Memory Requirements

The buffers used for holding H, Q_{ij} and R_{ji} values are two-dimensional arrays each of size $M \times N$. If we use bytes to represent parity check matrix H elements and 16-bit words for Q_{ij} and R_{ji}, then we require $5 * M * N$ bytes of memory to store H, Q_{ij} and R_{ji}. If $M = 588$ and $N = 576$, then we need 830 kB (see Appendix A.1 on the companion website for memory availability on the reference embedded processor) of memory to hold data values. All other buffers require less than 5 kB of data memory. In the next section, we discuss the techniques to reduce the memory requirements of the LDPC decoder.

4.6.5 Efficient LDPC Decoder Implementation

In the previous section, we saw the computational and memory requirements with an inefficient implementation of the LDPC decoder exceeding the budget of the reference embedded processor. In this section, we discuss techniques to implement the min-sum algorithm with less memory and computations. The low-density population of 1s in the parity check matrix not only gives the coding performance but also lowers high computational and memory requirements for LDPC codes decoding. The heavy computations and memory requirements in the LDPC decoder are due to the processing of the decoding algorithm on a two-dimensional array of $M \times N$. But in reality, we needed to process the data for only S non-zero elements of parity check matrix H, where $S << M \times N$.

If we can track the presence of 1s locations in the parity check matrix H during the decoding time, then it is possible to avoid that heavy two-dimensional processing and memory usage. To track the 1s locations during Tanner graph decoding, we use four look-up tables: V2C[ ][ ], vc[ ][ ], C2V[ ][ ], and cv[ ][ ]. The look-up table V2C[j][ ] contains the positions of bit nodes, which are connected to the j-th parity node and look-up table vc[j][ ] consists of the number of parity nodes to which the current bit node (which is connected to the j-th parity node) is connected before the j-th parity node. This is illustrated in Figure 4.24. Based on the figure, before the j-th parity node, the i-th bit node is connected to two parity nodes; so V2C[j][ ] = [$i-e, i, i+g$, 3] and vc[j][ ] = [1, 2, 1]. The last entry in the V2C[j][ ] look-up table represents the number of bits nodes that connect to the j-th parity node. Similarly, the look-up table C2V[i][ ] contains the position of parity nodes connected to the i-th bit node, and the look-up table cv[i][ ] consists of the number of bit nodes to which the current parity node (which is

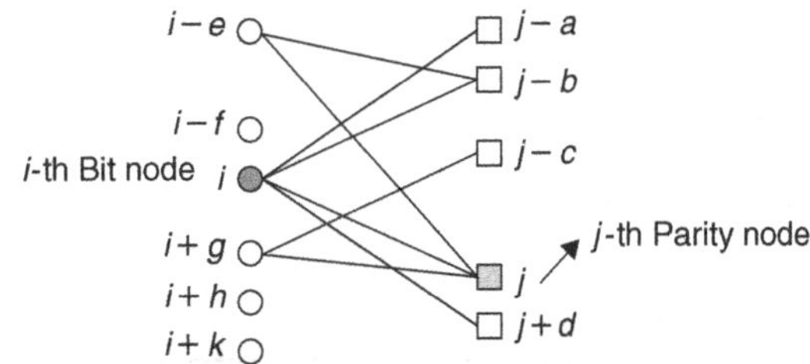

Figure 4.24: Illustration to fill entries of look-up tables.

connected to i-th bit node) is connected before the i-th bit node. Based on Figure 4.24, C2V[i][] = [$j-a, j-b, j, j+d$, 4] and cv[i][] = [0, 1, 1, 0]. The last entry in the C2V[i][] look-up table represents the number of parity nodes connected to the i-th bit node. With this tracking information, we don't need to hold the two-dimensional parity check matrix H elements.

With this, if we consider the parity check matrix H of size $M \times N$ with row weight w_r and column weight w_c, then the buffers Q_{ij} and R_{ji} are required to store only $M * w_r$ and $N * w_c$ values. If $M = 288$, $N = 576$, $w_r = 7$ and $w_c = 6$, then we need a memory of size $7 * (N * w_c + M * w_r) = 38304$ bytes to store Q_{ij} (in 16-bit words), R_{ji} (in 16-bit words), V2C[j][] (in 16-bit words), vc[j][] (in bytes), C2V[i][] (in 16-bit words) and cv[i][] (in bytes). Assuming 4 kB of memory used for other buffers, we require the data memory of 42 kB (which is reasonable) to implement the LDPC min-sum algorithm decoder.

The simulation code for Q_{ij}, R_{ji}, and LLR_i computation using this memory-efficient method is given in Pcodes 4.53, 4.54, and 4.55, respectively. As we are processing metrics only for non-zero elements parity check matrix, the number of computations is also greatly reduced. In Pcode 4.53, we spend 3 cycles per one iteration of the innermost loop and consume about $3 * w_r * M$ cycles to compute Q_{ij}s. In computing R_{ji} using Pcode 4.54,

```
for(j = 0;j < ldpc->m;j++){
    n = V2C[j][7];
    for(i = 0;i < n;i++){
        a = vc[j][i];
        b = V2C[j][i];
        Qij[b][a] = LLRi[b] - Rji[j][i];
    }
}
```

Pcode 4.53: Simulation code for efficient computation of Q_{ij}.

```
for(j = 0;j < ldpc->m;j++){
    n = V2C[j][7];
    for(i = 0;i < n;i++){
        sign = 0; mag = 32768;
        for(k = 0;k < n;k++){
            if (i!= k){
                m = V2C[j][k];
                a = vc[j][k];
                x = Qij[m][a];
                a = x < 0 ? 1 : 0;
                b = abs(x);
                if (mag > b) mag = b; // finding minimum
                sign = sign ^ a;      // computing product of signs
            }
        }
        mag = (6*mag) >> 3; // k = 0.8 or 6 in 5.3 format
        Rji[j][i] = (sign == 1) ? -mag : mag;
    }
}
```

Pcode 4.54: Simulation code for efficient computation of R_{ji}

```
for(i = 0;i < ldpc->n;i++){
    n = C2V[i][6];
    mag = 0;
    for(j = 0;j < n;j++){
        a = cv[i][j];
        b = C2V[i][j];
        mag = mag + Rji[b][a];
    }
    LLRi[i] = Lambda[i] + mag;
}
```

Pcode 4.55: Simulation code to efficiently compute LLR_i.

we spend 9 cycles in the innermost loop and the loop runs conditionally w_r times to compute one R_{ji}. Outside the innermost loop, we spend 6 cycles to initialize and to compute the final R_{ji} value. Thus, to compute all R_{ji} values, we consume $M(w_r(9^* w_r + 6) + 1)$ cycles. In Pcode 4.55, we spend 4 cycles in the inner most loop and the loop runs for w_c times. We consume a total of $N(4^* w_c + 3)$ cycles for LLR_i. With this, for $M = 288$, $N = 576$, $w_r = 7$, $w_c = 6$, and $L = 10$, we consume about 1,630,080 cycles for 288 bits or 5660 cycles per bit in decoding with the min-sum algorithm. In other words, decoding a 100-kbps bitstream requires only about 566 MIPS on the reference processor.

CHAPTER 5

Lossless Data Compression

Data compression (or source coding) enables the communication system to transfer more information by removing the redundancy present in the data (e.g., voice, audio, video). In other words, with data compression algorithms, it is possible to represent the given data with fewer number of information bits. Data compression algorithms are widely used in data storage and data communication applications. We use data compression algorithms to compress multimedia data at the transmitter side and corresponding decompression algorithms at the receiver side for getting back the transmitted data (which may not be exactly the same as the source-generated data). In Figure 5.1, the highlighted region corresponds to data compression (performed at the transmitter side) and decompression (performed at the receiver side) modules. In the communication system transceiver, the data compression block is placed at the beginning of the transmitter modules and the corresponding decompression block is placed at the end of the receiver modules so that the rest of the communication system works on compressed data to reduce the amount of data processing.

The communication system bandwidth is limited due to switching equipment, channel non-zero response and other channel impairments. The system's overall bandwidth determines the allowed bit rates for communication. However, with source coding techniques, it is possible to trade processing power with the communication system bandwidth. For example, in the case of multimedia (e.g., voice, audio, video, text) communications, data compression significantly reduces bit rates and thus the cost of media communications. It enables the broadcast of multimedia content in real time by reducing the data rate. The data compression and decompression blocks shown in Figure 5.1 contain many modules such as parsing (to parse headers and payload data), transforms (to remove redundancy in the data), motion estimation/compensation (to remove temporal redundancy in video frames), quantization (to eliminate insignificant data coefficients), entropy coding (to compress data parameters), and so on.

In this chapter, we concentrate only on entropy coding (or lossless data compression, with which we can get back the original data parameters after decoding) modules that are used in video data compression. The other modules of data compression or decompression blocks will be discussed in this volume's audio/video coding chapters.

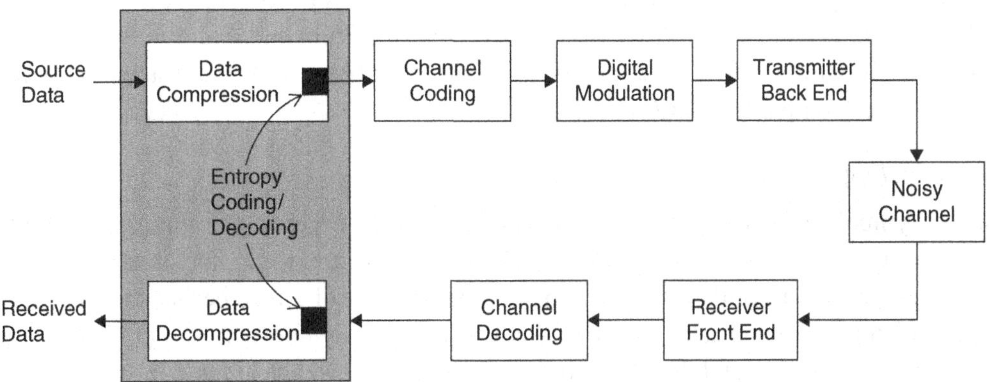

Figure 5.1: Digital communication system with data compression and decompression.

DOI: 10.1016/B978-1-85617-678-1.00005-3

5.1 Entropy Coding

In the data compression block, our entropy coding module is present at the end and we perform the corresponding entropy decoding in the receiver at the beginning of the data decompression block, which is highlighted with dark squares in Figure 5.1. Entropy coding algorithms output the bitstream by compactly representing various data parameters using their source information. As previously stated, entropy coding is a lossless process and is independent of the type of information (e.g., audio, video, text) that is being compressed. It is concerned solely with how the information is represented. In Example 5.1, we work with a simple entropy coding algorithm to see how an entropy coding system compactly represents the data information.

Example 5.1

We consider a source with symbol set S = {A,B,C,D,E,F,G,H}. Let us assume a probability set $P = \{p_a, p_b, p_c, p_d, p_e, p_f, p_g, p_h\}$ that governs the occurrence of symbols from the source S for their transmission. Now, assume that the data string generated for transmission from S following the symbol probability distribution P is M = BAAACAAAAABBDAAAAEAAAAFAAGCAAAAB. We have a total of 32 symbols for transmission.

Next, we assume two types of data coding schemes Type I and Type II as follows.

Type I coding: A:000, B:001, C:010, D:011, E:100, F:101, G:110, H:111

Type II coding: A:1, B:01, C:001, D:0001, E:00001, F:000001, G:0000001, H:00000001

for compactly representing the symbols.

With the Type I coding scheme, we need 96 bits to represent the data or an average of 3 bits/symbol to transmit the message.

With Type I coding: 001 000 000 000 010 000 000 000 000 000 001 001 011 000 000 000 000 100 000 000 000 000 101 000 000 110 010 000 000 000 000 001 (total bits: 96)

If we code the same message data by using the Type II scheme, we require only 56 bits or an average of 1.75 bits/symbol to transmit the message.

With Type II coding: 01 1 1 1 001 1 1 1 1 1 01 01 0001 1 1 1 1 00001 1 1 1 1 000001 1 1 0000001 001 1 1 1 1 01 (total bits = 56)

Here, with Type II coding, the average number of bits/symbol is less than with Type I coding. This is because the statistical nature of source S is modeled more accurately with the Type II coding scheme than with Type I. We will discuss this further in the next section. ■

In the literature, two types of entropy coding methods are widely used—Huffman (or variable length) coding and arithmetic coding. In previous generations of audio (e.g., MP3, WMV) and video codecs (e.g., the MPEG-2, H.263, WMV), variable length codes (VLCs) were widely used. Recent audio and video codecs (e.g., AAC, H.264) use arithmetic coding for lossless compression. With arithmetic coding, we achieve about 10 to 15% more compression when compared to VLC code.

5.1.1 Huffman Coding

Suppose that the symbol set S has N symbols and these symbols occur in the input string with respective probabilities $P_i, i = 1, 2, 3, \ldots, N$, so that $\sum P_i = 1$. The symbol occurrence is statistically independent. Then, based on the fundamentals of information theory, the optimal number of bits to be assigned for each symbol of the input string (which gets the character symbol at random from the symbol set S) is $Q_i = \log 2(1/P_i)$, where P_i is the probability of an i-th symbol. In other words, we require on average at least $H = -\sum P_i \log_2(P_i)$ bits per symbol to communicate the symbols from set S. Here H gives the average number of bits per symbol and is called the *entropy rate* of the symbol source S with the corresponding symbol probabilities P_i. The entropy rate of a source is a number that depends only on the statistical nature of the source. For example, if the probability of a symbol is 1/256, such as would be found in a random byte stream, the number of bits per symbol required is log2(256) or 8. As the probability goes up to 1/2, the optimum number of bits used to code the symbol would go down to 1.

The idea behind Huffman coding is simply to use shorter bit patterns for frequently occurring character symbols. Huffman coding assigns a code to each symbol, with the codes being as short as 1 bit or considerably longer than the input symbols, strictly depending on their probabilities. In Example 5.1, the Type II coding scheme is an example of Huffman coding. With Huffman coding, we cannot use $\log 2(1/P_i)$ for arbitrary values of P_i, as it outputs a noninteger number of bits. For this, we approximate the probabilities P_i by integer powers of ½ so that all the resulting Q_is are integers.

Now we discuss the assignment of bits to each symbol of the set S in a constructive way. Let us consider a different symbol set $S = \{U, V, X, Y, Z\}$ with the corresponding probability distribution set $P = \{0.4, 0.28, 0.22, 0.07, 0.03\}$. Note that the sum of probabilities of all N (=5) symbols is 1. Next, we build a binary tree with N stages. We start from the bottom of tree by considering the two least probable symbols. In this case, the two least probable symbols are Z and Y with probabilities 0.03 and 0.07. We always assign the bit "0" branch to the low-probability child node, and the bit "1" branch to the high-probability child node from the parent node. The probability of the parent node is the sum of probabilities of its child nodes. Next, we move one stage up and we consider the next highest probable symbol (i.e., X), and assign branch "1" if its probability is more than the probability of parent node for two lower-stage child nodes; otherwise, it is assigned branch "0." Continue like this until all characters of the symbol set are touched once. Finally, make sure that the final parent (or root) node probability is 1.00. Then, proceed to collect the bits of branches connecting from the root node to leaf nodes that represent the characters from the symbol set S. In our case, from Figure 5.2, we assign the bits to characters as given in Table 5.1.

With Huffman coding, it is not possible to code a symbol with a probability greater than 0.5 using a fraction of a bit. Thus, a minimum of 1 bit is required to represent a symbol with Huffman coding. Moreover, the adaptive Huffman coding algorithms are relatively time and memory consuming. We will discuss different variable length decoding algorithms used with the MPEG-2 and H.264 standards in Sections 5.2 and 5.3.

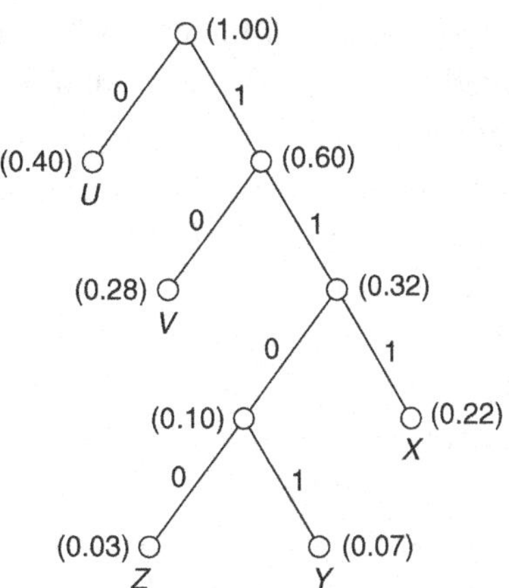

Figure 5.2: Building Huffman codes using a binary tree.

Table 5.1: Assignment of bits to symbols per probability

Symbol	Bits
U	0
V	10
X	111
Y	1101
Z	1100

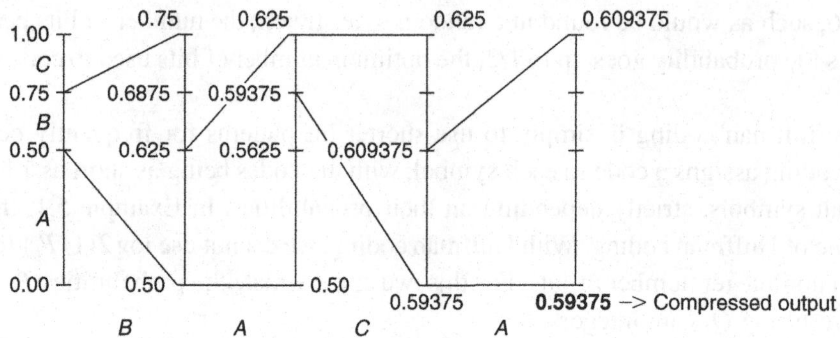

Figure 5.3: Illustration of arithmetic coding.

5.1.2 Arithmetic Coding

As discussed, if we have a symbol set with nonuniform probabilities P_i, then the data compression is possible and the number of bits we assign to data symbols equals to $Q_i = \log_2(1/P_i)$. With Huffman coding, we assign the length of bits to symbols after rounding the actual number of bits Q_i to the nearest integers. In other words, Huffman coding achieves the Shannon limit only if the symbol probabilities are all integer powers of ½. Thus, we require a minimum of 1 bit to represent a symbol even if its probability is more than half. This limits the performance of Huffman codes. In contrast, using arithmetic coding, it is possible to code a symbol with a probability of more than 0.5 using a fraction of a bit. This allows us to code the data very close to the ideal entropy of the source. Because of this, with arithmetic coding we can get better compression (about 10 to 15%) when compared to Huffman coding. However, arithmetic coding is more complex than Huffman coding.

In the arithmetic coding, an input message of any length is represented as a real number R in the range [0, 1). Unlike Huffman coding, which assigns a separate codeword for each character, arithmetic coding yields a single codeword for each encoded string of characters. The concept of arithmetic coding is explained in Example 5.2.

Although arithmetic coding is a complex coding method when compared to Huffman coding, the process of encoding and decoding a stream of symbols using arithmetic coding is not very complicated. The first step in arithmetic coding is to divide the numeric range [0,1) into N number of intervals, where N is the number of symbols in a character set. The size of each interval is related to the probabilities of corresponding symbols. In Example 5.2, the probability distribution of symbol set $\{A, B, C\} = \{0.5, 0.25, 0.25\}$. We divide the range [0,1) into 3 (=N) segments and mark the interval 0.0 to 0.5 for A, 0.50 to 0.75 for B, and 0.75 to 1.00 for C, respectively. The message to be compressed is, say, *BACA*. The first symbol to code is B, and thus we zoom the interval B of the range [0,1), and subdivide it again into three segments with the length of subsegments proportional to the probabilities of characters in the given symbol set in the same way as we did earlier. The next symbol to code is A, and we again zoom the subsegment A and divide it into three segments, and continue this process for the rest of symbols as shown in Figure 5.3. As we code more and more symbols of the long string, the length of the working interval becomes shorter and shorter. Finally, the arithmetic coded value of the string is given by the bottom value of the final subinterval. In Example 5.2, the complete arithmetic encoding and decoding of the symbol string is presented along with the encode and decode algorithms.

Example 5.2

Consider the symbol set {A,B,C} with probabilities ½, ¼, and ¼; the corresponding symbol intervals follow:

A	½	0.00 to 0.50
B	¼	0.50 to 0.75
C	¼	0.75 to 1.00

Symbol_Range(Symbol) = 0.00 to 0.50 for A, 0.50 to 0.75 for B, 0.75 to 1.00 for C
High_Range(Symbol) = 0.50 for A, 0.75 for B, 1.00 for C
Low_Range(Symbol) = 0.00 for A, 0.50 for B, 0.75 for C

Message to transmit: BACA

Encoding Algorithm

```
Value = 0.0;
high = 1.0;
i = 4;
while(i–)
{
        r = high-value;
        high = value + r*high_range(symbol);
        value = value + r*low_range(symbol);
}
output value as encoded_value;
```

Encoding Symbols

B: r = 1, high = 0.75, value = 0.5
A: r = 0.25, high = 0.625, value = 0.5,
C: r = 0.125, high = 0.625, value = 0.59375
A: r = 0.03125, high = 0.609375, value = 0.59375

Decoding Algorithm

```
value = encoded_value;
i = 4;
while(i–)
{
        symbol = symbol_range(value);
        r = high_range(symbol) - low_range(symbol);
        value = value-low_range(symbol);
        value = value / r;
}
```

Decoded Message

symbol = B
r = 0.25
value = 0.375
symbol = A
r = 0.50
value = 0.75
symbol = C
r = 0.25
value = 0
symbol = A

■

To avoid precision problems in arithmetic coding, the range of the arithmetic coder is frequently normalized. With binary symbols, the arithmetic coding can be implemented very efficiently, and this type of coding is popularly known as binary arithmetic coding.

Binary Arithmetic Coding

Binary arithmetic coding (BAC) is the most efficient way of implementing general arithmetic coding that is applied to data sequences with only two symbols (0 and 1), thereby making it easier to implement arithmetic coding operations both in hardware and software. Typically, any decision can be coded with multiple binary decisions as we can represent any number with a binary sequence of 0s and 1s. With binary arithmetic coding, we handle the following three steps.

Binary Symbols Probability The BAC works on binary symbols 0 and 1. However, it is more convenient to use variable symbol names for binary symbols, instead of 0 and 1 constants, to work with probabilities. In the BAC literature, the variable symbol names MPS (most probable symbol) and LPS (least probable symbol) are used for the binary decision 0 or 1. With BAC, knowing one symbol probability (p) is sufficient as the other symbol probability is obtained as $1-p$. Typically, as shown in Figure 5.4, we estimate the LPS probability and compute the MPS probability by subtracting the LPS probability from 1. In reality, the probabilities of symbols are not fixed, as they were in Example 5.2. As we code different types of symbols for different types of parameters, the probabilities of symbols keep changing. With BAC, we track only the LPS probabilities. Either by observing the previous symbols' probabilities or based on the context of symbols, we obtain the approximate probability information for the LPS. In addition, we fix the MPS decision bit for the context model and link it to the LPS probability. We obtain the LPS bit as 1-MPS.

We always get the LPS probability and the MPS decision bit from the context model. When we compress different types (e.g., headers, motion vectors, residual coefficients) of data then we will have that many contexts. For each context, we assign initial LPS probability and MPS decision bits. We update this context information (i.e., LPS probability and MPS bit value) after coding each binary decision. In this way, the binary arithmetic coder easily adapts without much computation.

Interval Subdivision To handle the precision problem with arithmetic coder interval size, we use a soft range for the interval range [0,1) by multiplying by a large integer, say, 2^{15}, and the interval becomes $[0, 2^{15}-1]$. The corresponding interval size is $R = 2^{15}$. If Qe $(=p)$ is the probability of the LPS, then the LPS subinterval R_LPS is obtained by multiplying the interval range R with LPS probability. Therefore,

$$R\_LPS = Qe * R$$
$$R\_MPS = R - R\_LPS = (1-p) * R$$

Symbol Coding To perform BAC on the binary symbol, we get the corresponding context $\{Qe, MPS \text{ bit}\}$ and then obtain the *R_LPS* and *R_MPS* by subdividing the interval using *Qe*. As MPS occur frequently, we reduce the number of computations for MPS decision coding when compared to LPS decision coding by arranging the *MPS* and *LPS* subintervals as shown in Figure 5.4. We assign a lower interval part to the MPS decision and by doing that the coding of the MPS decision becomes easy. If the binary decision is to code an *MPS* bit, then the *Code_Value* remains the same. In this case, we just update the context and assign *R_MPS* to *R*. But, if the binary decision is to code an LPS bit, then the value is updated by adding *R_MPS* to *Code_Value*. We update the contexts accordingly and assign *R_LPS* to the next working interval *R*. In some cases, *R_MPS* becomes less than *R_LPS* for a given *Qe*, in that case we swap *R_MPS* and *R_LPS* intervals or toggle the MPS bit in that context. The symbol coding with BAC follows:

MPS coding	**LPS coding**
$R = R\_MPS$	$Code\_Value = Code\_Value + R\_LPS$
	$R = R\_LPS$

Interval Normalization As we code more and more decisions, the range of the interval becomes smaller and smaller. And correspondingly, the number of bits required to represent *Code_Value* also increases. In that case, we normalize the interval by shifting left both *R* and *Code_Value*. During the normalization, we collect the shifted bits from *Code_Value* as those bits represent the compressed decisions.

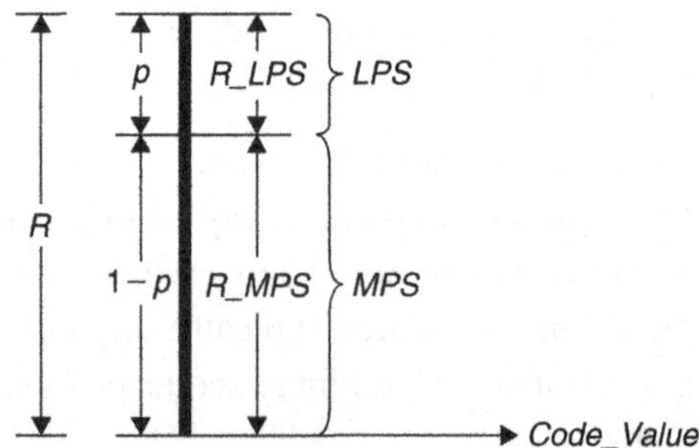

Figure 5.4: Binary arithmetic coder.

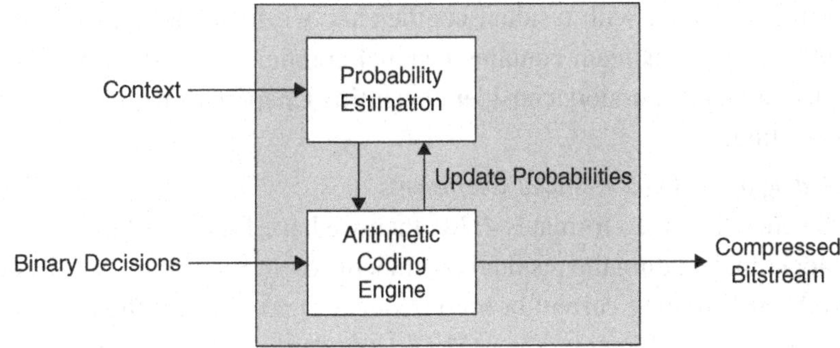

Figure 5.5: Adaptive binary arithmetic coder.

Adaptive Arithmetic Coding The adaptive binary arithmetic coding (ABAC) is one in which probabilities are adapted continuously with the coding of binary decisions. The schematic diagram of ABAC is shown in Figure 5.5.

The two most popular adaptive binary arithmetic coders are the M-coder and MQ-coder. The JPEG 2000 standard uses the MQ-coder for compressing the binary decisions, and the H.264 standard uses a variant of the M-coder for arithmetic coding of binary decisions. We will discuss binary arithmetic decoding algorithms used with the JPEG 2000 and H.264 in Sections 5.4 and 5.5.

5.2 Variable Length Decoding

As we discussed in Section 5.1.1, Huffman codes or VLCs are used to perform lossless data compression (or entropy coding) by assigning fewer bits to more frequently occurring data symbols and assigning more bits to rarely occurring data symbols. We use a variable length decoder (VLD) at the other side to decode the bitstream. But the question is whether we have any such application where these kinds of data symbols occur in reality. The answer is yes. There are many applications with these kinds of data symbols. In this chapter, we consider the video data in which we find this kind of unevenly probable symbols. In video coding (see Chapter 14 for more details on video coding technology), after applying the DCT to residual coefficients, we obtain the transform domain coefficients. We use VLC to encode the value and position of zigzag scanned quantized DCT coefficients at the encoder side using a predefined VLC codeword table. We use the corresponding VLD at the decoder side to decode the value and position of quantized DCT coefficients.

The MPEG-2 standard (MPEG-2: ISO/IEC, 1995) uses VLD to decode the received video bitstream. The standard specifies many codeword tables to encode/decode various types of slice parameters, macroblock parameters, and residual coefficients to/from the bitstream. In this section, an overview of the MPEG-2 residual VLD's most complex tasks is presented and its simulation and implementation techniques are discussed.

A few applications of the MPEG-2 codec are digital video broadcasting, digital subscriber lines, personal media players, HDTV, video surveillance, digital media storage (DVD), multimedia communications, and so on. Similar to VLD in the MPEG-2 standard, the MPEG-4 standard uses a different VLD, and the H.264 standard uses the CAVLC (context-based adaptive variable length coder) for lossless data compression. The MPEG-2 VLD is simpler when compared to the MPEG-4 and H.264 standards. Although the concept of VLD is more or less the same in all standards, the way the encoding and decoding procedures are used for encoding or decoding the parameters varies greatly from standard to standard. The performance of the MPEG-2 VLD is reasonable when compared to variable length coding performance of the MPEG-4 and H.264 standards.

5.2.1 MPEG-2 VLD

The MPEG-2 entropy coder uses variable length codes (VLCs) for lossless compression and decompression of video frame parameters. We use the VLD to decode the MPEG-2 bitstream. The MPEG-2 standard specifies many codeword tables to decode the various types of data which is encoded using VLC. With VLD, we decode the bitstream and get the encoded parameter information back by matching the received bit pattern with the appropriate MPEG-2 VLD codeword tables. Although the bitstream consists of many parameters and headers information along with residual coefficients, we focus on decoding 8×8 block residual coefficients, since 80 to 90% of the bitstream contains residual coefficient information. We use some video coding terminology in the following discussion; consider consulting Chapter 14 for more detail about video coding technology before proceeding.

Decoding of MPEG-2 Residual Coefficients

If the encoded video format is 4:2:0, then we have four 8×8 luma blocks and two 8×8 chroma blocks per macroblock. In decoding the residual coefficients of an 8×8 block, we decode DC (direct current or zero frequency) and AC (alternating current or high frequency) residual coefficients for both luma and chroma components. To decode these coefficients, the MPEG-2 standard specifies altogether five codeword tables. With the MPEG-2 VLD, the only difference between luma and chroma coefficients decoding is in decoding of the DC coefficient in the case of intra macroblock. Otherwise the same code can be used to decode either luma or chroma. In decoding the DC coefficients we use separate prediction values and codeword tables for luma blocks and chroma blocks. Although an 8×8 subblock contains 64 coefficients, most of them will be zeros. We decode all non-zero coefficients of an 8×8 subblock along with their locations using the MPEG-2 VLD. The flow diagram for decoding an 8×8 subblock with the MPEG-2 VLD is shown in Figure 5.6.

The basic parameters used in the MPEG-2 residual decoding are *macroblock_type* and *intra_vlc_format*. Depending on the *macroblock_type* and *intra_vlc_format* values, we select codeword tables for decoding residual coefficients. If the *macroblock_type* is intra, then we decode the residual DC coefficient (or first coefficient) using DC coefficients codeword tables and AC coefficients using another AC coefficient codeword table. If the *macroblock_type* is inter, then both DC and AC coefficients are decoded using the same codeword table. After decoding the first coefficient, we decode the rest of the AC coefficients in the loop which run up to 63 times. In each iteration we get the codeword from the VLD table and check whether all the coefficients are decoded (i.e., the end-of-block (EOB) is reached) or any coefficients have to be decoded further. If EOB is reached, we then quit the loop, otherwise we continue decoding of the coefficient. For each AC coefficient, we compute two values: the signed value and the run m (the number of zeros present from the previous non-zero coefficient to the present non-zero coefficient; note that this run value is meaningful only with respect to zigzag scanned positions; see MPEG-2: ISO/IEC, 1995). If $m > 0$, we first insert those many zeros in the coefficient buffer and then place the signed coefficient value. As shown in Figure 5.6, decoding AC coefficients of a block includes many condition checks and condition jumps.

We decode two parameters for each AC coefficient; signed value and run. Decoding of one AC coefficient using VLD involves the following four steps:

1. Accessing 16 bits of bitstream
2. Accessing the appropriate look-up table to get "run" and "value"
3. Decoding sign bit
4. Updating the bit position and word offset

In the MPEG2 VLD, to decode a residual coefficient, we have to analyze bit patterns of length from 2 bits to as large as 24 bits in the bitstream. Depending on the incoming bitstream bits, whichever bit pattern completely matches a codeword given in the table with a minimum length of bits, the corresponding row values (or VLD_SYMBOLS) of a table are chosen as the decoded values. In addition, we do not encode the information of number of bits (NUM_BITS) used for encoding the VLD_SYMBOLS, we determine NUM_BITS after decoding that particular codeword. Now, the question is how to search the codeword tables to find the right match? The brute-force solution for this problem is matching all size bit patterns to all codewords of a table and it is very costly in terms of cycles. The other solution for this bitstream decoding problem is bit-pattern matching by using look-up tables. If we use one look-up table for decoding all sizes of bit patterns, then the size of the look-up table becomes $(2^{24}) * 4 = 64{,}000$ kB. This is not a practical amount of on-chip data memory in many embedded processors.

VLD Decoding with Look-up Tables

The alternate solution for the MPEG-2 VLD decoding is to use a combination of look-up tables and analytic methods. In this approach we use many small look-up tables and apply some logic to match the bit patterns of

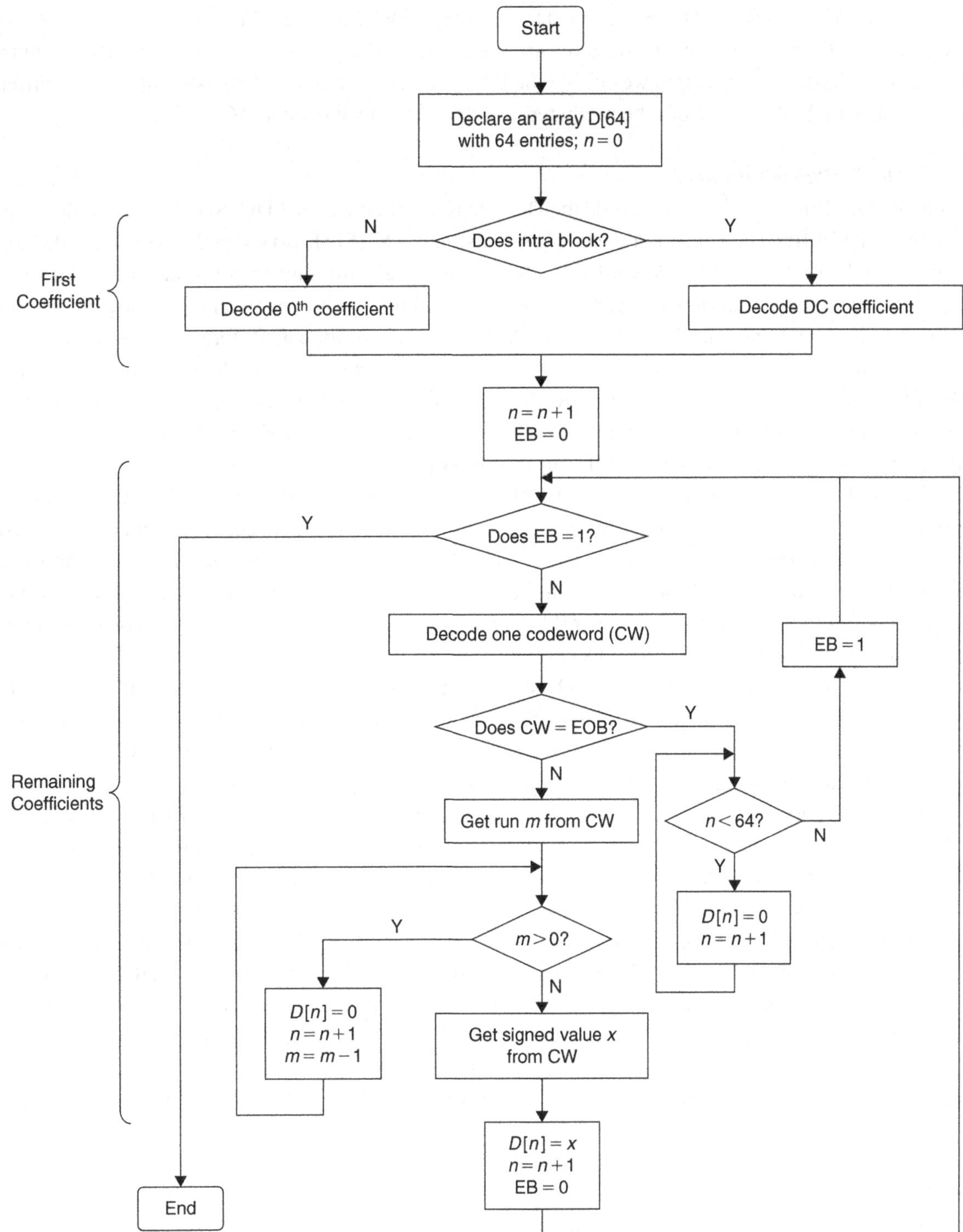

Figure 5.6: Flow diagram for decoding coefficients of MPEG-2 8×8 blocks with VLD.

all sizes. Apart from the escape codes (which are of 24-bit length and by analyzing the first 6 bits of a bit pattern we can tell whether it is an escape code or not), all other codes have maximum length of 17 bits including sign bit. If we take out the sign bit, then we have to analyze 16 bits. The advantage with these codes is that they are not random and they are systematically designed to uniquely represent all the possible positions and coefficient values of 8×8 blocks depending on their probability of occurrence.

Now we discuss a simple method for the decoding of one DC coefficient and one AC coefficient with an example. Let us assume that the current macroblock is intra, *intra_vlc_format* is zero and the received bitstream is 1101101001110000. At the time of encoding, in the case of the DC coefficient we encode both the DC difference and the number of bits (DC_SIZE) used to encode the DC difference. In the case of the AC coefficient we encode both run (to represent how many zeros are present from the previous non-zero coefficient) and value (with sign information). Therefore, first we decode the DC difference value (as we encode only the DC difference after subtracting actual DC value from the predicted value) and then we decode AC coefficients.

Decoding the DC Coefficient Codeword

In decoding the DC difference, first we decode the DC_SIZE and then we read DC_SIZE bits from the bitstream to get the signed DC difference value. For decoding the first part, DC_SIZE (to know the size of DC difference), if we scan through the luma DC codeword table for matching a minimum length codeword with the input bitstream, then we match the minimum length 110 codeword with input bitstream and this corresponds to value 4 (from the dct_dc_size_luminance look-up table) which is the size of the DC difference in terms of bits. Now we read next 4 bits (1101) from the bitstream as the DC difference value. As seen here, the decimal equivalent of the DC difference value is equal to 13. This DC difference of 13 is again manipulated to get the actual signed DC difference value before adding it to the prediction value to get the final DC coefficient. For decoding DC, we used a total of 7 bits so now we advance the bit position by 7 bits.

The remaining bit pattern after decoding DC is 001110000. In decoding the AC coefficient we decode both the signed coefficient and the number of zeros present in between the previous coefficient and current decoding coefficient. As we assumed the current macroblock was intra and *intra_vlc_format* was zero, then we select the corresponding codeword table to scan for the matching bitstream. The minimum length codeword we match with the bitstream from the codeword table is 001110 and that corresponds to a signed value of 1 and a run (the number of zeros between current and previous coefficients) of 3.

Next, we discuss the methodology to decode DC coefficients using small look-up tables. For this, we consider the design of a look-up table for decoding the DC_SIZE that is used to get a DC difference value. According to the MPEG-2 standard, to decode the DC_SIZE, we have to analyze a maximum of 9 bits. For this, if we use a look-up table, such a look-up table shall contain two parameters, DC_SIZE and number of bits in a codeword (NUM_BITS) to advance the bit position. We use 2 bytes to represent these two parameters in look-up table design. If we want to decode using a single look-up table without any extra logic, then we need 1024 ($2*2^9$) bytes. This problem can also be solved by a different approach which uses a look-up table (**VldTbA**[ ], provided at the simulation results) that contains only 96 bytes, but requires a few operations to fully decode DC_SIZE. With this 96-byte look-up table, the parameters DC_SIZE and NUM_BITS are decoded as follows. First, we analyze 4 bits from the bitstream and if the decimal equivalent of 4 bits is less than 15, then we are sure (from the MPEG-2 codeword table, dct_dc_size_luminance) that the DC_SIZE can be obtained with a look-up table of 32 ($2*2^4$) bytes. If the decimal equivalent is greater than or equal to 15, then we analyze 9 bits of bitstream to decode DC_SIZE. As seen in the codeword table, we know 4 MSB bits of codeword are all equal to 1, and if we mask these 4 bits then the effective address space is 5 bits. Therefore, the look-up table size for analyzing 9 bits is 64 bytes ($2*2^5$).

Decoding the AC Coefficient Codeword

Similarly, we analyze the procedure for decoding AC coefficients in the MPEG2 VLD. We choose one codeword table out of two AC coefficient codeword tables depending on *macroblock_type* and *intra_vlc_format* to decode the AC coefficient. We always extract a 16-bit string (excluding escape bits and sign bit) from the bitstream to decode any coefficient. For most of the VLD codewords of the same length, the length of prefix zeros is also constant. We first obtain the prefix zeros present in these 16 bits. For each prefix length, we choose a corresponding look-up table containing run and value. Given the length of prefix zeros, we remove the prefix zeros from the 16-bit string and we use the remaining bits (or nonprefix bits) value as an offset to the look-up table. If the length of nonprefix bits are different for a given prefix length, then we take care of this in the look-up table design and the bit position is updated according to the value of NUM_BITS. Thus, all the look-up tables designed to decode AC coefficients contain NUM_BITS information along with run and value for each codeword. All 10 look-up tables from **VldTb0**[ ] to **VldTb9**[ ] to decode AC coefficients are provided in the following section in the simulation results.

Next, we discuss the methodology to decode the AC coefficient using small look-up tables. We assume an AC coefficient whose codeword contains six prefix zero bits. As said, we first extract 16-bit strings from the bitstream. We check that the 16-bit string value is greater than or equal to 512 or not, to know whether the number of prefix zeros present in the 16-bit string is equal to 6 or more than 6. Once we know that the number of prefix zeros is 6, then we know from the MPEG-2 AC-coefficient VLD tables that we have only 8 codewords with 6 prefix zeros. We get the corresponding values (value, run, NUM_BITS) as decoded output with appropriate offset derived from the 16-bit data as [(offset>>6)-8]. Here the offset is shifted right by 6 bits to discard the 6 LSBs as the length of codeword with 6 prefix zeros is only 10 bits excluding sign bit. Out of 10 bits, 6 are prefix zeros. In addition, the 4th bit from the right is 1 in all codewords with 6 prefix zeros and we subtract 8 from 1xxx to clear this bit. Then only a 3-bit string remains in the offset, which represents eight unique entries in the look-up table **VldTb4**[ ].

5.2.2 MPEG-2 VLD Simulation

As seen in the previous discussion, it is clear that the bitstream is accessed from the bitstream buffer for decoding each coefficient. We call this a *bit FIFO* operation. We have two types of bit FIFO accesses for the bitstream buffer. In one case, we only extract certain number of bits from the buffer without updating the bit position immediately. For example, we extract 16 bits at the beginning of decoding any AC coefficient, but we are not sure whether we are going to use all 16 bits. We come to know how many bits were used to decode a coefficient only after obtaining NUM_BITS from the look-up table. Then we update the bit position with NUM_BITS. In another case, we know in advance how many bits we want to use to decode the value (as in decoding DC difference value using DC_SIZE bits). In this case, we update the bit position (and word pointer if the pointer update condition is satisfied) in the bit FIFO function itself. We use two different functions **Read_Bits**( ) and **Next_Bits**( ) to access the bit FIFO with and without bit position update. The simulation code for **Next_Bits**( ) and **Read_Bits**( ) is given in Pcodes 5.1 and 5.2. To extract K bits from the buffer, we read a continuous 32-bit string from the buffer and extract K bits from this string. In function **Read_Bits**( ), we decrement the bit position with the number of bits read from the buffer. Then we check whether the bit position is below zero and if it is, we increment the word (32 bits width) pointer by 1 and add 32 to the bit position. With the **Next_Bits**( ) function, we update the bit position outside the function after obtaining the NUM_BITS from the codeword read using fixed-length bits.

```
int Next_Bits(Mpeg2Vld *pVld, int n)
{
        unsigned int x, y, z;
        if (pVld->bit_pos >= n){
                x = Dat[pVld->word_offset];
                z = x << (32 - pVld->bit_pos);
                z = z >> (32 - n);
        }
        else {
                x = Dat[pVld->word_offset];
                z = x << (32 - pVld->bit_pos);
                z = z >> (32 - n); y = Dat[pVld->word_offset + 1];
                y = y >> (32 - n + pVld->bit_pos);
                z = z | y;
        }
        return z;
}
```

Pcode 5.1: Simulation code for Next_Bits( ).

DC Coefficient Decoding Simulation

The DC coefficients are present only in the intra frame (I-frame) macroblocks. Both luma and chroma component macroblocks contain the DC coefficients. Each 8×8 subblock of a macroblock contains one DC coefficient. A total of six 8×8 subblocks (four luma and two for two chroma components) are present in one macroblock, and hence we will have six DC coefficients per macroblock. However, luma and chroma subblocks use different VLD

```
int Read_Bits(Mpeg2Vld *pVld, int n)
{
        unsigned int x, y, z;
        if (pVld->bit_pos >= n) {
                x = Dat[pVld->word_offset];
                z = x << (32 - pVld->bit_pos);
                z = z >> (32 - n);
        }
        else {
                x = Dat[pVld->word_offset];
                z = x << (32 - pVld->bit_pos);
                z = z>> (32 - n);
                y = Dat[pVld->word_offset + 1];
                y = y >> (32 - n + pVld->bit_pos);
                z = z | y;
        }
        pVld->bit_pos = pVld->bit_pos - n;
        if (pVld->bit_pos <= 0) {
                pVld->bit_pos+= 32;
                pVld->word_offset++;
        }
        return z;
}
```

Pcode 5.2: Simulation code for Read_Bits( ).

codeword tables for decoding the DC coefficient. The simulation code for decoding one luma DC coefficient is given in Pcode 5.3. In this, first we extract 4-bit strings from the bitstream using the **Next_Bits**( ) function (as we discussed earlier we don't update the bit position within the **Next_Bits**( ) function), then check whether these 4 bits are sufficient for the current DC coefficient size, if they are, then we decode DC_SIZE, otherwise we read 9 bits to decode the DC_SIZE. In any case, we update the bit position after obtaining the NUM_BITS along with the DC_SIZE value as shown in Pcode 5.3. Once we know the DC_SIZE, then we extract the DC_SIZE bit value as DC_DIFFERENCE from the bitstream buffer using the **Read_Bits**( ) function. (Note: The **Read_Bits**( ) function updates bit position by itself and we do not update the bit position outside the function after reading the bits.) The actual DC coefficient is obtained after adding the prediction value to the signed DC_DIFFERENCE, which is computed from DC_SIZE and DC_DIFFERENCE.

```
if (pVld->intra_mb == 1) {                              // decode 1st coefficient
        offset = Next_Bits(pVld, 4);
        if (offset < 15)
                cw = VldTbA[offset];                    // DC_SIZE codeword
        else  {
                offset = Next_Bits(pVld, 9);
                offset = offset - 0x1e0;
                cw = VldTbA[16 + offset];               // DC_SIZE codeword
        }
        len = cw & 0xff;  // NUM_BITS
        pVld->bit_pos = pVld->bit_pos - len;
        if (pVld->bit_pos <= 0) {
                pVld->bit_pos+= 32; pVld->word_offset++;
        }
        size = cw >> 8;                                 // DC_SIZE
        if (size==0)
                diff = 0;
        else {
                diff = Read_Bits(pVld, size);    // DC_DIFFERENCE
                if ((diff & (1<<(size-1)))==0)
                        diff-= (1<<size) - 1; // signed DC_DIFFERENCE
        }
        *DcPred = *DcPred + diff;
        Sym[0] = *DcPred;
}
```

Pcode 5.3: Simulation code for decoding luma DC coefficient.

```
for (i = 1; ; i++) {
        offset = Next_Bits(pVld, 16);
        if (offset >= 512) {
                if (pVld->vlc_format == 1) {
                        if (offset >= 1024) cw = VldTb0[(offset>>8)-4];
                        else      cw = VldTb1[(offset>>6)-8];
                }
                else {
                        if (offset >= 16384) cw = VldTb2[(offset>>12)-4];
                        else if (offset >= 1024) cw = VldTb3[(offset>>8)-4];
                        else      cw = VldTb4[(offset>>6)-8];
                }
        }
        else if (offset>=256) cw = VldTb5[(offset>>4)-16];
        else if (offset>=128) cw = VldTb6[(offset>>3)-16];
        else if (offset>=64) cw = VldTb7[(offset>>2)-16];
        else if (offset>=32) cw = VldTb8[(offset>>1)-16];
        else (offset>=16) cw = VldTb9[offset-16];
        // continue with Pcode 5.6

}
```

Pcode 5.4: Simulation code for decoding intra macroblock VLD codewords.

```
for (i = 0; ; i++) {
        offset = Next_Bits(pVld, 16);
        if (offset>=16384) {
                if (i==0) cw = VldTbB[(offset>>12)-4];
                else      cw = VldTb2[(offset>>12)-4];
        }
        else if (offset >= 1024) cw = VldTb3[(offset>>8)-4];
        else if (offset >= 512) cw = VldTb4[(offset>>6)-8];
        else if (offset>=256) cw = VldTb5[(offset>>4)-16];
        else if (offset>=128) cw = VldTb6[(offset>>3)-16];
        else if (offset>=64) cw = VldTb7[(offset>>2)-16];
        else if (offset>=32) cw = VldTb8[(offset>>1)-16];
        else (offset>=16) cw = VldTb9[offset-16];
        // continue with Pcode 5.6
}
```

Pcode 5.5: Simulation code for decoding inter macroblock VLD codewords.

AC Coefficients Decoding Simulation

Depending on the *macroblock_type* and *intra_vlc_format* flag value, we choose one VLD codeword table for decoding AC coefficients. The simulation of decoding residual AC coefficients is divided into two parts. In the first part, we obtain the VLD codeword and in the second part we compute the run, value and NUM_BITS from the codeword. The first part of obtaining the codeword is a little bit different for luma and chroma components, as shown in Pcodes 5.4 and 5.5. But the basic idea of removal of the prefix zeros is the same in both cases. In both cases, we extract 16 bits from the bitstream buffer using the **Next_Bits**( ) function. We obtain the offset for the look-up table using the extracted 16 bits after removing the prefix zeros from the codeword. The entry containing run, value and NUM_BITS is accessed from the designed look-up tables using the offset. We extract the "run," "value," and NUM_BITS from the look-up output, and update the bit position using NUM_BITS. We inspect the "run" information for EOB, ESC or regular coefficients and accordingly we proceed. If the "run" information contains the information for the regular coefficient, then we will fill first the "run" number of zeros in the coefficient buffer followed by a signed coefficient. We compute the sign by accessing 1 bit from the bitstream buffer.

MPEG-2 VLD Simulation Results

Using the VLD codeword tables given in the MPEG-2 standard to decode the residual DCT coefficients, we design the look-up tables for decoding the coefficients. Here, we only design the look-up tables for decoding the coefficients of the luma component. The look-up table **VldTbA**[ ] is used to decode the DC coefficient of intra

```
len = cw>>16;
pVld->bit_pos = pVld->bit_pos - len;
if (pVld->bit_pos < 0) {
        pVld->bit_pos+= 32; pVld->word_offset++;
}
run = cw & 0xff;
if (run==64) {  // EOB
        while (i < 64) {
                Sym[i] = 0; i++;
        }
        return;
}
if (run==65) {  // escape
        run = Read_Bits(pVld, 6);
        val = Read_Bits(pVld, 12);
        if((sign = (val>=2048))) val = 4096 - val;
}
else {
        val = (cw & 0xff00)>>8; sign = Read_Bits(pVld, 1);
}
if (sign) val = -val;
while (run > 0) {
        Sym[i] = 0; i++; run = run - 1;
}
Sym[i] = val;
```

Pcode 5.6: Simulation code for decoding and storing the coefficients from codeword obtained using either Pcode 5.4 or Pcode 5.5.

subblocks whereas the look-up table **VldTbB**[ ] is used to decode the 0th coefficient of inter subblocks. Look-up tables **VldTb0**[ ] through **VldTb9**[ ] are used to decode the remaining 63 coefficients of the 8×8 subblock of either intra or inter macroblocks. All these look-up tables are derived from the MPEG-2 VLD codeword tables and all can be found on this book's companion website.

Simulation Results

We provide the simulation results for decoding the residual coefficients of one intra-luma macroblock assuming *intra_vlc_format* flag is 1. We use the following MPEG-2 encoded bitstream for four 8×8 subblocks of the luma intra macroblock.

```
Dat[6] = {0xace43d68, 0x58d2968f, 0x79626883, 0xd16a0360, 0x54205adb, 0x50000000};
```

We initialize the bitstream buffer parameters word offset with 0 and bit position with 31. After decoding each 8×8 subblock, the updated word offset, bit position, and decoded residual coefficients of 8×8 subblocks follow.

```
Decoded output of first luma block:
  pVld->word_offset = 0
  pVld->bit_pos = 9

  Sym[64] = 124, 0, 0, 0, 1, 2, 0, -1, 0, 0, 0, 0, 0, 0, 0, 0,
              0,  0, 0, 0, 0, 0, 0, 0, 0, 0, 0, 0, 0, 0, 0, 0,
              0,  0, 0, 0, 0, 0, 0, 0, 0, 0, 0, 0, 0, 0, 0, 0,
              0,  0, 0, 0, 0, 0, 0, 0, 0, 0, 0, 0, 0, 0, 0, 0;

Decoded output of second luma block:
  pVld->word_offset = 2
  pVld->bit_pos = 31

  Sym[64] = 129, 0, 0, 0, 0, 0, 0, 0, 0, 0, -1, 0, -2, 3, 0, 0,
            -1, 2, -1, 0, 0, 0, 0, 0, 0, 0, 0, 0, 0, 0, 0, 0,
             0, 0, 0, 0, 0, 0, 0, 0, 0, 0, 0, 0, 0, 0, 0, 0,
             0, 0, 0, 0, 0, 0, 0, 0, 0, 0, 0, 0, 0, 0, 0, 0;

Decoded output of third luma block:
  pVld->word_offset = 3
  pVld->bit_pos = 23
```

```
  Sym[64] = 151, -5, 0, 0, 0, 0, 0, 0, 0, 1, 0, 0, 0, -1, 2, 0,
            0, 0, 0, 0, 0, 0, 0, 0, 0, 0, 0, 0, 0, 0, 0, 0,
            0, 0, 0, 0, 0, 0, 0, 0, 0, 0, 0, 0, 0, 0, 0, 0,
            0, 0, 0, 0, 0, 0, 0, 0, 0, 0, 0, 0, 0, 0, 0, 0;

Decoded output of fourth luma block:
  pVld->word_offset = 5
  pVld->bit_pos = 29

  Sym[64] = 146,  0, 0, 0, 0, 0, 0, 0, 0, 0, 0, 0, 0, 0, 0, 0,
            -1, -7, 0, 0, 2, 0, 0, 0, 0, 0, 0, -1, 0, 0, -1, 0,
             1,  1, 0, 0, 0, 0, 0, 0, 0, 0, 0, 0, 0, 0, 0, 0,
            0,  0, 0, 0, 0, 0, 0, 0, 0, 0, 0, 0, 0, 0, 0, 0;
```

Computational Complexity of MPEG-2 VLD

The decoding of residual coefficients using the MPEG-2 VLD codeword tables is costly in terms of cycles. In decoding one coefficient, we read the bitstream two or three times, access different look-up tables, and also the decoding flow contains many conditional jumps. As the DC coefficient is present in intra macroblocks and there is only one coefficient, we are not going to discuss the complexity and optimization techniques for the DC coefficient. The number of AC coefficients present in a macroblock depends on the frame type and bit rate. As we saw in the simulation results, we may find five to six AC coefficients on average in medium bit rate applications. To decode residual AC coefficients, we use the simulation codes in Pcodes 5.4 and 5.6 or Pcodes 5.5 and 5.6.

Now, we analyze the maximum number of cycles consumed by the AC coefficients decoding loop. This loop decodes up to 63 AC coefficients in intra macroblocks and up to 64 coefficients in inter macroblocks. We decode two parameters—signed value and run—for each AC coefficient. As we discussed, the VLD simulation uses look-up tables with a few ALU operations. Decoding of one AC coefficient using the VLD involves the following four steps:

1. Access 16-bit string of bitstream using **Next_Bits**( ) function (10 cycles)
2. Access appropriate look-up table to get "run" and "value" (4 cycles)
3. Update the bit position and word offset (4 cycles)
4. Decode sign bit using **Read_Bits**( ) function (13 cycles)

If we look at the "for" loop code given in Pcode 5.4 or Pcode 5.5 to decode AC coefficients, it consists of many conditional jumps. If we assume that one conditional jump takes about 9 cycles on the reference embedded processor (see Appendix A, Section A.4, on this book's companion website for more details of cycle estimation on the reference embedded processor), then depending on the input data bits pattern we may take about 40 to 80 cycles to decode one AC coefficient. We also spend a variable number of cycles filling zeros into the coefficient array **Sym**[ ] when decoded "run" is not zero.

In decoding residual AC coefficient information as we discussed in Section 5.2.1, we can have prefix zeros up to 10 bits in a codeword and for that reason we scan for the number of prefix zeros by conditionally jumping after checking for a particular prefix length. Once we start decoding the VLD_SYMBOLS for an AC coefficient (i.e., run and value) by analyzing the 16 bits of bit pattern, we have to know how many bits (NUM_BITS) are actually used in decoding the VLD_SYMBOLS to advance the bit position. This information (NUM_BITS) also has to be coded for each codeword in the look-up table. With this, for each AC coefficient, our look-up table contains three entities (1) Run, (2) Value, and (3) NUM_BITS. If we represent each entity with 1 byte, then we need 3 bytes for each codeword of VLD tables. As we use 1-byte, 2-byte, or 4-byte words for easy memory access, we need 4 bytes for each codeword. If there are "n" remaining bits after removing the prefix zero bits and excluding the sign bit, then for covering all codewords with that particular number of prefix zeros, we need a look-up table size of $4*2^n$ bytes.

Once we know the look-up table output, we come to know the value of NUM_BITS and we advance the bit position by NUM_BITS. We check the "run" information to find out whether this particular bit pattern represents an escape code (ESC) or end of block (EOB) as "run" information contains abnormal values for these two cases. If the current bit pattern represents the escape code, we jump to decode escape information (run and signed value). If the bit pattern represents EOB, then we fill the remaining coefficient values with zeros and exit the loop. Otherwise, the coefficient array pointer incremented by "run" with filling zeros. Then the sign information (the coefficient value is negative if the next bit of bitstream is 1; otherwise, the coefficient value is positive if the next bit of bitstream is zero) is decoded from the bitstream using **Read_Bits**( ). The bit position is advanced by 1 bit with the **Read_Bits**( ) function. The decoded signed value is stored in the coefficient array pointed to by the array pointer, and the array pointer is increased by 1 to store the next coefficient value.

5.2.3 MPEG-2 VLD Optimization Techniques

As we discussed in the previous section, decoding an AC coefficient with the MPEG-2 VLD is a costly process in terms of cycles. If we have 10 AC coefficients in a particular 8×8 subblock then we may need on average 600 cycles to decode all the subblock coefficients. In this section we will discuss an efficient procedure (see Stein and Malepati, 2008) to decode AC coefficients and this approach reduces the cycles cost by approximately 80%, but this reduction in cycles is achieved at the cost of more memory. This efficient technique is considered after observing the statistics of MPEG-2 VLD test vectors. The following are the statistics of the MPEG-2 VLD for two test vectors.

1. About 90% of VLD symbols are coded with less than or equal to 10 bits.
2. The percentage of bits on average used for each VLD symbol is shown in Figure 5.7.
3. About 25 to 45% of the time any two successive VLD symbols are represented with less than or equal to 10 bits.
4. About 2 to 5% of the time any three successive VLD symbols are represented with less than or equal to 10 bits.

As seen in the previous statistics, 90% of the time we decode coefficients with less than or equal to 10 bits including sign information. Interestingly, out of 90%, 30% of coefficients use only 3 bits, 30 to 40% of the time two consecutive coefficients consume less than 10 bits, and 5% of the time three consecutive coefficients consume about 10 bits. This analysis prompts us to think about designing look-up tables for decoding multiple coefficients with only one access of the bitstream buffer and look-up table. If we consider the 10-bit offset, then we need a look-up table with 1024 ($=2^{10}$) entities. For each AC coefficient, we need three elements information (NUM_BITS, value, and run). We do not compute sign information separately for each coefficient; instead we embedded the sign information into "value" at the time of designing the look-up table. In this simulation, we pack up to three AC coefficients information in one look-up table entity as shown in Figure 5.8. In each entity of 32 bits or 4 bytes width, we will have the information about the number of coefficients packed, multiple coefficients run and signed value information and the total number of bits (NUM_BITS) consumed by all the coefficients packed in that entity. The look-up table size becomes 4096 ($= 4*2^{10}$) bytes for one AC-coefficient codeword table. In the MPEG-2 VLD, depending on *intra_vlc_format* value, we have two codeword tables to decode residual AC coefficients. Thus, we need a total of 8 kB of data memory for two look-up tables. In this implementation, all the codewords with more than 10 bits are treated as escape codes. In the case of escape codes, our look-up entry contains the pointer for the next small look-up table to decode the VLD symbol which

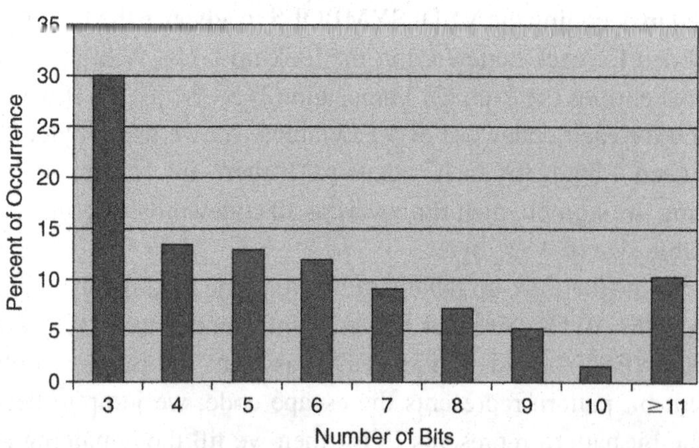

Figure 5.7: Histogram of MPEG-2 VLD symbol length versus percentage of their occurrence.

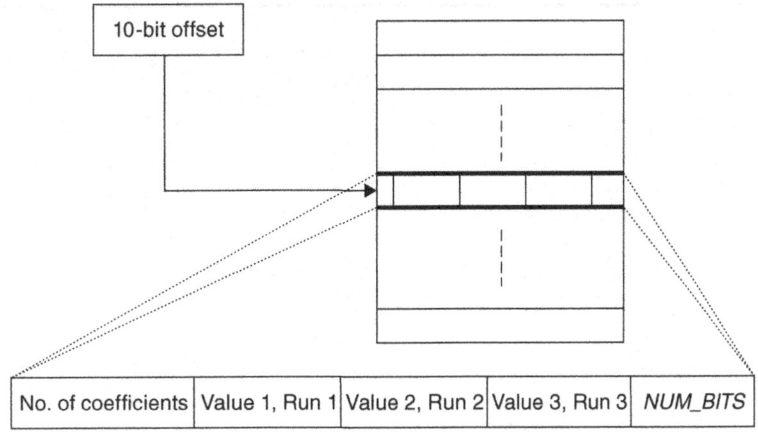

Figure 5.8: Look-up table design for efficient implementation of MPEG-2 VLD.

consumes less than or equal to 17 bits including sign bit. If the VLD symbol consumes more than 17 bits, then a separate code performs the decoding of that particular VLD symbol.

Although we decided on an offset length of 10 bits, we can also simultaneously access the data-register-width number of bits (usually 32) from the bitstream to the data register to reduce the number of bitstream buffer accesses and thus decode multiple coefficients with a single access. With this method of implementation, the following bit offset analysis and coefficient decoding are possible.

```
(10 bit, 10 bit, 10 bit) -> 3 to 9 coefficients (occur with high probability)
(10 bit, 10 bit, ESC) -> 2 to 6 coefficients (occur with high probability)
(10 bit, 17 bit, or ESC) -> 2 to 4 coefficients (occur with medium probability)
(17 bit or ESC, 10 bit) -> 1 to 4 coefficients (occur with medium probability)
(ESC)                   -> 1 coefficient (occur with low probability)
```

Based on the previous analysis, we can decode up to nine symbols with one bitstream access. The number of bitstream accesses, look-up table accesses, and the conditional jumps per 8×8 subblock AC coefficients decoding will be greatly reduced in this approach. The simulation code for the implementation of this efficient decoding is given in Pcodes 5.7 through 5.10. To reduce the cycles further, instead of filling the AC coefficient array with zeros conditionally for every coefficient and at the end of the block in "while" loops, we fill all 64 coefficients initially unconditionally with zeros and fill only the coefficient values at appropriate positions in the decoding loop by incrementing the coefficient array pointer using "run" information.

Computational Complexity with Efficient Implementation of VLD

With the efficient implementation, we access the bitstream buffer once for multiple symbols. In addition, as we extract 32 bits at a time from the bitstream buffer, it is simple and consumes fewer cycles (around 5, when compared to the less-than-32 bits case, which takes around 10 cycles as discussed). Updating the bit position twice for each coefficient is not required. Instead, the bit position is updated once for all symbols present in the 10-bit length pattern. With this efficient implementation, jumps occur only in cases of EOB (once for 8×8 block) and ESC (occurs rarely). On the reference embedded processor, an average of less than 100 cycles are used to decode 10 coefficients using this implementation, compared to 600 cycles using the standard implementation provided in Pcodes 5.4 through 5.6. On the flip side, we require about 8 kB of additional data memory to use this implementation.

Look-up Tables for Efficient Implementation of VLD

The simulation code given in Pcodes 5.7 through 5.10 can be used to decode the residual coefficients of 8×8 subblocks of both intra macroblocks as well as inter macroblocks with appropriate look-up table selection based on *intra_vlc_format* and *macroblock_type*. The look-up tables used with the efficient implementation of the MPEG-2 VLD can be found on the companion website.

The average number of coefficients present in a subblock will vary and it depends on the bit rate for the given frame resolution and frame rate. For example, the average number of coefficients present in a subblock will

```
for(i = 1; ; i++) {
        cw = Next_Bits(pVld, 32);                  // extract 32 bits from bitstream
        code = cw >> 22;                           // obtain 10 bit offset
        bitstr = Tb[code];                         // get one look-up table entity
        count = bitstr >> 30;
        if (count != 0) {
               val_inc = 5;
               if (count == 3) val_inc = 4;
               temp = 2;
               for(j = 0;j < count;j++) {
                        run = ((bitstr << temp))>>28);
                        temp+= 4;
                        value = ((int)(bitstr << temp) >> (32-val_inc));
                        temp+= val_inc;
                        i+= run;
                        Sym[i] = value;
                        i++;
               }
               i--;
               val = (bitstr << temp) >> 28;
               pVld->bit_pos = pVld->bit_pos - val;
               if (value == 0)
                        break;
               cw = cw << val;
               code = cw >> 22;                    // obtain second 10-bits offset
               bitstr = Tb[code];
               count = bitstr >> 30;
               // continue with Pcode 5.8
```

Pcode 5.7: Simulation code for efficient implementation of MPEG-2 VLD.

be less for the 6-Mbps bit rate than for the 10-Mbps bit rate for bitstreams with the same full D1 (720×480) resolution at 30 fps (frames per second).

5.3 H.264 VLC-Based Entropy Coding

In Section 5.2, we discussed the VLCs used with the MPEG-2 standard. The MPEG-2 uses static VLC tables to code different types of video parameters and data. The VLC scheme used for MPEG-2 entropy coding is non-adaptive since we do not use any context information in coding the symbols (except the *intra_vlc_format* flag to choose between two codeword tables). In this section, we will discuss more advanced VLC coding schemes that are used in the H.264 standard. The H.264 standard uses two types of VLC schemes to compress the bitstream: (1) universal VLCs (UVLCs), and (2) CAVLCs. We use VLC schemes in H.264 when the *entropy_coding_mode* flag is set to zero. The UVLC scheme is used to code different parameters (e.g., slice layer and macroblock layer headers, motion vectors, and coded block pattern), and the CAVLC scheme is used to code the residual coefficients. The following subsections present an overview of the UVLC and CAVLC schemes and their simulation techniques.

5.3.1 Overview of the H.264 VLC Schemes

With the H.264 coder (for more details, see Section 14.4), we code the following types of data elements: (1) sequence parameters, (2) picture parameters, (3) slice layer parameters, (4) macroblock layer parameters, and (5) residual coefficients. All data elements except residual coefficients are coded using either fixed-length codes or exponential Golomb codes. These VLC schemes are also known as UVLCs. The residual coefficients are coded using CAVLCs.

Fixed-Length Codes

We code the equiprobable data elements using a fixed-length code (FLC) of *n* bits since the coding of equiprobable elements does not offer any data compression. With FLC, we don't analyze the *n* bits length bit pattern and in

```
// continuation from Pcode 5.7
if (count != 0) {
        val_inc = 5;
        if (count == 3) val_inc = 4;
        temp = 2;
        for(j=0;j<count;j++) {
                run = ((bitstr << temp)>>28);
                temp+= 4;
                value = ((int)(bitstr << temp) >> (32-val_inc));
                temp+= val_inc;
                i+= run;
                Sym[i] = value;
                i++;
        }
        i--;
        val = (bitstr << temp) >> 28;
        pVld->bit_pos = pVld->bit_pos - val;
        if (value == 0)
                break;
        cw = cw << val;
        code = cw >> 22;          // obtain third 10 bits
        bitstr = Tb[code];
        count = bitstr >> 30;
        if (count != 0) {
                val_inc = 5;
                if (count == 3) val_inc = 4;
                temp = 2;
                for(j=0;j<count;j++) {
                        run = ((bitstr << temp)>>28);
                        temp+= 4;
                        value = ((int)(bitstr << temp) >> (32-val_inc));
                        temp+= val_inc;
                        i+= run;
                        Sym[i] = value;
                        i++;
                }
                i--;
                val = (bitstr << temp) >> 28;
                pVld->bit_pos = pVld->bit_pos - val;
                if (value == 0)
                        break;
        }
}
// continue with Pcode 5.9
```

Pcode 5.8: Simulation code for efficient implementation of MPEG-2 VLD.

most cases we directly obtain the coded information from the bitstream n bits and in some cases we use a look-up table that is accessed using the n bits as an offset. In other words, we read a fixed number of bits (here the bits are unsigned and we denote the bits reading function as u(n)) from bit FIFO and the *Code_Num* (or data parameter information) is given by either n bits block or output of the look-up table which is accessed using n bits block as an offset.

Exponential Golomb Codes

In the H.264 standard, the exponential Golomb codes (or exp-Golomb codes) are used to code a variety of data parameters. With exp-Golomb codes, a single infinite length codeword table is used to code different kinds of parameters. Instead of designing a different VLC table for each data parameter, the mapping to the codeword table is adapted according to the data statistics for coding a particular data parameter. The codewords of such a code progress in the logical order. One such codeword table with general form [m-zeros|1|m bits] is given in Table 5.2. Here, the length of the codeword is $2m+1$.

We construct each exp-Golomb codeword at the encoder with the formula $m = \lfloor \log_2(Code\_Num+1) \rfloor$. We frame m-zero bits with suffix bit "1" as [m-zeros|1]. Then, we obtain the m bits information from another formula m bits $= Code\_Num + 1 - 2^m$. With this, the final codeword is obtained as [m-zeros|1|m bits]. This exp-Golomb

```
            // continuation from Pcode 5.8
            else {
                    if (bitstr == 0)
                              continue;
                    else {
                              cw = cw << 10;
                              pVld->bit_pos = pVld->bit_pos - 10;
                              temp = bitstr >> 16;
                              code = cw >> (32-temp);
                              offset = bitstr & 0xffff;
                              offset = offset + (code<<1);
                              bitstr = Tba[offset];
                              offset = bitstr >> 8;
                              value = (int) (bitstr << 24) >> 24;
                              run = offset & 0x1f;
                              code = offset >> 5;
                              cw = cw << code;
                              pVld->bit_pos = pVld->bit_pos - code;
                              i+= run;
                              Sym[i] = value;
                    }
            }
  }
  else
  {
            if (bitstr == 0) {
                      cw = cw << 6;
                      run = cw >> 26;
                      i+= run;
                      cw = cw << 6;
                      value = cw >> 20;
                      pVld->bit_pos = pVld->bit_pos - 24;
                      if((sign = (value>=2048)))
                      value = 4096 - value;
                      if (sign) value = - value;
                      Sym[i] = value;
            }
            // continue with Pcode 5.10
```

Pcode 5.9: Simulation code for efficient implementation of MPEG-2 VLD.

code has the regular decoding properties. To decode the given codeword, first we compute the prefix zeros count (i.e., m), once we know the value of m, then we consider the following $m+1$ bits after prefix zeros and compute the *Code_Num* as [1|*m* bits]-1. For example, given the bitstream 000101000101, the prefix zeros present are 3. The 4 (i.e., $3+1$) bits following the prefix zero bits are [1010] and the $Code\_Num = [1010] - 1 = 9$.

The data parameter "v" is mapped to *Code_Num* before encoding and we name the exp-Golomb code accordingly. The four exp-Golomb codes used in the H.264 standard are (1) ue(v), unsigned exp-Golomb code, (2) se(v), signed exp-Golomb code (3) me(v), mapped exp-Golomb code, and (4) te(v), truncated exp-Golomb code. The parameter v is mapped to *Code_Num* for the previous schemes as follows.

$$\text{ue}(v)\text{: } Code\_Num = v \tag{5.1}$$

$$\text{se}(v)\text{: } Code\_Num = \begin{cases} 0 & \text{if } v = 0 \\ 2|v| & \text{if } v < 0 \\ 2v - 1 & \text{if } v > 0 \end{cases} \tag{5.2}$$

$$\text{me}(v)\text{: } Code\_Num = \text{LUT}[v] \tag{5.3}$$

where LUT is a predefined mapping look-up table.

$$\text{te}(v)\text{: } Code\_Num = \begin{cases} ue(v) & \text{if } v > 1 \\ !u(1) & \text{if } v = 1 \end{cases} \tag{5.4}$$

```
            // continuation from Pcode 5.9
            else {
                    cw = cw << 10; pVld->bit_pos = pVld->bit_pos - 10;
                    temp = bitstr >> 16;
                    code = cw >> (32-temp); offset = bitstr & 0xffff;
                    offset = offset + code;
                    bitstr = Tba[offset];
                    offset = bitstr >> 8; value = (int) (bitstr << 24) >> 24;
                    run = offset & 0x1f; code = offset >> 5;
                    cw = cw << code;
                    pVld->bit_pos = pVld->bit_pos - code; i+= run;
                    Sym[i] = value; code = cw >> 22;
                    bitstr = Tb[code];
                    count = bitstr >> 30;
                    if (count != 0) {
                            val_inc = 5;
                            if (count == 3) val_inc = 4;
                            temp = 2;
                            for(j=0;j<count;j++) {
                                    run = ((bitstr << temp)>>28);
                                    temp+= 4;
                                    value = ((int)(bitstr << temp) >> (32-val_inc));
                                    temp+= val_inc; i+= run;
                                    Sym[i] = value;
                                    i++;
                            }
                            i--;
                            val = (bitstr << temp) >> 28;
                            pVld->bit_pos = pVld->bit_pos - val;
                            if (value == 0)
                                    break;
                    }
                    else
                            continue;
            }
        }
        if (pVld->bit_pos <= 0) {
                pVld->bit_pos+= 32; pVld->word_offset++;
        }
}
if (pVld->bit_pos <= 0) {
        pVld->bit_pos+= 32; pVld->word_offset++;
}
```

Pcode 5.10: Simulation code for efficient implementation of MPEG-2 VLD.

Table 5.2: Exp-Golomb codeword table

Code_Num	Codeword
0	1
1	010
2	011
3	00100
4	00101
5	00110
6	00111
7	0001000
8	0001001
9	0001010
10	0001011
.....	....

Example 5.3

Consider the bitstream 01100101000111100110011010 0. We decode it with UVLC schemes u(n), ue(v), se(v), me(v), and te(v) using one scheme for one parameter. Let $n = 3$ for u(n), and the range of v is greater than 1 for te(v). Set the bit position to zero (*bit_pos* = 0) and the bits are read from the MSB side. We compute the data parameters as follows. In the case of se(v) decoding, if *Code_Num* is even then $v = -(Code\_Num)/2$, else $v = (Code\_Num + 1)/2$ and if $Code\_Num = 0$ then $v = 0$.

u(n): v = *Code_Num* = u(3) = 011 = 3.
Total bits used: 3
Updated *bit_pos*: 3
Remaining bitstream = 00101000111100110011 0100

ue(v): Prefix zeros m = 2
Next m+1 bits: 101
v = *Code_Num* = [101]−1 = 4
Total bits used: 5
Updated *bit_pos*: 8
Remaining bitstream = 000111100110011 0100

se(v): Prefix zeros m = 3
Next m+1 bits: 1111
Code_Num = [1111]−1 = 14
v = − *Code_Num*/2 = −7
Total bits used: 7
Updated *bit_pos*: 15
Remaining bitstream = 001100110100

me(v): Prefix zeros m = 2
Next m+1 bits: 110
Code_Num = [110]−1 = 5
v = LUT[*Code_Num*]
Total bits used: 5
Updated *bit_pos*: 20
Remaining bitstream = 0110100

te(v): Use ue(v) as v>1 is assumed
Prefix zeros m = 1
Next m+1 bits: 11
Code_Num = [11]−1 = 2
v = *Code_Num*
Total bits used: 3
Updated *bit_pos*: 23
Remaining bitstream: 0100

■

Context-Adaptive Variable Length Codes

In the H.264 standard, the CAVLC is used to code residual zigzag ordered 16 luma DC coefficients, 4 chroma DC coefficients, and 4×4 (luma or chroma) subblocks AC coefficients. With the CAVLC scheme, VLC tables for various syntax elements are changed depending on already coded syntax elements. Since the VLC tables are designed to match the corresponding statistics, the entropy coding performance is improved in comparison to schemes using a single VLC table such as in the MPEG-2 standard. The CAVLC tables are designed to take advantage of several characteristics of quantized residual data symbols. Typically, after transform, the magnitude of residual data symbols diminishes as we go from low frequency end to high frequency end. With quantization, most of the insignificant symbols are truncated to zero. At the medium bit rates, the residual data symbols contain many zeros after quantization. After the zigzag scan, the scanned array contains the DC and significant AC coefficients at the beginning of the array and most of the zeros fall after the significant symbols. An example of zigzag scanned and residual AC coefficients array $r[\,]$ for 4×4 subblock follows:

$$r = [7, -3, 0, 1, -1, 0, 0, 1, -1, 0, 0, 0, 0, 0, 0, 0] \tag{5.5}$$

As we discussed, the zigzag scanned and quantized residual symbol array contains a majority of zeros. In addition, the following cases are true with most of the quantized zigzag scanned, residual symbols array:

- The non-zero coefficients decay as we move from the start of the array toward its end.
- The majority of trailing non-zero coefficients are 1s.
- The number of non-zero coefficients of neighboring blocks are correlated.

Hence, the CAVLC is designed to compactly represent the residual data, which reflects the previous cases. A few important characteristics of the CAVLC follow:

1. Adapts the tables to code the total coefficients of the block depending on its neighbor blocks total coefficients
2. Uses *trailing 1s* to take care of non-zero trailing coefficients
3. Adapts various VLC tables to code non-zero coefficients from large coefficients to small coefficients
4. Adapts various VLC tables to code the total number of zeros present in-between all the coefficients
5. Adapts various VLC tables to code the number of zeros between two coefficients
6. Uses *run-level* coding to compactly represent the string of 0s

The H.264 CAVLC includes the following *decoding* steps:

- *Coeff_Token* (total coefficients and trailing 1s)
- Sign information for trailing 1s
- Signed-level information for remaining non-zero coefficients
- Total zeros present between all non-zero coefficients
- Run-before (the number of zeros present between two consecutive non-zero coefficients)

Coeff_Token

In the CAVLC, the combined coefficients and trailing 1s are treated as *Coeff_Token*. The coefficient total comprises the count of all non-zero coefficients present in a block. For example, in array $\boldsymbol{r}[\,]$, we have a total of six non-zero coefficients. In many cases, most of the trailing coefficients are 1s. However, we code up to three 1 coefficients as trailing 1s with the CAVLC. We treat only the last three 1 coefficients as trailing 1s even if we have more than three trailing 1s. For example, although we have four 1s in array $\boldsymbol{r}[\,]$, we treat the last three as trailing 1s and the remaining 1 as a normal coefficient. Thus, with respect to array $\boldsymbol{r}[\,]$, the total coefficients are six and the trailing 1s are three. There are many codeword tables specified in the H.264 standard to decode *Coeff_Token*. Depending on the context, we choose a particular look-up table to decode *Coeff_Token* from the bitstream. The context "nC" is determined based on the total coefficients present in corresponding up and left blocks. Using context "nC" we choose one codeword table and decode the *Coeff_Token* by searching for the bitstream bit pattern that matches with a minimum length codeword from the codeword table. We choose the corresponding *Coeff_Token* of the codeword (that matches with the bitstream) to get the total coefficients and trailing 1s.

Sign of Trailing 1s

Once we decode the *Coeff_Token*, we know whether there are any trailing 1s present in the block. If the trailing 1s are present, then we know their magnitudes are 1 and we need only their signs. Thus, we obtain the signs from the bitstream for all trailing 1s. If we read bit "1" from the bitstream, then the sign of the trailing 1 is minus, and if we read bit "0" then the sign of the trailing 1 is plus. We don't use any context information in decoding the signs for trailing 1s.

Levels

The signed levels of the remaining non-zero coefficients are decoded in reverse order starting with the highest frequency coefficient and working back toward the DC coefficient. There are seven VLC tables from VLC_0 to VLC_6 to choose from, based on context, depending on the previously decoded level's magnitude. The table VLC_0 is biased toward lower magnitudes, table VLC_1 is biased toward slightly higher magnitudes and so on, and finally table VLC_6 is biased toward larger magnitude levels. If the current decoded coefficient is greater than the predefined threshold, then we move VLC_m to VLC_n where $(m < n)$. An analytical method to decode the signed level (apart from trailing 1s) follows.

$SuffixLength = 0$

If total coefficients are greater than 10 and trailing 1s are less than three, then *SuffixLength* is set to 1.

1. Decode *LevelPrefix* (using bitstream and the *LevelPrefix* VLC table)
2. Determine the *LevelSuffixSize* (from *LevelPrefix* and *SuffixLength*)
3. Decode *LevelSuffix* with *LevelSuffixSize* bits (from the bitstream)
4. $LevelCode = (\min(15, LevelPrefix) << SuffixLength) + LevelSuffix$
5. Adjust *LevelCode* as follows:
   (a) If (LevelPrefix > 15) and (SuffixLength = 0), then LevelCode = LevelCode + 15
   (b) If (LevelPrefix > 16), then LevelCode = LevelCode + (1<<(LevelPrefix − 3)) − 4096
   (c) If trailing 1s are less than 3 and the first non-zero coefficient is decoding, then LevelCode = LevelCode + 2
6. Compute level from *LevelCode* as given:
   (a) Level = $(LevelCode + 2) >> 1$ if *LevelCode* is even
   (b) Level = $(-LevelCode - 1) >> 1$ if *LevelCode* is odd
7. Increment the *SuffixLength* if the current level magnitude is greater than the predefined threshold and repeat steps 1 to 7 for the remaining levels decoding

Total Zeros

The value *total_zeros* gives the total number of zeros present between the start of the zigzag scanned array and the last non-zero coefficient (which can be a trailing 1). For example, in array ***r***[ ], the value *total_zeros* is 3. Although we compute *run_before* (which gives the total number of zeros present between two consecutive non-zero coefficients) for placing each coefficient in the decoded array, there are two advantages in computing the *total_zeros*. The first advantage is that the decoding of *run_before* can be adapted with zeros-left information (which is obtained after subtracting the *run_before* of the previously decoded coefficient from *total_zeros*) and the second advantage is that there is no need to compute the *run_before* for the lowest frequency non-zero coefficient as zero left gives the indication of how many zeros are present from the start of the array to that coefficient position. The VLC table for decoding of *total_zeros* is adapted based on the total number of non-zero coefficients present in the block.

Run Before

The number of zeros preceding each non-zero coefficient is termed as *run_before* and is decoded in the reverse order (i.e., from the highest frequency non-zero coefficient toward the lowest frequency non-zero coefficient). For example, in array ***r***[ ], the *run_before* between −1 and 1 is 2, and the *run_before* between −3 and 1 is 1. We do not compute the *run_before* in the following two cases: (1) when the remaining *total_zeros* is zero (that indicates no zeros are present between the coefficients) and (2) when we reach the lowest frequency non-zero coefficient (for this zeros-left gives the count of preceding zeros). The VLC tables for decoding *run_before* are adapted using the zeros-left information (which is obtained after subtracting the *run_before* of previously computed coefficient from its zeros-left). At the start, we assign the *total_zeros* to zeros-left. Once we decode all the levels and run lengths (of zeros), then we store each level accordingly using run lengths.

Next, we will discuss the simulation details for decoding each step of the CAVLC. The H.264 standard specifies many codeword tables and functions to decode the residual coefficients as discussed previously. We consider the designing of look-up tables for a few codeword tables in the simulation and the rest of the look-up tables can be designed using similar approaches. The primary operation involved in decoding all of the steps is reading of bit pattern from the bitstream buffer. Assuming the VLC codes with codeword lengths more than 16 bits as escape codes (occurs very rarely), the bit FIFO is designed as follows.

We use a structure to hold the parameters and data to work with bit FIFO. The structure contains *current_word* (current word in a bit FIFO which is MSB aligned), *bit_pos* (current bit position), and *word_count* (pointer or index to bitstream buffer) as seen in the following:

```
struct {
unsigned int current_word;
int bit_pos;
int word_count;
} CAVLC_t;

CAVLC_t *pVLC;
```

At any time, to read n bits (less than or equal to 16) from the bit FIFO, we perform the following steps:

1. Extract n bits from the MSB side of the *current_word*.
2. Shift left the current word by n bits.
3. Increment the *bit_pos* by n bits.
4. If the bit FIFO contains less than 16 bits, read the next 16 bits from the buffer.

5.3.2 Simulation of the H.264 VLC Schemes

We use the 16-bit FIFO definition described previously in CAVLC simulations most of the time. For escape codes, we use the 32-bit FIFO discussed in Section 5.2. In this section, we design the look-up tables to efficiently simulate some of the CAVLC functions.

Decoding UVLC Codes

UVLC codes include both FLC and exp-Golomb codes. The FLC is a simple code that reads a fixed number of bits from bit FIFO. The simulation code for reading a fixed number of bits is given in Pcode 5.11. In computing signed or unsigned exp-Golomb codes, we first compute *Code_Num* value. Assuming the codes with more than 16 bits are escape codes, we compute *Code_Num* by scanning for lead zeros in a 16-length bit pattern. Say, if the lead zeros present in this case is m, we extract next $(m + 1)$ bits from the bitstream and its pattern looks like $[1|m$ bits$]$. The *Code_Num* is given by $[1|m$ bits$]-1$. Once we compute *Code_Num*, then the decoded unsigned and signed exp-Golomb code value "v" is obtained from Equations (5.1) and (5.2).

The simulation code for the decoding of unsigned and signed exp-Golomb codes is given in Pcodes 5.12 and 5.13.

```
w = (pVLC->current_word)>>(32-n);              // read n-bits from MSB side
pVLC->bit_pos = pVLC->bit_pos + n;             // increment bit position
pVLC->current_word = pVLC->current_word << n; // shift left bit FIFO by n-bits
if (pVLC->bit_pos > 16) {
        pVLC->bit_pos = pVLC->bit_pos - 16;
        a = bit_stream[pVLC->word_count++];
        a = a << pVLC->bit_pos;
        pVLC->current_word = pVLC->current_word | a;
}
return (w);
```

Pcode 5.11: Simulation code to read n-bits from bitstream buffer.

Decoding CAVLC Codes

As most CAVLC functions require context information, we first determine the context and choose the corresponding VLC table to decode the residual coefficients from the bitstream. We use the following functions in decoding residual coefficients.

Coeff_Token (Nonpredictable Bit-Pattern Lengths)

The *Coeff_Token* represents the total coefficients and trailing 1s present in the zigzag scanned array. We analyze a maximum of 16 bits in decoding the *Coeff_Token*. Depending on context "nC" and the bit pattern, we read n bits

```
w = pVLC->current_word >> 16; // consider 16-bits for scanning
k = 0;
while ((w & 0x8000) == 0) {
        w = w << 1; k++;          // obtain prefix zeros
};
pVLC->current_word = pVLC->current_word << k;
w = pVLC->current_word >> (32-k-1);
pVLC->bit_pos = pVLC->bit_pos + 2*k+1;
if (pVLC->bit_pos > 16){
        pVLC->bit_pos = pVLC->bit_pos - 16;
        a = bit_stream[pVLC->word_count++];
        a = a << pVLC->bit_pos;
        pVLC->current_word = pVLC->current_word | a;
}
return (w-1);
```

Pcode 5.12: Simulation code for unsigned exp-Golomb code ue(v).

```
w = pVLC->current_word >> 16; // consider 16-bits for scanning
k = 0;
while ((w & 0x8000) == 0) {
        w = w << 1; k++;          // obtain prefix zeros
};
pVLC->current_word = pVLC->current_word << k;
w = pVLC->current_word >> (32-k-1);
pVLC->bit_pos = pVLC->bit_pos + 2*k+1;
if (pVLC->bit_pos > 16){
        pVLC->bit_pos = pVLC->bit_pos - 16;
        a = bit_stream[pVLC->word_count++];
        a = a << pVLC->bit_pos;
        pVLC->current_word = pVLC->current_word | a;
}
if ((w&1) == 1) a = -(w-1)/2;
else a = w/2;

return (a);
```

Pcode 5.13: Simulation code for signed exp-Golomb code se(v).

(here n ranges from 1 to 16) from the bitstream and correlate with the codewords of the chosen VLC table. We select the minimum length codeword that matches with the bitstream and the associated *Coeff_Token* is chosen as the decoded total coefficients and trailing 1s. Although the codewords consists of prefix zeros followed by information bits, these codewords are nonprogressive and we do not have any constructive formula to get the number of bits present in a codeword. Thus, we search for all length bit patterns (from 1 to 16 bits) and choose the minimum length codeword that matches with the bitstream. However, this kind of search consumes many cycles on embedded processors as it involves many operations. Instead, we design a look-up table that gives the *Coeff_Token* and the actual number of bits used for the codeword and thereby we spend a minimum number of cycles in decoding the *Coeff_Token*. For this, we choose one *Coeff_Token* VLC table for nC less than 2, and obtain the look-up table values as described in the following.

The maximum number of prefix zeros present in the codeword of the *Coeff_Token* VLC table for nC less than 2, is 14. The *Coeff_Token* codeword looks like [p-zero bits|1|q bits] where $0 \leq p \leq 14$ and $0 \leq q \leq 3$. As seen here, we design a look-up table that contains the information of total coefficients, trailing 1s and the actual number of bits used $p+q+1$. Note that the value of $p+q+1$ never exceeds 16 or the value $p+q$ never exceed 15 which we can represent with 4 bits. The maximum number of total coefficients is 16 and we use 8 bits to represent it. The maximum number of trailing 1s is 3 and we use 4 bits of look-up table entry to represent it. A total of 16 bits (or 2 bytes) are used for each entry of the look-up table to hold the total coefficients, trailing 1s and $p+q$. For example, the codeword for *Coeff_Token*(1,3), which represents three total coefficients and a trailing 1, is 00000110. We have $p=5$ prefix zeros and $q=2$ bits and we have 8 bits in total for this codeword. The corresponding look-up table entry contains 0x8103. The general form of look-up table entry is [4 bits (actual bits used) | 4 bits (trailing 1s) | 8 (total coefficients)]. We design a look-up table for extreme values of p and q so that the look-up table can be accessed with a unique address. With this, we require 240 (=15*8*2) bytes of data memory to store one VLC table of the *Coeff_Token* for $0 \leq nC < 2$. The look-up table contains 15 segments (to take care of all possible p values) and each segment contains 8 entries (to take care of all possible q values). For example, in codeword 00000110, we have only $q = 2$ information bits, and we append one dummy bit for this in the design of the look-up table to make sure each segment contain exactly 8 entries. With this, the offset for a particular look-up table entry is given by $p * 8 + q$. The look-up table values of VLC codewords for $0 \leq nC < 2$ are available on the companion website.

The simulation code to obtain the *Coeff_Token* using look-up table **tcto_nc_less_than_2**[] is given in Pcode 5.14.

```
w = (pVLC->current_word) >> 16;                          // read 16-bits to w
p = 0;
while((w & 0x8000)==0) {w = w << 1; p++;}                // scan for lead zeros
if (nc < 2){
        q = w << 1;                                      // skip first '1' bit
        q = q >> 13;
        offset = p*8 + q;
        b = tcto_nc_less_than_2[offset];
        k = b >> 12;
        k = k + 1;                                       // p+q+1
        pVLC->bit_pos = pVLC->bit_pos + k;
        pVLC->current_word = pVLC->current_word << k;
        if (pVLC->bit_pos > 16){                         // bit FIFO
                pVLC->bit_pos = pVLC->bit_pos - 16;
                w = pVLC->buffer_pointer[pVLC->word_count++];
                w = w << pVLC->bit_pos;
                pVLC->current_word = pVLC->current_word | w;
        }
        *t_ones = (b & 0xfff) >> 8;
        *t_coeffs = b & 0xff;
}
```

Pcode 5.14: Simulation code for decoding *Coeff_Token* for *n*C < 2.

Level Prefix

The format for codewords of *LevelPrefix* is [$(n-1)$ zeros | 1] and contains a total of n bits. We treat the codes with $n > 16$ as escape codes. We scan 16 bits from the bitstream and find the number of prefix zeros. The *LevelPrefix* is the same as the number of prefix zeros present in the codeword. Depending on the bitstream pattern, we read n bits (where $1 \leq n \leq 16$ for nonescape codes) and output the corresponding *LevelPrefix* value. The simulation code for obtaining the *LevelPrefix* is given in Pcode 5.15.

```
w = (pVLC->current_word) >> 16;
k = 0;
while((w&0x8000) == 0){w = w << 1; k++;}
pVLC->bit_pos = pVLC->bit_pos+(k+1);
pVLC->current_word = pVLC->current_word << (k+1);
if (pVLC->bit_pos > 16){                         // bit FIFO
        pVLC->bit_pos = pVLC->bit_pos - 16;
        w = pVLC->buffer_pointer[pVLC->word_count++];
        w = w << pVLC->bit_pos;
        pVLC->current_word = pVLC->current_word | w;
}
*len = k;
```

Pcode 5.15: Simulation code to compute LevelPrefix.

Total Zeros

Like *Coeff_Token* codewords, the codewords of *total_zeros* contain unpredictable VLC codeword lengths. The general form of *total_zeros* codeword is [p-zeros |1/0|q bits], where $0 \leq p \leq 8$ and $0 \leq q \leq 2$. The VLC codeword tables of *total_zeros* are adapted depending on the context, which is the non-zero coefficients count "*tc*" in a block. If fewer coefficients are present in a block, then the total number of zeros present between coefficients is also lower. There is no need to compute the *total_zeros* if all the coefficients are present (i.e., total non-zero coefficients is the same as the maximum number of coefficients present in a block). If the total coefficients (obtained from the *Coeff_Token*) are less than the maximum coefficients of a block, we select the corresponding codeword table and decode the *total_zeros* using the bit pattern from the bitstream. We use a maximum 9 bits for decoding *total_zeros*. Depending on the bitstream pattern and the context (total coefficients), we read n bits ($n = 1$ to 9) from the bitstream and output the corresponding *total_zeros* value. We design a look-up table to perform *total_zeros* computation as follows. The general form of look-up entry w is organized as $w=$[4 bits (actual number of bits used, maximum value 9) | 4 bits (total zeros present, maximum value 15)] for decoding only 4×4 luma block *total_zeros*. The look-up table contains a total of 15 segments and each segment contains 36 entries. The particular entry of a 36-entry segment is accessed using the p and q, where p is lead zeros and q is the information bits of the codeword. The offset to access the look-up table entry follows:

$$\text{offset} = tc^*36 + p^*4 + q$$

The look-up table **total_zero_luma**[ ] values of *total_zeros* computation for a 4×4 luma block can be found on the website. The simulation code to compute *total_zeros* for a 4×4 luma block is given in Pcode 5.16.

```
w = (pVLC->current_word) >> 23;
p = 0;
while((w & 0x0100)==0) {w = w << 1; p++;}
q = w << 1;
q = (q >> 7) & 0x3;
offset = (t_coeffs-1)*36 + p*4 + q; // t_coeffs: non-zero coefficients of a 4x4 luma block
b = total_zeros_luma[offset];
k = b >> 4;
pVLC->bit_pos = pVLC->bit_pos + k;
pVLC->current_word = pVLC->current_word << k;
if (pVLC->bit_pos > 16){
        pVLC->bit_pos = pVLC->bit_pos - 16;
        w = pVLC->buffer_pointer[pVLC->word_count++];
        w = w << pVLC->bit_pos;
        pVLC->current_word = pVLC->current_word | w;
}
t_zeros = b & 0xf;
return (t_zeros);
```

Pcode 5.16: Simulation code to compute total_zeros for a 4×4 luma block.

Run Before

We read a maximum of 11 bits in decoding *run_before*. Depending on the bitstream pattern and the context (zeros left), we read n bits ($n = 1$ to 11) from the bitstream and output the corresponding *run_before* value. We use a look-up table to decode *run_before*. The look-up table design for decoding *run_before* is as follows. The look-up table entry w looks like $w=$[4 bits (actual bits used, maximum value 3 without escape codes) |4 bits (*run_ before*)]. If zeros-left is greater than 6 and if the lead zeros are greater than 2, then we treat those codes as escape codes. With this, scanning 3 bits of information from the bitstream is sufficient to decode *run_before* with nonescape codes. The look-up table contains a total of 7 segments (corresponding to 7 contexts) and each segment contains 8 entries. The look-up table entry for escape codes is zero as highlighted with a bold number in the file on the companion website. The offset for the look-up table is calculated as follows:

```
offset = zeros_left*8 + value (of 3 bits read from the bitstream)
```

The simulation code to decode *run_before* is given in Pcode 5.17; see the website for the look-up table **runbefore**[ ] values for decoding *run_before* with nonescape codes. The individual functions of the CAVLC involved in decoding residual coefficients have been discussed. The simulation code for the overall parsing process in decoding of a block of residual coefficients is given in Pcodes 5.18 and 5.19.

```
j = zeros_left; w = (pVLC->current_word)>>29;
if (j > 6) j = 7;
offset = (j-1)*8+w;
a = runbefore[offset];
k = a >> 4; rb = a & 0xf;
if (j == 7) {
        if (a == 0) {                                   // scan next 8-bits
                w = (pVLC->current_word)>> 21; k = 3;
                while((w & 0x800) == 0) { w = w << 1; k++;}
                rb = rb + 7;
        }
}
pVLC->bit_pos = pVLC->bit_pos + k;
pVLC->current_word = pVLC->current_word << k;
if (pVLC->bit_pos > 16){
        pVLC->bit_pos = pVLC->bit_pos - 16;
        w = pVLC->buffer_pointer[pVLC->word_count++];
        w = w << pVLC->bit_pos;
        pVLC->current_word = pVLC->current_word | w;
}
return (rb);
```

Pcode 5.17: Simulation code to decode run_before.

```
// decode total coefficients and trialing ones present in a 4x4 subblock
decode_tcoeffs_tones(pVLC, nc, &tcoeffs, &tones);
if (tcoeffs != 0){                  // decode sign information for trailing 1s
        k = 0; max_coeffs = 16; // initialize the local coefficient buffer to zero
        for(i=0;i<tcoeffs;i++) buf[i] = 0;
        if (tones != 0){
                for(i=0;i<tones;i++){
                        w = read_bits(pVLC,1);
                        coeff = (w == 0) ? 1 : -1;
                        buf[k++] = coeff;
                }
        }
        n = tcoeffs - tones;
        if (n != 0){ // decode level information
                suffix_length = 0;
                if ((tcoeffs > 10) && (tones < 3)) suffix_length = 1;
                for(i=k;i<tcoeffs;i++){                      // decode level prefix
                        level_prefix(pVLC, &prefix_length);
                        level_suffix_size = suffix_length; // determine level suffix size
                        if ((prefix_length==14) && (suffix_length==0)) level_suffix_size = 4;
                        if (prefix_length >= 15) level_suffix_size = prefix_length - 3;
                        if (level_suffix_size == 0) level_suffix = 0; // decode level suffix
                        else level_suffix = read_bits(pVLC, level_suffix_size);
                        tmp1 = (prefix_length < 15) ? prefix_length : 15;
                        tmp1 = tmp1 << suffix_length;
                        level_code = tmp1 + level_suffix; // determine level code
                        if ((prefix_length >= 15) && (suffix_length == 0)) level_code += 15;
                        if (prefix_length >= 16){
                                tmp2 = (1<<(prefix_length-3))-4096;
                                level_code = level_code + tmp2;
                        }
                        if ((i==tones) && (tones < 3)) level_code = level_code + 2;
                        if ((level_code & 1) == 0) buf[i] = (level_code+2)>>1;
                        else buf[i] = (-level_code-1)>>1;
                        if (suffix_length == 0) suffix_length = 1;
                        if (abs(buf[i])>sufvlc[suffix_length]) suffix_length+= 1;
                }
        }
        // Continued in Pcode 5.19
```

Pcode 5.18: Parsing process for decoding a block of residual coefficients.

```
        if (max_coeffs > tcoeffs){                              // decode total zeros
                t_zeros = total_zeros(pVLC, tcoeffs);
                if (t_zeros != 0){
                        k = tcoeffs+t_zeros-1;
                        for(i=0; i<tcoeffs-1;i++){
                                if (t_zeros > 0){               // decode run before
                                        coeff_buf[k] = buf[i]; // store the levels
                                        rb = run_before(pVLC, t_zeros);
                                         k = k - (rb + 1);
                                        t_zeros = t_zeros - rb;
                                }
                                else{
                                        coeff_buf[k] = buf[i];
                                        k = k - 1;
                                }
                        }
                        coeff_buf[t_zeros] = buf[i];
                }
                else {
                        for(i = 0;i < tcoeffs;i++)
                                coeff_buf[i] = buf[tcoeffs-1-i];
                }
        }
        else{
                for(i = 0;i < tcoeffs;i++)
                        coeff_buf[i] = buf[tcoeffs-1-i];
        }
}
```

Pcode 5.19: Parsing process for decoding a block of residual coefficients.

5.3.3 H.264 CAVLC Simulation Results

In this section, we present the simulation results for the H.264 CAVLC used to decode residual coefficients. We consider the decoding of a few luma 4×4 block residual coefficients with the following received bitstream.

```
bit_stream_buffer[] = {
0x74f0, 0x696a, 0x07f9, 0x8bd9, 0xe234, 0x4af6, 0x462c, 0xd89f,
0x3736, 0x0924, 0x1f01, 0x233c, 0xf458, 0x1bc1, 0x064a, 0xf879};
```

Next, we present the intermediate results (includes *Coeff_Token*, trailing 1 sign, signed levels, *total_zeros* and *run_before*) for the decoding process of multiple 4×4 luma blocks residual coefficients. The updated bit FIFO parameters {pVLC->*current_word*, pVLC-> *bit_pos*, pVLC->*word_count*} are shown whenever the FIFO is accessed to the read bits.

```
Initialization
FIFO: {0x74f0696a, 0, 2}
First luma 4x4 subblock
        -> Total coefficients and trailing 1s: Coeff_Token (t_coeffs, t_1s)
            Context: nC = 0
            Coeff_Token: (1, 1)
            Bits used: 2
            FIFO: {0xd3c1a5a8, 2, 2}

        -> Trailing 1s sign information
            sign: -ve
            Bits used: 1
            FIFO: {0xa7834b50, 3, 2}

        -> No levels to decode

        -> Total zeros information
            Context: 1 (t_coeffs)
            total_zeros: 0
            Bits used: 1
            FIFO: {0x4f0696a0, 4, 2}

        -> No run before to decode
```

```
        -> Output: [-1, 0, 0, 0, 0, 0, 0, 0, 0, 0, 0, 0, 0, 0, 0, 0]

Second luma 4x4 subblock
        -> Total coefficients and trailing 1s:
            Context: nC = 1
            Coeff_Token: (1, 1)
            Bits used: 2
            FIFO: {0x3c1a5a80, 6, 2}

        -> Trailing 1s sign information
            sign: +ve
            Bits used: 1
            FIFO: {0x7834b500, 7, 2}

        -> No levels to decode

        -> Total zeros information
            Context: 1 (t_coeffs)
            total_zeros: 1
            Bits used: 3
            FIFO: {0xc1a5a800, 10, 2}

        -> No run before to decode

        -> Output: [0, 1, 0, 0, 0, 0, 0, 0, 0, 0, 0, 0, 0, 0, 0, 0]

Third luma 4x4 subblock
        -> Total coefficients and trailing 1s:
            Context: nC = 0
            Coeff_Token: (0, 0)
            Bits used: 1
            FIFO: {0x834b5000, 11, 2}

        -> No trailing 1s sign information to decode

        -> No levels to decode

        -> No total zeros information to decode

        -> Output: [0, 0, 0, 0, 0, 0, 0, 0, 0, 0, 0, 0, 0, 0, 0, 0]

Fourth luma 4x4 subblock
        -> Total coefficients and trailing 1s:
            Context: nC = 1
            Coeff_Token: (0, 0)
            Bits used: 1
            FIFO: {0x0696a000, 12, 2}

        -> No trailing 1s sign information to decode

        -> No levels to decode

        -> No total zeros information to decode

        -> Output: [0, 0, 0, 0, 0, 0, 0, 0, 0, 0, 0, 0, 0, 0, 0, 0]

Fifth luma 4x4 subblock
        -> Total coefficients and trailing 1s:
            Context: nC = 0
            Coeff_Token: (3, 1)
            Bits used: 8
            FIFO: {0x96a07f90, 4, 3}

        -> Trailing 1s sign information
            sign: -ve
            Bits used: 1
            FIFO: {0x2d40ff20, 5, 3}
```

```
-> Levels to decode: 2
    First level
        - suffix_length = 0
        - Level prefix
            prefix_length: 2
            Bits used: 3
            FIFO: {0x6a07f900, 8, 3}
        - level_suffix_size = 0
            level_suffix: 0
        - level_code = 4
        - coeff = 3
    Second level
        - suffix_length = 1
        - Level prefix
            prefix_length: 1
            Bits used: 2
            FIFO: {0xa81fe400, 10, 3}
        - level_suffix_size = 1
            level_suffix: 1
            Bits used: 1
            FIFO: {0x503fc800, 11, 3}
        - level_code = 4
        - coeff = -2

-> Total zeros information
    Context: 3 (t_coeffs)
    total_zeros: 0
    Bits used: 4
    FIFO: {0x03fc8000, 15, 3}

-> No run before to decode

-> Output: [-2, 3,-1, 0, 0, 0, 0, 0, 0, 0, 0, 0, 0, 0, 0, 0]
```

Sixth luma 4x4 subblock

```
-> Total coefficients and trailing 1s:
    Context: nC = 0
    Coeff_Token: (3, 0)
    Bits used: 9
    FIFO: {0xf98bd900, 8, 4}

-> No trailing 1s sign information to decode

-> Levels to decode: 3
    First level
        - suffix_length = 0
        - Level prefix
            prefix_length: 0
            Bits used: 1
            FIFO: {0xf317b200, 9, 4}
        - level_suffix_size = 0
            level_suffix: 0
        - level_code = 2
        - coeff = 2
    Second level
        - suffix_length = 1
        - Level prefix
            prefix_length: 0
            Bits used: 1
            FIFO: {0xe62f6400, 10, 4}
        - level_suffix_size = 1
            level_suffix: 1
            Bits used: 1
            FIFO: {0xcc5ec800, 11, 4}
        - level_code = 1
        - coeff = -1
    Third level
        - suffix_length = 1
```

```
                    - Level prefix
                            prefix_length: 0
                            Bits used: 1
                            FIFO: {0x98bd9000, 12, 4}
                    - level_suffix_size = 1
                            level_suffix: 1
                            Bits used: 1
                            FIFO: {0x317b2000, 13, 4}
                    - level_code = 1
                    - coeff = -1

        -> Total zeros information
            Context: 3 (t_coeffs)
            total_zeros: 5
            Bits used: 4
            FIFO: {0x17b3c468, 1, 5}

        -> Run before
            Context: 5 (zeros-left)
            run_before: 5
            Bits used: 3
            FIFO: {0xbd9e2340, 4, 5}

    -> Output: [-1, -1, 0, 0, 0, 0, 0, 2, 0, 0, 0, 0, 0, 0, 0, 0]
```

5.3.4 H.264 CAVLC Optimization Techniques

In this section, we will discuss the computational complexity of the H.264 VLC and the optimization techniques for the parsing process of residual decoding. We estimate the computational complexity of the H.264 VLC in terms of clock cycles and memory used.

H.264 VLC Computational Complexity

As we discussed in Section 5.3.3, the simulation of the H.264 VLC involves many bit FIFO accesses and conditional jumps. With bit FIFO accesses, we have two cases: (1) updating only the FIFO parameters and (2) reading bits from the bitstream buffer along with FIFO updating parameters. We check to determine whether the number of bits present in the FIFO is less than 16, and then conditionally jump to read bits from the bitstream buffer to the FIFO if the bits present are less than 16. If we are not reading the bits from the bitstream buffer, then we consume only 4 cycles (2 cycles for FIFO update and 2 cycles for the conditional check and for taking the decision on the jump) to update the bit FIFO on the reference embedded processor by avoiding the conditional jump. See Appendix A, Section A.4, on the companion website for more details on cycles estimation on the reference embedded processor. If bits present in FIFO are less than 16, then we jump for reading bits from the bitstream buffer and jump back to continue the decoding. In this case we consume about 20 cycles. On average, we may read bits from the bitstream buffer once in four FIFO accesses. Hence, we consume on average about $(3*4+20)/4 = 8$ cycles to access bit FIFO instead of 13 cycles as in the MPEG-2 32-bit FIFO discussed in Section 5.2.

UVLC Computational Complexity

The three UVLC functions u(n), ue(v), and se(v) access bit FIFO, and it is the major cycle-consuming portion of the code. As seen in Pcode 5.11, the function u(n) consists of only bits extraction and bit FIFO update functionality, and its average cycles consumption is about 9 cycles. The other two functions—unsigned exp-Golomb code ue(v) and signed exp-Golomb code se(v)—consist of lead zero computation, which can be achieved in 2 cycles on the reference embedded processor. In addition, we perform a little bit of adjustment to the value read from FIFO to get the final *Code_Num*. On average, we consume about 12 and 15 cycles on the reference embedded processor to perform exp-Golomb code functions ue(v) and se(v), respectively.

CAVLC Computational Complexity

The CAVLC cycle estimation for decoding residual coefficients is a difficult task since it involves many contexts, functions, and jumps. We first estimate the cycle cost and memory consumption of individual CAVLC functions and then estimate the overall complexity.

Total Coefficients and Trailing 1s In computing the *Coeff_Token*, we have 6 VLC tables to choose from depending on context and luma or chroma blocks. For this, we require about 1.2 kB of data memory to store all look-up tables of *Coeff_Token* VLC codewords. In *Coeff_Token* computation, we have the following steps:

1. Choose the codeword table depending on context and luma or chroma blocks (2 cycles for choosing VLC table with an offset)
2. Scan bits and obtain lead zeros (3 cycles)
3. Offset computation and look-up table accesses (4 cycles)
4. Extract total coefficients, trailing 1s and actual bits used information (3 cycles)
5. Bit FIFO access (8 cycles)

With this, we may consume about 20 cycles to compute the *Coeff_Token* on the reference embedded processor.

Trailing 1s Sign Computation Computing the sign of the trailing 1s involves only bit FIFO access and making a decision on the sign information depending on bit "0" or "1" accessed from FIFO. We consume about 10 cycles to get the sign information for a single trailing 1.

Level Prefix Computation of the level prefix (i.e., *prefix_length*) involves the following two steps: scanning bits and obtaining lead zeros (3 cycles), and bit FIFO access (8 cycles). With this, we consume about 11 cycles to compute level prefix for decoding 1 level.

Level Suffix If *level_suffix_size* is not zero then we access bit FIFO to get the *level_suffix* value otherwise if the *level_suffix_size* is zero then the *level_suffix* value is set to zero. As it involves a conditional check and jump whenever we don't access bit FIFO, we consume either way about 10 cycles to compute *level_suffix*.

Total Zeros The *total_zeros* computation involves multiple VLC tables to choose from depending on context (here the context is total coefficients). We require about 0.6 kB of data memory to store the look-up table to compute *total_zeros* present between all non-zero coefficients of a block. In *total_zeros* computation, we have the following steps:

1. Choose the codeword table depending on context and luma or chroma blocks (2 cycles for choosing VLC table with an offset)
2. Scan bits and obtain lead zeros (3 cycles)
3. Offset computation and look-up table accesses (4 cycles)
4. Extract *total_zeros* and actual bits used information (2 cycles)
5. Bit FIFO access (8 cycles)

With this, we may consume about 19 cycles to compute *total_zeros* on the reference embedded processor.

Run Before We use 56 bytes of memory to store look-up tables in the *run_before* computation. We have the following steps in the *run_before* computation:

1. Adjust context (2 cycles)
2. Scan bits, offset computation, and look-up table access (5 cycles)
3. Escape code handling (2 cycles)
4. Execute *run_before* and the actual number of bits used, extraction (2 cycles)
5. Bit FIFO access (8 cycles)

With this, we consume about 19 cycles in computing *run_before*.

Parsing Residual Decoding Process The parsing of residual decoding is a complex process as given in Pcodes 5.18 and 5.19. In some cases we may obtain the *Coeff_Token* for the residual block as (0, 0), in which case we don't perform the rest of the functions as no coefficients are present in that residual block and we consume about 30 cycles. In some cases we may have only trailing 1s and so we don't perform levels decoding. If we have trailing 1s, we consume another 10 cycles per trailing 1 sign computation. In other cases, we may have more non-zero coefficients to decode. As given in Pcode 5.18, we have the following steps in decoding one non-zero coefficient:

1. Determine *suffix_length* (4 cycles)
2. Determine *suffix_level_size* (8 cycles)

3. Compute *prefix_length* (11 cycles)
4. Compute *suffix_level* (10 cycles)
5. Compute *level_code* (17 cycles)
6. Determine signed coefficient from *level_code* (3 cycles)
7. Update *suffix_length* (3 cycles)

Apart from this, we perform *total_zeros* computation and *run_before* computation to store coefficients as given in Pcode 5.19. If the total coefficient count is equal to maximum coefficients, we do not perform *total_zeros* and *run_before* operations and we skip (10 cycles) these two operations. Otherwise, we consume 20 cycles for *total_zeros* computation and 25 cycles per coefficient to perform *run_before* and to store that coefficient (following zig-zag/field scan rules). If *zeros-left* is zero, then we do not perform *run_before* and we skip (10 cycles) the *run_before* function in this particular case.

As seen in the previous cycle estimate, we consume about 56 cycles to decode one coefficient and 25 cycles to store that coefficient using *run_before*. With this, if we have three coefficients (a trailing 1 and two coefficients) in a 4×4 residual block, we may consume about 217 cycles (20 cycles for *Coeff_Token*, 10 cycles for trailing 1s sign, 112 cycles for decoding two coefficients and 75 cycles—20 cycles for *total_zeros* and 55 cycles for *run_before* and for other operations—for storing three coefficients) or about 13.5 cycles/pixel (as we have a total of 16 pixels in a 4×4 block). Although the CAVLC for decoding a coefficient is costly in terms of cycles, the average cycles per pixel will be small because the number of non-zero coefficients per block is small. We see fewer than three or four coefficients per 4×4 residual block most of the time with the D1 frame size at the 1-Mbps bit rate. Therefore, we consume about 10 cycles/pixel on average to decode the residual coefficients of D1 video frames at 1 Mbps using the CAVLC.

Optimization of the H.264 Parsing Process for CAVLC

In this section, we discuss some optimization techniques to reduce the cycle cost of the residual decoding process using the CAVLC. Unlike the MPEG-2 VLC, where we do not have any contexts and can decode multiple symbols in a single FIFO access, H.264 CAVLC decoding involves many contexts and it is very difficult to decode more than one coefficient at a time. However, we can optimize the CAVLC flow by avoiding the conditional flow wherever possible and by reducing the bit FIFO accesses whenever context is not present to choose a particular VLC table from multiple tables.

Especially in decoding signed level information, we have many conditional checks as we are handling all possible rarely occuring data paths with one flow. If we separate the loop into two parts by treating *prefix_length* > 13 as an escape code, then we can avoid many conditional checks and conditional moves. This optimized data flow is given in Pcode 5.20. In the case of computing the sign of trailing 1s, we access the bit FIFO three times if we have three trailing 1s as given in Pcode 5.18. Instead, we can also read 3 bits to a register from FIFO in one access and then extract the individual bits from the register in the loop as we do not have any context information in decoding trailing 1s sign information. In this way we save 50% of cycles in trailing 1s sign computation. In other words, we consume less than 15 cycles to get the sign information even if we have two or more trailing 1s.

In addition, in computing signed level using Pcode 5.20, we do not use any external context information in decoding *prefix_length* or *suffix_level* other than the updated *suffix_length* (t) for decoding *suffix_level*. Using six look-up tables (T_1 to T_6), we can minimize the cycle cost of signed level computation. The six look-up tables are designed based on the following rules.

When *prefix_length* < 15,

```
level = (prefix_length << (t-1) + 1 + suffix_level) * sign
```

where *suffix_level* is a value of unsigned $(t-1)$ bits, and the sign bit follows the $(t-1)$ suffix bits except for $t = 1$ (here the sign bit will be next to the "1" bit) and t is equal to the "n" in "T_n." In this case, the codeword looks like [prefix zeros][1][suffix bits][sign].

When prefix_level = 15,

```
level = (15 << (t-1) + 1 + 11_suffix_bits) * sign
codeword = [0000 0000 0000 000][1][11 suffix bits][sign]
```

```
for(i = k;i < tcoeffs;i++){
        level_prefix(pVLC, &prefix_length);                              // decode level prefix
        if (prefix_length < 14) { // decode level suffix
                if (suffix_length == 0) level_suffix = 0;
                else level_suffix = read_bits(pVLC, suffix_length);
                tmp1 = prefix_length << suffix_length;
                level_code = tmp1 + level_suffix;                        // determine level code
                if ((i==tones) && (tones < 3)) level_code = level_code + 2;
                if ((level_code & 1) == 0) buf[i] = (level_code+2)>>1;
                else buf[i] = (-level_code-1))>>1;
                if (suffix_length == 0) suffix_length = 1;
                if (abs(buf[i])>sufvlc[suffix_length]) suffix_length+= 1;
        }
        else { // escape
                level_suffix_size = suffix_length;                       // determine level suffix size
                if ((prefix_length == 14) && (suffix_length == 0)) level_suffix_size = 4;
                if (prefix_length >= 15) level_suffix_size = prefix_length - 3;
                if (level_suffix_size == 0) level_suffix = 0;     // decode level suffix
                else level_suffix = read_bits(pVLC, level_suffix_size);
                tmp1 = (prefix_length < 15) ? prefix_length : 15;
                tmp1 = tmp1 << suffix_length;
                level_code = tmp1 + level_suffix;                        // determine level code
                if ((prefix_length >= 15) && (suffix_length == 0)) level_code += 15;
                if (prefix_length >= 16){
                        tmp2 = (1<<(prefix_length-3))-4096;
                        level_code = level_code + tmp2;
                }
                if ((i==tones) && (tones < 3)) level_code = level_code + 2;
                if ((level_code & 1) == 0) buf[i] = (level_code+2)>>1;
                else buf[i] = (-level_code-1))>>1;
                if (suffix_length == 0) suffix_length = 1;
                if (abs(buf[i])>sufvlc[suffix_length]) suffix_length+= 1;
        }
}
```

Pcode 5.20: Optimization of signed level decoding process.

The tables updated (i.e., local context adaptation) as follows: Initially, t is set to zero except when ($total\_coeffs > 10$) and ($t\_ones < 3$), in this case t is set to 1. Afterwards, "t" is updated. If (abs(level) > C[t]), then $t = t + 1$, where the level is the decoded non-zero coefficient and C[] = {0,3,6,12,24,48,32768}.

When $t = 0$, this particular level is decoded as follows:

1. When ($prefix\_length < 14$),

```
level = [(prefix_length +2)>>1 ] * (-1)^prefix_length
```

2. When ($prefix\_length = 14$),

```
level = [(prefix_length +2)>>1 + 3 suffix bits] * sign
codeword = [prefix zeros][1][3 suffix bits][sign]
```

3. When ($prefix\_length = 15$),

```
level = [(prefix_length +1) + 11 suffix bits] * sign
codeword = [prefix zeros][1][11 suffix bits][sign]
```

With this optimization technique, we consume about 6 cycles/pixel on average to decode the residual coefficients of D1 video frames at 1 Mbps using the CAVLC.

5.4 MQ-Decoder

The JPEG 2000 standard (ISO and ITU JPEG2000, 2000) uses the MQ-coder for entropy coding to compress and decompress the data stream. In this section, we will discuss the overview, simulation and implementation of the MQ-decoder. All the notations used are similar to JPEG 2000 standard notations.

5.4.1 MQ Coder Overview

The MQ-coder is a context-based binary arithmetic coder. The basic parameters of the MQ-coder are interval range (A), code value (C), context parameters (I_{cx}, MPS_{cx}) and bit counter (CT). In the MQ-coder, unlike the binary arithmetic coder, we do not have multiplications or divisions to perform interval subdivision. The interval subdivision into least probable symbol (LPS) subinterval and most probable symbol (MPS) subinterval is achieved using a look-up table with the given probable state I_{cx} which is obtained from the context model. The value of range A is always kept in the interval [0.75, 1.5). This allows a simple approximation of the following interval subdivision calculations for given probability value "Qe" as the value of A is of the order unity.

$$\text{MPS subinterval} = A - (A^* Qe) = A - Qe$$
$$\text{LPS subinterval} = A^* Qe = Qe$$

The subinterval value for LPS is obtained from the look-up table. Whenever the value of A falls below 0.75 (or equivalent fixed point value of 0×8000), then both A and C are renormalized to keep the value of A around unity to perform the next subinterval division approximation.

A few applications of JPEG 2000 include digital photography, optical drive, digital cinema (motion JPEG), Internet, and so on. Similar to the MQ-coder in the JPEG 2000 standard, the H.264/AVC standard uses a variant of the M-coder known as the context-based adaptive binary arithmetic coder (CABAC). The H.264 arithmetic coder is simpler than the MQ-coder. The MQ-coder performs well when compared to VLCs and the bit savings is about 10% more, whereas the H.264 arithmetic coder performs well when compared to the MQ-coder in terms of throughput and bit savings by 15 to 20% and 2 to 5%.

In this section, assuming the availability of an MQ-coder-encoded bitstream, we will discuss bitstream decoding by using the MQ-decoder. As shown in Figure 5.9, the MQ-decoder consists of many ALU operations, look-up table accesses and conditional jumps. The flow of the MQ-decoder is a little bit similar to the CABAC flow, which we will discuss in Section 5.5. As in the CABAC, we can divide the MQ-decoder into three parts:

- Interval subdivision
- Parameter updating
- Normalization

Each part contains many steps as shown in Figure 5.9 with the numbers in the circles. In steps 1 and 2, we perform the interval subdivision. In interval subdivision, we get the LPS subinterval range from the look-up table using the offset obtained from the context model. Then we obtain the MPS subinterval after subtracting the LPS subinterval from A. Depending on the code value C, LPS subinterval QeI_{cx} and MPS subinterval A, we continue either an LPS decoding path or an MPS decoding path to update the parameters. We use steps 3 to 11 to update the parameters. In parameter updating, we update the code value (in the MSB halfword of C) and the context parameters and we compute decision D. We perform the renormalization process with steps 12 to 14 (not all at a time). With the renormalization process, we make sure that the value of A falls into the range [0.75, 1.5). During renormalization, we append the bits from the bitstream to the code value C (from the LSB side). Like the CABAC, the renormalization of the MQ-coder is also a multi-iterative process. The decoded binary decision is given by the value D. We will discuss the simulation details of the MQ-decoder in the following sections.

5.4.2 JPEG 2000 MQ-Decoder Simulation

The basic input and output parameters required for simulation of the JPEG 2000 arithmetic decoder are range (A), value (C), contexts (I_{cx}, MPS_{cx}), bit counter (CT), compressed data (*Dat*) and output decision (D). The following structure is used in the simulation of the MQ-decoder.

```
typedef struct jad_tag
{
        int A;
        int C;
        int CT;
        int Icx;
        int MPScx;
```

```
    unsigned char *BP;
    int D;
} JpegArtDec_t;

JpegArtDec_t JBA, *pJBA;
```

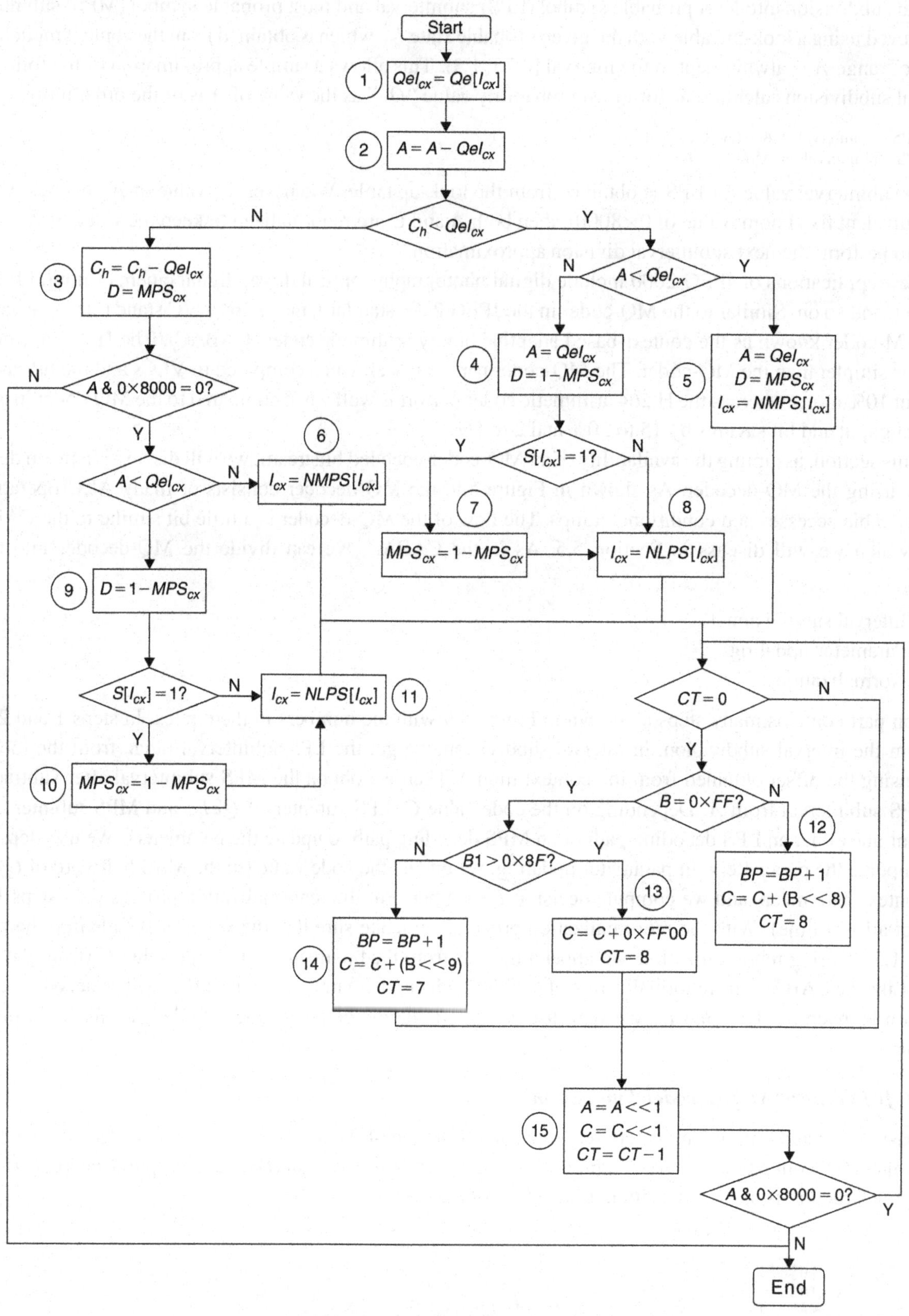

Figure 5.9: Flow chart diagram of JPEG 2000 MQ-decoder.

The values of A, C, and CT are initialized according to the JPEG 2000 standard, and the initialization code is given in Pcode 5.21.

```
pJBA = &JBA;
pJBA->C = (*(pJBA->BPST)) << 16;
if (*(pJBA->BPST) == 0xff) {
        if (*(pJBA->BPST+1) > 0x8f) {
                pJBA->C = pJBA->C + 0xff00;
                pJBA->CT = 8;
        }
        else {
                pJBA->BPST++;
                pJBA->C = pJBA->C + (*(pJBA->BPST) << 9);
                pJBA->CT = 7;
        }
}
else {
        pJBA->BPST++;
        pJBA->C = pJBA->C + (*(pJBA->BPST) << 8);
        pJBA->CT = 8;
}
pJBA->C = (pJBA->C) << 7;
pJBA->CT = pJBA->CT-7;
pJBA->A = 0x8000;
```

Pcode 5.21: Initialization of MQ-decoder.

The simulation code for interval subdivision and parameter updating is given in Pcode 5.22. To divide the interval range into LPS subinterval and MPS subinterval, first we obtain the LPS subinterval QeI_{cx} from the look-up table **Qe**[ ]. We obtain the MPS subinterval by subtracting the LPS subinterval from the total interval A. We update the parameters accordingly depending on the code value C and LPS subinterval QeI_{cx}. Given the current context (I_{cx}, MPS_{cx}), if the MPS subinterval A is less than the LPS subinterval QeI_{cx} and if the switch flag $S[I_{cx}]$ is set for context index I_{cx}, then we update the MPS value MPS_{cx} (i.e., 0 to 1 or 1 to 0) of the current index by inverting it. Next, we update the context index using LPS or MPS index tables depending on whether we are decoding LPS or MPS as shown in Figure 5.9.

The simulation code for renormalization of interval range A of the MQ-decoder is given in Pcode 5.23. In the renormalization process we consume the bits from the input bitstream. We shift left both the interval register A and code register C 1 bit at a time (or 1 bit per iteration). With each shift, we consume 1 bit from bit FIFO (present in the LSB halfword of C) and the bit count CT is reduced by 1. Whenever CT becomes zero, we append to FIFO a new data byte obtained from the bitstream buffer. The renormalization process may involve multiple iterations depending on the interval value A. Whenever interval range A goes beyond 0×8000 (or 0.75 in decimal notation), then we stop the renormalization process iterations and output the decoded decision value D.

MQ-Decoder Simulation Results

Here we present simulation results for the JPEG 2000 MQ-decoder. For a given JPEG 2000 arithmetic encoded bitstream, the initialized parameter values, output decision values and the decoder parameters after decoding 1 output decision, 5 output decisions, 10 output decisions and 20 output decisions follow. The encoded bitstream is present in buffer dat[ ], and the decoded binary decision output D is stored in the buffer sym[ ]. The following look-up tables are used in the MQ-decoder.

```
LPS probabilities or subintervals
  Qe[47] = {
  0x5601, 0x3401, 0x1801, 0x0ac1, 0x0521, 0x0221, 0x5601, 0x5401, 0x4801, 0x3801, 0x3001, 0x2401,
  0x1c01, 0x1601, 0x5601, 0x5401, 0x5101, 0x4801, 0x3801, 0x3401, 0x3001, 0x2801, 0x2401, 0x2201,
  0x1c01, 0x1801, 0x1601, 0x1401, 0x1201, 0x1101, 0x0ac1, 0x09c1, 0x08a1, 0x0521, 0x0441, 0x02a1,
  0x0221, 0x0141, 0x0111, 0x0085, 0x0049, 0x0025, 0x0015, 0x0009, 0x0005, 0x0001, 0x5601};
Next symbol probability estimation given the present symbol as MPS:
  nmps[47] = {
   1, 2, 3, 4, 5, 38, 7, 8, 9, 10, 11, 12, 13, 29, 15, 16, 17, 18, 19, 20, 21, 22, 23, 24,
   25, 26, 27, 28, 29, 30, 31, 32, 33, 34, 35, 36, 37, 38, 39, 40, 41, 42, 43, 44, 45, 45, 46};
Next symbol probability estimation given the present symbol as LPS:
```

```
QeIcx = Qe[pJBA->Icx];
pJBA->A = pJBA->A - QeIcx;
Ch = pJBA->C;
Ch = Ch >> 16;
if (Ch < QeIcx) {
        if (pJBA->A < QeIcx) {
                pJBA->A = QeIcx;
                pJBA->D = pJBA->MPScx;
                pJBA->Icx = nmps[pJBA->Icx];
        }
        else {
                pJBA->A = QeIcx;
                pJBA->D = 1 - pJBA->MPScx;
                if (S[pJBA->Icx] == 1)
                        pJBA->MPScx = 1 - pJBA->MPScx;
                pJBA->Icx = nlps[pJBA->Icx];
        }
        // continue with renormalization process (use Pcode 5.23)
}
else {
        Ch = Ch - QeIcx;
        pJBA->C = pJBA->C & 0xffff;
        pJBA->C = pJBA->C | (Ch << 16);
        if ((pJBA->A & 0x8000) == 0) {
                if (pJBA->A < QeIcx) {
                        pJBA->D = 1 - pJBA->MPScx;
                        if (S[pJBA->Icx] == 1)
                                pJBA->MPScx = 1 - pJBA->MPScx;
                        pJBA->Icx = nlps[pJBA->Icx];
                }
                else {
                        pJBA->D = pJBA->MPScx;
                        pJBA->Icx = nmps[pJBA->Icx];
                }
                // continue with renormalization process (use Pcode 5.23)
        }
        else
                pJBA->D = pJBA->MPScx;
}
```

Pcode 5.22: Simulation code for interval subdivision and parameter updating.

```
do {
    if (pJBA->CT == 0) {
            if (*(pJBA->BPST) == 0xff) {
                    if (*(pJBA->BPST +1) > 0x8f) {
                            pJBA->C = pJBA->C + 0xff00;
                            pJBA->CT = 8;
                    }
                    else {
                            pJBA->BPST++;
                            tmp = *(pJBA->BPST);
                            pJBA->C = pJBA->C + (tmp << 9),
                            pJBA->CT = 7;
                    }
            }
            else {
                    pJBA->BPST++;
                    tmp = *(pJBA->BPST);
                    pJBA->C = pJBA->C + (tmp << 8);
                    pJBA->CT = 8;
            }
    }
    pJBA->A = pJBA->A << 1;
    pJBA->C = pJBA->C << 1;
    pJBA->CT = pJBA->CT - 1;
} while((pJBA->A & 0x8000) != 0) ;
```

Pcode 5.23: Simulation code for renormalization of MQ-decoder.

```
  nlps[47] = {
  1, 6, 9, 12, 29, 33, 6, 14, 14, 14, 17, 18, 20, 21, 14, 14, 15, 16, 17, 18, 19, 19, 20, 21,
  22, 23, 24, 25, 26, 27, 28, 29, 30, 31, 32, 33, 34, 35, 36, 37, 38, 39, 40, 41, 42, 43, 46};
Switch flag to toggle the MPS of context
  S[47] = {
  1,0,0,0,0,0,1,0,0,0,0,0,0,0,0,1,0,0,0,0,0,0,0,0,0,0,0,0,0,0,
  0,0,0,0,0,0,0,0,0,0,0,0,0,0,0,0,0};
JPEG 2000 encoded bitstream data
  dat[] = {0x00, 0x00, 0xa4, 0xca, 0x2f, 0xff, 0x00, 0x00}
After JPEG 2000 arithmetic decoder initialization
  pJBA->A = 0x00008000
  pJBA->C = 0x00520000
  pJBA->CT = 1
  pJBA->Icx = 3
  pJBA->MPScx = 0
  sym[] = {0,0,0,0,0,0,0,0,0,0,0,0,0,0,0,0,0,0,0,0}
After decoding 1 decision by arithmetic decoder
  pJBA->A = 0x0000AC10
  pJBA->C = 0x05265000
  pJBA->CT = 5
  pJBA->Icx = C
  pJBA->MPScx = 0
  sym[] = {1,0,0,0,0,0,0,0,0,0,0,0,0,0,0,0,0,0,0,0}
After decoding 5 decisions by arithmetic decoder
  pJBA->A = 0x0000B004
  pJBA->C = 0x79905E00
  pJBA->CT = 7
  pJBA->Icx = 14
  pJBA->MPScx = 0
  sym[] = {1,1,1,0,0,0,0,0,0,0,0,0,0,0,0,0,0,0,0,0}
After decoding 10 decisions by arithmetic decoder
  pJBA->A = 0x0000C006
  pJBA->C = 0x51B9C000
  pJBA->CT = 2
  pJBA->Icx = 15
  pJBA->MPScx = 0
  sym[] = {1,1,1,0,0,0,0,0,1,0,0,0,0,0,0,0,0,0,0,0}
After decoding 20 decisions by arithmetic decoder
  pJBA->A = 0x0000A802
  pJBA->C = 0x76F00000
  pJBA->CT = 4
  pJBA->Icx = E
  pJBA->MPScx = 0
  sym[] = {1,1,1,0,0,0,0,0,1,0,0,0,1,1,0,1,1,1,1,1}
```

MQ-Decoder Computational Complexity

As seen in Figure 5.9, the flow of the JPEG 2000 arithmetic decoder is somewhat complex. We will analyze decoder complexity by considering the following possible cases. The steps in each case are specified with <>.

Case 1: In this case, the decoder steps in the path <Start, (1), (2), (3), and End> are considered. This is the shortest possible path. This path always decodes the MPS as output decision and does not require the process of renormalization.

Case 2: In this case, the decoder steps in the following six paths <Start, (1), (2), (3), (6), (15), and End>, <Start, (1), (2), (3), (9), (11), (15), and End>, <Start, (1), (2), (3), (9), (10), (11), (15), and End>, <Start, (1), (2), (5), (15), and End>, <Start, (1), (2), (4), (8), (15), and End> and <Start, (1), (2), (4), (7), (8), (15), and End> are considered. These paths include both the LPS and MPS decision decode and renormalization process. However, in the renormalization process we do not read bits from the bitstream as these correspond to the case where CT is greater than zero. In general (about 80% of the time), bits from the bitstream will not be read in the renormalization process.

Case 3: In this case, all the paths are the same as Case 2 except the presence of step (12) in all the paths to read bits from the bitstream buffer in the renormalization process when CT becomes zero. However, in this case the current byte value and next byte values of the bitstream pointed to by the buffer pointer is assumed not equal to 0xff. With this assumption, we can efficiently implement the renormalization process, as we will discuss later.

Case 4: In this case, all the considered paths of the decoder are the same as in Case 3 and the context is also same. The only difference is that one of the current bytes or next bytes of the bitstream buffer pointed to by the buffer pointer will be equal to 0xff.

As seen in the preceding four cases, we can see that the decoder complexity increases from Case 1 to Case 4. With this analysis, in the following section we will optimize the JPEG 2000 arithmetic decoder flow for number of cycles by keeping the memory usage the same for all cases.

5.4.3 Efficient Simulation of JPEG 2000 MQ-Decoder

In the optimization of the decoder, we first optimize each individual case described in the previous section and we later combine all the cases for single flow with a few conditional jumps. Here, the conditional jump is taken such that the average-to-peak cycles of decoding are reduced.

Optimization of Case 1

This path (Start, (1), (2), (3), and End) of the decoder is the shortest path and we do not have much scope for optimization. However, a small modification by combining the two conditions to one condition as shown in Pcode 5.24 will result in one conditional jump.

```
QeIcx = Jpeg_Art[pJBA->Icx + tmp];
Ch = pJBA->C;
Ch = Ch >> 16;
pJBA->A = pJBA->A - QeIcx;
if((Ch >= QeIcx) && ((pJBA->A&0x8000) == 0)) {
                                          // Case 2, Case 3, or Case 4
}
else {
         Ch = Ch – QeIcx;
         D = pJBA->MPScx;                 // Case 1
         pJBA->C = pJBA->C & 0xffff;
         pJBA->C = pJBA->C | (Ch << 16);
}
```

Pcode 5.24: Efficient implementation of Case 1 of the MQ-decoder.

Optimization of Case 2

The decoder flows in this case are much more complex than in Case 1. The common process for all the flows of Case 2 is the renormalization operation which is a conditional multi-iterative process and is very costly in terms of cycles. For example, if the interval A is 0x0ac1, then the four iterations are needed for the normalization process and if the bits are not going to read to value C (this is what assumed in Case 2), it requires about 68 $(= 4*(5+2*6))$ cycles (see Section A.4 on the companion website for more details on clock cycles estimation on the reference embedded processor). Many of the cycles to execute the renormalization process can be avoided if we first compute the normalization loop count "*CNT*" by counting the leading zeros in A, then shifting A and C by *CNT* and subtracting *CT* from *CNT*.

Next, a complex task common to all paths in Case 2 is obtaining the new values for I_{cx}, MPS_{cx} and D and new values for A and C before normalization. The new values for these parameters can be efficiently computed using a look-up table and conditional moves. In this way we can avoid most of the jumps. As shown in Pcode 5.25, the new values of A and C are obtained by conditional computation. Instead of accessing different look-up tables for computing new values for I_{cx} and MPS_{cx}, all look-up tables are combined to form a new look-up table. Depending on the conditions, an offset is chosen to select the appropriate look-up values. In this way, the output decision is also obtained from the look-up table. The look-up table's 16-bit codeword contains D (4 bits), MPS_{cx} (4 bits) and I_{cx} (8 bits). The values of the look-up table **Jpeg_Art**[] for obtaining all the previous specified parameters can be found on this book's companion website.

Optimization of Case 3

The optimization techniques used in Case 2 are all applicable to Case 3 too. The extra computations we perform in Case 3 are reading of the data bits from the bitstream buffer to value C in the renormalization process. If the

```
QeIcx = Jpeg_Art[pJBA->Icx ];
r1 = 3; r2 = 1; r3 = 1; r4 = 3; r5 = 2; r6 = 4;
Ch = pJBA->C;
Ch = Ch >> 16;
pJBA->A = pJBA->A - QeIcx;
if (pJBA->MPScx == 1) {
        r1 = r6; r2 = r5;
        r3 = r5; r4 = r6;
}
if (pJBA->A < QeIcx) {
        r1 = r2; r3 = r4;
}
if((Ch >= QeIcx) && ((pJBA->A&0x8000) == 0)) {
        if (Ch >= QeIcx) {
                Ch = Ch - QeIcx;
                r1 = r3;
                pJBA->C = pJBA->C & 0xffff;
                pJBA->C = pJBA->C | (Ch << 16);
        }
        else
                pJBA->A = QeIcx;
        tmp = Jpeg_Art[r1*47+pJBA->Icx];
        pJBA->Icx = tmp & 0xff;
        pJBA->MPScx = (tmp>>8)&1;
        pJBA->D = tmp >> 12;
        r1 = 0;
        while ((pJBA->A & 0x8000) == 0) {
                pJBA->A = pJBA->A << 1;
                r1++;
        }
        pJBA->C = pJBA->C << r1;     // Case 2
        pJBA->CT = pJBA->CT - r1;
        if (pJBA->CT <= 0) {
                if((*(pJBA->BPST) != 0xff) || (*(pJBA->BPST+1) != 0xff)) {
                                     // Case 3
                }
                else {
                                     // Case 4
                }
        }
}
else {
                                     // Case 1
}
```

Pcode 5.25: Efficient simulation of Case 2 of the MQ-decoder.

current byte and next byte are not 0xff, then we can efficiently implement reading bits by moving 16 bits at a time to C when CT becomes less than or equal to zero. Then add 16 to CT. In this way, we will read the buffer only after 16 bits of renormalization process. If one of the current bytes or the next byte is 0xff, then we continue with Case 4 optimization techniques. The efficient simulation code for reading bits to C in Case 3 is given in Pcode 5.26.

Optimization of Case 4

In Case 4, we use all the previously suggested techniques of Cases 1 through 3. In this case, we handle the normalization process in two parts to avoid a bit-by-bit process of normalization as given in the JPEG 2000 standard. In the first part, we read up to 8 bits to C when the normalization bits is less than or equal to 8. The second part handles instances in which the normalization bits are more than 8 to read up to 15 bits to C as shown in Pcode 5.27. Although Case 4 looks a little complex, this occurs rarely when compared to other cases.

Computational Complexity with Optimized MQ-Decoder

We estimate the computational complexity of the MQ-decoder in terms of memory and clock cycles consumed in executing the optimized MQ-decoder. We use 0.25 kB of extra data memory (see look-up table **Jpeg_art**[ ]) with the optimized MQ-decoder. Since Cases 1 and 3 of the MQ-decoder do not occur frequently and Case 4

```
if (pJBA->CT <= 0){
        if((*(pJBA->BPST) != 0xff) && (*(pJBA->BPST+1) != 0xff)){
                pJBA->BPST++;
                r1 = *(pJBA->BPST);
                r1 = r1 << 8;
                pJBA->BPST++;
                r2 = *(pJBA->BPST);
                r1 = r1 | r2;
                pJBA->C = pJBA->C | (r1 << (-pJBA->CT));
                pJBA->CT+= 16;
        }
        else {
                // Case 4
        }
}
```

Pcode 5.26: Efficient implementation of bit FIFO for Case 3 of the MQ-decoder.

```
if (pJBA->CT <= 0){
  if((*(pJBA->BPST) != 0xff) && (*(pJBA->BPST+1) != 0xff)){
      // Case 3
  }
  else {
     if (pJBA->CT >= -8) {
        if(*(pJBA->BPST) != 0xff) { pJBA->BPST++;
           pJBA->C = pJBA->C | (*(pJBA->BPST) << (8 - pJBA->CT)); pJBA->CT+= 8;
        }
        else {
           if (*(pJBA->BPST+1) > 0x8f) {
               pJBA->C = pJBA->C + (0xff00 << (8 - pJBA->CT)); pJBA->CT+= 8;
           }
           else {pJBA->BPST++;
               pJBA->C = pJBA->C | (*(pJBA->BPST) << (7 - pJBA->CT)); pJBA->CT+= 7;
           }
        }
     }
     else {
        if(*(pJBA->BPST) != 0xff) { pJBA->BPST++;
           pJBA->C = pJBA->C | (*(pJBA->BPST) << 16); pJBA->CT+= 8;
        }
        else {
           if (*(pJBA->BPST+1) > 0x8f) {
               pJBA->C = pJBA->C + (0xff00 << 16); pJBA->CT+= 8;}
           else { pJBA->BPST++;
               pJBA->C = pJBA->C | (*(pJBA->BPST) << 15); pJBA->CT+= 7;
           }
        }
        if(*(pJBA->BPST) != 0xff) { pJBA->BPST++;
           pJBA->C = pJBA->C | (*(pJBA->BPST) << (8 - pJBA->CT)); pJBA->CT+= 8;
        }
        else {
           if (*(pJBA->BPST+1) > 0x8f) {
               pJBA->C = pJBA->C + (0xff00 << (8 - pJBA->CT)); pJBA->CT+= 8;
           }
           else { pJBA->BPST++;
               pJBA->C = pJBA->C | (*(pJBA->BPST) << (7 - pJBA->CT)); pJBA->CT+= 7;
           }
        }
     }
  }
}
```

Pcode 5.27: Efficient implementation of Case 4 of the MQ-decoder.

occurs very rarely, we assume the average cycle cost of the MQ-decoder as the cycles required for Case 2 (since it occurs more frequently). As seen in Pcode 5.25, the approximate cycle cost to run Case 2 of the MQ-decoder on the reference embedded processor is about 45 cycles. We consume a minimum of 50 cycles and a maximum of around 150 cycles for Case 2 of the MQ-decoder without applying any optimization techniques. Thus, with optimization techniques, we can clearly reduce the average-to-peak cycles count by 100.

5.5 Context-Based Adaptive Binary Arithmetic Coding

The H.264 standard (ITU-T H.264, 2005) uses a variant of the M-coder for entropy coding to compress and decompress the datastream. This entropy coding is known as the context-based adaptive binary arithmetic coding, or CABAC. See Section 5.1 for more details on the binary arithmetic coder (BAC). The H.264 standard's main profile defines three CABAC core routines for compressing/decompressing the bitstream: encode/decode binary symbol, encode/decode equiprobable binary symbol, and encode/decode terminate symbol. Out of these three core routines, encode and decode symbol routines are the more complex ones. In this section, we present an overview of the H.264 arithmetic coder encode and decode symbol routines, and we estimate the computational complexity of CABAC encode and decode symbol routines. Although the H.264 reference software (see *http://iphome.hhi.de/suehring/tml/*) is available in the public domain, it is written very inefficiently and cannot be used as is for real-time applications. Thus, we discuss here efficient implementation techniques for H.264 CABAC encode and decode symbol routines.

A few applications of the H.264 standard include digital video broadcasting, digital subscriber lines, personal media players, HDTV, video surveillance, digital media storage, and multimedia communications. Similar to the CABAC in the H.264/AVC standard, the JPEG 2000 standard (see Section 5.4) uses the MQ-coder for bitstream compression. The H.264 arithmetic coder is simpler than the MQ-coder. The MQ-coder (JPEG 2000) performs well when compared to VLCs and the bit savings is about 10% greater, whereas the H.264 arithmetic coder performs well when compared to the MQ-coder in terms of throughput and bit savings by 15 to 20% and 2 to 5%, respectively.

5.5.1 H.264 CABAC Overview

The basic parameters used for the CABAC encode symbol function are *Range* (interval), *Value* or *Low* (code value), {*State, MPS*} (context parameters), and *Obits* (outstanding bits). In the H.264 CABAC, unlike in the binary arithmetic coder, we do not have multiplications or divisions to perform interval subdivision. The interval subdivision is achieved using a look-up table with the given *Range* and *State* (a quantized probability value, obtained from the context model). The *Symbol* (also called as binary decision or bin, obtained after binarization of syntax elements defined by the H.264 standard) is coded as *MPS* (most probable symbol) or *LPS* (least probable symbol), depending on the *Symbol* and present *MPS* value. The parameters *Range*, *Value*, *State* and *MPS* are updated after coding of each *Symbol*. To keep the precision of *Range* within limits, normalization of *Range* and *Value* is performed whenever the value of *Range* becomes less than 256 (see Figure 5.11 on page 271). We will discuss more about the H.264 CABAC encode symbol function in Section 5.5.2, Encode Symbol.

The basic parameters used for the CABAC decode symbol function are *Range*, *Value*, {*State*, *MPS*}, and compressed/encoded *bitstream*. We divide the current interval *Range* with given *State* (or quantized probability value) into *MPS* and *LPS* intervals. We get the *LPS* interval (rLPS) from the look-up table **RangeLPS**[ ] and we compute *MPS* interval by subtracting rLPS from current *Range*. Depending on the *MPS* interval and *Value*, we decode the symbol as *MPS* or *LPS*. We update *Range*, *Value* and {*State*, *MPS*} after decoding of every symbol. To keep the precision of *Range* within the limits, renormalization of *Range* and *Value* is performed whenever the value of *Range* becomes less than 256 and *Value* is filled with the *bitstream* during the renormalization process (see Figure 5.11).

5.5.2 CABAC Symbol Coding

In video coding, we have various types of parameters (e.g., slice layer parameters, macroblock layer parameters, prediction modes, motion vectors, residual coefficients) to encode (compress data) or decode (decompress data) using an entropy coder. The H.264 standard uses a special name for all these parameters: syntax elements. The H.264 standard defines various types of syntax elements along with the contexts {*State*, *MPS*} for coding different type of parameters. Over 460 contexts for different types of syntax elements are defined in the H.264 standard.

As the entropy coder CABAC of the H.264 works with binary data, we convert the syntax elements (nonbinary valued data) to binary *Symbols* (*bins*) using a binarization process (which is defined in the H.264 standard for each type of syntax elements) for encoding nonbinary syntax elements. In the same way, we apply a corresponding debinarization process for decoded *Symbols* to build the syntax element value for particular parameters. A context is a probability model for one or more *bins* of the binarized syntax element. This probability model may be chosen from a set of available models depending on the statistics of recently coded syntax elements. As an example, the syntax element value, *bins*, and associated context parameters {*State*, *MPS*} (which are not as per H.264 standard) for CABAC of the residual coefficient value 6 follow:

```
Syntax element (residual coefficient): 6
After binarization (Symbols or bins): 1 1 1 1 1 0
Contexts (for each bin): {21, 1}, {23, 0}, {24, 0}, {27, 1}, {28,0}, {29,1}
```

For each image slice (a video frame may contain multiple slices) encoding or decoding, we initialize *Range*, *Value*, and context {*State*, *MPS*} parameters of the CABAC. The associated context parameters of syntax elements are updated when coding those syntax elements. The H.264 CABAC encode and decode symbol process is shown in Figure 5.10. At the transmitter side, we perform the CABAC encoder operations (e.g., binarization, symbol coding, context model update) and generate compressed bitstream which we transmit after processing by a signal chain (include modules like channel coding, modulation, filtering, etc.) through a noisy channel. At the receiver, we receive the *bitstream* at the end of the receiver signal chain (includes filters, demodulation, data error correction, etc.). This *bitstream* corresponds to encoded bits. Signal chain blocks in the transmitter and receiver are not shown in Figure 5.10.

In the H.264 CABAC, the symbol coding engine consists of three steps: (1) interval subdivision, (2) CABAC parameters update, and (3) normalization process. In the interval subdivision, we divide the current interval *Range* into *LPS* and *MPS* intervals. With the CABAC symbol coding routine, we code the *Symbol* as either *LPS* or *MPS* and update the CABAC parameters correspondingly. After updating the CABAC parameters, we check the value of *Range* and if it is below 256, then we perform normalization of *Range* to make sure the *Range* is above 256. In doing normalization, we also normalize *Value* which produce (in encoder) or consume (in decoder) the *bitstream* during the normalization process.

Encode Symbol

The flow chart diagram of the H.264 CABAC encode symbol routine is shown in Figure 5.11. Inputs to the encode symbol function are *Range*, *Value*, {*State*, *MPS*} and *Obits* and outputs are the updated CABAC parameters and *bitstream*. According to *Range* and *State*, we get rLPS (an *LPS* interval range) using the look-up table **RangeLPS**[ ]. We compute *MPS* interval *Range* by subtracting rLPS from the current interval *Range*. Then, depending on the current *Symbol* and *MPS*, we code the *Symbol* as either *MPS* or *LPS* and update the parameters correspondingly. After updating the CABAC parameters, we check the value of *Range* and whether the *Range* is less than 256, then we perform the encoder normalization process. The H.264 CABAC encoder normalization process is a multi-iteration process as shown in Figure 5.11. In every iteration, we double the value of *Range* and compare it with 256 (to confirm whether *Range* is greater than or equal to 256 or not). If *Range* is greater

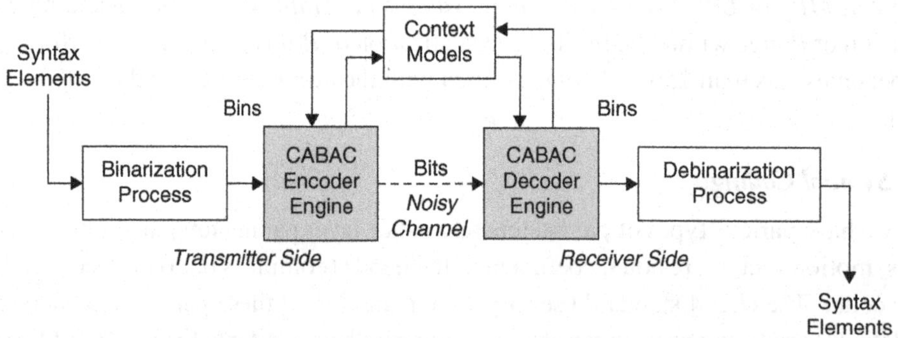

Figure 5.10: H.264 CABAC symbol coding process.

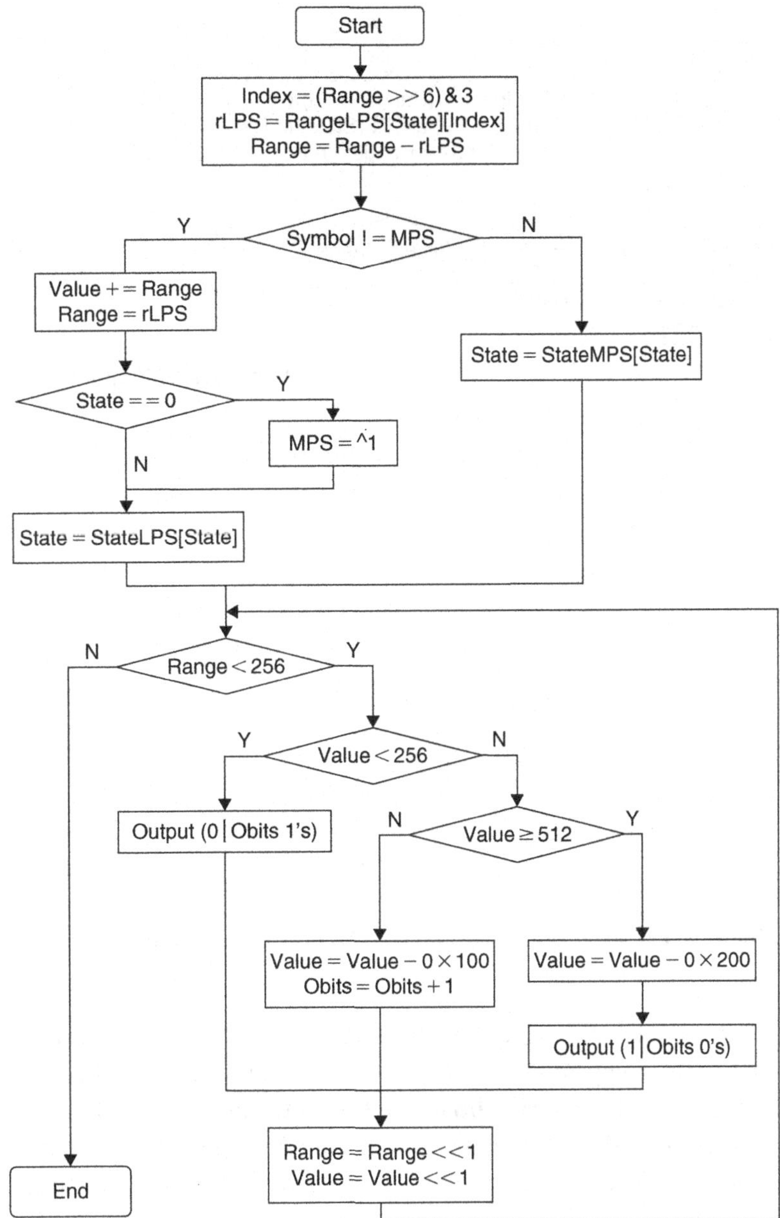

Figure 5.11: Flow chart diagram of the H.264 encode binary symbol.

than or equal to 256, then we quit the normalization process loop. During the normalization process, we also normalize *Value* and output bits, depending on *Value* (to avoid overflow) in each iteration.

Decode Symbol

The flow chart diagram of the H.264 CABAC decode symbol routine is shown in Figure 5.12. Inputs to the decode symbol function are *Range*, *Value*, {*State*, *MPS*} and *bitstream* and outputs are the updated CABAC parameters and decoded *Symbol*. Based on *Range* and *State*, we get the rLPS (an *LPS* interval range) using the look-up table **RangeLPS**[ ]. We compute the *MPS* interval *Range* by subtracting rLPS from the current interval *Range*. Then, depending on *Value* and *Range*, we decode either the *LPS* or *MPS* by updating the corresponding parameters. Then, we perform the normalization of *Range* and *Value* in multiple iterations if the value of *Range* is less than 256. During the normalization process, we update *Value* with the input *bitstream*.

CABAC Symbol Coding Simulation

We simulate CABAC symbol encoding (or decoding) using the flow chart diagrams shown in Figure 5.11 (or Figure 5.12). We use three look-up tables (defined by the H.264 standard) in CABAC symbol coding interval

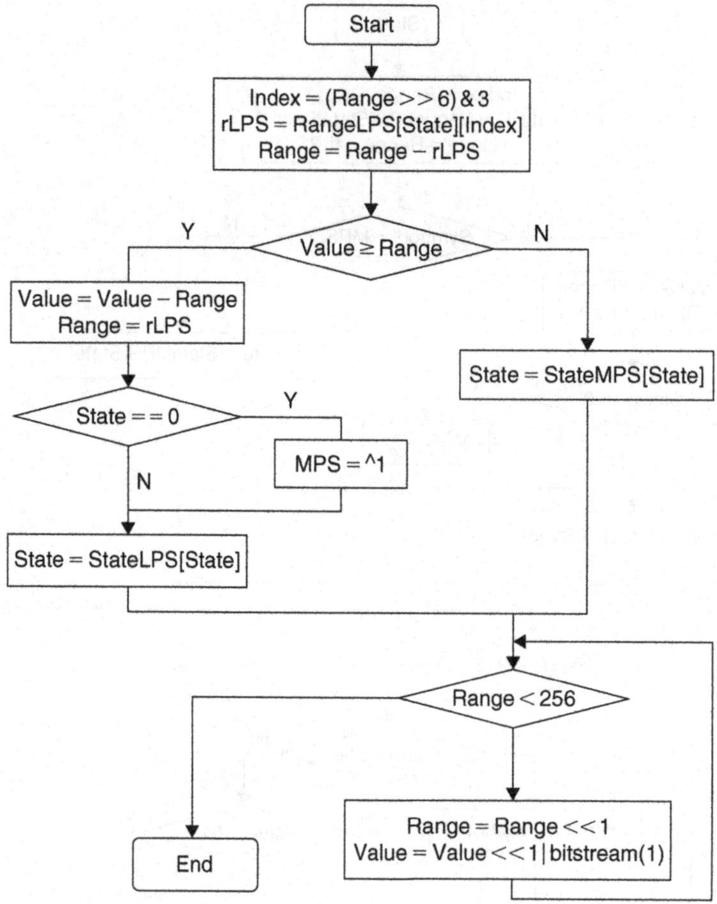

Figure 5.12: Flow chart diagram of CABAC decode symbol routine.

subdivision and parameters update; the values for the three look-up tables **RangeLPS**[ ], **StateLPS**[ ], and **StateMPS**[ ] can be found on the companion website. The simulation code for CABAC encode symbol is given in Pcode 5.28 and the simulation code for **write_bits**( ) (or **Output**( ) in Figure 5.11) is given in Pcode 5.29. The simulation code for the CABAC decode symbol is given in Pcode 5.30. We use the **read_bits**( )—or **bit_stream**( ) in Figure 5.12—function in the CABAC decode symbol routine to read bits from the *bitstream* buffer.

We use the following parameters structure in CABAC symbol coding:

```
typedef struct H264BacPars_tag
{
        int Range;
        int Low;
        int State;
        int MPS;
        int Obits;
        int Symbol;
        int byteoffset;
        int bitpos;
} H264BacPars_t;

H264BacPars_t BAC, *pBAC;
```

5.5.3 CABAC Symbol Coding Complexity

As seen in Figures 5.11 and 5.12, the CABAC symbol coding consists of many sequential and conditional operations (unlike other video coding block processing modules such as DCT transform, motion compensation and so on, where we don't have a conditional flow of operations). In some cases, the input of present operation depends on the output of the previous operation and we do not have much scope to interleave the program code.

```
pBAC = &BAC;
tmp = (pBAC->Range>>6)&3;
rLPS = RangeLPS[4*pBAC->State + tmp];
pBAC->Range = pBAC->Range - rLPS;
if (pBAC->Symbol == pBAC->MPS)
        pBAC->State = StateMPS[pBAC->State];
else {
        pBAC->Low = pBAC->Low + pBAC->Range;
        pBAC->Range = rLPS;
        if(pBAC->State == 0)
                pBAC->MPS = 1-pBAC->MPS;
        pBAC->State = StateLPS[pBAC->State];
}
while(pBAC->Range < 256) {
       if(pBAC->Low >= 512) {
               pBAC->Low-=512;
               write_bits(1,1);
               if(pBAC->Obits > 0) {
                       write_bits(0,pBAC->Obits);
                       pBAC->Obits = 0;
               }
       }
       else if(pBAC->Low < 256) {
                write_bits(0,1);
                if(pBAC->Obits > 0){
                        write_bits(1,pBAC->Obits);
                        pBAC->Obits = 0;
                }
       }
       else {
                pBAC->Obits++;
                pBAC->Low -= 256;
       }
       pBAC->Range = pBAC->Range << 1;
       pBAC->Low = pBAC->Low << 1;
}
```

Pcode 5.28: Simulation code for CABAC encode symbol.

```
tmp = dat[pBAC->byteoffset];
for (i=0;i<n;i++) {
    tmp = tmp << 1 | b;
    pBAC->bitpos = pBAC->bitpos - 1;
    if(pBAC->bitpos == 0) {
        dat[pBAC->byteoffset] = tmp;
        pBAC->byteoffset++;
        pBAC->bitpos = 8;
    }
}
dat[pBAC->byteoffset] = tmp;
```

Pcode 5.29: Simulation code for write_bits( ) function.

The first two parts, interval subdivision and parameters update, of the CABAC symbol encoder and decoder has similar flow in terms of computations. In the interval subdivision (see Pcode 5.28 or Pcode 5.30), we have to perform the following operations in dividing *Range*.

```
tmp1 = Range >> 6; tmp2 = 4*State;
tmp1 = tmp1 & 3;
index = tmp1 + tmp2;
rLPS = RangeLPS[index];    //LPS interval
Range = Range – rLPS;      //MPS interval
```

Dividing *Range* into *MPS* and *LPS* intervals takes around 9 to 10 cycles on the reference embedded processor as the rLPS value, after accessing from the look-up table, is used immediately in computing *Range*, which stalls the processor 3 to 4 cycles. The next step is coding the *Symbol* as *MPS* or *LPS*. This process involves

```
tmp = (pBAC->Range>>6)&3;
rLPS = RangeLPS[4*pBAC->State + tmp];
pBAC->Range = pBAC->Range - rLPS;
pBAC->Symbol = pBAC->MPS;
if (pBAC->Value < pBAC->Range)
        pBAC->State = StateMPS[pBAC->State]; //MPS decode
else {
        pBAC->Value = pBAC->Value - pBAC->Range;
        pBAC->Range = rLPS;
        pBAC->Symbol = 1 - pBAC->MPS;
        if (pBAC->State == 0)
                pBAC->MPS = 1-pBAC->MPS;
        pBAC->State = StateLPS[pBAC->State]; //LPS decode
}
while (pBAC->Range < 256){
        pBAC->Range = pBAC->Range << 1;
        pBAC->Value = (pBAC->Value << 1) | (read_bits(1));
}
//Output is pBAC->Symbol
```

Pcode 5.30: Simulation code for CABAC decode symbol.

one conditional jump to choose between *LPS* path or *MPS* path, update of *Range*, update of *Value*, conditional update of *MPS* and one memory access to update *State*. These operations consume around 10 to 15 cycles to update parameters. Based on the previous analysis, the first two parts of the CABAC symbol coding routines take around 25 cycles.

CABAC Encode Symbol Normalization

In the H.264 encode symbol routine given in Pcode 5.28, the normalization process has many conditional jumps in a "while loop." This process is costly in terms of cycles as it performs normalization 1 bit at a time with many jumps. In addition to this, writing encoded bits to memory using the **write_bits**( ) function (or **Output**( ); see Figure 5.11) with normalization of *Value* is a very complex operation. We have to perform the following operations every time for writing 1 bit to the memory buffer.

1. Read unfilled word from buffer (tmp = dat[wordoffset])
2. Shift the word left by 1 bit (tmp = tmp << (1)
3. OR the present bit "*b*" with the shifted word (tmp = tmp| b)
4. Store the ORed word to memory (dat[wordoffset] = tmp)
5. Reduce the bitpos by 1 (bitpos = bitpos – (1)
6. Check whether the bitpos is equal to zero (bitpos == 0)
7. If bitpos is zero, then increment the wordoffset by 1 and reset the bitpos to 32 (wordoffset = wordoffset + 1; bitpos = 32)

The procedure for writing bits to memory as just described is not part of the H.264 standard. But this function is needed to write the bits to the buffer. Typically, the data is stored to memory in bytes (8 bits), halfwords (16 bits) or words (32 bits) for easy addressing. When we want to store the encoded bits to a memory, first the bits are packed into bytes or words, and then they are stored in a memory. The procedure described previously packs the bits into 32-bit words and then stores them to the data buffer. We choose the 32-bit word instead of 8-bit byte because we are going to spend fewer cycles in storing words than bytes with fewer memory accesses (once for every 32 bits instead of 8 bits). To pack the bits to 32-bit words, we use the bit counter (or bitpos) to know how many bits are still needed to fill a 32-bit word. Every time we fill the word with a bit, we reduce the bit count by 1. When the bit count is zero, the word is full with 32 bits and that word is stored to the buffer and the bit counter is reset to 32.

To implement the previous procedure of packing bits to a word before storing to memory on the reference embedded processor, we need a minimum of 10 cycles. Now if we want to do two bits of normalization (i.e., the loop count is two) with outstanding bits (*Obits*) equal to zero, it takes around 30 to 40 cycles (including jumps and other operations) depending on *Value*. In addition to this, sometimes storing of *Obits* to memory in the normalization process will become a lengthy task as the upper limit on *Obits* count according to the standard is given by the number of encoding decisions present in a slice. This shows the complexity of the normalization process and the necessity of its optimization.

CABAC Decode Symbol Normalization

The decode symbol normalization is also a multi-iterative process. In each iteration, we shift left the values *Range* and *Value* by 1 bit and the LSB of *Value* is filled with 1 bit by reading 1 bit from the *bitstream* buffer. The complexity of reading bits from the memory buffer is the same as writing bits to the memory buffer. Therefore, a single iteration of the decode symbol normalization process consumes about 13 cycles (10 cycles for memory read and three cycles for left shifts and appending the bit to *Value*).

5.5.4 Efficient CABAC Symbol Coding

As seen in Section 5.5.3, the CABAC symbol coding consumes a minimum of 45 cycles for encoding and 35 cycles for decoding of one symbol. The compression ratio achieved with the H.264 CABAC coding engine is about 1.1. It means that the ratio of the number of input symbols to the number of output bits in the CABAC coder is approximately 1.1. If we work with 1 Mbps bit rate, then the H.264 CABAC symbol coding routine called approximately 1 million times per second and encode (or decode) symbol routine only consumes about 45 (or 35) MIPS of the embedded processor. In this section, we will discuss efficient simulation of the CABAC symbol coding routines.

Interval Subdivision and Parameters Update

On the reference embedded processor, the conditional jumps are too costly. Instead of jumping conditionally we can update parameters by moving the values conditionally. To reduce the number of conditional moves and memory accesses, we pack *State* and *MPS* and access through one look-up table (that consists of *State* for both *LPS* or *MPS* path and effective *MPS* value). Because of this, the new *State* look-up table becomes four times bigger when compared to original *State* (*LPS* or *MPS*) look-up tables. The look-up table design also includes the conditional update of *MPS* based on the current value of *State*. The offset calculation for look-up table access is based on *MPS* value and the condition with which we decide whether *MPS* or *LPS* path is used to code the *Symbol*. Thus, the encode symbol new *State* look-up table consists of a total of four parts. In each part, the codeword consists of next *State* information (LSB byte) and effective *MPS* value (MSB byte). The efficient simulation code for the first two parts of the encode decision routine is given in Pcode 5.31 and the new derived look-up table with (*MPS* | *State*) for the efficient CABAC encode symbol is available on the companion website.

```
tmp = pBAC->Range >> 6;
tmp = tmp & 3; offset = pBAC->State << 2;
offset = offset + tmp;
rLPS = RangeLPS[offset];
flag = (pBAC->MPS == pBAC->Symbol);
offset = flag << 7; tmp = pBAC->MPS << 6;
offset = offset + tmp;
pBAC->Range = pBAC->Range - rLPS;
if (!flag) pBAC->Low = pBAC->Low + pBAC->Range; if (!flag) pBAC->Range = rLPS;
tmp = StateTbl[pBAC->State + offset];
pBAC->State = tmp & 0xff; pBAC->MPS = tmp >> 8;
```

Pcode 5.31: Simulation code for CABAC encode symbol (without normalization).

We use a structure pointer pBAC = &BAC, where BAC = {*Range*, *Value*, *State*, *MPS*, *Obits*, *Symbol*, wordoffset, bitpos}, to handle the CABAC code parameters.

For the CABAC decode symbol routine, the aforementioned new *State* look-up up table can be used. As the decoder outputs *Symbol* information from present context *MPS* value, we can also embed this information into a new *State* look-up table by using the MSB of previous look-up table elements for *Symbol* or by adding 1 more byte to each element of the look-up table to represent *Symbol*. The simulation codes for the CABAC decode symbol (without normalization) is given in Pcode 5.32. As seen in Pcodes 5.31 and 5.32, the CABAC decode symbol routine flow is different from encode symbol routine flow and consumes five more cycles. With

```
tmp = pBAC->Range >> 6;
tmp = tmp & 3; offset = pBAC->State << 2;
offset = offset + tmp;
rLPS = RangeLPS[offset];
pBAC->Range = pBAC->Range - rLPS; //3 to 4 stalls
flag = (pBAC->Value >= pBAC->Range);
offset = flag << 7; tmp = pBAC->MPS << 6;
offset = offset + tmp;
if (!flag) pBAC->Value= pBAC->Value + pBAC->Range; if (!flag)pBAC->Range = rLPS;
tmp = StateTbl[pBAC->State + offset];
pBAC->State = tmp & 0xff; pBAC->Symbol = tmp >> 15;
tmp = tmp & 0x7fff;
pBAC->MPS = tmp >> 8;
```

Pcode 5.32: Simulation code for CABAC decode symbol (without normalization).

this simulation, we consume (without normalization process) approximately 14 cycles for the CABAC encode symbol routine and 20 cycles for the CABAC decode symbol routine on the reference embedded processor.

Normalization Process

In H.264 CABAC, we perform the normalization process to keep the value of *Range* greater than or equal to 256. Hypothetically, the "while" loop in the normalization can be avoided if we precompute the number of times the loop is going to repeat. Mathematically the while loop count is equal to the value of log2 [256/*Range*]. In other words, if we have an instruction which gives the lead zeros with respect to halfword or word boundary, then we can get the value of log2[256/*Range*]. In the simulation code, we precompute the loop count using a "while" loop. This loop count indirectly gives us the number of bits to normalize for the *Range* in the encode (or decode) symbol routine and the number of bits needs to write (or read) to (or from) the buffer (along with the outstanding bits in the case of the encode symbol routine) depending on *Value*. With this, in a single pass we can do the total normalization process.

Encode Symbol Normalization Process

The implementation of the "while" loop bit-by-bit normalization process of the encode symbol routine as it is on the reference embedded processor is not an acceptable implementation due to its heavy conditional flow. As described previously, we precompute the loop count for normalization to avoid iterative process. But the problem of writing a variable number of outstanding bits to memory will become complex in this case. The problem of storing outstanding bits will be there even if we use the bit-by-bit "while" loop implementation. With the precompute of the "while" loop count approach, the logic for writing the bits to the buffer will become more complicated because of arbitrary parameter values of loop count (or number of normalization bits), *Value* and *Obits* (the number of outstanding bits).

With the assumption of sufficient on-chip memory available, a look-up table based approach will eliminate most of the logic to implement the precompute loop count encode symbol normalization process. Now the question is how much on-chip memory is required for implementation of this look-up table based approach? Assuming the minimum value of *Range* that can go according to the H.264 standard as 2 (which means at most 7 bits of *Range* left shift is required), then the maximum loop count required is 7 (represented with 3 bits). This means that the analysis of 3 bits of loop count information, 8 bits of *Value* (as explained later the MSB of *Value* may flip based on the value of *Value* after normalization process) and variable number of outstanding bits is required. Assuming the number of outstanding bits as "n," the memory size required for the look-up table is $2\hat{}(3+8+\log2(n))*4*(n/8)$ bytes. According to the H.264 standard, the maximum limit on n is as high as 4,147,200 for a full D1-size video slice (which has $720\times480\times1.5\times8$ bits); implementing such a look-up table method is impractical. However, this methodology is a base for the efficient normalization approach that is described in the following.

The loop count and outstanding bits count are two important parameters used in the implementation of the look-up table based method. If we run the reference encoder with a few test vectors to get the statistics for these two parameters, then the histograms of those two parameters are obtained as shown in Figure 5.13. As seen in

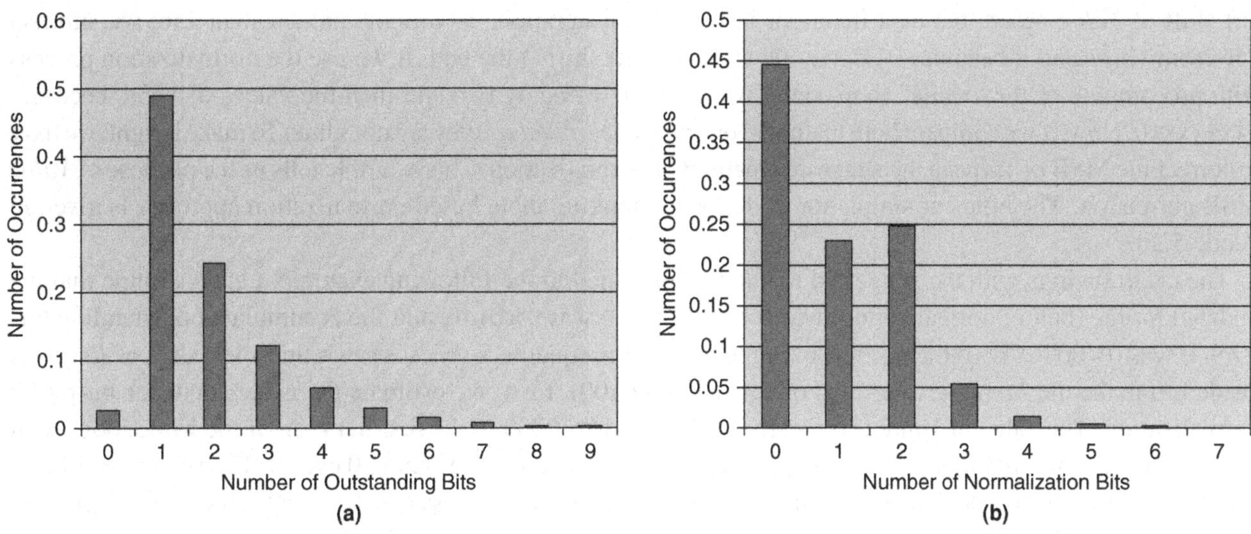

Figure 5.13: Histograms. (a) Outstanding bits. (b) Normalization bits.

the histograms, though the maximum number of outstanding bits according to the standard is much higher, the statistics show that the outstanding bits greater than 7 occur only in 2% of cases. Similarly, the normalization bits greater than 3 occur in only 3% of cases. Thus, if we consider 7 outstanding bits and 3 normalization bits for look-up table generation, almost 97% of the time we are going to use the look-up table for normalization process and the remaining 3% of the time we jump out and implement the costly bit-by-bit normalization process. The memory size required to implement the look-up table based approach for the previous parameters is $2^{(4+3+2)*}4*(7/8) = 2\,\text{kB}$. This makes a good trade-off between cycles and memory.

The look-up table codeword contains the following information: (1) updated *Obits* (4 bits), (2) actual bits information that go to the buffer (0 to 10 bits), (3) length of bits that go to the buffer (4 bits), and (4) a flag (1 bit) for *Value*'s MSB correction after normalization. Each codeword contains 19 bits of information and these bits may be packed such that they will be easily accessed from memory. The next example presents the functionality of the suggested method.

Example 5.4

Offset: 9 bits = loop count (2 bits) | *Obits* (3 bits) | *Value* (4 MSBs)
Codeword: *n* (4 bits) | bits (10 bits) | *Obits* (4 bits) | Flag (1 bit)
Look-up table size (or memory requirement): 512 entries (512*4 = 2 kB)
Loop count = 3, *Obits* = 6, *Value* (4 MSBs) = 1101
Offset = 0x1ed (Hex) = 11 110 1101 (bin)
Look-up table codeword: **1000** 0000 **1000 0001** 0000 **0001** 0000 0000

Iteration	*n*	Bits	*Obits*	Flag
1	7	1000000	0	1
2	8	10000001	0	0
3	8	10000001	1	0 → store to look-up

■

The purpose of *Value*'s MSB correction is more easily explained with an example. Let us consider the 10-bit value of *Value* as 1011xxxxxx with 4 MSBs of *Value* equal to 1011. If we normalize bit-by-bit as per the standard (as shown in Figure 5.11), after 2 bits of normalization we end up with *Value* as 01xxxxxx00. In the first iteration, as *Value* is greater than 512, we subtract 512 from *Value* and it becomes 011xxxxxx0 after one left shift of *Value* before the next iteration. In the second iteration, as *Value* is greater than 256, we subtract 256 from *Value* and it becomes 01xxxxxx00 after one left shift at the end. If we use the normalization process with precompute of the "while" loop count, we left shift *Value* by two and then the values of *Value* becomes 11xxxxxx0. Now, if we compare both methods' output values of *Value*, they are not same. To make it right, we have to correct the MSB of *Value* in the suggested method of normalization. This example tells us the purpose of *Value* MSB correction. The efficient simulation code for the look-up table based normalization approach is given in Pcode 5.33.

The cycle savings with the suggested method is explained in the following example. Let us assume that the updated *Range* (before normalization) was 0×0060, *Value* was 0×0140, and the accumulated outstanding bits (*Obits*) was 0×0006. Then the normalization loop count is equal to 2 (because two times left shift of *Range* is needed to make the *Range* greater than or equal to 0×0100). First, we estimate the cycle count for bit-by-bit normalization. The value of *Value* is between 0×0100 and 0×0200 in the first iteration of the while loop. As it involves two conditional jumps and four arithmetic operations, it takes around 20 cycles. The accumulated outstanding bits become 0×0007 in the first iteration. The value of *Value* is less than 0×0100 in the second iteration, so here we needed to write bit "0" to memory. In addition, we have to write 7 outstanding bits in this iteration. A total of 8 bits of storing (80 cycles), two conditional jumps (16 cycles) and four ALU operations (4 cycles) are present in the second iteration. This adds up to a total of 100 cycles. The estimate of total number of cycles consumed by bit-by-bit normalization for the previous example is about 120 cycles.

Now we estimate the cycle count for the suggested method. In this case, the loop count is computed in advance, and it takes 2 cycles (1 cycle for lead zeros and 1 cycle for correction) on the reference embedded processor. As the loop count and outstanding bits are within limits (which takes 3 cycles to confirm), we compute the offset

```
tmp = 0;
while (pBAC->Range < 256) {          //precompute loop count
  pBAC->Range = pBAC->Range << 1;
  tmp++;
}
if ((tmp<=3) && (pBAC->Obits <= 7)) { //single flow normalization process
   x1 = pBAC->Low >> 6; x2 = pBAC->Obits << 4;
   x1 = x1 + x2; x3 = tmp << 7;
   x1 = x1 + x3; pBAC->Low = pBAC->Low << tmp;
   //x1: offset for look-up table, x1[8:7]->nbits, x1[6:4]->obits, x1[3:0]-> MSB Value
   c = NormTbl[x1]; //c[31]-> flag, c[26:24]-> obits, c[19:16]-> length of bits, c[9:0]->actual bits
   //c[31:28]-> length of bits, c[27:16]-> actual bits, c[15:8]-> obits, c[0]->flag
   pBAC->Low = pBAC->Low & 0x1ff; flag = c & 1;
   pBAC->Low = pBAC->Low | (flag << 9); tmp = c << 16;
   x2 = tmp >> 24; x3 = c >> 28; x1 = c & 0x0fff0000;
   pBAC->Obits = x2; x1 = x1 >> 16;
   if (x3) { //write bits to memory
      pBAC->bitpos = pBAC->bitpos - x3; x2 = 32;
      tmp = datx[pBAC->wordoffset]; c = x1 << pBAC->bitpos;
      if (pBAC->bitpos < 0) c = x1 >> (-pBAC->bitpos);
      tmp = c | tmp; c = x2 + pBAC->bitpos;
      datx[pBAC->wordoffset] = tmp; x1 = x1 << c;
      datx[pBAC->wordoffset + 1] = x1;
      if (pBAC->bitpos <= 0) pBAC->wordoffset++;
      if (pBAC->bitpos <= 0) pBAC->bitpos+= 32;
   }
}
else {
  while (tmp > 0) {  //do bit-by-bit normalization as described in Pcode 5.28
   tmp = tmp - 1;
   if ((tmp<=3) && (pBAC->Obits <= 7))
         break;
  }
  //continue previously described normalization process when tmp and obits are within limits
}
```

Pcode 5.33: Simulation code for look-up table based encode symbol normalization process.

to access the look-up table. With this, we consume 10 cycles (6 for offset and 4 for loading) to get the look-up table value. Then unpacking of parameters to store in memory takes around 10 cycles. Then packing bits to the word for storing takes another 10 cycles. This adds up to a total of 35 cycles to perform the normalization for the previous example. We may not benefit by using the suggested method if the loop count is 1, and the accumulated outstanding bits are zero for the normalization process. The normalization look-up table **NormTbl**[ ] values, which are used in the suggested method, can be found on the companion website.

As we skip the normalization process when *Range* is greater than or equal to 256 (i.e., loop count = 0), the first 512 bytes of the look-up table are not used in the normalization process. To reduce the memory usage with the suggested method for efficient simulation of the H.264 binary arithmetic coder encode symbol routine, we can utilize these 512 bytes of memory to store **StateTbl**[ ] look-up values. With this change, the total memory usage of encode symbol routine including a look-up table of **RangeLPS**[ ] is equal to 2.25 kB.

Decode Symbol Normalization Process

With precompute of "while" loop count, the decode symbol normalization process will become very simple as the normalization of *Range* and *Value* and number of bits to be read from memory just depend on loop count. The simulation code for decode symbol normalization is given in Pcode 5.34.

```
r0 = 0;
while (pBAC->Range < 256) { //precompute loop count
        pBAC->Range = pBAC->Range << 1;
        r0++;
}
if (r0) {//read bits from memory
          pBAC->Value = pBAC->Value <<r0; r1 = 32;
          r2 = bit_stream[pBAC->wordoffset]; r3 = bit_stream[pBAC->wordoffset + 1];
          r4 = r1 - pBAC->bitpos; r5 = r1 - r0;
          r2 = r2 << pBAC->bitpos; r3= r3 >> r4;
          r2 = r2 + r3; pBAC->bitpos = pBAC->bitpos - r0;
          r2 = r2 >> r5;
          if (pBAC->bitpos <= 0) pBAC->wordoffset++;
          if (pBAC->bitpos <= 0) pBAC->bitpos+= 32;
          pBAC->Value = pBAC->Value | r2;
}
```

Pcode 5.34: Simulation code for decode symbol normalization process.

Further Optimization of Decode Symbol Normalization Process

On a limited MIPS embedded processor, the decoder software modules have to be optimized to the maximum extent to run in real time. The cycle cost (from Pcode 5.34) of reading bits (bit FIFO) from the memory buffer **bit_stream**[ ] is about 14 cycles. The cycle cost for reading bitstream can be reduced to 5 cycles by reading bits in terms of 16-bit blocks from the buffer instead of an arbitrary number of bits. By shifting *Value* 22 bits to the left and working with an upper halfword for *Value* (MSB aligned) manipulation and lower halfword for bit FIFO functionality, we can reduce the cycle cost of bits reading from buffer **bit_stream**[ ]. For this, we have to place *Range* and rLPS values in upper halfwords by shifting 22 bits. At the time of the initialization of *Value*, we initialize *Value* with 32 bits instead of 9 bits and set bit position as 16 instead of 23. Now, to access bit FIFO and updating **bit_stream**[ ] buffer parameters (bitpos and wordoffset), we spend about 7 cycles in simulation code as given Pcode 5.35.

5.5.5 Simulation Results

We assume few **Symbols** (or bins, which are obtained after binarization of syntax elements) to encode and decode using CABAC. In addition, we assume the corresponding context values {**State**, **MPS**} for **Symbols** coding as follows:

```
Ctx[20][2] = {{24,1},{18,1}, {14,1}, {21,0}, {12,0}, {4,1}, {1,0}, {0, 1}, {18, 1}, {10,0}, {5, 0},
{17,1}, {11,0}, {2, 1}, {16, 0}, {20, 0}, {7, 1}, {8, 0}, {3, 1}, {9, 1}};
```

```
r0 = 0;
while ( pBAC->Range < 256) { //precompute loop count
        pBAC->Range = pBAC->Range << 1;
        r0++;
}
pBAC->Value = pBAC->Value <<r0;
pBAC->bitpos = pBAC->bitpos - r0;
if (pBAC->bitpos <= 0) {
        pBAC->bitpos+= 16;
        r1 = bit_stream[pBAC->wordoffset++];
        r1 = r1 << pBAC->bitpos;
        pBAC->Value = pBAC->Value | r1;
}
```

Pcode 5.35: Efficient simulation of decode symbol normalization.

Encode Symbol

```
Input: Symbols[20] = {1,1,1,0,0,0,0,0,1,0,1,1,0,0,0,1,1,1,1,1}; //bins
Initialization:
  pBAC->Range = 0x1fe;
  pBAC->Value = 0;
  pBAC->Obits = 0;
  pBAC->bitpos = 32;
  pBAC->wordoffset = 0;
Intermediate outputs after encoding 1 symbol:
  pBAC->Range = 0x01b9
  pBAC->Value = 0x0000
  pBAC->Obits = 0
  pBAC->bitpos = 32
  pBAC->wordoffset = 0
Intermediate outputs after encoding 5 symbols:
  pBAC->Range = 0x0146
  pBAC->Value = 0x0000
  pBAC->Obits = 0
  pBAC->bitpos = 31
  pBAC->wordoffset = 0
Intermediate outputs after encoding 10 symbols:
  pBAC->Range = 0x0115
  pBAC->Value = 0x0060
  pBAC->Obits = 3
  pBAC->bitpos = 30
  pBAC->wordoffset = 0
Intermediate outputs after encoding 20 symbols:
  pBAC->Range = 0x01a8
  pBAC->Value = 0x0178
  pBAC->Obits = 0
  pBAC->bitpos = 17
  pBAC->wordoffset = 0
bitstream at end of 20 symbols encoding (includes a few dummy encoded bits):
  bit_stream[] = {0x001e78f1, 0x00000000, 0x00000000, 0x00000000,… }
```

Decode Symbol

```
Input: Encoded bitstream[].
  bit_stream[] = {0x001e78f1, 0x00000000, 0x00000000, 0x00000000,… }
Initialization:
  pBAC->Range = 0x01fe;
  pBAC->Value = 0x0079;
  pBAC->wordoffset = 0;
  pBAC->bitpos = 13;
Intermediate outputs after decoding 1 decision:
  pBAC->Range = 0x01b9;
  pBAC->Value = 0x0079;
  pBAC->wordoffset = 0;
  pBAC->bitpos = 13;
Intermediate outputs after decoding 5 decisions:
  pBAC->Range = 0x0146;
```

```
   pBAC->Value = 0x00f3;
   pBAC->wordoffset = 0;
   pBAC->bitpos = 12;
Intermediate outputs after decoding 10 decisions:
   pBAC->Range = 0x0115;
   pBAC->Value = 0x00dc;
   pBAC->wordoffset = 0;
   pBAC->bitpos = 8;
Intermediate outputs after decoding 20 decisions:
   pBAC->Range = 0x01a8;
   pBAC->Value = 0x006a;
   pBAC->wordoffset = 1;
   pBAC->bitpos = 30;
Decoded symbols:
   bins[20] = {1,1,1,0,0,0,0,0,1,0,1,1,0,0,0,1,1,1,1,1}; // Symbols
```

Part 2

Digital Signal and Image Processing

CHAPTER 6

Signals and Systems

Raw signals are processed using signal-processing algorithms (e.g., DFT, DCT, FIR filters, IIR filters, correlation, LMS and RLS adaptive filters, and so on, to be discussed in subsequent chapters) to get the desired signal output. Signal processing algorithms have many applications, including telecommunications, medical, aerospace, radar, sonar, and weather forecasting. Real-time processing of signals for many applications is possible with advances in semiconductor technology. This chapter addresses the fundamentals of signals and signal processing.

6.1 Introduction to Signals

A signal is a measure of physical phenomenon such as temperature, pressure, electric voltage, and radioactive decay, with respect to time or space. If we measure temperature during a day from 6 AM to 6 PM and plot the values, the plot may resemble Figure 6.1. Typically, the x-axis (or horizontal axis) is used to represent the independent variables (e.g., time, space) and the y-axis (or vertical axis) is used to represent the measured quantity (e.g., weight, amplitude) of dependent variables (e.g., temperature, voltage).

Figure 6.1 shows how the temperature measured from 6 AM to 6 PM on a particular day varies with time. We call such a measured quantity with respect to time a *signal*. The temperature signal cannot be calculated using a well-defined mathematical equation (because it depends on many factors such as weather, season, Earth orientation, etc.). Such signals are *random*. On the other hand, the behavior of signals that can be exactly predicted by mathematical equations is called *deterministic*. Examples of deterministic signals are sine waves, square waves, and staircase signals.

6.1.1 Deterministic Signals

Deterministic signals can be expressed precisely with mathematical formulas. In this subsection we will discuss various basic signals that appear in subsequent chapters focused on signal processing.

Sinusoidal Functions

Sinusoidal signals play an important role in signal processing applications. Here we discuss various representations of a sinusoidal signals. The simple representation of a sinusoidal signal (abbreviated as sin) is $y(t) = \sin(t)$. This means that the value of a sinusoid at time t is $y(t)$, and the plot of $y(t) = \sin(t)$ is shown in Figure 6.2.

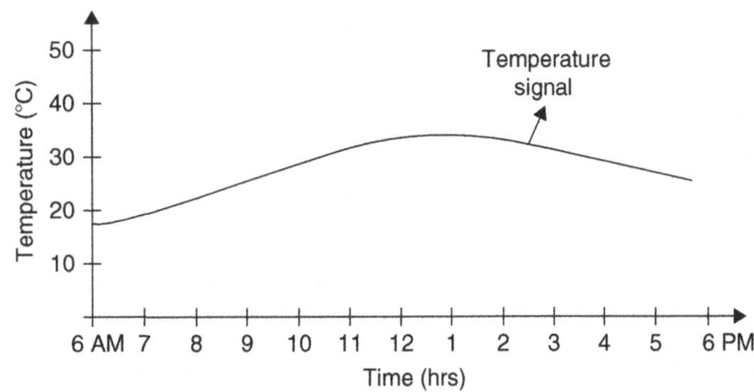

Figure 6.1: Signal representation of temperature (in °C) from 6 AM to 6 PM.

DOI: 10.1016/B978-1-85617-678-1.00006-5

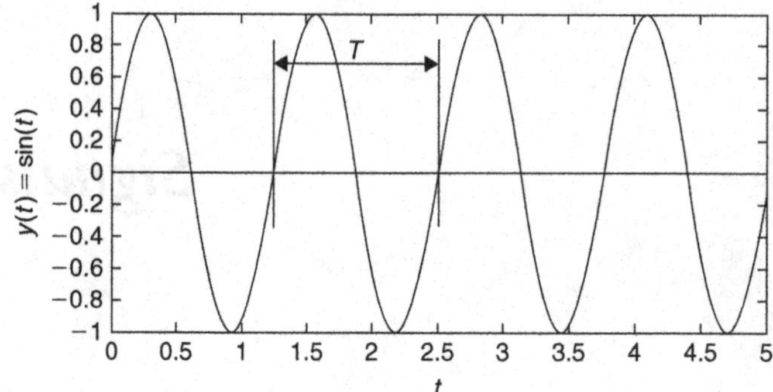

Figure 6.2: Sine waveform $y(t) = \sin(t)$.

As seen in Figure 6.2, the sine wave is periodic with period T, meaning that it repeats itself in regular intervals of time T. However, with the sine wave representation $y(t) = \sin(t)$, the sine wave period is not transparent in the equation. In addition, we cannot say how many times the sine wave repeats in one unit of the time interval. Therefore, we represent the sine wave in a more transparent way:

$$y(t) = \sin(2\pi ft) \tag{6.1}$$

Using the sine wave representation given in Equation (6.1), we obtain more information about the sine wave. For example, if we plot $y(t) = \sin(2\pi ft)$ for $f = 1$, 2, and 3 as shown in Figure 6.3(a), (b), and (c), we can clearly see that parameter f controls the number of cycles present in one unit of the time interval. With $f = 1$, we have one cycle of the sine wave in one unit of the time interval. With $f = 2$, we have two cycles of the sine wave in one unit of the time interval and so on. If T is the period of the sine wave, then $f = 1/T$ is the frequency of the sine wave. If time T is measured in seconds, then the quantity f gives the cycles per second. One cycle per second is equivalent to 1 hertz (Hz). With the sine wave representation in Equation (6.1), we can easily determine the number of cycles present in 1 second or we can know the frequency of the sine wave. The sine wave notation given in Equation (6.1) is commonly used in all signal processing algorithms.

A more general form of sinusoidal function can be expressed as follows:

$$x(t) = A\sin(2\pi ft + \phi) = A\sin(\omega t + \phi) \tag{6.2a}$$

where A is the peak amplitude, ϕ is the initial phase (or phase offset), and $\omega = 2\pi f$, is the angular frequency (measured in radians/second). The quantity $\omega t + \phi$ gives the instantaneous phase of the sinusoid in radians. Figure 6.4(a) and (b) show how the amplitude and phase offset modify the pure sinusoid function. When the phase value $\phi = \pi/2$, we have a special case and the resulting waveform is called a cosinusoid (or cos) function, as shown in Figure 6.4(c) with the dotted line. This means that $\sin(\omega t)$ lags $\cos(\omega t)$ by $\pi/2$ radians (or 90°) or $\cos(\omega t)$ leads $\sin(\omega t)$ by 90°.

Cosine and sine are often represented in complex number notation to perform signal processing tasks more efficiently. In particular, the multiplication and division operations on sinusoids become very easy with complex number representation. From the phasor (i.e., a rotating vector) diagram shown in Figure 6.4(d), the rectangular coordinates (a, b) are obtained from the polar coordinates $(A, \omega t)$ as $a = A\cos\omega t$ and $b = A\sin\omega t$. Using the famous Euler formula,

$$a + jb = A(\cos\omega t + j\sin\omega t) = Ae^{j\omega t} \tag{6.2b}$$

Based on Equation (6.2b), $a = A\cos\omega t = \mathrm{Re}(Ae^{j\omega t})$ and $b = A\sin\omega t = \mathrm{Im}(Ae^{j\omega t})$.

If $P = a + jb = Ae^{j\omega t}|_{t=t_n}$, then the amplitude $A = |P| = \sqrt{a^2 + b^2}$, and the instantaneous phase $\omega t_n = \angle P = \tan^{-1}\left(\frac{b}{a}\right)$. Note that A is the distance of the point P from the origin. For this reason, A is also called the *magnitude*.

The conjugate of P is called P^*, and we define the conjugate P^* as $P^* = a - jb = Ae^{-j\omega t}$. With this, the multiplication of two complex numbers (indirectly sinusoid values) $P_1 = A_1 e^{j\omega_1 t}$ and $P_2 = A_2 e^{j\omega_2 t}$ can be computed easily as $P_1 P_2 = A_1 A_2 e^{j(\omega_1 + \omega_2)t}$, and the division of two complex numbers P_1 and P_2 is computed as

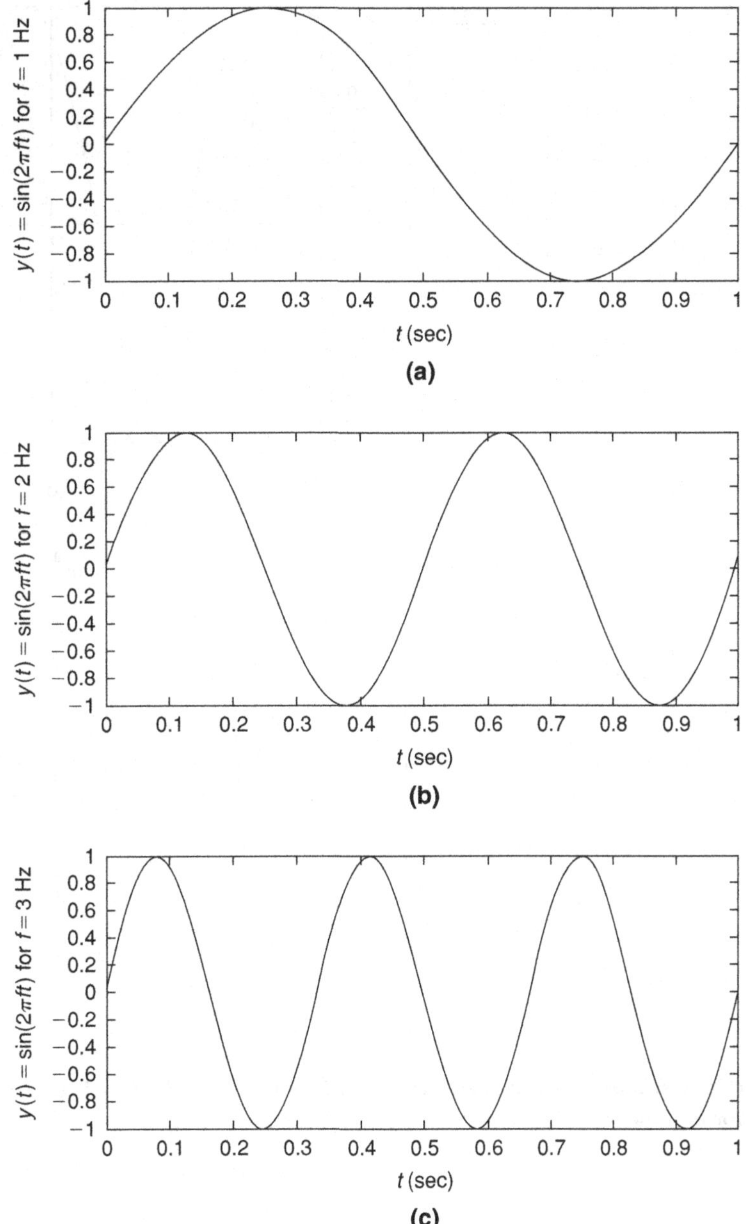

Figure 6.3: Plots of the sine wave: (a) $f = 1$ Hz, (b) $f = 2$ Hz and (c) $f = 3$ Hz.

$P_1/P_2 = P_1P_2^*/P_2P_2^* = (A_1/A_2)e^{j(\omega_1-\omega_2)t}$. As additions and subtractions are easy to perform using rectangular coordinates, we frequently switch between polar and rectangular coordinates in the computations involving sinusoids.

Selected Important Deterministic Signals

Dirac Delta Function or Impulse Function The Dirac delta function is an interesting and ideal function that is used for many theoretical purposes. The Dirac delta function $\delta(t)$ is defined as follows:

$$\delta(t) = \begin{cases} \infty & \text{if } t = 0 \\ 0 & \text{otherwise} \end{cases} \tag{6.3}$$

The signal diagram of the Dirac delta function is shown in Figure 6.5(a).

An important property of the Dirac delta function is that it integrates to 1 when we find the area under this function. This can be visualized as shown in Figure 6.5(b). The area of the rectangle shown is 1 (since area = width × height = $a \times 1/a = 1$). Now, what happens if a approaches zero? In the limiting case, we will

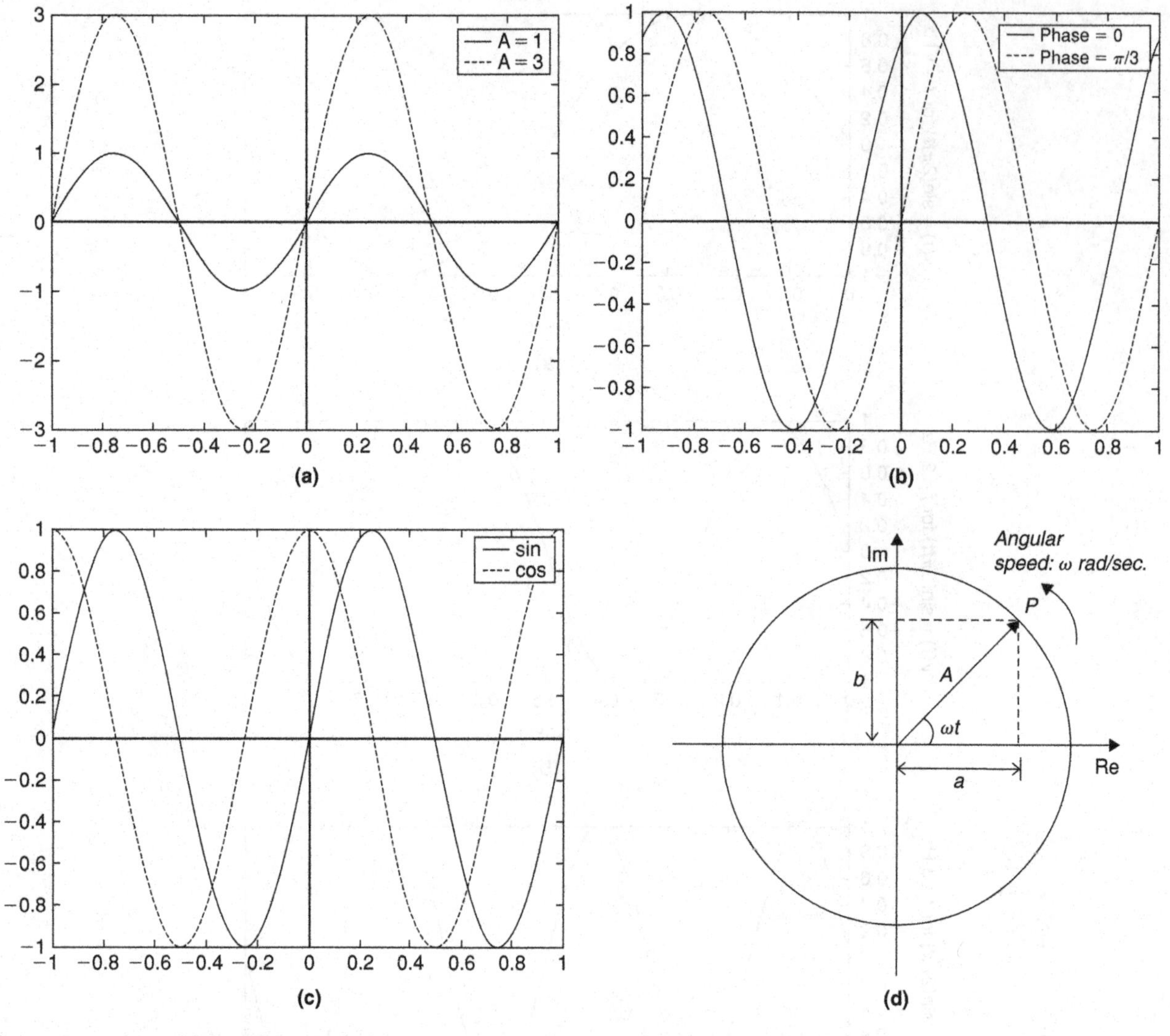

Figure 6.4: Sinusoid functions and phasor representation. (a) $f = 1, \phi = 0$. (b) $f = 1, A = 1$. (c) Relation between sine and cosine. (d) Phasor representation.

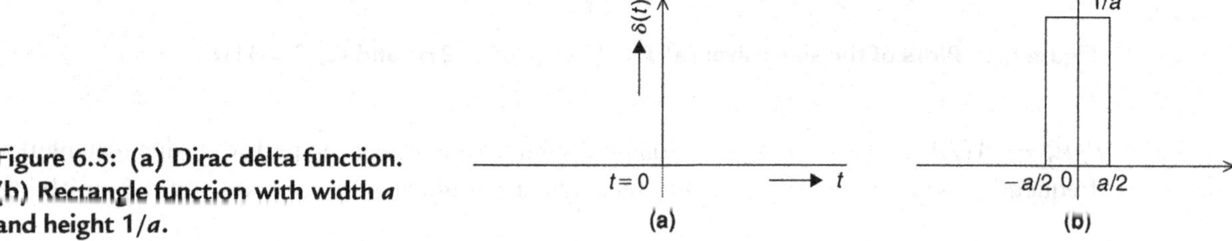

Figure 6.5: (a) Dirac delta function. (b) Rectangle function with width a and height $1/a$.

have the Dirac delta with the unit area. If we multiply any function $f(t)$ with the Dirac delta function $\delta(t)$ and integrate, we get $f(0)$, the value of function $f(t)$ at $t = 0$. Similarly, if we multiply $f(t)$ with $\delta(t-T)$, a shifted version of the Dirac delta by time T, and integrate, we get $f(T)$, the value of the function $f(t)$ at $t = T$.

Constant Function

A constant function $c(t)$, also referred to as DC value, is defined as follows:

$$c(t) = C \quad -\infty < t < \infty$$

Figure 6.6 shows a signal diagram of the constant function.

Rectangular Pulse

A rectangular pulse $r(t)$ with width T and constant height C is defined as

$$r(t) = \begin{cases} 0 & \text{if } t < -T/2 \\ C & \text{if } -T/2 \leq t \leq T/2 \\ 0 & \text{if } t > T/2 \end{cases} \tag{6.4}$$

and a schematic diagram of the rectangular pulse is shown in Figure 6.7.

Unit Step Function

A unit step function $u(t)$ is defined as

$$u(t) = \begin{cases} 0 & \text{if } t < 0 \\ 1 & \text{if } t \geq 0 \end{cases} \tag{6.5}$$

and a signal diagram of the unit step function is shown in Figure 6.8.

Signum Function

A signum function, sgn(t), is defined as follows:

$$\text{sgn}(t) = \begin{cases} -1 & \text{if } t < 0 \\ 0 & \text{if } t = 0 \\ 1 & \text{if } t > 0 \end{cases} \tag{6.6}$$

Figure 6.9 shows a signal diagram of the sgn(t) function. Any real value x can be expressed as the product of its absolute value and its signum function as $x = |x|\text{sgn}(x)$.

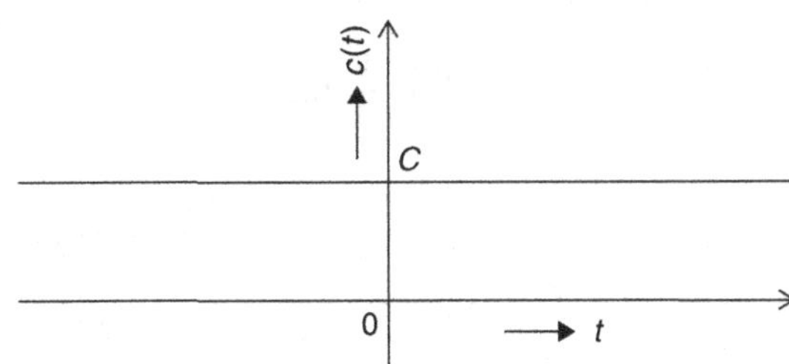

Figure 6.6: Signal diagram of constant function.

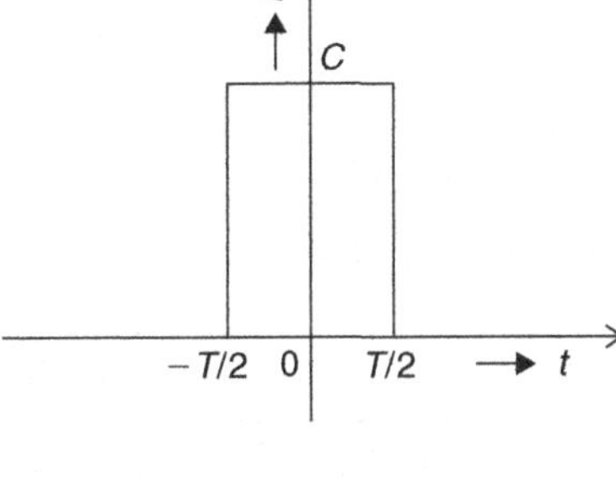

Figure 6.7: Signal diagram of rectangular pulse function.

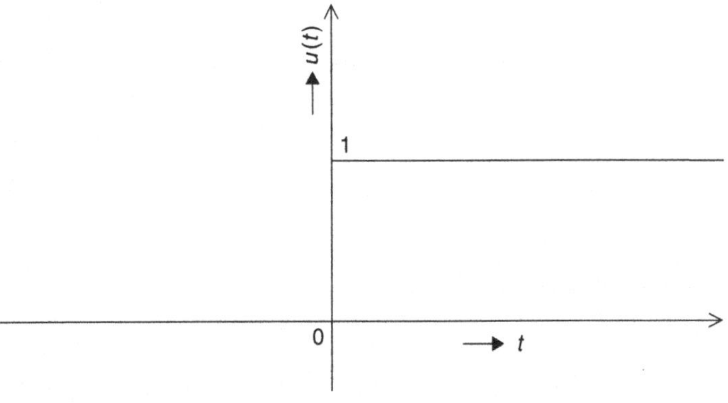

Figure 6.8: Signal diagram of unit step function.

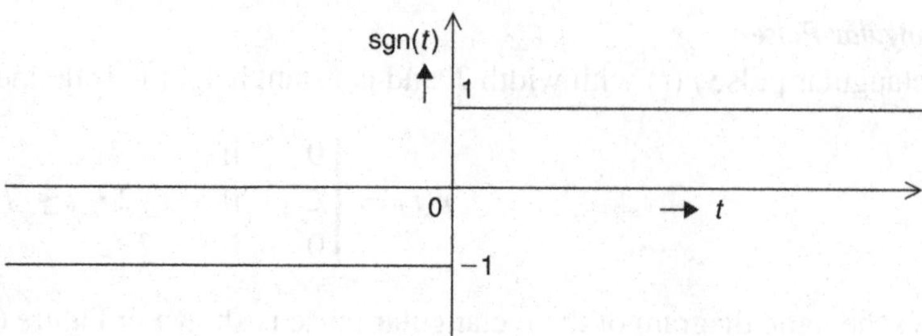

Figure 6.9: Signal diagram of signum function.

Sinc Function

The sinc function is widely used in signal processing and communication systems. Its two versions are the un-normalized sinc function, and the normalized sinc function, as given in Equations (6.7) and (6.8), respectively.

The un-normalized sinc function is defined as

$$\text{sinc}(t) = \frac{\sin(t)}{t}, \quad -\infty < t < \infty \tag{6.7}$$

As shown in Figure 6.10, the zero-crossings of the un-normalized sinc function are at multiples of $\pi(\approx 3.14)$. The normalized sinc function is defined as

$$\text{sinc}(t) = \frac{\sin(\pi t)}{\pi t}, \quad -\infty < t < \infty \tag{6.8}$$

As shown in Figure 6.11, the zero-crossings of the normalized sinc function occur at non-zero integer values. The normalized sinc function has important properties that make it ideal in relation to interpolation (since $\text{sinc}(0) = 1$ and $\text{sinc}(k) = 0$ for non-zero integers of k) and band-limited functions (if $x_k(t) = \text{sinc}(t-k)$, then $x_k(t)$ form an orthonormal basis for band-limited functions in $L^2(R)$ function space). The sinc function is also related to the Dirac delta function as follows:

$$\lim_{a->0} \frac{1}{a}\text{sinc}(t/a) = \delta(t) \tag{6.9}$$

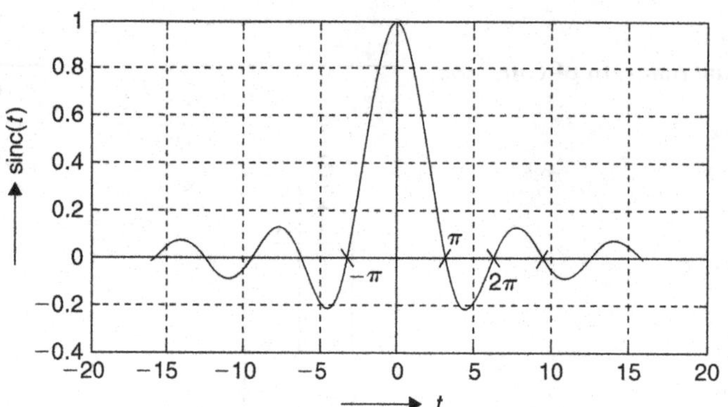

Figure 6.10: Unnormalized sinc(*t*) function.

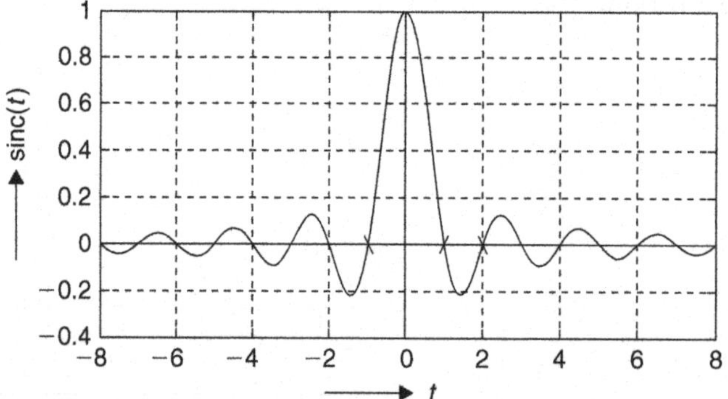

Figure 6.11: Plot of normalized sinc function.

6.1.2 Random Signals

Unlike deterministic signals, random signals are not so easy to handle. Random signals cannot be generated by simple, well-defined mathematical equations, and their future values cannot be predicted. Rather, we must use probability and statistics to analyze their behavior. The plot of one such random signal $y(t)$ is shown in Figure 6.12. As the random signal pattern varies from time to time, processing individual random signals does not make sense; instead we process *ensembles* (groups of random signals). At this juncture, you might ask: Why do I need to study random signals? Why do I need to process them? The answer is simple. In the real world (in nature), deterministic signals are always associated with random noise (see Section 9.1.2 for details on noise generation and measurement in a communication system environment).

To analyze deterministic signals, first we have to minimize the effect of noise, and for this we have to process (measure, classify, and eliminate) the random signals (or noise). To process the random signals, we use statistical measures such as mean, variance, standard deviation, and so on. Before going into statistical measure definitions, we introduce the concepts of random variable and random process. Examples are provided of random variables and random processes to present the overview of random signals. For definitions and fundamentals of random variables and processes, see Papoulis (1984) and Leon-Garcia (1994).

Random Variables

Typically, we process numerical data with digital computers. However, the output of an experiment (or events in a sample space) need not be a number. For example, if we conduct an experiment of tossing a coin, then the outcome of that experiment is a head or tail. The sample space (or all outcomes) of this coin experiment is $S = \{\text{head, tail}\}$. We cannot measure the output of the sample space of some experiments (e.g., {head, tail} of the coin experiment). Now, if we map these events (or subsets of the sample space) to a measurable space through a mapping function X, then we call such mapping function X a *random variable*. If we choose the measurable space as real numbers, then the random variable X maps the sample space to real numbers. For example, the head and tail events of a coin-tossing experiment may be mapped to $+0.5$ and -0.5 through random variable X. But, you may ask, why do we need a random variable?

If we toss a coin, how long will it take to get the first head? How can we answer such a question? The head may appear in the 1st, 2nd, 5th, or 10th toss, and so on. Clearly, we cannot answer such a question with a single number. However, using the random variable concept, we can answer the preceding coin-tossing experiment question in probabilistic terms.

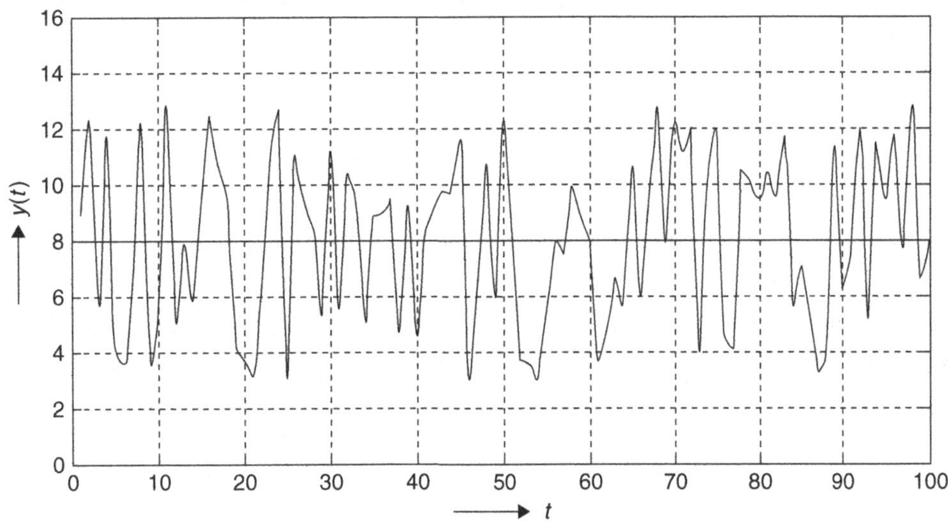

Figure 6.12: Plot of random signal.

Let X be a random variable mapping the event of first head in a coin-tossing experiment conducted N times. Let Ω_i be the outcome of a coin-toss experiment with probabilities

$$\Pr(\Omega_1 = \text{Head}) = p \text{ and } \Pr(\Omega_2 = \text{Tail}) = q = 1 - p \text{ with } \sum_{j=1}^{2} \Pr(\Omega_j) = 1$$

For an unbiased coin, $p = q = 0.5$. Assume, in the m-th experiment, that we get the first head. Then $\Pr(X = \text{first head}) = q^{m-1}p$. Similarly, in a dice-throwing experiment, we will have six outcomes of the dice facing up with 1, 2, 3, 4, 5, and 6. Now, assume that we want to know the probability that the event of a dice-throwing experiment never exceeds 4. We can answer this question in the same way as the coin-tossing experiment using the concept of a random variable with $\Pr(X$ less than or equal to 4) $= 2/3$ by assuming equal probabilities for all six outcomes.

Continuous and Discrete Random Variables

The outcome of an experiment need not be always discrete such as in the coin-tossing experiment. If we consider the lifetime of an electric bulb, then it can be any time until the bulb burns out. If the random variable represents the lifetime of an electric bulb, then that random variable takes continuous rather than discrete values. If a random variable can take only a finite number of distinct values, then it must be discrete. On the other hand, a continuous random variable is one that takes on an infinite number of possible values. Typically, discrete random variables apply to countable events, and continuous random variables apply to measurable events. The examples of discrete random variables include the number of heads showing up when we toss a coin 10 times, the number of defective bulbs in an electronics store, the number of passengers in a train, and so on. Examples for continuous random variable include the output voltage level of an electric circuit, the temperature at a given time, travel time between cities, and so on.

Probability Mass, Probability Density, and Cumulative Distribution Functions

In general, the random variable X is associated with a probability. Typically, the probability mass function (pmf) is used with discrete random variables, whereas the probability density function (pdf) is used for continuous random variables. The probability distribution of a discrete random variable is a list of probabilities associated with each possible outcome that are represented by a random variable. If X is a discrete random variable with associated probability mass function $f_X(x)$, and if x_i represents an i-th value in the range of random variable X then $f_X(x_i) = \Pr(X = x_i)$. For example, if we conduct an experiment of tossing a coin 10 times and the outcome of heads mapped to measurable space with random variable X, then the random variable takes 10 discrete values x_i, where $0 \le i \le 10$ and index i represents the count of heads in each experiment. The probability of x_k (i.e., to get k heads) is given by

$$\Pr(X = x_k) = \binom{10}{k} p^k (1-p)^{10-k}$$

where p is the probability of a head. For an unbiased coin (i.e., the probability of getting a head is equal to the probability of getting a tail is equal to 0.5), the pmf for the random variable X is shown in Figure 6.13. The probability of getting zero heads is $f_X(x_0) = \Pr(X = x_0) = \frac{1}{2^{10}}$, the probability of getting one head is $f_X(x_1) = \Pr(X = x_1) = \frac{10}{2^{10}}$, and so on. The pmf always satisfies the following two conditions:

$$0 \le f_X(x_i) \le 1$$

$$\sum_i f_X(x_i) = 1$$

Given a random variable X, the probability function $F_X(x) = \Pr(X \le x)$, where x is any real number in the interval $(-\infty, \infty)$, is called its cumulative distribution function (cdf). The function $F_X(x)$ is a nondecreasing

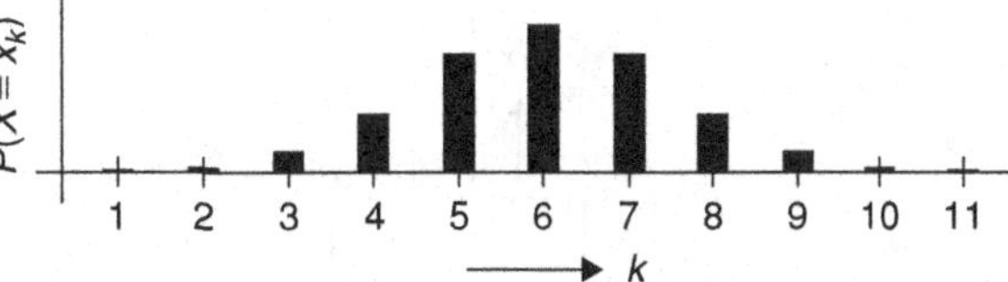

Figure 6.13: Probability mass function for getting heads in tossing a coin 10 times.

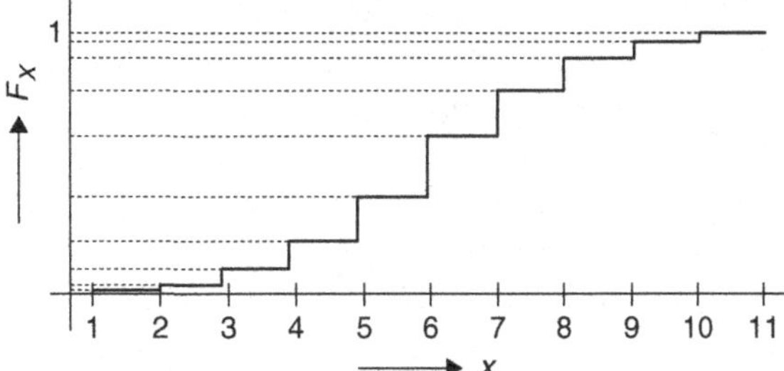

Figure 6.14: Cumulative distribution function for getting heads in tossing a coin 10 times.

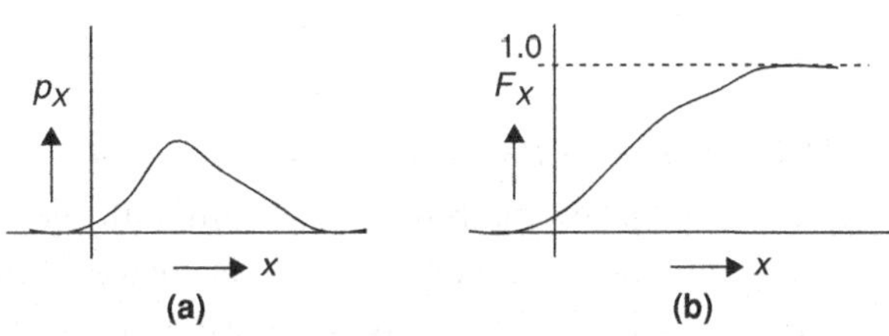

Figure 6.15: Continuous random variable. (a) pdf. (b) cdf.

function and satisfies the following conditions:

$$0 \leq F_X(x) \leq 1$$

$$F_X(-\infty) = 0 \text{ and } F_X(+\infty) = 1$$

$$\Pr(x_1 < X \leq x_2) = F_X(x_2) - F_X(x_1)$$

The cdf of the coin-experiment random variable, whose pmf appears in Figure 6.13, is shown in Figure 6.14. In the case of discrete random variables, the associated cdf always has jumps in the distribution curve as shown in Figure 6.14.

Like discrete random variables, continuous random variables are associated with the probability density function (pdf). As shown in Figure 6.15(a) and (b), both the pdf and cdf of a continuous random variable are smooth, unlike discrete random variable probability functions. In some practical problems, we may also encounter a random variable of mixed type. The cdf of such a random variable is a smooth, nondecreasing function in certain parts of the real line, and contains jumps at certain discrete values of x.

The pdf, $p_X(x)$, of the continous random variable can be obtained by differentiating the cdf $F_X(x)$. Thus, we have

$$p_X(x) = \frac{dF_X(x)}{dx}, \quad -\infty < x < \infty \tag{6.10}$$

$$F_X(x) = \int_{-\infty}^{x} p_X(y)dy, \quad -\infty < x < \infty \tag{6.11}$$

The two most popularly used probability distributions in signal processing are the uniform and Gaussian. The uniform distribution function is used to generate random numbers in a given interval. The pdf $p_X(x)$ and the cdf $F_X(x)$ of a uniform random variable are shown in Figure 6.16(a) and (b). The Gaussian distribution is widely used in digital media processing applications for noise modeling; the pdf and cdf of a Gaussian distributed random variable is shown in Figure 6.17(a) and (b), respectively.

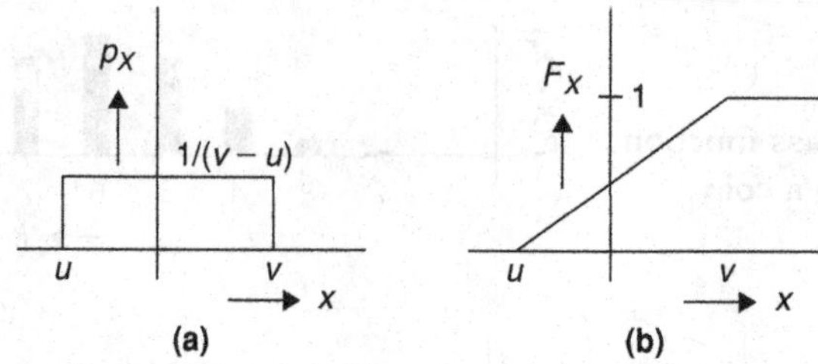

Figure 6.16: Uniform distribution: (a) pdf and (b) cdf.

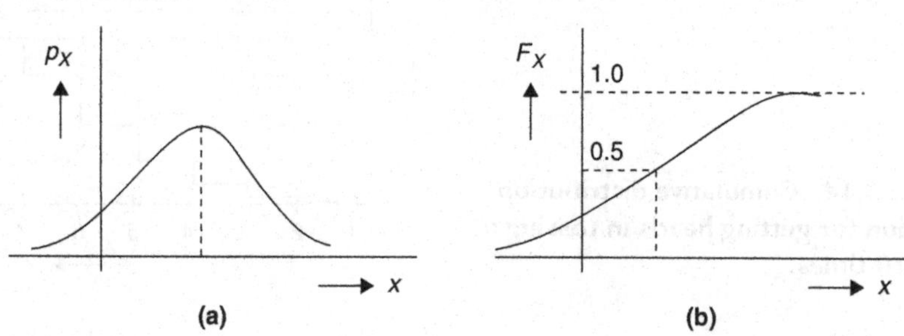

Figure 6.17: Gaussian distribution: (a) pdf and (b) cdf.

Multiple Random Variables and the Joint Probability Density Function

In practice, we encounter random phenomena resulting from multiple sources instead of just a single source. We measure the events or random variables of combined experiments using joint probabilities. Let us consider two random variables X_1 and X_2, each of which may be continuous, discrete, or mixed. The joint cdf for the two random variables is defined as

$$F_{X_1,X_2}(x_1,x_2) = \Pr(X_1 \le x_1, X_2 \le x_2) = \int_{-\infty}^{x_1}\int_{-\infty}^{x_2} p_{X_1,X_2}(y_1,y_2)dy_1dy_2 \tag{6.12}$$

or, equivalently,

$$p_{X_1,X_2}(x_1,x_2) = \frac{\partial^2}{\partial x_1 \partial x_2} F_{X_1,X_2}(x_1,x_2) \tag{6.13}$$

When the joint pdf $p_{X_1,X_2}(x_1,x_2)$ is integrated over one of the variables, we obtain the density function of the other variable as follows:

$$\int_{-\infty}^{\infty} p_{X_1,X_2}(x_1,x_2)dx_1 = p_{X_2}(x_2), \qquad \int_{-\infty}^{\infty} p_{X_1,X_2}(x_1,x_2)dx_2 = p_{X_1}(x_1) \tag{6.14}$$

The pdfs $p_{X_2}(x_2)$ and $p_{X_1}(x_1)$ obtained from the joint probability by integrating over the other random variable are called *marginal* pdfs.

Conditional Probability Density Functions

In some cases, we may have an idea about one random phenomenon in a combined experiment (e.g., *a priori* knowledge of symbol sets that are transmitted to the receiver). If one random variable X_1 is given, then we obtain the conditional pdf of another random variable X_2 as follows:

$$p_{X_2|X_1}(x_2|x_1) = \frac{p_{X_1,X_2}(x_1,x_2)}{p_{X_1}(x_1)} \tag{6.15}$$

Here, $p_{X_2|X_1}(x_2|x_1)$ is called the probability density of X_2 given X_1. We also express the joint pdf $p_{X_2,X_1}(x_2,x_1)$ in terms of the conditional pdfs as in the following:

$$p_{X_1,X_2}(x_1,x_2) = p_{X_2|X_1}(x_2|x_1)\cdot p_{X_1}(x_1) = p_{X_1|X_2}(x_1|x_2)\cdot p_{X_2}(x_2) \tag{6.16}$$

Bayes Theorem

Given Equation (6.16), we can write $P(x_1|x_2)$ as

$$p_{X_1|X_2}(x_1|x_2) = \frac{p_{X_2|X_1}(x_2|x_1).p_{X_1}(x_1)}{p_{X_2}(x_2)} \tag{6.17}$$

The Bayes theorem is a simple mathematical formula used for calculating conditional probabilities. Equation (6.17) represents the simplest form of the Bayes theorem. The theorem simply allows the new information to be used to update the conditional probability of a random variable in a combined experiment. For example, we can consider a digital communication system as a combined experiment representing the transmitted messages as mutually exclusive events with random variable X_1. Let us say that M messages are transmitted in a given time interval and $\Pr(x_{1i})$ represents the i-th message *a priori* probability. Assume that X_2 is a random variable of another event of the combined experiment, and X_2 represents the received noisy message that contains one of the M transmitted messages. Given X_2, the *a posteriori* probability of X_{1i} conditioned on having observed the received signal X_2 (i.e., $\Pr(x_{1i}|x_2)$) is obtained by using the generalized Bayes theorem as follows:

$$\Pr(x_{1i}|x_2) = \frac{\Pr(x_2|x_{1i}) \cdot \Pr(x_{1i})}{\Pr(x_2)} = \frac{\Pr(x_2|x_{1i}) \cdot \Pr(x_{1i})}{\sum_{j=1}^{M} \Pr(x_2|x_{1j})\Pr(x_{1j})} \tag{6.18}$$

Thus, if we assume that event X_2 arises with probability $\Pr(x_2|x_{1i})$ from each of the underlying messages $X_{1i}, i = 1, 2, \ldots, M$, we can use our observation of the occurrence of X_2 to update our *a priori* assessment of the probability of occurrence of each message, $\Pr(x_{1i})$, to an improved *a posteriori* estimate, $\Pr(x_{1i}|x_2)$.

Statistical Independence

What if the two random variables are not at all related (i.e., the occurrence of random variable X_1 has nothing to do with the occurrence of random variable X_2)? In this case, what happens to the conditional probability? If the occurrence of random variable X_1 does not depend on the occurrence of random variable X_2, then conditional pdfs $p_{X_1|X_2}(x_1|x_2) = p_{X_1}(x_1)$ and $p_{X_2|X_1}(x_2|x_1) = p_{X_2}(x_2)$. Based on Equation (6.16), $p_{X_1,X_2}(x_1, x_2) = p_{X_1}(x_1)p_{X_2}(x_2)$. Thus, if two random variables X_1 and X_2 are statistically independent, then their joint pdf $p_{X_1,X_2}(x_1, x_2)$ is given by the product of their individual pdfs $p_{X_1}(x_1)$ and $p_{X_2}(x_2)$. Similarly, for two statistically independent random variables X_1 and X_2, the joint cumulative distribution $F_{X_1,X_2}(x_1, x_2) = F_{X_1}(x_1)F_{X_2}(x_2)$. The notion of statistical independence can be easily extended to multiple random variables. If the N random variables $X_1, X_2, \ldots, X_N$ are statistically independent, then their joint pdf is a product of their individual pdfs as follows:

$$p_{X_1,X_2,\ldots X_N}(x_1, x_2, \ldots x_N) = p_{X_1}(x_1)p_{X_2}(x_2)\cdots p_{X_N}(x_N)$$

or equivalently,

$$F_{X_1,X_2,\ldots X_N}(x_1, x_2, \ldots x_N) = F_{X_1}(x_1)F_{X_2}(x_2)\cdots F_{X_N}(x_N)$$

Statistical Measures of Random Variables

Statistical measures play an important role in the overall characterization of an experiment and in the characterization of random variables defined on the sample space of an experiment. Popular statistical measures for single random variables are mean, variance and standard deviation; and for multiple random variables are correlation and covariance. These statistical measures are defined next.

The mean or expected value of a single continuous random variable X is defined as

$$E(X) = \mu_x = \int_{-\infty}^{\infty} x p_X(x) dx \tag{6.19}$$

where $E(.)$ denotes expectation used for statistical averaging. The expectation is also known as the first moment of a random variable X. In general, the n-th moment is defined as

$$E(X^n) = \int_{-\infty}^{\infty} x^n p_X(x)dx$$

If μ_x is the expected value of random variable X, then the n-th central moment is defined as

$$E[(X-\mu_x)^n] = \int_{-\infty}^{\infty} (x-\mu_x)^n p_X(x)dx \tag{6.20}$$

When $n = 2$, the second central moment is called the variance of a random variable, and is denoted by σ_x^2. Thus, the variance of random variable X is given by

$$\text{Var}(x) = \sigma_x^2 = \int_{-\infty}^{\infty} (x-\mu_x)^2 p_X(x)dx \tag{6.21}$$

Equation (6.21) can also be expressed in terms of first and second moments by expanding it as follows:

$$\sigma_x^2 = E(X^2) - \mu_x^2 \tag{6.22}$$

The variance of a random variable X gives the amount of spread from the mean value of distribution. If the variance of a random variable is large, then its probability distribution is also broader to that extent. The standard deviation σ_x is given by the square root of the variance.

Example 6.1

We can compute the statistical measures for the discrete random variable with pmf shown in Figure 6.13. Here, the random variable is the number of heads that show up when we toss a coin 10 times. With an unbiased coin, the probability of k heads in n experiments is given by

$$\Pr(X = k \text{ heads}) = \binom{n}{k} / 2^n$$

Table 6.1 shows the probability distribution values for $n = 10$.

The mean of the distribution follows:

$$\mu_x = \sum_{k=-\infty}^{\infty} x_k \Pr(X = x_k) = \sum_{k=0}^{10} x_k \Pr(X = x_k)$$

$$= \frac{0\times 1}{2^{10}} + \frac{1\times 10}{2^{10}} + \frac{2\times 45}{2^{10}} + \frac{3\times 120}{2^{10}} + \frac{4\times 210}{2^{10}} + \frac{5\times 252}{2^{10}} + \frac{6\times 210}{2^{10}}$$
$$+ \frac{7\times 120}{2^{10}} + \frac{8\times 45}{2^{10}} + \frac{9\times 10}{2^{10}} + \frac{10\times 1}{2^{10}} = 5$$

The distribution variance is obtained as follows:

$$\sigma_x^2 = \sum_{k=-\infty}^{\infty} (x_k-\mu_x)^2 \Pr(X = x_k) = \sum_{k=0}^{10} (x_k-\mu_x)^2 \Pr(X = x_k)$$
$$= (25+160+405+480+210+0+210+480+405+160+25)/2^{10} = 2.5$$

The standard deviation, then, is $\sigma_x = \sqrt{2.5} = 1.581$.

■

Table 6.1: Probability distribution for number of heads in a coin-tossing experiment

x_k = Number of Heads	$\Pr(X = x_k)$
0	$1/2^{10}$
1	$10/2^{10}$
2	$45/2^{10}$
3	$120/2^{10}$
4	$210/2^{10}$
5	$252/2^{10}$
6	$210/2^{10}$
7	$120/2^{10}$
8	$45/2^{10}$
9	$10/2^{10}$
10	$1/2^{10}$

Central Limit Theorem

The central limit theorem states that whenever a random sample z is taken from any distribution with mean μ and variance σ^2, then the sample mean $\hat{z}$ of n random samples will be approximately normal or Gaussian distributed with mean μ and variance σ^2/n. For example, the associated noise present in the desired signal at the receiver of a digital communication system is a result of accumulation of noise components from many sources, and the underlying distribution of this accumulated noise is close to Gaussian. This is one of the reasons for using the normal or Gaussian distribution to model the noise source most of the time. Typically, we model the normal distribution by averaging the statistically independent and identically distributed (i.i.d.) random variables with finite mean μ and finite variance σ^2. For example, by adding 12 times the samples from a uniform distribution defined over the interval [0, 12] and repeating the process many times, we create a normally distributed sample with $\mu = 6$ and $\sigma^2 = 1$. The pdf of the Gaussian distributed random variable with mean μ_x and variance σ^2 follows:

$$p_X(x) = N(\mu_x, \sigma^2) = \frac{1}{\sqrt{2\pi}\,\sigma} e^{-(x-\mu_x)^2/2\sigma^2}, \quad -\infty < x < \infty, \ \sigma > 0 \tag{6.23}$$

Random Process

In the previous discussion, we defined random variables as functions that map the sample space to a measurable real number space. In the same way, when we map the sample space to a measurable signal space instead of number space, we call such a mapping function $X(t)$ a random process. In the coin experiment, with the random process $X(t)$, we may map, for example, a head to a square wave and a tail to a triangle wave. We can view a random process as a collection of random variables or a collection of sample functions. At a particular time instance t_i, the random process $X(t)$ represents random variable $X(t_i)$. If we consider a process $s(t) = X.\sin(2\pi ft)$, and if X is a random variable, then for every possible value of X, there is a function of time called the *sample function* $s_x(t)$. Then, the collection of all such sample functions forms a random process. We call such a collection of functions an *ensemble*. Although the independent variable t is continuous, the underlying random process need not be continuous. If the associated random variable is discrete, then the corresponding random process is also discrete; if the random variable is continuous, then the corresponding random process is also continuous.

Distribution Functions for Random Processes

Random processes are easily studied by viewing them as a collection of random variables. Here, we consider the random process $X(t)$ at time t_i, $X(t_i)$, where $X(t_i)$ represents a random variable. The cumulative distribution function for random variable $X(t_i)$ is given by $F_{X(t_i)}(x_i) = \Pr[X(t_i) \le x_i]$. This relation can be generalized to the n-th–order case as follows:

$$F_{X(t_1),X(t_2),\ldots,X(t_n)}(x_1, x_2, \ldots, x_n) = \Pr[X(t_1) \le x_1, X(t_2) \le x_2, \ldots, X(t_n) \le x_n] \tag{6.24}$$

$$p_{X(t_1),X(t_2),\ldots,X(t_n)}(x_1, x_2, \ldots, x_n) = \frac{\partial^n F_{X(t_1),X(t_2),\ldots,X(t_n)}(x_1, x_2, \ldots, x_n)}{\partial x_1 \partial x_2 \cdots \partial x_n} \tag{6.25}$$

where $x_1, x_2, \ldots, x_n$ are n random variables considered at n time instances $t_1, t_2, \ldots, t_n$. In general, a complete statistical description of a random process requires knowledge of all order distribution functions. The random processes $X(t)$ and $Y(t)$ are said to be statistically independent if and only if

$$p_{X(t_1),X(t_2),\ldots,X(t_n),Y(t_1),Y(t_2),\ldots,Y(t_n)}(x_1, x_2, \ldots, x_n, y_1, y_2, \ldots, y_n)$$
$$= p_{X(t_1),X(t_2),\ldots,X(t_n)}(x_1, x_2, \ldots, x_n) p_{Y(t_1),Y(t_2),\ldots,Y(t_n)}(y_1, y_2, \ldots, y_n)$$

Stationarity of Random Processes

A random process $X(t)$ is said to be stationary if its statistical properties do not change with time. More precisely, a process $X(t)$ is said to be *stationary in the strict sense* if

$$p_{X(t_1),X(t_2),\ldots,X(t_n)}(x_1, x_2, \ldots x_n) = p_{X(t_1+\varepsilon),X(t_2+\varepsilon),\ldots,X(t_n+\varepsilon)}(x_1, x_2, \ldots, x_n) \tag{6.26}$$

for all orders n and all time shifts ε. That is, all order statistics of a stationary random process are invariant to any translation of the time axis. On the other hand, when the joint pdfs vary with time shifts, then that random process is *nonstationary*. Another kind of random process in which the statistics are neither stationary nor nonstationary, but periodically vary with period T, is called *cyclo-stationary*. For cyclo-stationary random processes, the following formula applies:

$$p_{X(t_1),X(t_2),\ldots,X(t_n)}(x_1, x_2, \ldots x_n) = p_{X(t_1+T),X(t_2+T),\ldots,X(t_n+T)}(x_1, x_2, \ldots, x_n) \tag{6.27}$$

where T is the period of n-th–order statistics.

In practice, we work with two kinds of stationary processes: *wide-sense stationary* and *ergodic*. A random process $X(t)$ is said to be wide-sense stationary if the following conditions are satisfied: its first-order statistics are constant, and its second-order statistics depend only on time difference instead of absolute time. A random process is said to be ergodic if all orders' statistical and time averages are interchangeable.

Statistical Averages for Random Processes

Statistical averages for random processes are defined in ways similar to how we defined statistical averages for random variables. We define next the popularly used first-order statistic mean and the second-order statistic autocorrelation for the random process $X(t)$. The expected value or mean $\mu(t)$ of a general random process $X(t)$ is defined as follows:

$$\mu(t_i) = E[X(t_i)] = \int_{-\infty}^{\infty} x_i \, p_{X(t_i)}(x_i) dx_i \tag{6.28}$$

In general, the value of the mean depends on the time instance t_i if the pdf of $X(t_i)$ depends on the time instance t_i. For a stationary process, the pdf is independent of time; consequently, the first-order statistic mean is also independent of time.

Next, we consider two random variables $X(t_1)$ and $X(t_2)$ at time instances t_1 and t_2. The autocorrelation between $X(t_1)$ and $X(t_2)$ is measured by the joint movement with the following equation:

$$R_{xx}(t_1, t_2) = E[X(t_1)X(t_2)] = \int_{-\infty}^{\infty}\int_{-\infty}^{\infty} x_1 x_2 p_{X(t_1),X(t_2)}(x_1, x_2) dx_1 dx_2 \tag{6.29}$$

When the random process $X(t)$ is stationary, the joint pdf $p_{X(t_1),X(t_2)}(x_1, x_2)$ is identical to the joint pdf $p_{X(t_1+\varepsilon),X(t_2+\varepsilon)}(x_1, x_2)$ for any arbitrary ε. This implies that the autocorrelation function of $X(t)$ does not depend on the specific time instances t_1 and t_2; instead, it depends on the time difference $\tau = t_1 - t_2$. Thus, for a stationary random process, the second-order statistic is $R_{xx}(t_1, t_2) = R_{xx}(t_1 - t_2) = R_{xx}(\tau)$. As previously defined, if the random process $X(t)$'s first-order statistic mean μ is independent of time, and the second-order statistic autocorrelation $R_{xx}(\tau)$ depends only on the time difference τ, then $X(t)$ is called a *wide-sense stationary* (WSS) process.

Time Averages for Random Processes

The statistical averages using an ensemble of sample functions assume an infinite-sized ensemble of signals. However, in practical applications, we only get finite ensemble sizes and finite-length signals rather than an infinite ensemble of signals. Thus, for practical handling of real-world signals, we define the time average mean μ_t of random processes as follows:

$$\mu_t = E[X(t)] = \lim_{T\to\infty} \frac{1}{2T} \int_{-T}^{T} X(t)dt \tag{6.30}$$

Similarly, the time autocorrelation function is defined as follows:

$$R_{xx}(\tau) = E[X(t)X(t+\tau)] = \lim_{T\to\infty} \frac{1}{2T} \int_{-T}^{T} X(t)X(t+\tau)dt \tag{6.31}$$

The time autocovariance function for random process $X(t)$ is defined as follows:

$$\gamma_{xx}(\tau) = E[(X(t) - \mu_t)(X(t+\tau) - \mu_t)] = \lim_{T\to\infty} \frac{1}{2T} \int_{-T}^{T} (X(t) - \mu_t)(X(t+\tau) - \mu_t)dt \tag{6.32}$$

The time cross-correlation function for two random process $X(t)$ and $Y(t)$ is defined as follows:

$$R_{xy}(\tau) = E[X(t)Y(t+\tau)] = \lim_{T\to\infty} \frac{1}{2T} \int_{-T}^{T} X(t)Y(t+\tau)dt \tag{6.33}$$

In practice, it is commonly assumed that a given signal is a sample function of an ergodic random process so that the averages can be computed from a single function. The Fourier transform (see next section) of the autocorrelation function of WSS random process gives the power spectral density (PSD) of the random process.

6.2 Time-Frequency Representation of Continuous-Time Signals

In Section 6.1 we introduced the concept of the signal and discussed various types of signals. All the signals discussed in the previous section are represented in the time domain. That is, the signal variations are represented with respect to time. Although we can clearly see the variations of physical phenomenon with respect to time in the time-domain representation of a signal, signal processing requires much more information than variation of signal amplitudes with respect to time. Using the time-domain signal information alone we cannot process the signal to get the desired signal. Sometimes by transforming the data from one domain to another, we may find more relevant information in the transformed domain data than in the original domain data. In addition, by eliminating the undesired components in one domain, we may get the desired data in another.

One way to process the raw signal to get a desired signal is by decomposing an arbitrary signal into known base components and choosing a subset of base components to form the desired signal. If we choose well-known sinusoidal components as base components to decompose the signal, then with the signal decomposition, we get the whole range of frequencies in the original signal. We obtain the desired signal by using a subset of frequencies. This emphasizes the frequency-domain representation of the signal. In addition, if the given signal contains fewer frequencies, we can compactly represent that signal in the frequency domain better than in the time domain.

6.2.1 Sinusoids and Frequency-Domain Representation

As discussed in Section 6.1, the sine wave representation $y(t) = \sin(2\pi ft)$ provides the frequency value of a sine wave. We can now easily represent any sine wave of the form $y(t) = A.\sin(2\pi ft + \phi)$, where A is the amplitude and ϕ is the phase delay, in the frequency domain with the x-axis representing the frequency value and the y-axis representing both magnitude and phase at a particular frequency. We use two separate plots to show the magnitude and phase. The time- and frequency-domain representations of the signal $y(t) = 5\sin(2\pi 3t + \pi/4) = 5\cos(2\pi 3t + 3\pi/4)$ are shown in Figures 6.18 and 6.19, respectively.

In Figure 6.18, the dotted curve represents the zero-phase sine wave, and the solid curve represents the sine wave with a phase difference of $\pi/4$ with respect to the zero-phase sine wave. The frequency-domain equivalent of Figure 6.18 is shown in Figure 6.19. Figure 6.19(a) indicates that a sinusoid of magnitude 5.0 is present at frequency index 3, and Figure 6.19(b) indicates that a sinusoid with a phase difference of $3\pi/4$ (with respect to the zero-phase cosinusoidal wave) is present at the frequency index 3. Thus, both figures represent the same sinusoid information in different domains. Actually, Figure 6.18 shows only the finite-length sine wave due to limited space, but it should be of infinite length to exactly match the equivalent frequency-domain information in Figure 6.19.

Consider another waveform $s(t)$ as shown in Figure 6.20. At first glance, the waveform of the figure seems random, but it is not. It repeats itself with interval T, which is approximately equal to 1. Actually, $s(t)$ is the sum of three sinusoids as follows:

$$s(t) = 5\sin(2\pi t + \pi/4) + 7\sin(2\pi 4t + \pi/8) + 4\sin(2\pi 9t + \pi/12) \tag{6.34}$$

The equivalent frequency-domain representation of the waveform in Equation (6.34) is shown in Figure 6.21. It consists of three frequencies at $f = 1$, $f = 4$, and $f = 9$ with phases $3\pi/4, 5\pi/8, 7\pi/12$, and amplitudes 5, 7, and 4, respectively.

As discussed previously, the time- and frequency-domain plots provide complementary information about the same signal. The question at this juncture is how to transform the signal from one domain to another domain. We use well-known Fourier methods to transform the signal from one domain to another. Depending on the type

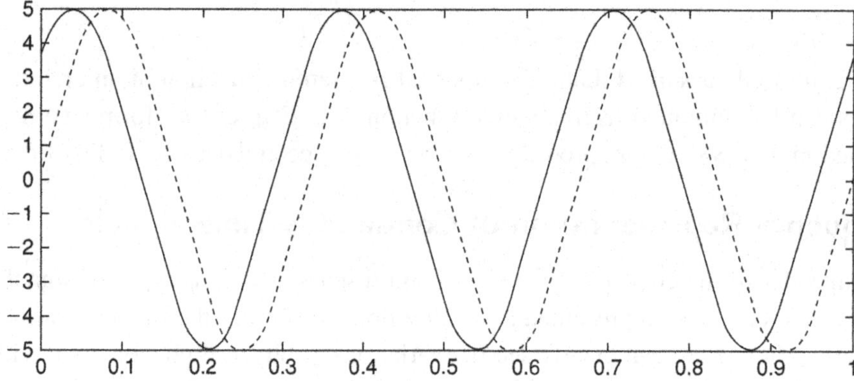

Figure 6.18: Time-domain plot for $y(t) = 5\sin(2\pi 3t + \pi/4)$.

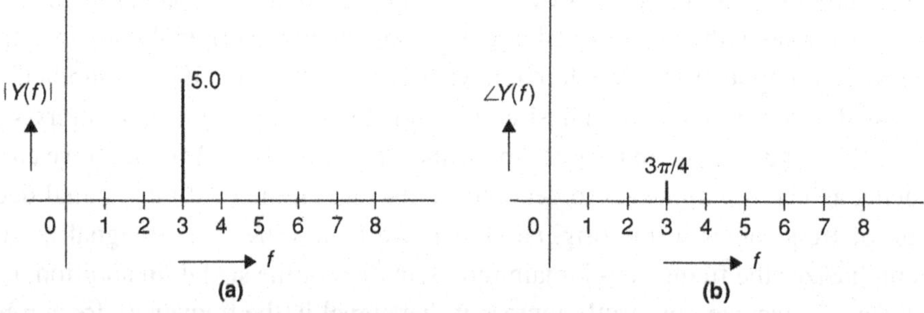

Figure 6.19: Frequency-domain representation for $y(t) = 5\sin(2\pi 3t + \pi/4)$. (a) Magnitude. (b) Phase.

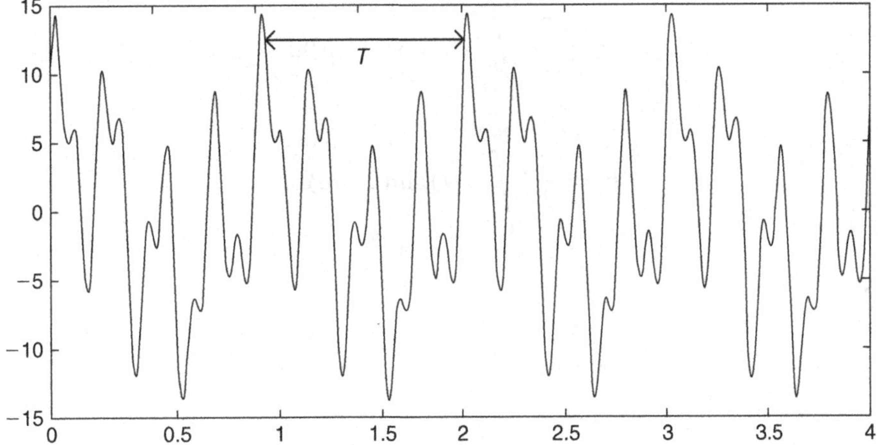

Figure 6.20: Plot of a multifrequency waveform.

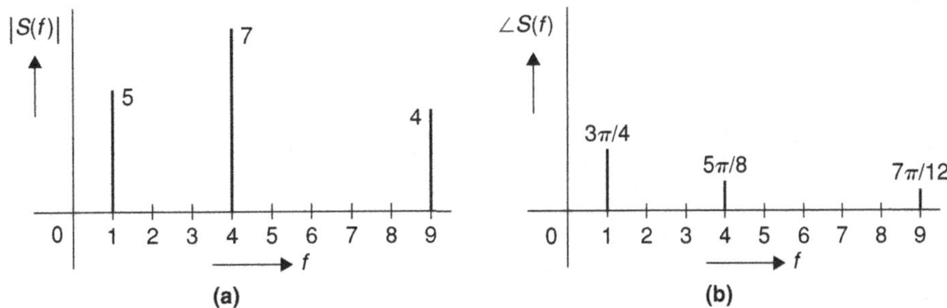

Figure 6.21: Frequency-domain representation of waveform $s(t)$ of Equation (6.34).

of signal (e.g., periodic, nonperiodic, continuous, discrete), we use the following four types of Fourier methods to transform the signal data:

- Fourier series (defined for periodic continuous-time signals)
- Fourier transform (defined for nonperiodic continuous signals)
- Discrete time Fourier transform (defined for nonperiodic discrete signals)
- Discrete Fourier transform (defined for periodic discrete signals)

In this section, we discuss the first two Fourier methods defined for continuous-time signals. The last two will be discussed in Section 6.4.

6.2.2 Fourier Series

Any periodic waveform $s(t)$ can be represented as the sum of an infinite number of sinusoidal and cosinusoidal terms together with a constant term as follows:

$$s(t) = c + \sum_{n=1}^{\infty} a_n \cos(2\pi fnt) + \sum_{n=1}^{\infty} b_n \sin(2\pi fnt) \tag{6.35}$$

where c is a constant (also called DC value), $f = 1/T$, and T is the signal period. Given $s(t)$, the coefficients a_n and b_n (also called AC values) and the constant term c are obtained as follows:

$$c = \frac{1}{T} \int_{-T/2}^{T/2} s(t)dt \tag{6.36}$$

$$a_n = \frac{2}{T} \int_{-T/2}^{T/2} s(t)\cos(2\pi fnt)dt \tag{6.37}$$

$$b_n = \frac{2}{T} \int_{-T/2}^{T/2} s(t)\sin(2\pi fnt)dt \tag{6.38}$$

Example 6.2

Assume the periodic square wave shown in Figure 6.22(a), where the period is 1. One period of the square wave is defined as follows:

$$s(t) = \begin{cases} 1 & 0 \le t < 0.5 \\ -1 & 0.5 \le t < 1 \end{cases}$$

Using Equation 6.36 we obtain the value of c as zero since the sum of $s(t)$ over one period of interval results in zero. By substituting $s(t)$ in Equations (6.37) and (6.38) and evaluating the integral over interval $[-T/2, T/2]$, we obtain the coefficients a_n as all zeros, and the coefficients b_n as follows:

$$b_n = \begin{cases} 0 & \text{if } n \text{ is even} \\ \dfrac{4}{\pi n} & \text{if } n \text{ is odd} \end{cases}$$

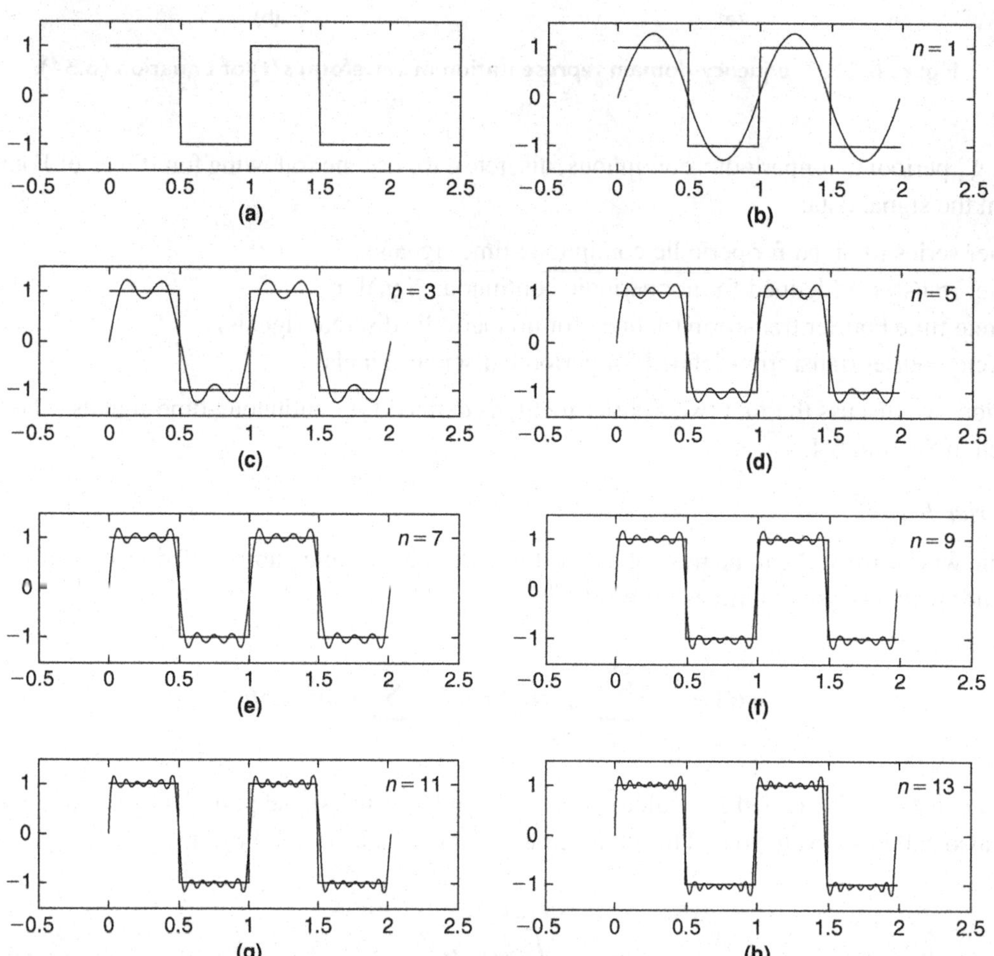

Figure 6.22: Fourier series representation of a periodic square wave.

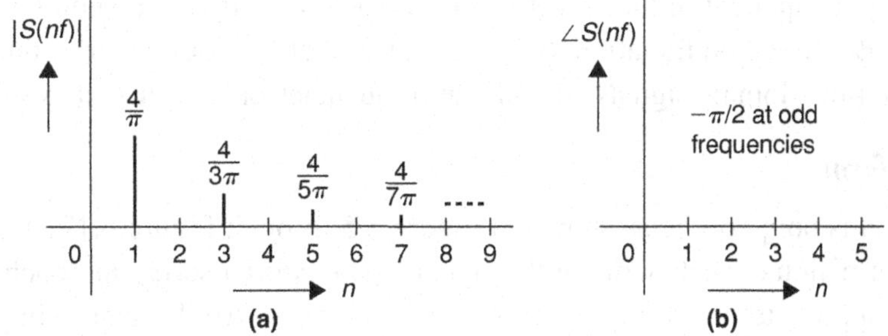

Figure 6.23: Frequency-domain representation of a square wave.

Then, based on Equation 6.35, the decomposition of the square wave in sinusoidal terms is given by

$$s(t) = \frac{4}{\pi} \sum_{odd\ n} \frac{\sin(2\pi fnt)}{n}, \quad 1 \le n < \infty$$

The frequency-domain representation of square wave $s(t)$ is shown in Figure 6.23.

■

As seen in Example 6.2, the square wave in Figure 6.22(a) can be represented by combining infinite sinusoids with odd frequencies only. We illustrated this in Figure 6.22 using the first few sinusoids with odd frequencies. Figure 6.22(b) through (h) represents the square wave $s(t)$ approximation using the sum of m sinusoids with frequencies $n = 2m - 1$ for $1 \le m \le 7$. As shown in Figure 6.22(h), we are close to the ideal square wave in representing it using the sum of the first eight odd-frequency sinusoids. However, we have ripples in the Fourier-series–represented square wave. The presence of ripples in the Fourier-series computed waveform is called the *Gibbs phenomenon*. We can only reduce the ripple width by adding more and more sinusoids, but cannot attenuate the peaks of the ripple. The reason for the presence of ripples in the Fourier-series approximated square wave is due to the discontinuous nature of square waves. If we have sharp edges or discontinuities in the periodic wave (e.g., square waveform, triangular waveform), then we cannot exactly represent the waveform using the Fourier-series representation. Because of this, the Fourier theory generalization was withheld from publication for decades. Nevertheless, we accept the Fourier-series representation for all periodic signals in the root mean square (RMS) error sense.

The Fourier-series representation in Equation (6.35) may be written more compactly by using exponential notation, and has the advantage of exponential mathematical manipulations. Equation (6.35) can be rearranged as follows:

$$s(t) = \sum_{n=-\infty}^{\infty} d_n e^{j2\pi fnt} \tag{6.39}$$

where

$$d_n = \frac{1}{T} \int_{-T/2}^{T/2} s(t) e^{-j2\pi fnt} dt \tag{6.40}$$

The values of d_n in Equation (6.40) are complex, containing both real and imaginary numbers. As the summation in Equation (6.39) includes negative values of n, we evaluate the integral for both negative and positive frequencies and the values of d_n are halved numerically to represent an equal sharing of the magnitudes between corresponding negative and positive frequencies. Using Equations (6.39) and (6.40), the relationship between d_n and c, a_n and b_n is obtained as follows:

$$d_0 = c, \quad |d_n| = \sqrt{a_n^2 + b_n^2}, \quad \phi_n = -\tan^{-1}(b_n/a_n)$$

Thus, each frequency component of the waveform is characterized by the magnitude $|S(nf)| = |d_n|$ and its phase angle $\angle S(nf) = \phi_n$. Based on Equation (6.40), it is clear that the Fourier series output is discrete and this means that the periodic time-domain signals contain the frequencies only at discrete values.

6.2.3 Fourier Transform

What if the given signal is nonperiodic as shown in Figure 6.5 through Figure 6.12? How do we compute the frequency-domain information of such nonperiodic signals? The Fourier series approach is defined for periodic signals and cannot be applied to nonperiodic signals. In Equation (6.40), by increasing the period value T to infinity, the quantity $f(= 1/T)$ becomes Δf as $T \to \infty$ and the quantity $S(nf)$ modifies to $S(f)$ as follows:

$$S(f) = \Delta f \int_{-\infty}^{\infty} s(t) e^{-j2\pi ft} dt \tag{6.41}$$

After normalization of Equation (6.41) with Δf, we have

$$\frac{S(f)}{\Delta f} = F(f) = \int_{-\infty}^{\infty} s(t) e^{-j2\pi ft} dt \tag{6.42}$$

We can compute $s(t)$ from Equation (6.42) by performing the inverse as follows:

$$s(t) = \int_{-\infty}^{\infty} F(f) e^{j2\pi ft} df \tag{6.43}$$

If we replace $2\pi f$ with ω in Equations (6.42) and (6.43), then we have the Fourier transform pair as follows:

$$F(\omega/2\pi) = \int_{-\infty}^{\infty} s(t) e^{-j\omega t} dt \tag{6.44}$$

$$s(t) = \frac{1}{2\pi} \int_{-\infty}^{\infty} F(\omega/2\pi) e^{j\omega t} d\omega \tag{6.45}$$

In practice, we avoid the constant term 2π in the index of $F(\omega/2\pi)$, and write $F(\omega)$ by assuming that the function $F(.)$ is defined for normalized frequencies. Equations (6.44) and (6.45) are called the Fourier transform pair. The time-frequency representation for nonperiodic signals, the Dirac delta function and rectangular pulse, are shown in Figure 6.24(a) and (b). If an arbitrary nonperiodic signal $s(t)$ contains frequencies up to $f_{\max}$, then $|S(f)|$, the magnitude of the Fourier transform of such a signal, resembles Figure 6.24(c).

6.3 Sampling of Continuous-Time Signals

In Section 6.1, we introduced the concept of signals and discussed various types of signals. All the signals presented in that section are continuous in time. However, we cannot process continuous-time signals with digital computers. Signal-processing computers handle only discrete signals in both time and amplitude. The quantization of the signal amplitude into finite discrete levels is a lossy process and we cannot recover this loss of information. On the other hand, sampling the signal with respect to time to get the discrete time samples can be a lossless process, and the original signal can be recovered if we sample the signals appropriately. In this section, we concentrate on appropriate sampling of continuous-time signals to get discrete-time signals, and then reconstructing the original signal from discrete samples. An example of a discrete-time signal $x[n]$ is shown in Figure 6.25, along with the actual analog signal $x(t)$. Given sampling period T, the samples are obtained from $x(t)$ as $x[n] = x(t)|_{t=nT}$. With sampling, the samples $x[n]$ are equal to the value of the corresponding analog signal $x(t)$ at the sampling time instances. Signal values in between the samples are undefined.

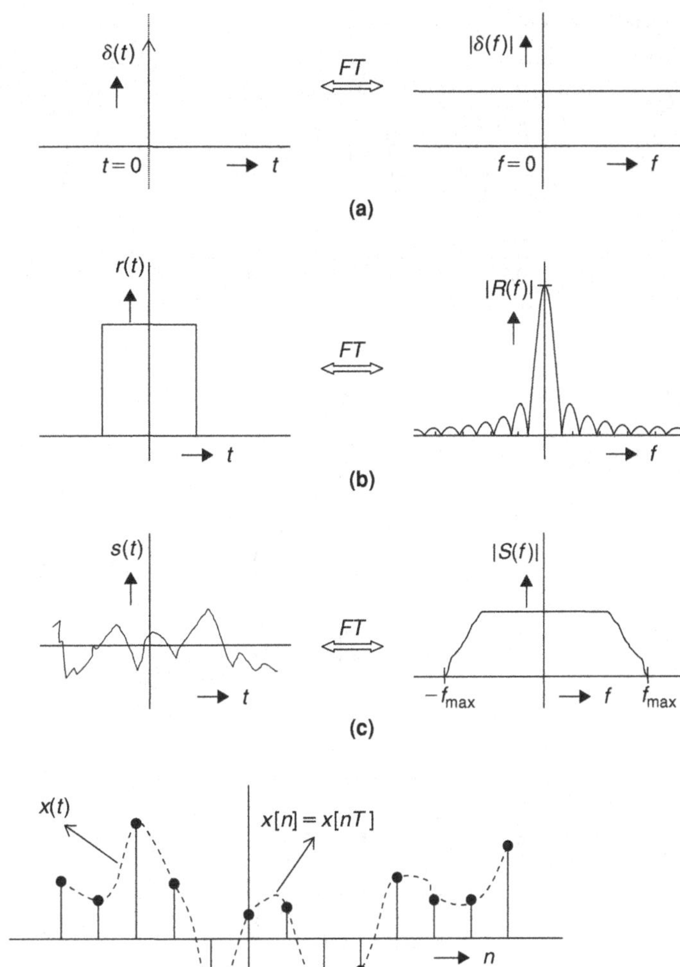

Figure 6.24: Time-frequency representation of nonperiodic signals. (a) Dirac delta function. (b) Rectangular pulse. (c) Arbitrary signal.

Figure 6.25: Plot of discrete-time signal.

Consider a 6-Hz sinusoidal signal as shown in Figure 6.26(a) with a solid curve. Since the sinusoid frequency is 6 Hz, it contains 6 cycles in 1-second intervals. The sinusoid shown in Figure 6.26(a) is plotted for 2 seconds and contains 12 cycles. We also show another sinusoid at a 2-Hz frequency (i.e., it contains only 4 cycles in a 2-second interval) in Figure 6.26(a) with a dotted curve. With sampling of continuous-time signal, we collect the samples at regular time intervals. For example, we sampled the 6-Hz signal at four samples per second in Figure 6.26(b) and at eight samples per second in Figure 6.26(c). Now the question is how many samples would be needed to obtain the original 6-Hz continuous-time sinusoidal signal? Is it possible to recover the original sinusoidal signal of 6 Hz using points sampled at four points per second or eight points per second? As seen in Figure 6.26(b) and (c), those four or eight points not only represent the 6-Hz sinusoid, but they also represent the 2-Hz sinusoid. Thus, there is ambiguity in deciding which sinusoidal curves those sampled points actually represent; we cannot recover the 6-Hz sinusoid signal using the four or eight points due to such ambiguity.

What if we chose a different set of sampling instances as shown in Figure 6.27? Is it possible then to recover the 6-Hz sinusoid with those sample points? In Figure 6.27(b), we sampled the signal at six regular time intervals, and those six points also represent the 3-Hz sinusoid apart from the 6-Hz sinusoid. The same ambiguity arises even with nine points as shown in Figure 6.27(c). Consequently, you may think sampling with 100 points (instead of 8 or 9 points) makes recovering the original 6-Hz sinusoid possible. Yes, we can recover that sinusoid if we sample the 6-Hz signal with 100 samples per second, but processing and storing those 100 samples is very costly when compared to 8 or 9 samples. Therefore, we are interested in the minimum number of samples required to represent the continuous-time signal, such that we can recover the original signal without ambiguity.

In the following, we discuss the famous sampling theorem that specifies the rate at which an analog signal should be sampled to ensure that all the relevant information contained in the signal is captured or retained via

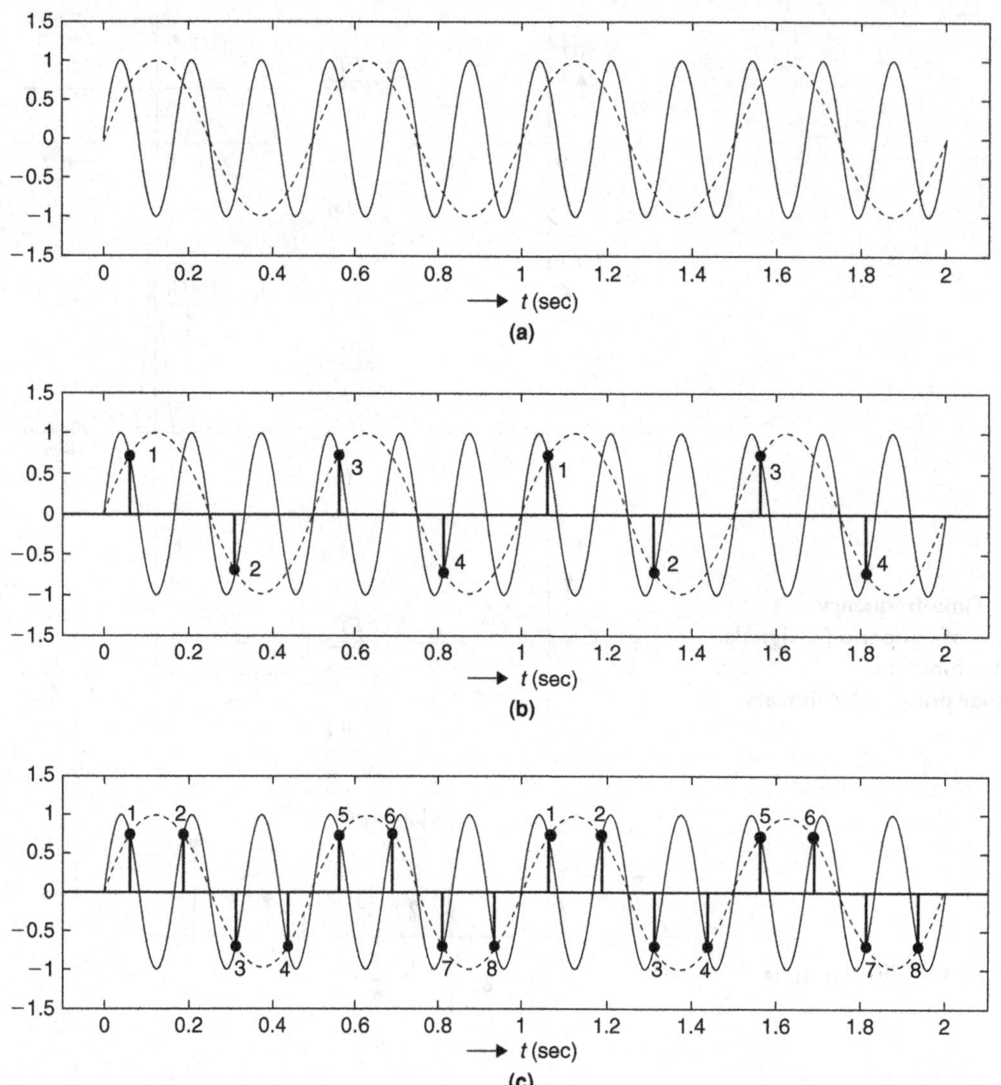

Figure 6.26: (a) Two sinusoids with frequencies 6 Hz (*solid line*) and 2 Hz (*dashed line*). (b) Sampling at four samples per second. (c) Sampling at eight samples per second.

sampling. Depending on whether the signal is low pass (as shown in Figure 6.28(a), which contains most of its energy at the lower frequencies) or bandpass (which contains most of its energy away from lower frequencies), we follow a slightly different procedure in applying the sampling theorem.

6.3.1 Nyquist Criterion: Sampling of Low-Pass Signals

According to the Nyquist criterion, if the highest-frequency component in a signal is $f_{\max}$ (Hz), then the signal should be sampled at the rate of at least $2f_{\max}$ samples per second to describe the signal completely. That is, the sampling frequency or rate F_s is given by

$$F_s \geq 2f_{\max} \tag{6.46}$$

We call the sample rate, F_s, the Nyquist rate. Now, if we look at the sampling of the sinusoid example, the maximum frequency of the sinusoid is 6 Hz as shown in Figure 6.26 or 6.27. This means that if we sample the 6-Hz sinusoid at 12 samples or more per second (i.e., greater than or equal to 2×6), then there will be no ambiguity in reconstructing the 6-Hz sinusoid after sampling. Sampling at less than the rate specified by the sampling theorem leads to *aliasing* of *image* frequencies into the desired frequency band; hence, the original signal cannot be recovered. The concept of image frequencies is explained next. For this, we consider a continuous-time

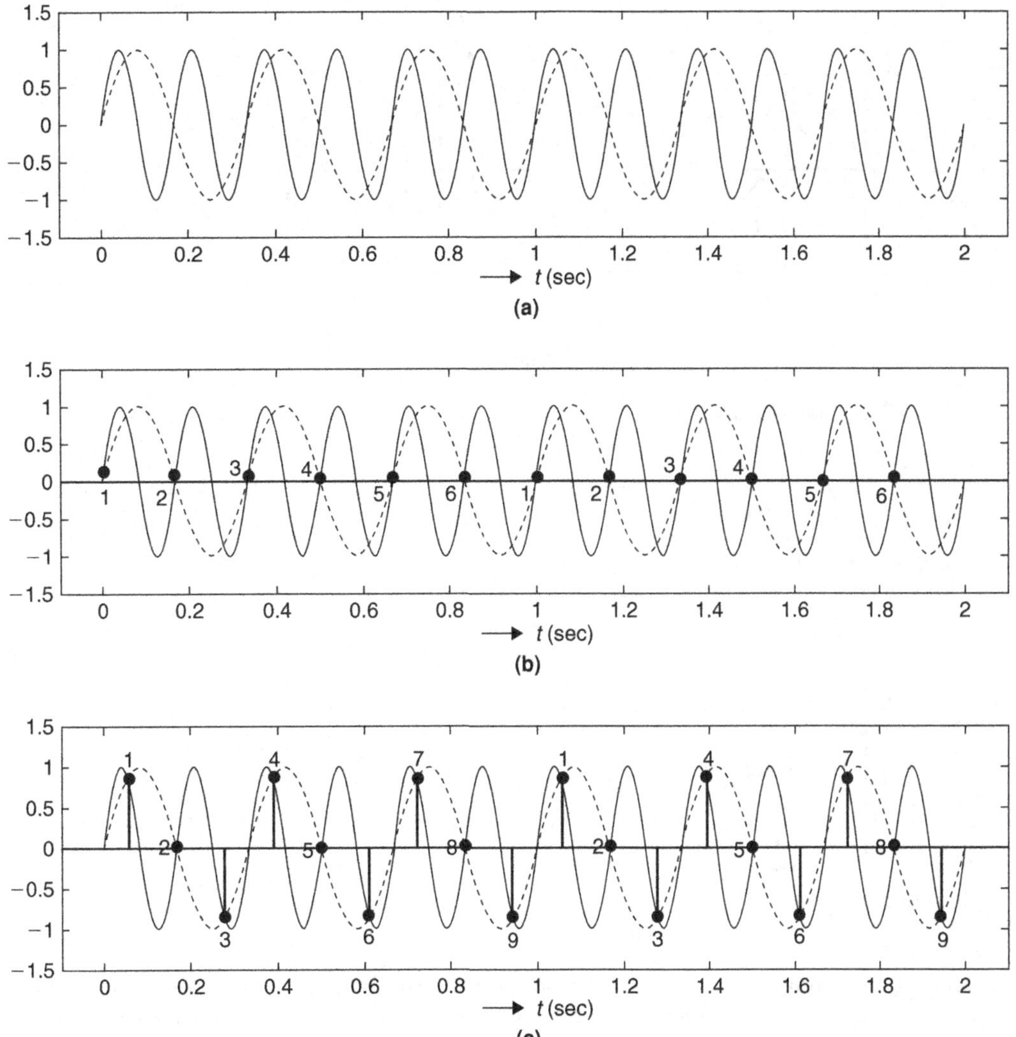

Figure 6.27: (a) Two sinusoids with frequencies 6 Hz (solid line) and 3 Hz (dotted line). (b) Sampling at six samples per second. (c) Sampling at nine samples per second.

signal as shown in Figure 6.28 along with its frequency-domain information (also called frequency *spectrum*). If we sample this continuous-time signal into discrete samples, then the frequency spectrum of discrete samples contains many replicas of the spectrum as shown in Figure 6.28(b). These are called image frequencies. The intuitive reasoning for the formation of images with the signal sampling is discussed next.

When we applied the Fourier series to a periodic signal, we got a discrete frequency spectrum. This means that when we have discrete content in one domain, we see the periodic information content in the other domain. In the same way, the sampling of a continuous-time signal to discrete samples causes the frequency spectrum to repeat itself. To obtain the original signal, we filter out these replicas. If we sample a continuous-time signal with less than the sampling rate as shown in Figure 6.28(c), then the repeating spectral images overlap in the frequency domain. In this case, we cannot obtain the original continuous signal as the filter cannot completely remove the spectral images.

In Figures 6.26 and 6.27, we saw that 2-Hz and 3-Hz sinusoids are formed when the 6-Hz sinusoid is sampled at less than 12 samples per second. This is because undersampling the 6-Hz signal causes overlapping in the frequency domain and forms an alias of higher-frequency signals at the lower frequencies. Thus, these 2-Hz and 3-Hz sinusoids are aliased signals of the actual 6-Hz signal when we undersample it. Even if we know the maximum frequency present in the desired signal, sampling the desired signal with the rate greater than twice the maximum frequency may not guarantee perfect reconstruction of the original signal due to noise. Noisy signals usually occupy wider frequency bands when compared to desired signals. In this case, even if we follow the

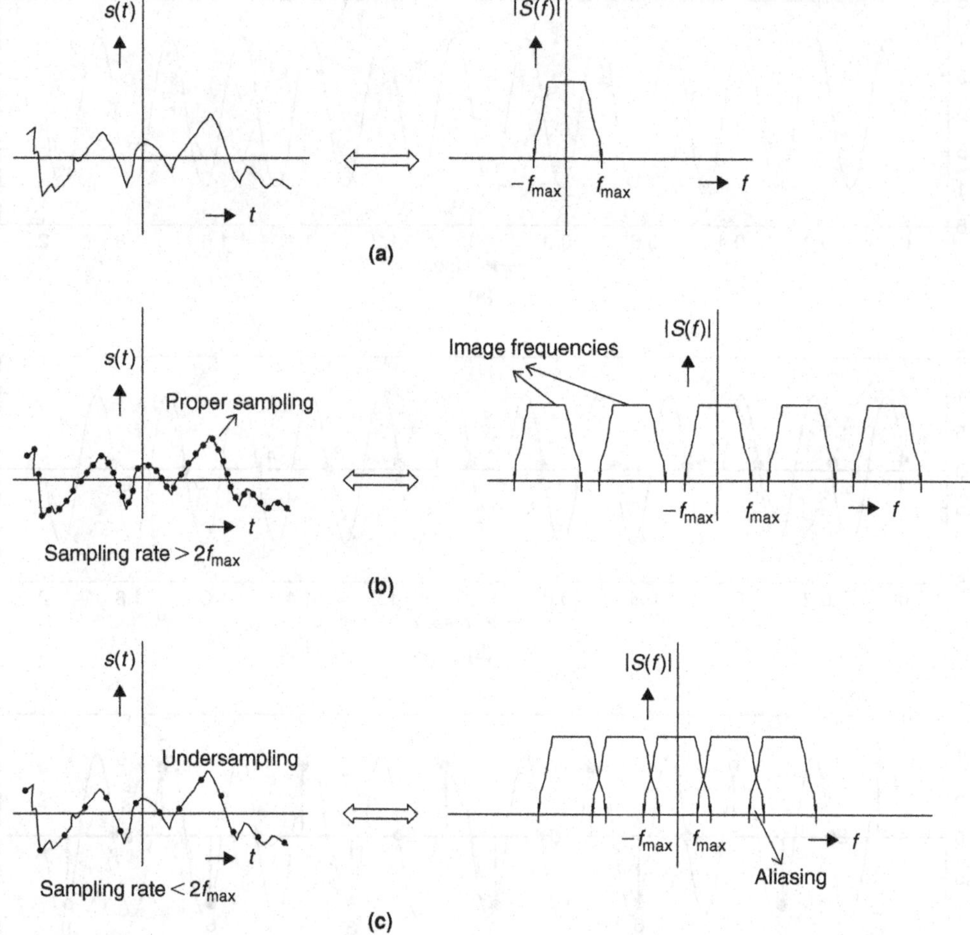

Figure 6.28: Sampling continuous-time signals. (a) Continuous-time signal and its frequency spectrum. (b) Proper sampled discrete signal and corresponding image frequency spectrums. (c) Undersampling and corresponding aliased frequency spectrum images.

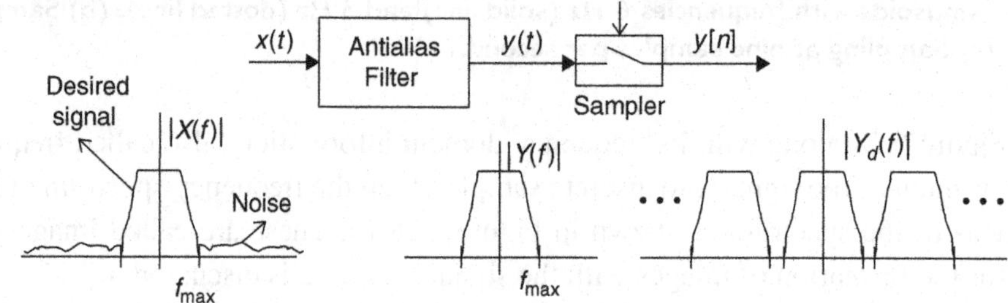

Figure 6.29: Sampling with an antialiasing filter.

sampling theorem, we may still see the frequency aliasing of sampled signals due to wideband noise. Thus, we filter the noise using an antialiasing filter before sampling the desired signal as shown in Figure 6.29.

6.3.2 Reconstruction of Signal from Discrete Samples

According to the sampling theorem, we can reconstruct continuous-time band-limited signals from samples obtained by sampling at least twice the maximum frequency present in the signal. If T is the sampling period associated with the sequence $x[n]$, then we construct the continuous-time signal $x(t)$ from its samples $x[n]$ as follows:

$$x(t) = \sum_{n=-\infty}^{\infty} x[n] \frac{\sin[\pi(t-nT)/T]}{\pi(t-nT)/T} \tag{6.47}$$

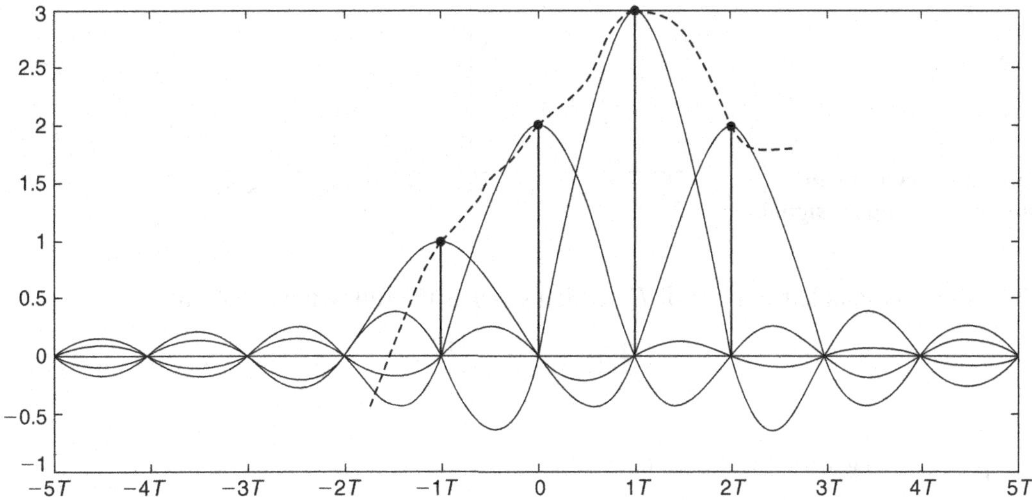

Figure 6.30: Reconstruction of continuous-time signal from discrete samples.

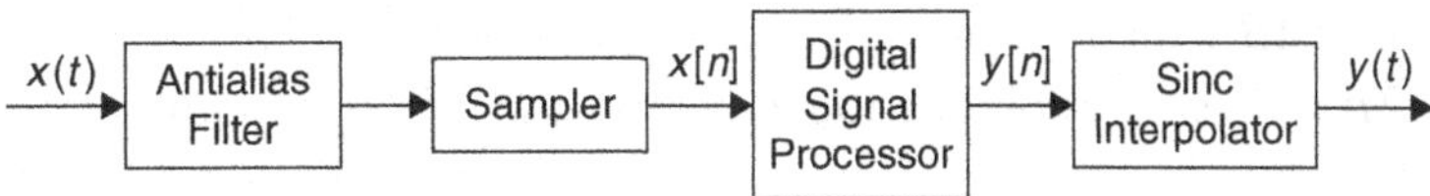

Figure 6.31: Discrete-time processing of continuous-time signals.

In Equation (6.47), we basically use the delayed versions of the normalized sinc function to reconstruct the continuous-time signal. With the normalized sinc function,

$$\frac{\sin(\pi t/T)}{\pi t/T}$$

we have a continuous signal with a non-zero value at only $t = 0$, and zero values at all time instances $t = nT$, where $n = (-\infty, \infty) - \{0\}$. Similarly, if we delay the sinc function by m samples in time as follows,

$$\frac{\sin[(\pi(t - mT)/T]}{\pi(t - mT)/T}$$

then we have a non-zero value only at $t = mT$, and zero values at all time instances $t = nT$, where $n = (-\infty, \infty) - \{m\}$. This is illustrated in Figure 6.30 using four samples $x[n] = [1, 2, 3, 2]$ at sampling instances $[-T, 0, T, 2T]$. As seen in Figure 6.30, the sinc function interpolates between the samples of $x[n]$ to construct a continuous-time signal $x_c(t)$. In fact, if there is no aliasing, then the sinc function can reconstruct a continuous-time signal that exactly represents $x(t)$.

Given a continuous-time signal, we can obtain discrete-time samples by sampling the continuous-time signal at the Nyquist rate in Equation (6.46). We can then perform signal processing on discrete samples using specialized tools, and then we get back the processed continuous-time signal by using the reconstruction formula in Equation (6.47). The basic signal processing system for real-world, continuous-time signals using a digital signal processor is shown in Figure 6.31.

6.3.3 Sampling of Bandpass Signals

Bandpass signals frequently occur in communication systems, where signals are modulated to occupy particular frequency bands for signal transmission, as shown in Figure 6.32. In such cases, the bandwidth of the signal B is often very small when compared to the maximum frequency (f_H) present, and sampling will be costly (to process, store, or reconstruct) using the Nyquist criterion. The bandpass sampling theorem is used in such

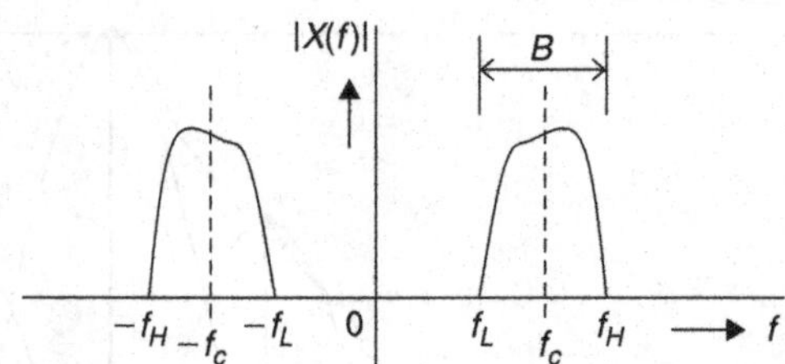

Figure 6.32: Frequency-domain representation of a bandpass signal.

situations. The signal is sampled at a rate of F_s, which satisfies the following equation:

$$\frac{2f_H}{n} \le F_s \le \frac{2F_L}{n-1} \tag{6.48}$$

where $n = \left\lceil \frac{f_H}{B} \right\rceil$, an integer rounded up to next integer.

The bandpass sampling theorem allows us to sample narrowband signals at a much reduced rate, while simultaneously permitting reconstruction of the signal without aliasing problems. In a special case where the edge frequencies f_L and f_H are integer multiples of the signal bandwidth B, then such a signal can be sampled at a theoretical minimum rate of $2B$ without aliasing. For example, if $B = 10\,\text{kHz}$, $f_L = 80\,\text{kHz}$, and $f_H = 90\,\text{kHz}$, then sampling at the rate $2B = 20\,\text{kHz}$ allows us to reconstruct the original continuous-time bandpass signal.

6.4 Time-Frequency Representation of Discrete-Time Signals

In Section 6.2, we used Fourier series and Fourier transforms for time-frequency representation of continuous-time signals. In this section, their counterparts to work with discrete-time signals are discussed. Like continuous-time signals, there are also two types of discrete-time signals: periodic and nonperiodic. A discrete-time signal $x[n]$ is said to be periodic if $x[n] = x[n+N]$ for some positive integer N. Here, the smallest integer value of N represents the $x[n]$ period. Note that the continuous-time sinusoid $\sin(\omega t)$ is periodic regardless of the value of ω. This is not the case with the discrete-time sinusoid $\sin(\Omega n)$. To make $\sin[\Omega(n+N)] = \sin(\Omega n)$, the following has to be satisfied:

$$\Omega N = 2\pi m \quad \text{or} \quad \frac{\Omega}{2\pi} = \frac{m}{N}$$

In brief, a discrete-time sinusoid $\sin(\Omega n)$ is periodic only if $\frac{\Omega}{2\pi}$ is a rational number.

6.4.1 Discrete-Time Fourier Transform

We obtain the frequency-domain information for discrete-time nonperiodic signals using the discrete time Fourier transform (DTFT) as follows:

$$X(\Omega) = \sum_{n=-\infty}^{\infty} x[n]e^{-j\Omega n} \tag{6.49}$$

The DTFT output $X(\Omega)$ is periodic as shown in Figure 6.33. Since $|e^{-j2\pi n}| = 1$, clearly the frequency information $X(\Omega)$ from Equation (6.49) is periodic with period 2π as derived here:

$$X(\Omega+2\pi) = \sum_{n=-\infty}^{\infty} x[n]e^{-j(\Omega+2\pi)n} = \sum_{n=-\infty}^{\infty} x[n]e^{-j\Omega n}e^{-j2\pi n} = \sum_{n=-\infty}^{\infty} x[n]e^{-j\Omega n} = X(\Omega) \tag{6.50}$$

In the following, the periodicity of this Fourier transform of the discrete-time signal is explained. The Fourier transform of an impulse train $d(t)$ is again a periodic impulse sequence with a different period as shown in Figure 6.34. Because discrete-time signals are obtained by multiplying the continuous-time signal with the impulse train, we obtain the Fourier transform of the discrete-time signal as periodic. In other words, if we have discrete information in one domain (time/frequency), then we will have periodic information in the other

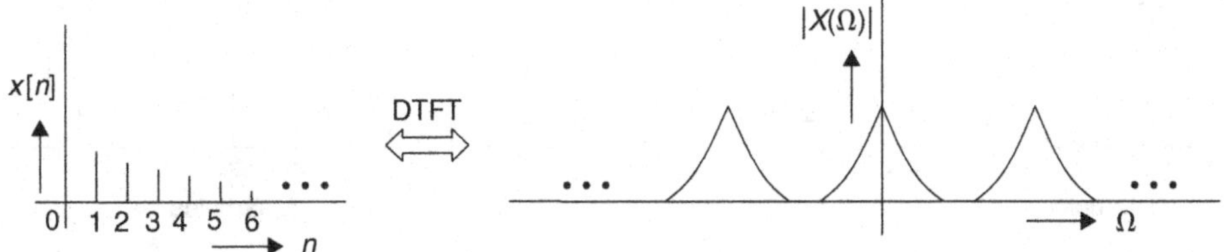

Figure 6.33: Discrete-time signals and periodic frequency-domain information.

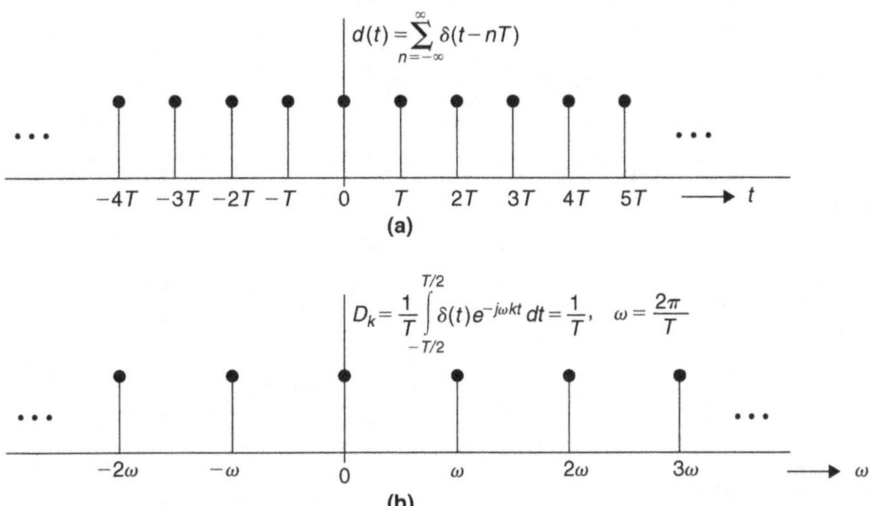

Figure 6.34: (a) Impulse train in time domain. (b) Equivalent frequency-domain information.

domain (frequency/time). Since the Fourier transform of discrete-time signals is periodic, the inverse transform is performed on one period, 2π, of the frequency spectrum:

$$x[n]=\frac{1}{2\pi}\int_{2\pi} X(\Omega)e^{j\Omega n}d\Omega \tag{6.51}$$

Equations (6.49) and (6.51) form a discrete-time Fourier transform pair.

6.4.2 Discrete Fourier Transform

Digital systems process and output only discrete signals; thus, the DTFT tool is not suitable for digital signal processing (DSP) because the output of DTFT is continuous. For this reason, we derive the discrete Fourier transform (DFT) equations from the DTFT to work with DSPs. Upon sampling the DTFT output frequency information in Equation (6.49), and taking samples at regular frequency intervals,

$$X[k\Omega_0]=\sum_{-\infty}^{\infty}x[n]e^{-j\Omega_0 kn},\quad \Omega_0=\frac{2\pi}{T} \tag{6.52}$$

In Equation (6.52), we usually ignore Ω_0 in the index and simply write $X[k\Omega_0]$ as $X[k]$. With sampling of frequency-domain information, we force periodicity in the time domain. If we have N samples in one period T, then $\Omega_0=\frac{2\pi}{N}$. With this, Equation (6.52) can be rewritten as follows:

$$X[k]=\sum_{n=0}^{N-1}x[n]e^{-j2\pi kn/N} \tag{6.53}$$

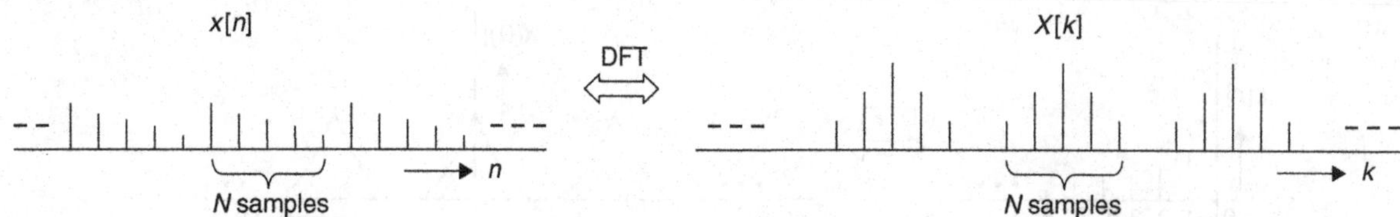

Figure 6.35: Graphic illustration of discrete Fourier transform.

Given Equations (6.51) and (6.53), the inverse for DFT follows:

$$x[n] = \frac{1}{N} \sum_{k=0}^{N-1} X[k] e^{j2\pi kn/N} \tag{6.54}$$

Equations (6.53) and (6.54) represent the DFT pair. Next, we verify the periodicity of the time-domain sequence $x[n]$ as follows:

$$x[n+N] = \frac{1}{N} \sum_{k=0}^{N-1} X[k] e^{j2\pi k(n+N)/N} = \frac{1}{N} \sum_{k=0}^{N-1} X[k] e^{j2\pi kn/N} e^{j2\pi k} = \frac{1}{N} \sum_{k=0}^{N-1} X[k] e^{j2\pi kn/N} = x[n]$$

Therefore, the DFT assumes a built-in periodicity in the time-domain information. A graphic illustration of the DFT is shown in Figure 6.35.

6.4.3 Discrete Cosine Transform

The discrete cosine transform (DCT) is commonly used to compress signal data. This is particularly important for the storage and transmission of image frames, as the images will have much spatial redundancy, and the DCT is good at eliminating the data correlations. Many types of DCT can be found in the literature; the following is the most commonly applied DCT pair in the image processing field:

$$X[k] = \beta[k] \sum_{n=0}^{N-1} x[n] \cos\left[\frac{\pi}{N}\left(n + \frac{1}{2}\right)k\right], \quad k = 0, 1, 2, \ldots, N-1 \tag{6.55}$$

$$x[n] = \sum_{k=0}^{N-1} \beta[k] X[k] \cos\left[\frac{\pi}{N}\left(n + \frac{1}{2}\right)k\right], \quad n = 0, 1, 2, \ldots, N-1 \tag{6.56}$$

where $\beta[0] = \sqrt{(1/N)}$ and $\beta[m] = \sqrt{(2/N)}$ for $m \neq 0$.

Implementation techniques for both DFT and DCT are discussed in the next chapter.

6.5 Linear Time-Invariant Systems

A system is any process that produces an output signal in response to an input signal. With specialized signal processing techniques, it is possible to express most of the systems in terms of mathematical models. This allows us to apply signal processing tools for system analysis and thereby improve system performance. In particular, we are interested in linear-time-invariant (LTI) systems, since many tools are available to analyze these systems. One important characteristic of an LTI system is that its output response to a sinusoidal input is also a sinusoid with some gain in amplitude and delay in phase. However, the frequency of the output sinusoid is the same as the input sinusoid (i.e., we get the same frequency sinusoid with a different gain and phase). All systems with input–output relationships described by linear differential equations are linear-time-invariant systems when the coefficients of such differential equations are constant. Next, we discuss the properties of stable, causal, linear-time-invariant systems.

Linearity. A system $H\{.\}$ is said to be linear if it follows the principles of superposition and homogeneity. If $y_1[n]$ and $y_2[n]$ are the output signals of system $H\{.\}$, when $x_1[n]$ and $x_2[n]$ are the respective input signals (i.e., $y_1[n] = H\{x_1[n]\}$ and $y_2[n] = H\{x_2[n]\}$), then the system $H\{.\}$ is linear if and only if

$$H\{ax_1[n]+bx_2[n]\} = aH\{x_1[n]\}+bH\{x_2[n]\} = ay_1[n]+by_2[n] \tag{6.55}$$

where a and b are arbitrary constants.

Time Invariance. Systems with parameters that do not change with respect to time are called time-invariant systems. With the time-invariant system $H\{.\}$, if the input $x[n]$ to a system $H\{.\}$ is delayed by N samples, then the corresponding output $y[n]$ is also delayed by N samples. That is, if $y[n] = H\{x[n]\}$, then $H\{x[n-N]\} = y[n-N]$.

Causality. A system is *causal* if for every choice of input signal delay N, the output signal $y[n]$ at the index $n = N$ depends only on the input signal $x[n]$ values for index $n \leq N$. That is, the output of a causal system depends on the current input and/or previous inputs, but not on future inputs.

Stability. A system $H\{.\}$ is stable in the BIBO (bounded-input, bounded-output) sense if and only if every bounded input sequence produces a bounded output sequence. In discrete time, the condition for BIBO stability is that the impulse response of the LTI system be absolutely summable, that is, $\sum_n |h[n]| < \infty$.

Continuous- and Discrete-Time Systems. Systems in which inputs and outputs are continuous-time signals are called continuous-time systems, usually denoted by $h(t)$. Similarly, systems whose inputs and outputs are discrete-time signals are called discrete-time systems, usually denoted by $h[n]$. Using the sampling theorem, we can obtain the corresponding discrete-time system from the given continuous-time system.

6.5.1 Impulse Response of LTI Systems

A major reason for interest in LTI systems is that these systems can be completely described by an impulse response. Why is an impulse response so important? We process the signals using systems and the processing of signals involves classification of signals and elimination of unwanted signals (or choosing the signal with a subset of frequency components). To process the signal with a system, we have to know the system (i.e., what frequency components the system attenuates and what frequencies it allows without attenuation). That is, we have to know the system frequencies and also the strength or amplitude and phase of each frequency. By passing a sinusoidal signal with a particular frequency through an LTI system, we can determine whether the system passes that particular frequency or attenuates it. Thus, by passing all the sinusoids within the required band of frequencies through an LTI system, we can describe the system in terms of frequencies in the band of interest. However, this is a huge task and it is not the most effective way to identify system behavior. Instead, if we input a unit impulse (whose frequency response is constant, meaning that it contains all frequencies, as shown in Figure 6.24(a)) to an LTI system, then its output response to a unit impulse provides the complete LTI system description. The response of a system to a unit impulse input is called an *impulse response*. The frequency content of a system's impulse response contains all system frequencies. Thus, the impulse response of LTI systems plays an important role in signal-processing applications. The graphic illustration of continuous- and discrete-time system impulse responses is shown in Figure 6.36. In working with DSPs, we use only discrete-time systems.

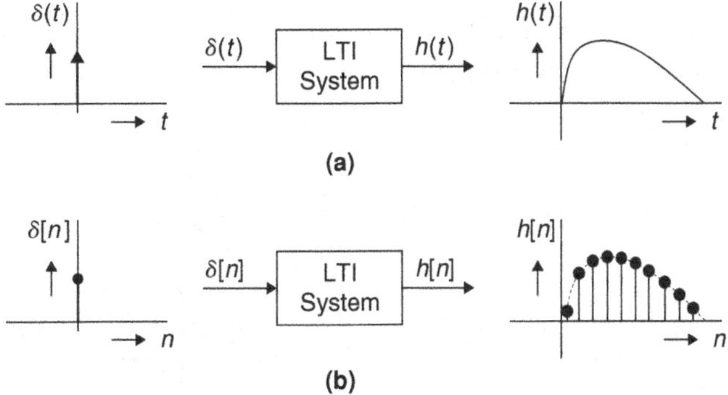

Figure 6.36: Impulse response examples of (a) continuous-time system and (b) discrete-time system.

6.5.2 Convolution

Once we know the impulse response of a system, we can then compute the response of that system to an arbitrary input signal by using the convolution operation. If $x(t)$ is the input signal and $h(t)$ is the impulse response of a given continuous-time system, then its output signal $y(t)$ is computed as follows:

$$y(t) = \int_{-\infty}^{\infty} x(\tau)h(t-\tau)d\tau \qquad (6.56)$$

In short, the continuous-time convolution operation in Equation (6.56) is represented as follows:

$$y(t) = x(t)^{*}h(t) \qquad (6.57)$$

where * represents the continuous-time convolution operation. For discrete-time systems, Equation (6.56) modifies to

$$y[n] = \sum_{k=-\infty}^{\infty} x[k]h[n-k] \qquad (6.58)$$

In brief, the discrete-time convolution operation in Equation (6.58) is represented as follows:

$$y[n] = x[n] \otimes h[n] \qquad (6.59)$$

where $\otimes$ represents the discrete-time convolution operation.

Based on Equations (6.58) and (6.59), an LTI system $H\{.\}$ response to an arbitrary input signal $x[k]$ can be expressed in terms of the impulse responses of the system to the input impulse train sequence $x[n] = \sum_k x[k]\delta[n-k]$ as follows:

$$y[n] = H\{x[n]\} = \sum_{k=-\infty}^{\infty} x[k]H\{\delta[n-k]\} \qquad (6.60)$$

The pictorial interpretation of Equation (6.60) is shown in Figure 6.37. A simple way to compute the convolution sum in Equation (6.58) is by first obtaining the mirror image of the impulse response $h[n]$ (i.e., the mirror image of $h[k]$ is $h[-k]$), and then correlating the input samples $x[k]$ with mirror image samples $h[n-k]$, where $-\infty < k < \infty$. This is illustrated in Example 6.3. If the length of input sequence $x[n]$ is M and the length of impulse response $h[n]$ is L, then the length of convolution output $y[n]$ is $N = M + L - 1$. The convolution operation is commutative, meaning that

$$y[n] = x[n] \otimes h[n] = h[n] \otimes x[n] \qquad (6.61)$$

6.5.3 DFT Based Convolution Computation

One important property of the convolution operation is that convolution in the time domain turns out to be a multiplication in the frequency domain as follows:

$$x[n] \otimes h[n] \Leftrightarrow X[k] \cdot H[k] \qquad (6.62)$$

where $X[k] = \text{DFT}\{x[n]\}$ and $H[k] = \text{DFT}\{h[n]\}$; that is, $Y[k] = X[k] \cdot H[k]$ or $H[k] = Y[k]/X[k]$. Here, $H[k]$ is called the system transfer function.

Based on Equation (6.62),

$$x[n] \otimes h[n] = \sum_{k=-\infty}^{\infty} x[k]h[n-k]$$

$$\text{DFT}\{x[n] \otimes h[n]\} = \text{DFT}\left\{\sum_{k=-\infty}^{\infty} x[k]h[n-k]\right\} \qquad (6.63)$$

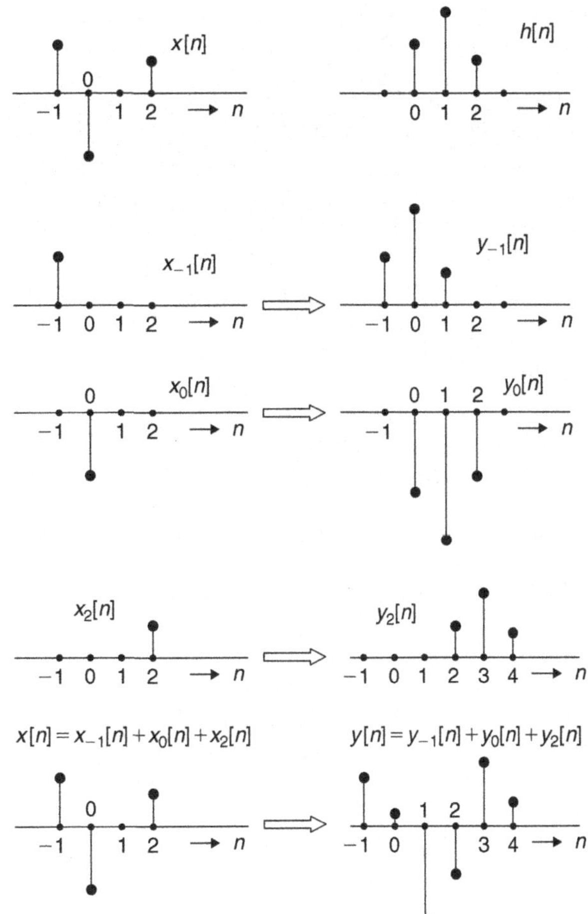

Figure 6.37: Discrete-time system response computation by convolution operation.

If the number of samples present in the input signal $x[n]$ is M, the number of samples present in the impulse response $h[n]$ is L, and if $N = M + L - 1$, then, after some manipulations, Equation (6.63) can be written as follows:

$$\text{DFT}\{x[n] \otimes h[n]\} = \text{DFT}\{x[n]\} \cdot \text{DFT}\{h[n]\} = X[k] \cdot H[k], \quad 0 \leq n \leq N-1, \ 0 \leq k \leq N-1$$

Now, by applying the IDFT on both sides of the previous equation, we have

$$x[n](\circ)h[n] = \text{IDFT}\{X[k] \cdot H[k]\}, \quad 0 \leq n \leq N-1, \ 0 \leq k \leq N-1 \tag{6.64}$$

where $(\circ)$ is a circular convolution operator. The circular convolution output $y[n]$ of the two sequences $x[n]$ and $y[n]$ is defined as follows:

$$y[n] = x[n](\circ)h[n] = \sum_{k=0}^{N-1} x[k]h[(n-k) \bmod N] \tag{6.65}$$

Based on Equation (6.65), we can see that the DFT-based convolution assumes periodicity in the input sequences. Consequently, to obtain the correct convolution output, we must use a DFT of $N = M + L - 1$ minimum length in the computation of convolution by the DFT method. For large values of M and L, computation of the convolution sum using (6.58) is very complex. Because we can compute the DFT faster using FFT algorithms (discussed in the next chapter), performing convolution on DSPs using Equation (6.65) can result in huge computational power savings. Examples for computing the convolution sum using Equations (6.58) and (6.65) are provided in Examples 6.3 and 6.4, respectively. Note that the end results in these examples are the same.

Example 6.3

Assume that the input signal $x[n] = [1, 2, -1, -3, -1, 1, 2, 4, 2, -1]$ and the impulse response $h[n] = [1, 3, 2]$. The convolution sum is computed as follows:

$$y[n] = \sum_{k=-\infty}^{\infty} x[k]h[n-k]$$

Given that $M = 10$ and $L = 3$, we will have a total of $N = M + L - 1 = 10 + 3 - 1 = 12$ samples in the convolution output. The output samples $y[n]$ are obtained as follows:

$x[k]$: $1, 2, -1, -3, -1, 1, 2, 4, 2, -1$
$h[0-k]$: $2, 3, 1$
$y[0] = 0 \cdot h[-2] + 0 \cdot h[-1] + 1 \cdot h[0] = 1$

$x[k]$: $1, 2, -1, -3, -1, 1, 2, 4, 2, -1$
$h[1-k]$: $2, 3, 1$
$y[1] = 0 \cdot h[-2] + 1 \cdot h[-1] + 2 \cdot h[0] = 1 \times 3 + 2 \times 1 = 5$

$x[k]$: $1, 2, -1, -3, -1, 1, 2, 4, 2, -1$
$h[2-k]$: $2, 3, 1$
$y[2] = 1 \cdot h[-2] + 2 \cdot h[-1] - 1 \cdot h[0] = 1 \times 2 + 2 \times 3 - 1 \times 1 = 7$

$x[k]$: $1, 2, -1, -3, -1, 1, 2, 4, 2, -1$
$h[3-k]$: $2, 3, 1$
$y[3] = 2 \cdot h[-2] - 1 \cdot h[-1] - 3 \cdot h[0] = 2 \times 2 - 1 \times 3 - 3 \times 1 = -2$

$x[k]$: $1, 2, -1, -3, -1, 1, 2, 4, 2, -1$
$h[4-k]$: $2, 3, 1$
$y[4] = -1 \cdot h[-2] - 3 \cdot h[-1] - 1 \cdot h[0] = -1 \times 2 - 3 \times 3 - 1 \times 1 = -12$

$x[k]$: $1, 2, -1, -3, -1, 1, 2, 4, 2, -1$
$h[5-k]$: $2, 3, 1$
$y[5] = -3 \cdot h[-2] - 1 \cdot h[-1] + 1 \cdot h[0] = -3 \times 2 - 1 \times 3 + 1 \times 1 = -8$

...

$x[k]$: $1, 2, -1, -3, -1, 1, 2, 4, 2, -1$
$h[10-k]$: $2, 3, 1$
$y[10] = 2 \cdot h[-2] - 1 \cdot h[-1] + 0 \cdot h[0] = 2 \times 2 - 1 \times 3 + 0 \times 1 = 1$

$x[k]$: $1, 2, -1, -3, -1, 1, 2, 4, 2, -1$
$h[11-k]$: $2, 3, 1$
$y[11] = -1 \cdot h[-2] + 0 \cdot h[-1] + 0 \cdot h[0] = -1 \times 2 + 0 \times 3 + 0 \times 1 = -2$

$y[n] = [1, 5, 7, -2, -12, -8, 3, 12, 18, 13, 1, -2]$

■

Example 6.4

Using the same input signal $x[n]$ and impulse response $h[n]$ as in Example 6.3, we compute the convolution sum using the DFT and IDFT pair as follows:

$x[n]$: $1, 2, -1, -3, -1, 1, 2, 4, 2, -1$

$$h[n]: \quad 1, 3, 2$$
$$M = 10, L = 3, N = M + L - 1 = 12$$

Hence, we use the 12-point DFT and 12-point IDFT in computing the convolution sum. Before applying the 12-point DFT, we make the lengths of arrays $x[n]$ and $y[n]$ equal to 12 by padding two zeros to $x[n]$ and nine zeros to $h[n]$ as follows:

$$x[n]: \quad 1, 2, -1, -3, -1, 1, 2, 4, 2, -1, 0, 0$$
$$h[n]: \quad 1, 3, 2, 0, 0, 0, 0, 0, 0, 0, 0, 0$$

$$X[k] = \text{DFT}\{x[n]\} = \sum_{n=0}^{N-1} x[n]e^{-j2\pi kn/N}$$

6.0000 + 0.0000i, −4.5981 + 5.9641i, 10.5000 − 6.0622i, 1.0000 − 1000i,
−4.5000 − 2.5981i, 0.5981 − 0.9641i, 0.0000 + 0.0000i, 0.5981 + 0.9641,
−4.5000 + 2.5981i, 1.0000 + 1.0000i, 10.5000 + 6.0622i, −4.5981 − 5.9641i

$$H[k] = \text{DFT}\{h[n]\} = \sum_{n=0}^{N-1} h[n]e^{-j2\pi kn/N}$$

6.0000 + 0.0000i, 4.5981 − 3.2321i, 1.5000 − 4.3301i, −1.0000 − 3.0000i,
−1.5000 − 0.8660i, −0.5981 + 0.2321i, 0.0000 + 0.0000i, −0.5981 − 0.2321i,
−1.5000 + 0.8660i, −1.0000 + 3.0000i, 1.5000 + 4.3301i, 4.5981 + 3.2321i

$Y[k] = X[k] \cdot Z[k] =$
36.0000 + 0.0000i, −1.8660 + 42.2846i, −10.5000 − 54.5596i, −4.0000 − 2.0000i,
4.5000 + 7.7942i, −0.1340 + 0.7154i, 0.0000 + 0.0000i, −0.1340 − 0.7154i,
4.5000 − 7.7942i, −4.0000 + 2.0000i, −10.5000 + 54.5596i, −1.8660 − 42.2846i

$$y[n] = \text{IDFT}\{Y[k]\} = \frac{1}{N}\sum_{k=0}^{N-1} Y[k]e^{j2\pi kn/N}$$

1.0000, 5.0000, 7.0000, −2.0000, −12.0000, −8.0000,
3.0000, 12.0000, 18.0000, 13.0000, 1.0000, −2.0000

■

6.6 Generalized Fourier Transforms

With Fourier methods, we are able to decompose an arbitrary signal in terms of sinusoids. Depending on the range of frequency components (or sinusoids) present in an LTI system impulse response, we get the corresponding output signal from the LTI system to an arbitrary input signal. However, as discussed previously, the Fourier transform of an arbitrary impulse response may contain infinite frequencies, and handling or representing such LTI systems would be too difficult. Moreover, most of the physical LTI systems (e.g., electric circuits, usually characterized by differential equations) have a particular kind of impulse response that decays with time, as shown in Figure 6.38. This kind of impulse response contains both sinusoids and exponentials of infinite length. To handle this type of signals and more compactly represent the systems with this kind of impulse response, as well as to better understand systems behavior, we use generalized Fourier transforms known as the Laplace transform and z-transform. Another motivation for introducing this generalization is that the Fourier transform does not converge for all sequences, and a generalization of the Fourier transform that encompasses a broader class of signals is useful. The Laplace transform is defined for continuous-time signals, whereas the z-transform is defined for discrete-time signals.

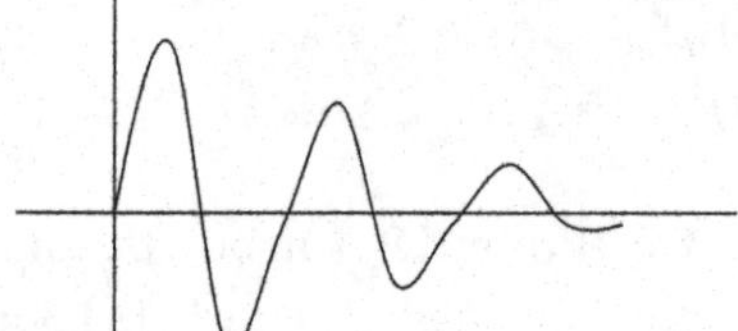

Figure 6.38: The impulse response shape of most real-world LTI systems.

6.6.1 Laplace Transform

For signal $x(t)$, the Laplace transform $X(s)$ is defined by

$$X(s) = \int_{-\infty}^{\infty} x(t)e^{-st}dt \tag{6.66}$$

where e^{-st} is called a complex exponential, which represents both sinusoid and exponential characteristics. With the Laplace transform, we are no longer in the frequency domain. We move to a two-dimensional s-plane, where $s = \sigma + j\omega$, which is formed with two parameters: σ (an exponential decay constant), which is represented using the x-axis, and ω (the sinusoid frequency), which is represented using the y-axis. The inverse Laplace transform produces the time-domain signal $x(t)$ from the s-plane response as follows:

$$x(t) = \frac{1}{j2\pi} \int_{c-j\infty}^{c+j\infty} X(s)e^{st}ds \tag{6.67}$$

The Laplace transform in Equation (6.66) may not converge for all values of s, and the region of s for which the integral in the equation converges is called the *region of convergence*. Based on Equation (6.66),

$$X(s) = \int_{-\infty}^{\infty} x(t)e^{-st}dt = \int_{-\infty}^{\infty} x(t)e^{-(\sigma+j\omega)t}dt = \int_{-\infty}^{\infty} x(t)e^{-\sigma t}e^{-j\omega t}dt$$

If $\sigma = 0$ (i.e., by evaluating the Laplace transform along the y-axis), then the preceding equation leads to our Fourier transform equation as follows:

$$X(j\omega) = \int_{-\infty}^{\infty} x(t)e^{-j\omega t}dt$$

Therefore, from a mathematical perspective, the Fourier transform is a particular case of the Laplace transform. The Fourier transform analyzes signals in terms of sinusoids, whereas the Laplace transform analyzes signals in terms of sinusoids and exponentials. In addition, the time-domain convolution operation on two signals maps to the multiplication of their respective Laplace-transform outputs in the s-domain.

Transfer Function

If X(s) is the Laplace transform of system input signal $x(t)$ and $Y(s)$ is the Laplace transform of system output signal $y(t)$, then the system transfer function $H(s)$ is obtained as follows:

$$H(s) = \frac{Y(s)}{X(s)} \tag{6.68}$$

Poles and Zeros of LTI Systems

For an LTI system, which is controlled by differential equations, the system transfer function can be expressed as follows:

$$H(s) = \frac{b_n s^n + b_{n-1}s^{n-1} + b_{n-2}s^{n-2} + \cdots + b_1 s + b_0}{s^n + a_{n-1}s^{n-1} + a_{n-2}s^{n-2} + \cdots + a_1 s + a_0} \tag{6.69}$$

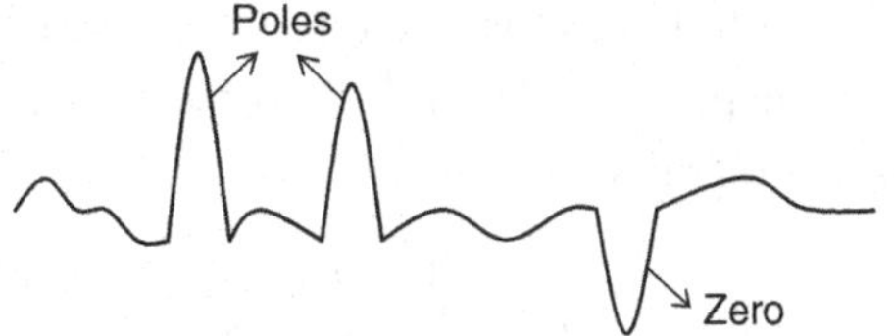

Figure 6.39: Illustration of poles and zeros in system frequency response.

If we factor both the numerator and denominator of Equation (6.69), then

$$H(s) = \frac{b_n(s - z_0)(s - z_1)\cdots(s - z_{n-1})}{(s - p_0)(s - p_1)\cdots(s - p_{n-1})} \tag{6.70}$$

where p_i's (the roots of denominator) are called the *poles* and z_i's (the roots of numerator) are called the *zeros* of LTI systems. Depending on the location of poles and zeros in the s-plane, we can uniquely represent an LTI system, and these few parameters (i.e., poles and zeros) can completely describe system characteristics. The system frequency response contains very large values at the pole locations, whereas it contains very small values at the zero locations. A graphic view of poles and zeros is shown in Figure 6.39 by taking a cross-section of the s-plane.

Typically, the number of zeros will be equal to, or less than, the number of poles. Factoring polynomials greater than the second order is difficult; thus, we use a cascade of second-order stages (which can be represented with second-order polynomials) to construct larger systems. For example, a 10th-order system can be obtained by cascading five second-order systems. For example, the impulse response of the second-order system in Equation (6.71) is easily obtained by rearranging the summation in Equation (6.72):

$$H(s) = \frac{k(s + z_0)}{(s + p_0)(s + p_1)} \tag{6.71}$$

$$H(s) = \frac{k_0}{(s + p_0)} + \frac{k_1}{(s + p_1)} \tag{6.72}$$

By taking the inverse Laplace transform of $H(s)$ in Equation (6.72), we obtain the impulse response as follows:

$$h(t) = (k_0 e^{-p_0 t} + k_1 e^{-p_1 t})u(t) \tag{6.73}$$

where $u(t)$ is the unit step function defined as in Equation (6.5).

As the locations of poles and zeros provide a complete description of system frequency response (the frequency response is equal to the values of $H(s)$ along the imaginary axis), the Laplace transform is popularly used to design the continuous-time LTI systems directly in the s-plane. In the next chapter, we will discuss the role of s-plane poles and zeros in the design of Butterworth, Chebyshev, and elliptic filters for given passband and stopband specifications.

6.6.2 z-Transform

The z-transform plays the same role in the analysis of discrete-time signals and LTI systems as the Laplace transform does in the analysis of continuous-time signals and LTI systems. In other words, the Laplace transform is a generalization of the Fourier transform, whereas the z-transform is a generalization of the discrete-time Fourier transform. In addition, the convolution in the time-domain results in the multiplication of the z-transform domain. The z-transform of a discrete-time signal $x[n]$ is defined as the power series,

$$X(z) = \sum_{n=-\infty}^{\infty} x[n]z^{-n} \tag{6.74}$$

where z is a complex variable. By substituting $z = re^{j\omega}$ in Equation (6.74), we have

$$X(re^{j\omega}) = \sum_{n=-\infty}^{\infty} x[n](re^{j\omega})^{-n} = \sum_{n=-\infty}^{\infty} (x[n]r^{-n})e^{-j\omega n} \tag{6.75}$$

Thus, Equation (6.75) can be interpreted as the discrete-time Fourier transform of the product of the original signal $x[n]$ and the exponential sequence r^{-n}. With the inverse z-transform, we obtain the discrete-time signal $x[n]$ from $X(z)$ using the contour integral as follows:

$$x[n] = \frac{1}{j2\pi} \oint_C X(z) z^{n-1} dz \tag{6.76}$$

where C is any contour that lies in the region of convergence (ROC) of the z-transform and encircles the origin.

Similar to how the Laplace transform deals with differential equations of LTI systems, the z-transform deals with the difference equations defining the behavior of an LTI system. However, the mathematics of the s-plane uses rectangular coordinates, whereas the z-transform uses polar coordinates. In addition, there are correspondences (if not one-to-one) from the s-plane to the z-plane as follows:

1. The y-axis in s-plane is mapped to the unit circle in the z-plane.
2. The left half of the s-plane is mapped to the interior of the unit circle.
3. The right side of the s-plane is mapped to the exterior of the unit circle.
4. The symmetry about the x-axis is reserved from the s-plane to the z-plane.

As the z-transform handles the sampled data, the z-plane can uniquely represent frequencies up to half the sampling rate, and the frequencies above that range are wrapped around the circles of the z-transform.

The z-transform is commonly used in the design of digital filters (see Chapter 7). Typically, we design recursive digital filters by starting with analog filters, and then we obtain the desired digital filter after a series of mathematical conversions. So, we basically map the pole-zero locations from the s-plane to the z-plane in deriving the recursive digital filters from analog filters. The locations of pole zeros in the s-plane are on the vertical lines, and after mapping to the z-plane, they lie on circles concentric with the origin.

CHAPTER 7

Transforms and Filters

In Chapter 6, the concepts of convolution and time-frequency representation of signals were introduced. In this chapter, we discuss how these concepts are implemented in digital systems using digital filters and fast transforms.

Transforms and filters are among the most powerful tools in the digital signal processing (DSP) field. Indeed, it is the development of fast versions of these computationally demanding algorithms, combined with advances in semiconductor technology, that allow us to perform most media processing tasks in real time.

Fast Fourier transform (FFT) algorithms are used to compute the discrete Fourier transform (DFT) with fewer computations. Digital filters are capable of achieving the performance that is close to desired system specifications. In addition, there are advantages of virtually eliminating errors in the filter (due to aging, temperature, etc., that usually degrade the performance of analog filters). One disadvantage of digital filters is that they are slower due to the "block" nature of the processing and cannot handle very high frequencies when compared to analog filters. In this chapter, we will discuss the simulation and implementation techniques of discrete transforms and digital filters.

Various transforms were introduced in Chapter 6, including the Fourier series, discrete Fourier transform, discrete cosine transform (DCT), Laplace, and z-transforms. These transforms uniquely map time-domain signals to their frequency-domain representations. The inverses of these transforms likewise map a signal's frequency-domain representation back to the time domain. Which transform we use depends on the signal's nature (periodic, nonperiodic, exponential sinusoid, etc.) and signal type (continuous-time, discrete-time).

Of all transforms discussed in Chapter 6, only the DFT and DCT can be implemented using digital systems (the others assume analog signals). The DFT is used in a wide range of signal-processing applications (e.g., telecommunications, medical, geophysics). The DCT is more heavily used in image and video compression applications (e.g., JPEG, MPEG-2, MPEG-4). The DFT and DCT are by far the most commonly used in media processing. Therefore, the discussion in this chapter is restricted to fast versions of these algorithms, and their fixed-point simulation and efficient implementation techniques.

A filter is a system that allows some frequency components of a signal to pass through while attenuating other components. Consider two extremes. One extreme is an amplifier, which allows all frequencies to pass through unattenuated. The other extreme would be an oscillator, which outputs only a single frequency. Filters lie somewhere in between. For example, linear-time-invariant (LTI) systems, as discussed in Section 6.5, are filters. In fact, all filters discussed in this chapter are assumed to be LTI systems. LTI filters are completely described by their impulse response, and the output of an LTI filter is obtained by convolving the filter input with its impulse response. A few applications of digital filters include telecommunications, medical signal processing, and audio/image/video processing.

The two main filter types are finite-impulse-response (FIR), and infinite-impulse-response (IIR) filters. In Sections 7.3 through 7.5 we briefly discuss FIR and IIR filters, examine their specifications, and explore digital filter design, simulation, and techniques for efficient implementation.

7.1 Fast Fourier Transform

In Section 6.4.2, we briefly discussed the DFT. Here, we discuss the complexity of the DFT, and then derive its faster, less complex variant, the FFT. If the sequence (or discrete-time signal) $x[n]$ consists of N samples, the

DOI: 10.1016/B978-1-85617-678-1.00007-7

DFT also produces a sequence of N samples, $X[k]$, spaced equally in the frequency domain:

$$X[k] = \sum_{n=0}^{N-1} x[n]e^{-j2\pi nk/N}, \quad k = 0, 1, 2, \ldots, N-1 \tag{7.1}$$

where $e^{-j2\pi nk/N} = \cos(2\pi nk/N) - j\sin(2\pi nk/N)$.

The DFT can be viewed as a correlation of the input signal with a set of sinusoids. Each sinusoid evaluates the frequency content of the input signal at the sinusoid's oscillation frequency. Equation (7.1) can also be expressed in terms of matrix multiplication:

$$X_{N\times 1} = W_{N\times N} \cdot x_{N\times 1} \tag{7.2}$$

where $x_{N\times 1} = [x_0, x_1, x_2, \ldots, x_{N-1}]^T$, $X_{N\times 1} = [X_0, X_1, X_2, \ldots, X_{N-1}]^T$, and the matrix

$$W_{N\times N} = \begin{bmatrix} 1 & 1 & 1 & \cdots & 1 \\ 1 & e^{-j2\pi\cdot 1\cdot 1/N} & e^{-j2\pi\cdot 1\cdot 2/N} & \cdots & e^{-j2\pi\cdot 1\cdot (N-1)/N} \\ 1 & e^{-j2\pi\cdot 2\cdot 1/N} & e^{-j2\pi\cdot 2\cdot 2/N} & \cdots & e^{-j2\pi\cdot 2\cdot (N-1)/N} \\ \vdots & \vdots & \vdots & \vdots & \vdots \\ 1 & e^{-j2\pi\cdot (N-1)\cdot 1/N} & e^{-j2\pi\cdot (N-1)\cdot 2/N} & \cdots & e^{-j2\pi\cdot (N-1)\cdot (N-1)/N} \end{bmatrix} \tag{7.3}$$

can be constructed from N components $W_k = e^{-j2\pi k/N}$, $k = 0, \ldots, N-1$, which we refer to as "twiddle factors."

DFT Computational Complexity

As seen in Equation (7.2), the matrix and vector multiplication in the DFT require N^2 operations, and each operation involves one complex multiplication and one complex addition. One complex multiplication requires four real multiplications and two real additions. One complex addition requires two real additions. Thus, one operation in the DFT computation involves four real additions and four real multiplications. We can now calculate the complexity of an N-point DFT, in terms of real operations, as $4N^2$ real multiplications and $4N^2$ real additions.

To illustrate how this maps to real hardware, consider the reference embedded processor. On the reference processor, multiplication and addition both consume 1 cycle (see Appendix A, Section A.4, on the companion website for more details on the cycle estimation). The processor also has two MAC (multiply and accumulate) units, which can perform two additions and two multiplications per cycle. Using these MAC units, an $N = 4096$-point DFT will consume approximately 33.5 million ($= 2 \times 4096 \times 4096$) cycles.

7.1.1 Fast Fourier Transforms

The FFT works by exploiting symmetry in the matrix W in Equation (7.3). Before going into the concepts involved in the FFT, let's examine the symmetry of W for $N = 6$, $N = 7$, and $N = 8$.

$$W_{6\times 6} = \begin{bmatrix} 1.0000 & 1.0000 & 1.0000 & 1.0000 & 1.0000 & 1.0000 \\ 1.0000 & 0.5000-0.8660i & -0.5000-0.8660i & -1.0000-0.0000i & -0.5000+0.8660i & 0.5000+0.8660i \\ 1.0000 & -0.5000-0.8660i & -0.5000+0.8660i & 1.0000+0.0000i & -0.5000-0.8660i & -0.5000+0.8660i \\ 1.0000 & -1.0000-0.0000i & 1.0000+0.0000i & -1.0000-0.0000i & 1.0000+0.0000i & -1.0000-0.0000i \\ 1.0000 & -0.5000+0.8660i & -0.5000-0.8660i & 1.0000+0.0000i & -0.5000+0.8660i & -0.5000-0.8660i \\ 1.0000 & 0.5000+0.8660i & -0.5000+0.8660i & -1.0000-0.0000i & -0.5000-0.8660i & 0.5000-0.8660i \end{bmatrix}$$

$$W_{7\times 7} = \begin{bmatrix} 1.0000 & 1.0000 & 1.0000 & 1.0000 & 1.0000 & 1.0000 & 1.0000 \\ 1.0000 & 0.6235-0.7818i & -0.2225-0.9749i & -0.9010-0.4339i & -0.9010+0.4339i & -0.2225+0.9749i & 0.6235+0.7818i \\ 1.0000 & -0.2225-0.9749i & -0.9010+0.4339i & 0.6235+0.7818i & 0.6235-0.7818i & -0.9010-0.4339i & -0.2225+0.9749i \\ 1.0000 & -0.9010-0.4339i & 0.6235+0.7818i & -0.2225-0.9749i & -0.2225+0.9749i & 0.6235-0.7818i & -0.9010+0.4339i \\ 1.0000 & -0.9010+0.4339i & 0.6235-0.7818i & -0.2225+0.9749i & -0.2225-0.9749i & 0.6235+0.7818i & -0.9010-0.4339i \\ 1.0000 & -0.2225+0.9749i & -0.9010-0.4339i & 0.6235-0.7818i & 0.6235+0.7818i & -0.9010+0.4339i & -0.2225-0.9749i \\ 1.0000 & 0.6235+0.7818i & -0.2225+0.9749i & -0.9010+0.4339i & -0.9010-0.4339i & -0.2225-0.9749i & 0.6235-0.7818i \end{bmatrix}$$

$$W_{8\times 8} =$$

$$\begin{bmatrix} 1.0000 & 1.0000 & 1.0000 & 1.0000 & 1.0000 & 1.0000 & 1.0000 & 1.0000 \\ 1.0000 & 0.7071-0.7071i & 0.0000-1.0000i & -0.7071-0.7071i & -1.0000-0.0000i & -0.7071+0.7071i & -0.0000+1.0000i & 0.7071+0.7071i \\ 1.0000 & 0.0000-1.0000i & -1.0000-0.0000i & -0.0000+1.0000i & 1.0000+0.0000i & 0.0000-1.0000i & -1.0000-0.0000i & -0.0000+1.0000i \\ 1.0000 & -0.7071-0.7071i & -0.0000+1.0000i & 0.7071-0.7071i & -1.0000-0.0000i & 0.7071+0.7071i & 0.0000-1.0000i & -0.7071+0.7071i \\ 1.0000 & -1.0000-0.0000i & 1.0000+0.0000i & -1.0000-0.0000i & 1.0000+0.0000i & -1.0000-0.0000i & 1.0000+0.0000i & -1.0000-0.0000i \\ 1.0000 & -0.7071+0.7071i & 0.0000-1.0000i & 0.7071+0.7071i & -1.0000-0.0000i & 0.7071-0.7071i & -0.0000+1.0000i & -0.7071-0.7071i \\ 1.0000 & -0.0000+1.0000i & -1.0000-0.0000i & 0.0000-1.0000i & 1.0000+0.0000i & -0.0000+1.0000i & -1.0000-0.0000i & -0.0000-1.0000i \\ 1.0000 & 0.7071+0.7071i & -0.0000+1.0000i & -0.7071+0.7071i & -1.0000-0.0000i & -0.7071-0.7071i & -0.0000-1.0000i & 0.7071-0.7071i \end{bmatrix}$$

Observing the matrix elements of $W_{6\times 6}$, $W_{7\times 7}$, and $W_{8\times 8}$, we find symmetry (except for sign) in both the horizontal and vertical directions. Similarly, in both $W_{6\times 6}$ and $W_{8\times 8}$, we also find periodicity (except for sign) in both horizontal and vertical directions. In matrix $W_{6\times 6}$, the elements repeat (except for sign) two times in any column or row (i.e., period $= N/2 = 6/2 = 3$). In matrix $W_{8\times 8}$, the elements repeat (except for sign) four times in any column or row (i.e., period $= N/4 = 8/4 = 2$). The $N/2$ period in matrix elements (or twiddle factors) is present in all DFT twiddle-factor matrices when N is even. Similarly, the $N/4$ period is present in all DFT twiddle-factor matrices where N is the power of 2 (i.e., for N equal to $4, 8, 16, 32, 64 \ldots$).

DFT Matrix Factorization

Why are the symmetry and periodicity of twiddle factors so important? They allow us to implement the DFT very efficiently. When we have repeated elements in a matrix, we can use divide-and-conquer methods to perform the matrix and vector multiplication (as seen in Equation (7.2)) with fewer multiplications. Consider, for illustration, a DFT matrix with $N = 8$. The 8-point DFT twiddle-factor matrix in terms of W_8 $(= e^{-j2\pi/8}$, the primitive eighth root of unity) is expressed as follows:

$$W_{8\times 8} = \begin{bmatrix} 1 & 1 & 1 & 1 & 1 & 1 & 1 & 1 \\ 1 & W_8^1 & W_8^2 & W_8^3 & W_8^4 & W_8^5 & W_8^6 & W_8^7 \\ 1 & W_8^2 & W_8^4 & W_8^6 & W_8^8 & W_8^{10} & W_8^{12} & W_8^{14} \\ 1 & W_8^3 & W_8^6 & W_8^9 & W_8^{12} & W_8^{15} & W_8^{18} & W_8^{21} \\ 1 & W_8^4 & W_8^8 & W_8^{12} & W_8^{16} & W_8^{20} & W_8^{24} & W_8^{28} \\ 1 & W_8^5 & W_8^{10} & W_8^{15} & W_8^{20} & W_8^{25} & W_8^{30} & W_8^{35} \\ 1 & W_8^6 & W_8^{12} & W_8^{18} & W_8^{24} & W_8^{30} & W_8^{36} & W_8^{42} \\ 1 & W_8^7 & W_8^{14} & W_8^{21} & W_8^{28} & W_8^{35} & W_8^{42} & W_8^{49} \end{bmatrix} \tag{7.4}$$

To begin, we divide the matrix $W_{8\times 8}$ into two parts, placing all even columns first followed by all odd columns. This is achieved by multiplying $W_{8\times 8}$ with the matrix $A_{8\times 8}$, defined as follows:

$$A = \begin{bmatrix} 1 & 0 & 0 & 0 & 0 & 0 & 0 & 0 \\ 0 & 0 & 0 & 0 & 1 & 0 & 0 & 0 \\ 0 & 1 & 0 & 0 & 0 & 0 & 0 & 0 \\ 0 & 0 & 0 & 0 & 0 & 1 & 0 & 0 \\ 0 & 0 & 1 & 0 & 0 & 0 & 0 & 0 \\ 0 & 0 & 0 & 0 & 0 & 0 & 1 & 0 \\ 0 & 0 & 0 & 1 & 0 & 0 & 0 & 0 \\ 0 & 0 & 0 & 0 & 0 & 0 & 0 & 1 \end{bmatrix}$$

The rearranged matrix, $W'_{8\times8} = W_{8\times8}A_{8\times8}$, and the elements of $W'_{8\times8}$ are given in the following:

$$W'_{8\times8} = \left[\begin{array}{cccc|cccc} 1 & 1 & 1 & 1 & 1 & 1 & 1 & 1 \\ 1 & W_8^2 & W_8^4 & W_8^6 & W_8^1 & W_8^3 & W_8^5 & W_8^7 \\ 1 & W_8^4 & W_8^8 & W_8^{12} & W_8^2 & W_8^6 & W_8^{10} & W_8^{14} \\ 1 & W_8^6 & W_8^{12} & W_8^{18} & W_8^3 & W_8^9 & W_8^{15} & W_8^{21} \\ \hline 1 & W_8^8 & W_8^{16} & W_8^{24} & W_8^4 & W_8^{12} & W_8^{20} & W_8^{28} \\ 1 & W_8^{10} & W_8^{20} & W_8^{30} & W_8^5 & W_8^{15} & W_8^{25} & W_8^{35} \\ 1 & W_8^{12} & W_8^{24} & W_8^{36} & W_8^6 & W_8^{18} & W_8^{30} & W_8^{42} \\ 1 & W_8^{14} & W_8^{28} & W_8^{42} & W_8^7 & W_8^{21} & W_8^{35} & W_8^{49} \end{array}\right] = \begin{bmatrix} P_{4\times4} & Q_{4\times4} \\ R_{4\times4} & S_{4\times4} \end{bmatrix} \tag{7.5}$$

After careful observation of the matrices $P_{4\times4}$ and $R_{4\times4}$, we can see that

$$W_8^2 = e^{-j2\pi2/8} = e^{-j2\pi/4} = W_4^1,\ W_8^4 = W_4^2,\ W_8^6 = W_4^3,\ W_8^{12} = W_4^6,\ W_8^{18} = W_4^9$$

$$W_8^8 = e^{-j2\pi8/8} = e^{-j2\pi} = 1 = W_4^4,\ W_8^{16} = W_4^8 = e^{-j2\pi8/4} = e^{-j2\pi2} = 1$$

$$W_8^{24} = 1,\ W_8^{10} = e^{-j2\pi10/8} = e^{-j2\pi(2+8)/8} = e^{-j2\pi2/8}.e^{-j2\pi8/8} = e^{-j2\pi1/4} = W_4^1$$

$$W_8^{20} = W_4^2,\ W_8^{30} = W_4^3,\ W_8^{12} = W_4^2,\ W_8^{24} = 1 = W_4^4,\ W_8^{36} = W_8^4 = W_4^2.1 = W_4^6,\ W_8^{14} = W_4^3$$

$$W_8^{28} = W_4^6 \text{ and } W_8^{42} = W_4^9$$

Thus, $P_{4\times4}$ and $R_{4\times4}$ represent 4-point, DFT twiddle-factor matrices as follows:

$$P_{4\times4} = W_{4\times4} = \begin{bmatrix} 1 & 1 & 1 & 1 \\ 1 & W_4^1 & W_4^2 & W_4^3 \\ 1 & W_4^2 & W_4^4 & W_4^6 \\ 1 & W_4^3 & W_4^6 & W_4^9 \end{bmatrix} \qquad R_{4\times4} = W_{4\times4} = \begin{bmatrix} 1 & 1 & 1 & 1 \\ 1 & W_4^1 & W_4^2 & W_4^3 \\ 1 & W_4^2 & W_4^4 & W_4^6 \\ 1 & W_4^3 & W_4^6 & W_4^9 \end{bmatrix}$$

Similarly, after examination of matrices $Q_{4\times4}$ and $S_{4\times4}$, we can rewrite them as follows:

$$Q_{4\times4} = \begin{bmatrix} 1 & 1 & 1 & 1 \\ W_8^1 & W_8^3 & W_8^5 & W_8^7 \\ W_8^2 & W_8^6 & W_8^{10} & W_8^{14} \\ W_0^3 & W_0^9 & W_0^{15} & W_0^{21} \end{bmatrix}$$

$$= \begin{bmatrix} 1 & 0 & 0 & 0 \\ 0 & W_8^1 & 0 & 0 \\ 0 & 0 & W_8^2 & 0 \\ 0 & 0 & 0 & W_8^3 \end{bmatrix} \begin{bmatrix} 1 & 1 & 1 & 1 \\ 1 & W_8^2 & W_8^4 & W_8^6 \\ 1 & W_8^4 & W_8^8 & W_8^{12} \\ 1 & W_8^6 & W_8^{12} & W_8^{18} \end{bmatrix}$$

$$= D_8 \begin{bmatrix} 1 & 1 & 1 & 1 \\ 1 & W_4^1 & W_4^2 & W_4^3 \\ 1 & W_4^2 & W_4^4 & W_4^6 \\ 1 & W_4^3 & W_4^6 & W_4^9 \end{bmatrix} = D_8 W_{4\times4}$$

$$S_{4\times4}=\begin{bmatrix} W_8^4 & W_8^{12} & W_8^{20} & W_8^{28} \\ W_8^5 & W_8^{15} & W_8^{25} & W_8^{35} \\ W_8^6 & W_8^{18} & W_8^{30} & W_8^{42} \\ W_8^7 & W_8^{21} & W_8^{35} & W_8^{49} \end{bmatrix} = W_8^4 \begin{bmatrix} 1 & 1 & 1 & 1 \\ W_8^1 & W_8^3 & W_8^5 & W_8^7 \\ W_8^2 & W_8^6 & W_8^{10} & W_8^{14} \\ W_8^3 & W_8^9 & W_8^{15} & W_8^{21} \end{bmatrix} = -\begin{bmatrix} 1 & 1 & 1 & 1 \\ W_8^1 & W_8^3 & W_8^5 & W_8^7 \\ W_8^2 & W_8^6 & W_8^{10} & W_8^{14} \\ W_8^3 & W_8^9 & W_8^{15} & W_8^{21} \end{bmatrix}$$

$$= -\begin{bmatrix} 1 & 0 & 0 & 0 \\ 0 & W_8^1 & 0 & 0 \\ 0 & 0 & W_8^2 & 0 \\ 0 & 0 & 0 & W_8^3 \end{bmatrix} \begin{bmatrix} 1 & 1 & 1 & 1 \\ 1 & W_8^2 & W_8^4 & W_8^6 \\ 1 & W_8^4 & W_8^8 & W_8^{12} \\ 1 & W_8^6 & W_8^{12} & W_8^{18} \end{bmatrix} = -D_8 W_{4\times4}$$

Thus, Equation (7.5) can be rewritten as follows:

$$W'_{8\times8} = \begin{bmatrix} W_{4\times4} & D_8 W_{4\times4} \\ W_{4\times4} & -D_8 W_{4\times4} \end{bmatrix} \tag{7.6}$$

Radix-2 FFT Algorithms

Once again, using matrix $A_{8\times8}$, we can rearrange the input data $x_{8\times8}$. Let $x'_{8\times1} = A_{8\times8}x_{8\times1}$ and let $X'_{8\times1} = W'_{8\times8}x'_{8\times1}$. Since $A_{8\times8}A_{8\times8} = I_{8\times8}$, based on Equations (7.4) and (7.6), we will have $X_{8\times1} = W_{8\times8}x_{8\times1} = W_{8\times8}A_{8\times8}A_{8\times8}x_{8\times1} = W'_{8\times8}x'_{8\times1} = X'_{8\times1}$. With this, by rearranging the input data $x_{8\times1}$, we can compute the 8-point DFT output $X_{8\times1}$ using two 4-point DFTs (using Equation (7.6)). The corresponding signal flow diagram is shown in Figure 7.1.

This factorization is not yet over, as we can further factorize the $W_{4\times4}$ into $W_{2\times2}$ in the same manner. That is, each 4-point DFT can be computed using two 2-point DFTs. The block diagram for computing an 8-point DFT using four 2-point DFTs is shown in Figure 7.2. The corresponding signal flow diagram for computing an 8-point DFT using 2-point DFTs is shown in Figure 7.3. As shown in Figure 7.2, we compute the 8-point DFT using four 2-point DFTs in three stages. Only in the first stage do we compute the 2-point DFTs; in the second and third stages we combine the outputs of previous stages with simple twiddle-factor multiplications (not shown in the block diagram) to get two 4-point DFT outputs and then one 8-point DFT output.

As seen in Figure 7.3, we compute the 8-point DFT in terms of 2-point DFTs in three stages (here the 2-point DFT is the smallest butterfly enclosed in a dashed curve as shown). In general, if N is a power of 2, then we compute the N-point DFT in $\log_2 N$ stages.

The number of complex multiplications in this approach is $N\log_2 N$, and half of these are multiplications by -1. Thus, we only require $(N/2)\log_2 N$ complex multiplications and $N\log_2 N$ complex additions to compute an N-point DFT. For $N = 4096$, this is only about 0.09 million cycles on the reference embedded processor. Compared to the DFT (which requires about 33.5 million cycles), this is 372 times faster!

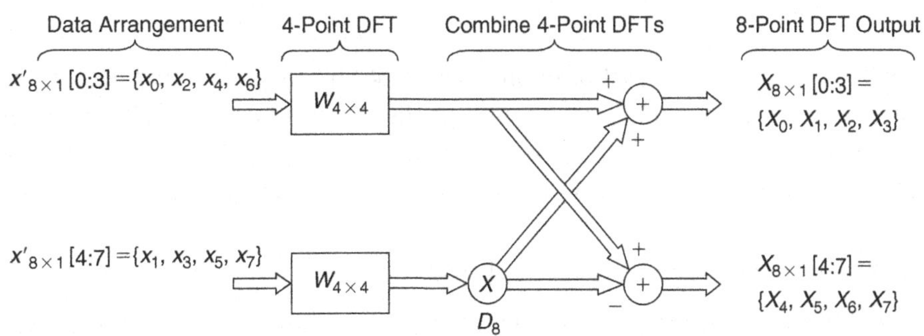

Figure 7.1: Signal flow diagram of 8-point DFT computation using two 4-point DFTs.

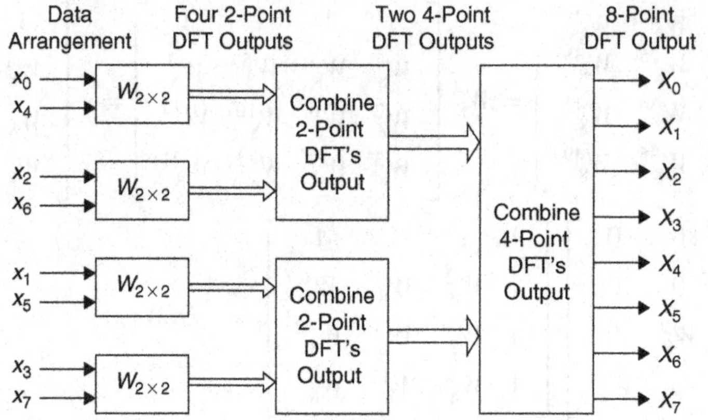

Figure 7.2: Block diagram to compute 8-point DFT using four 2-point DFTs.

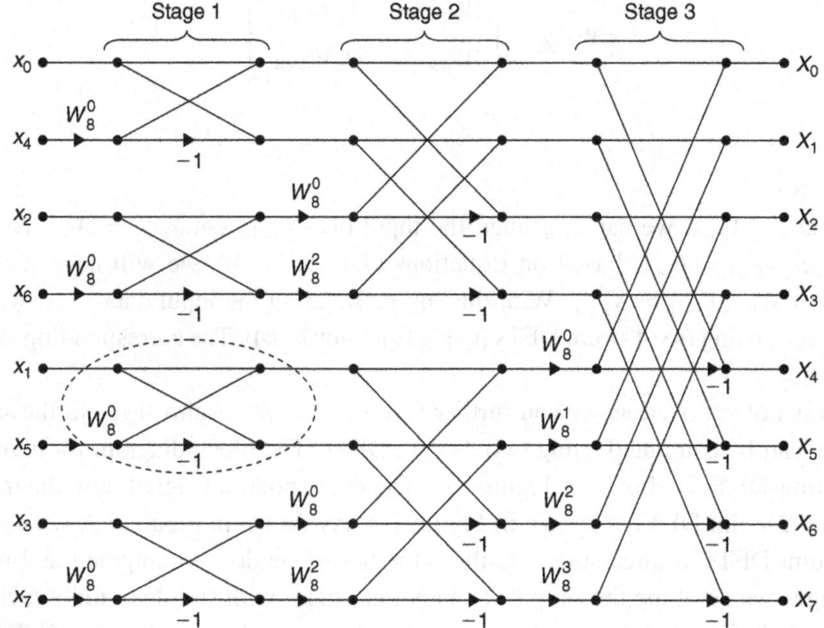

Figure 7.3: Signal flow diagram of decimation-in-time radix-2, 8-point DFT algorithm.

The multistage algorithm used to compute the 8-point DFT efficiently as shown in Figure 7.3 is referred to as a decimation-in-time (DIT) radix-2 algorithm. We also have an equivalent decimation-in-frequency (DIF) radix-2 algorithm for the N-point DFT. The signal flow diagram of DIF 8-point DFT is shown in Figure 7.4, and is exactly opposite to the flow of the DIT algorithm. The complexity of both algorithms is exactly the same.

An FFT is any algorithm that computes the DFT faster than the direct computation. Since the DFT is computed faster with radix-2 algorithms than with direct computation, we call these algorithms radix-2 FFT algorithms.

Bit Reversal

The FFT expects the input in the bit-reversal order in the case of DIT radix-2 or outputs the data in bit-reversal order in the case of DIF radix-2 algorithms. Therefore, we discuss the data sample's arrangement at the input of DIT radix-2 algorithm and extracting the appropriate output in the case of the DIF radix-2 algorithm. In the case of the DIT radix-2 algorithm, the inputs are rearranged ($\log_2 N - 1$) times in the following manner:

$$\{x_0, x_1, x_2, x_3, x_4, x_5, x_6, x_7\} \rightarrow \{[x_0, x_2, x_4, x_6], [x_1, x_3, x_5, x_7]\} \quad \longleftarrow \text{First-time decimation}$$

$$\rightarrow \{[(x_0, x_4), (x_2, x_6)], [(x_1, x_5), (x_3, x_7)]\} \quad \longleftarrow \text{Second-time decimation}$$

$$\rightarrow \{x_0, x_4, x_2, x_6, x_1, x_5, x_3, x_7\}$$

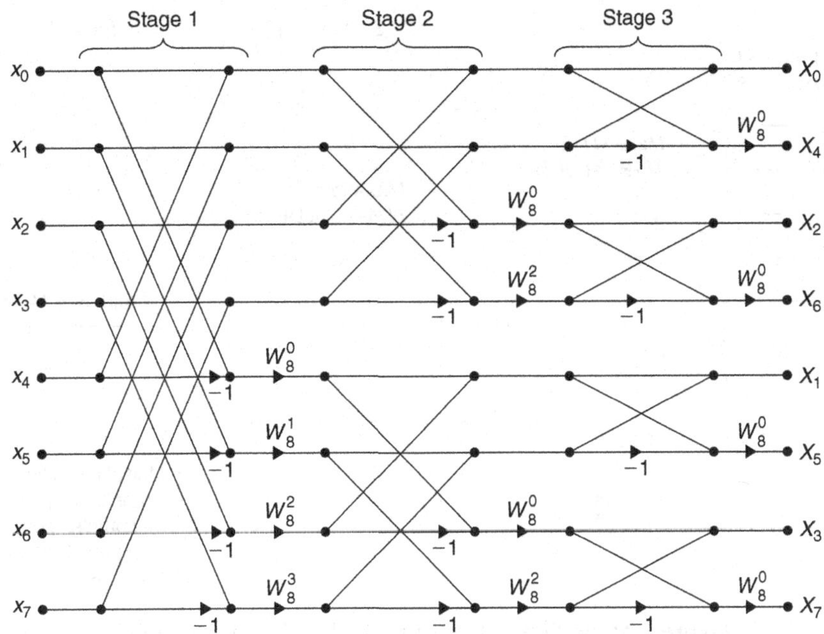

Figure 7.4: Signal flow diagram for decimation-in-frequency radix-2, 8-point DFT algorithm.

Table 7.1: Bit-reversal index for samples of decimation-in-time radix-2 FFT

Before Arrangement	After Arrangement
0 (000)	0 (000)
1 (001)	4 (100)
2 (010)	2 (010)
3 (011)	6 (110)
4 (100)	1 (001)
5 (101)	5 (101)
6 (110)	3 (011)
7 (111)	7 (111)

The DIF radix-2 algorithm outputs the frequency components in a particular order (permuted), and the actual DFT output is obtained by undoing this permutation. The actual and permuted sample indices for the 8-point DFT are provided in Table 7.1, and the corresponding binary numbers are shown in brackets. From these binary numbers, it is clear that the permuted index is obtained by reversing the bits of the actual index.

For example, in the case of the DIT radix-2 algorithm, the input sample (x_3) at index 3 (or binary 011) is moved to the index 6 (or binary 110), and the sample (x_4) at index 4 (or binary 100) is moved to the index 1 (or binary 001) after rearrangement.

Radix-4 FFT Algorithm

When the length of the DFT N is a power of 4, we can further reduce the number of complex operations using a radix-4 FFT algorithm. With a radix-4 FFT, we first divide the data into four datastreams and form a $4 \times N/4$ matrix. We compute four $N/4$-point DFTs and then multiply with twiddle factors and transpose the matrix (although this is a complex matrix, we transpose the matrix without conjugation). Then, we obtain the N-point DFT by computing 4-point DFTs on the transposed $(N/4) \times 4$ matrix. This process is repeated for the next stage by dividing each $N/4$-point DFT into four $N/16$ streams and it is continued until the length of the DFT reaches 4 as illustrated in Figure 7.5.

As an example, consider a 16-point DFT computed using a radix-4 FFT (i.e., $N = 16$). Let $x = \{x[n]\}$, $0 \le n \le N-1$ be the input vector with 16 discrete-time samples. We compute the 16-point DFT output $X = \{X[k]\}, 0 \le k \le N-1$, for input x using a radix-4 FFT algorithm as shown in Figure 7.5 We first divide $x[n]$ into four

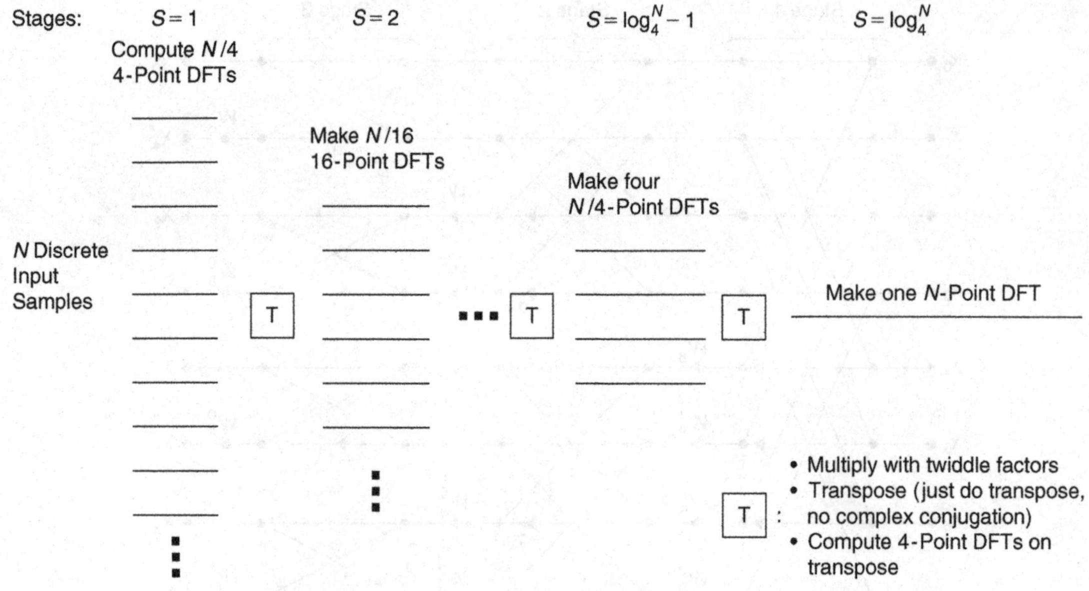

Figure 7.5: An illustration of radix-4 FFT computation.

sequences and form a $4 \times N/4$ two-dimensional array or matrix as $x(u, v) = x[4v + u]$, where $0 \le v \le N/4 - 1$ and $0 \le u \le 3$. The samples of $x(u, v)$ in two-dimensional space for $N = 16$ follow:

$$\begin{matrix} x[0], & x[4], & x[8], & x[12] \\ x[1], & x[5], & x[9], & x[13] \\ x[2], & x[6], & x[10], & x[14] \\ x[3], & x[7], & x[11], & x[15] \end{matrix}$$

If $X'(u, q)$ represents a row-wise $N/4$-point DFT of $x(u, v)$, then

$$X'(u, q) = \sum_{p=0}^{(N/4)-1} x(u, p) W_{N/4}^{pq} \tag{7.7}$$

For $N = 16$, Equation (7.7) becomes a 4-point DFT computation on rows of $x(u, v)$, and it can be expressed in a matrix form as shown in Equation (7.8):

$$\begin{bmatrix} X'(u,0) \\ X'(u,1) \\ X'(u,2) \\ X'(u,3) \end{bmatrix} = \begin{bmatrix} 1 & 1 & 1 & 1 \\ 1 & -j & -1 & j \\ 1 & -1 & 1 & -1 \\ 1 & j & -1 & -j \end{bmatrix} \begin{bmatrix} x(u,0) \\ x(u,1) \\ x(u,2) \\ x(u,3) \end{bmatrix} \tag{7.8}$$

The butterfly of a 4-point DFT equivalent to Equation (7.8) is shown in Figure 7.6. The 4-point DFT butterfly is also the basic butterfly in the radix-4 FFT algorithm.

Next, we multiply the $N/4$-point DFT output $X'(u, q)$ with twiddle factors W_N^{uq} and obtain $X''(u, q)$ as $X''(u, q) = W_N^{uq} X'(u, q)$, where $0 \le u \le 3$ and $0 \le q \le N/4 - 1$:

$$\begin{bmatrix} X''(0,0) & X''(0,1) & X''(0,2) & X''(0,3) \\ X''(1,0) & X''(1,1) & X''(1,2) & X''(1,3) \\ X''(2,0) & X''(2,1) & X''(2,2) & X''(2,3) \\ X''(3,0) & X''(3,1) & X''(3,2) & X''(3,3) \end{bmatrix} = \begin{bmatrix} W_{16}^0 X'(0,0) & W_{16}^0 X'(0,1) & W_{16}^0 X'(0,2) & W_{16}^0 X'(0,3) \\ W_{16}^0 X'(1,0) & W_{16}^1 X'(1,1) & W_{16}^2 X'(1,2) & W_{16}^3 X'(1,3) \\ W_{16}^0 X'(2,0) & W_{16}^2 X'(2,1) & W_{16}^4 X'(2,2) & W_{16}^6 X'(2,3) \\ W_{16}^0 X'(3,0) & W_{16}^3 X'(3,1) & W_{16}^6 X'(3,2) & W_{16}^9 X'(3,3) \end{bmatrix}$$

Now, we compute $N/4$ 4-point DFTs on $N/4$ columns of a $4 \times N/4$ matrix with elements $X''(u, q)$, and output it as a $4 \times N/4$ matrix with elements $X(p, q)$ as given in Equation (7.9). Then, the N-point DFT of x in the

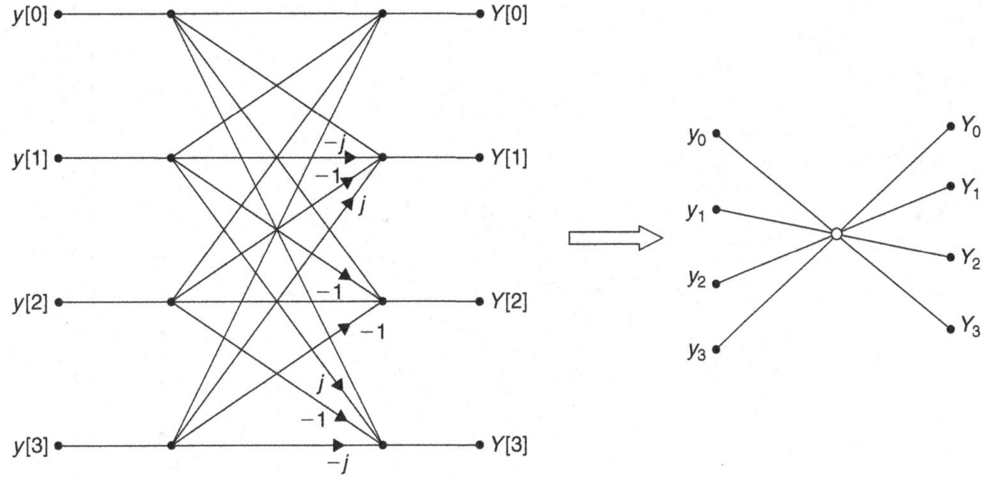

Figure 7.6: Radix-4 basic butterfly signal flow diagram.

digit-reversed order is obtained by converting two-dimensional indices to one-dimensional indices as $X[(N/4)p+q] = X(p,q)$.

$$X(p,q) = \sum_{m=0}^{3} X''(m,q)W_4^{mq}, \quad 0 \le p \le 3 \tag{7.9}$$

$$\begin{matrix} X(0,0), & X(0,1), & X(0,2), & X(0,3), \\ X(1,0), & X(1,1), & X(1,2), & X(1,3), \\ X(2,0), & X(2,1), & X(2,2), & X(2,3), \\ X(3,0), & X(3,1), & X(3,2), & X(3,3), \end{matrix} \Rightarrow \begin{matrix} X(0), & X(4), & X(8), & X(12), \\ X(1), & X(5), & X(9), & X(13), \\ X(2), & X(6), & X(10), & X(14), \\ X(3), & X(7), & X(11), & X(15) \end{matrix}$$

The one-dimensional output vector $X = \{X[0], X[4], X[8], X[12], X[1], X[5], X[9], X[13], X[2], X[6], X[10], X[14], X[3], X[7], X[11], X[15]\}$ is in digit-reversed order. If we apply $N/4$ 4-point DFTs in Equation (7.9) on $N/4$ rows of transposed matrix (just a transpose, not a complex conjugate transpose) $X''(q,u)$, then we get the DFT output X with indices in the correct order.

The 16-point radix-4 decimation-in-time algorithm with the input in normal order and the output in digit-reversed order is shown in Figure 7.7. The complexity of a radix-4 FFT algorithm in terms of number of operations is $N\log_2 N$ complex additions and $(3N/8)\log_2 N$ complex multiplications. That is, the number of complex additions of the radix-4 FFT is the same as a radix-2 FFT, but the number of complex multiplications in the radix-4 FFT is less than the number present in the radix-2 FFT. Thus, if N is a power of 4, then the use of the radix-4 FFT has computational advantages. However, having a DFT whose length N is a power of 4 is not always possible. In that case we can combine both radix-4 and radix-2 FFTs. Usually, the last stage of an FFT can be either a radix-4 stage or a radix-2 stage depending on the length of N. If $N = 2^n$ and $n > 3$, we use only a radix-4 FFT for all stages when n is even. Otherwise, we use radix-4 for all stages except for the last stage where we use a radix-2 FFT algorithm instead.

7.1.2 Radix FFT Fixed-Point Simulation

In this section, we discuss techniques to efficiently implement FFT algorithms on the reference embedded processor. There are three steps in the FFT implementation: (1) data arrangement, (2) butterfly computations, and (3) combining intermediate results. In the data arrangement step, we take linearly indexed samples and output them with indices in bit-reversed order. The simulation code to perform bit reversing is given in Pcode 7.1. This code reads the complex samples with linear indices from buffer ***x***[ ], and outputs the complex samples with the bit-reversed indices into the same input buffer ***x***[ ]. If we have sufficient on-chip data memory, for an FFT with length N, we can compute the bit-reversed indices offline and store them in a look-up table instead of computing

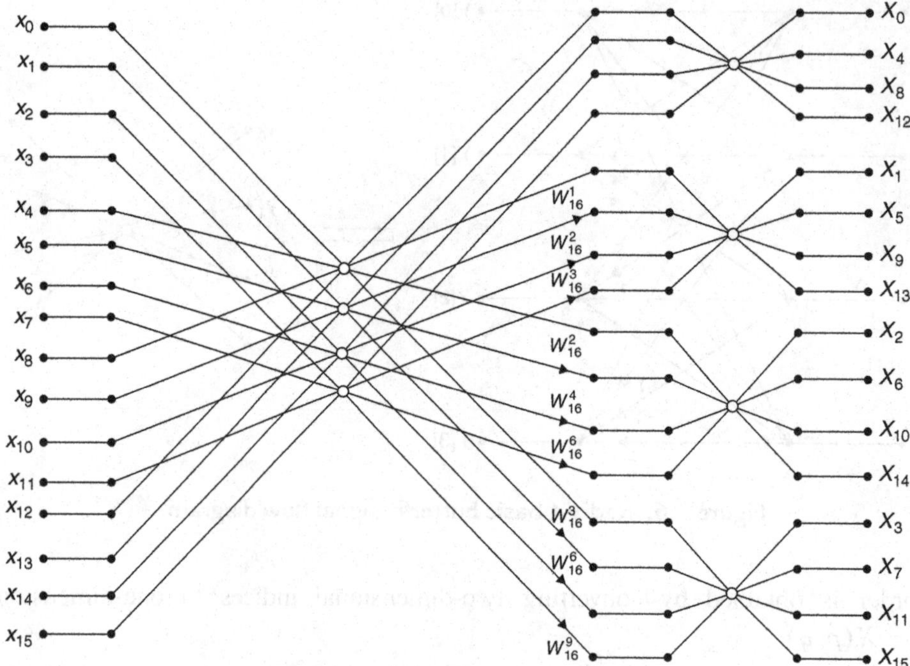

Figure 7.7: Sixteen-point DFT computation using decimation-in-time radix-4 FFT.

them in real time. Then, we access the samples in bit-reversed indexing fashion from samples in a buffer with linear indexing using the bit-reversed indices look-up table.

Now, with the $N = 2^n (n > 3)$ bit-reversed complex samples in $x[\,]$, we can simulate the combination of radix-4 and radix-2 complex FFT algorithms using 1.15 fixed-point computations (see Appendix B.1 on the companion website for more details on the fixed-point representation of real numbers).

In the DFT computation, we use the twiddle-factor matrix. We could calculate this matrix on the fly, but this would be costly because the twiddle-factor computation involves floating-point computations of a nonlinear function $e^{-j2\pi nk/N}$. Instead, we precompute the twiddle factors and store the values in the data memory in 1.15 format for various lengths of N.

```
//void bit_reverse(short *x, int n)

m = n << 1;j = 1;
for(i = 1;i < m;i+ = 2){
    if(j > i){
        tmp = x[j-1];x[j-1] = x[i-1];
        x[i-1] = tmp;tmp = x[j];
        x[j] = x[i];x[i] = tmp;
    }
    k = n;
    while(k > = 2 && j > k){
        j- = k;k >> = 1;
    }
    j+ = k;
}
```

Pcode 7.1: Simulation code to compute bit-reversed indexing.

The complex FFT simulation is divided into three parts. In the first part, we compute only 4-point complex DFTs. Using the routine given in Pcode 7.2, we compute a radix-4 FFT first stage using only additions and subtractions without any multiplications. In the second part, we compute multiple radix-4 middle stages. In these middle stages, we multiply the previous stage output with the twiddle-factor values before applying 4-point DFTs for the current stage. As the values in the first row of the twiddle-factor matrix are all 1s in all stages, we handle the first row separately without any twiddle-factor multiplications. All other rows are multiplied with twiddle factors first, and then the 4-point DFTs are computed. The simulation code for the second part of the FFT computation is given in Pcode 7.3. The **while**( ) loop in Pcode 7.3 runs $(\lfloor \log_4^N \rfloor - 1)$ times, where $\lfloor a \rfloor$ represents the integer part of real number a. The first **for**( ) loop computes 4-point DFTs for the first row of the data matrix. The second **for**( ) loop computes 4-point DFTs for other rows of the data matrix after multiplying with the twiddle factors. We perform twiddle-factor multiplication using 1.15 fixed-point computations.

In the third part of the FFT computation, depending on the DFT length N, we use either radix-2 or radix-4 butterflies to compute the last stage of the FFT. If N is a power of 4, we call the radix-4 algorithm given in Pcode 7.3. If N is only a power of 2, then we use the radix-2 algorithm as given in Pcode 7.4. In the radix-2 algorithm computation, we reuse the twiddle-factor values of the radix-4 algorithm by accessing the appropriate twiddle-factor values (except for sign). The sign information is compensated for within the addition/ subtraction operations. As each stage of the FFT introduces a gain to the output, we take care of this by scaling the intermediate outputs to avoid overflow in the outputs.

```
// void rad4_fft(short *x, short *tw, int n)
m = n >> 2;
                                // first part: first stage
r = 2; s = 4;                   // values are fixed for N = 512-point FFT computation
t = 6; p = 8;
k = -p;
for(i = 0; i < m; i++){         // 512 -> 128x4 (i.e., compute 128 4-point DFTs)
    k = k + p;
    a = x[k] + x[k+r];          b = x[k+1] + x[k+r+1];
    c = x[k] - x[k+r];          d = x[k+1] - x[k+r+1];
    e = x[k+s] + x[k+t];        f = x[k+s+1] + x[k+t+1];
    x[k] = (a + e) >> 1;        x[k+1] = (b + f) >> 1;
    a = (a - e) >> 1;           b = (b - f) >> 1;
    e = x[k+s] - x[k+t];        f = x[k+s+1] - x[k+t+1];
    x[k+s] = a;                 x[k+s+1] = b;
    x[k+r] = (c + f) >> 1;      x[k+r+1] = (d - e) >> 1;
    x[k+t] = (c - f) >> 1;      x[k+t+1] = (d + e) >> 1;
}
```

Pcode 7.2: Simulation code for first stage of radix-4 complex FFT algorithm.

In the radix-4 FFT stages given in Pcodes 7.2 and 7.3, we scaled down the output of the 4-point DFTs by a factor of 2 by right shifting 1 bit within the addition/subtraction operations. We can perform this scaling of intermediate outputs for free on the reference embedded processor (see Appendix A on the companion website) by shifting the addition/subtraction value left by 1 bit using optional mode.

7.1.3 Larger DFT Simulation

In many applications, the DFT length N is on the order of thousands of samples. For example, the DFT of length $N = 2048, 4096$, or 8192 is used in the DVB-H mobile TV application for performing OFDM (orthogonal frequency division modulation, used in many wireless standards). In such cases, the DFT computation uses large data buffers stored in memory, and the access pattern of the data from these buffers arbitrarily causes frequent closing and opening of DRAM pages, resulting in memory stalls. Thus, computation of longer-length DFTs requires special data arrangements to avoid memory stalls. If we divide the larger DFT into smaller DFTs, then this memory stall problem can be resolved. For this, we borrow the idea of the radix-4 FFT algorithm, which always divides the N-point DFT into four $N/4$-point DFTs. In the same way, we can efficiently compute the larger DFT using the matrix FFT.

With matrix FFT, we divide a long one-dimensional data array $x[n]$, where $0 \le n \le N-1$, into many shorter-length blocks $y(p, q) = x[qP + p]$, where $0 \le p \le P-1, 0 \le q \le Q-1$ and $N = PQ$, arranging them in a two-dimensional matrix. We then compute Q-point DFTs on P rows to get $Y(r, s)$. Next, we multiply $Y(r, s)$ with the twiddle factors and then compute P-point DFTs on Q columns to get $Z(u, v)$. Now, the DFT of the

```
// Second part: middle stages (continuation from Pcode 7.2)
m = n >> 4; q = 3; p = p << 2;
k = -p;
u = n>> 1;v = n >> 2;
u = u + v;
u = u >> 1;
l = u; r = r << 2;s = s << 2; t = t << 2;
while(m > 1){ // 128 -> 32x4, 32 -> 8x4, 8 -> 2x4 (for N = 512 case)
    for(i = 0;i<m;i++){ // 1x32 4-point DFTs, 1x8 4-point DFTs, 1x2 4-point DFTs (for N=512 case)
        k = k + p;
        a = x[k] + x[k+r]; b = x[k+1] + x[k+r+1]; c = x[k] - x[k+r]; d = x[k+1] - x[k+r+1];
        e = x[k+s] + x[k+t];              f = x[k+s+1] + x[k+t+1];
        x[k] = (a + e) >> 1;  x[k+1] = (b + f) >> 1; a = (a - e) >> 1; b = (b - f) >> 1;
        e = x[k+s] - x[k+t]; f = x[k+s+1] - x[k+t+1]; x[k+s] = a; x[k+s+1] = b;
        x[k+r] = (c + f) >> 1;       x[k+r+1] = (d - e) >> 1;
        x[k+t] = (c - f) >> 1;       x[k+t+1] = (d + e) >> 1;
    } // first row computed without multiplications as all twiddle factor values are 1s
    for(i = 0;i<q;i++){// 3, 15, 63 (for N = 512 case)
        k = k - m*p + 2;
        for(j = 0;j<m;j++){ // 3x32 4-point DFTs, 15x8 4-point DFTs, 63x2 4-point DFTs
            k = k + p;
            g = x[k+r]*tw[u];               h = x[k+r+1]*tw[u+1];
            g = (g - h + RC) >> 15;
            a = x[k] + g;                   c = x[k] - g;
            g = x[k+r]*tw[u+1];             h = x[k+r+1]*tw[u];
            g = (g + h + RC) >> 15;
            b = x[k+1] + g;                 d = x[k+1] - g;
            g = x[k+s]*tw[u+2];             h = x[k+s+1]*tw[u+3];
            g = (g - h + RC) >> 15;
            v = x[k+s]*tw[u+3];             h = x[k+s+1]*tw[u+2];
            h = (v + h + RC) >> 15;
            e = x[k+t]*tw[u+4];             v = x[k+t+1]*tw[u+5];
            e = (e - v + RC) >> 15;
            f = x[k+t]*tw[u+5];             v = x[k+t+1]*tw[u+4];
            f = (f + v + RC) >> 15;
            v = g + e;                               w = h + f;
            x[k] = (a + v) >> 1;            x[k+1] = (b + w) >> 1;
            a = (a - v) >> 1;               b = (b - w) >> 1;
            e = g - e;                      f = h - f;
            x[k+s] = a;                              x[k+s+1] = b;
            x[k+r] = (c + f) >> 1;          x[k+r+1] = (d - e) >> 1;
            x[k+t] = (c - f) >> 1;          x[k+t+1] = (d + e) >> 1;
        } // 4-point DFT computed after multiplying with twiddle factors
        u = u + 1;
    }
    l = l >> 2; u = l;   m = m >> 2; q = q << 2;
    q = q + 3;  p = p << 2;        r = r << 2; s = s << 2; t = t << 2;
    k = -p;
}
```

Pcode 7.3: Simulation code for middle stages of radix-4 complex FFT algorithm.

one-dimensional long array $x[n]$ is obtained as $X[k] = Z(uN/P + v)$, where $0 \le k \le N - 1, 0 \le u \le P - 1$ and $0 \le v \le Q - 1$.

For example, consider the computation of a DFT for data $x[n]$ of length $N = 8192$. We divide $N = 8192$ into two integers $P = 64$ and $Q = 128$, and arrange the data $x[n]$ in matrix form with 64 rows, each of 128 length. We first compute 64 128-point DFTs row-wise and then multiply the row-wise DFT computed matrix with twiddle factors. We then compute 128 64-point DFTs column-wise. In this way, we avoid memory stalls due to page misses.

When P and Q are relatively prime numbers (with $N = PQ$) and the twiddle factors are from a Galois field, multiplication of intermediate matrix DFT output with twiddle factors is not required in computing the N-point DFT. For example, using the Reed-Solomon erasures correction in Section 4.3, the 255-point DFT is computed with 15 17-point row DFTs followed by 17 15-point column DFTs. In this case, as 15 and 17 are relatively prime, we do not require the multiplication of intermediate matrix DFT output with twiddle factors.

```
q = q + 1;
q = q >> 1;
u = 2; k = 0;
for(i=0;i<q;i++){
    g = x[k+r]*tw[u];              h = x[k+r+1]*tw[u+1];
    g = (g - h + RC) >> 15;
    a = x[k] - g;
    x[k] = x[k] + g;
    g = x[k+r]*tw[u+1];            h = x[k+r+1]*tw[u];
    h = (g + h + RC) >> 15;
    b = x[k+1] - h;
    x[k+1] = x[k+1] + h;
    x[k+r] = a;                    x[k+r+1] = b;
    u+= 6;                         k+= 2;
}
for(i=0;i<q;i++){
    g = x[k+r]*tw[u];              h = x[k+r+1]*tw[u+1];
    g = (-g - h + RC) >> 15;
    a = x[k] - g;
    x[k] = x[k] + g;
    g = x[k+r]*tw[u+1];            h = x[k+r+1]*tw[u];
    h = (g - h + RC) >> 15;
    b = x[k+1] - h;
    x[k+1] = x[k+1] + h;
    x[k+r] = a;                    x[k+r+1] = b;
    u-= 6;                         k+= 2;
}
```

Pcode 7.4: Simulation code to compute the last stage of FFT (with radix-2 algorithm).

7.1.4 FFT Simulation Results

In this section, we provide the simulation results for a 16-point DFT and a 32-point DFT. We compute the 16-point DFT using two radix-4 stages and the 32-point DFT with two radix-4 stages and one radix-2 stage. We use only a three-fourth length (of N) of the twiddle factors ***tw***[ ] in the FFT computation since the first row of the twiddle factors are all 1s (when we arrange the twiddle factors in the matrix form). Given the DFT length N, the twiddle factors are computed using the following equations:

$$tw[3k] = W_N^{2k} = e^{-j2\pi 2k/N}$$
$$tw[3k+1] = W_N^{k} = e^{-j2\pi k/N}$$
$$tw[3k+2] = W_N^{3k} = e^{-j2\pi 3k/N}$$

We use two additional twiddle factors $\{0, -j\}$, $\{0, -j\}$ in computing the last stage with the radix-2 FFT. For fixed-point computation, we represent the twiddle factors in 1.15 format.

16-point DFT

Input: 16 complex samples

```
{11,9},{1,7},{16,5},{9,14},{13,11},{10,13},{14,10},{3,8},
{8,3},{7,12},{4,6},{6,1},{15,15},{12,2},{2,4},{5,16}
```

Bit-reversed index input:

```
{11,9},{8,3},{13,11},{15,15},{16,5},{4,6},{14,10},{2,4},
{1,7},{7,12},{10,13},{12,2},{9,14},{6,1},{3,8},{5,16}
```

Twiddle factors: 12 + 2 complex samples

```
{32767,0},{32767,0},{32767,0},{23170,-23170}
{30273,-12539},{2539,-30273},{0,-32767},{23170,-23170}
{-23170,-23170},{-23170,-23170},{12539,-30273},{-30273,12539}
{0,-32768},{0,-32768}
```

FFT first stage output: Radix-4 stage

```
{47,38},{-1,8},{-9,-14},{7,4},{36,25},{18,-13},{4,-3},{6,11},
{30,34},{5,-3},{-14,4},{-17,-7},{23,39},{-5,15},{7,-9},{11,11}
```

FFT second stage and final output: Radix-4 stage

```
{136,136},{18,-9},{-30,-4},{-16,-1},{6,6},{-20,39},{6,-14}, {22,15},
{30,-10},{-12,-19},{6,-32},{38,-15},{16,20},{10,21},{-18,-6}, {-16,17}
```

32-point DFT

Twiddle factors: 24 + 2 complex samples

```
{32767,0},{32767,0},{32767,0},{30273,-12539},
{32138,-6392},{27245,-18204},{23170,-23170},{30273,-12539},
{12539,-30273},{12539,-30273},{27245,-18204},{-6392,-32138},
{0,-32767},{23170,-23170},{-23170,-23170},{-12539,-30273},
{18204,-27245},{-32138,-6392},{-23170,-23170},{12539,-30273},
{-30273,12539},{-30273,-12539},{6392,-32138},{-18204,27245},
{0,-32768},{0,-32768}
```

Input: 32 complex samples

```
{15,26},{10,4},{7,13},{9,18},{20,23},{2,7},{22,9},{6,25},
{27,16},{32,17},{23,15},{4,32},{26,27},{12,10},{8,8},{3,24},
{5,11},{19,31},{31,2},{28,5},{18,30},{16,12},{17,14},{14,29},
{21,28},{25,6},{24,22},{30,21},{29,1},{1,3},{11,20},{13,19}
```

Bit-reverse of input:

```
{15,26},{5,11},{27,16},{21,28},{20,23},{18,30},{26,27},{29,1},
{7,13},{31,2},{23,15},{24,22},{22,9},{17,14},{8,8},{11,20},
{10,4},{19,31},{32,17},{25,6},{2,7},{16,12},{12,10},{1,3},
{9,18},{28,5},{4,32},{30,21},{6,25},{14,29},{3,24},{13,19}
```

FFT first stage output: Radix-4 stage

```
{68,81},{-2,9},{-28,-7},{22,21},{93,81},{28,-4},{-17,25},{-24,-10},
{85,52},{-31,12},{-9,-22},{-17,10},{58,51},{-7,-2},{20,-5},{17,-8},
{86,58},{2,-34},{-28,12},{-20,-20},{31,32},{-7,-16},{5,6},{-21,6},
{71,76},{-8,39},{3,-30},{-30,-13},{36,97},{-3,6},{4,11},{-13,-14}
```

FFT second stage output: Radix-4 stage

```
{304,265},{-14,15},{-43,-10},{22,79},{-24,-27},{-2,51},{-51,-20},{18,-19},
{18,59},{44,-43},{37,30},{42,11},{-26,27},{-36,13},{-55,-28},{6,13},
{224,263},{-2,4},{-36,-27},{-7,22},{34,-9},{52,-32},{-46,41},{-24,9},
{10,-83},{-26,-84},{-8,41},{5,-40},{76,61},{-16,-24},{-22,-7},{-54,-71}
```

FFT third stage and final output: Radix-2 stage

```
{528,528},{-15,19},{-87,-21},{28,101},{-6,-57},{0,-10},{-31,38},{22,6},
{-65,49},{-33,-1},{78,22},{6,29},{-37,-70},{-36,42},{-37,-13},{45,93},
{80,2},{-13,11},{1,1},{16,57},{-42,3},{-4,112},{-71,-78},{14,-44},
{101,69},{121,-85},{-4,38},{78,-7},{-15,124},{-36,-16},{-73,-43},{-33,-67}
```

7.2 Discrete Cosine Transform

The two-dimensional (2D) discrete cosine transform (DCT) is widely used in various image and video coding applications. For instance, the two-dimensional (2D) DCT is used in JPEG for still-image compression, in the H261/2/3 standards for video teleconferencing applications, in MPEG-2 for DVD, MPEG-4 for HDTV, and so on. The purpose of the DCT in image and video coding standards is to reduce spatial redundancy in images or video frames, thereby allowing us to encode them using fewer bits.

We could use the DFT (see Section 7.1) for image compression. However, we prefer the DCT for the following reasons:

- Image pixels are highly correlated and the redundant (i.e., correlated) components are nicely decorrelated with a DCT type-II.
- The DCT eliminates boundary discontinuities. This is important because boundary discontinuities introduce noticeable block edge artifacts.
- The DCT has higher energy compaction. In other words, the DCT packs more energy into a smaller number of frequency components. This translates into fewer bits needed to represent the image block.
- The DCT requires only real computations. When operating on real data, as is the case with pixel data, an N-point DCT has a frequency resolution similar to a $2N$-point DFT.

In this section, we first examine the DCT algorithm, deriving the popular type-II DCT and its matrix factorization. We then give a fixed-point implementation recipe for the DCT on the reference embedded processor, and discuss DCT input/output pruning. We also discuss the computational complexity and accuracy of fixed-point simulations with respect to floating-point simulations.

DCT Algorithm

The DCT obtains the frequency content of a signal/image in a similar manner as the discrete Fourier transform. There are eight variants of DCTs and four types out of eight are commonly used.

Extending the DCT to two dimensions (2D) is straightforward. We achieve 2D DCT by performing 1D DCT in the horizontal direction followed by another 1D DCT in the vertical direction. The DCT works on a block of data, and its proper implementation on an embedded processor reduces the overall cycle cost of image and video coding.

7.2.1 Discrete Cosine Transform

Of all discrete cosine transform variants, the type-II DCT (called DCT in this section) is the most commonly used for image/video compression. Since the 2D DCT is simply achieved using 1D DCTs (applied to row followed by column of 2D blocks or vice versa), here we will concentrate only on the 1D DCT (or just DCT) computations. The DCT equation (see Section 6.4.3) is given in the following:

$$X[k] = \sum_{n=0}^{N-1} x[n] \cos\left[\frac{\pi}{N}\left(n+\frac{1}{2}\right)k\right], \quad k = 0, 1, 2, \ldots, N-1 \tag{7.10}$$

To eliminate the scaling factor in the data after the inverse transform, we multiply the DCT Equation (7.10) with a variable constant β_i:

$$X[k] = \beta_k \sum_{n=0}^{N-1} x[n] \cos\left[\frac{\pi}{N}\left(n+\frac{1}{2}\right)k\right], \quad k = 0, 1, 2, \ldots, N-1 \tag{7.11}$$

where $\beta_0 = \sqrt{\frac{1}{N}}$ for $k = 0$ and $\beta_k = \sqrt{\frac{2}{N}}$ for $1 < k < N-1$.

The N-point DCT in Equation (7.11) can be represented in matrix form as

$$\boldsymbol{X} = \boldsymbol{Cd} \tag{7.12}$$

where $\boldsymbol{C}$ is an $N \times N$ matrix,

$$\begin{bmatrix} \beta_0 & \beta_0 & \beta_0 & \cdots & \beta_0 \\ \beta_1 \cos\left(\frac{\pi}{2N}\right) & \beta_1 \cos\left(\frac{3\pi}{2N}\right) & \beta_1 \cos\left(\frac{5\pi}{2N}\right) & \cdots & \beta_1 \cos\left(\frac{(2N-1)\pi}{2N}\right) \\ \beta_2 \cos\left(\frac{2\pi}{2N}\right) & \beta_2 \cos\left(\frac{6\pi}{2N}\right) & \beta_2 \cos\left(\frac{10\pi}{2N}\right) & \cdots & \beta_2 \cos\left(\frac{2(2N-1)\pi}{2N}\right) \\ \vdots & \vdots & \vdots & \vdots & \vdots \\ \beta_{N-1} \cos\left(\frac{(N-1)\pi}{2N}\right) & \beta_{N-1} \cos\left(\frac{(N-1)3\pi}{2N}\right) & \beta_{N-1} \cos\left(\frac{(N-1)5\pi}{2N}\right) & \cdots & \beta_{N-1} \cos\left(\frac{(N-1)(2N-1)\pi}{2N}\right) \end{bmatrix}$$

and $\boldsymbol{d} = [x_0, x_1, x_2, \ldots, x_{N-1}]^T$, an $N \times 1$ matrix with N elements of input data. From this point forward, we use the notation x_n instead of $x[n]$ to work with matrices. The inverse transform for the DCT in Equation (7.11), which is obtained with the type-III DCT (called IDCT), follows:

$$x_k = \sum_{n=0}^{N-1} X_n \beta_n \cos\left[\frac{\pi}{N}\left(k+\frac{1}{2}\right)n\right], \quad k = 0, 1, \ldots, N-1 \tag{7.13}$$

where $\beta_0 = \sqrt{\frac{1}{N}}$ and $\beta_n = \sqrt{\frac{2}{N}}$ for $1 < n < N-1$

The N-point IDCT in Equation (7.13) can be represented in matrix form as

$$\boldsymbol{x} = \boldsymbol{C}^T\boldsymbol{D} \tag{7.14}$$

where $\boldsymbol{D} = [X_0, X_1, X_2, \ldots, X_{N-1}]^T$, an $N \times 1$ matrix with N elements, and $\boldsymbol{C}$ is an $N \times N$ matrix whose elements are the same as in the DCT but transposed. One important property of the matrix $\boldsymbol{C}$ is that the multiplication of $\boldsymbol{C}$ with its transpose results in an identity matrix, that is, $\boldsymbol{C}\boldsymbol{C}^T = \boldsymbol{I}$. In other words, the inverse of matrix $\boldsymbol{C}$ is given by its transpose (i.e., $\boldsymbol{C}^{-1} = \boldsymbol{C}^T$). Matrices with this special property are referred to as *unitary matrices*.

In image compression and video coding applications, an 8-point DCT is commonly used. For $N = 8$, matrices $\boldsymbol{C}$ and $\boldsymbol{d}$ in the DCT Equation (7.13) follow:

$$\boldsymbol{C} =$$

$$\begin{bmatrix}
\beta_0 & \beta_0 & \beta_0 & \beta_0 & \beta_0 & \beta_0 & \beta_0 & \beta_0 \\
\beta_1\cos\left(\frac{\pi}{16}\right) & \beta_1\cos\left(\frac{3\pi}{16}\right) & \beta_1\cos\left(\frac{5\pi}{16}\right) & \beta_1\cos\left(\frac{7\pi}{16}\right) & -\beta_1\cos\left(\frac{7\pi}{16}\right) & -\beta_1\cos\left(\frac{5\pi}{16}\right) & -\beta_1\cos\left(\frac{3\pi}{16}\right) & -\beta_1\cos\left(\frac{\pi}{16}\right) \\
\beta_2\cos\left(\frac{2\pi}{16}\right) & \beta_2\cos\left(\frac{6\pi}{16}\right) & -\beta_2\cos\left(\frac{6\pi}{16}\right) & -\beta_2\cos\left(\frac{2\pi}{16}\right) & -\beta_2\cos\left(\frac{2\pi}{16}\right) & -\beta_2\cos\left(\frac{6\pi}{16}\right) & \beta_2\cos\left(\frac{6\pi}{16}\right) & \beta_2\cos\left(\frac{2\pi}{16}\right) \\
\beta_3\cos\left(\frac{3\pi}{16}\right) & \beta_3\cos\left(\frac{7\pi}{16}\right) & -\beta_3\cos\left(\frac{\pi}{16}\right) & -\beta_3\cos\left(\frac{5\pi}{16}\right) & \beta_3\cos\left(\frac{5\pi}{16}\right) & \beta_3\cos\left(\frac{\pi}{16}\right) & \beta_3\cos\left(\frac{7\pi}{16}\right) & -\beta_3\cos\left(\frac{3\pi}{16}\right) \\
\beta_4\cos\left(\frac{4\pi}{16}\right) & -\beta_4\cos\left(\frac{4\pi}{16}\right) & -\beta_4\cos\left(\frac{4\pi}{16}\right) & \beta_4\cos\left(\frac{4\pi}{16}\right) & \beta_4\cos\left(\frac{4\pi}{16}\right) & -\beta_4\cos\left(\frac{4\pi}{16}\right) & -\beta_4\cos\left(\frac{4\pi}{16}\right) & \beta_4\cos\left(\frac{4\pi}{16}\right) \\
\beta_5\cos\left(\frac{5\pi}{16}\right) & -\beta_5\cos\left(\frac{\pi}{16}\right) & \beta_5\cos\left(\frac{7\pi}{16}\right) & \beta_5\cos\left(\frac{3\pi}{16}\right) & \beta_5\cos\left(\frac{3\pi}{16}\right) & -\beta_5\cos\left(\frac{7\pi}{16}\right) & \beta_5\cos\left(\frac{\pi}{16}\right) & -\beta_5\cos\left(\frac{5\pi}{16}\right) \\
\beta_6\cos\left(\frac{6\pi}{16}\right) & -\beta_6\cos\left(\frac{2\pi}{16}\right) & \beta_6\cos\left(\frac{2\pi}{16}\right) & -\beta_6\cos\left(\frac{6\pi}{16}\right) & -\beta_6\cos\left(\frac{6\pi}{16}\right) & \beta_6\cos\left(\frac{2\pi}{16}\right) & -\beta_6\cos\left(\frac{2\pi}{16}\right) & \beta_6\cos\left(\frac{6\pi}{16}\right) \\
\beta_7\cos\left(\frac{7\pi}{16}\right) & -\beta_7\cos\left(\frac{5\pi}{16}\right) & \beta_7\cos\left(\frac{3\pi}{16}\right) & -\beta_7\cos\left(\frac{\pi}{16}\right) & \beta_7\cos\left(\frac{\pi}{16}\right) & -\beta_7\cos\left(\frac{3\pi}{16}\right) & \beta_7\cos\left(\frac{5\pi}{16}\right) & -\beta_7\cos\left(\frac{7\pi}{16}\right)
\end{bmatrix}$$

$$=$$

$$\begin{bmatrix}
\beta_0 & \beta_0 & \beta_0 & \beta_0 & \beta_0 & \beta_0 & \beta_0 & \beta_0 \\
\beta_1\cos\left(\frac{\pi}{16}\right) & \beta_1\cos\left(\frac{3\pi}{16}\right) & \beta_1\sin\left(\frac{3\pi}{16}\right) & \beta_1\sin\left(\frac{\pi}{16}\right) & -\beta_1\sin\left(\frac{\pi}{16}\right) & -\beta_1\sin\left(\frac{3\pi}{16}\right) & -\beta_1\cos\left(\frac{3\pi}{16}\right) & -\beta_1\cos\left(\frac{\pi}{16}\right) \\
\beta_1\sin\left(\frac{3\pi}{8}\right) & \beta_1\cos\left(\frac{3\pi}{8}\right) & -\beta_1\cos\left(\frac{3\pi}{8}\right) & -\beta_1\sin\left(\frac{3\pi}{8}\right) & -\beta_1\sin\left(\frac{3\pi}{8}\right) & -\beta_1\cos\left(\frac{3\pi}{8}\right) & \beta_1\cos\left(\frac{3\pi}{8}\right) & \beta_1\sin\left(\frac{3\pi}{8}\right) \\
\beta_1\cos\left(\frac{3\pi}{16}\right) & \beta_1\sin\left(\frac{\pi}{16}\right) & -\beta_1\cos\left(\frac{\pi}{16}\right) & -\beta_1\sin\left(\frac{3\pi}{16}\right) & \beta_1\sin\left(\frac{3\pi}{16}\right) & \beta_1\cos\left(\frac{\pi}{16}\right) & \beta_1\sin\left(\frac{\pi}{16}\right) & -\beta_1\cos\left(\frac{3\pi}{16}\right) \\
\beta_0 & -\beta_0 & -\beta_0 & \beta_0 & \beta_0 & -\beta_0 & -\beta_0 & \beta_0 \\
\beta_1\sin\left(\frac{3\pi}{16}\right) & -\beta_1\cos\left(\frac{\pi}{16}\right) & \beta_1\sin\left(\frac{7\pi}{16}\right) & \beta_1\cos\left(\frac{3\pi}{16}\right) & \beta_1\cos\left(\frac{3\pi}{16}\right) & -\beta_1\sin\left(\frac{\pi}{16}\right) & \beta_1\cos\left(\frac{\pi}{16}\right) & -\beta_1\sin\left(\frac{3\pi}{16}\right) \\
\beta_1\cos\left(\frac{3\pi}{8}\right) & -\beta_1\sin\left(\frac{3\pi}{8}\right) & \beta_1\sin\left(\frac{3\pi}{8}\right) & -\beta_1\cos\left(\frac{3\pi}{8}\right) & -\beta_1\cos\left(\frac{3\pi}{8}\right) & \beta_1\sin\left(\frac{3\pi}{8}\right) & -\beta_1\sin\left(\frac{3\pi}{8}\right) & \beta_1\cos\left(\frac{3\pi}{8}\right) \\
\beta_1\sin\left(\frac{\pi}{16}\right) & -\beta_1\sin\left(\frac{3\pi}{16}\right) & \beta_1\cos\left(\frac{3\pi}{16}\right) & -\beta_1\cos\left(\frac{\pi}{16}\right) & \beta_1\cos\left(\frac{\pi}{16}\right) & -\beta_1\cos\left(\frac{3\pi}{16}\right) & \beta_1\sin\left(\frac{3\pi}{16}\right) & -\beta_1\sin\left(\frac{\pi}{16}\right)
\end{bmatrix}$$

where $\beta_0 = 0.3536$ and $\beta_1 = 0.5$.

$$= \begin{bmatrix}
0.3536 & 0.3536 & 0.3536 & 0.3536 & 0.3536 & 0.3536 & 0.3536 & 0.3536 \\
0.4904 & 0.4157 & 0.2778 & 0.0975 & -0.0975 & -0.2778 & -0.4157 & -0.4904 \\
0.4619 & 0.1913 & -0.1913 & -0.4619 & -0.4619 & -0.1913 & 0.1913 & 0.4619 \\
0.4157 & -0.0975 & -0.4904 & -0.2778 & 0.2778 & 0.4904 & 0.0975 & 0.4157 \\
0.3536 & -0.3536 & -0.3536 & 0.3536 & 0.3536 & -0.3536 & -0.3536 & 0.3536 \\
0.2778 & -0.4904 & 0.0975 & 0.4157 & -0.4157 & -0.0975 & 0.4904 & -0.2778 \\
0.1913 & -0.4619 & 0.4619 & -0.1913 & -0.1913 & 0.4619 & -0.4619 & 0.1913 \\
0.0975 & -0.2778 & 0.4157 & -0.4904 & 0.4904 & -0.4157 & 0.2778 & -0.0975
\end{bmatrix}$$

$\boldsymbol{d} = [x_0, x_1, x_2, \ldots, x_7]^T$.

In the next section, we discuss the simulation of an 8-point DCT and IDCT.

7.2.2 DCT Simulation

The simulation code for an 8-point DCT is given in Pcode 7.5. It simply multiplies the 8×8 matrix $\boldsymbol{C}$ with an 8-element vector $\boldsymbol{d}$.

```
for(j = 0; j < 8; j++) {
    f = 0.0;
    for(k = 0; k < 8; k++)
            f+ = C[k][j]*d[k];
    X[j] = f;
}
```

Pcode 7.5: The simulation code for a floating point version of an 8-point DCT.

If $\boldsymbol{d} = [75, 68, 69, 65, 69, 75, 75, 77]^T$, then using Pcode 7.5, the computed DCT output is $\boldsymbol{X} = [202.5860, -5.9478, 8.1236, 3.9048, -0.3536, 0.6290, 3.9061, 1.2166]^T$. The same simulation code given in Pcode 7.5 can be used for an 8-point IDCT by simply changing the index values of matrix $\boldsymbol{C}$ from C[k][j] to C[j][k] (i.e., the transposing $\boldsymbol{C}$).

Now, we will discuss the complexity of the 8-point DCT code given in Pcode 7.5. Although the DCT code is only five instructions long, it will consume 15,000 or more cycles on the reference embedded processor (see Appendix A on the companion website), since the reference processor is a fixed-point processor, and it emulates floating-point computations without any dedicated instructions (see Appendix A, Section A.4, on the companion website for cycle estimation of arithmetic operations on fixed-point embedded processors).

Performing floating-point operations on a fixed-point embedded processor is too costly in terms of cycles. Computing an 8-point DCT as given in Pcode 7.5 requires 64 floating-point additions and 64 floating-point multiplications. On a reference embedded processor, if we assume that a floating-point multiplication consumes about 100 cycles and floating-point addition consumes about 145 cycles, then we consume about 15,680 $(= 64 \times 100 + 64 \times 145)$ cycles to perform an 8-point DCT. This is clearly not acceptable for real-time applications. In later sections, we will discuss efficient implementation techniques for an 8-point DCT that consumes about 100 cycles on a fixed-point embedded processor. This gives you an idea of how much can be done with a little optimization!

7.2.3 DCT Matrix Factorization

As discussed in Section 7.2.1, the coefficient matrix $\boldsymbol{C}$ used in DCT computation is a unitary matrix. The matrix $\boldsymbol{C}$ has symmetry about the middle columns (apart from the sign value) and many coefficients are repeated. Taking advantage of these features of $\boldsymbol{C}$, we factorize it as follows: based on Equation (7.12), $\boldsymbol{X} = \boldsymbol{Cd}$; also, $\boldsymbol{X}^T = \boldsymbol{d}^T\boldsymbol{C}^T$ (since $\boldsymbol{AB} = \boldsymbol{B}^T\boldsymbol{A}^T$). It is possible to factor $\boldsymbol{C}$ as a product of several sparse matrices. For $N = 8$, the matrix $\boldsymbol{C}^T$ can be factorized as $\boldsymbol{C}^T = \boldsymbol{C}_1\boldsymbol{C}_2\boldsymbol{C}_3\boldsymbol{C}_4\boldsymbol{W}$, where

$$\boldsymbol{C}_1 = \begin{bmatrix} 1 & 0 & 0 & 0 & 0 & 0 & 0 & 1 \\ 0 & 1 & 0 & 0 & 0 & 0 & 1 & 0 \\ 0 & 0 & 1 & 0 & 0 & 1 & 0 & 0 \\ 0 & 0 & 0 & 1 & 1 & 0 & 0 & 0 \\ 0 & 0 & 0 & 1 & -1 & 0 & 0 & 0 \\ 0 & 0 & 1 & 0 & 0 & -1 & 0 & 0 \\ 0 & 1 & 0 & 0 & 0 & 0 & -1 & 0 \\ 1 & 0 & 0 & 0 & 0 & 0 & 0 & -1 \end{bmatrix} \quad \boldsymbol{C}_2 = \begin{bmatrix} 1 & 0 & 0 & 1 & 0 & 0 & 0 & 0 \\ 0 & 1 & 1 & 0 & 0 & 0 & 0 & 0 \\ 0 & 1 & -1 & 0 & 0 & 0 & 0 & 0 \\ 1 & 0 & 0 & -1 & 0 & 0 & 0 & 0 \\ 0 & 0 & 0 & 0 & c_2 & 0 & 0 & -s_2 \\ 0 & 0 & 0 & 0 & 0 & c_1 & -s_1 & 0 \\ 0 & 0 & 0 & 0 & 0 & s_1 & c_1 & 0 \\ 0 & 0 & 0 & 0 & s_2 & 0 & 0 & c_2 \end{bmatrix}$$

$$\boldsymbol{C}_3 = \begin{bmatrix} 1 & 1 & 0 & 0 & 0 & 0 & 0 & 0 \\ 1 & -1 & 0 & 0 & 0 & 0 & 0 & 0 \\ 0 & 0 & c_3 & -s_3 & 0 & 0 & 0 & 0 \\ 0 & 0 & s_3 & c_3 & 0 & 0 & 0 & 0 \\ 0 & 0 & 0 & 0 & 1 & 0 & 1 & 0 \\ 0 & 0 & 0 & 0 & 0 & -1 & 0 & 1 \\ 0 & 0 & 0 & 0 & 1 & 0 & -1 & 0 \\ 0 & 0 & 0 & 0 & 0 & 1 & 0 & 1 \end{bmatrix} \quad \boldsymbol{C}_4 = \begin{bmatrix} 1 & 0 & 0 & 0 & 0 & 0 & 0 & 0 \\ 0 & 1 & 0 & 0 & 0 & 0 & 0 & 0 \\ 0 & 0 & 1 & 0 & 0 & 0 & 0 & 0 \\ 0 & 0 & 0 & 1 & 0 & 0 & 0 & 0 \\ 0 & 0 & 0 & 0 & -1 & 0 & 0 & 1 \\ 0 & 0 & 0 & 0 & 0 & p & 0 & 0 \\ 0 & 0 & 0 & 0 & 0 & 0 & p & 0 \\ 0 & 0 & 0 & 0 & 1 & 0 & 0 & 1 \end{bmatrix}$$

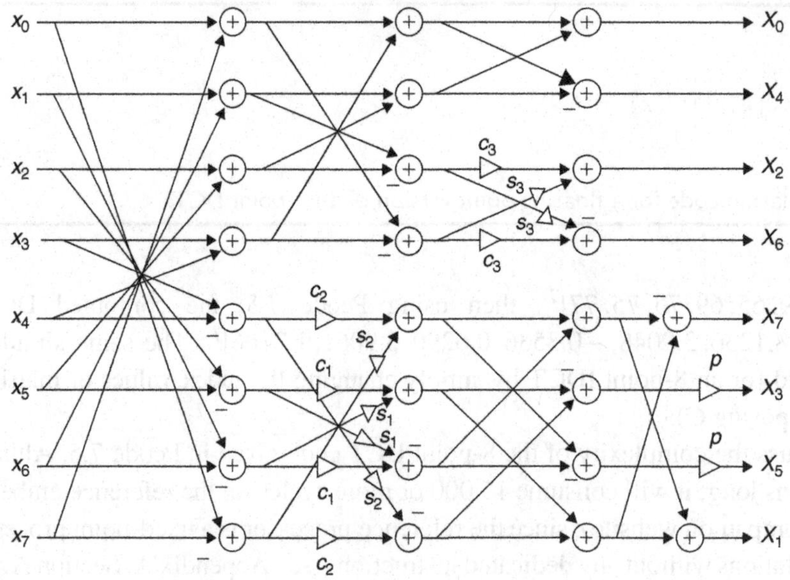

Figure 7.8: Signal flow diagram of 8-point DCT.

$$\boldsymbol{W} = q\begin{bmatrix} 1 & 0 & 0 & 0 & 0 & 0 & 0 & 0 \\ 0 & 0 & 0 & 0 & 0 & 0 & 0 & 1 \\ 0 & 0 & 1 & 0 & 0 & 0 & 0 & 0 \\ 0 & 0 & 0 & 0 & 0 & 1 & 0 & 0 \\ 0 & 1 & 0 & 0 & 0 & 0 & 0 & 0 \\ 0 & 0 & 0 & 0 & 0 & 0 & 1 & 0 \\ 0 & 0 & 0 & 1 & 0 & 0 & 0 & 0 \\ 0 & 0 & 0 & 0 & 1 & 0 & 0 & 0 \end{bmatrix}$$

$$c_1 = \cos\left(\frac{\pi}{16}\right), s_1 = \sin\left(\frac{\pi}{16}\right), c_2 = \cos\left(\frac{3\pi}{16}\right), s_2 = \sin\left(\frac{3\pi}{16}\right)$$

$$c_3 = \sqrt{2}\cos\left(\frac{3\pi}{8}\right), s_3 = \sqrt{2}\sin\left(\frac{3\pi}{8}\right), p = \sqrt{2}, q = \frac{1}{2\sqrt{2}}$$

The matrices $\boldsymbol{C}_1$ to $\boldsymbol{C}_4$ are low-density matrices with at most two non-zero elements per row or column, whereas the matrix $\boldsymbol{W}$ is a low-density matrix with only one element per row or column. Multiplying a vector with $\boldsymbol{W}$ only rearranges data in a vector and will not change any of its values. As matrix $\boldsymbol{W}$ is multiplied with the constant q, all elements of $\boldsymbol{W}$ will be affected in the same way. So, $\boldsymbol{X}^T = \boldsymbol{d}^T\boldsymbol{C}^T$, without matrix W, can be represented with a signal flow diagram as shown in Figure 7.8. Similarly, based on IDCT Equation (7.14), $\boldsymbol{x} = \boldsymbol{C}^T\boldsymbol{D} = \boldsymbol{D}^T\boldsymbol{C}$ and $\boldsymbol{C} = \boldsymbol{W}^T\boldsymbol{C}_4^T\boldsymbol{C}_3^T\boldsymbol{C}_2^T\boldsymbol{C}_1^T$, where the matrices $\boldsymbol{C}_1^T, \boldsymbol{C}_2^T, \boldsymbol{C}_3^T, \boldsymbol{C}_4^T$, and $\boldsymbol{W}^T$ are transposed matrices of $\boldsymbol{C}_1, \boldsymbol{C}_2, \boldsymbol{C}_3, \boldsymbol{C}_4$, and $\boldsymbol{W}$, respectively. The signal flow diagram of the IDCT without matrix $\boldsymbol{W}$ is shown in Figure 7.9. Using DCT matrix factorization and the signal flow diagram shown in Figure 7.8, the number of floating-point multiplications and additions present in DCT reduces to 14 and 26 (instead of 64 and 64). However, as these are floating-point operations, we still consume about 5170 (= 26 × 145 + 14 × 100) cycles to implement an 8-point DCT on a reference embedded processor. In the next section, we will discuss the simulation of a DCT and IDCT in fixed-point format, and compare the fixed-point simulation results with floating-point simulation results.

7.2.4 DCT Fixed-Point Simulation

In this section, we discuss the DCT and IDCT fixed-point simulations and compare the fixed-point simulation results with floating-point simulation results (see Appendix B, Section B.1, on the companion website for Q-format representation and fixed-point computations). The advantage of fixed-point calculation is that the fixed-point multiplication or addition consume only 1 cycle per operation on the reference embedded processor.

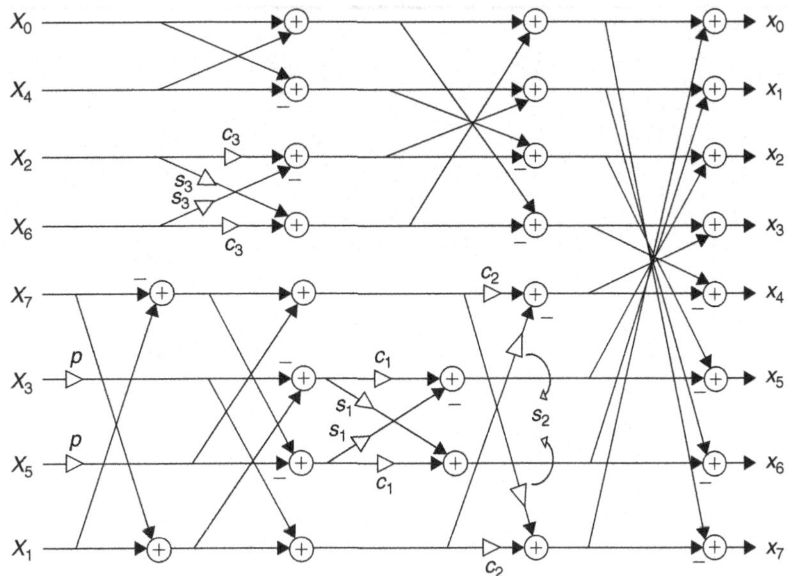

Figure 7.9: Signal flow diagram of 8-point IDCT.

As we discuss later, the difference between fixed-point simulation and the floating-point simulation output is negligible.

Fixed-Point Simulation

In this section, we discuss the fixed-point implementation of an 8-point DCT. We start by representing the DCT matrix values and scaling factors in 1.15 format (see Appendix B, Section B.1, on the companion website for fixed-point representation of real numbers) as follows:

$c_1 = 0\times 7d8a$, (the value of $\cos(\pi/16)$ in 1.15 format)
$s_1 = 0\times 18f9$, (the value of $\sin(\pi/16)$ in 1.15 format)
$c_2 = 0\times 6a6e$, (the value of $\cos(3\pi/16)$ in 1.15 format)
$s_2 = 0\times 471d$, (the value of $\sin(3\pi/16)$ in 1.15 format)
$c_3 = 0\times 22a2$, (the value of $\cos(3\pi/8)/\sqrt{2}$ in 1.15 format)
$s_3 = 0\times 539f$, (the value of $\sin(3\pi/8)/\sqrt{2}$ in 1.15 format)
$p = 0\times 5a82$, (the value of $1/\sqrt{2}$ in 1.15 format)
$q = 0\times 2d41$, (the value of $1/2\sqrt{2}$ in 1.15 format)

Based on Section 7.2.3, the values of factors p, c_3, and s_3 are greater than 1. As we cannot represent the values whose value is more than 1 in 1.15 format, first we divide the factors p, c_3, and s_3 by a factor of 2 (we multiply these coefficients by 2 during the computation), and then we represent the scaled-down values in 1.15 format. The fixed-point simulation code for an 8-point DCT and IDCT is given in Pcodes 7.6 and 7.7.

DCT Simulation Results

The DCT fixed-point simulation code runs many times faster than the DCT floating-point simulation code on the reference embedded processor. Fixed-point arithmetic operations consume 1 cycle each to execute on the reference embedded processor. But this speed-up is at the cost of less accurate results. We can improve the accuracy of a DCT output by scaling up the DCT input (i.e., by representing the DCT input in 12.4 format instead of 16.0 format). The DCT and IDCT output values for floating-point and fixed-point simulation are shown in Tables 7.2 and 7.3. The fixed-point simulation results provided in the tables are obtained by dividing the third-stage outputs of DCT and IDCT as seen in the code given in Pcodes 7.6 and 7.7 with $1/2\sqrt{2}$.

Precision, Accuracy, and Saturation

As can be seen in Tables 7.2 and 7.3, the output from the floating-point simulation code and fixed-point simulation code are not exactly the same. The reason for this is that the floating-point code uses double-precision data types,

```
// 1st stage of DCT signal flow diagram
r0 = in[0] + in[7]; r7 = in[0] - in[7];
r1 = in[1] + in[6]; r6 = in[1] - in[6];
r2 = in[2] + in[5]; r5 = in[2] - in[5];
r3 = in[3] + in[4]; r4 = in[3] - in[4];
// 2nd stage of DCT signal flow diagram
tmp1 = r0 + r3; r3 = r0 - r3;
tmp2 = r1 + r2; r2 = r1 - r2;
tmp3 = (r4 * c2) >> 15; tmp4 = (r7 * s2) >> 15;
r4 = (r4 * s2) >> 15; r7 = (r7 * c2) >> 15;
r7 = r7 - r4; r4 = tmp3 + tmp4;
tmp3 = (r5 * c1) >> 15; tmp4 = (r6 * s1) >> 15;
r5 = (r5 * s1) >> 15; r6 = (r6 * c1) >> 15;
r6 = r6 - r5; r5 = tmp3 + tmp4;
// 3rd stage of DC T signal flow diagram
r0 = tmp1 + tmp2; r1 = tmp1 - tmp2;
tmp1 = (r2 * c3) >> 14; tmp2 = (r2 * s3) >> 14;        // multiply by 2
tmp3 = (r3 * c3) >> 14; tmp4 = (r3 * s3) >> 14;        // multiply by 2
r2 = tmp1 + tmp4; r3 = tmp3 - tmp2;
tmp1 = r4 + r6; tmp2 = r5 + r7;
r6 = r4 - r6; r5 = r7 - r5;
r4 = tmp2 - tmp1; r7 = tmp2 + tmp1;
r5 = (r5 * p) >> 14; r6 = (r6 * p) >> 14;              // multiply by 2
// last stage
out[0] = (r0 * q) >>15; out[1] = (r7 * q) >>15;
out[2] = (r2 * q) >>15; out[3] = (r5 * q) >>15;
out[4] = (r1 * q) >>15; out[5] = (r6 * q) >>15;
out[6] = (r3 * q) >>15; out[7] = (r4 * q) >>15;
```

Pcode 7.6: Fixed point simulation code for an 8-point DCT.

```
// 1st Stage of IDCT signal flow diagram
r0 = in[0] + in[4]; r1 = in[0] - in[4];
r2 = (in[2] * c3) >> 14; r3 = (in[6] * c3) >> 14;     // multiply by 2
r4 = (in[2] * s3) >> 14; r5 = (in[6] * s3) >> 14;     // multiply by 2
r2 = r2 - r5; r3 = r3 + r4;
tmp1 = in[1] - in[7]; tmp2 = in[1] + in[7];
tmp3 = (in[3] * p) >> 14; tmp4 = (in[5] * p) >> 14;  // multiply by 2
r4 = tmp1 + tmp4; r6 = tmp1 - tmp4;
r5 = tmp2 - tmp3; r7 = tmp2 + tmp3;
// 2nd Stage of IDCT signal flow diagram
tmp1 = r0; tmp2 = r1;
r0 = tmp1 + r3; r3 = tmp1 - r3;
r1 = tmp2 + r2; r2 = tmp2 - r2;
tmp1 = (r5 * c1) >> 15; tmp2 = (r5 * s1) >> 15;
tmp3 = (r6 * c1) >> 15; tmp4 = (r6 * s1) >> 15;
r5 = tmp1 - tmp4; r6 = tmp3 + tmp2;
tmp1 = (r4 * c2) >> 15; tmp2 = (r4 * s2) >> 15;
tmp3 = (r7 * c2) >> 15; tmp4 = (r7 * s2) >> 15;
r4 = tmp1 - tmp4; r7 = tmp3 + tmp2;
// 3rd  Stage of IDCT signal flow diagram
tmp1 = r0 + r7; r7 = r0 - r7;
tmp2 = r1 + r6; r6 = r1 - r6;
tmp3 = r2 + r5; r5 = r2 - r5;
tmp4 = r3 + r4; r4 = r3 - r4;
// last stage
out[0] = (tmp1 * q) >> 15; out[7] = (r7 * q) >> 15;
out[1] = (tmp2 * q) >> 15; out[6] = (r6 * q) >> 15;
out[2] = (tmp3 * q) >> 15; out[5] = (r5 * q) >> 15;
out[3] = (tmp4 * q) >> 15; out[4] = (r4 * q) >> 15;
```

Pcode 7.7: Fixed point simulation code for an 8-point IDCT.

whereas the fixed-point code uses data types that are only 16 bits in length (i.e., the "short" data type in C). This difference in the output results can be reduced by increasing the precision of the fractional part of the decimal value. In fixed-point simulations, if we assign more bits to the fractional part to get more accurate results, then there is a possibility of totally unacceptable results due to saturation or overflow. The saturation of output with

Table 7.2: DCT simulation results

DCT Input	DCT Floating-Point Simulation Output	DCT Fixed-Point Simulation Output (with Input 16.0)	DCT Fixed-Point Simulation Output (with Input 12.4)
$x[0]=75$	$X[0]=202.5861$	$X[0]=202.5861$	$X[0]=202.5861$
$x[1]=68$	$X[1]=-5.9478$	$X[1]=-6.3640$	$X[1]=-6.0104$
$x[2]=69$	$X[2]=8.1236$	$X[2]=7.7782$	$X[2]=8.0433$
$x[3]=65$	$X[3]=3.9048$	$X[3]=4.2426$	$X[3]=3.8891$
$x[4]=69$	$X[4]=-0.3536$	$X[4]=-0.3536$	$X[4]=-0.3536$
$x[5]=75$	$X[5]=0.6289$	$X[5]=-0.7071$	$X[5]=0.5303$
$x[6]=75$	$X[6]=3.9061$	$X[6]=3.8891$	$X[6]=3.8891$
$x[7]=77$	$X[7]=1.2166$	$X[7]=1.4142$	$X[7]=1.1490$

Table 7.3: IDCT simulation results

IDCT Input	IDCT Floating-Point Simulation Output	IDCT Fixed-Point Simulation Output (with Input 16.0)	IDCT Fixed-Point Simulation Output (with Input 12.4)
$X[0]=202.5861$	$x[0]=75.0000$	$x[0]=73.8927$	$x[0]=74.8870$
$X[1]=-5.9478$	$x[1]=68.0000$	$x[1]=68.5894$	$x[1]=67.9927$
$X[2]=8.1236$	$x[2]=69.0000$	$x[2]=68.9429$	$x[2]=69.0534$
$X[3]=3.9048$	$x[3]=64.9999$	$x[3]=65.4074$	$x[3]=65.0538$
$X[4]=-0.3536$	$x[4]=68.9999$	$x[4]=69.6500$	$x[4]=69.0313$
$X[5]=0.6289$	$x[5]=74.9999$	$x[5]=73.1856$	$x[5]=74.9754$
$X[6]=3.9061$	$x[6]=75.0000$	$x[6]=74.9533$	$x[6]=74.9754$
$X[7]=1.2166$	$x[7]=76.9999$	$x[7]=76.7211$	$x[7]=76.9641$

fixed-point simulation is due to overflow of the integer part in arithmetic operations on the data that is represented by assigning fewer bits to its integer part. The number of required bits that we use for the fractional part and integer part depends on the range of values present in the input as well as the gain introduced by a particular algorithm.

We measure the accuracy of the results as the mean square error (MSE) between the fixed-point output and the floating-point output. The MSE is computed as follows:

$$\text{MSE} = \frac{1}{N}\sum_{n}(Y_1[n]-Y_2[n])^2$$

If we replace $Y_1[\ ]$ with the floating-point simulation output of the DCT and the IDCT (second columns in Tables 7.2 and 7.3) and $Y_2[\ ]$ with the fixed-point simulation output of the DCT and IDCT (third columns in Tables 7.2 and 7.3), then the MSE of the fixed-point simulation for DCT and IDCT is given by $\text{MSE}_{\text{DCT}} = 0.2789$ and $\text{MSE}_{\text{IDCT}} = 0.6921$, respectively.

If we want to get even more accurate results, we can increase the precision for both the input of DCT and IDCT via scaling. The DCT and IDCT flow diagrams shown in Figures 7.8 and 7.9 introduce a gain of $2\sqrt{2}$. To obtain more accurate results, we have to consider this gain in scaling up the inputs to the DCT and IDCT. If we increase the precision of the fractional part from 0 to 4 bits (i.e., convert the input data format from 16.0 to 12.4), then the MSE of the fixed-point simulation for the DCT and IDCT is computed using the fourth-column values (of Tables 7.2 and 7.3) and the MSE is given by $\text{DCT}_{\text{MSE}} = 0.0032$ and $\text{MSE}_{\text{IDCT}} = 0.0028$. Thus, we can see that the accuracy (measured with the MSE, smaller is better) of the fixed-point simulation results (given in Tables 7.2 and 7.3) is high in the case of fourth-column outputs (with 12.4 input format) when compared to third-column outputs (with 16.0 input format).

Fixed-Point Simulation Cycle Cost

The fixed-point simulation code given in Pcodes 7.2 and 7.3 is very efficient, and on a fixed-point embedded processor it runs many times faster when compared to the floating-point simulation code given in Pcode 7.1.

See Appendix A, Section A.4, on the companion website for cycle estimation on the reference embedded processor. As the data is handled as 16-bit data, multiplication of two fixed-point numbers (including the right shift for scaling) can be achieved with 1 cycle on the reference embedded processor (this is the case with most fixed-point embedded processors). If we assume that all arithmetic operations consume 1 cycle each on fixed-point embedded processors, then the fixed-point simulation code given in Pcodes 7.2 and 7.3 for the DCT and IDCT take approximately 50 cycles on a single ALU fixed-point embedded processors. The cycle consumption of the DCT and IDCT drops to 25 cycles on two ALU embedded processors. The cycle count drops further with the use of MAC units (e.g., the reference embedded processor has two MAC units).

7.2.5 DCT Input Pruning

In image or video processing applications, the DCT is also used as an interpolator function to scale up images. When the scaling ratio is large, the DCT interpolator outperforms the bilinear interpolation method. At the block level, the 2D DCT interpolator works as an optimum interpolator in the sense of generating better interpolated points. Typically, the upscaling of an image with a DCT interpolator is achieved by performing an input-pruned IDCT. In an input-pruned N-point IDCT, the number of inputs to the IDCT is less than N. In other words, with an input-pruned IDCT, the number of inputs ($< N$) and the number of IDCT outputs ($= N$) are different. For example, we use a 2D $N/2$-point DCT to an N-point IDCT transformation for scaling up images by a factor of 4. See Chapter 15 for more details on video scaling.

As an image or frame of video is processed in terms of blocks of pixels (either 4×4 or 8×8), the application of a 4×4 to 8×8 DCT interpolator is straightforward for use at the back end of a decoder. In addition, in some decoders, the DCT coefficients are readily available to work with for scaling. In that case, we do not compute the DCT of the data. If the DCT coefficients of a decoder are not usable (due to the feedback mechanism present in the decoder, such as intraprediction in H.264), then we have to compute the 4×4 DCT coefficients before scaling. The signal flow diagram for performing a 4-point DCT is shown in Figure 7.10 and its fixed-point simulation code is given in Pcode 7.8. The computation of a 4-point DCT using simple multiplications of cosine elements in a 4×4 matrix with 4 points in a data vector involves 16 floating-point multiplications and 16 floating-point additions. Using the DCT matrix factorization (obtained the same way as the 8-point DCT discussed in Section 7.2.3) and signal flow diagram as shown in Figure 7.10, we can perform a 4-point DCT with eight floating-point additions and six floating-point multiplications.

Once we have the 4×4 DCT coefficients, we use a 4×4 DCT to 8×8 IDCT function for interpolation in upscaling the video or images. This requires results of the computation of a 4-point DCT to an 8-point IDCT in both horizontal (row) and vertical (column) directions. One way of performing this is by taking 4 DCT points, and then appending 4 zeros and computing an 8-point IDCT. As discussed in Section 7.2.4, the 8-point IDCT code consumes about 50 instruction cycles. In this section, we provide efficient simulation code for a direct 4-point DCT to 8-point IDCT that takes only 32 instruction cycles on the reference embedded processor. The signal flow diagram of the 4-point DCT to 8-point IDCT is shown in Figure 7.11. The fixed-point simulation code of the 4-point to 8-point IDCT is given in Pcode 7.9.

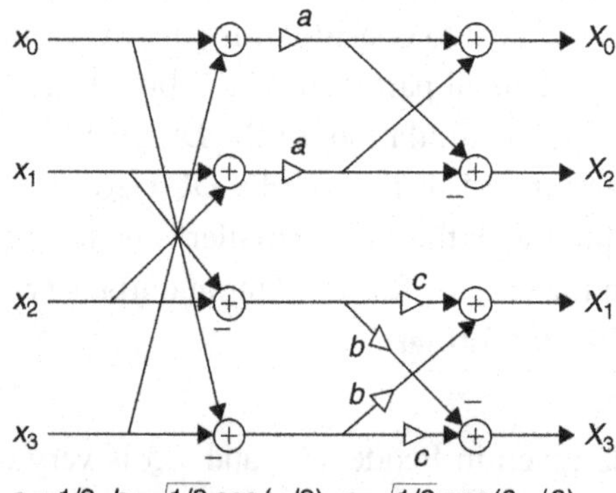

Figure 7.10: Signal flow diagram of 4-point DCT.

```
a = 0x4000;                              // 1/2
b = 0x539f;                              // sqrt(1/2)*cos(PI/8)
c = 0x2283;                              // sqrt(1/2)*cos(3*PI/8)

r0 = in[0]; r1 = in[1];
r2 = in[2]; r3 = in[3];
r4 = r0 + r3; r5 = r1 + r2;
r4 = (r4 * a) >> 15; r5 = (r5 * a) >> 15;
r6 = r4 + r5; r7 = r4 - r5;
out[0] = r6; out[2] = r7;
r4 = r0 - r3; r5 = r1 - r2;
r0 = (r4 * b) >> 15; r1 = (r4 * c) >> 15;
r2 = (r5 * b) >> 15; r3 = (r5 * c) >> 15;
r6 = r0 + r3; r7 = r1 - r2;
out[1] = r6; out[3] = r7;
```

Pcode 7.8: Simulation code for 4-point DCT.

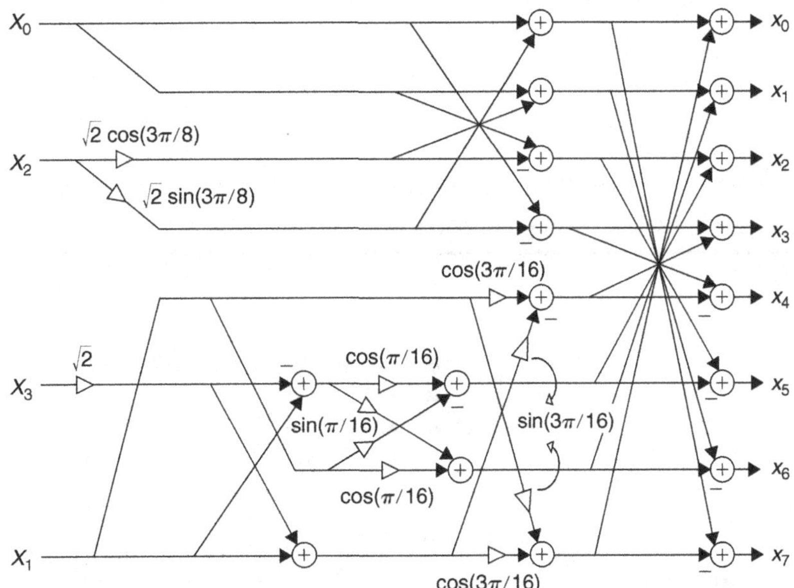

Figure 7.11: Signal flow diagram of 4-point DCT to 8-point IDCT.

7.2.6 DCT Output Pruning

We also use a DCT interpolator to downscale high-resolution images to lower resolution. Downscaling of video is required in many applications, especially to reduce the data bandwidth for transferring video or images over the Internet. Another application is viewing the DVD resolution video content on portable media players with QVGA (320 × 240) resolution. Given the 8 × 8 DCT coefficients, we have two ways to get the 4 × 4 IDCT. In the first approach, as shown in Figure 7.12, we take the top-left-corner 4 × 4 coefficients of an 8 × 8 block and perform a 4 × 4 IDCT on them by using a 4-point IDCT. In this case, we are ignoring the high-frequency content of an image. In Figure 7.12, the non-zero DCT coefficients are represented with solid circles and zero coefficients are shown with empty circles. If we consider only the top-left-corner 4 × 4 block of DCT coefficients, then we do not use the frequency information of five high-frequency DCT coefficients. If the bit rate of the video to be scaled is higher, then we will have more DCT coefficients outside the top-left 4 × 4 block of the 8 × 8 block. In high-bit-rate video, ignoring high-frequency DCT coefficients results in lower-quality downscaled images.

In the second approach, we use "output-pruned" IDCT for image or video downscaling. In particular, we use an 8 × 8 DCT to 4 × 4 IDCT. In this approach, we use all frequency content presented within the image block; the downscaled image quality is better with the output-pruned IDCT method since the downscaled image contains all the frequency content of whatever is present in the original image. However, the computational

```
c0 = 0x5a82;                                    // (1/sqrt(2)*32768) = 23170
c1 = 0x7d8a;                                    // cos(pi/16)*32768 = 32138
c2 = 0x18f9;                                    // sin(pi/16)*32768 = 6393
c3 = 0x6a6e;                                    // cos(3*pi/16)*32768 = 27246
c4 = 0x471d;                                    // sin(3*pi/16)*32768 = 18205
c5 = 0x22a2;                                    // cos(6*pi/16)/sqrt(2)*32768 = 8867
c6 = 0x539f;                                    // sin(6*pi/16)/sqrt(2)*32768 = 21407
// first stage
tmp1 = in[0]; r2 = (in[2] * c5) >> 14;
tmp2 = in[0]; r3 = (in[2] * c6) >> 14;
r4 = in[1]; tmp3 = (in[3] * c0) >> 14;
r5 = r4 - tmp3; r7 = r4 + tmp3;
r6 = r4;
// second stage
r0 = tmp1 + r3; r3 = tmp1 - r3;
r1 = tmp2 + r2; r2 = tmp2 - r2;
tmp1 = (r5 * c1) >> 15; tmp2 = (r5 * c2) >> 15;
tmp3 = (r6 * c1) >> 15; tmp4 = (r6 * c2) >> 15;
r5 = tmp1 - tmp4; r6 = tmp3 + tmp2;
tmp1 = (r4 * c3) >> 15; tmp2 = (r4 * c4) >> 15;
tmp3 = (r7 * c3) >> 15; tmp4 = (r7 * c4) >> 15;
r4 = tmp1 - tmp4; r7 = tmp3 + tmp2;
// third stage
out[0] = r0 + r7; out[7] = r0 - r7;
out[1] = r1 + r6; out[6] = r1 - r6;
out[2] = r2 + r5; out[5] = r2 - r5;
out[3] = r3 + r4; out[4] = r3 - r4;
```

Pcode 7.9: Simulation code for 4-point to 8-point IDCT.

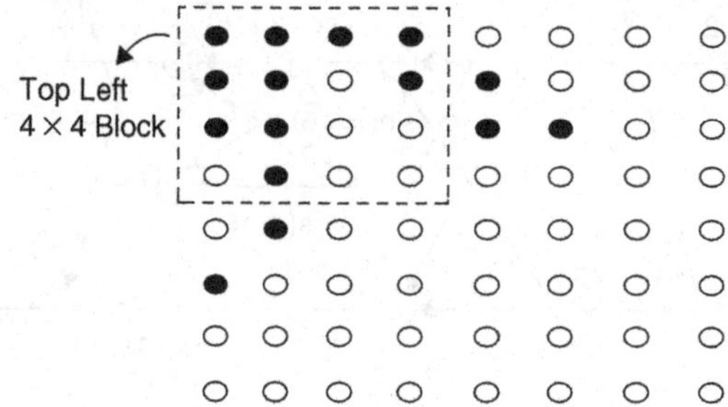

Figure 7.12: 8 × 8 image pixels. Filled: non-zero; empty: zero coefficients.

complexity of image or video downscaling with an output-pruned IDCT is greater, as this approach involves more computations. We may require a bilinear interpolator at the end to get an arbitrary-sized downscaled image with the DCT approaches.

In this section, we provide both 4-point IDCT and 8-point to 4-point IDCT methods for downscaling images by a factor of 2 in both the horizontal and vertical directions. The signal flow diagram of a 4-point IDCT is shown in Figure 7.13. The simulation code for a 4-point IDCT is given in Pcode 7.10. The computational complexity of a 4-point IDCT is the same as the 4-point DCT discussed in Section 7.2.5. With the signal flow diagram shown in Figure 7.13, we require eight floating-point additions and six floating-point multiplications to perform a 4-point IDCT.

With the output-pruned IDCT, we can compute the IDCT by using all eight DCT coefficients and we output 4 IDCT points as shown in Figure 7.14. The number of computations involved in an 8-point DCT to 4-point IDCT is 12 floating-point additions and 8 floating-point multiplications. The simulation code for an 8-point DCT to 4-point IDCT is given in Pcode 7.11.

With DCT scaling, it is also possible to enhance the edges of objects in an image. See Section 15.1 for the performance difference between the DCT and bilinear interpolation in scaling the luminance components of video frames.

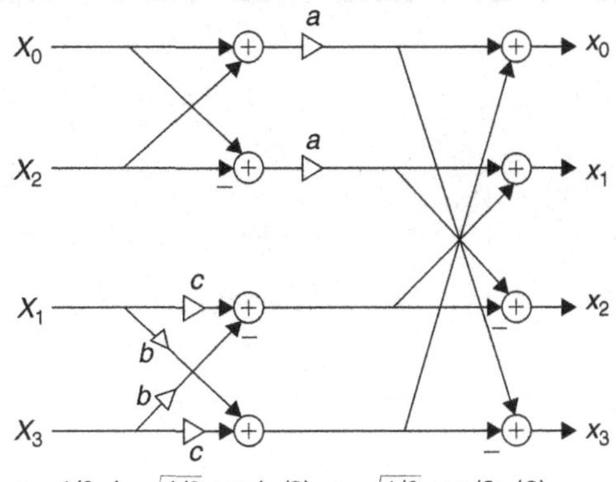

Figure 7.13: Signal flow diagram of 4-point IDCT.

```
a = 0x4000;                                  // 1/2
b = 0x539f;                                  // sqrt(1/2)*cos(PI/8)
c = 0x2283;                                  // sqrt(1/2)*cos(3*PI/8)
// first stage
r0 = (short) (in[0]+0.5);
r1 = (short) (in[1]+0.5);
r2 = (short) (in[2]+0.5);
r3 = (short) (in[3]+0.5);
// second stage
r4 = r0 + r2; r5 = r0 - r2;
r4 = (r4 * a) >> 15; r5 = (r5 * a) >> 15;
r2 = (r3 * c) >> 15; r0 = (r3 * b) >> 15;
r3 = (r1 * c) >> 15; r1 = (r1 * b) >> 15;
r6 = r4 + r1; r7 = r4 - r1;
r1 = r5 + r3; r4 = r5 - r3;
// third stage
out[0] = r6 + r2; out[3] = r7 - r2;
out[1] = r1 - r0; out[2] = r4 + r0;
```

Pcode 7.10: Simulation code for 4-point IDCT.

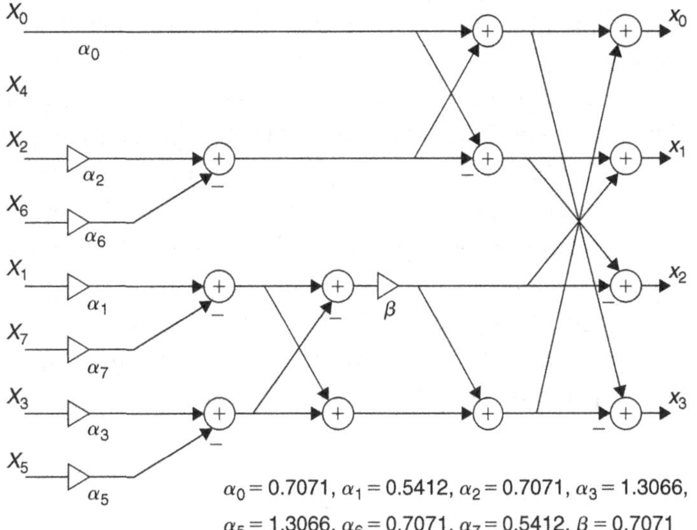

Figure 7.14: Signal flow diagram of 8- to 4-point DCT.

7.3 Filter Basics

We use filters for two purposes: signal separation and signal enhancement. The signal separation is needed to filter the noise when the desired signal is associated with noise, whereas signal enhancement is needed to improve signal quality when the desired signal-generating hardware malfunctions or components are distorted. For these purposes, we can use analog or digital filters. Analog filters are designed with physical components

```
c0 = 0x5a82;                                    // 0.7071 -> 23170 (1.15)
c1 = 0x4546;                                    // 0.5412 -> 17734 (1.15)
c2 = 0x539f;                                    // 1.3066/2 -> 21407 (1.15)
// first stage
r0 = ((short) (in[0]) * c0) >> 15;
tmp1 = ((short) (in[2]) * c0) >> 15; tmp2 = ((short) (in[6]) * c0) >> 15;
r2 = ((short) (in[1]) * c1) >> 15; r3 = ((short) (in[7]) * c1) >> 15;
r1 = tmp1 - tmp2; r2 = r2 - r3;
tmp1 = ((short) (in[3]) * c2) >> 14; tmp2 = ((short) (in[5]) * c2) >> 14;
r3 = tmp1 - tmp2;
// second stage
tmp1 = r0; tmp2 = r2;
r0 = tmp1 + r1; r1 = tmp1 - r1;
r2 = tmp2 - r3; r3 = tmp2 + r3;
r2 = (r2 * c0) >> 15;
r3 = r2 + r3;
// third stage
out[0] = r0 + r3; out[3] = r0 - r3;
out[1] = r1 + r2; out[2] = r1 - r2;
```

Pcode 7.11: Simulation code for 8-point DCT to 4-point IDCT.

(resistors, capacitors, inductors, op amps, etc.) as shown in Figure 7.15(a), whereas digital filters are defined with numbers alone as shown in Figure 7.15(b). Compared to analog filters, the digital filter designs offer sharp roll-offs, require no calibration, and have greater stability with time, temperature, and power supply variations. Simple software changes can alter a digital filter response in real time, creating so-called adaptive filters, whereas analog filters usually require hardware changes. Digital filters are increasingly finding their way into signal- and image-processing applications.

We illustrate the purpose of a filter with a simple example. In Figure 7.16(a), the frequency-domain characteristic $X(f)$ of signal $x(t)$, and whose spectrum occupies a frequency range between 0 and f_b, is shown. If the frequency components between f_a and f_b correspond to some undesired signal and if we want to eliminate this undesired signal from the desired signal $y(t)$ (whose frequency spectrum $Y(f)$ is between 0 and f_a), then we use a filter with the frequency response $H(f)$ as shown in Figure 7.16(b) to filter out the undesired signal component from the given input signal $x(t)$. The filtered signal with frequency spectrum $Y(f)$ is shown in Figure 7.16(c).

The filter shown in Figure 7.16(b) is a low-pass filter that passes the signal with frequency components up to f_a, and attenuates any signal whose frequency components are greater than f_a. Similarly, a high-pass filter shown in Figure 7.16(d) allows signals whose frequency components are above f_b to pass while it attenuates all other signals whose frequency components are below f_b. The bandpass filter shown in Figure 7.16(e) allows only signals whose frequency components lie between f_a and f_b to pass, and it attenuates the rest of the signals whose frequency component falls below f_a and above f_b.

Although filtering is often required for processing signals in the time domain, most designers understand the operation of a filter best in the frequency domain. When the spectrum of the input signal is multiplied by the frequency response of the filter we get an output signal with an altered spectrum as shown in Figure 7.16.

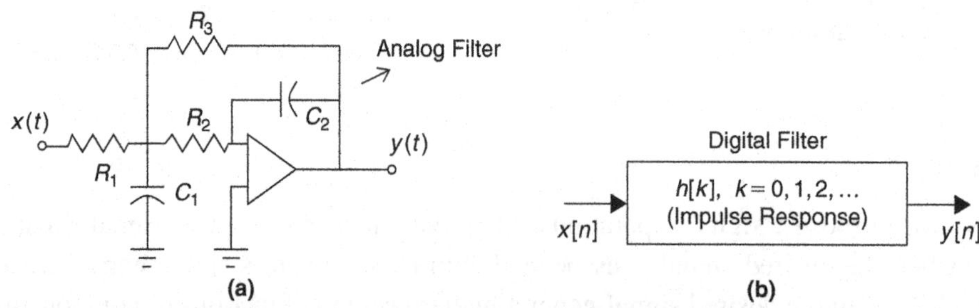

Figure 7.15: Filter schematics. (a) Analog filter. (b) Digital filter.

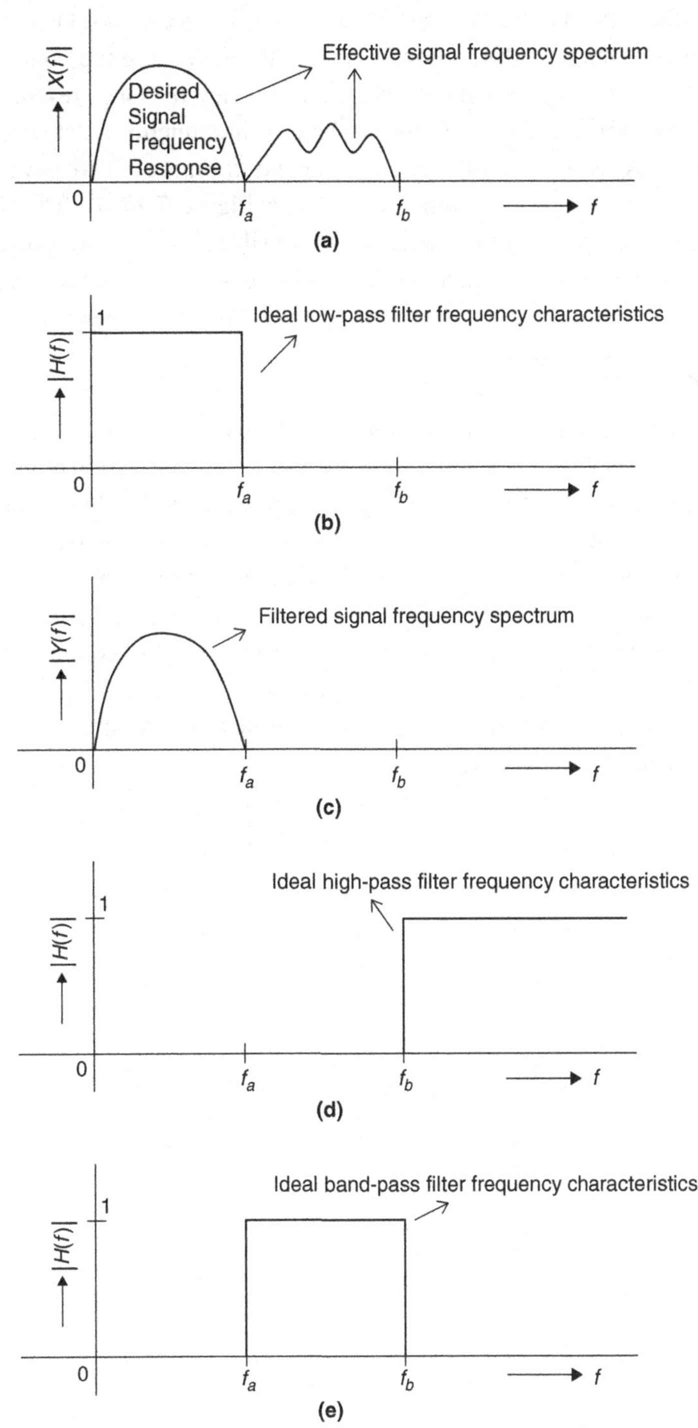

Figure 7.16: Illustration of the concept of filtering. (a) Input signal with undesired frequency components. (b) Ideal low-pass-filter frequency characteristics. (c) Filtered signal frequency spectrum. (d) Ideal high-pass-filter frequency characteristics. (e) Ideal bandpass-filter frequency characteristics.

As discussed in Section 6.5.3, the multiplication in the frequency domain is equivalent to convolution in the time domain. That is, if we convolve the input signal with the impulse response of the filter in the time domain, then we get the desired time-domain signal.

The filters shown in Figures 7.16(b), (d), and (e) are ideal with perfect low-pass, high-pass, and bandpass frequency characteristics. However, such filters cannot be realized in practice because they have an infinite-length impulse response (i.e., time-domain response), and therefore, DSP processors cannot handle such filters because the computational cost of implementation also becomes prohibitive.

As discussed previously, the time- and frequency-domain representations are related, and we can easily obtain the information in one domain given the information in another domain using the Fourier transforms. As shown in Figures 7.16(b), (d), and (e), the shape of an ideal filter's frequency response resembles a rectangular pulse, and its impulse response in the time domain is an infinite-length sinc function as shown in Figure 7.17(b).

If we truncate the impulse response to a finite length as shown in Figure 7.17(c), we no longer have an ideal frequency characteristic in the frequency domain, as shown in Figure 7.17(d). That is, good localization in both the frequency and time domains simultaneously is not possible. If we desire good frequency localization (i.e., ideal narrowband-frequency response), then we do not get good time-domain response localization (i.e., finite-length impulse response). This phenomenon is analogous to the Heisenberg uncertainty principle.

7.3.1 Filter Design Parameters

As discussed before, ideal filters exist only in theory and cannot be realized in practice. However, we can design filters that perform well for most day-to-day applications. From an implementation point of view, one of the most important parameters in filter design (in the time domain) is impulse-response length in terms of the number of samples (L). As L increases, the implementation complexity of the filter also increases. In the context of digital filters, we specify filter parameters in the frequency domain with respect to sampling frequency. This means that the filter parameters obtained for a particular sampling frequency do not represent the same filter characteristics for another sampling frequency. Four parameters typically specify the desired frequency response of a digital filter response in the frequency domain: f_p (passband cutoff frequency), f_s (stopband cutoff frequency), δ_1 (passband ripple), and δ_2 (stopband attenuation). The low- and high-pass digital filter specifications in the frequency domain are shown in Figure 7.18(a) and (b), respectively.

Example 7.1

As digital filter parameters make sense only for a given sampling frequency, we first obtain the sampling frequency (F_s) of the input discrete signal in determining filter parameters. Then we choose the passband (f_p) and stopband (f_s) frequencies with respect to sampling frequency for required low-pass filtering. Designers usually define the passband ripple in decibel units as $20\log_{10}^{(1+\delta_1)}$, while the stopband ripple is also in decibels at $-20\log_{10}^{\delta_2}$. The length of the filter, L, determines the transition bandwidth of the filter $\Delta f = f_s - f_p$. Given the roll-off or transition bandwidth, Δf (this also depends on the type of window used, to be discussed in Section 7.4), the approximate value of the filter length, L, is obtained as $L \approx 4/\Delta f$. With this, an example of low-pass filter parameter values follows.

Sampling frequency (f_s)	44.1 kHz*
Passband frequency (f_p)	18 kHz (or normalized frequency = 0.408)
Stopband frequency (f_s)	21 kHz (or normalized frequency = 0.4762)
Transition bandwidth (Δf)	21 to 18 = 3 kHz (or normalized frequency = 0.068)
Passband ripple	0.001 dB
Stopband ripple	−96 dB
Filter length (L)	58 coefficients ($L \approx 4/\Delta f$)
*High-fidelity audio signals are typically sampled at this frequency.	

■

In this chapter, we restrict our discussion to the digital filters based on LTI systems that are completely described by the discrete-time impulse response. Depending on a filter's impulse-response length, two types of filters are suggested: FIR and IIR. We briefly discuss the design of FIR and IIR filters, and mainly concentrate on the implementation of FIR and IIR filters given their coefficients. We will discuss design, simulation, and implementation techniques for FIR filters and IIR filters in Sections 7.4 and 7.5.

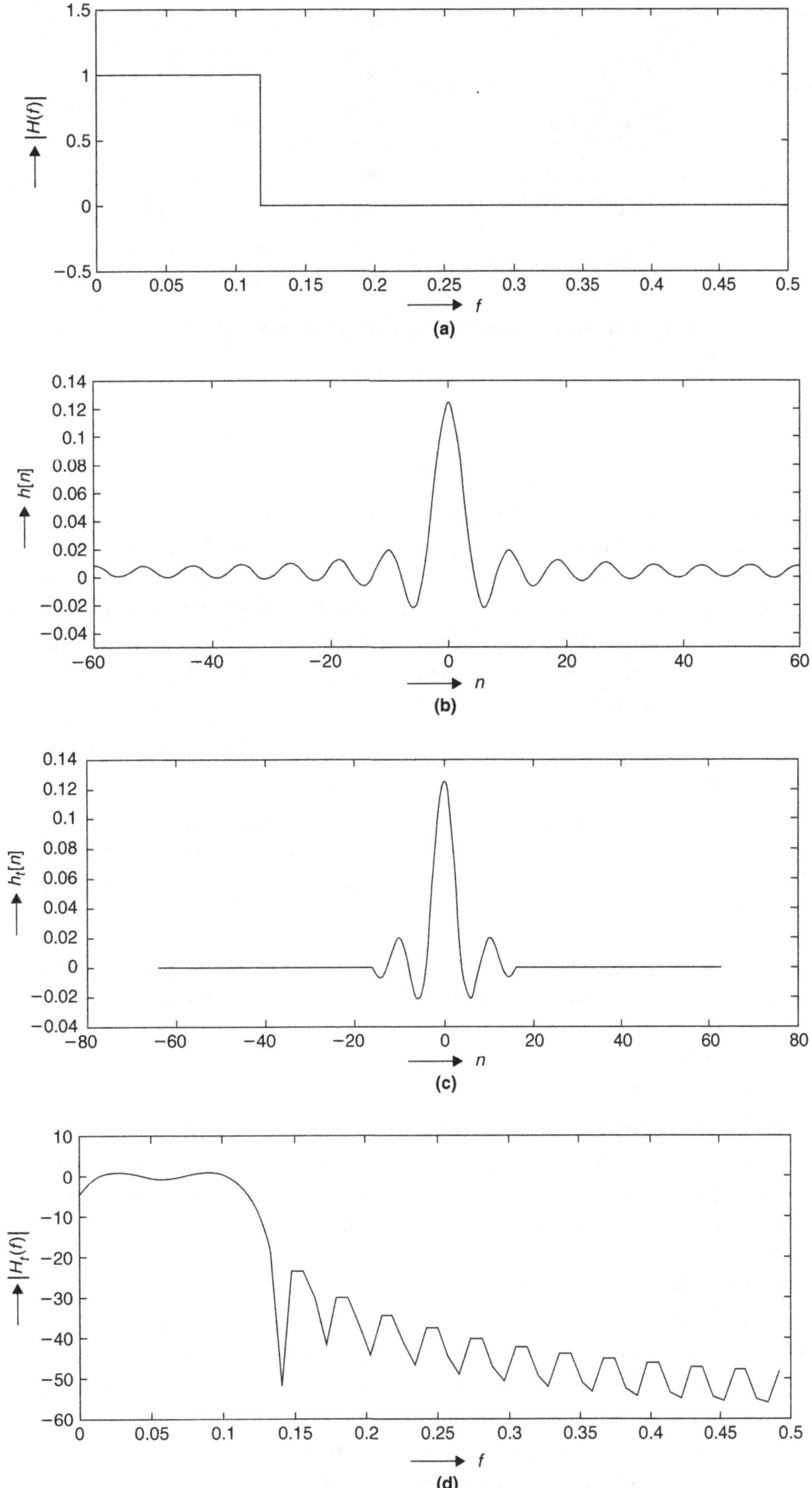

Figure 7.17: Impulse response truncation and its effect on frequency response. (a) Ideal low-pass-frequency response. (b) Corresponding infinite-length impulse response. (c) Truncated impulse response. (d) Non-ideal frequency response.

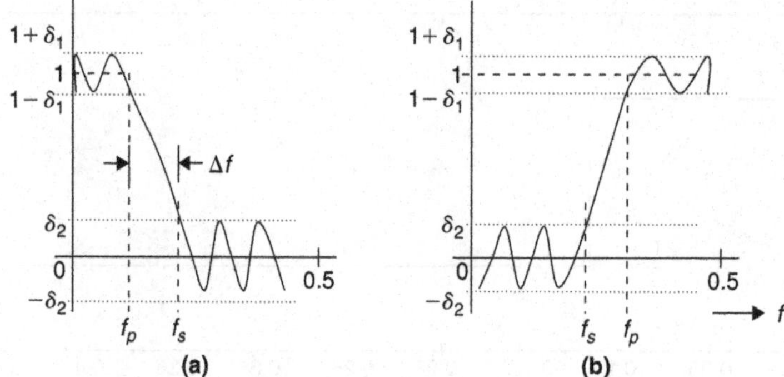

Figure 7.18: Frequency-domain specifications. (a) Description of low-pass filter parameters. (b) Description of high-pass filter parameters.

7.3.2 FIR versus IIR

Important Features of FIR Filters

Linear Phase: With linear-phase response, the phase delay of the output signal increases linearly with the frequency of the input signal. A linear-phase response becomes particularly important in applications such as speech processing, sonar, radar, and so on. We can design FIR filters with linear-phase response by maintaining the symmetry in the impulse response. Digital IIR filters, on the other hand, have nonlinear-phase response (however, we can achieve linear phase with special IIR filter designs). Linear-phase response is difficult to achieve with analog filters. The term "linear phase" has nothing to do with system linearity. Both FIR and IIR filters are linear filters from a system standpoint.

Stability: FIR filters have no poles in their z-plane transfer function, and thus outputs are always finite and stable. IIR filters, in contrast, require careful design to ensure stability.

Low Sensitivity to Coefficient Errors: FIR filters are less sensitive to coefficient errors. This permits FIR filters to be implemented with small word sizes (12 to 16 bits). Conversely, IIR filters are highly sensitive to coefficient errors, and this may cause the filter to become unstable. Typical IIR filters need between 16 to 24 bits per coefficient.

Adaptive Filtering: Adaptive FIR filters are comparatively easy to implement via changes to the filter coefficients in real time to adapt the filter's characteristics to external conditions.

Important Features of IIR Filters

Highest Efficiency: IIR filters require fewer filter coefficients to obtain required frequency characteristics, thereby minimizing the number of operations in filtering the data and maximizing throughput.

Least Memory Storage: Because IIR filters have fewer coefficients, they require less memory. Typically, we use less than 10 coefficients for IIR filters to achieve a given performance level and we may use hundreds of coefficients for FIR filters to achieve similar performance.

7.3.3 Digital Filtering and Finite-Word-Length Effects

The digital filter is nothing but a set of coefficients (or real numbers), and the filtering comprises transformation of data. Thus, digital filtering involves basic mathematical operations (i.e., additions/subtractions and multiplications/divisions) on the input data using filter coefficients. In general, the filter input and filter coefficients are real numbers, and we require infinite-length precision data registers in digital computers to handle them (since the real numbers are continuous in amplitude). However, the width of arithmetic registers in any digital computer is limited and real numbers must be represented with a finite number of bits. For this, we quantize the continuous amplitude data to discrete amplitudes to work with digital computers. In practice, we quantize the continuous amplitude data to 2^M discrete levels of information using M bits (where M is a finite number). With quantization, the finite precision values are obtained either by rounding or truncation of actual data values. This results in a quantization error and we usually prefer rounding over truncation as rounding errors have better statistical properties. Coefficient quantization has the adverse effect of modifying the desired frequency response, and it may increase the peak passband ripple. We may also see a reduction in the maximum attenuation of the stopband ripples.

We represent finite precision data in floating-point or fixed-point format (see Appendix B, Section B.1, on the companion website). We use floating-point hardware to execute floating-point arithmetic operations. Since floating-point processors typically run at lower clock rates and cost more than fixed-point processors, we prefer fixed-point hardware processors over floating-point processors for many applications. The precision of most fixed-point embedded processor registers is 16 or 32 bits. We use an $m.n$ fixed-point format (where $m+n=16$ or 32 depending on the 16- or 32-bit processor architecture) to represent quantized values. We choose m and n depending on the dynamic range of coefficients or data, filter gain, and filter structure. Some examples for fixed-point formats include 1.15, 4.12, 1.31, 8.24, and so on.

The goal of a fixed-point implementation is to maximize the filter performance and minimize finite-word-length effects, which include quantization errors and register overflow. Quantization errors occur whenever we limit the precision of data and can arise in two ways: quantization of continuous amplitude data (as discussed earlier), and quantization of arithmetic operations output. As an example of the latter, assume that we represent two numbers in 1.15 format using 16 bits to work on a 16-bit processor; the precision of the multiplication output is the sum of the precisions of the two numbers used in the multiplication operation. In our example, it is 2.30. To hold/store the output in 16-bit architecture, we reduce the precision of the multiplication output to 16 bits by right shifting. This results in round-off error, which in turn affects the output SNR of the filter. The extent of the errors introduced depends on the type of arithmetic used and the filter structure.

Register overflow occurs whenever the dynamic range of the filter's data or coefficients exceeds the dynamic range of the fixed-point processor registers. This happens during filtering when we sum fixed-point numbers. Register overflow can be avoided by scaling the data and coefficients or by using the two's complement arithmetic, which saturates the result to the extreme end values whenever register overflow occurs. However, saturation does not always yield the right results as it blindly avoids the register overflow. Another way of eliminating register overflow is to use extended-precision arithmetic registers. Extended-precision registers provide additional headroom that allows holding the intermediate outputs with higher precision. For example, the precision of accumulators present in the reference embedded processor is 40 bits, which is 8 bits more when compared to 32-bit precision of arithmetic registers.

7.3.4 Digital Filters: Advantages and Disadvantages

With digital filtering, computations must be completed in a given sampling period to achieve real-time filtering. In addition, finite-length-word effects must be taken care of during implementation of digital filters. These issues do not arise in the case of analog filters.

Digital Filtering Advantages

Some of the advantages of digital filters (when compared to analog filters) follow:

- High accuracy and performance
- Linear phase and constant group delay (can be achieved with FIR filters)
- No drift due to component variations
- Flexibility, or adaptive filtering capabilities
- Easy to simulate and design

Digital Filtering Limitations

Digital filters have some limitations:

- May not handle high-bandwidth signals due to DSP speed limitations
- Analog filters are still needed for antialiasing and high-frequency filtering
- Lack of high-speed analog-to-digital converters (ADCs) for sampling of continuous-time signals

7.4 Finite Impulse-Response Filters

Mathematically, the FIR filter is nothing but a linear-time-invariant transformation. The filter's input and output signals are related by the convolution sum as follows:

$$y[n]=\sum_{k=0}^{L-1} h[k]x[n-k] \tag{7.15}$$

where $x[\,]$ is input signal to the filter, $y[\,]$ is output signal from the filter, and $h[\,]$ is the impulse response of the filter. Impulse-response length of the filter $h[\,]$ is L samples, where L is a finite number, and hence these filters are called FIR filters. The concept of convolution operation is illustrated in Figure 6.37. Using Equation (7.15), we basically take the mirror image of $x[k]$ (i.e., $x[-k]$) and correlate it with the impulse response $h[\,]$ to get the filtered samples $y[\,]$. If all L samples of $h[\,]$ have the same value $1/L$, then the Equation (7.15) reduces as follows:

$$y[n]=\frac{1}{L}\sum_{k=0}^{L-1} x[n-k] \tag{7.16}$$

With Equation (7.16), we basically obtain the current filtered sample by summing the current sample to previous $L-1$ samples and multiplying by a constant $1/L$. Then we increase n by 1 and repeat the preceding process and continue like this until we finish all the input samples. This type of filter is called a *moving-average* filter. The moving-average filter performs well in smoothing time-domain signals. The degree of smoothing depends on the length of filter L. This is shown in Figure 7.19 in filtering a noisy sinusoid for three filter lengths.

The moving-average filter can be efficiently computed using a recursive equation given as follows:

$$y[n]=y[n-1]+x[n]-x[n-L] \tag{7.17}$$

With Equation (7.17), to get the first filtered sample, we compute the sum of the current sample and previous $L-1$ samples and multiply by $1/L$. To obtain n-th filtered samples, we add the previous filtered sample $y[n-1]$ to $z[n]$, where $z[n]$ is obtained by subtracting the $(n-L)$th-input sample $x[n-L]$ from the current input sample

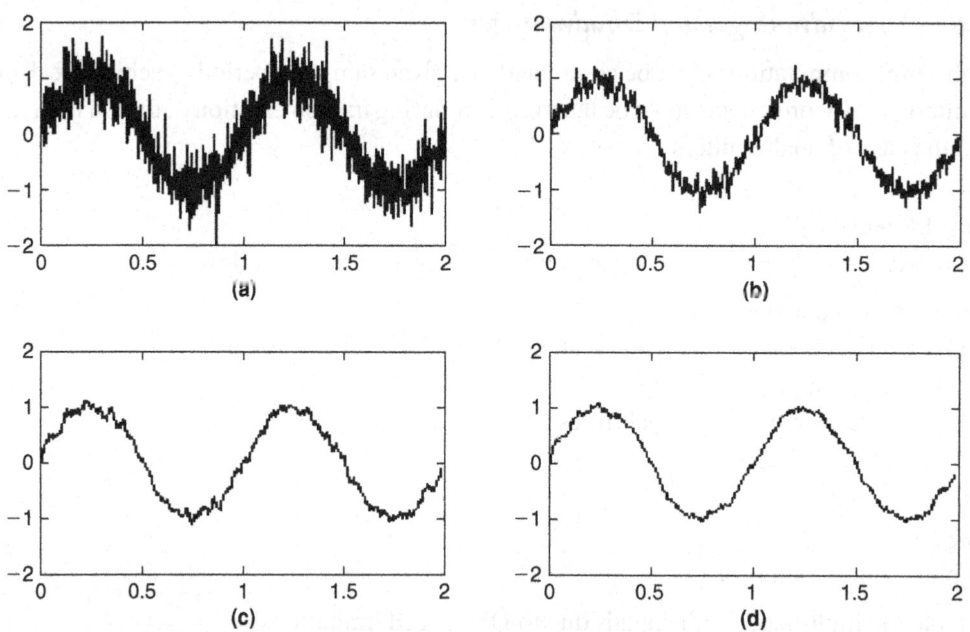

Figure 7.19: Smoothing of time-domain signal using moving-average filter. (a) Noisy sinusoid, moving average. (b) Five samples in (a). (c) Fifteen samples in (a). (d) Twenty-five samples in (a).

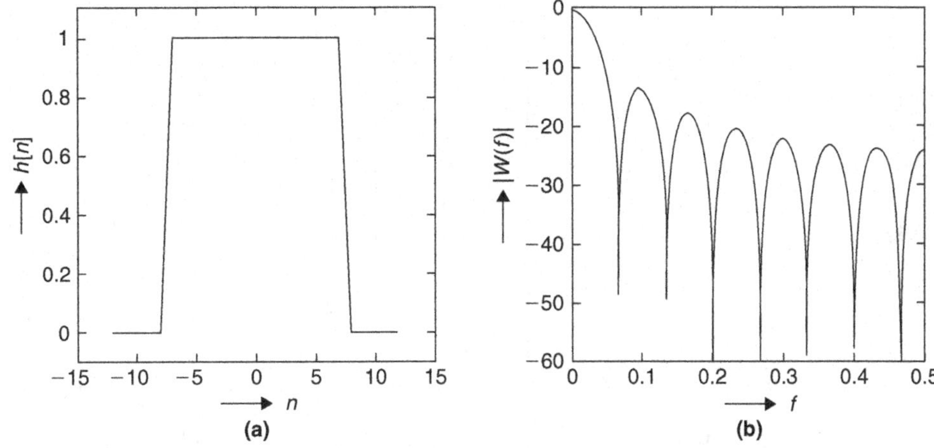

Figure 7.20: Time- and frequency-domain characteristics of a moving-average filter.

$x[n]$. In this way, we use one addition and one subtraction in computing the moving-average filter irrespective of its length.

Although the moving-average filter performs well in smoothing time-domain signals, it performs inadequately in separating the frequency components (i.e., in extracting or attenuating the specified frequency bands). The time- and frequency-domain responses of the moving-average filter are shown in Figure 7.20. As shown in the figure, the moving-average filter is a discrete rectangular pulse with height $1/L$. If we look at the frequency response of the moving-average filter, it has very poor low-pass filter characteristics with slow roll-off and poor stopband attenuation. The expression for frequency response of the moving-average filter with length L samples follows:

$$H(f) = \frac{1}{L}\frac{\sin(\pi f L)}{\sin(\pi f)} \tag{7.18}$$

The frequency-response characteristics of the moving-average filter can be improved by using different weights (instead of the constant $1/L$) for filter coefficients $h[\,]$ in Equation (7.15).

7.4.1 Windowing

Applying a proper window to the impulse response minimizes abrupt changes in the truncated impulse response. If we just cut the impulse response at both ends (i.e., by multiplying by the rectangular window) to obtain the shorter impulse response, we introduce an abrupt change in values of the impulse-response samples, and this leads to very poor frequency-response characteristics. For example, we applied a rectangular window to an ideal sinc response in Figure 7.17(c) to get the shorter sinc response, and the ghastly frequency-response characteristics of the filter can be seen in Figure 7.17(d). The same also applies to the moving-average filter because it is obtained by multiplying an impulse train by a rectangular window. Two commonly used windows to obtain acceptable frequency-response characteristics for FIR filter design are discussed next.

Hamming Window

The following equation represents the Hamming window function:

$$w[n] = 0.54 - 0.46\cos\left(\frac{2\pi n}{N}\right), \quad -\frac{N-1}{2} \leq n \leq \frac{N-1}{2} \tag{7.19}$$

where N is window length.

The time-domain (window is shifted right by 15 samples for $N = 31$) and frequency-domain characteristics of the Hamming window are shown in Figure 7.21. A few characteristics of a Hamming window are: the passband ripple is about 0.0194 dB, stopband attenuation is about 53 dB, and the main lobe relative to the side lobe is

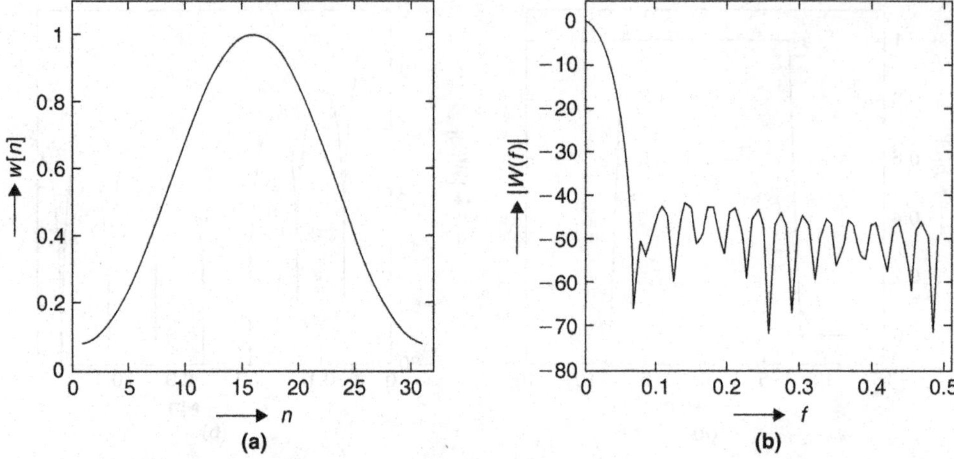

Figure 7.21: Time- and frequency-domain characteristics of Hamming window.

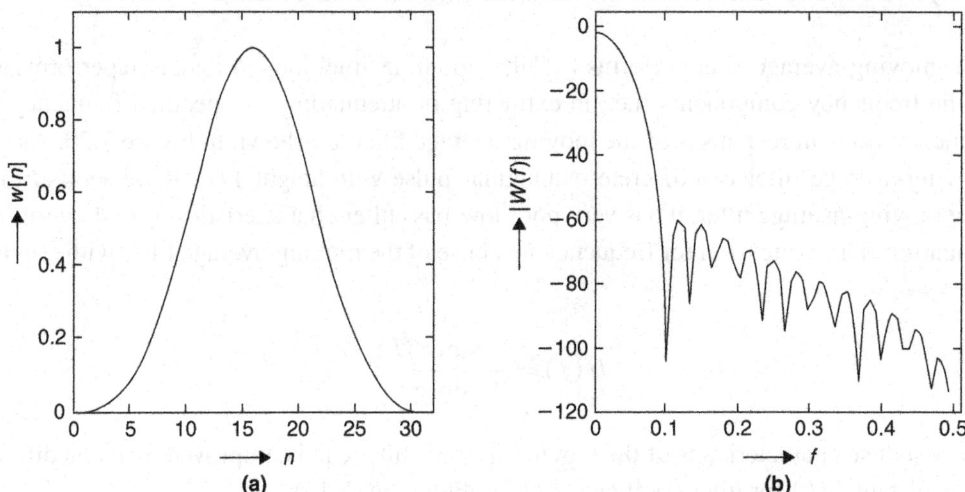

Figure 7.22: Time- and frequency-domain characteristics of Blackman window.

about 41 dB. Given filter length N, the transition width Δf is obtained as follows:

$$\Delta f = \frac{3.3}{N} \tag{7.20}$$

Blackman Window

The time-domain characteristics of a Blackman window function are represented in the following equation:

$$w[n] = 0.42 - 0.5\cos\left(\frac{2\pi n}{N-1}\right) + 0.08\cos\left(\frac{4\pi n}{N-1}\right), \quad -\frac{N-1}{2} \le n \le \frac{N-1}{2} \tag{7.21}$$

where N is window length.

The time-domain (window is shifted right by 15 samples for $N = 31$) and frequency-domain characteristics of the Blackman window are shown in Figure 7.22. A few characteristics of a Blackman window follow: the passband ripple is about 0.0017 dB, stopband attenuation is about 75 dB, and the main lobe relative to the side lobe is about 57 dB. Given filter length N, the transition width Δf is obtained as follows:

$$\Delta f = \frac{5.5}{N} \tag{7.22}$$

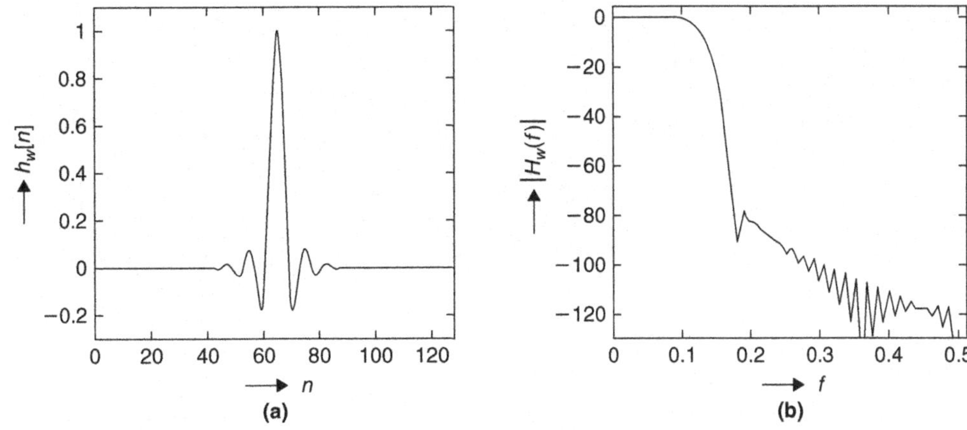

Figure 7.23: The time-frequency response characteristics of Blackman windowed low-pass filter.

As shown in Figure 7.23, we can see amazing results in the frequency-response characteristics (from a practical point of view) of a low-pass filter when we apply a Blackman window to the time-domain impulse response (i.e., sinc function) of an ideal low-pass filter shown in Figure 7.17(b).

Example 7.2

Consider the following low-pass-filter frequency-domain characteristics:

Passband cut-off frequency f_p	2.2 kHz
Transition width	0.6 kHz
Stopband attenuation	>50 dB
Sampling frequency	8.8 kHz

Obtain the coefficients of a FIR low-pass filter using the Hamming window. For a given cut-off frequency f_c, the ideal low-pass-filter impulse response (i.e., sinc functions) follows:

$$h_{lp}[n] = \begin{cases} \frac{\sin(2\pi f_c n)}{\pi n}, & n \neq 0 \\ 2f_c, & n = 0 \end{cases}$$

The filter coefficients are then obtained as follows:

$$h[n] = h_{lp}[n]w[n], \quad -\frac{N-1}{2} \leq n \leq \frac{N-1}{2}$$

where $w[n]$ is the Hamming window.

The length of filter N is determined as follows. The normalized transition width $\Delta f = 0.6/8.8 = 0.0682$. Based on Equation (7.21), $N = 3.3/\Delta f = 3.3/0.0682 = 48.4$. Given that we prefer N to be an odd number, we choose $N = 49$. With the smearing effect of the window on the filter response, usually the cut-off frequency is centered on the transition band and the effective frequency cut-off is determined from the passband frequency and transition width as follows:

$$f_c = f_p + \Delta f/2 = 2.2 + 0.6/2 = 2.5 \text{ kHz}$$

The normalized cut-off frequency is $f_c = 2.5/8.8 = 0.2841$. With the symmetric filter property, we only need to compute half the filter coefficients, with the other half automatically derived from the computed coefficients. That is, if we compute coefficients $h[n]$ from $n = 0$ to $n = (N-1)/2 = (48)/2 = 24$, we can get the filter coefficients $h[n]$ from $n = 0$ to 48 in the following way: $h[24], h[25] = h[23]$, $h[26] = h[22], \ldots, h[48] = h[0]$. With this, all the filter coefficients are obtained as follows:

$$h[24] = 2f_c = 2 \times 0.2841 = 0.5682$$

$$h[23] = h[25] = h_{lp}[25]w[25] = \frac{\sin(2\pi f_c 25)}{25\pi}[0.54 - 0.46\cos(2\pi 25/48)] = 0.3099$$

$$h[22] = h[26] = h_{lp}[26]w[26] = \frac{\sin(2\pi f_c 25)}{25\pi}[0.54 - 0.46\cos(2\pi 26/48)] = -0.0651$$

$$\vdots$$

$$h[0] = h[48] = h_{lp}[48]w[48] = \frac{\sin(2\pi f_c 48)}{48\pi}[0.54 - 0.46\cos(2\pi 48/48)] = -9.7594 \times 10^{-4}$$

■

The subject of FIR filter design theory is very broad, and the purpose of the concepts underlying FIR filter design is to obtain the appropriate filter coefficients that best satisfy the frequency-response characteristics with a minimum number of coefficients. We assume that the FIR filter coefficients are available for the desired time- and frequency-domain responses. Next, we discuss FIR filter implementation techniques.

7.4.2 FIR Filter Realization

Filter difference equations (e.g., the convolution sum equation given in Equation (7.15)) are represented using special signal flow diagrams called filter realization structures. There are many filter realization structures for a given difference equation, each with specific advantages and disadvantages. All filter realization structures consist of a delay unit, an adder, and a multiplier, as shown in Figure 7.24(a) through (c). In this section, we discuss three widely used FIR filter realizations: the direct-form or transversal, linear-phase, and DFT-based structures.

FIR Transversal Realization

A transversal FIR filter realization is a signal flow diagram that corresponds to the filter difference equation given in Equation (7.15). The transversal realization of a FIR filter is shown in Figure 7.25. With a transversal FIR filter structure, the computation of each output sample $y[n]$ requires (1) $L-1$ delay units to store the previous $L-1$ input samples, (2) L memory locations to store L filter coefficients, (3) L multipliers, and (4) $L-1$ adders.

As seen in Figure 7.25, the current output sample $y[n]$ is obtained from a weighted sum of the current input sample $x[n]$ and $L-1$ previous input samples (i.e., $x[n-1]$ to $x[n-L+1]$). With this realization, we can implement a FIR filter very efficiently on an embedded processor, as all the indexing in accessing the input data and filter coefficients is linear.

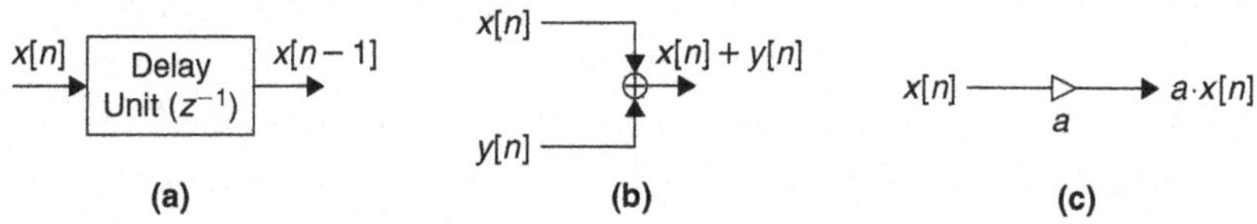

Figure 7.24: Building blocks of filter realization structure. (a) Delay unit. (b) Adder. (c) Multiplier.

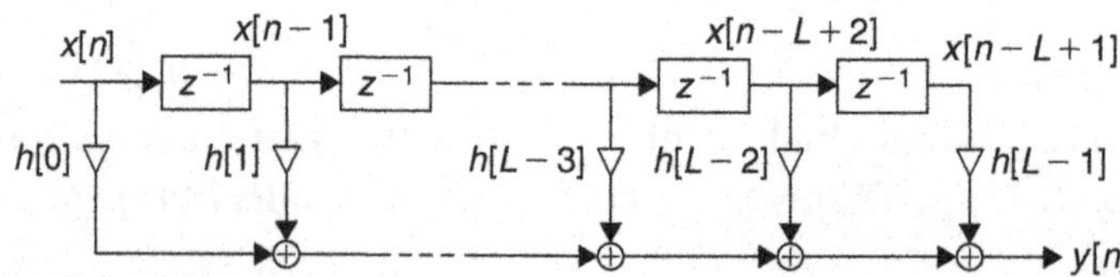

Figure 7.25: Transversal realization of FIR filter.

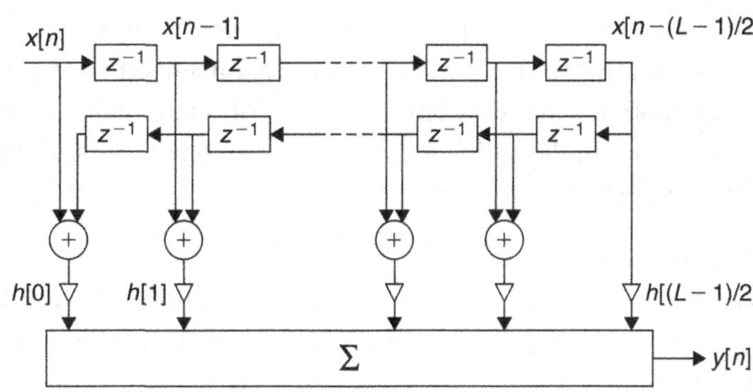

Figure 7.26: Linear-phase realization of FIR filter.

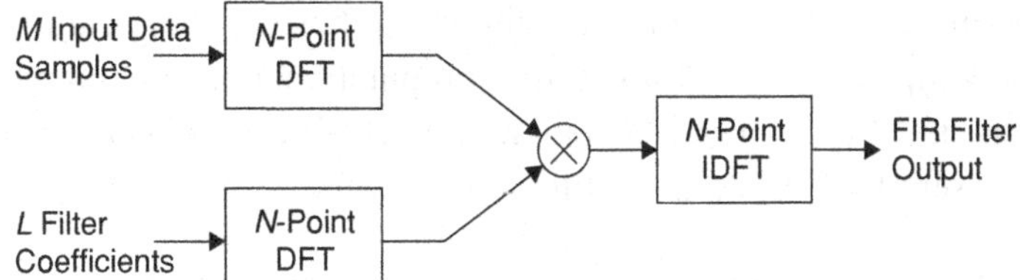

Figure 7.27: DFT-based FIR filter implementation.

Linear-Phase Realization

For a linear-phase realization, we modify the FIR filter difference equation as follows:

$$y[n] = \sum_{k=0}^{(N-1)/2-1} h[k]\{x[n-k] + x[n-(L-1-k)]\} + h[(L-1)/2]x[n-(L-1)/2] \tag{7.23}$$

The signal flow diagram of the linear-phase realization is shown in Figure 7.26. With a linear-phase realization, we can compute the filter output with fewer multiplications as the filter coefficients are symmetric about the center (i.e., $h[n] = h[n-(L-1)]$). Although the linear-phase structure allows us to compute the filter output with fewer multiplications, the index order of input samples to the filter is not linear anymore and its efficient implementation is not straightforward.

DFT-Based Structure

Since the convolution in the time domain is equivalent to multiplication in the frequency domain (see Section 6.5.3), we can also use the DFT for performing the filter operation. This realization structure is popularly used for a FIR filter implementation, especially when the filter impulse response is long. As a DFT can be implemented very efficiently with FFT algorithms (see Section 7.1), the computation of a longer convolution for a FIR filter can be avoided with use of a DFT structure as shown in Figure 7.27. Given the input data of M-length samples and filter-impulse response of length L samples, we must use minimum N-point DFT with the DFT structure to obtain linear convolution output, where $N = M + L - 1$.

7.4.3 FIR Filter Fixed-Point Simulation

In this section, we discuss simulation and implementation techniques for a FIR filter using the transversal realization structure. The floating-point simulation of a transversal structure is given in Pcode 7.12. Although the

```
for(n = 0;n < N;n++) {
        y[n] = 0;
        M = n < (L-1) ? n:(L-1);           // maximum filter output samples
        for(k = 0;k < M;k++)
                y[n] = y[n] + h[k] * x[n-k];
}
```

Pcode 7.12: Floating point simulation code for a FIR transversal realization.

simulation code given in Pcode 7.12 is simple, it is computationally very inefficient. First, it uses floating-point values in the computation; hence it runs very slowly on a fixed-point embedded processor. Even if we convert to fixed-point computations, this simulation code is still inefficient as it does not utilize the structural features of transversal realization. In the following, we discuss a few tasks for efficient implementation of the fixed-point FIR filter using a transversal structure.

Fixed-Point Computation

The most common fixed-point formats used with digital filtering are 1.15 and 1.31 (usually along with extended arithmetic registers) (see Appendix B, Section B.1, on the companion website for more details on fixed-point data formats). We may require scaling of the filter coefficients if the maximum value present in the coefficients is greater than or equal to 1. If the dynamic range of the filter coefficients is larger, then we prefer the 1.31 format over the 1.15 format to retain the lower-amplitude coefficients after scaling. While we obtain better results with the 1.31 format compared to 1.15 format, the computational power and memory required with the 1.31 format are greater. In the fixed-point implementation of a FIR filter as given in Pcode 7.13, we are restricted to 16-bit precision to represent both the data and filter coefficients.

```
for(n = 0;n < N;n+=4) {
    y[n] = 0; y[n+1] = 0;
    y[n+2] = 0; y[n+3] = 0;
    M = i < (L-1) ? i : (L-1);
    for(k = 0;k < = M;k+=4) {
        a = (x[n-k] * h[k]) >> 15; b = (x[n-1-k] * h[k+1]) >> 15;
        c = (x[n-2-k] * h[k+2]) >> 15; d =(x[n-3-k] * h[k+3]) >> 15;
        a = a + b; c = c + d;
        y[n] = a + c;

        a = (x[n+1-k] * h[k]) >> 15; b = (x[n-k] * h[k+1]) >> 15;
        c = (x[n-1-k] * h[k+2]) >> 15; d =(x[n-2-k] * h[k+3]) >> 15;
        a = a + b; c = c + d;
        y[n+1] = a + c;

        a = (x[n+2-k] * h[k]) >> 15; b = (x[n+1-k] * h[k+1]) >> 15;
        c = (x[n-k] * h[k+2]) >> 15; d = (x[n-1-k] * h[k+3]) >> 15;
        a = a + b; c = c + d;
        y[n+2] = a + c;

        a = (x[n+3-k] * h[k]) >> 15; b = (x[n+2-k] * h[k+1]) >> 15;
        c = (x[n+1-k] * h[k+2]) >> 15; d = (x[n-k] * h[k+3]) >> 15;
        a = a + b; c = c + d;
        y[n+3] = a + c;
    }
}
```

Pcode 7.13: Fixed point simulation code for FIR filter kernel.

Reuse of Data and Coefficients

In Pcode 7.13, we read the same data and coefficients multiple times from respective buffers. In other words, we access the same data and coefficients up to L times in computing L output samples as shown in Figure 7.28, where L is the filter length. However, we can reuse the data for computing multiple filter outputs by unrolling both the inner and outer loops. By unrolling the inner and outer loops, we can (1) reduce the data and coefficient memory buffer access, (2) compute the many MAC operations in parallel, and (3) reduce the cycles spent in loop overheads. In Pcode 7.13, we unrolled both the inner and outer loops four times, and both input data samples and filter coefficients are reused for computing four filter outputs.

Real-Time Filtering

Previously, we assumed a buffer of data samples and computed the filtered data output for that buffer of data samples. In practice, things are not that simple. We must filter the data in real time for most applications. With

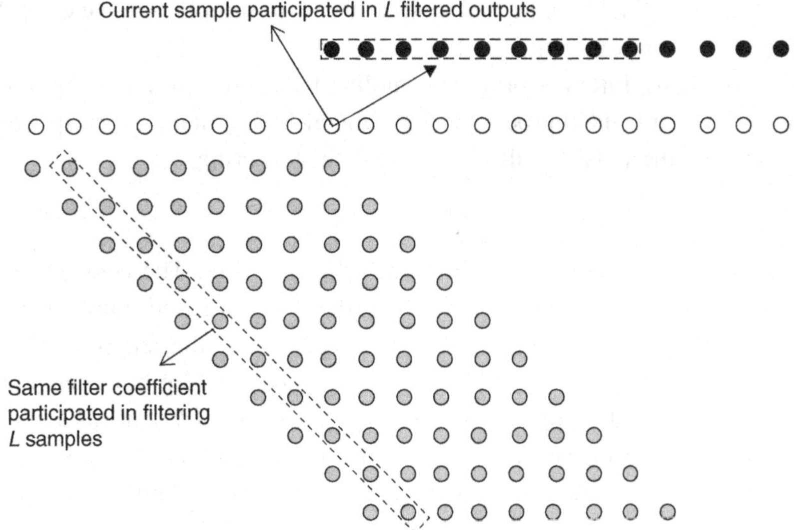

Figure 7.28: Illustration of data and coefficient reuse in filtering data samples.

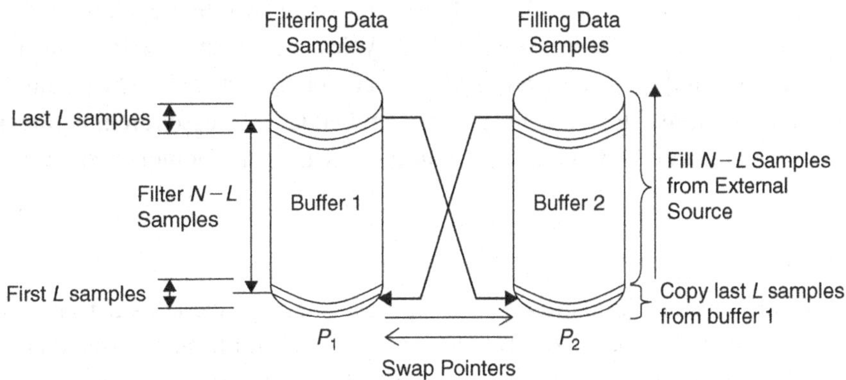

Figure 7.29: Ping-Pong buffer scheme.

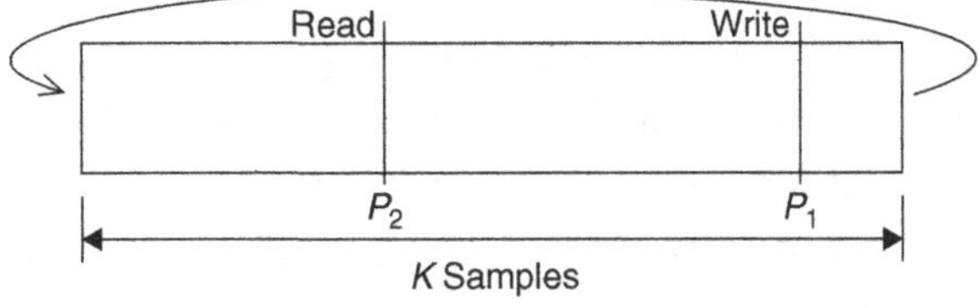

Figure 7.30: Schematic of circular buffer.

real-time filtering, the current data sample is filtered before arrival of next data sample. However, we do not handle the data in terms of single samples; instead we work on a buffer of data samples (to efficiently utilize processor resources). In brief, we must filter the current data sample buffer by the time that the next data buffer is filled with data samples. For this, we use two approaches: (1) a Ping-Pong buffer scheme using two data buffers, as shown in Figure 7.29, and a circular buffer scheme as shown in Figure 7.30. The Ping-Pong buffer scheme is useful for C-implementation, whereas the circular buffer scheme is useful at assembly-level implementation on embedded processors that support circular indexing.

Ping-Pong Buffer Scheme

With the Ping-Pong buffer scheme, when filtering the data of buffer 1, buffer 2 is filled with data samples. Once we finish filtering buffer-1 data samples, we swap the pointers of both buffers and filtering is continued with the buffer-2 data samples while filling buffer 1 with data samples. This process continues as long as the filter is enabled. To perform filtering continuously without missing samples, the middle $N - L$ samples in the current buffer are always filtered while filling the other buffer from the L-th sample, and we copy the last L samples of the current buffer to the beginning of the other buffer.

If buffer overflow occurs when a filter is working on another buffer, we cannot perform real-time filtering due to the limited bandwidth of an embedded processor (in terms of MIPS, memory, peripherals, etc.). Sometimes inefficient implementation of a filter also results in non–real-time filtering.

Circular Buffer Scheme

Circular indexing is used to make a circular buffer from a linear buffer. The concept of circular indexing is used in most embedded processors. With circular indexing, the write and read pointers P_1 and P_2 of the buffer automatically wrap around after incrementing K samples, where K is the length of the circular buffer. The schematic diagram of a circular buffer is shown in Figure 7.30. By making both data and coefficient buffers circular, we can perform filtering of all samples with one loop and avoid all overheads associated with data copy, pointer swap, and multiple loops setting overhead, and so on. For continuous filtering, we do not need to copy the data samples from one place to another; instead simple adjustment of the buffer read pointer P_2 allows us to perform continuous filtering.

Computational Complexity

The computational complexity (in terms of cycles and memory) of a FIR filter depends solely on filter length L. If we use the 1.15 format, we consume approximately $L/2$ cycles to perform filtering of a single sample on the reference embedded processor (as the reference embedded processor consists of two MAC units). See Appendix A on the companion website for more details on the reference embedded processor architecture. Given that we use 16 bits to represent both the data and coefficients, the amount of L1 data memory required is about $2(L+K)$ bytes.

7.4.4 Simulation Results

In this section, we will present the simulation results for FIR filtering. We consider an analog signal whose maximum frequency is less than or equal to 64 Hz. That is, we must sample such a signal at least 128 times per second to process it in the digital domain and recover the signal from the processed digital signal. With this, the normalized frequency of 0.5 in the digital domain is equivalent to the analog frequency of 64 Hz.

Low-Pass Filter

We consider a low-pass filter whose passband/cutoff frequency is 15 Hz (or the normalized cutoff frequency is 0.1172), and its shortened impulse response is obtained by applying the Blackman window to the impulse response of the ideal low-pass filter with a 15-Hz cutoff frequency. The time-frequency characteristics of this low-pass filter are shown in Figure 7.31.

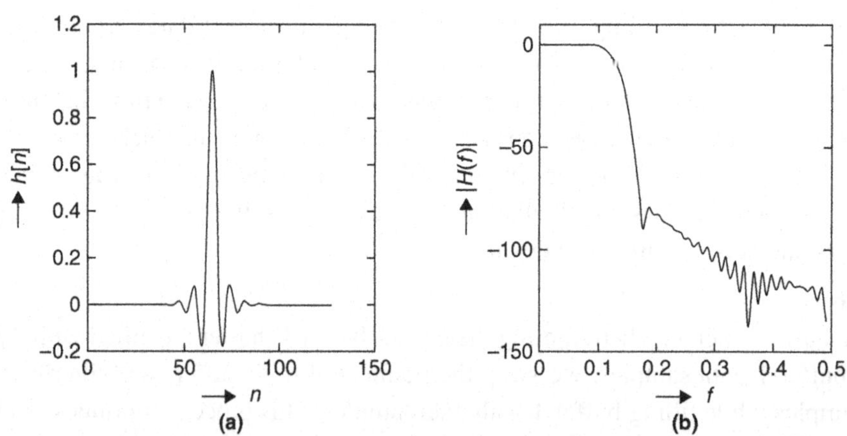

Figure 7.31: Low-pass filter characteristics. (a) Time domain. (b) Frequency domain.

Desired Signal Generation

The desired signal is formed by adding two sine waves with frequencies 8 Hz (or the equivalent normalized frequency equal to 0.0625) and 10 Hz (or the equivalent normalized frequency equal to 0.0781) as shown in Figure 7.32(a). Its corresponding frequency-domain information is shown in Figure 7.32(b).

Noise Signal Generation

We consider two test cases for FIR filtering. In the first case, the desired signal is associated with narrowband noise; and in the second case, the desired signal is associated with wideband noise.

1. *Narrowband noise u[n] (bandwidth = 5 Hz)*: Obtained by adding five sine waves from 40 Hz to 44 Hz (or equivalent normalized frequency range is 0.3125 to 0.3438). The time-frequency information of the noisy signal $z[n]$ ($= x[n] + u[n]$, where $x[n]$ is a desired signal and $u[n]$ is a narrowband noise signal) is shown in Figure 7.33.

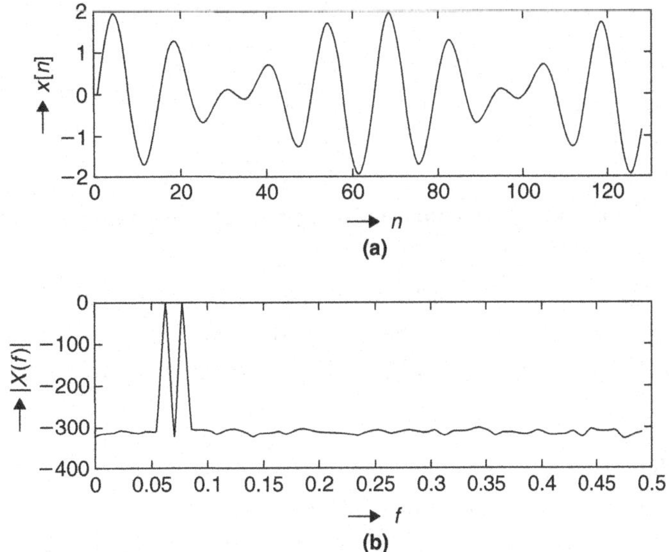

Figure 7.32: Desired signal information. (a) Time domain. (b) Frequency domain.

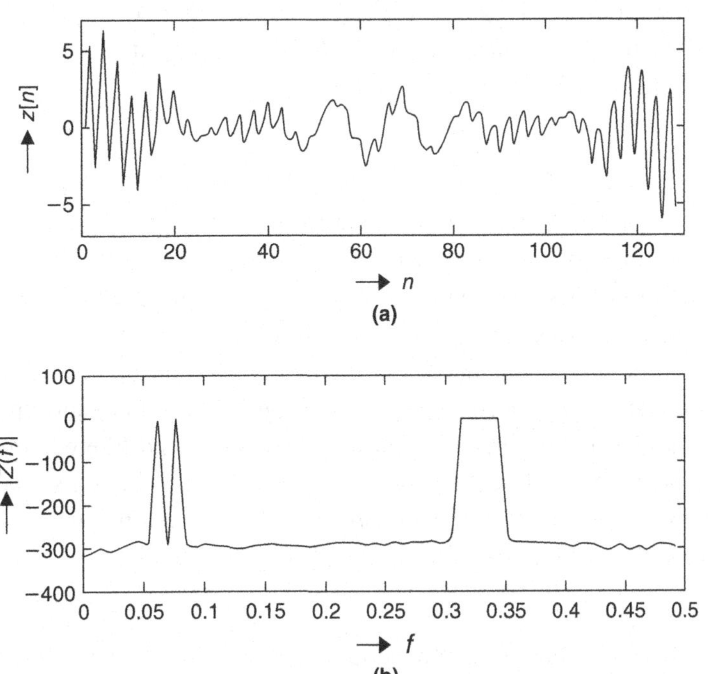

Figure 7.33: Plot of narrowband noise signal. (a) Time domain. (b) Frequency domain.

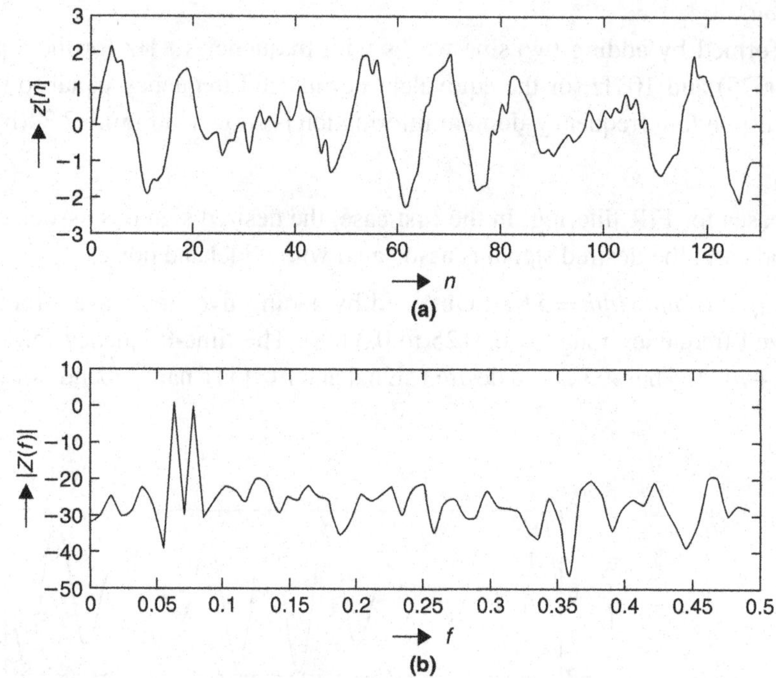

Figure 7.34: Plot of wideband noise signal. (a) Time domain. (b) Frequency domain.

2. *Wideband noise $v[n]$ (bandwidth = 64 Hz)*: Obtained with Gaussian distributed random variable. The range of the equivalent normalized frequencies present in wideband noise is 0.0 to 0.5. The time-frequency information of a noisy signal $z[n](= x[n] + v[n]$, where $x[n]$ is a desired signal and $v[n]$ is a wideband noise signal) is shown in Figure 7.34.

Filtering Noisy Signals with the FIR Filter

We filter the noisy signals by passing them through a FIR filter whose impulse response $h[n]$ is shown in Figure 7.31. The FIR filtering can be achieved either by convolution (using Pcode 7.13, page 358) or FFT (see Section 7.1). If the number of samples present in the input signal is M and the length of the impulse response is L, then the length of the filter output is $M + L - 1$ samples. The filtered samples (corresponding to M input samples) are given by the middle M samples in the convolution or FFT output (i.e., starting from the sample at index $(L - 1)/2$ to the sample at index $(M + L - 1) - (L - 1)/2$).

Narrowband Noise Filtering

The frequency spectrum of the narrowband noise-signal filter output is shown in Figure 7.35(a). As expected, the noise band in the filter output (from 0.3125 to 0.3438 on the normalized frequency scale, shown with a dashed line in Figure 7.35(a)) is attenuated by 100 dB with respect to the input-signal noise band. This attenuation factor is the same as that of a low pass filter in the stopband at those frequencies, as shown in Figure 7.31(b). In addition, the noise signal (solid line) and filtered signal (dashed line), and original signal (solid line) and filtered signal (dashed line) of the time domain are shown in Figure 7.35(b) and Figure 7.35(c), respectively. We can determine FIR filter performance by inspecting the original signal (solid line) and filtered signal (dashed line) in Figure 7.35(c). We cannot see the difference because both original and filtered signals are overlapping and they are almost the same. The MSE difference between the original and filtered signal is 2.3556×10^{-8} (with double-precision computations). Using 16-bit precision for both filter coefficients and input data (not shown), the MSE difference between the original and filtered signals is 5.9×10^{-3}.

Wideband Noise Filtering

The wideband noise signal $z[n]$ is constructed by adding Gaussian-distributed white noise (whose frequency spectrum is almost flat at all the frequencies between 0 to 64 Hz) to original signal $x[n]$. The filtered signal $y[n]$

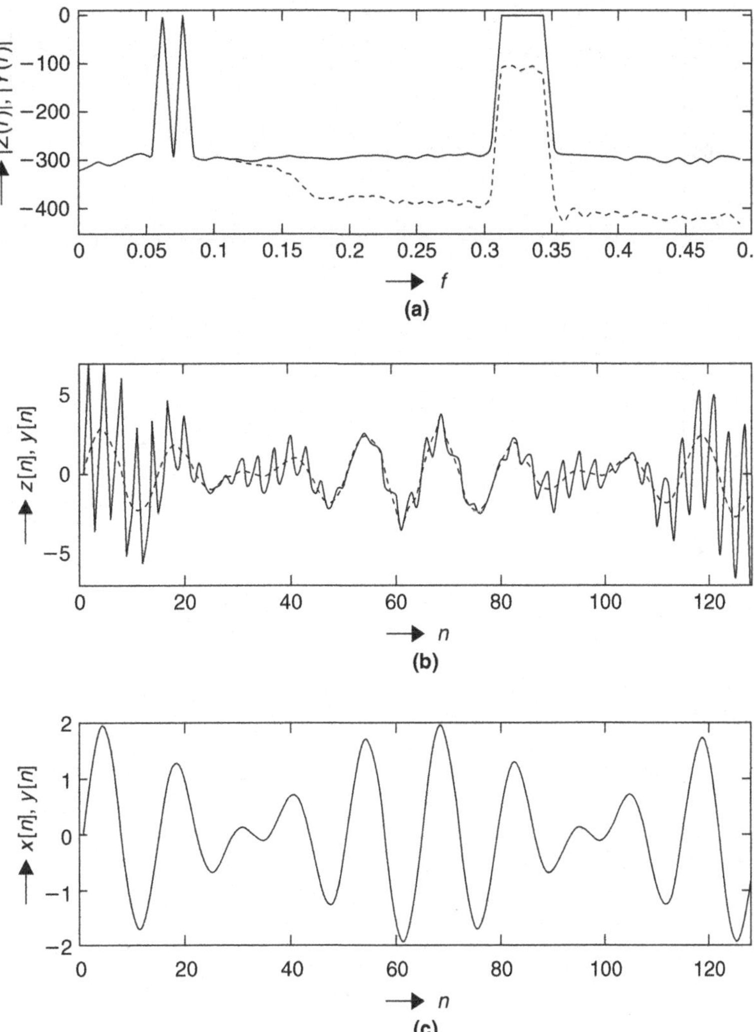

Figure 7.35: Narrowband noise filtering with FIR low-pass-filter. (a) Frequency domain. Solid line, before filtering; dashed line, after filtering. (b) Time domain. Solid line, before filtering; dashed line, after filtering. (c) Time domain. Solid line, original signal; dashed line, filtered signal.

is obtained by convolving the noise signal $z[n]$ with the filter impulse response $h[n]$ shown in Figure 7.31(a). The frequency spectra of the noisy signal (*solid line*) and filtered signal (*dashed line*) are shown in Figure 7.36(a). In addition, the noise signal (*solid line*) and filter output (*dashed line*), and the original signal (*solid line*) and filter output (*dashed line*) of the time domain are shown in Figure 7.36(b) and Figure 7.36(c), respectively. As the filter allows the noise components in the passband, we can make out the difference between the original and filtered signals in this case.

7.5 Infinite Impulse-Response Filters

Although we obtain desired time-frequency characteristics using FIR filters, their higher performance is at the cost of greater computational complexity. Here we discuss another class of filters—the IIR filters, with which we get the satisfactory performance results at very low computational complexity. FIR filters are implemented using convolution, whereas IIR filters are implemented using *recursion* (hence IIR filters are also called recursive filters). We will discuss details of IIR recursive implementation later. IIR filters are useful because they avoid a longer convolution in implementing digital filters. Unlike FIR filters, which lack analog counterparts, IIR

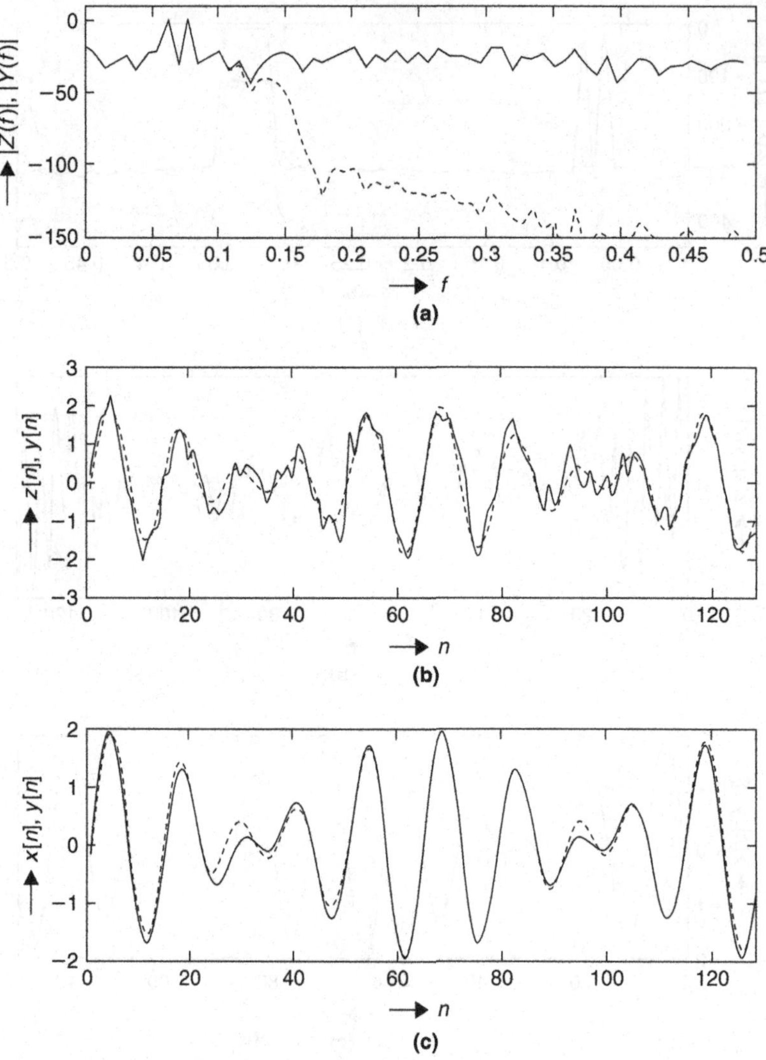

Figure 7.36: Wideband noise filtering with FIR low-pass-filter. (a) Frequency domain. Solid line, before filtering; dashed line, after filtering. (b) Time domain. Solid line, before filtering; dashed line, after filtering. (c) Time domain. Solid line, original signal; dashed line, filtered signal.

filters have traditional analog counterparts (e.g., Chebyshev, elliptic), and can be analyzed and synthesized using familiar traditional filter design techniques. IIR filter design based on analog filters uses generalized Fourier transform tools (i.e., Laplace transform and z-transform as discussed in Section 6.6). In particular, filter design uses pole-zero location information to determine the time-frequency response characteristics of IIR filters. In this section, we provide an overview of IIR filter design based on analog filter design techniques, their realization, simulation, and implementation techniques, and practical issues associated with the implementation of IIR filters.

7.5.1 IIR Filter Design

Digital IIR filters are commonly designed based on weighted least-squares, min-max, analog filter, and modeling designs. In this section, we concentrate only on digital IIR filter design based on analog filters. In this approach, IIR filter specifications are derived from their analog counterparts. Digital IIR filter coefficients are obtained in two steps: (1) picking an appropriate analog filter design, and (2) mapping filter specifications from the analog to the digital domain. There are many choices in the two-step process of obtaining digital IIR filter coefficients from analog filter designs. The main features of a few analog filters and analog-to-digital specification mapping methods are briefly discussed.

Analog-Filter Design Methods

The subject of analog filter design is very broad, and covering all concepts related to IIR filter design is beyond the scope of this book. Here we discuss a few IIR filters that have comparable performance (from the application point of view) with respect to moving-average and windowed-sinc FIR filters.

Single-Pole Analog Filters Like moving-average FIR filters, single-pole IIR filters also have good time-domain characteristics, and these filters perform well in smoothing time-domain noisy signals. The single-pole filter is not good at frequency-selective filtering. Time- and frequency-domain characteristics of a single-pole filter for a particular pole location are shown in Figure 7.37. Unlike FIR filters, the IIR filter impulse response is not symmetric, as shown in Figure 7.37(a); hence IIR filters are nonlinear-phase filters. The single-pole IIR filter has very poor passband and stopband characteristics, as shown in Figure 7.37(b).

Chebyshev Filters Like windowed sinc FIR filters, Chebyshev IIR filters are used to perform frequency-selective filtering. The Chebyshev filters achieve a faster roll-off by allowing the ripple in the passband (type-I) or stopband (type-II) of their frequency response. Although Chebyshev filters cannot match the performance of windowed sinc filters, the former are more efficient and more than adequate for many applications. Chebyshev filters provide a trade-off between the roll-off and ripple. A particular class of filters with zero ripples is called maximally flat or Butterworth filters. Butterworth filters have slower roll-off compared to Chebyshev filters. Another variation of Chebyshev filters in which the ripples exist in both passband and stopband are called elliptic filters. Elliptic filters provide the fastest roll-off for a given number of poles (or filter order), but are much harder to design.

The location of poles and zeros in the s-plane determines the complete frequency characteristics of analog filters (e.g., Chebyshev filters), as shown in Figure 7.38. The expressions for squared magnitude response along with the pole–zero location information for commonly used low-pass analog filters are provided in Table 7.4. The frequency-domain characteristics of four low-pass digital IIR filters (obtained from the correspondent analog filters by using mapping methods provided in Table 7.5) are shown in Figure 7.39. All four filters are designed with the following specifications: filter order $N = 6$, passband cut-off frequency $f_p = F_s/8$ (where F_s is sampling frequency), passband ripple $= 0.5$ dB, and stopband attenuation $= 20$ dB. For a given set of specifications, the elliptic filters provide good magnitude response with smallest filter order. However, Butterworth filters are preferred due to better phase response.

Mapping Methods

Three of the most common methods of converting analog IIR filter to equivalent digital IIR filter are the impulse invariant, the matched z-transform, and the bilinear z-transform. Mapping functions and advantages and disadvantages for all three methods are presented in Table 7.5.

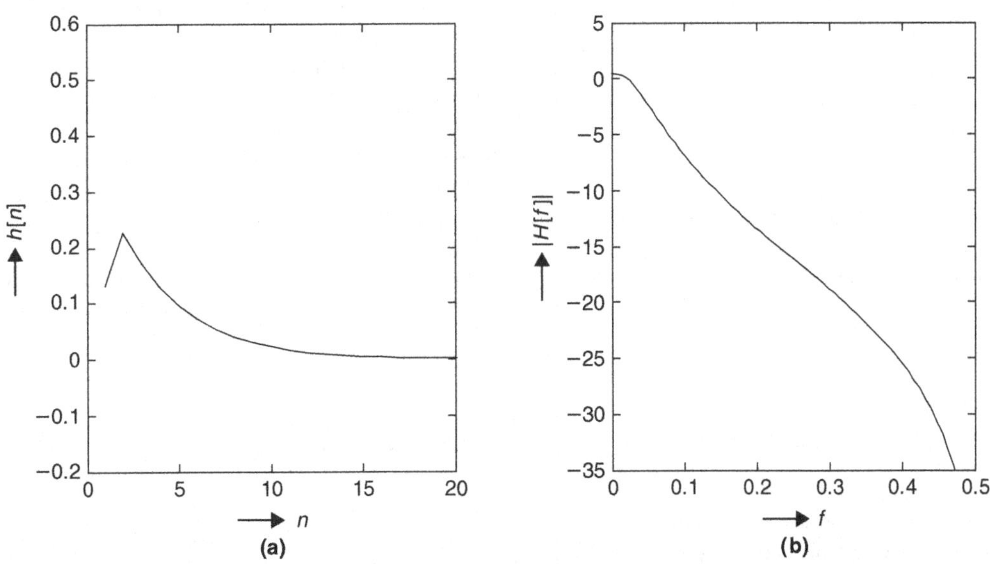

Figure 7.37: Time-frequency characteristics of IIR filter with single pole.

Table 7.4: Commonly used low-pass analog filter information

Analog Low-Pass Filters	Information (e.g., Magnitude Response, Pole-Zero Locations)
Butterworth	Contains only poles specified by the squared magnitude response $\lvert H(\omega)\rvert^2 = \frac{1}{1+(\omega/\omega_c)^{2N}}$, where ω_c is the cutoff frequency and N is the filter order. The order N is obtained as $N \geq \frac{\log\{(A_s-1)/(A_p-1)\}}{2\log(\omega_s/\omega_c)}$, where A_s and A_p are stopband attenuation and passband ripple (in amplitude, not in dB value), and ω_s is stopband frequency. No ripples in both passband and stopband, as shown in Figure 7.39(a). All poles are located in equally spaced positions on a circle of radius ω_c as shown in Figure 7.38(a)
Chebyshev type-I	Contains only poles specified by the squared magnitude response $\lvert H(\omega)\rvert^2 = \frac{1}{1+\varepsilon^2 C_N^2(\omega/\omega_c)}$, where N is the order of filter, ε is related to passband ripple, and $C_N(x)$ are Chebyshev polynomials $C_N(0) = 1$ and $C_N(x) = 2xC_{N-1}(x) - C_{N-2}(x)$. Ripples are present only in the passband, as shown in Figure 7.39(b). All poles are located on the ellipse as shown in Figure 7.38(b).
Chebyshev type-II	Contains both poles and zeros, and the magnitude square frequency response is given by $\lvert H(\omega)\rvert^2 = \frac{1}{1+1/[\varepsilon^2 C_N^2(\omega/\omega_c)]}$ (i.e., it contains the inverse Chebyshev polynomial). Ripples present only in the stopband, as shown in Figure 7.39(c). For a particular 6th-order filter, the s-plane pole-zero locations are shown in Figure 7.38(c).
Elliptic	Contains both poles and zeros, and the magnitude square frequency response is given by $\lvert H(\omega)\rvert^2 = \frac{1}{1+\varepsilon^2 G_N^2(\omega/\omega_c)}$, where $G_N(x)$ is a Chebyshev rational function. Ripples in both the passband and stopband, as shown in Figure 7.39(d). For a particular 6th-order filter, the s-plane pole-zero locations are shown in Figure 7.38(d).

Table 7.5: Analog to digital mapping methods

Mapping Method	Mapping Function and Limitations
Impulse invariant method: In this method, we basically compute continuous-time impulse response from the analog filter transfer function, sample it with sampling interval T, and then compute the z-transform of the samples to obtain the system function and z-domain frequency response.	MF: $\sum_{k=1}^{Q} \frac{A_k}{s-p_k} \to \sum_{k=1}^{Q} \frac{A_k}{1-e^{p_k T} z^{-1}}$, where T is the sampling period. As we sample the impulse response, the time-frequency-domain characteristics remain the same if we sample with reasonable sampling frequency. Higher-order transfer functions have to be factored into many first-order transfer functions to apply the mapping function. The antialiasing filter is required to work with high-pass or bandpass filters.
Matched z-transform method: In this method, the s-domain poles and zeros are mapped to z-domain poles and zeros.	MF: $(s-a) \to (1-e^{aT}z^{-1})$, where T is the sampling period. Requires knowledge of poles and zeros. The higher-order transfer function has to be factored into first-order transfer functions to obtain poles and zeros information.
Bilinear z-transform method: The most common method used in obtaining digital IIR filter coefficients from analog IIR filter. With bilinear z-transform, the imaginary axis of s-plane maps to the unit circle in the z-plane, the left half of the s-plane maps to inside the unit circle, and the right half of the s-plane maps to outside the unit circle.	MF: $s = k\frac{z-1}{z+1}$, $k = 1$ *or* $2/T$, where T is the sampling period. Does not need any factorization. Due to nonlinear mapping of frequencies, as $\omega = k\tan\left(\frac{\Omega T}{2}\right)$, $k = 1$ *or* $2/T$, where ω is the analog frequency and Ω is the digital frequency, the frequencies warp in this mapping method. This effect is normally compensated for by prewarping the analog filter before applying the bilinear transformation.

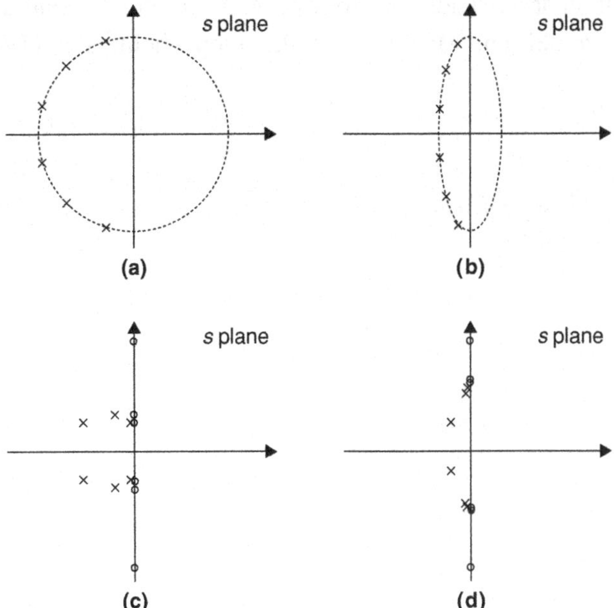

Figure 7.38: *S*-plane pole-zero locations of 6th-order low-pass IIR filters: (a) Butterworth, (b) Chebyshev type-I, (c) Chebyshev type-II, and (d) elliptic.

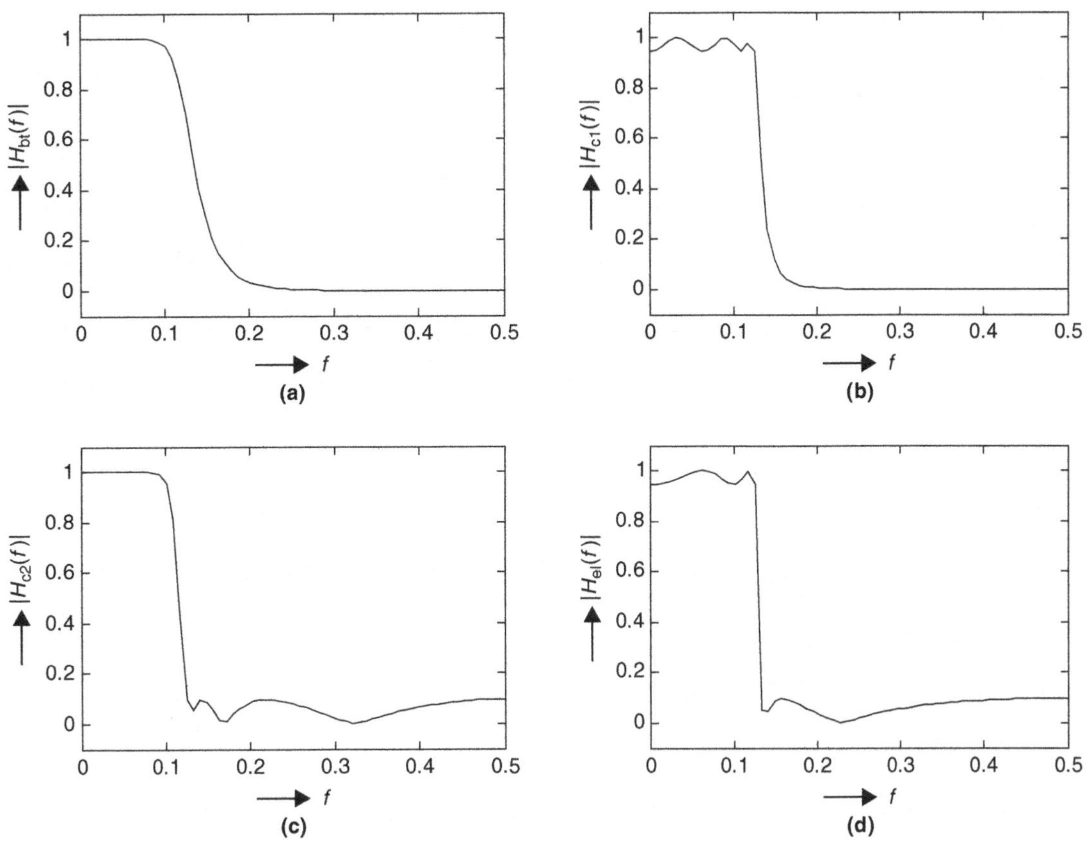

Figure 7.39: Frequency-domain characteristics of 6th-order low-pass IIR filters: (a) Butterworth, (b) Chebyshev type-I, (c) Chebyshev type-II, and (d) elliptic.

For more details on analog filter design and for converting analog filter information to digital filter information, see Rabiner and Gold (1975), Proakis and Manolakis (1992), Oppenheim et al. (1999), and Ifeachor and Jervis (2002).

Example 7.3

Obtain low-pass digital IIR filter coefficients from analog filter design, assuming Butterworth characteristics and meeting the following digital filter specifications:

Passband	0–750 Hz
Stopband	2–4 kHz
Passband ripple	5 dB
Stopband attenuation	20 dB
Sampling frequency	8 kHz

Use the bilinear z-transform method to convert the analog domain to discrete domain. With bilinear transformation, the frequencies are warped in the analog-to-digital filter conversion. As the passband and stopband frequencies are specified for the digital filter, we first determine the corresponding prewarp analog frequencies as follows:

$$\omega_c \text{ or } \omega_p = \tan\left(\frac{\Omega_p T}{2}\right) = \tan\left(\frac{2\pi \times 750}{2 \times 8000}\right) = 0.3033$$

$$\omega_s = \tan\left(\frac{\Omega_s T}{2}\right) = \tan\left(\frac{2\pi \times 2000}{2 \times 8000}\right) = 1$$

The order of the filter N for Butterworth characteristics is determined as follows:

$$N \geq \frac{\log\{(A_s - 1)/(A_p - 1)\}}{2\log(\omega_s/\omega_c)}$$

$$\text{Passband ripple } (A_p)\text{: } 10^{5/10} = 3.1623$$

$$\text{Stopband attenuation } (A_s) = 10^{20/10} = 100$$

Then, $N \geq \frac{\log(2.1623/99)}{2\log(1/0.3033)} = \frac{1.6607}{2\times 0.5181} = 1.6027$. We use $N = 2$ as it must be an integer.

Given the order of the Butterworth filter as 2, the corresponding analog filter transfer function follows:

$$H(s) = \frac{1}{(s/\omega_c)^2 + \sqrt{2}s/\omega_c + 1} = \frac{\omega_c^2}{s^2 + \sqrt{2}s\omega_c + \omega_c^2}$$

Applying bilinear z-transform mapping leads to

$$H(z) = H(s)|_{s=\frac{z-1}{z+1}} = \frac{\omega_c^2}{\left(\frac{z-1}{z+1}\right)^2 + \sqrt{2}\omega_c\left(\frac{z-1}{z+1}\right) + \omega_c^2} = \frac{\omega_c^2(z+1)^2}{(z-1)^2 + \sqrt{2}\omega_c(z^2-1) + \omega_c^2(z+1)^2}$$

After simplification and dividing the top and bottom by z^2, the preceding equation reduces to

$$H(z) = \frac{\omega_c^2}{1 + \sqrt{2}\omega_c + \omega_c^2} \times \frac{1 + 2z^{-1} + z^{-2}}{1 + \frac{2(\omega_c^2 - 1)z^{-1}}{1+\sqrt{2}\omega_c+\omega_c^2} + \frac{(1-\sqrt{2}\omega_c+\omega_c^2)z^{-2}}{1+\sqrt{2}\omega_c+\omega_c^2}}$$

Substituting the value of $\omega_c = 0.3033$ in the preceding equation results in

$$H(z) = \frac{0.0605(1 + 2z^{-1} + z^{-2})}{1 - 1.1940z^{-1} + 0.3150z^{-2}}$$

The corresponding frequency-domain characteristic of the digital IIR filter is shown in Figure 7.40. ■

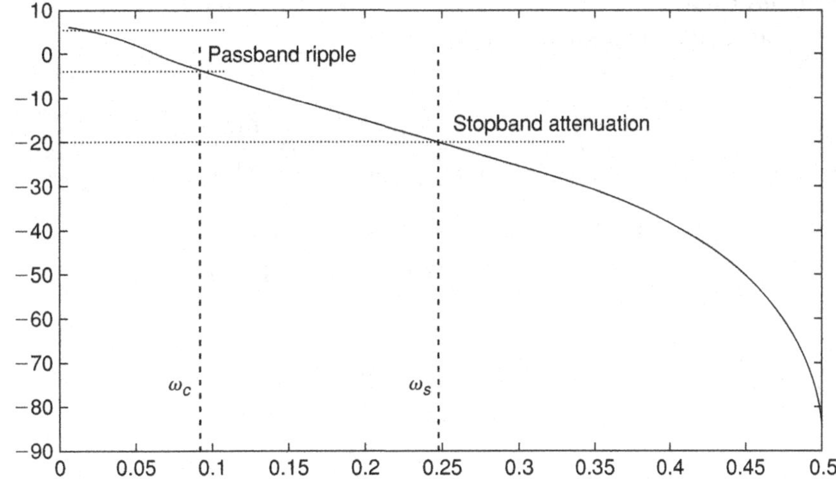

Figure 7.40: Frequency-domain characteristics for low-pass filter in Example 7.3.

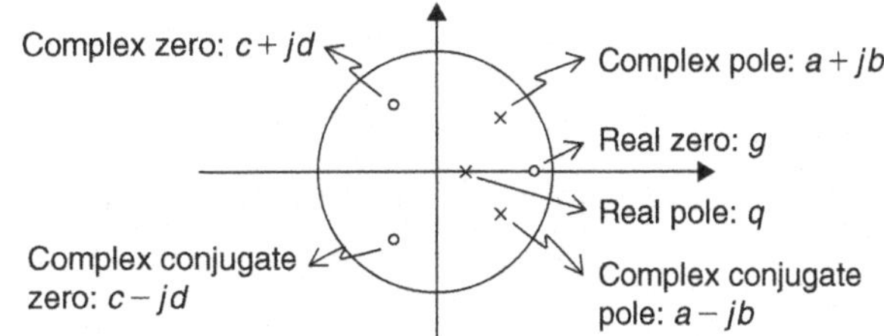

Figure 7.41: Pole-zero locations for real impulse response.

Thus far, we discussed the digital IIR filter design based on its counterpart analog filter. Next, we discuss IIR filter implementation aspects given the system function of the digital IIR filter.

Pole-Zero Locations

The locations of poles and zeros completely determine the time-frequency characteristics of IIR filters. The general system function for the digital IIR filter follows:

$$H(z) = \frac{b_0 + b_1 z^{-1} + b_2 z^{-2} + \cdots + b_N z^{-N}}{1 + a_1 z^{-1} + a_2 z^{-2} + \cdots + a_M z^{-M}} \tag{7.24}$$

If we factor the numerator and denominator of the system function in Equation (7.24) into first-order polynomials, then we have

$$H(z) = G\frac{(z-z_1)(z-z_2)\cdots(z-z_N)}{(z-p_1)(z-p_2)\cdots(z-p_M)} \tag{7.25}$$

where G is the filter gain. The z_i values, $1 \leq i \leq N$, are zeros, and p_i values, $1 \leq i \leq M$, are poles of system function $H(z)$. If the poles and zeros of $H(z)$ are symmetric with respect to the horizontal axis in the z-plane, then the corresponding impulse response (i.e., inverse z-transform of $H(z)$) contains only real values. That means the complex zeros and poles should occur in conjugate pairs as shown in Figure 7.41 to have real impulse response.

Assuming M_1 and N_1 real poles and zeros, and M_2 and N_2 complex conjugate pole and zero pairs, then Equation (7.25) can be rearranged as follows:

$$H(z) = G\frac{\prod_{k=1}^{M_1}(z-z_k)\prod_{k=1}^{M_2}(z-z_k)(z-z_k^*)}{\prod_{k=1}^{N_1}(z-p_k)\prod_{k=1}^{N_2}(z-p_k)(z-p_k^*)} \tag{7.26}$$

where $M = M_1 + 2M_2$ and $N = N_1 + 2N_2$.

Recursive Computation of IIR Filters

Equation (7.24) can be compactly represented as follows:

$$H(z) = \frac{\sum_{k=0}^{N} b_k z^{-k}}{1 + \sum_{k=1}^{M} a_k z^{-k}} = \frac{Y(z)}{X(z)} \tag{7.27}$$

$$\sum_{k=0}^{N} b_k z^{-k} X(z) = \left(1 + \sum_{k=1}^{M} a_k z^{-k}\right) Y(z) \tag{7.28}$$

Taking the inverse z-transform on both sides of Equation (7.28) leads to

$$\sum_{k=0}^{N} b_k x[n-k] = y[n] + \sum_{k=1}^{M} a_k y[n-k]$$

or

$$y[n] = \sum_{k=0}^{N} b_k x[n-k] - \sum_{k=1}^{M} a_k y[n-k] \tag{7.29}$$

Equation (7.29) is a recursive equation that produces an infinite-length sequence when the input is an impulse function. Consequently, these filters are called IIR filters. Based on Equations (7.27) and (7.29), the z-transform of the IIR-filter impulse response can always be expressed as a rational function (i.e., $H(z) = Y(z)/X(z)$).

Stability of IIR Filters

The IIR filters are not always stable due to their recursive or feedback nature. IIR filter poles must lie within the unit circle for stable filtering. As shown in Figure 7.42(a) through (e), the rate of decay of the single-pole, IIR-filter impulse response slows down as the pole location moves toward the unit circle. The impulse response grows outward as shown in Figure 7.42(f) when the pole moves outside the unit circle. We cannot produce stable output data for stable input data with this outgrown impulse response and in this case we say that the filter is unstable. What happens if system zeros lie outside the unit circle? The position of zeros only affects frequency-response characteristics and does not affect system stability. In the case of systems with multiple poles and zeros as given in Equation (7.26), even if one pole moves outside the unit circle, then the system become unstable.

If we use double-precision floating-point operations in the implementation of IIR filters, we can guarantee filter stability by taking care of pole locations (i.e., by making sure all poles lie within the unit circle) at the time of filter design. However, this is not always the case when we implement IIR filters with fixed point processors. For efficiency and cost reasons, designers generally prefer fixed-point processors over floating-point processors. If proper care is not taken in the fixed-point implementation of IIR filters, then we may end up with totally unacceptable filter output due to finite-word-length effects associated with fixed-point computing.

7.5.2 IIR Filter Realization

In practice, we use various filter realization techniques (e.g., direct form, cascade, parallel, canonical, lattice) to control arithmetic round-off errors. In this section, we focus on direct-form and cascade realization of IIR filters. For $M = N$, Equation (7.29) can be realized using a direct-form structure as shown in Figure 7.43.

When the filter order is high, direct-form realization of the filter shown in Figure 7.43 is very sensitive to finite-word-length effects. Numerical errors due to finite-word-length effects cause the systems to behave nonlinearly. In practice, $H(z)$ is broken down into smaller sections to minimize the finite-word-length effects, typically

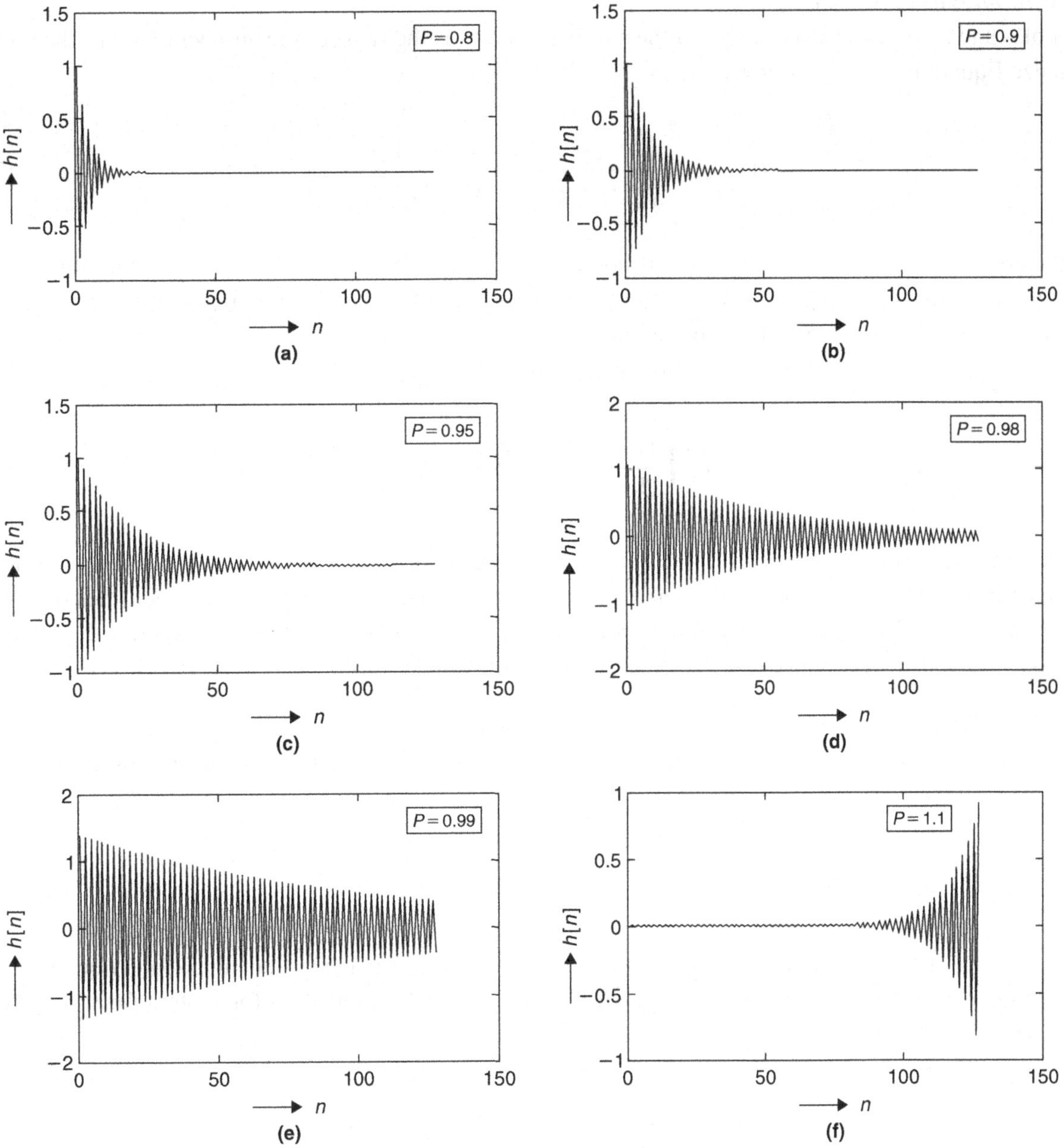

Figure 7.42: Impulse responses of single-pole system for various pole locations.

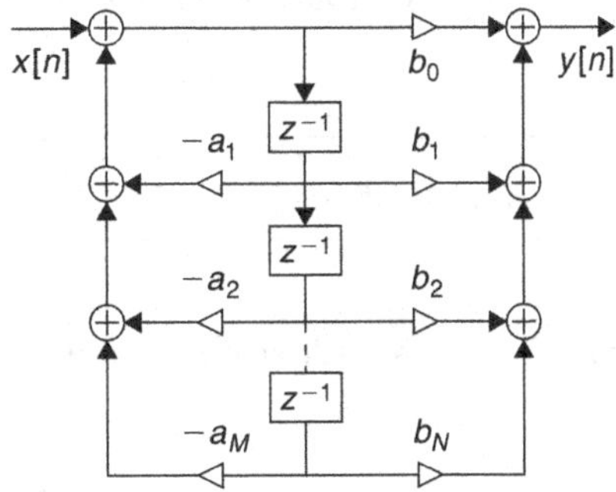

Figure 7.43: Direct-form realization of IIR recursive equation.

first- or second-order blocks that are then connected in cascade or in parallel. Based on Equation (7.26), it is straightforward to realize the higher-order system function in terms of cascaded first- or second-order structures. The coefficients of these small-order structures can be real if all poles and zeros of higher-order system functions are symmetric with respect to the horizontal axis.

Cascade Realization of IIR Filters

If the poles and zeros are symmetric and if the number of poles is the same as the number of zeros, then we can reorganize Equation (7.26) as follows:

$$H(z) = G\prod_{k=1}^{N_1}\frac{(z-z_k)}{(z-p_k)}\prod_{n=1}^{N_2}\frac{(z-z_n)(z-z_n^*)}{(z-p_n)(z-p_n^*)} \tag{7.30}$$

If the complex zero $z_n = a_n + jb_n$, then its complex conjugate zero $z_n^* = a_n - jb_n$. With this, we can write $(z-z_n)(z-z_n^*)$ as $(z-z_n)(z-z_n^*) = z^2 - (z_n + z_n^*)z + z_n z_n^* = z^2 - 2a_n z + (a_n^2 + b_n^2) = z^2 - f_n z + g_n$, where $f_n = 2a_n$ and $g_n = a_n^2 + b_n^2$. Similarly, if complex pole $p_n = c_n + jd_n$, then $(z-p_n)(z-p_n^*) = z^2 - u_n z + v_n$, where $u_n = 2c_n$ and $v_n = c_n^2 + d_n^2$. Now, Equation (7.30) is modified as follows:

$$H(z) = G\prod_{k=1}^{N_1}\frac{(1-z_k z^{-1})}{(1-p_k z^{-1})}\prod_{n=1}^{N_2}\frac{(1-f_n z^{-1}+g_n z^{-2})}{(1-u_n z^{-1}+v_n z^{-2})} \tag{7.31}$$

The system function in Equation (7.31) contains first- and second-order polynomials with real coefficients and such a system function can be realized as a cascade of many first- and second-order system function blocks as shown in Figure 7.44. Cascade realizations are usually the least sensitive to finite-word-length effects. For details on various IIR filter realizations and finite-word-length effects, see Oppenheim (1999).

Biquad IIR Filters

The second-order filters shown in Figure 7.44 are also called biquad filters. The general system function of the biquad filter follows:

$$H(z) = \frac{b_0 + b_1 z^{-1} + b_2 z^{-2}}{1 + a_1 z^{-1} + a_2 z^{-2}} \tag{7.32}$$

The second-order system functions in Equation (7.31) and the biquad filter system function in Equation (7.32) are the same except for gain. Based on Equation (7.26), the recursive equation for system function given in Equation (7.32) follows:

$$y[n] = \sum_{k=0}^{2} b_k x[n-k] - \sum_{k=1}^{2} a_k y[n-k] \tag{7.33}$$

The corresponding direct-form realization of the biquad filter is shown in Figure 7.45.

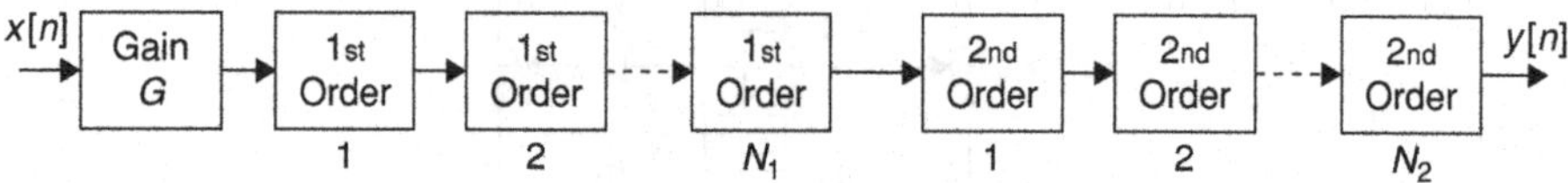

Figure 7.44: Cascade realization of IIR filters.

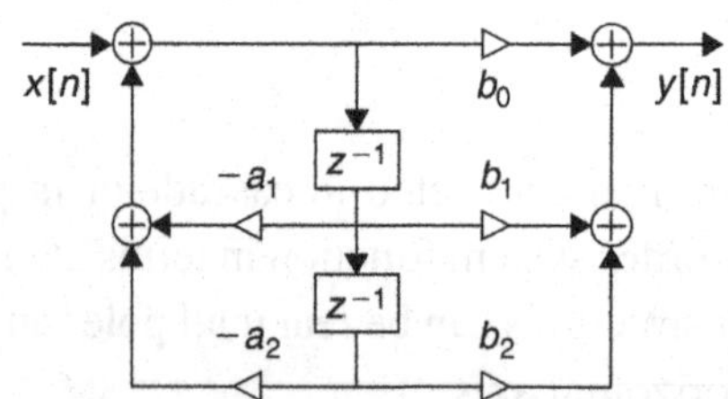

Figure 7.45: Direct-form realization of a biquad filter.

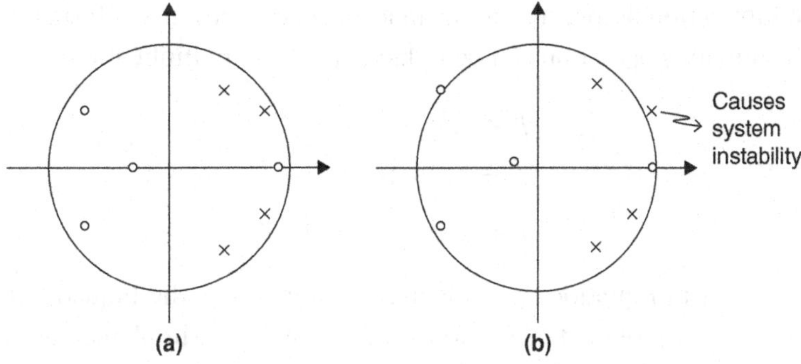

Figure 7.46: Illustration of the finite-word-length effects on pole-zero locations.

The higher-order filter implementation using biquad filters executes a little bit slower but generates smaller arithmetic round-off errors than the direct implementation shown in Figure 7.43. The biquads can be scaled separately and then cascaded to minimize the quantization errors and recursive accumulation of errors. In the direct implementation of Figure 7.43, the coefficients and data are usually scaled all at once, which gives rise to large errors. Another disadvantage of direct implementation is that the poles of such single-stage high-order polynomials become increasingly sensitive to arithmetic round-off errors. Although care is taken in filter design so that poles lie inside the unit circle of the z-plane, the filter input may see the poles and zeros as if they moved from their actual positions due to quantization errors. This is illustrated in Figure 7.46. If the quantization errors cause the poles to move outside the unit circle, then we obtain unacceptable filter outputs due to system instability. The second-order polynomials (or biquads) are less sensitive to finite-word-length effects, and error accumulation is also reduced because of shorter data flow in biquad sections.

7.5.3 Biquad IIR Filter Fixed-Point Simulation

Finite-word-length effects can be minimized by implementing higher-order polynomials in terms of small-order polynomials. In addition, the quantization errors can be minimized by increasing the precision of arithmetic registers. As discussed, the best way to avoid register overflow is by scaling input data and filter coefficients and by using extended-precision registers (if available) for holding intermediate accumulated results. For scaling, we must first find the absolute maximum in the given data (say p) and in the coefficients (say q); then we divide the entire data array with integer P and the entire coefficient array with integer Q, where $P > p$ and $Q > q$.

Next, we choose the appropriate Q-format fixed-point representation to implement the IIR filters. As 16-bit multiplications can be easily performed on 32-bit fixed-point processors, we generally use the 1.15 format to represent scaled input data and filter coefficients. However, if the precision of 16 bits is insufficient for a particular filter implementation (i.e., to meet stringent specifications and to represent vulnerable pole locations), we use the 1.31 format to represent data and coefficients. The question now becomes how we perform 32-bit multiplications on a processor (e.g., the reference embedded processor) that has 32-bit width arithmetic registers and 48-bit extended-precision accumulators. One way of performing this 32-bit multiplication on 32-bit processors is described here. Let a, b, c, and d represent four registers with 32-bit precision, and f and g represent two registers with 48-bit extended precision. If $b|a$ and $d|c$ represent two 32-bit numbers u and v (here $y|x$ represents the 32-bit number MSB 16 bits (y) and LSB 16 bits (x)), then we perform two 32-bit number multiplications in terms of 16-bit quantities $(dc)\times(ba)$ as follows:

$$f = (ac) \gg 16$$

$$g = (ad + bc)$$

$$g = (f + g) \gg 16$$

$$f = (bd + g) \ll 1$$

where f contains the multiplication output in 1.31 format. If we compromise a little bit on accuracy, then the four multiplications in the previous operation can be reduced to three multiplications as follows:

$$f = ad + bc$$
$$g = f \gg 16$$
$$f = (bd + g) \ll 1$$

The recursive equation given in Equation (7.33) is used to implement the biquad IIR filter. We borrow the concepts of real-time FIR filtering provided in Section 7.4.3 for real-time implementation of biquad IIR filters. Either the Ping-Pong buffer model or circular buffer model can be used for real-time IIR filtering. With biquad filters, we use three input data samples and two output data samples in computing the current output sample. There are five coefficients in the biquad filter, and we denote them as a_1, a_2, b_0, b_1, and b_2. We scale down both filter coefficients and input samples if needed to make sure that all values are below 1. We represent both input data and filter coefficients in the fixed-point format. The 1.15 and 1.31 fixed-point implementations of the biquad filter are given in Pcodes 7.14 and 7.15, respectively. In the next section, we compare simulation results to see how much improvement we can get by increasing precision from 16 to 32 bits.

We have not addressed the register overflow in Pcode 7.14 or 7.15 (see page 374) during filtering, as we did not perform scaling for data or coefficients and we used the same fixed-point format for filter inputs, intermediate outputs, and final outputs. As the IIR filters use the feedback structure and the current output sample is computed by addition and subtraction of few terms, there is a chance of register overflow in the output that we give as input again in the 1.15 fixed-point format to compute the next output. This causes error accumulation in filtering due to feedback, and we may obtain unacceptable results if we do not properly scale the filter coefficients and input. Sometimes we use different fixed-point formats for input samples, for intermediate outputs, and for final outputs to minimize finite-length-word effects.

For example, in Pcode 7.14, by using the 1.15 format for inputs, the 4.12 format for intermediate outputs (i.e., right shift only 12 bits instead of 15 bits), and the 1.15 format for final output (scale it down to obtain 1.15 from 4.12), we avoid the register overflow in all biquad sections. However, this leads to more quantization errors due to less precision of intermediate outputs. We determine which fixed-point format is appropriate for a particular application based on the SNR that we want at the filter output.

```
a1 = fc[0]; a2 = fc[1]; b0 = fc[2]; b1 = fc[3]; b2 = fc[4];
out[0] = 0; out[1] = 0;
for(i = 2;i < L;i++){
  a = in[i]; b = in[i-1];
  e = (a*b0) >> 15; f = (b*b1) >> 15;
  a = out[i-1]; b = out[i-2];
  e = e - ((a*a1) >> 15); f = f - ((b*a2) >> 15);
  a = in[i-2];
  e = e + ((a*b2) >> 15);
  e = e + f;
  out[i] = e;
}
```

Pcode 7.14: Implementation of biquad IIR filter using 1.15 data format.

Computational Complexity

The number of filter coefficients associated with IIR filters is very small when compared to FIR filters, and hence the number of computations and memory size are much smaller in the case of IIR filters. However, given the filter order, the computational complexity of the IIR filter depends on fixed-point representation of data. For example, the number of computations and the amount of memory required for 1.31 fixed-point IIR implementation is greater compared to the 1.15 fixed-point IIR implementation. We consume almost double the memory and approximately four times the number of clock cycles for 1.31 fixed-point IIR filters compared to 1.15 fixed-point IIR filters. If L is the input data length, then we require about $2L$ bytes (using the circular buffer model) of data memory to implement the biquad IIR filter using the 1.15 fixed-point data format. To

```
out[0] = 0; out[1] = 0;
for(i = 2;i < L;i++){
  a = in[i]; c = fc[2];
  b = a >> 16; d = c >> 16; // MSB
  a = a & 0xffff; c = c & 0xffff;
  e = a * d; f = b * c;
  e = e + f;
  f = (a * c) >> 16; e = (e + f) >> 16;
  f = b * d; g = f + e;

  a = in[i-1]; c = fc[3];
  b = a >> 16; d = c >> 16;
  a = a & 0xffff; c = c & 0xffff;
  e = a * d; f = b * c;
  e = e + f;
  f = (a * c) >> 16; e = (e + f) >> 16;
  f = b * d; g = g + (f + e);

  a = in[i-2]; c = fc[4];
  b = a >> 16; d = c >> 16;
  a = a & 0xffff; c = c & 0xffff;
  e = a * d; f = b * c;
  e = e + f;
  f = (a * c) >> 16; e = (e + f) >> 16;
  f = b * d; g = g + (f + e);

  a = out[i-1]; c = fc[0];
  b = a >> 16; d = c >> 16;
  a = a & 0xffff; c = c & 0xffff;
  e = a * d; f = b * c;
  e = e + f;
  f = (a * c) >> 16; e = (e + f) >> 16;
  f = b * d; g = g - (f + e);

  a = out[i-2]; c = fc[1];
  b = a >> 16; d = c >> 16;
  a = a & 0xffff; c = c & 0xffff;
  e = a * d; f = b * c;
  e = e + f;
  f = (a * c) >> 16; e = (e + f) >> 16;
  f = b * d; g = g - (f + e);
  out[i] = (g << 1);
}
```

Pcode 7.15: Implementation of biquad IIR filter using 1.31 data format.

implement the biquad filter in 1.15 fixed-point format, we consume approximately four cycles per sample on the reference embedded processor as it has two MAC units (see Appendix A on the companion website for details on reference embedded processor architecture). In these four cycles, we do not include the cycles for memory access as they are done parallel to the compute units. In addition, the operation (>> 15) is done for free on the reference embedded processor.

7.5.4 Simulation Results

In this section, we present simulation results for the biquad IIR filter. In the following, we consider $L = 64$, the length of the real-input data sample array $x[\,]$ with double precision.

```
x[] = {
 -0.73419553272114,  0.69405470315228, -0.84314100608659,  0.42060603379301,
 -0.51497013058388,  0.28366075710274, -0.76249083362512,  0.00732434885485,
 -0.58049161351719, -0.16355848979111,  0.03552863713489, -0.06948245208239,
 -0.28186206405527,  0.54475523288876,  0.04860020926975,  0.10269344548893,
  0.23900047593625, -0.91868755888719,  0.10931397941616,  0.02989635686007,
  0.48129131846464,  0.22630493931331, -0.62535401079048, -0.06404540081684,
 -0.21027908942413,  0.28991869866662, -0.18376371097574, -0.04607275562230,
 -0.34467910818770,  0.03057475436452,  0.09694153826073,  0.33563844814254,
 -0.02416783891113, -0.26440282666954,  0.44496738170435,  0.89073350344725,
```

```
 0.18027758692862, -0.05091551453884,  0.66804249350107, -0.36076559293720,
-0.42021964837270, -0.13223144391175, -0.04760000000000,  0.19154078804663,
 0.12776795614633, -0.72556957909998, -0.18972954048883,  0.40266274104115,
-0.16628001546795,  0.35163798899788, -0.35120788406922,  0.15174746297898,
 0.03905005003068, -0.09937556376360,  0.17213090531081, -0.02292825444822,
-0.72290233148861,  0.16326757381837,  0.07208180757915, -0.01150832752460,
 0.07739777241019,  0.39472396921568, -0.81561204524936,  0.69420288575391};
```

The following system function is used for a biquad filter:

$$H(z) = \frac{0.675436 - 0.892374z^{-1} + 0.223344z^{-2}}{1 - 0.446897z^{-1} + 0.312345z^{-2}}$$

Based on Equation (7.32), the filter coefficients a_1, a_2, b_0, b_1, and b_2 follow:

```
a1 = -0.446897; a2 = 0.312345;
b0 = 0.675436;  b1 = -0.892374; b2 = 0.223344;
```

We do not require any scaling for input data samples and filter coefficients as all data is less than 1. The corresponding biquad filter double-precision output **y**[ ] follows:

```
y[] = {
-0.49590209383903,  0.90234937876447, -0.79467255749613,  0.55452142418984,
-0.41545177790717,  0.38621432902562, -0.58079842143537,  0.36853886544915,
-0.22281034840190,  0.19449363218240,  0.19681566440432, -0.08795837245195,
-0.22122306494244,  0.53256461804274, -0.20915182775101, -0.11215212035432,
 0.09585021138778, -0.73299116989775,  0.58951692184313,  0.20986023925516,
 0.23247062122988, -0.23161855732137, -0.69296240191518,  0.32799702080286,
 0.13847754331020,  0.32860193150835, -0.32620265851882, -0.05079779789430,
-0.15355068526684,  0.26518898833673,  0.12768463035671,  0.12125429422500,
-0.27988101758672, -0.24500876263810,  0.50902121010294,  0.44951068113125,
-0.53182590730524, -0.37439903543690,  0.53571490566407, -0.49483844488573,
-0.20116004923176,  0.26976687190430,  0.17538495311387,  0.13643612229281,
-0.08906583580072, -0.64373152600100,  0.28800305277561,  0.60900503181259,
-0.33180601570965,  0.13732243683096, -0.42314175592357,  0.26244796092886,
 0.06197356355373, -0.12235570598558,  0.13962764322551, -0.09067028101991,
-0.51350154892085,  0.54909326130500,  0.14731278403655, -0.14130513011438,
-0.03051523695858,  0.22547148622623, -0.77555500415086,  0.86786173773460};
```

Biquad Filter 1.15 Implementation

The input is converted to 1.15 format by multiplying all elements in array **x**[ ] with 2^{15}. The corresponding 1.15 fixed-point data values array **x_1_15**[ ] is given next.

```
x_1_15[] = {
-24058,  22742,  -27628,  13782,   -16874,   9294,
-24985,  240,    -19021, -5359,     1164,   -2276,
-9236,   17850,   1592,   3365,     7831,   -30103,
 3582,   979,     15770,  7415,    -20491,  -2098,
-6890,   9500,   -6021,  -1509,    -11294,   1001,
 3176,   10998,  -791,    -8663,    14580,   29187,
 5907,  -1668,    21890, -11821,   -13769,  -4332,
-1559,   6276,    4186,  -23775,   -6217,    13194,
-5448,   11522,  -11508,  4972,     1279,   -3256,
 5640,  -751,    -23688,  5349,     2361,   -377,
 2536,   12934,  -26725,  22747};
```

The values of filter coefficients a_1, a_2, b_0, b_1, and b_2 in 1.15 format follow:

```
a1 = -14643; a2 = 10234;
b0 = 22132;  b1 = -29241; b2 = 7318;
```

The biquad filter output **y_1_15**[ ] in 1.15 format is computed using Pcode 7.14 as follows:

```
y_1_15[] = {
-16250, 29567, -26040, 18170, -13614, 12654, -19032,  12076,
-7301,  6373,   6449, -2882,  -7250,  17450, -6854,  -3674,   3141,  -24019, 19316,
 6875,  7617,  -7590, -22705,  10747, 4536,   10766, -10689, -1665,  -5033,  8688,
 4183,  3973,  -9171, -8029,   16678, 14728, -17427, -12267,  17553, -16216,
-6592,  8840,   5747,  4470,  -2919, -21093,  9436,   19953, -10873,  4500, -13865,
 8600,  2030,  -4009,  4574,  -2972, -16827,  17992,  4826,  -4630,  -1001,  7386,
-25413, 28437
```

The corresponding decimal values ***y*_16** [ ] are obtained by dividing ***y*_1_15**[ ] with 2^{15}.

```
y_16[] = { -0.49591064453125, 0.90231323242188,
-0.79467773437500,  0.55450439453125, -0.41546630859375,  0.38616943359375,
-0.58081054687500,  0.36853027343750, -0.22280883789063,  0.19448852539063,
 0.19680786132813, -0.08795166015625, -0.22125244140625,  0.53253173828125,
-0.20916748046875, -0.11212158203125,  0.09585571289063, -0.73300170898438,
 0.58947753906250,  0.20980834960938,  0.23245239257813,-0.23162841796875,
-0.69290161132813,  0.32797241210938,  0.13842773437500,  0.32855224609375,
-0.32620239257813, -0.05081176757813, -0.15359497070313,  0.26513671875000,
 0.12765502929688,  0.12124633789063, -0.27987670898438, -0.24502563476563,
 0.50897216796875,  0.44946289062500, -0.53182983398438, -0.37435913085938,
 0.53567504882813, -0.49487304687500, -0.20117187500000,  0.26977539062500,
 0.17538452148438,  0.13641357421875, -0.08908081054688, -0.64370727539063,
 0.28796386718750,  0.60891723632813, -0.33181762695313,  0.13732910156250,
-0.42312622070313,  0.26245117187500,  0.06195068359375, -0.12234497070313,
 0.13958740234375, -0.09069824218750, -0.51351928710938,  0.54907226562500,
 0.14727783203125, -0.14129638671875, -0.03054809570313,  0.22540283203125,
-0.77554321289063,  0.86782836914063};
```

Biquad Filter 1.31 Implementation

We convert the input to 1.31 format by multiplying all elements in array ***x***[ ] with 2^{31}. The corresponding 1.31 fixed-point data values array ***x*_1_31**[ ] is given next.

```
x_1_31[] ={
-1576672900, 1490471125, -1810631523,  903244579,  -1105889934,  609156837,
-1637436596, 15728919,   -1246596247, -351239182,   76297167,   -149212429,
-605294173,  1169852954,  104368154,   220532494,   513249613,  -1972866510,
 234749983,  64201937,    1033565236,  485986156,  -1342937512, -137536450,
-451570906,  622595664,  -394629564,  -98940489,   -740192748,   65658785,
 208180368,  720778079,  -51900038,   -567800746,   955560176,   1912835633,
 387143170, -109340234,   1434610330, -774738211,  -902414823,  -283964863,
-102220221,  411330710,   274379596,  -1558148806, -407441085,   864711652,
-357083614,  755136831,  -754213188,   325875195,   83859343,   -213407398,
 369648304, -49238051,   -1552420935,  350614445,   154794503,  -24713945,
 166210450,  847663269,  -1751513530,  1490789345};
```

The values of filter coefficients a_1, a_2, b_0, b_1, and b_2 in 1.31 format follow:

```
a1= -959703999;   a2 = 670755780;
b0 = 1450487765; b1 = -1916358572; b2 = 479627587;
```

The biquad filter output ***y*_1_31**[ ] in 1.31 format is computed using Pcode 7.15 as follows:

```
y_1_31[] = {
-1064941640,  1937780528, -1706546328,  1190825686, -892175900,
 829388954,  -1247255116,  791431184,  -478481582,   417671892,   422658420,
-188889168,  -475072918,   1143673806, -449150128,  -240844846,   205836760,
-1574086548,  1265977952,  450671432,   499226856,  -497397066,  -1488125428,
 704368238,   297378258,   705667274,  -700514874,  -109087440,  -329747584,
 569489014,   274200650,   260391612,  -601039906,  -526152312,   1093114724,
 965316838,  -1142087438, -804015804,   1150438998, -1062657468, -431987920,
 579319944,   376636320,   292994342,  -191267426,  -1382402924,  618481844,
 1307828342, -712547994,   294897690,  -908690002,   563602706,   133087216,
-262756876,   299848080,  -194712944,  -1102736182,  1179168796,  316351788,
-303450462,  -65530980,    484196328,  -1665491688,  1863718888};
```

The corresponding decimal values ***y*_32** [ ] are obtained by dividing ***y*_1_31**[ ] with 2^{31}.

```
y_32[] = {
-0.49590209499002,  0.90234937518835,
-0.79467255994678,  0.55452142190188, -0.41545177809894,  0.38621432799846,
-0.58079842291772,  0.36853886395693, -0.22281034942716,  0.19449363090098,
 0.19681566394866, -0.08795837312937, -0.22122306656092,  0.53256461676210,
-0.20915182679892, -0.11215212102979,  0.09585021063685, -0.73299116827548,
 0.58951692283154,  0.20986023917794,  0.23247062042356, -0.23161855805665,
-0.69296240247786,  0.32799702044576,  0.13847754243761,  0.32860193122178,
-0.32620265800506, -0.05079779773951, -0.15355068445206,  0.26518898736686,
 0.12768462765962,  0.12125429324806, -0.27988101635128, -0.24500876292586,
 0.50902120955288,  0.44951068144292, -0.53182590659708, -0.37439903430641,
 0.53571490477771, -0.49483844451606, -0.20116005092859,  0.26976687088609,
 0.17538495361805,  0.13643612246960, -0.08906583581120, -0.64373152516782,
```

```
 0.28800305165350,  0.60900502931327, -0.33180601615459,  0.13732243794948,
-0.42314175609499,  0.26244796160609,  0.06197356432676, -0.12235570512712,
 0.13962764292955, -0.09067028015852, -0.51350155007094,  0.54909325949848,
 0.14731278084219, -0.14130513276905, -0.03051524050534,  0.22547148540616,
-0.77555500343442,  0.86786173656583};
```

From the three output arrays, double-precision output **y[ ]**, 1.15 fixed-point output **y_16[ ]**, and 1.31 fixed-point output **y_32[ ]**, we can see that the double-precision filter output is very close to 32-bit precision filter output when compared to 16-bit precision filter output. The root-mean-square error (RMSE) with the 16-bit precision biquad filter is 3.0157649×10^{-5}, whereas the RMSE with the 32-bit precision biquad filter is 1.3189298×10^{-9}.

7.5.5 Goertzel Algorithm

As discussed in Section 7.1, the N-point FFT algorithm efficiently computes N DFT coefficients given N input samples. In some applications (such as dual-tone multifrequency or DTMF), we do not require all the DFT coefficients. In such cases, the Goertzel algorithm can be used to compute few DFT coefficients (or frequencies) of the input signal $x[n]$ using a second-order IIR filter. The recursive expression for computing k-th DFT coefficient can be derived from the following standard DFT equation. Based on Equation (7.1),

$$X[k]=\sum_{n=0}^{N-1}x[n]W_N^{nk},\ \text{where } W_N=e^{-j2\pi/N} \tag{7.34}$$

$$X[k]=\sum_{n=0}^{N-1}x[n]W_N^{-kN}W_N^{nk},\quad \because W_N^{-kN}=1 \tag{7.35}$$

$$X[k]=\sum_{n=0}^{N-1}x[n]W_N^{-(N-n)k} \tag{7.36}$$

$$\begin{aligned}&=x[0]W_N^{-Nk}+x[1]W_N^{-(N-1)k}+x[2]W_N^{-(N-2)k}+\cdots+x[N-1]W_N^{-k}\\&=\left(\cdots\left(\left(\left(x[0]W_N^{-k}+x[1]\right)W_N^{-k}\right)+x[2]\right)W_N^{-k}\right)+\cdots+x[N-1]\right)W_N^{-k}\\&=y_k[n]|_{n=N}\end{aligned} \tag{7.37}$$

where

$$y_k[n]=W_N^{-k}y_k[n-1]+x[n],n=0,\ 1,\ 2,\ldots,N\ \text{with } x[N]=0 \tag{7.38}$$

The system function governing the previous difference equation can be expressed as follows:

$$\begin{aligned}\frac{Y_k[z]}{X[z]}&=\frac{1}{1-W_N^{-k}z^{-1}}=\frac{1-W_N^kz^{-1}}{\left(1-W_N^{-k}z^{-1}\right)\left(1-W_N^kz^{-1}\right)}=\frac{1-W_N^kz^{-1}}{1-2\cos\frac{2\pi k}{N}z^{-1}+z^{-2}}\\&=\left(\frac{1}{1-2\cos\frac{2\pi k}{N}z^{-1}+z^{-2}}\right)\left(1-W_N^kz^{-1}\right)=\frac{S_k[z]}{X[z]}\frac{Y_k[z]}{S_k[z]}\end{aligned} \tag{7.39}$$

where

$$\frac{S_k[z]}{X[z]}=\frac{1}{1-2\cos\frac{2\pi k}{N}z^{-1}+z^{-2}},\quad \frac{Y_k[z]}{S_k[z]}=1-W_N^kz^{-1} \tag{7.40}$$

The final expressions for implementation of Goertzel algorithms are obtained from Equation (7.40) as follows:

$$s_k[n]=x[n]+2\cos\left(\frac{2\pi k}{N}\right)s_k[n-1]-s_k[n-2],\quad n=0,1,2,\ldots,N \tag{7.41}$$

$$X[k]=y_k[N]=s_k[N]-W_N^ks_k[N-1] \tag{7.42}$$

Based on Equation (7.42), we are only interested in the IIR filter output to compute the DFT coefficient. Thus, we need not compute the FIR filter $Y_k[z]/S_k[z]$ output for each input sample $s_k[n]$. The square-value magnitude of the k-th DFT coefficient can be obtained as follows:

$$|X[k]|^2 = X[k]X^*[k] = s_k^2[N] + s_k^2[N-1] - 2\cos\left(\frac{2\pi k}{N}\right) s_k[N]s_{k-1}[N] \tag{7.43}$$

Goertzel Algorithm Fixed-Point Implementation

For the k-th tone detection, we compute the magnitude square of the k-th DFT coefficient using the Goertzel algorithm and detect the tone by applying the appropriate threshold on the magnitude square value. Equations (7.41) and (7.43) are used for the simulation. For the given application, the values of k and N are available in advance. Thus, we can precompute the value $2\cos(2\pi k/N)$ in advance. The actual implementation of the algorithm is simple, and it involves only MAC and update operations as described in the following pseudocode.

Start $n = 1:N$
$a = x[n] + k^* b - c$; $//k = 2\cos(2\pi k/N)$
$c = b$;
$b = a$;
End

The value of $s_k[n]$ in Equation (7.41) grows in the recursive computation when the signal contains the k-th-frequency component. Thus, we cannot use the 1.15 or 1.31 fixed-point format for $s_k[n]$. The final amplitude of $s_k[n]$ depends on block size N. For this reason, we use the 16.16 format in the simulation for all coefficients, intermediate variables, and input samples. The simulation code for the 16.16 fixed-point implementation of the Goertzel algorithm is given in Pcode 7.16. We use the extended precision (64-bit) variable **q** in the simulation for simplifying the multiplication process of two 16.16 format numbers.

```
int detect_tone(int a, int n)                // a: 2cos(2*pi*k/N) in 16.16 format, n: block size
{
        int i,x,y,z;
        long long q;

        y = z = 0;
        for(i = 0;i<n;i++){
            q = (long long)a*y;              // 2*cos(2*pi*k/N)*s[n-1]
            q = q >> 16;
            x = inp_x[i]+(int)q-z;           // s[n] = x[n]+2*cos(2*pi*k/N)*s[n-1]-s[n-2]
                                             // input inp_x[i] comes in 16.16 format
            z = y;                           // s[n-2] = s[n-1]
            y = x;                           // s[n-1] = s[n]
        }
        q = (long long) a*y;
        q = q >> 16;
        q = (long long) q*z;
        x = q >> 16;
        q = (long long) y*y;
        y = q >> 16;
        q = (long long) z*z;
        z = q >> 16;
        x = y+z-x;                           // magnitude square
        x = x >> 16;
        return x;

}
```

Pcode 7.16: Simulation code for fixed-point Goertzel algorithm.

By unrolling the IIR filter loop, we can further reduce the number of operations in the Goertzel algorithm implementation. The explicit move operations can be avoided with the following unrolling:

Start $n = 1:N/2$
$a = x[n] + k^* b - c$
$b = x[n] + k^* a - b$
End

The corresponding simulation code for the filter loop is provided in Pcode 7.17. Depending on block size N (odd or even number), we may need to repeat one more iteration after the loop, as shown in the Pcode.

```
for(i = 0;i<n-1;i+=2){
    s = (long long) a*y;                    // 2*cos(2*pi*k/N)*s[n-1]
    s = s >> 16;
    x = inp_s[j++] + (int) s-x;             // s[n] = x[n]+2*cos(2*pi*k/N)*s[n-1]-s[n-2]

    s = (long long) a*x;                    // 2*cos(2*pi*k/N)*s[n-1]
    s = s >> 16;
    y = inp_s[j++] + (int) s-y;             // s[n] = x[n]+2*cos(2*pi*k/N)*s[n-1]-s[n-2]
}
                                            // last iteration for odd values of N
s = (long long) a*y;                        // 2*cos(2*pi*k/N)*s[n-1]
s = s >> 16;
x = inp_s[j++] + (int) s-x;                 // s[n] = x[n]+2*cos(2*pi*k/N)*s[n-1]-s[n-2]
z = y;                                      // s[n-2] = s[n-1]
y = x;                                      // s[n-1] = s[n]
```

Pcode 7.17: Efficient implementation of Goertzel algorithm.

Goertzel Algorithm Computational Complexity

The computation for $s_k[n]$ takes one add and one MAC per sample. In DTMF detection, we are only concerned with the magnitude square of the k-th DFT coefficient, that is, $|X[k]|^2$, as given in Equation (7.43). Unlike DFTs, which require storing of many twiddle factors, we need not store any coefficients in the Goertzel algorithm. We use only one coefficient "a" in the computation as given in Pcode 7.17, and this can be held in a data register.

On the reference embedded processor, we consume about 6 cycles (of which 4 cycles are used for multiplication of two 16.16 format numbers) per iteration in the IIR filter loop of the Goertzel algorithm. If $N = 200$, then we require about 1200 cycles to detect one frequency tone in the given signal using the Goertzel algorithm.

CHAPTER 8

Advanced Signal Processing

In Chapters 6 and 7, we discussed the basic signal processing tools such as the discrete Fourier transform (DFT), discrete cosine transform (DCT), and digital filters. Most of these tools assume that the signals being processed are stationary (or wide-sense stationary). In other words, if the second-order statistics (i.e., correlation or power spectral density) of signals or underlying systems that produce the signals are constant, then we can effectively process those signals with basic tools such as DFT, DCT, and digital filters. If the signal statistics vary with time, then we cannot process such signals with basic tools. For this, we need advanced tools, the topic of this chapter.

In Section 8.1, we discuss adaptive signal-processing algorithms—widely used in digital communications, and automotive, aerospace, control, and medical applications to operate effectively in an unknown environment and to track time variations of statistics of underlying system or input data.

In Section 8.2, we discuss multirate signal-processing techniques with which we can save processing time, reduce bandwidth requirements, and overcome a few other issues of single-rate systems. Multirate systems differ from single-rate processing systems in that the sample rate is altered at various places within the system. The aim of multirate techniques is to operate, at each point in the system, at the lowest sampling rate possible, without introducing aliasing effects. The multirate signal-processing tools such as decimators, interpolators, and polyphase filters are briefly discussed.

Fourier transforms use sinusoidal functions as base functions to analyze arbitrary signals. As sinusoids are well-localized in frequency, but not in time, achieving both time and frequency localization of an arbitrary signal to the required extent is not possible with Fourier transforms. To represent the frequency behavior of an arbitrary signal locally in time, the signal should be analyzed by base functions that are localized both in time and frequency. In Section 8.3, we introduce the wavelet transform bases (that overcome the shortcomings of the Fourier transform's sinusoidal bases), which are generated by translations and dilations of a prototype wave called a *mother wavelet*. In addition, we discuss the discrete wavelet transform and its implementation aspects.

8.1 Adaptive Signal Processing

Before discussing adaptive signal-processing algorithms, we consider a few examples to understand more about the limitations of the static digital filter. Let us consider the following three cases (from Chapter 9): (1) filter to shape the transmitting signals (e.g., raised cosine filter to shape modulated signal), (2) filter to undo effects of a stationary source that generates the signals (e.g., channel equalization in wired communications), and (3) filter to undo effects of a nonstationary source that generates the signals (e.g., channel equalization in wireless communications). We further divide case 3 into two scenarios: equalization of a slow time-varying channel, and equalization of a fast time-varying channel. Here, the terms *slow* and *fast* are relative with respect to duration of the sample block considered for processing. In other words, if channel statistics remain constant (i.e., variations are negligible) within a given block of channel output samples, then we treat such a channel as slow time-varying or quasistationary; otherwise, the channel statistics are fast time-varying or nonstationary (i.e., the channel statistics are not constant within the block of samples considered for processing). Next, we explain the purpose of adaptive signal processing in digital communication systems by considering the three cases.

Case 1: In this case, given the sampling frequency and roll-off factor parameter, we can design offline a raised cosine digital filter that meets the specifications and filters the modulated signals resulting in zero intersymbol

DOI: 10.1016/B978-1-85617-678-1.00008-9

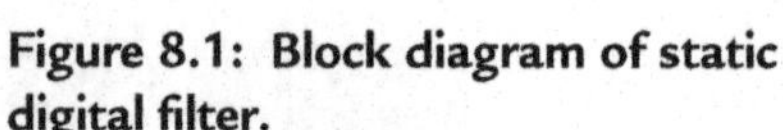
Figure 8.1: Block diagram of static digital filter.

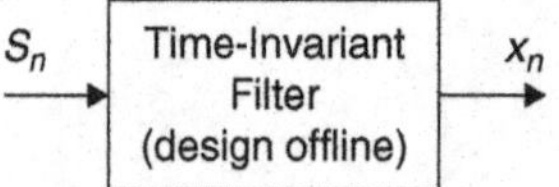

interference (ISI) at the receiver under ideal channel conditions. With this filtering operation via a static digital filter (see Figure 8.1), we get the expected filter output.

Case 2: In this case, there are no fixed specifications for filter design. Instead, we estimate the channel (a source that outputs the sequence as a received sequence) using a training sequence, design the equalizer filter based on the estimated channel by following given criteria, and filter the channel-generated samples to undo the effect of the channel on transmitted samples. This is illustrated in Figure 8.2.

We transmit a training sequence at the beginning of communication. With the received training sequence and using the reference training sequence (available at receiver), we then estimate the channel. Once we obtain the equalizer filter coefficients from the estimated channel, we perform filtering on the received data samples by assuming that the channel characteristics do not change during the established communication-link period.

Case 3: If channel statistics change with time, then a single time estimation of channel and equalizer design to undo the channel effects will not be effective, as the equalizer weights computed at one point in time do not represent inverse channel characteristics at any other point in time. In other words, the scheme illustrated in Figure 8.2 cannot be used with time-varying channels. As shown in Figure 8.3, the equalizer filter coefficients are adapted according to the current channel conditions. In this scheme, the training sequence is transmitted periodically. The time period between two training sequences will be determined after rigorously studying channel operating conditions. Here, we will have two modes to generate the error signal for adaptation: training mode and decision-directed mode. Whenever the receiver perceives a training sequence, we use the reference training sequence to generate the error; otherwise, we use decisions from the detector to generate the error signal.

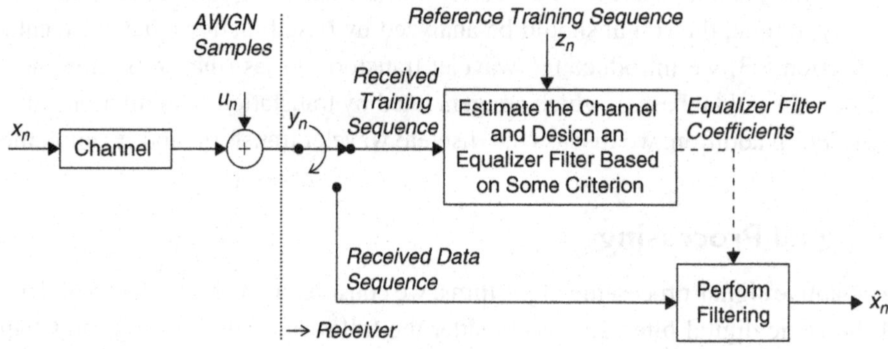

Figure 8.2: Static-channel estimation and equalization.

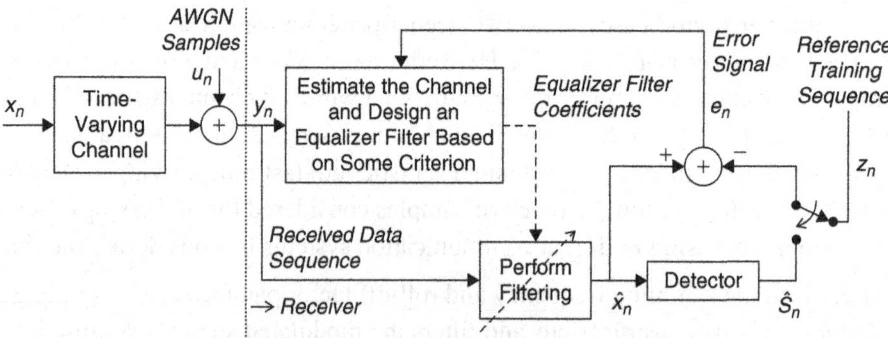

Figure 8.3: Block diagram of adaptive equalizer.

Once the error signal is available, we use that error signal for updating the equalizer coefficients to track the channel changes.

As discussed later, we use less computationally complex iterative algorithms to generate adaptive filter weights. The algorithm generating the filter coefficients takes time to converge (known as *convergence time*) in obtaining coefficients that accurately represent channel conditions. If the convergence time of an algorithm is greater than the time at which the channel varies, then that adaptive scheme cannot cope with the channel variations and the resulting adaptive filter will not be effective.

In the literature, adaptive filtering based on Wiener filter theory or least squares is widely used with stationary and quasistationary signals or systems, whereas Kalman filter theory is applied to nonstationary systems. Due to its high computational complexity, Kalman filtering is not preferred, especially in low-end applications. In the following, we discuss adaptive filter algorithms based on Wiener filter and least-squares filter theories. We consider the previous channel estimation and equalization applications as examples in discussing adaptive filtering algorithms.

Given the input sequence $\{x_n\}$, L channel coefficients $\{h_n\}$, and additive white Gaussian noise (AWGN) samples $\{u_n\}$, we can represent the AWGN channel output samples $\{y_n\}$ in the three following ways:

- Convolution model representation

$$\begin{aligned} y_n &= x_n \otimes h_n + u_n \\ &= \sum_{k=0}^{L-1} h_k x_{n-k} + u_n \end{aligned} \tag{8.1}$$

- Vector model representation

$$y_n = \underline{h}^T \underline{x}_n + u_n \tag{8.2}$$

where $\underline{h} = [h_0\ h_1\ h_2 \ldots h_{L-1}]^T$ and $\underline{x}_n = [x_n\ x_{n-1}\ x_{n-2} \ldots x_{n-L+1}]^T$

- Matrix model representation

$$\underline{y}_n = H \underline{x}_n + \underline{u}_n \tag{8.3}$$

where

$$\underline{y}_n = [y_n\ y_{n-1}\ y_{n-2} \ldots y_{n-N}]^T, \quad \underline{x}_n = [x_n\ x_{n-1}\ x_{n-2} \ldots x_{n-N-L+1}]^T, \quad \underline{u}_n = [u_n\ u_{n-1}\ u_{n-2} \ldots u_{n-N}]^T$$

and

$$H = \begin{bmatrix} h_0 & h_1 & h_2 & \cdots & h_{L-1} & 0 & 0 & \cdots & 0 & 0 \\ 0 & h_0 & h_1 & h_2 & \cdots & h_{L-1} & 0 & \cdots & 0 & 0 \\ \vdots & \vdots & \vdots & \vdots & \vdots & \vdots & \vdots & \vdots & \vdots & \vdots \\ 0 & 0 & \cdots & 0 & h_0 & h_1 & h_2 & \cdots & h_{L-1} & 0 \\ 0 & 0 & \cdots & 0 & 0 & h_0 & h_1 & h_2 & \cdots & h_{L-1} \end{bmatrix}$$

The transversal filter structure is commonly used in most adaptive filtering applications. One such M-length transversal filter structure is shown in Figure 8.4.

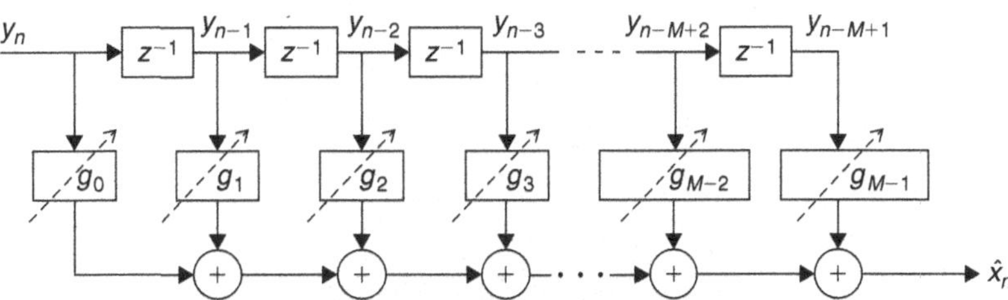

Figure 8.4: Structure of adaptive transversal filter.

8.1.1 Wiener Filters

The Wiener filter solution is stated as follows: For stationary input signals, design a linear filter to minimize the mean-square value of the error signal defined as the difference between the reference signal and actual filter output signal. The Wiener filter solution is said to be optimum in the mean-square sense.

MMSE Criterion

With the minimum mean-square error (MMSE) criterion, we minimize the mean-square error (MSE) value. In Figure 8.3, with the training mode, the error signal e_n is obtained by taking the difference between the actual output signal $\hat{x}_n$ and the reference signal z_n as

$$e_n = \hat{x}_n - z_n \tag{8.4}$$

Then the MSE is defined as

$$\text{MSE} = E\,|e_n|^2 = E\,|\hat{x}_n - z_n|^2 \tag{8.5}$$

where $E|.|$ represents the expectation operator.

Using the transversal filter structure as shown in Figure 8.4, the filter output signal $\hat{x}_n$ is obtained by computing the convolution sum as follows:

$$\hat{x}_n = \sum_{m=0}^{M-1} g[m] y_{n-m} \tag{8.6}$$

(*Note:* In Equation (8.6), we use notation $g[m]$ instead of g_m for representing the filter coefficients.)

Using the vector model representation, Equation (8.6) can be expressed as

$$\hat{x}_n = \underline{y}_n^T \underline{g} \tag{8.7}$$

where $\underline{g} = (g[0]\ g[1]\ g[2] \cdots g[M-1])^T$ and $\underline{y}_n = [y_n\ y_{n-1}\ y_{n-2} \cdots y_{n-M+1}]^T$. Given Equations (8.5) and (8.7),

$$\text{MSE} = J(\underline{g}) = E\left|\underline{y}_n^T \underline{g} - z_n\right|^2 \tag{8.8}$$

$$\begin{aligned} &= E\left[\left(\underline{g}^T \underline{y}_n - z_n\right)\left(\underline{y}_n^T \underline{g} - z_n\right)\right] \\ &= \underline{g}^T E\left[\underline{y}_n \underline{y}_n^T\right]\underline{g} - \underline{g}^T E\left[\underline{y}_n z_n\right] - E\left[z_n \underline{y}_n^T\right]\underline{g} + E\,|z_n|^2 \\ &= \underline{g}^T R_{yy}[n]\underline{g} - \underline{g}^T \underline{r}_n - \underline{r}_n^T \underline{g} + \sigma_z^2 \end{aligned} \tag{8.9}$$

where $R_{yy}[n] = E[\underline{y}_n \underline{y}_n^T]$, the autocorrelation matrix of the filter input vector; $\underline{r}_n = E[\underline{y}_n z_n]$, the cross-correlation vector between the input vector and reference data; and $\sigma_z^2 = E\,|z_n|^2$, the variance of the reference sequence, assuming that z_n has a zero mean.

Based on Equation (8.9), if the filter input vector $\underline{y}_n$ and the reference vector z_n are jointly stationary, then the MSE is precisely a second-order function of the filter coefficient vector $\underline{g}$. The MSE function is a bowl-shaped surface with a unique minimum as shown in Figure 8.5 (for $M = 2$), and our aim is to design the filter so that it operates at the bottom of the bowl-shaped error surface.

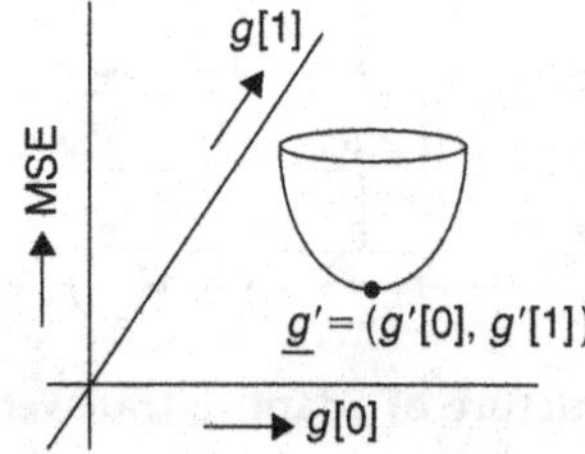

Figure 8.5: MSE error-performance surface of two-tap transversal filter.

The optimum filter coefficient vector $\underline{g}'$ is obtained by differentiating the MSE function $J(\underline{g})$ with respect to the filter coefficient vector $\underline{g}$ and setting the result to zero. By differentiating the MSE function in Equation (8.9) with respect to $\underline{g}$,

$$\frac{dJ(\underline{g})}{d\underline{g}} = 2R_{yy}[n]\underline{g} - 2\underline{r}_n \tag{8.10}$$

In Equation (8.10), when $\frac{dJ(\underline{g})}{d\underline{g}}$ becomes zero, we reach the bottom of the error surface (i.e., the minimum MSE), and the corresponding coefficient vector (known as the *optimum* coefficient vector) is obtained as follows:

$$2R_{yy}[n]\underline{g}' - 2\underline{r}_n = 0 \Rightarrow R_{yy}[n]\underline{g}' = \underline{r}_n \tag{8.11}$$

or

$$\underline{g}' = R_{yy}^{-1}[n]\underline{r}_n \tag{8.12}$$

Then, from Equations (8.9) and (8.11), the minimum MSE is given by

$$J_{\min} = J(\underline{g}') = \sigma_z^2 - \underline{r}_n^T \underline{g}' \tag{8.13}$$

Equation (8.11) is called the *normal equation* for the following reason:

$$\begin{gathered} E\left[\underline{y}_n \underline{y}_n^T\right]\underline{g}' = E\left[\underline{y}_n z_n\right] \text{ or} \\ E\left[\underline{y}_n\left(\underline{y}_n^T \underline{g}' - z_n\right)\right] = \underline{0} \Rightarrow E\left[\underline{y}_n e_n'\right] = \underline{0} \end{gathered} \tag{8.14}$$

where $e_n' = \underline{y}_n^T \underline{g}' - z_n$ and $\underline{0}$ is the zero vector.

Equation (8.14) states that when the filter operates in its optimum condition, each element of the input vector $\underline{y}_n$ and the estimation errors e_n' are orthogonal. Similarly, when the filter operates in its optimum condition, the filter output x_n' and the estimation error e_n' are also orthogonal. It is for this reason that Equation (8.11), which defines the optimum filter, is called the normal equation.

Computation of the optimum filter coefficient vector $\underline{g}'$ using Equation (8.12) involves finding the inverse of the correlation matrix, which is computationally very expensive as the filter length increases. To reduce the computational complexity of the MMSE filter, we use an iterative algorithm, the steepest-descent method, to obtain the filter coefficient vector $\underline{g}$ with fewer computations.

Steepest-Descent Method

In real-world applications, the transversal filter coefficient vector $\underline{g}$ is usually obtained with an iterative procedure that avoids the explicit computation of the inverse of correlation matrix. The simplest iterative procedure is the steepest-descent method, which involves the following steps:

1. Given the filter length M, set the initial coefficient vector $\underline{g}_0$ to the null vector of length M.
2. In the i-th iteration, we compute the gradient vector (defined as the gradient of the MSE function, $J(\underline{g})$, evaluated with respect to coefficient vector) using the existing coefficient vector $\underline{g}_i$.
3. We update the coefficient vector to $\underline{g}_{i+1}$ by making a change in the $\underline{g}_i$ in a direction opposite to the gradient vector (since the error surface $J(\underline{g})$ contains a single global minimum and the gradient gives the direction in which the function $J(\underline{g})$ increases the most, adjusting the coefficient vector in the opposite direction to that of gradient vector eventually updates any arbitrarily initialized coefficient vector toward the optimum coefficient vector after a few iterations).
4. Repeat steps 2 and 3 until we achieve $J_{\min}$, at which point the coefficient vector assumes its optimum value $\underline{g}'$.

Let Δ_i denote the gradient vector value at the i-th iteration, which is obtained by differentiating the MSE function $J(\underline{g}_i)$ with respect to the coefficient vector $\underline{g}_i$. Based on Equation (8.10),

$$\Delta_i = \frac{dJ(\underline{g}_i)}{d\underline{g}_i} = 2R_{yy}[i]\underline{g}_i - 2\underline{r}_i \tag{8.15}$$

According to the steepest-descent method, the updated value of the coefficient vector of $(i+1)$th iteration is computed from the i-th iteration coefficient vector using the following simple recursive relationship:

$$\underline{g}_{i+1} = \underline{g}_i + \frac{\mu}{2}(-\Delta_i) \tag{8.16}$$

where μ is the step-size parameter required for convergence of this iterative procedure. Based on Equations (8.15) and (8.16),

$$\underline{g}_{i+1} = \underline{g}_i + \mu\left(\underline{r}_i - R_{yy}[i]\underline{g}_i\right), \quad i = 0, 1, 2, 3, \ldots \tag{8.17}$$

To ensure convergence of the iterative procedure, the step-size μ is chosen to be a small positive number. In such a case, the gradient vector Δ_i converges toward zero and the coefficient vector $\underline{g}_i$ converges toward the optimum coefficient vector $\underline{g}'$. The step size μ controls the convergence time and minimum MSE that can be achieved with the steepest-descent algorithm. For smaller step-size values, the algorithm converges slowly and may contain a small steady-state error, whereas with a larger step size, the algorithm converges faster and may contain a large steady-state error. Since the steepest-descent method works as a feedback system as shown in Figure 8.6, the system can become unstable and the bounds on the step size guaranteeing stability can be determined with respect to eigenvalues of the correlation matrix $R_{yy}[i]$. The necessary and sufficient condition for the stability and convergence of the steepest-descent algorithm is that the step-size parameter μ must satisfy the following condition

$$0 < \mu < \frac{2}{\lambda_{max}} \tag{8.18}$$

where λ_{max} is the largest eigenvalue of the correlation matrix $R_{yy}[i]$.

Given that the computation of $\lambda_{max}(< \sum_{m=0}^{M-1} \lambda_m)$ is expensive, we use the trace of $R_{yy}[i]$ instead of λ_{max} in choosing the step-size parameter μ upon satisfying the following condition:

$$0 < \mu < \frac{2}{trace\left(R_{yy}[i]\right)} \tag{8.19}$$

where

$$trace\left(R_{yy}[i]\right) = sum[diag\left(R_{yy}[i]\right)] = \sum_{m=0}^{M-1} \lambda_m = \sum_{m=0}^{M-1} |y[i-m]|^2 = input\ power$$

One more metric that affects the convergence behavior of the steepest-descent algorithm is the eigenvalue spread of the correlation metric $R_{yy}[i]$, ρ_R. The eigenvalue spread ρ_R is defined as the ratio of the largest and

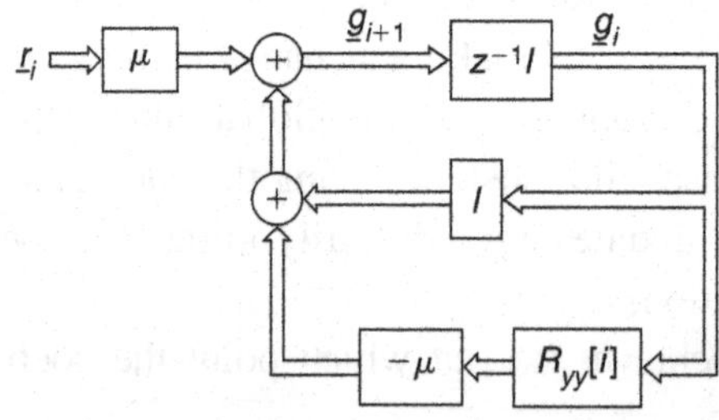

Figure 8.6: Signal flow diagram of steepest-descent algorithm.

smallest eigenvalues associated with the correlation metric $R_{yy}[n]$, that is,

$$\rho_R = \lambda_{max}/\lambda_{min} \tag{8.20}$$

The best convergence behavior of steepest descent can be obtained when all eigenvalues are equal (i.e., $\rho_R = 1$ or $\lambda_{max} = \lambda_{min}$). In this case, the filter inputs are samples of the white noise process and they are perfectly uncorrelated. As the eigenvalue spread ρ_R of the correlation matrix increases, the convergence speed of the steepest-descent method deteriorates. In that case, one way to speed up the algorithm convergence rate is by preprocessing the input with the whitening filter (or predictor) to get uncorrelated samples. This is called *prewhitening* of input data.

Next, we provided the simulation results for the optimal Wiener filter and steepest-descent method. We consider two cases with eigenvalue spread, $\rho_R = 2.96$ and 1.296. The error difference plot with the optimal Wiener filter for the case when the eigenvalue spread $\rho_R = 2.96$ is shown in Figure 8.7(a), and the plots of error versus the number of iterations of the steepest-descent algorithm with step size $\mu = 0.0003$ and 0.003 are shown Figure 8.7(b) and (c), respectively. The plot of filter coefficient convergence with the number of iterations is shown in Figure 8.8. The solid curves represent the convergence of filter coefficients when $\mu = 0.003$, and the dotted curves represent the convergence of filter coefficients when $\mu = 0.0003$. As seen in the simulation results shown in Figures 8.7 and 8.8, the error and filter coefficients converge toward the optimum solution with the steepest-descent algorithm as the number of iterations increases.

Similarly, the error plot with the optimal Wiener filter solution for the case of eigenvalue spread $\rho_R = 1.296$ is shown in Figure 8.9(a), and the error versus number of iterations plots of the steepest-descent algorithm with step size $\mu = 0.0003$ and 0.003 are shown in Figure 8.9(b) and (c), respectively. The plot for filter coefficient convergence with the number of iterations for the case when eigenvalue spread $\rho_R = 1.296$ is shown in Figure 8.10. The solid curves represent the convergence of filter coefficients when $\mu = 0.003$, and the dotted curves represent the convergence of filter coefficients when $\mu = 0.0003$. Figures 8.9 and 8.10 show the improved convergence behavior of the steepest-descent algorithm when the eigenvalue spread is close to unity. For the fixed eigenvalue spread, smaller values of μ result in slower convergence of the steepest descent with reduced steady-state error,

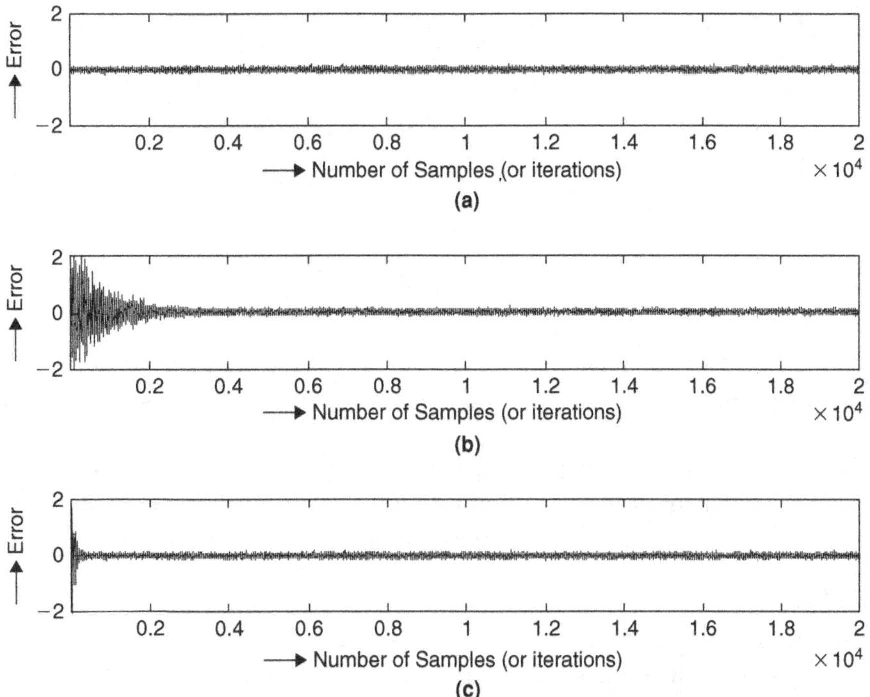

Figure 8.7: Error estimate with MMSE filtering for $\rho_R = 2.96$. (a) Using optimal MMSE filter. (b) Using steepest-descent algorithm with $\mu = 0.0003$. (c) Using steepest-descent algorithm with $\mu = 0.003$.

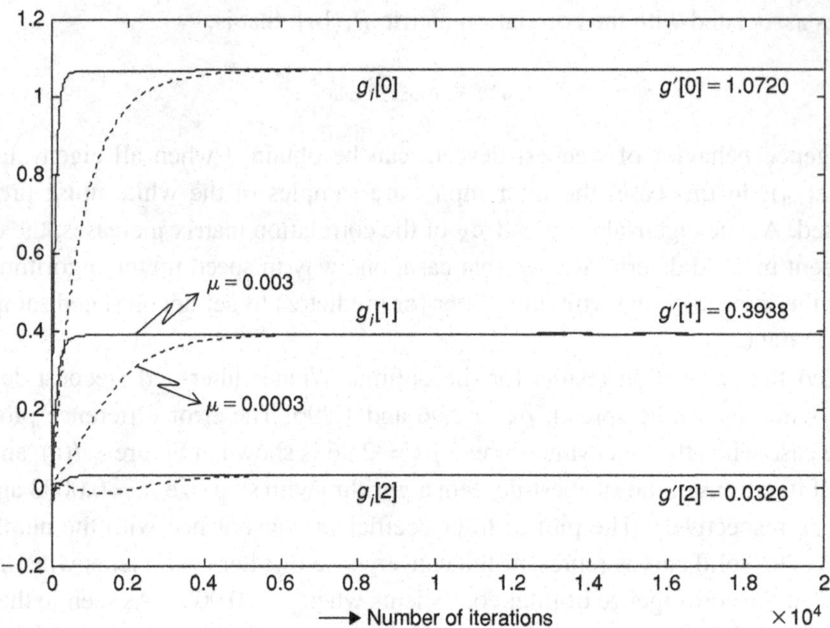

Figure 8.8: Convergence of filter coefficients with steepest-descent algorithm for $\rho_R = 2.96$. Faster convergence with $\mu = 0.003$ (solid curves) and slow convergence with $\mu = 0.0003$ (dotted curves).

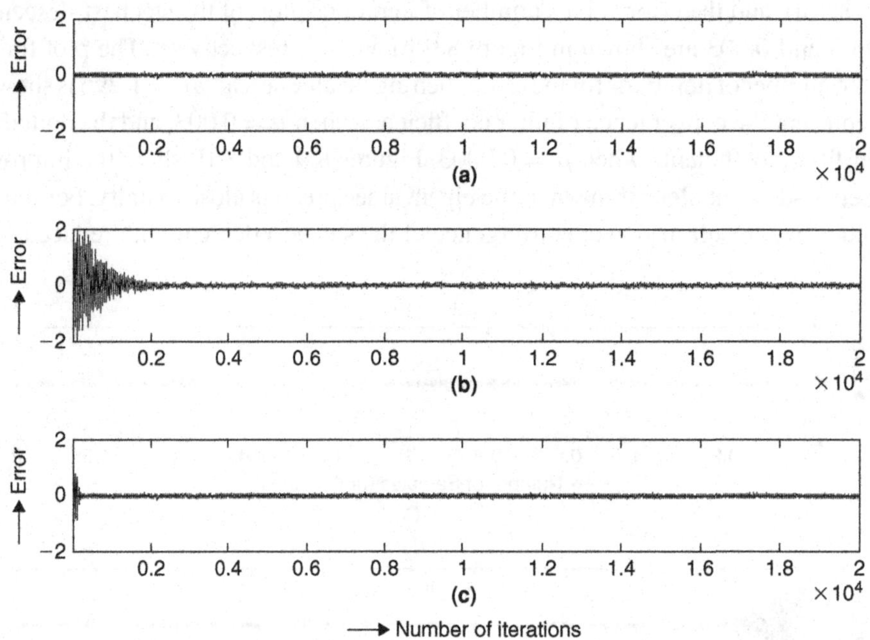

Figure 8.9: Error estimate with MMSE filtering for $\rho_R = 1.296$. (a) Using optimal MMSE filter. (b) Using steepest-descent algorithm with $\mu = 0.0003$. (c) Using steepest-descent algorithm with $\mu = 0.003$.

whereas larger values of μ result in faster convergence of steepest descent with more steady-state error. In summary, the convergence behavior of the algorithm is highly sensitive to variations in the step-size parameter μ and the eigenvalue spread ρ_R of the correlation matrix of the transversal filter input data.

Least-Mean Square Algorithm

As discussed previously, the optimum filter coefficients of a transversal, finite impulse-response (FIR) Wiener filter can be obtained by solving the normal equations described by Equation (8.12) provided that the required statistics of the underlying signals are available. Since solving normal equations by matrix inversion is computationally costly, an alternative way of finding the transversal filter coefficient vector is to use an iterative search (e.g., steepest-descent) algorithm given in Equation (8.17) that starts at some arbitrary initial point in the tap-weight

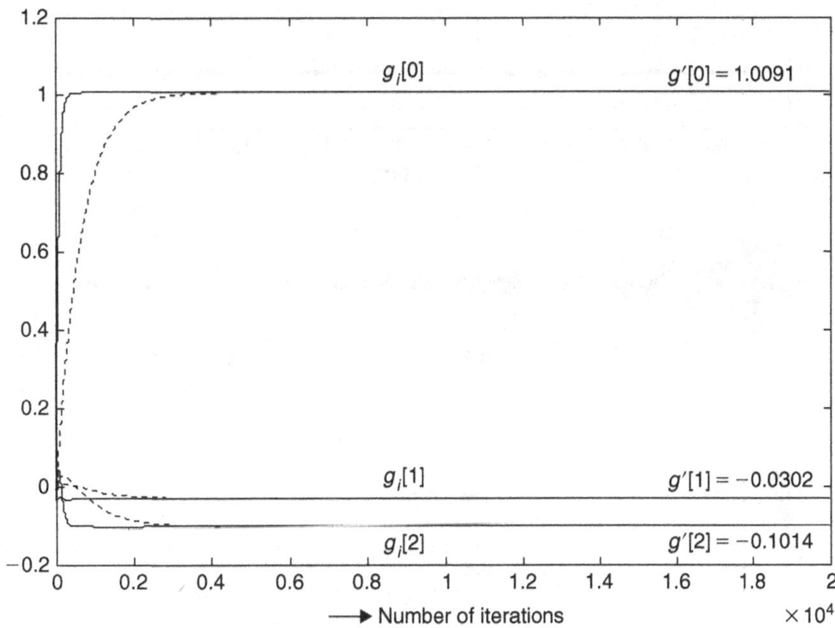

Figure 8.10: Convergence of filter coefficients with steepest-descent algorithm for $\rho_R = 1.296$. Faster convergence with $\mu = 0.003$ (solid curves) and slower convergence with $\mu = 0.0003$ (dotted curves).

vector space and progressively moves toward the optimum point in a few steps. Both the steepest-descent algorithm and optimal Wiener filter solution assume the availability of autocorrelation ($R_{yy}[n]$) of the input data samples and cross-correlation ($\underline{r}_n$) statistics of the input data and the reference data samples. We estimate these statistics before computing the filter coefficients. However, the estimation of correlation matrices introduces delay in the system; moreover, it is not the appropriate solution for dealing with time-varying systems. Instead, the simplest estimators of $R_{yy}[i]$ and $\underline{r}_i$ for adaptive processing are instantaneous (instead of ensemble or time averages), based on sample values of filter input data and reference data:

$$\hat{R}_{yy}[i] = \underline{y}_i \underline{y}_i^T \tag{8.21}$$

$$\hat{\underline{r}}_i = \underline{y}_i z_i \tag{8.22}$$

Based on Equations (8.17), (8.21), and (8.22),

$$\hat{\underline{g}}_{i+1} = \hat{\underline{g}}_i + \mu \underline{y}_i \left[z_i - \underline{y}_i^T \hat{\underline{g}}_i \right] \tag{8.23}$$

$$\hat{\underline{g}}_{i+1} = \hat{\underline{g}}_i + \mu \underline{y}_i e_i \tag{8.24}$$

where $e_i = z_i - \underline{y}_i^T \hat{\underline{g}}_i$, which is computed based on the current estimate of the filter coefficient vector $\hat{\underline{g}}_i$. The algorithm described by Equation (8.24) is known as the *least-mean square* (LMS) algorithm. For convergence of LMS, the step-size parameter μ is set within the bounds defined by Equation (8.19); this is also the necessary and sufficient condition for overall stability of the LMS algorithm.

As seen in Equation (8.24), the filter coefficient vector is updated in accordance with an algorithm that adapts to the incoming data. Given that we use the instantaneous noisy estimates in LMS for computing the gradient vector, we can get the converged filter coefficients $\hat{\underline{g}}$ only after a large number of iterations. Since the LMS algorithm is recursive in nature, the algorithm itself effectively averages out the larger variances of instantaneous estimates during the course of adaptation. However, because of the instantaneous noisy gradient vectors, the converged filter coefficients $\hat{\underline{g}}$ fluctuate about the optimum Wiener solution $\underline{g}'$. In other words, the LMS-algorithm filter coefficients converge in the mean sense.

We consider two cases with the eigenvalue spread $\rho_R = 2.96$ and 1.296, which are the same as those used for illustrating the steepest-descent method's convergence properties. The plot of error difference with the optimal

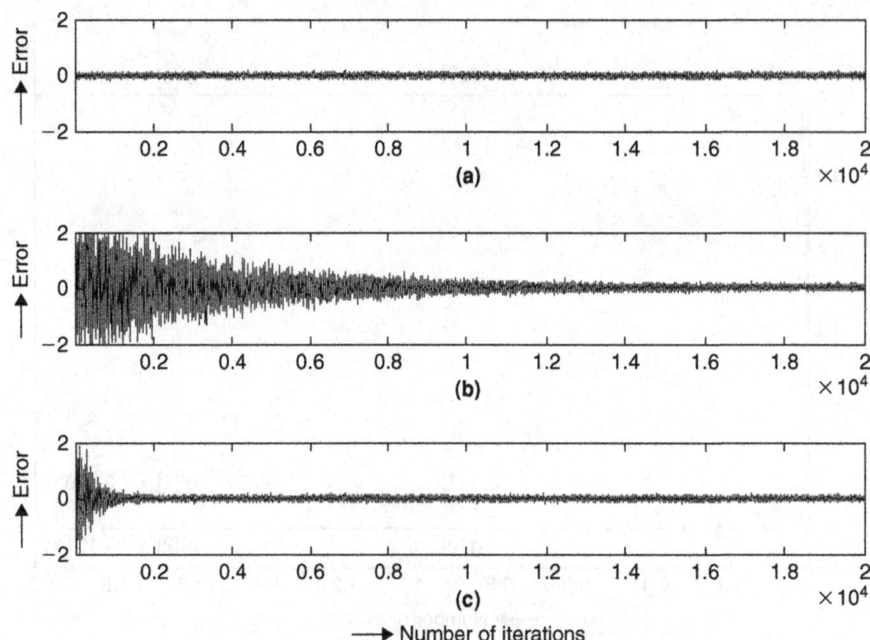

Figure 8.11: Error estimate for inputs with $\rho_R = 2.96$. (a) Using optimal MMSE filter. (b) Using LMS algorithm with $\mu = 0.0003$. (c) Using LMS with $\mu = 0.003$.

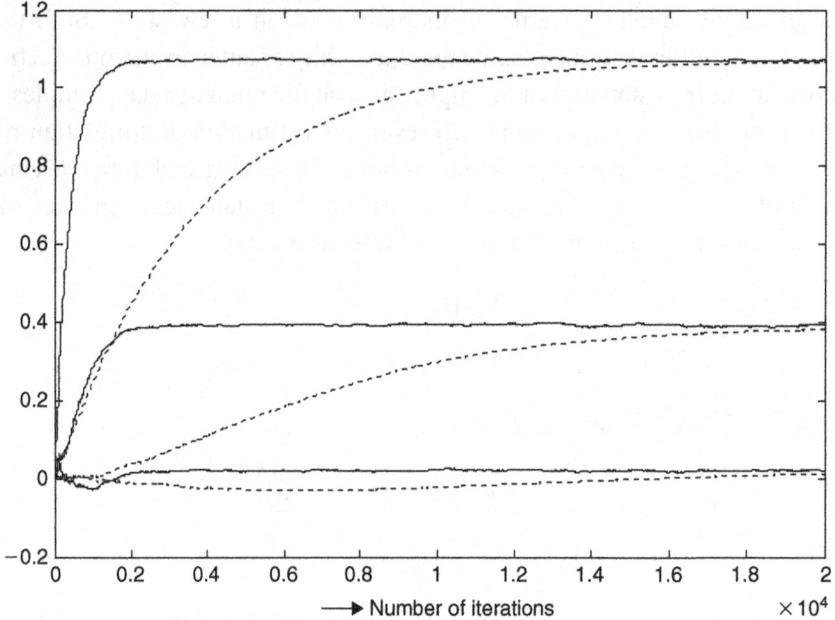

Figure 8.12: Convergence of filter coefficients with LMS algorithm for $\rho_R = 2.96$. Faster convergence with $\mu = 0.003$ (solid curves) and slower convergence with $\mu = 0.0003$ (dotted curves).

Wiener filter for the case when the eigenvalue spread $\rho_R = 2.96$ is shown in Figure 8.11(a), and the plots of error versus the number of iterations of the LMS algorithm with step size $\mu = 0.0003$ and 0.003 are shown in Figure 8.11(b) and (c), respectively. The plot of filter coefficients convergence with the number of iterations is shown in Figure 8.12. The solid curves represent the convergence of filter coefficients when $\mu = 0.003$ and the dotted curves represent the convergence of filter coefficients when $\mu = 0.0003$. The convergence behavior of LMS for the small eigenvalue spread of $\rho_R = 1.296$ is shown in Figures 8.13 and 8.14. Figures 8.8 and 8.12 clearly show the slow convergence behavior of the LMS algorithm when compared to the steepest-descent algorithm. Like the steepest-descent algorithm, when the eigenvalue spread ρ_R is large, the LMS algorithm slows down, in that a large number of iterations are required for it to converge toward optimal solution.

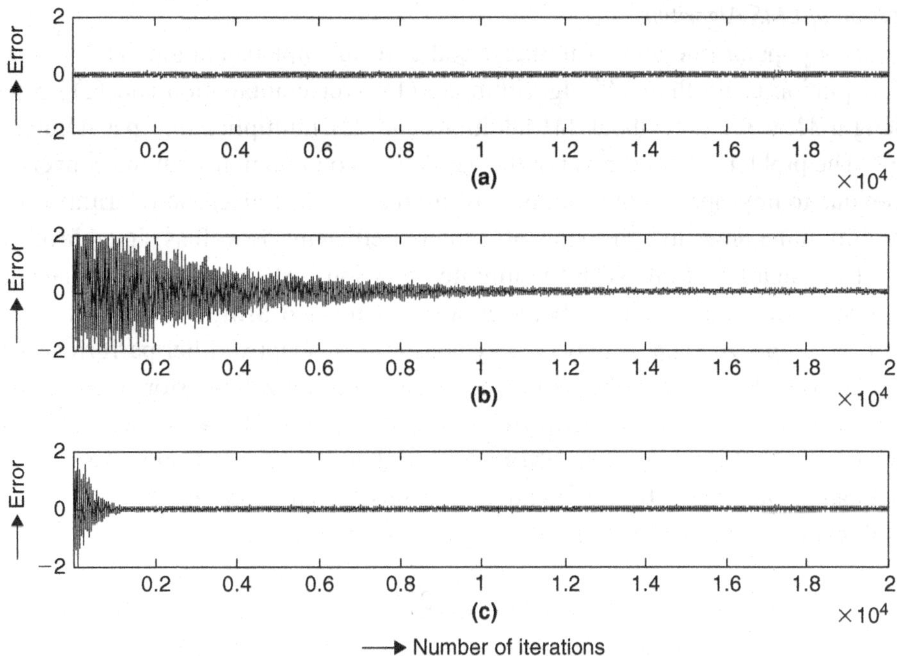

Figure 8.13: Error estimate for inputs with $\rho_R = 1.296$. (a) Using optimal MMSE filter. (b) Using LMS algorithm with $\mu = 0.0003$. (c) Using LMS with $\mu = 0.003$.

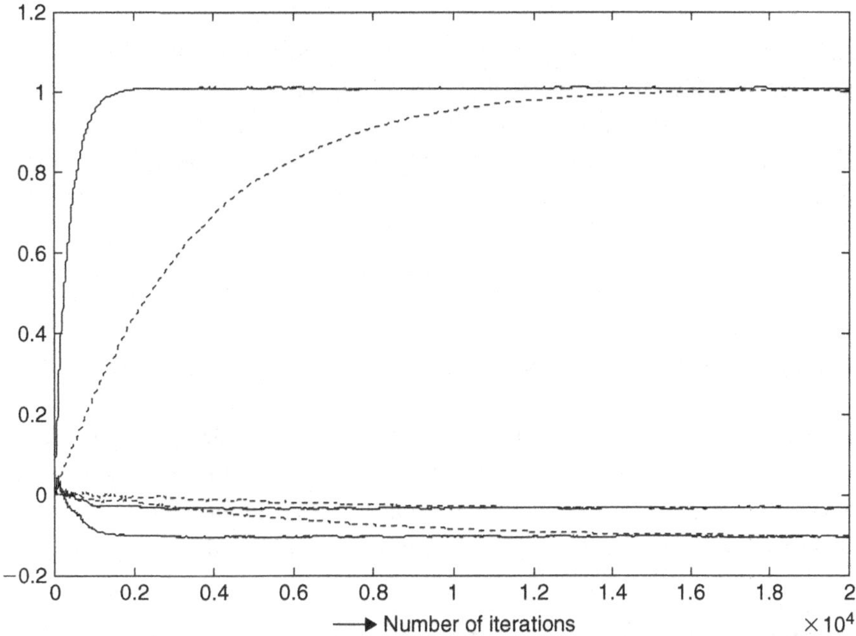

Figure 8.14: Convergence of filter coefficients with LMS algorithm for $\rho_R = 1.296$. Faster convergence with $\mu = 0.003$ (solid curves) and slower convergence with $\mu = 0.0003$ (dotted curves).

Adaptive channel equalization (see Section 9.4) is required for channels whose characteristics change with time. The channel equalizer must track such time variations in the channel response and adapt its coefficients to reduce the time-varying ISI. If the LMS algorithm is chosen due to its low computational complexity for adapting the channel equalizer to undo time-varying channel conditions, then the convergence time of the LMS algorithm must be smaller than channel coherence time (i.e., the time period during which the channel characteristics remain constant). But for channels that vary rapidly with time, the LMS cannot keep up with the time variations. Increasing the step size μ beyond a certain point causes the algorithm to diverge. This limits the applicability of LMS in fast-fading channels.

Digital Implementation of LMS Algorithm

The LMS algorithm is popular due to its simplicity and ease of implementation. The two steps involved in filter coefficient adaptation using the LMS algorithm are (1) error computation and (2) coefficient updating. Given the filter length M, we require about $2M$ additions and $2M$ multiplications per iteration to perform the previous two steps. The problem, however, is not the number of computations, but the convergence behavior of the LMS algorithm due to improper scaling and quantization errors with fixed-point arithmetic implementation (see Section 8.4). With finite precision, the adjustable filter coefficients as well as signal levels in the algorithm are quantized to a least-significant bit. With the infinite-precision LMS algorithm, a small step size μ value reduces the excess MSE (i.e., the difference between actual error and MMSE), whereas with finite-precision LMS, a decrease in the step-size value μ may or may not improve adaptive filter performance. Sometimes the algorithm virtually stops making any further adjustments due to quantization errors (see Figure 8.64(b) late in chapter). In particular, when the correction term $\mu e_i \underline{y}_i$ in Equation (8.24) is less than half the filter coefficient quantization interval, then performance of an LMS adapted filter would not improve because the adaptation is terminated by the quantization effect. If B is the number of bits used to represent the filter coefficients, then the LMS algorithm will continue to adapt if the following condition is satisfied:

$$|\mu e_i \underline{y}_i| \geq 2^{-B-1} \tag{8.25}$$

A practical solution for combating finite precision error is to use more bits for the filter coefficients than for the data. For more detail on the finite precision effects in the digital implementation of the LMS algorithm, see Gitlin and Weinstein (1979).

Normalized LMS

With conventional LMS, tuning the step size μ can become especially difficult if there is much variation in the filter input $\underline{y}_n$ values. Depending on the variance of $\underline{y}_n$, the effective updated step sizes become inherently large when $\underline{y}_n$ has large values and small when $\underline{y}_n$ has small values. Such variations in $\underline{y}_n$ values can be compensated for by choosing the step size β according to the incoming data. In other words, we normalize the step size μ with the filter input power to mitigate input data variations as follows:

$$\hat{\underline{g}}_{i+1} = \hat{\underline{g}}_i + \frac{\mu}{(\alpha + ||\underline{y}_i||^2)} \underline{y}_i e_i = \hat{\underline{g}}_i + \beta \underline{y}_i e_i \tag{8.26}$$

where $\beta = \mu/(\alpha + ||\underline{y}_i||^2)$ and $\alpha > 0$ is a constant used to avoid possible numerical problems when $||\underline{y}_i||$ is close to zero.

The algorithm described in Equation (8.26) is known as the *normalized LMS*, and it has much more predictable convergence behavior. The normalized LMS algorithm is convergent in the mean-square sense if $0 < \beta < 2$. In communications systems, one way to achieve the normalized filter input values is to use the automatic gain control (AGC) to scale the input signal before the equalization is performed.

Other LMS Algorithm Variants

A simple version of LMS is called the *sign LMS* (SLMS), in which the sign quantized error or input data (instead of actual input/error values) are used to update the filter coefficients. Like the SLMS, the reduction in complexity for LMS-algorithm gradient-vector computing is obtained by quantizing the error and data to the nearest power of 2. This is called the *log-log LMS* algorithm, and the convergence behavior of log-log LMS is far better than the signed LMS algorithm. For long adaptation processes, the *block LMS* (BLMS) is used to make the LMS faster. In the block LMS, the input sequence is divided into blocks and the filter coefficients are updated block-wise. In some adaptive applications (e.g., active noise control; see Section 17.1.5), the filtered signal undergoes few phase changes (due to the presence of a secondary path) before we subtract it from the reference signal to obtain the error signal. In that case, the input signal must be filtered (using the estimated secondary-path impulse response) to compute the error for updating the filter coefficients. We compensate the phase delays of the secondary path by filtering the input signal. The LMS algorithm that uses a filtered input signal for updating the filter coefficients is known as the *filtered LMS* (FLMS).

8.1.2 Least-Squares Filters

In the previous section, we used the MMSE criterion to obtain the transversal filter coefficients. The MMSE criterion assumes the availability of statistics, autocorrelation of filter input data, and cross-correlation of filter input data and reference data. In this section, we discuss least-squares criteria that do not require such statistical information to obtain the filter coefficients. With the least-squares approach, we directly work with the raw data rather than statistics based on the data. To illustrate the basic idea of least squares, consider the filter input vector $\underline{y}_n = [y_n\ y_{n-1}\ y_{n-2} \dots y_{n-M+1}]^T$ and reference data vector $\underline{z}_n = [z_n\ z_{n-1}\ z_{n-2} \dots z_{n-M+1}]^T$. Assume a transversal filter of length M (as shown in Figure 8.4) with the filter coefficient vector $\underline{g} = [g_0\ g_1\ g_2 \dots g_{M-1}]^T$. By utilizing $\underline{z}_n$ as the desired response, we define the residual error e_n as the difference between the reference sample z_n and the filter output $\hat{x}_n = \underline{g}^T \underline{y}_n$, that is,

$$e_n = z_n - \hat{x}_n \tag{8.27}$$

Using the least-squares approach, the best filter model in the least-squares sense is the instance of the model for which the sum of squared residual errors has its least or lowest value. In other words, in the method of least squares, we choose the transversal filter coefficient vector $\underline{g}$ so as to minimize an index of performance that consists of the sum of error squares,

$$J(\underline{g}) = \sum_{n=N_1}^{N_2} |e_n|^2 \tag{8.28}$$

Let us consider $(N_2 - N_1+1)$-length residual error vector $\underline{e}$:

$$\underline{e} = \left[e_{N_1}\ e_{N_1+1}\ e_{N_1+2} \cdots e_{N_2-1}\ e_{N_2}\right]^T \tag{8.29}$$

where

$$\begin{aligned} e_{N_1+i} &= z_{N_1+i} - \hat{x}_{N_1+i} \\ &= z_{N_1+i} - \underline{g}^T \underline{y}_{N_1+i} \end{aligned} \tag{8.30}$$

Based on Equations (8.29) and (8.30),

$$\underline{e}^T = \underline{z}^T - \underline{g}^T Y^T \tag{8.31}$$

where

$$\underline{z} = \left[z_{N_1}\ z_{N_1+1}\ z_{N_1+2} \cdots z_{N_2}\right]^T \tag{8.32}$$

$$\begin{aligned} Y^T &= \left[\underline{y}_{N_1}\ \underline{y}_{N_1+1} \cdots \underline{y}_{N_2}\right] \\ &= \begin{bmatrix} y_{N_1} & y_{N_1+1} & \cdots & y_{N_2} \\ y_{N_1-1} & y_{N_1} & \cdots & y_{N_2-1} \\ \vdots & \vdots & \ddots & \vdots \\ y_{N_1-M+1} & y_{N_1-M+2} & \cdots & y_{N_2-M+1} \end{bmatrix} \end{aligned} \tag{8.33}$$

Based on Equations (8.28) and (8.31),

$$\begin{aligned} J(\underline{g}) &= \underline{e}^T \underline{e} \\ &= (\underline{z}^T - \underline{g}^T Y^T)(\underline{z} - Y\underline{g}) \\ &= \underline{z}^T \underline{z} - \underline{z}^T Y \underline{g} - \underline{g}^T Y^T \underline{z} + \underline{g}^T Y^T Y \underline{g} \end{aligned} \tag{8.34}$$

To get the optimum filter coefficient vector $\hat{\underline{g}}$ that minimizes the error squares sum, $J(\underline{g})$, we differentiate $J(\underline{g})$ with respect to $\underline{g}$ and set the result to zero as

$$\frac{\partial J(\underline{g})}{\partial \underline{g}} = -2Y^T\underline{z} + 2Y^TY\underline{g}$$

or

$$\frac{\partial J(\hat{\underline{g}})}{\partial \hat{\underline{g}}} = -2Y^T\underline{z} + 2Y^TY\hat{\underline{g}} = 0 \tag{8.35}$$

which means

$$Y^TY\hat{\underline{g}} = Y^T\underline{z} \tag{8.36}$$

Equation (8.36) is called the deterministic normal equation for the linear least-squares problem. The solution of the normal equations yields the optimum vector $\hat{\underline{g}}$, as follows:

$$\hat{\underline{g}} = (Y^TY)^{-1}Y^T\underline{z} \tag{8.37}$$

In linear algebra, the normal equations described by Equation (8.36) are used to find an approximate solution to an overdetermined system of linear equations. Here, we derive the same normal equations using the concepts of linear algebra to provide a geometric interpretation of the least-squares solution, which in turn provides invaluable insight into the problem. Let us consider an overdetermined system $A\underline{x} = \underline{b}$ described by m equations with n unknowns, where $m > n$. In general, we cannot have a solution $\underline{x}$ that satisfies $A\underline{x} = \underline{b}$ when $m > n$. In that case, the vector $\underline{b}$ is not in the column space (i.e., linear combinations of columns) of matrix A, C(A). This is illustrated in Figure 8.15. Assume that the columns of A are independent and that the dimensionality of column space is n or the rank of matrix A is n. The approximate solution $\hat{\underline{x}}$ for $A\underline{x} = \underline{b}$ with minimum error $\underline{e}$ can be obtained by projecting the vector $\underline{b}$ onto the C(A). The term $\hat{\underline{b}}$ is the projection vector of $\underline{b}$ and $A\hat{\underline{x}} = \hat{\underline{b}}$. The error between the given vector $\underline{b}$ and projection $\hat{\underline{b}}$ is $\underline{e} = \underline{b} - \hat{\underline{b}}$, and the error vector $\underline{e}$ is perpendicular to C(A). In other words, the error vector $\underline{e} = \underline{b} - A\hat{\underline{x}}$ is perpendicular to all columns of matrix A, meaning that

$$\begin{aligned} \underline{a}_1^T(\underline{b} - A\hat{\underline{x}}) &= \underline{0} \\ \underline{a}_2^T(\underline{b} - A\hat{\underline{x}}) &= \underline{0} \\ &\vdots \\ \underline{a}_n^T(\underline{b} - A\hat{\underline{x}}) &= \underline{0} \end{aligned} \tag{8.38}$$

Equation (8.38) can also be represented in matrix form as

$$A^T(\underline{b} - A\hat{\underline{x}}) = \underline{0} \tag{8.39}$$

or

$$A^TA\hat{\underline{x}} = A^T\underline{b} \tag{8.40}$$

Equations (8.36) and (8.40) are exactly the same except for variables. Consequently, we conclude that the least-squares optimal filter coefficient vector $\hat{\underline{g}}$ produces the minimum-length error vector when compared to the error length produced by any other coefficient vector $\underline{g}$.

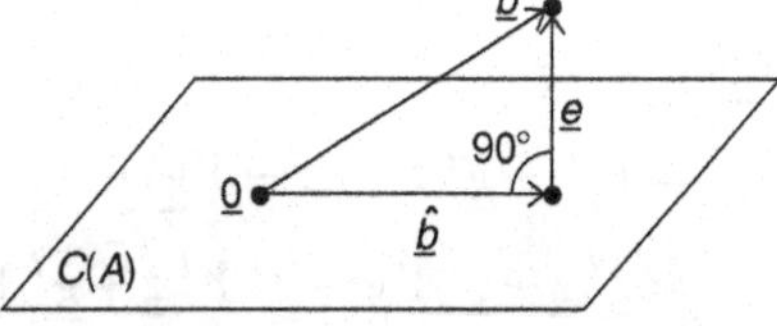

Figure 8.15: Geometric interpretation of $A\underline{x} = \underline{b}$.

Based on Equation (8.37), the least-squares solution involves computation of the matrix inverse and is computationally very complex. Next, we discuss the recursive way of obtaining the least-squares solution.

Recursive Least-Squares Algorithm

With the recursive least-squares (RLS) algorithm, we update the least-squares estimate of coefficient vector $\underline{\hat{g}}$ at time instance n on arrival of new data using the coefficient vector at time $n-1$,

$$\underline{\hat{g}}_n = \underline{\hat{g}}_{n-1} + \Delta\underline{\hat{g}}_n \tag{8.41}$$

where $\Delta\underline{\hat{g}}_n$ is the correction term that is a function of input data and error data. We obtain the correction term as follows. Let $R_{yy} = Y^T Y$ and $\underline{r}_{yz} = Y^T \underline{z}$; then by rewriting Equation (8.37),

$$\underline{\hat{g}} = R_{yy}^{-1} \underline{r}_{yz} \tag{8.42}$$

At any given time instance n, the correlation functions R_{yy} and $\underline{r}_{yz}$ can be expressed as

$$\underline{r}_{yz}[n] = \sum_{i=0}^{n} \underline{y}_i z_i \tag{8.43}$$

$$R_{yy}[n] = \sum_{i=0}^{n} \underline{y}_i \underline{y}_i^T \tag{8.44}$$

To limit the contribution of previous instance samples, we may embed a weighting factor or forgetting factor λ in Equations (8.43) and (8.44) as follows:

$$\underline{r}_{yz}[n] = \sum_{i=0}^{n} \lambda^{n-i} \underline{y}_i z_i \tag{8.45}$$

$$R_{yy}[n] = \sum_{i=0}^{n} \lambda^{n-i} \underline{y}_i \underline{y}_i^T \tag{8.46}$$

The cross-correlation function at time instance n, $\underline{r}_{yz}[n]$ in Equation (8.45) can be expressed in terms of the cross-correlation function at time instance $n-1$ as

$$\begin{aligned} \underline{r}_{yz}[n] &= \sum_{i=0}^{n} \lambda^{n-i} \underline{y}_i z_i = \sum_{i=0}^{n-1} \lambda^{n-i} \underline{y}_i z_i + \lambda^0 z_n \underline{y}_n \\ &= \lambda \sum_{i=0}^{n-1} \lambda^{n-1-i} \underline{y}_i z_i + z_n \underline{y}_n = \lambda \underline{r}_{yz}[n-1] + z_n \underline{y}_n \end{aligned} \tag{8.47}$$

Similarly, the autocorrelation function at time instance n, $R_{yy}[n]$, can be expressed in terms of $R_{yy}[n-1]$:

$$R_{yy}[n] = \lambda R_{yy}[n-1] + \underline{y}_n \underline{y}_n^T \tag{8.48}$$

If A and B are $M \times M$ positive-definite matrices, D is an $N \times N$ matrix, and C is an $M \times N$ matrix, which are related by

$$A = B^{-1} + CD^{-1}C^T \tag{8.49}$$

then, according to the *matrix inverse lemma*, we may express the inverse of matrix A as follows:

$$A^{-1} = B - BC(D + C^T BC)^{-1} C^T B \tag{8.50}$$

Applying the matrix inverse lemma to Equation (8.48), we obtain

$$R_{yy}^{-1}[n] = \lambda^{-1} R_{yy}^{-1}[n-1] - \frac{\lambda^{-2} R_{yy}^{-1}[n-1] \underline{y}_n \underline{y}_n^T R_{yy}^{-1}[n-1]}{1 + \lambda^{-1} \underline{y}_n^T R_{yy}^{-1}[n-1] \underline{y}_n} \tag{8.51}$$

Denoting

$$\Omega[n] = R_{yy}^{-1}[n] \text{ and } \beta[n] = \frac{\lambda^{-1}\Omega[n-1]\underline{y}_n}{1+\lambda^{-1}\underline{y}_n^T\Omega[n-1]\underline{y}_n}$$

we may rewrite Equation (8.51) as

$$\Omega[n] = \lambda^{-1}\Omega[n-1] - \lambda^{-1}\beta[n]\underline{y}_n^T\Omega[n-1] \quad (8.52)$$

We can obtain the correction term $\Delta\hat{\underline{g}}_n$ in Equation (8.41) using Equations (8.42) and (8.52) as follows:

$$\begin{aligned}
\hat{\underline{g}}_n &= \Omega[n]\underline{r}_{yz}[n] = \Omega[n]\left(\lambda\underline{r}_{yz}[n-1] + z_n\underline{y}_n\right) \\
&= \Omega[n]\left(\lambda R_{yy}[n-1]\hat{\underline{g}}_{n-1} + z_n\underline{y}_n\right) \\
&= \Omega[n]\left(\left(R_{yy}[n] - \underline{y}_n\underline{y}_n^T\right)\hat{\underline{g}}_{n-1} + z_n\underline{y}_n\right) \\
&= \hat{\underline{g}}_{n-1} - \Omega[n]\underline{y}_n\underline{y}_n^T\hat{\underline{g}}_{n-1} + \Omega[n]z_n\underline{y}_n \\
&= \hat{\underline{g}}_{n-1} + \Omega[n]\underline{y}_n\left(z_n - \underline{y}_n^T\hat{\underline{g}}_{n-1}\right) \\
&= \hat{\underline{g}}_{n-1} + \Omega[n]\underline{y}_n\alpha_n
\end{aligned} \quad (8.53)$$

where $\alpha_n = z_n - \underline{y}_n^T\hat{\underline{g}}_{n-1}$ is the *a priori* estimation error.

Using the definition of $\beta[n]$ and Equation (8.52), we can express Equation (8.53) as follows:

$$\hat{\underline{g}}_n = \hat{\underline{g}}_{n-1} + \alpha_n\beta[n] \quad (8.54)$$

Finally, the correction term is given by $\Delta\hat{\underline{g}}_n = \alpha_n\beta[n]$. An important feature of the RLS algorithm described by Equations (8.52) to (8.54) is that the inverse of correlation matrix $R_{yy}[n]$ is replaced by a simple division.

The RLS algorithm to update the filter coefficient vector by satisfying the least-squares error criteria is summarized in the following. Initialize the algorithm by setting $\Omega[0] = \delta^{-1}I$, $\hat{\underline{g}}_0 = \underline{0}$, where δ = positive constant (choose small value for high signal-to-noise ratio [SNR], and large value for low SNR), and I is an $M \times M$ identity matrix. Choose λ such that $0 < \lambda^{n-i} \leq 1$ for $i = 1, 2, \ldots, n$. Then,

Compute $\underline{\omega}_n = \Omega[n-1]\underline{y}_n$

Compute $\beta[n] = \dfrac{\underline{\omega}_n}{\lambda + \underline{y}_n^T\underline{\omega}_n}$

Compute $\alpha_n = z_n - \underline{y}_n^T\hat{\underline{g}}_{n-1}$

Update $\hat{\underline{g}}_n = \hat{\underline{g}}_{n-1} + \alpha_n\beta[n]$

Compute $\Omega[n] = \lambda^{-1}\Omega[n-1] - \lambda^{-1}\beta[n]\underline{y}_n^T\Omega[n-1]$

The signal flow diagram that describes the flow of previous RLS algorithm equations is shown in Figure 8.16.

Convergence of RLS Algorithm

At high SNR, the RLS algorithm converges in the mean square in about $2M$ iterations, where M is the number of coefficients in the transversal filter. Unlike the LMS algorithm, the rate of convergence of the RLS algorithm is insensitive to variations in the eigenvalue spread of the correlation matrix $R_{yy}[n]$ of filter input data. However, ill-conditioned least-squares problems may lead to poor convergence behavior. As the number of iterations increases, the RLS algorithm-produced coefficient vector $\hat{\underline{g}}_n$ converges to the Wiener solution $\underline{g}'$. The performance of the RLS algorithm in terms of convergence rate, tracking, stability, and steady-state error depends on the forgetting factor. When the forgetting factor is very close to 1, the algorithm achieves low steady-state error and good stability, but its tracking capabilities are reduced. A smaller value of the forgetting factor improves the tracking capabilities but increases steady-state errors and affects stability.

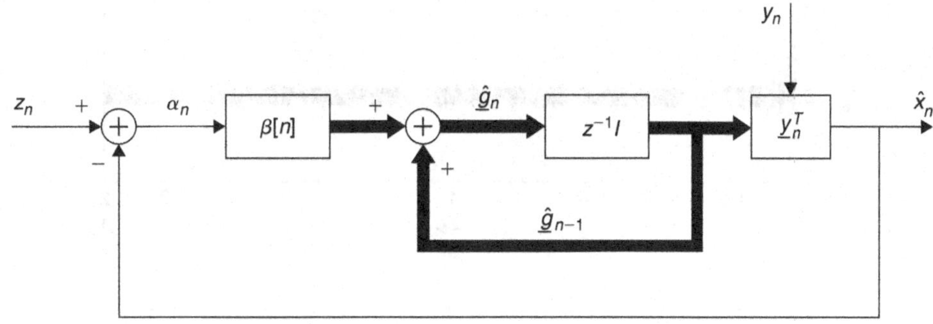

Figure 8.16: Signal-flow graph representation of the RLS algorithm.

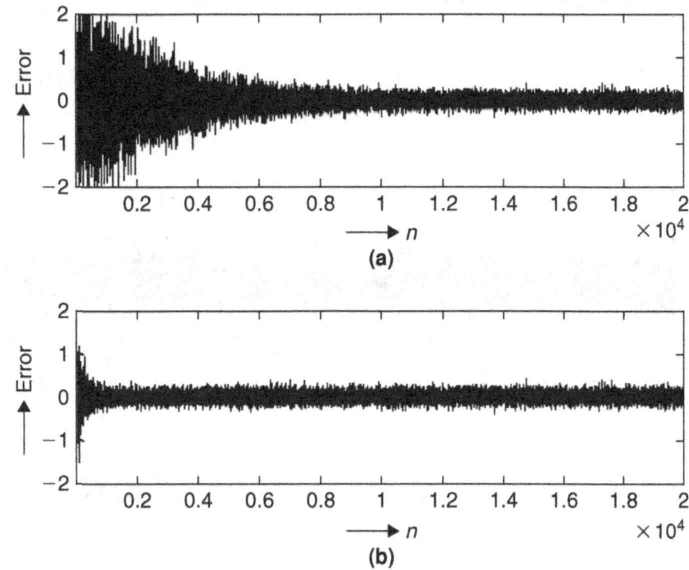

Figure 8.17: Convergence of estimation error. (a) With LMS using step size $\mu = 0.0003$ and eigenvalue spread $\rho_R = 1.296$. (b) With RLS using forgetting factor $\lambda = 1.0$.

For $M = 3$, SNR $= 20$ dB, and eigenvalue spread $\rho_R = 1.296$, the plot of estimation error with the LMS algorithm is shown in Figure 8.17(a). The step size used with LMS is $\mu = 0.0003$. The convergence of *a priori* estimation error with the RLS algorithm for $M = 3$, SNR$= 20$ dB, and $\lambda = 1.0$ is shown in Figure 8.17(b). From Figure 8.17, we can clearly see the superior performance of the RLS algorithm over the LMS algorithm in terms of convergence speed and steady-state error. Figure 8.18 shows the *a priori* estimation error convergence with the RLS algorithm for diverse values of the forgetting factor. As expected, when the value of the forgetting factor approaches zero, the RLS algorithm converges very fast with a large steady-state error.

In contrast, the RLS algorithm produces quite opposite results with *a posteriori* estimation error (i.e., the error obtained after filtering the input with updated filter coefficients). In other words, the smaller the forgetting factor value, the faster the convergence with low steady-state error. The convergence of *a posteriori* estimation error with the RLS algorithm for various values of forgetting factors is shown in Figure 8.19.

Computational Complexity of RLS Algorithm

The faster convergence of the RLS algorithm over the LMS algorithm is achieved at the expense of increased computations per iteration. The complexity of the RLS algorithm per iteration is $O(M^2)$, whereas the complexity of the LMS algorithm per iteration is $O(M)$. To reduce the computational complexity of the RLS algorithm, several fast algorithms have been introduced by Cioffi and Kailath (1984) and Cioffie (1990).

8.1.3 Linear Prediction

Linear prediction is an important topic in the field of digital signal processing. Given $M+1$ input data samples, $x_n, x_{n-1}, x_{n-2}, \ldots, x_{n-M}$, the difference between the processes of sample filtering and prediction is that the

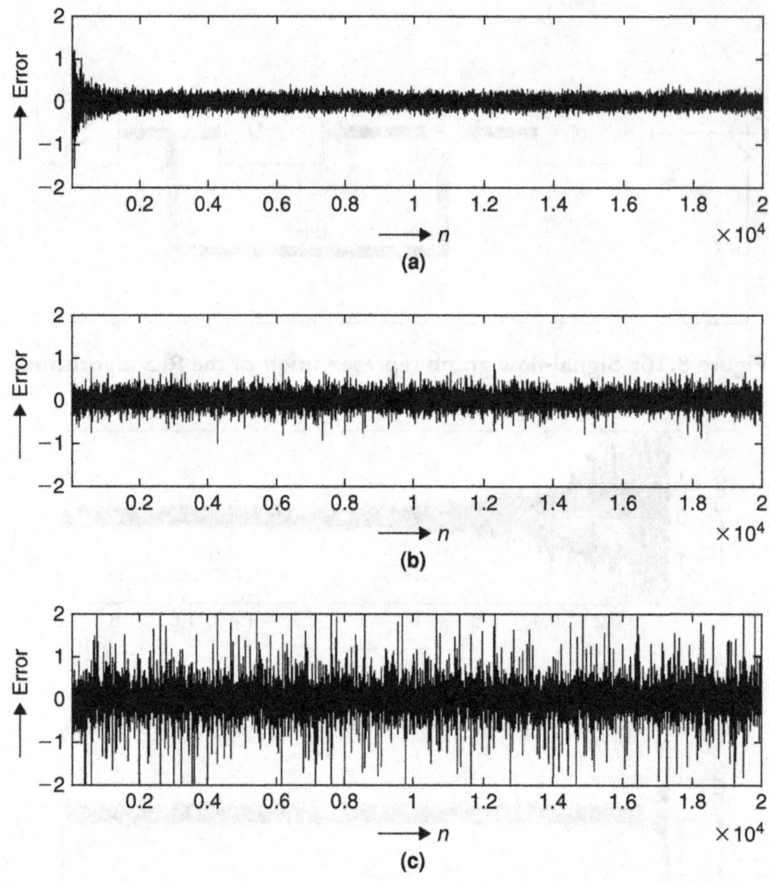

Figure 8.18: Convergence of *a priori* estimation error with RLS algorithm for various values of forgetting factor. (a) $\lambda = 1.0$. (b) $\lambda = 0.5$. (c) $\lambda = 0.1$.

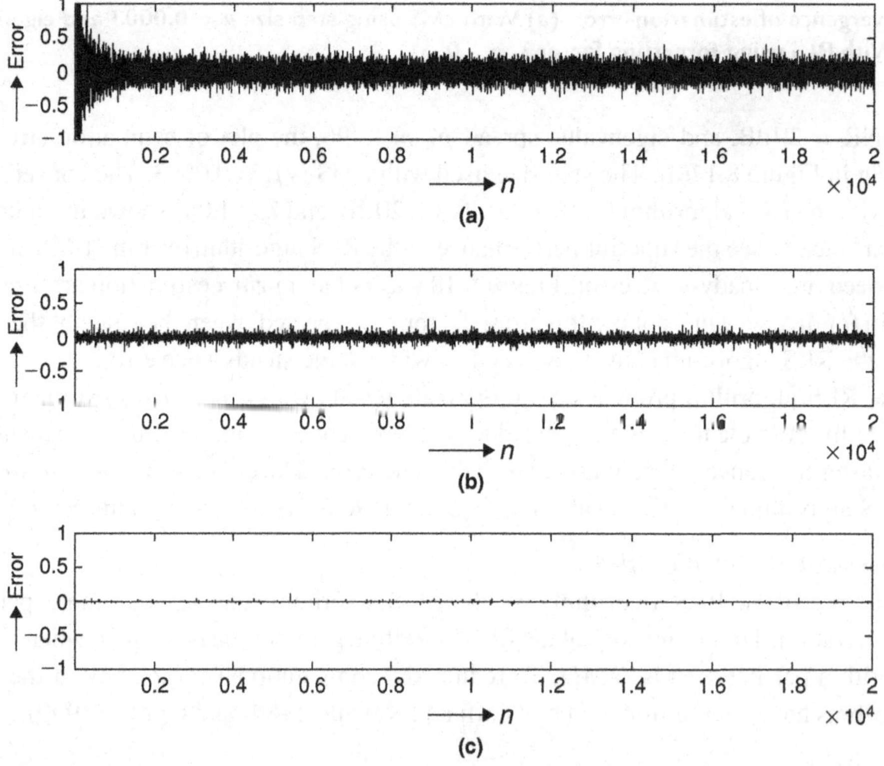

Figure 8.19: Convergence of *a posteriori* estimation error with RLS algorithm for various values of forgetting factor. (a) $\lambda = 1.0$. (b) $\lambda = 0.5$. (c) $\lambda = 0.1$.

former produces the output at time index n by using the data samples measured up to and including time instance n, whereas the latter produces the sample at instance m (where $m = n + v - 1$) by using the data samples measured up to time instance n and including time instance n. As discussed in Chapter 7, the M-th-order digital FIR filters produce output y_n at time instance n using current and previous M input data samples, $\{x_k\}_{k=n-M}^{k=n}$. Similarly, the M-th-order digital IIR filter produces output y_n at time instance n using the current input data sample and previous M input data samples, $\{x_k\}_{k=n-M}^{k=n}$, and previous N output data samples, $\{y_k\}_{k=n-N}^{k=n-1}$. In the case of linear prediction, we output a sample y_m at time instance m (where $m = n + v - 1$) using the previous $M + 1$ input data samples $\{x_k\}_{k=n-M}^{k=n}$ and using previous N output data samples $\{y_k\}_{k=n-N}^{k=n-1}$. In other words, we predict the sample y_m (which is v samples ahead) using the *linear combination* of the input sample at time instant n, and using few previous input and output samples as described with the difference equation,

$$y_m = G\sum_{l=0}^{M} b_l x_{n-l} - \sum_{k=1}^{N} a_k\, y_{n-k} \tag{8.55}$$

where $\{a_k\}$ and $\{b_l\}$(with $b_0 = 1$) are called predictor coefficients, G is the gain, and $\varepsilon_m = x_m - y_m$ is termed the prediction error. In this section, we discuss the *one-step* predictor (i.e., $v = 1$, or $m = n$), which is widely used in digital-media-compression applications.

Given a particular sample $\{y_n\}$, the problem is to determine the one-step predictor coefficients $\{a_k\}$ and $\{b_l\}$, and the gain G. The predictor can also be specified in the frequency domain by taking the z-transform on both sides of Equation (8.55). If $H[z]$ is the system function of the predictor, then

$$H[z] = \frac{B[z]}{A[z]} = G\frac{1+\sum_{l=1}^{M} b_l z^{-l}}{1+\sum_{k=1}^{N} a_k z^{-k}} \tag{8.56}$$

The process described by Equation (8.56) is also called the autoregressive moving-average (ARMA) process (or pole–zero model). If $M = 0$, then the resulting process is called the autoregressive (AR) process (or all-pole model); if $N = 0$, it is called the moving-average (MA) process (or all-zero model). Of all models, the AR model is the most widely used in practice because any process can be approximated with fewer AR model coefficients.

Linear-prediction-based source coding is widely used in speech compression applications. In general, speech compression can be achieved with waveform-based or model-based methods. Linear-predictive-coding (LPC)–based speech compression is the most widely used model-based source-coding technique. To analyze the speech signals, we consider a simplified vocal tract model of speech production as shown in Figure 8.20. With linear-prediction-based speech compression, instead of transmitting the digitized speech as is, we transmit the perceptual parameters of speech (e.g., pitch, gain, voiced/unvoiced, vocal tract model, codebook addresses for residual error, etc.) to reduce the data bandwidth requirements. The source that generates speech is not stationary, and hence the spectral characteristics of speech vary with time. However, in practice, we assume that the spectral characteristics of speech are stationary over segments between 20 and 50 ms, and hence process it segment by segment. We

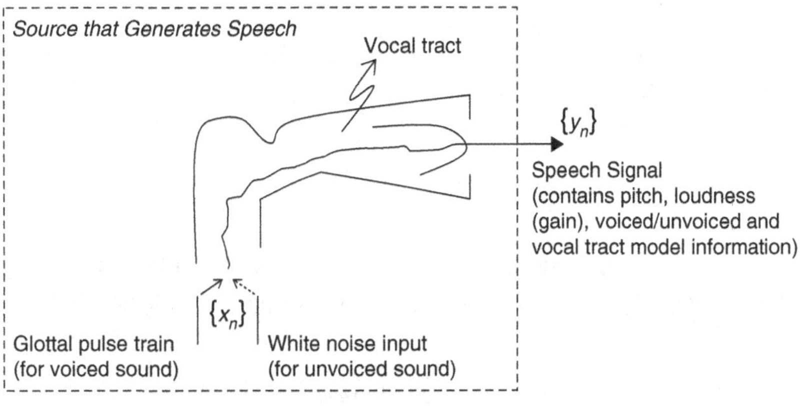

Figure 8.20: Simplified model for speech signal production.

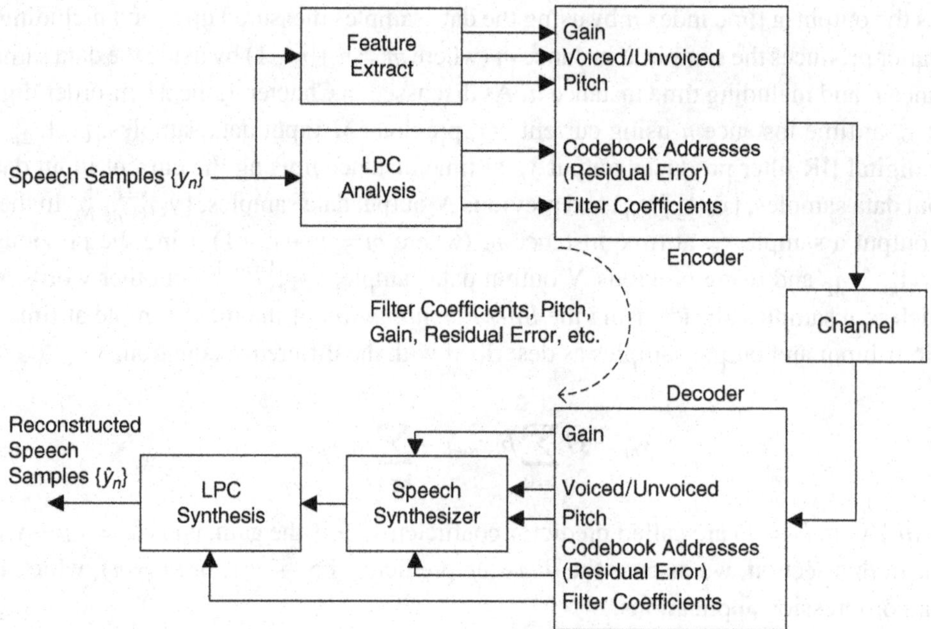

Figure 8.21: Linear-prediction-based speech compression.

model the vocal tract using a linear filter, and the filter coefficients are updated periodically to cope with the source variations that generate speech.

The LPC system comprises an analysis filter at the transmitter and a synthesis filter at the receiver as shown in Figure 8.21. Redundancy in a speech signal is removed by passing the signal through a speech analysis filter. The output of the analysis filter is termed *residual error*. Because the residual error has a lower standard deviation and is less correlated than the speech itself, fewer bits are required to represent the quantized residual error. This residual error along with the filter coefficients and other parameters are encoded and transmitted to the receiver. At the receiver, the speech is reconstructed by passing the decoded residual error signal through the synthesis filter (whose coefficients are decoded from the received bitstream). Since the speech signals are quasi-wide-sense stationary, the filter model is valid only over short periods. The filter coefficients have to be updated with time. The LPC filter spectral response is very sensitive to coefficient quantization; hence, these coefficients are transformed to a different set of parameters, called *line spectral pairs* (LSP), that are insensitive to quantization. Our interest in this section is focused on the linear prediction module (i.e., generating the filter coefficients and residual error).

With LPC, we assume that the speech samples have been generated by an all-pole discrete-time filter having the transfer function,

$$H[z] = \frac{G}{1 + \sum_{k=1}^{N} a_k z^{-k}} \tag{8.57}$$

With such an N-th order all-pole filter, the output sequence y_n is obtained as linear combinations of past values and current input x_n, as described in Equation (8.58).

$$y_n = Gx_n - \sum_{k=1}^{N} a_k \, y_{n-k} \tag{8.58}$$

In many applications (e.g., in speech production), the input x_n is wholly unknown. In such cases, the sample y_n can be predicted approximately by using a linear combination of past samples:

$$\hat{y}_n = -\sum_{k=1}^{N} a_k \, y_{n-k} \tag{8.59}$$

Then the error ε_n between the actual sample y_n and the predicted sample $\hat{y}_n$ is given by $\varepsilon_n = y_n - \hat{y}_n$:

$$\varepsilon_n = y_n + \sum_{k=1}^{N} a_k \, y_{n-k} \tag{8.60}$$

The predictor coefficients $\{a_k\}$ are obtained by minimizing the mean-square value of the prediction error ε_n. The minimum mean-square value E_N (where N represents the order of filter) is obtained with the optimum filter coefficients $\{a'_k\}$. Based on Equation (8.14), for the optimum condition, the error sequence ε_n is orthogonal to y_{n-k}, that is,

$$E\left[\varepsilon_n \, y_{n-k}\right] = 0, \quad 1 \le k \le N \tag{8.61}$$

Equation (8.61) results in the following normal equations:

$$R\,\underline{a'} = \underline{r} \tag{8.62}$$

where

$$R = \begin{bmatrix} r(0) & r(1) & \cdots & r(N-1) \\ r(1) & r(0) & \cdots & r(N-2) \\ \vdots & \vdots & \ddots & \vdots \\ r(N-1) & r(N-2) & \cdots & r(0) \end{bmatrix} \tag{8.63}$$

$$\underline{a'} = [a'_1 \, a'_2 \cdots a'_N]^T \text{ and } \underline{r} = -[r(1)\, r(2) \cdots r(N)]^T \tag{8.64}$$

Assuming that the signal is stationary over the segment of L samples, the elements $r(i)$ of matrix R can be approximately computed as follows:

$$r(i) = \sum_{n=0}^{L-1-i} y_n \, y_{n+i} \tag{8.65}$$

To solve the normal equations in Equation (8.62) for optimum predictor coefficients $\{a'_k\}$, traditional techniques such as Gauss elimination or QR decomposition can be used and the complexity of either of those methods is $O(N^3)$. However, because the matrix R is a Toeplitz matrix, the complexity of solving normal equations can be reduced to $O(N^2)$ with the Levinson-Durbin algorithm, to be discussed later in this section.

Once the predictor coefficients are found, Equation (8.60) can be used to compute the prediction error sequence ε_n. Then the gain, G, of the speech generation model is obtained by computing the variance of prediction error:

$$G^2 = E_N = r(0) + \sum_{k=1}^{N} a_k r(k) \tag{8.66}$$

Based on Equation (8.60), the analysis filter generates the error sequence $\{\varepsilon_n\}$ by taking the sequence $\{y_n\}$ as input. In contrast, the synthesis filter reconstructs the sequence $\{y_n\}$ by taking the error sequence $\{\varepsilon_n\}$ as input. This is shown in Figure 8.22(a) and (b). Based on Equation (8.60), the transfer function $A[z]$ is obtained as follows:

$$A[z] = 1 + \sum_{k=1}^{N} a_k z^{-k} \tag{8.67}$$

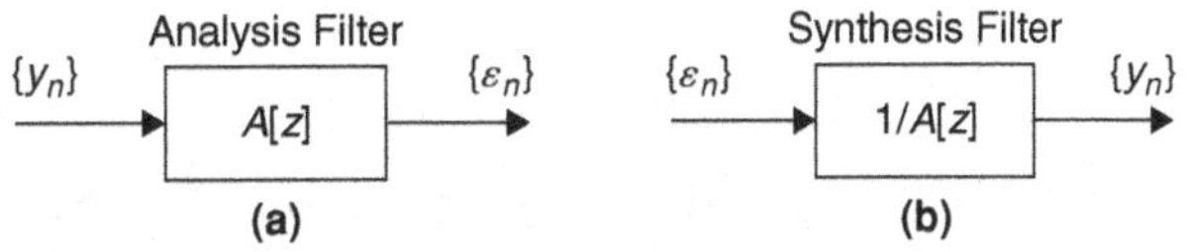

Figure 8.22: LPC. (a) Analysis filter. (b) Synthesis filter.

The Levinson-Durbin algorithm, using the Toeplitz properties of matrix R, proceeds to find the predictor coefficients $\{a_k\}$ recursively, beginning with a first-order predictor and iteratively increasing the order of the predictor filter up to the order N. Based on Equation (8.66), the final expression for prediction error variance becomes

$$E_N = r(0) + a_1 r(1) + a_2 r(2) + \cdots + a_N r(N) \tag{8.68}$$

We start with the 0-th order filter (or $i = 0$), and E_i can be expressed in this case as

$$E_0 = r(0) \tag{8.69}$$

For $i = 1$,

$$E_1 = r(0) + a_1^{(1)} r(1) \tag{8.70}$$

The superscript 1 in $a_1^{(1)}$ indicates the coefficient value when the prediction order $i = 1$. Based on Equation (8.62), the solution is simply

$$a_1^{(1)} = -r(1)/r(0) = -r(1)/E_0 = p_1 \tag{8.71}$$

Based on Equations (8.70) and (8.71),

$$E_1 = r(0) + p_1 r(1) = r(0)\left(1 - p_1^2\right) = E_0\left(1 - p_1^2\right) \tag{8.72}$$

For $i = 2$,

$$E_2 = r(0) + a_1^{(2)} r(1) + a_2^{(2)} r(2) \tag{8.73}$$

or

$$\begin{bmatrix} r(0) & r(1) & r(2) \\ r(1) & r(0) & r(1) \\ r(2) & r(1) & r(0) \end{bmatrix} \begin{bmatrix} 1 \\ a_1^{(2)} \\ a_2^{(2)} \end{bmatrix} = \begin{bmatrix} E_2 \\ 0 \\ 0 \end{bmatrix} \tag{8.74}$$

Assume that the solution can be expressed as

$$\begin{bmatrix} 1 \\ a_1^{(2)} \\ a_2^{(2)} \end{bmatrix} = \begin{bmatrix} 1 \\ a_1^{(1)} \\ 0 \end{bmatrix} + p_2 \begin{bmatrix} 0 \\ a_1^{(1)} \\ 1 \end{bmatrix} \tag{8.75}$$

Then, based on Equations (8.74) and (8.75),

$$\begin{bmatrix} r(0) & r(1) & r(2) \\ r(1) & r(0) & r(1) \\ r(2) & r(1) & r(0) \end{bmatrix} \left\{ \begin{bmatrix} 1 \\ a_1^{(1)} \\ 0 \end{bmatrix} + p_2 \begin{bmatrix} 0 \\ a_1^{(1)} \\ 1 \end{bmatrix} \right\} = \begin{bmatrix} E_2 \\ 0 \\ 0 \end{bmatrix} \tag{8.76}$$

$$\Rightarrow \begin{bmatrix} E_1 \\ 0 \\ q_2 \end{bmatrix} + p_2 \begin{bmatrix} q_2 \\ 0 \\ E_1 \end{bmatrix} = \begin{bmatrix} E_2 \\ 0 \\ 0 \end{bmatrix} \tag{8.77}$$

where

$$q_2 = r(2) + a_1^{(1)} r(1) \tag{8.78}$$

Based on Equation (8.77), the values of p_2 and E_2 are given by

$$p_2 = -q_2/E_1 \tag{8.79}$$

$$E_2 = E_1 + p_2 q_2 = E_1 - E_1 p_2^2 = E_1(1 - p_2^2) \tag{8.80}$$

With this, the predictor coefficients for $i = 2$ can be obtained from Equation (8.76) as

$$a_1^{(2)} = a_1^{(1)} + p_2 a_1^{(1)} \quad (8.81)$$

$$a_2^{(2)} = p_2 \quad (8.82)$$

The recursive solution for computing the predictor coefficients for $i > 2$ can be performed with the following steps:

$$(1)\quad q_i = r(i) + \sum_{j=1}^{i-1} q_j^{(i-1)} r(i-j) \quad (8.83a)$$

$$(2)\quad p_i = -q_i / E_{i-1} \quad (8.83b)$$

$$(3)\quad a_i^{(i)} = p_i \quad (8.83c)$$

$$(4)\quad a_j^{(i)} = a_j^{(i-1)} + p_i a_{i-j}^{(i-1)}, \quad j = 1, 2, \ldots, i-1 \quad (8.83d)$$

$$(5)\quad E_i = E_{i-1}\left(1 - p_i^2\right) \quad (8.83e)$$

Based on these results, we perform $2i + 1$ MAC (multiply and accumulate) operations in computing the Levinson-Durbin i-th iteration using the above steps. Thus, the total number of MAC operations to compute the prediction coefficients for the prediction order N becomes

$$\sum_{i=1}^{N} (2i + 1) = N(N + 2)$$

In other words, the complexity of the Levinson-Durbin method is $N^2 + O(N)$ operations. The intermediate quantities p_i, $1 \le i \le N$, are known as *reflection coefficients*. For the stability of the linear prediction filter, the reflection coefficients must satisfy the following condition:

$$|p_i| < 1, \quad 1 \le i \le N \quad (8.84)$$

The reflection coefficients $\{p_i\}$ can easily be obtained from Equations (8.83c) and (8.83d), given the prediction coefficients $\{a_j^{(i)}\}$, $1 \le j \le i - 1$.

8.1.4 Lattice Filters

Lattice filters are widely used in prediction applications. In this section, LPC is implemented in a lattice form using reflection coefficients. As the absolute values of reflection coefficients are never greater than 1, the lattice structures are always stable. In addition, the reflection coefficients guarantee the stability of the filter on quantization as they have a well-defined dynamic range. Consequently, reflection coefficient–based lattice structures are often used to represent a vocal tract filter.

In the previous section, we discussed the computation of N prediction coefficients recursively using the Levinson-Durbin algorithm. The N prediction coefficients are equivalent to N reflection coefficients since the prediction coefficients and reflection coefficients are related as given in Equations (8.83c) and (8.83d). Based on Equation (8.60), the error (also called forward prediction error) expressions of $(N - 1)$th- and N-th-order filters can be expressed as follows:

$$\varepsilon_n^{(N-1)} = y_n + \sum_{k=1}^{N-1} a_k^{(N-1)} y_{n-k} \quad (8.85)$$

$$\varepsilon_n^{(N)} = y_n + \sum_{k=1}^{N} a_k^{(N)} y_{n-k} \quad (8.86)$$

In the same way, if we predict the backward sample y_{n-N} based on N ahead samples $y_n, y_{n-1}, \ldots, y_{n-N+1}$, the backward prediction errors $\delta_n^{(N-1)}$ and $\delta_n^{(N)}$ of $(N-1)$th and N-th-order filters can be expressed as follows:

$$\delta_n^{(N-1)} = y_{n-N+1} + \sum_{k=1}^{N-1} a_k^{(N-1)} y_{n-N+1+k} \tag{8.87}$$

$$\delta_n^{(N)} = y_{n-N} + \sum_{k=1}^{N} a_k^{(N)} y_{n-N+k} \tag{8.88}$$

Based on Equations (8.83c), (8.83d), and (8.86),

$$\begin{aligned}
\varepsilon_n^{(N)} &= y_n + \sum_{k=1}^{N} a_k^{(N)} y_{n-k} = y_n + \sum_{k=1}^{N-1} a_k^{(N)} y_{n-k} + a_N^{(N)} y_{n-N} \\
&= y_n + \sum_{k=1}^{N-1} \left(a_k^{(N-1)} + p_N a_{N-k}^{(N-1)}\right) y_{n-k} + p_N y_{n-N} \\
&= y_n + \sum_{k=1}^{N-1} a_k^{(N-1)} y_{n-k} + p_N \sum_{k=1}^{N-1} a_{N-k}^{(N-1)} y_{n-k} + p_N y_{n-N} \\
&= \varepsilon_n^{(N-1)} + p_N \left[\sum_{k=1}^{N-1} a_{N-k}^{(N-1)} y_{n-k} + y_{n-N}\right] \\
&= \varepsilon_n^{(N-1)} + p_N \left[y_{n-N} + \sum_{k=1}^{N-1} a_k^{(N-1)} y_{n-N+k}\right]
\end{aligned} \tag{8.89}$$

From Equations (8.87) and (8.89),

$$\varepsilon_n^{(N)} = \varepsilon_n^{(N-1)} + p_N \delta_{n-1}^{(N-1)} \tag{8.90}$$

Similarly, based on Equations (8.83c), (8.83d), (8.87), and (8.88),

$$\delta_n^{(N)} = \delta_{n-1}^{(N-1)} + p_N \varepsilon_n^{(N-1)} \tag{8.91}$$

We can represent Equations (8.90) and (8.91) compactly using the following matrix notation:

$$\begin{bmatrix} \varepsilon_n^{(N)} \\ \delta_n^{(N)} \end{bmatrix} = \begin{bmatrix} 1 & p_N \\ p_N & 1 \end{bmatrix} \begin{bmatrix} \varepsilon_n^{(N-1)} \\ \delta_{n-1}^{(N-1)} \end{bmatrix} \tag{8.92}$$

Equation (8.92) describes the lattice filter i-th stage as shown in Figure 8.23(a). The lattice implementation of the LPC analysis filter using reflection coefficients is shown in Figure 8.23(b). Basically, we compute N reflection coefficients from the given segment of speech samples and obtain the residual error ε_n by passing the speech samples y_n through the N-th order analysis filter. At the receiver, we use the corresponding synthesis filter to construct the speech samples $\hat{y}_n$ from the quantized residual error $\hat{\varepsilon}_n$. The lattice implementation of the LPC synthesis filter using reflection coefficients is shown in Figure 8.24. For the synthesis filter, the input comprises quantized error (i.e., $\varepsilon_n^{(N)} = \hat{\varepsilon}_n$), and the output comprises reconstructed speech samples, $\hat{y}_n = \varepsilon_n^{(0)}$. The i-th stage of synthesis filter is governed by the following set of linear equations:

$$\varepsilon_n^{(N-1)} = \varepsilon_n^{(N)} - p_N \delta_{n-1}^{(N-1)} \tag{8.93}$$

$$\delta_n^{(N)} = \delta_{n-1}^{(N-1)} + p_N \varepsilon_n^{(N-1)} \tag{8.94}$$

The intermediate prediction errors in a lattice are orthogonal to each other and as a consequence of the orthogonality, the various sections of the lattice exhibit a form of independence that allows us to add or delete one or

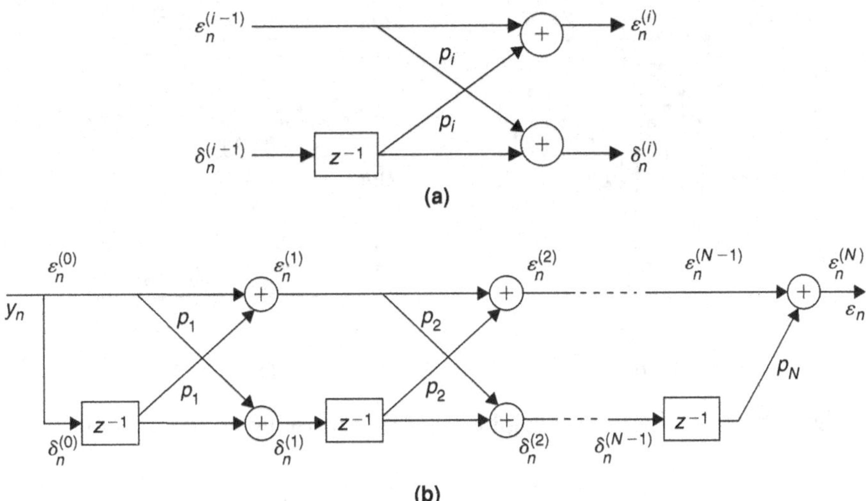

Figure 8.23: Lattice filter realization. (a) *i*-th stage. (b) *N*-th-order LPC filter.

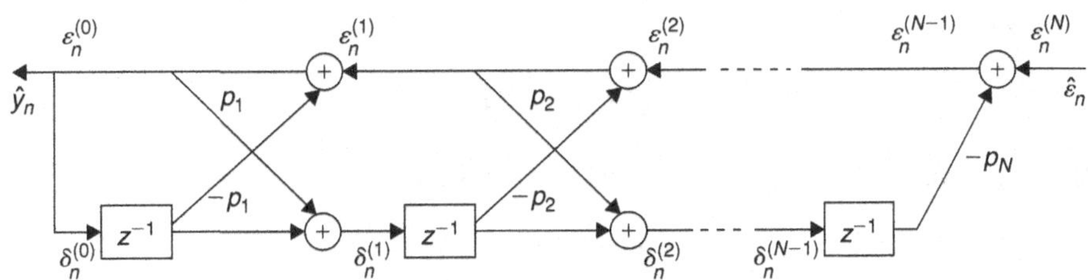

Figure 8.24: Lattice filter realization of *N*-th-order LPC synthesis filter.

more of the last stages without affecting the parameters of the remaining stages. The power of the prediction error decreases with increasing lattice order. Typically, the first few reflection coefficients are of greater magnitude, which drop to values close to zero in later stages. Although the operation of lattice filters is usually described in the prediction context, the application of lattice filters is not limited to prediction applications. For example, since backward prediction errors are orthogonal to each other, we can perform orthogonal transformation (in the way similar to Gram-Schmidt orthogonalization) with the lattice filter on input samples to get the uncorrelated output samples from N stages of the backward predictor.

8.2 Multirate Signal Processing

To this point, we have discussed digital processing when data was sampled at a frequency greater than or equal to the Nyquist frequency. The same sampling rate is assumed across all modules. However, in many applications, sampling signals at different frequencies at different stages of a digital system may be required. For example, audio signals are handled at 48 kHz in studio work, while the CD (compact disc) production rate is 44.1 kHz and the broadcast rate is 32 kHz. One obvious way to change the sampling rate is to switch from the digital to the analog domain and sampling the analog signal again with a new sampling frequency. This approach, however, may result in signal degradation, and it also requires high-quality antialiasing analog filters. Using multirate techniques is the alternative method for changing the sampling rate. Multirate processing is basically an efficient digital technique for changing the signal sampling frequency. Many applications take advantage of multirate processing techniques to avoid the use of expensive antialiasing analog filters to reduce computational costs and to efficiently handle the signals sampled at different frequencies.

8.2.1 Downsampler and Upsampler

The two important building blocks of multirate signal processing are the downsampler (or decimator) and upsampler (or interpolator). The downsampler is used to decrease the sampling rate of a signal, whereas the

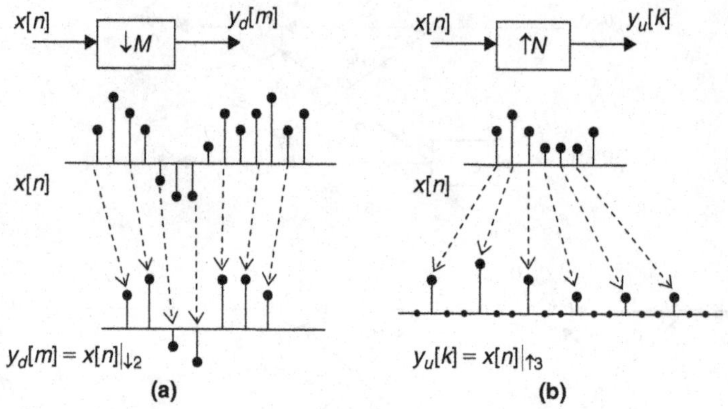

Figure 8.25: Multirate building blocks. (a) Downsampler. (b) Upsampler.

upsampler is used to increase the sampling rate. We use the symbol $\downarrow M$ to denote the downsampler that decreases the sampling rate by M-fold, and $\uparrow N$ to denote the upsampler that increases the sampling rate by N-fold. This is illustrated in Figure 8.25. Mathematically, we can express the output $y_d[m]$ of the downsampler in terms of its input $x[n]$ as follows:

$$y_d[m] = x[Mn] \tag{8.95}$$

Similarly, the output $y_u[k]$ of the upsampler can be expressed in terms of its input $x[n]$,

$$y_u[k] = \begin{cases} x[n/N] & \text{if } n = kN \\ 0 & \text{if } n \neq kN \end{cases} \tag{8.96}$$

where k, M, and N are integers.

We are also curious about what is going to happen in the frequency domain with the sample rate conversion forced on the input sequence $x[n]$ with either the downsampler or upsampler. Based on (Vaidyanathan, 1992), the expressions for $Y_d(\Omega)$ and $Y_u(\Omega)$ in terms of $X(\Omega)$ are given by

$$Y_d(\Omega) = \frac{1}{M}\sum_{k=0}^{M-1} X\left(\frac{\Omega - 2\pi k}{M}\right) \tag{8.97}$$

$$Y_u(\Omega) = X(\Omega N) \tag{8.98}$$

The effects of downsampling or upsampling of a digital signal in the frequency domain are seen in Equations (8.97) and (8.98). As discussed in Chapter 6, the discrete-time Fourier transform $X(\Omega)$ of a signal $x[n]$ is periodic with period 2π as shown in Figure 8.26(a). When we downsample the digital signal, we lose the information during the process unless the input signal $x[n]$ is a proper band-limited signal. This results in *aliasing error* as shown in Figure 8.26(b). Aliasing can be prevented if $x[n]$ is a low-pass signal band-limited to the region $|\Omega| < \pi/M$. With upsampling of a digital signal, we do not lose information. Instead, the spectrum is compressed and multiple copies of the compressed spectrum, called *images*, are created, as shown in Figure 8.26(c). This necessitates a low-pass filtering of the signal after upsampling. This low-pass filtering results in interpolation (or filling the spaces between samples shown in Figure 8.25(b)) of samples in the time domain. Thus, in general, we require a low-pass digital filter called the *decimation filter* before the downsampler as shown in Figure 8.27(a) to ensure that the input to the downsampler is properly band-limited; and we use an *interpolation filter* as shown in Figure 8.27(b) after the upsampler to suppress the images. The downsampling and upsampling operations are the two fundamental operations in multirate signal processing. With these operations, we can increase or decrease sampling frequency without significant errors due to aliasing and quantization.

In some applications, we may need to change the sampling rate by a noninteger factor P. In such cases, we express the noninteger factor P by an approximate rational number N/M where M and N are integers.

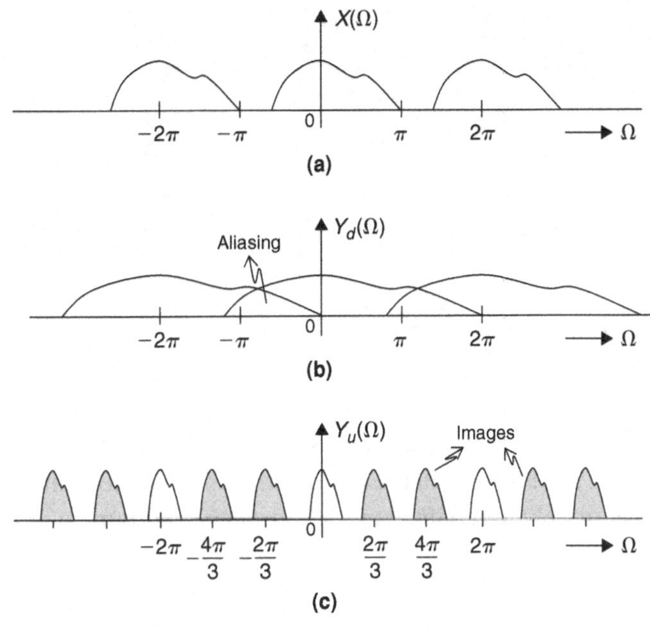

Figure 8.26: Effects of downsampler and upsampler in frequency domain. (a) Actual spectrum. (b) After downsampling by 2. (c) After upsampling by 3.

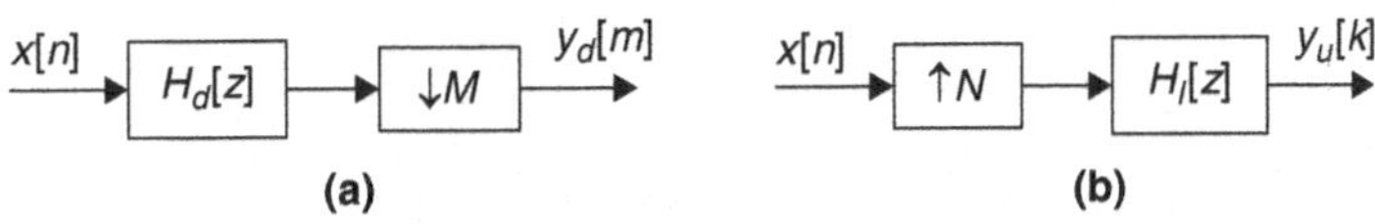

Figure 8.27: Multirate signal processing building blocks. (a) Downsampler preceded by decimation filter $H_d[z]$. (b) Upsampler followed by interpolation filter $H_i[z]$.

Figure 8.28: Multirate system with noninteger sampling factor.

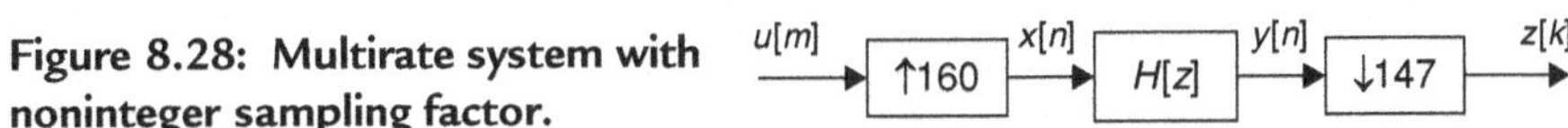

It is necessary that the upsampler process precedes the downsampler; otherwise, the downsampling process would remove some useful signal components. For example, to obtain 48-kHz audio samples from CD 44.1-kHz samples, the CD samples are upsampled by a noninteger factor of $P = 48/44.1 = 160/147$; that is, $N = 160$ and $M = 147$. Here, we can combine the interpolation filter $H_I[z]$ and decimation filter $H_d[z]$ into a single filter with the system function $H[z] = H_I[z]H_d[z]$, as shown in Figure 8.28.

Assuming a direct-form implementation of the FIR filter $H[z]$, the multirate system in Figure 8.28 can be redrawn as shown in Figure 8.29; this multirate system is computationally very inefficient for the following reasons. First, the delay line is fed with an input sample followed by $N-1$ zeros because of input upsampling by factor N. In other words, for each input sample $u[m]$ fed in, N samples of $y[n]$ are computed. Clearly, filtering of zero-value samples is unnecessary. Similarly, the filter output $y[n]$ is downsampled by a factor M, and this involves discarding $M-1$ samples from input $y[n]$ of the downsampler for each output sample $z[k]$. Since for each sample that is kept, the next $M-1$ samples of $y[n]$ are discarded, performing filtering of those samples of $y[n]$ that are discarded is unnecessary. Next, we discuss the polyphase decomposition of the system function with which we can efficiently implement the decimation and interpolation filters of multirate signal processing.

8.2.2 Polyphase Filters

The ideal setup for efficient implementation of a multirate system such as the one shown in Figure 8.29 would be to first downsample the input by factor M, followed by filtering with $H[z]$ and then upsampling the filter output

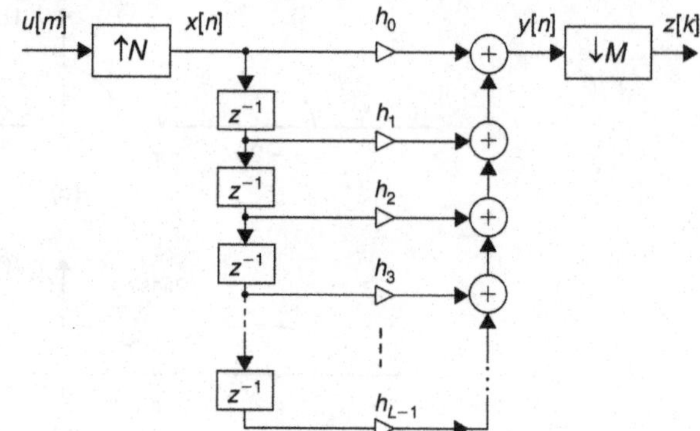

Figure 8.29: FIR filter implementation of multirate system.

by factor N. To achieve this, we use a technique called *polyphase decomposition* to implement the downsampler and upsampler. Multirate systems can be efficiently implemented with this polyphase decomposition. By separating the even-numbered coefficients of h_i from the odd-numbered coefficients in $H[z]$, we can write $H[z]$ as follows:

$$H[z] = \sum_n h_{2n} z^{-2n} + z^{-1} \sum_n h_{2n+1} z^{-2n} \tag{8.99}$$

$$H[z] = A_0[z^2] + z^{-1} A_1[z^2] \tag{8.100}$$

where

$$A_0[z] = \sum_n h_{2n} z^{-n}, \quad A_1[z] = \sum_n h_{2n+1} z^{-n} \tag{8.101}$$

The idea of decomposing the system function $H[z]$ into two subsystem functions, $A_0[z]$ and $A_1[z]$, can be extended to any integer M number of subsystem functions. In other words, we can express $H[z]$ as

$$H[z] = \sum_{k=0}^{M-1} z^{-k} A_k[z^M] \tag{8.102}$$

where

$$A_k[z] = \sum_n h_{Mn+k} z^{-n}, \quad 0 \le k \le M-1 \tag{8.103}$$

Equation (8.102) is called type-1 polyphase decomposition, with $A_k[z]$ representing the polyphase components of $H[z]$. This type-1 polyphase decomposition of the decimation filter is illustrated in Figure 8.30. As shown in Figure 8.30(c), because we first downsample the signal and then filter the downsampled sequence, the number of multiplications and additions required to perform the decimation filtering is much lower compared to straightforward implementation of the downsampler. In a similar manner, a more efficient structure can be obtained for the interpolation filter using the following type-2 polyphase decomposition:

$$H[z] = \sum_{k=0}^{N-1} z^{-(N-1-k)} B_k[z^N] \tag{8.104}$$

where

$$B_k[z] = C_{N-1-k}[z], \; C_i[z] = \sum_n h_{Nn+i} z^{-n}, \quad 0 \le k \le N-1, \; 0 \le i \le N-1 \tag{8.105}$$

Using the type-2 polyphase decomposition as given in Equation (8.104), we can implement the interpolation filter shown in Figure 8.27(b) very efficiently as shown in Figure 8.31.

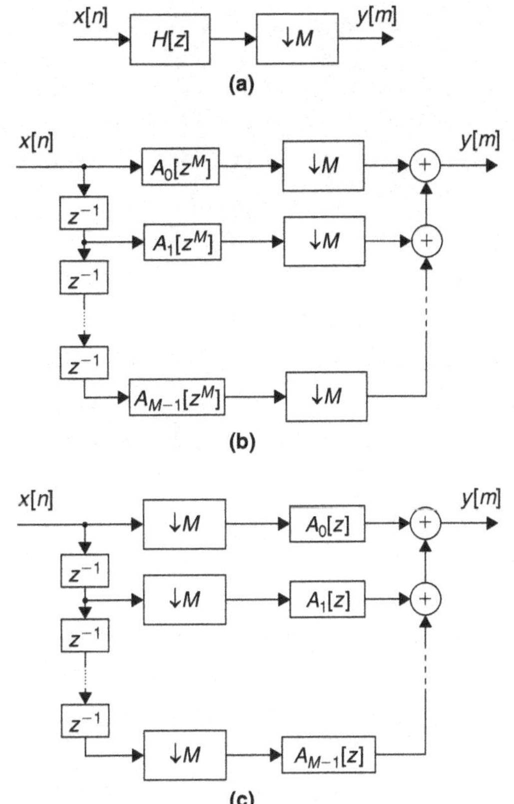

Figure 8.30: This is the polyphase implementation of M-fold decimation filter. (a) Actual decimation filter. (b) Polyphase decomposition of filter. (c) Swapping of downsampler and system functions (using noble identity property [Vaidyanathan, 1992]).

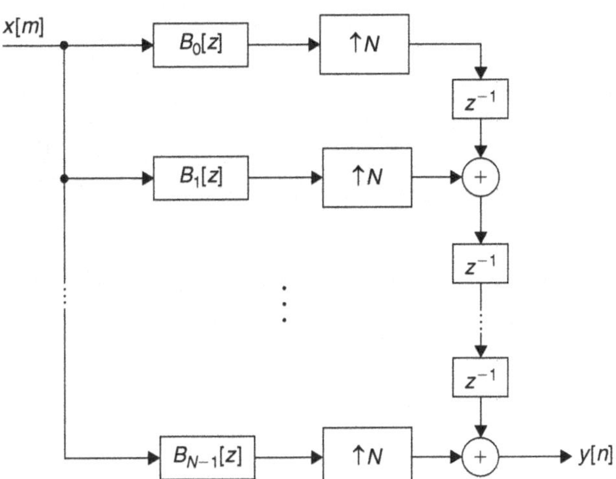

Figure 8.31: This is the polyphase implementation of interpolation filter.

Example 8.1

Given filter length $L = 9$ and upsampling factor $N = 3$, show that the schematics in Figures 8.27(b) and 8.31 essentially output the same samples with the following five input samples: $x = \{x_0, x_1, x_2, x_3, x_4\}$. Assume that the $L\ (= 9)$ filter coefficients are $h = \{h_0, h_1, h_2, \ldots, h_8\}$.

Case 1: Direct-Form Implementation

Using Figure 8.27(b), the upsampler output is obtained by inserting $N(= 3)$ zeros between every two input samples, that is,

$$x' = \{x_0, 0, 0, x_1, 0, 0, x_2, 0, 0, x_3, 0, 0, x_4\}$$

The upsampled sequence y is obtained by convolving the two sequences x' and h as follows:

$$
\begin{array}{lll}
y_0 = h_0x_0, & y_1 = h_1x_0, & y_2 = h_2x_0 \\
y_3 = h_0x_1 + h_3x_0, & y_4 = h_1x_1 + h_4x_0, & y_5 = h_2x_1 + h_5x_0 \\
y_6 = h_0x_2 + h_3x_1 + h_6x_0, & y_7 = h_1x_2 + h_4x_1 + h_7x_0, & y_8 = h_2x_2 + h_5x_1 + h_8x_0 \\
y_9 = h_0x_3 + h_3x_2 + h_6x_1, & y_{10} = h_1x_3 + h_4x_2 + h_7x_1, & y_{11} = h_2x_3 + h_5x_2 + h_8x_1 \\
y_{12} = h_0x_4 + h_3x_3 + h_6x_2, & y_{13} = h_1x_4 + h_4x_3 + h_7x_2, & y_{14} = h_2x_4 + h_5x_3 + h_8x_2 \\
y_{15} = h_3x_4 + h_6x_3, & y_{16} = h_4x_4 + h_7x_3, & y_{17} = h_5x_4 + h_8x_3 \\
y_{18} = h_6x_4, & y_{19} = h_7x_4, & h_{20} = h_8x_4
\end{array}
$$

Although we see a few MAC operations per output y_n in the preceding calculations, in the actual implementation there are $L(=9)$ MAC operations. In this way, we avoid conditional computation. For example, the output sample y_{10} is computed using the convolution sum without any conditional checks as follows:

$$y_{10} = h_0 \cdot 0 + h_1x_3 + h_2 \cdot 0 + h_3 \cdot 0 + h_4x_2 + h_5 \cdot 0 + h_6 \cdot 0 + h_7x_1 + h_8 \cdot 0$$

Case 2: Polyphase Implementation

Here, we compute the upsampler outputs with polyphase decomposition of the interpolation filter. Based on Equation (8.105), the filters $B_0[z]$, $B_1[z]$, and $B_2[z]$ follow:

$$B_0[z] = h_2 + h_5z^{-1} + h_8z^{-2}, \quad B_1[z] = h_1 + h_4z^{-1} + h_7z^{-2}, \quad B_2[z] = h_0 + h_3z^{-1} + h_6z^{-2}$$

Next, the convolution of input x and polyphase filters $B_i[z]$ are obtained as follows:

$$
\begin{array}{ll}
B_0: & h_2x_0,\ h_2x_1 + h_5x_0,\ h_2x_2 + h_5x_1 + h_8x_0,\ h_2x_3 + h_5x_2 + h_8x_1, \\
 & h_2x_4 + h_5x_3 + h_8x_2,\ h_5x_4 + h_8x_3,\ h_8x_4 \\
B_1: & h_1x_0,\ h_1x_1 + h_4x_0,\ h_1x_2 + h_4x_1 + h_7x_0,\ h_1x_3 + h_4x_2 + h_7x_1, \\
 & h_1x_4 + h_4x_3 + h_7x_2,\ h_4x_4 + h_7x_3,\ h_7x_4 \\
B_2: & h_0x_0,\ h_0x_1 + h_3x_0,\ h_0x_2 + h_3x_1 + h_6x_0,\ h_0x_3 + h_3x_2 + h_6x_1, \\
 & h_0x_4 + h_3x_3 + h_6x_2,\ h_3x_4 + h_6x_3,\ h_6x_4
\end{array}
$$

The upsampled filter outputs with proper delay as shown in Figure 8.31 are tabulated as follows:

B_0	B_1	B_2	y_n
0	0	h_0x_0	h_0x_0
0	h_1x_0	0	h_1x_0
h_2x_0	0	0	h_2x_0
0	0	$h_0x_1+h_3x_0$	$h_0x_1+h_3x_0$
0	$h_1x_1+h_4x_0$	0	$h_1x_1+h_4x_0$
$h_2x_1+h_5x_0$	0	0	$h_2x_1+h_5x_0$
0	0	$h_0x_2+h_3x_1+h_6x_0$	$h_0x_2+h_3x_1+h_6x_0$
0	$h_1x_2+h_4x_1+h_7x_0$	0	$h_1x_2+h_4x_1+h_7x_0$
$h_2x_2+h_5x_1+h_8x_0$	0	0	$h_2x_2+h_5x_1+h_8x_0$
0	0	$h_0x_3+h_3x_2+h_6x_1$	$h_0x_3+h_3x_2+h_6x_1$
0	$h_1x_3+h_4x_2+h_7x_1$	0	$h_1x_3+h_4x_2+h_7x_1$
$h_2x_3+h_5x_2+h_8x_1$	0	0	$h_2x_3+h_5x_2+h_8x_1$
0	0	$h_0x_4+h_3x_3+h_6x_2$	$h_0x_4+h_3x_3+h_6x_2$
0	$h_1x_4+h_4x_3+h_7x_2$	0	$h_1x_4+h_4x_3+h_7x_2$
$h_2x_4+h_5x_3+h_8x_2$	0	0	$h_2x_4+h_5x_3+h_8x_2$
0	0	$h_3x_4+h_6x_3$	$h_3x_4+h_6x_3$
0	$h_4x_4+h_7x_3$	0	$h_4x_4+h_7x_3$

$h_5x_4 + h_8x_3$	0	0	$h_5x_4 + h_8x_3$
0	0	h_6x_4	h_6x_4
0	h_7x_4	0	h_7x_4
h_8x_4	0	0	h_8x_4

Both the direct-form and polyphase implementation of the upsampler provide the same outputs. From the computational point of view, the direct-form implementation requires L MAC operations per output, whereas polyphase implementation requires only L/N MAC operations per output.

■

Using the polyphase structures of decimation and interpolation filters, we can efficiently implement the multirate system shown in Figure 8.29. For simplicity, we choose $M = 4$ and $N = 3$. The successive redrawings in Figure 8.32 show how the polyphase decomposition techniques lead to efficient implementation of noninteger sampling conversion. As long as factors M and N are relatively prime, we can swap the consecutive downsampler and upsampler operations without losing information. The final structure for noninteger sampling conversion is shown in Figure 8.32(d).

For $M = 4$ and $N = 3$, we modified the multirate structure (which require LN MAC operations to compute one output sample $y[m]$, where L is the length of the filter) shown in Figure 8.29 to the most efficient structure as shown in Figure 8.32(d) by moving all the downsamplers to the left of all the computational units and the upsamplers to the right of all the computational units. This restructuring is applicable for any arbitrary M and N as long as they are relatively prime. With this restructuring, noninteger sampling conversion based on polyphase decomposition requires only L/N MAC operations per output sample. For large values of M or N, we can significantly reduce the number of computations per output sample by implementing the decimation or interpolation filters in multiple stages (Vaidyanathan, 1992).

8.2.3 Quadrature Mirror Filter Banks

Before discussing quadrature mirror filter (QMF) banks, we consider an example of processing two signals whose spectra $S(f)$ and $X(f)$ are shown in Figure 8.33. Assume that the spectrum $S(f)$ is strictly band-limited to B Hz, and the spectrum $X(f)$ contains frequencies up to $2B$ Hz. As shown in Figure 8.33(b), most of the energy in the signal spectrum $X(f)$ is in its lower frequency region (below B Hz), with only a very small percentage in the B- to $2B$-Hz region. In addition, assume that both signals are sampled with the same sampling frequency, say $4B$ Hz. Let $s[n]$ and $x[n]$ be the corresponding sampled signals. For various cost reasons (i.e., processing cost, transmitting cost, storage cost, etc.), assume that both sequences $s[n]$ and $x[n]$ are downsampled by a factor of 2 to minimize the cost of handling the sequences. Let $s_d[m]$ and $x_d[m]$ represent the downsampled sequences. Since the sequence $s_d[m]$ is strictly band-limited to B Hz (and contains $2B$ samples per second), we can completely recover the sequence $s[n]$ from its downsampled sequence $s_d[m]$. In the case of sequence $x[n]$, it is not possible to recover it from the downsampled sequence $x_d[m]$ because of aliasing.

However, since the energy of $x[n]$ frequency components is much lower in the B- to $2B$-Hz region, we can efficiently represent the signal $x[n]$ with a lower number of bits on average by assigning fewer bits to those high-frequency signal components. Thus, the average number of bits required to represent the overall signal will be reduced. To accomplish this, we decompose the signal $x[n]$ using *subband decomposition*; the technique of decomposing the source signal into constituent subbands and separately coding each subband samples efficiently is known as *subband coding*. Typically, subband decomposition is implemented with so-called *filter banks*.

A filter bank is an array of subband filters with either a common input or summed output. If the subband filters of filter bank are used to decompose the common input signal $x[n]$ into a set of subband signals $x_k[n]$, then such subband filters $H_k[z]$ are called *analysis filters*. If the subband filters of the filter bank are used to combine a set of subband signals $y_k[n]$ into a single signal $y[n]$ at its output, then such subband filters $F_k[z]$ are called *synthesis filters*. In general, the number of analysis filters is equal to the number of synthesis filters. If M subband filters are used for analysis or synthesis filters, the system is called an M-channel filter bank. Typically,

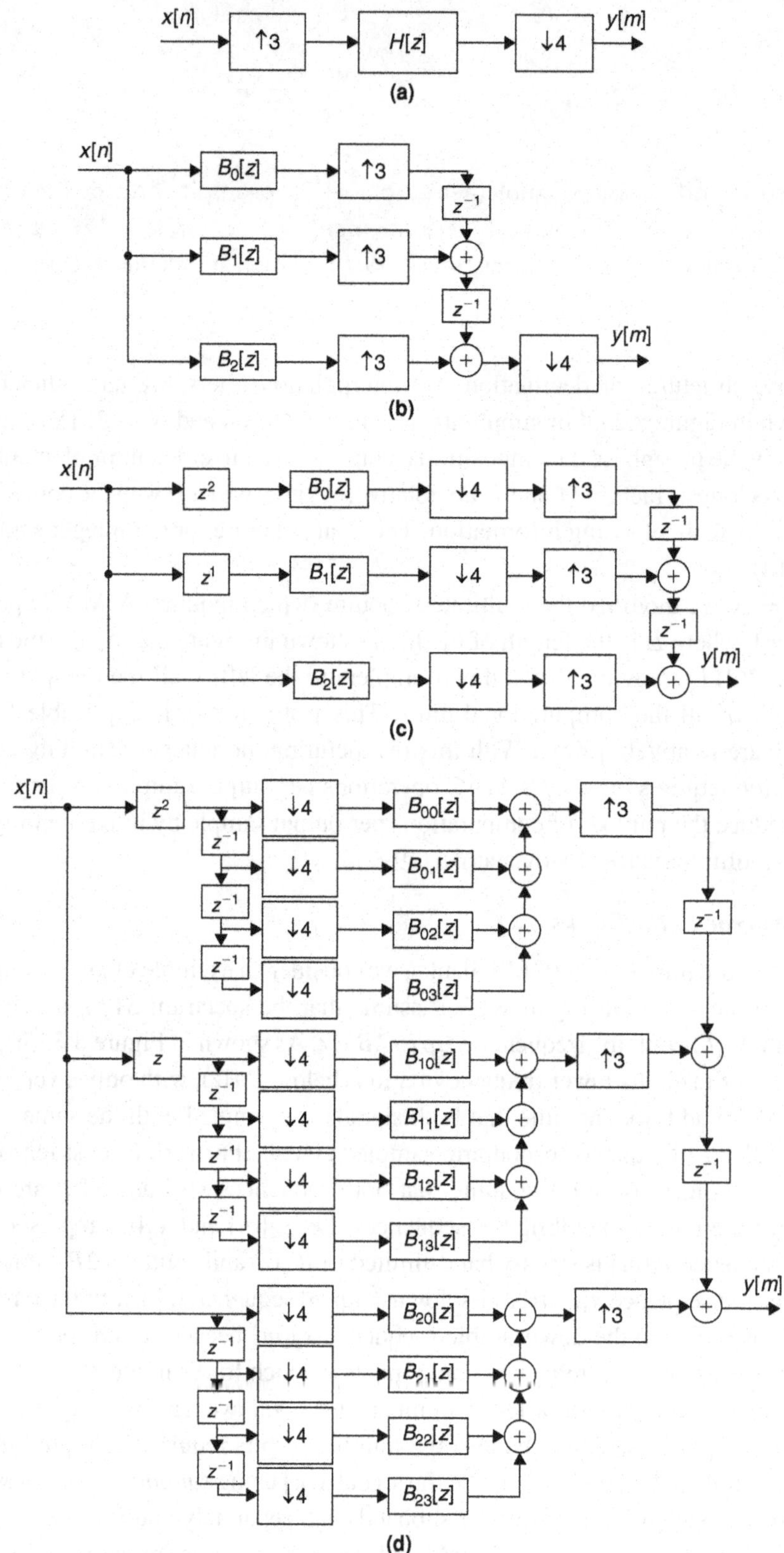

Figure 8.32: Polyphase implementation of noninteger sampling conversion.

in an M-channel filter bank, the M-analysis filters are followed by M-fold downsamplers and the M-synthesis filters are preceded by M-fold upsamplers, as shown in Figure 8.34.

Next, we discuss various frequency response characteristics of a filter bank for subband decomposition. Ideal frequency response characteristics for filter banks are shown in Figure 8.35(a). However, designing the filters with ideal frequency-response characteristics is impractical. In practice, the filters have non-zero transition

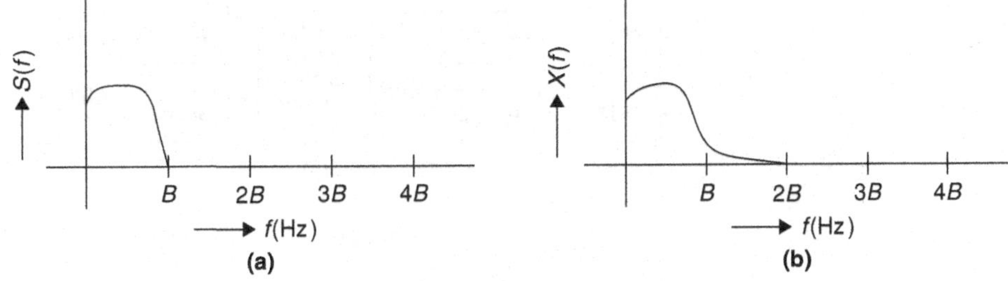

Figure 8.33: Frequency spectra. (a) Band-limited to B Hz. (b) Frequencies up to $2B$ Hz.

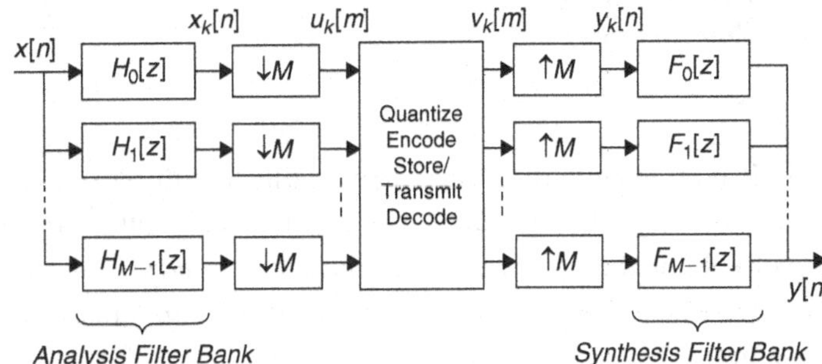

Figure 8.34: M-channel filter bank.

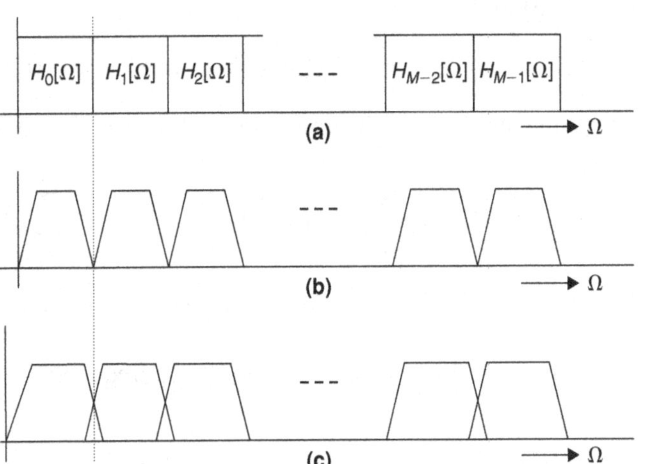

Figure 8.35: Various frequency-response characteristics of filter bank for signal subband decomposition.

bandwidth and stopband gain. Thus, the signals $x_k[n]$ are not band-limited and their decimation results in aliasing. The filters with frequency-response characteristics as shown in Figure 8.35(b) are realizable. Assuming that stopband attenuations are sufficiently large, the effect of aliasing is not severe with such realization. However, sub-band filters with frequency responses as seen in Figure 8.35(b) introduce severe attenuation of the input signal around the transition frequencies. The alternative solution is to allow overlapping of frequency responses, which minimizes signal attenuation around the transition frequencies. The drawback to this type of realization is that it introduces aliasing error, even if the filters are designed with good stopband attenuation characteristics. However, such aliasing due to overlapping can be canceled in the reconstruction process by using properly designed synthesis filters.

Here, we consider a simple two-channel filter bank for subband coding as shown in Figure 8.36(a). A discrete-time signal $x[n]$ is passed through analysis filters $H_0[z]$ and $H_1[z]$, whose frequency responses are shown in Figure 8.36(b). The frequency responses of low-pass filter $H_0[z]$ and high-pass filter $H_1[z]$ are mirror symmetric at about $\pi/2$; hence this filter bank is known as the quadrature mirror filter (QMF) bank.

The subband signals $x_k[n]$ are then downsampled by a factor of 2. Since the bandwidth of decomposed signals $x_k[n]$ is half when compared to that of the original signal $x[n]$, we do not lose any information with the downsampling process. Downsampled subband signals $u_k[m]$ are quantized and encoded by using the special characteristics of the signals, such as energy levels and perceptual characteristics. The coded subband signals are

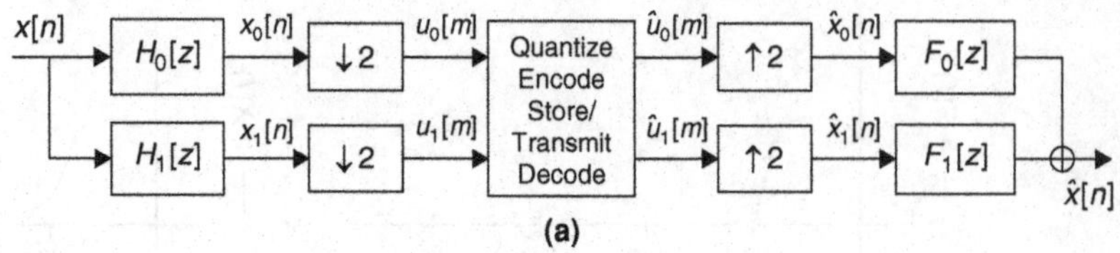

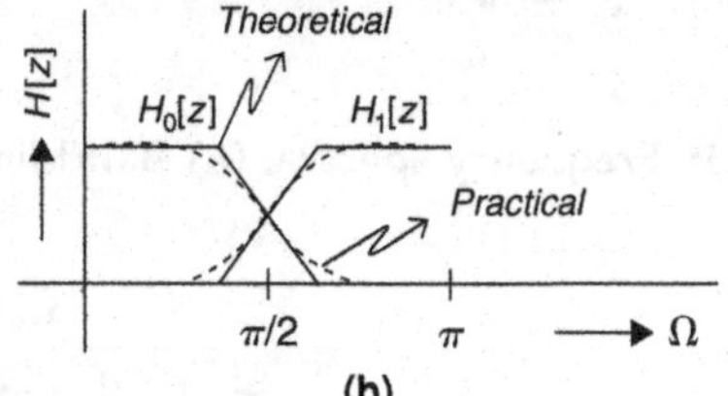

Figure 8.36: Simple multirate system. (a) Two-channel filter bank. (b) Overlapping filter frequency responses.

then multiplexed and transmitted. At the receiver, the demultiplexed subband signals are decoded first to obtain $\hat{u}_k[m]$ before upsampling. Then the upsampled subband signals $\hat{x}_k[m]$ are passed through the reconstruction or synthesis filters to obtain the estimate $\hat{x}[n]$ of the transmitted signal $x[n]$. The reconstructed signal $\hat{x}[n]$ may not be the same as $x[n]$ due to the presence of noise sources (e.g., quantization, aliasing, distortions due to filtering, etc.) in the system.

Based on Figure 8.36(a),

$$X_k[z] = H_k[z]X[z], \quad k = 0, 1 \tag{8.106}$$

The frequency-domain equivalent of the downsampled signal (Vaidyanathan, 1992) follows:

$$\begin{aligned} U_k[z] &= \frac{1}{M}\sum_{m=0}^{M-1} X_k\left[z^{1/M}e^{-j2\pi m/M}\right] = \frac{1}{2}\sum_{m=0}^{1} X_k\left[z^{1/2}e^{-j2\pi m/2}\right] \\ &= \frac{1}{2}\left(X_k\left[z^{1/2}\right] + X_k\left[-z^{1/2}\right]\right) \end{aligned} \tag{8.107}$$

Ignoring the effects of quantization, the expression for the frequency-domain equivalent of the upsampled signal $\hat{x}_k[n]$ follows:

$$\hat{X}_k[z] = \hat{U}_k[z^2] = \frac{1}{2}(X_k[z] + X_k[-z]) = \frac{1}{2}(H_k[z]X[z] + H_k[-z]X[-z]) \tag{8.108}$$

From Figure 8.36(a), the reconstructed signal is obtained as seen in Equation (8.109).

$$\begin{aligned} \hat{X}[z] &= \sum_{k=0}^{M-1} F_k[z]\hat{X}_k[z] \\ &= F_0[z]\hat{X}_0[z] + F_1[z]\hat{X}_1[z] \end{aligned} \tag{8.109}$$

Based on Equations (8.108) and (8.109),

$$\begin{aligned} \hat{X}[z] = &\frac{1}{2}(H_0[z]F_0[z] + H_1[z]F_1[z])X[z] \\ &+\frac{1}{2}(H_0[-z]F_0[z] + H_1[-z]F_1[z])X[-z] \end{aligned} \tag{8.110}$$

The second term in Equation (8.110) accounts for aliasing and imaging due to downsampling and upsampling of the signal, and we can cancel the aliasing and imaging terms by choosing the synthesis filters such that $H_0[-z]F_0[z] + H_1[-z]F_1[z]$ is zero; that is, by choosing the synthesis filters $F_0[z] = H_1[-z]$ and $F_1[z] = -H_0[-z]$, it is possible to completely cancel the aliasing effects. With this, Equation (8.110) is simplified to

$$\hat{X}[z] = \frac{1}{2}(H_0[z]F_0[z] + H_1[z]F_1[z])X[z] = P[z]X[z] \tag{8.111}$$

Although the aliasing is canceled in the reconstructed signal $\hat{x}[n]$, Equation (8.111) still suffers from amplitude and phase distortions due to the $P[z]$ factor. Unless $P[z]$ is a constant magnitude with a linear phase (i.e., $P[z] = cz^{-\Delta}$), a perfectly reconstructed signal is not possible. When a QMF bank is free from aliasing, amplitude, and phase distortions, it is called a QMF bank with perfect reconstruction (PR) property. By choosing the filter $H_1[z] = H_0[-z]$, that is, the impulse responses as $h_1[l] = (-1)^l h_0[l]$, $l = 0, 1, 2, \ldots, L-1$, we can obtain all four filters of the PR QMF bank using a single filter $H_0[z]$. The perfectly reconstructed signal $\hat{x}[n]$ is still not exactly the same as the transmitted signal $x[n]$ due to the presence of irreversible quantization errors and unavoidable additive noise.

Example 8.2

Determine the four filters of the QMF bank with PR property given the prototype filter $H_0[z] = 1 + z^{-1}$. In addition, verify the perfect reconstruction property of the QMF bank.

The QMF bank's four filters follow:

Analysis filters: $H_0[z] = 1 + z^{-1}$, $H_1[z] = H_0[-z] = 1 - z^{-1}$
Synthesis filters: $F_0[z] = H_1[-z] = 1 + z^{-1}$, $F_1[z] = -H_0[-z] = -1 + z^{-1}$
Aliasing component: $H_0[-z]F_0[z] + H_1[-z]F_1[z] = H_0[-z]H_0[z] - H_0[z]H_0[-z] = 0$

$$P[z] = \frac{1}{2}(H_0[z]F_0[z] + H_1[z]F_1[z]) = \frac{1}{2}[(1+z^{-1})^2 - (1-z^{-1})^2]$$
$$= \frac{1}{2}(4z^{-1}) = 2z^{-1}$$

That is, $P[z]$ is a simple delay with a gain of 2. Thus, the resulting QMF bank is the perfect reconstruction filter bank.

An illustration of subband coding of a signal using the QMF bank designed with the prototype filter $H_0[z] = 1 + z^{-1}$ is shown in Figure 8.37. The original signal for coding is shown in Figure 8.37(a). Figure 8.37(b) through (j) indicate the outputs of various processes. The output of analysis filters is shown in Figure 8.37(b) and (c); the downsampled subband signals, Figure 8.37(d) and (e); the quantized subband signals, Figure 8.37(f) and (g); the receiver upsampled signals, Figures 8.37(h) and (i); and the reconstructed signal, Figure 8.37(j).

■

In practice, polyphase decomposition methods (discussed in the previous section) are commonly used to efficiently implement QMF filter banks. If we express the prototype filter $H_0[z]$ using type-1 polyphase decomposition as $H_0[z] = A_0[z^2] + z^{-1}A_1[z^2]$, then the other filters of the QMF bank with the PR property can be derived as $H_1[z] = A_0[z^2] - z^{-1}A_1[z^2]$, $F_0[z] = A_0[z^2] + z^{-1}A_1[z^2]$, and $F_1[z] = -A_0[z^2] + z^{-1}A_1[z^2]$. The final structure for efficient polyphase implementation of a two-channel QMF bank is shown in Figure 8.38.

8.3 Wavelet Signal Processing

Signals or images are decomposed to analyze their content, eliminate the undesired components, and compactly represent them for storing or transmitting purposes. For this, we project the signal from a finite or infinite dimensional space to another finite dimensional space using orthogonal basis functions. One way of analyzing an arbitrary signal is by decomposing the signal into the number of frequency components using the Fourier transform (i.e., decomposition of the signal using Fourier bases). As discussed in Chapter 6, the Fourier bases are sinusoidal functions $\sin(2\pi f_i t)$ and $\cos(2\pi f_j t)$. A discrete signal $x[n]$ described by Equation (8.112) is shown in Figure 8.39(a), and its Fourier transform output is shown in Figure 8.39(b). This signal $x[n]$ contains four frequencies: $f_1 = 5\,\text{Hz}$, $f_2 = 10\,\text{Hz}$, $f_3 = 15\,\text{Hz}$, and $f_4 = 20\,\text{Hz}$:

$$x[n] = \sin(2\pi f_1 n/F_s) + \sin(2\pi f_2 n/F_s) + \sin(2\pi f_3 n/F_s) + \sin(2\pi f_4 n/F_s) \tag{8.112}$$

where $n = 0, 1, 2, \ldots, 4095$, $F_s = 1\,\text{kHz}$.

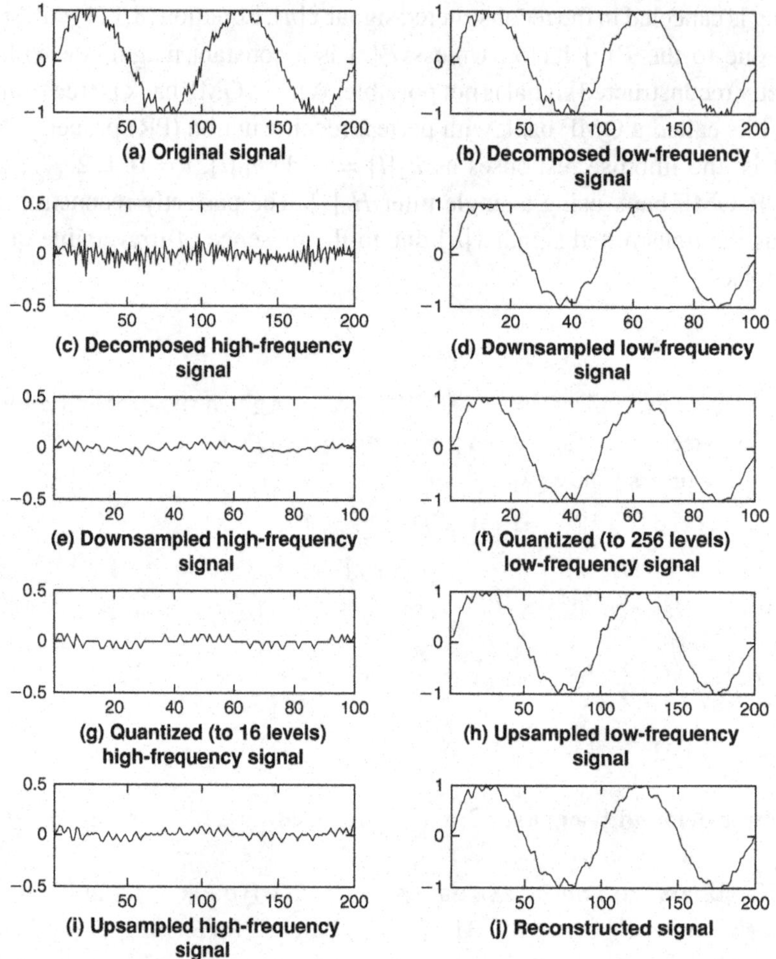

Figure 8.37: Illustration of subband decomposition, quantization, and reconstruction.

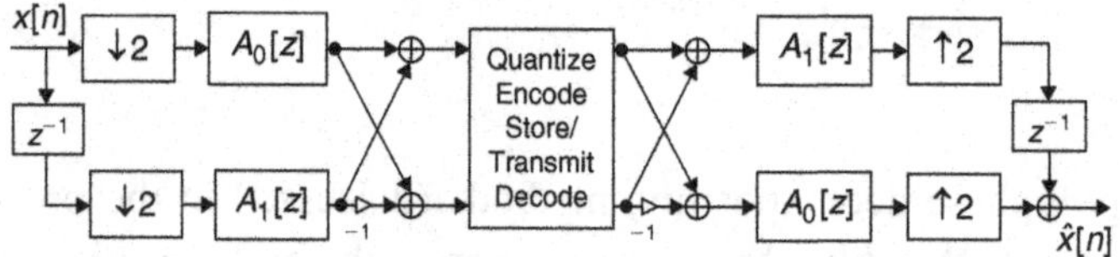

Figure 8.38: The polyphase implementation of two-channel QMF bank.

The Fourier transform provides all frequencies contained in the input signal $x[n]$, and does not provide any information about frequencies in a given segment (or window) of the signal. For example, let us consider another signal described by Equation (8.113), shown in Figure 8.40(a). As seen in Figure 8.40(b), the signal $y[n]$ also contains the same four frequencies (i.e., 5 Hz, 10 Hz, 15 Hz, and 20 Hz) as that of $x[n]$, although the time-domain representations of $x[n]$ and $y[n]$ signals are entirely different. This is because the Fourier basis (which is extended to infinity as shown in Figure 8.44(a), page 419) assumes that the signals under consideration contain the frequency components all the time. In other words, the Fourier transform assumes that the signals are stationary. This is one of the limitations of the Fourier transform. At any given time, we cannot obtain good time and frequency localization of a signal using a Fourier transform. With the Fourier transform, we can have either good time localization with poor frequency localization as shown in Figure 8.41(a), or good frequency localization with poor time localization as shown in Figure 8.41(b).

$$y[n] = \begin{cases} \sin(2\pi f_1 n/F_s) & 0 \le n < 1024 \\ \sin(2\pi f_2 n/F_s) & 1024 \le n < 2048 \\ \sin(2\pi f_3 n/F_s) & 2048 \le n < 3072 \\ \sin(2\pi f_4 n/F_s) & 3072 \le n < 4096 \end{cases} \tag{8.113}$$

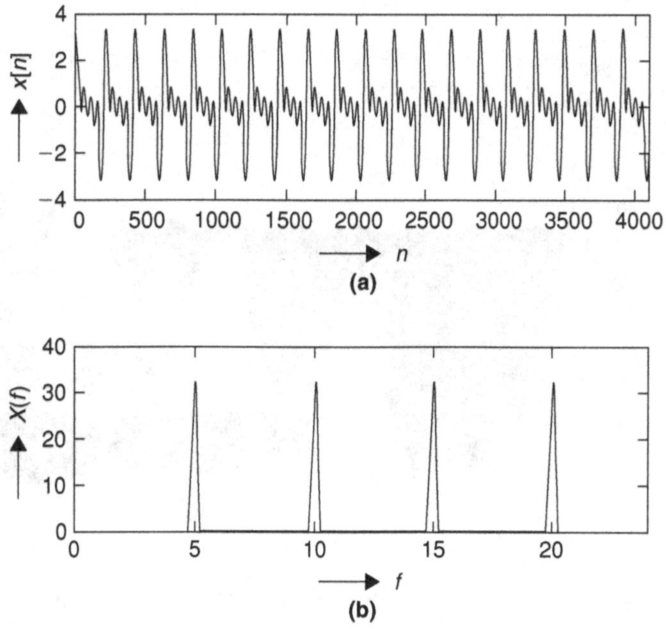

Figure 8.39: Stationary sinusoidal signal. (a) Time domain. (b) Frequency domain.

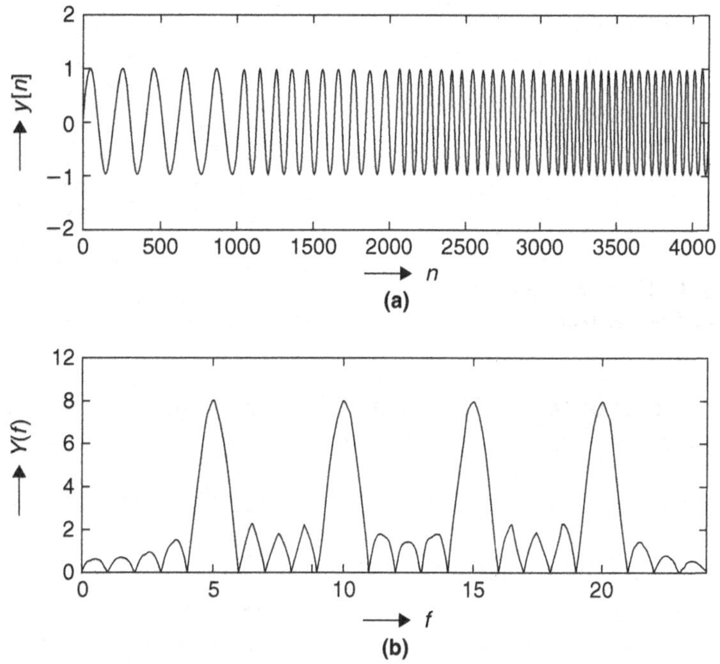

Figure 8.40: Non-stationary sinusoidal signal. (a) Time domain. (b) Frequency domain.

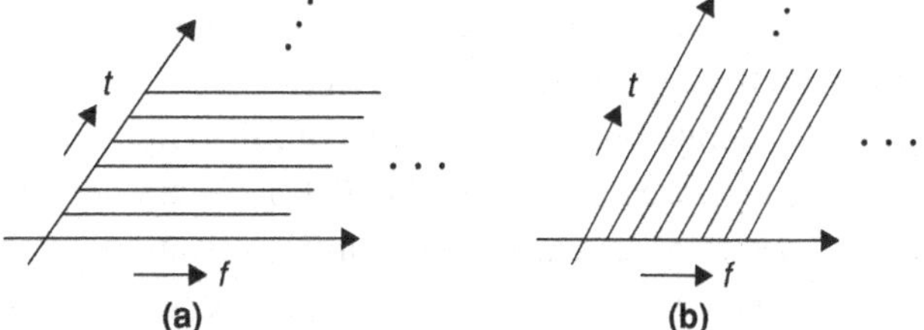

Figure 8.41: Fourier transform time-frequency grid. (a) Good time localization with poor frequency localization. (b) Poor time localization with good frequency localization.

Short-Time Fourier Transform

The time-frequency localization problem of Fourier transform can be overcome using the so-called *short-time Fourier transform* (STFT) or *windowed Fourier transform.* In this transform, the signal $y[n]$ shown in Figure 8.40(a) is divided into a few segments (or windows) and the Fourier transforms of those segments are computed using Equation (8.113). The time-frequency information of each segment is plotted separately in the two dimensions as shown in Figure 8.42, which provides simultaneous time and frequency localization.

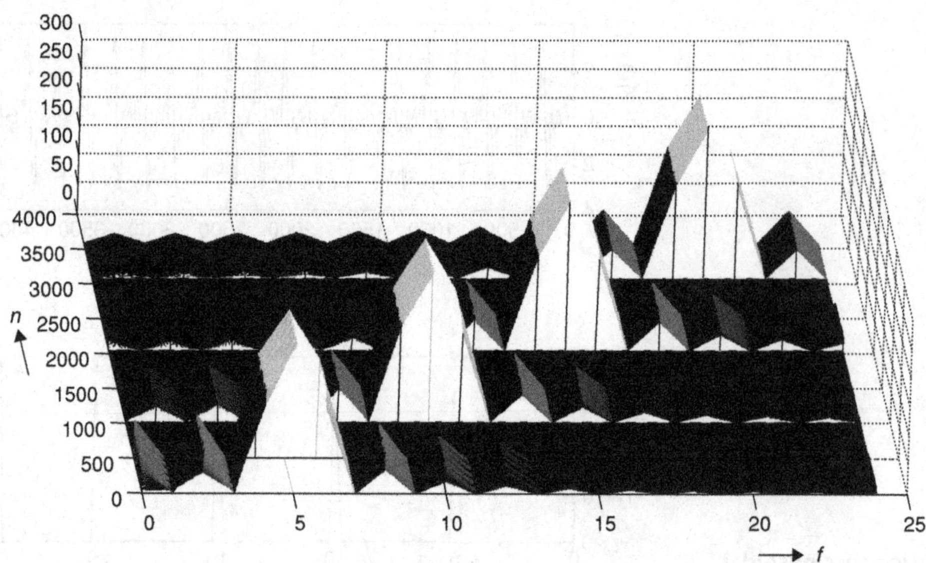

Figure 8.42: STFT of $y[n]$ in 2D space.

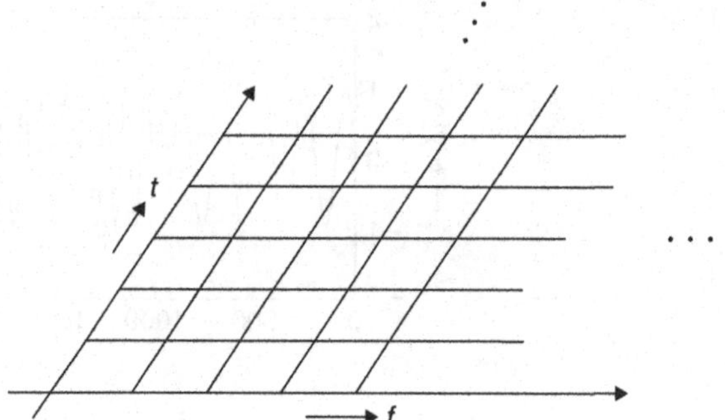

Figure 8.43: Time-frequency grid for short-time Fourier transform.

As seen in Equation (8.114), the length of the window determines the frequency resolution:

$$Y_{\text{STFT}}[k,m] = \sum_{n=m}^{m+N-1} x[n]w[n-m]e^{-j2\pi k(n-m)/N} \tag{8.114}$$

where $w[n]$ is a sliding window.

The time-frequency localization characteristics of STFT are shown in Figure 8.43, which clearly displays $y[n]$ signal frequencies at various instants in time. However, the STFT has a few shortcomings. As the STFT uses the windowed Fourier basis (i.e., truncated sinusoidal waves with a window, as shown in Figure 8.44(b)), we cannot obtain accurate frequency estimates over all frequency ranges because of the windowing. In any given window, the STFT can analyze high-frequency components very accurately and its low-frequency components estimate will not be that accurate due to the absence of full-length low-frequency components in that window. In addition, the time localization we obtain with the STFT occurs only at the cost of frequency-localization loss.

In practice, the very nature of the signals in many applications is that the slowly varying longer signals are associated with small bursts of high-frequency signals. Processing these types of signals with the STFT may not provide accurate results. In contrast to the STFT, which uses a single analysis window, the *wavelet transform* to be discussed next uses multiple windows, and in particular, shorter windows at high frequencies and longer windows at low frequencies.

Time and frequency resolution cannot be arbitrarily small because their product is lower bounded as follows:

$$\text{Time Bandwidth Product: } \Delta t \Delta f \geq \frac{1}{4\pi} \tag{8.115}$$

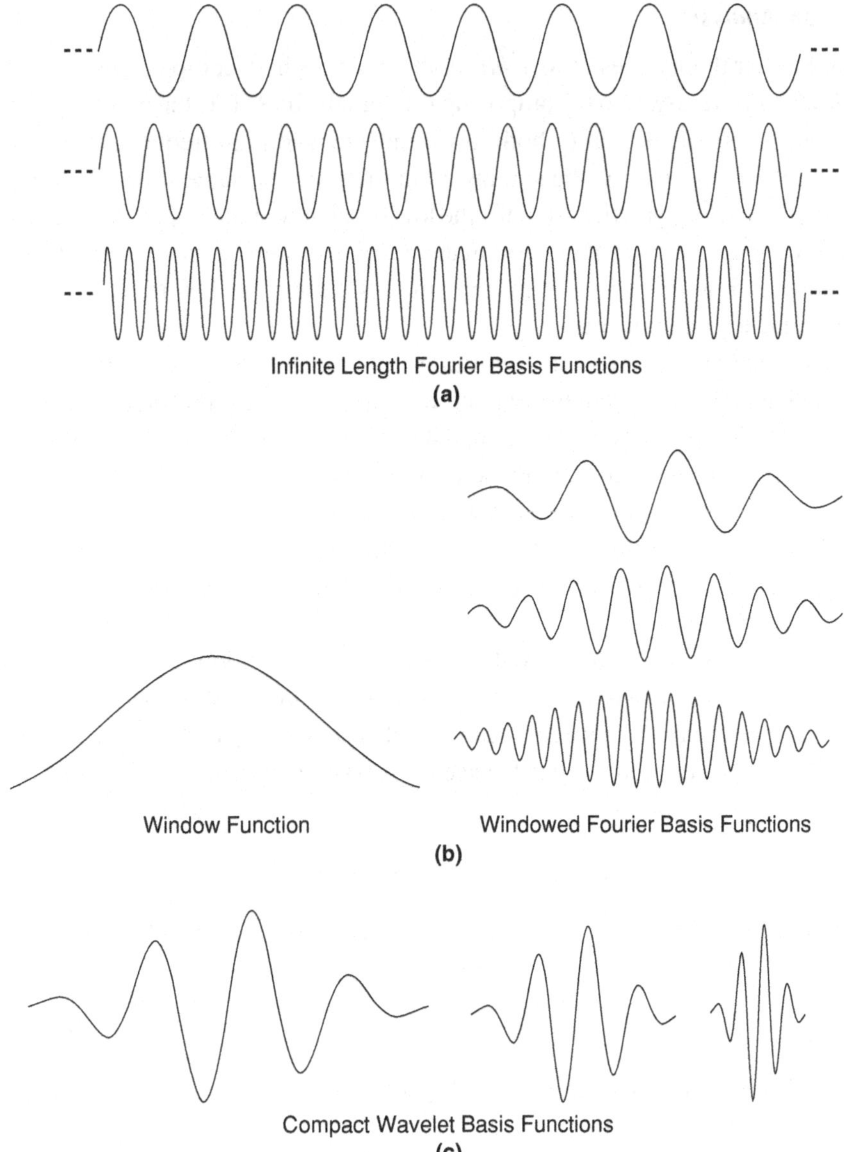

Figure 8.44: Various transform function bases. (a) Fourier transform basis. (b) STFT basis. (c) Wavelet transform basis.

This is referred to as the Heisenberg inequality for Fourier transforms. It means that one can only trade time resolution for frequency resolution or vice versa. A limitation of the STFT is that, because a single window is used for all frequencies, the resolution of the analysis is the same at all locations in the time-frequency grid (i.e., once the window is chosen, the time-frequency resolution is fixed for the entire time-frequency plane, as shown in Equation (8.115)). To overcome the resolution limitation of the STFT, one can imagine letting the resolution Δt and Δf vary in the time-frequency plane in order to obtain the multiresolution analysis. This can be visualized by adjusting the lower-bound equation:

$$\text{Time Bandwidth Product: } \left(\frac{\Delta t}{k}\right)(k\Delta f) \geq \frac{1}{4\pi} \tag{8.116}$$

By varying the parameter k, we can trade time resolution for frequency resolution or vice versa. An intuitively appealing way to achieve this is short high-frequency basis functions and long low-frequency basis functions. This is exactly what is achieved with the wavelet transform. In particular, the wavelet transform is of interest for the analysis of nonstationary signals.

8.3.1 Multiresolution Analysis

In the same way that Fourier theory uses *classic harmonic analysis* in decomposing signals, the wavelet theory uses so-called *multiresolution analysis* in decomposing the signals. In STFT, the windowed signals are analyzed in terms of all harmonic components, that is, both low frequency and high frequency components are analyzed with the same time resolution. In reality, the signals do not require the same time resolution for all frequency components. For example, in many practical signals, the low frequency signals span the entire duration of a signal, whereas high frequency signals occur in a transient manner. In such cases, it makes sense to use a multiresolution *time-scale* grid as shown in Figure 8.45 to adapt low time resolutions for low frequency signals and high time resolutions for high frequency components.

We use time scale instead of time frequency in multiresolution analysis. This is because the wavelet theory analyzes the signals using different wavelets obtained by scaling a single prototype wavelet called the *mother wavelet*. Wavelets are small waves as shown in Figure 8.44(c). The scale parameter inversely relates to frequency, that is, smaller scales represent the higher frequencies and larger scales represent the lower frequencies. This time-scale grid results in very good time resolution with poor frequency resolution at high frequencies, and very good frequency resolution with poor time resolution at low frequencies. In other words, it is possible to achieve nonuniform time-frequency localization with a multiresolution time-scale grid that has better characteristics for analyzing the very nature of signals.

To formulate the multiresolution analysis mathematically, we start with scaling (or complete) subspaces C_j and wavelet (or difference) subspaces D_j as shown in Figure 8.46, where $j \in Z$. The wavelet subspaces D_{j+a} comprise the difference between scaling subspaces C_{j+a} and C_{j+a+1}. The scaling subspaces are increasing in dimension. In addition, each subspace C_j is contained in the next higher-order subspaces C_{j+i}, that is,

$$C_{-\infty} \subset \cdots C_{-j-1} \subset C_{-j} \subset \cdots \subset C_{-2} \subset C_{-1} \subset C_0 \subset C_1 \subset C_2 \subset \cdots \subset C_j \subset C_{j+1} \subset \cdots \subset C_\infty$$

The following relationship holds true with the scaling subspaces and wavelet subspaces as pictorially presented in Figure 8.46:

$$C_{j+2} = C_{j+1} \oplus D_{j+1} = C_j \oplus D_j \oplus D_{j+1} = C_{j-1} \oplus D_{j-1} \oplus D_j \oplus D_{j+1}$$

and so on, where the symbol $\oplus$ denotes a union of subspaces.

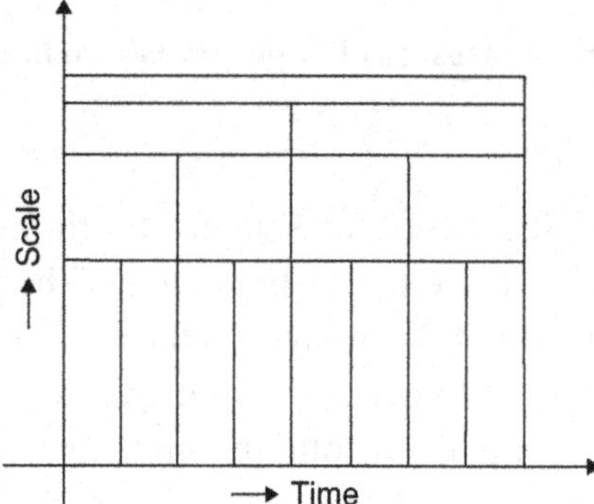

Figure 8.45: Multiresolution time-scale grid.

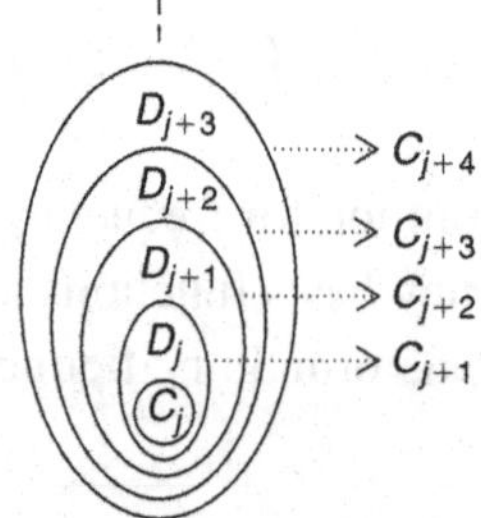

Figure 8.46: Pictorial view of scaling subspaces and wavelet subspaces.

Let $L^2(R)$ denote a space of measurable and integrable square functions f, that is, if $f(t) \in L^2(R)$, then

$$\int |f(t)|^2 < \infty \tag{8.117}$$

Assume that the function $f(t)$ belonging to the whole space $L^2(R)$ has formed from the sum of its elementary functions $f_j(t)$, which belong to the subspaces of $L^2(R)$. We further assume that the elementary functions belong to the scaling subspaces C_j (i.e., $f_j(t) \in C_j$), which means,

$$C_{-\infty} = 0 \subset \cdots C_{-j-1} \subset C_{-j} \subset \cdots \subset C_{-2} \subset C_{-1} \subset C_0 \subset C_1 \subset C_2 \subset \cdots \subset C_j \subset C_{j+1} \subset \cdots \subset C_\infty = L^2(R)$$

In addition, the subspaces C_j are such that $\bigcup_j C_j$ is dense in $L^2(R)$, $\bigcap_j C_j = \{0\}$ and $C_j \bigcap D_j = \{0\}$.

It also means that the elementary functions $f_j(t)$ are obtained by projecting the $f(t)$ onto the subspaces C_j. With this, an estimate of the function $f(t)$ can be obtained by summing the elementary functions of subspaces up to C_J as follows:

$$\hat{f}(t) = \sum_{j \le J} \beta_j f_j(t) \tag{8.118}$$

In Equation (8.118), $\hat{f}(t) \to f(t)$ as $J \to \infty$. This implies that a portion of $f(t)$ will be in each subspace C_j upon the decomposition of $f(t)$. The addition of each of these pieces provides increasingly finer detail to the reconstructed signal $\hat{f}(t)$. Logically, we can think of this as lower-dimension subspaces containing the coarse or approximate information about $f(t)$, while higher-dimension subspaces contain finer details of the function $f(t)$.

The functions $\varphi(t)$ in subspaces C_i behave according to the following laws:

- Dilation law: If $\varphi(t) \in C_i$, then $\varphi(\alpha^j t) \in C_{i+j}$.
- Translation law: If $\varphi(t) \in C_i$, then $\varphi(t-k) \in C_i$.

According to the dilation law, if $\phi(t) = \phi(\alpha^0 t) \in C_0$, then $\phi(\alpha^j t) \in C_j$ and $\phi(a^{-j} t) \in C_{-j}$. For this reason, the function $\phi(t)$ is called a *scaling function*. Defining the set of functions $\phi_{j,k}(t)$ as in

$$\phi_{j,k}(t) = 2^{j/2}\phi(2^j t - k), \quad j, k \in Z \tag{8.119}$$

we can produce multiresolution subspaces C_j. We have chosen the scaling factor $\alpha = 2$ to achieve a type of multiresolution analysis shown in Figure 8.45. The factor $2^{j/2}$ in Equation (8.119) indicates equal energy in functions $\phi_{j,k}(t)$ at different scales j. If function $\phi(t)$ is defined such that the value of $\phi_{0,0}(t) = \phi(t)$ outside the interval [0, 1) is zero, then $\phi_{0,k}(t) = \phi(t-k)$ for different integer shift values of k forms the orthogonal basis of subspace C_0, that is,

$$\int_{-\infty}^{\infty} \phi(t)\phi(t-k)dt = \delta(k) \tag{8.120}$$

If the subspace C_0 represents the band-limited functions in the interval $(-\pi/2, \pi/2)$, then as seen in Equation (8.119), the bandwidth of functions in C_1 extends to the interval $(-\pi, \pi)$ due to signal compression by a factor of 2 in C_1. This is illustrated in Figure 8.47(a). Since the subspace C_0 is contained in C_1, we can express the function $\phi(t)$ of subspace C_0 using the linear combination of the functions $\phi(2t-k)$ of subspace C_1. In other words, given Figure 8.47(a), it is clear that the $\phi(t)$ can be obtained by passing $\phi(2t)$ through a halfband low-pass filter $\{g_k\}$ shown in Figure 8.47(b), expressed as

$$\phi(t) = \sqrt{2} \sum_k g_k \phi(2t-k) \tag{8.121}$$

Since $C_1 = C_0 \oplus D_0$, the subspace D_0 in C_1 can be interpreted as band-limited function space with frequencies in the interval $(-\pi, -\pi/2) \cup (\pi/2, \pi)$. In the signal domain, the corresponding band-limited function $\psi(t)$ of

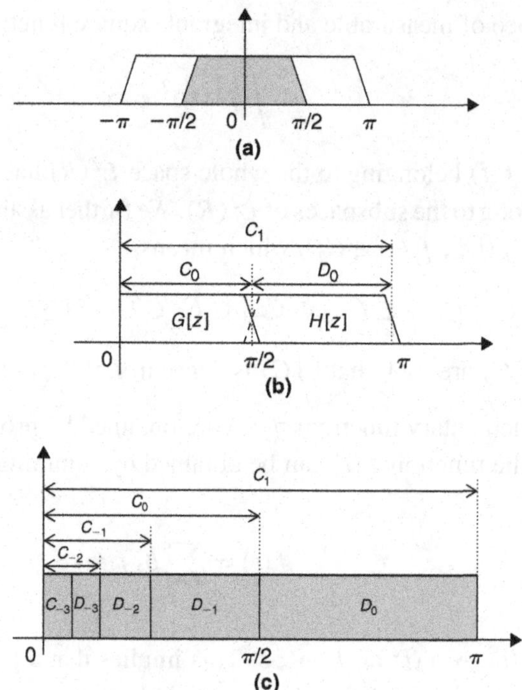

Figure 8.47: Frequency-domain division with multiresolution analysis.

the space D_0 is obtained by passing the $\phi(2t-k)$ through the corresponding halfband high-pass filter $\{h_k\}$, and is expressed as

$$\psi(t) = \sqrt{2}\sum_k h_k\,\phi(2t-k) \tag{8.122}$$

It can be shown that $\psi(t)$, called the *wavelet function*, and its translated forms an orthogonal basis for D_0, that is,

$$\int_{-\infty}^{\infty} \psi(t)\psi(t-k)dt = \delta_k \tag{8.123}$$

Since C_0 and D_0 cover disjointed regions of C_1, the functions $\phi(t)$ and $\psi(t)$ are orthogonal to each other for different shift values (i.e., their dot product is zero):

$$<\phi(t-m), \psi(t-n)> = \int_{-\infty}^{\infty} \phi(t-m)\psi(t-n)dt = 0 \qquad \forall m, n \tag{8.124}$$

Given $\psi(t)$ of D_0, we can define a set of functions to cover the difference space D_j:

$$\psi_{j,k}(t) = 2^{j/2}\psi(2^j t-k), \quad j, k \in Z \tag{8.125}$$

The functions $\{\psi_{j,k}(t)\}$ are orthogonal for all scaling parameter values j and shift parameter values k. For various shift values of k, the sets $\{\phi_{j,k}(t)\}$ and $\{\psi_{j,k}(t)\}$ form the orthogonal basis for subspaces C_j and D_j. Although the formulas in Equations (8.119) through (8.125) for scaling functions and wavelet functions happen to be similar, their functionalities are entirely different. In analyzing the signals of subspace C_1, the dilated scaling functions contain the approximate information of C_1, whereas the dilated wavelet functions contain the detailed information of C_1.

Example 8.4

Given the Haar scaling function and wavelet function in C_0 and D_0, obtain the set of scaling functions for C_0 and C_1 and the set of wavelet functions for D_0 and D_1. Plot the corresponding scaling and wavelet functions. Obtain the filter coefficients $\{h_k\}$ and $\{g_k\}$ for generating the scaling function $\phi(t)$ and wavelet function $\psi(t)$ from $\phi(2t)$. In addition, verify the orthogonality properties of scaling and wavelet functions.

The Haar scaling function in C_0 is defined in the following graphic:

$$\phi(t) = \begin{cases} 1 & 0 \le t < 1 \\ 0 & \text{otherwise} \end{cases}$$

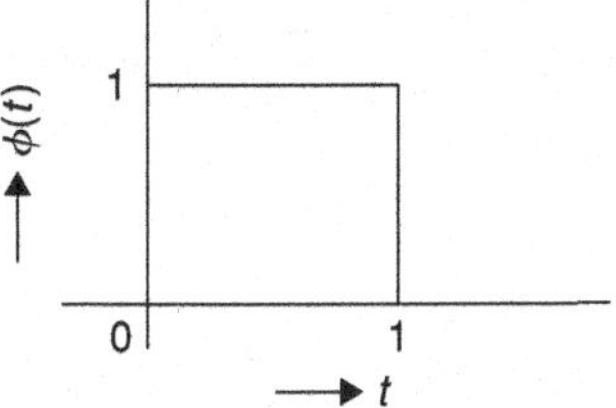

The corresponding Haar wavelet function in D_0 is defined as follows:

$$\psi(t) = \begin{cases} 1 & 0 \le t < 0.5 \\ -1 & 0.5 \le t < 1 \\ 0 & \text{otherwise} \end{cases}$$

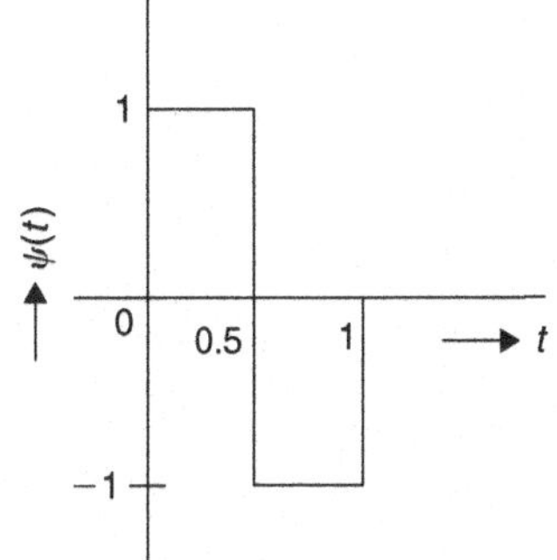

Based on Equation (8.119), the shifted scaling functions in C_0 can be obtained as follows:

$$\phi_{0,k}(t) = \phi(t-k) = \begin{cases} 1 & k \le t < k+1 \\ 0 & \text{otherwise} \end{cases}$$

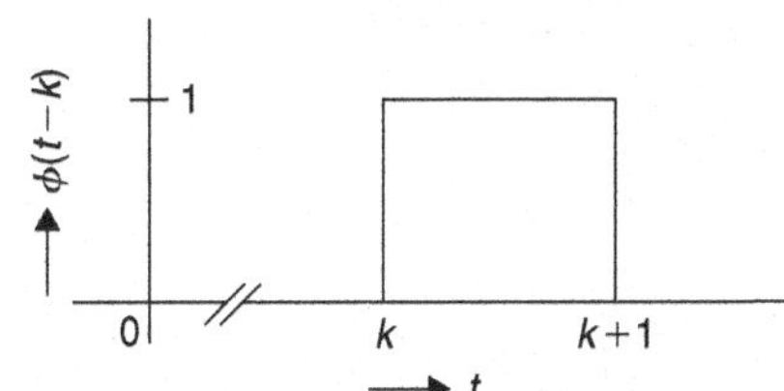

Similarly, the scaling functions of subspace C_1 are

$$\phi_{1,k}(t) = \sqrt{2}\phi(2t-k) = \begin{cases} \sqrt{2} & k/2 \le t < (k+1)/2 \\ 0 & \text{otherwise} \end{cases}$$

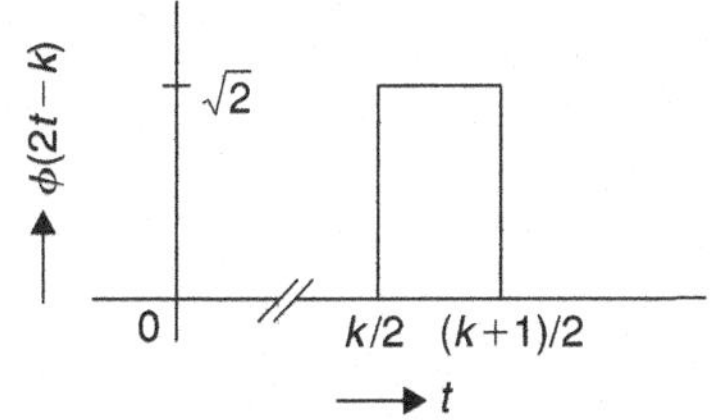

The wavelet functions of subspace D_0 are obtained from Equation (8.125) as follows:

$$\psi_{0,k}(t) = \psi(t-k) = \begin{cases} 1 & k \le t < (k+1/2) \\ -1 & (k+1/2) \le t < k+1 \\ 0 & \text{otherwise} \end{cases}$$

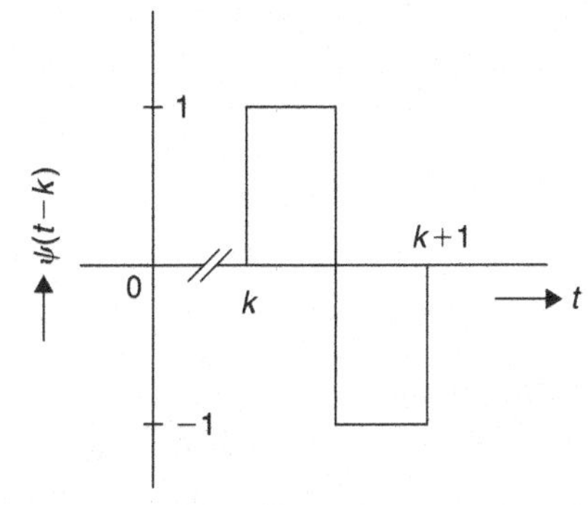

The wavelet functions of subspace D_1 follow:

$$\psi_{1,k}(t) = \sqrt{2}\psi(2t-k) = \begin{cases} \sqrt{2} & \frac{k}{2} \le t < \left(\frac{k}{2}+\frac{1}{4}\right) \\ -\sqrt{2} & \left(\frac{k}{2}+\frac{1}{4}\right) \le t < \left(\frac{k}{2}+\frac{1}{2}\right) \\ 0 & \text{otherwise} \end{cases}$$

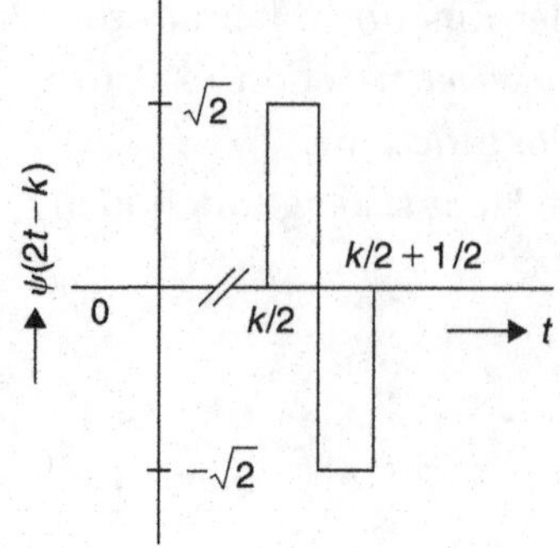

Filter Coefficients Calculation

The filter coefficients $\{g_k\}$ are obtained as follows:

$$\begin{aligned}\phi(t) &= \frac{1}{\sqrt{2}}\phi(2t) + \frac{1}{\sqrt{2}}\phi(2t-1) \\ &= \sqrt{2}\left[\frac{1}{2}\phi(2t) + \frac{1}{2}\phi(2t-1)\right]\end{aligned}$$

Based on Equation (8.121), $\phi(t) = \sqrt{2}\sum_k g_k\phi(2t-k)$. This implies that $g_0 = \frac{1}{2}$ and $g_1 = \frac{1}{2}$.

Similarly, the wavelet function $\psi(t)$ can be expressed as follows:

$$\begin{aligned}\psi(t) &= \frac{1}{\sqrt{2}}\phi(2t) - \frac{1}{\sqrt{2}}\phi(2t-1) \\ &= \sqrt{2}\left[\frac{1}{2}\phi(2t) - \frac{1}{2}\phi(2t-1)\right]\end{aligned}$$

Based on Equation (8.122),

$$\psi(t) = \sqrt{2}\sum_k h_k\phi(2t-k)$$

This expression means that $h_0 = \frac{1}{2}$ and $h_1 = -\frac{1}{2}$. Clearly, the moving-average nature of scaling filter coefficients forms a low-pass filter and the moving-difference nature of wavelet filter coefficients forms a high-pass filter.

Orthogonal Properties

Since the functions $\phi_{0,k}(t)$ in C_0 are disjointed for different shift values of k, the dot-product of $\phi_{0,k}(t)$, and $\phi_{0,m}(t)$ is zero as long as $k \neq m$, that is,

$$< \phi_{0,k}(t), \phi_{0,m}(t) > = \delta(k-m)$$

However, the scaling functions $\phi(t-k)$ and $\sqrt{2}\phi(2t-m)$ of C_0 and C_1 need not be disjointed $\forall k, m$; hence they are not orthogonal to each other.

In the case of wavelet functions, although the functions $\psi(t-k)$ and $\sqrt{2}\psi(2t-m)$ overlap, because of positive and negative areas, the dot product of wavelet functions $\forall k, m$ is always zero. Thus, the wavelet function is orthogonal to all its dilations and translations:

$$< \psi_{0,k}(t), \psi_{0,m}(t) > = \delta(k-m), \quad < \psi_{0,k}(t), \psi_{1,m}(t) > = 0$$

■

Wavelet Basis Functions

The Haar wavelets considered in Example 8.4 are the simplest of all known wavelet functions. Haar scaling and wavelet functions are not smooth, and hence are not suitable for practical applications. Unlike the Fourier

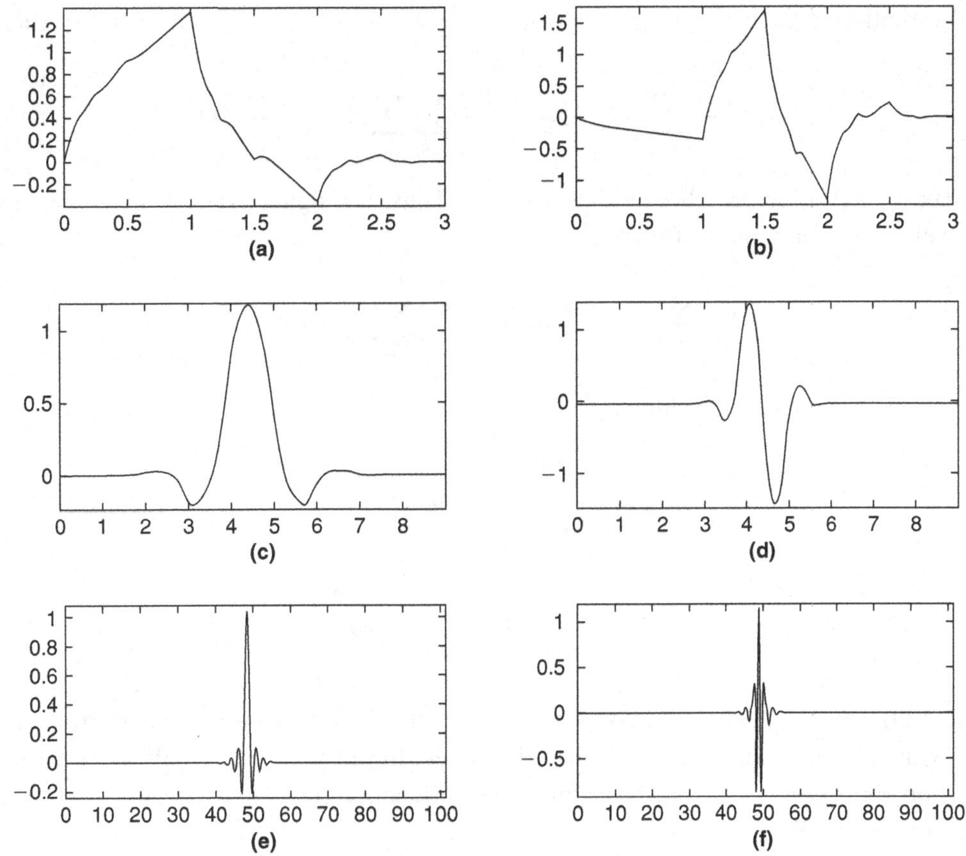

Figure 8.48: Selected scaling and wavelet functions used in practice. (a) Daubechies-2 scaling function. (b) Daubechies-2 wavelet function. (c) Biorthogonal-1.5 scaling function. (d) Biorthogonal-1.5 wavelet function. (e) Meyer scaling function. (f) Meyer wavelet function.

transform (which has only infinite-length sinusoidal functions as a basis), the wavelet transform has many varieties of compact basis functions that can be used as the mother wavelet. Since the mother wavelet produces all wavelet functions used in transformation through shifting and scaling, it determines the characteristics of the resulting wavelet transform. Particular basic functions for the mother wavelet are chosen depending on the application. A few common scaling and wavelet functions are shown in Figure 8.48.

8.3.2 Discrete Wavelet Transform

The aim of signal analysis is to extract relevant information from a signal by transforming it. Both Fourier and wavelet transforms represent a signal through a linear combination of their basic functions. An important feature of both wavelet and Fourier transforms is the orthogonality of their basic functions, which allows for a unique representation of the signal being analyzed. The multiresolution approach to wavelets discussed in the previous section enables us to characterize the class of functions $\psi(t) \in L^2(R)$ that generate an orthonormal basis. Wavelets $\psi(t)$ exist such that $\psi_{j,k}(t) = 2^{j/2}\psi(2^j t - k)$, $j, k \in Z$ is an orthonormal basis of $L^2(R)$. The change in the parameter j scales the mother wavelet $\psi(t)$, whereas the change in parameter k shifts the mother wavelet by k positions. The scaling parameter j is inversely related to the frequency of the signal. Unlike the Fourier basis, wavelet bases are well localized in both time and frequency. By correlating the given signal $x(t)$ with the wavelet basis $\psi_{j,k}(t)$ at different dilations (or scales) j and translations (or shifts) k, we analyze the signal $x(t)$. If $x(t) \in L^2(R)$, then the portion of $x(t)$ in the subspace $C_j \subset L^2(R)$ can be represented as

$$x_j(t) = \sum_{k=-\infty}^{\infty} c_\phi[j,k]\phi_{j,k}(t) \tag{8.126}$$

Using multiresolution analysis $C_j = C_0 \oplus D_0 \oplus D_1 \oplus D_2 \oplus \cdots \oplus D_{j-1}$, we can rewrite Equation (8.126) as

$$x_j(t) = \sum_k c_\phi[0,k]\phi_{0,k}(t) + \sum_{i=0}^{j-1}\sum_k d_\psi[i,k]\psi_{i,k}(t) \tag{8.127}$$

The quantity $||x(t) - x_j(t)||$ approaches zero as $j \to \infty$. Thus, the signal $x(t)$ can be expressed in terms of scaling and wavelet basis functions as follows:

$$x(t) = \sum_k c_\phi[0,k]\phi_{0,k}(t) + \sum_{i=0}^{\infty}\sum_k d_\psi[i,k]\psi_{i,k}(t) \tag{8.128}$$

The coefficients $c_\phi[0,k]$ and $d_\psi[i,k]$ follow:

$$c_\phi[0,k] = \int_{-\infty}^{\infty} x(t)\phi_{0,k}(t)dt \tag{8.129}$$

$$d_\psi[i,k] = \int_{-\infty}^{\infty} x(t)\psi_{i,k}(t)dt \tag{8.130}$$

Equations (8.129) and (8.130) are referred to as the wavelet series expansion of an arbitrary signal $x(t)$ and Equation (8.128) is the corresponding inverse wavelet series. In practice, the signals of interest are sampled. With discretization of the input signal and basic functions in Equations (8.128) to (8.130), an equivalent discrete wavelet series expansion follows:

$$x[n] = \frac{1}{\sqrt{N}}\left(\sum_k c_{0,k}\phi_{0,k}[n] + \sum_{i=0}^{I-1}\sum_k d_{i,k}\psi_{i,k}[n]\right), \quad n = 0, 1, 2, \ldots, N-1, \; I = \log_2(N) \tag{8.131}$$

$$c_{0,k} = \frac{1}{\sqrt{N}}\sum_n x[n]\phi_{0,k}[n] \tag{8.132}$$

$$d_{i,k} = \frac{1}{\sqrt{N}}\sum_n x[n]\psi_{i,k}[n], \quad i = 0, 1, 2, \ldots, I-1 \tag{8.133}$$

By choosing the number of samples $N = 2^I$, we can perform the transformation with only I dilations of the mother wavelet. A fast implementation of analysis and synthesis equations of discrete wavelet series expansion is referred to as a *discrete wavelet transform* (DWT). The computation of a DWT naturally fits into the multistage two-channel filter bank. Next, we describe the filter bank implementation of the DWT.

Based on Equations (8.125) and (8.133),

$$d_{i,k} = \frac{1}{\sqrt{N}}\sum_n x[n]\psi_{i,k}[n] = \frac{1}{\sqrt{N}}\sum_n x[n]2^{i/2}\psi[2^i n - k] \tag{8.134}$$

Based on Equation (8.122),

$$\psi[m] = \sqrt{2}\sum_p h_p\phi[2m - p] \tag{8.135}$$

By substituting $m = 2^i n - k$ in Equation (8.135),

$$\begin{aligned}\psi[2^i n - k] &= \sqrt{2}\sum_l h_l\phi[2(2^i n - k) - l] \\ &= \sqrt{2}\sum_l h_l\phi[2^{i+1}n - 2k - l]\end{aligned} \tag{8.136}$$

By substituting $l = m - 2k$ in Equation (8.136),

$$\psi[2^i n - k] = \sqrt{2}\sum_m h_{m-2k}\phi[2^{i+1}n - m] \tag{8.137}$$

Based on Equations (8.134) and (8.137),

$$\begin{aligned} d_{i,k} &= \frac{1}{\sqrt{N}}\sum_n x[n]2^{i/2}\sqrt{2}\sum_m h_{m-2k}\,\phi[2^{i+1}n - m] \\ &= \sum_m h_{m-2k}\frac{1}{\sqrt{N}}\sum_n x[n]2^{(i+1)/2}\phi[2^{i+1}n - m] \\ d_{i,k} &= \sum_m h_{m-2k}c_{i+1,m} \end{aligned} \tag{8.138}$$

Similarly, we can obtain the coefficients $c_{i,k}$ from $c_{i+1,m}$ as follows:

$$c_{i,k} = \sum_m g_{m-2k}c_{i+1,m} \tag{8.139}$$

The structure of Equations (8.138) and (8.139) is a direct consequence of multiresolution subspace $C_{j+1} = C_j \oplus D_j$. These expressions take us from the coefficients $c_{i+1,k}$ of the scaling basis in the subspace C_{j+1} to the coefficients $c_{i,k}$ and $d_{i,k}$ of the scaling and wavelet basis in subspaces C_j and D_j. This is the recursion that makes the transform computation described in Equations (8.132) and (8.133) fast. Equations (8.138) and (8.139) can be interpreted in the following manner. The convolution of $c_{i+1,m}$ with h_m followed by downsampling by a factor of 2 results in $\sum_m h_{2k-m}c_{i+1,m}$. If we use a time-reversal filter response, $\{h_{-m}\}$, in the convolution operation, we can obtain $d_{i,k} = \sum_m h_{m-2k}c_{i+1,m}$. Similarly, convolving $c_{i+1,m}$ with $\{g_{-m}\}$, we obtain $c_{i,k}$. We can obtain $c_{i-1,p}$ and $d_{i-1,p}$ from $c_{i,k}$ by repeating the same process once again. We repeat this process for $I (= \log_2 N)$ stages to compute the DWT. This is shown in Figure 8.49 with the multistage two-channel filter bank. The DWT output is a collection of finer coefficients $\{d_{i,k}\}$ at each stage together with the coarser coefficients $\{c_{i,k}\}$ at the final stage. Note that the noncausal nature of the filter $\{h_{-m}\}$ and $\{g_{-m}\}$ does not create a problem in practice if we use FIR filters. If L is the length of filters, then we can make the filters causal by delaying the input by $L - 1$ samples.

The frequency characteristic of a multistage two-channel filter bank is shown in Figure 8.50. The downsampling of filter output by a factor of 2 can also be explained from a frequency-spectrum perspective. As we pass the input sequence $x[n]$ through low-pass halfband $\{g_{-k}\}$ and high-pass halfband $\{h_{-k}\}$ filters, the bandwidth of outputs $c_{j,k}$ and $d_{j,k}$ from low-pass and high-pass filters halves after filtering. Hence, we do not lose any information with downsampling of these filter outputs by a factor of 2.

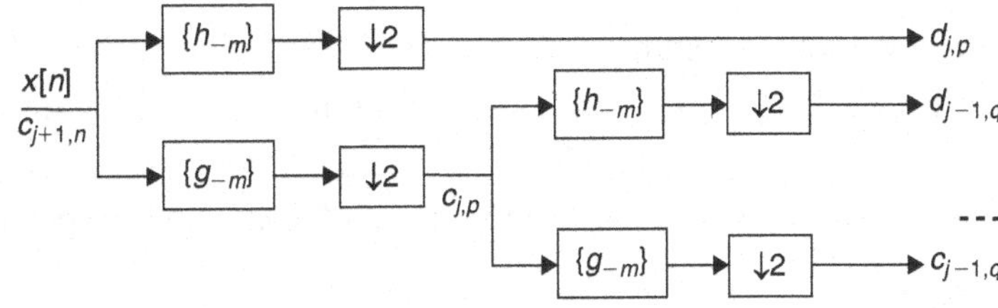

Figure 8.49: Analysis of filter bank for computing DWT.

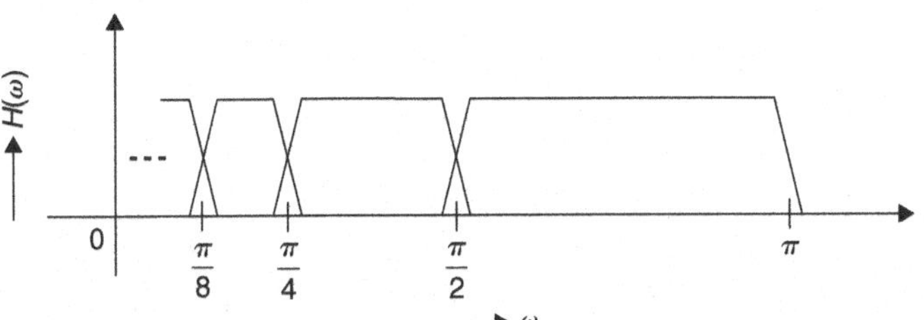

Figure 8.50: Typical frequency characteristics of wavelet filter bank.

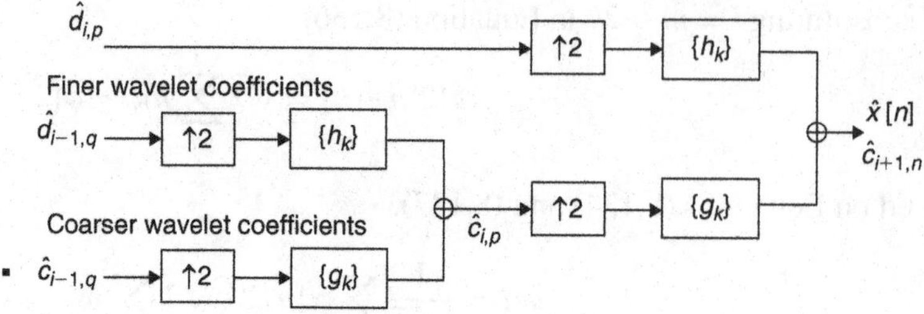

Figure 8.51: Synthesis filter bank for computing IDWT.

To compute the inverse DWT (IDWT), we use the synthesis filter bank as shown in Figure 8.51. We start from the coarser approximation coefficients and obtain an approximate signal $\hat{x}[n]$ by adding finer and finer detail coefficients. At the i-th level, the synthesis formula can be expressed as

$$c_{i,n} = \sum_k g_{n-2k}\, c_{i-1,k} + \sum_k h_{n-2k}\, d_{i-1,k} \tag{8.140}$$

This synthesis formula can be interpreted as upsampling of coarser and finer coefficients at the $(i-1)$th level and then filtering the upsampled sequence with corresponding synthesis filters $\{g_k\}$ and $\{h_k\}$ to obtain the i-th-level coarser coefficients, $c_{i,n}$.

The choice of filters is crucial in achieving perfect reconstruction of the original signal. Typically, the down-sampling operation introduces aliasing during the wavelet analysis. As discussed in Section 8.2.3, by carefully choosing filters for the decomposition (or analysis) and reconstruction (or synthesis) systems, we can cancel out the effects of aliasing. The choice of filters not only determines whether perfect reconstruction is possible, but also determines the shape of the wavelet that we use to perform the analysis. We cannot choose arbitrary wavelets for transforming the signal if we want to accurately reconstruct the original signal from transformed coefficients. Instead, we choose a wavelet shape determined by the perfect reconstruction filter banks. The various filter coefficients for low-pass and high-pass filters in the two-channel filter bank produce different shapes of scaling and wavelet functions. For example, choosing the decomposition low-pass filter,

$$\{g_{-k}\}: G_D[z] = -0.1294 + 0.2241z^{-1} + 0.8365z^{-2} + 0.4830z^{-3}$$

and other filter system functions,

$$\{h_{-k}\}: H_D[z] = z^{-(L-l-1)} G_D[-z], \quad L = 4, l = 0, 1, 2, 3$$
$$\{g_k\}: G_R[z] = -H_D[-z]$$

and

$$\{h_k\}: H_R[z] = G_D[-z]$$

the perfect reconstruction conditions described in the Section 8.2.3 can be satisfied. Iteratively upsampling $\{g_k^{(i)}\}$ (where $\{g_k^{(0)}\} = \{g_k\}$) by a factor of 2 and convolving with the low-pass filter $\{g_k\}$, and iteratively upsampling $\{h_k^{(i)}\}$ (where $\{h_k^{(0)}\} = \{h_k\}$) and convolving with the low-pass filter $\{g_k\}$ produce the Daubechies-2 scaling function and wavelet function, shown in Figures 8.52 and 8.53, respectively.

Example 8.5

Consider a nonstationary sinusoidal signal defined as

$$x[n] = \begin{cases} \sin(2\pi f_1 n/F_s) & 0 \le n < 1024 \\ \sin(2\pi f_2 n/F_s) & 1024 \le n < 2048 \\ \sin(2\pi f_3 n/F_s) & 2048 \le n < 3072 \\ \sin(2\pi f_4 n/F_s) & 3072 \le n < 4096 \end{cases}$$

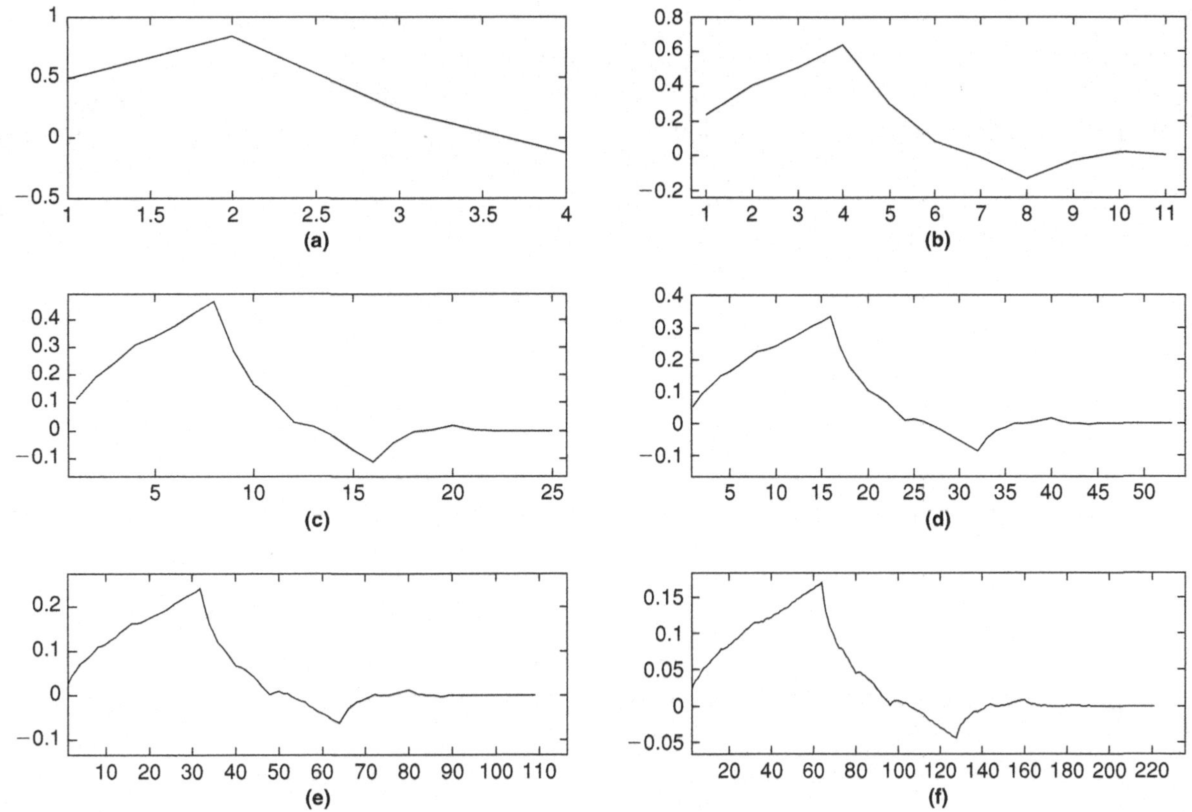

Figure 8.52: Iterative computation of Daubechies-2 scaling function. (a) $\{g_k^{(0)}\} = \{g_k\}$. (b) $\{g_k^{(1)}\}$. (c) $\{g_k^{(2)}\}$. (d) $\{g_k^{(3)}\}$. (e) $\{g_k^{(4)}\}$. (f) $\{g_k^{(5)}\}$.

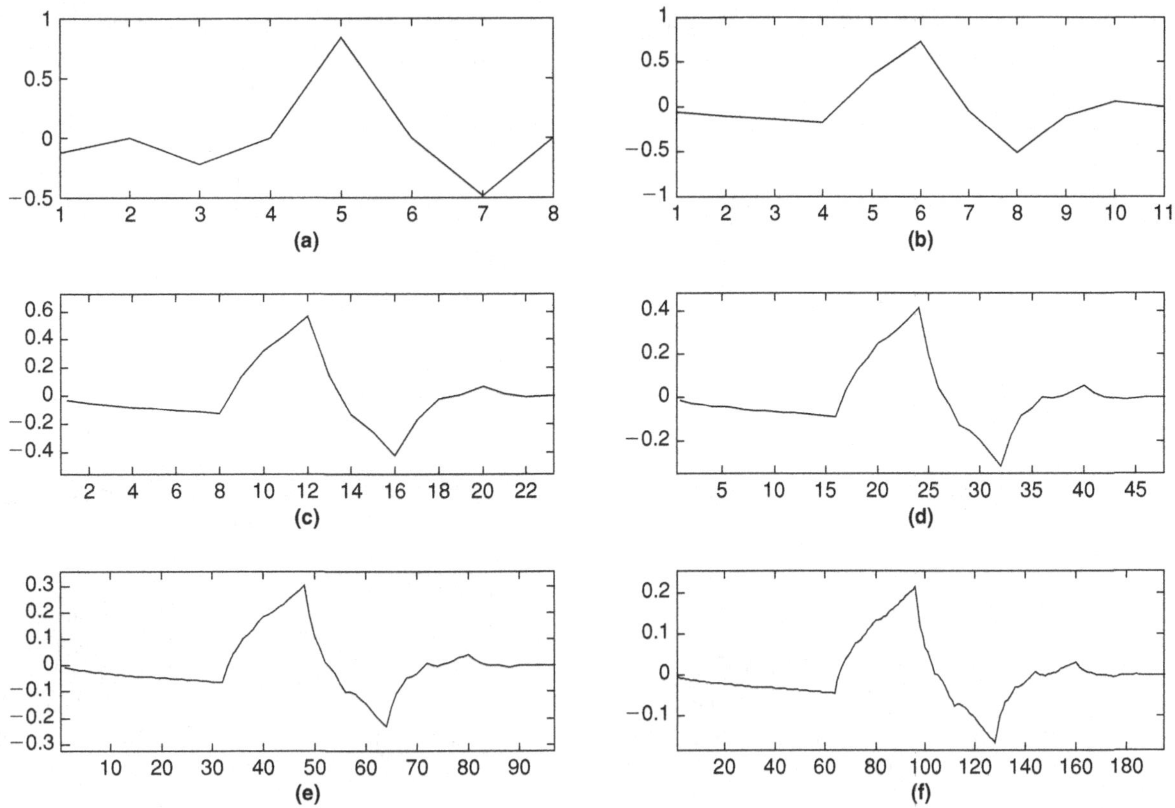

Figure 8.53: Iterative computation of Daubechies-2 wavelet function. (a) $\{h_k^{(0)}\} = \{h_k\}$. (b) $\{h_k^{(1)}\}$. (c) $\{h_k^{(2)}\}$. (d) $\{h_k^{(3)}\}$. (e) $\{h_k^{(4)}\}$. (f) $\{h_k^{(5)}\}$.

with $f_1 = 5\,\text{Hz}$, $f_2 = 10\,\text{Hz}$, $f_3 = 15\,\text{Hz}$, and $f_4 = 20\,\text{Hz}$. Using the Daubechies-4 family of scaling and wavelet functions, decompose $x[n]$ up to four levels using Equations (8.138) and (8.139) and plot them. Then reconstruct the signal using Equation (8.140) and plot the reconstructed and error signals.

The low-pass filter $G_D[z]$ coefficients that determine the shape of the Daubechies-4 scaling function are given by $g_{-n} = \{-0.0106, 0.0329, 0.0308, -0.1870, -0.0280, 0.6309, 0.7148, 0.2304\}$.

The other filters $H_D[z]$, $G_R[z]$, and $H_R[z]$ coefficients that satisfy the perfect reconstruction property can be obtained as follows:

$$h_{-n} = \{-0.2304, 0.7148, -0.6309, -0.0280, 0.1870, 0.0308, -0.0329, -0.0106\}$$

$$g_n = \{0.2304, 0.7148, 0.6309, -0.0280, -0.1870, 0.0308, 0.0329, -0.0106\}$$

$$h_n = \{-0.0106, -0.0329, 0.0308, 0.1870, -0.0280, -0.6309, 0.7148, -0.2304\}$$

At the beginning, the coarser signal at level $j+1$ is $c_{j+1,n} = x[n]$. The coarser signal at the scale j, $c_{j,n}$ is obtained by convolving $c_{j+1,n}$ with $\{g_{-n}\}$ and downsampling the result by a factor of 2. Then we obtain the finer signal at the scale j, $d_{j,n}$, by convolving $c_{j+1,n}$ with $\{h_{-n}\}$ and downsampling the result by a factor of 2. The plot of $d_{j,n}$ is shown in Figure 8.54(f). Similarly, we obtain the finer signal at the scale $j-1$, $d_{j-1,n}$, by convolving $c_{j,n}$ with $\{h_{-n}\}$ and downsampling the result by a factor of 2. The plot of $d_{j-1,n}$ is shown in Figure 8.54(e). In the same way, we obtain the finer signal $d_{j-2,n}$ from $c_{j-1,n}$ and $\{h_{-n}\}$. The plot of $d_{j-2,n}$ is shown in Figure 8.54(d). Finally, we compute $c_{j-3,n}$ and $d_{j-3,n}$ from $c_{j-2,n}$. The plots of $c_{j-3,n}$ and $d_{j-3,n}$ are shown in Figure 8.54(b) and 8.54(c), respectively. Next, we reconstruct the signal recursively from $c_{j-3,n}$ and $d_{j-3,n}$ using Equation (8.140). The reconstructed signal $\hat{c}_{j+1,n}$ is

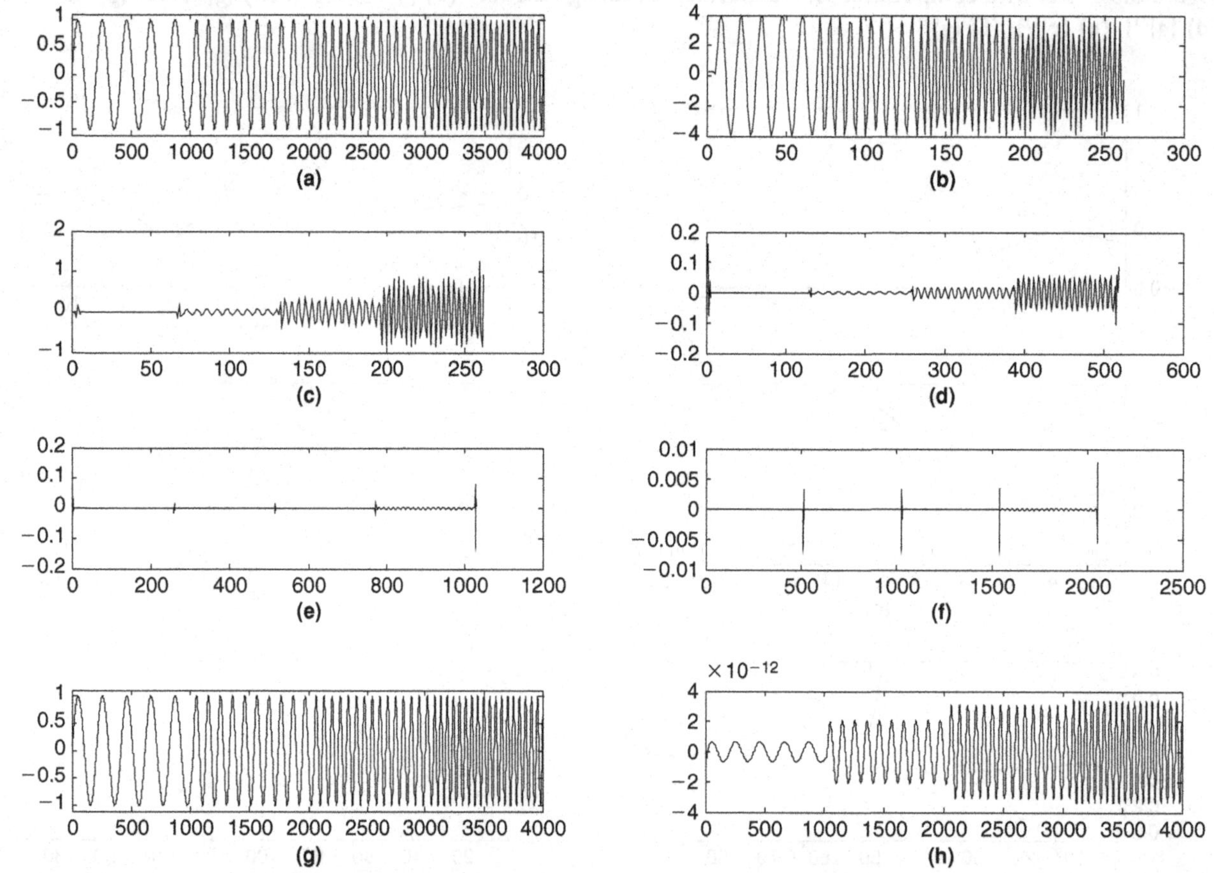

Figure 8.54: Wavelet decomposition of nonstationary sinusoidal signal. (a) Original signal $x[n]$ at scale $j+1$. (b) Coarser signal at scale $j-3$. (c) Finer signal at level $j-3$. (d) Finer signal at level $j-2$. (e) Finer signal at level $j-1$. (f) Finer signal level j. (g) Reconstructed signal. (h) Error between original signal and reconstructed signal.

shown in Figure 8.54(g). Finally, the error between the original signal $c_{j+1,n}$ and the reconstructed signal $\hat{c}_{j+1,n}$ is shown in Figure 8.54(h).

■

Complexity of DWT

As the DWT is computed with a multistage two-channel filter bank, the complexity of the filtering operation for a given filter length and input data length is the sole determinant of DWT complexity. For example, if L is the length of the filter, N is the length of the input, and Q is the complexity of the 0-th stage two-channel filter bank, then the complexity of the first-stage, two-channel filter bank becomes $Q/2$ as the length of input to the two-channel filter bank becomes $N/2$, the complexity of the second stage is $Q/4$ as the input length becomes $N/4$, and so on. Thus, the overall complexity (excluding overheads) of DWT $= Q+Q/2+Q/4+Q/8+\cdots = Q(1+1/2+1/4+1/8+\cdots) \leq 2Q$

8.4 Simulation and Implementation Techniques

The core operation for most of the algorithms discussed in this chapter happens to be a FIR filtering operation whose implementation aspects are thoroughly discussed in Chapter 7. For this reason, instead of simulating all the algorithms here, a few algorithms are identified for simulation and moved to the Exercises section on the companion website. The interested reader can work through the exercises and think about efficiently implementing a particular algorithm using the FIR filter simulation techniques in Chapter 7. As the adaptive algorithms contain feedback loops, their fixed-point implementation requires engineering experience. In this section, we discuss a few techniques to implement the widely used LMS adaptive algorithm on the fixed-point reference embedded processor.

8.4.1 *Implementation of LMS Algorithm*

As discussed previously, the LMS algorithm consists of three simple steps:

$$x_n = \underline{f}[n]\underline{u}[n] \tag{8.141}$$

$$e_n = z_n - x_n \tag{8.142}$$

$$\underline{f}[n+1] = \underline{f}[n] + \mu\underline{u}[n]e_n \tag{8.143}$$

where $\underline{f}[n] = \left[f_0^{(n)}, f_1^{(n)}, \ldots, f_{M-1}^{(n)}\right]$, $\underline{u}[n] = [u_n, u_{n-1}, \ldots, u_{n-M+1}]^T$ and z_n is the reference input.

With the floating-point simulation in Pcode 8.1, as long as the step-size parameter μ satisfies the condition in Equation (8.19), the filtering will be stable. However, in the fixed-point implementation of the LMS algorithm, even if we choose the step size by satisfying Equation (8.19), the scaling of various data at various stages of the algorithm modifies the effective step-size parameter and this may result in an unstable system due to feedback (see Figure 8.63, page 435). Thus, the fixed-point implementation of the LMS is sometimes viewed as an engineering art rather than a science.

```
float e[2000], f[7];
void lms_flt(int N, int M) // LMS function call: N -> data length and  M-> filter length
{
        int i,j,k;
        float mu = 0.0156;                          // step size
        float sum;
        for(j = M - 1;j < N;j++){
            sum = 0.0;
            for(i = j,k = 0;i >= (j - M + 1);i--,k++)
                sum = sum + flt_u[i]*f[k];          // convolution
            e[j] = flt_z[j] - sum;                  // error
            for(k = 0;k < M;k++)
                f[k] = f[k] + mu*e[j]*flt_u[j - k]; // filter weights update
        }
}
```

Pcode 8.1: Floating-point simulation for LMS algorithm.

The flow diagram for floating-point implementation of the LMS algorithm described by Equations (8.141) to (8.143) is shown in Figure 8.55. Here, the LMS algorithm is used for system identification, and hence the input $\underline{u}[n]$ of the LMS filter is the same as the input to the unknown system H. For simulation purposes, we assume that the impulse-response vector of the unknown system is $\underline{h} = [1.0, 0.67, 0.33]$. Let the $\underline{f}$ and $\underline{g}$ vectors denote the filter weights (i.e., impulse response of the identified system) obtained with LMS floating-point and fixed-point simulation, respectively. The input signal $u[n]$ is a unit variance Gaussian distributed random signal of length 2000 (samples) as shown in Figure 8.56. The reference signal $z[n]$ is obtained by convolving input $u[n]$ with the system impulse response $\underline{h}$, and is shown in Figure 8.57. The error signal and filter weight convergence obtained with the LMS floating-point simulation are shown in Figures 8.58 and 8.59. The step

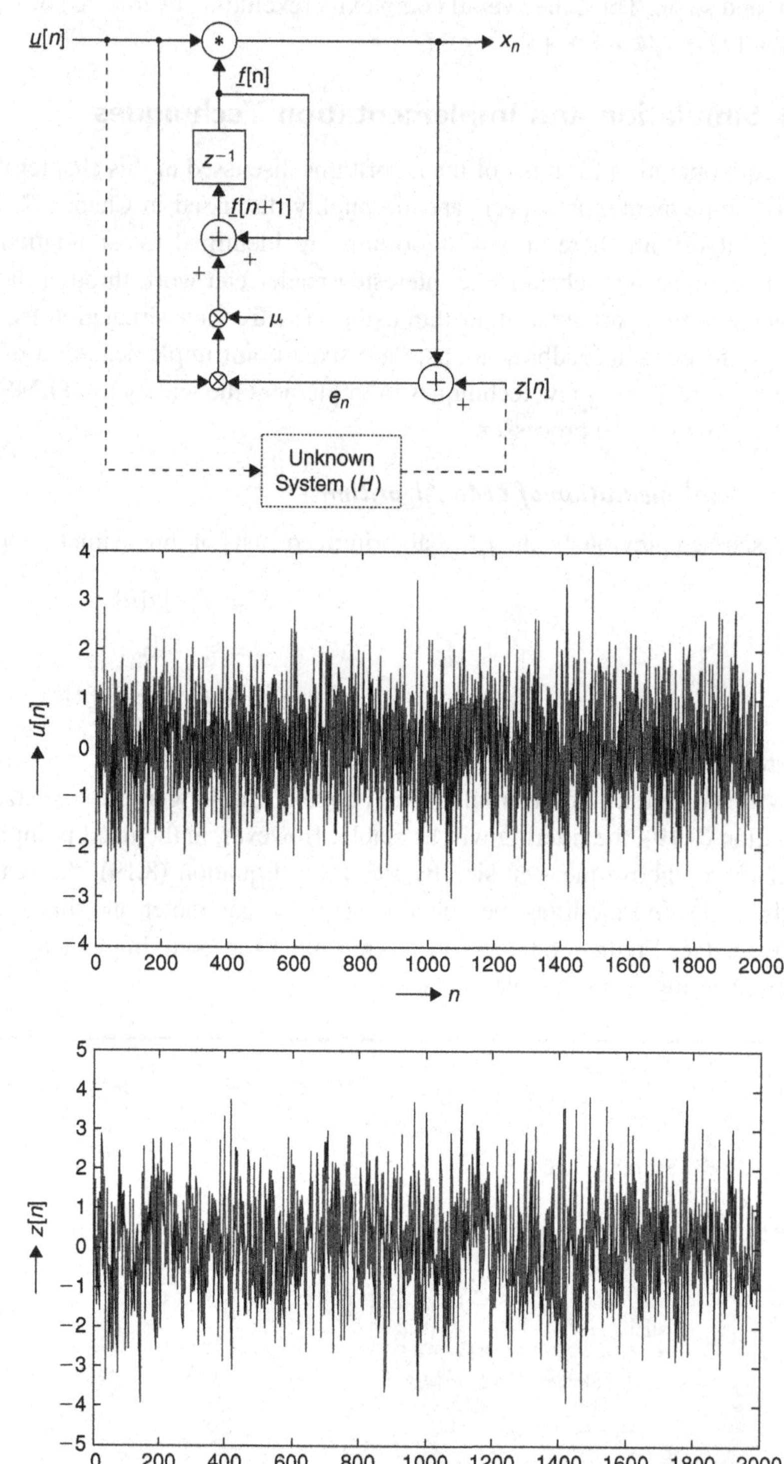

Figure 8.55: Flow diagram of floating-point LMS diagram.

Figure 8.56: Input to LMS algorithm (unit-variance Gaussian-distributed signal).

Figure 8.57: Reference input to LMS algorithm.

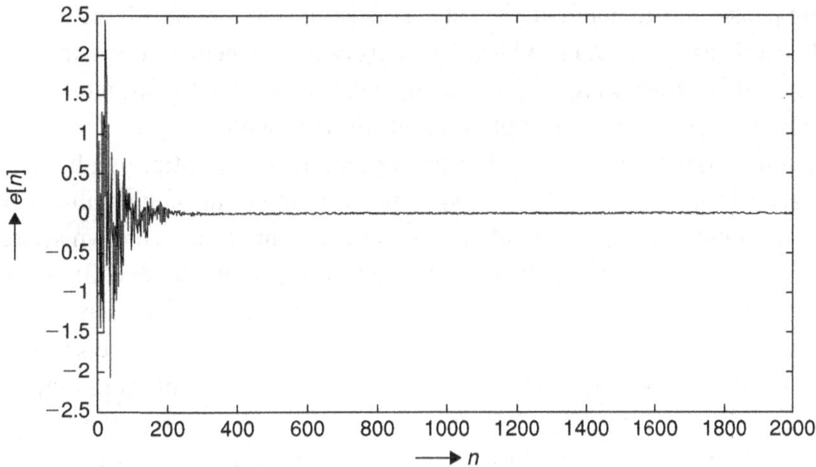

Figure 8.58: Error convergence with floating-point simulation.

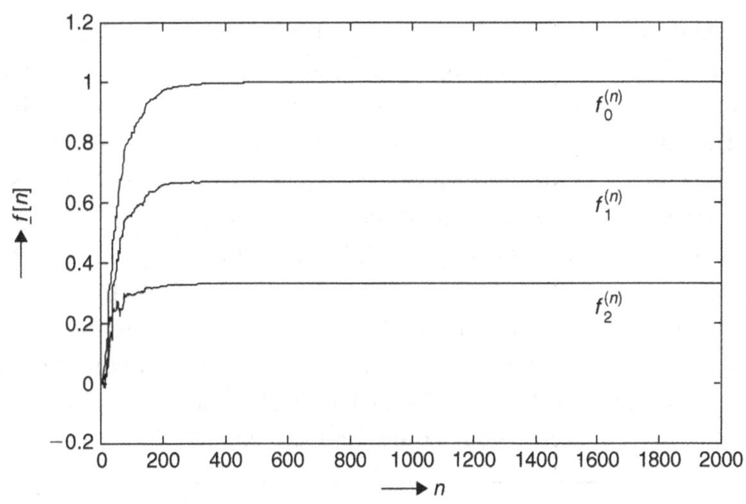

Figure 8.59: Convergence of filter weights with LMS floating-point simulation (first three significant values are plotted).

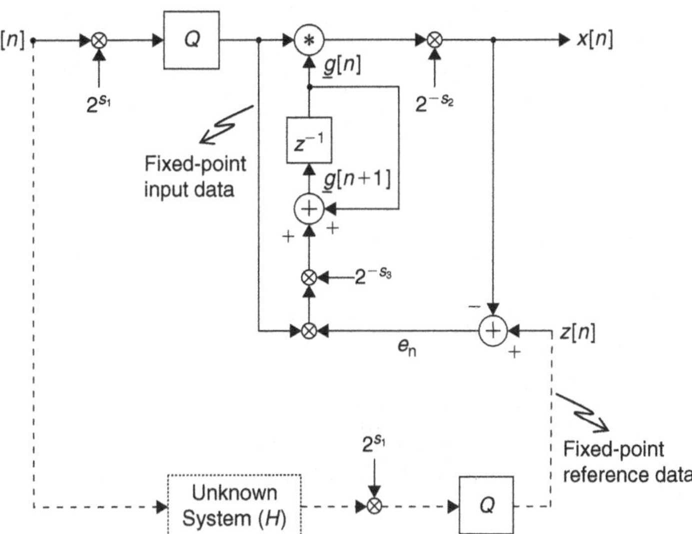

Figure 8.60: Signal-flow diagram for fixed-point implementation of LMS algorithm.

size used is $\mu = 1/64$, and the converged filter weight values after processing $n = 2000$ samples (or iterations) with filter length $M = 7$ are $f = [1, 0.670000017, 0.329999954, -3.26260041e-09, -4.98232966e-09, 1.18865406e-08, -3.16232551e-08]$.

Next, we discuss fixed-point implementation (see Figure 8.60) to run the LMS algorithm on the reference embedded processor (see Appendix A on the companion website). Given that the reference processor can efficiently perform filtering with 16-bit data, we represent both signals and filter coefficients in 16 bits. We use a total of three scaling parameters to maintain the data at different stages of the algorithm to avoid data overflow and realize stable filtering. Since both data and filter weights can be signed numbers, the MSB is always used to indicate the sign of the data or filter weight. In addition, we allow 2 bits of margin to take care of variations in the input signals. With this, we have only 13 out of 16 bits to work with.

The input and reference signals are converted to fixed-point data by multiplying by 2^{s_1} and rounding to the nearest integer (i.e., quantizing signals to finite levels). In practice, the value of the scaling parameter for the input and reference signals need not be the same. It all depends on the gain of the unknown system H. We determine the scale parameter s_1 as follows. Assuming the amplitude levels of unit-variance Gaussian-distributed signals can go as high as 7 (theoretically it can take any value), we require 3 bits to represent the integer portion of the signals. We are left then with 10 bits for the fraction, and thus we choose 10 for the scale parameter s_1.

By scaling the convolution output by 2^{-s_2}, we ensure that the result of filtering output is within the range $[-2^{15}, 2^{15}-1]$ with a margin of 1 or 2 bits. We choose $s_2 = 13$, assuming that the convolution output grows to 26 bits as the convolution is a MAC (multiply and accumulate) operation on 13-bit input and 13-bit filter coefficients.

Then, scaling of the gradient, which is the output of multiplying the error and input signals, by 2^{-s_3} ensures that the gradient estimate is within range. Because the error signal is the difference between the output signal $x[n]$ and reference signal $z[n]$, its amplitude can be represented by fewer than 13 bits. By assuming that the error signal requires about 50% of total bits when compared to the reference signal, the gradient estimate can grow to 20 bits. This means that to get the filter weights with 13-bit precision, we must multiply the gradient by 2^{-7}. Further, we also multiply the gradient by the step size $\mu(= 1/64)$, and this effectively scales the gradient by a factor 2^{-13}. Thus, we choose 13 for the third scaling parameter s_3.

The fixed-point simulation code for the LMS algorithm is given in Pcode 8.2. The error convergence with fixed-point simulation is shown in Figure 8.61. Figure 8.62 shows the filter weight convergence with fixed-point implementation of the LMS algorithm. The converged filter weight values after $n = 2000$ samples with filter length $M = 7$ is $g = [8192, 5488, 2703, -1, 0, 1, 1]$. By normalizing the filter weights g with 2^{13}, we get the filter coefficients $[1.0000, 0.6699, 0.3299, -0.0001, 0.0000, 0.0001, 0.0001]$, which are very close to the filter coefficients that are obtained with floating-point simulation.

```
                              // fix_u[] array contain the fixed-point input data
                              // fix_z[] array contain the fixed-point reference data
short g[7];
short ee[2000];
void lms_fix(int N, int M)
{
      int i,j,k;
      int s1,s2,s3,sum;
      s1 = 10;                // data is converetd to fixed point by multiplying by (1 << s1)
      s2 = 13; s3 = 13;
      for(j = M - 1;j < N;j++){
         sum = 0;
         for(i = j,k = 0;i >= (j - M + 1);i--,k++)
            sum = sum + (fix_u[i]*g[k]);
         ee[j] = fix_z[j] - ((sum + 4096) >> s2);        // round by adding (1 << (s2 - 1))
         for(k = 0;k < M;k++){
            sum = (ee[j]*fix_u[j - k] + 4096) >> s3;   // round by adding (1 << (s3 - 1))
            g[k] = g[k] + sum;
         }
      }
}
```

Pcode 8.2: Fixed-point simulation code of LMS algorithm.

As discussed previously, improper scaling in fixed-point implementation of the LMS algorithm may lead to unstable filtering. For example, the error diverges as shown in Figure 8.63 if we run the program in Pcode 8.2 by choosing scaling parameters $s_1 = 10$, $s_2 = 13$, and $s_3 = 9$. This is where engineering experience plays a role. One more important thing is that the error convergence of the fixed-point LMS algorithm also depends on register width (i.e., precision) of the embedded processor. Based on Equation (8.25), it is clear that the LMS algorithm

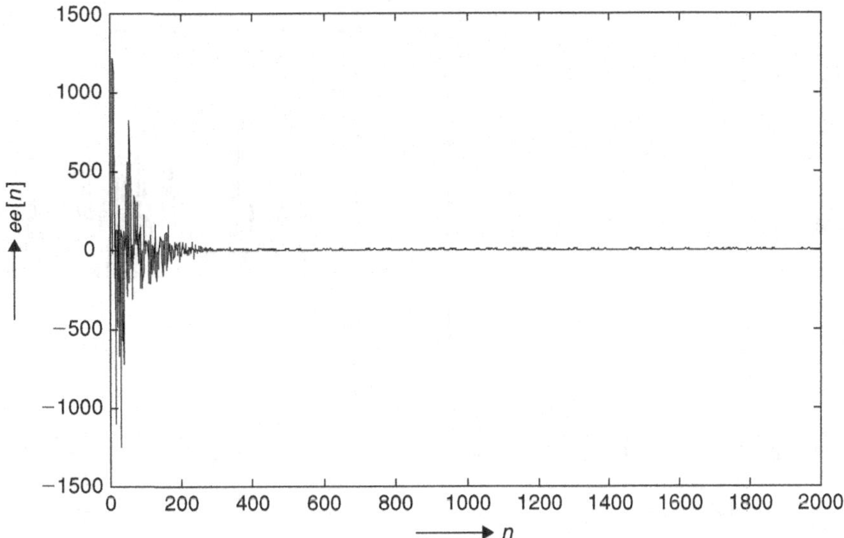

Figure 8.61: Error convergence with fixed-point LMS algorithm.

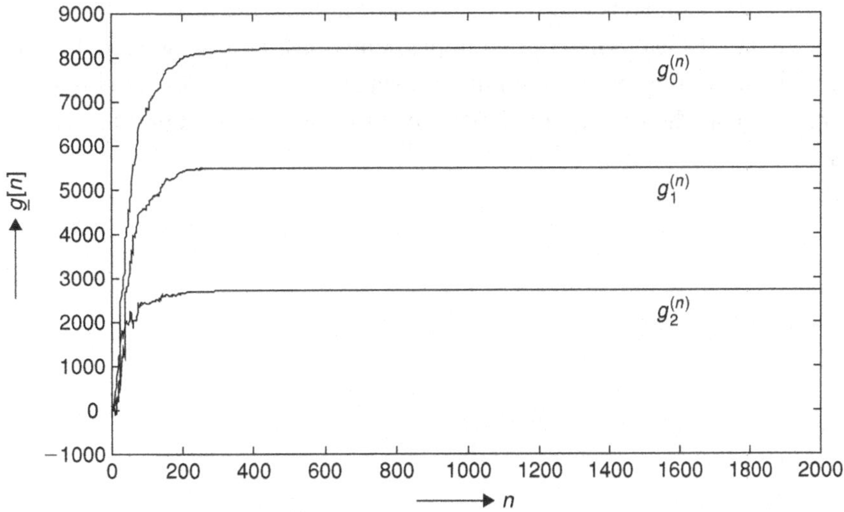

Figure 8.62: Filter-weight convergence with fixed-point LMS algorithm.

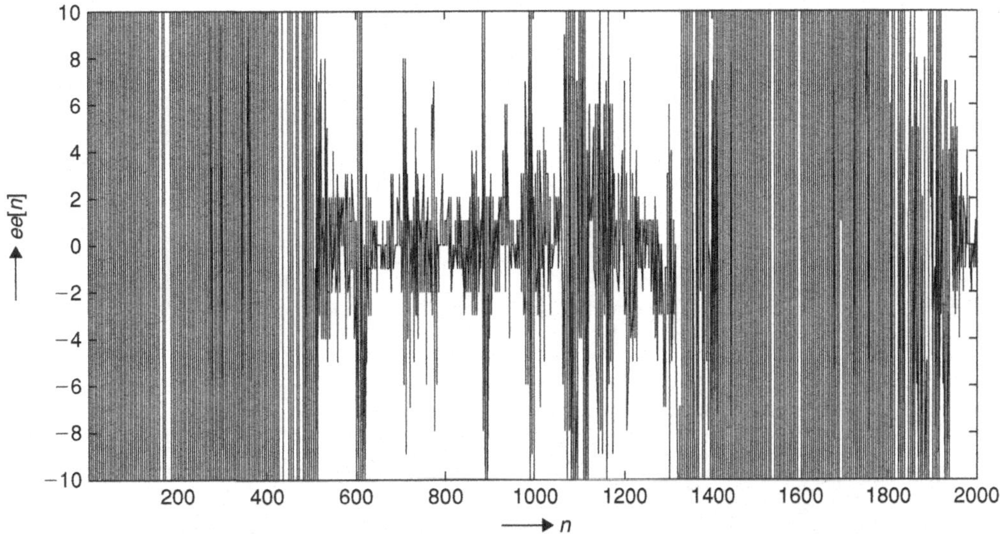

Figure 8.63: Error divergence with fixed-point LMS due to improper scaling.

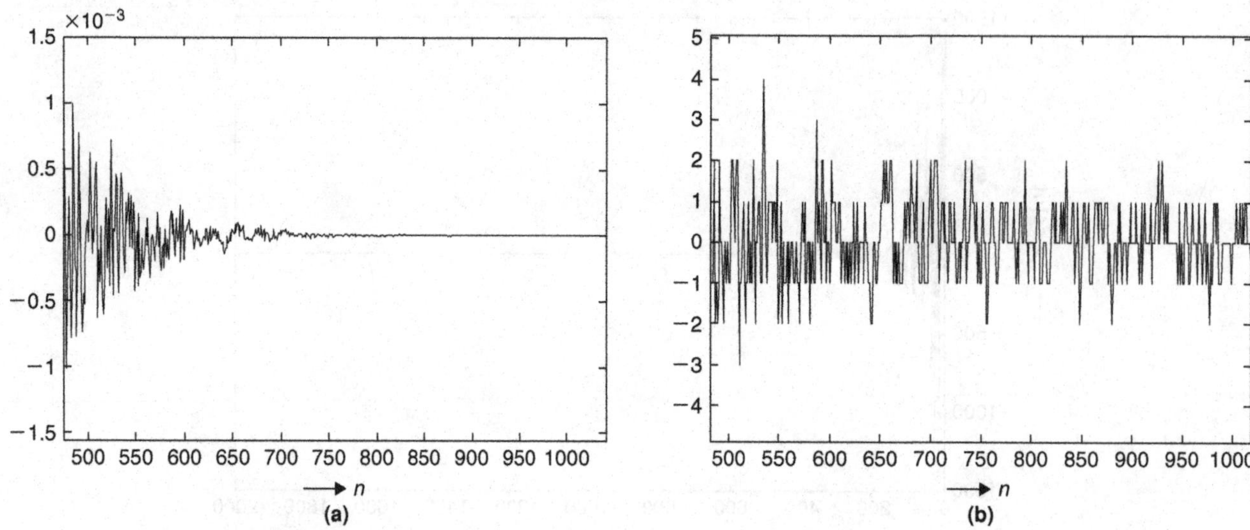

Figure 8.64: Error convergence with LMS algorithm. (a) Floating-point simulation. (b) Fixed-point simulation.

will stop adapting for error magnitudes below a certain threshold as the number of bits used to represent the filter coefficients is finite (i.e., 13 in our fixed-point implementation). This is shown in Figure 8.64 after $n = 500$ iterations. The error with the floating-point simulation converges to zero as shown in Figure 8.64(a), whereas the convergence of error stopped as shown in Figure 8.64(b) due to finite precision of filter weights in the fixed-point implementation case.

CHAPTER 9

Digital Communications

9.1 Introduction

In digital communications, we basically deal with the transmission of data in digital form from one source to one or more destinations through physical channels (e.g., copper wire, space). In everyday life, we frequently encounter two types of communications: (1) one-to-one or point-to-point communication (e.g., telephone), and (2) one-to-many or broadcast communication (e.g., radio, TV). The data generated at the source can be any information, such as voice, text, audio, and video. At present, multimedia network communications and the Internet play a major role in all our lives.

The general structure of the TCP/IP protocol-based network communication system, shown in Figure 9.1, consists of many layers and interfaces. Discussion of all layers, protocols, and interfaces of the system shown in Figure 9.1 is outside the scope of this book. In this chapter, we limit our discussion to digital communication modules that work on every bit of data and make the data suitable for transmission on physical channels. Most of these communication modules pertain to the physical layer. Figure 9.2 shows a simplified communication system after stripping off the protocol stack, network routing, and interfaces.

A brief description of the physical layer modules in the digital communication system shown in Figure 9.2 follows.

Information source: Captures the information (e.g., voice, images or any physical phenomenon) and digitizes it with an appropriate sampling rate.

Data compression block: Compresses and represents the data with a minimum number of bits to transmit more information using less channel bandwidth. In Chapter 5, we discussed and simulated various video data entropy coding algorithms.

Channel coding block: Adds redundancy to data bits before transmitting them in order to perform forward error correction at the receiver side (see Chapters 3 and 4).

Digital modulator block: Maps the individual or group of bits to symbols that are suitable for transmission over communication channels.

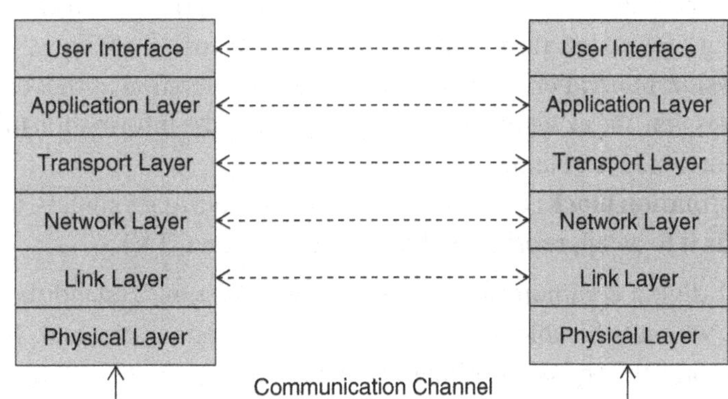

Figure 9.1: General structure of a TCP/IP protocol-based communication system.

DOI: 10.1016/B978-1-85617-678-1.00009-0

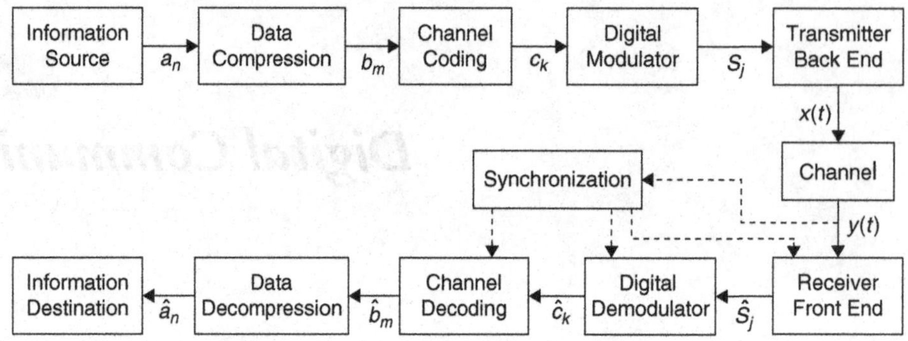

Figure 9.2: Simplified structure of a digital communication system.

Transmitter back end: Serves as the interface between the data processing blocks and physical channel. In some cases, a radio frequency (RF) modulator is located in the transmitter back-end block and places the data symbols onto high-frequency carriers. The processed signals at the transmitter back end are then passed to the receiver front end through physical channels.

Channel: The physical medium used to send the signals from the transmitter to the receiver, such as twisted-pair wirelines, fiber optic cables, and space. Communication signals are corrupted due to channel impairments during signal transmission through these physical channels. A few channel impairments include noise from human-made sources, noise from natural phenomena (due to lightning, high temperatures), non-zero channel response, and so on. Apart from the channels, the switching equipment at both the transmitter and receiver ends also adds noise to signals. The non-zero response of both switching equipment and physical channel limits the effective transmission bandwidth of the communication system. Due to such channel impairments and limited bandwidth, we cannot reliably transmit data over any communication channel at whatever rate we wish. In other words, reliable communication is not possible beyond the information rate C, known as channel capacity. We discuss more on channel capacity later.

Receiver front end: Receives, demodulates, and samples signals. This block consists of all the synchronization circuitry needed for the demodulator and sampler, as well as filters to remove undesired out-of-band signals received by the receiver.

Synchronization methods: Required in most communication systems to align the timing (with respect to the data samples or frames) of receivers to the corresponding transmitters.

Digital demodulator block: Performs the exact opposite operation as that of the modulator block. When the error correction module is embedded in the digital modulator (e.g., trellis-coded modulation [TCM]), both demodulation and error decoding are simultaneously performed with this block.

Channel decoding block: Corrects the errors in the received data using redundancy added at the transmitter side. In Chapters 3 and 4, we discussed and simulated various error detection and forward error correction algorithms (e.g., RS codes, turbo codes) to minimize error data frames.

Data decompression block: Performs the exact opposite operation as that of the data compression block. Upon data decompression, the exact or approximate replica of the information that was compressed and transmitted at the transmitter side is obtained.

Information destination block: Reconstructs the analog data (e.g., signals, text, or images) using decompressed data and sends it to an appropriate end device (e.g., phone, TV).

To understand digital communications systems, we must understand the environment in which they operate. Specifically, we must be able to model the communications channel. Modeling it allows us to determine channel capacity and transmission reliability. It also allows us to determine the most effective modulation scheme. To this end, we discuss the concepts of channel capacity, noise, and modulation schemes in the next section.

In subsequent sections, we discuss other communication system modules that heavily use signal-processing algorithms to mitigate channel effects. The topics of information source, transmitter back end, receiver front end, and information destination blocks are outside the scope of this book.

9.1.1 Channel Capacity

In information theory, channel capacity is defined as the upper bound on the amount of information that can reliably be transmitted over a communication channel. Before deriving the capacity of a channel, we discuss some theoretical concepts with respect to discrete random variables (see Section 6.1.2 for more on random variables).

Let X be a discrete random variable taking values from a set $S_X = \{x_1, x_2, \ldots, x_n\}$ with probability $\Pr(X = x_i) = f_X(x_i)$, where $f_X(x_i)$ is the probability mass function of the discrete random variable X. Then, the average self-information or entropy $H(X)$ of a discrete random variable X is defined as

$$H(X) = -\sum_i f_X(x_i) \log_2 f_X(x_i) \text{ bits} \tag{9.1}$$

In Equation (9.1), entropy $H(X)$ represents the measure of uncertainty of a random variable X in terms of bits.

Let $g(.)$ be a probabilistic function and $Y = g(X)$. Let S_Y denote the set of possible outcomes from $g(.)$ when it takes inputs from set S_X. Given the random variable Y, the conditional entropy of X follows:

$$\begin{aligned} H(X|Y) &= \sum_j f_Y(y_j) H(X|Y = y_j) \\ &= \sum_j f_Y(y_j) \left[-\sum_i f_{X|Y}(x_i|y_j) \log_2 f_{X|Y}(x_i|y_j) \right] \\ &= -\sum_i \sum_j f_Y(y_j) f_{X|Y}(x_i|y_j) \log_2 f_{X|Y}(x_i|y_j) \\ &= -\sum_i \sum_j f_{X,Y}(x_i, y_j) \log_2 f_{X|Y}(x_i|y_j) \text{ bits} \end{aligned} \tag{9.2}$$

The average mutual information $I(X;Y)$ between random variables X and Y is the difference between the entropy of X and the conditional entropy of X given Y. Thus, $I(X;Y)$ is given by

$$\begin{aligned} I(X;Y) &= H(X) - H(X|Y) \\ &= -\sum_i f_X(x_i) \log_2 f_X(x_i) + \sum_i \sum_j f_{X,Y}(x_i, y_j) \log_2 f_{X|Y}(x_i|y_j) \\ &= -\sum_i f_X(x_i) \log_2 f_X(x_i) + \sum_i \sum_j f_{X,Y}(x_i, y_j) \log_2 \left[\frac{f_{Y|X}(y_j|x_i) f_X(x_i)}{f_Y(y_j)} \right] \\ &= -\sum_i f_X(x_i) \log_2 f_X(x_i) + \sum_i \sum_j f_{X,Y}(x_i, y_j) \left[\log_2 f_X(x_i) + \log_2 \frac{f_{Y|X}(y_j|x_i)}{f_Y(y_j)} \right] \\ &= -\sum_i f_X(x_i) \log_2 f_X(x_i) + \sum_i f_X(x_i) \log_2 f_X(x_i) + \sum_i \sum_j f_{X,Y}(x_i, y_j) \log_2 \frac{f_{Y|X}(y_j|x_i)}{f_Y(y_j)} \\ &= \sum_i \sum_j f_{X,Y}(x_i, y_j) \log_2 \frac{f_{Y|X}(y_j|x_i)}{f_Y(y_j)} \text{ bits} \end{aligned} \tag{9.3}$$

If we represent a communication channel with the probability function $g(.)$ and the random variables X and Y represent input and output of a channel, then the maximum mutual information between X and Y gives the channel capacity C as

$$C = \max_{f_X(x_i)} I(X;Y) \tag{9.4}$$

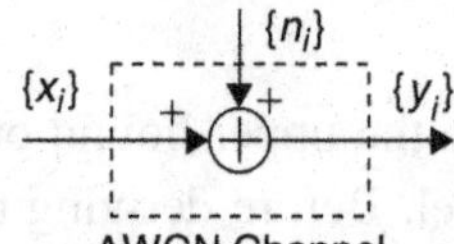

Figure 9.3: AWGN channel model.

Given Equations (9.1) through (9.4), the channel capacity is obtained as

$$C = \max_{f_X(x_i)} \sum_i \sum_j f_{X,Y}(x_i, y_j) \log_2 \frac{f_{Y|X}(y_j|x_i)}{f_Y(y_j)} \tag{9.5}$$

In Example 9.1, the channel capacity for an additive, white Gaussian noise (AWGN) channel model is derived. Figure 9.3 shows such a channel model. (See Section 9.1.2 for more detail on AWGN.) If a symbol enters the channel every T seconds, then the channel capacity in bits/second is given by C/T.

■ Example 9.1

With an additive white Gaussian noise (AWGN) channel, we model the channel as Gaussian distributed noise with flat frequency response within the operative band of W Hz. This communication system with inputs $\{x_i\}$ and outputs $\{y_i\}$ can be realized as shown in Figure 9.3.

$$y_i = x_i + n_i \tag{9.6}$$

where the noise samples n_i are Gaussian zero-mean with variance $\sigma_n^2 = N_0/2$.

Then the conditional probability mass function (pdf), $f_{Y|X}(y_i|x_i)$, is given by

$$f_{Y|X}(y_i|x_i) = \frac{1}{\sqrt{2\pi\sigma_n^2}} e^{-(y_i - x_i)^2/2\sigma_n^2} \tag{9.7}$$

Given Equation (9.5), the maximum of $I(X;Y)$ over the input pdf's $f_X(x_i)$ is obtained when $\{x_i\}$ are zero-mean, statistically independent, Gaussian random variables; that is,

$$f_X(x_i) = \frac{1}{\sqrt{2\pi\sigma_x^2}} e^{-\frac{x_i^2}{2\sigma_x^2}} \tag{9.8}$$

where σ_x^2 is the variance of input $\{x_i\}$. Then, given N input samples $\{x_1, x_2, \ldots, x_N\}$ for transmission in time T seconds, channel capacity based on Equation (9.5) follows:

$$C = \frac{N}{2} \log_2 \left(1 + \frac{2\sigma_x^2}{N_0}\right) \text{ bits} \tag{9.9}$$

Since $T = N/(2W)$ and $P_{av} = N\sigma_x^2/T$ (with average power-limited inputs), the channel capacity (C) per second follows:

$$C = W \log_2 \left(1 + \frac{P_{av}}{WN_0}\right) \text{ bits/second} \tag{9.10}$$

The normalized channel capacity is given by

$$C/W = \log_2 \left(1 + \frac{P_{av}}{WN_0}\right) \text{ bits/second/hertz} \tag{9.11}$$

If E_b denotes energy per bit, then $P_{av} = CE_b$. Then the normalized channel capacity in terms of E_b/N_0 is represented as

$$C/W = \log_2 \left(1 + \frac{C}{W}\frac{E_b}{N_0}\right) \text{ bits/second/hertz} \tag{9.12}$$

■

9.1.2 Noise Generation and Measurement

In a communication system, we typically receive data that is different from the data transmitted due to the addition of noise to the data signals during transmission. The accumulated noise comes from different sources, such as thermal noise (resulting from electron collision in conducting materials), interference noise (due to many transmission signals running in parallel at a particular time), lightning noise (because of the natural lightning phenomena during storms), switching noise (due to imperfect switching equipment at transmitter and receiver sides), quantization noise (result of analog/digital conversion), intersymbol interference (ISI) (due to limited channel bandwidth), and so on. Figure 9.4 displays a few noise sources in baseband digital communication systems. Each noise component has its own distribution and they are random and independent. The presence of noise restricts us from achieving reliable communication beyond the channel capacity. Achieving reliable communication even below the channel capacity is possible only with very complex channel coding and modulation techniques. Receiver performance (with channel decoders and demodulators) depends on the signal strength that we are able to maintain at the receiver input.

As receiver modules introduce some gain to the signals during processing, the performance of a particular module depends on signal strength at that particular module. Suppose we measure the signal-to-noise ratio (SNR) at one stage of the receiver; if we compute module performance at another stage of the receiver using this SNR, then those performance curves (or bit-error-rate [BER] curves) may not reflect module performance. Consequently, we have to measure the SNR at each stage of the receiver in order to obtain correct performance indicators for individual receiver modules.

But, as shown in Figure 9.4, the type of data present at one receiver module is different from the data at another module. In other words, the data at different stages of the receiver is not of the same type. For example, the data at the receiver front-end input is a continuous modulated signal, compared to the discrete sample form at the channel equalization input, and data symbol form at the inner channel decoder input, and data bits form at the outer channel decoder input. Signal strength is measured with different metrics at the input of the various receiver modules by considering the appropriate data rate (as it affects bandwidth and noise power); and thereby we avoid in previous modules upon determining the performance of the present receiver module.

Thermal Noise

In this section, we consider thermal noise generated by conducting materials such as resistors, and obtain a few relationships to measure noise strength and to compute the ratio of signal power to noise power at different stages

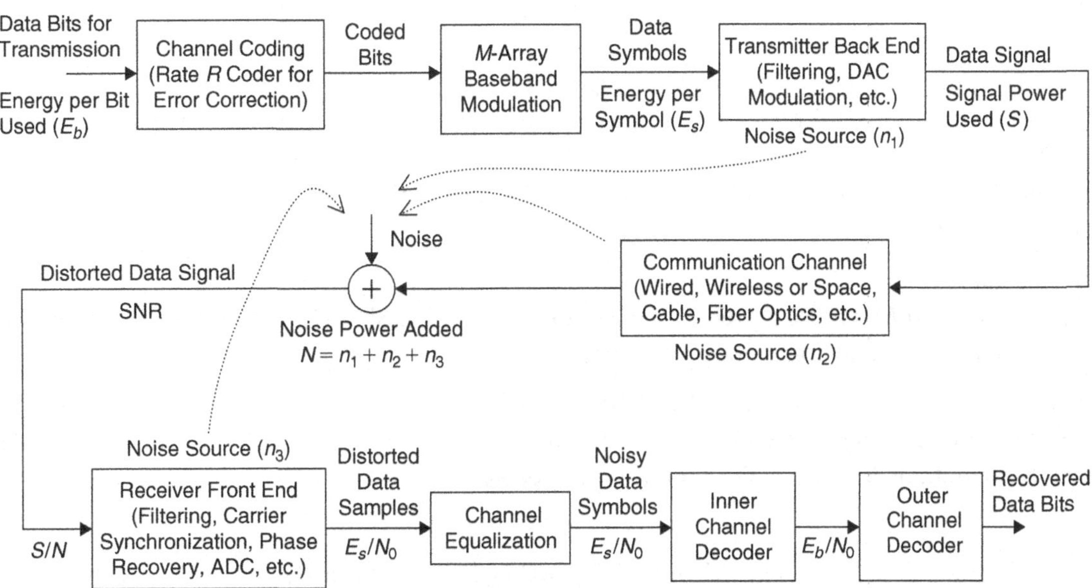

Figure 9.4: General digital communication system along with a few noise sources.

of the receiver. The noise root-mean-square voltage (E) across the resistor is given by

$$E = (4 \cdot K \cdot T \cdot R \cdot B)^{1/2} \text{ volts} \tag{9.13}$$

where K is the Boltzman constant in joules per kelvin, T is temperature in kelvins, R is resistance value in ohms, and B is the bandwidth of frequencies (in Hz) involved in this process. Noise power (N) is defined as the noise energy per unit time, as in

$$N = E^2 \text{ watts} \tag{9.14}$$

The noise power spectral density ($N_0/2$) is defined as noise power per unit bandwidth:

$$N_0/2 = N/B = 4 \cdot K \cdot T \cdot R \text{ watts/Hz} \tag{9.15}$$

The noise voltage spectral density (V) follows:

$$V = (4 \cdot K \cdot T \cdot R)^{1/2} = (N_0/2)^{1/2} \text{ volts/(Hz)}^{1/2} \tag{9.16}$$

White Noise

For white noise, spectral density is a constant $N_0/2$ across all frequencies (i.e., it contains the noise components with the same energy at all frequencies as in white color, which contains all colors). To compute the noise power N for a given bandwidth B,

$$N = (N_0/2)^* B \tag{9.17}$$

Gaussian Noise

If many noise sources are present in the system, then the effective noise power becomes the sum of all individual noise powers. The distribution of this accumulated noise (according to the central limits theorem) converges to the Gaussian distribution. If $n_1, n_2, \ldots, n_m$ are the powers of noises $u_1, u_2, \ldots, u_m$, which come from m different and independent sources, then the effective noise power (N) is

$$N = n_1 + n_2 + \cdots + n_m \tag{9.18}$$

and as m approaches infinity, the distribution of accumulated noise $U = u_1 + u_2 + \cdots + u_m$ becomes Gaussian. As shown in Figure 9.4, although we have many noise sources, we only see the effective noise power at the receiver. Therefore, in simulations, we use one noise to represent all noise effects and we call that noise additive white Gaussian noise (AWGN), assuming that the effective noise is random and occupies all frequencies (hence it is white) in the band of interest.

Complex Noise

In the case of a complex signal, there are two independent noise channels; if their noise powers are n_a and n_b, then the effective noise power for complex noise is $N = n_a + n_b$. If s^2 is the variance (which is the same as the power of the signal when the signal mean is zero), N_0 is spectral density (power per unit bandwidth), and B is bandwidth, then in the case of real noise, $s^2 = N = (N_0/2)B$, and in the case of complex noise, $s^2 = N = (N_0/2)\,B + (N_0/2)\,B = (N_0 B)$.

Signal-to-Noise Ratio

If S is signal power and N is noise power, then the ratio S/N is called SNR (signal-to-noise ratio). Typically, we use SNR $= S/N$ in the case of continuous-time signals.

E_s/N_0 If the complex signal is discrete, then SNR is defined in terms of discrete sample energies. If energy per complex sample is E_s and the sample rate is F_s, then the power of the complex signal is $S = E_s F_s$. If we are using a bandwidth of B Hz, then the complex noise power is $N = N_0 B$. The ratio of signal-to-noise power follows:

$$\text{SNR} = S/N = E_s F_s / N_0 B = E_s/N_0 (\because F_s = B) \tag{9.19}$$

$$\text{SNR} = E_s/N_0 \tag{9.20}$$

In the case of real signals,

$$\text{SNR} = E_s/(N_0/2) \tag{9.21}$$

E_b/N_0 If we use the *M*-array modulation (see Section 9.1.3 for more details on modulation methods) with mapping of *k* bits per symbol (without using any channel coding), then in complex sequences, $E_b/N_0 = \text{SNR}/k = (E_s/N_0)/k$, and in real sequences, $E_b/(N_0/2) = \text{SNR}/k = (E_s/(N_0/2)/k$. With coding, we embed the code rate (R) in the preceding formula. Then, with complex sequences $E_b/N_0 = (E_s/N_0)/(R^*k)$ and in real sequences, $E_b/(N_0/2) = (E_s/(N_0/2))/(R^*k)$. Once we understand all the previous relationships, then we can generate noise with necessary power to add to the signal in determining the performance of individual receiver modules during the simulation time.

Noise Generation Using MATLAB

In MATLAB, the command **randn**() generates zero-mean unit variance (or power) for the normal or Gaussian distributed noise sequence. Now, using **randn**(), assume that we want to generate a noise sequence with the required noise power for a given E_b/N_0. Assume that $u = \text{sqrt}(s^2) * \textbf{randn}()$, where s^2 is a variance of u, is a noise sequence which satisfies E_b/N_0 measured at the inner channel decoder (corresponding to rate R encoder) in Figure 9.4; assume also that the *M*-array modulation is used with unit average symbol energy (or $E_s = 1$). In this process, $k = \log_2(M)$ bits are loaded per symbol. We would like to know the value of s^2 in terms of all parameters E_b/N_0, R, k, and E_s.

Per unit bandwidth, in the case of real sequences $E_b/(N_0/2) = \text{SNR}/(k * R)$, or

$$\begin{aligned} \text{SNR} &= k * R * E_b/(N_0/2) \\ S/N &= E_s/(N_0/2) = k * R * E_b/(N_0/2) \\ E_s/s^2 &= k * R * E_b/(N_0/2) \\ s^2 &= E_s/(k * R * E_b/(N_0/2)) = 1/(k * R * E_b/(N_0/2)) = 1/\left(2 * k * R * E_b/N_0\right) \end{aligned} \tag{9.22}$$

If E_b/N_0 is specified in decibel means, we have to convert to non-decibel quantities before substituting into the preceding formula. This is done as follows:

$$x\,(\text{in dB}) = 10^* \log 10(E_b/N_0) \tag{9.23}$$

$$E_b/N_0 = 10^{x/10} \tag{9.24}$$

In complex sequences, the following factors must be considered. Although MATLAB generates zero-mean, unit-variance, random Gaussian distributed numbers with the **randn**() command, some adjustment has to be done for a complex sequence to generate a unit-variance complex sequence $v = \text{sqrt}(s^2) * u$, where $u = \textbf{randn}() + j * \textbf{randn}\,()$ is a complex sequence, which is generated from two independent noise sequences obtained by using the **randn**() command. At this point, u is no longer a unit-power sequence (which has a variance of 2), and it has to be adjusted to unit power to use with the preceding formula to compute v. Therefore, we generate u to have unit variance as follows:

$$u = (\textbf{randn}() + j^*\textbf{randn}())/\textbf{sqrt}(2) \tag{9.25}$$

Next, s^2 is obtained with the following formula to get an appropriate complex noise sequence v that is going to be added to a complex data signal in determining the performance of a decoder module. For complex sequences,

$$s^2 = 1/(k^* R^* E_b/N_0) \tag{9.26}$$

Here E_b/N_0 is a non-decibel value.

Noise Generation Using C

The simulation code to generate complex Gaussian-distributed L noise samples is given in Pcode 9.1. Given the E_b/N_0 (in decibels), we first convert it to its equivalent non-dB value using Equation (9.24) and compute the sigma with the modulation parameter k and code rate R using Equation (9.26). We generate uniformly distributed random values using the "C" library function **rand()/RAND_MAX.** Once we have uniformly distributed random values, we can generate Gaussian distributed samples either by repeated addition of uniformly distributed random values (due to the central limit theorem) or using the Box-Muller transformation. If x_1 and x_2 are uniformly and independently distributed between 0 and 1, then y_1 and y_2 as defined by Box-Muller transformation have a Gaussian distribution with mean $\mu = 0$ and variance $\sigma^2 = 1$.

$$y_1 = \sqrt{2 \ln \frac{1}{x_1}} \cos(2\pi x_2) \tag{9.27}$$

$$y_2 = \sqrt{2 \ln \frac{1}{x_1}} \sin(2\pi x_2) \tag{9.28}$$

The simulation code given in Pcode 9.1 generates complex AWGN samples using Equations (9.27) and (9.28).

```
EbNo = 9;                                      // in dB
x = EbNo/10.0; y = pow(10.0f, x);
k = 3; R = 2/3;
sigma = sqrt(Es/(k*R*y)); mean = 0;            // Signal power Es = 1
for(i = 0;i < L;i++){
     x = (float)rand()/ RAND_MAX;              // uniform distributed random number x1
     if (x == 1.0) x = x - 0.0000001f;
     y = sigma * sqrt(2.0 * log(1.0/(x)));
     x = (float)rand()/ RAND_MAX;              // uniform distributed random number x2
     if (x == 1.0) x = x - 0.0000001f;
     z = mean + y*cos(2*PI *x);                // Gaussian distributed random number y1
     cn[0] = z/sqrt(2);
     z = mean + y*sin(2*PI *x);                // Gaussian distributed random number y2
     cn[1] = z/sqrt(2);
}
```

Pcode 9.1: Simulation code to generate complex noise samples.

9.1.3 Modulation Techniques

Modulation is a process by which some characteristics of a carrier signal are varied in accordance with the message signal. Here the carrier signal is referred to as the "modulated signal," and the message signal is referred to as the "modulating signal." Typically, the frequency of the carrier signal is very high when compared to the message signal. At this point you may be wondering why such modulation is required. The simple answer is that the modulated signals are more suitable for transmitting on a communication channel than the message signal itself. For example, in wireless communications, we can transmit the signals in the available frequency band and also minimize the antenna size by modulating the signals. The modulation schemes are broadly classified into two categories—analog and digital. The message signals are continuous (or analog) in the case of analog modulation, whereas they are discrete (or digital) for digital modulation. However, the carrier signals themselves are continuous in both cases. Examples of analog modulation schemes include amplitude modulation (AM), phase modulation (PM), and frequency modulation (FM), and examples of digital modulation schemes include pulse amplitude modulation (PAM), quadrature amplitude modulation (QAM), and phase shift keying (PSK).

With modulation schemes, we can efficiently use the available bandwidth (or improve spectral efficiency); minimize cross-talk interference, noise, and ISI; and work with trade-offs of power, bandwidth, and cost. There are more than one type of modulation scheme to choose from depending on channel characteristics, frequency band of operation, and application type, among other factors. Each modulation scheme has its own advantages and disadvantages, and all modulation schemes cannot be used with all applications. Discussing all analog and digital modulation techniques is beyond the scope of this book. In this section, we briefly discuss some widely used digital modulation schemes such as PAM, PSK, and QAM.

With baseband pulse amplitude modulation (PAM), we map a bit sequence b_k to a set of symbols a_m, and then each symbol is multiplied with a baseband pulse $p(t)$ to form a continuous-time signal $d(t) = \sum_m a_m p(t - mT)$.

Assume that the pulse $p(t)$ and the channel $h(t)$ are band-limited to W Hz (i.e., $P(f) = H(f) = 0$ for $|f| > W$). The signal $d(t)$ is transmitted to a receiver over channel $h(t)$. The frequency characteristics of the channel and the shape of baseband pulse $p(t)$ determine the overall spectrum of the transmitted signal. In an ideal baseband channel (i.e., $H(f) = 1$ for $|f| \leq W$), the receiver output $y(t)$ can be expressed as $y(t) = \sum_m a_m p(t - mT) + n(t)$, where $n(t)$ is the noise component. We pass the signal $y(t)$ through a demodulator to get back the transmitted symbols, a_m. In an AWGN channel, the optimum demodulation is achieved using the matched filter (Proakis, 1995). If a signal $y(t)$ is corrupted with AWGN, then the filter with impulse response $c(t)$ matched to $y(t)$ maximizes the demodulator output SNR at sampling instances kT. In this case, the matched filter impulse response is simply $c(t) = p(T - t)$. With imperfect sampling, we see the interference of current symbols with neighboring symbols due to the time overlap of band-limited pulses. This is called inter-symbol interference. In Section 9.1.4, we introduce the raised cosine filter, and discuss how zero ISI is achieved with this pulse-shaping filter assuming that the channel has ideal frequency response characteristics in the frequency band of operation.

With bandpass digital modulation, we further multiply the baseband pulse $p(t)$ with the carrier signal by varying the carrier's amplitude, phase, or frequency parameters, or by varying combinations of two or more parameters. Vector space representation of signals is used in dealing with the bandpass digital modulation schemes (see Lathi, 2000, for details on representation of signals as vectors).

With vector space representation, we represent the N-dimensional signal $x(t)$ using the linear combination of K basis functions $u_k(t)$. Let $\hat{x}(t)$ be the K-dimensional approximation of the original signal $x(t)$; the K coefficients x_k are obtained by minimizing the mean square error (MSE) between $x(t)$ and $\hat{x}(t)$. Let $e_{\min}$ be the minimum MSE due to approximation. When $e_{\min} = 0$,

$$x(t) = \sum_{k=1}^{K} x_k u_k(t) \tag{9.29}$$

If we can represent a finite energy signal by a series expansion of the form as in Equation (9.29), then such a finite energy signal $x(t)$ can be represented with a point in the K-dimensional vector space as $P_X = (x_1, x_2, x_3, \ldots, x_K)$. For example, using sinusoidal basis functions, the bandpass pulse-amplitude modulated (PAM) signal given in Equation (9.30) can be represented with a one-dimensional vector space.

Pulse Amplitude Modulation

In this section, we consider the bandpass PAM scheme and derive expressions for obtaining the probability of error with the demodulation of noisy PAM data received over AWGN channels. The same ideas can be applied to obtain the probability of error for other digital modulation schemes as well. A bandpass PAM communicating signal can be expressed (Proakis, 1995) as follows:

$$x_n(t) = A_n p(t) \cos 2\pi f_c t, \quad n = 1, 2, \ldots, N, \quad 0 \leq t \leq T \tag{9.30}$$

The energy of such a PAM signal in one interval [0, T] is

$$E_n = \int_0^T x_n^2(t) dt = \frac{1}{2} A_n^2 E_p \tag{9.31}$$

where E_p denotes the energy of pulse $p(t)$ in the interval [0, T]. The $x_n(t)$ term in Equation (9.30) can then be represented as in Equation (9.29):

$$x_n(t) = x_n u(t) \tag{9.32}$$

where

$$u(t) = \sqrt{\frac{2}{E_p}} p(t) \cos 2\pi f_c t \tag{9.33}$$

and

$$x_n = A_n \sqrt{\frac{1}{2} E_p} \tag{9.34}$$

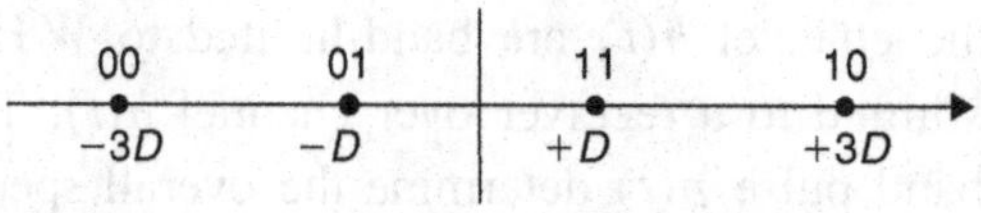

00 01 11 10
$-3D$ $-D$ $+D$ $+3D$

Figure 9.5: A 4-PAM signal constellation.

Now, if we map k-bit blocks to symbols, we will have $N = 2^k$ levels. The signal amplitudes take the following discrete levels:

$$A_n = (2n - 1 - N)d, \quad n = 1, 2, \ldots, N \tag{9.35}$$

For example, with $k = 2$ bit blocks, there will be $N = 4$ levels corresponding to four combinations of 2 bits—00, 01, 11, and 10. This is referred to as a 4-PAM scheme. The amplitude values A_n for a 4-PAM scheme follow:

$$A_1 = -3d, \quad A_2 = -d, \quad A_3 = d, \quad A_4 = 3d$$

These four levels are plotted as points in the one-dimensional plane as shown in Figure 9.5, where $D = d\sqrt{E_p/2}$. We refer to the points of vector space corresponding to the modulated waveform signals as "constellation points." The bits are assigned to points but not in a linear fashion; instead the bits are assigned such that the consecutive bit patterns differ by 1 bit, known as Gray coding. With this type of bit assignment, there are fewer bit errors (when compared to linear bit assignment) in the demodulation process at the receiver.

The Euclidean distance between any two constellation points is given by

$$d^{(E)} = |x_m - x_n|^2 = d\sqrt{2E_p}|m - n| \tag{9.36}$$

If $|m - n| = 1$, then the constellation points are adjacent, and with this we get the minimum Euclidean distance of constellation as follows:

$$d^{(E)}_{\min} = d\sqrt{2E_p} = 2D \tag{9.37}$$

The average energy of constellation is

$$E_{av} = \frac{1}{N}\sum_{n=1}^{N} E_n \tag{9.38}$$

Given Equations (9.31), (9.35), and (9.38),

$$E_{av} = \frac{1}{6}(N^2 - 1)d^2 E_p \tag{9.39}$$

The average power of PAM signals, then, is given by

$$P_{av} = \frac{1}{T}\left[(N^2 - 1)\, d^2 E_p/6\right] \tag{9.40}$$

With AWGN channels, the demodulator output for the m-th transmitted symbol follows:

$$y_m = x_m + n_m = \sqrt{\frac{1}{2}E_p}A_m + n_m \tag{9.41}$$

where n_m is the noise sample and has zero mean and variance $\sigma_n^2 = N_0/2$.

If $|y_m - x_m| = |n_m| > d^{(E)}_{\min}/2$, then the optimum detector output $\hat{x}_m$ will be in error and the probability of symbol error (P_{se}) (Proakis, 1995), in this case is given by

$$\begin{aligned} P_{se} &= \frac{N-1}{N} P(|y_m - x_m| > d\sqrt{E_p/2}) \\ &= \frac{N-1}{N}\frac{2}{\sqrt{\pi N_0}} \int_{d\sqrt{E_p/2}}^{\infty} e^{-t^2/N_0}\, dt \end{aligned} \tag{9.42}$$

By substituting $t = t\sqrt{N_0/2}$ in Equation (9.42), P_{se}

$$= \frac{(N-1)}{N}\frac{2}{\sqrt{2\pi}}\int_{\sqrt{d^2E_p/N_0}}^{\infty} e^{-t^2/2}dt$$
$$= \frac{2(N-1)}{N}Q\left(\sqrt{\frac{d^2E_p}{N_0}}\right) \tag{9.43}$$

where

$$Q(a) = \frac{1}{\sqrt{2\pi}}\int_a^{\infty} e^{-t^2/2}dt, \qquad a \geq 0$$

Given Equations (9.39) and (9.43), the probability of symbol error in terms of E_b/N_0 follows:

$$P_{se} = \frac{2(N-1)}{N}Q\left(\sqrt{\frac{(6\log_2 N)}{(N^2-1)}\frac{E_b}{N_0}}\right) \tag{9.44}$$

The bit-error-rate (BER) performance of the 16-PAM scheme is shown in Figure 9.9.

Quadrature Amplitude Modulation

PAM modulation uses one carrier to map k bits of information to $N = 2^k$ possible levels. With quadrature amplitude modulation (QAM), we map two separate k-bit blocks from the information sequence onto two quadrature carriers $\cos 2\pi f_c t$ and $\sin 2\pi f_c t$. The QAM signal waveform is expressed as follows:

$$x_n(t) = A_n^I p(t)\cos 2\pi f_c t - A_n^Q p(t)\sin 2\pi f_c t \tag{9.45}$$

$$x_n(t) = x_{n1}u_1(t) + x_{n2}u_2(t) \tag{9.46}$$

where

$$u_1(t) = \sqrt{\tfrac{2}{E_p}}p(t)\cos 2\pi f_c t,\ u_2(t) = -\sqrt{\tfrac{2}{E_p}}p(t)\sin 2\pi f_c t \tag{9.47}$$

$$x_n = [x_{n1}, x_{n2}] = [A_n^I\sqrt{E_p/2},\ A_n^Q\sqrt{E_p/2}] \tag{9.48}$$

We represent two quadrature $N = 2^k$ amplitude levels A_n^I and A_n^Q using two separate k-bit patterns from the bit sequence as follows:

$$A_n^I \text{ or } A_n^Q = \{(2n-1-N)d, n = 1, 2, \ldots, N\}$$

For the even value of k, the QAM scheme can be obtained with two quadrature PAM schemes. We get a 16-point constellation diagram as shown in Figure 9.6 by representing each one of four quadrature component levels with $k = 2$ bits. In other words, we can map a total of 4 bits using 16 QAM. The 4-bit values are assigned to QAM points in a particular order such that the hamming distance between neighboring points is always 1. With this bit assignment, we probably see a 1-bit error even if we misdetect the symbol due to channel noise.

In Figure 9.6, we choose the value of $D(= A_n^I\sqrt{E_p/2}$ or $A_n^Q\sqrt{E_p/2})$ by making the average energy of the constellation as 1, and the average energy of the constellation is calculated using the distance of points from the origin as follows:

$$E_{av} = \frac{4\times 2D^2 + 8\times 10D^2 + 4\times 18D^2}{16} = \frac{160D^2}{16} = 10D^2$$
$$1 = 10D^2 \text{ or } D = 1/\sqrt{10}$$

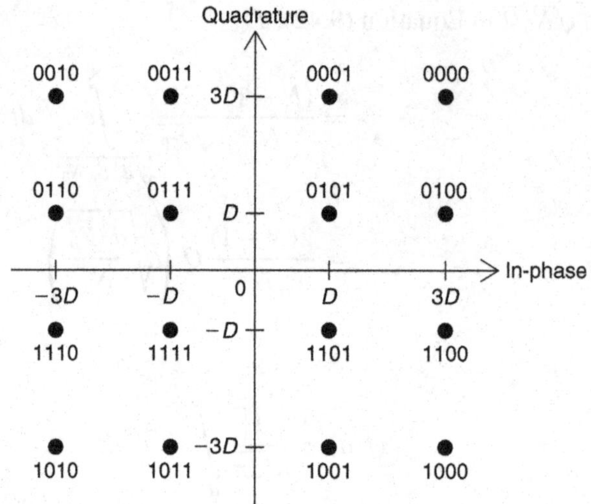

Figure 9.6: A 16-QAM constellation diagram.

Given Equation (9.48), the minimum distance between any two QAM constellation points follows:

$$d_{\min}^{(E)} = d\sqrt{2E_p} = 2d\sqrt{E_p/2} = 2D \tag{9.49}$$

The upper bound on the symbol error probability for the rectangular QAM schemes in the AWGN channels (Proakis, 1995) is given as

$$P_{se} \leq 4Q\left(\sqrt{\frac{3k}{N-1}\frac{E_b}{N_0}}\right) \tag{9.50}$$

Phase Shift Keying

With phase shift keying (PSK) schemes, we modify the phase of the carrier with information bits. We convey k bits of information using $N(=2^k)$ phases of carrier, and the corresponding signal waveforms are represented as follows:

$$\begin{aligned} x_n(t) &= p(t)\cos\left[2\pi f_c t + \frac{2\pi}{N}(n-1)\right] \\ &= p(t)\cos\frac{2\pi}{N}(n-1)\cos 2\pi f_c t - p(t)\sin\frac{2\pi}{N}(n-1)\sin 2\pi f_c t \end{aligned} \tag{9.51}$$

$$x_n(t) = x_{n1}u_1(t) + x_{n2}u_2(t) \tag{9.52}$$

where

$$u_1(t) = \sqrt{\frac{2}{E_p}}p(t)\cos 2\pi f_c t \tag{9.53}$$

$$u_2(t) = -\sqrt{\frac{2}{E_p}}p(t)\sin 2\pi f_c t \tag{9.54}$$

and

$$x_n = [x_{n1}, x_{n2}] = \left[\sqrt{\frac{E_p}{2}}\cos\frac{2\pi}{N}(n-1), \sqrt{\frac{E_p}{2}}\sin\frac{2\pi}{N}(n-1)\right], \quad n = 1, 2, \ldots, N \tag{9.55}$$

In Equation (9.55), $\phi_n = \frac{2\pi}{N}(n-1), n = 1, 2, \ldots, N$, are the N possible phases of the carrier that convey k bits of information. The constellation diagram of PSK for $N = 16$ is shown in Figure 9.7.

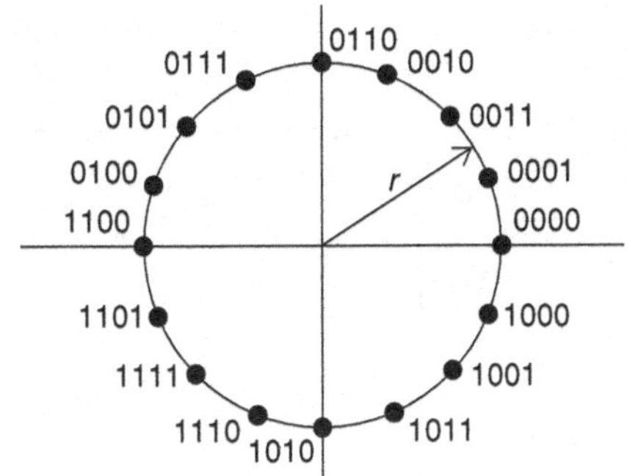

Figure 9.7: A 16-PSK constellation diagram.

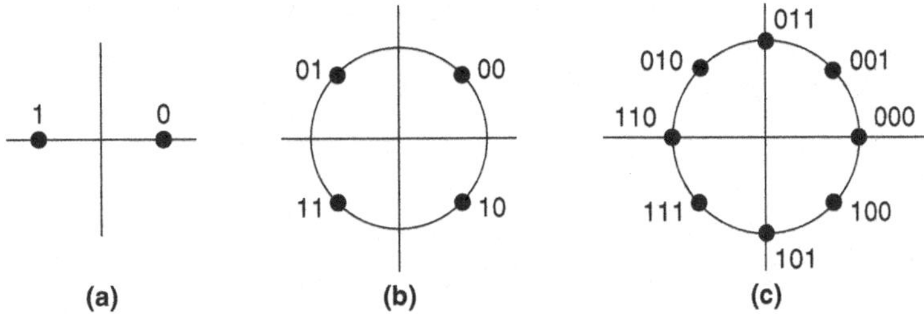

Figure 9.8: Constellation diagrams. (a) BPSK. (b) QPSK. (c) 8-PSK.

As all PSK points are positioned on the circle of radius r as shown in Figure 9.7, the average energy of the PSK constellation is r^2. By choosing $r = 1$, we can get the average energy of the PSK constellation as unity. The minimum distance between any two points of PSK constellation is

$$d_{\min}^{(E)} = \sqrt{E_p\left(1 - \cos\frac{2\pi}{N}\right)} \tag{9.56}$$

The approximate symbol error probability for PSK schemes in AWGN channels is given as

$$P_{se} \approx 2Q\left(\sqrt{2k\frac{E_b}{N_0}}\sin\frac{\pi}{N}\right) \tag{9.57}$$

In practice, we widely use 2-PSK or BPSK (binary-phase shift keying), 4-PSK or QPSK (quadrature phase shift keying), and 8-PSK schemes. The constellation diagrams of these modulation schemes are shown in Figure 9.8. The 2-PSK and 4-PSK modulation schemes are the same as 2-PAM and 4-QAM in terms of constellations and error performance.

The BER performance curves of the 16-PAM, 16-QAM, and 16-PSK schemes are shown in Figure 9.9. From BER curves at BER $= 10^{-6}$ it is clear that 16-QAM requires 4.2 dB less power when compared to the 16-PSK scheme. Thus, we prefer N-QAM schemes over N-PSK schemes for larger values of N. If $N = 4^k$, then N-QAM modulation constellation points are obtained with two orthogonal one-dimensional $\sqrt{N}$-PAM schemes. In other words, the BER performance of N-PAM is the same as for the N^2-QAM scheme. For example, the BER performance of 16-PAM and 256-QAM schemes is the same. Although we can double the number of transmitted bits with QAM schemes when compared to PAM schemes at a given SNR, the bandwidth efficiency of QAM and PAM schemes are the same because QAM signals are transmitted via double sideband (DSB), whereas PAM signals can be transmitted via single sideband (SSB). In all of the previous modulation schemes, increasing k by 1 bit requires an extra 4 dB of power to have the same BER performance.

Orthogonal Modulation Schemes

There are many orthogonal modulation techniques based on time, frequency, or code division. Here, we consider orthogonal modulation based on a frequency-division scheme in which a channel with a frequency bandwidth of F is subdivided into N frequency slots, each with a width Δf. We transmit N components of the N-dimensional

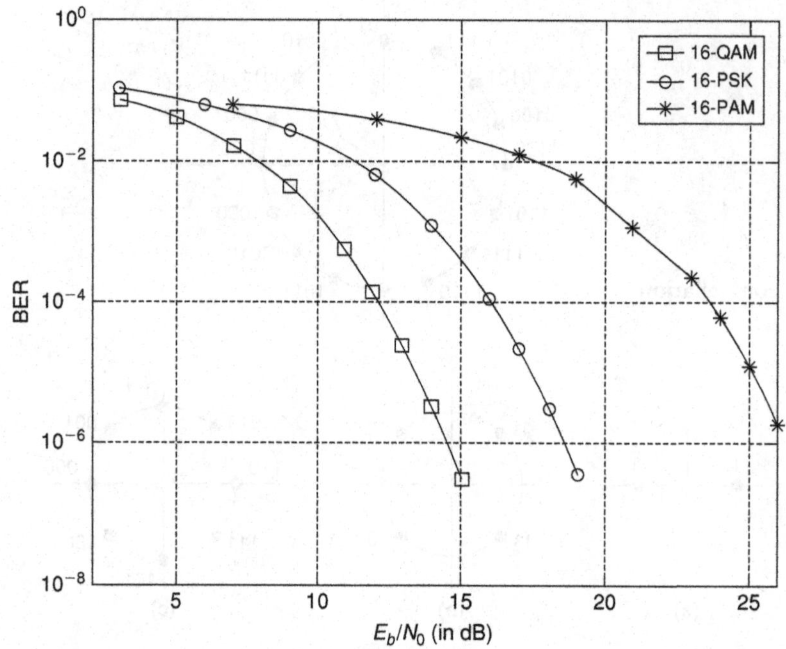

Figure 9.9: BER performance curves of 16-PAM, 16-PSK, and 16-QAM schemes.

signal vector over the channel by simultaneously modulating the amplitudes of N carriers of N frequency slots. Consider N frequency-shift keying (FSK) signals with equal energy E as follows:

$$\begin{aligned} x_n(t) &= \sqrt{\frac{2E}{T}}\cos[2\pi(f_c + n\Delta f)t], \quad n = 1, 2, \ldots, N, \quad 0 \le t \le T \\ &= \sqrt{\frac{2E}{T}}\cos(2\pi f_c t + 2\pi n\Delta f t) \\ &= \mathrm{Re}\left[x_n^{(l)}(t)e^{j2\pi f_c t}\right] \end{aligned} \tag{9.58}$$

where $x_n^{(l)}(t)$ is the corresponding baseband signal equivalent of $x_n(t)$, and is defined as

$$x_n^{(l)}(t) = \sqrt{\frac{2E}{T}}e^{j2\pi n\Delta f t}, \quad n = 1, 2, \ldots, N, \quad 0 \le t \le T \tag{9.59}$$

The magnitude of $x_n^{(l)}(t)$ is $\sqrt{2E/T}$, which is independent of t, and hence all these N signals have equal energy of E. If we compute the cross-correlation of $x_n^{(l)}(t)$, then the real part of cross-correlation is given by

$$R_{ab} = \frac{\sin 2\pi T(a-b)\Delta f}{2\pi t(a-b)\Delta f} \tag{9.60}$$

Given Equation (9.60), it is clear that the cross-correlation coefficient R_{ab} is zero whenever $\Delta f = 1/2T$ and $a \neq b$. With $\Delta f = 1/2T$, the N-FSK signals are orthogonal and equivalent to the N-dimensional vectors with $\sqrt{2E}$ as the distance between signals as represented here:

$$\begin{aligned} x_1 &= [\sqrt{E}\ \ 0\ \ 0\ \ \ldots\ \ 0] \\ x_2 &= [0\ \ \sqrt{E}\ \ 0\ \ \ldots\ \ 0] \\ &\vdots \\ x_N &= [0\ \ 0\ \ \ldots\ \ 0\ \ \sqrt{E}] \end{aligned} \tag{9.61}$$

With the N-FSK orthogonal modulation, we send the information on one of the N frequency components in any given interval of time T as described in Equation (9.61). Now, upon considering the orthogonal signals described by Equation (9.61), it is evident that we are using N frequency components to transmit one symbol of information; hence this system is very inefficient from a bandwidth point of view. However, it is possible to transmit a symbol at very low power with this scheme. Hence these systems are power efficient. For a given BER requirement, we can trade system power with bandwidth. In other words, we can reduce the power requirement by increasing the number of frequency components N. If we transmit k bits of information with each symbol, then $N = 2^k$. The upper bound on the probability of symbol error with N-FSK orthogonal signals in AWGN channels is given by

$$P_{se} \leq NQ\left(\sqrt{k\frac{E_b}{N_0}}\right) \tag{9.62}$$

Comparison of Various Modulation Schemes

Next, we compare different modulation schemes in terms of spectral efficiency, power efficiency, and cost. Spectral efficiency is defined as channel capacity per unit bandwidth, and we measure it in terms of bits per second per hertz. Power is another important factor that we take into account. We specify power in terms of energy per bit, E_b/N_0 (in decibels). The next important criterion in choosing the modulation scheme is the hardware cost to implement particular modulation and corresponding demodulation schemes. For example, the cost of BPSK or 2-PAM demodulators is very small compared to 16-PSK. A comparison of widely used modulation schemes N-QAM, N-PSK, and N-FSK in terms of spectral efficiency, power efficiency, and cost is given in Table 9.1. Figure 9.10 shows the performance of various modulation schemes at BER $= 10^{-5}$.

Table 9.1: Comparison of several modulation methods

Method/Metric	Spectral Efficiency	Power Efficiency	Cost
N-PSK	Good	Poor	High
N-QAM	Good	Poor	Medium
N-FSK	Poor	Good	Low

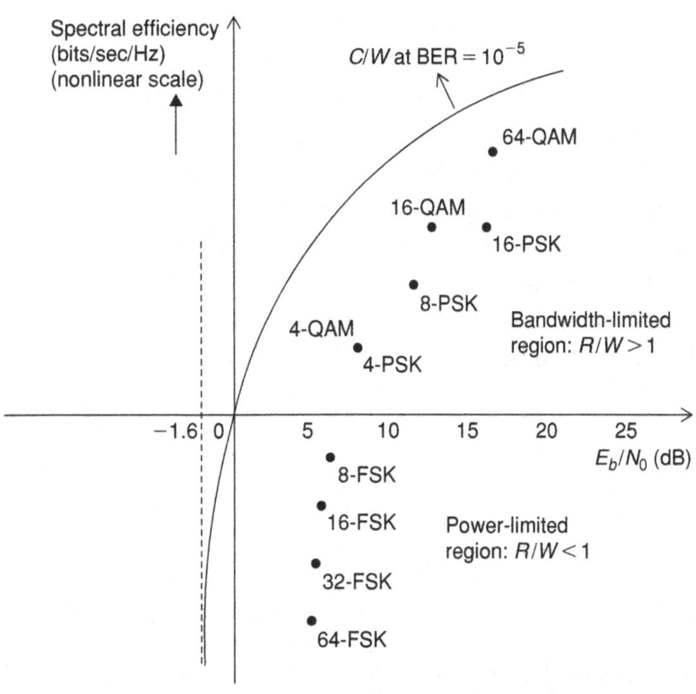

Figure 9.10: Comparison of various modulation schemes at BER $= 10^{-5}$.

9.1.4 Raised Cosine Modulation Filter

Assuming ideal channel frequency-response characteristics in the band of operation, the sampled matched filter output can be expressed as

$$y_m = a_m + \sum_{\substack{n=-\infty \\ n\neq m}}^{\infty} a_n x_{m-n} + z_m \tag{9.63a}$$

where $x(t)$ and $z(t)$ are the responses of the matched filter for inputs $p(t)$ and $n(t)$. The first term, a_m, in Equation (9.63a) is the desired information at the m-th sampling instant, and the second term (due to ISI) and third term (due to noise) are the undesired terms. It is possible to eliminate the ISI term with the following Nyquist condition:

$$x_m = x(t = mT) = \begin{cases} 1 & m = 0 \\ 0 & m \neq 0 \end{cases} \tag{9.63b}$$

One such pulse that satisfies the Nyquist condition for zero ISI in Equation (9.63b) is the normalized sinc pulse. However, the sinc pulse is noncausal and is not suitable for transmission. Also, as the rate of convergence of sinc toward zero is slow, any error in sampling instances may lead to non-zero ISI. Here we discuss another type of pulse, namely the Nyquist pulse or raised cosine filter. The frequency- and time-domain characteristics of the raised cosine filter are given by

$$X_{rc}(f) = \begin{cases} T & \left(0 \le |f| \le \dfrac{1-\alpha}{2T}\right) \\ \dfrac{T}{2}\left\{1+\cos\left[\dfrac{\pi T}{\alpha}\left(|f| - \dfrac{1-\alpha}{2T}\right)\right]\right\} & \left(\dfrac{1-\alpha}{2T} \le |f| \le \dfrac{1+\alpha}{2T}\right) \\ 0 & \left(|f| > \dfrac{1+\alpha}{2T}\right) \end{cases} \tag{9.64a}$$

$$x_{rc}(t) = \frac{\sin(\pi t/T)}{\pi t/T}\,\frac{\cos(\pi \alpha t/T)}{1 - 4\alpha^2 t^2/T^2} \tag{9.64b}$$

where α is the roll-off factor and takes values in the range of $0 \le \alpha \le 1$.

The time- and frequency-domain characteristics of the raised cosine filter for $T = 0.1$ are shown in Figure 9.11. The time response of the filter goes through zero with a period that exactly corresponds to the symbol spacing, T. Adjacent symbols do not interfere with each other at the symbol times because the response equals zero at all symbol times except the center one. The raised cosine filters heavily filter the signal without blurring the symbols together at the symbol times. This is important for transmitting information without errors caused by ISI. The bandwidth occupied by the signal beyond the Nyquist frequency $1/2T$ is referred to as excess bandwidth, and is usually expressed as a percentage of the Nyquist frequency. For example, when $\alpha = 0.0$, the excess bandwidth is 0%; when $\alpha = 0.5$, the excess bandwidth is 50%; and when $\alpha = 1.0$, the excess bandwidth is 100%. Typically, the filter is split, half being in the transmitter path and half in the receiver path. In this case, root raised cosine filters are used in each part, so that their combined response is that of the raised cosine filter. In the special case where the channel is ideal (i.e., $H(f) = 1, |f| \le 1/T$),

$$X_{rc}(f) = P_{rc}^{T}(f)P_{rc}^{R}(f) = |P_{rc}^{T}(f)|^2 \tag{9.65}$$

or

$$P_{rc}^{T}(f) = \sqrt{X_{rc}(f)}e^{-j2\pi f\tau} \tag{9.66}$$

and

$$P_{rc}^{R}(f) = \sqrt{X_{rc}(f)}e^{j2\pi f\tau} \tag{9.67}$$

where τ is some nominal delay that is required to ensure physical reliability of the filter.

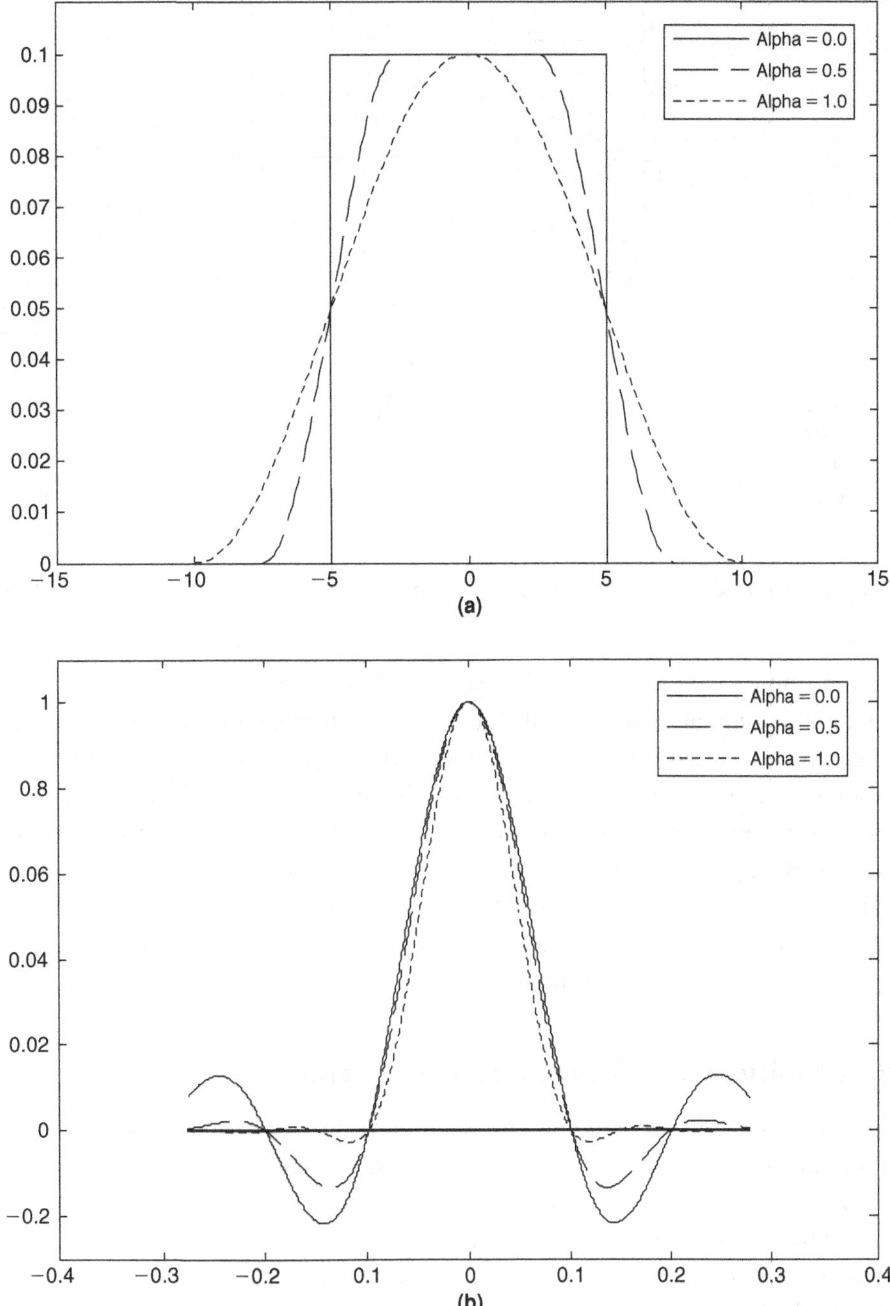

Figure 9.11: Time-frequency domain characteristics of a raised cosine filter for $T = 0.1$. (a) Frequency-domain characteristics for $\alpha = 0$, 0.5, and 1.0. (b) Time-domain characteristics for $\alpha = 0$, 0.5, and 1.0.

9.1.5 Eye Diagrams

As discussed previously, raised cosine filters are widely used for pulse shaping before transmission of modulated symbols. Let's consider an example of transmitting BPSK symbols. The constellation of BPSK symbols is shown in Figure 9.8(a). With BPSK, we transmit symbol "1" for bit "0" and symbol "– 1" for bit "1". If we use rectangular pulses (with positive and negative amplitudes) to transmit the symbols – 1 and 1 as shown in Figure 9.12(a), then we require infinite frequency bandwidth to transmit the symbols, as the rectangular pulse contains infinite frequencies. Because of this, we use a pulse-shaping filter to transmit symbols "1"and "– 1" as shown in Figure 9.12(b).

The eye diagram is an oscilloscope display of repetitively sampled transmitted signal. With eye diagrams, we see many transmitted pulses in two or more symbol time intervals in an overlapped fashion. The eye diagrams

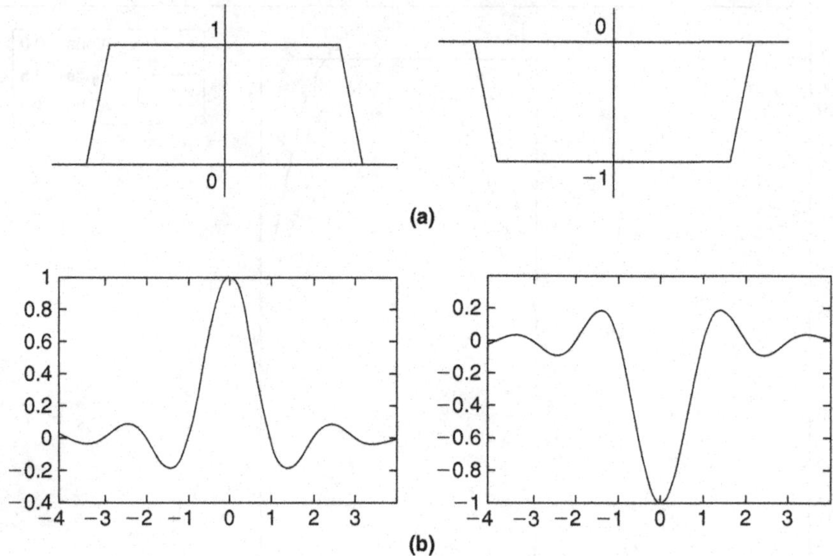

Figure 9.12: Two pulse shapes for transmitting BPSK symbols 1 and −1: (a) rectangular and (b) raised cosine.

of BPSK symbols transmitted with the ideal pulse and raised cosine pulse are shown in Figure 9.13. The eye diagram is a useful tool for qualitative analysis of signals used in digital communications. Like the constellation points, the eye diagrams also provide information on channel imperfections, SNR, clock timing jitter, skew, and so on. For example, the spread and rotation of constellation points (see Figure 9.14(a)) indicate the SNR and sampling time error at the receiver end. Similarly, eye diagrams for received noise signals indicate overall channel conditions. Greater eye closure indicates low SNR, more signal distortion, more jitter in clock timing, and so on. The width of the eye opening provides information on the time interval over which the received signal can be sampled without error from noise and ISI. As seen in Figures 9.14(b) and (c), choosing the α value for the raised cosine pulse affects receiver performance.

9.2 Single- and Multicarrier Communication Systems

As digital communication systems are making the transition from voice-centric communication to interactive Internet data and multimedia types of applications, the demand for higher data-rate transmission is increasing tremendously. For example, in the early days of voice communication systems (i.e., voiceband modems), data rates were about 32 kbps, whereas we require 10 times or more data transmission rates to transmit present-day multimedia services (e.g., voice, audio, video, text, image). We use more channel bandwidth and higher constellation sizes to achieve this high-speed data communication. In the communication system design, a few parameters that play important roles include the channel time-frequency characteristic, data rates, transmission power levels, and receiver complexity. Given a particular channel time-frequency characteristic, the communication system designer must decide how to efficiently use the available channel bandwidth to transmit the information reliably within the constraints of transmission power and receiver complexity.

In this section, we discuss how high-speed communications are achieved using single- and multicarrier communication systems. One of the main problems associated with the nonideal (i.e., spectrally shaped) channels is ISI. Since the information is transmitted serially at a very high baud rate (i.e., the number of signals transmitted per second), the time dispersion (i.e., distortion to the signal that occurs when the coherence bandwidth of the channel is less than the modulation bandwidth) leads to ISI, where the energy from one symbol spills over into another symbol. Traditionally, ISI is removed using a channel equalizer, which may be implemented in the time or frequency domain. The higher data rates, with narrower symbol durations, experience significant time dispersion and require highly complex equalizers. To transmit information through a spectrally shaped channel, one option is to employ a single-carrier system with very complex equalizers. We discuss various channel equalization techniques in detail in a later section.

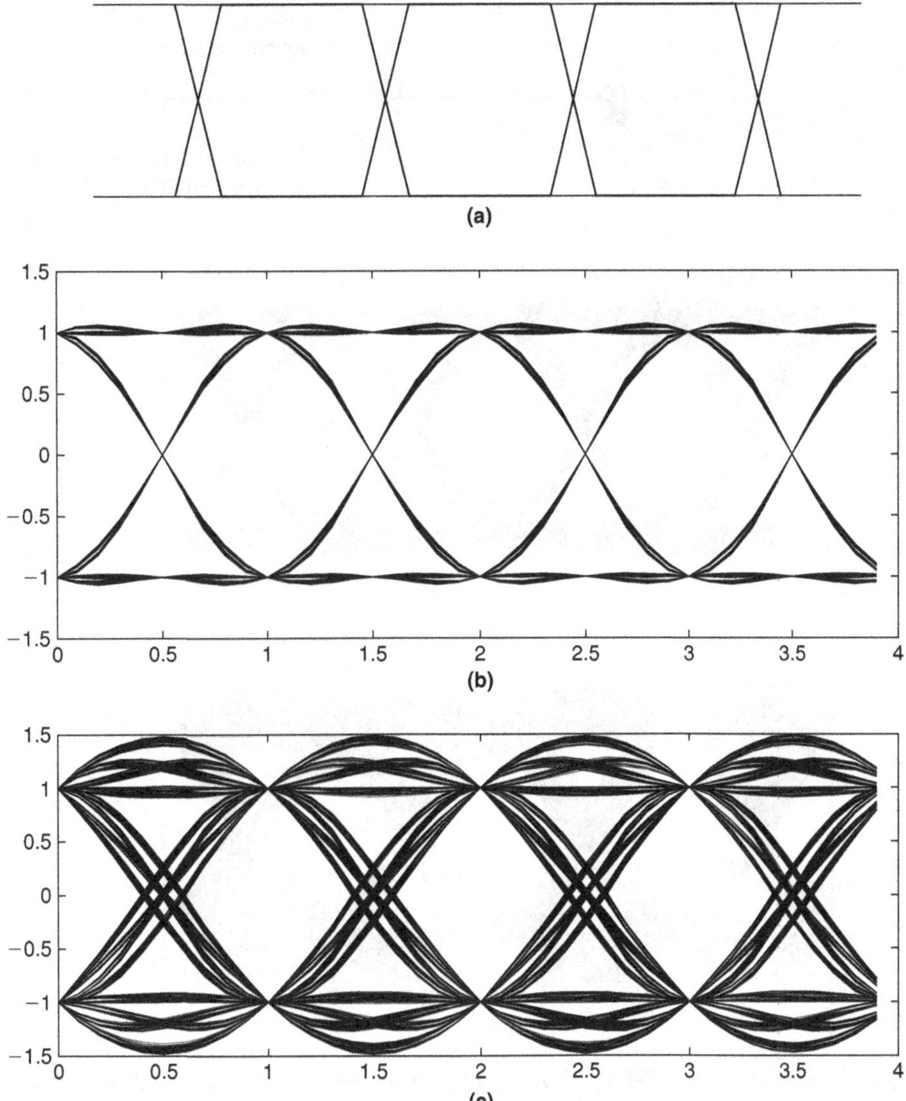

Figure 9.13: Eye diagram for BPSK transmitted signals. (a) With rectangular pulse. (b) With raised cosine filter, $\alpha = 1$. (c) With raised cosine filter, $\alpha = 0.5$.

Multicarrier modulation (MCM) techniques, on the other hand, overcome the problem of transmitting data over channels that are severely distorted. From the ISI point of view, the MCM technique is a divide-and-conquer approach to combat the problem of ISI. In MCM, we transmit the data by dividing the high bit-rate bitstream into several parallel low bit-rate bitstreams and modulating those low bit-rate bitstreams onto many orthogonal carriers. In other words, with MCM the channel is partitioned into a large number of small-bandwidth channels called subchannels, and if a subchannel is narrow enough, the channel gain in the subchannel is approximately a complex constant. In such cases, the ISI can be easily eliminated with a single tap filter, and the information is transmitted over the narrowband subchannels without any ISI. Note that the multicarrier does not mean multiple physical carriers; it is only the transceiver (i.e., transmitter and receiver pair) that views a single datastream transmitting on multiple-frequency subbands (or subchannels).

Next, we discuss the techniques of both the single- and the multicarrier systems to achieve high-speed data communications.

9.2.1 Single-Carrier Communication Systems

In single-carrier communication systems, the data signals are modulated on a single carrier and transmitted. At the receiver, the down-converted baseband signals are processed to get the estimate of baseband modulated data

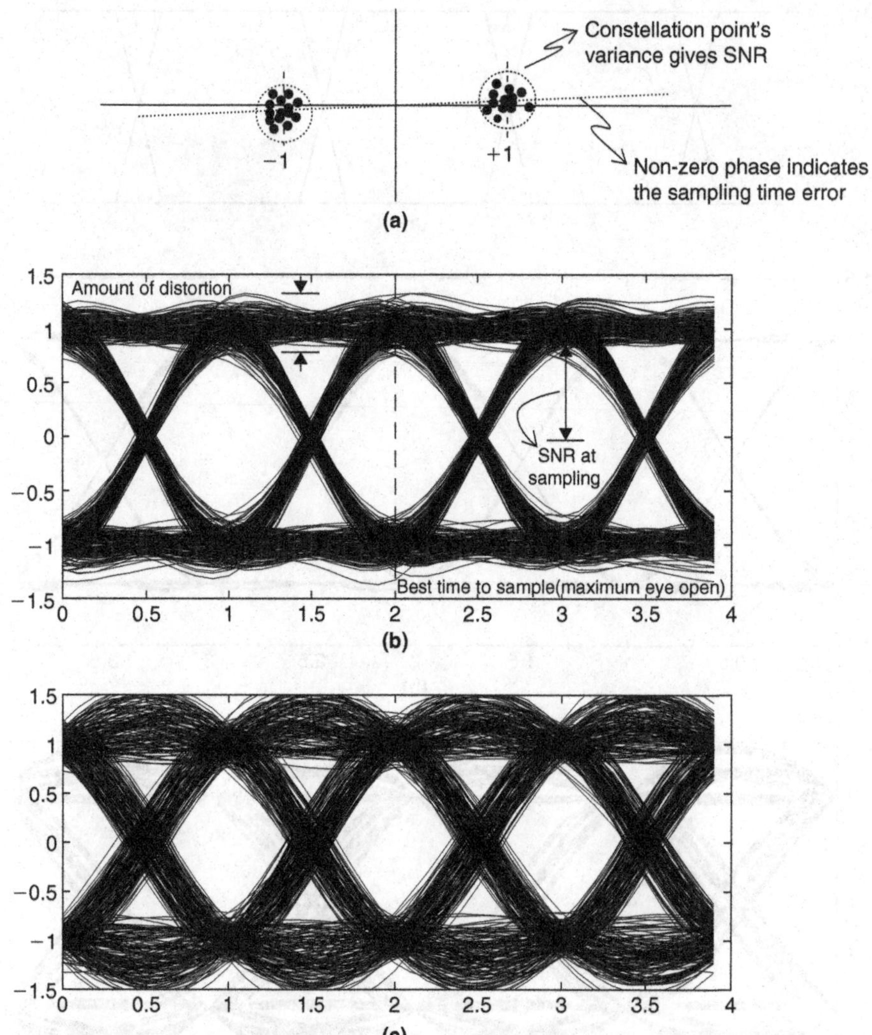

Figure 9.14: Views of received noisy BPSK symbols. (a) Represented by constellation points. (b) Represented by eye diagrams of raised cosine pulse, $\alpha = 1$. (c) Represented by eye diagrams of raised cosine filter, $\alpha = 0.5$.

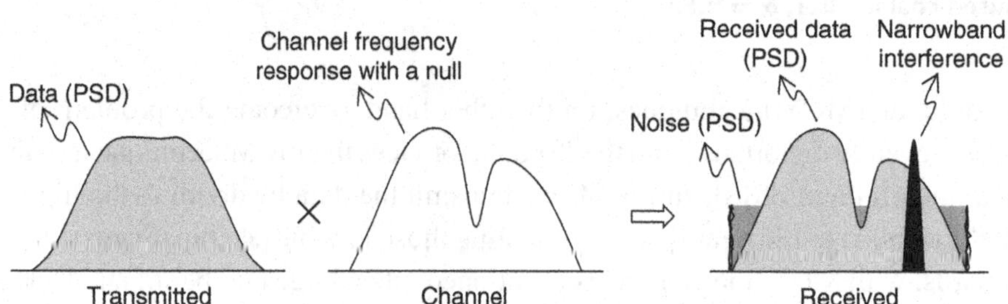

Figure 9.15: Single-carrier communication system with associated power spectral densities at transmitter and receiver ends.

symbols by minimizing the effects of a dispersive and noisy channel. As shown in Figure 9.15, at the receiver, the received-signal power spectral density (PSD) consists of channel attenuated data PSD along with undesired PSDs such as noise, interference, and so on. Because of these channel imperfections, it may not be possible to get back the exact transmitted data, instead, we try to get the estimate of transmitted data after applying a series of signal processing and error correction algorithms on the received data. The baseband equivalent of a modern single-carrier communication system with major building blocks is shown in Figure 9.16. Here, we briefly explain the functionality of transmitter and receiver modules.

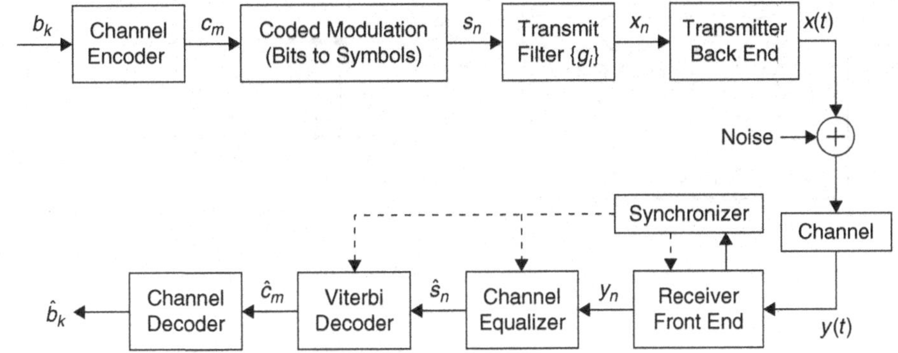

Figure 9.16: Major building blocks present in baseband equivalent of single-carrier modern digital communication system.

Transmitter Modules

First, we compress the source data (e.g., voice, audio, video, text) before transmitting to minimize the data bandwidth, and encrypt it to protect it from eavesdroppers. The data bits $\{b_k\}$ are compressed (see Chapter 5) and encrypted (see Chapter 2) before arriving at the channel encoder. The channel encoder (see Chapter 3) adds redundancy to bits $\{b_k\}$ and forms codeword bits $\{c_m\}$ with forward error correction capability. The bits $\{c_m\}$, after passing through the inner coder (shown as a coded modulation block, see Chapter 3), are again added with redundancy of one more layer of error correction capability, and then these coded bits are mapped to baseband symbols $\{s_n\}$ by the inner coder. The baseband symbols are compatible with the requirements imposed by the transmission channel. These baseband symbols $\{s_n\}$ are then shaped by the transmit filter $\{g_i\}$ to minimize the cross-interference with other channel data. The filtered data samples $\{x_n\}$ are then passed through the transmitter back-end block (which contains DAC, filters, etc.) before transmitting through the noise-dispersive channel.

Receiver Modules

The receiver front end (which contains band-limiting filters, ADC, etc.) along with the synchronization block (see Section 9.5) produces the discrete samples $\{y_n\}$ from received signal $y(t)$. These received samples $\{y_n\}$ correspond to transmitted samples $\{x_n\}$, and are corrupted by the impaired channel. As shown in Figure 9.15, the received signal spectrum is attenuated by the channel, and corrupted with noise and narrow band interference. We use a channel equalizer (see Section 9.4), which is a filter design based on the estimated channel (see Section 9.3), to undo the channel attenuation effects. The channel equalizer is one of the major blocks in a single-carrier communication system receiver, and many complex signal processing algorithms are used to perform channel estimation and equalization. The outputs of the channel equalizer $\{\hat{s}_n\}$ are estimates of the transmitted baseband symbols $\{s_n\}$ and contain many errors due to noise, interference, and residual errors resulting from imperfect channel equalization; hence the symbols $\{\hat{s}_n\}$ are mostly unreliable. The convolutional decoder (or Viterbi decoder, see Chapter 3 for more detail) works on those corrupted noisy symbols $\{\hat{s}_n\}$ and produces more reliable codeword bits $\{\hat{c}_m\}$. Then, the channel decoder (e.g., RS coder; see Chapter 3 for more detail) performs forward error correction and produces bits $\{\hat{b}_k\}$ with a low bit error rate (BER). The bits $\{\hat{b}_k\}$ are the estimate of transmitted compressed and encrypted bits $\{b_k\}$. The bits $\{\hat{b}_k\}$ are then decrypted and decompressed by using corresponding modules (not shown in the figure) before being fed to customer-end devices.

In the next section, we discuss a multicarrier system in which the block modulation and equalization structures are significantly different than in single-carrier systems. Channel equalization in multicarrier systems is achieved with relatively low complexity. We achieve very good spectral efficiency with multicarrier systems at the cost of complex modulators and synchronization circuitry.

9.2.2 Multicarrier Communication Systems

An alternative approach to designing a bandwidth-efficient system in the presence of channel distortion is to divide the available channel bandwidth into a number of subchannels such that each subchannel is nearly

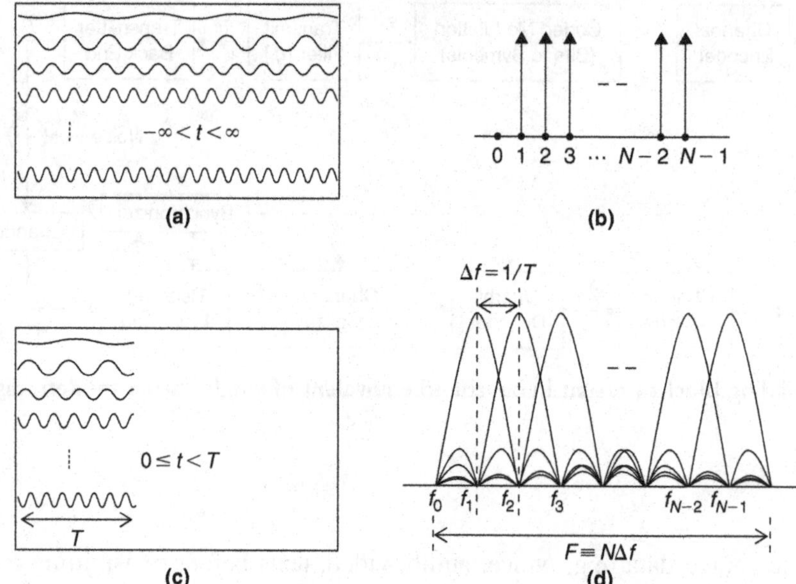

Figure 9.17: Illustration of multicarrier modulation. (a) Sinusoids with infinite duration. (b) Power-density spectra of infinite-duration waveforms. (c) Sinusoids with finite duration. (d) Power-density spectra of finite-duration carriers.

ideal. The technique of dividing the channel into a number of subchannels and modulating data over a carrier corresponding to each subchannel is called multicarrier modulation (MCM). The total number of bits transmitted is the sum of the number of bits transmitted in each subchannel. The MCM principle is to superimpose several carrier-modulated waveforms in parallel subchannels in order to increase the data rate of a channel given a fixed transmission power level. If available power is distributed over the subchannels using the SNR of each subchannel, then high spectral efficiency can be achieved. In contrast to single-carrier modulation, multicarrier modulation:

- Avoids full channel equalization
- Uses available bandwidth efficiently by controlling power and number of bits in each subchannel
- Is robust against impulse noise and fast fading due to long symbol duration
- Avoids narrowband distortion by simply disabling one or more subchannels

The concept of multicarrier modulation is illustrated in Figure 9.17. If we modulate the data onto frequency carriers with infinite duration, then the frequency spectra of such a modulated signal is discrete as shown in Figure 9.17(b). In practice, the modulated sinusoidal components are truncated in time as shown in Figure 9.17(c), and the power-density spectrum of such truncated carriers consists of $|\sin(\pi f)/\pi f|^2$-shaped spectra as shown in Figure 9.17(d). When we transmit the data symbol on the carriers with finite duration T, the width of subbands $f_n - f_{n-1} = \Delta f$ is wider than single frequency f_n width, and the frequencies must satisfy $f_n - f_{n-1} = 1/T$ for orthogonality between carriers. Note that the width of subband Δf is very small compared to the total frequency band $F \equiv N\Delta f$ used for transmission as shown in Figure 9.17(d). A schematic block diagram of the multicarrier communication system is shown in Figure 9.18. At the output of the MCM block, the signal $x(t)$ can be obtained as

$$x(t) = \sum_{n=0}^{N-1} X_n e^{j2\pi f_n t}, \quad \text{where } f_n = n\Delta f \tag{9.68a}$$

Let us consider

$$z(t) = \int_0^T e^{j2\pi f_n t}(e^{j2\pi f_{n-1} t})^* dt = \int_0^T e^{j2\pi (f_n - f_{n-1})t} dt = \int_0^T e^{j2\pi \Delta f t} dt$$

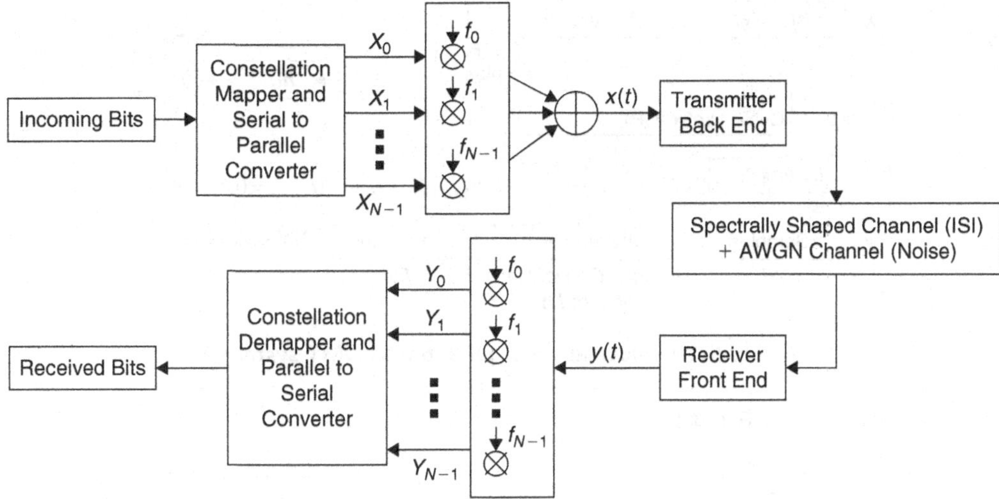

Figure 9.18: Block diagram of multicarrier communication system.

If $\Delta f = 1/T$, then the inner product of two adjacent carriers, $z(t)$, is 0. In other words, if $f_n - f_{n-1} = 1/T$, then the modulated waveforms are orthogonal to each other. This important property of MCM allows us to demodulate the data at the receiver by correlation. If we sample the signal with sampling interval Δt (i.e., $T = N\Delta t$), then based on Equation (9.68a),

$$x(m\Delta t) = \sum_{n=0}^{N-1} X_n e^{j2\pi f_n t_m}, \quad \text{where } t_m = m\Delta t \tag{9.68b}$$

$$x_m = \sum_{n=0}^{N-1} X_n e^{j2\pi n\Delta f m\Delta t} = \sum_{n=0}^{N-1} X_n e^{j\frac{2\pi nm\Delta t}{N\Delta t}} = \sum_{n=0}^{N-1} X_n e^{j2\pi nm/N} = IDFT\{X_n\} \tag{9.69}$$

The two most commonly used transceiver systems that employ MCM schemes are discrete multitone (DMT) systems and orthogonal frequency-division multiplexing (OFDM) systems. The term "DMT" is used in the wireline community (e.g., ADSL, VDSL), whereas the term "OFDM" is used in the wireless community (e.g., DVB, WLAN). Next, we discuss the basic principles and techniques used in DMT and OFDM systems.

9.2.3 DMT Transceiver

DMT modulation is the discrete implementation technique of multicarrier modulation. The idea is to use a set of orthogonal subcarriers in the frequency domain so that variable numbers of bits are allocated to different subcarriers according to the subcarrier channel gain.

DFT-Based DMT Modulation

One way of implementing DMT is using discrete Fourier transform (DFT) basis as subcarriers. A DFT-based DMT system is illustrated in Figure 9.19; its block diagram appears in Figure 9.20.

In Figure 9.19, system output vector $\boldsymbol{y}$ is a linear convolution of input vector $\boldsymbol{x}$ and channel vector $\boldsymbol{h}$. The middle N samples of vector $\boldsymbol{y}$ (of length $N + \upsilon + L - 1$) are the circular convolution of $\boldsymbol{x}$ and $\boldsymbol{h}$. The circular convolution result is due to the addition of cyclic prefix (CP) of υ samples (where υ is greater than or equal to the channel impulse-response length of L samples) to the input vector $\boldsymbol{x}$ of N samples (so that the input becomes periodic within the extent of the channel time spread). Basically, we add the cyclic prefix as a guard interval to avoid the ISI. But we can also avoid this ISI by simply adding zero samples. Then why do we use the cyclic prefix? We add the cyclic prefix because it serves more than one purpose—it avoids intercarrier interference (ICI) among DFT carriers and preserves the orthogonality of DFT carriers (by forming circular convolution) after passing through the dispersive channel. This type of system can be realized in the frequency domain with the blocks shown in Figure 9.20. Here, the IDFT basis is used as the modulator basis and the DFT basis as the

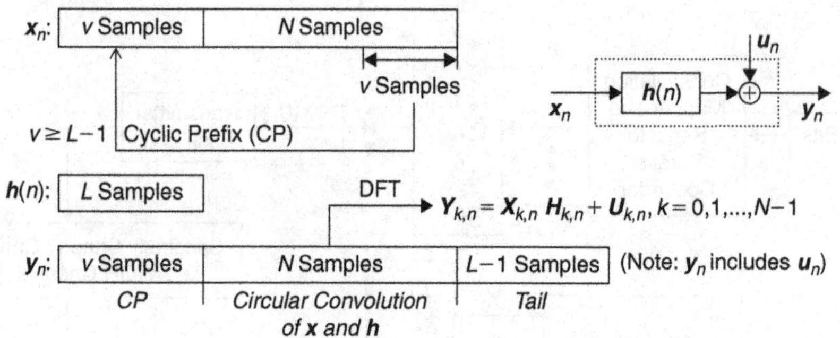

Figure 9.19: Illustration of DFT-based DMT system.

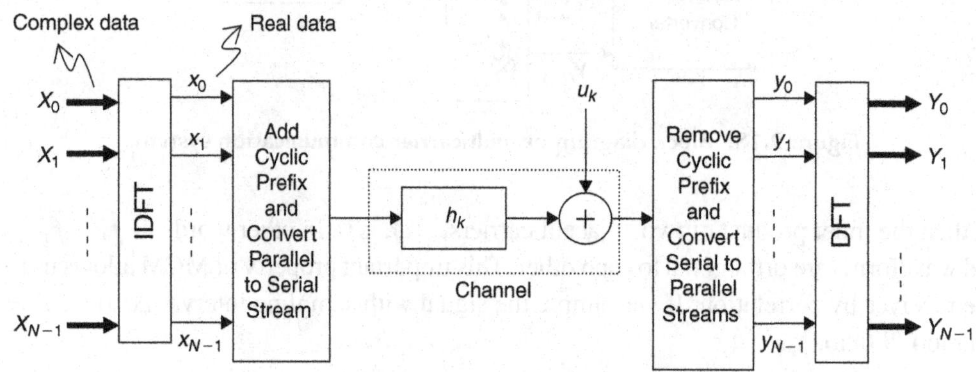

Figure 9.20: Block diagram of DFT-based DMT system.

demodulator basis. The N modulator basis follow:

$$f_m(n) = \frac{1}{\sqrt{N}} e^{j\frac{2\pi mn}{N}}, \quad 0 \leq n \leq N-1 \quad \text{for } m = 0, 1, \ldots, N-1 \tag{9.70}$$

A serial-to-parallel data buffer divides the input bitstream into blocks of b bits. The b bits in each block are parsed into $(N/2-1)$ groups, where the i-th group is allocated b_i bits such that

$$b = \sum_{i=1}^{N/2-1} b_i \tag{9.71}$$

Note that the subcarriers $f_0(n)$ and $f_{N/2}(n)$ in Equation (9.70) are the real subcarriers, which are not used in practice. It is reasonable to view the DMT as being composed of $N/2$ orthogonal quadrature amplitude modulation (QAM) channels, each operating at the same symbol rate, Δf, with a different QAM constellation size. For example, the i-th channel will have 2^{b_i} possible signal points. In Figure 9.20, X_i denotes the i-th encoded QAM signal point at the output of the constellation encoder. To obtain real-value, time-domain transmitting samples, we use the following Hermitian symmetry:

$$X_{N-k} = X_k^*, \quad k = 1, 2, \ldots, N/2-1 \tag{9.72}$$

The N-length, DMT modulated data sequence, $\{x_k\}$, for a given block of N symbols $[X_0, X_1, \ldots, X_{N-1}]$, is given by

$$x_k = \frac{1}{\sqrt{N}} \sum_{i=0}^{N-1} X_i e^{j2\pi ki/N}, \quad k = 0, 1, \ldots, N-1 \tag{9.73}$$

Note that the signal points X_0 and $X_{N/2}$ are of zero amplitude. The N-sample input and output of the IDFT block are called DMT blocks. The last v samples of the DMT block, where v is greater than or equal to the channel impulse-response length minus one, are cyclically prefixed to the block, thereby making it an $(N+v)$-length block. This is illustrated in Figure 9.19. The cyclic prefix is added to avoid the ISI introduced by the

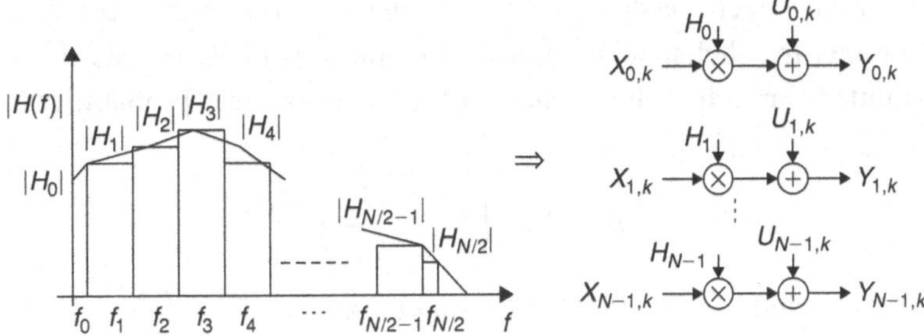

Figure 9.21: Viewing channel as subchannels when DMT modulation is used.

dispersive channel. This $(N + v)$-length block is converted into $(N + v)$ serial samples by using a parallel to serial converter and then transmitted. (In practice, these samples are passed through D/A, channel, and A/D. The D/A and A/D clocks are to be synchronized both in frequency and phase.) At the receiver, from each block of $(N + v)$ received samples, the first v samples are discarded. The resulting process can be viewed as a circular convolution of the N-length DMT block with N-length channel impulse response (padded with the required $N - L$ number of zeros). This implies that the DFT of the N-length received block (after removing the first v samples) is the product of the DFT of the N-length IDFT output DMT block and the DFT of the channel impulse response, assuming no noise. Note that the DFT of the N-length IDFT output is the input DMT symbol block $[X_0, X_1, \ldots, X_{N-1}]$. Thus, in the presence of noise,

$$Y_{i,k} = H_i X_{i,k} + U_{i,k}, \quad i = 0, 1, \ldots, N-1 \tag{9.74}$$

where $\{H_i\}_{i=0}^{N-1}$ denote the N DFT coefficients of the channel impulse response $h(n)$, and $\{U_i\}_{i=0}^{N-1}$ denote the N DFT coefficients of the N-length noise sequence $\{u_n\}$. Here, $Y_{i,k}$ denotes the i-th output of the DFT demodulator in the k-th DMT symbol block. Similarly $X_{i,k}$ denotes the i-th input of the IDFT modulator, and $U_{i,k}$ represents the i-th noise sample of the k-th DMT block. Let the noise variance per dimension be σ^2.

When N is large, the continuous transfer function of the channel response $H(f)$ can be approximated by narrow rectangles, as shown in Figure 9.21. The N outputs of the DFT block correspond to N outputs of the orthogonal subchannels, that is, there is no interference between them. Each subchannel is approximately flat in that no transmission distortion is present other than the multiplication with H_i and the addition of noise U_i. Clearly, as the number of subchannels N increases, the approximation that each subchannel is nearly flat becomes very accurate. However, carrier and symbol synchronization are critical in multicarrier systems. Improper synchronization results in loss of orthogonality between carriers, which in turn results in a catastrophic error system.

Bit Loading

Depending on the channel frequency response, a particular number of bits is assigned to a given subchannel. This assignment of bits to each subchannel is called "bit loading." Although assignment of bits to each subchannel using the bit-loading concept is suboptimal when compared to Shannon's water pouring solution of power distribution, bit-loading concepts are mathematically very attractive and easily implementable. Using bit loading, bits are assigned to each subchannel such that the symbol error probability (P_e) in all the subchannels is same. For this, we use different constellations for each subchannel to have the same minimum distance at the output of the demodulator. For nonrectangular QAM constellations, the symbol error probability P_{se} follows:

$$P_{se} < (2^{b_i} - 1)\, Q(d_{\min}/2\sigma) \tag{9.75}$$

If the minimum distance used for the i-th subchannel at the input of the IDFT is $d_{\min,i}$, then the minimum distance of the symbol constellation at the output of the DFT block, denoted $d_{\min}$, is related to $d_{\min,i}$:

$$d_{\min}^2 = \left|H_i^2\right| d_{\min,i}^2. \tag{9.76}$$

We choose b_i, the number of bits for the i-th subchannel, such that the 2^{b_i}-QAM constellation has a minimum distance $d_{\min,i}$ with average symbol energy as unity. With QAM, the minimum number of bits used per subchannel is 2. As the minimum distance between constellation points and the average energy per symbol are directly related, we use estimated SNR_i of the i-th subchannel to allocate the number of bits to that i-th subchannel. The number of bits that can be transmitted through each subchannel for a certain error probability can be calculated using the following formula:

$$b_i = \log_2\left(1 + \frac{SNR_i}{\Gamma}\right) \tag{9.77}$$

where Γ is called the *SNR gap* and is equal to 9.8 dB for an error rate of 10^{-7}. The Γ of 9.8 dB is the reference point for the uncoded system with a 0-dB performance margin (i.e., $\gamma_{margin} = 0\,\text{dB}$). For $\gamma_{margin} > 0\,\text{dB}$, we embed γ_{margin} into the bit-loading equation as follows:

$$b_i = \log_2\left(1 + \frac{SNR_i}{\Gamma + \gamma_{margin}}\right) \tag{9.78}$$

We use the following iterative algorithm to compute b_i for a given SNR_i, a total number of bits B_{total} per DMT symbol, and a minimum performance margin $\gamma_{\min} = g$ dB.

1. $\gamma_{margin} = 0$, $B_{\text{total}} = round(sum(b_i)$ and $U_{\text{ch}} = N$, where N is the maximum number of usable carriers.
2. Calculate b_i', and U_{ch} as follows:
   Get $b_i' = round(b_i)$.
   If $b_i' = 0$, then $U_{\text{ch}} = U_{\text{ch}} - 1$.
3. Get $B_{\text{temp}} = \sum_{i=1}^{N} b_i'$ if $B_{\text{temp}} = 0$, and then stop and declare the channel bad.
4. Compute the new γ_{margin}:
   $$\gamma_{margin} = \gamma_{margin} + 10\log_{10}\left(2^{\frac{B_{\text{temp}} - B_{\text{total}}}{U_{\text{ch}}}}\right)$$
5. If $\gamma_{margin} > \gamma_{\min}$, then stop and declare b_i' to be the bit-loading vector.
6. Decrease B_{total} by k adaptively and repeat steps 2 to 5.

The channel frequency response and corresponding bit-loading diagram are illustrated in Figure 9.22.

Performance of DMT with Bit Loading: Simulation Results

DMT system performance with bit loading can be clearly seen when the channel has a deep spectral null in its frequency response (as shown in Figure 9.22), or when the narrowband interference is present or the impulse noise disturbs the transmitted sequence. Simulations have been carried out for a channel with a deep spectral null and for the downstream case of CSA loop-4. The performance of DMT with bit loading for both cases is shown in Figure 9.23.

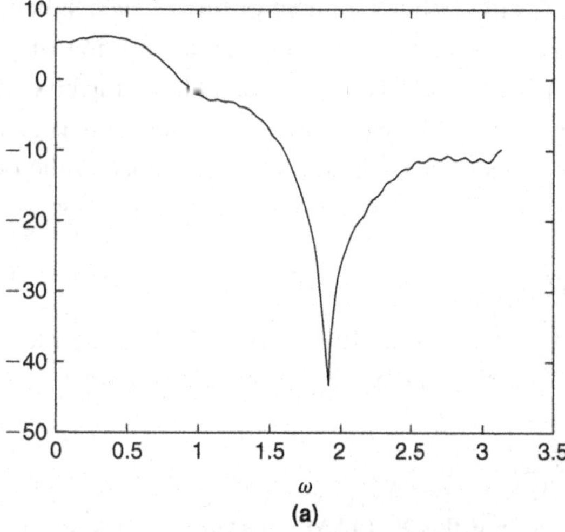

(a)

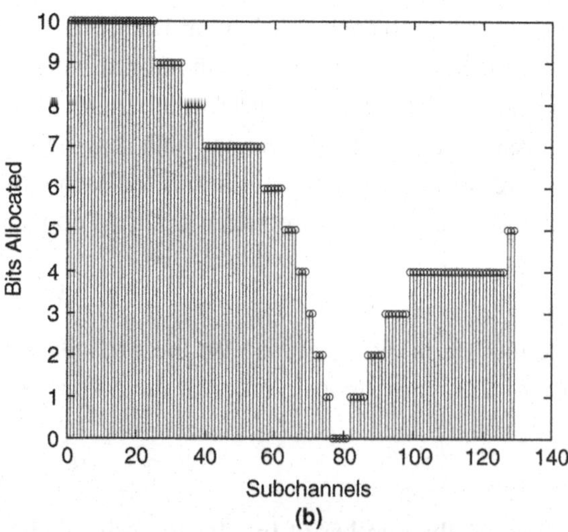

(b)

Figure 9.22: (a) Channel frequency response. (b) Bit-loading diagram.

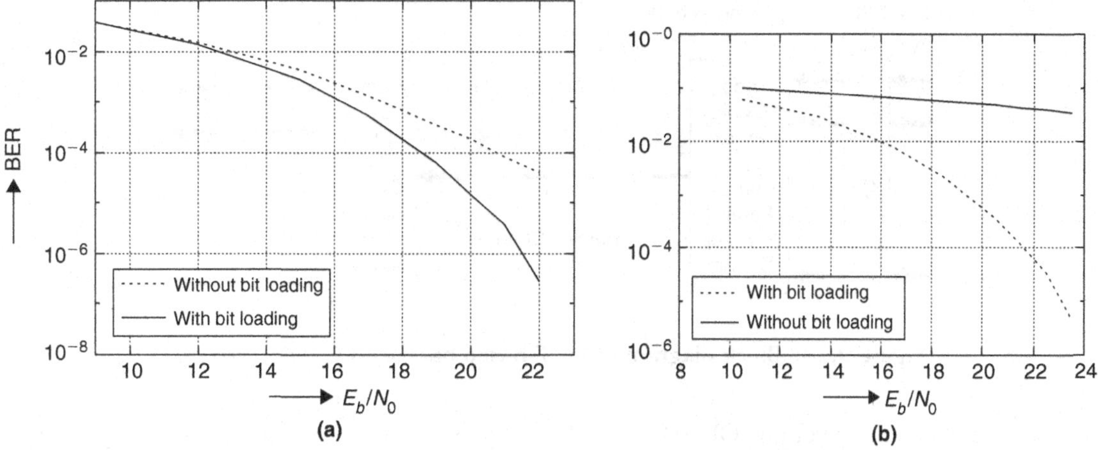

Figure 9.23: (a) DMT system performance with and without bit loading for the case of CSA loop-4. (b) DMT system performance with and without bit loading for the case of channel with deep null in frequency response.

The BER curves show that there is about a 3-dB gain with bit loading in the case of CSA loop-4, and the necessity for bit loading in the case of a channel with deep nulls in its frequency response. For both cases, we used white Gaussian noise as one of the channel impairments. To implement the bit loading, we need a channel estimate. The simulations have been carried out based on the assumption that the channel estimation is already available (see Section 9.3 for more details on channel estimation).

9.2.4 OFDM Transceivers

Although both DMT and OFDM schemes use the basic principle of MCM (i.e., dividing the transmission bandwidth into many narrow subchannels and transmitting low bit-rate data on many parallel subchannels), there are small differences between the two modulation schemes as noted here.

- The DMT schemes are used with low-pass channels (e.g., twisted-pair wireline), whereas OFDM schemes are used with bandpass channels (e.g., wireless channels).
- We output the real sequence with DMT schemes by making the IDFT input symbols symmetric, whereas the OFDM schemes output a complex sequence (i.e., OFDM-modulated output contains both real and imaginary parts) to transmit the data samples on I and Q channels of the bandpass communication system.
- We have information about the channel in the case of DMT at the transmitter; thus we perform bit loading to improve spectral efficiency, whereas we cannot perform bit loading with OFDM schemes because we lack information about the channel at the transmitter. Therefore, we transmit a fixed number of bits per subchannel (i.e., small constellation sizes are used) across all subchannels in the OFDM, whereas we transmit a variable number of bits per subchannel in the case of the DMT depending on the SNR of the subchannels (which we know at the transmitter as it receives the channel estimation information via the feedback channel).

The schematic diagram of the baseband OFDM system is shown in Figure 9.24. Given the N-length constellation points vector $\{X_m\}$, the OFDM-modulated data sample vector $\{x_n\}$ of length N samples is obtained as follows:

$$x_n = \frac{1}{\sqrt{N}} \sum_{m=0}^{N-1} X_m e^{j2\pi nm/N}, \quad 0 \le n \le N-1 \tag{9.79}$$

We form an $N+v$ length sample vector $\{s_k\}$ by adding a cyclic prefix of length v samples as guard data to the N-length OFDM symbol vector $\{x_n\}$ as follows:

$$s = \left[x_{N-v}, x_{N-v+1}, \ldots, x_{N-1}, x_0, x_1, \ldots, x_{N-1}\right] \tag{9.80}$$

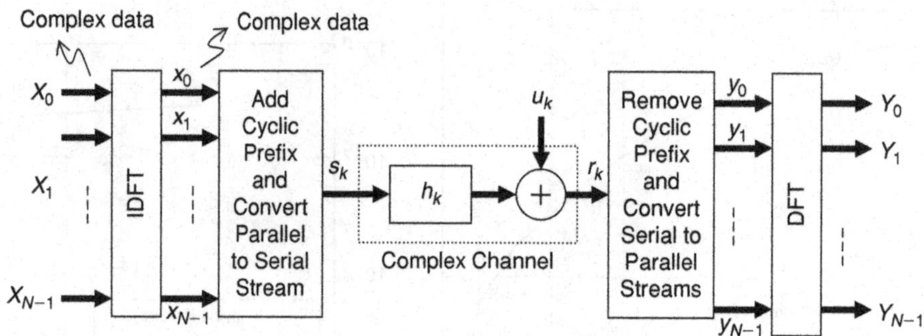

Figure 9.24: Block diagram of DFT-based baseband OFDM system.

Assuming a constant channel over one OFDM symbol interval, we can express the channel output vector $\{r_k\}$ as

$$r_k = s_k * h_k + u_k, \quad 0 \le k < N + v + L - 1 \tag{9.81}$$

where * represents the linear convolution operation and L is length of channel $\{h_k\}$.

Here, the first v samples of $\{r_k\}$ correspond to the cyclic prefix and the last $L-1$ samples of $\{r_k\}$ correspond to the convolution operation tail. We form the input $\{y_n\}$ to the demodulator by extracting middle N samples from $\{r_k\}$ in Equation (9.81). The N samples of $\{y_n\}$ correspond to the circular convolution of the modulator output $\{x_n\}$ and channel $\{h_n\}$. With no ICI, assuming proper synchronization, the demodulator output can be expressed as

$$Y_{i,j} = H_i X_{i,j} + U_{i,j} \tag{9.82}$$

Here, $Y_{i,j}$ denotes the i-th output of the DFT demodulator in the j-th OFDM symbol block.

However, in the mobile communications environment, channel frequency variations due to delay spread, and channel time variations due to Doppler spread introduce ISI and ICI that degrade OFDM system performance. With ICI, the expression for the demodulator output in Equation (9.82) is no longer valid.

9.3 Channel Estimation

As the channel attenuates and delays different frequencies by different amounts, the transmitted signal experiences distortions when passing through a channel. The distortion of one symbol due to adjacent symbols is known as ISI, whereas the distortion in data on one carrier due to data on other carriers is called ICI. Further distortions in transmitted data occur due to thermal and cross-talk noise. Due to these distortions, the decoder may make incorrect decisions, resulting in data errors. Upon compensating these distortions introduced by the channel, we can achieve higher data transmission rates with low data errors. To combat channel distortions, first we must measure or estimate the distortions. In this section, we discuss channel estimation techniques with DMT and OFDM transceivers.

9.3.1 Channel Estimation in DMT Systems

In DMT transceivers, a cyclic prefix of length v, where v is the length of the channel impulse response minus 1, is inserted between the transmitted symbols to avoid ISI and ICI. This cyclic prefix carries no information. Since the v samples do not carry any new information about the transmitted signal, the transmission rate of a DMT transceiver is decreased by a factor of $N/(N+v)$. But by choosing v, a small deterministic value, we can still maintain high data rates. However, the channel length is generally large. To reduce the inefficiency of the DMT transmission system due to the use of a long cyclic prefix, the use of a time-domain equalizer (TEQ) to shorten the effective channel impulse response to a standard cyclic prefix length has been the most popular equalization approach in DMT receivers. As the equalizer designs assume the channel to be known, next we discuss channel and noise estimation in DMT systems.

The block diagram of channel estimation in DMT systems is shown in Figure 9.25. The inputs to the system consist of symbols from the 4-QAM constellation with unit average energy. These symbols are modulated on

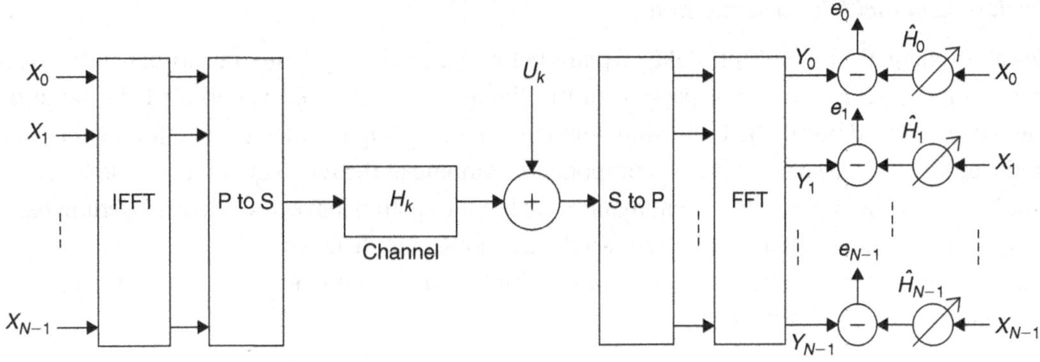

Figure 9.25: Block diagram of channel estimation in DMT systems.

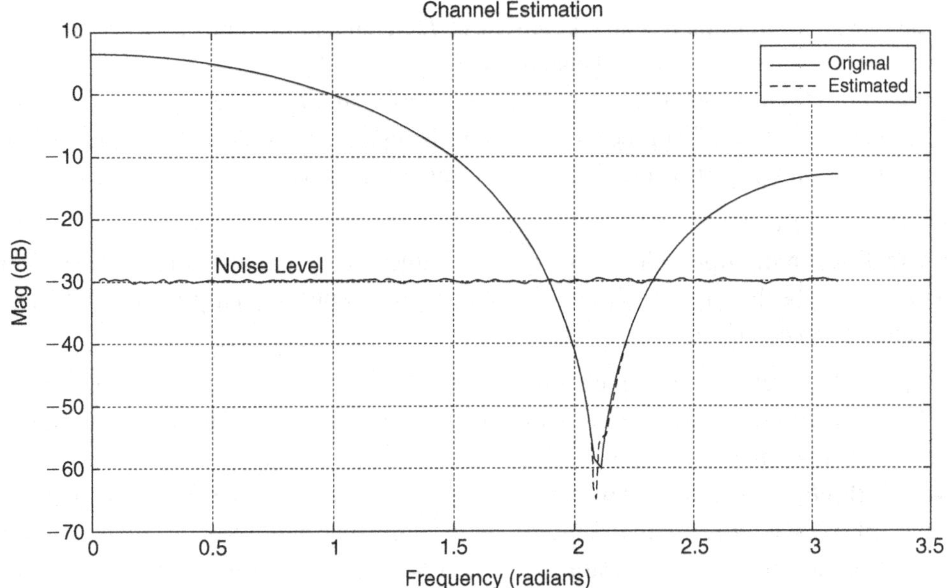

Figure 9.26: Frequency response and subchannel noise level.

carriers by means of an IDFT operation. The modulated symbols are passed through a parallel-to-serial converter and are given to the channel as input samples. The channel output with additive stationary noise is converted from serial to parallel and given to the demodulated block. From this received noisy data, and with knowledge of the input, we can estimate channel and noise characteristics by formulating the MSE cost function and minimizing MSE.

Here, the same DMT symbol block is repeated so that the output of the channel is a cyclic convolution of each N-sample block with the impulse response. The minimum MSE (MMSE) estimate of channel $\hat{H}_k$ for a periodic input is given by

$$\hat{H}_k = \frac{E[Y_k X_k^*]}{E[|X_k|^2]} = \frac{\frac{1}{L}\sum_{l=1}^{L} Y_{k,l} X_{k,l}^*}{\frac{1}{L}\sum_{l=1}^{L} X_{k,l} X_{k,l}^*} \tag{9.83}$$

$$E(|e_k|^2) = \frac{1}{L}\sum_{l=1}^{L} |e_{k,l}|^2 \equiv \frac{1}{L}\sum_{l=1}^{L} |Y_{k,l}|^2 - \left|\frac{1}{L}\sum_{l=1}^{L} Y_{k,l}\right|^2 \tag{9.84}$$

Figure 9.26 shows estimation of a channel $\{h(n) = [.227\ .460\ .688\ .460\ .227]\}$ and noise at SNR $= 30$ dB with $L = 100$ DMT blocks (ensembles) using Equations (9.83) and (9.84).

9.3.2 Wireless Channel Characterization

A typical wireless channel with multiple delayed paths between a stationary radio transmitter and moving receiver is illustrated in Figure 9.27. The major paths result in the arrival of delayed versions of the same transmitted signal at the receiver. In addition, the radio signal undergoes scattering on a local scale for each major path and results in reflected paths. These irresolvable components combine at the receiver and give rise to a phenomenon known as multipath fading. Due to this phenomenon, each major path behaves as a discrete fading path and such a fading process is commonly characterized by Rayleigh and Rician distributions.

A typical wireless channel is characterized with multiple time-varying amplitudes and it can be expressed, with τ_i representing the delay of the i-th path, as

$$h(t,\tau) = \sum_{i=0}^{L-1} h_i(t)\delta(\tau - \tau_i) \tag{9.85}$$

Given Equation (9.85), the multipath channel consists of L channel amplitudes corresponding to L paths. The amplitude $h_0(t)$ corresponds to the first arrival path and the remaining $L-1$ amplitudes $\{h_j(t), j = 1, 2, \ldots, L-1\}$ correspond to $L-1$ delayed paths. Due to mobile-unit motion, the $h_i(t)$s comprise a wide-sense stationary (WSS), narrowband complex Gaussian process, which are independent for different paths. The real part of the wireless channel described by Equation (9.85) can be visualized as shown in Figure 9.28.

Delay Spread and Doppler Spread

In order to compare different multipath channels, we use parameters that quantify the multipath fading channels. Four parameters that describe the nature of fading of a multipath channel are *delay spread*, *coherence bandwidth*, *Doppler spread*, and *coherence time*.

Delay spread (τ_{max}): In wireless communications, the signal usually arrives via multiple paths with different path gains. The time difference between the arrival moment of the first multipath component and the last multipath component is called delay spread.

Coherence bandwidth (B_c): A statistical measure of the range of frequencies over which the channel can be considered flat. In other words, it's the range of frequencies that pass through the channel with the same spectral attenuation and linear phase distortion. Coherence bandwidth is inversely proportional to delay spread.

Doppler spread (B_d): A measure of spectral broadening caused by the time rate of change of the mobile radio channel, it is defined as the range of frequencies over which the received Doppler spectrum is essentially non-zero.

Coherence time (T_c): This is a statistical measure of time duration over which the multipath channel gain is essentially invariant. Coherence time is inversely proportional to Doppler spread.

The parameters' delay spread and coherence bandwidth describe the time-dispersive nature of the channel in a local area; however, they do not offer information about the time-varying nature of the channel caused by

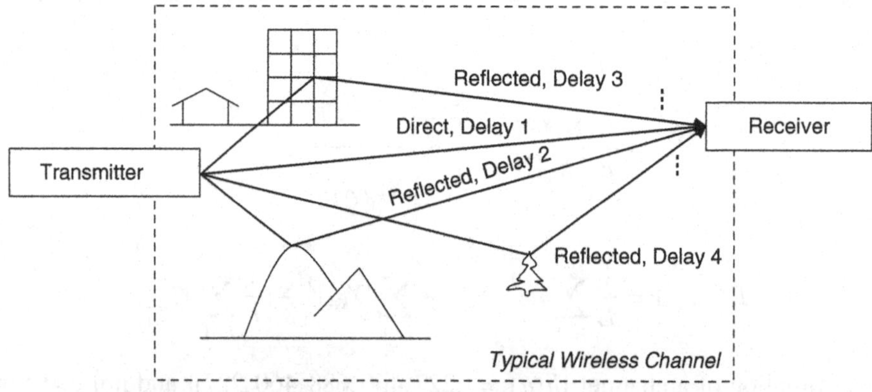

Figure 9.27: Typical wireless channel with multiple delayed paths.

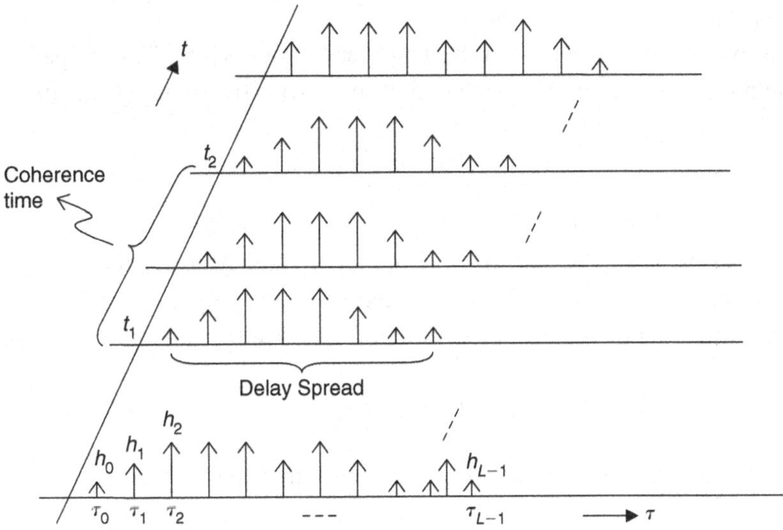

Figure 9.28: Visualization of wireless channel in time domain.

relative motion of the transmitter and receiver. The parameters' Doppler spread and coherence time describe the time-varying nature of a wireless channel in a small-scale region due to the motion of transmitter, receiver, or obstacles. The delay spread and coherence time parameters are defined in the time domain, whereas the coherence bandwidth and Doppler spread are defined in the frequency domain. The interpretation of the delay spread and coherence time parameters are shown in Figure 9.28.

Calculation of Delay Spread and Coherence Bandwidth

The power delay profile of the channel is used to determine the delay spread. The power of the i-th path of a quasistationary (i.e., $T_c > 0$) multipath channel follows:

$$\rho_i = E\left\{|h_i|^2\right\} \tag{9.86}$$

The values of ρ_i for $0 \leq i \leq L-1$ are referred to as the multipath power spread or power delay profile of the channel. The RMS delay spread τ_{RMS} follows:

$$\tau_{RMS} = \sqrt{\frac{\sum_i (\tau_i - \mu_\tau)\rho_i}{\sum_i \rho_i}} \tag{9.87}$$

where μ_τ is the mean-access delay and is computed as

$$\mu_\tau = \frac{\sum_i \tau_i \rho_i}{\sum_i \rho_i} \tag{9.88}$$

In practice, we do not have any knowledge of path gains h_is and delays τ_is, and we cannot compute the metric RMS delay spread τ_{RMS} using Equation (9.87). Instead, we estimate the RMS delay spread using the received data symbols. The RMS delay spread τ_{RMS} value is useful for estimating the channel more accurately. Coherence bandwidth can be computed from the RMS delay spread using the fact that the signal components passing through the channel coherence bandwidth will have a larger correlation. Typically,

$$B_c \approx \frac{1}{50\tau_{RMS}} \text{ (for frequency correlation function} > 0.9) \tag{9.89}$$

$$B_c \approx \frac{1}{5\tau_{RMS}} \text{ (for frequency correlation function} \approx 0.5) \tag{9.90}$$

Calculation of Doppler Spread and Coherence Time

The amount of spectral broadening depends on the Doppler frequency, f_d. The f_d parameter is related to the relative speed v between the transmitter and receiver and the carrier frequency f_c, as in

$$f_d = \frac{v f_c}{c} \tag{9.91}$$

where the constant c is the speed of light.

Coherence time (T_c) can be computed from the Doppler frequency using the fact that signal components arriving with a time separation greater than T_c are affected differently by the channel. If the coherence time is defined as the time over which the time correlation function is above 0.5, then the T_c is approximately given by

$$T_c \approx \frac{9}{16\pi f_m} \tag{9.92}$$

where f_m is the maximum Doppler shift. A widely used rule of thumb for calculating the T_c is given as

$$T_c \approx \frac{0.423}{f_m} \tag{9.93}$$

OFDM Channel and Correlation Functions

Given the wireless channel $h(t, \tau)$, its time-varying frequency response can be calculated as

$$\begin{aligned} H(t, f) &= \int_{-\infty}^{\infty} h(t, \tau) e^{-j2\pi f\tau} d\tau \\ &= \sum_{i=0}^{L-1} h_i(t) e^{j2\pi f \tau_i} \end{aligned} \tag{9.94}$$

With sampling of the time-frequency axis, the channel frequency response at the m-th tone of the n-th OFDM symbol in the time-frequency grid of the OFDM system can be expressed as

$$\begin{aligned} H[n, m] &= H(nT_f, m\Delta f) \\ &= \sum_{i=0}^{L-1} h_i(nT_f) e^{-j2\pi m \Delta f \tau_i} \end{aligned} \tag{9.95}$$

where T_f and Δf are the symbol duration and the inter-subcarrier spacing of the OFDM system, respectively.

The channel correlation function in the time-frequency space for different OFDM symbols and tone separations can be obtained as follows:

$$\begin{aligned} R_{HH}[k, l] &= E\left\{H[n+k, m+l] H^*[n, m]\right\} \\ &= \sigma_H^2 R_t[k] R_f[l] \end{aligned} \tag{9.96}$$

where

$$\sigma_H^2 = \sum_{i=0}^{L-1} \rho_i$$

is the total average power of the channel response, and ρ_i is the average power of the i-th propagation path. Given Equation (9.96), note that the correlation function of $H(t, f)$ can be separated into the multiplication of time-domain correlation $R_t[k]$ and frequency-domain correlation $R_f[l]$ functions. The function $R_t[k]$ depends on the motion of the mobile unit (or vehicle speed) or equivalently, the Doppler frequency f_d.

Assuming a Jakes model, the simplified form of the time-domain correlation function can be expressed as follows:

$$R_t[k] = J_0(2\pi k F_d) \tag{9.97}$$

where $J_0(.)$ is the zero-order Bessel function of the first kind and $F_d = f_d T_f$, the normalized Doppler frequency (i.e., f_d is normalized with the OFDM symbol rate, $1/T_f$).

The frequency correlation function $R_f[l]$ depends on the multipath delay spread. We consider the exponential decaying, multipath power delay profile (PDP) (which is the most commonly accepted model for indoor channels). Such channels are characterized by

$$\rho_i = E\left\{|h_i|^2\right\} = e^{-i/\tau'_{RMS}} \tag{9.98}$$

where $\tau'_{RMS} = \tau_{RMS}/T_s$ is the RMS delay spread relative to the sampling interval T_s of the OFDM system. For an exponentially decaying PDP, the $R_f[l]$ is given by

$$R_f[l] = \frac{1}{1 + j2\pi\tau'_{RMS}l/N} \tag{9.99}$$

where N is the total number of subcarriers used to transmit an OFDM symbol.

9.3.3 Channel Estimation in OFDM Systems

OFDM technology is widely used in wireless applications such as wireless LAN, DVB, WiMAX, and so on. The wireless channel estimation in the frequency domain can be obtained by employing the frequency domain interpolation of regularly spaced transmitted pilot symbols as shown in Figure 9.29. With combo-type pilot symbols, the channel variations from one OFDM block to a subsequent OFDM block can be easily obtained by frequency-domain interpolation. Next, we discuss the techniques to estimate the delay spread and Doppler spread, which are very useful parameters in accurate channel estimation.

Channel Delay Spread Estimation

In typical OFDM systems, a guard interval may be specified to account for delay spread. Generally, the channel length may be unknown, so typical channel estimation schemes may *a priori* assume that channel length is equal to guard interval (or cyclic prefix). However, under some operating circumstances, the actual delay spread encountered may not be the same as the guard interval, in which case it is not reasonable to assume that the channel length is equal to the guard interval. Therefore, it may be desirable to provide a system that estimates an actual delay spread encountered by the system, and utilize that estimated delay spread to provide a more accurate channel estimate.

In Athaudage and Jaylath (2003), a novel RMS delay–spread estimation technique for wireless OFDM system is proposed. This technique utilizes a frequency correlation function evaluated over the cyclic-prefix of the OFDM signal to estimate the delay spread. The RMS delay spread is estimated by means of an MMSE fitting between the observed samples correlation and its theoretical expectation.

The frequency selectivity of the channel is often characterized by the correlation function $R_f[l]$. The $R_f[l]$ shows the correlation between the channel response of two subcarriers, which are l subcarriers apart in the OFDM spectrum. In the OFDM channel estimation, the $R_f[l]$ is utilized at the receiver to interpolate the channel

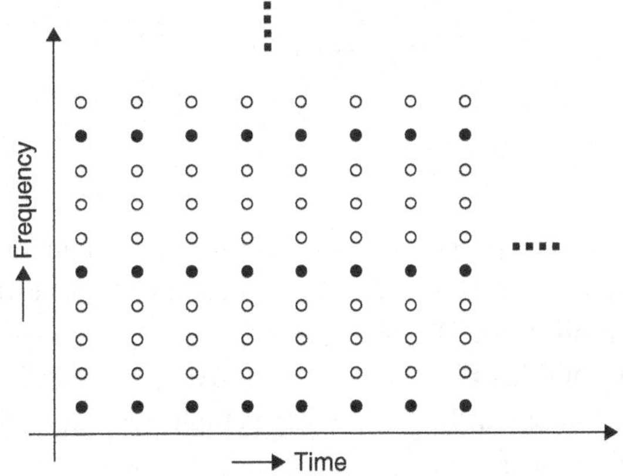

Figure 9.29: Combo-type pilot arrangement for OFDM channel estimation.

response at unknown subcarrier locations using the channel estimates at pilot carrier locations. Here, we consider a wireless channel with an exponentially decaying multipath PDP for the delay spread estimation, and the $R_f[l]$ for such channel is given in Equation (9.99).

As mentioned previously, the RMS delay spread value τ_{RMS} is *a priori* unknown. The use of a likely value of a fixed number of samples for τ'_{RMS} results in a suboptimal channel estimation and equalization process. Accurate knowledge of τ'_{RMS} is required at the receiver to ensure that the proper correlation function $R_f[l]$ is used for channel estimation.

Given a received multipath OFDM signal $y[n]$ corresponding to channel input $x[n]$, as in

$$y[n] = \left[\sum_{i=0}^{L_c-1} h_i x[n-\tau_i]\right] e^{j2\pi n\varepsilon/N} + u[n] \tag{9.100}$$

where ε is the normalized frequency offset and $u[n]$ is the additive white Gaussian noise component, the τ'_{RMS} is estimated by searching for the value of τ'_{RMS} that minimizes the MSE between the theoretical correlation measure $|R_J[N]|$ and observed correlation measure $|R^I_J[n]|$, where $1 \le J \le L_c$. The $|R_J[N]|$ for the channel given in Equation (9.98) follows:

$$|R_J[N]| = \frac{\sigma_s^2}{1-\beta}\left[J + \frac{\beta^{L_c+1}(1-\beta^{-J})}{1-\beta}\right] \tag{9.101}$$

where σ_s^2 is the OFDM signal variance and $\beta = e^{-1/\tau_{RMS}}$. The observed correlation measure $|R^I_J[n]|$ is computed from the received samples $y[n]$ as

$$|R^I_J[n]| = \frac{1}{I}\sum_{i=0}^{I-1}\sum_{j=0}^{J-1} y(n+iN_c-j)y^*(n+iN_c-j-N) \tag{9.102}$$

where $N_c = N + L_c$, I is the number of OFDM symbols used.

Given that we do not have *a priori* knowledge of the symbol timing and frequency offset, we estimate them by using the magnitude and phase of $|R^I_J[n]|\big|_{J=L_c}$, as in

$$\hat{T} = \arg\max_n |R^I_{L_c}[n]| \tag{9.103}$$

$$\hat{\varepsilon} = \frac{1}{2\pi}\angle R^I_{L_c}[n] \tag{9.104}$$

The MMSE criterion can be then expressed as follows:

$$\hat{\beta} = \arg\min_{0\le\beta\le\beta_{\max}} Q(\beta) \tag{9.105}$$

where

$$Q(\beta) = \frac{1}{L_c}\sum_{J=1}^{L_c}\left(|R_J(N)| - |R^I_J(N)|\right)^2 \tag{9.106}$$

and $\beta_{\max} = e^{-1/L_c}$

Doppler Spread Estimation

Doppler spread gives a measure of the fading rate of the wireless channel, which can be used to adjust the OFDM channel estimation rate and create specifically designed channel estimators to combat ICI induced by loss of orthogonality. Due to mobility, the Doppler spread causes the channel to be modeled with a time-variant finite-impulse response filter. If mobility is low (i.e., a small Doppler spread), then the rate of channel estimation can be lowered and throughput increased. If the mobility is high (i.e., high Doppler spread), then an increase of the estimation rate can help to lower the BER.

Many approaches are suggested in the literature for estimating Doppler spread from the received symbols, such as level crossing rate (LCR) or zero-crossing rate (ZCR) of signal envelope–based estimation, covariance-based estimation, and correlation-based estimation. The accuracy of Doppler spread estimation based on crossing rates is less efficient with shorter estimation windows at high Doppler values and low SNR values. On the other hand, the computational complexity of covariance-based Doppler estimation is significantly high. Here, we discuss correlation-based Doppler spread estimation. In Doukas and Kalivas (2006), a Doppler estimation technique based on the time correlation function of channel estimates over two OFDM symbols is proposed for low-mobility OFDM channels. The time correlation function using demodulated OFDM symbols can be expressed as

$$R_t[p] = \frac{1}{S-|p|} \sum_{i=0}^{S-1-|p|} Y_{i,k} Y^*_{i+|p|,k} \tag{9.107}$$

where S is the number of participating OFDM symbols and p is the time difference of OFDM symbols.

Assuming the Jakes model in Equation (9.97),

$$\frac{R_t[1]}{R_t[0]} = \frac{J_0(2\pi f_d T_f)}{J_0(0)} = J_0(2\pi f_d T_f) \tag{9.108}$$

Then, using Equations (9.107) and (9.108),

$$\frac{Y_{0,k} Y^*_{1,k}}{(|Y_{0,k}|^2 + |Y_{1,k}|^2)/2} = J_0(2\pi f_d T_f)$$

or

$$f_d = \frac{1}{2\pi T_f} J_0^{-1} \left[\frac{2 Y_{0,k} Y^*_{1,k}}{|Y_{0,k}|^2 + |Y_{1,k}|^2} \right] \tag{9.109}$$

Pilot Symbol–Aided Channel Estimation

Given Equation (9.100), the OFDM receiver has to know the subchannel gains H_i to obtain the estimate of transmitted symbols from the received noisy symbols. A dynamic channel estimation is necessary before the demodulation of OFDM signals since wireless channels are frequency selective and time varying. For OFDM systems, the channel estimation can be performed by either inserting pilot tones into all of the subcarriers with a specific OFDM symbol period or inserting regularly spaced pilot tones into a few subcarriers of all OFDM symbols. The former, known as the block-type pilot arrangement, is applicable to slow time-varying channels, whereas the latter, known as the combo-type pilot arrangement, is applicable to fast time-varying channels. The same framework described earlier for DMT channel estimation can be used for channel estimation of block-type pilot arrangement OFDM systems. Next, we discuss channel estimation techniques for combo-type pilot arrangement OFDM systems.

Let x_p be the pilot information known at both the transmitter and the receiver. It is uniformly inserted at the transmitter to the subcarriers according to the following equation:

$$X[k] = X[nM+m] = \begin{cases} x_p & m = 0 \\ data & m = 1, 2, \ldots, M-1 \end{cases} \tag{9.110}$$

where $M = N/N_p$, N is the total number of carriers, and N_p is the number of pilot carriers. With this, we can estimate the channel frequency response at N_p pilot carriers as

$$\hat{H}_p[kM] = \frac{Y_p[kM]}{X_p[kM]}, \quad k = 0, 1, \ldots, N_p - 1 \tag{9.111}$$

Then, an efficient interpolation technique is used to estimate the channel at the data subcarriers by using the channel information $\hat{H}_p$ at the pilot subcarriers. Commonly used interpolation techniques include linear, second-order, spline cubic, low-pass, and time-domain. For example, the channel estimation $H_d[m]$ at the data carrier m, where $kL < m < (k+1)L$, using linear interpolation is given by

$$\begin{aligned}\hat{H}_d[m] &= \hat{H}_d[kL+l], \quad 0 \le l < L \\ &= \hat{H}_p[kL] + (\hat{H}_p[(k+1)L] - \hat{H}_p[kL])\frac{l}{L}\end{aligned} \tag{9.112}$$

However, the OFDM channel estimation using Equation (9.112) does not use already available side information such as channel RMS delay spread and Doppler spread in the interpolation process, and hence the resulting channel estimation will not be optimum from the performance and computational complexity points of view. In Hoeher et al. (1997), pilot-symbol aided channel estimation based on 2D Weiner filtering of the time-frequency grid using the maximum delay spread and maximum Doppler spread as side information was discussed. The channel estimation-based on 2D Weiner filtering is formulated as

$$\hat{H}_d[n,m] = \sum_{n',m' \in S_p} w[n,m,n',m']\hat{H}_p[n',m'], \quad 0 \le n \le N_t - 1, 0 \le m \le M-1 \tag{9.113}$$

where $\hat{H}_p$ is the channel frequency response at pilot positions; $w[]$, 2D Weiner filter coefficients; N_t, number of OFDM symbols considered; M, number of subcarriers; and S_p, set of pilot carriers in 2D grid.

Equation (9.113) can be expressed with the matrix notation as

$$\hat{H}_d[n,m] = \underline{w}[k,l]\underline{\hat{H}}_p \tag{9.114}$$

Coefficient values for the optimized Weiner filter $\underline{w}_o[n,m]$ in the sense of MMSE can be obtained using the autocorrelation matrix $R_{\hat{H}_p\hat{H}_p}$ of observed samples and the cross-correlation vector $R_{\hat{H}_pH}[n,m]$ of observed and reference samples as in

$$\underline{w}_o^T[n,m] = R^T_{\hat{H}_pH}[n,m]R^{-1}_{\hat{H}_p\hat{H}_p} \tag{9.115}$$

where T represents the transpose operation.

The order of the Weiner filter decides the computational complexity of channel estimation, and we use the estimated delay spread and Doppler spread parameters in determining the optimal order for the Weiner filter. In Classen et al. (1995), two one-dimensional Weiner filtering (time-domain filtering followed by frequency domain filtering) is suggested for channel estimation. Here, too, for interpolating the time-frequency grid in the two directions, the sampling factors for both directions are chosen based on the maximum Doppler frequency and maximum delay spread.

9.4 Channel Equalization

As the channel attenuates and delays various frequencies by different amounts, the transmitted signal experiences distortions when passing through a channel. The distortion of one symbol due to adjacent symbols is known as ISI, whereas the distortion in data on one carrier due to data on the other carriers is called ICI. Further distortions in transmitted data result due to thermal and cross-talk noise. In single-carrier systems, the received sequence $y[n]$ can be expressed in terms of transmitted sequence $x[n]$ and channel $h[n]$ as

$$y[n] = \underbrace{h[m]x[n]}_{\text{useful data}} + \underbrace{\sum_{k \ne m} h[k]x[n-k]}_{\text{ISI}} + \underbrace{u[n]}_{\text{noise}} \tag{9.116}$$

If these distortions are severe, then the decoders at the receiver may make incorrect decisions resulting in data errors. By compensating these distortions introduced by the channel, we can achieve higher data transmission rates with low data errors. For this, we must perform "channel equalization" on the received data.

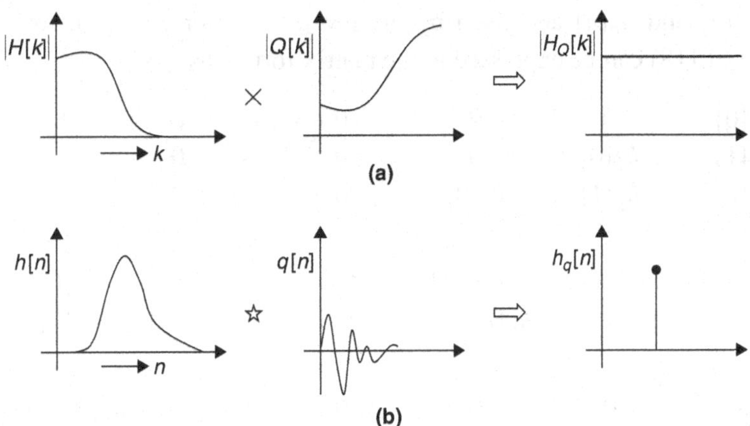

Figure 9.30: Illustration of channel equalization concept.

In theory, a channel equalizer should have a frequency response that is exactly the inverse of the channel. This is illustrated in Figure 9.30. When we multiply the frequency response of channel $H[k]$ with the frequency response of an equalizer $Q[k]$, since the equalizer frequency response and the channel frequency response are inversely related we get the flat frequency response $H_Q[k]$ as shown in Figure 9.30(a). The same occurs when we look at the time domain as shown in Figure 9.30(b); after convolving the impulse response of channel with that of equalizer, we get an impulse as the effective time-domain response of channel and equalizer. As the impulse has zero delay spread or time dispersion, there is no ISI after equalization of the data symbol. However, this is an ideal case and happens only in theory. In practice, we will have a few problems. First, we cannot design an equalizer with 100% inverse characteristics as that of the channel, and thus a small amount of ISI will occur. Second, the received data always contains noise and when we perform equalization on the noisy data, the noise component is also amplified. This affects the demodulator output and leads to incorrect data decisions. Thus, in practice we make a trade-off among ISI, noise, and implementation complexity.

In practice, an equalizer is normally implemented with a digital adaptive filter to combat the time-varying nature of communication channels. An adaptation process is used to identify the optimal channel equalizer coefficients and keep tracking possible variations of channel characteristics. For more details on adaptive filtering algorithms (such as LMS and RLS) and their implementation techniques, see Chapter 8. Channel equalization consists of two steps: (1) determination of equalizer response given the estimated channel impulse response, and (2) performing the equalization of data by passing the data through the equalizer. Here, we briefly discuss two types of equalization approaches—linear equalization and decision feedback equalization. In the later sections, we discuss the application of these equalization techniques in DMT and OFDM systems.

9.4.1 Linear Equalization

With linear equalization, the equalized output is obtained after passing the received signal through a linear filter. Next, we discuss two commonly used criteria to determine the linear filter coefficients.

Zero-Forcing Equalizer

In zero-forcing equalization (ZFE), the linear-filter frequency response is chosen as the exact inverse of channel frequency response, as in

$$H_E[k] = \frac{1}{H_C[k]} \tag{9.117}$$

The time-domain equivalent of Equation (9.117) is expressed as

$$\sum_i h_c[i]h_e[j-i] = \begin{cases} 1 & \text{if } i = j \\ 0 & \text{if } i \neq j \end{cases} \tag{9.118}$$

where $h_c[n]$ and $h_e[n]$ are given by the inverse Fourier transform of $H_C[k]$ and $H_E[k]$. The condition in Equation (9.118) can be expressed in the matrix format as

$$\begin{bmatrix} h_c[0] & 0 & 0 & 0 & \cdots & 0 & 0 \\ h_c[1] & h_c[0] & 0 & 0 & \cdots & 0 & 0 \\ h_c[2] & h_c[1] & h_c[0] & 0 & \cdots & 0 & 0 \\ \vdots & \vdots & \vdots & \vdots & \vdots & \vdots & \vdots \\ h_c[N-1] & h_c[N-2] & h_c[N-3] & h_c[N-4] & \cdots & h_c[1] & h_c[0] \\ 0 & h_c[N-1] & h_c[N-2] & h_c[N-3] & \cdots & h_c[2] & h_c[1] \\ \vdots & \vdots & \vdots & \vdots & \vdots & \vdots & \vdots \\ 0 & 0 & 0 & 0 & \cdots & 0 & h_c[N-1] \end{bmatrix} \begin{bmatrix} h_e[0] \\ h_e[1] \\ \vdots \\ h_e[N/2] \\ \vdots \\ h_e[N-2] \\ h_e[N-1] \end{bmatrix} = \begin{bmatrix} 0 \\ 0 \\ \vdots \\ 1 \\ \vdots \\ 0 \\ 0 \end{bmatrix} \tag{9.119}$$

We can express Equation (9.119) in simplified notation as

$$H_c\overline{h}_e = \overline{a} \tag{9.120}$$

Because the matrix H_c is not a square matrix, the solution for h_e can be expressed as

$$\overline{h}_e = (H_c^T H_c)^{-1} H_c^T \overline{a} \tag{9.121}$$

where $\overline{h}_e = [h_e[0], h_e[1], \ldots h_e[N-1]]^T$ gives the coefficients of the equalization filter.

The zero-forcing equalizer minimizes ISI, but ignores any impact that channel noise may have on the system. In other words, ZFE corrects for distortion due to the ISI term in Equation (9.116) but ignores the effects of the additive noise component $u[n]$. Because the ZFE criterion ignores the noise associated with the channel, ZFE filters can end up amplifying the noise.

Minimum Mean Square Equalizer

The MMSE criterion aims to minimize the power of the symbol or decision error, considering both ISI and additive noise associated with the channel. Assuming the equalizer coefficient vector $\overline{h}_e$, the instantaneous error between the desired data sequence and the equalizer output is expressed as

$$e_k = x_{k-m} - \overline{y}_k^T \overline{h}_e \tag{9.122}$$

where x_{k-m} = the desired data sequence after there is a channel delay of m sampling instances, $\overline{y}_k^T = [y_k, y_{k-1}, \ldots, y_{k-N+1}]$ is the received sequence vector, and $\overline{h}_e^T = [h_e[1], h_e[2], \ldots, h_e[N]]$ is the equalizer coefficient vector.

Given the channel-impulse response (i.e., estimated channel coefficients), the received sequence y_k at the k-th sampling instant can be expressed with the convolution of the desired sequence vector $\overline{x}$ and the channel impulse response vector $\overline{h}_c$ as

$$y_k = \overline{x}_k^T \overline{h}_c + u_k \tag{9.123}$$

where $\overline{x}_k^T = [x_k, x_{k-1}, \ldots, x_{k-N+1}]$ is the desired transmitted sequence, $\overline{h}_c^T = [h_c[1], h_c[2], \ldots, h_c[N]]$ is the channel impulse response vector, and u_k is the associated noise sample at the k-th sampling instant.

Based on Equation (9.122), the MSE with the equalizer $\overline{h}_e$ is given by

$$E[e_k^2] = E\left[(x_{k-m} - \overline{y}_k^T \overline{h}_e)^2\right] \tag{9.124}$$

Using the MMSE criterion (i.e., by taking the derivative on both sides of Equation (9.124) with respect to the equalizer coefficient vector $\overline{h}_e$ and setting the derivative to zero; see Section 8.1.1 for more detail on the MMSE criterion), we get the optimum equalizer coefficient vector $\overline{h}_e^{opt}$ as follows:

$$\overline{h}_e^{opt} = E[x_{k-m}\overline{y}_k^T]/E[\overline{y}_k\overline{y}_k^T] \tag{9.125}$$

The equalizer coefficients can be adapted with the error converging in the least mean square (LMS) sense as

$$\overline{h}_e^{(k+1)} = \overline{h}_e^{(k)} + \alpha \overline{y}_k [x_{k-m} - \overline{y}_k^T \overline{h}_e^{(k)}] \tag{9.126}$$

where α is the step size and should satisfy the following condition for error convergence,

$$\alpha < \frac{1}{trace[Y]}, \text{ where } Y = E[\overline{y}_k \overline{y}_k^T] \tag{9.127}$$

In adaptive signal processing, the tuning of the LMS algorithm by choosing the appropriate step size α tends to be more of an art than a science. For more details on the LMS algorithm and the importance of choosing the right step size α for fast convergence of an adaptive process, please refer Section 8.1.1. Channel equalization based on the MMSE criterion yields much better performance when compared to the zero-forcing criterion, especially at low SNRs.

9.4.2 Decision Feedback Equalization

Assuming that the symbol decisions are correct after decision making, we can significantly improve the equalizer performance by introducing the feedback path in the equalizer structure as shown in Figure 9.31. The basic idea of decision feedback equalization (DFE) is that if the values of the symbols previously detected are known, then the ISI contributed by these symbols can be canceled out exactly at the output of the forward filter by subtracting past symbol values with appropriate weighting. This kind of equalization with nonlinear structure (due to feedback path) can be implemented without a significant increase in computational complexity. The feedback filter weights can be adjusted to fulfill a criterion such as the MMSE.

The equalized samples in the DFE structure are given by

$$\hat{s}[n-d] = \sum_{m=0}^{M-1} h[m] r[n-m] - \sum_{k=1}^{K-1} g[k] \tilde{s}[n-d-k] \tag{9.128}$$

where the symbol values $\tilde{s}[n]$ are the output of the detector, and d is the delay through the communication channel, including the delay introduced by the forward filter $h[n]$.

Equation (9.128) can also be written with the vector notation as

$$\hat{s}_{n-d} = R_n^T H - \tilde{S}_{n-d-1}^T G \tag{9.129}$$

where

$$H = [h_0\ h_1\ \cdots\ h_{M-1}]^T, G = [g_1\ g_2\ \cdots\ g_{K-1}]^T, R_n^T = [r_n\ r_{n-1}\ \cdots\ r_{n-M+1}] \text{ and}$$

$$\tilde{S}_{n-d-1}^T = [\tilde{s}_{n-d-1}\ \tilde{s}_{n-d-2}\ \cdots\ \tilde{s}_{n-d-K+1}]$$

The instantaneous error between the desired signal and the DFE output is

$$e_n = \tilde{s}_{n-d} - \hat{s}_{n-d} = \tilde{s}_{n-d} - R_n^T H + \tilde{S}_{n-d-1}^T G \tag{9.130}$$

where $\tilde{s}_{n-d}$ is the desired data symbol after d symbol intervals of channel delay, and e_n is the error between the desired symbol and the decision feedback equalizer output.

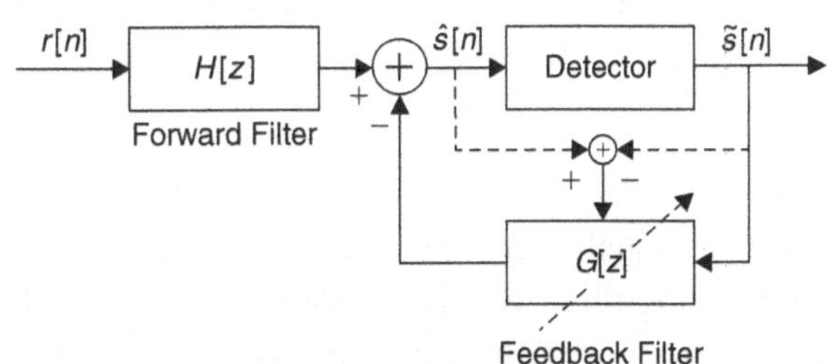

Figure 9.31: Structure of decision feedback equalizer.

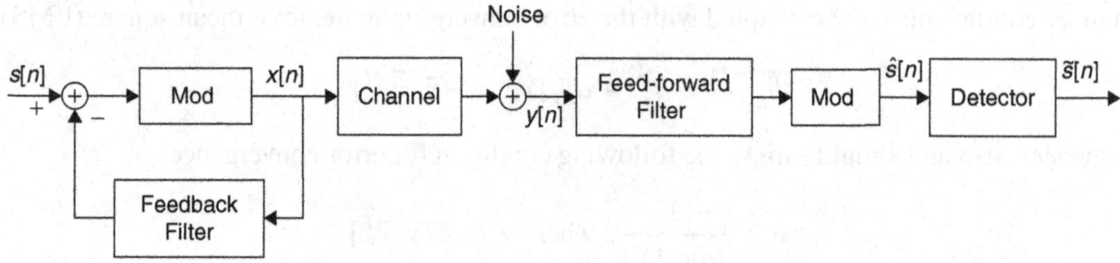

Figure 9.32: DFE structure with precoding.

The expected value of the square error with a given set of equalizer coefficient vectors H and G is

$$E[e_n^2] = E\left[(\tilde{s}_{n-d} - R_n^T H + \tilde{S}_{n-d-1} G)^2\right] \tag{9.131}$$

Using the MMSE criterion, the optimum coefficient values for the coefficient vectors H and G are given by

$$H_{opt}^T = \left(E[R_n R_n^T] - E[R_n \tilde{S}_{n-d-1}^T] E[\tilde{S}_{n-d-1} R_n^T]\right)^{-1} E[\tilde{s}_{n-d} R_n^T] \tag{9.132}$$

$$G_{opt}^T = H_{opt}^T E[R_n \tilde{S}_{n-1}^T] \tag{9.133}$$

As the DFE coefficient vectors are obtained using the MMSE criterion, we also refer to channel equalization using Equations (9.132) and (9.133) as the MMSE-DFE equalization.

The basic assumption for the DFE structure is that all detector decisions are correct, and as long as correct decisions are made in the detector, the DFE feedback loop remains stable. If the detector outputs wrong decisions, then the DFE starts generating poor equalized symbols, which in turn can cause more detector errors, causing worse equalization outputs. Thus, a wrong estimation of the symbols could propagate errors through DFE structure and it might take many symbol intervals for the DFE to recover from the error propagation. One way to address the problem of error propagation is to use precoding methods such as Tomlinson-Harashima precoding (THP). With THP, the feedback filter is moved into the transmitter to filter the original data symbols as shown in Figure 9.32. For details on precoding based on MMSE-DFE, see Wesel and Cioffi (1995).

9.4.3 Channel Equalization in DMT Systems

As previously discussed, the DMT schemes are widely used in the high-speed wired communication systems such as ADSL and VDSL. Since the statistics of wired channels vary quite slowly and may even have the same characteristics during the entire transmission period, we can perform channel estimation and equalizer coefficient computation once at the beginning of the transmission. We may use adaptive methods for updating equalizer coefficients to embed the small variations of the channel characteristics during the transmission period. As discussed in Section 9.3.1, we use a block-type pilot arrangement for channel estimation in DMT systems.

Given the channel estimates, the DMT systems usually apply two types of equalizers—one in the time domain equalizer (TEQ) and the other in the frequency domain (FEQ)—on received data to eliminate ISI and ICI from the data as shown in Figure 9.33. To compensate for residual ISI that occurs when the channel impulse response duration exceeds the chosen cyclic prefix duration, the TEQ may be used in the receiver. The TEQ is designed to shorten the channel impulse-response length to within the cyclic prefix duration. Thus, a shorter cyclic prefix (v) can be employed to avoid ISI and ICI without significant degradation in transmission efficiency. Then, after demodulation, an FEQ is used to extract the transmitted data symbols by compensating for the effect of channel gains.

Time-Domain Equalization

The concept of time-domain equalization can be easily understood from Figure 9.34. The TEQ is worked as a channel memory-truncating filter. Before the demodulator, it will produce a target channel, which is the convolution of an actual channel and TEQ, with much shorter memory than the actual channel memory.

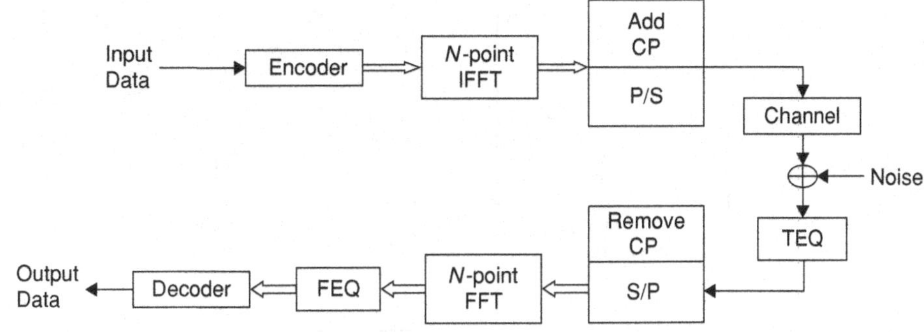

Figure 9.33: Block diagram of DMT system along with TEQ and FEQ.

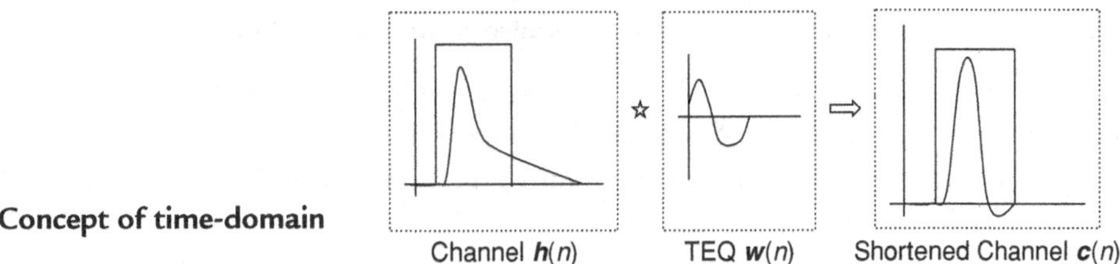

Figure 9.34: Concept of time-domain equalization.

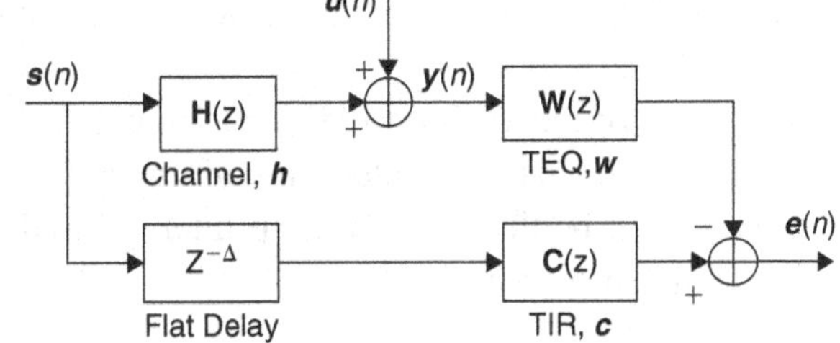

Figure 9.35: TEQ design based on MMSE approach.

There are many approaches to designing time-domain equalizers, and each has advantages and disadvantages. A few TEQ design criteria follow:

- MMSE
- Maximizing shortening SNR (MSSNR)
- Maximizing channel capacity (MCC)
- Minimizing ISI (MINISI)

TEQ Design Based on MMSE Approach The MMSE design method formulates the square of the difference between the target impulse response and the shortened impulse response as the error as shown in Figure 9.35 and minimizes it. The MMSE design method maximizes the SNR at the TEQ output. The frequency response of the equalizer tends to be a narrow bandpass filter placed at a center frequency, which has high SNR. The equalizer increases the output SNR by filtering out the low SNR regions of the channel frequency response.

In this approach, we need to find a filter $\boldsymbol{w}$ with N_w taps such that the cascade of the channel $\boldsymbol{h}$ and the TEQ $\boldsymbol{w}$ yields a shortened impulse response **c**, which has duration limited to $(v + 1)$ samples. The MMSE-based TEQ solution involves computation of the minimum eigenvalue of a matrix that is dependent on channel and noise parameters. We use either the unit energy or unit tap constraint to avoid a trivial solution. If we formulate an MSE (with the minimum eigenvalue) that depends on effective channel delay, then the optimum TEQ corresponds to the optimum channel delay. For more analysis on the MMSE TEQ design method, see Arslan (2000).

TEQ Design Based on MSSNR Approach In this method, we treat the TEQ design problem as a problem of channel shortening rather than as an equalization problem. The goal is to find a TEQ that minimizes the energy of the shortened impulse response (SIR) outside the target window by keeping the energy inside constant. Here, we formulate shortened SNR (SSNR) with the energy ratio (energy of SIR inside the target window to the energy of SIR outside the target window) that depends on the effective delay of the shortened impulse response. The TEQ

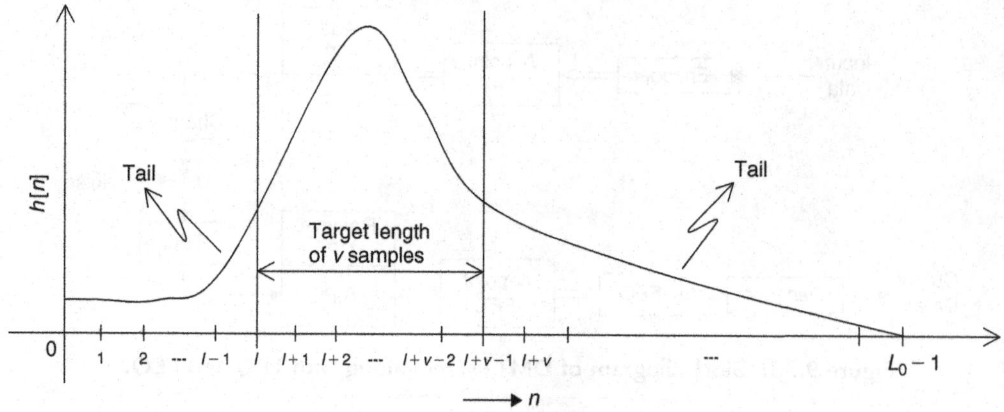

Figure 9.36: Arbitrary-length channel impulse response with L_0 coefficients.

solution based on maximizing the SSNR (MSSNR) involves eigenvalue decomposition, and the optimum TEQ solution corresponds to the optimum delay. There are iterative methods to obtain the optimal TEQ in the sense of MSSNR.

In the following, we discuss a computationally efficient divide-and-conquer TEQ (DC-TEQ) design proposed in Lu et al. (2000). Let $\underline{h}^{(0)}$ be the initial channel impulse response with L_0 channel coefficients as shown in Figure 9.36. Let v be the target impulse-response length. Let K be the length of the TEQ impulse response $g[n]$. The

DC-TEQ method divides the K taps of the TEQ into $(K-1)$ 2-tap filters, and iteratively designs each 2-tap filter by maximizing the energy inside the target window and minimizing the energy outside the target window.

Let $\{[1 \;\; g_1], [1 \;\; g_2], \ldots, [1 \;\; g_{K-1}]\}$ be the $(K-1)$ 2-tap filters. Based on Figure 9.36, the initial channel impulse response with length L_0 may be expressed as

$$\underline{h}^{(0)} = \left[h_0^{(0)}\, h_1^{(0)} \cdots h_{I-1}^{(0)}\, h_I^{(0)}\, h_{I+1}^{(0)} \cdots h_{I+v-1}^{(0)} \;\; h_{I+v}^{(0)} \cdots h_{L_0-1}^{(0)}\right] \tag{9.134}$$

Then, the first iteration output of the effective channel impulse-response vector $\underline{h}^{(1)}$of length $L_1 = L_0$+1 after convolving $\underline{h}^{(0)}$with the 2-tap vector $\underline{g}^{(1)}$, where $\underline{g}^{(1)} = [1 \;\; g_1]$, is given by

$$\underline{h}^{(1)} = \left[h_0^{(1)}\, h_1^{(1)} \cdots h_{I-1}^{(1)}\, h_I^{(1)}\, h_{I+1}^{(1)} \cdots h_{I+v-1}^{(1)} \;\; h_{I+v}^{(1)} \cdots h_{L_1-1}^{(1)}\right] \tag{9.135}$$

where $h_j^{(1)} = h_j^{(0)} + g_1 h_{j-1}^{(0)}$.

Similarly, the i-th iteration output of the effective channel impulse-response vector $\underline{h}^{(i)}$ of length $L_i = L_{i-1}+1$ after convolving $\underline{h}^{(i-1)}$ with the 2-tap vector $\underline{g}^{(i)}$, where $\underline{g}^{(i)} = [1 \;\; g_i]$, is given by

$$\underline{h}^{(i)} = \left[h_0^{(i)}\, h_1^{(i)} \cdots h_{I-1}^{(i)}\, h_I^{(i)}\, h_{I+1}^{(i)} \cdots h_{I+v-1}^{(i)} \;\; h_{I+v}^{(i)} \cdots h_{L_i-1}^{(i)}\right] \tag{9.136}$$

where $h_j^{(i)} = h_j^{(i-1)} + g_i h_{j-1}^{(i-1)}$.

$S = \{0, 1, 2, \ldots, I-1, I+v, I+v+1, \ldots, L_i - 1\}$ represents the set of indices of the channel response outside the target window. The energy of the tail portion of channel after the i-th iteration is given by

$$E_{tail}^{(i)} = \sum_{k \in S} \left[h_k^{(i)}\right]^2 = \sum_{k \in S} \left[h_k^{(i-1)} + g_i h_{k-1}^{(i-1)}\right]^2 \tag{9.137}$$

We find the minimum of the quadratic function of g_i in Equation (9.137) by differentiating with respect to g_i, setting the derivative to zero, and solving for g_i yields as follows:

$$g_i = -\frac{\sum_{k \in S} h_k^{(i-1)} h_{k-1}^{(i-1)}}{\sum_{k \in S} \left[h_{k-1}^{(i-1)}\right]^2} \tag{9.138}$$

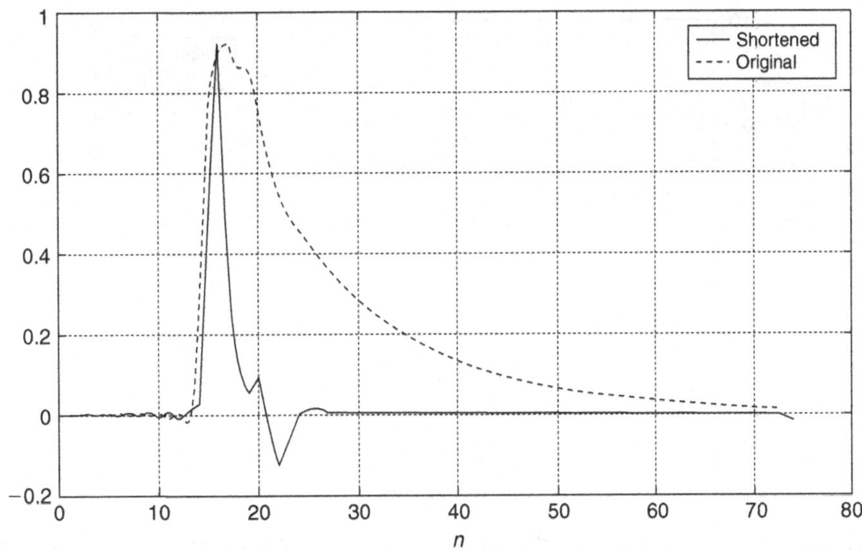

Figure 9.37: Actual impulse response of CSA loop-4 and its shortened impulse response by TEQ.

The computation of g_i in Equation (9.138) requires two vector multiplications and one scalar division. Figure 9.37 shows the actual impulse response of CSA-4 and a shortened impulse response by MSSNR approach TEQ. For more information and for the computation analysis of the TEQ design approaches described here, see Arslan (2000).

TEQ Simulation Results

In this section, we compare performance of the DMT system (shown in Figure 9.33) with and without TEQ. Figure 9.38 shows the performance gain with TEQ. It is clear from the BER curves that the time-domain equalizer is necessary in multicarrier modulation applications, where a standard cyclic prefix length is used to avoid ISI and ICI. At BER $= 10^{-1}$, we have a performance gain of 2 dB with TEQ. The parameters of the DMT system used to obtain the BER curves follow:

- Total number of bits/DMT block: 408 bits
- Channel: CSA loop-4
- Cyclic prefix length: 16
- TEQ length: 5
- Total number of DMT blocks transmitted: 10,000
- Design approach used: MSSNR

The results show that without TEQ, we cannot achieve a BER below 10^{-2}. But, in practical systems, the BER is maintained in the range 10^{-7} to 10^{-9}. To achieve these performance rates, we should use time-domain equalizers.

Frequency-Domain Equalizer

Once the effective channel impulse response, $c(n)$, is found, the frequency-domain equalizer (FEQ) coefficients Q_k are given by the inverse of the N-point DFT of $c(n)$, as in

$$Q_k = \frac{1}{\sum_{n=0}^{N-1} c(n)e^{-j2\pi nk/N}} \tag{9.139}$$

In block-type pilot-based channels, the estimators are usually calculated once per block and are used until the next pilot symbols arrive. This block-type pilot arrangement is used with wired or slow-fading wireless systems, where the channel statistics change very slowly. For such channels, channel estimation with decision feedback improves performance significantly, as the estimator adapts to small channel variations. The receiver first estimates the channel conditions using the pilots, and obtains $\{\hat{H}_k\}, 0 \leq k \leq N-1$ using Equation (9.83).

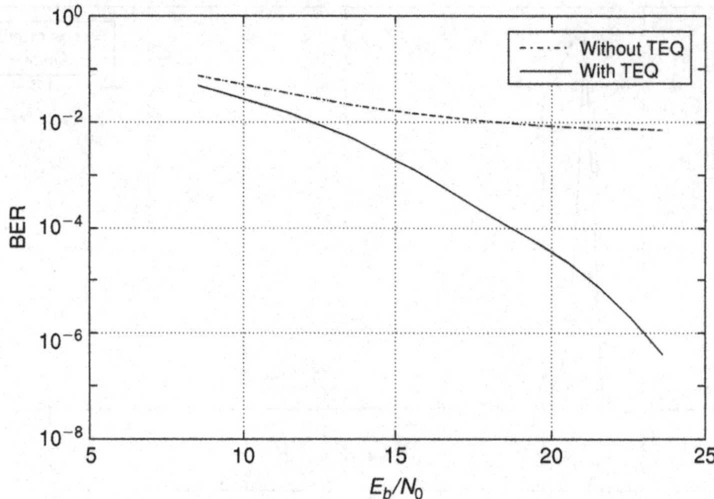

Figure 9.38: Performance of DMT system (see Figure 9.33) with and without TEQ (designed by MSSNR approach).

Then, we shorten the channel impulse response using TEQ to make the channel delay less than the cyclic prefix length. Let

$$\hat{H}_k^Q = \frac{1}{Q_k} = \sum_{n=0}^{N-1} c[n]e^{-j2\pi nk/N}$$

where $c[n] = \hat{h}[n] * w[n]$ is the shortened channel impulse response. Then the decision feedback equalization for the k-th subcarrier can be described as follows:

1. Estimate the transmitted symbols using the current channel estimate as

$$\hat{X}[k] = Y[k]/\hat{H}_k^Q, \quad k = 0, 1, \ldots, N-1 \tag{9.140}$$

2. Get the $X[k]$ after demapping $\hat{X}[k]$ to the binary data and mapping back again using the signal mapper.
3. The channel estimate $\hat{H}_k^Q$ is updated by using the detector output decision $X[k]$, as in

$$\hat{H}_k^Q = \frac{Y[k]}{X[k]}, \quad k = 0, 1, 2, \ldots, N-1 \tag{9.141}$$

Since the decision feedback equalizer assumes that the detector output decisions $X[k]$ are correct, we cannot use the preceding scheme with the fast-fading wireless channels. The fast-fading channel will cause the complete loss of estimated channel parameters.

9.4.4 Channel Equalization in OFDM Systems

As previously discussed, the wireless community uses OFDM techniques to efficiently implement the multicarrier modulation scheme. The OFDM handles frequency-selective fading resulting from delay spread by expanding symbol duration. The increased symbol duration together with insertion of the guard interval mitigates the ISI caused by time-dispersive fading channels. As the amount of channel dispersion (i.e., delay spread) increases, symbol duration should also increase for two reasons—for a near-constant channel in each subchannel and better transmission efficiency (i.e., relatively small guard interval when compared to OFDM symbol duration). However, the longer symbol duration increases the ICI caused by Doppler spread in time-variant channels. The coherence time of the channel reduces as the Doppler spread increases, and the assumption of a constant channel in the single OFDM symbol interval is not valid anymore. Thus, these channel variations within the OFDM symbol destroy the orthogonality between the subcarriers and result in ICI.

In the OFDM, ICI is generated due to frequency offset because of imperfect synchronization, due to Doppler spread (because of motion between the transmitter and receiver), or a combination of frequency offset and Doppler spread. The frequency offset between the transmitter and receiver oscillators causes the loss of orthogonality between the carriers and results in ICI. Thus, OFDM systems are very sensitive to synchronization errors. We discuss synchronization techniques for multicarrier modulation schemes in Section 9.5. In this section, we discuss ICI mitigation techniques that assume perfect synchronization between the transmitter and receiver oscillators and treat the source of ICI due to the presence of Doppler spread.

ICI Cancellation

Using the discrete baseband equivalent the OFDM system model as shown in Figure 9.24 and assuming that the channel delay spread is less than the inserted guard interval and the perfect synchronization between transmitter and receiver, the received symbols Y_k on the k-th subcarrier after demodulation can be expressed as

$$Y_k = \underbrace{H_{k,k} X_k}_{\text{Desired}} + \underbrace{\sum_{\substack{l=0 \\ l \neq k}}^{N-1} H_{k,l} X_l}_{\text{ICI}} + \underbrace{W_k}_{\text{Noise}} \tag{9.142}$$

where X_k is the transmitted symbol on the k-th subcarrier, $H_{k,k}$ is the channel gain at the k-th carrier frequency, $W_k = \sum_{n=0}^{N-1} w[n] e^{-j2\pi nk/N}$, and $w[n]$ are AWGN noise samples.

In Equation (9.142), the middle term on the right-hand side is the ICI contribution due to channel time variations within the OFDM symbol. In the discrete baseband channel model, let $p_i[n]$ represent the i-th fading tap with delay τ_i, and by defining $P_i[k]$ as the FFT of $p_i[n]$,

$$P_i[k] = \sum_{n=0}^{N-1} p_i[n] e^{-j2\pi kn/N}, \quad 0 \leq k \leq N-1 \tag{9.143}$$

With this, the channel matrix $H_{k,l}$ can be expressed as

$$H_{k,l} = \frac{1}{N} \sum_{i=0}^{L-1} P_i[l-k] e^{-j2\pi li/N}, \quad 0 \leq l, k \leq N-1 \tag{9.144}$$

where $L < L_c$, L is the number of channel taps, and L_c is the cyclic prefix length.

When $l = k$ in Equation (9.144),

$$H_{k,k} = \frac{1}{N} \sum_{i=0}^{L-1} P_i[0] e^{-j2\pi ki/N},$$

where $P_i[0] = \sum_{n=0}^{N-1} p_i[n]$ is an average value of the i-th path of the channel in one OFDM symbol duration. If ICI is not present, then $H_{k,l} = 0$ for $l \neq k$ and we can easily compensate channel multiplicative distortion using a single-tap frequency-domain equalizer as in

$$\hat{X}_k = \frac{Y_k}{H_{k,k}} = X_k + W_k/H_{k,k} \tag{9.145}$$

However, in the presence of ICI, first we have to cancel or mitigate the effect of the ICI before performing frequency-domain equalization. Given Equations (9.142) and (9.144), we have

$$Y = HX + W \tag{9.146}$$

where $Y = [Y_0, Y_1, \ldots, Y_{N-1}]^T$, $X = [X_0, X_1, \ldots, X_{N-1}]^T$, $W = [W_0, W_1, \ldots, W_{N-1}]^T$, and

$$H = \begin{bmatrix} H_{0,0} & H_{0,1} & \cdots & H_{0,N-1} \\ H_{1,0} & H_{1,1} & \cdots & H_{1,N-1} \\ \vdots & \vdots & & \vdots \\ H_{N-1,0} & H_{N-1,1} & \cdots & H_{N-1,N-1} \end{bmatrix} \rightarrow \begin{bmatrix} R_1 & R_2 & R_3 \\ R_2 & R_1 & R_2 \\ R_3 & R_2 & R_1 \end{bmatrix} \tag{9.147}$$

where the matrix elements $H_{k,l}$ are obtained using Equation (9.144).

To solve X in Equation (9.146), we need to estimate the channel matrix H and calculate its matrix inverse. Since H can be a large-sized matrix, it is difficult to compute in real time. In Jeon et al. (1999), assuming slow multipath fading channel-tap variations in any given OFDM symbol duration, an efficient method for computing the inverse of the H matrix is proposed. If the time variations of $p_i[n]$ for all L paths during one OFDM symbol are small, then all L channel paths can be approximated using straight lines with small slope values. In Figure 9.39(b), an illustration of the linear approximation for the i-th tap of a slowly varying channel is shown. With this assumption, the ICI contribution from the channel matrix elements in the region $R3$ as defined in Equation (9.147) is negligible, as most of the energy is concentrated in the neighborhood of the DC component. This is illustrated with the time-frequency grid in Figure 9.40. Assuming all zeros in the region $R3$, we can simplify the estimation of channel matrix H and computation of its inverse.

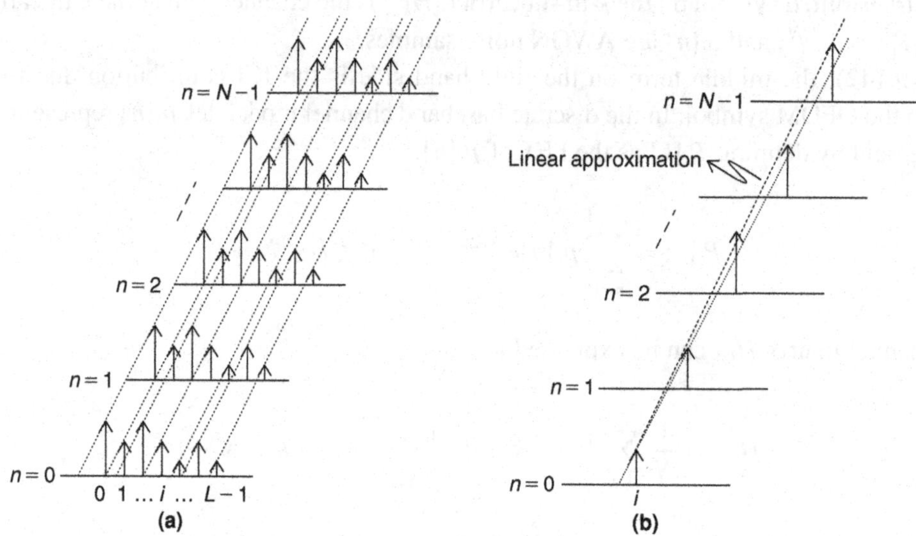

Figure 9.39: Wireless channel tap-delay model. (a) Quasi-stationary channel (i.e., time invariant in one OFDM symbol duration). (b) Slow time-varying channel.

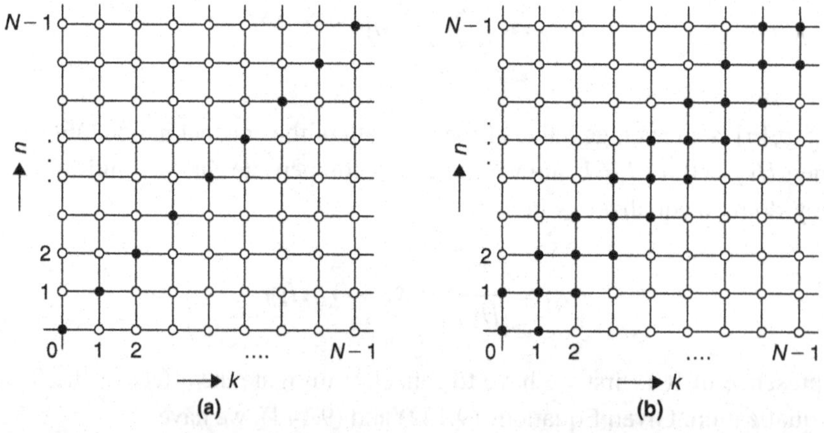

Figure 9.40: Wireless OFDM channel time-frequency grid. (a) Quasi-stationary channel (i.e., time invariant in one OFDM symbol duration). (b) Slow time-varying channel.

In Mostofi and Cox (2005), the channel matrix H is estimated assuming linear approximation to fading channel paths. To perform linearization, knowledge of the channel path at one time instant in the symbol is necessary. Using the pilot carriers, we estimate the average value for each channel path and assign this value to mid-channel response within one OFDM symbol duration. With this, the $p_i[n]$ mid-value (i.e., for $n = N/2 - 1$) can be obtained as in

$$p_i\left[\frac{N}{2}-1\right] = \frac{1}{L_p}\sum_{k=0}^{L_p-1} \hat{H}_{\mu_k,\mu_k} e^{j2\pi ik/L_p}, \quad 0 \le i \le L_p - 1 \tag{9.148}$$

where $\mu_k, 0 \le k \le L_p - 1$ are L_p ($> L_c$) pilot positions, and $\hat{H}_{\mu_k,\mu_k}$, the channel frequencies at pilot tones, are estimated as follows:

$$\hat{H}_{\mu_k,\mu_k} = \frac{Y_{\mu_k}}{X_{\mu_k}} = H_{\mu_k,\mu_k} + (\text{noise} + \text{ICI}) \tag{9.149}$$

Let α_i denote the slope of the i-th channel tap in the current OFDM symbol. Then, assuming the linear model, the $p_i[n]$, the i-th channel tap at n-th instant, can be calculated as

$$p_i[n] = p_i\left[\frac{N}{2}-1\right] + \alpha_i\left(n - \frac{N}{2} + 1\right) \tag{9.150}$$

The main diagonal elements of channel matrix $H_{k,k}$ are merely the N-point DFT of q_i. So,

$$H_{k,k} = \sum_{i=0}^{N-1} q_i e^{-j2\pi ik/N} \tag{9.151}$$

where

$$q_i = \begin{cases} p_i\left[\frac{N}{2}-1\right] & \text{for } 0 \le i \le L \\ 0 & \text{for } L < i < N \end{cases} \tag{9.152}$$

Computation of the off-diagonal elements of the channel matrix H can be simplified using Equations (9.143), (9.144), and (9.150) as follows:

$$H_{k,k+a} = \left(\frac{1}{N}\sum_{n=0}^{N-1}(n+1-N/2)e^{-j2\pi na/N}\right)\left(\sum_i \alpha_i e^{-j2\pi(k+a)i/N}\right), \quad a = \pm 1 \tag{9.153}$$

$$= C^{(off\ diagonal)} H^{(diagonal)} \tag{9.154}$$

where

$$C^{(off\ diagonal)} = \begin{bmatrix} 0 & c_1 & 0 & 0 & \cdots & 0 & 0 \\ c_{-1} & 0 & c_1 & 0 & \cdots & 0 & 0 \\ 0 & c_{-1} & 0 & c_1 & \cdots & 0 & 0 \\ 0 & 0 & c_{-1} & 0 & \cdots & 0 & 0 \\ \vdots & \vdots & \vdots & \vdots & \ddots & \vdots & \vdots \\ 0 & 0 & 0 & 0 & \cdots & 0 & c_1 \\ 0 & 0 & 0 & 0 & \cdots & c_{-1} & 0 \end{bmatrix} \tag{9.155}$$

$$H^{(diagonal)} = diag(FFT[\alpha_0, \alpha_1, \ldots]) \tag{9.156}$$

$$c_a = \frac{1}{N}\sum_{n=0}^{N-1}(n+1-N/2)e^{-j2\pi na} = (N-1) \times \begin{cases} 0.5, & a = 0 \\ -\frac{1}{1-e^{-j2\pi a/N}}, & a \ne 0 \end{cases} \tag{9.157}$$

and

$$\alpha_i = \frac{p_i^{(curr)}\left[\frac{N}{2}-1\right] - p_i^{(prev)}\left[\frac{N}{2}-1\right]}{N+L_c} \tag{9.158}$$

In Equation (9.158), $p_i^{(curr)}$ and $p_i^{(prev)}$ represent the *i*-th channel fading-tap coefficient in the mid-intervals of the current and previous OFDM symbols. In Equation (9.154), the elements of off-diagonal matrix C are constant, and they can be computed in advance as they depend only on the OFDM system parameters. With this, the estimated channel matrix in Equation (9.146) can be expressed as

$$\hat{H} = H_{k,k} + C^{(off\ diagonal)} H^{(diagonal)} \tag{9.159}$$

With the off-diagonal matrix $C^{(off\ diagonal)}$ in Equation (9.155), the estimated channel matrix $\hat{H}$ contains non-zero elements only in two off-diagonal array positions apart from the main diagonal array as expressed in Equation (9.160).

$$\hat{H} = \begin{bmatrix} h_{00} & h_{01} & 0 & 0 & 0 & 0 & 0 & \cdots & 0 & 0 \\ h_{10} & h_{11} & h_{12} & 0 & 0 & 0 & 0 & \cdots & 0 & 0 \\ 0 & h_{21} & h_{22} & h_{23} & 0 & 0 & 0 & \cdots & 0 & 0 \\ 0 & 0 & h_{32} & h_{33} & h_{34} & 0 & 0 & \cdots & 0 & 0 \\ \vdots & \vdots & \vdots & \vdots & \vdots & \vdots & \vdots & \ddots & \vdots & \vdots \\ 0 & 0 & 0 & 0 & 0 & 0 & 0 & \cdots & h_{N-3N-2} & 0 \\ 0 & 0 & 0 & 0 & 0 & 0 & 0 & \cdots & h_{N-2N-2} & h_{N-2N-1} \\ 0 & 0 & 0 & 0 & 0 & 0 & 0 & \cdots & h_{N-1N-2} & h_{N-1N-1} \end{bmatrix} \tag{9.160}$$

The matrix elements of $\hat{H}$ are rearranged to obtain the new matrix Π as follows:

$$\Pi = \begin{bmatrix} h_{00} & h_{01} & 0 & 0 & 0 & 0 & \cdots & 0 & 0 & 0 \\ h_{10} & h_{11} & h_{12} & 0 & 0 & 0 & \cdots & 0 & 0 & 0 \\ 0 & h_{21} & h_{22} & 0 & 0 & 0 & \cdots & 0 & 0 & 0 \\ 0 & 0 & 0 & h_{11} & h_{12} & 0 & \cdots & 0 & 0 & 0 \\ 0 & 0 & 0 & h_{21} & h_{22} & h_{23} & \cdots & 0 & 0 & 0 \\ 0 & 0 & 0 & 0 & h_{32} & h_{33} & \cdots & 0 & 0 & 0 \\ \vdots & \vdots & \vdots & \vdots & \vdots & \vdots & \ddots & \vdots & \vdots & \vdots \\ 0 & 0 & 0 & 0 & 0 & 0 & 0 & h_{N-3N-3} & h_{N-3N-2} & 0 \\ 0 & 0 & 0 & 0 & 0 & 0 & 0 & h_{N-2N-3} & h_{N-2N-2} & h_{N-2N-1} \\ 0 & 0 & 0 & 0 & 0 & 0 & 0 & 0 & h_{N-1N-2} & h_{N-1N-1} \end{bmatrix} \tag{9.161}$$

$$\Pi = \begin{bmatrix} \Pi_0 & & & 0 \\ & \Pi_1 & & \\ & & \ddots & \\ 0 & & & \Pi_{N-1} \end{bmatrix}$$

Then, the input–output relationship of the multipath channel is expressed using Equations (9.146) and (9.161) as

$$Y' = \Pi X' + W' \tag{9.162}$$

where

$$X' = [X'_0\, X'_1 \cdots X'_{N-3}]^T,\ X'_i = [X_i\, X_{i+1}\, X_{i+2}],\ Y' = [Y'_0\, Y'_1 \cdots Y'_{N-3}]^T,\ Y'_i = [Y_i\, Y_{i+1}\, Y_{i+2}],$$
$$W' = [W'_0\, W'_1 \cdots W'_{N-3}],\ \text{and}\ W'_i = [W'_i\, W'_{i+1}\, W'_{i+2}]$$

Ignoring the noise sample contribution in Equation (9.163),

$$X' = \Pi^{-1} Y' \tag{9.163}$$

where

$$\Pi^{-1} = \begin{bmatrix} \Pi_0^{-1} & & & 0 \\ & \Pi_1^{-1} & & \\ & & \ddots & \\ 0 & & & \Pi_{N-1}^{-1} \end{bmatrix} \tag{9.164}$$

Note that the size of the matrix inversion is lowered to 3×3, implying that the transmitted sequence can be obtained with moderate computational complexity. Finally, the estimated transmitted symbols $\hat{X}_2, \hat{X}_3, \ldots, \hat{X}_{N-3}$ can be obtained by selecting the elements in the middle of X'_i, where $1 \leq i \leq N-4$. The remaining symbols $\hat{X}_0, \hat{X}_1$ are estimated by taking the first two elements of X'_0, and $\hat{X}_{N-2}, \hat{X}_{N-1}$ are estimated by taking the last two elements of X'_{N-3}.

The relative Doppler frequency change, Δf_D, which indicates the degree of time variation of channel in any given OFDM symbol, is defined by the ratio of the OFDM symbol duration to the inverse of Doppler frequency (i.e., $T.f_D$). As long as Δf_D is less than 0.1, the linear approximation holds good, and we will get acceptable channel estimation results using the preceding method, as proposed in Jeon (1999).

9.4.5 Viterbi Equalizer

In Section 9.4.1, we discussed two criteria—namely zero forcing and MMSE—for designing channel equalizers. In this section, we introduce the third approach—namely, maximum likelihood sequence estimation (MLSE). The MLSE is a procedure for estimating a sequence of bits from a sequence of channel observations given the channel model. The MLSE is optimal in the sense of having the lowest probability of detecting the incorrect sequence. In the presence of ISI, the Viterbi algorithm provides an efficient way of computing the MLSE. The equalizers based on the MLSE criterion along with the Viterbi algorithm are known as Viterbi equalizers. As discussed in Section 3.9, the Viterbi algorithm finds the sequence at a minimum Euclidean distance from the received signal using the predefined model's trellis. We used the convolutional coder as a predefined model in Section 3.9 for error correction, whereas in this section a communication channel is used as a predefined model for channel equalization.

As discussed previously, the complexity of the Viterbi algorithm increases exponentially with the increase of predefined model memory (e.g., the constrained length of convolutional coder determines the complexity of the Viterbi decoder in error correction). In channel equalization, the amount of ISI (i.e., channel spread or memory) present in the channel outputs determines Viterbi equalizer complexity. However, complexity can be reduced by giving the Viterbi algorithm an approximate channel model with a shorter channel spread than that of the original channel. For this, we use an equivalent model as shown in Figure 9.35 to shorten the channel before using the Viterbi algorithm for channel equalization. The class of receivers employing this technique of linear prefiltering of received data followed by equalization using the Viterbi algorithm is known as combined linear Viterbi equalizers (CLVEs). The block diagram of a CLVE receiver is shown in Figure 9.41.

Since we know the L taps of shorted channel as $\{h_i\}_{i=0}^{L-1}$ after channel estimation and prefiltering, given a sequence of symbols $\{s_n\}$, the receiver can create noise-free channel output symbols as follows:

$$y_n^{NF} = \sum_{i=0}^{L-1} h_i s_{n-i} \tag{9.165}$$

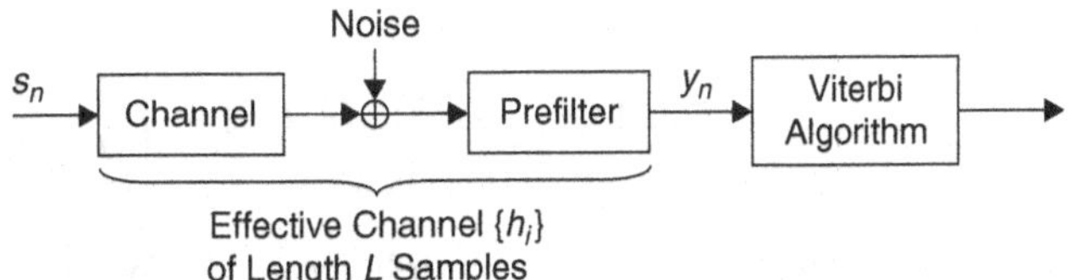

Figure 9.41: Block diagram of CLVE.

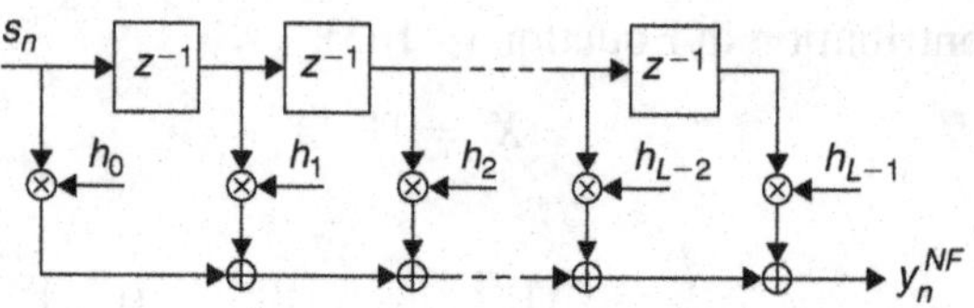

Figure 9.42: FIR filter realization of effective channel response.

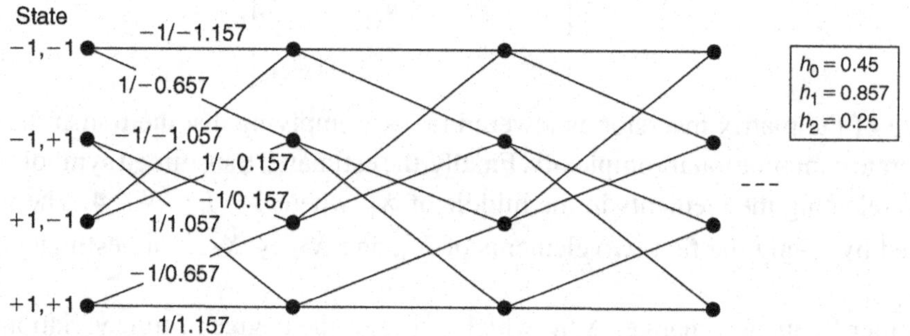

Figure 9.43: Steady-state trellis diagram of FIR channel for $L = 3$.

Let $\{y_n\}$ represent the received noisy channel observations at the prefilter output. The squared Euclidean distance d^{SED} of $\{y_n^{NF}\}$ from $\{y_n\}$ is given by

$$d^{SED} = \sum_n \left| y_n - y_n^{NF} \right|^2 = \sum_n \left| y_n - \sum_{i=0}^{L-1} h_i s_{n-i} \right|^2 \tag{9.166}$$

The MLSE decision then is the sequence of symbols $\{\hat{s}_m\}$ minimizing the distance d^{SED}; that is,

$$\{\hat{s}_m\} = \arg \min_{\{s_m\}} \sum_n \left| y_n - \sum_{i=0}^{L-1} h_i s_{n-i} \right|^2 \tag{9.167}$$

We solve Equation (9.167) with the trellis generated by using the shorted channel model as shown in Figure 9.42. The steady-state trellis diagram of the FIR channel for $L = 3$ is shown in Figure 9.43. Here the constraint length of the channel model is the same as the length of the channel L, and the memory size of the model is $L - 1$ samples. The number of states present in the trellis corresponding to such a channel model is 2^{L-1}. Thus, the complexity of the Viterbi equalizer grows with the constraint length L of the channel.

Application of Viterbi Equalizer in GSM Systems

Next, we consider an application of the Viterbi equalizer in GSM (global system for mobile communications) systems. The GSM communication protocol establishes the training sequence in the data packets to determine the channel characteristics. In order to cope with the time-varying nature of mobile radio channels, GSM supports block adaptivity by introducing a training sequence into the most frequently used normal burst (NB) as shown in Figure 9.44. The duration of one normal burst slot is 0.577 ms. Each NB slot contains 58 message bits on each side of 26 bits mid-amble, which is called a training sequence. The total number of bits per NB (including 6 tail bits and 9.25 dummy bits) is 156.25, and so a 1-bit duration in GSM is about $T = 3.6928\,\mu s$. The middle 16-bit r_s of the 26-bit mid-amble r_t is also used for synchronization purposes. These synchronization pattern bits are chosen such that the autocorrelation $R_s[n]$ of the resulting binary modulated sequence $r_s[k]$ is

$$R_s[n] = \sum_{k=0}^{15} r_s[k] r_s[k+n] = \begin{cases} 16, & n = 0 \\ 0, & n \neq 0 \end{cases} \tag{9.168}$$

at least in the range of expected maximum echo delay $\tau = nT$ for $|n| < 5$.

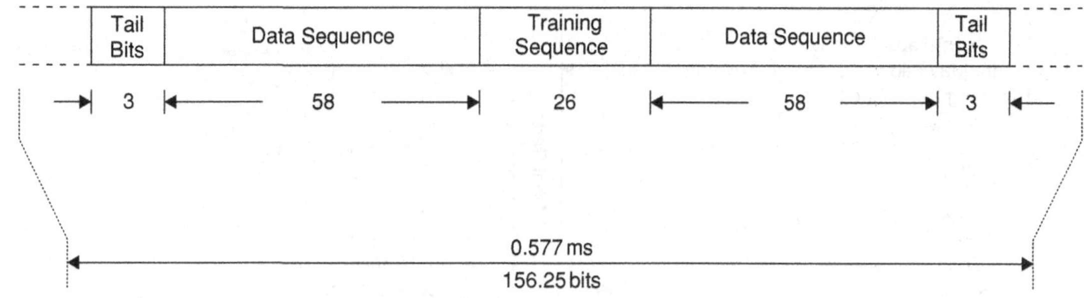

Figure 9.44: Structure of normal burst in GSM systems.

The training sequence $r_t[n]$ enables the receiver to perform channel estimation and equalization. Let $y_t[n]$ represent the channel output corresponding to the training sequence. Then,

$$y_t[n] = h[n] \otimes r_t[n] \tag{9.169}$$

where $h[n]$ is the sampled effective response of channel $h_c(t)$ and the transmitted pulse $p(t)$ that is used to shape the signals for minimizing the interference during the transmission. Here, we assume that the fading behavior of the channel $h[n]$ remains constant in the given NB slot duration. In other words, there should no fast-fading degradation during an NB slot time when the receiver is using knowledge from the mid-amble to compensate for the channel's fading behavior.

At the receiver, the received sequence is passed through a matched filter with an impulse response $h_m[n]$, which is matched to $r_t[n]$ (i.e., $h_m[n] = r_t[-n]$). The matched filter output $y_t^{MF}[n]$ can be written as

$$\begin{aligned} y_t^{MF}[n] &= h_m[n] \otimes y_t[n] \\ &= h_m[n] \otimes r_t[n] \otimes h[n] \\ &= r_t[-n] \otimes r_t[n] \otimes h[n] \\ &= R_t[n] \otimes h[n] \end{aligned} \tag{9.170}$$

where $R_t[n]$ is the autocorrelation of the training sequence $r_t[n]$. In GSM, the training sequences (ETS, 1998) are engineered so that $R_t[n]$ result in a highly peaked function. Therefore, the matched filter output $y_t^{MF}[n]$ is a good estimate of the complex channel $h[n]$. That is,

$$\hat{h}[n] \approx y_t^{MF}[n] \tag{9.171}$$

The mathematical approximation to the metric in Equation (9.167) can be expressed with matched filter outputs as input to the metric calculation (i.e., matched filter metric) as follows:

$$\{\hat{b}_n\} = \arg\max_{\{b_n\}} \sum_m b_m \mathrm{Re}\left[y_d^{MF}[m] - \sum_{k=1}^{L-1} S_k b_{m-k} \right] \tag{9.172}$$

where

$$y_d^{MF}[n] = \sum_{k=0}^{L-1} \hat{h}^*[k] y_d[k+n] \tag{9.173}$$

$$S_i = \sum_{k=0}^{L-1} \hat{h}[k] \hat{h}^*[k+i], \quad i = 1, 2, \ldots, L-1 \tag{9.174}$$

Given that we know that b_n are binary modulated symbols (i.e., $+1$ or -1), we can precompute 2^{L-1} possible values of

$$\mathrm{Re}\left[\sum_{k=1}^{L-1} S_k b_{m-k} \right]$$

in Equation (9.172) and store them in a look-up table. The tail bits at both ends of the NB define the start and end states for the Viterbi algorithm. The necessary functional blocks to simulate Equation (9.172) are shown

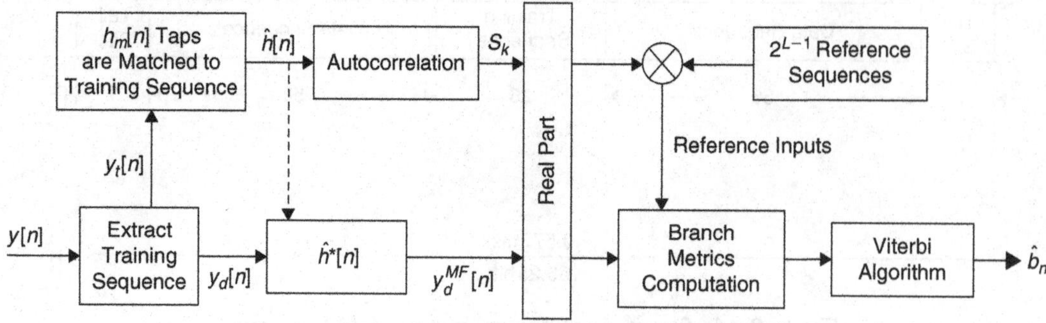

Figure 9.45: Functional blocks of Viterbi equalizer.

in Figure 9.45. We use a special filter (not shown) to truncate the estimated channel impulse response $\hat{h}[n]$ to a few taps (usually four to six channel taps are present after truncation). This means that in GSM, the Viterbi algorithm performed on 8-, 16-, or 32-state trellises depends on the number of taps present in the truncated channel response.

9.4.6 Turbo Equalizer

So far, we have discussed the design of the receiver where the module's channel equalization (CE) and channel decoding (CD) are treated as two separate entities. However, in the literature, it has been shown that the receiver design with modules CE and CD as a single entity performs well when compared to the receiver design in which CE and CD are two design entities. If we treat modules CE and CD as two entities, then the CD gets only decision outputs without *a priori* probability information from the CE. In order to best take advantage of the CD, the CE has to provide decisions along with their reliability information. As CD algorithms such as turbo or LDPC decoding provide likelihood information as an output, in turn, we can feed back this extrinsic information to the CE and make the total process iterative. This type of equalizer structure is known as "turbo equalization" since the extrinsic information is passed back and forth between the CE and CD in the same way as in turbo code decoding.

Turbo equalization is motivated by turbo code breakthroughs, and has emerged as a promising technique for drastic reduction of ISI effects in frequency-selective wireless channels. However, the trellis-based turbo equalizer can be a heavy computational burden for wireless systems with limited processing power, especially in cases where the wireless channel has a long delay spread (or larger ISI). In this section, we discuss two turbo-equalization schemes—an ML/MAP criterion-based scheme with exponential computational complexity and an MMSE criterion-based scheme with linear complexity. The difference between ML/MAP and MMSE schemes is that the former relies on the nonlinear trellis-based processing whereas the latter can be achieved with simple linear operations such as matrices processing.

We use the same transmitter structure with interleaver block shown in Figure 9.46 to discuss the turbo-equalizer receiver design based on MAP and MMSE criteria. The source bits $\{b_k\}$ are encoded to produce the codeword bits $\{c_n\}$. Next, the bits $\{c_n\}$ are mapped to symbols $\{s_n\}$ using the BPSK modulator. The symbols are interleaved to produce the symbol sequence $\{x_n\}$ before transmitting through the channel corrupted by AWGN noise and ISI. Let $\{y_n\}$ represent the received symbols corresponding to the transmitted sequence $\{x_n\}$. At the receiver, we will assume a coherent symbol-spaced receiver front end as well as precise knowledge of the signal phase and symbol timing such that the channel can be approximated by an equivalent, discrete-time, baseband model. We use the same channel decoder structure (except for mapping functions) with both MAP and MMSE turbo-equalizer algorithms.

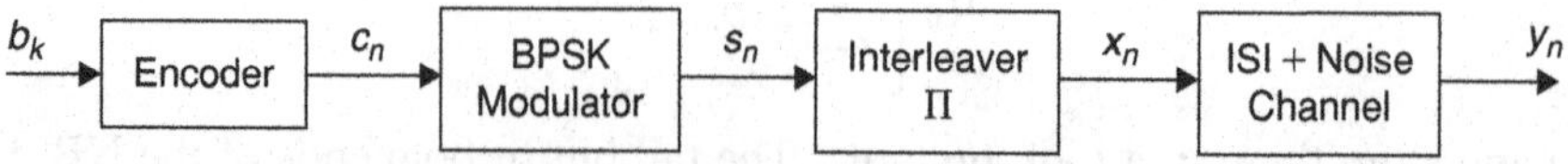

Figure 9.46: Transmitter structure with interleaver block for data transmission.

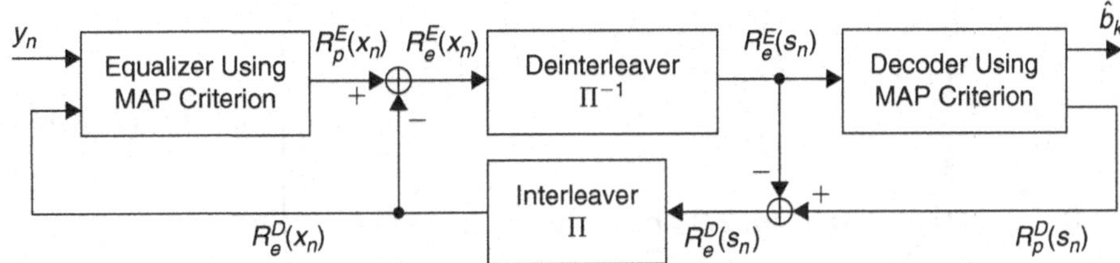

Figure 9.47: Turbo-equalizer architecture based on MAP criterion.

Turbo Equalization Based on MAP Criterion

Given the received sequence $\underline{y} = \{y_n\}$, the MAP algorithm of the equalizer computes the log-likelihood ratios (LLRs), $R_p^E(x_n)$, using *a posteriori* probabilities $\Pr\{x_n = +1|\underline{y}\}$ and $\Pr\{x_n = -1|\underline{y}\}$ as follows:

$$\begin{aligned} R_p^E(x_n) &\equiv \ln \frac{\Pr\{x_n=+1|\underline{y}\}}{\Pr\{x_n=-1|\underline{y}\}} = \ln \frac{\Pr(\underline{y}|x_n=+1)}{\Pr(\underline{y}|x_n=-1)} + \ln \frac{\Pr\{x_n=+1\}}{\Pr\{x_n=-1\}} \\ &= R_e^E(x_n) + R_a^E(x_n) \end{aligned} \tag{9.175}$$

where $R_e^E(x_n)$ is the extrinsic information about x_n contained in the received sequence $\{y_n\}$, and $R_a^E(x_n)$ is the *a priori* information of x_n and is independent from channel observations $\{y_n\}$. The $R_e^E(x_n)$ is generated using the given received sequence $\{y_n\}$ and the *a priori* information of all symbols except n-th symbol (i.e., $R_a^E(x_m), m \neq n$). After deinterleaving the extrinsic information $R_e^E(x_n)$, we have the output of the deinterleaver $R_e^E(s_n)$ to use as *a priori* information for the channel decoder.

Given the *a priori* information $\underline{r} = \{r_n\} = R_e^E(s_n) = \Pi^{-1}[R_e^E(x_n)]$, the MAP algorithm of the decoder computes the LLRs using *a posteriori* probabilities $\Pr\{s_n = +1|\underline{r}\}$ and $\Pr\{s_n = -1|\underline{r}\}$ as

$$\begin{aligned} R_p^D(s_n) &\equiv \ln \frac{\Pr\{s_n=+1|\underline{r}\}}{\Pr\{s_n=-1|\underline{r}\}} = \ln \frac{\Pr(\underline{r}|s_n=+1)}{\Pr(\underline{r}|s_n=-1)} + \ln \frac{\Pr\{s_n=+1\}}{\Pr\{s_n=-1\}} \\ &= R_e^D(s_n) + R_a^D(s_n) \end{aligned} \tag{9.176}$$

where $R_e^D(s_n)$ is the extrinsic information about s_n contained in $\{r_n\}$, and $R_a^D(s_n)$ is the *a priori* information of s_n. After interleaving the extrinsic information $R_e^D(s_n)$, we have the output of interleaver $R_e^D(x_n)$ to use as *a priori* information for the equalizer. The *a priori* information $R_e^D(x_n) = \Pi[R_e^D(s_n)]$ is not available to the equalizer for the first iteration, and we set $R_e^D(x_n)$ to zero for all symbols assuming that they are equiprobable. Once we reach the maximum iteration count Q, we extract the decoded bits $\hat{b}_k$ from the decoder by applying the threshold on the LLRs, $R_p^D(s_n)$. The turbo equalizer based on Equations (9.175) and (9.176) is shown in Figure 9.47. For more information on LLR computation using the trellis diagram, see Section 3.10. An example of steady-state trellis diagram representation of the FIR channel is shown in Figure 9.43.

Turbo Equalization Based on MMSE Criterion

In contrast to the MAP approach, the MMSE-based approach performs only simple linear filter operations on the received block of symbols $\{y_n\}$ to get the estimate of x_n, $\hat{x}_n$, and then apply a mapping function on $\hat{x}_n$ to produce extrinsic information, $R_e^E(\hat{x}_n)$. Let us assume an MMSE linear equalizer as shown in Figure 9.48, consisting of a filter with time-varying filter coefficients $\underline{\lambda}_n = [\lambda_{n,-M_2}, \lambda_{n,-M_2+1}, \ldots, \lambda_{n,-1}, \lambda_{n,0}, \lambda_{n,1}, \ldots, \lambda_{n,M_1-1}, \lambda_{n,M_1}]^T$ of length $M = M_1 + M_2 + 1$. The design rule for the filter coefficients $\underline{\lambda}_n$ is to minimize the MMSE cost function $E\{|x_n - \hat{x}_n|^2\}$. Let $L = L_1 + L_2 + 1$ be the length of the channel impulse response with the coefficient vector $\underline{h} = [h_{-L_2}, h_{-L_2+1}, \ldots, h_{-1}, h_0, h_1, \ldots, h_{L_1-1}, h_{L_1}]$. Then the received symbol vector $\underline{y}_n$ can be expressed as

$$\underline{y}_n = H\underline{x}_n + \underline{u}_n \tag{9.177}$$

where

$\underline{y}_n \equiv [y_{n+M_2}, y_{n+M_2-1}, \ldots, y_{n+1}, y_n, y_{n-1}, \ldots, y_{n-M_1+1}, y_{n-M_1}]^T$, an M×1 vector

$\underline{x}_n \equiv [x_{n+L_2+M_2}, x_{n+L_2+M_2-1}, \ldots, x_{n+1}, x_n, x_{n-1}, \ldots, x_{n-L_1-M_1+1}, x_{n-L_1-M_1}]^T$, an (L+M−1)×1 vector

$\underline{u}_n \equiv [u_{n+M_2}, u_{n+M_2-1}, \ldots, u_{n+1}, u_n, u_{n-1}, \ldots, u_{n-M_1+1}, u_{n-M_1}]^T$, an M×1 vector

$$H \equiv \begin{bmatrix} h_{-L_2} & h_{-L_2+1} & \cdots & h_{L_1} & 0 & 0 & 0 & 0 & \cdots & 0 \\ 0 & h_{-L_2} & h_{-L_2+1} & \cdots & h_{L_1} & 0 & 0 & 0 & \cdots & 0 \\ \vdots & \vdots & \vdots & \ddots & \vdots & \vdots & \ddots & \vdots & \vdots & \vdots \\ 0 & 0 & 0 & 0 & 0 & 0 & h_{-L_2} & h_{-L_2+1} & \cdots & h_{L_1} \end{bmatrix}, \text{ an } M \times (L+M-1) \text{ matrix}$$

The MMSE estimated symbol $\hat{x}_n$ is calculated as follows:

$$\hat{x}_n = \underline{\lambda}_n^{HT} \underline{y}_n + v_n \tag{9.178}$$

where the vector $\underline{\lambda}_n$ and the scalar v_n are complex valued parameters subject to optimization, and $(.)^{HT}$ is the Hermitian transpose.

The block diagram of the MMSE-based turbo equalizer is shown in Figure 9.49. The extrinsic information $R_e^D(x_n)$ from the channel decoder is demapped to obtain *a priori* information χ_n that is suitable to work with the MMSE criterion. Once the estimated symbols $\hat{x}_n$ are available, the extrinsic information $R_e^E(\hat{x}_n)$ from the equalizer is obtained by using the mapping function. The complete description of MMSE estimation, mapping, and demapping functions involves the manipulation of many mathematical equations. See Tuchler et al. (2002) for a complete mathematical description of the MMSE-based turbo equalizer. Only the final results for the MMSE-based equalizer follows.

Demapping

$$\chi_n \equiv \tanh\left(\frac{R_e^D(x_n)}{2}\right) \tag{9.179}$$

where

$$\underline{\chi}_n = [\chi_{n+L_2+M_2}, \chi_{n+L_2+M_2-1}, \ldots, \chi_{n+1}, \chi_n, \chi_{n-1}, \ldots, \chi_{n-L_1-M_1+1}, \chi_{n-L_1-M_1}]^T$$

is an $(L+M-1)\times 1$ vector.

MMSE Estimation

$$\hat{x}_n = \underline{\lambda}_n^{HT}(\underline{y}_n - H\underline{\chi}_n + \chi_n \underline{d}) \tag{9.180}$$

where

$$\underline{d} \equiv H\underline{s}, \quad \underline{s} \equiv [\underline{0}_{1\times(L_2+M_2)} \;\; 1 \;\; \underline{0}_{1\times(L_1+M_1)}]^T, \; \underline{0}_{1\times K}$$

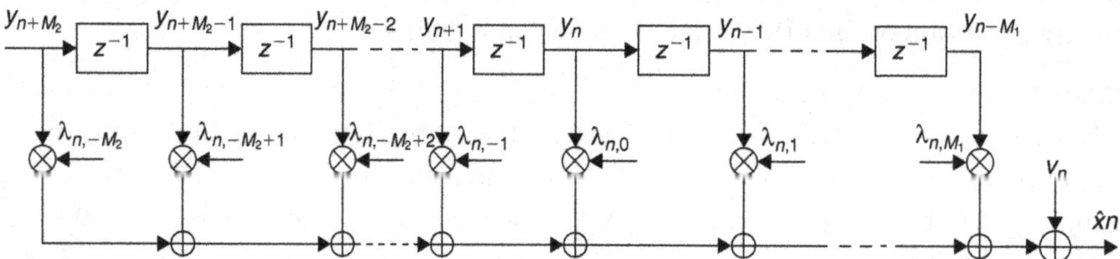

Figure 9.48: MMSE symbol estimator with time-variant filter coefficients.

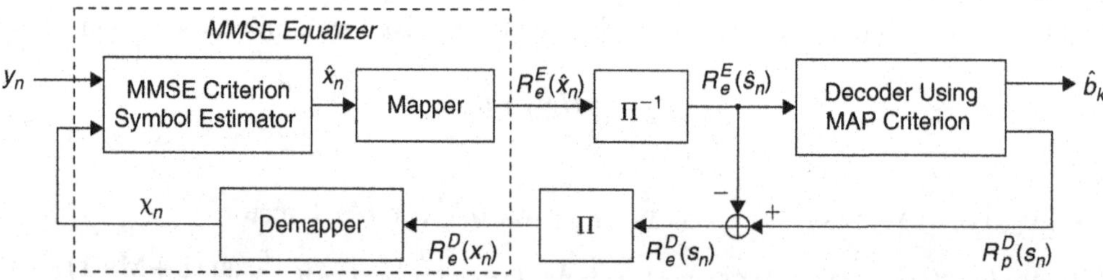

Figure 9.49: Turbo-equalizer architecture based on MMSE criterion.

is a $1 \times K$ zero vector,

$$\underline{\lambda}_n \equiv Z^{-1}\underline{d}$$
$$Z \equiv \sigma_u^2 I_N + H\Sigma_n H^{HT} + |\chi_n|^2 \underline{d}\,\underline{d}^{HT}$$

where

$$\Sigma_n \equiv diag[(1-|\chi_{n+L_2+M_2}|^2), (1-|\chi_{n+L_2+M_2-1}|^2), \ldots, (1-|\chi_{n+1}|^2), (1-|\chi_n|^2),$$
$$(1-|\chi_{n-1}|^2), \ldots, (1-|\chi_{n-L_1-M_1+1}|^2), (1-|\chi_{n-L_1-M_1}|^2)]$$

in which I_N is the $N \times N$ identity matrix, and σ_u^2 is the estimated channel noise variance.

For the first iteration, the *a priori* information is not available, and we set $\chi_n = 0, \forall n$ assuming the symbols x_n as equiprobable. Thus, for the first iteration, we can simplify the computation of Z as

$$Z \equiv \sigma_u^2 I_N + HH^{HT}$$

Mapping

$$R_e^E(\hat{x}_n) = \frac{2\hat{x}_n}{1-\underline{d}^H \underline{\lambda}_n} \tag{9.181}$$

9.5 Synchronization

In a digital communication system, synchronization is an essential receiver function. Accurate timing information must be known to the demodulator to produce reliable estimates of the transmitted data sequence. In the previous sections, we assumed precise knowledge about the symbol phase and timing information, although this assumption is often not explicitly stated. To have meaningful communication between the transmitter and receiver, synchronization at various levels should first be established, depending on the type of communication system. For example, in carrier-based communication systems, the carrier frequency is generated at the transmitter by the RF oscillator and the receiver also generates the replica of the carrier signal for demodulation purpose. We use a local RF oscillator at the receiver to generate the carrier signal.

For generation of the exact frequencies of both carrier signals at the transmitter and receiver, we must impose a severe accuracy specification on the oscillators and this inflates the cost. If communication systems employ less-accurate oscillators, then there will be a difference in the transmitter-generated carrier frequency and receiver-generated carrier frequency, and this in turn results in a frequency offset between transmitted and received generated-replica carrier signals. We estimate this frequency offset and correct it to minimize the errors in the demodulated baseband signal. Similarly, the receiver should know about sample timing and phase (to have proper samples to work with), and frame boundaries (to process proper data blocks) to optimally perform receiver functions such as channel equalization, error correction, and so on.

Synchronization in communications systems has two steps—offset parameter (e.g., frequency offset, timing offset, phase offset) estimation and correction. Typically, the offset estimation module is a signal-processing algorithm that estimates the error between the actual transmitted signal parameter and the receiver regenerated signal parameter. Once the offset is estimated by a corresponding algorithm, information is fed to the control unit, usually a phase-locked loop (PLL) or equivalent function module, to generate signals with the desired frequency, phase, and timing. In this section, we are restricted to parameter offset estimation algorithms, as the subject of PLL control units is beyond this book's scope. At the receiver, accurate frequency, timing, and phase recovery are critical to obtain near optimal performance. In practice, we encounter two types of synchronizer structures—data aided (DA), which use receiver decisions or a training sequence in computing the symbol timing estimates, and nondata aided (NDA), which operate independent of the transmitted information sequence. In noisy environments, the NDA structures are more robust when compared to DA structures.

9.5.1 Frequency Offset Estimation

In practice, we deal with two types of communication systems—single- and multicarrier systems. In single-carrier communication, we modulate the baseband signal on a carrier with RF frequency and transmit the information.

In a multicarrier system, the modulated OFDM signals are once again modulated onto an RF carrier to transmit the information in a particular range of available broad wireless frequency spectra. Next, we discuss frequency offset estimation for both single- and multicarrier systems.

Single-Carrier Systems

Frequency offset estimation for various single-carrier communication systems has been discussed in the literature (Kay, 1989; Luise, 1995; Mengali and Morelli, 1997; Kuo and Fitz, 1997). Here, we discuss the frequency offset estimation in widely used burst-mode digital transmission systems such as time-division multiple access (TDMA) systems. Let us consider an M-ary PSK modulation and AWGN channel with two-sided power spectral density (PSD) $N_0/2$. Assuming the correct sampling time instants, we can express the received sequence as

$$y[k] = s_k e^{j(2\pi f_e kT+\phi)} + n[k] \tag{9.182}$$

where $\{s_k\}$ are M-PSK symbols, f_e is the frequency offset, ϕ is constant phase offset, T is the sampling interval, and $n[k]$ are complex-valued AWGN samples. Since s_k are unit amplitude symbols, we can eliminate the effect of s_k on $y[k]$ by multiplying Equation (9.182) by s_k^* on both sides. With this,

$$r[k] = e^{j(2\pi f_e kT+\phi)}(1+u[k]) \tag{9.183}$$

where $r[k] = y[k]s_k^*$ and $u[k] = n[k]s_k^* e^{-j(2\pi f_e kT+\phi)}$.

Now, computing the autocorrelation of sequence $r[k]$ of length N for different lags yields

$$\begin{aligned} R[m] &= \frac{1}{N-m}\sum_{k=m}^{N-1} r[k]r^*[k-m] \\ &= e^{j2\pi m f_e T}(1+\eta[m]) \end{aligned} \tag{9.184}$$

where

$$\eta[m] \equiv \frac{1}{N-m}\sum_{k=m}^{N-1}(u[k]+u^*[k-m]+u[k]u^*[k-m])$$

The frequency offset f_e is then estimated as

$$\hat{f}_e = \frac{1}{2\pi T}\arg\left\{\sum_{m=1}^{N-1} R[m]R^*[m-1]\right\} \tag{9.185}$$

Once we obtain the frequency offset using Equation (9.185), the effect of the frequency offset in the received sequence $y[k]$ is nullified by multiplying Equation (9.182) by the term $e^{-j2\pi f_e kT}$.

Multicarrier Systems

As previously discussed, we use cyclic prefix-based discrete multitone (DMT) or orthogonal frequency division multiplexing (OFDM) techniques to implement spectrally efficient multicarrier systems. OFDM system performance mostly depends on the performance of synchronization algorithms used to find frequency offset, phase offset, OFDM symbol timing, and so on. Although the modulated subcarriers overlap spectrally, they can be easily recovered as long as the channel does not destroy orthogonality among the subcarriers. However, DMT and OFDM systems are very sensitive to frequency offset caused by the oscillator instabilities and Doppler shifts induced by the channel. The frequency offset in OFDM systems results in loss of orthogonality between subcarriers, and this in turn results in symbol amplitude reduction after demodulating the signal from the subcarriers. As the carriers are inherently closely spaced in frequency compared to channel bandwidth, the tolerable frequency offset becomes a very small fraction of the channel bandwidth. For discussion of frequency offset estimation in OFDM systems, see, for instance, Nogami and Nagashima (1995), Schmidl and Cox (1997), and Van de Beek et al. (1997). In the following, we discuss a simple approach to estimate such frequency offset.

Let $\{x_n\}, n = 0, 1, 2, \ldots, N-1$ represent the OFDM modulated sequence obtained from N baseband modulated symbols $\{X_k\}, k = 0, 1, 2, \ldots, N-1$. In other words, the sequence $\{x_n\}$ is obtained after taking N-point

IDFT of $\{X_k\}$. Let L and L_c, where $L_c \geq L-1$, represent the channel $\{h_l\}$ length and cyclic prefix length, respectively. Let $\{x_i'\}$ represent the $N+L_c$-length cyclic prefix-extended sequence of $\{x_n\}$, and let $\{y_i'\}$ represent the received noisy sequence after passing $\{x_i'\}$ through the time-dispersive channel $\{h_l\}$. Let $\{y_n\}$ represent N-length received noise sequence formed by removing the L_c cyclic prefix samples from $\{y_i'\}$. With this, the noisy sequence $\{y_n\}$ can be expressed as

$$y_n = \frac{1}{N}\left[\sum_{k=0}^{N-1} X_k H_k e^{j2\pi n(k+\varepsilon)/N}\right] + u_n \tag{9.186}$$

where H_k is the channel gain at the k-th carrier, ε is the relative frequency offset (which is defined as the ratio of the actual frequency offset, f_e, to the intercarrier spacing, Δf), and u_n are the AWGN samples. If we repeat the OFDM symbol with the same information, then based on Equation (9.186), the samples y_n and y_{n+N}, as long as $0 \leq n \leq N-1$, are related by

$$y_{n+N} = y_n e^{j2\pi\varepsilon} + u_{n+N} \tag{9.187}$$

Using this observation in Moose (1994), the maximum likelihood estimate (MLE) of ε, $\hat{\varepsilon}$, is proposed by repeating the OFDM symbol. Thus, the MLE estimate of relative frequency offset $\hat{\varepsilon}$ follows:

$$\hat{\varepsilon} = \frac{1}{2\pi}\tan^{-1}\left\{\left[\sum_{i\in S} \mathrm{Im}(Y_{1,i}Y_{0,i}^*)\right] \Big/ \left[\sum_{i\in S} \mathrm{Re}(Y_{1,i}Y_{0,i}^*)\right]\right\} \tag{9.188}$$

where

$$Y_{0,k} = \sum_{n=0}^{N-1} y_n e^{-j2\pi nk/N}, \quad Y_{1,k} = \sum_{n=0}^{N-1} y_{n+N} e^{-j2\pi nk/N} \tag{9.189}$$

and the set $S = \{0, 1, 2, \ldots, K-1, 0, 0, 0, \ldots, 0, N-K, N-K+1, \ldots, N-1\}$ contains only low-frequency carrier indices to avoid the contribution of high-frequency carrier offsets, as they are more erroneous.

9.5.2 Symbol Synchronization

We sample the received continuous-time signal to process the signal in the digital domain; for this we must know the exact start of the sample or symbol time. In single-carrier systems, the exact sample timing can be found by searching for the maximum "eye opening" in the down-converted, baseband modulated signal. Since the DMT or OFDM modulated sequences are random in nature, the concepts used to calculate the sample timing for the DMT signal are significantly different, as there is no "eye opening" where a best sampling time can be found. In OFDM systems, we use the term "symbol" to represent the OFDM block, and it contains N time samples (or $N+L_c$, including the cyclic prefix) as shown in Figure 9.50(a). Thus, for OFDM symbol synchronization, we require information on the start of sample time as well symbol time.

The N-length OFDM modulated sequence $x[n]$ can be obtained by taking IFFT for N baseband modulated signals $\{X_k\}$ as follows:

$$x[n] = \frac{1}{N}\sum_{k=0}^{N-1} X_k e^{j2\pi kn/N}, \quad n = 0, 1, 2, \ldots, N-1 \tag{9.190}$$

The autocorrelation of the OFDM sequence $x(n)$ has an important property, that $x(n)$ behaves like white Gaussian noise in the band of operation, as shown in Figure 9.51. The autocorrelation of OFDM modulated $x(n)$ follows:

$$\begin{aligned} r_{xx}(m) &= \sum_{n=0}^{N-1} x(n)x^*(n+m) \\ &= \begin{cases} \sigma_X^2 & \text{if } m = 0 \\ 0 & \text{if } m \neq 0 \end{cases} \end{aligned} \tag{9.191}$$

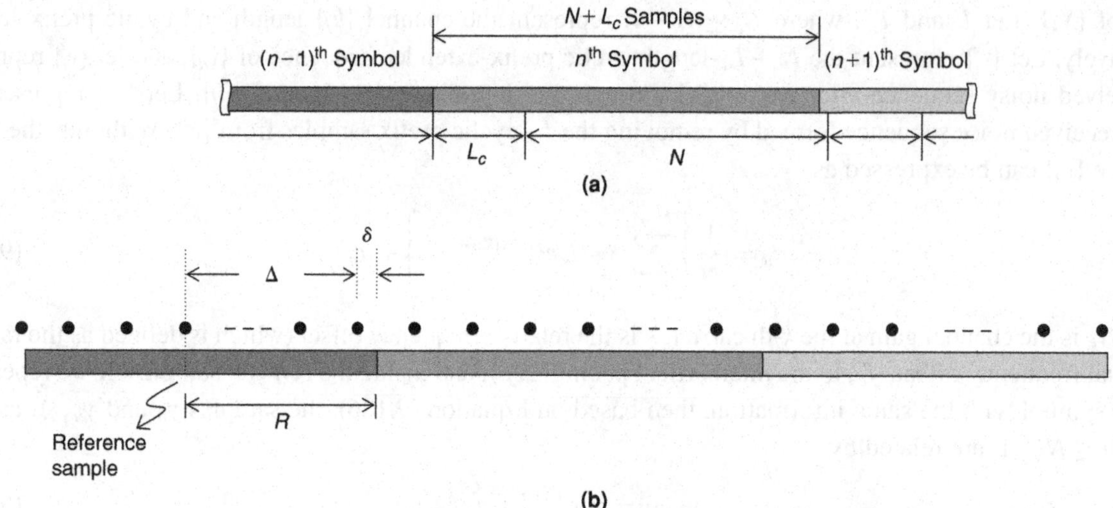

Figure 9.50: DMT symbol synchronization. (a) Transmitted. (b) Received.

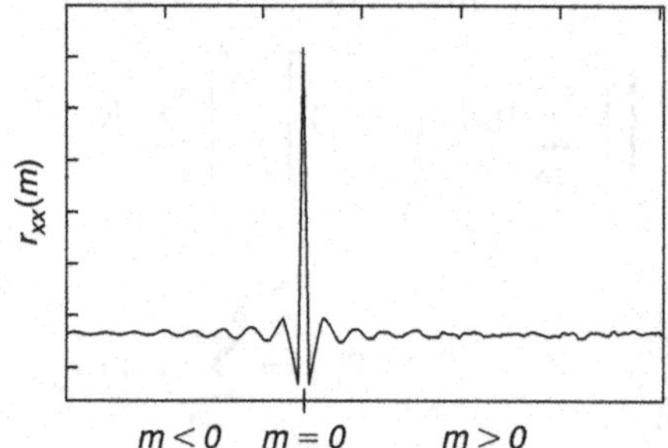

Figure 9.51: Autocorrelation of OFDM-modulated sequence $x(n)$.

In Keller et al. (2001) and Speth et al. (1997), many correlation-based algorithms using the cyclic prefix were suggested to achieve OFDM symbol synchronization. These correlation-based methods work well under AWGN channel conditions at high SNRs. Their performance degrades significantly with frequency-selective (or multipath fading) channels and with the increase of the Doppler frequency. In addition, correlation-based methods perform poorly at low SNRs. Moreover, achieving fine synchronization is very difficult with correlation-based techniques as the strong noise component attenuates the correlation peak at low SNRs. In Landstrom et al. (2001) and Muller-Weinfurtner (1998), maximum likelihood (ML) and MMSE-based algorithms for OFDM symbol synchronization are proposed, and they are computationally expensive in general. At low SNRs under AWGN and moderately dispersive conditions, the sophisticated algorithms ML and MMSE show considerable performance gains.

In this section, we describe both coarse- and fine-symbol synchronization techniques to identify an OFDM/DMT symbol boundary by taking advantage of the redundant (or cyclic prefix) or training data (pilot tones) present in OFDM/DMT symbols. We use correlation-based and simplified ML-based algorithms for obtaining coarse symbol synchronization. The same techniques can be applied for both OFDM and DMT coarse symbol synchronization. However, fine synchronization algorithms used for DMT are slightly different from OFDM due to the time-varying nature of wireless channels.

Let us assume that the channel introduces a delay equal to DT (where T is the sampling interval and D is a noninteger) as shown in Figure 9.50(b). The receiver estimates D and splits the delay into two parts—Δ, to be estimated by a coarse symbol synchronization algorithm, and δ, to be estimated by a fine symbol synchronization algorithm. In distortionless AWGN channels, we can estimate Δ to the nearest integer value of D, and in that case $0 \leq \delta < 1$. The symbol synchronizer detects the block of samples that belong to the same received symbol and controls which N samples are fed to the demodulator (or FFT module). The fine symbol synchronization guarantees timing alignment (zero phase/clock offset) of the receiver sampling clock with the transmitter sampling clock (assuming zero-frequency offset between the clocks).

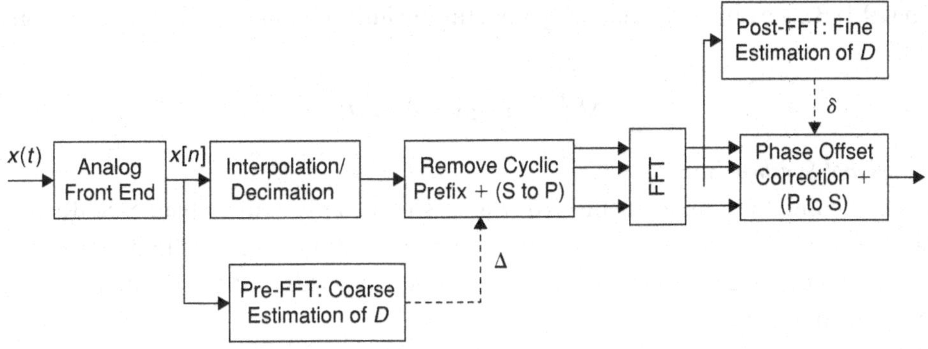

Figure 9.52: Symbol synchronization with DMT systems.

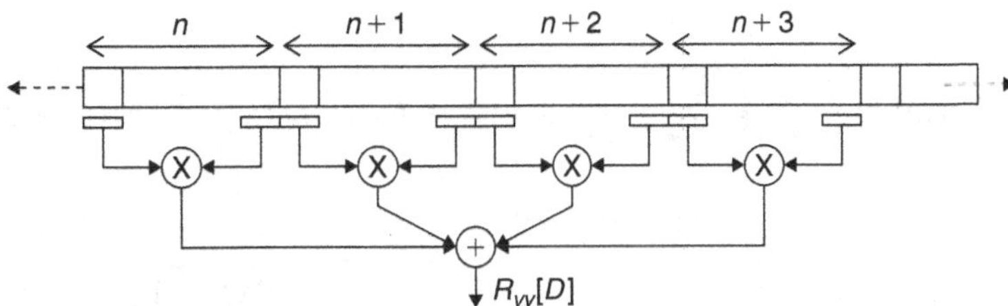

Figure 9.53: Symbol timing estimation by correlation.

Before FFT, we achieve coarse symbol synchronization with estimation of Δ, and this allows us to perform demodulation. After FFT, we perform fine symbol synchronization by estimating δ using the training symbols. As shown in Figure 9.52, we align sample time instances in the digital domain (instead of using PLL) by performing interpolation and decimation on the received samples.

Coarse Symbol Synchronization

Given that we are not using any training data with the correlation-based or ML-based algorithms, these methods come under NDA schemes. The autocorrelation property of the OFDM modulated sequence $x[n]$ given in Equation (9.191) and the redundant cyclic prefix in the transmitted sequence are mostly useful for achieving coarse symbol synchronization at the receiver. Let $y[n]$ be the received discrete baseband equivalent of the OFDM sequence corresponding to the transmitted sequence $x[n]$, which can be expressed as

$$y[n] = \sum_{i=0}^{L-1} h_i x[n - \tau_i] + w[n] \tag{9.192}$$

where $\{h_i\}$ are L channel coefficients, τ_i are channel delays, and $w[n]$ are AWGN samples. The length of channel L is assumed to be less than the cyclic prefix length L_c. The coarse symbol synchronization techniques discussed in this section assume that the channel is quasistationary (i.e., channel characteristics remain unchanged during one OFDM symbol interval) and that there is a zero-frequency offset between transmitter and receiver clocks.

Correlation-Based Coarse Symbol Synchronization

We estimate coarse-symbol timing by using the correlation of observed data and reference data (here reference data can be a shifted version of received data) as follows:

$$R_{yy}[D] = \sum_n \left(\sum_{m=0}^{L_c-1} y[(m + n(N + L_c) + D)T] y^*[(m + n(N + L_c) + N + D)T] \right) \tag{9.193}$$

The algorithm in Equation (9.193) correlates the received sample sequence $y[n]$ with the N-samples shifted version of the same sequence. As the OFDM symbols contain a cyclic prefix of length L_c, L_c consecutive samples are pair-wise correlated with L_c other consecutive samples, N samples ahead, in the received OFDM sequence. The value of D, for which $R_{yy}[D]$ attains the maximum, gives the estimation of coarse symbol timing, Δ. Figure 9.53 shows how $R_{yy}[D]$ can be computed at the receiver for a fixed value of δ.

Given Equation (9.193), we obtain the coarse symbol timing information Δ^{CR} from correlation metric $R_{yy}[D]$ as follows:

$$\Delta^{CR} \approx \arg\max_{D} R_{yy}[D] \tag{9.194}$$

ML-Based Coarse Symbol Synchronization

As the performance of correlation-based methods degrades significantly at low-channel SNRs or with dispersive channel conditions, ML-based methods are preferred over correlation-based methods for coarse symbol synchronization. In Van de Beek et al. (1997), assuming zero-frequency offset, the following ML estimation metric for coarse symbol synchronization is derived:

$$\Lambda[D] = Re\{R_{yy}[D]\} - \alpha P_{yy}[D] \tag{9.195}$$

where

$$P_{yy}[D] = \frac{1}{2}\sum_{n}\left(\sum_{m=0}^{L_c-1} |y[(m+n(N+L_c)+D)T]|^2 + |y[(m+n(N+L_c)+N+D)T]|^2\right) \tag{9.196}$$

$$\alpha = \frac{SNR}{SNR+1} \tag{9.197}$$

Given Equation (9.195), the ML estimation of coarse symbol timing Δ, Δ^{ML}, is

$$\Delta^{ML} = \arg\max_{D} \Lambda[D] \tag{9.198}$$

As discussed previously, the ML-based coarse symbol synchronization is computationally very expensive. In Van de Beek et al. (1995), a low-complexity ML-based, coarse symbol synchronization method is proposed, and using this approach, we incorporate the sign-quantized information in building the coarse-symbol timing metric $\Lambda^s[D]$, as follows:

$$\Lambda^s[D] = \sum_{n}\sum_{m=0}^{L_c-1} (2g_m^D - 1) \tag{9.199}$$

where

$$g_m^D = \begin{cases} 1 & \text{if } \mathrm{sgn}(y[(m+n(N+L_c)+D)T]) = \mathrm{sgn}(y[(m+n(N+L_c)+N+D)T]) \\ 0 & \text{if } \mathrm{sgn}(y[(m+n(N+L_c)+D)T]) \neq \mathrm{sgn}(y[(m+n(N+L_c)+N+D)T]) \end{cases} \tag{9.200}$$

The sign-quantized ML estimation of coarse symbol timing Δ, Δ^{SML}, is then obtained as follows:

$$\Delta^{SML} = \arg\max_{D} \Lambda^s[D] \tag{9.201}$$

The performance of metrics $\Lambda^s[D]$ and $R_{yy}[D]$ for the single Tu6 channel with 150-Hz Doppler at $SNR = 0$ dB is shown in Figure 9.54(a) and (b).

There is usually some tolerance for symbol timing error when a cyclic prefix is used to avoid ISI and ICI. As long as the error between actual delay D and estimated coarse symbol timing value Δ is less than the difference between channel length (L) and cyclic prefix length (L_c), we will have a scope to correct the residual timing error with the fine symbol synchronization algorithms.

Fine Symbol Synchronization

Once we estimate the coarse symbol timing with the estimation error within the range, we work in the frequency domain to compensate for residual symbol timing error using fine symbol synchronization techniques. In DMT systems, the time characteristics of the twisted-pair channel vary quite slowly, and there are very few pilot tones to work with, whereas in OFDM systems, multipath channel characteristics change rapidly and we also have many pilot tones to take advantage of in residual symbol timing error estimation. Thus, the fine symbol synchronization techniques used for the DMT system are slightly different from the ones used with OFDM systems.

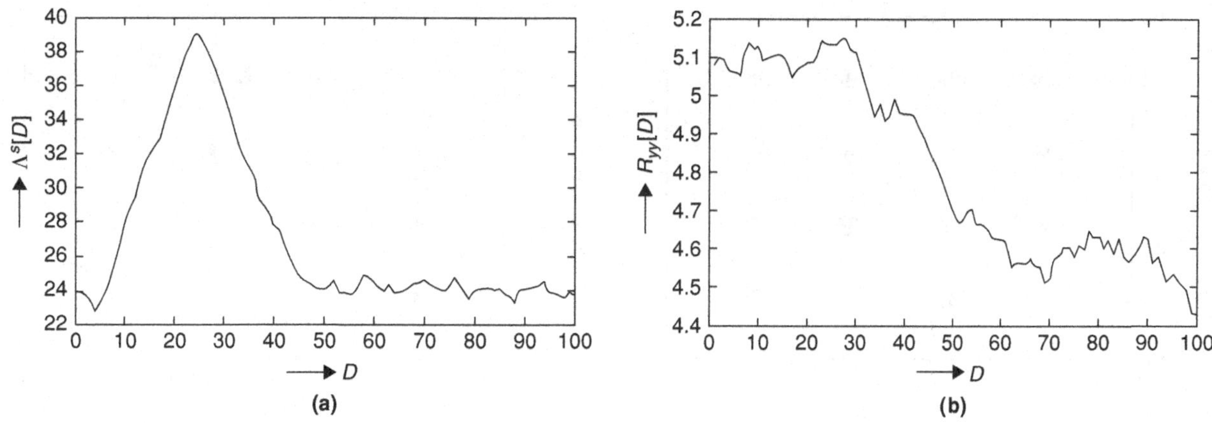

Figure 9.54: Performance of coarse symbol timing-recovery metrics. (a) Sign-quantized ML-based metric. (b) Correlation-based metric.

DMT Systems

In DMT systems, with zero frequency offset it is possible to estimate the coarse symbol timing Δ to the nearest integer value of the delay D introduced by the channel. In other words, the residual symbol timing error δ is a fraction and lies in the range $0 \leq \delta < 1$. If we represent the discrete time equivalent of the channel when sampling with phase δ by $h(\delta)$, then the *k-th* output of the DFT (or demodulator) can be expressed as $a_k^n H_k(\delta)$, where $H(\delta)$ is the DFT of $h(\delta)$. The effect of a sample phase shift δ results in a rotation of the DFT outputs. In brief, this means,

$$a_k^n H_k(\delta) = a_k^n H_k(0) e^{j2\pi k\delta/N} \tag{9.202}$$

This shows that a sample phase shift can be compensated in the digital domain by rotating each DFT output over an angle proportional to the carrier index and the phase shift δ.

The phase shift δ can be estimated from the pilot tone with a known phase. Let K be the pilot tone carrier index; its phase is assumed to be zero or some constant, and its amplitude is 1 at the time of transmission. At the receiver, after estimating the coarse symbol timing, we know what samples should go to the demodulator, DFT. Then, using the DFT output $Y[k]$, the phase deviation of the n-th DMT symbol pilot tone can be computed using the following relationship:

$$\phi_n = \tan^{-1} \frac{\text{Im}(Y[K])}{\text{Re}(Y[K])} \tag{9.203}$$

However, the phase ϕ_n computed using Equation (9.203) is not exactly equal to the actual phase shift δ, as the transmitted signal is corrupted by background noise (AWGN); it is a random variable with some non-zero variance and the mean is equal to probable actual phase shift δ. So, the actual phase shift is given by the ensemble average of ϕ_n. Therefore,

$$\delta = \sum_n \phi_n \tag{9.204}$$

Then, with the estimated sample timing or phase offset δ, we can correct the sampling phases of each output of the DFT by using the following formula:

$$Z[m] = Y[m] e^{-jm\delta/K} \tag{9.205}$$

where $Z[m]$ represents the demodulated output with corrected phase offset (or residual symbol timing error).

Now we provide few simulation results for the DMT system fine-symbol synchronization assuming that the residual symbol timing error δ is a fraction in the range $0 \leq \delta < 1$. Figure 9.55(a) shows the 16-point QAM constellation diagram of the transmitted signal on a particular carrier at an SNR of 28 dB. Figure 9.55(b) shows the rotation of constellation points due to the presence of a 20% phase shift in the received signal. Figure 9.56(a) shows the derotation of constellation points after the phase offset correction using a single

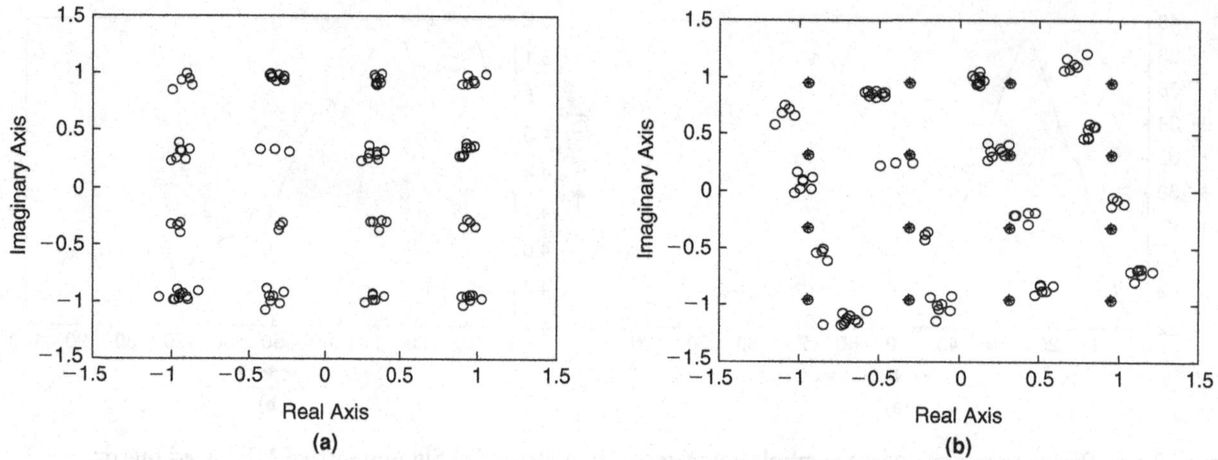

Figure 9.55: Constellation diagram of data on a particular carrier at SNR = 28 dB. (a) Received sequence with zero-phase offset. (b) Rotation of constellation points due to 20% phase offset in received sequence.

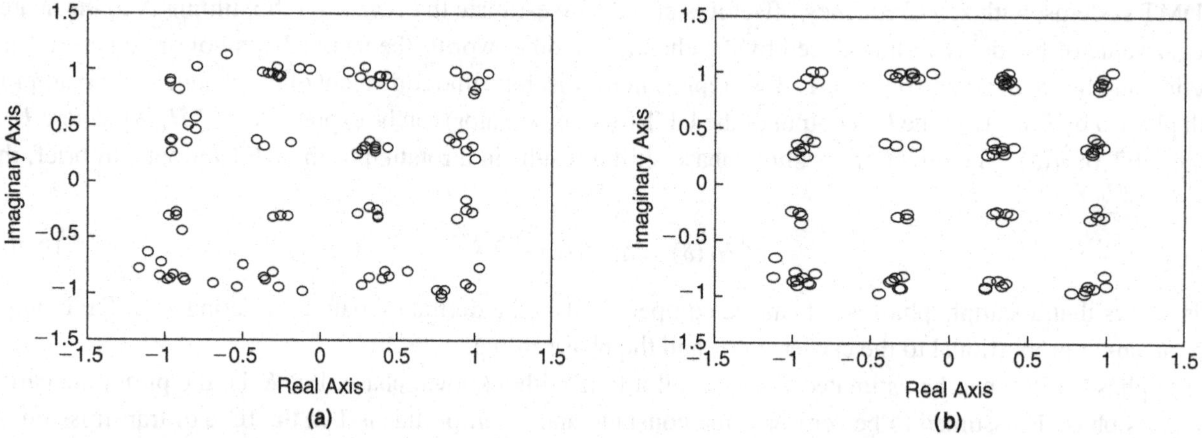

Figure 9.56: Constellation diagram of derotated data on a particular carrier at SNR = 28 dB after 20% phase-offset correction. (a) Using a single estimate. (b) Using an average of eight estimates.

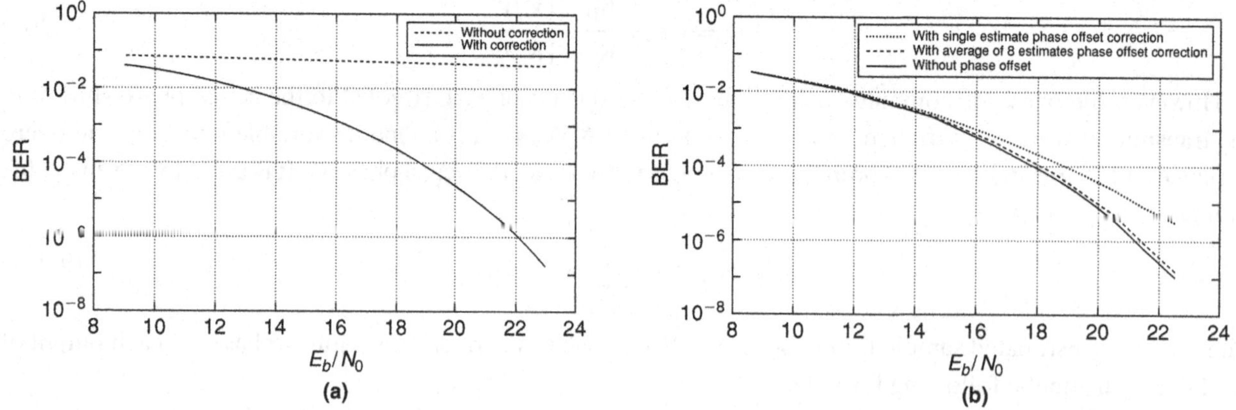

Figure 9.57: Performance of DMT system. (a) With and without 10% phase correction. (b) With 10% phase correction using a single estimate and an average of eight estimates (solid curve represents zero-phase offset).

estimate. Figure 9.56(b) shows the derotation of constellation points after the phase offset correction using an average of eight estimates. Figure 9.57(a) shows performance of the DMT system with and without phase offset correction. Finally, Figure 9.57(b) shows DMT system performance with phase offset correction using a single estimate and an average of eight estimates.

OFDM Systems

In Speth et al. (1997, 1999), the following simplified metric based on the ML principle for OFDM fine symbol synchronization is derived:

$$\Lambda_H(m) = \sum_{k \in P} |\tilde{H}_{l,k}(m)|^2 \tag{9.206}$$

where P is the set of subcarriers bearing the scattered pilots and $\tilde{H}_{l,k}(m)$ is the channel transfer function at pilot positions belonging to P. In the DVB-H, these scattered pilots P are transmitted with boosted power level 4/3, and therefore the channel at these pilot positions will not be severely affected by channel impairments. $\Lambda_H(m)$ is the accumulated energy of the channel at pilot positions P. The fine symbol synchronization is the offset d where $\Lambda_H(d)$ is the maximum. Given that we are assuming the residual symbol timing error spans more than one sample interval in OFDM systems, we use the notation d instead of δ for residual error. Since the metric is fully coupled with the channel, its performance degrades significantly at low SNRs with multipath and high Doppler.

To reduce the effect of channel conditions, only the real part of the channel transfer function at pilot positions P is considered for the metric. This new metric $\Lambda_{HR}(m)$ is defined as

$$\Lambda_{HR}(m) = \sum_{k \in P} |real\{\tilde{H}_{l,k}(m)\}| \tag{9.207}$$

Performance of the metrics $\Lambda_H(m)$ and $\Lambda_{HR}(m)$ with the known starting position of pilots is shown in Figure 9.58(a) and (b). With the metric given in Equation (9.207), a significant peak is achievable in the worst channel conditions. In addition, computationally this metric is very simple, as it involves only real-number additions.

With the fine-symbol timing metric given in Equation (9.207), we must know the scattered pilots starting index. In the DVB-H standard, OFDM symbol number indicates the starting position of scattered pilots in the OFDM symbol. The position p_k of scattered pilots is given by the expression

$$p_k = K_{\min} + 3(l \bmod 4) + 12p \tag{9.208}$$

where l is the OFDM symbol index (ranging from 0 to 67) in a DVB-H frame, $p \geq 0$, $p_k \in [K_{\min}, K_{\max}]$, $K_{\min} = 0$, and $K_{\max} = 1704$, 3408, and 6816, for 2k, 4k, and 8k modes, respectively.

The scattered pilots are used for channel estimation; the starting index of scattered pilots is also required here. To know the starting position of scattered pilots in the OFDM symbol, we must identify the index of the OFDM symbol as given in Equation (9.208). But the OFDM symbol index is only obtained with the TPS data, which in turn is obtained after channel estimation.

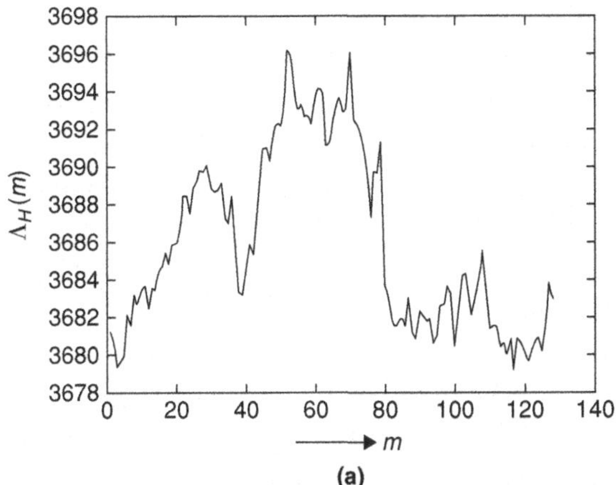

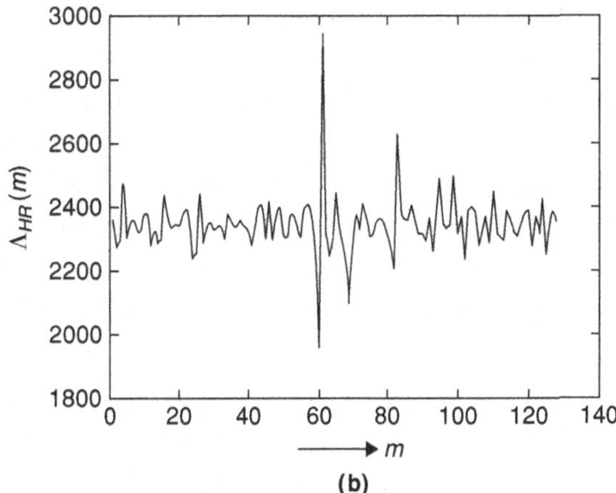

Figure 9.58: Performance of ML-based, fine symbol synchronization metrics. (a) ML with absolute number additions. (b) ML with real number additions.

In Schwoerer (2004), without waiting for channel estimation and TPS data extraction, which takes about 80 to 85 ms in $8k$ mode, two scattered pilot synchronization algorithms—power based and correlation based—are proposed to get the starting position in about 10 ms. However, these algorithms involve complex multiplications and absolute squaring computations. Instead, the fine symbol synchronization metric given in Equation (9.207) can be used for fast scattered pilot-position synchronization. The modified power-based, fast scattered pilot synchronization can be obtained with only additions as follows:

$$\begin{aligned} P_{m,0} &= \sum_{p=0}^{P_{max}} |real\{\tilde{H}_{l,12p}(m)\}| \\ P_{m,1} &= \sum_{p=0}^{P_{max}} |real\{\tilde{H}_{l,12p+3}(m)\}| \\ P_{m,2} &= \sum_{p=0}^{P_{max}} |real\{\tilde{H}_{l,12p+6}(m)\}| \\ P_{m,3} &= \sum_{p=0}^{P_{max}} |real\{\tilde{H}_{l,12p+9}(m)\}| \end{aligned} \tag{9.209}$$

where $P_{max} = 141, 283$, and 567 for $2k$, $4k$, and $8k$, respectively.

Let P_0, P_1, P_2 and P_3 correspond to the maximums of $P_{m,0}$, $P_{m,1}$, $P_{m,2}$ and $P_{m,3}$ over m. Then the starting position of scattered pilots in the OFDM symbol is given by $3I$, where the value of I is given by

$$I = \arg\max_i P_i \tag{9.210}$$

The fine symbol synchronization metric $\Lambda_{HR}(m)$ computed using Equation (9.207) may not always result in a clear peak, as scattered pilot positions are not known in advance. Here, an alternate fine symbol synchronization metric $\Lambda_{HRn}(m)$ is computed with the learning of the scattered pilot position from $P_{m,0}$, $P_{m,1}$, $P_{m,2}$ and $P_{m,3}$ as follows:

$$\Lambda_{HRn}(m) = \max(P_{m,0}, P_{m,1}, P_{m,2}, P_{m,3}) \tag{9.211}$$

In this way, both fine symbol synchronization and fast scattered pilot synchronization can be achieved with one-time computations.

Symbol Synchronization Computational Complexity

In the OFDM-symbol coarse, fine, and fast scattered-pilot synchronization metrics, almost all the operations are additions. Typically, more than one OFDM symbol is used in achieving the symbol synchronization. The following computational complexity analysis assumes that the OFDM symbol synchronization is achieved with a single OFDM symbol.

Coarse Symbol Synchronization In coarse symbol synchronization, the metric $\Lambda^s(D)$ is usually computed with the two windows of L samples separated by N samples by summing the matched sign-quantized values over L samples and moving the windows one sample at a time over N samples while increasing D by 1. This requires overall LN additions and LN right-shift operations apart from comparison operations. To reduce the number of operations, coarse symbol synchronization is achieved in two steps as shown in Figure 9.59.

First, compute the metric $\Lambda^s(D)$ at $D = 100 \cdot a$, where $a = 0, 1 \ldots (N + L + 100)/100$. Then find the value of u where $\Lambda^s(100 \cdot u)$ is maximum. Next, compute the metric $\Lambda^s(D)$ again in the range $(u-2)100$ to $(u+2)100$ at $m = (u-2)100 + 10b$, where $b = 0, 1 \ldots (u+2)10$. Now, find the value of v where $\Lambda^s(10 \cdot v)$ is maximum. Then the total offset index D for the coarse symbol synchronization is $(u-2)100 + v10$. In this way, the coarse symbol synchronization is achieved within ± 20 samples, and the total number of additions or right shifts reduces to $L(N + L + 100)/100 + 40L$. In the same two-step method, the correlation-based metric $R_{yy}[D]$ requires $L(N + L + 100)/100 + 40L$ complex multiplications and $L(N + L + 100)/100 + 40L$ additions.

Fine Symbol Synchronization Typically, the fine symbol synchronization algorithms work with the data after demodulation, which involves DFT. In this analysis, DFT computations are not considered. Assuming the availability of demodulated complex symbols, the proposed fine OFDM-symbol synchronization algorithm

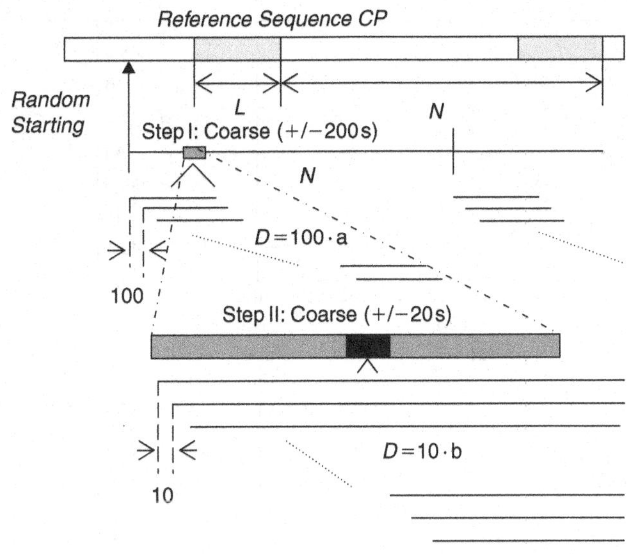

Figure 9.59: Two-step coarse symbol synchronization.

involves only real additions. The number of additions required is given by $R \cdot P_{\max}$ where $P_{\max}$ is the number of scattered pilots present in the OFDM symbol and R is the number of points for which the metric is computed.

Scattered Pilot Synchronization Fast scattered pilot synchronization also involves the DFT operation and is not considered in this analysis. Assuming the availability of demodulated complex symbols, the scattered pilot synchronization algorithm involves only addition. The number of additions is given by $4RP_{\max}$, where $P_{\max}$ is the number of scattered pilots present in the OFDM symbol and R is the range of samples the window moved.

Simulation Results

The simulations are carried out with single Tu6 and double Tu6 channels and the entities for the same follow:

Single Tu6

$$h_i = [10^{-3/20}, 1, 10^{-2/20}, 10^{-6/20}, 10^{-8/20}, 10^{-10/20}]$$

$$\tau_i = [0,\ 2,\ 5,\ 15,\ 21, 46]$$

$$D_f^{(i)} = [90,\ 150,\ 89,\ 99,\ 101,\ 100]$$

$$M = 8$$

Double Tu6

$$h_i = [10^{-3/20}, 1, 10^{-2/20}, 10^{-6/20}, 10^{-8/20}, 10^{-10/20}, 10^{-18.5/20}, \\ 10^{-15.5/20}, 10^{-17.5/20}, 10^{-21.5/20}, 10^{-23.5/20}, 10^{-25.5/20}]$$

$$\tau_i = [1,\ 3,\ 6,\ 16,\ 22, 47,\ 1793,\ 1795,\ 1798,\ 1809,\ 1816,\ 1843]$$

$$D_f^{(i)} = [90,\ 150,\ 78,\ 99,\ 120,\ 51,\ 70,\ 120,\ 48,\ 69,\ 90,\ 21]$$

$$M = 16$$

where h_i, τ_i, $D_f^{(i)}$ and M correspond to the channel gains, delays for each channel gain, Doppler frequency with each channel gain in Hz, and the iteration count for the Jakes model, respectively. The values of the parameters N and L used are 8192 and 2048, respectively.

The two-step coarse symbol synchronization is simulated as described in Figure 9.59. For the single Tu6 channel at SNRs 5 dB and −5 dB, the plots in Figure 9.60 show the presence of clear peaks with the sign-quantized, ML-based method when compared to the correlation-based method. Figure 9.61 shows the performance of the fine symbol synchronization algorithm metrics $\Lambda_H[m]$ and $\Lambda_{HR}[m]$ at SNRs 5 dB and −5 dB with the double Tu6 channel. The overall performance of symbol synchronization algorithms is evaluated at various SNRs with respect to the existing algorithms for both single Tu6 and double Tu6 and for AWGN channels. The

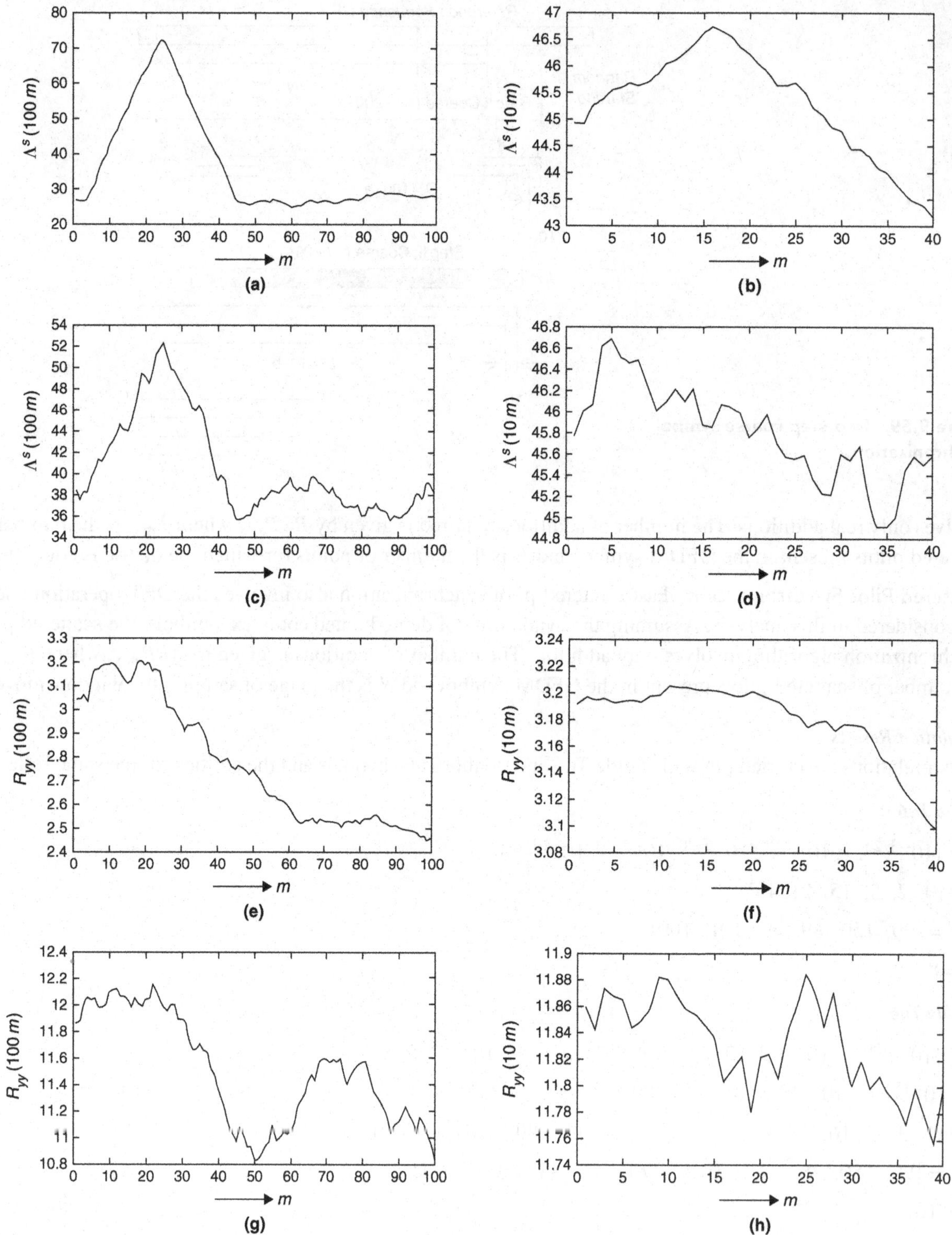

Figure 9.60: Coarse symbol synchronization using sign-quantized, ML-based, and correlation-based metrics with a single Tu6 channel. (a), (e) Step-I CS with single Tu6 channel at SNR = 5 dB. (b), (f) Step-II CS with single Tu6 channel at SNR = 5 dB. (c), (g) Step-I CS with single Tu6 channel at SNR = −5 dB. (d), (h) Step-II CS with single Tu6 channel at SNR = −5 dB.

simulations are carried out over 100 times for every SNR, and the success rate of symbol synchronization or correct detection of the symbol boundary is counted. Figure 9.62(a) shows the performance of the sign-quantized ML metric and correlation-based metric achieved in two steps for the OFDM coarse symbol synchronization within ±20 samples. The performance of OFDM fine symbol synchronization for the same offset with the metrics

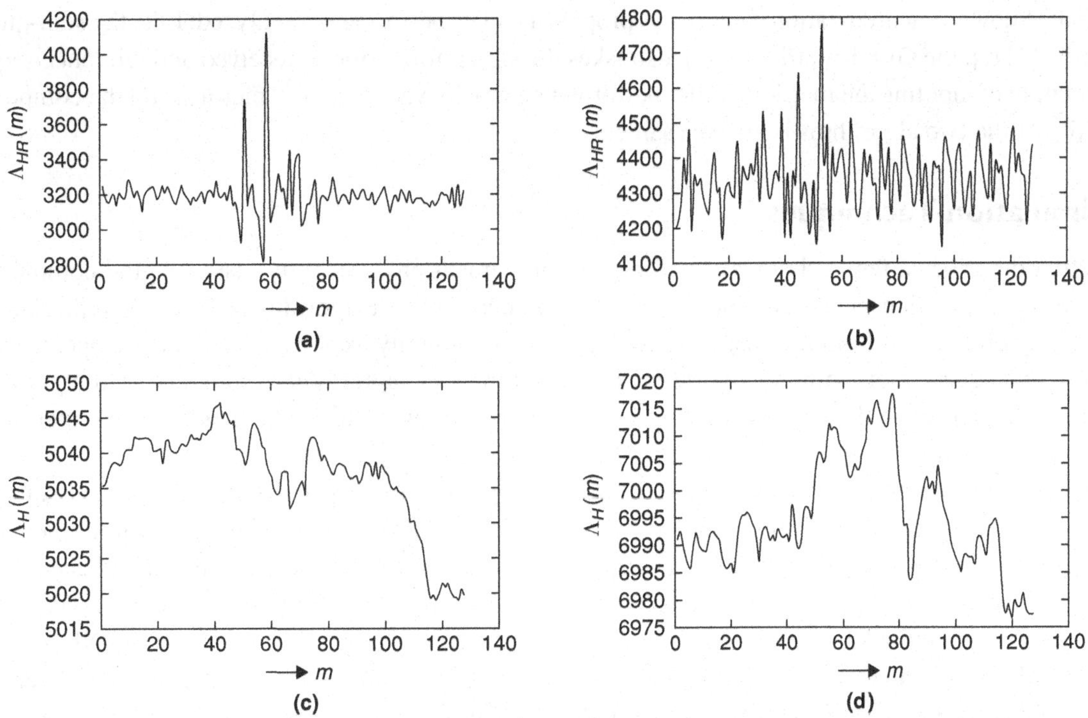

Figure 9.61: Fine symbol synchronization using sign-quantized, ML-based, and correlation-based metrics with a double Tu6 channel, (a) FS with metric $\Lambda_{HR}(m)$ at SNR = 5 dB. (b) FS with metric $\Lambda_{HR}(m)$ at SNR = –5 dB. (c) FS with metric $\Lambda_H(m)$ at SNR = 5 dB. (d) FS with metric $\Lambda_H(m)$ at SNR = –5 dB.

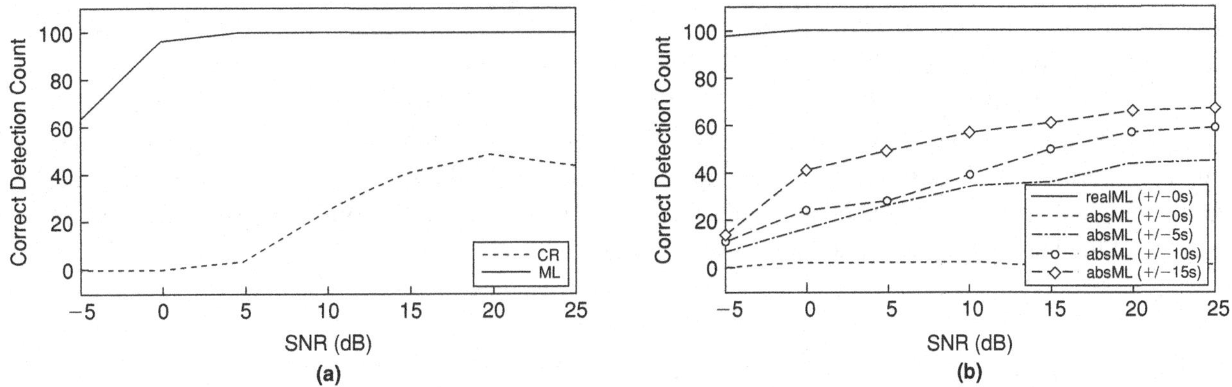

Figure 9.62: Performance of symbol synchronization metrics at various SNRs. (a) CS with $\Lambda^s[D]$ (or sign-quantized ML) and $R_{yy}[D]$ (or correlation) metrics for 2Tu6 channel. (b) FS with $\Lambda_{HR}(m)$ (or ML with real part) and $\Lambda_H(m)$ (or ML with absolute values) metrics for Tu6 channel.

$\Lambda_H(m)$ and $\Lambda_{HR}(m)$ for a given fixed, coarse symbol synchronization offset is shown in Figure 9.62(b). From this, improved performance is clear with the sign-quantized ML metric, $\Lambda^s[D]$, and the ML with real-channel metric, $\Lambda_{HR}(m)$, over the correlation metric, $R_{yy}[D]$, and ML with the absolute channel metric, $\Lambda_H(m)$, in achieving coarse and fine OFDM-symbol synchronization.

Frame Synchronization

In DMT or OFDM systems, a frame is formed with many DMT or OFDM symbols (e.g., in DVB-H systems, one frame is formed with 68 OFDM symbols); thus we may be required to identify frame boundaries for extracting the correct frame data/overhead information. In DVB-H systems, the standard specifies the synchronization word as part of the TPS (transmission parameter signaling), and we can use this synchronization pattern as a reference to identify the frame boundaries. In Chiani and Martini (2005, 2006), an algorithm based on the generalized likelihood ratio test (GLRT) for finding the frame boundaries in AWGN channels with unknown data distribution and with the known synchronization pattern was proposed and its performance analyzed. Like the sign-quantized ML metric $\Lambda^s[D]$, the GLRT metric $\Lambda^g[D]$ also takes the sign information of received and reference sequences into account in computing the metric. Similar performance is achieved with both metrics, and the computational complexity of the two algorithms is also the same.

9.6 Simulation Techniques

This section describes a few techniques to efficiently implement previously discussed digital communication algorithms. As simulation techniques and C code are provided for most algorithms elsewhere in this book, here we focus only on a few techniques to efficiently implement commonly used basic mathematic operations, such as division and square root, with the algorithms discussed in this chapter. The commonly used algorithms are identified and reappear in the exercise section on the companion website so that readers can experiment and practice implementation.

Implementation of nonlinear mathematical operations (e.g., division, square root, and one over square root) on the fixed-point processor is really an interesting task. The two important issues we face in implementation of this type of operation are implementation complexity (in terms of cycles and memory) and accuracy (how close the fixed-point implementation output is when compared to floating-point implementation). Typically, we implement these operations by successive approximation algorithms (e.g., Newton Raphson [NR]) by choosing the initial "seed" value. We use the analytic method or look-up table to obtain a good initial seed value. Here, we follow the look-up table method to get that value. The output accuracy of fixed-point implementation depends on many factors—initial seed value, number of iterations, data format chosen, and precision of processor registers.

9.6.1 Division

We can perform the division P/Q of two numbers P and Q, by first computing $1/Q$, and then multiplying the result by P. We compute $1/Q$ using the NR successive approximation method. The algorithm used with NR to compute $y = 1/x$ is given as $y_{i+1} = y_i(2 - xy_i)$ with y_0 equal to the initial seed value from the look-up table.

For an arbitrary value of x, we require more memory for the look-up table to store more accurate initial seed values. By normalization of input (i.e., denominator Q) to the NR algorithm, we can minimize the memory requirement, and at the same time obtain better initial seed values. With the normalization, we make sure that the range of the input is between 1 and 2 as described here:

$$\begin{aligned} 2^n &\le Q < 2^{n+1} \\ 2^n &\le 2^n q < 2^{n+1} \end{aligned} \tag{9.212}$$

where q is a real number and

$$1 \le q < 2 \tag{9.213}$$

or

$$\frac{1}{2^n} \ge 2^{-n} y > \frac{1}{2^{n+1}} \text{ where } y = \frac{1}{q}, \quad 1 \ge y > 0.5 \tag{9.214}$$

Thus, $P/Q \approx 2^{-n} Py$. The question is how to find y with a minimum number of operations. The final accuracy of division P/Q depends on how accurately we obtain the value of y using NR. With each iteration, we double the accuracy of y. For example, if we choose the initial seed value y_0 with 7 bits of accuracy, then with one iteration of NR method, we will have y_1 with 14 bits of accuracy and after two iterations we will have y_2 with 28 bits of accuracy. Here, we have a trade-off between accuracy and complexity (i.e., cycles, memory). With 128 initial seed values and two NR iterations, we can have division output with accuracy up to 28 bits. For initial seed values, the y in the range [1, 0.5) is divided into 128 equal segments and assigned to 128 look-up table entries. The precomputed 128 initial seed values in 1.31 format is given in the table **_div_int_seeds**[].

```
unsigned int DivInt(unsigned int a, unsigned int b)
{
        int i;
        unsigned int c,d,e,f,g,h;
        i = 0;
        while ((b&0x80000000) == 0){        // lead zeros
                b = b << 1;i++;
        }
        c = b; c = c >> 24; i-= 28;
        d = _div_int_seeds[c-128];          // get initial seed value
        // first iteration
        c = b & 0xffff; e = d & 0xffff;
        f = d >> 16; h = b >> 16;
        g = h * f; h = h * e; c = c * f; // w * c
        h = (h+32768) >> 16; c = (c+32768) >> 16;
        g = g + c + h;
        h = 0x80000000-g; // 2-w*c
        c = h & 0xffff; e = d & 0xffff;
        f = d >> 16; h = h >> 16;
        g = h * f; h = h * e; c = c * f; // c*(2-w*c)
        h = (h + 32768) >> 16; c = (c + 32768) >> 16;
        h = g + c + h;
        d = h << 2;
        // second iteration
        c = b & 0xffff; e = d & 0xffff;
        f = d >> 16; h = b >> 16;
        g = h * f; h = h * e; c = c * f; // w*c
        h = (h +32768) >> 16; c = (c +32768) >> 16;
        g = g + c + h;
        h = 0x80000000-g;                   // 2-w*c
        c = h & 0xffff; e = d & 0xffff;
        f = d >> 16; h = h >> 16;
        g = h * f; h = h * e; c = c * f; // c*(2-w*c)
        h = (h +32768) >> 16; c = (c +32768) >> 16;
        h = g + c + h;
        // multiply with numerator
        c = h & 0xffff; e = a & 0xffff;
        f = a >> 16; h = h >> 16;
        g = h * f; h = h * e; c = c * f; // P*(1/q)
        h = (h +32768) >> 16; c = (c +32768) >> 16;
        h = g + c + h;
        if (i<0){                           // P*(1/q)*2^-n
                i = -i;
                h = h >> i;
        }
        else
                h = h << i;
        return h;
}
```

Pcode 9.2: Fixed point simulation code for unsigned integer 32-bit division.

The simulation code for this division is given in Pcode 9.2. Each iteration of the NR method for division consumes 4 cycles on the reference embedded processor, and about 24 cycles are required to perform the total division operation with two NR iterations using the normalized denominator value.

9.6.2 Square Root

The square root of a number x, $\sqrt{x}$, can be obtained as $x/\sqrt{x}$. We can use the NR method to compute $\sqrt{Q}$ efficiently in the same way as previously discussed:

$$2^{2n} \leq Q < 2^{2(n+1)} \text{ (if } Q > 1) \tag{9.215}$$

$$2^{2(-n-1)} \leq Q < 2^{-2n} \text{ (if } Q < 1 \text{ and } Q > 0) \tag{9.216}$$

Here, we discuss the process for the case $Q > 1$, similar equations can be derived for the $Q < 1$ case as well:

$$2^{2n} \le 2^{2n} q < 2^{2(n+1)}$$

where q is a real number, and

$$1 \le q < 4 \tag{9.217}$$

or

$$2^n \le 2^n y < 2^{n+1}$$

where

$$y = \sqrt{q}, \quad 1 \le y < 2 \tag{9.218}$$

Then, $\sqrt{Q} \approx 2^n y$. For this, we first compute $z = 1/\sqrt{q}$ and then compute y as $y = q \times z$. To obtain just 1 over the square root of Q, we compute it as $\sqrt{1/Q} \approx 2^{-n} z$. The NR algorithm used for computing 1 over the square root is $z_{i+1} = z_i(3 - qz_i^2)/2$. Here, also we get the initial seed value z_0 from the look-up table. The 192 initial seed values stored in the look-up table are given in **_sqrt_int_seeds**[]. The simulation code for computing 1 over the square root is given in Pcode 9.3.

9.6.3 Matrix Inversion

The literature contains many approaches to find the inverse of a given matrix depending on its properties. In signal processing and digital communications, we often encounter matrices that are formed with the correlation of data. These matrices are special in the sense that they are symmetric and positive definite. Given a symmetric, positive definite matrix $A \in C^{N \times N}$, a special factorization method, called *Cholesky decomposition*, factorizes the matrix into lower- and upper-triangular matrices with a relatively small number of computations. Instead of finding arbitrary lower and upper triangular matrices L and U, as in LU decomposition method, the Cholesky decomposition constructs a lower triangular matrix L whose transpose can itself serve as the upper triangular part. In other words, $LL^H = A$, where $(.)^H$ is a Hermitian transpose operation. If $A = [a_{ij}]$ and $L = [l_{ij}]$ where $l_{ij} = 0$ for $i < j$, then elements l_{ij} are computed as

$$l_{ii} = \sqrt{a_{ii} - \sum_{k=1}^{i-1} l_{ik} l_{ik}^*}, \quad \text{for } i = j \tag{9.219}$$

$$l_{ji} = \frac{1}{l_{ii}} \left(a_{ji} - \sum_{k=1}^{j-1} l_{ik} l_{jk}^* \right), \quad \text{for } i > j \tag{9.220}$$

The simulation code given in Pcode 9.4 computes a lower triangular matrix L using Equations (9.219) and (9.220) for matrix A with real elements.

After computing the lower triangular matrix L, the two problems—solving the linear system equation and finding the matrix inverse—can be solved in a more or less similar way. Let $A \in R^{N \times N}$ be a symmetric and positive definite matrix; then $Ax = b$ and $LL^T x = b$:

$$Ly = b, \quad \text{where } y = L^T x \tag{9.221}$$

The system $Ly = b$ is solved by forward substitution, whereas $L^T x = y$ is solved by back substitution methods. The simulation code for forward substitution is given in Pcode 9.5; the simulation code for backward substitution is similar to that of forward substitution but uses different indexing. The computational complexity of linear system solving via Cholesky decomposition (for $N = 18$) is given in Table 9.2.

Similarly, the inverse of lower triangular matrix L can be easily computed. Let $G = L^{-1}$; elements of the inverse matrix G, g_{ji}, are obtained from $L = [l_{ji}]$ as follows:

$$g_{ji} = \begin{cases} 1/l_{ii} & \text{if } i = j \\ -\dfrac{1}{l_{jj}} \sum_{k=i}^{j-1} l_{jk} g_{ki} & \text{if } i < j \end{cases} \tag{9.222}$$

```
unsigned int SqrtInt(unsigned int b)
{
        int i;
        unsigned int a,c,d,e,f,g,h;
        a = b; i = 0;
        while ((b & 0 x 80000000) == 0){      // lead zeros,
                b = b << 1;
                i++; }                         // or i = 32-(int) (log2(b) + 1);
        c = b >> 25;
        d = _div_int_seeds[c-64];              // get initial seed value
        // first iteration
        c = b & 0xffff; e = d & 0xffff;
        f = d >> 16; h = b >> 16;
        g = h * f; h = h * e; c = c * f;      // w*c
        h = (h+32768) >> 16; c = (c+32768) >> 16;
        g = g + c + h;
        g = g << 1;
        c = g & 0xffff; e = d & 0xffff;
        f = d >> 16; h = g >> 16;
        g = h * f; h = h * e; c = c * f;      // w*c*c
        h = (h+32768) >> 16; c = (c+32768) >> 16;
        h = g + c + h;
        h = 0xc0000000-h;                      // 3-w*c*c
        c = h & 0xffff; e = d & 0xffff;
        f = d >> 16; h = h >> 16;
        g = h * f; h = h * e; c = c * f;      // c*(3-w*c*c)
        h = (h + 32768) >> 16; c = (c + 32768) >> 16;
        h = g + c + h;
        d = h << 1;
        // second iteration
        c = b & 0xffff; e = d & 0xffff;
        f = d >> 16; h = b >> 16;
        g = h * f; h = h * e; c = c * f;      // w*c
        h = (h+32768) >> 16; c = (c+32768) >> 16;
        g = g + c + h;
        g = g << 1;
        c = g & 0xffff; e = d & 0xffff;
        f = d >> 16; h = g >> 16;
        g = h * f; h = h * e; c = c * f;      // w*c*c
        h = (h+32768) >> 16; c = (c+32768) >> 16;
        h = g + c + h;
        h = 0xc0000000-h;                      // 3-w*c*c
        c = h & 0xffff; e = d & 0xffff;
        f = d >> 16; h = h >> 16;
        g = h * f; h = h * e; c = c * f;      // w*c*(3-w*c*c)
        h = (h + 32768) >> 16; c = (c + 32768) >> 16;
        h = g + c + h;
        h = h << 1;
        // multiply with numerator
        c = h & 0xffff; e = a & 0xffff;
        f = a >> 16; h = h >> 16;
        g = h * f; h = h * e; c = c * f;      // P*(1/q)
        h = (h +32768) >> 16; c = (c +32768) >> 16;
        h = g + c + h;
        i = 32-i;                              // z*2^-n
        i = i >> 1;
        h = d >> i;
        return h;
}
```

Pcode 9.3: Fixed point simulation code for one over square root.

The simulation code for computing G, the inverse of L, appears in Pcode 9.6. The inverse of the upper triangular matrix L^T is given by G^T (i.e., $G^T = (L^T)^{-1}$). Thus,

$$\begin{aligned} A &= LL^T \\ A^{-1} &= (LL^T)^{-1} = (L^T)^{-1}L^{-1} = G^T G \end{aligned} \tag{9.223}$$

```
for(i = 0; i < N; i++) {
        sum = 0.0;
        if (i > 0) {
            for(k = 1; k < i; k++){
                temp2 = A[i][k];
                sum = sum + temp2*temp2;
            }
        }
        d = A0[i][i] - sum;
        A[i][i] = sqrt(d);
        d = 1/A[i][i];
        for(j = i + 1; j < N; j++){
            sum = 0.0;
            for(k = 0; k < i; k++){
                temp2 = A[i][k];
                temp3 = A[j][k];
                sum = sum + temp2*temp3;
            }
            sum = A0[j][i] - sum;
            A[j][i] = sum*d;
        }
}
```

Pcode 9.4: Simulation code for lower triangular matrix computation using Cholesky decomposition.

```
y[0] = b[0]/L[0][0];
for(i = 1;i < N;i++) {
        sum = 0.0;
        for (j = 0; j < i; j++)
                sum = sum + L[i][j]*y[j];
        y[i] = (b[i] - sum)/L[i][i];
}
```

Pcode 9.5: Simulation code for linear system solving with forward substitution.

Table 9.2: Computational complexity (number of operations) of linear system solving via Cholesky decomposition

Operations ($N = 18$)	Cholesky Decomposition	Linear System Solving
Addition/subtraction	1140	342
Multiplication	1140	342
1/square root	18	–
Division	–	18

```
for(j = 0;j < N;j++){
        G[j][j] = 1.0/L[j][j];
        for(i = 0;i < j;i++){
                sum = 0.0;
                for(k = i;k < j;k++)
                        sum = sum - L[j][k]*G[k][i];
                G[j][i] = sum/L[j][j];
        }
}
```

Pcode 9.6: Simulation code for computing inverse of lower triangular matrix.

CHAPTER 10

Image Processing Tools

Image processing tools play an important role in medical imaging, digital photography, computer graphics, video processing, multimedia communications, and so forth. These tools are basically algorithms used to process the image to meet the needs of given applications, such as improving image quality, creating special effects, compressing images for storage or fast transmission, and correcting abnormalities in captured images (sometimes the capturing device itself introduces artifacts in the image due to hardware limitations or lens distortion). Image processing tools are also used in classifying images, detecting objects in the image, and extracting useful information from the captured images. In this chapter, we discuss and simulate common tools such as color conversion, color enhancement, brightness and contrast correction, edge enhancement, noise reduction, edge detection, scaling, object corner detection, dilation and erosion, and the Hough transform.

Typically, the raw image can be represented in any format (e.g., RGB, YUV, HSV). Various color formats for processing images are used, and applications often require switching from one format to another in different stages of an algorithm. For example, images are commonly processed in the YUV domain, and then converted to RGB for display. We capture images in RGB format, and we compress digital images in the YUV domain. In displaying the image, we convert the decompressed image to RGB format before display. Color format conversion, then, is an important tool for many applications.

If the color of a particular image is dull, we use a color enhancement tool. In a color-enhanced image, the green portions of the image become greener and the yellow portions become yellower and so on. In the RGB domain, color enhancement is achieved by the histogram equalization technique (details of histogram equalization are discussed later). Color enhancement also makes the image brighter, and enhancement in the RGB domain results in brightness and contrast correction in the YUV domain. If the image is in YUV format, then applying a histogram equalization technique on the luminance component enhances image brightness and contrast.

Edge enhancement to sharpen images is achieved by augmenting high-frequency components of the image. In enhancing the edges, we first filter the high-frequency portions of image and then we enhance the high-frequency content of the image by boosting its values in a controlled manner. Sometimes the image itself may contain unnecessarily noisy high-frequency components that make the image annoying. Smoothing filters are used to remove high-frequency content. In later sections, we discuss average and median smoothing filters to remove high-frequency content. Image scaling is used in many applications to change image resolution and aspect ratio. A few previously mentioned image-processing tools are also used in image scaling to maintain image quality after scaling. Detection of edges, corners, lines, circles, and so on, in images has many applications (e.g., image stabilization, object detection, and lens distortion correction).

10.1 Color Conversion

All image processing algorithms may not be applicable for a particular image format. For example, color correction is performed in the RGB domain. If we perform color correction in the YUV domain, then we lose the actual color information in the corrected image. Although there are many image formats, YUV and RGB formats are widely used in many image processing applications. The following equations are used in converting an image from one format to another:

YUV to RGB:

$$y = Y - 16 \tag{10.1}$$

DOI: 10.1016/B978-1-85617-678-1.00010-7

$$u = U - 128 \tag{10.2}$$

$$v = V - 128 \tag{10.3}$$

$$\begin{aligned} R &= y^*1.164 + v^*1.596 \\ G &= y^*1.164 - v^*0.813 - u^*0.391 \\ B &= y^*1.164 + u^*2.018 \end{aligned} \tag{10.4}$$

RGB to YUV:

$$\begin{aligned} Y &= R^*0.257 + G^*0.504 + B^*0.098 + 16 \\ U &= -R^*0.148 - G^*0.291 + B^*0.439 + 128 \\ V &= R^*0.439 - G^*0.368 - B^*0.071 + 128 \end{aligned} \tag{10.5}$$

This format conversion of YUV to RGB may lead to overflow and underflow of pixel values. To avoid this, we clip calculation results so that the pixel values always lie in the range 0 to 255. The fixed-point simulation codes for YUV and RGB color conversion are given later in this chapter in Pcodes 10.2 and 10.3.

10.2 Color Enhancement

In this section, we discuss the histogram equalization technique of color enhancement in the RGB domain. As we know, if the color component is represented with 8-bit precision, then the values 0 to 255 are used to represent a particular color component. We say that the image colors are well represented when the color components occupy the total range of 0 to 255. If the color components of an image do not occupy the full range (i.e., 0 to 255), then we have the scope to enhance the colors of that image. With the histogram equalization technique, first we find the minimum (X_{min}) and maximum (X_{max}) values of a particular color component, and then we translate that color component to have minimum value at zero by subtracting the X_{min} from its values, and finally, multiply the color component by $255/(X_{max} - X_{min})$ to obtain the maximum color component 255. This process is illustrated in Figure 10.1. The same process is applied for all three color components of an image. This process enhances image colors (green becomes greener, yellow becomes more yellow, etc.), and we also see image brightness and contrast enhancement in the YUV domain. The simulation code for image color enhancement using histogram equalization is given later in the chapter in Pcode 10.4.

The histogram for one color component in the original image is shown in Figure 10.1(a); clearly the pixels of this color component do not span the full range of values (0 to 255). Therefore, we have scope for enhancing that particular color component. The shifted histogram by subtracting X_{min} from all pixel values of that color component is shown in Figure 10.1(b). In Figure 10.1(c), the subtracted pixel values are multiplied by $255/(X_{max} - X_{min})$ to enhance that color component by stretching the histogram maximum value to 255. This process is called histogram equalization. The original test image used to enhance color components is shown in Figure 10.2(a) and the corresponding color corrected image is shown in Figure 10.2(b).

10.3 Brightness and Contrast Adjustment

Raising pixel values toward 255 increases the intensity or brightness of image. In other words, we eliminate the dullness of image by raising pixel values toward 255. Increasing the contrast means increasing the difference between dark and bright pixels. This makes the bright part of an image brighter and the dark part darker. For example, by increasing the contrast of an image containing objects along with shadows, the objects become brighter and the shadows become darker. We usually perform image brightness and contrast adjustment in the YUV domain. Typically, by applying the histogram equalization technique (discussed in the previous section) to the luminance component of image, we achieve the image brightness and contrast correction. Figure 10.3(a) shows the image before correction and Figure 10.3(b) shows the image after correction. The simulation code for

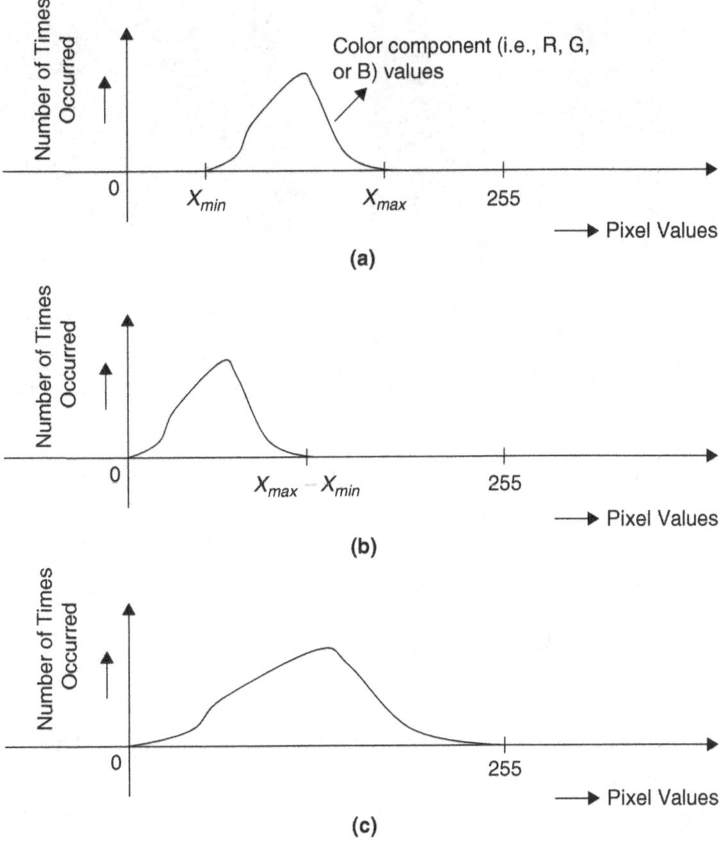

Figure 10.1: Histogram equalization of image color components. (a) Original image color component histogram. (b) Shifted histogram. (c) Equalized histogram.

Figure 10.2: (a) Original image. (b) Color-enhanced image.

Figure 10.3: (a) Before correction. (b) After correction.

(a)

(b)

Figure 10.4: (a) Before edge enhancement. (b) After edge enhancement.

correcting brightness and contrast of an image based on luminance component histogram equalization is given in Pcode 10.5 later in the chapter.

10.4 Edge Enhancement/Sharpening of Edges

In applications such as digital photography, we perform edge enhancement to maintain sharp edges in an image. With edge enhancement, we increase the contrast of the image along the edges. The edge enhancement is done by strengthening the high-frequency components of an image. One way of enhancing edges is by adding weighted high-frequency components of an image to itself. The following equation gets the high-frequency components of an image and adds the weighted high-frequency components to the image:

$$X[m][n] = X[m][n] + k^* H_F \tag{10.6}$$

where k is a weighting factor and H_F is a high-frequency component obtained by the following filtering operation:

$$H_F = 4^* X[m][n] - X[m-1][n] - X[m+1][n] - X[m][n-1] - X[m][n+1] \tag{10.7}$$

or the corresponding mask given by

$$HF = \begin{bmatrix} 0 & -1 & 0 \\ -1 & 4 & -1 \\ 0 & -1 & 0 \end{bmatrix} \tag{10.8}$$

Figure 10.4(a) and (b) show the original image and the edge-enhanced image. The simulation code for obtaining the edge enhancement is given in Pcode 10.6.

10.5 Image Filtering

Sometimes we introduce artifacts in the image at the time of processing it. The artifacts may be due to quantization, scaling, overflow or underflow of pixels. Typically, we use two kinds of filters in image processing to reduce the noise effects: average and median filters. With an average filter, we average the current and its surrounding pixels and update the current pixel with an average value. With a median filter, we sort the current and all neighboring pixel values in ascending or descending order, and then select the middle value as the current pixel. The filtering process using the average and median filters is shown in Figure 10.5.

- Average filter: $(217+227+231+211+216+169+198+139+126)/9 = 193$
- Median filter: 126, 139, 169, 198, **211**, 216, 217, 227, 231 (sorted in ascending order)

In Figure 10.5, we use 3×3 average and median filters to smooth the pixels of a noisy image. We apply the filter by placing the center of the window at the current pixel that we want to filter. With the average filter, we get

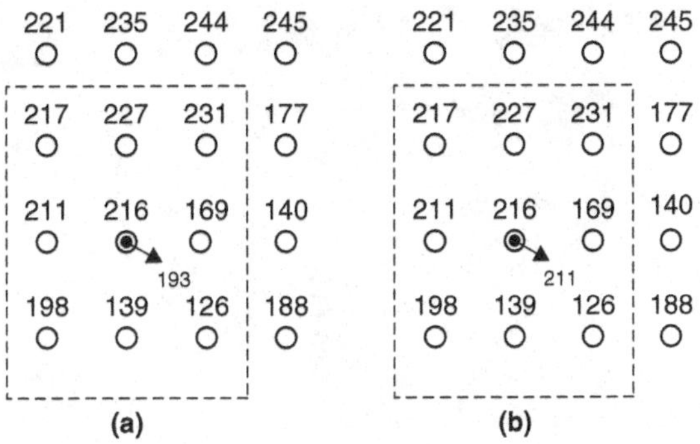

221 235 244 245 | 221 235 244 245
217 227 231 177 | 217 227 231 177
211 216 169 140 | 211 216 169 140
193 | 211
198 139 126 188 | 198 139 126 188

(a) (b)

Figure 10.5: 3 × 3 average and median filter output at highlighted pixel position.

Figure 10.6: Scaled image without filtering.

Figure 10.7: Scaled image after applying average filter.

193 as the output for an actual pixel value of 216, whereas with the median filter we get 211 as the output. After filtering the current pixel, we move the window in raster scan order by 1 pixel to filter the next pixel value and we continue like this to filter all pixels in smoothing the image. The median filter is preferred over the average filter in reducing noise as the average filter makes the image more blurry. With the average filter, we lose a lot of edge information as it averages out the edge pixels with nonedge pixels. The scaled image without applying filters is shown in Figure 10.6; the staircase artifacts result from scaling. The filtered scaled image with the average and median filters is shown in Figures 10.7 and 10.8. In Figures 10.6 through 10.8, it is apparent that the median filter performs well in reducing image artifacts.

10.6 Edge Detection

The edge detector is an important tool in image processing applications as edges represent the local boundaries of objects in an image. Edge detectors filter out less relevant information while preserving important structural properties. With edge detection, we can reduce the amount of work to process an image by (1) avoiding its

Figure 10.8: Scaled image after applying median filter.

redundant portions, (2) extracting and processing only specific objects, or (3) classifying and processing only selected portions of an image. The presence of objects (or edges) in some portions of an image causes intensity variations in those portions of the image.

We compute intensity variations either by using pixel gradients (i.e., rate of change of pixels' intensity obtained from its first derivative) or by finding zero-crossings in the second derivative of pixel values. This is illustrated in Figure 10.9 where first and second derivatives are applied to the 1D function $s(x)$ representing the intensity variation.

Many edge-detection algorithms are discussed in the literature. In this section, we briefly discuss edge detection using the Sobel operator, Laplace edge detector, and Canny edge detector. We use three photographs—Lena, wallpaper, and Lord Ganesh—as test images, shown in Figure 10.10. The first test image, shown in Figure 10.10(a), contains fewer proper edges, whereas the second and third test images shown in Figures 10.10(b) and (c) have many edges. Next we discuss the performance of Sobel, Laplacian, and Canny detectors in detecting the edges of the three test images.

10.6.1 Edge Detection Based on Sobel Operators

With Sobel operators, we find the approximate absolute gradient magnitude at each pixel in an input grayscale 2D image. The Sobel edge detector uses a pair of 3×3 convolution masks, one estimating the gradient in the x-direction (i.e., horizontal) and the other estimating the gradient in y-direction (i.e., vertical). The Sobel operators for x and y directions are given as follows:

+1	0	−1
+2	0	−2
+1	0	−1

x−Sobel operator

+1	+2	+1
0	0	0
−1	−2	−1

y−Sobel operator

If G_x and G_y represent the gradients in x and y directions, then the pixel gradient G is obtained as $G = \sqrt{G_x^2 + G_y^2}$. We compute the x and y gradients (i.e., G_x and G_y) for the current intensity pixel $I(i, j)$ by applying the x and y Sobel operators at the current pixel. In computing the gradients, we place the Sobel operators such that the current intensity pixel $I(i, j)$ aligns with the center coefficient of 3×3 masks. In a large image with $M \times N$ pixel resolution, we compute the pixel gradients by moving the 3×3 masks one pixel at a time in the raster scan order. This is illustrated in Figure 10.11. If G is the gradient of pixel p_5, then G is computed using Sobel operators as in

$$G = \sqrt{G_x^2 + G_y^2} \tag{10.9a}$$

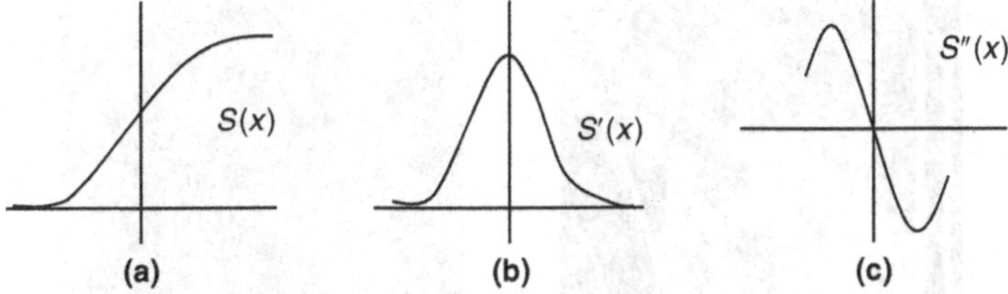

Figure 10.9: (a) Sample one-dimensional intensity variation function $s(x)$. (b) First derivative showing peak at maximum rate of change of intensity. (c) Second derivative showing the zero-crossing at maximum rate of change of intensity.

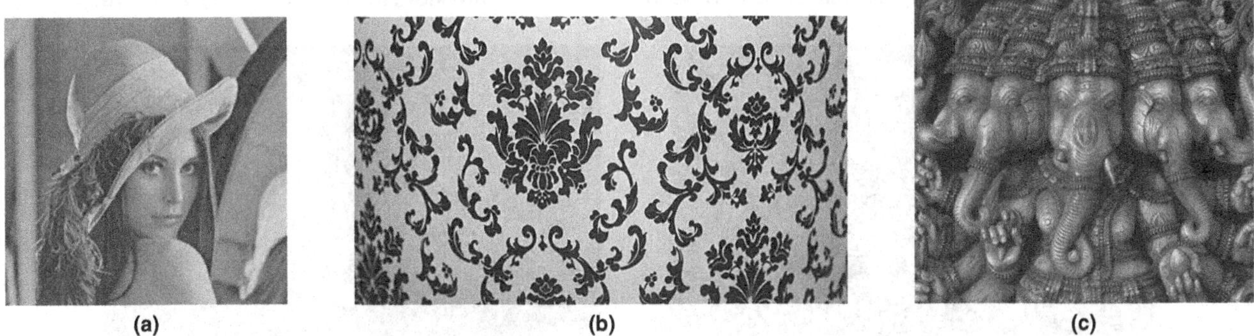

Figure 10.10: Test images for edge detection. (a) Lena. (b) Wallpaper. (c) Lord Ganesh.

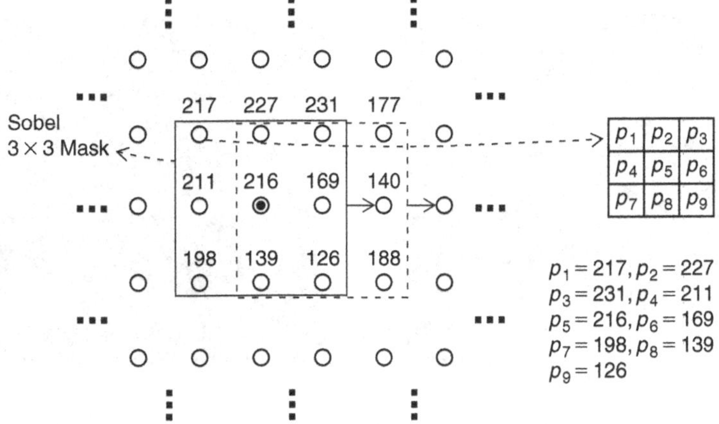

Figure 10.11: Illustration of pixel gradient computation in large image.

where

$$G_x = (p_3 + 2^* p_6 + p_9) - (p_1 + 2^* p_4 + p_7) \tag{10.9b}$$

$$G_y = (p_1 + 2^* p_2 + p_3) - (p_7 + 2^* p_8 + p_9) \tag{10.9c}$$

By following the preceding equations, the gradient value G for the pixel (with value 216) as highlighted in Figure 10.11 is equal to 331.9. After computing the gradients for all pixels, we obtain a binary image with only prominent edges information by applying a threshold (T) value to gradients. Figures 10.12 through 10.14 show the output of the Sobel edge detector when applied to the Lena, wallpaper, and Lord Ganesh images using various threshold values.

10.6.2 Laplace Edge Detector

The edge detection based on the Sobel operator uses the pixels' first derivatives (i.e., gradients), whereas the Laplace edge detector uses the zero-crossings of second derivatives of pixels in identifying the edges. The

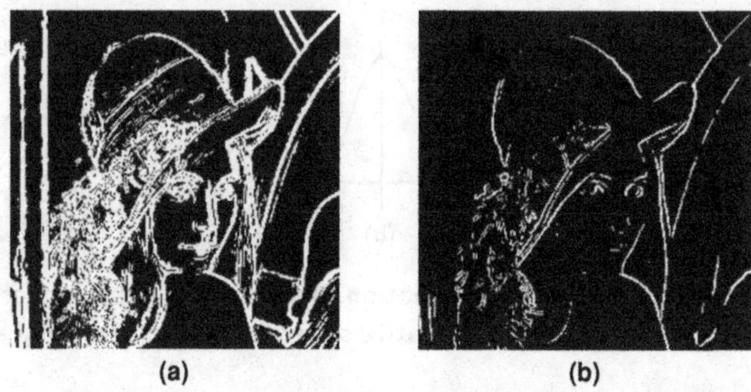

(a) (b)

Figure 10.12: Lena image, Sobel edge detection with various thresholds. (a) $T = 64$. (b) $T = 240$.

(a) (b)

Figure 10.13: Wallpaper image, Sobel edge detection with various thresholds. (a) $T = 64$. (b) $T = 240$.

(a) (b)

Figure 10.14: Lord Ganesh image, Sobel edge detection with various thresholds. (a) $T = 64$. (b) $T = 240$.

Laplacian of a 2D function $I(x, y)$ is a second-order derivative and is defined as

$$\nabla^2 I = \frac{\partial^2 I}{\partial x^2} + \frac{\partial^2 I}{\partial y^2} \tag{10.10}$$

where

$$\frac{\partial^2 I}{\partial x^2} = I(x+1, y) + I(x-1, y) - 2I(x, y) \tag{10.11}$$

$$\frac{\partial^2 I}{\partial y^2} = I(x, y+1) + I(x, y-1) - 2I(x, y) \tag{10.12}$$

Given Equations (10.10), (10.11) and (10.12),

$$\nabla^2 I = [I(x+1, y) + I(x-1, y) + I(x, y+1) + I(x, y-1)] - 4I(x, y) \tag{10.13}$$

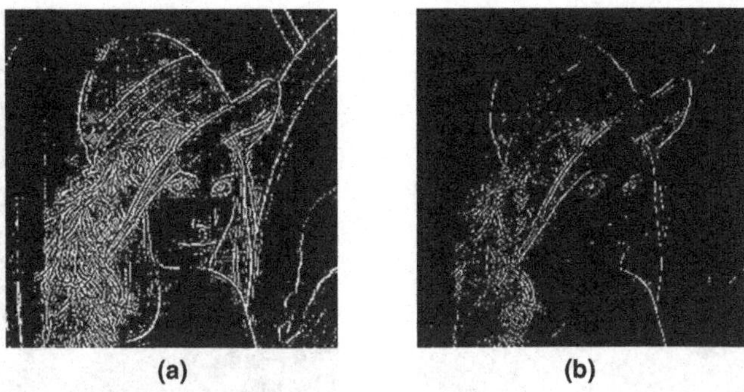

(a) (b)

Figure 10.15: Lena image, Laplacian edge detection with various thresholds. (a) $T = 16$. (b) $T = 64$.

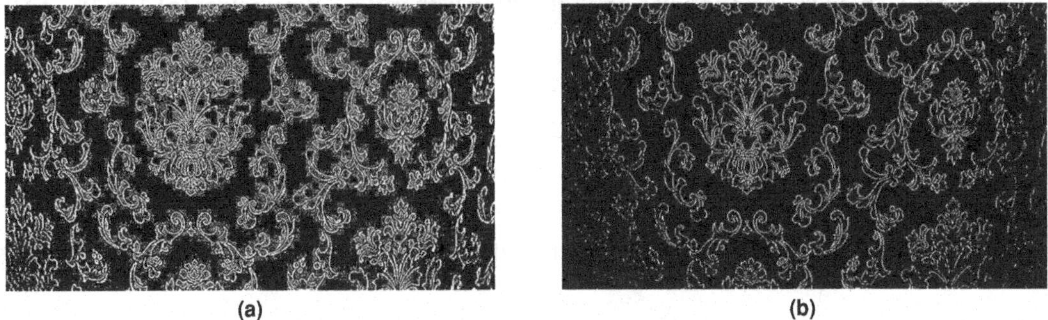

(a) (b)

Figure 10.16: Wallpaper image, Laplacian edge detection with various thresholds. (a) $T = 16$. (b) $T = 64$.

Equation (10.13) is the same as Equation (10.7) except for the sign, and we implement Equation (10.13) using the following mask L_{xy}.

$$L_{xy} = \begin{bmatrix} 0 & 1 & 0 \\ 1 & -4 & 1 \\ 0 & 1 & 0 \end{bmatrix} \tag{10.14}$$

Computation of the image's edge information using the Laplace edge detector is similar to the Sobel operator as shown in Figure 10.11; the only difference is that the Laplace edge detector uses a single mask in edge computation whereas the Sobel operator uses two masks. Thus, we cannot obtain the angle information using the Laplace edge detector. Here we also use the threshold value (T) to get binary images with prominent edges. Figures 10.15 through 10.17 show edge information in the Lena, wallpaper, and Lord Ganesh images obtained using the Laplace edge detector. The Laplacian operator highlights gray-level discontinuities in an image and deemphasizes regions with slowly varying gray levels. As the Laplacian operator increases the contrast at the locations of gray-level discontinuities, adding the Laplacian edges to the actual image enhances the edges while preserving the slowly varying background. Figure 10.4 shows the edge enhancement obtained using Laplacian operator.

10.6.3 Canny Edge Detector

Canny developed a totally different approach to edge detection. The Canny edge detection operator uses a multistage algorithm to detect a wide range of edges in images. This is an optimum edge detection algorithm, and the detector is optimal in the sense of the following three criteria:

- *Good detection*: The detector marks as many real edges in the image as possible.
- *Good localization*: Edges marked should be as close as possible to the edges in the real image.
- *Minimal response*: There is only one response per edge under white noise conditions.

The Canny edge detector uses the following five steps to satisfy the preceding criteria:

1. Noise reduction using Gaussian filter
2. Computation of gradients (the Sobel operator can be used for this purpose)

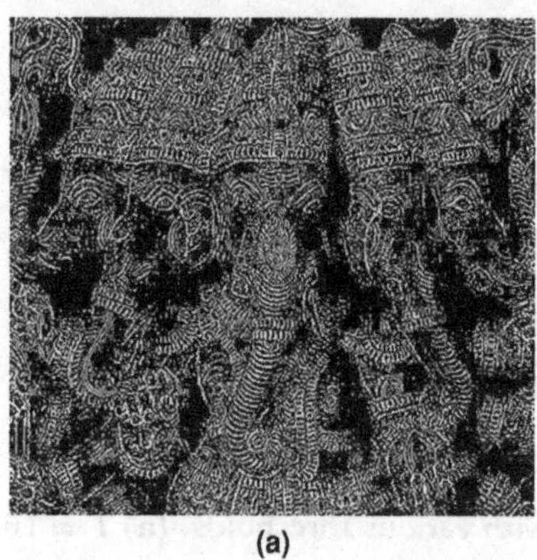
(a)

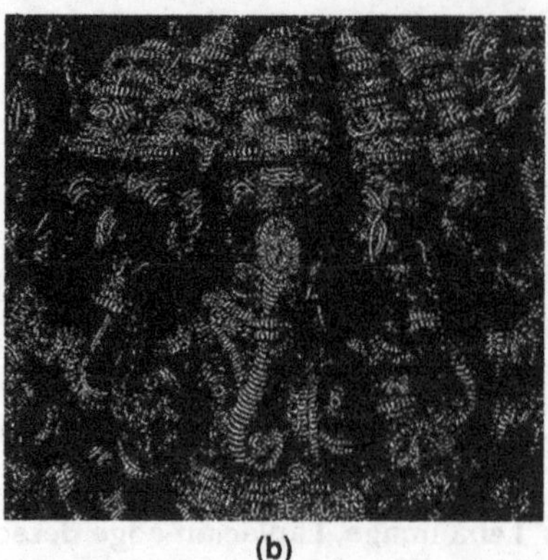
(b)

Figure 10.17: Lord Ganesh image, Laplacian edge detection with various thresholds. (a) $T = 16$. (b) $T = 64$.

3. Computation of quantized orientation of edges
4. Nonmaximum suppression
5. Hysteresis thresholding

Noise Reduction

We use the following Gaussian function to generate the filter coefficients for minimizing noise effects in edge detection:

$$G_\sigma(m,n) = \frac{1}{\sqrt{2\pi\sigma^2}} \exp\left(-\frac{m^2+n^2}{2\sigma^2}\right) \tag{10.15}$$

where σ^2 is the variance of Gaussian function.

Given that $m = n = k$, we obtain a $k \times k$ Gaussian filter. For $\sigma = 1.0$, 1.5, and 2.0, three Gaussian filters approximate discrete coefficients obtained from Equation (10.15):

$$G_{1.0} = \frac{1}{159}\begin{bmatrix} 0 & 2 & 3 & 2 & 0 \\ 2 & 7 & 11 & 7 & 2 \\ 3 & 11 & 18 & 11 & 3 \\ 2 & 7 & 11 & 7 & 2 \\ 0 & 2 & 3 & 2 & 0 \end{bmatrix} \quad G_{1.5} = \frac{1}{171}\begin{bmatrix} 2 & 5 & 6 & 5 & 2 \\ 5 & 9 & 12 & 9 & 5 \\ 6 & 12 & 15 & 12 & 6 \\ 5 & 9 & 12 & 9 & 5 \\ 2 & 5 & 6 & 5 & 2 \end{bmatrix} \quad G_{2.0} = \frac{1}{230}\begin{bmatrix} 5 & 8 & 9 & 8 & 5 \\ 8 & 11 & 13 & 11 & 8 \\ 9 & 13 & 14 & 13 & 9 \\ 8 & 11 & 13 & 11 & 8 \\ 5 & 8 & 9 & 8 & 5 \end{bmatrix}$$

We smooth the image by convolving the image with filter coefficients G_σ. Figure 10.18 shows the Gaussian-filtered Lena image for various sigma values. The amount of smoothing achieved by changing sigma values is seen in the encircled areas.

Gradient Computation

We use the Sobel operators given in Equations (10.9b) and (10.9c) for computing the pixel gradients. If G_x and G_y represent the x-gradient and y-gradient, respectively, of a pixel, then from Equation (10.9a) the pixel gradient is given by $G = \sqrt{G_x^2 + G_y^2}$. Computing the exact pixel gradient on fixed-point processors is a complex task as it involves square root computations. However, we tackle this problem by computing the approximate value for G using simple methods. Two commonly used approaches are given in Equations (10.16a) and (10.16b).

$$G = |G_x| + |G_y| \tag{10.16a}$$

$$G = \max(G_x, G_y) \tag{10.16b}$$

The value computed using Equations (10.16a) and (10.16b) gives reasonable gradient information only when the difference between G_x and G_y is large. In another approach, we get the approximate value for the square root of the sum $G_x^2 + G_y^2$. There are many algorithms in the literature to obtain the approximate value of the square root. Using the following method (Philipsson, 2002), we can get the approximate square root value to nearest integer d.

(a)

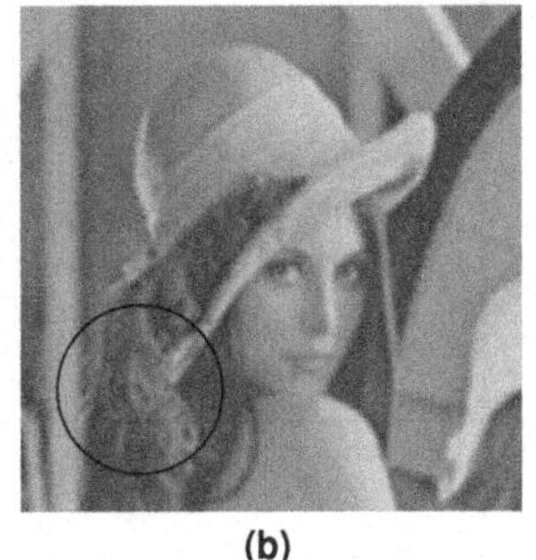
(b)

(c)

Figure 10.18: Lena original image after processing with Gaussian filter using sigma. (a) 1.0. (b) 1.5. (c) 2.0.

1. Get $y = G_x^2 + G_y^2$
2. Get the number of bits in y, say m
3. Get $n = m >> 1$
4. Get $a = x >> n, b = 1 << n$
5. Get $c = a + b$
6. Finally, $d = c >> 1$, where d contains the approximate square root value (to the nearest integer for most but not all cases) for the sum $G_x^2 + G_y^2$

Edge Orientation Computation

The pixel gradient direction is computed from the pixel gradients G_x and G_y as follows:

$$\phi = \tan^{-1}\left(\frac{G_y}{G_x}\right) \tag{10.17}$$

The edge orientation is always perpendicular to its pixel gradient direction. As the Canny edge detector uses only quantized angles, we can efficiently compute the quantized gradient directions using the iterative CORDIC algorithm (Volder, 1959) in a few iterations. Using the CORDIC algorithm, we find the orientation of the vector by rotation of the vector with the known angles in multiple iterations.

CORDIC Algorithm

Let $z_0 = (x_0, y_0)$ represent the initial point P rectangular coordinates, and assume that the point P is in the first quadrant as shown in Figure 10.19. In the complex plane (because we are going to solve the problem in the complex plane!), its equivalent polar coordinates are given by $z_0 = re^{j\phi}$. Assume that the vector is rotated by a known angle θ_0 and that the new point $z_1 = (x_1, y_1)$ is obtained as follows:

$$z_1 = z_0 e^{j\theta_0} = (x_0 + jy_0)(\cos\theta_0 + j\sin\theta_0) = (x_0\cos\theta_0 - y_0\sin\theta_0) + j(x_0\sin\theta_0 + y_0\cos\theta_0)$$

The preceding expression can be represented in matrix form:

$$\begin{bmatrix} x_1 \\ y_1 \end{bmatrix} = \begin{bmatrix} \cos\theta_0 & -\sin\theta_0 \\ \sin\theta_0 & \cos\theta_0 \end{bmatrix} \begin{bmatrix} x_0 \\ y_0 \end{bmatrix} \tag{10.18}$$

$$\begin{bmatrix} x_1 \\ y_1 \end{bmatrix} = \cos\theta_0 \begin{bmatrix} 1 & -\tan\theta_0 \\ \tan\theta_0 & 1 \end{bmatrix} \begin{bmatrix} x_0 \\ y_0 \end{bmatrix} \tag{10.19}$$

If $\theta_0 = -45°$ (i.e., rotate vector z_0 by 45° in the clockwise direction), then

$$\begin{bmatrix} x_1 \\ y_1 \end{bmatrix} = \cos\theta_0 \begin{bmatrix} 1 & 1 \\ -1 & 1 \end{bmatrix} \begin{bmatrix} x_0 \\ y_0 \end{bmatrix} \tag{10.20}$$

or

$$x_1 = (x_0 + y_0)\cos\theta_0, \quad y_1 = (-x_0 + y_0)\cos\theta_0$$

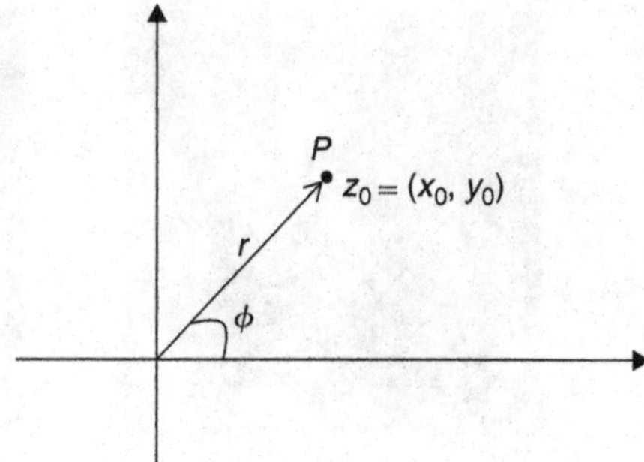

Figure 10.19: Rectangular and polar coordinate representation of point P.

If $y_1 = 0$, then the actual orientation of given vector is $\theta_0 = 45°$. However, this need not be the case. If $y_1 \neq 0$, then we again rotate the z_1 by a known angle θ_1 and obtain z_2. Given Equation (10.19),

$$\begin{bmatrix} x_2 \\ y_2 \end{bmatrix} = \cos\theta_1 \begin{bmatrix} 1 & -\tan\theta_1 \\ \tan\theta_1 & 1 \end{bmatrix} \begin{bmatrix} x_1 \\ y_1 \end{bmatrix} \tag{10.21}$$

This time we choose θ_1 such that $\tan\theta_1 = \pm 1/2$. That is, if $y_1 > 0$, we choose $\theta_1 = -26.5651°$; else if $y_1 < 0$, then we choose $\theta_1 = 26.5651°$. Thus,

$$\begin{aligned} &\text{if} \quad y_1 > 0, \quad x_2 = (x_1 + y_1/2)\cos\theta_1, \quad y_2 = (-x_1/2 + y_1)\cos\theta_1 \\ &\text{else if} \quad y_1 < 0, \quad x_2 = (x_1 - y_1/2)\cos\theta_1, \quad y_2 = (x_1/2 + y_1)\cos\theta_1 \end{aligned}$$

We continue this process until $y_n = 0$ by choosing $\theta_n = \tan^{-1}[\pm(1/2)^n]$ every time. If $y_n = 0$, then the orientation of vector ϕ is obtained as $\phi = \theta_0 + \theta_1 + \theta_2 + \cdots \theta_n$. During this process, we also obtained the magnitude of the vector r as x_n. To avoid the multiplications and divisions, we precompute the value $\cos\theta_0 \cos\theta_1 \cdots \cos\theta_{n-1}$, and multiply once to get x_n as $x_n = x_{n-1}\cos\theta_0\cos\theta_1 \cdots \cos\theta_{n-1}$. In addition, we can compute x_i or y_i with right shifting x_{i-1} or y_{i-1} by n since $\tan\theta_n = (1/2)^n$.

Example 10.1

If P: (9, 56), then find the approximate magnitude r and quantized angle ϕ of point P using the CORDIC algorithm in four iterations.

Given that the signs of both coordinates are positive, the point P lies in the first quadrant.

$$z_0 = (x_0, y_0) = (9, 56)$$

First iteration: $\tan\theta_0 = 1$ (since $y_0 > 0$)

$x_1 := x_0 + y_0,\ y_1 := -x_0 + y_0$ (here we are not using "=" since we didn't perform multiplication of x_0 and y_0 with $\cos\theta_0$)

$$z_1 = (x_1, y_1) := (65, 47)$$

Second iteration: $\tan\theta_1 = 1/2$ (since $y_1 > 0$)

$$x_2 := x_1 + y_1/2,\ y_2 := -x_1/2 + y_1$$

$$z_2 = (x_2,\ y_2) := (88, 14)$$

Third iteration: $\tan\theta_2 = 1/4$ (since $y_2 > 0$)

$$x_3 := x_2 + y_2/4,\ y_3 := -x_2/4 + y_2$$

$$z_3 = (x_3,\ y_3) := (91, -8)$$

Fourth iteration: $\tan\theta_3 = -1/8$ (since $y_3 < 0$)

$$x_4 := x_3 - y_3/8, \quad y_4 := x_3/8 + y_3$$

$$z_4 = (x_4, y_4) := (92, 3)$$

The approximate value of magnitude r follows:

$$r = x_4 \cos\theta_0 \cos\theta_1 \cos\theta_2 \cos\theta_3 = 92 \times 0.6088 = 56.01$$

$$\phi = \theta_0 + \theta_1 + \theta_2 + \theta_3 = 45 + 26.5651 + 14.0362 - 7.1250 = 78.4763$$

The actual polar coordinates of point (9, 56) are $r = 56.72$ and $\phi = 80.87$.

■

From Example 10.1, it is clear that the iterative CORDIC algorithm computes the pixel gradient's approximate magnitude

$$G = \sqrt{G_x^2 + G_y^2}$$

and orientation

$$\phi = \tan^{-1}\left(\frac{G_y}{G_x}\right)$$

in four iterations. This accuracy is more than sufficient for the Canny edge detection application. Because a single iteration involves two right shifts and two addition operations, we can implement the CORDIC algorithm on the reference embedded processor with four cycles per iteration.

Analytic Method for Computing Quantized Edge Orientation

The problem of quantized edge orientation computation can also be solved using the analytic method described in the following. As shown in Figure 10.20, we want to find one of four quantized angles for each pixel given the x-gradient G_x and y-gradient G_y of the pixel. For this, we generate a look-up table **gradient_directions**[] with a 5-bit number as an offset to work with the analytic method. The 5 bits of the offset represent truth flags for following five conditions:

0th bit: $|G_y| \leq 0.4|G_x|$
1st bit: $|G_y| > 2.4|G_x|$
2nd bit: $(|G_y| > 0.4|G_x|)$ && $(|G_y| \leq 2.4|G_x|)$
3rd bit: $G_x < 0$
4th bit: $G_y < 0$

We precompute the look-up table **gradient_directions**[] values based on the preceding five conditions or based on Figures 10.20(a) through (d). The 32 look-up table values are given as follows:

```
gradient_directions[32] = {//look-up table
0, 0, 90, 0, 45, 0, 0, 0, 0, 0, 90, 0, 135, 0, 0, 0,
0, 0, 90, 0, 135,0, 0, 0, 0, 0, 90, 0, 45, 0, 0, 0};
```

Once the look-up table values are generated, the quantized gradient direction Q is obtained from the look-up table with an offset computed using the following pseudocode. We build the offset by checking the preceding five conditions for the given x-gradient G_x and y-gradient G_y.

```
x = Gx;  y = Gy;
a = 0.4 * abs(x); b = 2.4 * abs(x);
i = 0;
if (y < 0)
        i = 1;
end
```

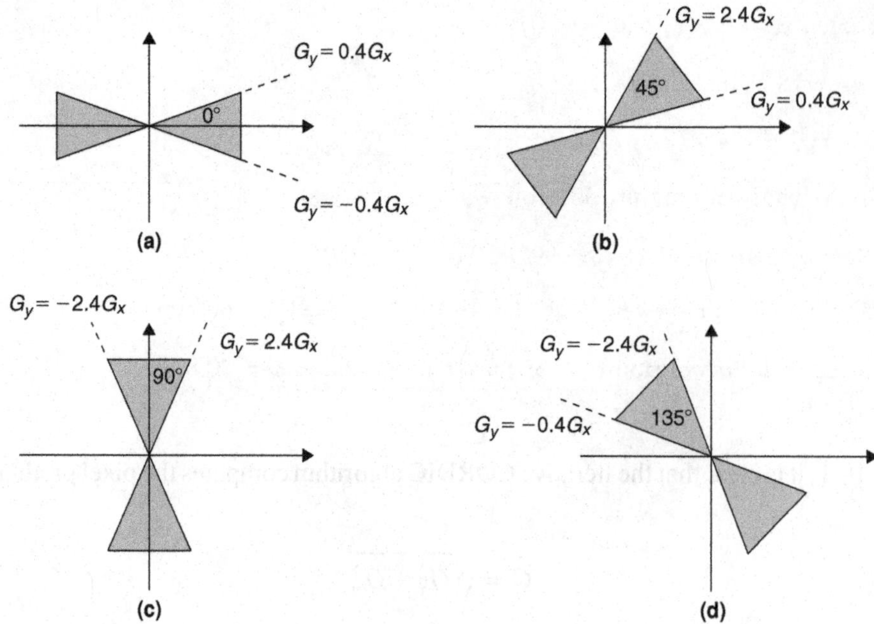

Figure 10.20: Analytic approach for quantized angle computation. (a) Quantized range for 0°. (b) Quantized range for 45°. (c) Quantized range for 90°. (d) Quantized range for 135°.

```
i = i << 1;
if (x < 0)
        i |= 1;
end
i = i << 1;
if ((abs(y) > a) && (abs(y) <= b))
        i |= 1;
end
i = i << 1;
if (abs(y) > b)
        i |= 1;
end
i=i <<1;
if (abs(y) <= a)
        i |= 1;
end
Q = gradient_directions[i];
```

Since the pixel gradients G_x and G_y of Example 10.2 belong to the shaded region of Figure 10.20(c), the corresponding quantized gradient direction is obtained as 90°.

Example 10.2

Given $G_x = -9$ and $G_y = 56$, compute the quantized gradient direction Q.

$$x = G_x = -9, y = G_y = 56$$

0th bit: 0 (since $|G_y| > 0.4^* |G_x|$)
1st bit: 1 (since $|G_y| > 2.4^* |G_x|$)
2nd bit: 0 (since $|G_y| > 2.4^* |G_x|$)
3rd bit: 1 (since $G_x < 0$)
4th bit: 0 (since $G_y > 0$)
offset $= 01010_b = 10_d$

$$Q = \textbf{gradient\_direction}[\text{offset}] = 90°$$

■

Nonmaximum Suppression

Nonmaximum suppression makes all edges one pixel thick. Given the image gradients, a search is then carried out to determine whether the gradient magnitude assumes a local maximum in the gradient direction. If $g[j][i]$ is the current pixel gradient, and $g[j+1][i]$, $g[j-1][i]$, $g[j][i-1]$, $g[j-1][i-1]$, $g[j+1][i-1]$, $g[j][i+1]$, $g[j-1][i+1]$, and $g[j+1][i+1]$ are the neighbor pixels gradients, then the following pseudocode performs nonmaximum suppression:

```
q[][] = g[][];
for j = 1:M
          for i = 1:N
                    if (g[j][i] != 0)
                              if (Q == 0) // i.e., if -22.5 < φ ≤ 22.5
                                        if (g[j][i] < g[j][i-1] || g[j][i] < g[j][i+1])
                                                  q[j][i] = 0;
                                        end
                              end
                              if (Q == 45) // i.e., if 22.5 < φ ≤ 67.5
                                        if ((g[j][i] < g[j-1][i+1]) || (g[j][i] < g[j+1][i-1]))
                                                  q[j][i] = 0;
                                        end
                              end
                              if (Q == 90) // i.e., if 67.5 < φ ≤ 112.5
                                        if ((g[j][i] < g[j-1][i]) || (g[j][i] < g[j+1][i]))
                                                  q[j][i] = 0;
                                        end
                              end
                              if (Q == 135) // i.e., if 112.5 < φ ≤ 157.5
                                        if ((g[j][i] < g[j+1][i+1]) || g[j][i] < g[j-1][i-1]))
                                                  q[j][i] = 0;
                                        end
                              end
                    end
          end
end
```

With nonmaximum suppression, we basically suppress the gradient information $g[j][i]$ if $g[j][i]$ is less than the gradients of either of its neighbors with the same orientation as $g[j][i]$. This is because gradient direction is perpendicular to the edge orientation, and therefore the edge points are suppressed in the gradient direction. This is illustrated in Figure 10.21. We get better results if we use nearest-neighbor points (obtained by interpolation of neighbor points) with nonmaximum suppression. Figure 10.22 shows the thinning effect of nonmaximum suppression on the edges.

Hysteresis Threshold

A binary image is obtained after applying hysteresis thresholds. The aim of hysteresis thresholding is to realize an improved balance between false positives and false negatives by exploiting connectedness in the object boundaries. The pixels with larger gradients are more likely to correspond to edges than those with small gradients. If we use a single threshold limit, the edge values fluctuating above and below the threshold will

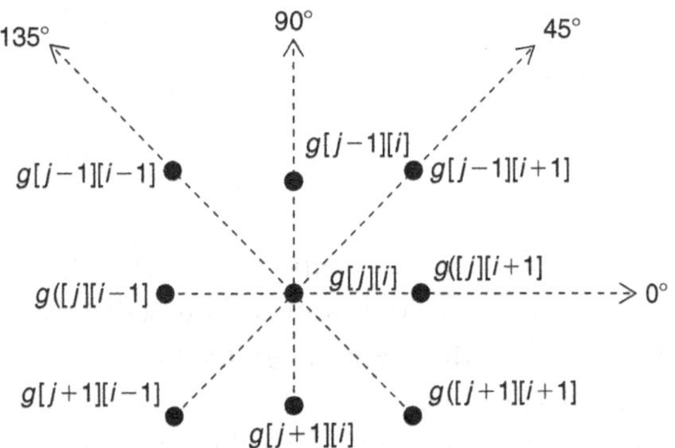

Figure 10.21: Illustration of nonmaximum suppression.

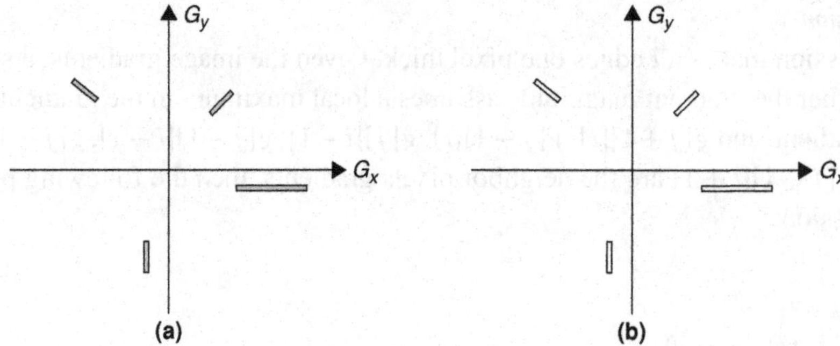

Figure 10.22: Nonmaximum suppression. (a) Wide edges before suppression. (b) Thin edges after suppression.

appear broken (referred to as *streaking*). Hysteresis minimizes streaking by setting limits on upper and lower edge values. Given upper- and lower-threshold values *max_t* and *min_t*, respectively, the following pseudocode performs hysteresis thresholding:

```
for j=1:M
    for i=1:N
        if (g[j][i] > max_t)
            g[j][i] = 1;
        end
        if ((g[j][i] < max_t)&&(g[j][i] > min_t))
            g[j][i] = 2;
        end
        if (g[j][i] < min_t)
            g[j][i] = 0;
        end
    end
end
flag = 1;
while (flag)
    flag = 0;
    for j=1:M
        for i=1:N
            if (g[j][i] > 0)
                if (g[j][i] == (2)
                    if((g[j-1][i]) == (1) || (g[j-1][i-1]) == (1) ||
                    (g[j][i-1] == (1) || (g[j+1][i-1] == (1) ||
                    (g([j+1][i] == (1) || (g[j+1][i+1] == 1) ||
                    (g[j][i+1] == 1) ||  (g[j-1][i+1] == 1))
                        g[j][i] = 1;
                        flag = 1;
                    end
                end
            end
        end
    end
end
for j=1:M
    for i=1:N
        if (g[j][i] == 2)
            g[j][i] = 0;
        end
    end
end
```

With the preceding pseudocode, we immediately accept the gradient at the current pixel position as edge if the gradient value is greater than the upper threshold limit and immediately reject if the gradient value is less than the lower threshold limit. The gradients that lie between the two thresholds are accepted as edges if they are connected to pixels which exhibit strong connectedness.

Now, we apply the Canny edge detection method to the three test images and see its performance when compared to Sobel and Laplacian. We use different sigma and threshold values to see the behavior of the Canny

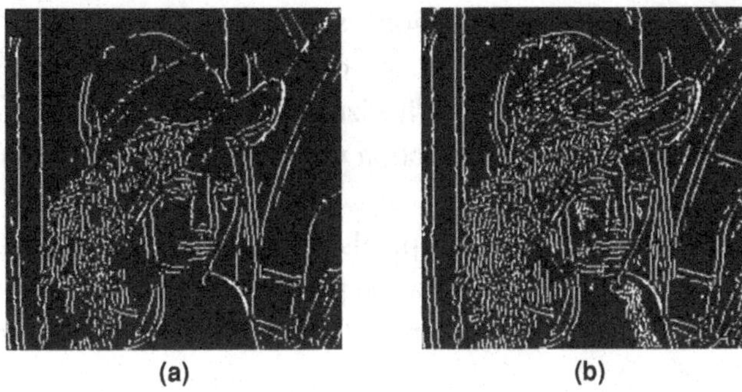

Figure 10.23: Lena image, Canny edge detection with various parameters: (a) $T1 = 16$, $T2 = 32$, Sig = 1.0. (b) $T1 = 8$, $T2 = 16$, Sig = 2.0.

Figure 10.24: Wallpaper image, Canny edge detection with various parameters. (a) $T1 = 16$, $T2 = 32$, Sig = 2.0. (b) $T1 = 8$, $T2 = 16$, Sig = 2.0.

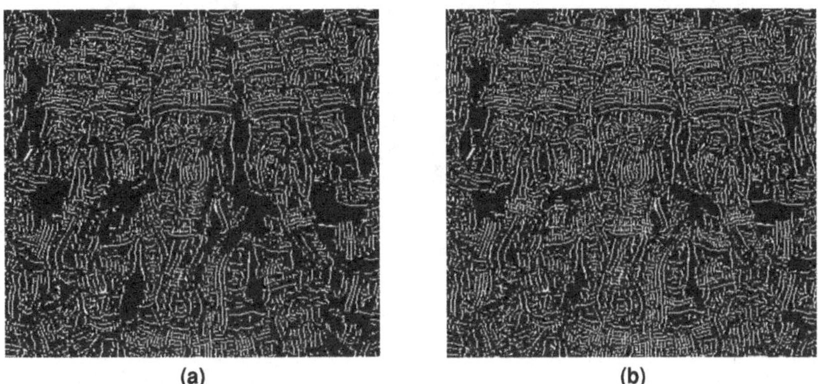

Figure 10.25: Lord Ganesh image, Canny edge detection with various parameters. (a) $T1 = 16$, $T2 = 32$, Sig = 2.0. (b) $T1 = 8$, $T2 = 16$, Sig = 2.0.

edge detector. From Figures 10.23 through 10.25, we can see the superior performance of the Canny edge detector.

10.7 Image Scaling

Images are scaled for purposes of changing aspect ratio, transmission of images over a communication link with less bandwidth, storing images with less memory, and for better viewing. The main functionality in the image scaling is the interpolation of image pixels. The quality of the scaled image depends on the type of interpolator used for the scaling. There are many interpolator functions suggested in the literature for scaling the images. In this section, we discuss two simple interpolation methods, namely (1) *nearest neighbor* and (2) *bilinear* interpolator functions to scale the image. In Section 15.1, we discuss more complex interpolator functions in scaling the luminance and chrominance components of video frames.

Consider a QVGA image (i.e., 320 × 240 resolution), and assume scaling by a 3/2 factor in the horizontal direction and by a factor of 2 in the vertical direction. We obtain a 480 × 480 resolution image. To achieve this, we produce three pixels for every two pixels in the horizontal direction with factor 3/2 scaling, whereas two pixels are produced for each pixel in the vertical direction with factor 2 scaling, as illustrated in Figure 10.26(a) and (b).

For image scaling, we need to know which image pixels participate in the generation of new pixels, and how to compute the new pixel value once we come to know the participating pixels. To find the pixels that participate in the scaling or to generate the new pixels, we require both the scaling factor and interpolation method used.

10.7.1 Nearest-Neighbor Interpolation

As the name indicates, we reuse the nearest pixel value for the new interpolated pixel in the nearest-neighbor interpolation. We consider a 4 × 4 block (i.e., 16 pixels) from the original image as shown in Figure 10.27(a). Those 16 pixel values are represented by $A, B, C, D, E, F, G, H, I, J, K, L, M, N, O$, and P. When we perform scaling by a factor of 3/2 in the horizontal direction and by a factor of 2 in the vertical direction, the 4 × 4 block of pixels in the original image maps to a 6 × 8 block of pixels as shown in Figure 10.27(b). In the horizontal direction with factor 3/2 scaling, the interpolated pixel position u is placed at 2/3 distance from pixel A and at 1/3 distance from pixel B. Similarly, the pixel v is placed at 1/3 distance from pixel B and 2/3 distance from pixel C. With the nearest-neighbor criterion, we assign the pixels u and v with pixel value B (since the pixel B is nearer to pixels u and v) as shown in Figure 10.27(b).

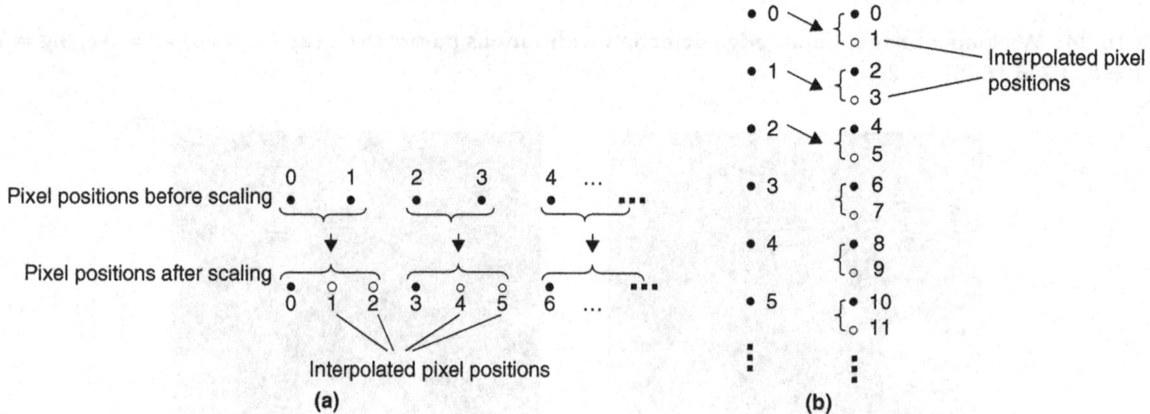

Figure 10.26: Illustration of image scaling. (a) Horizontal scaling with factor 3/2. (b) Vertical scaling with factor 2.

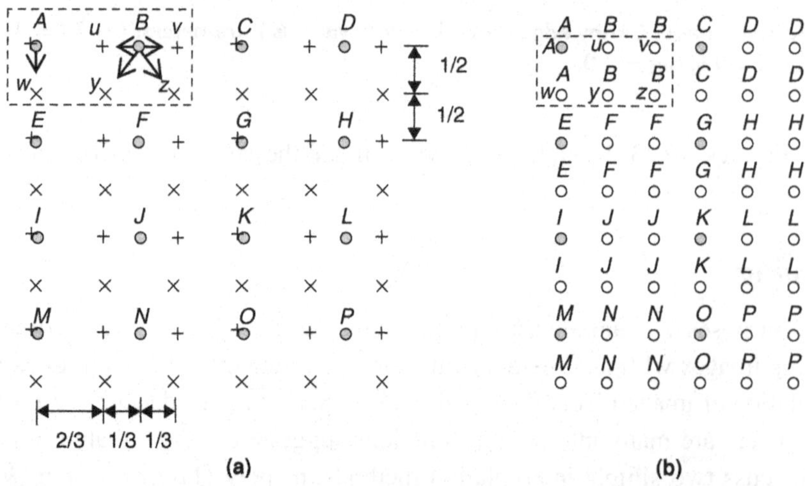

Figure 10.27: Image pixel interpolation using nearest-neighbor method. (a) Original 16 pixels. (b) Interpolated pixels with nearest-neighbor method.

Similarly, we get all other interpolated pixel values in the horizontal direction. In the vertical direction with factor 2 scaling, the interpolated pixel w, is placed at equal distances from original pixels A and E. As the distance of x from A and E is the same, we can choose either A or E pixel value for pixel w, and we choose A, as shown in Figure 10.27(b). Similarly, we obtain all interpolated pixels in the vertical direction. The scaling may be performed with full horizontal scaling first followed by full vertical scaling next or with full vertical scaling first followed by horizontal scaling next or both horizontal and vertical scaling at the same time. The test image used in the simulation of scaling methods is shown in Figure 10.28. Figure 10.29 shows the scaled image using nearest-neighbor interpolation.

The nearest-neighbor interpolation function is a simple rectangular function in 1D-spatial domain, defined as

$$h_{nn}(x) = \begin{cases} 1, & 0 \leq |x| < 0.5 \\ 0, & \text{otherwise} \end{cases} \tag{10.22}$$

Spatial- and frequency-domain characteristics of the nearest-neighbor interpolator are shown in Figure 10.30. As shown in the figure, the nearest-neighbor interpolator has very poor stopband characteristics.

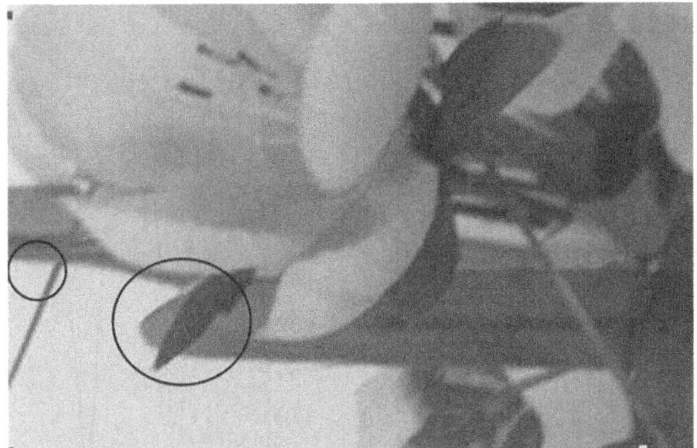

Figure 10.28: Flower image to be scaled.

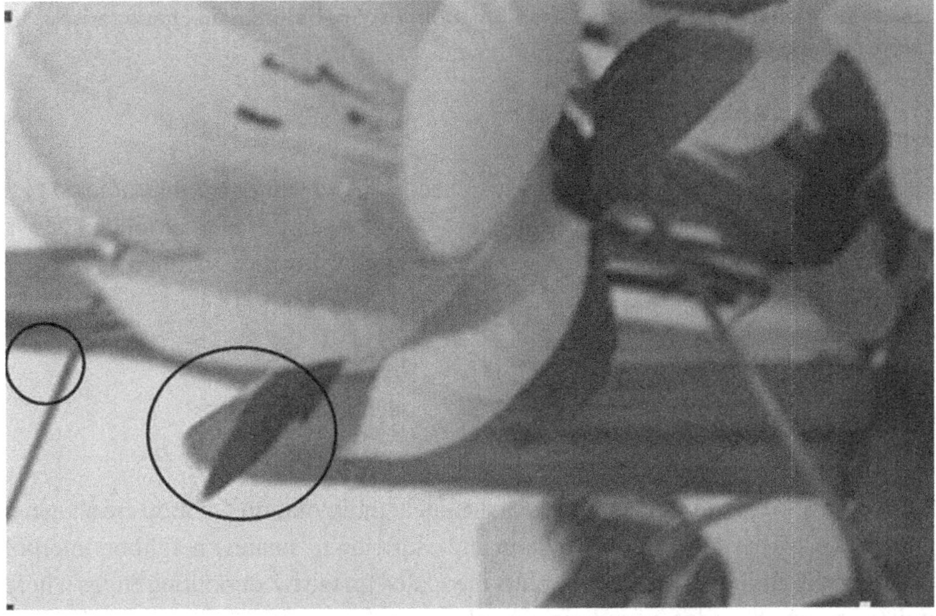

Figure 10.29: Scaled image with nearest-neighbor interpolation.

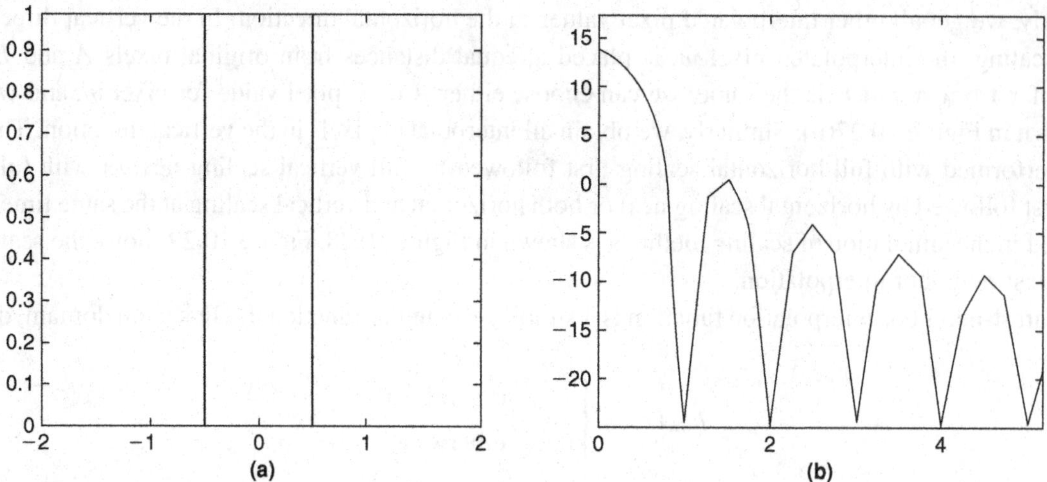

Figure 10.30: One-dimensional nearest-neighbor interpolation function. (a) Spatial-domain characteristic. (b) Frequency-domain characteristic.

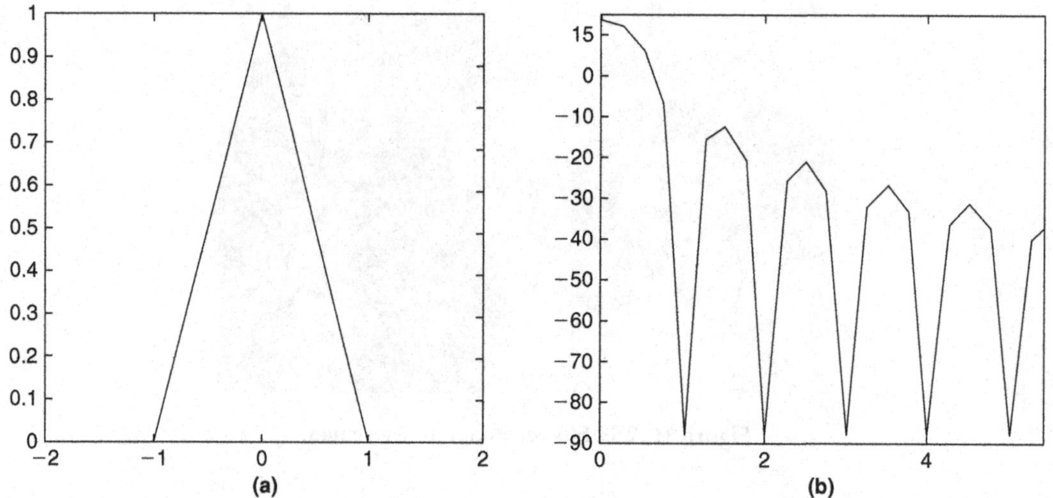

Figure 10.31: One-dimensional bilinear interpolation function. (a) Spatial-domain characteristic. (b) Frequency-domain characteristic.

10.7.2 Bilinear Interpolation

Unlike nearest-neighbor interpolation where we reuse the actual pixel values for interpolated pixel positions, in the bilinear interpolation we obtain the weighted average of pixel values for interpolated new pixels. The 1D linear interpolation function can be characterized with the triangular function, defined as

$$h_{bl}(x) = \begin{cases} 1 - |x|, & 0 \leq |x| < 1 \\ 0, & \text{otherwise} \end{cases} \tag{10.23}$$

The 1D spatial-frequency domain characteristics of the linear interpolation function are shown in Figure 10.31. Stopband characteristics of the bilinear interpolator are superior to nearest-neighbor interpolator stopband characteristics; however, the bilinear interpolator blurs the scaled image by smoothing edges whereas the nearest-neighbor interpolator retains the edge boundaries. As shown in Figure 10.32, the interpolated pixel value E is obtained by averaging the four neighboring pixels A, B, C, and D with appropriate weights calculated using

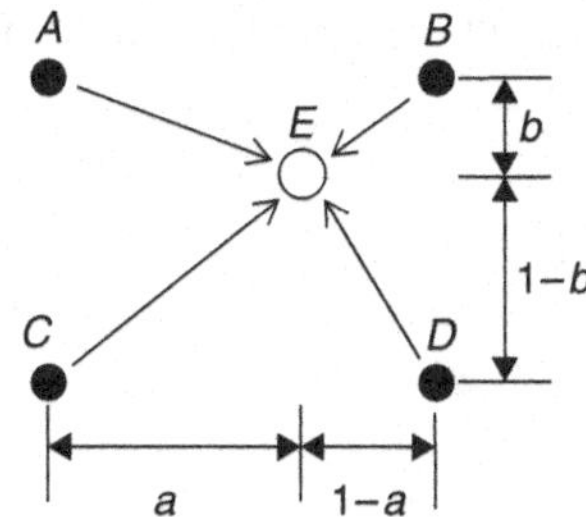

Figure 10.32: Illustration of bilinear interpolation.

Equation (10.23). The weights are obtained by using the respective distance of the new pixel position from the original pixel positions:

$$\begin{aligned} E &= (1-b)[(1-a)A + aB] + b[(1-a)C + aD] \\ &= h_0 A + h_1 B + h_2 C + h_3 D \end{aligned} \tag{10.24}$$

where

$$h_0 = (1-a)(1-b),\ h_1 = a(1-b),\ h_2 = (1-a)b,\ h_3 = ab$$

To scale the image with bilinear interpolation, we must determine which original pixels should participate in generating the new pixel and the corresponding coefficients to perform the interpolation. When $b = 0$, we perform interpolation only in the horizontal direction with coefficients $h_0 = (1-a)$ and $h_1 = a$; when $a = 0$ we perform interpolation only in the vertical direction with coefficients $h_0 = (1-b)$ and $h_2 = b$.

Line-Based Bilinear Interpolation

In video frame scaling using line-based bilinear interpolation, we interpolate pixels line by line horizontally and vertically in two passes. The pixel values of scalar output will be the same whether we perform horizontal scaling first followed by vertical scaling or vice versa, as bilinear interpolation is a linear operation. Which approach is better in terms of cycles depends on the scaling ratios used in each direction. If the horizontal scaling ratio is bigger than the vertical scaling ratio, then performing horizontal scaling first followed by vertical scaling consumes less cycles and vice versa.

In line-based bilinear interpolation, we obtain one row of image pixels at a time from L3 memory to L1 memory to perform horizontal scaling, and store them in L3 after scaling (as we cannot keep the full image in the L1 memory because L1 size is limited). In this manner, we continue scaling for all rows. Next, we get one column of horizontally scaled pixels from L3 memory to L1 memory to perform vertical scaling. After performing interpolation of one column of pixels, we DMA out the interpolated pixels. See Chapter 16 for more detail on the embedded processor architecture, memory, DMA, and so on.

Assume that the scaling is accomplished by performing horizontal scaling first followed by vertical scaling. In up scaling the image from resolution $M_1 \times M_2$ to resolution $N_1 \times N_2$ using bilinear interpolation, we determine the index of original pixels that participate in the interpolation and the coefficient values as follows.

Let x represent the pixels from the original image and y represent the pixels of scaled image. Then,

```
r = M1/N1  (i.e., horizontal scaling ratio)
i = 0;  s = 0;
y[k] = x[i];
s = s + r;
i = ⌊s⌋; a = s − i;
y[k+1] = x[i]*(1-a) + x[i+1]*a;
s = s + r;
i = ⌊s⌋; a = s − i;
y[k+2] = x[i]*(1-a) + x[i+1]*a;
s = s + r;
i = ⌊s⌋; a = s − i;
y[k+3] = x[i]*(1-a) + x[i+1]*a;
...
s = s + r;
i = ⌊s⌋; a = s − i;
y[N1 − 1] = x[i]*(1-a) + x[i+1]*a;
```

We perform the vertical scaling by taking the horizontally scaled pixels y as original pixels and obtain the up scaled image pixels z as follows:

```
r = M2 / N2  (i.e., vertical scaling ratio)
j = 0;  s = 0;
z[k] = y[j];
s = s + r;
j = ⌊s⌋; b = s - j;
z[k+1] = y[j]*(1-b) + y[j+1]*b;
s = s + r;
j = ⌊s⌋; b = s - j;
z[k+2] = y[j]*(1-b) + y[j+1]*b;
s = s + r;
j = ⌊s⌋; b = s - j;
z[k+3] = y[j]*(1-b) + y[j+1]*b;
...
s = s + r;
j = ⌊s⌋; b = s - j;
z[N2 - 1] = y[j]*(1-b) + y[j+1]*b;
```

On-the-fly computation of new pixel position indices i and j and the coefficients a and b in the preceding scaling process can be avoided by using look-up tables if the scaling ratios are known in advance.

Block-Based Bilinear Interpolation

In video and image coding, data processing is typically carried out on a block basis. The block sizes 4×4, 8×8, and 16×16 are commonly used in many coding standards. If we have the block-based scaling module, it is easy to plug in the scalar at the back end of the codec. We can then reduce the number of data transfers between L1 and L3 memories in video scaling implementation on embedded processors. This technique reduces the DMA bandwidth, which leads to less embedded-processor power consumption. The implementation procedure for block-based bilinear interpolation is shown in Figure 10.33.

In the line-based approach, we duplicate the pixels at the extreme ends of the image to fill the gap, which is not interpolated due to insufficient pixels at those edges. In block-based bilinear interpolation, we face this situation for every block with insufficient pixels at the right-most and bottom-most edges. To interpolate edge pixels, we always use neighbor block pixels as shown in Figure 10.33. In line-based interpolation, we can take care of edge conditions separately as they occur once per line. But, in the block-based approach, this edge condition occurs for every row or column of the block, which is relatively frequent when compared with a line-based approach. One way of implementing this block-based approach efficiently is to copy the neighbor block pixels to the current pixel buffer and running the loop without any condition checks or jumps. Given an $M \times N$ block, we work with a somewhat larger buffer size of $(M+1) \times (N+1)$ to accommodate neighbor-block pixels.

In the line-based approach, we have two options to handle the top-line pixels. In the first option, we always bring two lines from L3 and in the second option we always bring the current-line pixels from L3 and top-line

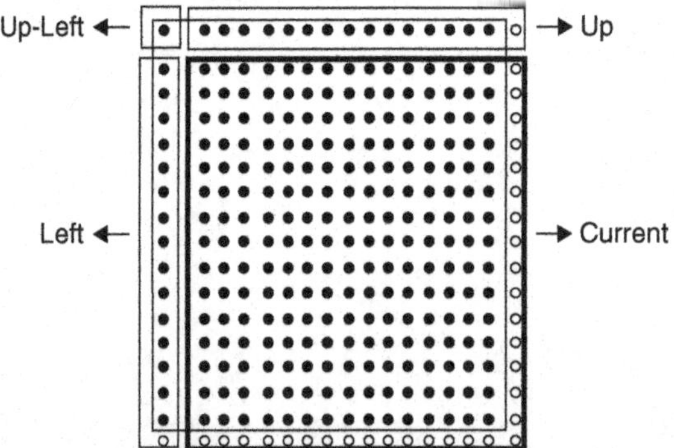

Figure 10.33: Block-based bilinear interpolation.

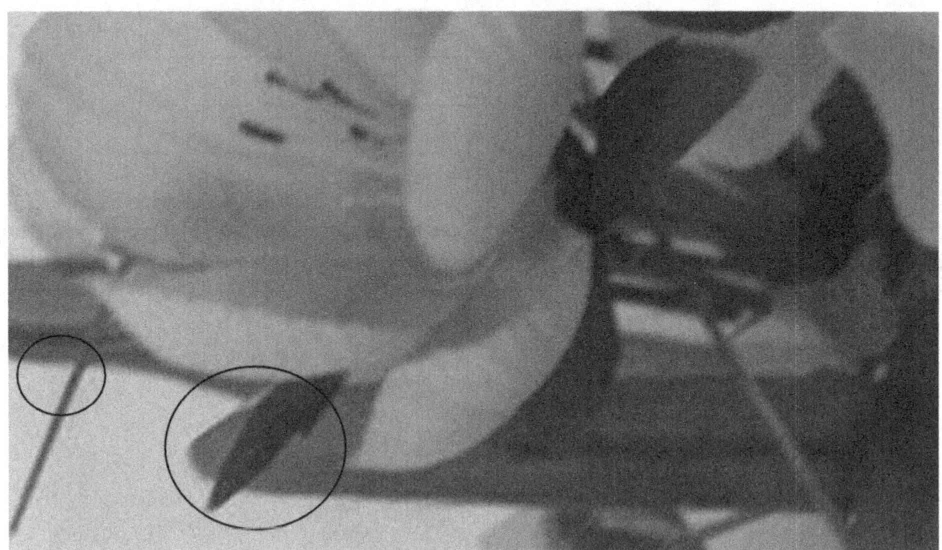

Figure 10.34: Scaled image with bilinear interpolation.

pixels from the delay line in L1 memory. In this block-based approach, we scale a small block of pixels that are usually present in L1 memory (after performing the decoding operation). We move the block of scaled pixels back to L3.

The bilinear interpolation is widely used in many image-scaling applications because it is less computationally complex. Bilinear interpolation performs well as long as the scaling factor is greater than 0.5 and less than 2. We see more staircase kinds of artifacts in the up scaled image when the scaling factor increases. Figure 10.34 shows the scaled image of Figure 10.28 with bilinear interpolation. From Figures 10.29 and 10.34, we can clearly see the improved performance of bilinear interpolation. Staircase artifacts of nearest-neighbor scaling are seen in the encircled area of Figure 10.29.

In practice, bilinear interpolation is used to scale an image's chrominance component. As the scaling artifacts are clearly seen in the intensity (or luminance) component (since the human visual system is more sensitive to luminance), we use high-end interpolation methods to scale the luminance component. More complex and advanced image scaling algorithms (e.g., scaling with bicubic and B-spline, DCT based scaling, edge orientation–based scaling, etc.) are discussed in Section 15.1.

10.8 Erosion and Dilation

The basic morphological operations erosion and dilation produce opposite results when applied to grayscale or binary images. Erosion shrinks image objects while dilation expands them. These operations apply a structuring element to an input image, creating an output image of the same size by modifying the objects within the image. The functionality of morphological operations depends on the structuring element and associated rules. A few examples of structuring elements are shown in Figure 10.35.

Dilation

Dilation uses the following rules for grayscale and binary images:

- *Grayscale image rule*: The value of the output pixel is the maximum value of all pixels in the input pixel's neighborhood (i.e., within the structuring element mask).
- *Binary image rule*: The output pixel value is set to 1 if any of the input pixels are 1 in the neighborhood (i.e., within the structuring element mask).

Dilation generally increases the size of objects, filling holes and broken areas, and connecting areas that are separated by spaces smaller than the size of the structuring element. In grayscale images, dilation increases the

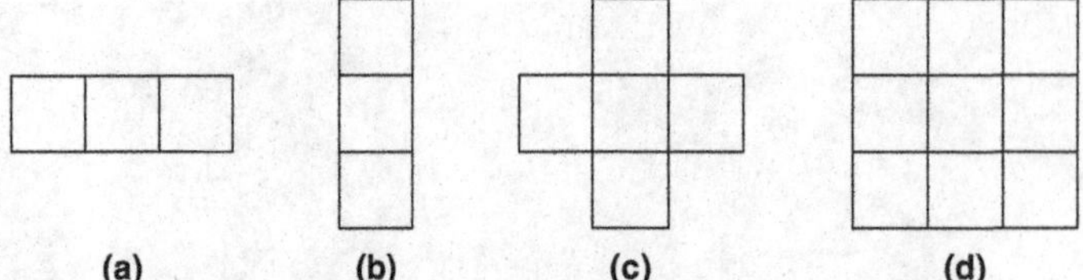

Figure 10.35: Structuring elements: The input pixel at the center is connected to (a) Two neighboring pixels horizontally. (b) Two neighboring pixels vertically. (c) Four neighboring pixels both horizontally and vertically. (d) Eight neighboring pixels in all directions.

Figure 10.36: Test image used for demonstration of dilation and erosion operators.

Figure 10.37: Grayscale image intensity variation with dilation. (a) Original image. (b) Intensity variations with three dilation operations.

brightness of objects by taking the neighborhood maximum when passing the structuring element over the image. In binary images, dilation connects areas that are separated by spaces smaller than the structuring element, and adds pixels to the boundary of each image object. To further expand the image objects in the case of binary images or to further increase the intensity of image objects, the dilation operation is repeated multiple times. The test image used for demonstrating dilation and erosion is shown in Figure 10.36. Figures 10.37 and 10.38 show the brightness variation and expansion of image objects with the dilation operation.

Erosion

Erosion uses the following rules for grayscale and binary images:

- *Grayscale image rule*: The value of the output pixel is the minimum value of all the pixels in the input pixel's neighborhood (i.e., within the structuring element mask).
- *Binary image rule*: The output pixel value is set to 0 if any of the input pixels are 0 in the neighborhood (i.e., within the structuring element mask).

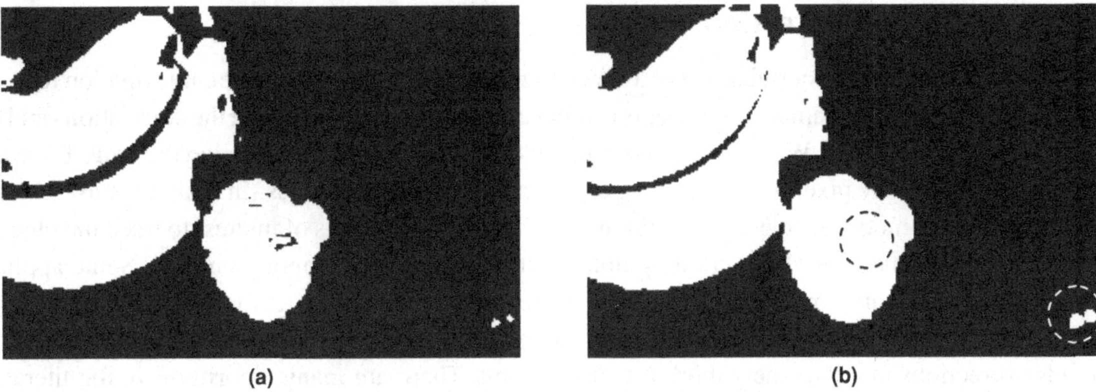

Figure 10.38: Binary image object size variation with dilation. (a) Original binary image with a few objects of Figure 10.36. (b) After three dilation operations.

Figure 10.39: Grayscale image intensity variation with erosion. (a) Original image. (b) Intensity variations with three erosion operations.

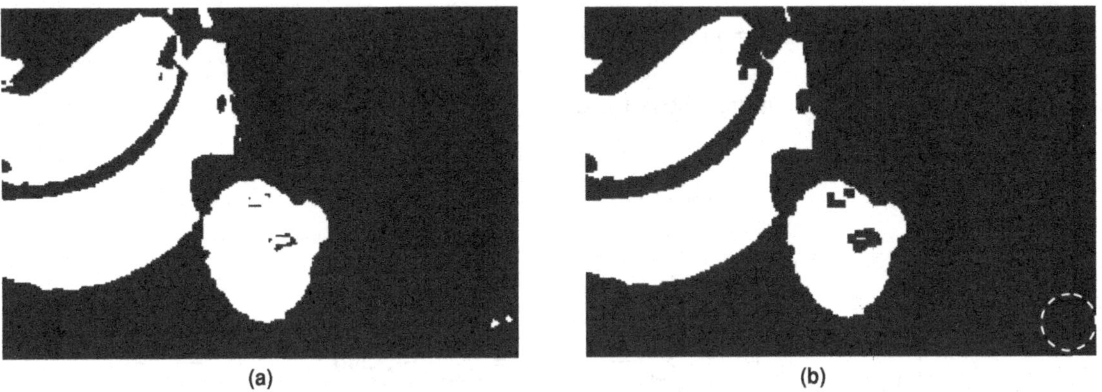

Figure 10.40: Binary image object size variation with erosion. (a) Original binary image of with a few objects of Figure 10.36. (b) After three erosion operations.

Erosion generally decreases the size of objects and removes small anomalies by subtracting objects with a radius smaller than the structuring element. In grayscale images, erosion reduces the brightness of objects by taking the neighborhood minimum when passing the structuring element over the image. In binary images, erosion completely removes objects smaller than the structuring element and removes boundary pixels from larger image objects. To further shrink the objects in the case of binary images or to further reduce the intensity of image objects in the case of grayscale images, we repeat the erosion operation multiple times. Figures 10.39 and 10.40 show the brightness variation and shrinkage of image objects upon using the erosion operation.

10.9 Objects Corner Detection

In many applications we use the correlations of a few images to process and extract the information (e.g., object motion, object depth, shooting camera movements). There are many ways to calculate the correlations and extract the information from the images. We can obtain correlations between two images by using the brute-force method (in which we examine every pixel in the two images for matching), object edges (in which we use object edge information to track the motion), object corner points (in which we use points of interest to track the object), and so on. Finding correlations with object corner points drastically reduces computation time. Some applications of object corner detection are object motion tracking, stereo vision, object recognition, and image registration.

A corner point can be defined as the intersection of two edges or a point for which there are two dominant and different edge directions in a local neighborhood of the point. There are many algorithms in the literature for detecting object corners. In this section, we discuss the widely used Harris/Plassey operator to detect points of interest. Although it has poor localization and is expensive to compute, the Harris operator is generally considered the best operator with respect to detecting true corners.

The Harris operator uses pixel intensity variations to identify object corners. Pixel intensity variation in two dimensions can be measured as follows:

$$U_{m,n}(x,y) = \sum_{\forall i} \left(m \frac{\partial I_i}{\partial x} + n \frac{\partial I_i}{\partial y} \right)^2 \tag{10.25}$$

where the index i belongs to the pixel indices in the given window centered at pixel (x, y).

Equation (10.25) can be rewritten as

$$\begin{aligned} U_{m,n}(x,y) &= \sum_{\forall i} \left(m^2 \frac{\partial I_i^2}{\partial x} + n^2 \frac{\partial I_i^2}{\partial y} + 2mn \frac{\partial I_i}{\partial x} \frac{\partial I_i}{\partial y} \right) \\ &= m^2 \sum_{\forall i} \frac{\partial I_i^2}{\partial x} + n^2 \sum_{\forall i} \frac{\partial I_i^2}{\partial y} + 2mn \sum_{\forall i} \frac{\partial I_i}{\partial x} \frac{\partial I_i}{\partial y} \\ &= m^2 V_{xx} + n^2 V_{yy} + 2mn V_{xy} \end{aligned} \tag{10.26}$$

Equation (10.26) can be written in the matrix form as

$$U_{m,n}(x,y) = [m \quad n] \, A \begin{bmatrix} m \\ n \end{bmatrix} \tag{10.27}$$

where

$$A = \begin{bmatrix} V_{xx} & V_{xy} \\ V_{xy} & V_{yy} \end{bmatrix}, \; V_{xx} = \sum_{\forall i} \frac{\partial I_i^2}{\partial x}, \quad V_{yy} = \sum_{\forall i} \frac{\partial I_i^2}{\partial y}, \text{ and } V_{xy} = \sum_{\forall i} \frac{\partial I_i}{\partial x} \frac{\partial I_i}{\partial y}$$

Here the matrix A contains all the differential operators describing the geometry of the image surface at the pixel (x, y) of interest, and the eigenvalues of A, λ_1 *and* λ_2, will be proportional to the principal curvatures of the image surface. The following inferences can be made about pixel (x, y) based on the magnitudes of the eigenvalues:

- If both λ_1 and λ_2 are close to zero, then there are no features of interest at this pixel (x, y).
- If λ_1 is close to zero and λ_2 is a large positive value, then the pixel (x, y) belongs to an object edge.
- If both λ_1 and λ_2 are distinct and large positive values, then the pixel (x, y) belongs to an object corner.

The Harris operator uses the cornerness measure $C(x, y)$, which is obtained from elements of matrix A:

$$C(x,y) = \det(A) - k[\text{trace}(A)]^2 \tag{10.28}$$

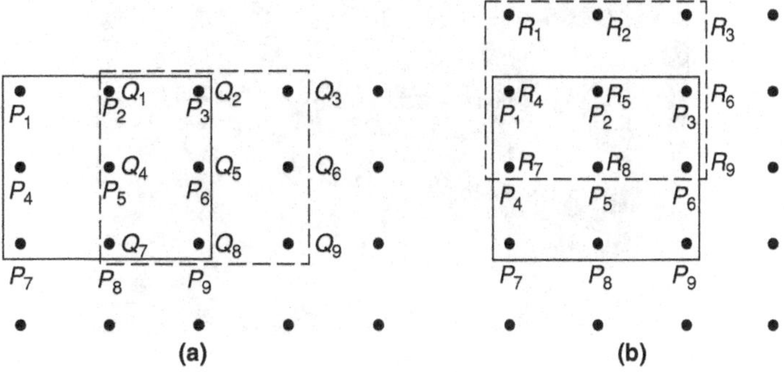

Figure 10.41: Approximate intensity variation calculation. (a) In horizontal direction. (b) In vertical direction.

where

$$\det(A) = \lambda_1\lambda_2 = V_{xx}V_{yy} - V_{xy}^2$$

$$\text{trace}(A) = \lambda_1 + \lambda_2 = V_{xx} + V_{yy}$$

and k = constant (for best results we choose k between 0.04 and 0.06). Now, thresholding the cornerness measure $C(x, y)$ using the appropriate threshold T provides image object corners.

Next, we discuss a simple procedure to compute approximate directional intensities V_{xx}, V_{yy}, and V_{xy}. We can obtain the approximate horizontal intensity variation V_{xx} using pixel P_is and Q_is placed with one pixel displacement as shown in Figure 10.41. The weighted horizontal intensity variation is obtained as in

$$V_{xx} = \sum_{i=1}^{9} w_i \frac{\partial I_i^2}{\partial x} \approx \sum_{i=1}^{9} w_i (P_i - Q_i)^2 = \sum_{i=1}^{9} w_i (Q_i - P_i)^2 \tag{10.29}$$

where w_i are coefficients of the 2D Gaussian filter,

$$w = \begin{bmatrix} w_1 & w_2 & w_3 \\ w_4 & w_5 & w_6 \\ w_7 & w_8 & w_9 \end{bmatrix} = \begin{bmatrix} 0.04 & 0.12 & 0.04 \\ 0.12 & 0.36 & 0.12 \\ 0.04 & 0.12 & 0.04 \end{bmatrix}$$

Similarly, the weighted vertical intensity variation V_{yy} is obtained with pixel P_is and R_is as shown in Figure 10.41(b):

$$V_{yy} = \sum_{i=1}^{9} w_i \frac{\partial I_i^2}{\partial y} \approx \sum_{i=1}^{9} w_i (P_i - R_i)^2 = \sum_{i=1}^{9} w_i (R_i - P_i)^2 \tag{10.30}$$

$$V_{xy} = \sum_{i=1}^{9} w_i \frac{\partial I_i}{\partial x} \frac{\partial I_i}{\partial y} \tag{10.31}$$

where

$$\frac{\partial I_i}{\partial x} \approx (P_i - Q_i), \ \frac{\partial I_i}{\partial y} \approx (P_i - R_i)$$

Consider these test images: Analog Devices Inc. logo, house and blocks, and tree leaves, as shown in Figure 10.42(a) through (c). The Harris-Plessey corner detection results for the test images are shown in Figure 10.43(a) through (c), respectively.

It is desirable for a corner detector to satisfy the following criteria: detection of all true corners, localization of corner points, robustness to noise, high repeatability rate, and computational efficiency. However, we do not have a single algorithm to satisfy all these requirements. Some algorithms are good at performance but computationally expensive and some are good at computational efficiency, but we may not obtain required performance. Corner detection algorithms such as CSS, Trajkovic and Hedley with 8 neighbors, and SUSAN provide both performance and computational efficiency.

(a)

(b)

(c)

Figure 10.42: Test images for corner detection. (a) Analog Devices Inc. logo. (b) House and blocks. (3) Tree leaves.

10.10 Hough Transform

The Hough transform is popularly known as a method for detecting lines and circles. The line and circle detection is used in many image processing applications such as detecting and tracking image objects of different shapes. In this section, we provide an overview of the Hough transform in line detection, its computational complexity, and a few efficient implementation methods for real-time applications.

We can generate a straight line easily using a few parameters. For example, we can generate a line with two points (x_1, y_1) and (x_2, y_2), or we can generate a line with one point (x_1, y_1) and slope m, or with polar coordinates using magnitude r and angle ϕ. However, given points in a 2D plane, it is a difficult task for computers to find whether they lie on a line. In 1962, Paul Hough suggested one way of modeling this problem in a systematic way. Using the Hough approach, we parameterize the straight line by mapping the line to a single point as shown in Figure 10.44. When we draw a perpendicular line from the origin to line $y = mx + c$, the perpendicular line makes a certain angle ϕ with the horizontal line and meets the given line at distance r from the origin. These two parameters are unique and no other line can have the perpendicular line with the same parameters. In this way, we map the points on a straight line in the x and y domain to a single point in the *magnitude* and *angle* domain. Now, any point (x, y) on the line L satisfies the following equation:

$$r = x\cos\phi + y\sin\phi \tag{10.32}$$

Given a particular point (x_1, y_1), there are an infinite number of lines (or their perpendicular lines with infinite lengths r and infinite angles ϕ) that pass through point (x_1, y_1). If this is the case, then how does one find (r, ϕ)

(a)

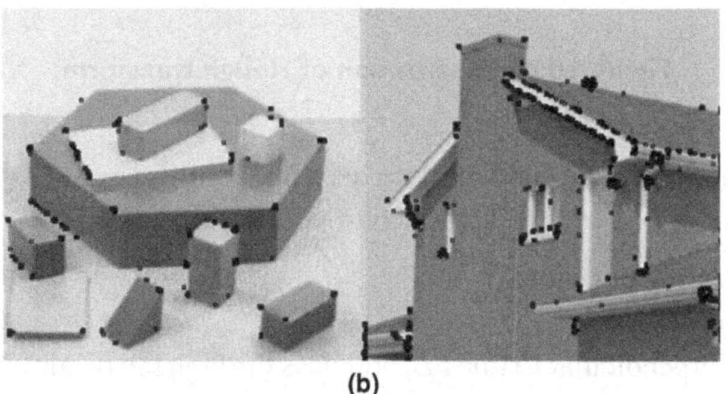

(b)

(c)

Figure 10.43: Harris-Plessey corner detection output results. (a) Analog Devices Inc. logo. (b) House and blocks. (3) Tree leaves.

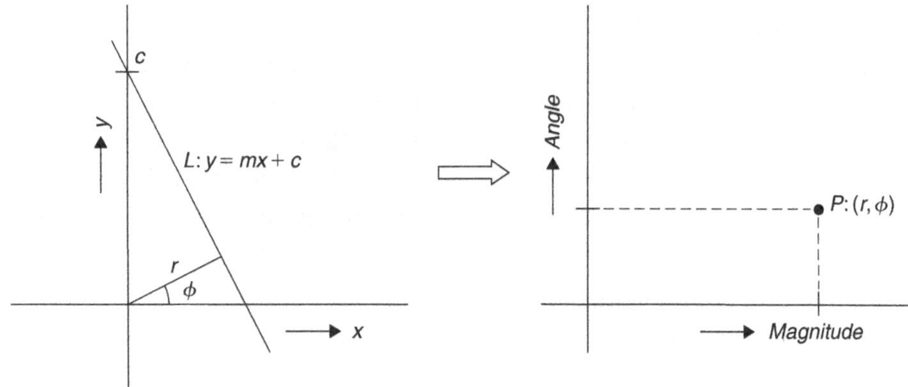

Figure 10.44: Hough approach of representing a line with a point.

that satisfies line L? One approach is to assume finite possibilities (e.g., a finite resolution image has finite pixels, and thus finite amplitudes and finite angles) and find (r, ϕ) for only those finite possibilities. We map all given points (x_i, y_i) to (r_i, ϕ_i), and in this process all points $\left(x_i^{(L)}, y_i^{(L)}\right)$ that belong to line L map to a single point (r_L, ϕ_L). This is illustrated in Figure 10.45. We mapped a given $N_L = 30$ points of line L to the (r, ϕ) plane;

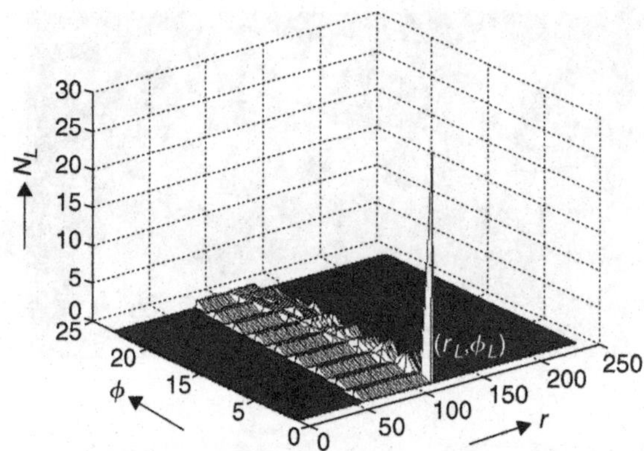

Figure 10.45: Illustration of Hough transform.

we see a maximum of accumulated points at one place and that point is (r_L, ϕ_L). But still, how can we identify these finite points (r_i, ϕ_i) given (x_i, y_i)? One approach to find (r_i, ϕ_i) follows:

1. Identify all lines L_i passing through (x_i, y_i).
2. Compute the slopes m_i of L_i.
3. Find lines Z_i that are perpendicular to lines L_i and pass through the origin. As the slopes of perpendicular lines are given by $(-1/m_i)$, the equations for perpendicular lines are given by $y = (-1/m_i)x$.
4. Find the intersecting points of lines L_i and Z_i. Assume that both lines intersect at point (u_i, v_i).
5. Obtain the magnitude r_i as the distance between (0, 0) and (u_i, v_i) $r_i = \sqrt{u_i^2 + v_i^2}$.
6. Obtain the angle ϕ_i as $\phi_i = \tan^{-1}\left(-\frac{1}{m_i}\right) = \tan^{-1}\left(\frac{v_i}{u_i}\right)$.

Computational Complexity of Hough Transform

Even if we assume finite possibilities, the computations involved in the Hough transform are very high when we want to detect lines in an $M \times N$-pixel–resolution image. Using the preceding approach, we require 40 to 50 fixed-point operations to compute one point (r_i, ϕ_i) from (x_i, y_i). For example, if we consider a QVGA image (i.e., 320×240 pixels), and assume that we quantize the angle to 360 finite angles, then we will have 360 points of (r_i, ϕ_i) for one point (x_i, y_i). In other words, the number of fixed-point operations present in computing the Hough transform for one QVGA image is about 1.4 billion ($= 50 \times 360 \times 320 \times 240$). Consequently, this is not a practical approach for detecting lines in an image.

Efficient Implementation of Hough Transform

As the edges obtained from an image contain line information, we can reduce the computations in the Hough transform drastically by working on binary images instead of grayscale images. There are fewer points (x_i, y_i) to work with in the case of binary images if we use a higher threshold level to obtain these images. Assume that we have 1000 points in the binary image; using the Hough transform, we require only 18 million ($= 50 \times 1000 \times 360$) operations. We can further reduce the complexity of the Hough transform by using the following techniques:

- Symmetry properties
- Look-up tables for cosine and sine values
- Embedded CORDIC algorithm

Hough Transform Using Look-up Tables

As the perpendicular lines with 180° phase difference can be distinguished with the sign information, we do not compute Hough transform for all 360°. Instead, we compute it for angles in the range (−90° to 90°] and use the sign information of r in Equation (10.32) to get all other angles. Instead of computing the angle and magnitude by using the multiple iteration CORDIC algorithm, we use look-up tables for storing the precomputed cosine and sine values in the range (−90° to 90°) and use them to compute the amplitude information r using Equation (10.32). In the look-up table method, we can compute a point (r_i, ϕ_i) using two multiplications and

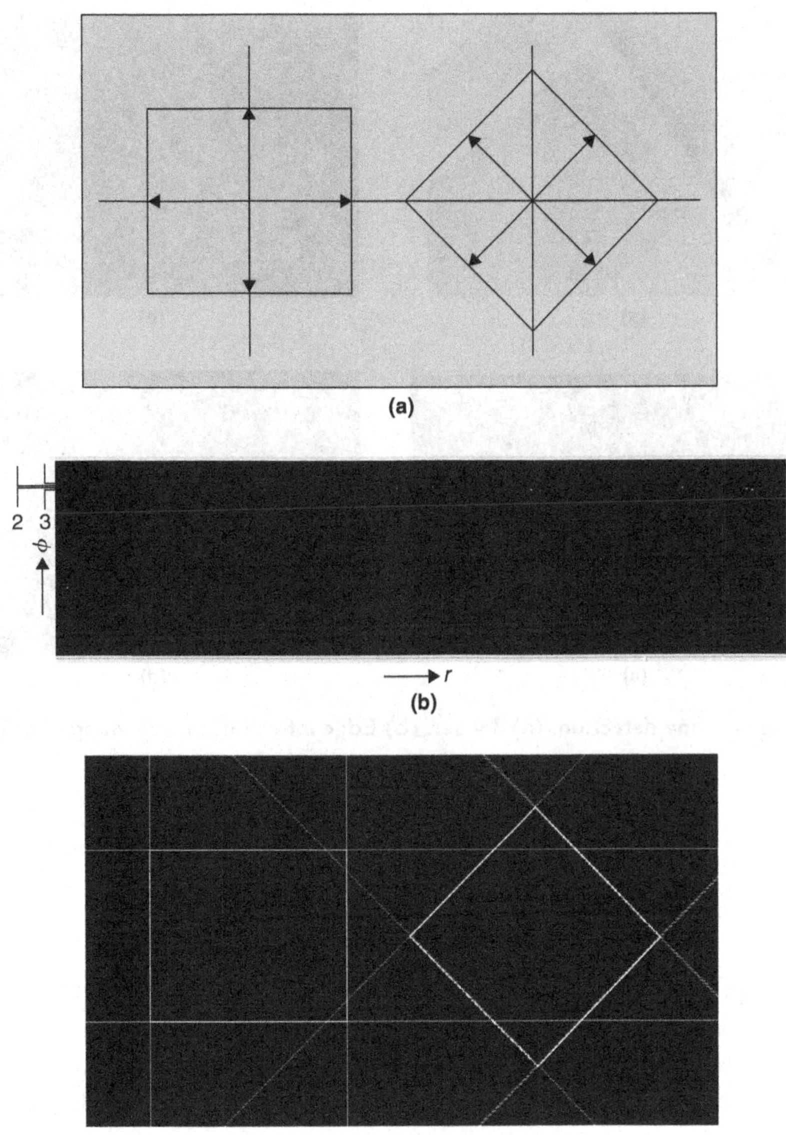

(a)

(b)

(c)

Figure 10.46: Line detection. (a) Synthetic image. (b) Mapped points. (c) Detected lines.

one addition. As we have two MAC units on the reference embedded processor, we consume 2 cycles per point being mapped. In other words, we consume about 0.36 million cycles for mapping all 1000 pixels of a binary image to parameter space $<r, \phi>$ with quantized angle ϕ_i resolution equal to 1°. The simulation results of line detection in synthetic and real images using the Hough transform is shown in Figures 10.46 and 10.47.

Circle and Ellipse Detection

The Hough transform concept can be extended to circle and ellipse detection as we can map circle and ellipse coordinates to the parameter space using the following equations.

For circle detection,

$$x = r\cos\phi, \quad y = r\sin\phi \tag{10.33}$$

In Equation (10.33), we fix the angle ϕ and compute the amplitude r as:

$$r = \frac{x+y}{\cos\phi + \sin\phi} \tag{10.34}$$

For ellipse detection,

$$x = a\cos\phi, \quad y = b\sin\phi \tag{10.35}$$

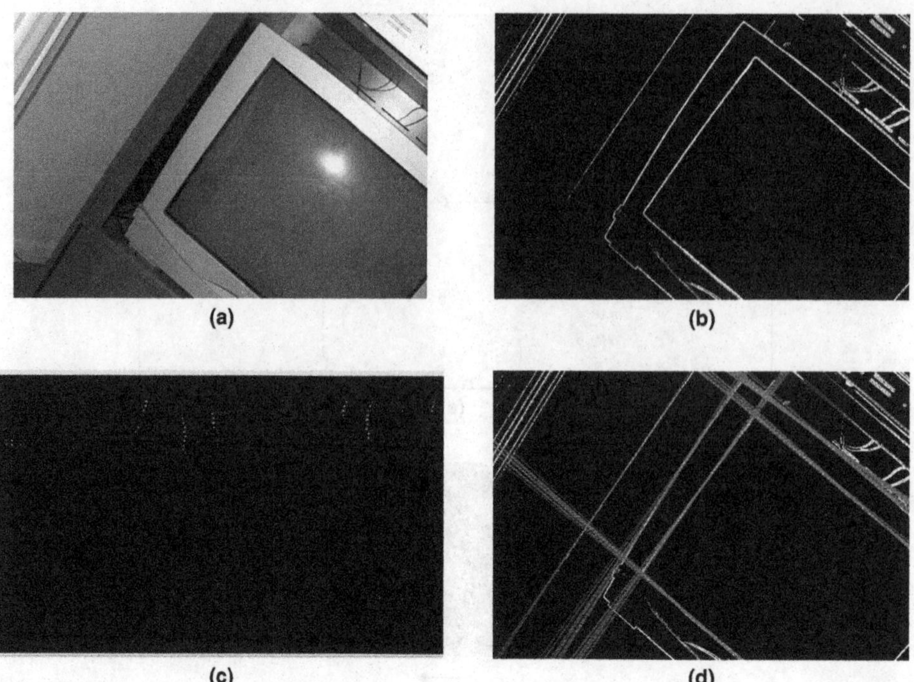

Figure 10.47: Real image for line detection. (a) TV set. (b) Edge information. (c) Mapped points after threshold. (d) Detected lines.

In Equation (10.35), we fix the angle ϕ and compute the amplitudes a and b as follows:

$$a = \frac{x}{\cos\phi}, \quad b = \frac{y}{\sin\phi} \tag{10.36}$$

We can implement both circle and ellipse detection efficiently using the look-up table method. In the case of circle detection, we map the point (x, y) coordinates to the parameter space $<r, \phi>$ using Equation (10.34) by precomputing the values $1/(\cos\phi + \sin\phi)$, whereas in the case of ellipse detection, we map the point (x, y) coordinates to the parameter space $<a, b, \phi>$ using Equation (10.36) by precomputing the values $1/\cos\phi$ and $1/\sin\phi$.

10.11 Simulation of Image Processing Tools

We can represent any image format pixel values in two dimensions. We use YUV format in the simulations, as most of the image processing tools can be applied in the YUV format. The simulation code for reading/writing the $M \times N$ resolution YUV 4:2:0 image from/to memory is given in Pcode 10.1. In C, *fread* or *fwrite* commands are more efficient when we read/write a large number of bytes and read/write full-image pixels instead of one row or column at a time. In real-time applications, we use the DMA for moving the image data to/from memory.

10.11.1 Color Conversion

Images are typically processed in the YUV domain. But display systems require the RGB format to output to the screen. For this, we must convert YUV to RGB using Equation (10.4). The fixed-point simulation code for converting YUV to RGB and RGB to YUV is given in Pcodes 10.2 and 10.3, respectively. In the case of YUV to RGB, the coefficients are represented in 3.13 fixed-point format, whereas in the case of RGB to YUV the coefficients are represented in 1.15 fixed-point format due to the different dynamic range of the coefficients. Fixed-point values follow.

YUV to RGB:

9535 (3.13 format of 1.164), 13074 (3.13 format of 1.596), 6660 (3.13 format of 0.813),
2613 (3.13 format of 0.391) and 16531 (3.13 format of 2.018).

```
// reading image A from memory
if (!(fp1 = fopen("image_a.yuv","rb"))){
   return(-1);
}
fread(hBufY,1,M*N,fp1); /* Y */
fread(BufU,1,M*N/4,fp1); /* Cb */
fread(BufV,1,M*N/4,fp1); /* Cr */
fclose (fp1);
// writing image B to memory
if (!(fp2 = fopen("image_b.yuv","wb"))){
   return(-1);
}
fwrite(hBufY,1,M*N,fp2); /* Y */
fwrite(BufU,1,M*N/4,fp2); /* Cb */
fwrite(BufV,1,M*N/4,fp2); /* Cr */
fclose (fp2);
```

Pcode 10.1: Simulation code for reading/writing images.

```
//void yuv2rgb()
//R = (Y-16)*1.164 + (V-128)*1.596;
//G = (Y-16)*1.164 - (V-128)*0.813 - (U-128)*0.391;
//B = (Y-16)*1.164 + (U-128)*2.018;

for(j = 0;j < M;j++)
       for(i = 0;i < N;i++){
               p = j*N+i; q = (j/2)*N+i/2;
               x0 = BufY[p]-16; y0 = BufV[q]-128;
               u = (9535*x0) >> 13; v = (13074*y0) >> 13;
               u = u + v;
               if (u < 0) u = 0;
               if (u > 255) u = 255;
               BufR[p] = (unsigned char) u;
               u = (9535*x0) >> 13; v = (6660 * y0) >> 13;
               y0 = BufU[q]-128;
               u = u - v; v = (2613 * y0) >> 13;
               u = u - v;
               f (u < 0) u = 0;
               if (u > 255) u = 255;
               BufG[p] = (unsigned char) u;
               u = (9535*x0) >> 13; v = (16531*y0) >> 13;
               u = u + v;
               if (u < 0) u = 0;
               if (u > 255) u = 255;
               BufB[j*N+i] = (unsigned char) u;
       }
}
```

Pcode 10.2: Fixed-point simulation code to convert from YUV to RGB.

RGB to YUV:

8421 (1.15 format of 0.257), 16515 (1.15 format of 0.504), 3211 (1.15 format of 0.098), 4850 (1.15 format of 0.148), 9535 (1.15 format of 0.291), 14385 (1.15 format of 0.439), 12059 (1.15 format of 0.368) and 2327 (1.15 format of 0.071)

10.11.2 Color, Brightness, and Contrast Correction

Histogram equalization is performed in the RGB domain to enhance colors. It also adjusts brightness and contrast in the YUV domain. The histograms are generated for each color component, and equalization is performed as shown in Figure 10.1. We can also apply this histogram equalization technique in the YUV domain to enhance brightness and contrast of images. In histogram equalization, we perform the following steps:

1. Obtain the histogram
2. Find minimum and maximum pixel values

```
//void rgb2yuv()
//Y = R*0.257 + G*0.504 + B*0.098 + 16
//U = -R*0.148 - G*0.291 + B*0.439 + 128
//V = R*0.439 - G*0.368 - B*0.071 + 128

for(j = 0;j < M;j++){
    p = j*N; q = (j+1)*N;
    for(i = p;i < q;i++){
        r = BufR[i]; g = BufG[i]; b = BufB[i];
        x0 = (8421 * r) >> 15; y0 = (16515 * g) >> 15;
        x0 = x0 + y0 + 16; y0 = (3211 * b) >> 15;
        x0 = x0 + y0;
        if (x0 < 0) x0 = 0;
        if (x0 > 255) x0 = 255;
        BufY[i] = x0;
    }
}
for(j = 0;j < M/2;j++){
    for(i = 0;i < N/2;i++){
        p = (j << 1)*N+(i << 1);
        q = j*(N >> 1)+i;
        r = BufR[p]; g = BufG[p]; b = BufB[p];
        x0 = (14385 * b) >> 15; y0 = (9535 * g) >> 15;
        x0 = x0 - y0 + 128; y0 = (4850 * r) >> 15;
        x0 = x0 - y0;
        if (x0 < 0) x0 = 0;
        if (x0 > 255) x0 = 255;
        BufU[q] = x0;

        x0 = (14385 * r) >> 15; y0 = (12059 * g) >> 15;
        x0 = x0 - y0 + 128; y0 = (2327 * r) >> 15;
        x0 = x0 - y0;
        if (x0 < 0) x0 = 0;
        if (x0 > 255) x0 = 255;
        BufV[q] = x0;
    }
}
```

Pcode 10.3: Fixed-point simulation code for RGB to YUV conversion.

3. Subtract all pixels from the minimum
4. Find the ratio $r = 255/(\text{maximum-minimum})$
5. Multiply all pixels with factor r

The simulation code for red color correction is given in Pcode 10.4, and for brightness and contrast enhancement, in Pcode 10.5.

10.11.3 Edges Enhancement

We enhance the edges by augmenting high-frequency components of the image. We compute the high-frequency components using the Laplacian mask:

$$\begin{bmatrix} 0 & -1 & 0 \\ -1 & 4 & -1 \\ 0 & -1 & 0 \end{bmatrix}$$

Whenever we apply a mask (to filter, to find edges, etc.), we handle boundaries by appropriately filtering, skipping, or copying them, depending on the operation. In Pcode 10.6, since we do not have much information to find the frequencies at the boundaries, we just copy the pixel values to the destination folder without augmenting the frequencies. For the rest of the pixels, we first compute high-frequency components and add them to actual pixels before storing to memory.

```
// Red color enhancement

for(j = 0;j < M;j++){
          p = j*N; q = (j+1)*N;
          for(i = p;i < q;i++)
                    Hist[BufR[i]]+= 1;
}
y0 = 0;
for(p = 0;p < 255;p++) {
          y0+= Hist[p];
          if (y0 > 25) break;
}
x = 0;
for(j = 0;j < M;j++){
          p = j*N; q = (j+1)*N;
          for(i = p;i < q;i++) {
              x0 = (int) BufR[i] - p;
              if (x0 < 0) x0 = 0;
              if (x0 > 255) x0 = 255;
              BufR[i] = x0;
          }
}
for(j = 254;j > 0;j--)
          if (Hist[j] > 0) break;
              x = (float) 255.0/(255-p + 254-j);
for(j = 0;j < M;j++){
          p = j*N; q = (j+1)*N;
          for(i = p;i < q;i++)
                    BufR[i] = (unsigned char) ((float) BufR[i]*x + 0.5);
}
```

Pcode 10.4: Simulation code for red color enhancement.

```
// Brightness and contrast enhancement

for(j = 0;j < M;j++){
          p = j*N; q = (j+1)*N;
          for(i = p;i < q;i++)
                    Hist[BufY[i]]+= 1;
}
y0 = 0;
for(p = 0;p < 255;p++) {
          y0+= Hist[p];
          if (y0 > 25) break;
}
x = 0;
for(j = 0;j < M;j++){
      p = j*N; q = (j+1)*N;
      for(i = p;i < q;i++) {
          x0 = (int) BufY[i] - p;
          if (x0 < 0) x0 = 0;
          if (x0 > 255) x0 = 255;
          BufY[i] = x0;
      }
}
for(j = 254;j > 0;j--)
          if (Hist[j] > 0) break;
              x = (float) 255.0/(255-p + 254 - j);
for(j = 0;j < M;j++){
          p = j*N; q = (j+1)*N;
          for(i = p;i < q;i++)
              BufY[i] = (unsigned char) ((float) BufY[i]*x + 0.5);
}
```

Pcode 10.5: Simulation code for brightness and contrast enhancement.

```
// edges enhancement
for(j = 0;j < 1;j++) { // copy top row
        p = j*N; q = (j+1)*N;
        for(i = p;i < q;i++)
                BufX[i] = BufY[i];
}
 for(j = 0;j < M;j++) { // copy left column
        p = j*N;
        BufX[p] = BufY[p];
}
for(j = 1;j < M-1;j++) {
    p = j*N+1; q = (j+1)*N-1;
    for(i = p;i < q;i++) {
          x0 = BufY[i];         y0 = BufY[i-1];
          x0 = x0 << 2;
          x0 = x0 - y0;         y0 = BufY[i+1];
          x0 = x0 - y0;         y0 = BufY[i-N-1];
          x0 = x0 - y0;         y0 = BufY[i+N+1];
          x0 = x0 - y0;
          x0 = (int) BufY[i] + (int) x*0.3;
          if (x0 < 0) x0 = 0;
          if (x0 > 255) x0 = 255;
          BufX[i] = (unsigned char) x0;
    }
}
for(j = 0;j < M;j++){
        p = j*N; q = (j+1)*N;
        for(i = p;i < q;i++)
            BufY[i] = BufX[i];
}
```

Pcode 10.6: Simulation code for edge enhancement.

10.11.4 Image Filtering

In this section, we simulate both the 3×3 Gaussian filter and 3×3 median filter for smoothing images. The general form of the 3×3 Gaussian filter mask is

$$\frac{1}{K}\begin{bmatrix} a & b & a \\ b & c & b \\ a & b & a \end{bmatrix}$$

where $K = 4a + 4b + c$. We precompute the value of $G = 1/K$ and represent G in 1.15 format. The simulation code for the 3×3 Gaussian filter is given in Pcode 10.7.

```
for(j = 1;j < M-1;j++){
    p = j*N+1; q = (j+1)*N-1;
    for(i = p;i < q;i++){
        x0 = BufY[i] * c;
        y0 = BufY[i-N-2] + BufY[i-N] + BufY[i+N] + BufY[i+N+2];
        y0 = y0 * a;
        x0 = x0 + y0;
        y0 = BufY[i-1] + BufY[i+1] + BufY[i-N-1] + [i+N+1];
        y0 = y0 * b;
        x0 = x0 + y0;
        x0 = (x0 * G) >> 15;
        BufX[i] = (unsigned char) x0;
    }
}
```

Pcode 10.7: Simulation code for 3×3 Gaussian filter.

In the case of the 3×3 median filter, we compute the median of nine pixels present in the 3×3 mask by sorting the pixels in ascending or descending order. The simulation code for the 3×3 median filter is given in Pcode 10.8. See Section 15.2 for efficient implementation of the 3×3 median filter.

```
for(j = 1;j < M-1;j++) {
    p = j*N+1; q = (j+1)*N-1;
    for(i = p;i < q;i++) {
        MedE[0] = BufY[i-N-2]; MedE[1] = BufY[i-N-1]; MedE[2] = BufY[i-N];
        MedE[3] = BufY[i-1]; MedE[4] = BufY[i]; MedE[5] = BufY[i+1];
        MedE[6] = BufY[i+N]; MedE[7] = BufY[i+N+1]; MedE[8] = BufY[i+N+2];
           for(r = 0;r < 9;r++) {
              x0 = MedE[0]; n = 0;
              for(m = 1;m < 9;m++)
                  if (x0 < MedE[m]) {
                      x0 = MedE[m]; n = m;
                      }
                      MedF[r] = MedE[n];
                      MedE[n] = 0;
           }
        BufX[i] = MedF[4];
    }
}
```

Pcode 10.8: Simulation code for 3 × 3 median filter (bubble sort approach).

10.11.5 Edge Detection

Edge detection based on the Sobel or Laplacian operator is a simple algorithm and involves only gradient magnitude computation. The simulation code for the Sobel and Laplacian edge detectors is given in Pcodes 10.9 and 10.10, respectively.

In contrast, the Canny edge detector is a more complex multistep algorithm. It involves image smoothing, gradient magnitude and angle computation, nonmaximum suppression, and hysteresis thresholding. We use a

```
for(j = 1;j < M-1;j++){
          p = j*N+1; q = (j+1)*N-1;
          for(i = p;i < q;i++){
                x0 = BufY[i-N] + (BufY[i+1] << 1) + BufY[i+N+2] -
                             (BufY[i-N-2] + (BufY[i-1] << 1) + BufY[i+N] );
                y0 = BufY[i-N-2] + (BufY[i-N-1] << 1) + BufY[i-N] -
                             (BufY[i+N] + (BufY[i+N+1] << 1) + BufY[i+N+2]);
                x0 = abs(x0); y0 = abs(y0);
                grad = x0 > y0 ? x0 : y0;                // approximate gradient computation
                if (grad > 255) grad = 255;
                BufX[i] = (unsigned char) grad;
          }
}
for(j = 0;j < M;j++){
          p = j*N; q = (j+1)*N;
          for(i = p;i < q;i++) {
              BufY[i] = BufX[i] > 128 ? 255 : 0;          // thresholding
```

Pcode 10.9: Simulation code for Sobel edge detector.

```
for(j = 1;j < M-1;j++){
    p = j*N+1; q = (j+1)*N-1;
    for(i = 1;i < N-1;i++){
          x0 = BufY[i-N-1] + BufY[i-1] + BufY[i+N+1] + BufY[i+1];
          y0 = (BufY[i] << 2); x0 = x0 - y0;
          if (x0 < 0) x0 = 0;
          if (x0 > 255) x0 = 255;
          BufX[i] = x0;
    }
}
for(j = 0;j < M;j++){
          p = j*N; q = (j+1)*N
          for(i = p;i < q;i++)
              BufY[i] = BufX[i] > 32 ? 255 : 0
}
```

Pcode 10.10: Similation code for Laplacian edge detector.

```
for(j = 2;j < M-2;j++){
        p = (j-2)*N; q = (j-1)*N; r = j*N;
        s = (j+1)*N; t = (j+2)*N;
        for(i = 2;i < N-2;i++){
                y0 = (BufY[p+i-2] + BufY[p+i+2] + BufY[t+i-2] + BufY[t+i+2]) << 2;
                x0 = (BufY[p+i-1] + BufY[p+i+1] + BufY[t+i-1] + BufY[t+i+1] + BufY[q+i-2] +
                    BufY[q+i+2] + BufY[s+i-2] + BufY[s+i+2]);
                y0 = y0 + (x0 << 2) + (x0 << 1);
                x0 = BufY[p+i] + BufY[r+i+2] + BufY[r+i-2] + BufY[t+i];
                y0 = y0 + (x0 << 3) - x0;
                x0 = BufY[q+i-1] + BufY[q+i+1] + BufY[s+i-1] + BufY[s+i+1];
                y0 = y0 + (x0 << 3) + x0;
                x0 = BufY[q+i] + BufY[r+i+1] + BufY[r+i-1] + BufY[s+i];
                y0 = y0 + (x0 << 3) + (x0 << 2) - x0;
                y0 = y0 + BufY[r+i]*12;
                x0 = (y0*G) >> 15;          // G = 1.15 format of 1/184
                if (x0 > 255) x0 = 255;
                BufX[r+i] = (unsigned char) x0;
        }
}
```

Pcode 10.11: Simulation code for image smoothing using 5 × 5 Gaussian filter.

5 × 5 Gaussian filter to smooth the images. The simulation code for smoothing images using the 5 × 5 Gaussian filter is given in Pcode 10.11. We compute the x-gradient (G_x) and y-gradient (G_y) using Sobel operators after smoothing the image. Once we know the values of G_x and G_y, we compute both pixel gradient magnitude and angle using the CORDIC algorithm or any other methods to compute the gradient and angle. We can get an approximate value of magnitude and quantized angle in four iterations of the CORDIC algorithm. Here we compute the gradient and angle separately using simple methods. We use the same approach as in Pcode 10.9 to get the magnitude. The quantized angle is obtained by using the look-up table method as given in Pcode 10.12. The values of the look-up table **edge_orientations**[ ] used in quantized gradient-angle computation follow.

```
edge_orientations[32] = {
0, 0, 90, 0, 45, 0, 0, 0, 0, 0, 90, 0, 135, 0, 0, 0,
0, 0, 90, 0, 135,0, 0, 0, 0, 0, 90, 0, 45, 0, 0, 0};
```

Simulation code for nonmaximum suppression and hysteresis thresholding is given in Pcodes 10.13 and 10.14, respectively.

```
x0 = abs(Gx); y0 = abs(Gy);
a = (g * x0) >> 13;         // g is 3.13 format of 0.4
b = (h * x0) >> 13;         // h is 3.13 format of 2.4
i = 0;
if (Gy < 0) i = 1;
i = i << 1;
if (Gx < 0) i |= 1;
i = i << 1;
if ((y0 > a) && (y0 <= b)) i |= 1;
i = i << 1;
if (y0 > b) i |= 1;
i = i << 1;
if (y0 <= a) i |= 1;
angle = edge_orientations[i];
```

Pcode 10.12: Simulation code for computing quantized angle.

10.11.6 Image Scaling

In this section, we present the simulation code for nearest-neighbor and the bilinear interpolation. See Section 15.1 for simulations of advanced interpolation methods. The simulation code for the nearest-neighbor

```
for(j = 0;j < M;j++){
          p = j*N; q = (j+1)*N;
          for(i = p;i < q;i++)
          BufX[i] = BufY[i];
}
for(j = 0;j < M;j++){
    p = j*N; q = (j+1)*N;
    for (i = 0;i < N;i++){
      if (BufY[i] != 0){
             if (dirc[i] == 0){
                    if ((BufY[i] < BufY[i-1]) || (BufY[i] < BufY[i+1]))
                  BufX[i] = 0;
             }
             else if (dirc[i] == 45){
                    if ((BufY[i] < BufY[i+N]) || (BufY[i] < BufY[i-N]))
                BufX[i] = 0;
             }
             else if (dirc[i] == 90){
                    if ((BufY[i] < BufY[i-N-1]) || (BufY[i] < BufY[i+N+1]))
                BufX[i] = 0;
             }
             else if (dirc[i] == 135){
                    if ((BufY[i] < BufY[i-N-2]) || (BufY[i] < BufY[i+N+2]))
                BufX[i] = 0;
             }
      }
    }
}
for(j = 0;j < M;j++){
          p = j*N; q = (j+1)*N;
          for(i = p;i < q;i++)
          BufY[i] = BufX[i];
}
```

Pcode 10.13: Simulation code for nonmaximum suppression.

```
// apply thresholds
t1 = 16;                                    // minimum threshold
t2 = 64;                                    // maximum threshold
for(j = 0;j < M;j++) {
    p = j*N; q = (j+1)*N;
    for(i = p;i < q;i++){
        if (BufY[i] > t2)
            BufY[i] = 255;
        else if ((BufY[i] < t2) && (BufY[i] > t1))
                BufY[i] = 128;
        else
                BufY[i] = 0;
    }
}
f = 1;
while (f){
        f = 0;
        for (j = 0;j < M;j++){
                   p = j*N; q = (j+1)*N;
                   for(i = p;i < q;i++){
                             if (BufY[i] > 0){
                                      if(BufY[i] == 128){
                                               if ((BufY[i-1] == 255) && (BufY[i+1] == 255) &&
(BufY[i-N-1] == 255) && (BufY[i+N+1] == 255) && (BufY[i-N-2] == 255) && (BufY[i+N]== 255) &&
(BufY[i+N] == 255) && (BufY[i+N+2] == 255)){
                               BufY[i] = 255;
                               f = 1;
                      }
                 }
            }
        }
    }
}
for(j = 0;j < M;j++){
          p = j*N; q = (j+1)*N;
          for(i = p;i < q;i++)
    if (BufY[i] == 128)
        BufY[i] = 0;
}
```

Pcode 10.14: Simulation code for hysteresis thresholding.

interpolation method in order to double the image size in both horizontal and vertical directions is given in Pcode 10.15.

```
for(j = 0;j < 2*M;j+=2){        // luma component scaling
    p = j*2*N; q = (j+1)*2*N; r = (j >> 1)*N;
    for(i = 0;i < 2*N;i+ = 2){
        BufX[p+i] = BufY[r+(i >> 1)];
        BufX[p+i+1] = BufY[r+(i >> 1)];
        BufX[q+i] = BufY[r+(i >> 1)];
        BufX[q+i+1] = BufY[r+(i >> 1)];
    }
}
for(j = 0;j < M;j+=2){         // chroma component scaling
    p = j*N; q = (j+1)*N; r = (j >> 1)*(N >> 1);
    for(i = 0;i < N;i+ = 2){
        BufA[p+i] = BufU[r+(i >> 1)];
        BufA[p+i+1] = BufU[r+(i >> 1)];
        BufA[q+i] = BufU[r+(i >> 1)];
        BufA[q+i+1] = BufU[r+(i >> 1)];
    }
    for(i = 0;i < N;i+ = 2){
        BufB[p+i] = BufV[r+(i >> 1)];
        BufB[p+i+1] = BufV[r+(i >> 1)];
        BufB[q+i] = BufV[r+(i >> 1)];
        BufB[q+i+1] = BufV[r+(i >> 1)];
    }
}
```

Pcode 10.15: Nearest-neighbor interpolation to double the image size both in horizontal and vertical direction.

We must also determine the pixel index offsets for the source image (i.e., which pixels participate in the interpolation to get the current pixel in the output image) with arbitrary scaling of images. Computation of index offset values on the fly for every pixel of original and scaled images is a time-consuming process. Instead, we use a look-up table to hold the index offset values. We can scale the image by scaling all rows followed by all columns or vice versa. In this process, if we know index offsets for one row or one column, then we can use the same index offsets for all other rows or columns. Given the interpolation method and scaling ratio, we can compute the look-up table values. For example, the computed index offset values for nearest-neighbor interpolation with a scaling ratio of 3:2 and for the bilinear interpolation method with a scaling ratio of 5:4 is shown in Figures 10.48 and 10.49, respectively.

When using circular buffering, storing the index values for one interval period is sufficient. We access appropriate offsets by configuring the circular index register parameters. The simulation code for nearest-neighbor interpolation to arbitrarily scale the luma component of the image is given in Pcode 10.16.

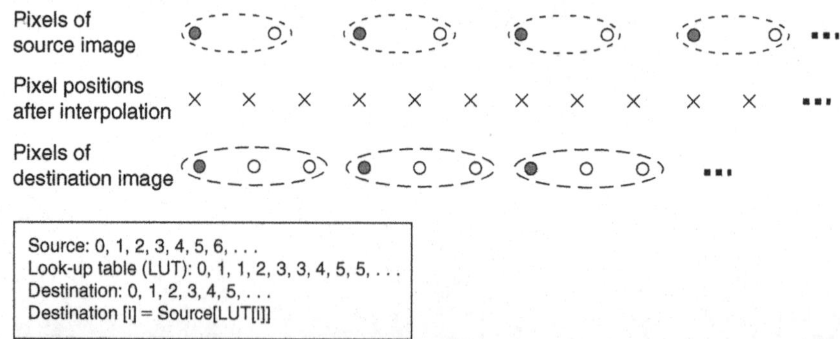

Figure 10.48: Illustration of source and destination pixel placement for scaling ratio of 3:2 (i.e., generate three pixels from given two pixels) using nearest-neighbor approach.

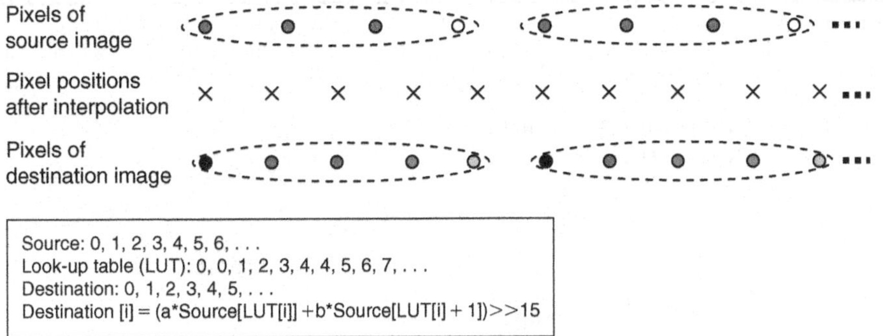

Figure 10.49: Illustration of source and destination pixel placement for scaling ratio of 5:4 (i.e., generate five pixels from given four pixels) using bilinear interpolator approach.

```
for(j = 0;j < M;j++){                  // luma component horizontal scaling
         p = j*K; q = (j+1)*K;         // K = (N/rH), rH: horizontal scaling ratio
         t = 0;
         for(i = p;i < q;i++)
                  BufX[i] = BufY[HLUT[t++]];
}
for(i = 0;i < K;i++)
         for(j = 0;j < R;j++)          // R = (M/rV), rV: vertical scaling ratio
             BufY[j*K+i] = BufX[VLUT[j]*K+i];
```

Pcode 10.16: Nearest-neighbor interpolation to scale the luminance component of image with arbitrary scaling ratios in both horizontal and vertical directions.

```
for(j = 0;j < 2*M;j+= 2){
    p = j*(N << 1); q = (j+1)*(N << 1);
    r = (j >> 1)*N; s = ((j >> 1)+1)*N;
    for(i = 0;i < 2*N;i+= 2){
        BufX[p+i] = BufY[r+(i >> 1)];
        BufX[p+i+1] = (BufY[r+(i >> 1)]+BufY[r+(i >> 1)+1]) >> 1;
        BufX[q+i] = (BufY[r+(i >> 1)]+BufY[s+(i >> 1)]) >> 1;
        BufX[q+i+1] = (BufY[r+(i >> 1)]+BufY[r+(i >> 1)+1]+
                      BufY[s+(i >> 1)]+BufY[s+(i >> 1)+1]) >> 2;
    }
}
for(j = 0;j < M;j+=2){
    p = j*N; q = (j+1)*N;
    r = (j >> 1)*(N >> 1); s = ((j >> 1)+1)*(N >> 1);
    for(i = 0;i < N;i+= 2){
        BufA[p+i] = BufU[r+(i >> 1)];
        BufA[p+i+1] = (BufU[r+(i >> 1)]+BufU[r+(i >> 1)+1]) >> 1;
        BufA[q+i] = (BufU[r+(i >> 1)]+BufU[s+(i >> 1)]) >> 1;
        BufA[q+i+1] = (BufU[r+(i >> 1)]+BufU[r+(i >> 1)+1]+
                      BufU[s+(i >> 1)]+BufU[s+(i >> 1)+1]) >> 2;
                      BufB[p+i] = BufV[r+(i >> 1)];
        BufB[p+i+1] = (BufV[r+(i >> 1)]+BufV[r+(i >> 1)+1]) >> 1;
        BufB[q+i] = (BufV[r+(i >> 1)]+BufV[s+(i >> 1)]) >> 1;
        BufB[q+i+1] = (BufV[r+(i >> 1)]+BufV[r+(i >> 1)+1]+
                      BufV[s+(i >> 1)]+BufV[s+(i >> 1)+1]) >> 2;
    }
}
```

Pcode 10.17: Simulation code to double the size of image using bilinear interpolation method.

Simulation code to double the image size and to arbitrarily scale the luminance component of an image using bilinear interpolation is given in Pcodes 10.17 and 10.18. Before calling this module, we should generate the look-up table with index offsets in both horizontal and vertical directions.

```
for(j = 0;j < M;j++){                          // luma component horizontal scaling
    p = j*K; q = (j+1)*K;                      // K = (N/rH), rH: horizontal scaling ratio
    t = 0;
    for(i = p;i < q;i++) {
        r = HLUT[t++];  a = HLUT0[j]; b = HLUT1[j];
        BufX[i] = (a*BufY[r] + b*BufY[r+1]) >> 15;
    }
}
for(i = 0;i < K;i++)
    for(j = 0;j < R;j++) {                     // R = (M/rV), rV: vertical scaling ratio
        r = VLUT[j];  a = VLUT0[j]; b = VLUT1[j];
        BufY[j*K+i] = (a*BufX[r*K+i] + b*BufX[(r+1)*K+i]) >> 15;
    }
```

Pcode 10.18: Bilinear interpolation to scale the luminance component of image with arbitrary scaling ratios in both horizontal and vertical directions.

10.11.7 Dilation and Erosion

Dilation and erosion operations are performed based on rules specified for grayscale and binary images. The dilation-operation simulation code for grayscale and binary images is given in Pcode 10.19, and the simulation code for erosion applied to grayscale and binary images is given in Pcode 10.20.

```
if (binary_image) {
        for(j = 1;j < M-1;j++) {
                p = j*N+1; q = (j+1)*N;
                for(i = p;i < q;i++){
                        if (BufY[i] == 0){
                                x0 = BufY[i-N-2] + BufY[i-1] + BufY[i+N] + BufY[i+N+1] +
                                        BufY[i+N+2] + BufY[i+1] + BufY[i-N] +
                                        BufY[i-N-1];
                                if (x0 > 0)
                                        BufX[i] = 255;
                        }
                }
        }
}
else {
        for(j = 1;j < M-1;j++){
                p = j*N+1; q = (j + 1)*N;
                for(i = p;i < q;i++){
                        x0 = BufY[i]; y0 = BufY[i-N-2];
                        if (x0 > y0) x0 = y0;
                        y0 = BufY[i-1];
                        if (x0 > y0) x0 = y0;
                        y0 = BufY[i+N];
                        if (x0 > y0) x0 = y0;
                        y0 = BufY[i-N-1];
                        if (x0 > y0) x0 = y0;
                        y0 = BufY[i+N+1];
                        if (x0 > y0) x0 = y0;
                        y0 = BufY[i-N];
                        if (x0 > y0) x0 = y0;
                        y0 = BufY[i+1];
                        if (x0 > y0) x0 = y0;
                        y0 = BufY[i+N+2];
                        if (x0 > y0) x0 = y0;
                        BufX[i] = x0;
                }
        }
}
```

Pcode 10.19: Simulation code for dilation operation.

```
if (binary_image) {
   for(j = 1;j < M-1;j++) {
            p = j*N + 1; q = (j+1)*N;
            for(i = p;i < q;i++){
                     if (BufY[i] == 255){
                              x0 = BufY[i-N-2] + BufY[i-1] + BufY[i+N] + BufY[i+N+1] +
                                   BufY[i+N+2] + BufY[i+1] + BufY[i-N] + BufY[i-N-1];
                              if (x0 < 2040) // 8x255 -> 2040
                                       BufX[i] = 0;
                     }
            }
   }
}
else {
    for(j = 1;j < M-1;j++) {
             p = j*N+1; q = (j+1)*N;
             for(i = p;i < q;i++){
                      x0 = BufY[i]; y0 = BufY[i-N-2];
                      if (x0 < y0) x0 = y0;
                      y0 = BufY[i-1];
                      if (x0 < y0) x0 = y0;
                      y0 = BufY[i+N];
                      if (x0 < y0) x0 = y0;
                      y0 = BufY[i-N-1];
                      if (x0 < y0) x0 = y0;
                      y0 = BufY[i+N+1];
                      if (x0 < y0) x0 = y0;
                      y0 = BufY[i-N];
                      if (x0 < y0) x0 = y0;
                      y0 = BufY[i+1];
                      if (x0 < y0) x0 = y0;
                      y0 = BufY[i+N+2];
                      if (x0 < y0) x0 = y0;
                      BufX[i] = x0;
             }
    }
}
```

Pcode 10.20: Simulation code for erosion operation.

10.11.8 Corner Detection

In this section, we simulate the Harris–Plassey operator to detect corners. For this, the cornerness measure $C(x, y)$ is obtained from elements of 2×2 matrix A. The elements of matrix A represent intensity variations of the image as discussed in Section 10.9.

$$A = \begin{bmatrix} V_{xx} & V_{xy} \\ V_{xy} & V_{yy} \end{bmatrix}$$

$$C(x, y) = \det(A) - k[\text{trace}(A)]^2$$

where

$$\det(A) = \lambda_1 \lambda_2 = V_{xx} V_{yy} - V_{xy}^2$$

$$\text{trace}(A) = \lambda_1 + \lambda_2 = V_{xx} + V_{yy}$$

and $k =$ constant (for best results we choose k between 0.04 and 0.06).

We obtain object corners after applying threshold T to the cornerness measure. The simulation code for detecting object corners using the Harris–Plassey operator is given in Pcode 10.21.

```
for(j = 2;j < M-2;j++)
    for(i = 2;i < N-2;i++){
        x0 = 0;
        for(p = 0;p < 3;p++)
            for(q = 0;q < 3;q++)
                x0 = x0 + (int) ((BufY[(j+p)*N+i+q] - BufY[(j+p)*N+i+q+1])*
                                         (BufY[(j+p)*N+i+q] -
                BufY[(j+p)*N+i+q+1])* w[p*3+q]);
                              BufA[j*N+i] = x0;
    }
for(j = 2;j < M-2;j++)
    for(i = 2;i < N-2;i++){
        x0 = 0;
        for(p = 0;p < 3;p++)
            for(q = 0;q < 3;q++)
                x0 = x0 + (int) ((BufY[(j+p)*N+i+q] - BufY[(j+p+1)*N+i+q])*
                (BufY[(j+p)*N+i+q] - BufY[(j+p+1)*N+i+q]) * w[p*3+q]);
                        BufB[j*N+i] = x0;
    }
for(j = 2;j < M-2;j++)
    for(i = 2;i < N-2;i++){
        x0 = 0;
        for(p = 0;p < 3;p++)
            for(q = 0;q < 3;q++)
                x0 = x0 + (int) (abs((BufY[(j+p)*N+i+q] -
                                           BufY[(j+p)*N+i+q+1])*(BufY[(j+p)*N+i+q]-
                BufY[(j+p+1)*N+i+q])) * w[p*3+q]);
                        BufC[j*N+i] = x0;
    }
for(j = 0;j < M;j++)
    for(i = 0;i < N;i++){
        x0 = BufA[j*N+i] * BufB[j*N+i] - (BufC[j*N+i]*BufC[j*N+i]);
        y0 = (BufA[j*N+i] + BufB[j*N+i])*(BufA[j*N+i] + BufB[j*N+i]);
        BufC[j*N+i] = x0 - 0.04*y0;
    }
for(j = 0;j < M;j++)
    for(i = 0;i < N;i++)
        BufD[j*N+i] = BufC[j*N+i] > T ? 255 : 0; // T: threshold
```

Pcode 10.21: Similation code of Harris/Plassey operator for corner detection.

10.11.9 Hough Transform

The Hough transform is efficiently implemented by using the look-up table method. In the look-up table method, we precompute look-up table values for $\cos\phi$ and $\sin\phi$ in the range $(-90, 90)$ and implement with two multiplications and one addition.

The simulation code for detecting the lines using the look-up table based Hough transform method is given in Pcode 10.22.

```
for(t = 0;t < 180;t++){
    for(j = 0;j < M;j++){
        p = j*N; q = t*3*K;
        for(i = 0;i < N;i++)
            if (BufY[p+i] != 0){
                  x0 = i-(N >> 1); y0 = j-(M >> 1);
                  r = (x0*cos_lut[t]) >> 15 +(y0*sin_lut[t]) >> 15;
                  r = r + K;
                  hBufY[q+r]+ = 1; // counting the mapped points
            }
    }
}
```

Pcode 10.22: Look-up table based Hough transform computation for line detection.

CHAPTER 11

Advanced Image Processing Algorithms

As discussed in Chapter 10, the pixels of a discrete image can be obtained by 2D sampling of the corresponding analog image captured by a camera sensor. The previous chapter focused on many basic image processing tools to perform image enhancement, edge detection, scaling, filtering, and so on, by processing images at their basic element level (i.e., at the pixel level). In this chapter, we discuss certain advanced image processing tools in detail, including image rotation, image stabilization, object detection, and image compression, based on the assumption that the digital image pixels are available in the appropriate format. In addition, we discuss C-simulation techniques for commonly used image processing algorithms.

11.1 Image Rotation

Real-time image rotation is a core operation in many applications such as medical image processing, computer vision (CV), and image registration. Many applications such as radiology and photographic analysis require very high-quality image rotation. In addition, high-throughput algorithms for image rotation are a common requirement in real-time image processing. Typically, we rotate images about their center as shown in Figure 11.1. The rotation of a 2D image about its Cartesian origin can be accomplished by moving each pixel of the source image to the destination image with the rotation of pixel position by angle ϕ. For example, the position (c, d) of pixel P in the destination image is computed from the position (a, b) of pixel P in the source image using the rotation angle ϕ.

The mathematical expressions for computing the pixel positions (c, d) in the rotated image can be obtained as follows: Let P be the pixel value of the 2D source image located at the position A: (a, b) shown in Figure 11.2. We can express location A: (a, b) using polar coordinates A: (r, θ), where $r = \sqrt{a^2+b^2}$ and $\theta = \tan^{-1}(b/a)$. Given polar coordinates (r, θ), we can obtain Cartesian coordinates (a, b) as in $a = r\cos\theta$ and $b = r\sin\theta$. Using a complex coordinate system, the position A can be expressed as

$$\begin{aligned} A &= a + jb \\ &= r\cos\theta + j\sin\theta \\ &= re^{j\theta} \end{aligned} \tag{11.1}$$

Let (c, d) denote a rotated pixel position C obtained after rotating pixel P at position A by an angle ϕ shown in Figure 11.2. As before, the position C can be expressed using a complex coordinate system:

$$\begin{aligned} C &= re^{j(\theta+\phi)} \\ &= r[\cos(\theta+\phi) + j\sin(\theta+\phi)] \\ &= r[\cos\theta\cos\phi - \sin\theta\sin\phi + j(\sin\theta\cos\phi + \cos\theta\sin\phi)] \end{aligned} \tag{11.2}$$

Equation (11.2) can be simplified using polar to Cartesian coordinate expressions $a = r\cos\theta$ and $b = r\sin\theta$:

$$\begin{aligned} C &= a\cos\phi - b\sin\phi + j(b\cos\phi + a\sin\phi) \\ &= c + jd \end{aligned} \tag{11.3}$$

DOI: 10.1016/B978-1-85617-678-1.00011-9

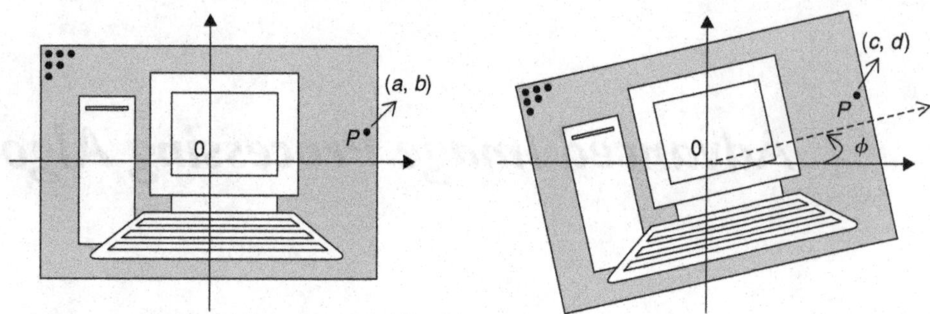

Figure 11.1: An illustration of synthetic image rotation by angle ϕ.

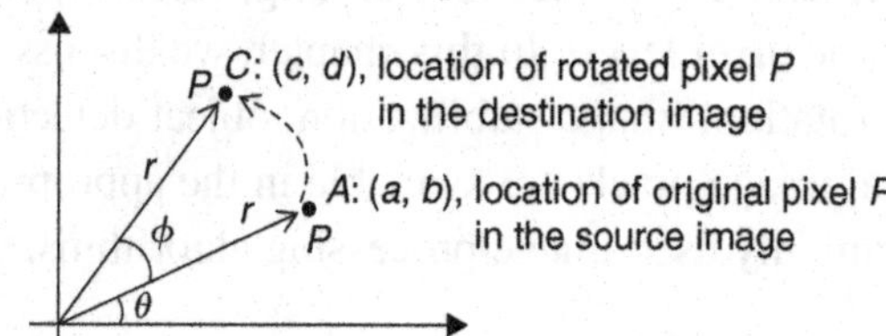

Figure 11.2: Rotation of pixel by angle ϕ.

where

$$c = a\cos\phi - b\sin\phi \tag{11.4}$$

$$d = a\sin\phi + b\cos\phi \tag{11.5}$$

The expressions in Equations (11.4) and (11.5) define the basic rotation transformation. Given the pixel position A: (a, b) and rotation angle ϕ, the rotated pixel position C: (c, d) can be obtained using compact matrix notations:

$$\begin{bmatrix} c \\ d \end{bmatrix} = \begin{bmatrix} \cos\phi & -\sin\phi \\ \sin\phi & \cos\phi \end{bmatrix} \begin{bmatrix} a \\ b \end{bmatrix} \tag{11.6}$$

We need not compute a full transformation for every pixel to obtain its rotated position. As we scan the pixels in raster scan order (i.e., reading row by row), at the start of the b-th row we compute the rotated pixel position $(c_0^{(b)}, d_0^{(b)})$ from the source pixel position (a, b), where a indicates the column position and b indicates the row position, using Equation (11.6). We then obtain the subsequent rotated position indices $(c_{n+1}^{(b)}, d_{n+1}^{(b)})$ by simply following an iterative procedure:

$$c_{n+1}^{(b)} = c_n^{(b)} + \cos\phi \tag{11.7}$$

$$d_{n+1}^{(b)} = d_n^{(b)} + \sin\phi \tag{11.8}$$

where

$$c_0^{(b)} = a\cos\phi - b\sin\phi \quad \text{and} \quad d_0^{(b)} = a\sin\phi + b\cos\phi.$$

In this chapter, we use a real test image shown in Figure 11.3 for examining various image rotation algorithms. This particular image was chosen as a test image because it consists of edges in various directions, and the rotation of image affects the edges of the various directions differently.

11.1.1 Issues in Image Rotation

Although we can rotate images using the simple expressions given in Equations (11.4) and (11.5) or using the equivalent matrix transformation given in Equation (11.6), obtaining a high-quality rotated image is challenging. If we simply move the pixel at position (a, b) in the source image to the pixel position (c, d) in the destination

Figure 11.3: Test image for rotation.

Figure 11.4: Image rotation showing holes in rotated image via forward mapping approach.

image using the preceding transformation, we may get the rotated image with many *holes* on the 2D sampled grid due to discontinuity of indices c and d after transformation. In other words, no pixel is mapped to those particular positions after performing the rotation transformation. For example, if we rotate the test image with $\phi = 15°$ by simply copying the pixels from the source image to the rotated destination image, we obtain a visually unpleasant rotated image with many holes, as shown in Figure 11.4. In this approach, we basically scan the source image pixels in raster scan order, compute the rotated pixel position indices c and d from the source pixel indices a and b and the angle ϕ, and then copy the corresponding pixel values from the source to the destination image. This approach is also called image rotation by *forward mapping*.

Holes in the destination image can be avoided by scanning the pixel positions the other way. That is, instead of scanning the source image pixel positions and copying those pixels to the rotated positions, we scan the pixel positions in the rotated image, map back to the pixel position in the source by reverse transformation, and then copy the corresponding pixel values from the source image to the destination image as shown in Figure 11.5. As we continuously scan the destination image, we avoid the presence of holes in the rotated image. This is called *inverse mapping*. Hereinafter we use only inverse mapping to rotate images since it does not leave holes in the rotated image.

As shown in Figure 11.5(b), the problem with the inverse mapping approach is that the pixel positions obtained by inverse transformation do not fall exactly onto the existing pixel positions of the source image. For example, as shown in Figure 11.5, for a given angle ϕ, the pixel at position P in the destination image (i.e., rotated image)

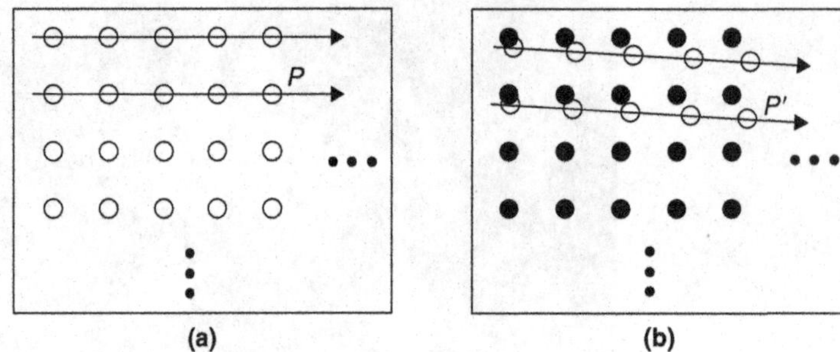

Figure 11.5: Image rotation with inverse mapping approach. (a) Destination image. (b) Source image.

is mapped to the pixel position P' in the source image after inverse transformation. But there is no pixel value at position P' because it does not fall on the grid of the source image. This means we should make the pixel value at P' and move that newly created pixel to the position P in the rotated image. There are many ways to obtain the pixel values at noninteger positions (i.e., off the grid) given the pixel values at integer positions using interpolation (see Section 10.7). Methods such as nearest-neighbor, bilinear, and cubic B-spline are commonly used to obtain new pixel values at intermediate pixel positions.

11.1.2 Image Rotation with Nearest-Neighbor

As discussed in Section 10.7.1, in the nearest-neighbor approach, we pick the pixel that is the nearest neighbor to the pixel position P' as the new pixel value and move that new pixel to the pixel position P in the rotated image. The test image is rotated two different angles, 15° and 125°, using the nearest-neighbor method; the corresponding rotated images are shown in Figure 11.6(a) and (b), respectively. Although the holes are avoided in the rotated image with inverse mapping, we can see many staircase-type artifacts in the rotated image. These artifacts arise due to overlapping of many pixels of the source image at a single pixel position in the destination image after rotating, known as the *aliasing* effect. The main reason for this aliasing is the result of infinite-precision pixel indices after rotation transformation and the presence of only finite sampling intervals in the 2D sampled grid. The elimination of aliasing in rotated images with fewer computations is a hot topic in the image processing field.

11.1.3 Image Rotation Using Bilinear Interpolation

In the literature, many techniques have been proposed to minimize aliasing in rotated images. One such technique is to use interpolation—instead of simply copying the value of the nearest available pixel for the "exact" position obtained by inverse mapping, we use several neighboring pixels for interpolation and then write the interpolated pixel value to the rotated position. This is illustrated in Figure 11.7. Let G denote the inverse-mapped pixel position in the source image. In the nearest-neighbor approach, we just copy the pixel value at position A (which is the closest to pixel position G) to the rotated pixel position in the destination image. In the interpolation approach, we compute the approximate pixel value g at pixel position G by means of interpolation, and then move the pixel value g to the rotated pixel position in the destination image. The easiest method to obtain the interpolated pixel value for inverse mapped position G is to apply bilinear interpolation for the neighboring 4 pixels as shown in Figure 11.7 (see Section 10.7.2 for more detail on bilinear interpolation).

Images that are rotated by the bilinear interpolation method are shown in Figure 11.8. The two rotated images by angles of 15° and 125° are shown in Figure 11.8(a) and (b), respectively. Here we can see the improved quality of the rotated images with bilinear interpolation when compared to the nearest-neighbor approach. Even though we are able to minimize the aliasing effect with bilinear interpolation when compared to the nearest-neighbor approach, there is still a significant amount of aliasing in the rotated images. You may ask at this juncture whether one could obtain even better quality upon using higher-order interpolators (e.g., cubic B-spline, sinc). The aliasing effect can, in fact, be further minimized with higher-order interpolators. While it is not possible to completely eliminate this aliasing with higher-order interpolators, we can

Figure 11.6: Image rotation with nearest-neighbor approach. (a) Rotated 15°. (b) Rotated 125°.

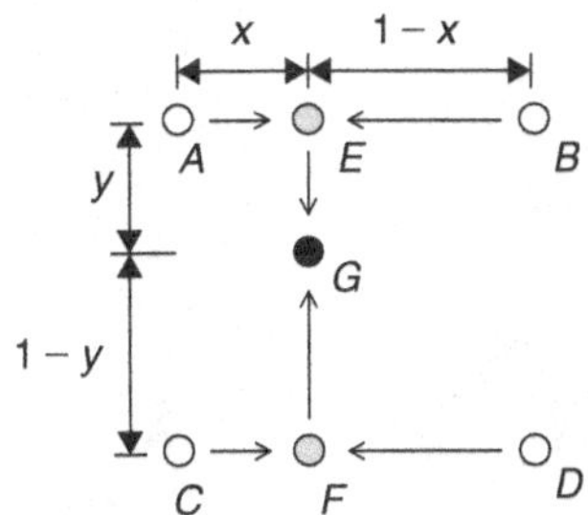

Figure 11.7: Bilinear interpolation of image pixels.

Figure 11.8: Image rotation by bilinear interpolation. (a) Rotated 15°. (b) Rotated 125°.

obtain relatively high-quality rotated images such that the artifacts are so negligible that the human eye cannot perceive them.

11.1.4 Image Rotation with Cubic B-Spline Interpolation

In this section, we discuss rotation of images with cubic B-spline interpolation (see Section 15.2.1 for more detail on this method). In cubic B-spline interpolation, we work on a 4×4 area of pixels as shown in Figure 11.9. The interpolation is carried out by first computing intermediate gray-colored pixels a, b, c, and d from corresponding row pixels a_1 to a_4, b_1 to b_4, c_1 to c_4, and d_1 to d_4, and then computing the required pixel p at the target position from intermediate pixels a, b, c, and d. The coefficients f_1 to f_4 and g_1 to g_4 that are used in interpolating

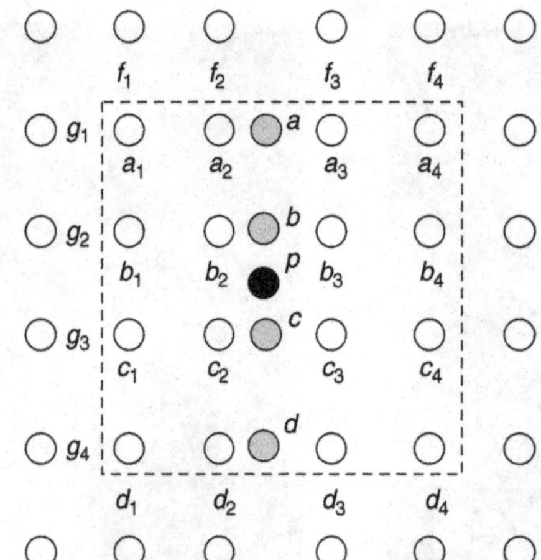

Figure 11.9: Cubic B-spline interpolation of image pixels.

Figure 11.10: Image rotation using cubic B-spline interpolation. (a) Rotated 15°. (b) Rotated 125°.

the pixels are first obtained using a cubic B-spline approximation function, given in Equation (15.8). Then the interpolated pixels are calculated as follows:

$$a = f_1 a_1 + f_2 a_2 + f_3 a_3 + f_4 a_4 \tag{11.9}$$

$$b = f_1 b_1 + f_2 b_2 + f_3 b_3 + f_4 b_4 \tag{11.10}$$

$$c = f_1 c_1 + f_2 c_2 + f_3 c_3 + f_4 c_4 \tag{11.11}$$

$$d = f_1 d_1 + f_2 d_2 + f_3 d_3 + f_4 d_4 \tag{11.12}$$

$$p = g_1 a + g_2 b + g_3 c + g_4 d \tag{11.13}$$

Note that the same coefficients f_1 to f_4 are used in computing all four rows of intermediate pixels a, b, c, and d. This is because the distances of the corresponding row pixels with respect to intermediate pixels a, b, c, and d are the same. As shown in Figure 11.10, the quality of rotated images with cubic B-spline interpolation is far better when compared to the bilinear interpolation method. The aliasing artifacts are not visible in the rotated images as shown in Figures 11.10(a) and (b). The higher-quality rotated images that are achieved with the cubic B-spline method are at the cost of increased computation. Next, we discuss the computational complexity of image rotation based on the cubic B-spline method.

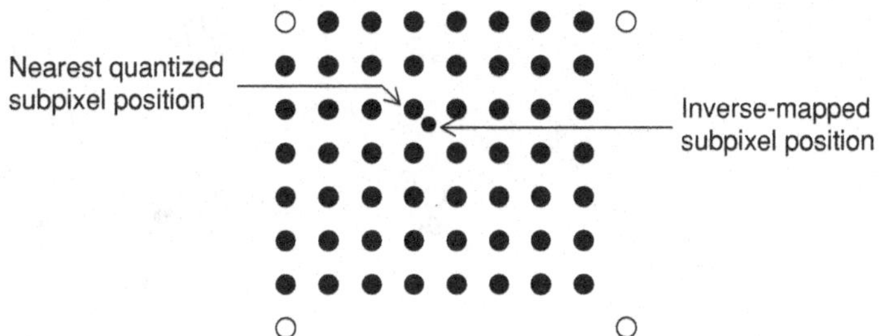

Figure 11.11: Quantization of 2 x 2 pixel space for look-up table method.

Computational Complexity with Cubic B-Spline Interpolation

As shown in Figure 11.9 and based on Equations (11.9) through (11.13), given the coefficient values, the computation of one interpolated pixel using the cubic B-spline interpolation method requires about 20 MAC (multiply and accumulate) operations. In addition, since the inverse mapped pixel position with respect to neighboring pixel positions vary from one pixel to another, we must compute the eight coefficient values using Equation (15.8) for every inverse mapped pixel position. This is computationally very costly. Instead, we use the look-up table method, which avoids coefficient computation. In the look-up table method, we quantize the 2×2 pixel space to 1/8th resolution as shown in Figure 11.11. For each quantized subpixel position, we precompute and store the eight cubic B-spline filter coefficients. If we represent each filter coefficient in 1.15 format, then the look-up table size would be 1 kB($= 64 \times 8 \times 2$). With 1/4th quantization resolution, we require only 256 bytes($= 16 \times 8 \times 2$) of data memory. The filter coefficients of the inverse mapped subpixel position are given by its nearest quantized subpixel position.

Still, the image rotation with cubic B-spline is costly, as it requires 20 MAC operations. Next, we discuss another method with which we can get similar quality rotated images while performing the image rotation with only nine MAC operations.

11.1.5 Image Rotation with 3 x 3 *Gaussian Filter*

Two-dimensional Gaussian filters are widely used for smoothing images in image processing applications. In Section 10.6.3, we used the Gaussian filter to minimize noise effects in performing Canny edge detection. Here we treat aliasing as noise and use the Gaussian filter for interpolation. The 2D Gaussian window generated using Equation (10.15) with $\sigma = 0.75$ is shown in Figure 11.12. We obtain the 3×3 filter coefficients $\{h_i\}$ by placing the center of the window at the inverse mapped pixel position. The scaled filter coefficients $\{g_i\}$ are obtained as shown in Figure 11.13 by substituting the relative distances of actual pixel P_i from the inverse mapped pixel Q into the Gaussian function given in Equation (10.15). In this instance, we can also use the look-up table method as described in the previous section to avoid computation of filter coefficients.

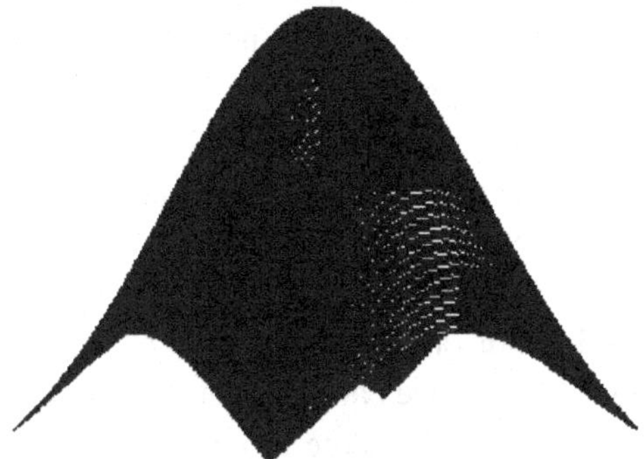

Figure 11.12: Gaussian window with $\sigma = 0.75$.

The normalized weights $\{h_i\}$ are computed from $\{g_i\}$ as follows:

$$h_i = \frac{g_i}{\sum_{i=1}^{9} g_i} \tag{11.14}$$

Figure 11.13: Image rotation with 3 x 3 Gaussian filter.

Figure 11.14: Image rotation using 3 x 3 Gaussian filter. (a) Rotated 15°. (b) Rotated 125°.

Then, the approximate pixel value Q is obtained at the inverse mapped pixel position from the neighboring 3×3 pixels P_i with nine MAC operations:

$$Q = h_1 P_1 + h_2 P_2 + h_3 P_3 + h_4 P_4 + h_5 P_5 + h_6 P_6 + h_7 P_7 + h_8 P_8 + h_9 P_9 \quad (11.15)$$

Rotated images obtained from 3×3 Gaussian filtering are shown in Figure 11.14.

11.1.6 Real-Time Implementation of Image Rotation Algorithm

In image rotation, we have two steps. The first step is obtaining the inverse-mapped pixel position, and the second step comprises performing interpolation to create a new pixel at the inverse mapped position. We compute the inverse mapped position using Equations (11.7) and (11.8). For this, we must have the cosine value for the given rotation angle ϕ. The computation of the exact cosine value using fixed-point processors (e.g., the reference embedded processor) is very costly in terms of cycles.

In practice, not all applications require the rotation of images for arbitrary angles. If we know in advance the rotation angles, then we can precompute the cosine values for those angles and store them as a look-up table. Otherwise, the best thing we can do is to quantize the entire range of rotation with a given resolution and precompute the cosine values for those quantized angles and store them in memory. The amount of memory required to store cosine values depends on the quantization resolution and the range of the rotation angle. If we have cosine values in the range 0 to 90°, we can then get the cosine values in other quadrants by just using the symmetry of cosine values. In addition, the same look-up table can be used to compute the sine values since $\sin(x) = \cos(90 - x)$.

Typically, it is sufficient to use 1° resolution for most of the practical applications. In that case, we precompute the cosine values from 0 to 90° in increments of 1° and store them in memory as a look-up table. As the reference embedded processor is 16-bit MAC operations friendly, we use 1.15 fixed-point format to represent the cosine values. The cosine values for 0 to 90° in 1.15 fixed-point format are given in the look-up table **CosLut**[] (see companion website for the values). In addition, image rotation based on 3×3 Gaussian filter requires only 9 MAC operations and gives similar quality (as shown in Figure 11.14) as cubic B-spline interpolation. In this section we simulate image rotation based on a 3×3 filter. The 3×3 Gaussian filter weight in 1.15 format for obtaining interpolated pixels at the inverse mapped pixel position with subpixel space 1/8-th quantization resolution is given in the look-up table **LutRot**[] (see companion website for the values).

The fixed-point simulation code for rotating a QVGA (320×240) gray image in the range $-90°$ to $90°$ at $1°$ resolution is given in Pcode 11.1. As we rotate the images with respect to center of image, the loop indices move from -160 to 159 and -120 to 119 instead of 0 to 319 and 0 to 239. At the beginning of the row, we compute the coordinates of the inverse mapped pixel position using Equations (11.4) and (11.5), and then for all other pixels in the row, the inverse mapped pixel position is obtained using Equations (11.7) and (11.8). When the inverse mapped pixel position falls outside the source image boundaries, then we skip the computation of that pixel rotation. For this, we check the inverse mapped pixel regardless of whether its coordinates are within the boundaries of the source image. On the reference embedded processor (see Appendix A on the companion website), the cost of image rotation with the program code given in Pcode 11.1 is about 30 cycles/pixel and we require about 1.5 kB of memory for both program and data. Another important issue in the implementation of image rotation is the availability of pixel data to process in real time. The preceding cycles estimate assumes that the corresponding pixel data is available in on-chip data memory, and there should be no delay in accessing the image pixels.

```
xx = abs(theta);
dxx = cos_lut[xx]; dyy = cos_lut[90-xx];        // cosine from look-up table
if (theta < 0) dyy = -dyy;
for(j = 119;j >=-120;j--){
        xx = -160*dxx + j*dyy;                                          // Equation (11.4)
        yy = 160*dyy + j*dxx;                                           // Equation (11.5)
        for(i =-160;i <= 159;i++){
                r = xx >> 12; s = yy >> 12;
                if ((r >=-1264)&&(r < 1264)&&(s >= -944)&&(s < 944)){  // skip out of image
                        m = r >> 3; n = s >> 3;                        // portions
                        p = M/2-n-1; q = N/2 + m-1;
                        m = m << 3; n = n << 3;
                        m = r - m; n = s - n;
                        r = abs(m); s = abs(n);
                        s = s*72 + r*9;
                        A1 = lut_rot[s];   A2 = lut_rot[s+1];          // filter weights from
                        A3 = lut_rot[s+2]; A4 = lut_rot[s+3];          // look-up table
                        A5 = lut_rot[s+4]; A6 = lut_rot[s+5];
                        A7 = lut_rot[s+6]; A8 = lut_rot[s+7];
                        A9 = lut_rot[s+8];
B5 = (A5 * BufY[p*N+q]+16384) >> 15;          // filtering or interpolation
B1 = (A1 * BufY[(p-1)*N+(q-1)]+16384) >> 15; B2 = (A2*BufY[(p1)*N+q]+16384) >> 15;
B3 = (A3 * BufY[(p-1)*N+(q+1)]+16384) >> 15; B4 = (A4*BufY[p*N+(q-1)]+16384) >> 15;
B6 = (A6 * BufY[p*N+(q+1)]+16384) >> 15; B7 = (A7*BufY[(p+1)*N+(q-1)]+16384) >> 15;
B8 = (A8 * BufY[(p+1)*N+q]+16384) >> 15; B9 = (A9*BufY[(p+1)*N+(q+1)]+16384) >> 15;
                    r = B1+B2+B3+B4+B5+B6+B7+B8+B9;                    // Equation (11.15)
                    BufD[(119-j)*N+(160+i)] = (unsigned char) r;       // store pixel in
                }                                                      // in rotated position
                xx = xx + dxx;                                         // Equation (11.7)
                yy = yy - dyy;                                         // Equation (11.8)
        }
}
```

Pcode 11.1: Simulation code for fixed-point implementation of image rotation.

As the images occupy more memory, they are usually stored in slow SDRAM (L3) memory and a few pixels of the image are brought to on-chip memory (L1) for processing each time and the rotated pixels are moved back to L3 after processing. There are two approaches to achieve this: enabling a data cache or enabling direct memory access (DMA). Although we can enable a data cache at program compilation without any extra effort, it is not as efficient as the DMA method. Next, we discuss image rotation by moving pixel data from L3 to/from

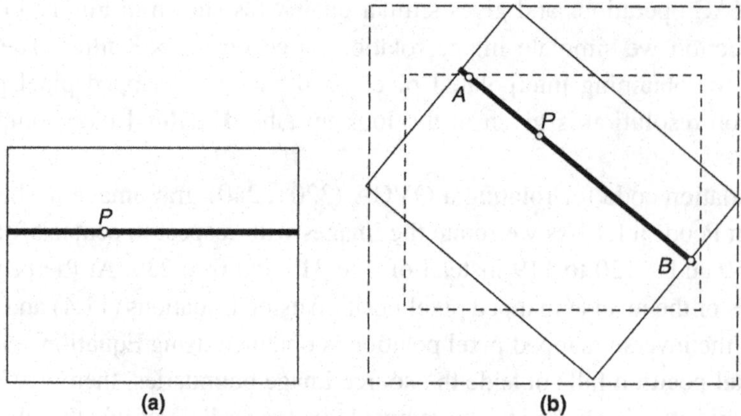

Figure 11.15: Illustration of row-based image rotation. (a) Destination image. (b) Source image.

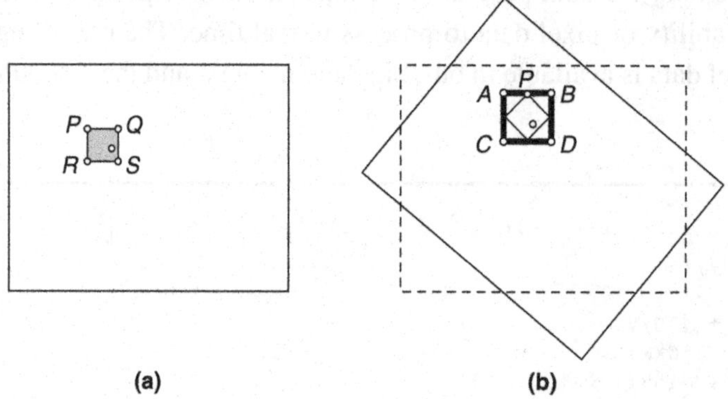

Figure 11.16: Illustration of block-based image rotation. (a) Destination image. (b) Source image.

L1 using DMA. The reference processor DMA (see Appendix A on the companion website) allows us to bring either a line of pixels (1D-DMA) or a block of pixels (2D DMA) from L3.

As illustrated in Figure 11.15, in the image rotation, the pixels of the source image at a given location are not exactly mapped to the same location in the destination image. If we scan a line of pixels in the destination image, the corresponding inverse-mapped pixel locations can fall anywhere in the source image depending on the angle of rotation. For example, a line with pixel P on it in the destination image is mapped to line AB in the source image with a given rotation angle. The line AB is neither a row nor a column. That means we cannot get the pixels on or around the line AB using 1D-DMA. The only way is to use 2D-DMA and bring the block of pixels that belong to the rectangle specified by line AB as its diagonal. However, this brings a huge amount of pixels into L1 memory and that much data may not fit. Another approach is to work on a block of pixels, as shown in Figure 11.16; this can be implemented using 2D DMA with much less L1 memory. In this approach, we always consider a square block of pixels (say, the area of pixels defined by $PQRS$) in the destination image and get the source image's appropriate pixels (defined by the area $ABCD$) from L3 using 2D DMA. Then obtain the block of pixels $PQRS$ in the rotated image from the pixels $ABCD$ by inverse mapping.

11.2 Digital Image Stabilization

Image stabilization (IS) is the process of removing effects of unwanted camera movements from the captured video sequence. The video sequences acquired by video cameras are usually affected by undesired motion produced by an unstable camera platform. These undesired fluctuations of video will affect visual quality. The challenge of image stabilization systems is how to compensate for shaking of the camera without affecting

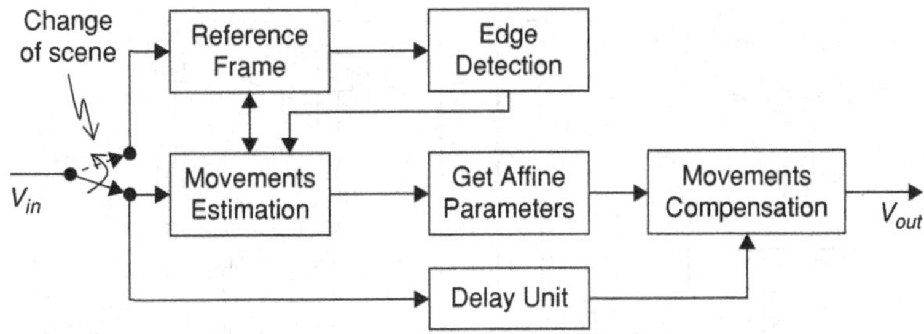

Figure 11.17: Schematic diagram of digital image stabilization.

the actual moving objects in the image sequence. Digital image stabilization (DIS) is the process of removing undesired motion effects present in the captured video to generate a compensated image sequence using digital image processing techniques without mechanical devices such as gyro sensors. In this section, we discuss a DIS algorithm that detects such movements in the video sequence and compensates for them in order to obtain stabilized video frames.

The DIS algorithm compensates for camera movement in the captured sequence by assuming that these undesired effects in the video sequence are due to unexpected translations (both vertically and horizontally) or rotations at the time the video is captured. The DIS system is generally composed of two basic modules: the undesired movement estimation unit and the compensation unit. In DIS, we fix one video frame (usually a good frame at the beginning of video sequence) as a reference frame and estimate the undesired movements of subsequent frames with respect to the reference frame and then compensate those movements by processing the video frames with estimated parameters. We use the affine transform (see Equations (11.16) through (11.20)) to compensate for both translation and rotation effects.

Because the video frames contain both high-frequency regions as well as low-frequency regions, we can efficiently estimate those unwanted movements by concentrating on the high-frequency regions. In other words, we use a few sections of the image with strong edge information. The DIS system with basic blocks is shown in Figure 11.17.

11.2.1 DIS Modules

As shown in Figure 11.17, the basic DIS modules are reference frame processing, motion estimation, affine parameters computation, and motion compensation. The following sections briefly discuss the DIS modules.

Reference Frame Processing

Given the input video sequence shown in Figure 11.17, we will have a switch to choose the reference frame path or sequence stabilization path. Whenever a change of scene occurs in the video sequence, we update the reference frame from the input video sequence and perform some processing (e.g., finding edges information, locating macroblocks with strong edges) on the new frame. We choose the relevant portions (in terms of 16×16 macroblocks) of the reference frame with strong edges for estimating unwanted video movements. We call these 16×16 blocks strong macroblocks. This is illustrated in Figure 11.18 with a synthetic image.

Motion Estimation

The motion of the current input frame is estimated by subdividing the frame into macroblocks (i.e., 16×16 block of pixels) and correlating the present reference frame's strong macroblock pixels with the input frame's pixels. The current input-frame motion with respect to the reference frame can be in any direction, and with our DIS algorithm this motion is approximated with three motion parameters: (1) horizontal motion, (2) vertical motion, and (3) rotation. The horizontal and vertical motion together is called *translation*.

Translation Estimation To get the translation motion vector (TMV) of the current frame with respect to the reference frame, N macroblocks, referred to as *trans_macroblocks*, with the largest gradient value (which is

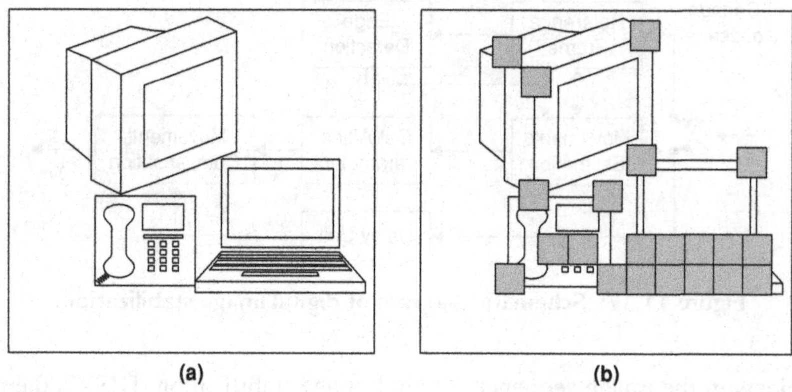

Figure 11.18: Illustration of strong macroblocks in a synthetic image.

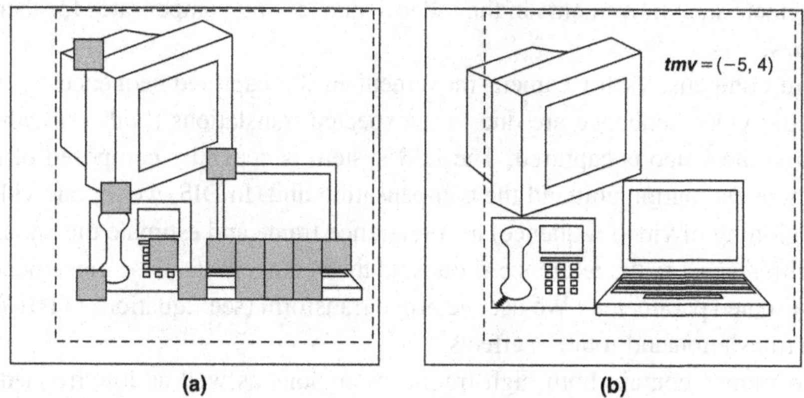

Figure 11.19: Translation estimation. (a) trans_macroblocks selection. (b) *tmv* estimation.

obtained as the sum of gradients of all pixels in the macroblock) are chosen from the strong macroblocks set of the reference frame. This is shown in Figure 11.19 for the synthetic image. The motion vectors for trans_macroblocks are obtained by correlating the trans_macroblocks of the reference frame with the current input frame. The global motion vector or translation motion vector, $tmv = (T_x, T_y)$, is now computed by taking the median of the trans_macroblocks motion vector's x and y coordinates separately. This allows us to correct the translation of the current input frame with respect to the reference frame using *tmv* before estimating the affine parameters (using Equations (11.18) through (11.21)).

Rotation Estimation For rotation estimation, the use of trans_macroblocks to estimate the rotation parameters (for the affine transform) may result in incorrect values because the motion due to rotation from the image center to its corners will vary a lot. If we use the macroblocks close to the frame center for estimating the rotation parameters, the results may not be consistent from frame to frame. So, to get the proper affine transform parameters, M macroblocks, referred to as *rot_macroblocks*, having the largest gradient values and away from frame center, are selected as shown in Figure 11.20. We obtain the rotation motion vector $rmv = (R_x, R_y)$ from the motion vectors of rot_macroblocks. The parameters R_x and R_y can be computed in the same way as *tmv* by taking the median of the motion vectors' x and y coordinates. Note that the rot_macroblocks motion vectors are used in computing *rmv*.

Affine Transform Parameters Computation

The affine transform given here detects unwanted frame motion using the image translation (R_x, R_y) and rotation parameters $(a_{11}, a_{12}, a_{21}, a_{22})$ as inputs:

$$G_x = a_{11}x + a_{12}y + R_x \tag{11.16}$$

$$G_y = a_{21}x + a_{22}y + R_y \tag{11.17}$$

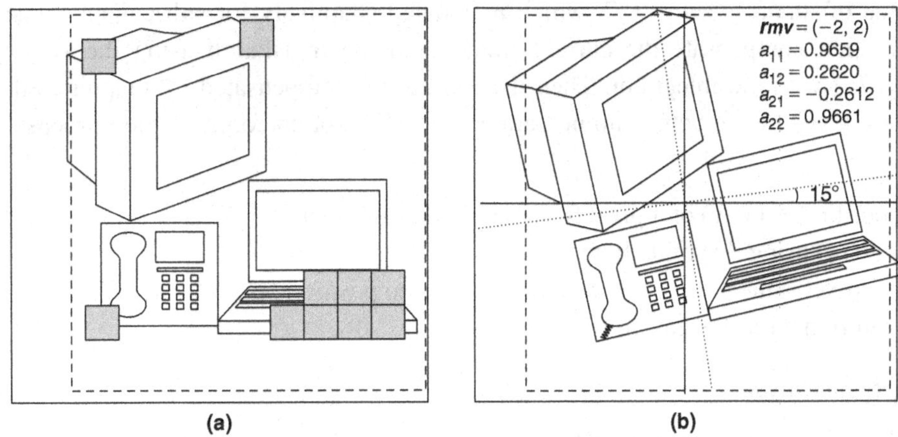

Figure 11.20: Rotation estimation. (a) Selection of rot_macroblocks. (b) Affine parameters estimation.

where (x, y) is the source pixel position relative to the center of the image, and (G_x, G_y) is the destination pixel position relative to the image center.

After removing the translation (R_x, R_y) from the motion vectors of rot_macroblocks, the rotation parameters $(a_{11}, a_{12}, a_{21}, a_{22})$ are estimated by minimizing the mean-squared difference between the affine model and the actual motion vector field. The final expressions for computing a_{11}, a_{12}, a_{21}, and a_{22} follow:

$$a_{11} = \frac{1}{\det}\left(\sum_{x,y} xV_x \sum_{x,y} y^2 - \sum_{x,y} yV_x \sum_{x,y} xy\right) \tag{11.18}$$

$$a_{12} = \frac{1}{\det}\left(\sum_{x,y} yV_x \sum_{x,y} x^2 - \sum_{x,y} xV_x \sum_{x,y} xy\right) \tag{11.19}$$

$$a_{21} = \frac{1}{\det}\left(\sum_{x,y} xV_y \sum_{x,y} y^2 - \sum_{x,y} yV_y \sum_{x,y} xy\right) \tag{11.20}$$

$$a_{22} = \frac{1}{\det}\left(\sum_{x,y} yV_y \sum_{x,y} x^2 - \sum_{x,y} xV_y \sum_{x,y} xy\right) \tag{11.21}$$

where

$$\det = \sum_{x,y} x^2 \sum_{x,y} y^2 - \left(\sum_{x,y} xy\right)^2 \tag{11.22}$$

and (V_x, V_y) are the motion vector results after subtracting (R_x, R_y) from the rot_macroblocks motion vectors.

Motion Compensation

The motion compensation (MC) of the current frame is achieved by applying the affine transform described in Equations (11.16) and (11.17) to the individual pixels of the current frame. To avoid the shakiness from frame to frame due to motion compensation with estimated inaccurate parameters because of a few abnormal inputs, an integrator is used for smoothing the frame-to-frame transition. If $P[n]$ is the estimated parameter with frame number n, then the parameter $Q[n]$ used to compensate for frame number n is derived as

$$Q[n] = Alpha^* Q[n-1] + (1 - Alpha)^* P[n]$$

The initial value of *Alpha* is set as 0.7, which is updated adaptively for subsequent frames. With motion compensation, we first compensate the current frame with the translation using the smoothed translation vector ***tmv*** $= (T_x, T_y)$ with the integrator. Then the frames are compensated by mapping all the pixels with the affine transform using the smoothed affine parameters. The motion compensation process is performed as follows:

1. Take the coordinates (x, y) of a pixel from the current frame n.
2. Obtain (G_x, G_y) using the affine transform.
3. Transfer the pixel value at (x, y) in the current frame to position (G_x, G_y) in the new frame, which is the compensated frame for the current frame.

11.2.2 DIS Implementation

The functional block diagram for DIS is shown in Figure 11.21. We update the reference frame (RF) from the input video sequence whenever the scene change detector (SCD) identifies a change of scene. When the reference frame is updated, we then perform a series of operations such as edge detection and determination of strong macroblocks (sMB), trans_macroblocks (tMB), and rot_macroblocks (rMB) for the new reference frame. The sMBs are selected by choosing the appropriate threshold value T to avoid image portions with insignificant edges. We use two threshold values T_1 and T_2 to get tMBs and rMBs from sMBs. We then estimate the *tmv* using the tMBs motion vectors and pass-through integrator $(1/s_1)$ to get the smoothed *tmv*. Next, we perform motion compensation (tMC) on the input frame using *tmv*. This motion-compensated frame is then used in computing the motion vectors for rot_macroblocks, which are then used for obtaining the affine transform (AT) parameters. To minimize the shakiness from frame to frame, we pass the affine parameters through the second integrator $(1/s_2)$ as shown in Figure 11.21. Finally, motion compensation (rMC) is performed using affine parameters to obtain the stabilized output video.

Scene Change Detector

The scene change detector updates the reference frame whenever there is a scene change in the video using a threshold in the motion estimation process. The threshold is the lower limit on the number of translation macroblocks. If the number of translation macroblocks is less than the threshold, then the current frame varies a lot from the reference frame and the scene change detector signals the system to update the reference frame with the current frame.

The DIS flow chart diagram is shown in Figure 11.22. We initially set SCD equal to 1 so that the first frame is considered the reference frame. For subsequent frames, we determine the SCD based on the previous frame's tMV count. We exit the loop upon reaching the end-of-frame (EOF) count.

Integrator performance is shown in Figure 11.23. The dotted curve is the input to the integrator and the solid curve is the output from the integrator. This smoothing of motion vectors by the integrator minimizes fluctuations

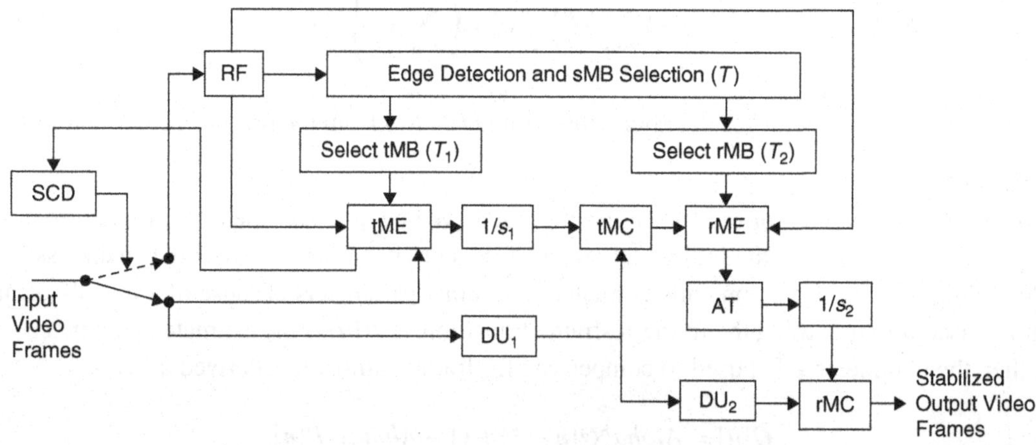

Figure 11.21: Functional block diagram of digital image stabilization.

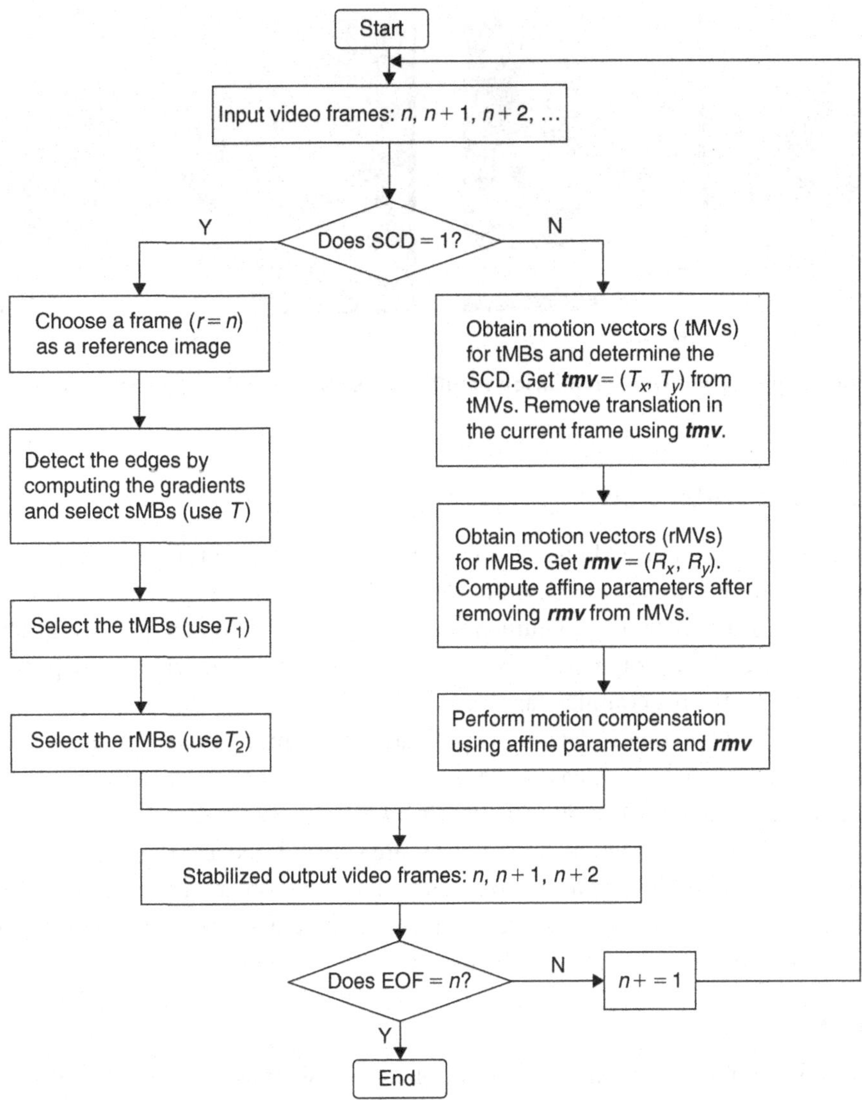

Figure 11.22: DIS flow chart diagram.

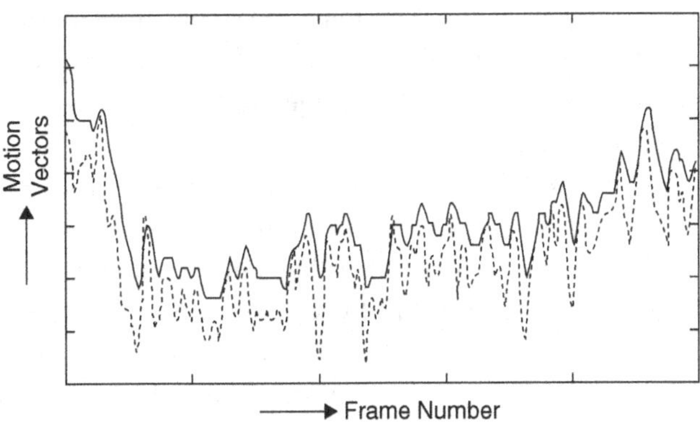

Figure 11.23: Smoothing motion vectors with integrator (the *dotted curve* is the input to the integrator and the *solid curve* is the output of the integrator).

present in the stabilized image. Figure 11.24 demonstrates image stabilization with the DIS algorithm. The test video sequence with unstabilized video tracking is shown in Figure 11.24(a) and the corresponding stabilized video is shown in Figure 11.24(b).

(a)

(b)

Figure 11.24: Digital image stabilization simulation results. (a) Unstabilized video sequence. (b) Stabilized video sequence.

11.3 Image Objects Detection

Object detection algorithms are the backbone of a wide variety of image processing applications. Commonly used image object detection techniques are based on object features, shape, pattern, motion, color, and so on. Some approaches utilize advance tools (e.g., neural networks, principal component analysis, template matching, Hough transform) in detecting image objects. Image variations such as scale, orientation, pose, and illumination make the object detection problem a complex task.

In this section, we focus on two object detection applications: (1) human face detection in color images, and (2) vehicle license plate detection. In both cases, we use feature-based object detection techniques to detect the image objects. In this approach, detection is achieved in two steps. First, the objects are classified using the perceptual nature of the objects. For example, human faces are skin colored and the license plates are rectangular shaped. In the second step, we use the features of objects to detect the object. For example, the relative position of facial features such as eyes, nose, and lips serves as a device in detecting human faces. Similarly, the license plate aspect ratio is an important feature that can be used in detecting plates.

11.3.1 Face Detection

Human face detection is an important component of applications such as video surveillance, computer vision, image database management, digital photography, and so on. People are usually identified via face recognition. Detecting people (i.e., faces) in static digital images is a very challenging problem because it is very difficult to define a single model that describes all people. In addition, a single model may not be sufficient to detect the same face at different scales and in different poses, illuminations, and so on. Here we discuss a face detection method that assumes all images are at the same scale and all faces are in the straight frontal pose. The face detection algorithm discussed in this section works with color images in the presence of slightly varying illumination conditions as well as complex backgrounds.

Skin color is a prominent perceptual feature of human faces. Furthermore, color information is invariant vis-à-vis face orientations. Although skin color varies by ethnicity, several studies have shown that the major differences in the skin color model lie in intensity rather than color components. Modeling skin color requires choosing an appropriate color space and identifying a cluster associated with color in that space. We use the *YUV* color space (see Section 10.1) since it is perceptually uniform and separates luminance (Y) and chrominance (UV) components. Here we assume that the UV components of the skin-tone color are independent of the Y component.

Skin Color Detection

Typically, we use many test images to statistically determine the skin color region boundaries. The skin color model is not only useful in localizing the skin regions, but also reduces the computational complexity of face detection by a huge amount. As we discuss later, human faces are detected by filtering only the skin region portions of the image. Therefore, accurate identification of the skin color regions in a given image is very important for high face detection rate with less complexity. The region of skin color that is obtained by projecting the various

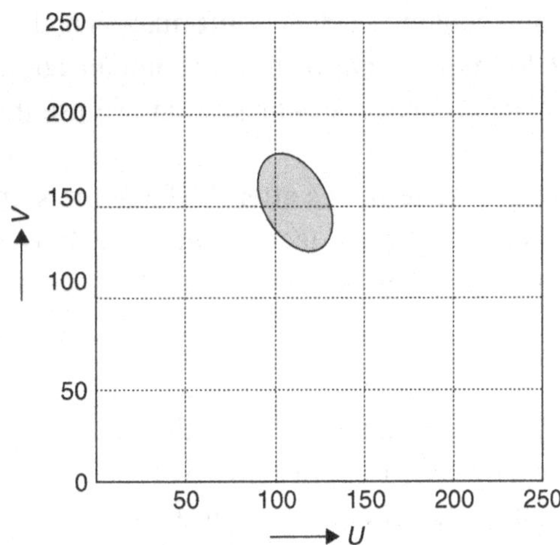

Figure 11.25: Range of *U* and *V* components for skin-tone colors.

Figure 11.26: Skin object localization using skin-color model.

images *UV* components on a 2D plane is shown in Figure 11.25. From this, the skin color regions *Skin_UV* are identified using the following condition on the *U* and *V* components of a given image:

$$Skin\_UV = (90 < U < 135) \text{ AND } (130 < V < 160) \tag{11.23}$$

After the skin color classification is done for every pixel of the image with *U* and *V* pixel values using Equation (11.23), the image is marked with the skin and nonskin regions using a binary image representation as shown in Figure 11.26. The grayscale binary image contains only 2 pixel values, 0 and 255. In generating the skin color segmented image shown in the figure, we represented the nonskin color portion of the image with 0 and the skin-color portion of the image with 255. We often apply *erosion* followed by *dilation* morphological operations (see Section 10.8) to avoid non–skin-color parts of the human face, such as eyeballs, eyebrows, and facial hair. As expected, we are clearly able to localize the skin regions using the skin-color model.

Edge Computation

As seen in the binary image shown in Figure 11.26, there are many other parts of the body, such as hands and the neck, that are skin-colored objects apart from the face. The facial regions of a skin-color binary image can be extracted by searching for facial features in the image using the skin-color segmentations as side information. We achieve this in two steps. In the first step, we obtain the skin-color segments along with their features. In the second step, we extract the regions of interest by applying the appropriate filter. One way to obtain the skin-color portion of the image along with their features is to compute the image edges and by ANDing this edge information with the skin-color binary image. The reason for using image edges instead of the image itself is that the useful facial features are rich with edges and contain relatively more information. The smooth portions of the face, such as forehead and chin, contain much less information and thus are not used as primary features in detecting faces. See Section 10.6 for more details on how to compute edge information using various methods given the luminance component (Y) of an image. In this section, we use the Sobel operator to compute image edges.

Figure 11.27 shows the effective grayscale image after ANDing the skin color binary image with the edge information. This grayscale image shows the clear facial features such as eyes, nose, mouth, and so on. With this, although there are other skin color portions, we can localize the faces by searching for these facial features using the appropriate filter.

Face Detection Using Facial Features

Among the various facial features, the eyes, nose, and mouth are the most prominent features for detecting human faces. The principle of a feature-based approach is that these features on a human face have a fixed relative position and this geometrical relationship is more invariant to changes in facial expressions than other properties such as intensity. A filter, as shown in Figure 11.28, can be designed to identify these facial features in detecting faces. This filter can be described with the edge information of three rectangles—$ABCD$, $efgh$, and $pqrs$. Let us define the regions T and W as $W = efgh + pqrs$ and $T = ABCD - efgh - pqrs$. Region W contains strong edges and region T contains much less edge information.

If we scan the image in raster scan order (in steps of block size $L \times L$ instead of a pixel to reduce computations) and compute the metrics T and W by accumulating all the edge information in those regions, then it is possible to identify facial features using the appropriate threshold values Z_1 and Z_2. Here, the threshold values Z_i and the size of rectangles $ABCD$, $efgh$, and $pqrs$ all depend on the image object scale factor. If we have images with the same scaling factor (i.e., images obtained by fixing the camera zoom and its distance from objects), we can use the same filter parameters and threshold value in detecting faces in all the images. We search for the facial features in the grayscale image shown in Figure 11.27 by processing the image with the facial feature filter shown in Figure 11.28. We mark a particular region as a face whenever the following condition is satisfied:

$$\begin{aligned} Obj &= Face, \quad \text{if}(W > Z_1) \text{ AND } (T < Z_2) \\ Obj &= Nonface \quad \text{otherwise} \end{aligned} \tag{11.24}$$

Figure 11.27: Effective grayscale image with skin segments and edges.

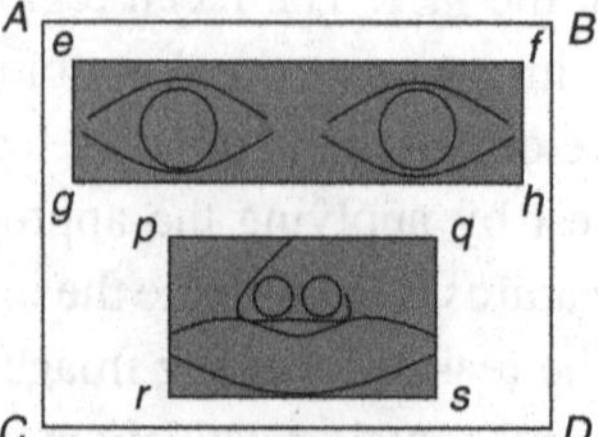

Figure 11.28: Filter design for extracting frontal face features.

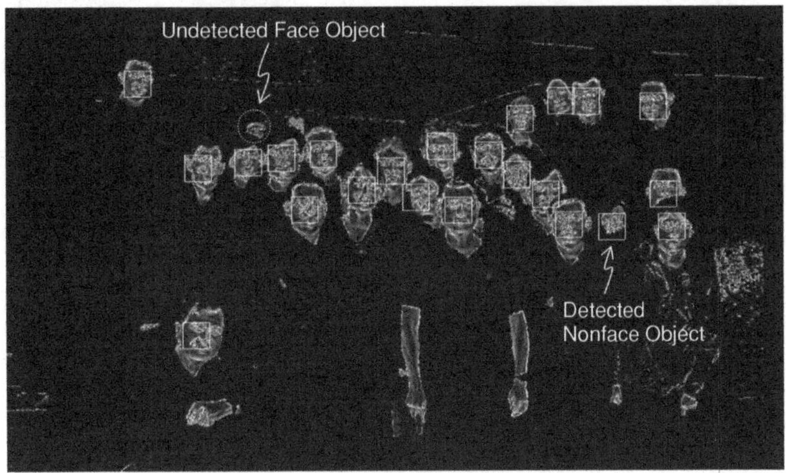

Figure 11.29: Detected faces using skin color model and face filter.

The detected faces using the criterion in Equation (11.24) are shown in Figure 11.29. The parameters used are, $AB = 32, AC = 48, ef = 28, eg = 10, pq = 22, pr = 15$, and $Z_1 = Z_2 = 50{,}000$. The detected faces are marked with a square. Most of the faces are detected with the previously described filter. There is one undetected face object and one detected nonface object in the image (as highlighted). This algorithm can detect multiple faces with a wide range of facial variations. Further, this algorithm can detect the faces of light- to dark-skinned people, as we considered a range of *UV* component values in localizing skin-color objects.

11.3.2 License Plate Detection

License plate recognition (LPR) technology uses image processing algorithms to identify vehicles by automatically reading their license plates. Typical applications of LPR include parking management, traffic monitoring, automatic toll payment, and surveillance. LPR systems consist of two modules—license plate detection (LPD) and character recognition. In this section, we discuss the detection of car license plate in the static images. The subject of optical character recognition is outside the scope of this book.

Many algorithms can be found in the literature for the license plate detection problem and few of them are based on spectral analysis (using the Fourier transform), line detection (using Hough transform), edge detection, template matching, and so on. However, all algorithms have advantages and disadvantages. Some are good at performance, while others are robust or can be implemented with fewer computations. In addition, these algorithms work based on certain assumptions, such as fixed license-plate aspect ratio, complete visibility of the plate, and location of plate. Since the dimensions of license plates vary, the plate placement on the vehicle depends on a particular vehicle model, and since parked vehicles can be located in various surroundings, no single license plate detection algorithm will work in all circumstances. Next, we discuss various approaches to plate detection as well as their complexity.

Plate Detection by Spectral Analysis

In this approach, we compute the Fourier transform for an image's rows and columns. As shown in Figure 11.30, if a particular row or column contains characters, then the periodogram (which is obtained by squaring the Fourier transform magnitude) of such a row or column contains high component values when compared to the periodogram of other rows or columns with no characters. Upon accumulating the periodograms of individual rows or columns, we will see peaks in the accumulated values as shown in Figure 11.31. Since the license plate contains characters, we can locate the plate by looking for peaks in the accumulated values.

Next, we discuss the complexity and robustness of this license plate detection algorithm. Although the rows or columns that contain the license plate have frequencies with high component values due to the presence of letters, characters outside the license plate may also exist, as shown in Figure 11.31. Consequently, a "false positive" is possible, that is, locating a license plate where one does not exist. Using the aspect ratio of the license plate

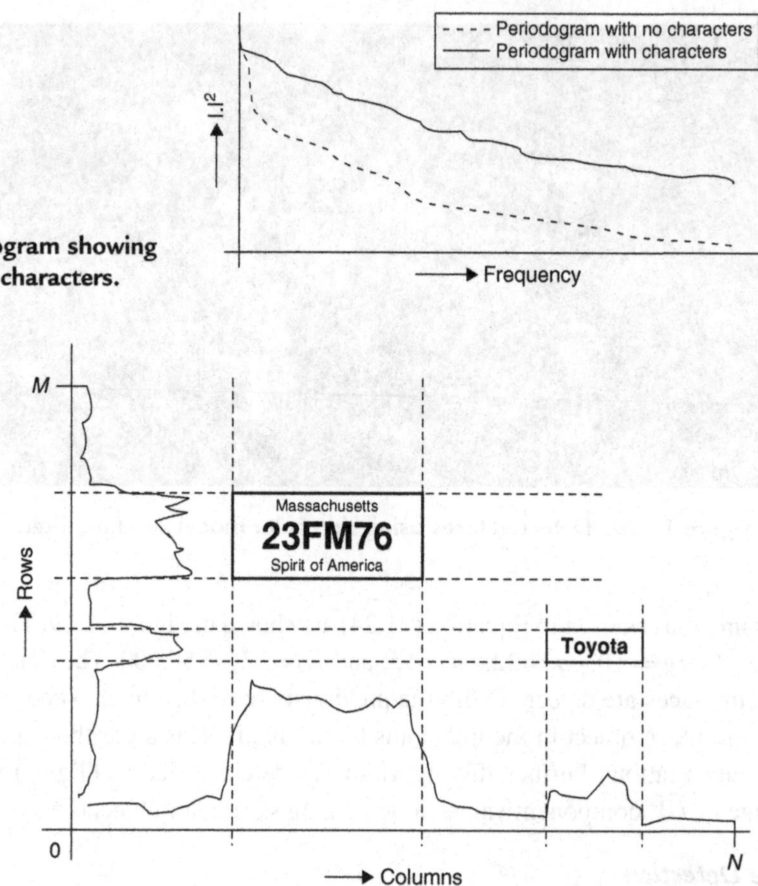

Figure 11.30: Periodogram showing row with and without characters.

Figure 11.31: Plate detection by accumulation of row and column periodograms.

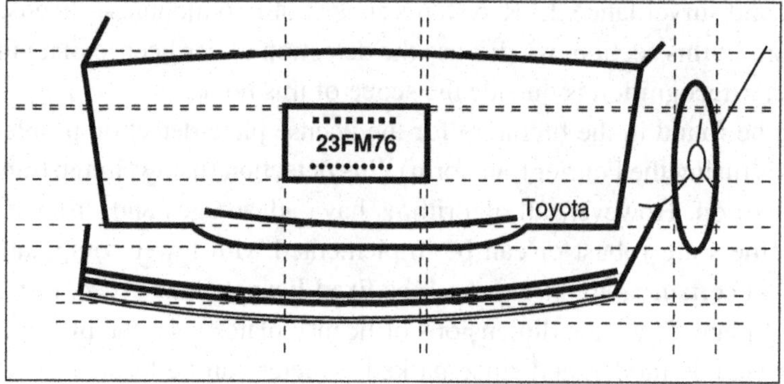

Figure 11.32: License plate detection using Hough transform.

minimizes this false detection rate. This algorithm is computationally very costly for real-time applications, as we need to compute a Fourier transform for every row and column of the image.

License Plate Detection by Hough Transform

The rectangular shape of license plates is an obvious noticeable characteristic. As the edges of the license plates form straight lines, we can use the Hough transform (see Section 10.10) to detect lines. However, the Hough transform detects many line edges on a vehicle in addition to license plate line edges. To minimize false detection, we use the aspect ratio (usually it is 2:1) of the license plate to localize the rectangular shape as shown in Figure 11.32.

Unfortunately, this technique is not effective when the license plate borders do not produce high enough straight edges due to lower-level luminance around the plate borders. For example, when the border color matches the vehicle color, the Hough transform may fail to detect license plate lines. Moreover, Hough transform

Figure 11.33: Test image for license plate detection.

computations for nonhorizontal lines may be required depending on plate orientation. As discussed in Section 10.10, the computation of Hough transforms for all orientations is computationally very costly.

License Plate Detection by Edge Information

In this approach, we use edge detection methods to localize the car license plate. Consider the test image shown in Figure 11.33 for license plate detection. This image is a very simple one for license plate detection because the plate is clearly visible and no complex background is present. However, there is lot of information apart from the license plate in the image. Most algorithms look for high-frequency content (e.g., lines, edges, letters) to detect the license plate. This image also contains letters and lines outside the license plate.

Image Smoothing by Gaussian Filtering

Our principal aim in license place detection is to localize the plate by segmenting the image regions with license plate features. The images are filtered to avoid false-positive localizations due to the presence of high-frequency noisy components. The 5×5 Gaussian filter described in Section 10.6.3 is used to smooth the images before computing the edges by Sobel operators. In this approach, no color information is used for license plate detection; only grayscale images are processed for localization purposes. The grayscale test image and its 5×5 Gaussian-filter-smoothed image are shown in Figure 11.34(a) and (b), respectively.

Edge Computation by Sobel Operator

In Section 10.6.1, we discussed edge detection using the Sobel operator. The detected edges (which are represented with a binary image obtained using an appropriate threshold value) for the test image and Gaussian smoothed image by the Sobel operator are shown in Figure 11.34(c) and (d), respectively. A lot of edge information unrelated to the license plate is detected by the Sobel operator, and thus localizing the plate is difficult. In Figure 11.34(e) and (f), the edges information is computed using only the y-Sobel operator. The amount of edge information obtained with the y-Sobel operator is more or less the same as the two-directional Sobel operator. This occurs because most of the edges in the test image are in the horizontal direction.

Upon computing the x-Sobel operator only, the binary image shows very strong edge information in the license plate region and much less edge information in all other places as shown in Figure 11.34(g) and (h). This is because characters contain edges in all directions. The x-Sobel operator finds only the edges of characters in the vertical direction and masks all edges in other directions.

License Plate Localization by Edge Accumulation

After computing edges with the x-Sobel operator, the next step in this plate detection algorithm is to localize the license plate boundaries. As the x-Sobel operator outputs the character edges and lines as shown in Figure 11.34(h), we can easily identify the license plate regions by searching for more edge information in the binary image. Since the width of the license plate is greater than its height and all vertical edges are present in the license plate region, we first accumulate the edges row-wise as shown in Figure 11.35 to identify the

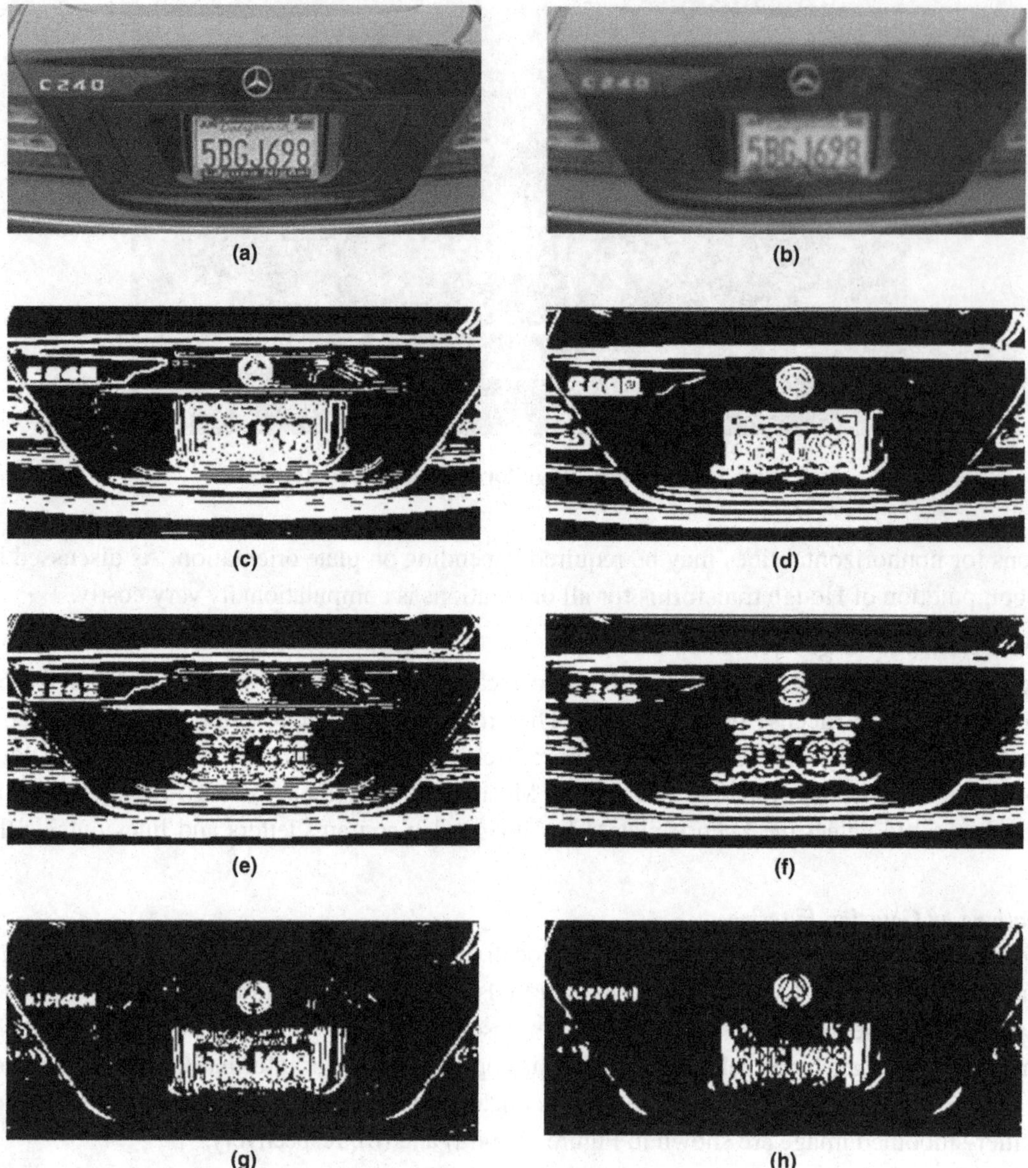

Figure 11.34: License plate detection using edge detection techniques. (a) Test image. (b) Gaussian filtered test image. (c) After applying Sobel operator on (a). (d) After applying Sobel operator on (b). (e) After applying *y*-Sobel operator on (a). (f) After applying *y*-Sobel operator on (b). (g) After applying *x*-Sobel operator on (a). (h) After applying *x*-Sobel operator on (b).

row locations of the plate. We see a peak in the license plate region after filtering the accumulated edges. The height of the license plate is computed by determining the number of rows around the peak with the strong edge information. We get the plate height based on the number of rows by counting all the rows whose accumulated edge value is above 50% of peak value. This is illustrated in Figure 11.35. Similarly, we obtain the width of the license plate by counting all the columns whose accumulated edge value is above 50% of the peak value as shown in Figure 11.36. Here, we accumulate the edges using only plate row pixels.

Localization Using License Plate Aspect Ratio

From Figure 11.34(h), we can also localize a license plate using its aspect ratio. Since the aspect ratio of the plate will be the same irrespective of camera zoom and vehicle distance, we can find its location by accumulating edge information in a box whose aspect ratio is the same as the license plate's aspect ratio. We determine the plate location by searching for the maximum accumulated edges in the box area. This process is repeated many times for various box sizes because we do not know the size of the license plate in advance.

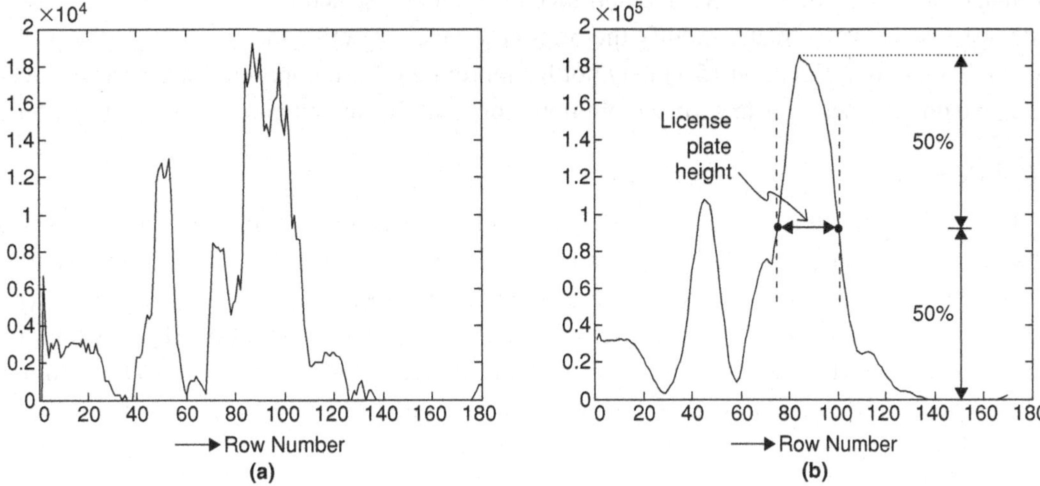

Figure 11.35: Row-wise accumulation of edges. (a) Simple accumulation of edges. (b) Accumulation of edges followed by smoothing of accumulated values.

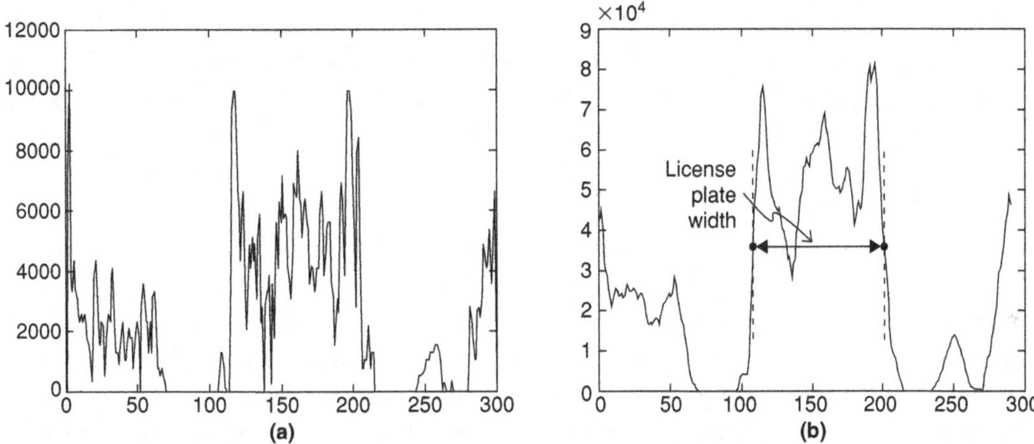

Figure 11.36: Column-wise accumulation of edges. (a) Simple accumulation of edges. (b) Accumulation of edges followed by smoothing the accumulated values.

11.4 2D Image Filters

In image processing applications, two-dimensional (2D) image filters play an important role in producing the desired images. Typically, the image filters are implemented using 2D masks. As discussed in Chapter 10, we use 2D masks for two purposes: reducing noise levels and extracting and enhancing image features (e.g., edges, objects, corners). In this section, we discuss simulation and implementation techniques of 2D image filters for smoothing images. When processing image pixels in the digital domain, a kind of random data (noise) from many sources is added to the image pixels. A few noise sources follow:

- Channel (used for transmission or storing of images)
- Quantization (result of analog-to-digital conversion in the time domain)
- Removal of high-frequency content (quantization in the frequency domain)
- Scaling (or resampling) of image pixels
- Compression and decompression

Two-dimensional filters are applied to minimize these noise components in the image pixels. In this section, we discuss an efficient way of applying typical 2D average and Gaussian filters to minimize noise levels, as well as techniques to efficiently implement them on the embedded processor. The most commonly used median filter implementation techniques are presented in Section 15.3.1.

Filtered images after applying 2D average and median filters on scaled images are shown in Figures 10.7 and 10.8. Because such filters greatly modify the original image, objective measures (e.g., the peak signal to noise ratio [PSNR] given in Equation 15.1) may not be appropriate for comparing filter performance. Instead, we use subjective quality measures (e.g., mean opinion score [MOS]) to compare image quality after filtering.

11.4.1 2D Filters

Generally, 2D filters are of the form $Q \times Q$ (where Q is an odd integer and $Q > 1$) matrix with Q^2 taps. Commonly used Q values are 3, 5, or 7. Later we discuss techniques to efficiently implement the 3×3 average filter and the 5×5 Gaussian filter. With 2D filters, the center pixel of the $Q \times Q$ block is filtered upon applying a $Q \times Q$ filter matrix as shown (for $Q = 3$) in Figure 11.37. We perform 2D filtering by computing 2D convolution of image pixels and filter taps. If the filter taps are symmetric, then the filtered output is also obtained by accumulating the element-wise product of pixels and filter taps. For example, we compute the filtered pixel x_5' using the symmetric 3×3 filter as follows:

$$x_5' = \begin{bmatrix} x_1 & x_2 & x_3 \\ x_4 & x_5 & x_6 \\ x_7 & x_8 & x_9 \end{bmatrix} * \begin{bmatrix} a & b & a \\ b & c & b \\ a & b & a \end{bmatrix} = ax_1 + bx_2 + ax_3 + bx_4 + cx_5 + bx_6 + ax_7 + bx_8 + ax_9$$

With an average filter, the filtered pixel is obtained by averaging all pixels present in the $Q \times Q$ block. The Gaussian filtered pixel is obtained by calculating the weighted average of all pixels in the $Q \times Q$ block, where the weight values are given by the taps of the $Q \times Q$ Gaussian filter. Efficient implementation techniques for 2D average and Gaussian filters are discussed in Sections 11.4.3 and 11.4.4, respectively.

11.4.2 2D Image Filter Implementation

Since images are represented with 2D data, we process the images in 2D space. Although the filtering algorithms are mathematically simple, there is a huge amount of data to be accessed and filtered per image. In this section, we discuss efficient techniques to implement 2D image filters with limited resources on the embedded processor. See Appendix A on the companion website for details on computation unit, memory, and data bus bandwidths supported by the reference embedded processor. Assuming limited resources of the embedded processor, we implement 2D image filters efficiently for real-time applications. This section covers selected aspects of applying the filter to the entire image. In practice, we process the image or video in terms of blocks or rows by scanning the image in a raster-scan order. For this, we have to store the entire image in embedded system memory and we may need a lot of memory to store larger images. Typically, we store the entire image (which is approximately 0.5 MB for 720×480 resolution) in off-chip memory and a small amount of image data in terms of blocks or rows (e.g., 256 bytes in 16×16 block) to bring to on-chip memory for filtering. We use the embedded processor DMA

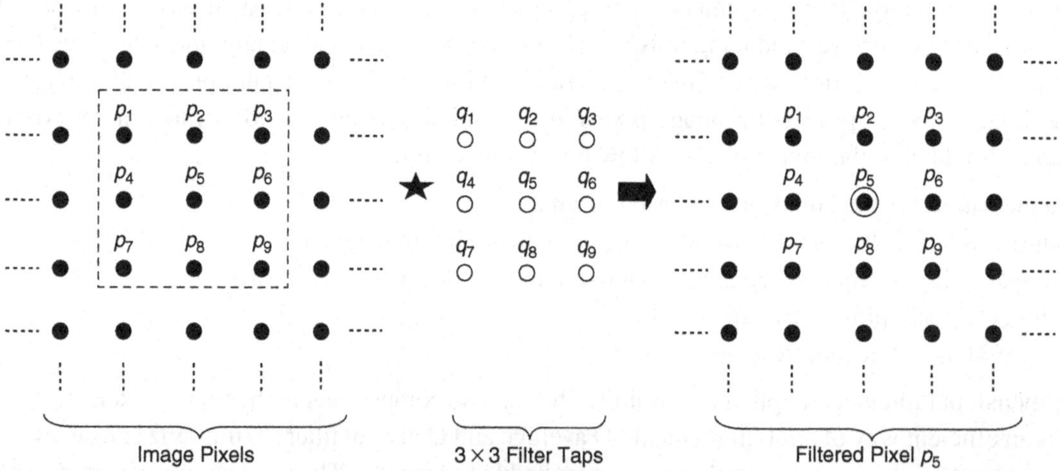

Figure 11.37: Two-dimensional image filtering.

controller without interrupting the processor core to move a block or row of pixels from off-chip memory to on-chip memory for filtering the image and moving the filtered block from on-chip memory to off-chip memory to store the filtered image (see Appendix A, Section A.3, on the companion website for more detail on DMA usage).

As the 2D filter works on $Q \times Q$ block of data, implementing 2D filters efficiently may require working with more than one $Q \times Q$ data block. We place both image block and filter coefficients in L1 memory for fast execution at the processor clock rate. As DMA is used to move the image data from L3 memory (slow, but big in size) to L1 memory (fast, but small in size), setting up DMA every time is costly in terms of cycles. We move data in bulk quantities to L1 to reduce DMA overhead. If we transfer too much data to L1, we may end up with a few problems such as L1 memory shortage and DMA waits. With experience, we learn to make decisions for efficiently handling DMA data transfers. We use either 1D DMA for working with rows or 2D DMA for working on blocks. If we work with rows, we bring one full row (of N pixels each) at a time to L1 memory, and if we work with blocks, we bring $K \times K$ block (where $K > Q$) of pixels to L1 memory. In row-based filtering, at any point of time, we need Q rows for the filtering process and hence we bring Q rows for first-row filtering and from the second row onward, we use the previous $Q - 1$ rows (which are already in L1 memory) and bring the next row to L1 using DMA.

To implement 2D image filters efficiently, we take advantage of 2D filter tap properties in performing the filtering process. Sometimes we reuse the intermediate outputs of previous pixel filtering for filtering the current pixel. As filter taps from one type of filter to another vary a lot (in terms of values, symmetry, and properties), we follow various techniques in implementing filters.

As edge pixels do not have sufficient neighbors to apply filtering, we cannot perform the same filtering on edge pixels as on nonedge pixels. We perform edge pixel filtering in two ways. First, we can filter the edge pixels with whatever neighbors are available to that pixel (a costly technique, as it involves a few condition checks). In the second instance, we basically duplicate edge pixels as they are without performing a filtering operation. Since we do not concentrate much on the edges, we prefer the second method of duplicating pixels instead of filtering the edge pixels. In other words, we duplicate four sides of the edge pixels and apply the filter only for nonedge pixels. Next, we discuss implementation aspects of row-based and block-based 2D filtering.

Row-Based Image Filter Implementation

In row-based image filter implementation, we consume fewer cycles (due to less overhead) and more memory (as we need Q rows of pixels in L1 at any point in time). As an example, consider the row-based 3×3 2D filtering process shown in Figure 11.38. We place a 2D filter at the beginning (ignore edge pixel filtering) and we move the filter mask to the right by 1 pixel and continue until the end of the row. If a row contains N pixels, then we filter the middle $N - 2$ pixels. In the meantime, we bring the next row from L3 to L1 using DMA in the

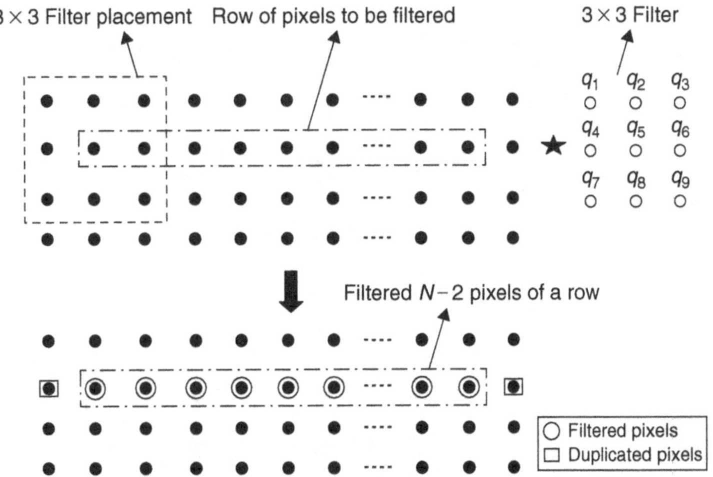

Figure 11.38: Row-based 2D filter implementation.

background. Then we DMA out filtered pixels of the current row to L3. Next, we move the 2D filter one row down and continue the same process. In this manner, we continue filtering all the pixels of an image.

The computational complexity of row-based 2D filtering is estimated as follows: Assume that we are working with an $N \times M$ size image and we duplicate all four edge pixels instead of filtering (which consumes about $2 * (N + M)$ cycles). In addition, assume that we consume H cycles as overhead in switching from the current row to the next row. If filtering of 1 pixel consumes G cycles, then we consume about $2 * (N + M) + (M - 2) * H + (N - 2) * (M - 2) * G$ cycles on the reference embedded processor to filter the entire image with row-based implementation. The DMA waits (which may arise in moving the data from L3 to L1 and L1 to L3) are ignored in the process of cycle estimation.

Block-Based Image Filter Implementation

We filter a $K \times K$ block of pixels at a time in block-based image filtering as shown in Figure 11.39. Block-based filtering is preferred, particularly when the filtering is needed at the back end of video or image decoders (to avoid data transfer overhead between L1 and L3 using DMA), as decoders work on blocks and the data block will be available for filtering in L1 immediately after decoding. In this approach, we will have a problem in filtering the block edges, as we do not have sufficient pixel information to apply the filter. Moreover, we cannot ignore block edges (or cannot duplicate edge pixels) for every block. If we do so, we end up with many unfiltered pixels.

If we want to filter one block at a time to avoid extra data transfers and memory, we have to find ways to filter the pixels at the following positions for all $K \times K$ blocks:

- Top left corner pixel
- Left-most column pixel
- Top-most row pixel
- Right-most column pixel
- Bottom-most row pixel

If we always filter the first three cases of pixels in a $K \times K$ block using the $Q \times Q$ 2D filter, then we automatically cover the last two cases for all $K \times K$ blocks except for right-most column $K \times K$ blocks and bottom-most row

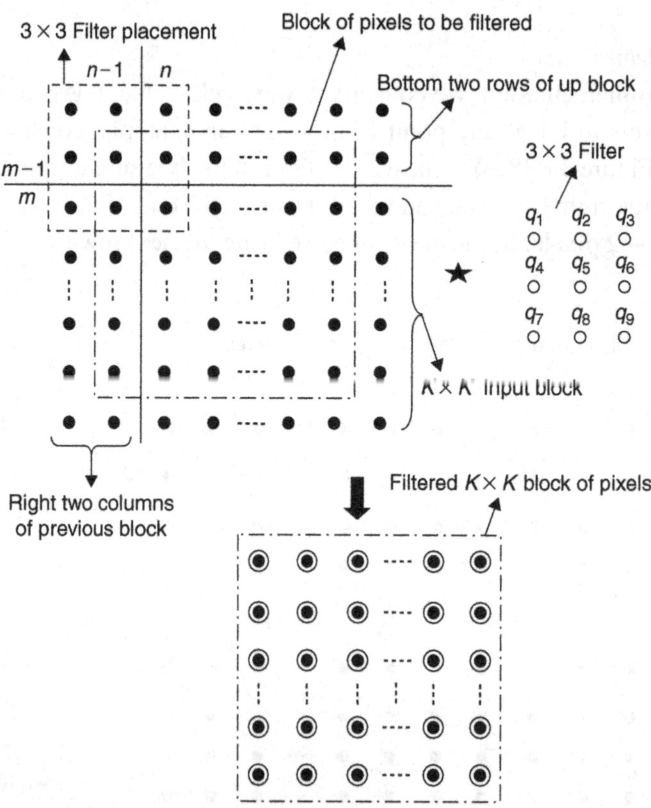

Figure 11.39: Implementation of block-based 2D image filter.

$K \times K$ blocks of an image. We duplicate $(Q-1)/2$ bottom rows and $(Q-1)/2$ right-column pixels of an image, as they are not viewed much. Let us assume m and n denote the image row and column indexes, respectively, for $K \times K$ blocks, and we proceed by filtering the $K \times K$ blocks in raster scan order. We use the following procedure to always filter the first three cases and output $K \times K$ block pixels. As shown in Figure 11.39, to filter the bottom-most row of pixels of the up $K \times K$ block (with index $[n, m-1]$) just above the current $K \times K$ block (with index $[n, m]$) and the top-most row pixels of the current $K \times K$ block, we maintain a delay line buffer to hold the $(Q-1)/2$ bottom-most row pixels of $[n, m-1]$ $K \times K$ block. Similarly, to filter the right-most column pixels of the previous $K \times K$ block $[n-1, m]$ and the left-most column pixels of the current $K \times K$ block, we maintain another buffer to hold the $(Q-1)/2$ right-most column pixels of the previous $K \times K$ block $[n-1, m]$. The current $K \times K$ block pixels are loaded from off-chip memory to the on-chip memory buffer using DMA. Therefore, we need three types of buffers (i.e., a buffer to hold the previous block's right-most column pixels, a buffer to hold the up block's bottom-most row of pixels, and a buffer to hold the current $K \times K$ block pixels) in total to apply the 2D filter for the entire image with this block-by-block approach, as shown in Figure 11.39. A $K \times K$ block of filtered pixels is outputted and moved to off-chip memory via DMA.

In block-based filtering, we place a $Q \times Q$ filter (we used a 3×3 filter in Figure 11.39) at the top-left corner and filter the block either row- or column-wise. With block-based filtering, if we assume D cycles as overhead for switching from one row/column filtering to another row/column filtering of a block, and if we consume G cycles to filter each pixel, then we consume about $[(KG+D)K](N/K)(M/K)$ cycles to filter a total image of $N \times M$ size.

11.4.3 Average Filter

In this section, we discuss efficient simulation of 3×3 average filters. As the 3×3 average filter works on the 3×3 pixel block, we efficiently implement the 3×3, 2D average filter by reusing intermediate outputs of previously filtered pixels. As shown in Figure 11.40, for filtering each pixel using the 3×3 average filter, instead of summing all 9 pixels at a time and multiplying by 1/9 (costing approximately 10 cycles), we compute the intermediate 3-pixel sum (we reuse two out of three intermediate sums) and then add all three pixel sums and multiply by 1/9. Nine sums and one multiplication are performed for filtering the first pixel. Four sums and one multiplication, then, are sufficient for filtering the remaining pixels. In Figure 11.40, values A, B, C, and D are computed by adding three column pixels.

The filtered pixel p_1 is computed as $p_1 = (A+B+C) * (1/9)$ and filtered pixel p_2 is computed as $p_2 = (B+C+D) * (1/9)$. To compute the intermediate results, we spend 2 cycles for two additions in the computation of each A, B, C, D, and so on. For filtering pixel p_2, we already have B and C; we need to compute D (involving two additions). Finally p_2 is obtained with two more additions (for computing $B+C+D$). The simulation code for performing the row-based 3×3 average filter is given in Pcode 11.2.

11.4.4 Gaussian Filter

Unlike an average filter in which filtering involves the simple addition of pixels, using a Gaussian filter involves a weighted sum of pixels. The approximate weights for the 5×5 Gaussian filter with $\sigma = 1.4$ follow:

$$\frac{1}{159}\begin{bmatrix} 2 & 4 & 5 & 4 & 2 \\ 4 & 9 & 12 & 9 & 4 \\ 5 & 12 & 15 & 12 & 5 \\ 4 & 9 & 12 & 9 & 4 \\ 2 & 4 & 5 & 4 & 2 \end{bmatrix}$$

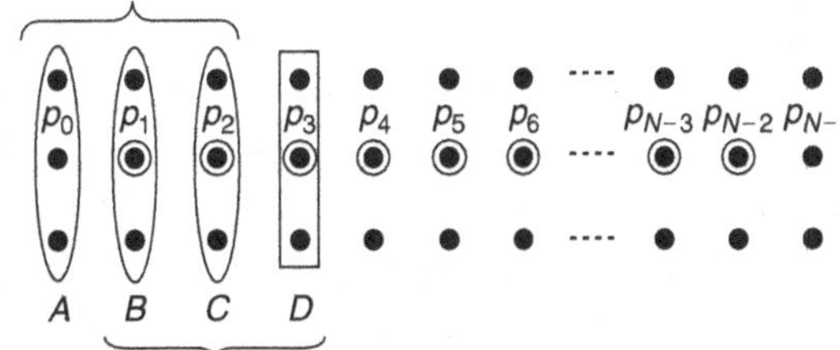

Figure 11.40: Efficient row-based implementation of the 3x3 2D average filter.

```
R = 0x0e39;
For(j = 1;j < M-1;j++) {
    i = 1;
    r0 = BufY[(j-1)*N+i-1]; r3 = BufY[(j-1)*N+i];
    r1 = BufY[j*N+i-1]; r4 = BufY[j*N+i];
    r2 = BufY[(j+1)*N+i-1]; r5 = BufY[(j+1)*N+i];
    r0 = r0 + r1; r3 = r3 + r4;                        // 2 additions
    r1 = BufY[(j-1)*N+i+1]; r4 = BufY[j*N+i+1];
    A = r0 + r2; B = r3 + r5;                          // 2 additions
    r2 = BufY[(j+1)*N+i+1]; r5 = BufY[(j-1)*N+i+2];
    r1 = r1 + r4; Q = A + B;                           // 2 additions
    C = r1 + r2; BufP[0] = B;                          // 1 addition
    Q = Q + C;  BufP[1] = C;                           // 1 addition, 8 additions  in total
    BufZ[j*N+i] = (Q*R) >> 15;                         // R contains 1.15 format of 1/9
    For(i=2;i < N-1;i++) {
        r0 = BufY[j*N+i+1]; A = BufP[0];
        r1 = BufY[(j+1)*N+i+1]; B = BufP[1];
        r0 = r0 + r1; Q = A + B;                       // 2 additions
        C = r0 + r5; BufP[0] = B;                      // 1 addition
        Q = Q + C; BufP[1] = C;                        // 1 addition
        BufZ[j*N+i] = (Q*R) >> 15; r5 = BufY[(j-1)*N+i+2];
    }
}
```

Pcode 11.2: Simulation code for 3 x 3 average filter.

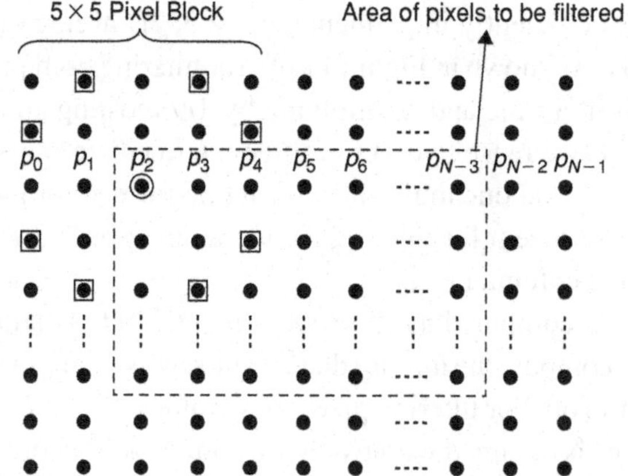

Figure 11.41: Efficient row-based implementation of 5×5 2D Gaussian filter.

Computing one filtered output using a 5 × 5 Gaussian filter involves about 24 additions, 25 multiplications, and 1 division. Discussed here are two approaches to reduce the number of computations for the 5 × 5 Gaussian filter using its symmetry properties. As most of the filter taps repeat many times, we can substantially reduce the number of multiplications. We can implement the 5 × 5 Gaussian filter with the previous matrix filter coefficients using 24 additions, 6 multiplications, and 1 division. First, we add all pixels for which the filter coefficient is the same, and then multiply the sum with the corresponding filter coefficient. For example, we have eight pixel positions as shown in Figure 11.41, highlighted with square boxes, for which the filter coefficient value is 4. Instead of multiplying eight times with 4 and then adding all of them, we first add all of them and then multiply the sum by 4. In this way, we eliminate most multiplications.

However, this approach does not save any cycles on the reference embedded processor since multiplication and addition operations consume 1 cycle each. Even though the number of multiplications required is reduced to 6, we still require 25 cycles to perform 25 additions. As the reference embedded processor consists of two MAC units, we can perform 5 × 5 Gaussian filtering efficiently by filtering 2 pixels at a time using vector instructions. This is illustrated in Figure 11.42.

Although we use two MAC units in computing 1 pixel at a time, we have more overhead in this case. By filtering 2 pixels at a time, we compute the convolution in 25 cycles for 2 pixels. In other words, we consume

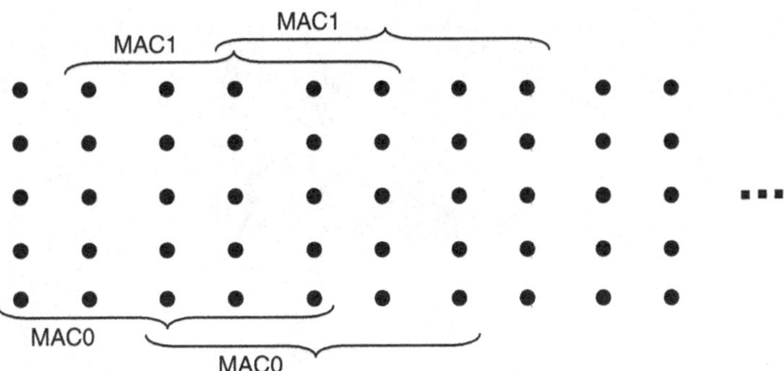

Figure 11.42: Efficient implementation of 5 x 5 Gaussian filter.

```
// duplicate two top and bottom rows edge pixels
// duplicate two left and right column edge pixels

R = 0x00ce; // 1.15 format of 1/159
For(j = 2;j < M-2;j++) {
    p = j * N; q = (j + 1)*N; r = (N << 1);
    For(i = p + 2;i < q - 2;i++) {
        r0 = BufY[p-r-4]; r1 = BufY[p-r-3]; r2 = Coeff[0];
        r3 = r0 * r2; r4 = r1 * r2; r0 = BufY[p-N-3]; r1 = BufY[p-N-2]; r2 = Coeff[1];
        r3+= r0 * r2; r4+= r1 * r2; r0 = BufY[p-2]; r1 = BufY[p-1]; r2 = Coeff[2];
        r3+= r0 * r2; r4+= r1 * r2; r0 = BufY[p+N-1]; r1 = BufY[p + N]; r2 = Coeff[3];
        r3+= r0 * r2; r4+= r1 * r2; r0 = BufY[p+r]; r1 = BufY[p + r + 1]; r2 = Coeff[4];
        r3+= r0 * r2; r4+= r1 * r2; r0 = BufY[p-r-3]; r1 = BufY[p-r-2]; r2 = Coeff[5];
        r3+= r0 * r2; r4+= r1 * r2; r0 = BufY[p+N-2]; r1 = BufY[p + N - 1]; r2 = Coeff[6];
        r3+= r0 * r2; r4+= r1 * r2; r0 = BufY[p-1]; r1 = BufY[p]; r2 = Coeff[7];
        r3+= r0 * r2; r4+= r1 * r2; r0 = BufY[p+N]; r1 = BufY[p + N + 1]; r2 = Coeff[8];
        r3+= r0 * r2; r4+= r1 * r2; r0 = BufY[p+r+1]; r1 = BufY[p + r + 2]; r2 = Coeff[9];

        r0 = (r0 * R) >> 15;          // 1 division with 1/159
        BufZ[j*N+i] = r0;
    }
}
```

Pcode 11.3: Simulation code for 5 × 5 Gaussian Filter.

12.5 cycles per pixel. The feeding of data to compute units also becomes easy. MAC0 always computes the convolution sum for the first pixel and MAC1 always computes the convolution sum for the second pixel. After filtering the first 2 pixels, we move the window 2 pixels and continue with the same process.

The simulation code for a 5 × 5 Gaussian filter is given in Pcode 11.3. With the 5 × 5 Gaussian filter, we do not have sufficient pixels to filter two top- and bottom-most rows and two left- and right-most columns. We duplicate those pixels at the edge locations.

With the block-based approach, to filter image pixels using the 5 × 5 Gaussian filter, we have to maintain two bottom rows of the up block and two right columns of the previous block as history. The pixel area covered for filtering is the same in both row- and block-based approaches. The edge pixels (two left- and right-most column edge pixels and two top- and bottom-most row edge pixels of the image) are duplicated in the filtered image.

11.5 Fisheye Distortion Correction

In photography, when we use a wide-angle lens, the pictures may look distorted as shown in Figure 11.43. This is called "fisheye" distortion. The purpose of using a wide-angle lens is to extend the view angle with a short focal length. In the early days, wide-angle lenses were used in astronomy or underwater applications. At present, many commercial applications also use wide-angle lens cameras. In particular, fisheye cameras are increasingly used in automobile rear-view imaging systems due to their cost-effectiveness.

In the fisheye distorted images, the edges of objects away from the center of focus look curved. The degree of curvature depends on the view angle that the lens is made for. For a viewer of fisheye images, such distortion can

Figure 11.43: Images with fisheye lens.

(a)

(b)

Figure 11.44: (a) Fisheye-distorted image. (b) Distortion-corrected image.

be both unusual and confusing. Therefore, correcting the images captured by fisheye cameras to approximately rectilinear versions before presenting them to viewers is desirable. To correct fisheye distortion, we first estimate the amount of distortion present in a particular image and then we dewrap the image by remapping the pixel positions to eliminate the fisheye distortion. One such fisheye-distortion corrected image is shown in Figure 11.44. There are many fisheye correction algorithms discussed in the literature; some are based on neural networks or training, lens calibration, and parametric and nonparametric approaches. Next, we discuss fisheye distortion correction assuming that the camera lens is fixed; hence the amount of distortion is known in advance for correction in the digital domain.

Since the fisheye distortion is corrected by remapping the source image distorted pixel positions to destination image rectilinear pixel positions, we can easily perform distortion correction using the look-up table method in the case of fixed camera geometry. All mapping locations of the entire image using appropriate inverse equations are precomputed and stored in the look-up table. Consider a setting where two main parameters of the image are given: fisheye lens field of view, *FOV*, and image width, *W*.

Assuming that x_d and y_d are the destination image pixel x and y coordinates, and x_s and y_s are the source image pixel x and y coordinates, the inverse equations for remapping the fisheye-distorted pixels are given by

$$x_s = \frac{2x_d \sin\left(\tan^{-1}(\eta/2)\right)}{\eta} \tag{11.25}$$

$$y_s = \frac{2y_d \sin\left(\tan^{-1}(\eta/2)\right)}{\eta} \tag{11.26}$$

where

$$\eta = \frac{\sqrt{x_d^2 + y_d^2}}{F} \text{ and} \tag{11.27}$$

$$F = \frac{image\_width}{4\sin(FOV/2)} \tag{11.28}$$

As shown in Figure 11.45, the remapping positions need not be integer pixel positions in the source image; consequently, we use an appropriate interpolation method to obtain pixel values at noninteger locations. Here, we can use interpolation methods similar to those discussed for image rotation applications in Section 11.1. For example, use of a 3×3 Gaussian filter requires a block of 3×3 pixels for interpolation as shown in Figure 11.45. Since the remapping pixel locations of the source are not exactly mapped to integer numbers, it will be costly to hold real numbers in the memory. Instead, we quantize the source image pixel grid to either one-fourth or one-eighth subpixel resolution and store all remapping pixel location values in the off-chip memory by appropriately representing them in the integer format.

In the look-up table method, we compute mapping positions offline once in the lifetime of a given camera's fisheye lens. In automotive rear-view imaging system applications, all the parameters needed for look-up table generation are known beforehand, such as camera geometry and display system characteristics. The current problem is accessing the appropriate memory location for remapping the pixel positions. Since the mapping of pixel locations from the source image to destination image is not a one-to-one operation, programming the embedded processor DMA descriptors for appropriately moving the right pixel data from off-chip memory to on-chip memory is challenging.

Memory and DMA bandwidth requirements can be reduced using a block-based approach and interpolation of pixel coordinates. We can use, say, 16×16 blocks, storing only coordinates of the blocks' corners in on-chip memory, and set up DMA descriptors to transfer the rectangular area covering the entire block. Then we can linearly interpolate pixel coordinates for inner pixels of the block and read the pixel values from the rectangle.

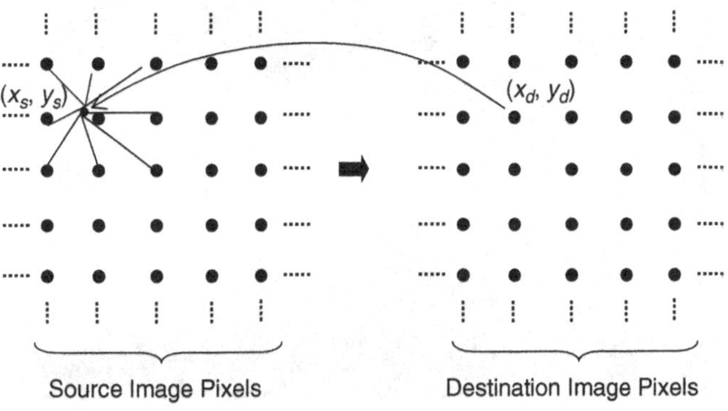

Figure 11.45: Pixel remapping with appropriate interpolation of pixels.

11.6 Image Compression

Before discussing image compression techniques, first we must understand how digital images are represented. How much storage capacity or transmission bandwidth is required for storing or transmitting a digital image as is? As discussed, the basic element of a digital image is the *pixel*. When we say an image of size $M \times N$, its width is M pixels and height is N pixels, and it contains a total of MN pixels. An image can be represented in more than one format. Image formats include *RGB*, *YUV*, *HSV*, and so on. With the *RGB* format, for example, each pixel of the image is represented with three color components—red, green, and blue. If we represent each color with 8 bits (i.e., 256 levels), then we require 24 bits for representing R, G, and B components of a pixel. Similarly, with *YUV* 4:4:4 representation (the Y component indicates luminance or intensity and UV components indicate chrominance or colors), we require 24 bits for representing a pixel.

Consider an image of size 700×660 as shown in Figure 11.46; it contains a total of 462,000 pixels, and $462,000 \times 3 = 1.386$ megabytes (MB) of memory are required to store that image for future use. Thus, uncompressed images require considerable storage capacity and transmission bandwidth. Despite rapid progress in mass-storage capacity and digital communication system performance, the demand for storage capacity and transmission bandwidth continues to outstrip the capabilities of available technologies. This naturally suggests compact representation of images—in other words, compressing digital images. For example, with a compression ratio of 16:1, the space, bandwidth, and transmission time requirements can be reduced by a factor of 16, with acceptable perceptual image quality.

In general, there are several high-level approaches to image compression, most of which take advantage of human perception limitations. For instance, we can reduce the color bandwidth (from YUV 4:4:4 to YUV 4:2:0) in an image to reduce storage space without losing quality because our eyes are much more sensitive to intensity than to color. Spatial techniques reduce the compressed image size by accounting for visual similarities within image regions, such that a small amount of information can be made to represent a large object or portion of a scene. In other words, image compression research aims at reducing the number of bits needed to represent an image by removing as much redundancy as possible.

Image compression can be performed with "lossy" or "lossless" techniques, depending on the type of application. Lossless compression implies that the original content can be wholly reconstructed, whereas lossy compression allows some degradation in reconstruction quality in order to achieve much higher compression ratios. Under normal viewing conditions, no visible loss is perceived with lossy compression techniques. The lossless variety can only achieve a modest amount of compression (say, 2:1), whereas lossy compression schemes are capable of achieving much higher compression (usually more than 10:1).

A common characteristic of most images is that neighboring pixels are correlated and therefore contain redundant information. With image compression techniques, we remove the redundant data at various levels

Figure 11.46: Example digital image.

(at the pixel, transform coefficient, and binary symbol levels), and thereby reduce the number of bits required to represent image content. JPEG (joint photographic experts group) and JPEG2000 compression techniques are widely used for still images compression.

11.6.1 JPEG

Since its standardization in 1994, JPEG is very popular for use in applications such as digital cameras and the Internet to compress images for storage and transmission purposes. The basic building blocks of the JPEG image compression standard (ISO/IEC 10918-1, 1994) to perform the preceding tasks of removing redundancy are shown in Figure 11.47. JPEG typically achieves 10:1 compression with negligible perceptible loss in image quality. As JPEG (in particular baseline JPEG method) is a lossy compression method, it should not be used in applications where the exact reproduction of data is required, such as medical imaging and astronomical observation. In the following, we focus a bit more on the basic building blocks of the baseline JPEG coder.

In general, the images captured by digital cameras are in *RGB* format. But for better compression, the *RGB* format image is first converted to *YUV* format. See Section 10.1 for more details on *RGB* to *YUV* conversion. The *YUV* color space conversion allows greater compression without a significant effect on perceived image quality. Since the *YUV* color space decouples the intensity part and associated colors, and our human eyes are more sensitive to the intensity component than to color components, greater perceptual image quality for the same compression ratio is possible with compression of *YUV* images instead of *RGB*-format images.

Transform Coding

Transform coding has become the de facto standard paradigm in image compression, where the discrete cosine transform (DCT) is used because of its efficient decorrelation and energy compaction properties. With DCT, we divide the input image into 8×8 pixel blocks and then calculate the DCT of each 8×8 block. For more detail on computing the 8×8 DCT and for its efficient implementation techniques, see Section 7.2. An example follows of 8×8 block image pixels and related DCT computed coefficients. As expected, the DCT transforms most of the energy to a few low-frequency coefficients; these components are located inside the triangle in Figure 11.48(b).

Since DCT packs most of the energy in the 8×8 pixel block into the first few low-frequency components, the reconstructed image with the first few DCT coefficients still has good perceptual image quality. For example, the reconstructed image with only the first one-fourth of the DCT coefficients is shown in Figure 11.49(b); human eyes cannot perceive a quality difference between the original image shown in Figure 11.49(a) and the DCT-reconstructed image shown in Figure 11.49(b).

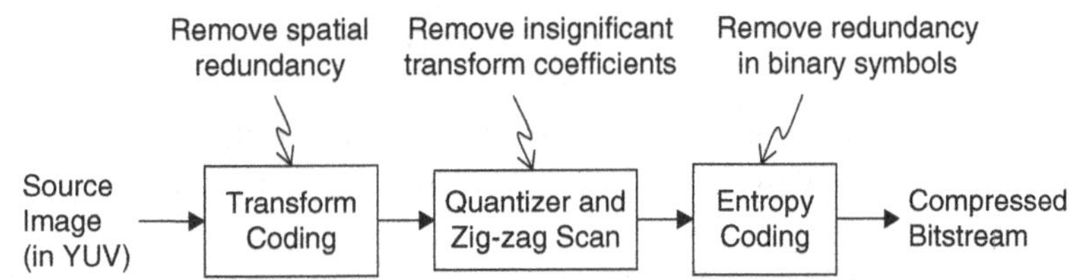

Figure 11.47: Block diagram of baseline JPEG image-compression system.

96	98	99	99	99	99	99	99
97	98	99	99	99	99	99	99
97	99	100	100	100	97	97	98
98	100	101	100	100	97	96	97
98	96	96	98	101	98	100	101
96	94	96	98	101	97	98	98
92	91	93	96	99	95	95	96
87	87	89	93	96	93	93	94

(a)

776	−6	−6	−1	4	−1	−1	2
15	5	1	−2	−4	0	0	−1
−10	−4	−1	0	0	0	0	0
5	−2	1	1	0	0	0	0
−1	0	0	0	0	0	0	0
0	3	−1	−1	0	0	0	0
0	0	0	0	0	0	0	0
0	−2	1	0	0	0	0	0

(b)

Figure 11.48: Transformation of an 8×8 block of pixels using 8×8 DCT. (a) Spatial-domain pixels. (b) Frequency-domain pixels.

(a)

(b)

Figure 11.49: Image compression with DCT. (a) Original image. (b) Reconstructed image with one-fourth of DCT coefficients.

Quantization

The output of transform coding is directly fed to the quantization block. The purpose of quantization is to achieve further compression by representing DCT coefficients with no greater precision than is necessary to achieve the desired image quality. Thus, the quantizer simply reduces the number of bits needed to store the transformed coefficients by reducing the precision of those values. Quantization is *many-to-one* mapping, and therefore is fundamentally a *lossy* process. Both *uniform* and *nonuniform* quantizers can be used depending on the problem at hand. If the quantization is performed on each individual coefficient, then it is referred to as *scalar quantization*, whereas if quantization is performed on a group of coefficients, then it is referred to as *vector quantization*. With scalar quantization, we divide each DCT coefficient by its corresponding quantizer step size, followed by rounding to the nearest integer.

$$d_{ij}^{Q} = \left\lceil \frac{d_{ij}}{Q_{ij}} \right\rfloor \tag{11.29}$$

Remember that the human eye is much more attuned to low-frequency information than high-frequency details. Therefore, small errors in high-frequency representation are not easily noticed, and eliminating certain high-frequency components entirely is often perceptually acceptable. The JPEG quantization process takes advantage of this to reduce the amount of DCT information that needs to be coded for a given 8×8 block.

Zig-Zag Scan

After quantization, most of the high-frequency component values become zero, and to efficiently code non-zero quantized DCT coefficients, we rearrange the coefficients by a special scan known as *zig-zag* scanning, shown in Figure 11.50.

With zig-zag scanning, we can rearrange the coefficients into a 1D array sorted from the DC value to the highest-order frequency component. With this scanning, most of the zero coefficients fall at the end of the sequence as shown in Figure 11.51.

All of the DC coefficients (one from each 8×8 DCT output block) are grouped together in a separate list. The DC coefficient is a measure of the average value of the 8×8 block image pixels. Because there is usually strong correlation between the DC coefficients of adjacent 8×8 block pixels, the quantized DC coefficient is encoded using a differential prediction model (DPCM). With DPCM, we can increase the probability that the code value we encode will be small, and thus reduce the number of bits overall for coding the DC coefficients. Thus, the DC coefficients will be encoded as one group and each set of AC values will be encoded separately as another group.

Entropy Coding

The entropy coding block achieves additional compression losslessly by encoding the quantized DCT coefficients more compactly based on their statistical characteristics. It uses a model to accurately determine the probabilities for each quantized value and produces an appropriate code based on these probabilities so that the resultant output codestream will be smaller than the binarized DCT coefficients input stream. The two most commonly used entropy methods are Huffman coding and arithmetic coding. For more detail on Huffman coding and arithmetic

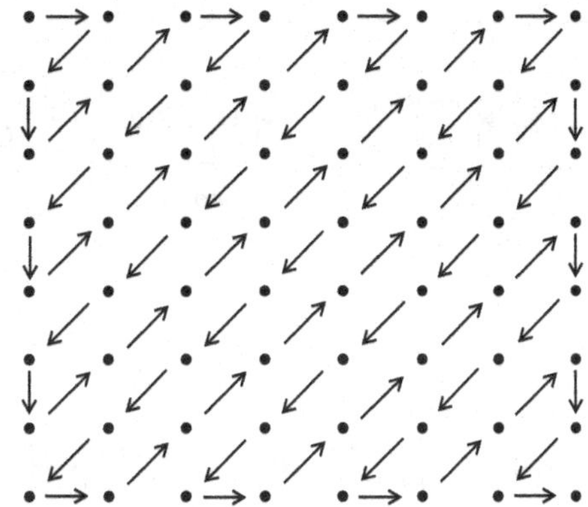

Figure 11.50: Zig-zag scanning of DCT coefficients.

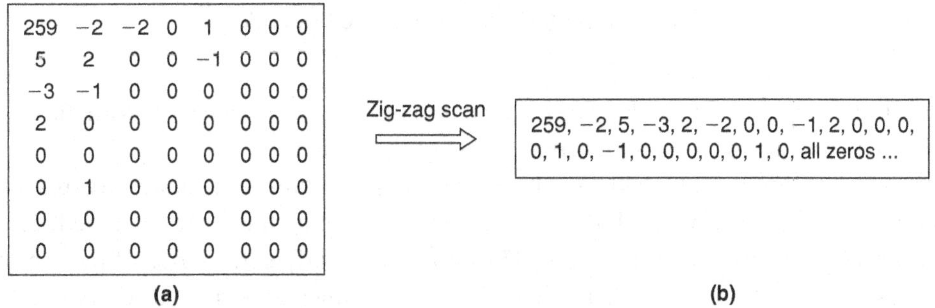

Figure 11.51: (a) An 8×8 DCT output in two dimensions. (b) Mapping from 2D to 1D using zig-zag scanning.

coding, and for efficient techniques to implement them, see Chapter 5. While arithmetic coding provides better compression than Huffman coding because it uses adaptive techniques that make it easier to achieve the entropy rate, the additional processing required may not justify the fairly small increase (5 to 10%) in compression. It is important to note that a properly designed quantizer and entropy coder are absolutely necessary along with optimum signal transformation to obtain optimal compression.

11.6.2 JPEG 2000

JPEG2000, also known as J2K, is a successor to JPEG; it addresses some of JPEG fundamental limitations while remaining backward compatible with it. The J2K standard (JPEG and JBIG, 2000) provides a set of features that are of importance to many high-end and emerging applications by taking advantage of new technologies. The J2K image-compression system has a rate-distortion advantage (provides the minimum bit rate required for allowed image distortion) over the original JPEG. More important, it also allows extraction of various resolutions, pixel fidelities, regions of interest, and more, all from a single compressed bitstream. J2K has a long list of features, a subset of which follow: superior low bit-rate performance, progressive transmission by pixel accuracy and resolution, region-of-interest coding, random codestream access and processing, compressed domain processing, lossless and lossy compression, and limited memory implementations. These features allow an application to manipulate or transmit only the essential information with the highest quality to any target device from any J2K compressed-source image. The block diagram of the J2K codec is shown in Figure 11.52. Each functional block in the decoder either exactly or approximately inverses the effects of its corresponding block in the encoder. Next, the individual modules of the J2K encoder are briefly discussed. For more description of the J2K compression method, see Christopoulos et al. (2000).

Preprocessing

In the preprocessing stage, the source image is decomposed into components (e.g., *RGB* components or *YUV* components). Then the image components are divided into nonoverlapping rectangular tiles. The tile blocks are compressed independently with J2K, as if they were entirely distinct images. Tiling reduces memory requirements, and since they are also reconstructed independently, they can be used for decoding specific parts of the image instead of the entire image. Arbitrary tile sizes are allowed, up to and including the entire image

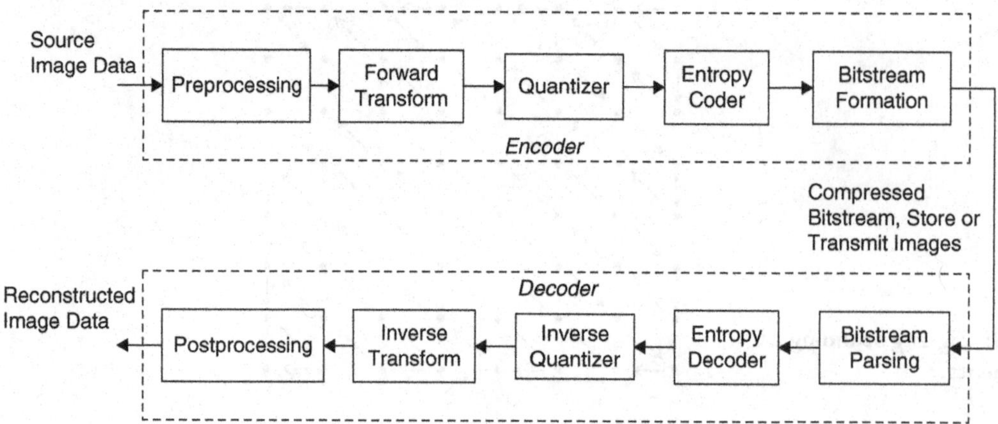

Figure 11.52: Block diagram of the J2K codec.

(i.e., entire image as a single tile). Each tile of a component must be of the same size, with the exception of tiles around the border (i.e., right-most and bottom-most sides) of the image.

The J2K coder expects its input sample data to have a nominal dynamic range that is approximately centered around zero. Suppose that a pixel has Q bits/pixel, and if the sample values are unsigned, then the nominal dynamic range is clearly not centered around zero. Thus, the nominal dynamic range of the samples is adjusted by subtracting a bias of 2^{Q-1} from each pixel value. If the pixel values of an image component are signed, the nominal dynamic range is already centered around zero, and no further processing is required.

Forward Transform: 2D Discrete Wavelet Transform

Despite all the advantages of JPEG compression schemes based on DCT, such as simplicity, satisfactory performance, and availability of hardware for efficient implementation, they are not without shortcomings. Since the input image needs to be divided into 8×8 blocks, correlation across block boundaries is not eliminated. This results in noticeable and annoying *blocking artifacts*, particularly at low bit rates (or at higher compression ratios) as shown in Figure 11.53(b), which is reconstructed by considering only first 1/16th of 8×8 DCT coefficients. The J2K codec is based on wavelet/subband coding techniques. See Section 8.3 for more detail on the wavelet transform.

The tile components are decomposed into different decomposition levels using a wavelet transform. The decomposed subbands consist of coefficients that describe the horizontal and vertical spatial frequency characteristics of the original tile component. Power of 2 decompositions is allowed in the form of dyadic decomposition as shown in Figure 11.54. Figure 11.54(d) shows an illustration of n-level dyadic decomposition of a tile component into 2D subbands. Each application of 2D dyadic decomposition of tile components yields four subbands: (1) horizontally and vertically high-pass (HH), (2) horizontally low-pass and vertically high-pass (LH), (3) horizontally high-pass and vertically low-pass (HL), and (4) horizontally and vertically low-pass (LL). The input tile component is considered to be the LL_n band. At each decomposition (or resolution level), the LL band is further decomposed (except if it is the LL_0 band). For example, the LL_{n-1} band is decomposed to yield the LL_{n-2}, LH_{n-2}, HL_{n-2}, and HH_{n-2} subbands.

Unlike DCT-based image compression, the performance of a wavelet-based, J2K image coder depends to a large degree on the choice of the wavelet. The wavelet transform used in J2K can be *reversible* or *irreversible*. The default irreversible transform (real to real) is implemented by means of the Daubechies 9-tap/7-tap filter. The default reversible transformation (integer to integer) is implemented by means of the 5-tap/3-tap filter. The wavelet filters are designed so that the coefficients in each subband are almost uncorrelated from the coefficients in the other subbands. The wavelet transform achieves better energy compaction than the DCT, and hence can help in providing better compression for the same PSNR. To perform the forward wavelet transform, the standard uses a 1D subband decomposition of a 1D set of samples into low-pass samples and high-pass samples. The basic building block for such a transform is the 1D two-channel perfect reconstruction (PR), uniformly maximally decimated filter bank, which has the general form shown in Figure 11.55.

Figure 11.53: DCT block artifacts. (a) Original image. (b) Reconstructed image with first 1/16th of DCT coefficients.

Figure 11.54: Image compression using wavelet transform. (a) Original image. (b) With one-level dyadic decomposition. (c) With two-level dyadic decomposition. (d) Illustration of *n*-level dyadic decomposition of tile component into 2D subbands.

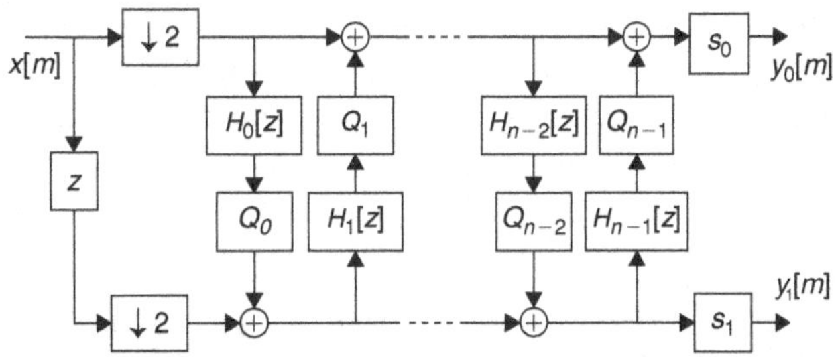

Figure 11.55: 1D realization of two-channel analysis filter bank.

Parameters for the 9/7 transform follow:

$$n=4,\ H_0[z]=\beta_0(z+1),\ H_1[z]=\beta_1(1+z^{-1}),\ H_2[z]=\beta_2(z+1),\ H_3[z]=\beta_3(1+z^{-1})$$

$$\beta_0\approx-1.586134,\quad \beta_1\approx-0.052980,\quad \beta_2\approx 0.882911,\quad \beta_3\approx 0.443506$$

$$Q_i(x)=x,\quad i=0,1,2,3\quad s_0\approx 1.230174,\quad s_1=1/s_0$$

Parameters for the 5/3 transform are given by

$$n=2,\ H_0[z]=-\frac{1}{2}(z+1),\ H_1[z]=\frac{1}{4}(1+z^{-1}),\ Q_0(x)=-\lfloor -x \rfloor,\ \ Q_1(x)=\left\lfloor x+\frac{1}{2}\right\rfloor,\ \ s_0=s_1=1$$

If a particular transform was applied to the tile component during encoding, the corresponding inverse transform is applied at the decoder. Due to the effects of finite precision arithmetic, the inverse transform process is not guaranteed to be exactly as the data input at the forward transform unless reversible 5/3 transforms are employed.

Quantization

After tile component transformation, the resulting coefficients are subjected to uniform scalar quantization employing a fixed dead zone about the origin. This is accomplished by dividing the magnitude of each coefficient by a quantization step size and rounding down. A different quantizer is employed for the coefficients of each subband. These step sizes can be chosen in a way to achieve a given quality level or target bit rate. When the integer-to-integer transform (i.e., lossless coding) is employed, the quantization step size is essentially set to 1 (which effectively bypasses quantization). In this case, quality or precise rate control is achieved through bitstream truncation. In the case of real-to-real transform mode (which implies lossy coding), the quantizer step sizes are in conjunction with rate control. The relative values of step-size parameters, used by the encoder, are conveyed to the decoder via the coded bitstream.

After quantization, each subband is divided into nonoverlapping rectangular blocks. Three spatially consistent rectangles, one from each subband at a given resolution level, comprise a *packet partition* location. These packet partitions are also referred to as *precincts*. Each packet partition location is further divided into nonoverlapping rectangles, called *code blocks*. This is illustrated in Figure 11.56.

Entropy Coding

Code blocks are the fundamental entries for the entropy coding module. Coding is performed independently on each code block. The coding is carried out in many passes on binarized coefficients and a *bitplane* is formed from the output of each pass. Considering a quantized code block to be an array of signed integers, the bitplanes are coded across the coefficients of the code block, one bitplane at a time starting from the most significant bitplane with non-zero element to the least significant bitplane.

The individual bitplanes of a code block are coded with three coding passes. The three coding passes are significance pass, refinement pass, and clean-up pass. Which pass a coefficient bit is coded in depends on conditions for that pass. In general, the significant pass includes the coefficients that are predicted to become significant and their sign bits, as appropriate. The magnitude pass includes bits from already significant coefficients. The clean-up pass includes all the remaining coefficients and sign coding, as appropriate.

All three types of coding passes scan the coefficients of a code block in the same fixed order as shown in Figure 11.57. This scan pattern is basically a column-wise raster within the height strips of the four coefficients. At the end of each strip, scanning continues at the beginning of the next strip, until an entire code block is covered as shown in Figure 11.57. For most significant bitplane coding, starting from the top left, the first 4 bits of the

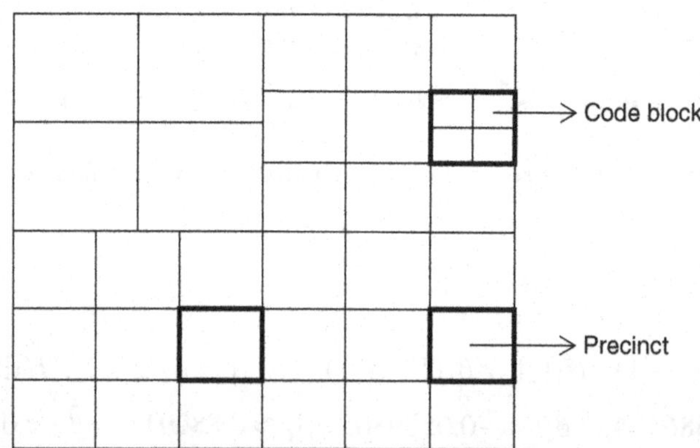

Figure 11.56: Dividing the subbands into precincts and code blocks.

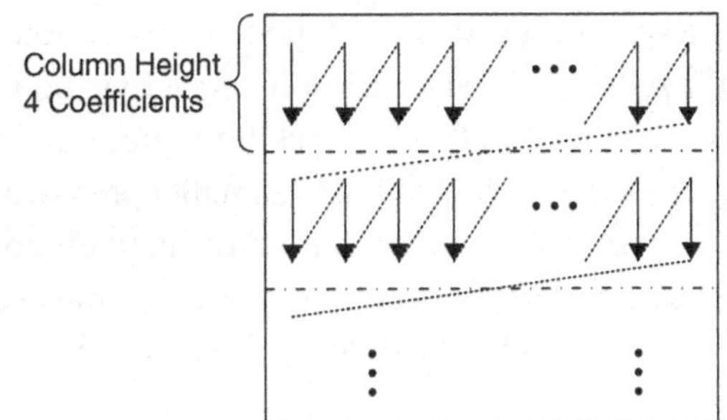

Figure 11.57: Coefficient scan order within a code block.

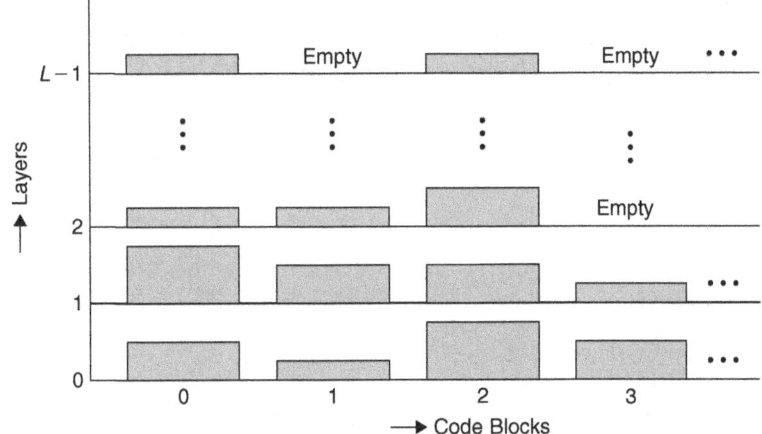

Figure 11.58: Illustration of code block data contribution to bitstream layers.

first column are scanned. Then the first 4 bits of the second column are scanned, until the width and height of the code block is covered. Other bitplanes are similarly coded.

The first coding pass for each bitplane is the significance pass. If a coefficient has not yet been found to be significant, the significance of the coefficient is coded with a single binary symbol. If the coefficient happens to be significant, then its sign is coded using a single binary symbol. The second coding pass for each bitplane is the refinement pass. If the coefficient was found to be significant in a previous bitplane, the next most significant bit of that coefficient is coded using a single binary symbol. The last coding pass for each bitplane is the clean-up pass. This pass codes significance and sign information (if needed) for coefficients that have not yet been found to be significant and are predicted to remain insignificant during bitplane processing.

The coding is carried out as context-dependent, binary arithmetic coding of bitplanes. The arithmetic coder employed is the MQ-coder, which is discussed in Section 5.4. Since context-based arithmetic coding is employed, a means for context selection is necessary. The contexts are selected by examining state information for the connected neighbors of the current coefficient. J2K uses up to nine contexts to code any given type of binary symbol information. The context models are always reinitialized at the beginning of each code block. Similarly, the arithmetic codeword is always terminated at the end of each code block.

Bitstream Formation

The encoded data of each code block is distributed in one or more layers in the codestream as shown in Figure 11.58. The coded data for each code block of a tile is organized into L layers, numbered from 0 to $L-1$. Each layer contains the additional information from each code block. Some contributions may be empty, and in general the number of bits contributed by a code block is variable. The coding passes containing the most important data are included in the lower layers, while the coding passes associated with finer details are included in the higher layers. In the case of lossy compression, some coding passes may be discarded, in which case rate control must decide which passes to include in the final codestream. In the lossless case, all coding passes must be included. Each layer successively and monotonically improves image quality, so that the decoder will be able to decode the code block contributions contained in each layer in sequence.

The coded data representing a specific tile, layer, component, resolution, and precinct appear in the codestream in a contiguous segment called a *packet*. Packet data is aligned at byte boundaries. Only code blocks that contain samples from relevant subbands confined to the precinct are represented in the packet. Since coding pass data from different precincts is coded in separate packets, using smaller precincts reduces the amount of data contained in each packet. If less data is contained in a packet, a bit error is likely to result in less information loss. Thus, using a smaller precinct size leads to improved *error resilience*, while *coding efficiency* is degraded due to the increased overhead of having a larger number of packets, as each packet contains its own header information.

J2K Decoder

At the decoder, we perform the exact opposite operations to decode the J2K compressed bitstream. The decoder performs the following operations in sequence to decompress the images: parse bitstream with scalability options, decode the bitstream with arithmetic decoder, get wavelet coefficients with dequantization, and perform inverse transformation and implement post-processing to reconstruct the image.

Part 3

Digital Speech and Audio Processing

CHAPTER 12

Speech and Audio Processing

In this chapter, we begin with a discussion of sound and audio signals, and then explore how audio data is presented to the processor from a variety of audio converters.

We will also describe the formats in which audio data is stored and processed. In particular, we will review the compromises associated with selecting data sizes. This is important because it dictates the data types used and may also rule out some processor choices if the desired quality level is too high for a particular device to achieve. Furthermore, data size selection helps in making trade-offs between increased dynamic range and additional processing power.

Next is a discussion of software building blocks for embedded audio systems. Efficient data movement is essential, so we will examine data buffering as it applies to speech and audio algorithms.

Lastly, we cover some fundamental algorithms and then finish up with a brief discussion on various speech compression standards and the voice-over Internet protocol (VoIP). Audio coding methods are discussed in Chapter 13.

Audio and speech coding is used in digital audio broadcasting (DAB), VoIP phone, media players, military applications, cinema, home entertainment systems, and distance learning, among many other applications.

12.1 Sound Waves and Signals

Sound is a longitudinal displacement wave that propagates through a medium, such as air. Sound waves are defined in terms of amplitude and frequency attributes.

Amplitude describes the sound pressure displacement above and below the equilibrium atmospheric level. In other words, the amplitude of a sound wave is a gauge of pressure change, measured in decibels (dB). The lowest sound amplitude that the human ear can perceive is called the "threshold of hearing," denoted by 0 dBSPL. On this SPL (sound pressure level) scale, the reference pressure is defined as 20 micropascals (20 μPa). The general equation for dBSPL, given a pressure change x, is

$$\text{dBSPL} = 20 * \log(x\,\mu\text{Pa}/20\,\mu\text{Pa})$$

Table 12.1 shows decibel levels for common sounds relative to the threshold of hearing (0 dBSPL). The main point of Table 12.1 is that the range of tolerable audible sounds is about 0 to 120 dB (when used to describe ratios without reference to a specific value, the correct notation is dB without the SPL suffix). Therefore, all engineered sound systems can use 120 dB as the upper bound of the dynamic range. Dynamic range will be related to data formats for digital media processing in the following discussion.

Frequency, the other key feature of sound, is denoted in hertz (Hz), or cycles per second. We can hear sounds in the frequency range between 20 and 20,000 Hz, but as we age the highest frequency that we can hear decreases.

12.1.1 Converting Sound Waves to Electrical Signals

To create an analog signal that represents a sound wave, we must use a transducer to convert the mechanical pressure energy into electrical energy. A more common name for this audio source transducer is a microphone. All transducers can be described with a sensitivity (or transduction) curve. In the case of microphones, this curve dictates how well it translates pressure into an electrical signal. Ideal transducers have a linear sensitivity curve. Therefore, a voltage level is directly proportional to a sound wave's pressure.

DOI: 10.1016/B978-1-85617-678-1.00012-0

Table 12.1: Decibel (dBSPL) values for selected common sounds

Source (distance)	dBSPL
Threshold of hearing	0
Normal conversation (3 to 5 feet away)	60 to 70
Busy traffic	70 to 80
Loud factory	90
Power saw	110
Jet engine (100 feet away)	150

Since a microphone converts a sound wave into voltage levels, we now need to use a new decibel scale to describe amplitude. This scale, called dBV, is based on a reference point of 1 V. The equation describing the relationship between a voltage level x and dBV is

$$\text{dBV} = 20 * \log(x \text{ volts}/1.0 \text{ volts})$$

An alternative analog decibel scale is based on a reference of 0.775 V and uses dBu units. To create an audible mechanical sound wave from an analog electrical signal, we again need to use a transducer. In this case, the transducer is a pair of speakers or headphones.

12.1.2 Audio and Speech Signals

The signal whose frequency spectrum is in the audible range (i.e., 20 Hz to 20 kHz) is considered an audio signal. Essentially, we are concerned with two types of audio signals: speech signals as used in variety of telecommunications and music signals such as used in broadcast and media player applications. Other audio signals include machine/electronic sounds, vehicle horns, bird sounds, and so on. Audio signals are compressed using the characteristics of the human auditory system and data compression techniques. Audio compression techniques are discussed in Chapter 13.

Speech signals can be considered a subset of audio signals. Speech signals contain information about the time-varying characteristics of the excitation source and the vocal tract system. Speech signals are nonstationary and at best they can be considered quasistationary over short time periods (typically 10 to 30 ms). The spectral properties of speech are thus defined over short segments. Resolution in both the temporal and spectral domains is essential for extracting the characteristics of speech signals. Speech can generally be classified as voiced, unvoiced, or mixed. Voiced speech is quasiperiodic in the time domain and harmonically structured in the frequency domain, while unvoiced speech is random-like in the time domain and occupies a broad spectrum in the frequency domain. Speech signals contain significant energy, from 200 Hz to 3.2 kHz. As mentioned previously, these signals are compressed using the characteristics of the human speech production system and auditory system, and data compression techniques. Various speech processing and compression algorithms are briefly addressed later in this chapter.

12.2 Digital Representation of Audio Signals

Assuming that we have already converted sound energy into electrical energy, the next step is to digitize the analog signals. Because audio itself is analog in nature, digital systems employ sampling and quantization to convert the analog audio into digital audio.

12.2.1 Sampling and Quantization

A digital representation expresses the audio signals as a sequence of symbols, usually *binary* numbers. This permits signal processing using *digital circuits* such as *DSP processors* and *computers*. In order to convert the continuous-time analog signal to a discrete-time digital representation, it must be *sampled* and *quantized*. This is accomplished with an analog-to-digital converter (A/D converter or ADC). As one might expect, in order to create an analog signal from a digital one, a digital-to-analog converter (D/A converter or DAC) is used. Since many audio systems are really intended for a full-duplex media flow, the ADC and DAC are available in a single package and called an "audio codec." These audio codecs are usually implemented with hardware chips. As discussed in Chapter 13 on audio compression, this audio codec should not be confused with audio coding codecs, which are algorithms that compress audio signals. Audio coding codecs can be implemented in software or hardware.

All A/D and D/A conversions should obey the Shannon-Nyquist sampling theorem. In short, this theorem dictates that an analog signal must be sampled at a rate (Nyquist sampling rate) equal to or exceeding twice its bandwidth (Nyquist frequency) in order to be perfectly reconstructed in the eventual D/A conversion. Sampling below the Nyquist sampling rate will introduce aliases (see Section 6.3), which are low-frequency "ghost" images of frequencies above the Nyquist frequency. If we take a sound signal that is band limited at 0 to 20 kHz, and sample it at $2 \times 20\,\text{kHz} = 40\,\text{kHz}$, then the Nyquist theorem assures us that the original signal can be reconstructed perfectly without any signal loss. However, sampling this 0- to 20-kHz band-limited signal at any frequency less than 40 kHz will introduce distortions due to aliasing.

No practical system will sample at exactly twice the Nyquist frequency, however. For example, restricting a signal to a specific band requires an analog low-pass filter, but these filters are never ideal. So the lowest sampling rate used to reproduce music is 44.1 kHz, not 40 kHz, and many high-quality systems sample at 48 kHz in order to capture the 0- to 20-kHz range of hearing even more faithfully. As mentioned earlier, speech signals are only a subset of the frequencies that we can hear; the energy content below 4 kHz is enough to store an intelligible reproduction of the speech signal. For this reason, telephony applications typically use only 8-kHz sampling ($= 2 \times 4\,\text{kHz}$). Table 12.2 summarizes common sampling rates.

The most common digital representation for audio is a PCM (pulse-code–modulated) signal. In this representation, an analog amplitude is encoded with a digital level for each sampling period. The resulting digital wave is a vector of snapshots taken to approximate the input analog wave. All A/D converters have finite resolution, so they introduce quantization noise that is inherent in digital audio systems. Figure 12.1 shows a PCM representation of an analog sine wave (Figure 12.1(a)) converted using an ideal A/D converter, in which the quantization manifests itself as the "staircase effect" (Figure 12.1(b)). You can see that the lower resolution leads to a worse representation of the original wave (Figure 12.1(c)).

For instance, assume that a 24-bit A/D converter is used to sample an analog signal whose range is −2.828 V to 2.828 V (5.656 Vpp). The 24 bits allow for 2^{24} (16,777,216) quantization levels. Therefore, the effective voltage

Table 12.2: Commonly used sampling rates

System	Sampling Frequency
Telephone	8000 Hz
Compact disc	44,100 Hz
Professional audio	48,000 Hz
DVD audio	96,000 Hz (for 5.1 channel audio)

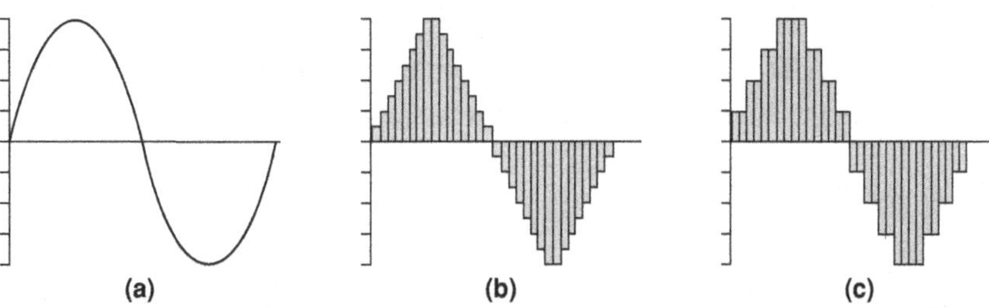

Figure 12.1: PCM representation: (a) Analog signal. (b) Digitized PCM signal. (c) Digitized PCM signal using fewer precision bits.

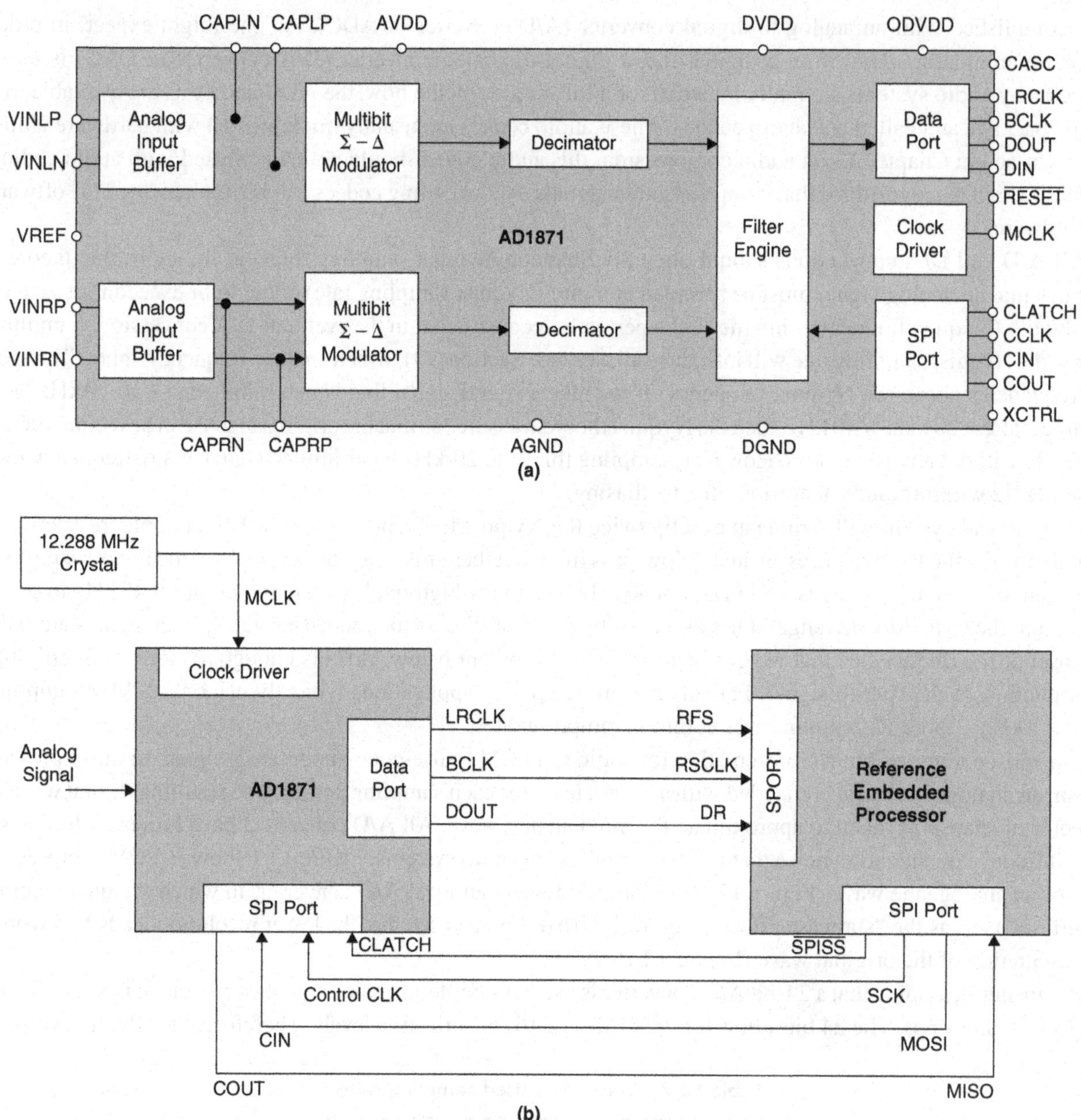

Figure 12.2: (a) Functional block diagram of AD1871 audio ADC. (b) Glueless connection of a reference embedded processor to AD1871.

resolution is 5.656 V/16,777,216 = 337.1 nV. In later sections, we see how codec resolution affects the dynamic range of audio systems.

12.2.2 Audio Converters

There are many ways to perform A/D conversion. One traditional approach is a successive approximation scheme, which uses a comparator to test the analog input signal against a number of interim D/A conversions to arrive at the final answer.

Audio ADCs

Most audio ADCs today, however, are sigma-delta converters. Instead of employing successive approximations to create wide resolutions, sigma-delta converters use 1-bit ADCs. More detail about delta modulation is provided in Section 12.4. In order to compensate for the reduced number of quantization steps, they are oversampled at a frequency much higher than the Nyquist frequency. Conversion from this supersampled 1-bit stream into a slower, higher-resolution stream is performed using digital filtering blocks inside these converters in order to accommodate the more traditional PCM stream processing. For example, a 16-bit, 44.1-kHz, sigma-delta ADC might oversample at 64x, yielding a 1-bit bitstream at a rate of 2.8224 MHz. A digital decimation filter (discussed in Section 8.2.1) converts this supersampled stream to a 16-bit one at 44.1 kHz.

Because they oversample analog signals, sigma-delta ADCs relax performance requirements of the analog low-pass filters that band limit input signals. They also have the advantage of spreading out noise over a wider spectrum than traditional converters.

Audio DACs

Traditional approaches to D/A conversion include weighted resistor, R-2R ladder, and zero-cross distortion (Pohlmann, 2000). Just as in the A/D case, sigma-delta designs rule the D/A conversion space. They can take a 16-bit 44.1-kHz signal and convert it into a 1-bit 2.8224-MHz stream using an interpolation filter (see Section 8.2.1). The 1-bit DAC then converts the supersampled stream to an analog signal.

A typical embedded digital audio system may employ a sigma-delta audio ADC and a sigma-delta DAC; therefore, the conversion between a PCM signal and an oversampled stream is done twice. For this reason, Sony and Philips have introduced an alternative to PCM, called direct-stream digital (DSD), in their Super Audio CD (SACD) format. This format stores data using the 1-bit, high-frequency (2.8224 MHz), sigma-delta stream, bypassing the PCM conversion. The disadvantage is that DSD streams are less intuitive than PCM, and they require a separate set of digital audio algorithms, so we focus only on PCM in this chapter and in Chapter 13.

Connecting to Audio Converters

A good choice for a low-cost audio ADC is the Analog Devices AD1871, which features 24-bit conversion at 96 kHz using sigma-delta technology.

An ADC Example

The functional block diagram of the AD1871 is shown in Figure 12.2(a). This converter has left (VINLx) and right (VINRx) input channels, which is really just another way of saying it can handle stereo data. The digitized audio data is streamed out serially through the data port, usually to a corresponding serial port on a signal processor (e.g., SPORT interface on a reference embedded processor). There is also a serial peripheral interface (SPI) port provided for the host processor to configure the AD1871 via software commands. These commands include ways to set the sampling rate, word width, and channel gain and muting, among other parameters.

As the block diagram in Figure 12.2(b) implies, interfacing the AD1871 ADC to a reference embedded processor is a glueless connection. The analog part of the circuit is simplified, since only the digital signals are important in this discussion. The oversampling rate of the AD1871 is supplied with an external crystal. The reference embedded processor shown has two serial ports (SPORTs) and an SPI port used for connecting to the AD1871. The SPORT, configured in I²S mode, is the data link to the AD1871, whereas the SPI port acts as the control link.

I²S (Inter-IC-Sound) The I²S protocol is a standard developed by Philips for the digital transmission of audio signals. This standard allows for audio equipment manufacturers to create components that are compatible with each other.

In a nutshell, I²S is simply a three-wire serial interface used to transmit stereo data. As shown in Figure 12.3(a), it specifies a bit clock (*middle*), a data line (*bottom*), and a left/right synchronization line (*top*) that selects whether a left or right channel frame is currently being transmitted. In essence, I²S is a time-division-multiplexed (TDM) serial stream with two active channels. TDM is a method of transferring more than one channel (e.g., left and right audio) over a physical link.

In the AD1871 setup, the ADC can reduce the 12.288-MHz sampling rate it receives from the external crystal to drive the SPORT clock (RSCLK) and frame synchronization (RFS) lines. This configuration ensures that the sampling and data transmission are in sync.

SPI (Serial Peripheral Interface) The SPI interface, shown in Figure 12.3(b), was designed by Motorola for connecting host processors to a variety of digital components. The entire interface between an SPI master and

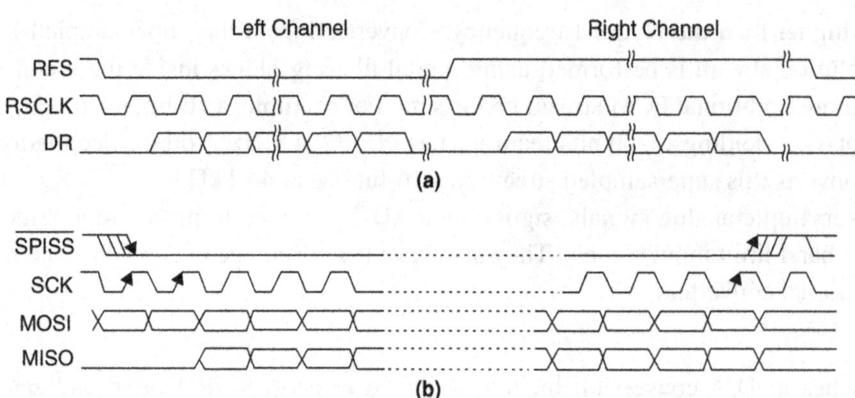

Figure 12.3: Timing diagrams. (a) Data signals transmitted by AD1871 using I²S protocol. (b) SPI interface used to control AD1871.

an SPI slave consists of a clock line (SCK), two data lines (MOSI and MISO), and a slave select (SSEL) line. One of the data lines is driven by the master (MOSI), and the other is driven by the slave (MISO). In the example shown in Figure 12.2(b), the reference embedded processor's SPI port interfaces gluelessly to the SPI block of the AD1871.

Audio codecs with a separate SPI control port allow a host processor to change the ADC settings on the fly. Besides muting and gain control, one of the really useful settings on ADCs like the AD1871 is the ability to place it in power-down mode. For battery-powered applications, this is often an essential function.

Audio Codecs

Connecting an audio DAC to a host processor is an identical process to the ADC connection just discussed. In a system that uses both an ADC and a DAC, the same serial port can hook up to both if it supports bidirectional transfers. But if you are tackling full-duplex audio, then you are better off using a single-chip audio codec that handles both the analog-to-digital and digital-to-analog conversions. A good example of such a codec is the Analog Devices AD1836, which features three stereo DACs and two stereo ADCs, and is able to communicate through a number of serial protocols, including I^2S.

I^2S is not the only audio specification. Another popular one is AC'97, which Intel Corporation created to standardize all PC audio and to separate the analog circuitry from the less noise-susceptible digital chip. In its simplest form, an AC'97 codec uses a five-pin TDM scheme where control and data are interleaved in the same signal. Various time slots in the serial transfer are reserved for a specific data channel or control word. Most processors with serial ports that support TDM mode can demultiplex an AC'97 signal at the expense of some software overhead. A good example of an AC'97 codec is the Analog Devices AD1847.

Speech Codecs

Since speech processing has slightly relaxed requirements compared to high-fidelity music systems, you may find it worthwhile to look into codecs designed specifically for speech. Among many good choices is the dual-channel 16-bit Analog Devices AD73322 (Analog Devices Inc., 2004), which has a configurable sampling frequency from 8kHz all the way to 64kHz. Figure 12.4 shows the functional diagram of AD73322 and its connection to DSP.

PWM Output Thus far, the discussion has focused on digital PCM representation and the audio DACs used to get those digital signals to the analog domain. But there is a way to use a different kind of modulation, called pulse-width modulation (PWM), to drive an output circuit directly without any need for a DAC, when a low-cost solution is required.

In PCM, amplitude is encoded for each sample period, whereas it is the duty cycle that describes amplitude in a PWM signal. PWM signals can be generated with general-purpose I/O pins, or they can be driven directly by specialized PWM timers, available on many processors. To make PWM audio achieve decent quality, the PWM carrier frequency should be at least 12 times the bandwidth of the signal, and the resolution of the timer

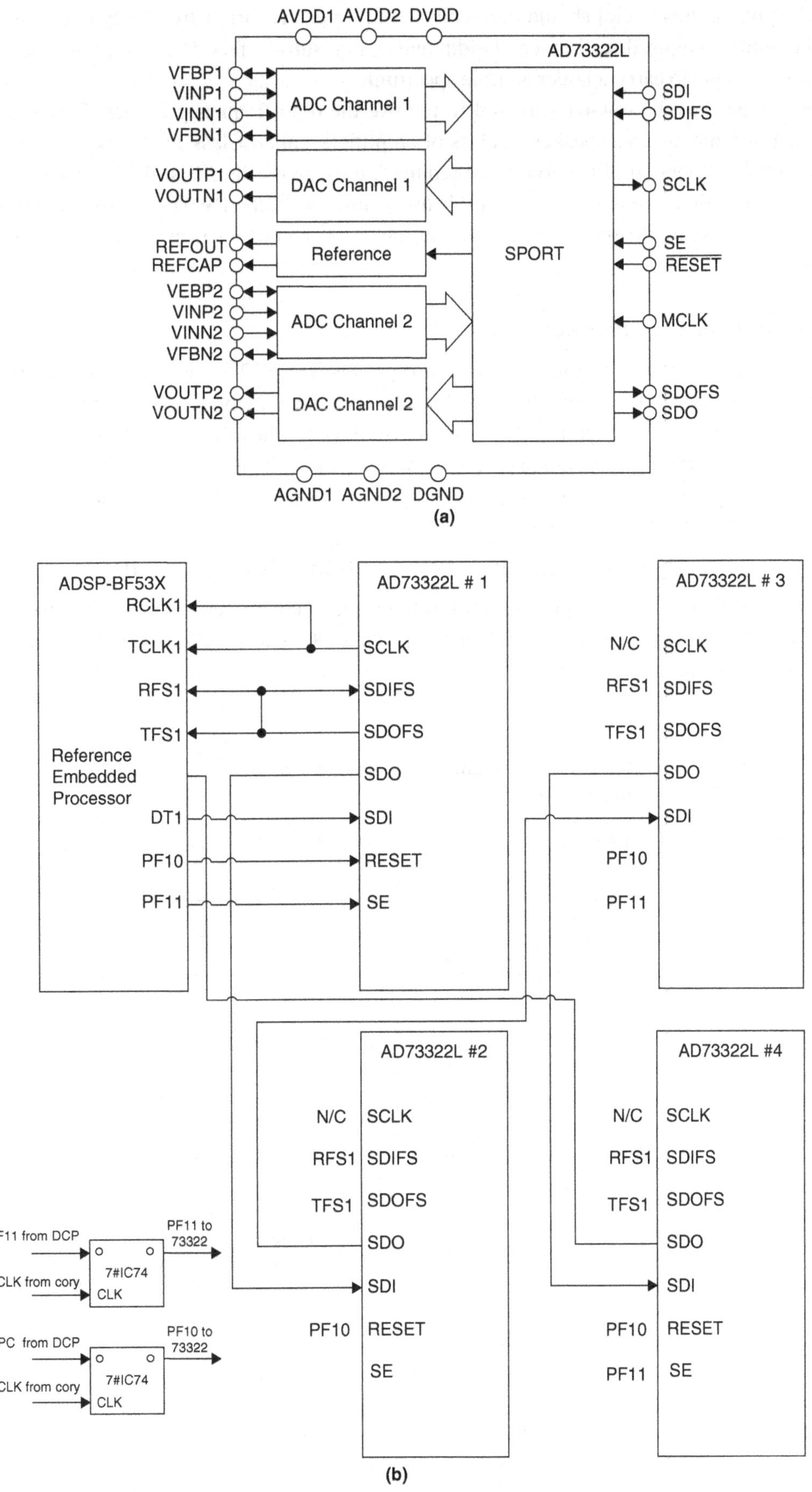

Figure 12.4: (a) AD73322L. (b) Eight-channel CODEC-DSP connection.

(i.e., granularity of the duty cycle) should be 16 bits. Because of the carrier frequency requirement, traditional PWM audio circuits were used for low-bandwidth audio, like subwoofers. However, with today's high-speed processors, it is possible to carry a larger audible spectrum.

The PWM stream must be low-pass filtered to remove the high-frequency carrier. This is usually done in the amplifier circuit that drives a speaker. A class of amplifiers, called Class *D*, has been used successfully in such a configuration. When amplification is not required, a low-pass filter is sufficient as the output stage. In some low-cost applications, where sound quality is not as important, the PWM streams can connect directly to a speaker. In such a system, the mechanical inertia of the speaker's cone acts as a low-pass filter to remove the carrier frequency.

12.2.3 Dynamic Range and Precision

In this section, we focus on the dynamic range of audio systems. Table 12.3 lists a few fairly established products along with their assigned signal quality, measured in dB. So what exactly do those numbers represent? Let us begin with some definitions. Use Figure 12.5 as a reference signal for the following "cheat sheet" of the essentials.

As mentioned earlier, the dynamic range for the human ear (the ratio of the loudest to the quietest signal level) is about 120 dB. In systems where noise is present, dynamic range is described as the ratio of the maximum signal level to the noise floor. In other words,

$$\text{Dynamic Range (dB)} = \text{Peak Level (dB)} - \text{Noise Floor (dB)} \tag{12.1}$$

The noise floor in a purely analog system comes from the electrical properties of the system itself. In addition, digital audio signals also acquire noise from the circuitry of ADCs and DACs, as well as from the quantization errors due to the sampling of analog data.

Table 12.3: Dynamic range comparison of selected audio systems

Audio Device	Typical Dynamic Range
AM radio	48 dB
Analog TV	60 dB
FM radio	70 dB
16-bit audio codecs	90 to 95 dB
CD player	92 to 96 dB
Digital audio tape (DAT)	110 dB
20-bit audio codecs	110 dB
24-bit audio codecs	110 to 120 dB

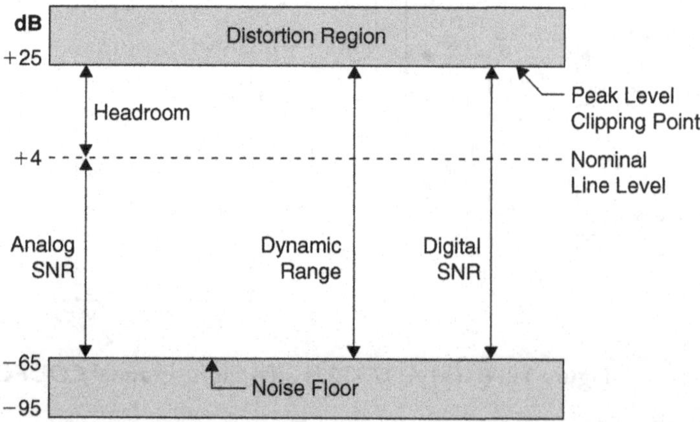

Figure 12.5: Relationship among important terms in audio systems.

Another important term is the signal-to-noise ratio (SNR). In analog systems, this means the ratio of the nominal signal to the noise floor, where "line level" is the nominal operating level. On professional equipment, the nominal level is usually 1.228 Vrms, which translates to +4 dBu. The headroom is the difference between nominal line level and the peak level where signal distortion starts to occur. The definition of SNR is a bit different in digital systems, where it is defined as the dynamic range.

Without going into a long derivation, let us simply state what is known as the "6-dB rule," which holds the key to the relationship between dynamic range and computational word width. The complete formulation is shown in Equation 12.2, but it is used in shorthand to mean that the addition of 1 bit of precision will lead to a dynamic range increase of 6 dB. Note that the 6-dB rule does not take into account the analog subsystem of an audio design, so imperfections in the transducers on both the input and the output must be considered separately.

$$\text{Dynamic Range (dB)} = 6.02n + 4.77 - 20\log_{10}\left[\frac{S_{\max}}{\sigma_s}\right] \approx 6n\,\text{dB} \tag{12.2}$$

where $n =$ the number of precision bits, $S_{\max}$ represent the maximum amplitude of signal $s[n]$, and σ_s is the variance of $s[n]$.

The 6-dB rule dictates that the more bits we use, the higher the quality of the system we can attain. In practice, however, there are only a few realistic choices. Most devices suitable for digital media processing come in three word-width flavors: 16-, 24-, and 32-bit. Table 12.4 summarizes the dynamic range for these types of processors.

Given the 6-dB rule, it is worth noting that nonlinear quantization methods are typically used for speech signals. A telephone-quality linear PCM encoding requires 12 bits of precision. However, our ears are more sensitive to audio changes at small amplitudes than at high amplitudes. Therefore, the linear PCM sampling is overkill for telephone communications. The logarithmic quantization used by the *A-law* and *μ-law* companding standards achieves a 12-bit PCM level of quality using only 8 bits of precision. More detail on μ-law quantization is provided in Section 12.4.1 during discussion of speech compression methods. To make our lives easier, some processor vendors have implemented A-law and μ-law companding into the serial ports of their devices. This relieves the processor core from performing logarithmic calculations.

After reviewing Table 12.4, recall once again that the dynamic range for the human ear is around 120 dB. Because of this, 16-bit data representation is inadequate for high-quality audio. This is why vendors introduced 24-bit processors that extended the dynamic range of 16-bit systems. The 24-bit systems are a bit nonstandard from a C-compiler standpoint, so many audio designs these days use 32-bit processing.

Choosing the right processor is not the end of the story, because the total quality of an audio system is dictated by the level of the "lowest-achieving" component. Besides the processor, a complete system includes analog components like microphones and speakers, as well as the converters to translate signals between the analog and digital domains. The analog domain is outside of the scope of this discussion, but the audio converters cross into the digital realm.

Assume that you want to use the AD1871, the same ADC as shown in Figure 12.2(a), for sampling audio. The data sheet for this converter explains that it is a 24-bit converter, but its dynamic range is not 144 dB, but rather 105 dB. The reason for this is that a converter is not a perfect system, and vendors publish only the useful dynamic range in their documentation.

If we were to hook up a 24-bit processor to the AD1871, then the SNR of the complete system would be 105 dB. The noise floor would amount to 144 dB − 105 dB = 39 dB. Figure 12.6 is a graphical representation

Table 12.4: Dynamic range of selected fixed-point architectures

Computation Word Width	Dynamic Range (Using 6-dB Rule)
16-bit fixed-point precision	96 dB
24-bit fixed-point precision	144 dB
32-bit fixed-point precision	192 dB

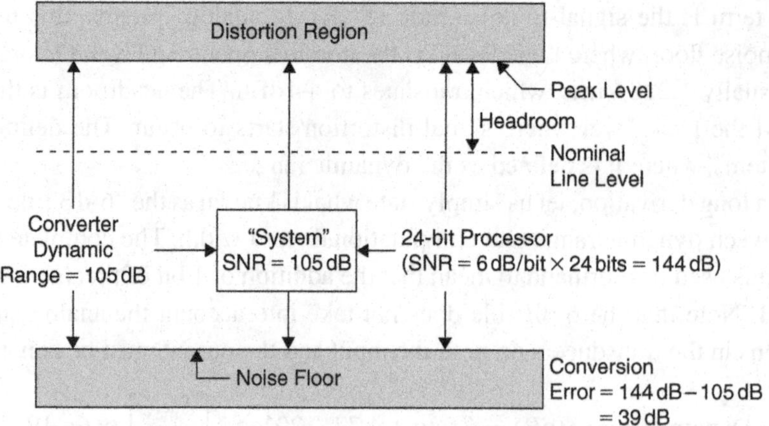

Figure 12.6: Audio system's SNR is equal to weakest component's SNR.

of this situation. However, there is still another component of a digital audio system that we have not discussed yet: computation on the processor's core.

Passing data through a processor's computation units can potentially introduce a variety of errors. One is quantization error. This can be introduced when a series of computations causes a data value to be either truncated or rounded (up or down). For example, a 16-bit processor may be able to add a vector of 16-bit data and store this in an extended length accumulator. However, when the value in the accumulator is eventually written to a 16-bit data register, then some of the bits are truncated.

Take a look at Figure 12.7 to see how computation errors can affect a real system. If we take an ideal 16-bit A/D converter (Figure 12.7(a)), then its SNR would be $16 \times 6 = 96$ dB. If quantization errors did not exist, then 16-bit computations would suffice to keep the SNR at 96 dB. Both 24-bit and 32-bit systems would dedicate 8 and 16 bits, respectively, to the dynamic range below the noise floor. In essence, the extra bits would be wasted.

However, all digital audio systems introduce some round-off and truncation errors. If we can quantify this error to take, for example, 18 dB (or 3 bits), then it becomes clear that 16-bit computations will not suffice in keeping the system's SNR at 96 dB (Figure 12.7(b)). Another way to interpret this is to say that the effective noise floor is raised by 18 dB, and the total SNR is decreased to $96\,\text{dB} - 18\,\text{dB} = 78\,\text{dB}$. This leads to the conclusion that having extra bits below the noise floor helps to deal with the nuisance of quantization.

Numeric Formats for Audio There are many ways to represent data inside a processor. The two main processor architectures used for audio processing are fixed point and floating point. Fixed-point processors are designed for integer and fractional arithmetic, and they usually natively support 16-bit, 24-bit, or 32-bit data. For more details on fixed-point (or Q-format) representation of real numbers and for fixed-point arithmetic, see Appendix B, Section B.1, on the companion website. Floating-point processors provide very good performance with native support for 32- or 64-bit floating-point data types. However, they are typically more costly and consume more power than their fixed-point counterparts, and most real systems must strike a balance between quality and engineering cost.

Fixed-Point Arithmetic

Processors that can perform fixed-point operations typically use a 2 complement binary notation for representing signals. A fixed-point format can represent both signed and unsigned integers and fractions. The signed fractional format is most common for digital signal processing on fixed-point processors. The difference between integer and fractional formats lies in the location of the binary point. For integers, the binary point is to the right of the least significant bit, whereas the binary part of fractions is usually to the right of the sign bit. Figure 12.8(a) shows integer and fractional formats (see Appendix B, Section B.1, on the companion website). While the fixed-point convention simplifies numeric operations and conserves memory, it presents a trade-off between dynamic range and precision. In situations that require a large range of numbers while maintaining high resolution, a radix point that can shift based on magnitude and exponent is desirable.

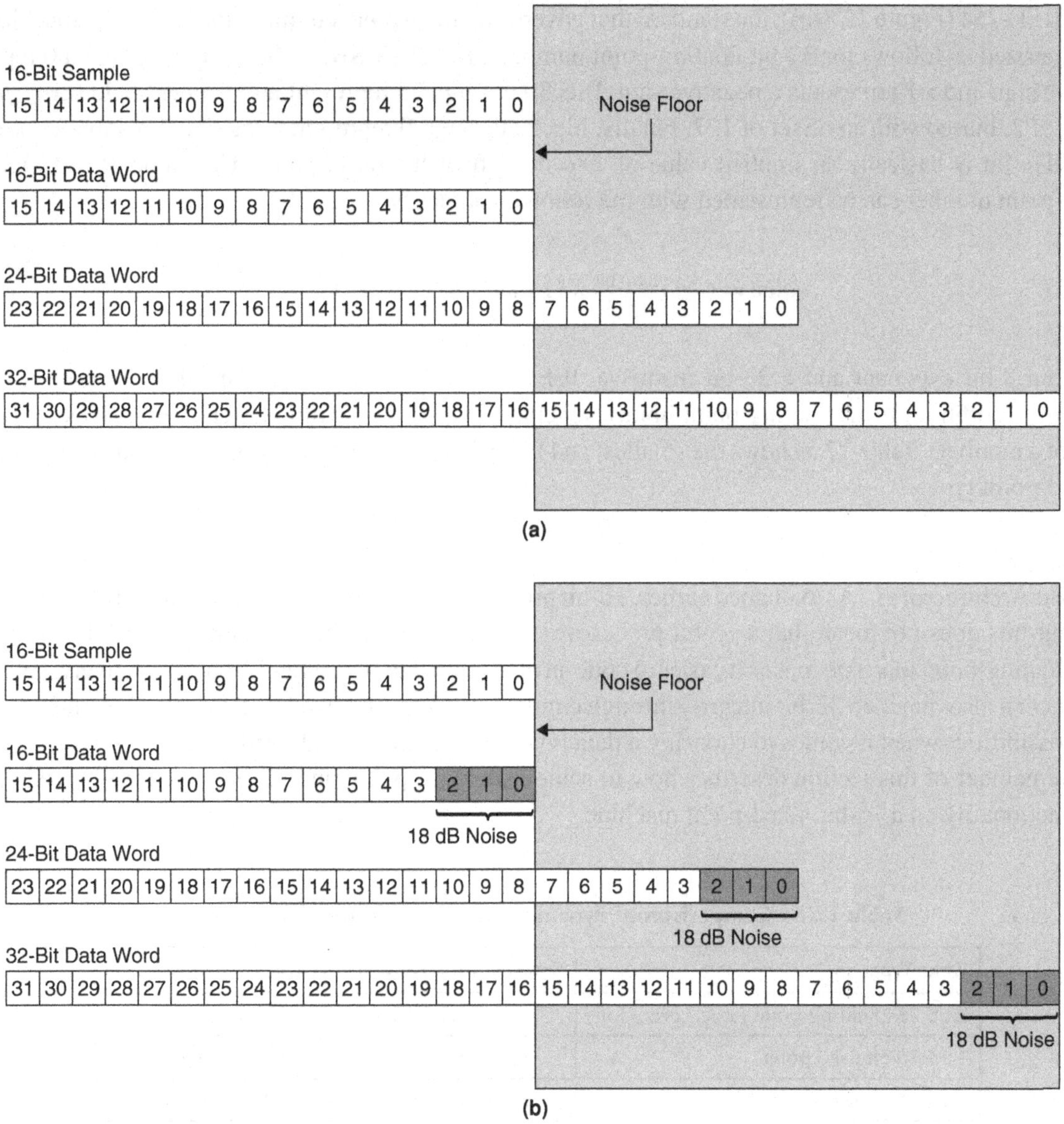

Figure 12.7: (a) Allocation of extra bits with various word-width computations for ideal 16-bit, 96-dB SNR system, when quantization error is neglected. (b) Allocation of extra bits with various word-width computations for ideal 16-bit, 96-dB SNR system, when quantization noise is present.

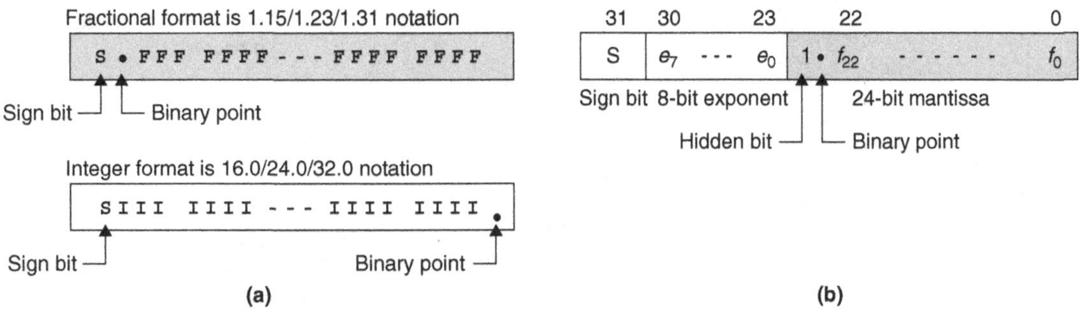

Figure 12.8: (a) Fractional and integer formats. (b) IEEE 754 32-bit, single-precision floating-point format.

Floating-Point Arithmetic

Using the floating-point format, very large and very small numbers can be represented in the same system. Floating-point numbers are quite similar to scientific notation of rational numbers. They are described with a mantissa and an exponent. The mantissa dictates precision, and the exponent controls dynamic range.

The IEEE-754 (Figure 12.8(b)), the standard that governs floating-point computations of digital machines, can be summarized as follows for 32-bit floating-point numbers. Bit 31 (MSB) is the *sign bit*, where a 0 represents a positive sign and a 1 represents a negative sign. Bits 30 through 23 represent an exponent field (*exp_ field*) as a power of 2, biased with an offset of 127. Finally, bits 22 through 0 represent a fractional mantissa (*mantissa*). The hidden bit is basically an implied value of 1 to the left of the radix point. The value of a 32-bit, IEEE floating-point number can be represented with the following equation:

$$\text{Value} = (-1)^{\text{sign\_bit}} \times (1.\text{mantissa})*2^{(\text{exp\_field}-127)} \qquad (12.3)$$

With an 8-bit exponent and a 23-bit mantissa, IEEE-754 reaches a balance between dynamic range and precision. In addition, IEEE floating-point libraries include support for additional features such as $\pm\infty$, 0, and NaN (not a number). Table 12.5 shows the smallest and largest values attainable from the common floating-point and fixed-point types.

Emulation on Fixed-Point Processors

On 16-Bit Architectures As explained earlier, 16-bit processing does not provide enough SNR for high-quality audio, but this does not mean that a 16-bit processor should be rejected for an audio system. For example, a 32-bit, floating-point machine makes it easier to code an algorithm that preserves 32-bit data natively, but a 16-bit processor can also maintain 32-bit integrity through emulation at a much lower cost. Figure 12.9 illustrates some of the possibilities when it comes to choosing a data type for an embedded algorithm.

The remainder of this section describes how to achieve floating-point, and 32-bit, extended-precision fixed-point functionality on a 16-bit, fixed-point machine.

Table 12.5: Comparison of dynamic range for selected data formats

Data Type	Smallest Positive Value	Largest Positive Value
IEEE 754 floating-point (single precision)	$2^{-126} \approx 1.2 \times 10^{-38}$	$2^{128} \approx 3.4 \times 10^{38}$
1.15 16-bit fixed point	$2^{-15} \approx 3.1 \times 10^{-5}$	$1-2^{-15} \approx 9.9 \times 10^{-1}$
1.23 24-bit fixed point	$2^{-23} \approx 1.2 \times 10^{-7}$	$1-2^{-23} \approx 9.9 \times 10^{-1}$

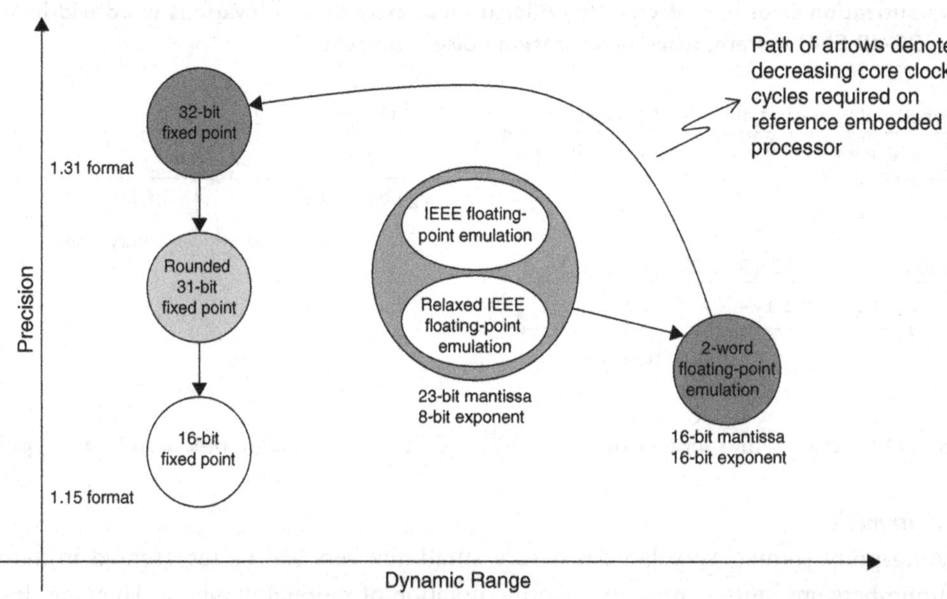

Figure 12.9: Depending on application goals, many data types can satisfy system requirements.

Floating-Point Emulation on Fixed-Point Processors

On most 16-bit fixed-point processors, IEEE-754 floating-point functions are available as library calls from either C/C++ or assembly language. These libraries emulate the required floating-point processing using fixed-point multiply and ALU logic. This emulation requires additional cycles to complete. However, as fixed-point, processor-core clock speeds venture into the 500-MHz to 1-GHz range, the extra cycles required to emulate IEEE-754–compliant floating-point math become less significant.

It is sometimes advantageous to use a "relaxed" version of IEEE-754 in order to reduce computational complexity. This means that the floating-point arithmetic does not implement the standard features such ∞ and NaN.

A further optimization is to use a more native type for the mantissa and exponent. Take, for example, the reference-embedded-processor architecture, which has a register file set that consists of sixteen 16-bit registers that can be used instead as eight 32-bit registers. In this configuration, on every core clock cycle, two 32-bit registers can source operands for computation on all four register halves. To make optimized use of the reference embedded processor register file, a two-word format can be used. In this way, one word (16 bits) is reserved for the exponent and the other word (16 bits) is reserved for the fraction.

Double-Precision Fixed-Point Emulation

There are many applications in which 16-bit fixed-point data is not sufficient, but where emulating floating-point arithmetic may be too computationally intensive. For these applications, extended-precision, fixed-point emulation may be enough to satisfy system requirements. Using a high-speed, fixed-point processor will ensure a significant reduction in the amount of required processing. Two popular extended-precision formats for audio are 32-bit and 31-bit fixed-point representations.

32-Bit Accurate Emulation

The 32-bit arithmetic is a natural software extension for 16-bit fixed-point processors. For processors whose 32-bit register files can be accessed as two 16-bit halves, the halves can be used together to represent a single 32-bit, fixed-point number. The reference embedded processor's hardware implementation allows for single-cycle 32-bit addition and subtraction. For instances where a 32-bit multiply will be iterated with accumulation (as is the case in some algorithms discussed in subsequent sections), we can achieve 32-bit accuracy with 16-bit multiplications in just 3 cycles. Each of the two 32-bit operands (R0 and R1) can be broken up into two 16-bit halves (R0.H/R0.L and R1.H/R1.L).

As seen in Figure 12.10, the following operations are required to emulate the 32-bit multiplication R0 × R1 with a combination of instructions using 16-bit multipliers.

- Four 16-bit multiplications to yield four 32-bit results.
    1. R1.L × R0.L
    2. R1.L × R0.H

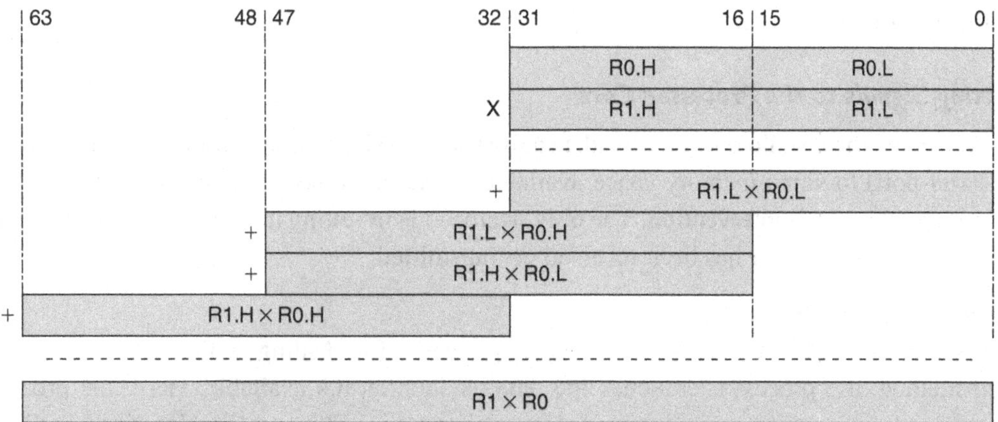

Figure 12.10: 32-bit multiplication with 16-bit operations.

3. R1.H × R0.L
4. R1.H × R0.H

- Three operations to preserve bit place in the final answer (the >> symbol denotes a right shift). Since we are performing fractional arithmetic, the result is 1.63 (1.31 × 1.31 = 2.62 with a redundant sign bit). Most of the time, the result can be truncated to 1.31 in order to fit in a 32-bit data register. Therefore, the result of the multiplication should be in reference to the sign bit, or the most significant bit. This way the right-most least significant bits can be safely discarded in a truncation.
  1. (R1.L × R0.L) >> 32
  2. (R1.L × R0.H) >> 16
  3. (R1.H × R0.L) >> 16

  The final expression for a 32-bit multiplication is

$$((R1.L \times R0.L) \gg 32 + (R1.L \times R0.H) \gg 16) + ((R1.H \times R0.L) \gg 16 + R1.H \times R0.H)$$

On the reference-embedded-processor architecture, these instructions can be issued in parallel to yield an effective rate of a 32-bit multiplication in 3 cycles.

31-Bit Accurate Emulation

We can reduce a fixed-point multiplication requiring at most 31-bit accuracy to just 2 cycles. This technique is especially appealing for audio systems, which usually require at least 24-bit representation, but where 32-bit accuracy may be a bit excessive. Using the "6-dB rule," 31-bit accurate emulation still maintains a dynamic range of around 186 dB, which is plenty of headroom even with all the quantization effects.

From the multiplication diagram shown in Figure 12.10, it is apparent that the multiplication of the least significant halfword R1.L × R0.L does not contribute much to the final result. In fact, if the result is truncated to 1.31, then this multiplication can only have an effect on the least significant bit of the 1.31 result. For many applications, the loss of accuracy due to this bit is balanced by the speeding up of the 32-bit multiplication through eliminating one 16-bit multiplication, one shift, and one addition.

The expression for 31-bit accurate multiplication is

$$((R1.L \times R0.H) + (R1.H \times R0.L)) \gg 16 + (R1.H \times R0.H)$$

On the reference-embedded-processor architecture, these instructions can be issued in parallel to yield an effective rate of 2 cycles for each 32-bit multiplication.

12.3 Signal Processing with Embedded Processor

There are a number of ways to get the signal data into the processor core. For example, a foreground program can poll a serial port for new data, but this type of transfer is uncommon in embedded media processors because it makes inefficient use of the core.

12.3.1 Getting Signals to the Processor Core

A processor connected to an audio codec, instead, usually uses a DMA engine to transfer the data from the codec link (like a serial port) to some memory space available to the processor. This transfer of data occurs in the background without the core's intervention. The only overhead is in setting up the DMA sequence and handling the interrupts once the data buffer has been received or transmitted.

Block Processing versus Sample Processing

Sample processing and block processing are two approaches for dealing with digital audio data. In the sample-based method, the processor crunches the data as soon as it's available. Here, the processing function incurs overhead during each sample period. Many filters (e.g., FIR and IIR, described in Chapter 7) are implemented this way, because the effective latency is low.

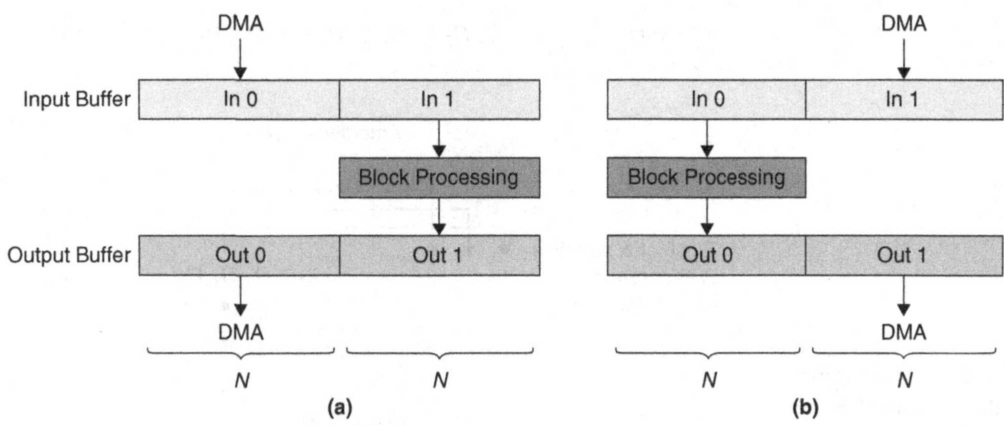

Figure 12.11: Double-buffering scheme for stream processing. (a) DMA accessing In0 and Out0 buffers while core works on In1 and Out1 (b) DMA accessing In1 and Out1 buffers while core works on In0 and Out0 buffers.

Block processing, on the other hand, is based on filling a buffer of a specific length before passing the data to the processing function. Some filters are implemented using block processing because it is more efficient than sample processing. For one, the block method sharply reduces the overhead of calling a processing function for each sample. Also, many embedded processors contain multiple ALUs that can parallelize the computation of a block of data. What's more, some algorithms are, by nature, meant to be processed in blocks. A well-known one is the Fourier transform (and its practical counterpart, the fast Fourier transform, or FFT, see Section 7.1), which accepts blocks of temporal or spatial data and converts them into frequency-domain representations.

Double Buffering

In a block-based processing system that uses DMA to transfer data to and from the processor core, a "double buffer" must exist to arbitrate between the DMA transfers and the core. This is done so that the processor core and the core-independent DMA engine do not access the same data at the same time, causing a data coherency problem. To facilitate the processing of a buffer of length N, simply create a buffer of length $2 \times N$. For a bidirectional system, two buffers of length $2 \times N$ must be created. As shown in Figure 12.11(a), the core processes the **In1** buffer and stores the result in the **Out1** buffer, while the DMA engine is filling **In0** and transmitting the data from **Out0**.

Figure 12.11(b) shows that once the DMA engine is done with the left half of the double buffers, it starts transferring data into **In1** and out of **Out1**, while the core processes data from **In0** and into **Out0**. This configuration is sometimes called "Ping-Pong buffering," because the core alternates between processing the left and right halves of the double buffers.

Note that in real-time systems, the serial port DMA (or another peripheral's DMA tied to the audio sampling rate) dictates the timing budget. For this reason, the block-processing algorithm must be optimized in such a way that its execution time is less than or equal to the time it takes the DMA to transfer data to/from a half of a double-buffer.

2D DMA

When data is transferred across a digital link like I^2S, it may contain several channels. These may all be multiplexed on one data line going into the same serial port. In such a case, 2D DMA (see Appendix A, Section A.3, on the companion website) can be used to deinterleave the data so that each channel is linearly arranged in memory. Take a look at Figure 12.12 for a graphical depiction of this arrangement, where samples from the left and right channels are demultiplexed into two separate blocks. This automatic data arrangement is extremely valuable for those systems that employ block processing.

12.3.2 Signal Processing

There are three fundamental building blocks in audio processing. They are the summing operation, multiplication, and time delay. Many more complicated effects and algorithms can be implemented using these three elements.

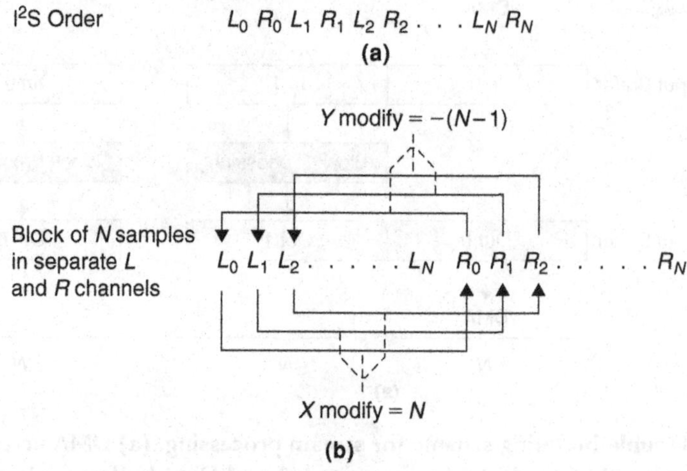

Figure 12.12: 2D DMA engine: (a) Used to deinterleave I²S stereo data. (b) Data interleaved into separate left and right buffers.

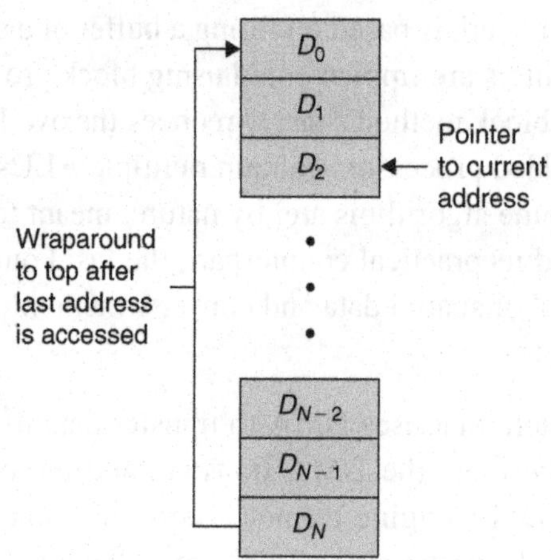

Figure 12.13: Layout of circular buffer in memory.

Basic Operations

A summer has the obvious duty of adding two signals together. A multiplication can be used to boost or attenuate an audio signal. On most media processors, multiple summer and/or multiplier blocks can be executed in a single cycle. A time delay is a bit more complicated. In many audio algorithms, the current output depends on a combination of previous inputs and/or outputs. The implementation of this delay effect is accomplished with a delay line, which is really nothing more than an array in memory that holds previous data. For example, an echo algorithm might hold 500 ms of input samples for each channel. The current output value can be computed by adding the current input value to a slightly attenuated previous sample. If the audio system is sample based, then the programmer can simply keep track of an input pointer and an output pointer (spaced at 500 ms worth of samples apart), and increment them after each sampling period.

Since delay lines are meant to be reused for subsequent sets of data, the input and output pointers will need to wrap around from the end of the delay line buffer back to the beginning. In C/C++, this is usually done by appending the modulus operator (%) to the pointer increment. This wraparound may incur no extra processing cycles if you use a processor that supports circular buffering (see Figure 12.13). In this case, the beginning and length of a circular buffer must be provided only once. During processing, the software increments or decrements the current pointer within the buffer, but the hardware takes care of wrapping around to the beginning of the buffer if the current pointer falls outside of the bounds. Without this automated address generation, the programmer would have to manually keep track of the buffer, thus wasting valuable processing cycles.

An echo effect derives from an important audio building block called the comb filter, which is essentially a delay with a feedback element. When multiple comb filters are used simultaneously, they can create the effect of reverberation.

Signal Generation

In some audio systems, a signal (e.g., a sine wave) might need to be synthesized. Taylor-series function approximations can emulate trigonometric functions. Moreover, uniform random number generators are handy for creating white noise.

However, synthesis might not fit into a given system's processing budget. On fixed-point systems with ample memory, you can use a look-up table instead of generating a signal. This has the side effect of taking up precious memory resources, so hybrid methods can be used as a compromise. For example, you can store a coarse look-up table to save memory. During runtime, the exact values can be extracted from the table using interpolation, an operation that can take significantly less time than computing using a full Taylor series approximation. This hybrid approach provides a good balance between computation time and memory resources.

Digital Filtering

Digital filters are used in audio systems for attenuating or boosting the energy content of a sound wave at specific frequencies. The most common filter forms are high-pass, low-pass, band-pass, and notch. Any of these filters can be implemented in two ways. These are the finite impulse response filter (FIR) and the infinite impulse response filter (IIR), and they constitute building blocks to more complicated filtering algorithms like parametric equalizers and graphic equalizers. See Section 7.4 for detail on FIR-filter implementation techniques and Section 7.5 for detail on IIR-filter implementation techniques.

Fast Fourier Transform

Quite often we can do a better job describing an audio signal by characterizing its frequency composition. A Fourier transform takes a time-domain signal and rearranges it into the frequency domain; the inverse Fourier transform achieves the opposite, converting a frequency-domain representation back into the time domain. Mathematically, there are some nice relationships between operations in the time domain and those in the frequency domain. Specifically, a time-domain convolution (or an FIR filter) is equivalent to a multiplication in the frequency domain. This tidbit would not be too practical if it were not for a special optimized implementation of the Fourier transform called the fast Fourier transform (FFT). In fact, it is often more efficient to implement an FIR filter by transforming the input signal and coefficients into the frequency domain with an FFT, multiplying the transforms, and finally transforming the result back into the time domain with an inverse FFT. See Section 7.1 for detail on FFT implementation techniques.

There are other transforms that are used often in audio processing. Among them, the most common is the modified discrete cosine transform (MDCT), which is the basis for many audio compression algorithms. We will discuss more on MDCT in the next chapter.

12.4 Speech Compression

Speech compression is the field concerned with obtaining compact digital representation of voice signals for the purpose of efficient transmission or storage. Speech compression probably deserves a chapter of its own, and we will not delve too deeply here.

12.4.1 Speech Signals

The speech signals contain information about the time-varying characteristics of the excitation source and the vocal tract system. Speech can generally be classified as voiced, unvoiced, or mixed. Voiced speech is quasiperiodic in the time domain and harmonically structured in the frequency domain as shown in Figure 12.14(a) and (b), while unvoiced speech is random-like in time domain and occupies a broad spectrum in the frequency domain as shown in Figure 12.14(c) and (d). The voiced speech is produced by exciting the vocal tract with quasiperiodic glottal air pulses generated by vibrating the vocal cords. Unvoiced speech is produced by forcing air through a constriction in the vocal tract. Low bit-rate voice codecs utilize this important characteristic of the speech production system, and compress the speech by modeling the speech as a two-state excitation model together with the time-varying linear filter for mitigating the vocal tract. Model parameters are updated periodically to track

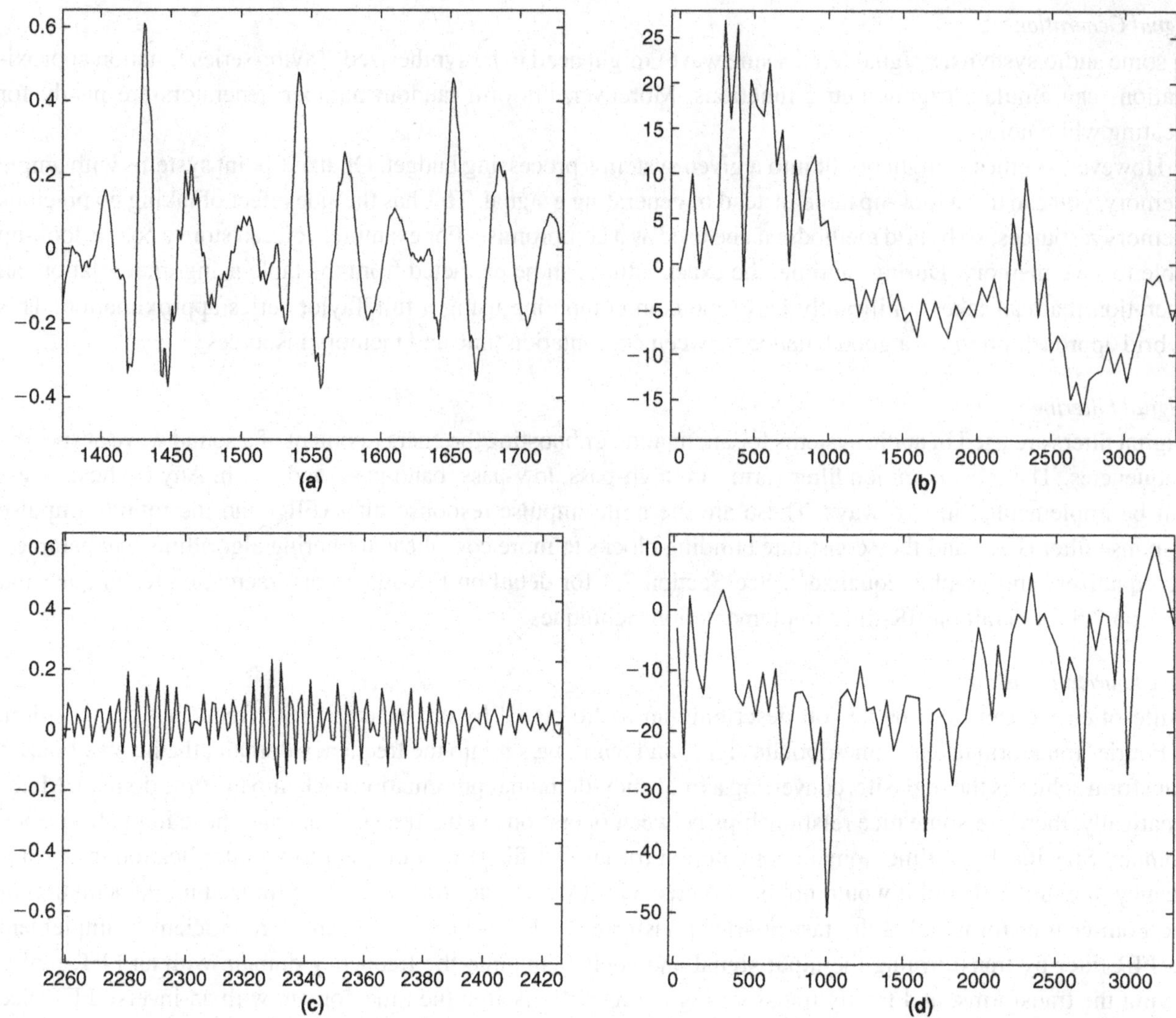

Figure 12.14: (a) Voiced speech. (b) Spectrum of voiced speech. (c) Unvoiced speech. (d) Spectrum of unvoiced speech.

the quasiperiodic statistics of the speech signals. Since model parameters vary relatively slowly compared to the speech signal itself, we achieve speech signal compression by representing the speech segment with few model parameters and transmitting those parameters to the receiver. The receiver uses the received model parameters to reproduce the synthetic speech.

The most common use for speech compression is in voice telecommunications. Most of the energy in typical speech signals is stored within less than 4 kHz of bandwidth, thus making speech a subset of audio signals. However, many speech compression techniques are based on modeling the human vocal tract, so these cannot be used for general audio compression.

Speech compression is used widely in real-time communications systems like cell phones and in packetized voice connections like Internet phones. Most of these applications require that the speech signal is in digital format so that it can be processed, stored, or transmitted under software control.

Since speech is more band limited than full-range audio, it is possible to use audio codecs, taking the smaller bandwidth into account. Almost all speech codecs do, indeed, sample voice data at 8 kHz. However, we can do better than just take advantage of the smaller frequency range. Since only a subset of the audible signals within the speech bandwidth is ever vocally generated, we can drive bit rates even lower. The major goal in speech encoding is a highly compressed stream with good intelligibility and short delays to make real-time full-duplex communication possible.

12.4.2 Speech Compression Objectives and Requirements

The objective in speech coding is to represent speech with a minimum number of bits while maintaining its perceptual quality. A speech compression algorithm is evaluated based on the following factors: quality of reconstructed speech, achievable bit rates, algorithm complexity, coding delay, and robustness of the algorithm to channel errors.

Reconstructed Speech Quality

In digital communication systems, speech quality is classified into four categories: broadcast (highest), network, communication, and synthetic (lowest). The requirement on level of speech quality varies from application to application. Typically, we use a mean opinion score (MOS) of 1 to 5 for evaluating the speech quality. The MOS are based on listener ratings. The MOS of 1 refers to poor and 5 refers to excellent. Different speech coding algorithms at different bit rates would achieve the required speech quality.

Bit Rate

The speech signals can be coded (for different applications) with bit rates in the range of 1 to 64 kbps. Usually, broadcast quality speech can be achieved with bit rates at around 64 kbps, and network-quality speech can be produced with bit rates above 16 kbps. The communication quality speech can be produced with bit rates above 4 kbps. The speech coders operating well below 4 kbps tend to produce speech of synthetic quality. In general, high-quality speech coding at low bit rates is achieved using high-complexity compression algorithms.

Coding Delay

The speech quality experience by the end user depends on many factors and one of them is end-to-end delay. Various kinds of delays are present in digital speech transmission and some of them are transmission, packetization, processing, and algorithmic. Transmission delay is beyond our control and it is variable in nature. On the other hand, algorithmic and processing delays depend on the type of algorithm used for speech coding and the type of processor architecture chosen for a particular application. End-to-end delay must be minimized for high speech quality.

Robustness to Channel Errors

In general, communication channels introduce errors in the received speech signals. As some of the compression methods code parameters instead of the signal itself and transmit, the decoding of erroneous compressed speech data at the receiver may sometimes result in a catastrophic error in the reconstructed speech. Usually, we use forward error correction (FEC) techniques (see Chapters 3 and 4) to minimize errors in the received data.

12.4.3 Speech Compression Methods

In the literature, speech compression methods are broadly divided into three classes: waveform coding, vocoder (voice coder), and hybrid coding methods as shown in Figure 12.15. The performance (quality versus bit rate) of these codecs is shown in Figure 12.16.

12.4.4 Waveform Coders

Waveform coding techniques are not speech-specific. The waveform coders focus on representing the speech waveform as such without exploiting the underlying speech model. Typically, waveform coders produce

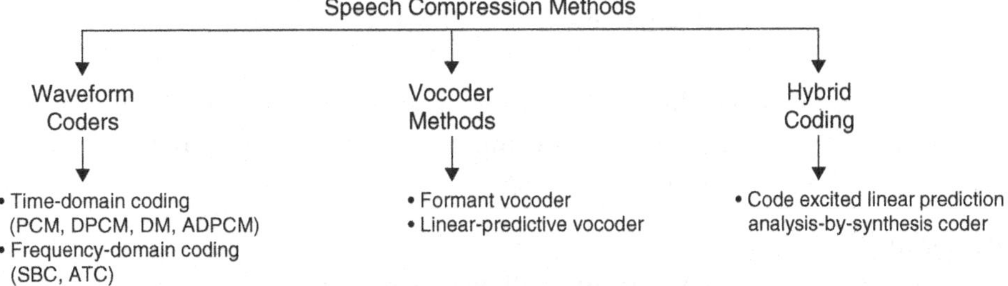

Figure 12.15: Various speech compression approaches.

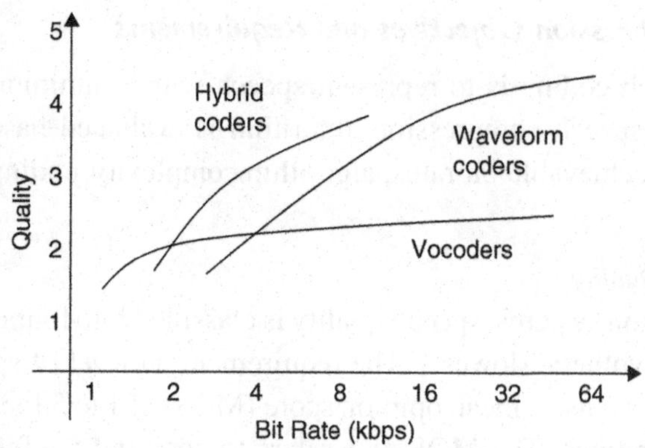

Figure 12.16: Speech codec performance (quality versus bit rate).

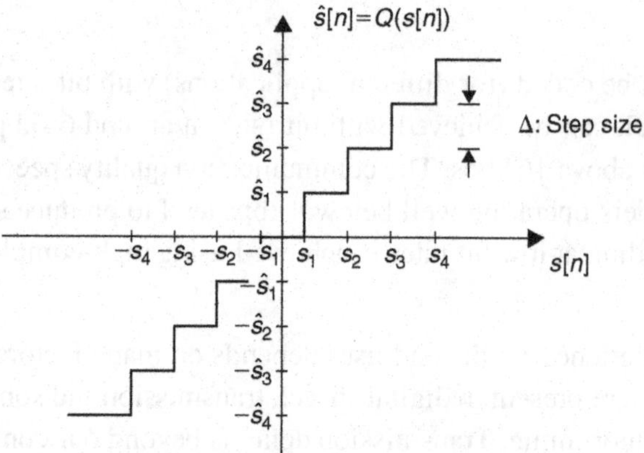

Figure 12.17: Eight-level, mid-tread quantizer.

high-quality decoded speech at bit rates in the range 16 to 64 kbps. The simplest waveform coding is PCM (pulse code modulation), which merely involves sampling and quantizing the input waveform. The sampled signal values $s[n]$ are real numbers and can be useful only for theoretical study purposes. The continuous amplitude (or infinite precision) real samples must be quantized to work with digital computers. The quantizer simply takes the real value samples $s[n]$ as input and assigns an output $\hat{s}[n]$ according to the discrete mapping $Q(s)$. An illustration of an eight-level, mid-tread quantizer is shown in Figure 12.17.

For samples within the range, the quantization error $e[n]$ satisfies the following condition:

$$-\frac{\Delta}{2} < e[n] < \frac{\Delta}{2} \tag{12.4}$$

where Δ is the quantizer step size. For a b-bit quantizer, if the peak-to-peak signal range is $2S_{\max}$, the step size Δ is given by

$$\Delta = 2S_{\max}/2^b \tag{12.5}$$

The signal-to-quantization noise ratio (in dB) of the b-bit uniform quantizer (assuming the quantization noise as uncorrelated and uniformly distributed white noise) is obtained as follows:

$$\text{SNR} = 6.02b + 4.77 - 20\log_{10}\left(\frac{S_{\max}}{\sigma_s}\right) \tag{12.6}$$

A telephone-quality linear PCM encoding with uniform quantization requires 12 bits of precision. However, our ears are more sensitive to audio changes at small amplitudes than at high amplitudes. Therefore, the linear PCM sampling is overkill for telephone communications.

Nonuniform Quantization

In the logarithmic scale, a nonuniform quantization allows quantization intervals to increase with amplitude, and it ensures that low-amplitude signals can be digitized with a minimum loss of fidelity. The nonuniform quantization used by the *A-law* and μ-law companding standards achieves a 12-bit PCM level of quality using only 8 bits of precision. A μ-law quantized speech sample is obtained by the process described in Equation 12.7. A block diagram of the PCM waveform codec with a nonuniform quantizer is shown in Figure 12.18.

$$s_l[n] = g(s[n]) = S_{\max}\frac{\log(1+\mu\,|s[n]|\,/S_{\max})}{\log(1+\mu)}\mathrm{sign}(s[n]) \tag{12.7}$$

For μ-law quantization, the SNR (in dB) is given by

$$\mathrm{SNR} = 6b + 4.77 - 20\log_{10}(1+\mu) - 10\log_{10}\left(1+\left[\frac{S_{\max}}{\mu\sigma_s}\right]^2 + \sqrt{2}\frac{S_{\max}}{\mu\sigma_s}\right) \tag{12.8}$$

Figure 12.19 shows the input-output mapping and SNR versus $S_{\max}/\sigma_s$ characteristics for uniform and μ-law quantizers. The μ-law matches the logarithmic curve with a piece-wise linear approximation rather than computing thc logarithm of the input sample directly. Eight straight line segments along the curve produce a close approximation to the logarithmic function. Each segment is known as a chord, and each chord is divided into equally sized quantization intervals called *steps*. An encoded 8-bit codeword of a μ-law quantizer (for $\mu = 255$, shown in Figure 12.20 adapted by U.S. and Japan standards) is composed of 1 sign bit concatenated with a 3-bit chord and a 4-bit step. The μ-law binary encoding and decoding, which is described in the Table 12.6, is well-suited for hardware or software implementation.

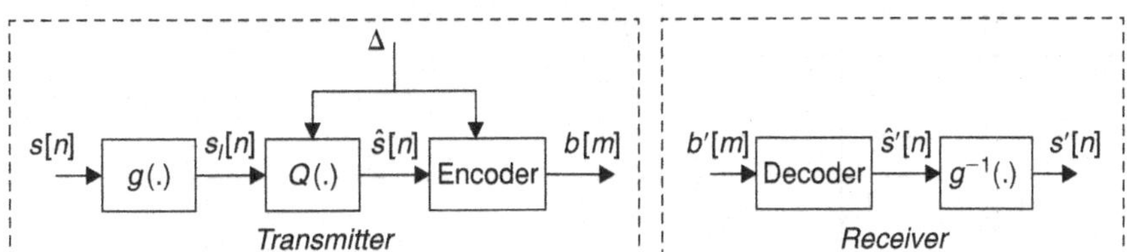

Figure 12.18: Block diagram of PCM with nonuniform quantization.

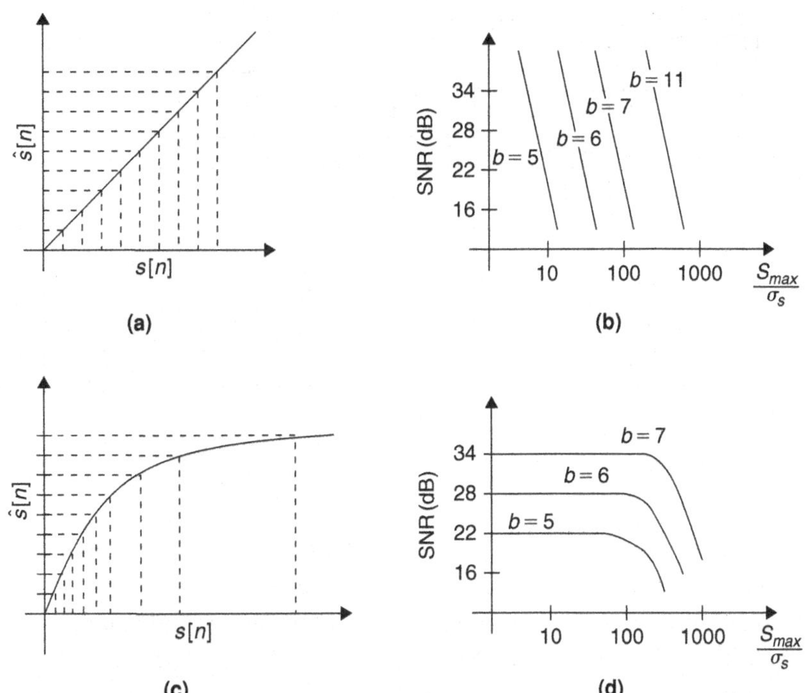

Figure 12.19: Comparison of uniform and μ-law quantization. (a) Uniform quantizer input-output mapping. (b) SNR versus $S_{\max}/\sigma_s$ characteristics of uniform quantizer. (c) μ-Law quantizer input-output mapping. (d) SNR versus $S_{\max}/\sigma_s$ characteristics of μ-law quantizer.

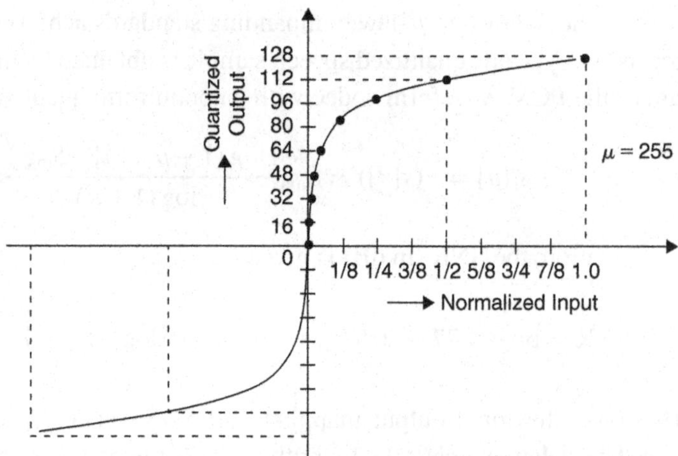

Figure 12.20: μ-Law companding curve for $\mu = 255$.

Table 12.6: Coding of μ-Law Quantized Samples

Encoding

	Input														Encoded Output (Sign|Chord|Step: 1|3|4 Bits)							
Bits:	12	11	10	9	8	7	6	5	4	3	2	1	0	Bits:	7	6	5	4	3	2	1	0
	0	0	0	0	0	0	0	1	a	a	a	a	x		s	0	0	1	a	a	a	a
	0	0	0	0	0	0	1	a	a	a	a	x	x		s	0	1	0	a	a	a	a
	0	0	0	0	0	1	a	a	a	a	x	x	x		s	0	1	1	a	a	a	a
	0	0	0	0	1	a	a	a	a	x	x	x	x		s	1	0	0	a	a	a	a
	0	0	0	1	a	a	a	a	x	x	x	x	x		s	1	0	1	a	a	a	a
	0	0	1	a	a	a	a	x	x	x	x	x	x		s	1	1	0	a	a	a	a
	0	1	a	a	a	a	x	x	x	x	x	x	x		s	1	1	1	a	a	a	a
	1	a	a	a	a	x	x	x	x	x	x	x	x		s	0	0	0	a	a	a	a

Decoding

Received Codeword (Chord|Step), Sign Bit Ignored								Decoded Output													
Bits:	6	5	4	3	2	1	0	Bits:	12	11	10	9	8	7	6	5	4	3	2	1	0
	0	0	0	a	a	a	a		0	0	0	0	0	0	0	1	a	a	a	a	1
	0	0	1	a	a	a	a		0	0	0	0	0	0	1	a	a	a	a	1	0
	0	1	0	a	a	a	a		0	0	0	0	0	1	a	a	a	a	1	0	0
	0	1	1	a	a	a	a		0	0	0	0	1	a	a	a	a	1	0	0	0
	1	0	0	a	a	a	a		0	0	0	1	a	a	a	a	1	0	0	0	0
	1	0	1	a	a	a	a		0	0	1	a	a	a	a	1	0	0	0	0	0
	1	1	0	a	a	a	a		0	1	a	a	a	a	1	0	0	0	0	0	0
	1	1	1	a	a	a	a		1	a	a	a	a	1	0	0	0	0	0	0	0

ADPCM and ADM

The encoding and decoding process for A-law is similar to that of μ-law. With nonuniform quantization (i.e., using either the A-law or μ-law), the PCM coded speech at the bit rate of 64 kbps (i.e., 8 bits/sample and 8 kilosamples per second) can give a reconstructed speech which is almost indistinguishable from the original. The more efficient waveform coders such as DPCM (differential PCM), DM (delta modulation), ADM (adaptive DM), and ADPCM (adaptive DPCM), utilize the redundancy present in the speech waveform by exploiting the correlation between adjacent samples. These waveform coders perform better than ordinary PCM for rates at and below 32 kbps. The coding schemes DPCM and DM use differential quantization, whereas the schemes ADM and ADPCM incorporate the adaptive differential quantizers. The block diagrams for these four systems are shown in Figures 12.21 through 12.24. DM is a subclass of DPCM where the error signal is encoded with only 1 bit (i.e., DM incorporates a two-level quantizer).

DM and DPCM are low-complexity coders and perform better than ordinary PCM for rates at and below 32 kbps. In all four systems—DPCM, DM, ADM, and ADPCM—the block labeled $P[z]$ is a linear predictor.

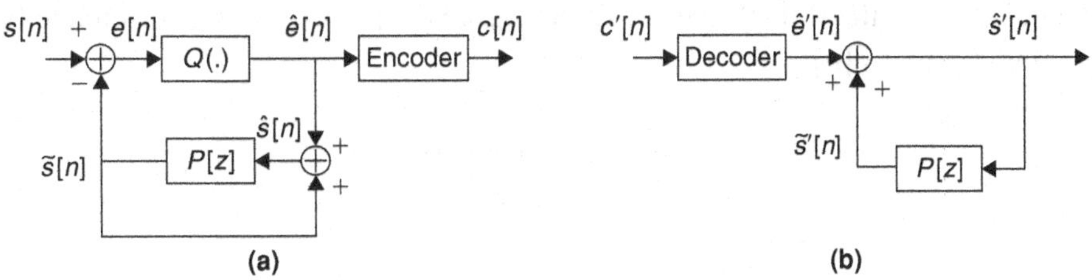

Figure 12.21: Block diagram of DPCM system. (a) Encoder. (b) Decoder.

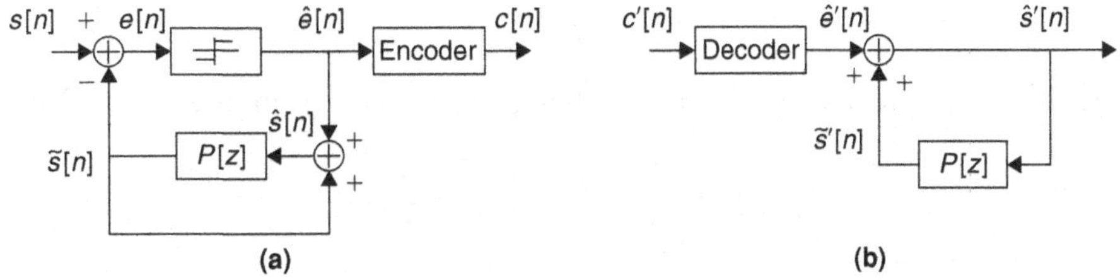

Figure 12.22: Block diagram of DM system. (a) Encoder. (b) Decoder.

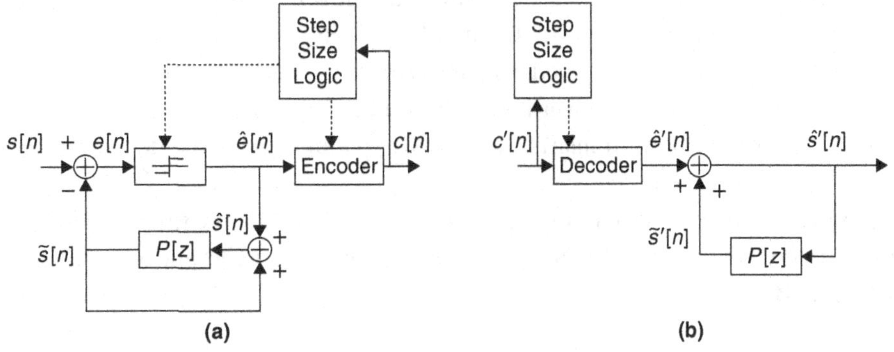

Figure 12.23: Block diagram of ADM system. (a) Encoder. (b) Decoder.

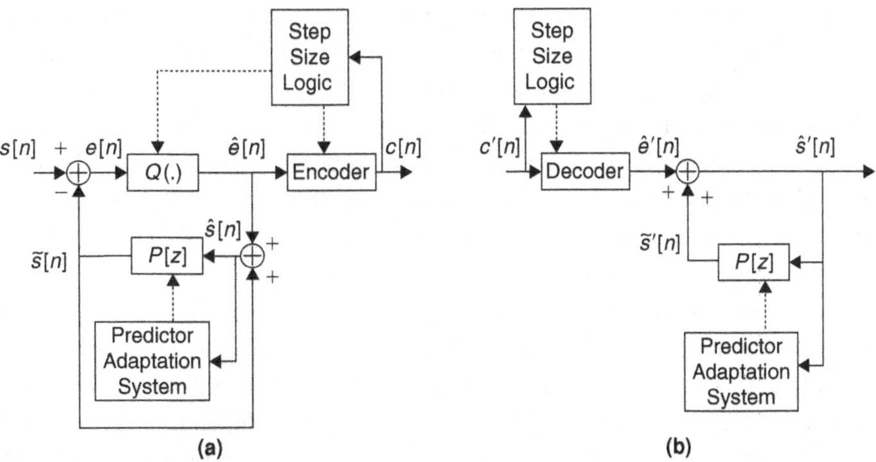

Figure 12.24: Block diagram of ADPCM system. (a) Encoder. (b) Decoder.

The signal $\tilde{s}[n]$ is predicted from p past samples of the signal $\hat{s}[n]$. The predicted signal $\tilde{s}[n]$ is obtained as follows:

$$\tilde{s}[n] = \sum_{k=1}^{p} \alpha_k \hat{s}[n-k], \text{ where } \alpha_k\text{'s are predictor coefficients} \tag{12.9}$$

The input to the quantizer is the differential (or error) signal $e[n]$, which is the difference between the input signal $s[n]$ and predicted signal $\tilde{s}[n]$:

$$e[n] = s[n] - \tilde{s}[n] \tag{12.10}$$

$$\hat{e}[n] = e[n] + q[n] \tag{12.11}$$

where $q[n]$ is the quantization error signal. Since $\hat{s}[n] = \tilde{s}[n] + \hat{e}[n]$, from Equations (12.10) and (12.11), we have

$$\hat{s}[n] = s[n] + q[n] \tag{12.12}$$

Based on Equation (12.12), the SNR of the differential quantization system is computed as

$$\text{SNR} = \frac{\sigma_s^2}{\sigma_q^2} = \frac{\sigma_s^2}{\sigma_e^2}\frac{\sigma_e^2}{\sigma_q^2} = G_p \text{SNR}_q \tag{12.13}$$

where G_p is the prediction gain and SNR_q is the quantizer SNR.

If the prediction is good, then the G_p in Equation (12.13) will be greater than 1 and the variance of the error signal $e[n]$ is much less than the original signal $s[n]$. This will allow us to use smaller step size Δ, and therefore to represent the quantized signal $\hat{e}[n]$ with a smaller number of bits.

In ADM and ADPCM, the step size is allowed to adapt to the time-varying statistics of speech. The adaptation can be forward or backward. We used backward adaptation in the systems shown in Figures 12.23 and 12.24. With backward adaptation, we need not transmit the step-size parameters as the decoder itself can derive them from the bitstream.

As shown in Figure 12.24, the predictor is also allowed to adapt and track the time-varying statistics of speech. Typically, adapting the step size improves the SNR by 6 dB over ordinary PCM and adapting the predictor further improves the SNR by 4 dB.

Transform Domain Coding

Frequency-domain coding approaches such as subband coding (SBC) and adaptive transform coding (ATC) exploit the redundancy of the signal in the transform domain. By coding different subbands (or frequencies) independently, we can allocate more bits to perceptually important subbands so that the noise in these frequency regions is maintained low, while in other subbands we allocate fewer bits and allow high coding noise, as the noise at these frequencies is perceptually less important.

The SBC uses the filter bank techniques to split the input speech into a number of frequency bands. The block diagram of SBC codec is shown in Figure 12.25. The design of the filter bank is a very important consideration in the design of an SBC. In the absence of quantization noise, perfect reconstruction of speech can be achieved using QMF (quadrature mirror filter) banks. See Section 8.2.3 for more details on QMF. Typically, SBC codecs operate at bit rates in the range 16 to 32 kbps.

ATC, on the other hand, uses unitary transforms (e.g., DCT) to split the block of speech samples into a number of frequency components (or transform coefficients). The potential for bit-rate reduction in ATC lies in the fact that unitary transforms tend to generate near-uncorrelated transform coefficients that can be coded independently. The number of bits used to code each transform coefficient is adapted depending on the spectral properties of the speech. The block diagram of ATC codec is shown in Figure 12.26. The bit rates supported by ATC are also in the range of 16 to 32 kbps.

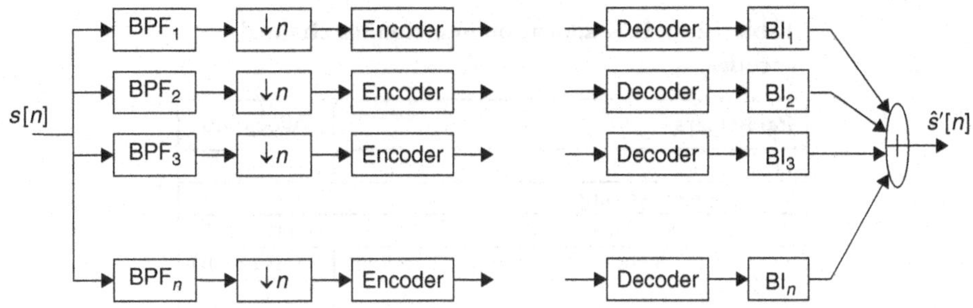

Figure 12.25: Block diagram of subband speech codec. BPF, bandpass filter; BI, bandpass interpolation.

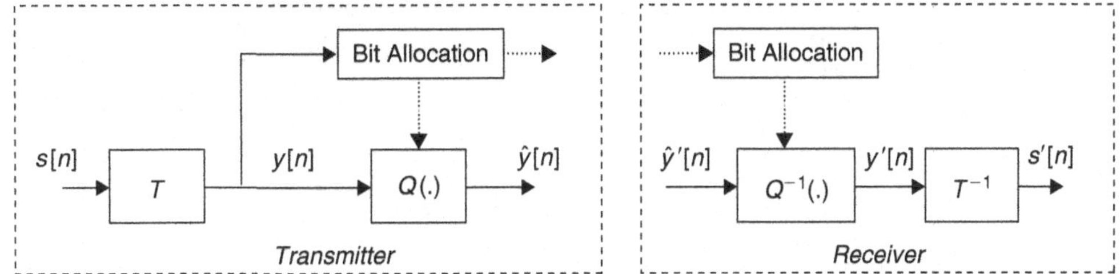

Figure 12.26: Block diagram of adaptive transform coding codec.

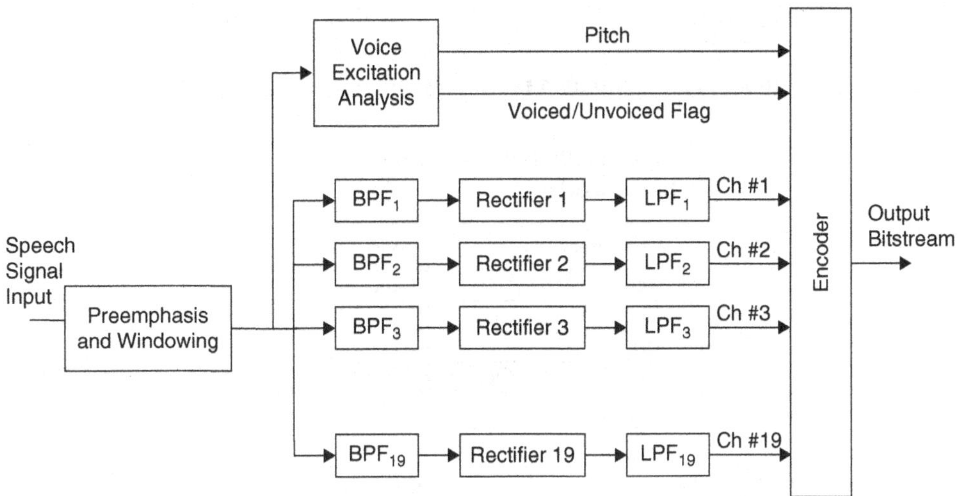

Figure 12.27: Block diagram of Holmes channel vocoder (only the encoder is shown).

12.4.5 Vocoders

Vocoders, on the other hand, are speech-specific coders and rely on speech models. As the vocoders rely on a speech source model, performance generally degrades for nonspeech signals. The vocoders focus on producing perceptually intelligible speech without necessarily matching the waveform. They operate at very low bit rates in the range 2 to 4 kbps and the decoder reconstructed speech sounds synthetic.

Two well-known vocoder methods are channel and linear predictive coder (LPC). These vocoders operate at bit rates as low as 2.4 kbps. Next, we briefly address these methods as well as the corresponding *open-loop speech synthesis* process.

Channel Vocoder

The channel vocoder relies on representing the speech spectrum as the product of vocal tract and excitation spectra. The block diagram of the Holmes channel vocoder (Holmes, 1980) is shown in Figure 12.27. The excitation analysis system consists of pitch estimation and voiced/unvoiced speech flag computation. A vocal tract envelop representation is obtained using a bank of bandpass filters. This vocoder can be efficiently implemented in the digital domain using discrete Fourier transform techniques.

Table 12.7: Bits allocation in a Holmes channel vocoder

Parameters	Allocation
Pitch	6 bits
Voiced/unvoiced flag	1 bit
Absolute level of first channel coefficient	3 bits
Remaining 18 channels (differential coding)	2 bits (each)
Signaling	2 bits
Total	48 bits

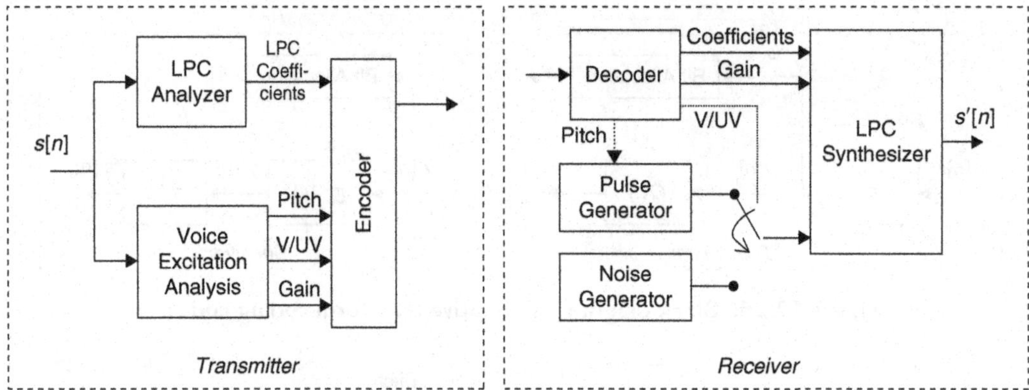

Figure 12.28: Simplified block diagram of an LPC vocoder.

Table 12.8: Bits allocation in an LPC vocoder

Parameters	Allocation
Pitch	6 bits
Voiced/unvoiced flag	1 bit
Gain	5 bits
10 Predictor coefficients	6 bits (each)
Total	72 bits

In the Holmes vocoder, each 20-ms speech segment is represented with 48 bits of information. Table 12.7 describes the parameters required to transmit with the Holmes vocoder and the allocation of bits for individual parameters. The bit rate of this vocoder is 2400 bps (48 * 50 frames/sec).

LPC Vocoder

LPC vocoders are more commonly used in practice for low bit-rate applications. Unlike the channel vocoder (which analyzes a speech signal in the frequency domain), the LPC vocoder performs speech analysis in the temporal domain. LPC vocoders use algorithms to predict the present speech sample from past samples. See Section 8.1.3 for more detail on the linear prediction method and its application in speech compression.

The idea behind using LPC for speech coding is grounded in the observation that the human vocal tract can be roughly modeled with linear filters. Voiced sounds can be modeled as linear filters driven by a fundamental frequency, whereas unvoiced ones are modeled with random noise sources. Using these models, we can describe human utterances with just a few parameters. This allows the LPC to predict signal output based on previous inputs and outputs. A simplified block diagram of the LPC vocoder is shown in Figure 12.28. The LPC vocoder also consists of a voice excitation analysis block to estimate the pitch, voiced/unvoiced flag, and gain information.

Eight to 14 linear predictive parameters are usually required to model the human vocal tract. Typically, these parameters are updated every 10 to 30 ms. In the LPC vocoder, we use 72 bits to represent each speech segment. Table 12.8 describes the parameters that are required to transmit with the LPC vocoder and the allocation of bits for individual parameters. The bit rate of this vocoder is about 2400 bps at the frame rate of 33 frames per second.

Open-Loop Speech Synthesis

In the open-loop speech analysis/synthesis coders, the parameters of the model are estimated directly from the speech signal. In this, the two-state voice excitation model used for speech synthesis can be very simple. Many of the low-rate channel and LPC vocoders employ this simple two-state excitation (impulse train/white noise). Although this simple excitation model is associated with strikingly low bit rates, it is also responsible for synthetic-quality speech.

As shown in Figure 12.28, the decoder (or open-loop synthesis) parameters are directly obtained from the compressed speech bitstream. Given the V/UV flag, pitch, and gain information at periodic intervals (or on a frame basis), the unvoiced sounds are produced by exciting the system with white noise, and voiced sounds are produced by a periodic impulse train excitation, where the spacing between impulses is the pitch period. The V/UV switch selects the voiced or unvoiced segment of speech and the gain parameter G controls the amplitude level of speech signal in that segment. The synthesized speech is obtained at the output of a time-varying digital filter whose filter coefficients are derived from the decoded bitstream.

V/UV, Gain, and Pitch Detection

The vocoder methods heavily depend on the voice excitation analysis block, which detects voice activity, gain, and pitch information. For digital coding applications, the pitch period and gain must be quantized. Typically, we use 6 bits to represent pitch, 5 bits for gain (with the logarithmic scale), and 1 bit for the voice activity flag. The following briefly discusses estimation of these parameters.

Voice Activity Detection

As the speech signals are quasistationary in nature, we transmit the speech in multiple small segments (or frames) over which the underlying model parameters of speech are assumed to be nearly constant. By detecting the voice activity in those small speech segments, we can reduce the bit rates by transmitting only the voice excitation and vocal tract filter parameters instead of actual speech information. The unvoiced speech is produced by exciting the system with white noise and voiced speech is produced by a periodic pulse train excitation. The transmission of a simple flag conveys the information to the receiver that the current speech segment is voiced or unvoiced and the receiver takes the appropriate action to synthesize the corresponding speech segment. Next, we briefly discuss two popular voice-activity detection techniques.

Short-Time Energy The short-time energy, E_n, for the speech segment starting at index n is defined as

$$E_n = \sum_{m=-\infty}^{\infty} w^2[m]s^2[n-m] \tag{12.14}$$

where $w[n]$ is a window function (see Section 7.4.1).

Since the amplitude levels of unvoiced speech is relatively low when compared to voiced speech samples, the short-time energy E_n is significantly low in the unvoiced region compared to the energy in the voiced region as shown in Figure 12.29. Thus, given an appropriate threshold on short-time energy, we can determine the particular speech segment as voiced or unvoiced.

Short-Time Zero-Crossing Rate Given that the speech segment $s_n[]$ starts at index n, the short-time zero-crossing rate is defined as the average number of times the speech signal changes sign within the time window. The rate is obtained as follows:

$$Z_n = \sum_{m=-\infty}^{\infty} 0.5|\text{sgn}(x[m]) - \text{sgn}(x[m-1])| \tag{12.15}$$

where

$$x[m] = s_n[m] \otimes w[m], \tag{12.16}$$

$w[]$ is a window function and $\otimes$ represents the convolution operation. The definition of the function sgn() is

$$\text{sgn}(x) = \begin{cases} 1 & x \geq 0 \\ -1 & x < 0 \end{cases} \tag{12.17}$$

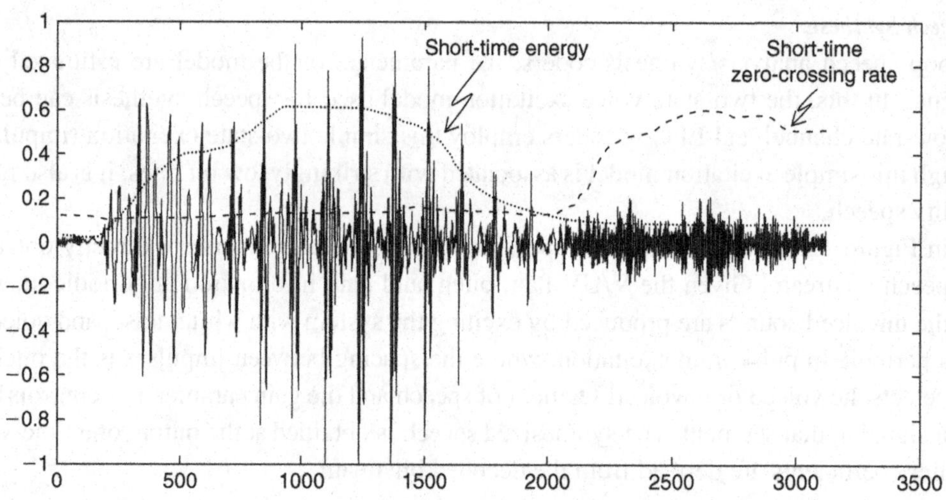

Figure 12.29: Typical speech waveform.

Since unvoiced speech signals are random in nature, the zero-crossing rate for the unvoiced speech segment interval is relatively high compared to the zero-crossing rate in the voiced interval, as shown in Figure 12.29. By using an appropriate threshold, we can determine the voice activity with the zero-crossing rate method in the given speech segment.

Gain Estimation

The gain of unvoiced and voiced segments is typically determined such that the energy of the synthetic speech segment matches that of the analysis segment. For this purpose, the short-time energy E_n given in Equation (12.14) can be used to estimate the gain parameter. This short-time energy can also be obtained from the autocorrelation function value $R^n_{ss}[k]$ at lag $k = 0$.

Pitch Estimation

One of the important features of the speech signal is its fundamental frequency (F_0), more commonly its inverse value, referred to as pitch period $P_0(= 1/F_0)$, which is useful in most speech processing applications. The fundamental frequency of voiced speech can be anywhere in the range of 50 Hz to 500 Hz. As the fundamental frequency varies slowly, we estimate the pitch period for each speech segment on a frame-by-frame basis.

A pitch detector is an essential component in various speech processing systems. Many low–bit-rate speech codecs require pitch information for speech synthesis. The pitch detector, besides providing pitch information to the speech synthesis block for generating voiced speech, can also be used in voice activity detection, speaker recognition, and text-to-speech systems, among other applications. Various pitch detection methods have been proposed in the literature; here we briefly discuss pitch detection based on autocorrelation and cepstrum methods.

Autocorrelation Method The autocorrelation approach is widely used in many applications for detecting human-voice pitch information. This method is based on detecting the highest value of the autocorrelation function in the region of interest. Given N samples of a speech segment, the short-time autocorrelation function is computed as

$$R_{ss}[m] = \frac{1}{N} \sum_{n=0}^{N-1-m} s[n]\,s[n+m], \qquad 0 \le m \le M \tag{12.18}$$

The variable m in Equation (12.18) is called the lag, and the pitch is equal to the value of m for which $R_{ss}[m]$ results in a maximum value. Usually, the range of M is 16 to 160 samples at an 8-kHz sampling rate. This range of lags corresponds to fundamental frequency values that lie in the 50- to 500-Hz interval. The autocorrelation output of voiced speech (shown in Figure 12.14(a)) is shown in Figure 12.30.

The major limitation of the autocorrelation function is that it can contain many peaks other than those due to the fundamental frequency. For voiced speech, many peaks may be present in the autocorrelation function

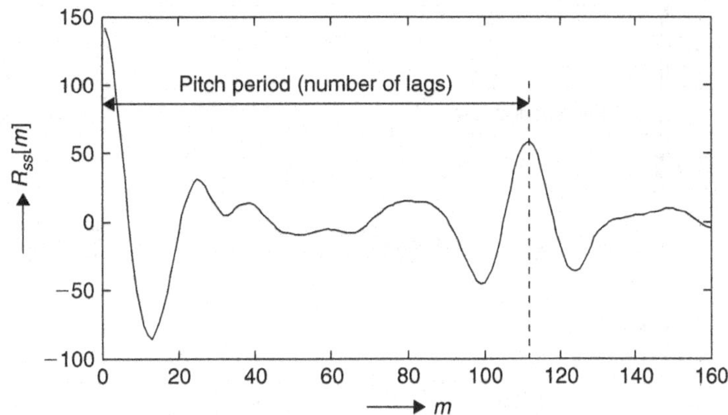

Figure 12.30: Autocorrelation of speech segment with lags 0 to 160.

due to vocal-tract formant resonance frequencies. The peak selection must be robust in pitch detection; we use preprocessing techniques and large window sizes to minimize the false detection rate.

Upon using center-clipping techniques in preprocessing, the increased distinctiveness of true period peaks in the autocorrelation function can be seen. The relationship between input signal $s[n]$ and the center-clipped signal $x[n]$ is expressed as follows:

$$x[n] = center\_clip(s[n]) = \begin{cases} s[n] - C_T, & s[n] \geq C_T \\ 0, & |s[n]| < C_T \\ s[n] + C_T, & s[n] \leq C_T \end{cases} \tag{12.19}$$

where C_T is the clipping threshold.

Cepstrum Method Cepstrum computation transforms the multiplicative relationship between voice source and vocal tract effects into an additive relationship. With cepstrum, it is possible to separate the voice excitation source part from the speech signal and find more accurate pitch information. For pitch determination, the real part of cepstrum is sufficient, and is computed as

$$\tilde{s}\,[n] = real\left(\frac{1}{N}\sum_{k=0}^{N-1} \hat{S}\,[k]\, e^{j2\pi kn/N}\right), \quad n = 0, 1, \ldots, N-1 \tag{12.20}$$

where

$$\hat{S}\,[k] = \log\left(\left|\sum_{n=0}^{N-1} s[n]\, e^{-j2\pi nk/N}\right|\right), \quad k = 0, 1, \ldots, N-1 \tag{12.21}$$

The term "cepstrum" derives from the notion that it turns the spectrum inside out. The x-axis of the cepstrum has units of quefrency (measured in seconds). To obtain excitation of the fundamental frequency from the cepstrum, we look for a peak in the quefrency region as shown in Figure 12.31 corresponding to the fundamental frequencies of typical speech. The block diagram of cepstrum-based pitch detection is shown in Figure 12.32.

12.4.6 Hybrid Coders

With hybrid coders, speech compression is achieved by combining the features of waveform coding techniques (by providing for the matching of input speech signal) and vocoder techniques (by representing the formant and pitch structure of speech), and by exploiting human auditory system characteristics (by incorporating perceptual weighting). The analysis-by-synthesis approach is used in most hybrid codecs.

In analysis-by-synthesis methods, the excitation parameters are determined by minimizing the difference between the reconstructed speech (by the decoder present in the encoder block) and original speech. The most traditional hybrid speech coding approach is code-excited linear prediction (CELP). CELP is based on linear prediction coding (LPC) models of the vocal tract (see Section 8.1.3) and a supplementary residue codebook.

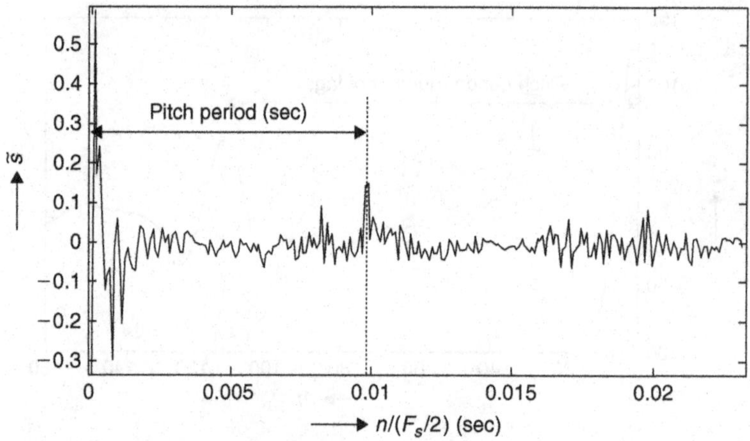

Figure 12.31: Pitch detection by computing the cepstrum of the speech segment.

Figure 12.32: Computing the cepstrum using DFT.

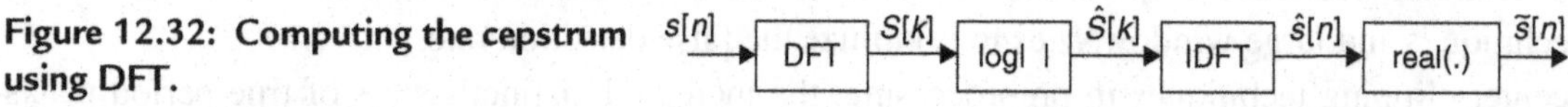

Table 12.9: Selected Speech Codecs

Speech Coding Standard	Bit Rate	Governing Body
GSM-FR	13 kbps	ETSI
GSM-EFR	12.2 kbps	ETSI
GSM-AMR	4.75, 5.15, 5.90, 6.70, 7.40, 7.95, 10.2, 12.2 kbps	3GPP
G.711	64 kbps	ITU-T
G.723.1	5.3, 6.3 kbps	ITU-T
G.729	6.4, 8, 12.8 kbps	ITU-T
Speex	2 to 44 kbps	Xiph.org

In real-time duplex communications systems, one person speaks while the other one listens. Since the person's listening is not contributing anything to the signal, some codecs implement features like voice activity detection (VAD) to recognize silence, and comfort noise generation (CNG) to simulate the natural level of noise without actually encoding it at the transmitting end.

12.4.7 Speech Compression Standards

Progress in speech coding, particularly in the late 1980s, enabled a number of organizations to standardize various speech compression methods for diverse application (e.g., military, wireline, wireless communications) requirement (in terms of quality, bit rates, delay, etc.). The result of these efforts was more than a dozen speech compression standards. Table 12.9 shows selected widely used speech compression standards, supported bit rates, and oversight organizations. These standards are briefly discussed in the following.

GSM

GSM speech codecs, used in cell phone systems around the world, are overseen by the European Telecommunications Standards Institute (ETSI). There has been an evolution of standards in this domain. The first was the GSM full rate (GSM-FR). This standard uses a CELP variant called the regular pulse excited linear predictive coder (RPE-LPC). The speech signal input is broken up into 20-ms frames. Each of those frames is encoded as 260 bits, thereby producing a total bit rate of 13 kbps. Free GSM-FR implementations are available for use under certain restrictions.

The GSM enhanced full rate (GSM-EFR) was developed to improve the quality of speech encoded with GSM-FR. It operates on 20-ms frames at a bit rate of 12.2 kbps, and it works in noise-free and noisy environments. Because GSM-EFR is based on the patented Algebraic Code Excited Linear Prediction (ACELP) technology, one must purchase a license before using it in end products.

The 3rd-Generation Partnership Project (3GPP), a group of standards bodies, introduced the GSM adaptive multirate (GSM-AMR) codec to deliver even higher-quality speech over lower bit-rate data links by using an ACELP algorithm. It uses 20-ms data chunks, and allows for multiple bit rates at eight discrete levels between 4.75 kbps and 12.2 kbps. GSM-AMR supports VAD and CNG for reduced bit rates.

"G-Dot" Standards

The International Telecommunication Union (ITU) was created to coordinate standards in the communications industry, and the ITU Telecommunication Standardization Sector (ITU-T) is responsible for many speech codec recommendations, known as the G.x standards.

G.711 G.711, introduced in 1988, is a simple standard when compared with the other options presented here. The only compression used in G.711 is companding (using either μ-law or A-law standards), which compresses each data sample to 8 bits, yielding an output bit rate of 64 kbps.

G.723.1 G.723.1 is an ACELP-based, dual–bit-rate codec, released in 1996, that targets VoIP (see Section 12.5) applications such as teleconferencing. The encoding frame for G.723.1 is 30 ms. Each frame can be encoded in 20 or 24 bytes, thus translating to 5.3- and 6.3-kbps streams, respectively. The bit rates can be effectively reduced through voice activity detection and comfort noise generation. The codec offers good immunity against network imperfections like lost frames and bit errors. This speech codec is part of video-conferencing applications described by the H.324 family of standards.

G.729 Another speech codec released in 1996 is G.729, which partitions speech into 10-ms frames, making it a low-latency codec. It uses an algorithm called the conjugate structure ACELP (CS-ACELP). G.729 compresses 16-bit signals sampled at 8 kHz via 10-ms frames into a standard bit rate of 8 kbps, but it also supports 6.4- and 11.8-kbps rates. Voice activity detection and comfort noise generation are also supported.

Speex

Speex is another codec released by Xiph.org, with the goal of being a totally patent-free speech solution. Like many other speech codecs, Speex is based on CELP with residue coding. The codec can take 8-, 16-, and 32-kHz linear PCM signals and code them into bit rates ranging from 2 to 44 kbps. Speex is resilient to network errors, and it supports voice activity detection. Besides allowing variable bit rates, another unique feature of Speex is stereo encoding. Source code is available from Speex.org in both a floating-point reference implementation and a fixed-point version.

The MIPS and memory required to implement some of the described earlier speech codecs on the reference embedded processor is given in Table 12.10.

Table 12.10: MIPS and memory requirements to implement voice codecs on reference embedded processor

Voice Codec	Encoder/Decoder	Data Memory (kB)	Program Memory (kB)	MIPS	Encoder (I/O)
G.711 with PLC	Encoder	0.25	3.35	0.09	*Input*: 14-bit left-justified PCM samples at 8 kHz *Output*: Bitstream at 64 kbps
	Decoder	2.83	3.35	0.14 (1.09 for PLC)	
G.723.1A	Encoder	24	32	10.4	*Input*: 16-bit PCM samples at 8 kHz *Output*: G.723 bitstream at 5.3 or 6.3 kbps
	Decoder	21.5	32	0.93	
G.729AB	Encoder/Decoder	13	30	6.77	*Input*: PCM samples at 8 kHz *Output*: 8-kbps G.729AB bitstream

12.5 VoIP and Jitter Buffer

VoIP is one of the most powerful technologies revolutionizing the telecom industry. This technology allows us to make voice calls using a broadband Internet connection instead of the regular *public switched telephone network* (PSTN) connection. VoIP services convert analog voice into a digital signal and transmit this digitized voice in terms of data packets over the IP network. The transition from circuit-switched to packet-switched networking, occurring now at breakneck speed, is encouraging applications that go far beyond simple voice transmission, embracing other forms of data and allowing all of them to travel over the same infrastructure.

By their nature, networks cause great variation in the data transmission delay. This variation, known as *jitter*, is removed by buffering the packets long enough to ensure that the slowest packets arrive in time to be decoded in the correct sequence. Naturally, a larger jitter buffer contributes to greater overall system latency. In this section, we briefly discuss VoIP technology and jitter buffer schemes to handle delays.

12.5.1 VoIP Overview

Today's voice networks—such as the PSTN—utilize digital switching technology to establish a dedicated link between the caller and the receiver. While this connection offers only limited bandwidth, it does provide an acceptable quality level without the burden of a complicated encoding algorithm. The VoIP alternative uses the *Internet protocol* (IP) to send digitized voice traffic over the Internet or private networks. An IP *packet* consists of a train of digits containing a control header and a data payload. The header provides network navigation information for the packet, and the payload contains the compressed voice data. While circuit-switched telephony deals with the entire message, VoIP-based data transmission is packet based, so that chunks of data are packetized (separated into units for transmission), compressed, and sent across the network—and eventually reassembled at the designated receiving end. The key point is that there is no need for a dedicated link between transmitter and receiver in VoIP communication.

Figure 12.33(a) shows a simplified representation of a possible IP telephony network connections. Figure 12.33(b) shows the key components of a VoIP system: signaling process, encoder/decoder, transport mechanism, and switching gateway.

The *signaling* process involves creating, maintaining, and terminating connections between nodes. To reduce network bandwidth requirements, audio and video are encoded before transmission and decoded during reception. This compression and conversion process is governed by various codec standards for both audio and video streams.

The compressed packets move through the network governed by one or more *transport* protocols. A *switching gateway* ensures that the packet set is interoperable at the destination with another IP-based system or a PSTN system. At its final destination, the packet set is decoded and converted back to an audio/video signal, at which point it is played through the receiver's speakers and/or display unit.

Packetizing voice data involves adding header and trailer information to data blocks. Packetization *overhead* (additional time and data introduced by this process) must be reduced to minimize added latencies (time delays through the system). Therefore, the process must achieve a balance between minimizing transmission delay and using network bandwidth most efficiently—smaller size allows packets to be sent more often, while larger packets take longer to compose. On the other hand, larger packets amortize header and trailer information across a bigger chunk of voice data, so they use network bandwidth more efficiently than do smaller packets.

VoIP Protocols

The OSI (open systems interconnection) seven-layer model (see Figure 12.34) specifies a framework for networking. If there are two parties to a communication session, data generated by each starts at the top, undergoes required configuration and processing through the layers, and is finally delivered to the physical layer for transmission across the medium. At the destination, processing occurs in the reverse direction, until the packets are finally reassembled and the data is provided to the other user.

Session Control: H. 323 versus SIP

The first requirement in a VoIP system is a *session-control protocol* to establish presence and locate users, as well as to set up, modify, and terminate sessions. There are two protocols in wide use today. Historically, the first of

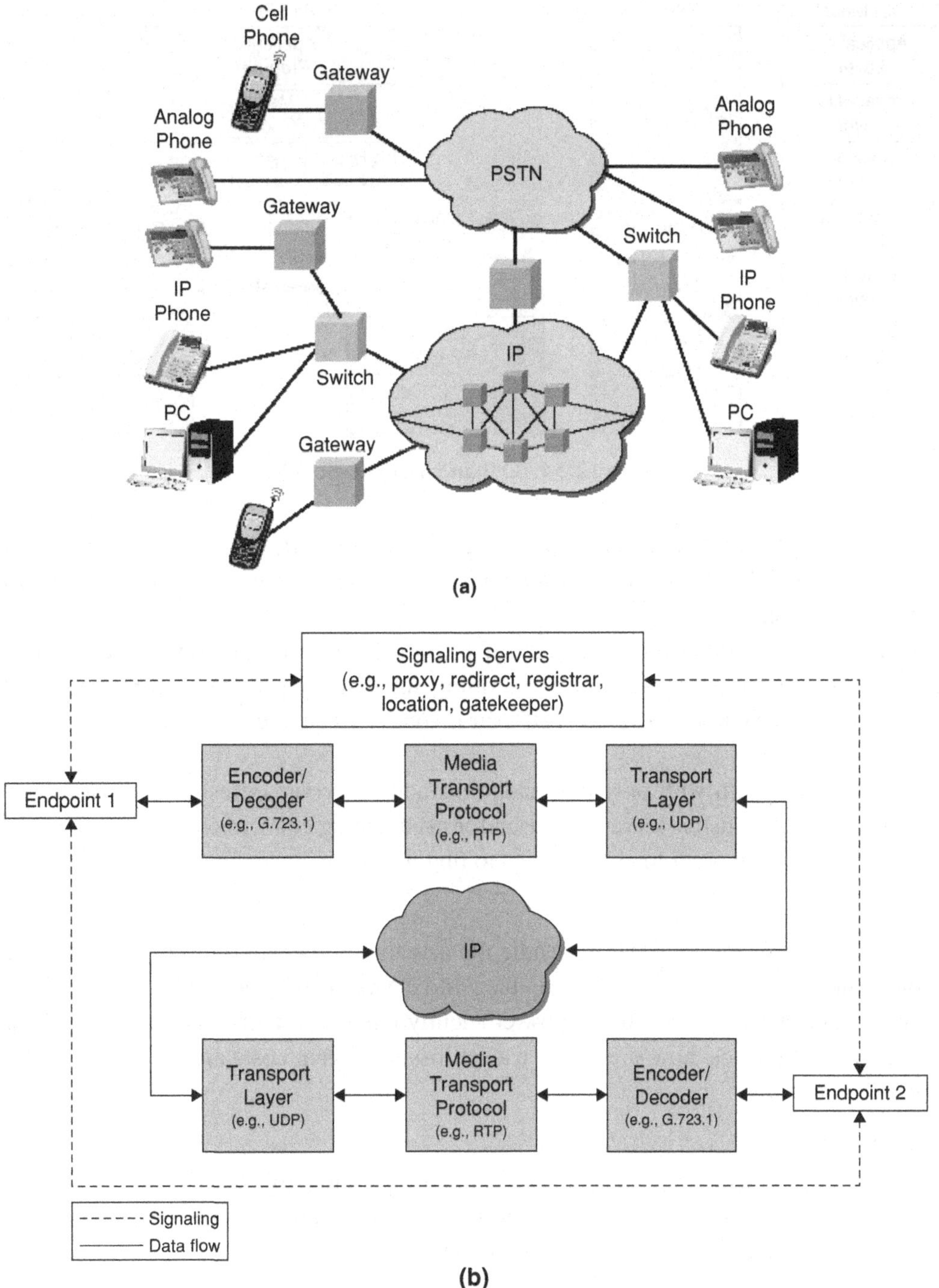

Figure 12.33: (a) Simplified representation of possible IP telephony network connections. (b) Signaling and transport flows between endpoints.

these protocols was H.323 (to be exact, the task of session control and initiation lies in the domain of H.225.0 and H.245, which are part of the H.323 umbrella protocol), but SIP (session initiation protocol) is rapidly becoming the main standard. Let's take a look at the role played by each.

ITU H.323

H.323 is an ITU standard originally developed for real-time multimedia (voice and video) conferencing and supplementary data transfer. It has rapidly evolved to meet the requirements of VoIP networks. It is technically a container for a number of required and optional network and media codec standards. The connection signaling part of H.323 is handled by the H.225 protocol, while feature negotiation is supported by H.245.

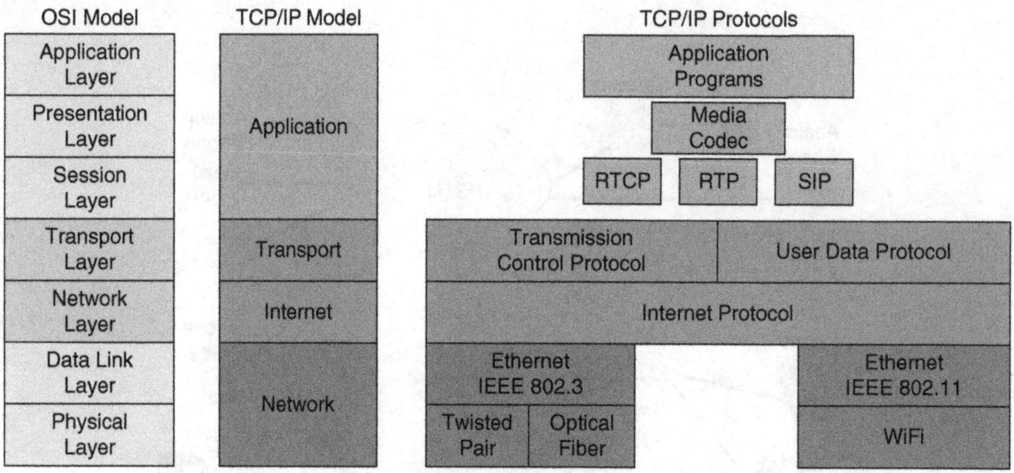

Figure 12.34: OSI and TCP/IP models.

SIP SIP is defined by the Internet Engineering Task Force (IETF) under RFC 3261. It was developed specifically for IP telephony and other Internet services, and although it overlaps H.323 in many ways, it is usually considered a more streamlined solution.

SIP is used with the session description protocol (SDP) for user discovery; it provides feature negotiation and call management. SDP is essentially a format for describing initialization parameters for streaming media during session announcement and invitation. The SIP/SDP pair is somewhat analogous to the H.225/H.245 protocol set in the H.323 standard.

SIP can be used in a system with only two endpoints and no server infrastructure. However, in a public network, special proxy and registrar servers are used for establishing connections. In such a setup, each client registers itself with a server, in order to allow callers to find it from anywhere on the Internet.

Media Codecs

At the top of the VoIP stack are protocols to handle the actual media being transported. There are potentially quite a few voice, audio, and video codecs that can feed into the media transport layer. A number of factors help determine how desirable a codec is, including how efficiently it makes use of available system bandwidth, how much coding delay it introduces, how it handles packet loss, and what costs are associated with it, including intellectual-property royalties.

Transport Layer Protocols

The preceding signaling protocols are responsible for configuring multimedia sessions across a network. Once the connection is set up, media flows between network nodes are established by utilizing one or more data-transport protocols, such as the user datagram protocol (UDP) or TCP.

UDP The UDP is a network protocol covering only packets that are broadcast out. There is no acknowledgment that a packet has been received at the other end. Since delivery is not guaranteed, voice transmission will not work very well with UDP alone when there are peak loads on a network. That is why a media transport protocol, such as the real-time transport protocol (RTP), usually runs on top of UDP.

TCP TCP uses a client/server communication model. The client requests (and is provided) a service by another computer (a server) in the network. Each client request is handled individually, unrelated to any previous one. This ensures that "free" network paths are available for other channels to use.

TCP creates smaller packets that can be transmitted over the Internet and received by a TCP layer at the other end of the call, such that the packets are "reassembled" back into the original message. The IP layer interprets the address field of each packet so that it arrives at the correct destination.

Unlike UDP, TCP guarantees complete receipt of packets at the receiving end. However, it does this by allowing packet retransmission, which adds latencies that are not helpful for real-time data. For voice, a late packet due to retransmission is as bad as a lost packet. Because of this characteristic, TCP is usually not considered an appropriate transport for real-time streaming media transmission. Figure 12.34 shows how the TCP/IP Internet model and its associated protocols compare with and utilize various layers of the OSI model.

Media Transport

As noted before, sending media data directly over a transport protocol is not very efficient for real-time communication. Because of this, a *media transport layer* is usually responsible for handling this data in an efficient manner.

RTP RTP provides delivery services for real-time packetized audio and video data. It is the standard way to transport real-time data over IP networks. The protocol resides on top of UDP to minimize packet header overhead, but at a cost—there is no guarantee of reliability or packet ordering. Compared to TCP, RTP is less reliable, but it has less latency in packet transmission, since its packet header overhead is much smaller than for TCP (see structure of RTP frame in Figure 12.35).

In order to maintain a given quality-of-service (QoS) level, RTP utilizes time stamps, sequence numbering, and delivery confirmation for each packet sent. It also supports a number of error-correction schemes for increased robustness, as well as some basic security options for encrypting packets. Figure 12.36 compares performance and reliability of UDP, RTP, and TCP.

RTP Control Protocol The RTP control protocol (RTCP) is a complementary protocol used to communicate control information, such as number of packets sent and lost, jitter, delay, and endpoint descriptions. It is most useful for managing session time bases and for analyzing the QoS of an RTP stream. It also can provide a backchannel for limited retransmission of RTP packets.

Delays and Echo Cancellation

Packetization is a good match for transporting data (e.g., a JPEG file or email) across a network, because the delivery falls into a non–time-critical "best-effort" category. The network efficiently moves data from multiple sources across the same medium. For voice applications, however, "best effort" is not adequate, because variable-length delays as the packets make their way across the network can degrade the quality of the decoded voice signal at the receiving end. For this reason, VoIP protocols, via QoS techniques, focus on managing network bandwidth to prevent delays from degrading voice quality. The effect due to these delay variations or jitter can be minimized by using a jitter buffer, which imposes a certain delay to each packet before playing back the packet stream at a constant rate. More detail about the jitter buffer appears in the next section.

As mentioned before, *latency* represents the time delay through the IP system. *One-way latency* is the time from when a word is spoken to when the person on the other end of the call hears it. *Round-trip latency* is simply the sum of the two one-way latencies. The lower the latency value, the more natural a conversation will sound. For the PSTN phone systems, this round-trip latency is less than 150 ms.

For VoIP systems, a one-way latency of up to 200 ms is considered acceptable. The largest contributors to latency in a VoIP system are the network and the gateways at either end of the call. The voice codec adds

IP Header	UDP Header	RTP Header	RTP Payload

Figure 12.35: Header structure and payload of RTP frame.

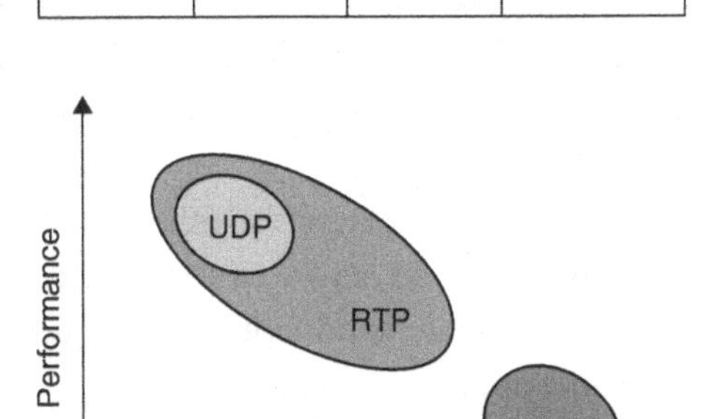

Figure 12.36: Performance versus reliability.

some latency, but this is usually small by comparison (< 20 ms). When the delay is large in a voice network application, the main challenges are to cancel echoes and eliminate overlap. *Echo cancellation* directly affects perceived quality; it becomes important when the round-trip delay exceeds 50 ms. Voice overlap becomes a concern when the one-way latency is more than 200 ms.

Because most of the time elapsed during a voice conversation is "dead time"—during which no speaker is talking—codecs take advantage of this silence by not transmitting any data during these intervals. Such "silence compression" techniques detect voice activity and stop transmitting data when there is no voice activity, instead generating "comfort" noise to ensure that the line does not "sound" dead when no one is talking.

In a standard PSTN telephone system, echoes that degrade perceived quality can happen for a variety of reasons. The two most common causes are impedance mismatches in the circuit-switched network ("line echo") and acoustic coupling between the telephone's microphone and speaker ("acoustic echo"). Line echoes are common when there is a two-wire-to-four-wire conversion in the network (e.g., where analog signaling is converted into a T1 system). Because VoIP systems can link to the PSTN, they must be able to deal with line echo, and IP phones can also fall victim to acoustic echo. Echo cancellers can be optimized to operate on line echo, acoustic echo, or both. Effectiveness of the cancellation depends directly on the quality of the algorithm used.

An important parameter for an echo canceller is the length of the packet on which it operates. Put simply, the echo canceller keeps a copy of the signal that was transmitted. For a given time after the signal is sent, it seeks to correlate and subtract the transmitted signal from the returning reflected signal—which is, of course, delayed and diminished in amplitude. To achieve effective cancellation, it usually suffices to use a standard correlation window size (e.g., 32 ms, 64 ms, or 128 ms), but larger sizes may be necessary.

VoIP Advantages and Applications

Because the high-speed network as a whole (rather than a dedicated channel) is used as the transport mechanism, a major advantage of VoIP systems is the lower cost per communication session. Moreover, VoIP calls allow network operators to avoid most interconnect charges associated with circuit-switched telephony networks; the additional infrastructure required to complete a VoIP phone call is minimal because it uses the network already in place for the home or business personal computer (PC). Yet another reason for lower costs is that data-network operators often have not used all available bandwidth, so that the additional VoIP services currently incur an inconsequential additional cost-overhead burden. Use of the packet-switched network for voice increases bandwidth utilization compared with the traditional connection-oriented approach and can lead to lower call costs.

VoIP users tend to think of their connection as being "free," since they can call anywhere in the world, as often as they want, for just pennies per minute. Although they are also paying a monthly fee to their Internet service provider, it can be amortized over both data and voice services.

Besides the low-cost relative to the circuit-switched domain, many new features of IP services become available. For instance, incoming phone calls on the PSTN can be automatically rerouted to a user's VoIP phone, as long as it is connected to a network node. This arrangement has clear advantages over a global enabled cell phone, since there are no roaming charges involved. From the VoIP standpoint, the end user's location is irrelevant; it is simply seen as just another network connection point. This is especially useful where wireless local-area networks (LANs) are available; IEEE Standard 802.11-enabled VoIP handsets allow conversations at worldwide Wi-Fi hotspots without the need to worry about mismatched communications infrastructure and transmission standards.

Everything discussed thus far in relation to VoIP extends to other forms of data-based communication as well. After all, once data is digitized and packetized, the nature of the content does not much matter, as long as it is appropriately encoded and decoded with adequate bandwidth. Consequently, the VoIP infrastructure facilitates an entirely new set of networked real-time applications, such as:

- Videoconferencing
- Remote video surveillance
- Multicasting

- Instant messaging
- Gaming

VoIP Disadvantages

Because VoIP relies on an Internet connection, the VoIP service will be affected by the quality and reliability of broadband Internet service. Because VoIP devices operate with electricity, there is no service during a power outage. In emergency situations, tracing the location of call origination is difficult with VoIP services.

12.5.2 Jitter Buffer

There are two reasons to use VoIP services instead of PSTN: lower cost and increased functionality. However, the advantages of VoIP services come with few disadvantages. One of the major issues with VoIP services is QoS. Given that a dedicated link between sender and receiver does not exist, voice quality is not guaranteed.

Many factors determine voice quality, including the choice of codec, packet loss, echo control, jitter delay, and overall network design. In this section, we discuss jitter delay and its handling. Selected sources of delay in VoIP communications and corresponding delay values are given in Table 12.11.

The nature of packet-switched networks causes unpredictable and variable delays (or jitter) to speech packets, often resulting in unintelligible speech at the receiving end. Applications sending real-time datastreams over unreliable IP networks have a lot of problems to overcome, including variable and long delays, and lost and out-of-sequence packets. This is illustrated in Figure 12.37.

Jitter Buffer Overview

Of all delays, network delay is the most unpredictable (see Table 12.11), and it must be taken care of to achieve QoS. Using an optimum jitter handling algorithm is an essential part of any VoIP system to address this unpredictable network latency.

It is possible to absorb delay variations by adding a *jitter buffer*. With a jitter buffer, it is also possible to reorder the packets within the time duration that corresponds to the buffer size. Figure 12.38 shows the placement of a jitter buffer in the IP packet communication receiver. The greater the size of the buffer, the higher the delay

Table 12.11: Selected delay sources in VoIP transmission

Source	Delay (ms)
Encoding delay	18
Packetization/depacketization	20
Queuing	1
Uplink delay (at transmitter)	10
Network delay	Variable (x)
Downlink delay	10
Jitter buffer	63
Decoder delay	2
Capture/playout delay	1
Total	$125+x$

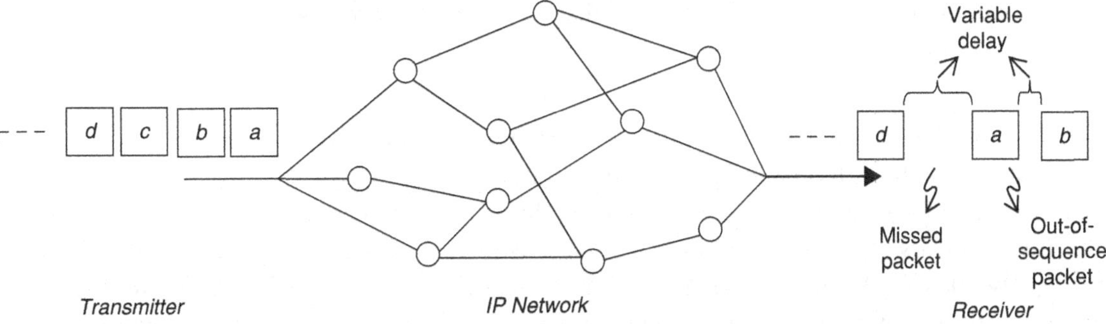

Figure 12.37: Receiving out-of-order IP packets due to diverse latencies of network paths.

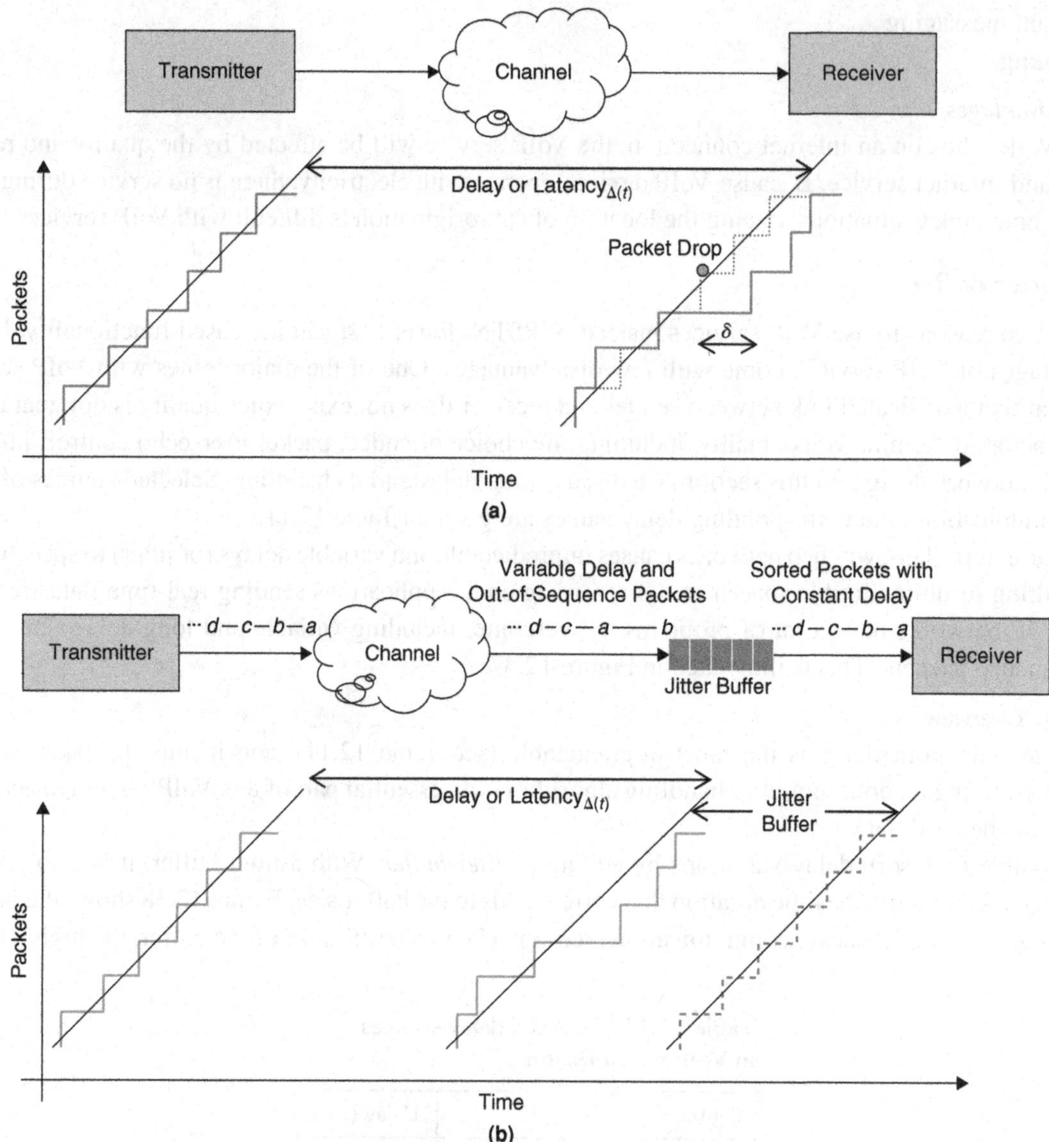

Figure 12.38: IP packet communication. (a) Packet drops due to variable network latencies. (b) Avoiding packet drops with inclusion of jitter buffer.

variations it can accommodate. The higher the jitter buffer delay, the greater the overall latency (i.e., end-to-end delay). For real-time applications like VoIP, minimal latency is required. These two conflicting requirements are addressed by an adaptive jitter buffer (AJB).

The jitter buffer design can be static or dynamic. The static alternative assumes that the jitter buffer is too large or too small, thereby causing voice quality to suffer due to excessive delay or packet loss. On the other hand, dynamic buffer design allows the increase or decrease of buffer size based on interarrival delay variation statistics of the last few packets.

AJB

As previously described, if the size of the jitter buffer is too small, it leads to deterioration of voice quality in communications, such as discontinuity in voice reproduction due to packet loss. On the other hand, if the buffer size is too big, the overall delay is very high and this leads to unpleasant delayed voice communication. Therefore, it is necessary to optimize the number of packets to be accumulated in the buffer in accordance with jitters in the network such that the minimum number of packets for retaining voice quality in communications is accumulated, thereby minimizing the transmission delay resulting from packet accumulation in the buffer. This can be achieved with the AJB as shown in Figure 12.39. One way to adapt is to insert/remove more silence

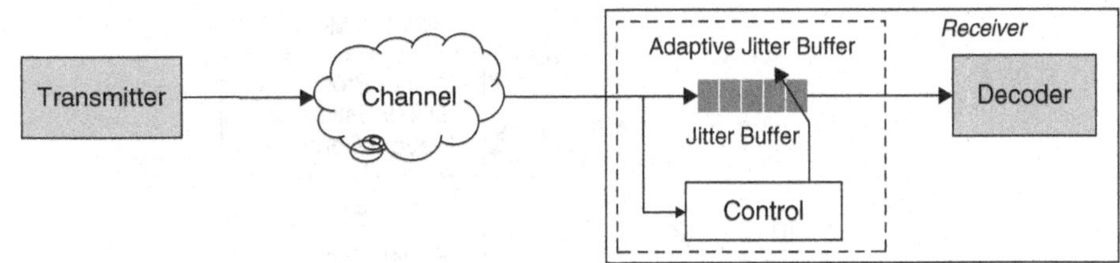

Figure 12.39: Block diagram of adaptive jitter buffer.

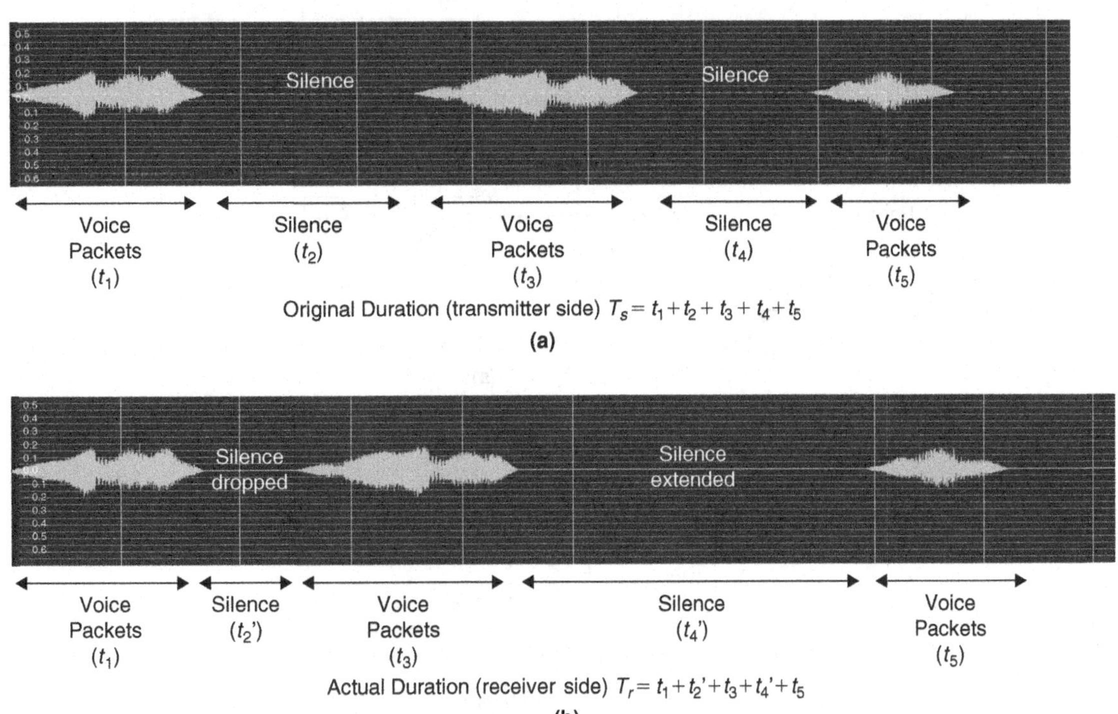

Figure 12.40: Illustration of adaptive jitter buffer handling jitter in VoIP. (a) Speech with original silence periods at transmitter. (b) Jitter buffer adaptation with insert or removal of silence.

between two "speech packets," as there is a greater likelihood of silence packets in VoIP systems. If the buffer underflows, the duration of silence is extended to the stretch time. If the buffer overflows, the duration of silence is reduced to skew time as illustrated in Figure 12.40. However, this type of adaptation may not be possible with all speech codecs.

Therefore, the key to intelligent AJB design is to know how long to expand the buffer (i.e., wait for delayed packets), when to shrink the buffer (i.e., skip the packets), and by how much (i.e., how many packets to be skipped) without deteriorating the voice quality.

Jitter Buffer Design

A jitter buffer comprises three entities as shown in Figure 12.41: control module, buffer manager, and buffer memory. The manager is responsible for managing the jitter buffer memory, including storage and retrieval of packet data. The control module is responsible for processing received packets, delay estimation, and playout scheduling (i.e., informing the buffer manager which packet in the buffer is to output at what time instance).

The packet processor parses RTP header information and extracts parameters such as sequence number, time stamp (which indicates when the voice packets needs to be sent to the player), payload type, payload size, and so on.

The delay estimator estimates the packet delay based on the extracted time stamp and actual packet arrival time. Figure 12.42(a) shows four periodically generated voice packets a, b, c, and d at the transmitter, and the

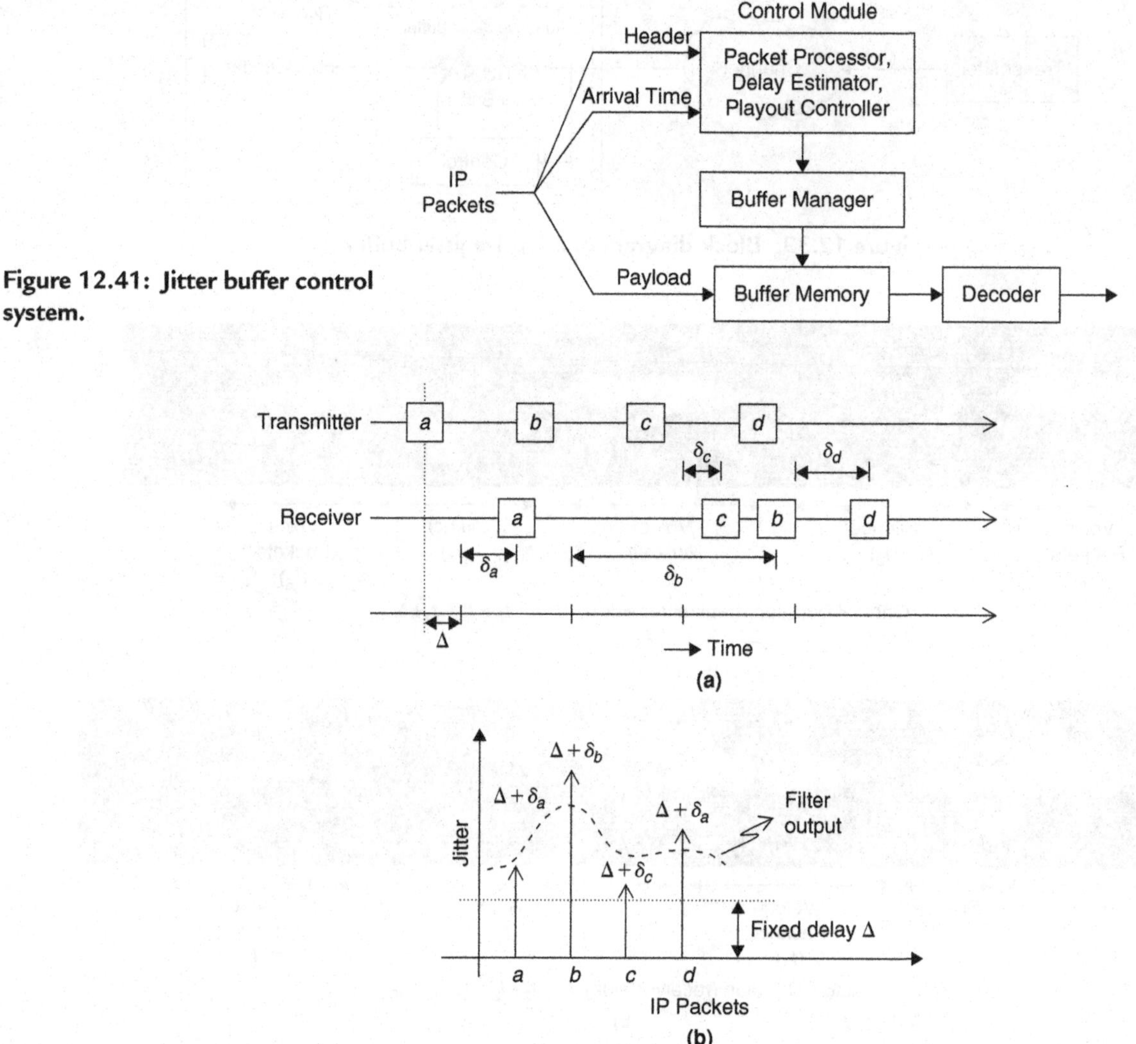

Figure 12.41: Jitter buffer control system.

Figure 12.42: (a) Illustration of IP packet communication with network delays. (b) Plot showing individual packet delays and smoothed filter output.

corresponding received packets with arbitrary delays $\Delta_i = \Delta + \delta_i|_{i=a,b,c,d}$, where Δ corresponds to the common fixed delay associated with all IP packets. Figure 12.42(b) shows the delay versus IP packet received.

To improve voice quality, instead of using the individual packets delays Δ_i, we use the statistics of delays of the current and previously arrived packets to update the buffer parameters. A one-tap linear recursive filter can be used to obtain the average delay $\hat{\Delta}_i$ and its variation $\hat{V}_i$ (Ramjee et al., 1994). At the start of the session, there are no statistics on which the delay can be estimated. Therefore, the delay needs to be set to a certain value at start-up. This value can be a delay set by the user or a value agreed during the connection negotiation.

Upon completion of the header processing, the RTP packet sequence number is checked. If it is less than the currently expected playout sequence number, then this packet is too late and is immediately discarded. Otherwise, the time stamp, packet payload, and playout delay are passed to the playout controller, and the playout table updated. When the playout control adds a new packet to the buffer, a linear search is performed to determine where in the list the current packet ought to be inserted. During this linear search through the list, the time stamp of the current packet is compared with the packets in the list, and the current packet is inserted into a place based on the time stamp value. The packet addition process effectively sorts the playout order of the packets, and no further search is required during the playout.

The playout control is responsible for playing out the buffered packets at the specified time instances in the correct order. It utilizes the entries in the playout table to determine which packet is to be played out next. The

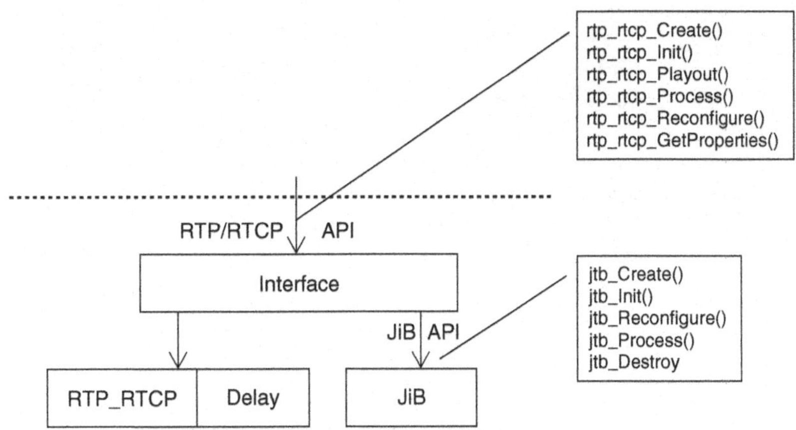

Figure 12.43: Jitter buffer interface in an RTP stack.

controller fetches the next packet in sequence from the playout table, and the frames within the packet are played out at the playout instances as indicated by the time stamp value.

Once all frames within a packet have been played out, the expected sequence number counter is incremented by 1, and the packet entry is cleared from the playout table. Finally, the entire block of memory used to buffer that packet in the jitter buffer is freed.

Jitter Buffer in RTP Stack

The real-time media is transferred as an RTP payload. An RTP header contains information related to the RTP payload, such as sequence number, time stamp, data type, size, and so on. RTP itself does not provide a mechanism to ensure timely delivery or provide other QoS guarantees. For this, as discussed previously, a jitter buffer is embedded in the RTP stack at the receiver to improve the QoS. Figure 12.43 shows the interface used in the RTP stack to embed the jitter buffer.

For more detail on the VoIP, RTP stack, and jitter buffer description, see Nagireddi (2008).

CHAPTER 13

Audio Coding

Audio functionality plays a critical role in digital media processing. While audio requires less processing power in general than video processing, it should be considered equally important. Recent applications such as wireless, Internet, and multimedia communication systems have created a demand for high-quality digital audio delivery at low bit rates. Audio coding or compression algorithms are used to obtain compact digital representation of high-fidelity audio signals for the purpose of efficient transmission or storage.

In this chapter, we discuss audio coding techniques. We begin with the concepts and technologies behind various audio coding techniques in Sections 13.1 and 13.2. Next is a discussion about the modules comprising the Moving Picture Experts Group-4 (MPEG-4) advanced audio coding (AAC) codec and encoder and decoder architectures in Section 13.3. Section 13.4 focuses on various commercially available audio codecs and provides implementation complexity (in terms of cycles and memory). Finally, we discuss a few audio post-processing techniques to enhance the audio listening experience in Section 13.5.

Audio codecs are used for source encoding and decoding of audio information. Like any other source coding, audio codecs remove redundancies without altering the perceptible information content. Codecs are designed for two different parameters—sampling rate and bit rate. The sampling rate is the rate of uncompressed input samples; bit rate is the rate of compressed output bit information. Audio signals contain frequencies in the range of 20 to 20,000 Hz, and typically audio signals are sampled at 44.1 kHz or 48 kHz. For stereo audio with 16 bits per sample and at a sampling rate of 44.1 kHz, we require a bit rate of about $1.41 (= 2 \times 16 \times 44.1 \times 10^3)$ Mbps to transmit or store the digital audio. This bit rate increases to 4.32 Mbps with the addition of synchronization and error correction overheads. Although high, these data rates were used successfully in first-generation digital audio applications such as CD (compact disc) audio.

However, end-user expectations have created a demand for high-quality digital audio delivery at low bit rates. Recent applications such as wireless and Internet communication systems are designed for lower bit rates. The basic requirements for low bit-rate audio coding are robustness against variations in audio level and its spectrum, minimum coding delay, robustness against random and burst errors, and graceful degradation in audio quality with an increased bit-error rate due to packet losses in packet communications.

13.1 Psychoacoustics and Perceptual Coding

In this section, we briefly discuss the principles underlying audio compression. Unlike speech signals (which can be compressed easily by source modeling), audio signals come from many sources and no simple source model exists to compress audio. We use the psychoacoustic principles of the human auditory system (the ultimate receiver) to compress the audio signals.

Audio codecs assume that the audio is for human listening. There are certain listening characteristics of normal human hearing that can be exploited to achieve audio compression. Almost all audio coders use the following characteristics in compressing audio signals: absolute threshold of hearing, critical bands, and masking.

13.1.1 Absolute Threshold of Hearing

The human ear can sense only frequencies in the range of 20 Hz to 20 kHz, and maximum sensitivity is in the range of 4 kHz. Responses to various frequencies are studied in detail, and this response is called the absolute threshold of hearing (ATH). The ATH characterizes the amount of energy needed in a pure tone such that it can

DOI: 10.1016/B978-1-85617-678-1.00013-2

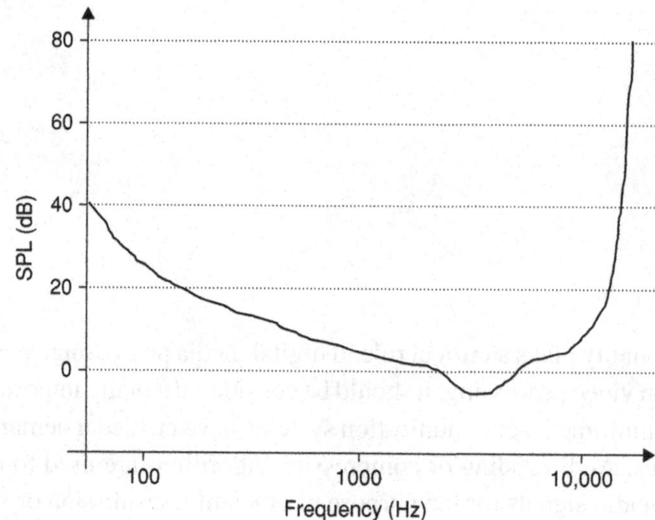

Figure 13.1: Absolute threshold of hearing: SPL versus frequency.

be detected by a listener in a noiseless environment. The ATH is typically expressed in terms of dB SPL (see Section 12.1 for more details on dB SPL). The human auditory system is not a linear organ. For example, the threshold of hearing is 40 dB for a 50-Hz sine tone and 28 dB for an 80-Hz sine. Figure 13.1 shows a plot of the ATH characteristic measured in the range 50 to 20,000 Hz.

What is the purpose of this ATH plot? Well, it gives us the maximum coding distortion that can be introduced in a particular frequency band so that a smaller number of bits can be used to represent the signal component in that particular band. This threshold can be mapped to different Bark bands or even to scalefactor bands to perform psychoacoustic analysis. The terms *Bark* and *scalefactor* are further described later.

13.1.2 Critical Bands

The auditory system processes incoming audio spectral content with auditory filters having different passband frequencies, referred to as *critical bands*. The critical bandwidth is a function of frequency that quantifies the auditory filter passband. Although many experiments were done and many models conceived, there is no unique way to determine the critical bandwidth. For an average listener, the approximate critical bandwidth (Painter and Spanias, 2000) is given by the following Munich critical-bandwidth model:

$$BW_c(f) = 25 + 75\left[1 + 1.4\,(f/1000)^2\right]^{0.69} \tag{13.1}$$

This may be approximated by the one-third octave model using the following expression:

$$CBW_{1/3}(f) = 232 \times (f/1000) \tag{13.2}$$

Figure 13.2 shows critical bandwidth characteristics for the Munich and one-third octave models.

Alternatively, center frequencies are used to represent critical bandwidths. The spacing between center frequencies is nonuniform with hertz spacing; for this reason we use the *Bark scale* to measure critical bandwidths. One critical bandwidth is measured as one Bark. Table 13.1 presents the Munich model based on a few critical bandwidths, corresponding center frequencies, and the Bark scale values. The idealized (or rectangular) critical band filter magnitude responses based on Munich-model critical bandwidths are shown in Figure 13.3.

13.1.3 Masking

Another well-studied behavior of human ear is its masking characteristic. Masking refers to a process where one sound is rendered inaudible because of the presence of another sound. For example, a strong frequency can mask a weaker frequency if they appear close in the spectrum with sufficient energy difference. This phenomenon is called *frequency masking*. The stronger signal (*masker*) masks the weaker signal (*maskee*). The masker and maskee can be tone or noise, which results in four combinations: tone-masking tone (TMT), tone-masking noise (TMN),

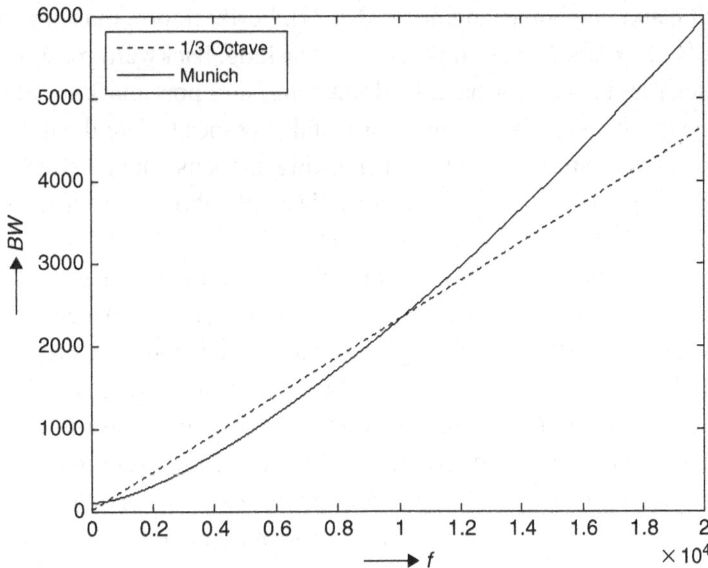

Figure 13.2: Critical bandwidths based on Munich and one-third octave models.

Table 13.1: Critical bandwidths, center frequencies, and bark values for auditory filters that span audio spectrum

Bark Number	Center Frequency (Hz)	Critical Bandwidth (Hz)
0	50	0–100
1	150	100–200
2	250	200–300
3	350	300–400
4	450	400–510
5	570	510–630
–	–	–
23	13,500	12,000–15,500
24	19,500	15,500–

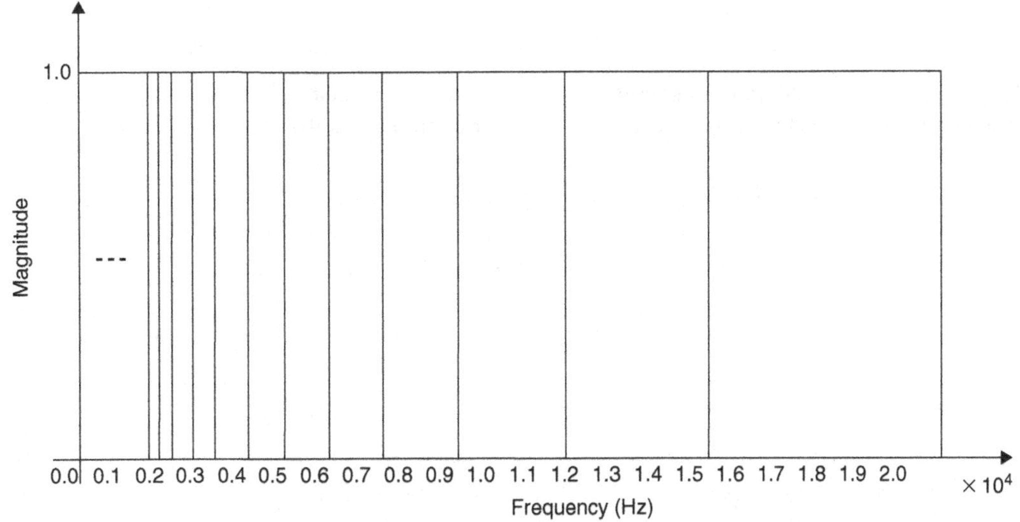

Figure 13.3: Idealized responses for critical band-filter magnitude.

noise-masking tone (NMT), and noise-masking noise (NMN). Furthermore, masking has temporal characteristics, and therefore it can also be classified as simultaneous masking, backward masking, and forward masking.

Figure 13.4(a) illustrates premasking (or backward masking) and post-masking (or forward masking). Premasking happens when the masker signal can mask a signal that comes before the masker itself. This can occur when a soft signal is followed by a strong signal. Post-masking happens when the masker signal masks a signal that comes after the masker. Typically, premasking tends to last only about 3 to 5 ms, whereas post-masking will extend anywhere from 30 to 300 ms, depending on the masker.

Simultaneous masking may occur whenever two or more tones are simultaneously presented to the auditory system. It is a frequency-domain phenomenon where a low-level signal can be made inaudible by a simultaneously occurring stronger signal, and this is effective as long as both tones lie in the same critical band. This is illustrated in Figure 13.4(b). Most audio coding algorithms utilize this feature (in particular TMN) of the auditory system to mask unwanted signal components such as quantization noise, aliasing distortion, or transmission errors.

Temporal masking can be used to reduce effective pre-echo. Pre-echo is a coding artifact that is very annoying for block-based transform coders in nonstationary input conditions, such as attacks. If the block size is large, for an attack signal the transform-domain quantization error that spreads across the entire block introduces more error in the early silent portion of the attack. If the temporal masking effect (as shown in Figure 13.5) is considered while coding, more error is acceptable in the masked area, which provides more bits to code the rest of the waveform. This is the basic principle of the temporal noise shaping (TNS) tool.

Masking occurs not only within the critical band but also spreads to neighboring bands. A spreading function $SF(x)$ can be defined, where x is the frequency and has units of Barks. This function provides a masking threshold produced by a single masker for neighboring frequencies. The simplest function would be a triangular function with slopes of +25 and −10 dB/Bark, but a more sophisticated one is highly nonlinear and depends on both

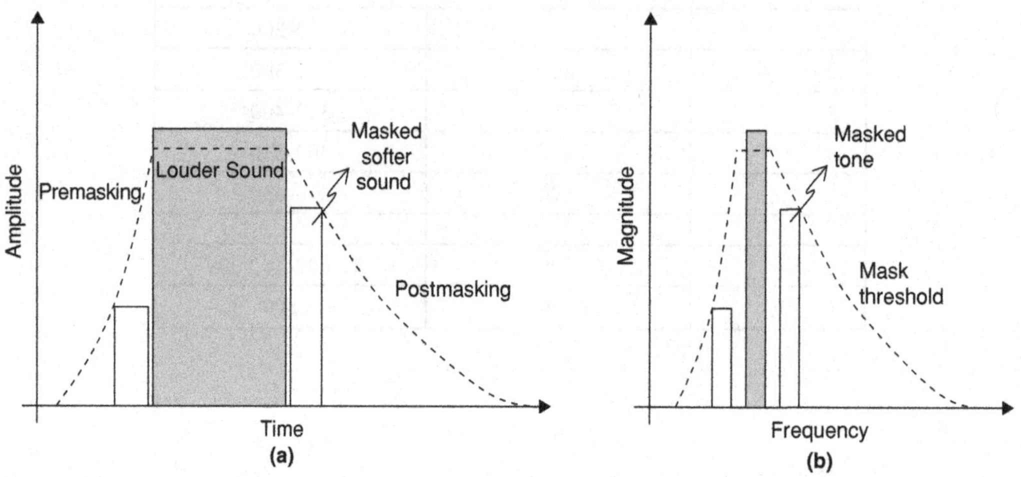

Figure 13.4: (a) Temporal masking: loud sounds at a specific time can mask softer sounds in the temporal vicinity. (b) Simultaneous masking: loud sounds at a specific frequency can mask softer sounds at nearby frequencies.

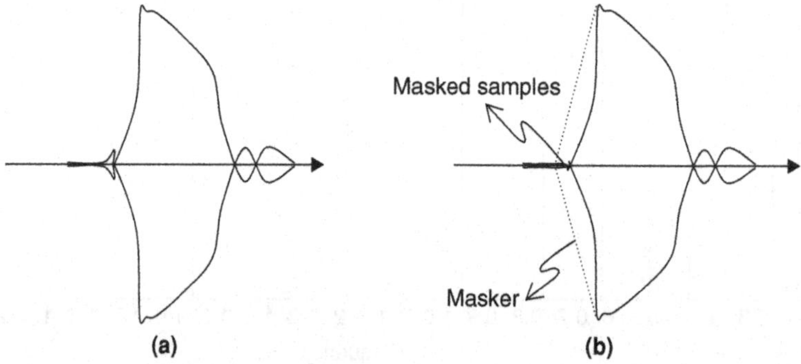

Figure 13.5: Temporal noise shaping. (a) Pre-echo before masking. (b) After masking.

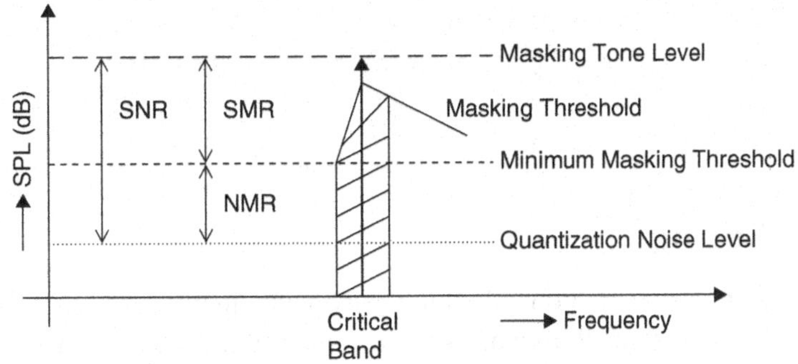

Figure 13.6: Illustration of SNR, SMR, and NMR.

frequency and amplitude of the masker. A convenient analytical expression for $SF(x)$ is given by

$$SF(x) = 15.81 + 7.5(x + 0.474) - 17.5\sqrt{1 + (x + 0.474)^2}\ \text{dB} \quad (13.3)$$

The *masking threshold*, in the context of source coding (also known as threshold of just noticeable distortion – JND), can be measured, and low-level signals under this threshold will not be audible. Without a masker, a signal is still inaudible if its sound pressure level is below the absolute threshold of hearing.

Defining SNR_q as the SNR resulting from q-bit quantization, the perceivable distortion in a given subband is measured by the *noise-to-mask ratio* (NMR) defined as follows:

$$NMR_q = SMR - SNR_q \quad (13.4)$$

where SMR is *signal-to-mask ratio*. The relationship among SNR, SMR, and NMR is illustrated in Figure 13.6. Within a critical band, coding noise will not be audible as long as NMR_q is negative.

Example 13.1 describes the importance of the masking for achieving efficient audio coding.

Example 13.1

Assume that the input to an audio codec has four non-zero spectral lines: $X = \{S_1\ S_2\ S_3\ S_4\}$. If the average bits/spectral line = 10 bits, compare the bits used for encoding the frame if frequency masking is used. Assume different relative power levels including the masker spread.

Spectral lines are illustrated in Figure 13.7. The curved line is the absolute threshold of hearing, which can also be treated as a static mask. The slanted lines are dynamic masking thresholds contributed by different masker spreads. S_4 is always less than the absolute hearing threshold. Consequently, this need not be transmitted, resulting in a savings of 10 bits.

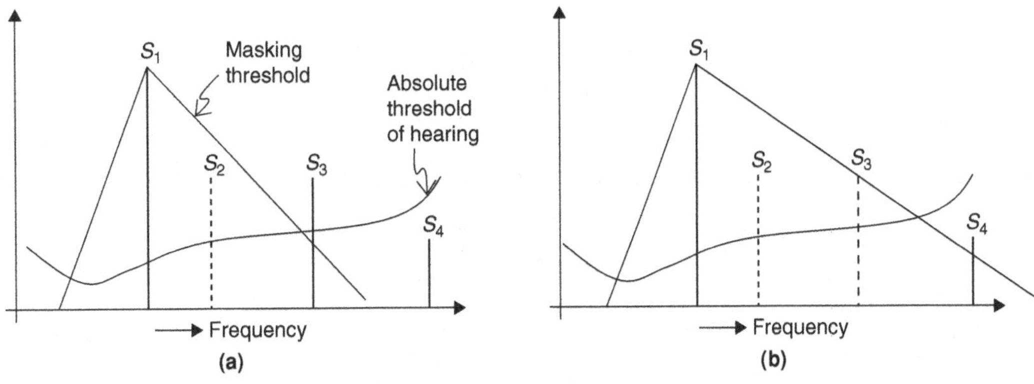

Figure 13.7: Spectral levels and masking thresholds. (a) Narrow masker spread. (b) Wider masker spread.

In Figure 13.7(a), the masker spread is masking S_2. Thus, S_2 is also redundant and need not be coded, resulting in an additional savings of 10 more bits. That is, total bits required are going to be reduced by 20 bits. In Figure 13.7(b), masker spread is wider and masks S_2 and S_3. So, S_2 and S_3 are redundant and need not be coded; total bits required are reduced by 30 bits.

■

13.2 Audio Signals Coding

To achieve the required compression without affecting perceived quality, perceptual redundancies must be removed to the greatest possible extent. Removal of these three redundancies decreases the data rate without affecting perceived quality: (1) interchannel, (2) intrachannel, and (3) psychoacoustic.

In the previous section, we discussed various psychoacoustic principles for coding audio signals by removing redundancies that are irrelevant to the auditory system. Redundancies can be removed in various signal domains, such as the time domain or frequency domain. Once redundancies are removed from the input signals, then the signals can be quantized and coded efficiently as bitstreams. In this section, we discuss inter- and intra-channel redundancies, and various aspects of audio encoders.

13.2.1 Interchannel Techniques

Interchannel redundancies can be removed by looking for common information in different channels. Stereo audio coding heavily depends on removal of interchannel redundancies. Two popular stereo coding techniques are joint stereo and parametric stereo coding.

Joint Stereo Coding

Joint stereo coding is one of the most commonly used techniques in audio coding. There are two types of joint stereo coding—midside (MS) stereo and intensity stereo (IS). For MS stereo, at the encoder side, mid and side samples are calculated from left and right samples using the following equations:

$$\text{mid } M_i = \frac{R_i + L_i}{\sqrt{2}} \tag{13.5}$$

$$\text{side } S_i = \frac{R_i - L_i}{\sqrt{2}} \tag{13.6}$$

Mid and side samples are encoded. MS coding is an efficient coding method for stereo channels when there is a great degree of correlation between two channels. At the decoder side, the left and right are computed using the following equations:

$$\text{left } L_i = \frac{M_i + S_i}{\sqrt{2}} \tag{13.7}$$

$$\text{right } R_i = \frac{M_i - S_i}{\sqrt{2}} \tag{13.8}$$

For IS, at the encoder side, the mono samples are calculated from left and right samples using following equations:

$$\text{mono } M_i = \frac{R_i + L_i}{\sqrt{2}} \tag{13.9}$$

$$\text{intensity } I_b = \sqrt{\frac{\sum L_i^2}{\sum R_i^2}} \tag{13.10}$$

Only mono samples are encoded. The intensity factor is computed for a collection of samples called *bands*. The I_b is quantized and encoded as a band parameter.

At the decoder side, left and right are computed using the following equations:

$$left\ L_i = M_i * \frac{I'_b}{1+I'_b} \tag{13.11}$$

$$right\ R_i = M_i * \frac{1}{1+I'_b} \tag{13.12}$$

where I'_b is the inverse quantized intensity factor. A block diagram of intensity stereo coding is shown in Figure 13.8.

Parametric Stereo Coding

Parametric stereo coding constitutes a major step toward enhancing the efficiency of audio compression for low bit-rate stereo audio data. This coding achieves about 40% more compression than conventional stereo coding methods (e.g., MS stereo coding). A block diagram of the parametric stereo coding system is shown in Figure 13.9.

At the encoder side, we down-mix the stereo data to monaural data and extract corresponding parameters. The monaural data samples are encoded by the conventional audio encoder and the parameters are encoded by the parameter encoder. Then we multiplex the two bitstreams before transmitting. At the decoder side, we perform inverse operations to get back the stereo audio data. The decoder uses a stereo synthesizer to reconstruct the stereo data from the decoded monaural samples and the side parameter information.

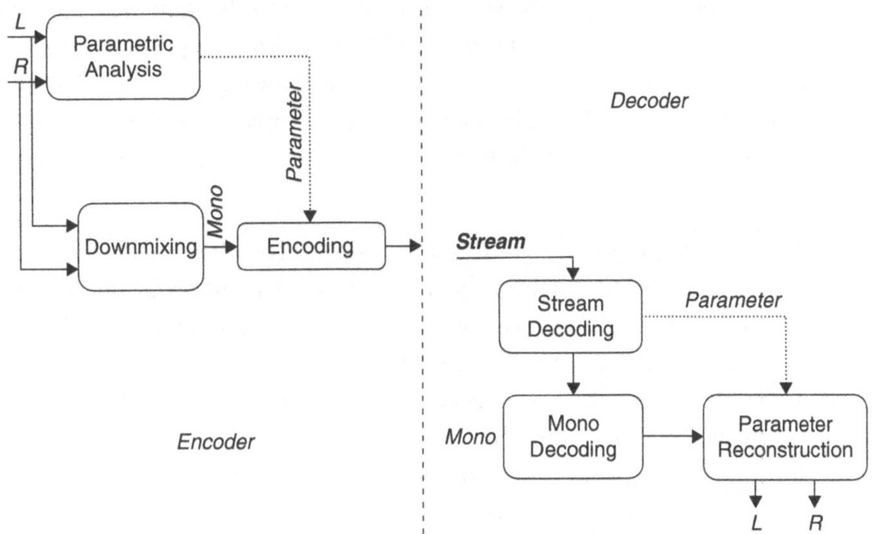

Figure 13.8: Block diagram of IS coding.

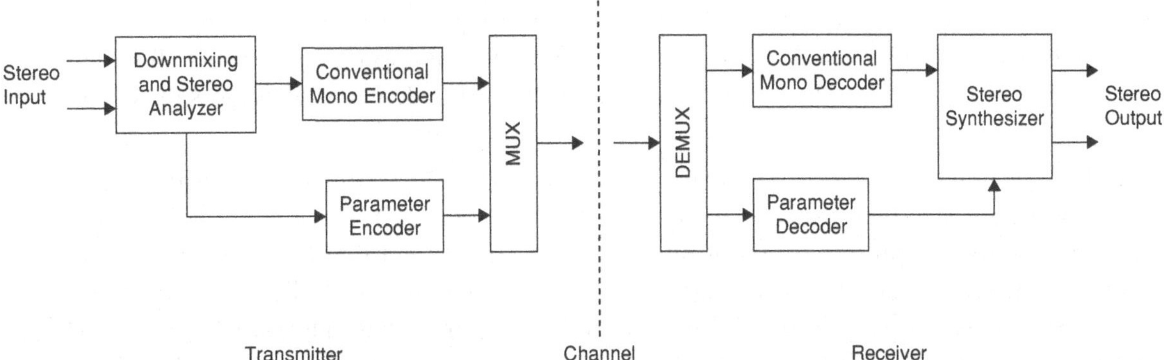

Figure 13.9: Simplified block diagram of parametric stereo coder.

The parameter stereo coding provides high audio quality at bit rates as low as 24 kbps. For more details on parametric stereo coding, see Breebaart et al. (2005).

13.2.2 Intrachannel Techniques

The information rate can be improved by removing redundancies in a given channel. Intrachannel redundancies can be removed with time-domain techniques, transform-domain techniques, or a combination of both. Lossless coding techniques such as Huffman coding can effectively remove the redundancies present in the quantized data symbols.

Time-Domain Techniques

DPCM and ADPCM Coding The simplest form of time-domain information reduction is DPCM. In this technique, the difference between real-time samples is quantized and encoded. As further enhancement to the DPCM, ADPCM improves coding gain by adding adaptive prediction. The difference between the samples is predicted, and the difference between the real sample and predicted speech samples are quantized and encoded. See Section 12.4.4 for more details on DPCM and ADPCM coding techniques.

Linear Predictive Coding Linear predictive coding (LPC) is a widely used technique in speech coding; it is a classical example of parametric coders. See Sections 8.1.3 and 12.4.5 for more detail on LPC. In comparison to nonparametric spectral modeling techniques such as filter banks or transforms, LPC is more powerful in compressing the spectral information into a few filter coefficients. However, LPC-based coders are considered suboptimal for audio signals since these signals do not fit the assumed audio source model. This is because the audio signals are typically multichannel and obtained from different instruments.

Audio compression is achieved by studying the perception of sound by the human ear rather than by modeling sound-producing sources. Warped linear prediction coding (WLPC) is a technique that utilizes the characteristics of human hearing for audio compression, and it is a preferred solution for wideband audio coding. Since a WLPC system can be adjusted so that the spectral resolution closely approximates the frequency resolution of human hearing, it is a clear step forward in applying LPC to model the human ear's perception of audio signals.

Frequency-Domain Techniques

Filter Banks Filter banks can be employed to analyze audio samples. The filter bank can be used to exploit signal redundancy and psychoacoustic irrelevancy in the frequency domain. The subband coders commonly use a filter bank structure. The filter bank divides the audible signal spectrum into a number of frequency subbands, and provides the frequency-localized signal power within each subband. The output of each filter is then decimated, quantized, and encoded into the bitstream. Psychoacoustic signal analysis is used to allocate an appropriate number of bits for the quantization of each subband.

At the receiver, the bitstream is decoded into samples, upsampled, and summed to reconstruct the signal. The analysis and synthesis filters are carefully designed to cancel aliasing and imaging distortions. With perfect reconstruction filter banks, the reconstructed audio samples will be identical to the original audio samples as long as no quantization and channel errors are present in the process. For more details on signal processing with filter banks, see Section 8.2.

DFT In this technique, the audio signal is transformed to the frequency domain by taking the discrete Fourier transform (DFT) of the input signal and only significant portions of the spectrum are coded. But this method is not very efficient as it introduces the imaginary part in the transform domain and doubles the output samples. And there are more blocking artifacts if the quantization error is increased.

MLT and MDCT Modulated lapped transforms (MLTs) are a family of orthogonal transforms that allow an orthogonal time-frequency representation of signals without blocking artifacts caused by sharp block edges. They were first introduced in the context of filter banks by Princen and Bradley (1986), and generalized by Malvar (1999). Because MLT basis vectors are derived from local (windowed) discrete cosine functions, they are well adapted for the representation of audio signals, which are sum of sinusoids (partials), with slowly varying amplitude and frequency. The MLT represents the perfect-reconstruction cosine-modulated filter bank based on the concept of time-domain alias cancellation (TDAC).

The MLT has also been referred to as an oddly stacked, modified, discrete cosine transform (MDCT). The MDCT is used in MPEG 1/2 for layer 3, Dolby AC-3, MPEG 2/4 AAC, and Windows Media Player. The MDCT maps an array of K real numbers, $x[0], x[1], \ldots, x[K-1]$, into an array of $K/2$ real numbers (here we assumed K as even number) as

$$X_m = \sum_{k=0}^{K-1} x[k]\cos\left[\frac{\pi}{2K}(2k+1+K/2)(2m+1)\right], \quad m = 0, 1, \ldots, K/2-1 \tag{13.13}$$

If $\{X_m\}$ is an array of $K/2$ elements, then the inverse MDCT of $\{X_m\}$ is an array of K elements, and is obtained as

$$y_k = \frac{4}{K}\sum_{m=0}^{K/2-1} X_m \cos\left[\frac{\pi}{2K}(2k+1+K/2)(2m+1)\right], \quad k = 0, 1, 2, \ldots, K-1 \tag{13.14}$$

The final time-domain output $x[k]$ is obtained from y_k by overlap and add method as illustrated in Figure 13.10(b). A portion of the audio signal $x[k]$ is shown in Figure 13.11(a); the MDCT computed to the corresponding audio signal with $K/2 = 128$ (i.e., a total of 80 windowed segments of length, 128 samples each) is shown in Figure 13.11(b).

Fast Implementation of MDCT Using FFT The MDCT (with input length N and output length $N/2$, where N is divisible by 4) can be calculated using $N/4$ point FFT with some pre- and post-rotation of the sample points. The summary of MDCT fast implementation using $N/4$-point FFT follows (see Duhamel et al. [1991] for details). Define

$$\tilde{x}[k] = \begin{cases} -x\left[k+\frac{3N}{4}\right], & 0 \le k \le N/4-1 \\ x\left[k-\frac{N}{4}\right], & N/4 \le k < N-1 \end{cases} \tag{13.15}$$

and

$$x'[k] = (\tilde{x}[2k] - \tilde{x}[N-2k-1]) + j(\tilde{x}[N/2+2k] - \tilde{x}[N/2-2k+1]) \tag{13.16}$$

where $0 \le k \le N/4-1$. Obtain $x''[k]$ by multiplying $x'[k]$ with $e^{-j\frac{2\pi}{N}(k+\frac{1}{8})}$,

$$x''[k] = x'[k]e^{-j\frac{2\pi}{N}(k+\frac{1}{8})} \tag{13.17}$$

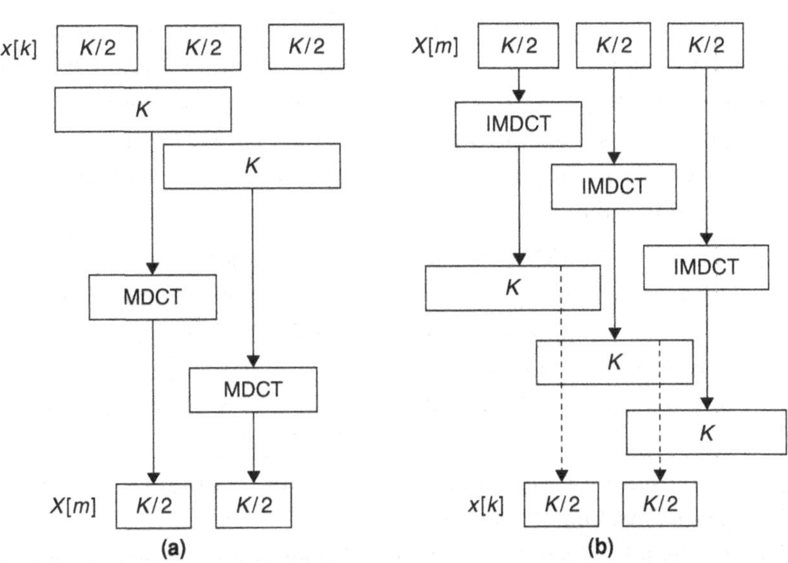

Figure 13.10: MDCT. (a) Forward transform. (b) Inverse transform and reconstruction by overlap and add method.

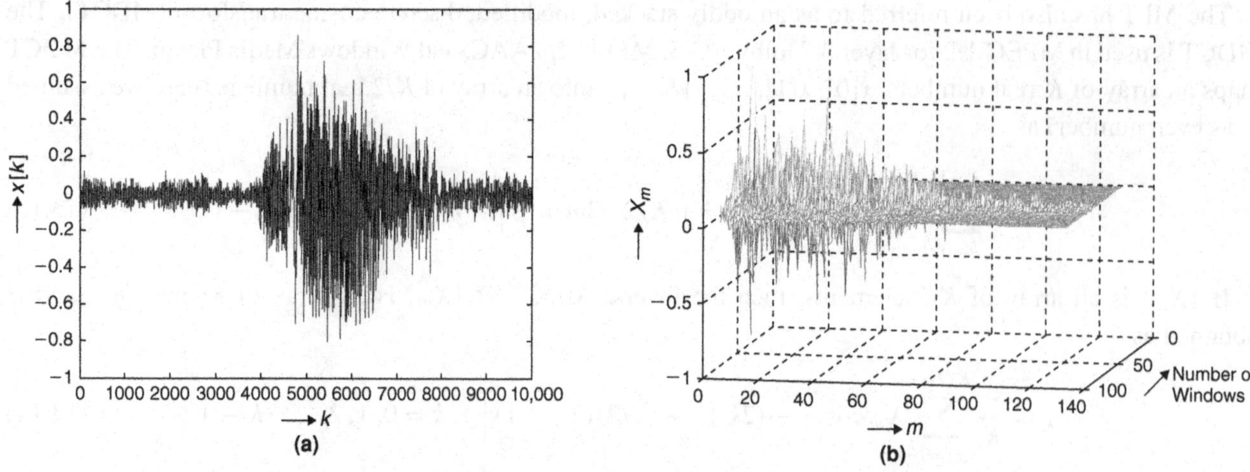

Figure 13.11: (a) Portion of audio signal. (b) MDCT output with $K/2 = 128$.

Then, compute $N/4$-point FFT and obtain the frequency-domain equivalent of $x''[k]$, $X''[m]$ as

$$X''[m] = FFT\left(x''[k]\right), \quad 0 \le k \le N/4-1, 0 \le m \le N/4-1 \tag{13.18}$$

Obtain $X'[m]$ by multiplying $X''[m]$ with $e^{-j\frac{2\pi}{N}\left(m+\frac{1}{8}\right)}$,

$$X'[m] = X''[m]e^{-j\frac{2\pi}{N}\left(m+\frac{1}{8}\right)} \tag{13.19}$$

Finally, the $N/2$-length MDCT output $X[m]$ is obtained as follows:

$$\begin{aligned} X[2m] &= \mathrm{Re}\left(X'[m]\right), \quad m = 0, 1, 2, \ldots, N/4-1 \\ X[2m+1] &= \mathrm{Im}\left(X'[N/4-m-1]\right), \quad m = 0, 1, 2, \ldots, N/4-1 \end{aligned} \tag{13.20}$$

In similar fashion, we can compute the IMDCT using the FFT transform.

13.2.3 General Structure of an Audio Encoder

Based on the audio coding techniques discussed so far, we can design an audio encoder. Building blocks of an audio encoder are shown in Figure 13.12. Most audio codecs perform frame-based encoding. Incoming audio is buffered to get N consecutive samples, called the *audio frame*. One audio frame will contain an equal number samples from all channels. After processing, the encoder outputs one *audio packet* corresponding to a single audio frame. The audio frame is represented in samples and audio packet is represented in bits. In most cases, frame and packet sizes are fixed for a given encoder configuration. One frame of audio samples is processed at a time to remove spatial and temporal redundancies.

Psychoacoustic Model: Computes SMRs, estimates masking thresholds, and so on.

Time-Domain Processing: Removes interchannel redundancies, applies windowing, and so on.

Transform: Maps time-domain samples to number of frequency components. Filter bank or MDCT is commonly used to transform the audio samples.

Transform-Domain Processing: Performs temporal noise shaping (TNS), perceptual noise substitution (PNS), and so on.

Quantization: Quantizes transform-domain coefficients such that resulting quantization noise is lower than the psychoacoustic-model masking thresholds.

Entropy Coding: Encodes quantized data using either Huffman or arithmetic coding methods.

Side Information Processing: Encodes psychoacoustic analysis parameters, filter coefficients, control information, and so on.

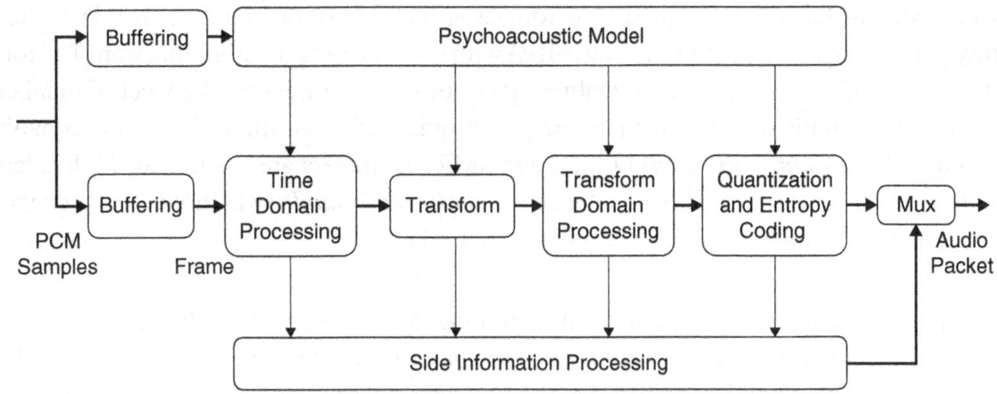

Figure 13.12: Block diagram of audio encoder.

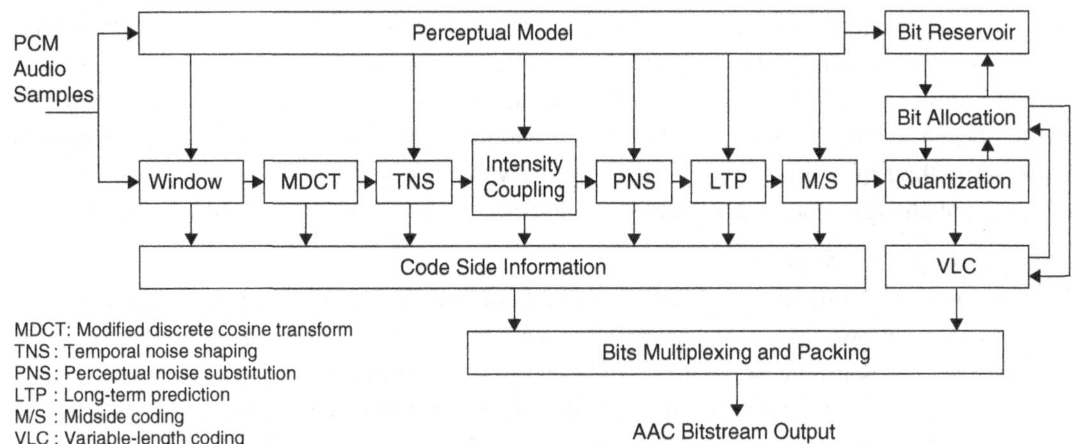

Figure 13.13: MPEG-4 AAC encoder block diagram.

13.3 MPEG-4 AAC Codec

In this section, we discuss MPEG AAC building blocks that utilize the audio-coding principles discussed thus far. The MPEG-4 AAC codec, part of the ISO/IEC MPEG standard is a powerful coding algorithm, in terms of perceived audio quality for single-channel and multichannel audio content. AAC delivers indistinguishable quality stereo audio (from the original or CD) at bit rates of 128 kbps. The AAC is widely used in PC multimedia and Internet broadcast applications. Different trade-offs between quality and complexity are provided by the three MPEG-4 AAC profiles, namely, the main profile, low-complexity profile, and scalable sample rate profile. Although the AAC requires a patent license for manufacturing or developing AAC codec, it is not a proprietary format and no payments are required to stream or distribute files in AAC format.

13.3.1 MPEG-4 AAC Encoder

The block diagram of the MPEG-4 AAC encoder is shown in Figure 13.13. The AAC encoder receives PCM audio samples and transfers them to the perceptual model and MDCT blocks.

Psychoacoustic Model

The MPEG-4 AAC algorithm, like other perceptual encoders (e.g., MP3, MPEG-2 AAC), uses psychoacoustic principles to achieve target compression efficiency. The psychoacoustic model is used to calculate the signal-to-mask ratio (SMR), masking thresholds, bit allocation information, window type, and so on. The psychoacoustic model runs in the frequency domain and we use a separate transform (e.g., FFT) to obtain the spectrum for the purpose of psychoacoustic analysis.

For psychoacoustic analysis, the spectrum is divided into many spectral partitions, and the energy of each spectral partition is calculated. Also, the unpredictability measure for each partition is calculated (which provides the portion of the spectrum that cannot be predicted from the spectra of two previous blocks). Then the energy and unpredictability measure of each partition are convolved with the cochlea-spreading function. The tonality index is then calculated from the convolved unpredictability measure (which measures the level of tonal components of the spectral partitions and is used to calculate the power ratio of the partition). Using the convolved energy and the power ratio, the *masking thresholds* (T_{mask}) and SMR parameters are calculated. Both calculations are adapted from the original spectral partitions to the actual *scalefactor bands* (which we define later). The T_{mask} gives the maximum allowed quantization noise for scalefactor band.

Windowing

The MPEG-4 AAC encoder applies windowing to the incoming samples for MDCT block. Two types of windows, the *long window* (with 2048-sample length) and the *short window* (with 256-sample length) are used. There is an overlap of 50% between consecutive windows (i.e., 1024 samples overlap in the long window and 128 samples overlap in the short window). Depending on the nature of the input audio samples (e.g., transient, steady state), we switch between the two window types. When switching from one length to another length window, a different type of window is used to facilitate a smooth transition. In other words, a *start window* is used when changing from a long to short window and a *stop window* is used when changing from a short to long window.

Figure 13.14 shows a typical window sequence applying for MPEG-4 AAC input audio samples. Adaptive window switching provides dynamic changing of the window length and shape. The psychoacoustic model defines a simple method of switching by comparing the values of *perceptual entropy* from two consecutive blocks. If significant change in perceptual entropy is detected, then a change of the block mode is triggered.

Modified Discrete Cosine Transform

The modified discrete cosine transform (MDCT) converts the samples from the time domain to the frequency domain. This transform allows for signal decorrelation, and therefore minimizes the redundancies present in the signal. Moreover, using a combination of the MDCT and psychoacoustic model, the irrelevant components (to the human auditory system) of the original signal are identified and eliminated. By eliminating signal correlations and irrelevant portions of signal spectrum, bits required to code the audio signals are significantly reduced. For more detail on MDCT and its fast computation using FFT, see Section 13.2.2.

Several neighboring spectral coefficients are grouped into so-called *scalefactor bands* (SFBs), which share the same scalefactor for quantization. The number of coefficients for a given scalefactor band depends on the sampling rate and window length. Prior to quantization, a number of processing tools operate on the spectral coefficients in order to improve coding performance.

Temporal Noise Shaping

Temporal noise shaping (TNS) is used to control the pre-echo, an artifact common to all transform-domain compression algorithms. Pre-echoes occur when a signal with a sharp attack begins near the end of a transform block immediately following a low-energy region. In this case, the inverse transform spreads the quantization

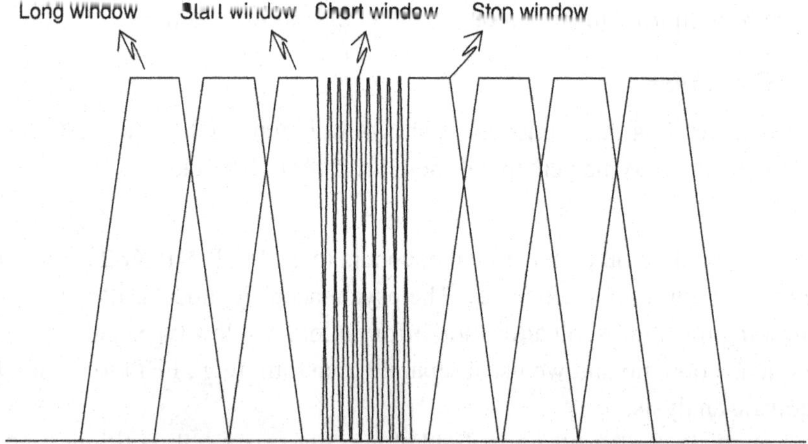

Figure 13.14: Example of window-switching sequence.

noise over an entire block, and it may become audible, as it is not present in the encoder psychoacoustic analysis. One way to compensate pre-echo is by using a short window length. However, frequent use of short blocks reduces coding efficiency. Another way to compensate for pre-echo is by using the TNS tool. The TNS tool uses frequency-domain linear prediction (LP) to shape the noise in the time domain. In other words, filtering the frequency spectrum at the decoder with LP coefficients attenuates the pre-echo quantization noise generated by transient signals.

Stereo Coding

The joint stereo coding tools, *intensity coupling* and *M/S coding*, exploit the redundancies in the stereo channel and help to improve audio compression efficiency. The intensity coupling process is used to reduce the number of bits needed for encoding stereo audio by coding two channels as a single channel. The individual spectral envelopes for both the channels are transmitted as side information for reconstructing the stereo channel signals at the decoder with appropriate gain factors.

The M/S decision is used for stereo signals, and determines whether the stereo channels should be encoded as the usual left and right channels, or as middle and side channels. When a coding benefit is realized, M/S transforms the left/right signals into sums and differences prior to quantization.

Perceptual Noise Substitution

Perceptual noise substitution (PNS) is used to efficiently code noisy signals. The PNS tool codes noisy spectral components as white noise by replacing the noise spectral coefficients with a white-noise constant energy level. The algorithm scans the frequency spectrum within the given range and checks for noise-like regions. A spectral band is classified as noise-like if it is neither tonal nor has considerable energy changes over time.

Long-Term Prediction

The long-term prediction (LTP) tool is used to enhance the coding of tonal signals by applying a prediction process to time-domain block data and transmitting just the error. This tool exploits the redundancy between tonal signals of successive data blocks. The predicted signal for the current frame is calculated from the inverse quantized time-domain signal from previous frames.

Scalefactors and Quantization

For the quantization, the MDCT coefficients are converted into a kind of floating-point representation. The coefficients are represented with the mantissa and exponent. Here, the exponent is called the *scalefactor*, since it is a factor that determines the resolution of the quantization scale. Each SFB is assigned a single scalefactor. Scalefactors are encoded and transmitted as side information.

For each MDCT coefficient X_i, its quantized value X_i^Q is obtained as

$$X_i^Q = \text{sgn}(X_i)\left\lfloor |X_i|^{3/4}\, 2^{\frac{3}{16}[sf(j)-csf]} + 0.4054 \right\rfloor \tag{13.21}$$

where $sf(j)$ is the scalefactor of the j-th SFB to which the current MDCT coefficient X_i belongs, and csf is the common scalefactor, which is computed as follows:

$$csf = 40 + \left\lfloor \frac{16}{3}\log_2\left(\left|\frac{\max\{X_i\}^{3/4}}{8191}\right|\right)\right\rfloor \tag{13.22}$$

The common scalefactor (csf) and the scalefactor $sf(j)$ determine the quantization level for the j-th SFB. Distortion in a j-th SFB caused by quantization is given by

$$Dist_j^Q = \sum_{i=j_{start}}^{j_{end}} \left|X_i - X_i^{IQ}\right|^2 \tag{13.23}$$

where j_{start} and j_{end} are lower and upper limits of the j-th SFB, respectively, and X_i^{IQ} is the inverse quantized value obtained as

$$X_i^{IQ} = \left(X_i^Q\right)^{4/3} 2^{-\frac{1}{4}[sf(j)-csf]} \tag{13.24}$$

Bit Allocation and Bit Reservoir

In AAC, quantization is responsible for allocating the noise while adhering to psychoacoustic demands set by the perceptual model. A two-loop iterative quantizer is designed such that the inner loop maintains the bit rate and the outer loop maintains perceptual performance by adjusting the bit allocation in each SFB.

The properties of audio signals vary with time. However, most audio applications expect a constant bit rate after encoding the audio signals. For that purpose, the AAC standard defines a *bit reservoir* for storing or spending the extra bits. A bit reservoir is used to achieve a constant bit rate by buffering the extra bits for coding signals with greater detail and by clearing the buffer when encoding signals with less information using fewer bits.

Entropy Coding

Huffman coding is used for noiseless coding of the quantized spectral values to further reduce the number of bits needed to encode the audio signals. The MPEG-4 AAC Huffman coding uses multiple codebooks with multiple dimensions to code the quantized data. One or more SFBs are grouped into a *section* and coded using the same codebook.

Bitstream Format

The bitstream packer assembles the coded data and control information into bitstream frames for transmission. Each frame represents 1024 PCM samples per channel. The length of the AAC frames varies from frame to frame because of the bit reservoir technique. The structure of the AAC encoded frame is shown in Figure 13.15. The AAC bitstream frame consists of three mandatory fields (*nonshaded*) and five nonmandatory fields (*shaded*). Two headers are specified in the AAC standard: audio data interchange format (ADIF) and audio data transport stream (ADTS). The ADIF header is used for file-based applications, while the ADTS header is used for streaming applications.

The AAC frame nonheader field contains the following information: program configuration (specifies sample rate, output channel assignment, and so on), audio (at least one audio element must be present), coupling channel element (used for intensity coding), data (contains auxiliary nonaudio information), fill (pads data if the frame size is not big enough to reach the target bit rate), and terminator (allows for parsing and synchronization of the bitstream).

13.3.2 MPEG-4 AAC Decoder

A simplified block diagram of MPEG-4 AAC decoder is shown in Figure 13.16. The first step in decoding is to establish frame alignment. Once the frame alignment is found, the bitstream is demultiplexed. This includes unpacking of the encoded quantized spectral data, scalefactors, stereo coding side information, TNS LPC coefficients, PNS flag, and gain information.

Huffman decoded data must be inverse quantized and then scaled. We then perform stereo decoding using the decoded stereo side information. Before applying IMDCT, we perform TNS by filtering the decoded stereo data using LPC coefficients. For the noiselike portion of audio, we perform PNS. Finally, we compute the inverse MDCT to obtain time-domain samples. After the IMDCT transform, the time-domain samples are passed through the overlap and add block to reconstruct the PCM audio samples. Once we decode the complete audio frame, the decoded audio samples are moved to the playback buffer.

In Chapter 5, we discussed the decoding procedure for Huffman or variable-length codes for MPEG-2 video bitstream decoding. The same Huffman decoding techniques can be used for decoding MPEG-4 AAC. For this, we first design look-up tables in advance from the codeword tables given in the AAC standard. Table entries contain the level, run length, and codeword length in terms of the number of bits. For decoding, first we extract the fixed number of bits from the bit FIFO (first-in-first-out) bitstream. We use the look-up table

Figure 13.15: MPEG-4 AAC encoded frame structure.

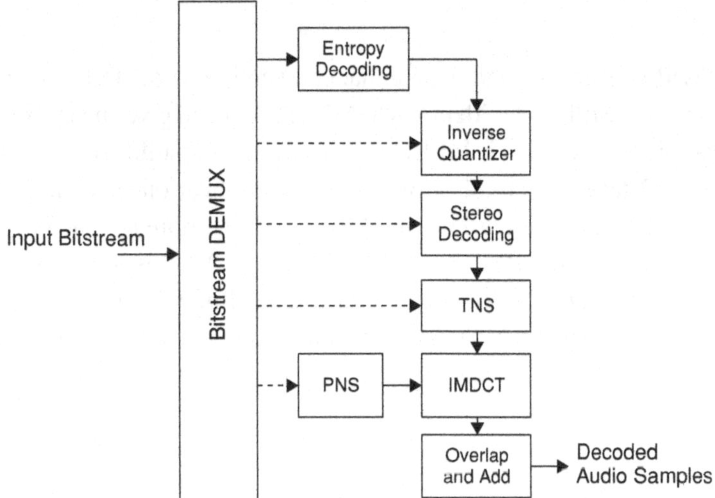

Figure 13.16: Block diagram of MPEG-4 AAC decoder.

to get the level, run length, and codeword length. The bit FIFO pointer is updated using the codeword length value. The inverse quantization process of the AAC decoder can also be performed efficiently using the look-up table.

13.4 Popular Audio Codecs

Many audio coding standards were developed since 1990 to support various application requirements (e.g., channel/storage bandwidth, quality, coding delay). In this section, we briefly address various audio codecs.

MPEG-1

MPEG-1 is defined by ISO/IEC 11172-3 and is a simplified version of MUSICAM (Masking-Pattern Adapted Universal Subband Integrated Coding and Multiplexing). MUSICAM is a primary audio format used for digital video broadcast and the direct satellite system. MPEG-1 operates pretty well at 192 or 256 kbps per channel. MPEG-1 has three layers—1, 2, and 3—with increasing coding complexity.

All three layers use 32-bank filter banks to perform time-frequency analysis at the encoder side. Processing after the time-frequency analysis distinguishes the three layers. There are also differences in psychoacoustic analysis. The bitstreams encoded in one layer cannot be decoded by another layer.

Layer 1 quantizes the filter bank output based on primitive psychoacoustic analysis. The quantized samples are encoded to form the bitstream. Layer 3 uses 384 samples for encoding one frame. Because the lengths and quantization parameters are also implicitly coded in the bitstream, the bitstream overhead is more in layer 1. Layer 2 takes three times more samples for analysis than layer 1, and performs grouping of samples to reduce the overhead. Layer 2 quantization is different from that of layer 1. Layer 2 reuses quantization parameters across more samples to further reduce the overhead.

Layer 3 is the most complex of the three. Layers 1 and 2 use the type I psychoacoustic model from the ISO/IEC 11172-3 recommendation, whereas layer 3 uses the type II model. MPEG-1 layer 3 is also called MP3. MP3 is probably the most popular lossy audio compression codec available today. The MP3 format was released in 1992 as a complement to the MPEG-1 video standard from the Moving Pictures Experts Group. MPEG forms part of the ISO/IEC, an information center jointly operated by the International Organization for Standardization and the International Electrotechnical Commission. MP3 was developed by the German Fraunhofer Institut Integrierte Schaltungen (Fraunhofer IIS), which holds a number of patents for MP3 encoding and decoding.

MP3 uses "polyphase filters" to separate the original signal into subbands. Then, the MDCT transform converts the signal into the frequency domain, where the psychoacoustic model quantizes the frequency coefficients. CD-quality MP3 encoding can operate at a 128- to 196-kbps rate, thus achieving up to a 12:1 compression ratio.

MPEG-2

MPEG-2 is defined by ISO/IEC 13818-3, and is an enhanced version of MPEG-1 to support multichannel and other sampling rates and bit rates. MPEG-2 is identical to MUSICAM and gives near-CD quality at 96 to 192 kbps. It is fully backward compatible with MPEG-1. MPEG-2 (backward compatible) defines its multichannel versions of layers 1, 2, and 3. MPEG-2 layer 2 is used in broadcasting applications such as DAB. MPEG-2 layer 3 is obsolete and superseded by nonbackward-compatible (NBC) and the more advanced version, AAC.

The MPEG-2 AAC is defined by ISO/IEC 138318-7. MPEG-2 AAC is a high-quality multichannel audio coding system, which is used for HDTV, DVD, and cable and satellite television. It encodes multiple channels of audio into a low bit-rate format. The high compression rate is achieved due to encoding multiple channels as a single entity.

MPEG-4 AAC

MPEG-4 AAC (as discussed in Section 13.3) is the enhancement to MPEG-2 AAC, with many new codec and system supports like low complexity (LC-AAC), high efficiency (HE-AAC), scalable sample rate (AAC-SSR), and bit-sliced arithmetic coding (BSAC). It is approximately 30% more bit-rate efficient than the MP3 algorithm, and outperforms its predecessors achieving indistinguishable CD audio quality at 128 kbps for stereo audio. AAC supports sample rates that range from 8 to 96 kHz and bit rates of 32 to 160 kbps (for mono) and 64 to 320 kbps (for stereo). It encompasses the error protection tool and error resilience techniques. Although the AAC requires patent license for manufacturing or developing of AAC codec, it is not a proprietary format and there is no fee to stream or distribute files in AAC format.

MPEG-4 ALS

MPEG-4 audio lossless (ALS) is an extension of the MPEG-4 audio coding family. Its operation is similar to FLAC (free lossless audio codec).

MPEG-4 ALS data packing is efficient for audio data. It allows getting high-quality records at significantly reduced data rates. MPEG-4 ALS mainly uses linear prediction coding (LPC), Golomb Rice coding and run-length encoding (RLE) for its operation. MPEG-4 ALS provides fast lossless audio compression techniques for consumer and professional use. An important benefit of MPEG 4-ALS coding is that it provides certain features that are not available in other lossless compression formats:

- Support for uncompressed digital audio format
- Support for PCM resolutions of up to 32-bit at any sampling rate
- Support for up to 65,536 channels
- Optional storage in MPEG-4 file format

WMA 9 Lossless

WMA 9 lossless is the codec abbreviation for Windows Media Audio 9. Its extension is .wma, and it is considered an audio file format. It is a lossless audio codec with an audio sampling rate of 96 kHz using 24 bits, which makes it ideal for archive or backup storage. The data compression ratio is 2:1 or 3:1, depending on the complexity of the source. It is compatible with various operating systems and backward compatible with previous WMA standards. In addition, it has a digital rights management (DRM) platform (for copyright protection of digital media).

WMA

WMA, the abbreviation for Windows Media Audio, is Microsoft's proprietary codec. The WMA codec supports sampling rates of 44.1 or 48 kHz and bit rates from 64 to 192 kbps using 16-bits PCM sample resolution. It supports constant bit-rate (CBR) and variable bit-rate (VBR) modes. With the development of WMA10 Pro, many features were added to enhance the functionality of this codec. It can support 24-bit/96-kHz stereo, 5.1-channel or even 7.1-channel surround sound. WMA10 Pro offers streaming, progressive download, and download-and-play delivery at 128 to 768 kbps. This makes it applicable for a wide range of playback devices and methods. WMA10 Pro is patented and supports DRM. Verification of performance results was conducted by National Software Testing Labs.

Vorbis

Vorbis is a free and open-source, lossy audio-compression codec developed by the Xiph Foundation. The development of Vorbis was stimulated by the announcement of MP3 licensing. Many video games and consumer electronics audio are stored in Vorbis format.

At a standard input sampling rate of 44.1 kHz, the encoder produces a digitized output sequence from 32 to 500 kbps, with VBR and various quality settings. It uses an MDCT transform for converting data from the time domain into the frequency domain. After the data is broken into noise floor and residue components, it is quantized and entropy coded using a codebook based on a vector quantization algorithm.

From a technical viewpoint, Vorbis outperforms MP3, according to many subjective tests, and it is therefore in the class of the newer codecs such as WMA and AAC. Vorbis also fully supports multichannel compression, thereby eliminating redundant information carried by the channels, as discussed previously.

AC3

The Acoustic Coder 3 (AC3) is a high-quality audio codec (audio coding format) elaborated by Dolby Laboratories. AC3 achieves large compression ratios by encoding multiple channels of audio into a low bit rate, and encoding multiple channels as a single-entity format. It uses a hybrid backward/forward, adaptive bit allocation approach, which is necessary for advanced television.

Dolby Digital, one of the AC-3 versions, encodes up to 5.1 channels of audio. AC-3 has been adopted as an audio compression scheme for many consumer and professional applications. It is a mandatory audio codec for DVD video, Advanced Television Standards Committee (ATSC), digital terrestrial television and Digital Living Network Alliance (DLNA), and home networking, as well as an optional multichannel audio format for DVD audio.

RealAudio 10

RealAudio10 is the proprietary codec of Real Networks. It supports bit rates from 12 to 800 kbps, and provides extremely high audio quality at the widest possible bandwidth range. To achieve such superior quality, the Real Audio codec is used for bit rates that are less than 128 kbps, but at bit rates higher than 128 kbps, it incorporates the AAC codec. Real Audio is widespread in the portable and mobile devices market as well as in streaming, on-demand, and download solutions.

FLAC

The Free Lossless Audio Code (FLAC) is another open standard from the Xiph Foundation. As the name implies, this code does not throw out any information from the original audio signal. This, of course, comes at the expense of much smaller achievable compression ratios. The typical compression range for FLAC is 30 to 70%.

MIPS (million instructions per second) and memory requirements for implementation of various audio codecs on the reference embedded processor are given in Table 13.2.

13.5 Audio Post-Processing

Audio post-processing can be used to improve the user listening experience or for compatibility of the audio player in multiple ways. Supporting multiple compression formats in audio players is no longer a special feature but rather a standard one. The added value in audio systems today comes in the form of quality enhancements that increase listening pleasure. Audio post-processing techniques such as equalization, stereo enhancement, surround sound, noise removal, visual effects, and so on, add value to audio players. The post-processing module called

Table 13.2: MIPS and memory requirements for audio codec implementation on reference embedded processor

Audio Codec	Encoder/ Decoder	Data Memory (kB)	Program Memory (kB)	MIPS	Encoder Sample Rate/Bit Rate
MP3	Encoder	30	32	45 (at 44.1 kHz, 128 kbps)	32/44.1/48 kHz, 32–320 kbps
	Decoder	25	32	20 (at 128 kbps, 48 kHz)	
MPEG-4 HE-AAC-v2	Encoder	110	130	74 (at 44.1 kHz, 36 kbps)	32/44.1/48 kHz, 16–36 kbps
	Decoder	123	105	36 (at 48 kbps, 48 kHz)	
WMA	Encoder	156	60	35 (at 44.1 kHz, 128 kbps)	44.1/48 kHz, 64–320 kbps
	Decoder	78	42	60 (at 128 kbps, 48 kHz)	
AC-3	Encoder	117	68	136 (at 48 kHz, 448 kbps)	All sampling frequencies, 32–640 kbps
	Decoder	39	26	44.1 (at 48 kHz, 384 kbps)	
Vorbis	Decoder	48	31	40.6 (at 48 kHz, 128 kbps)	All sampling frequencies, upto 500 kbps
Audio post-processing	Sample rate conversion	12.5	6	46 (for 32 kHz to 48 kHz)	*Input:* 8/11.025/12/16/22.05/ 24/32/44.1/48 kHz *Output:* 32/44.1/48/64/88.2/ 96/128/174/192 kHz

sample rate conversion (SRC) is often used for compatibility of players with other digital systems. Most audio post-processing involves some kind of filtering. We use either FIR or IIR digital filters (see Chapter 7) to perform filtering. Next, we briefly discuss a few audio post-processing modules.

13.5.1 Audio Sample Rate Conversion

There are times converting a signal sampled at one frequency to a different sampling rate is necessary. One situation where this is useful is decoding an audio signal sampled at, say 11.025 kHz, but when the DAC you are using does not support that sampling frequency. Another scenario is when a signal is oversampled, and converting it to a lower frequency can lead to a reduction in computation time. The process of converting the sampling rate of a signal from one rate to another is called sample rate conversion, or SRC.

Increasing the sample rate is called *interpolation*, and decreasing it is called *decimation*. Decimating a signal by a factor of M is achieved by keeping only every M-th sample and discarding the rest. Interpolating a signal by a factor of L is accomplished by padding the original signal with $L-1$ zeros between each sample and filtering the resultant images. See Section 8.2 for more details on decimation and interpolation processes.

Even though interpolation and decimation factors are integers, we can apply them in series to an input signal and get a rational conversion factor. When we upsample by factor 5 and then downsample by factor 3, we get the resulting factor as $5/3 = 1.67$. Figure 8.29 shows SRC through upsampling and downsampling. We use an antialiasing filter in the decimation process and an anti-imaging filter in the interpolation process to filter the out-of-band signals. Note that it is possible to combine the anti-imaging and antialiasing filter into a single component for computational savings.

The SRC is efficiently implemented by using polyphase decomposition techniques. See Section 8.2.2 for more details on efficient implementation of decimation and interpolation using polyphase decomposition.

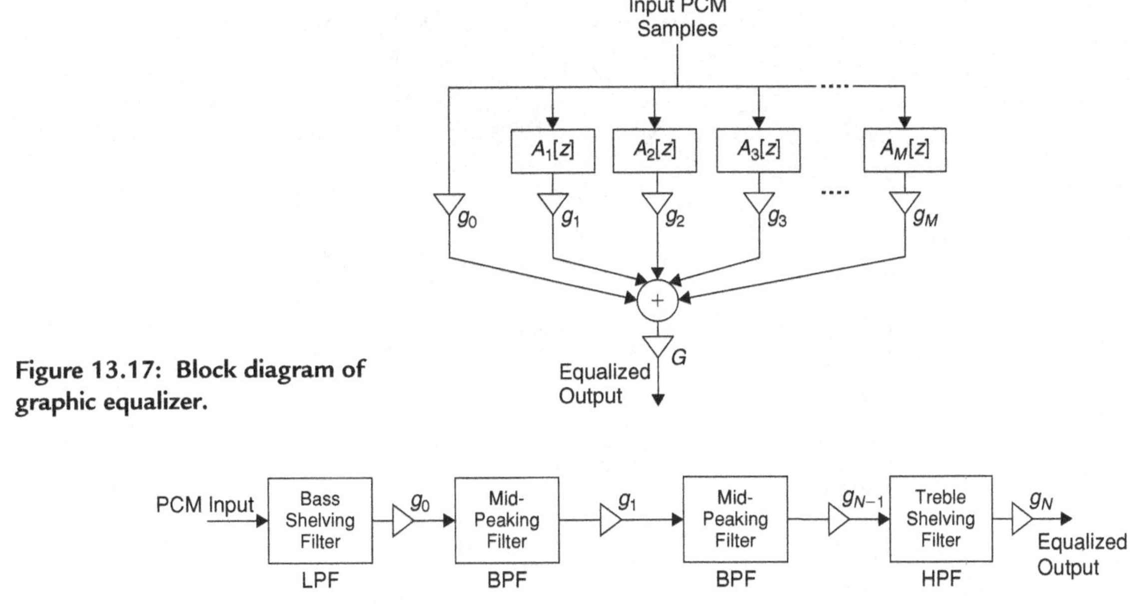

Figure 13.17: Block diagram of graphic equalizer.

Figure 13.18: Parametric equalizer for boosting bass, mid, and treble frequencies.

13.5.2 Audio Equalization

Audio equalizers can be used for high-fidelity audio control. Audio equalizer applications include home theater audio, car audio, PC audio, and so on. On the stage, music effects from different instruments may be highlighted using equalization techniques. They may also be used to enhance audio content to suit particular listeners' preferences or to match a particular acoustic environment.

Audio equalizers, by modifying the frequency envelope, compensate the distortion introduced by the sound reproduction system. A regular audio equalizer includes several audio filters with appropriate gain control as shown in Figure 13.17 to tune different parts of the frequency spectrum. Each filter controls a particular frequency band. Usually, the entire audio spectrum is divided into 5 to 31 bands, and that many bandpass filters are used to control the audio frequency spectrum. Often the equalizer design uses octave spacing to cover the entire audio frequency spectrum.

With low bit-rate audio and in poor-quality audio reproduction systems, audio players need corrections at the bass and treble frequencies. The bass adjusts the signal's low-frequency spectrum, whereas the treble adjusts the signal's high-frequency spectrum. In parametric equalizers, many mid-frequency peaking filters are used to control the mid audio spectrum apart from bass and treble. A cascade of bass (shelf filter), mid (peaking filter), and treble (shelf filters) are present in a typical parametric equalizer design as shown in Figure 13.18.

13.5.3 Stereo Enhancement

A stereo signal can be viewed as comprising two main components: left+right and left−right channel. The stereo image field is a function of amplitude, phase, time, and spectral content differences between left and right channels in a stereo sound system. The true stereo sound field covers the entire listening area equally.

Stereo enhancement is typically achieved by widening (to a 180-degree arc in front of the audience) the stereo sound field. The listener receives cleaner and richer sound effects with stereo enhancement. A general stereo enhancement system is shown in Figure 13.19. There are many techniques to achieve stereo enhancement (National Semiconductor, 2007): channel gains adjustment (where one channel gain is altered with respect to the other stereo channel), delaying (where one channel is delayed with respect to the other stereo channel), phase offsetting (where one channel is made out of phase with respect to the other stereo channel), frequency emphasis (where more high frequencies are placed in one channel when compared to the other stereo channel), and so on. The stereo enhancement may not always result in better sound perception. In some cases, the listener tends to prefer unenhanced stereo version to the enhanced stereo version.

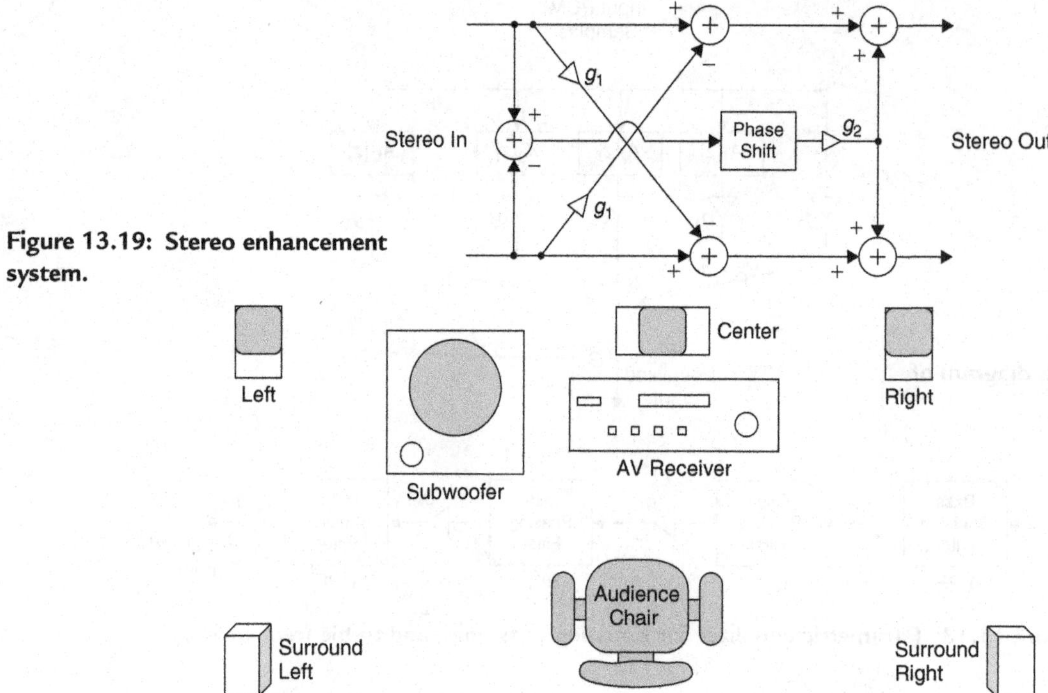

Figure 13.19: Stereo enhancement system.

Figure 13.20: Speaker positioning of home theater 5.1-channel system.

13.5.4 Surround Sound

Surround sound is commonly used in movie theater applications. The surround sound technology is also widely used in home theater, portable audio, virtual reality games, and PC audio. A surround-sound component makes the audio seem to surround the user. Several surround-sound technologies are available today, such as Dolby Pro Logic, Dolby Digital, DTS, Dolby TrueHD, and DTS-HD.

In Dolby Pro Logic, the center and surround channels are matrixed into the left-and-right channel information for storage/transmission, and they are separated out by the decoder before playing out, whereas Dolby Pro Logic II is designed to simulate the surround effect from a two-channel source (e.g., playing CDs and stereo sound tracks on surround speakers).

With Dolby digital and DTS, multichannel audio is encoded into digital bitstreams and transmitted via multiple discrete channels. This type of surround-sound system keeps all the channels separate from start to finish, producing a clear surround effect. The most common format is 5.1 channels; it includes front left, center, and right channels; rear left-and-right surround channels; and a low-frequency effects (LFE) subwoofer channel as shown in Figure 13.20. Dolby digital technology is used in many commercial DVDs and in HDTV broadcasting.

In some cases, the decoded audio channel may not be compatible with the audio reproduction system. For example, AC-3 audio codec codes multiple audio channels into a single bitstream. If we decode AC-3 5.1-channel audio and want to play out on stereo speakers, then we must down-mix 5.1-channel audio to stereo audio before playing it.

A virtual surround-sound technology uses only one or two speakers and still creates the perception of surround sound. This type of system provides surround sound virtually by utilizing the properties of the human auditory system. The core virtual surround-sound technology depends on head-related transfer function (HRTF) filters that can position a particular sound source at a particular azimuth and elevation angle. The HRTF implementation consists of two filters for producing output for each ear. The virtual surround sound is popularly used in PC stereo audio and portable audio with headphones.

Part 4

Digital Video Processing

CHAPTER 14

Video Coding Technology

14.1 Introduction

Before the mid-1990s, nearly all video was in analog form. Then the advent of MPEG compression, the proliferation of streaming media on the Internet, and the FCC adoption of a digital television (DTV) standard brought the benefits of digital representation into the video world. These advantages over analog include better signal-to-noise performance, improved bandwidth utilization (fitting several digital channels into each existing analog channel), and reduction in storage space through digital compression techniques.

Figure 14.1 shows a typical end-to-end video processing system. A video source feeds into a media processor (e.g., reference embedded processor) where it might be compressed via a software encoder before being stored locally or sent over the network. In an opposite flow, a compressed stream is retrieved from a network or mass storage. It is then decompressed via a software decoder and sent to display panels (e.g., CRT, TFT-LCD).

In analog video inputs, a video decoder chip converts an analog video signal (e.g., NTSC, PAL, CVBS, S-video) into a digital form (usually of the ITU-R BT.601/656, YCbCr, or RGB variety). This is a complex, multistage process as shown in Figure 14.2. It involves extracting timing information from the input, separating luma from chroma, separating chroma into Cr and Cb components, sampling the output data, and arranging it into an appropriate format. A serial interface such as SPI or I^2C configures the decoder's operating parameters.

A video encoder converts a digital video stream into an analog video signal. It typically accepts a YCbCr or RGB video stream in either ITU-R BT.656 or BT.601 format and converts it to a signal compliant with one of

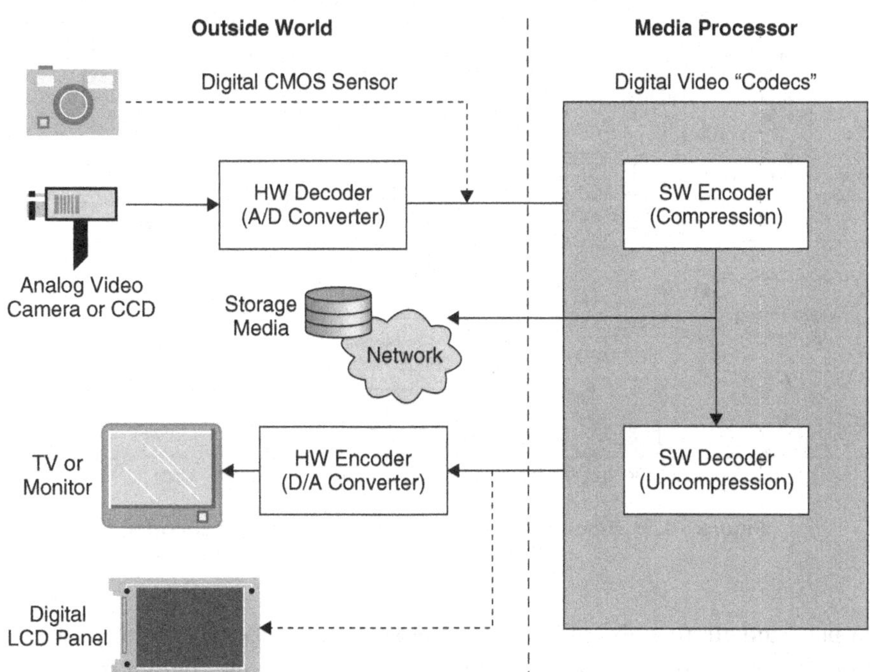

Figure 14.1: System video flow for analog/digital sources and displays.

DOI: 10.1016/B978-1-85617-678-1.00014-4

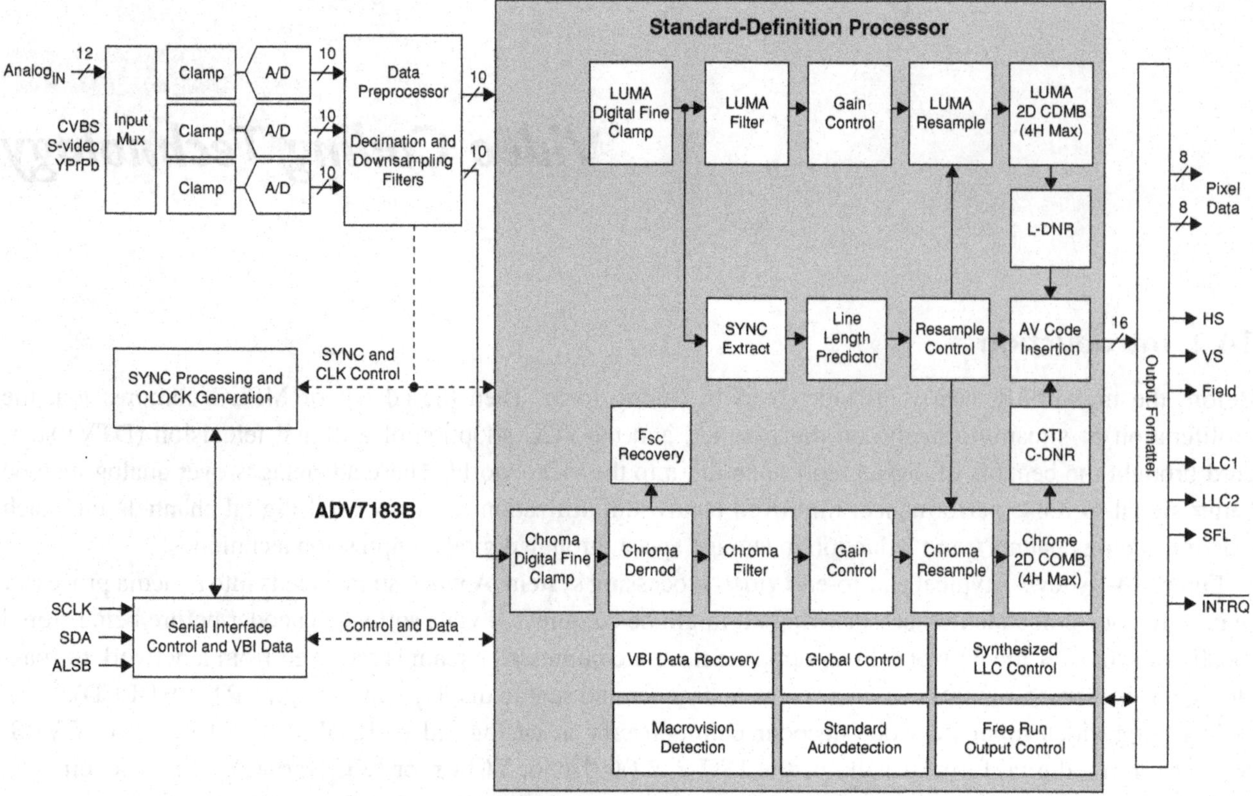

Figure 14.2: Block diagram of an ADV7183B video decoder.

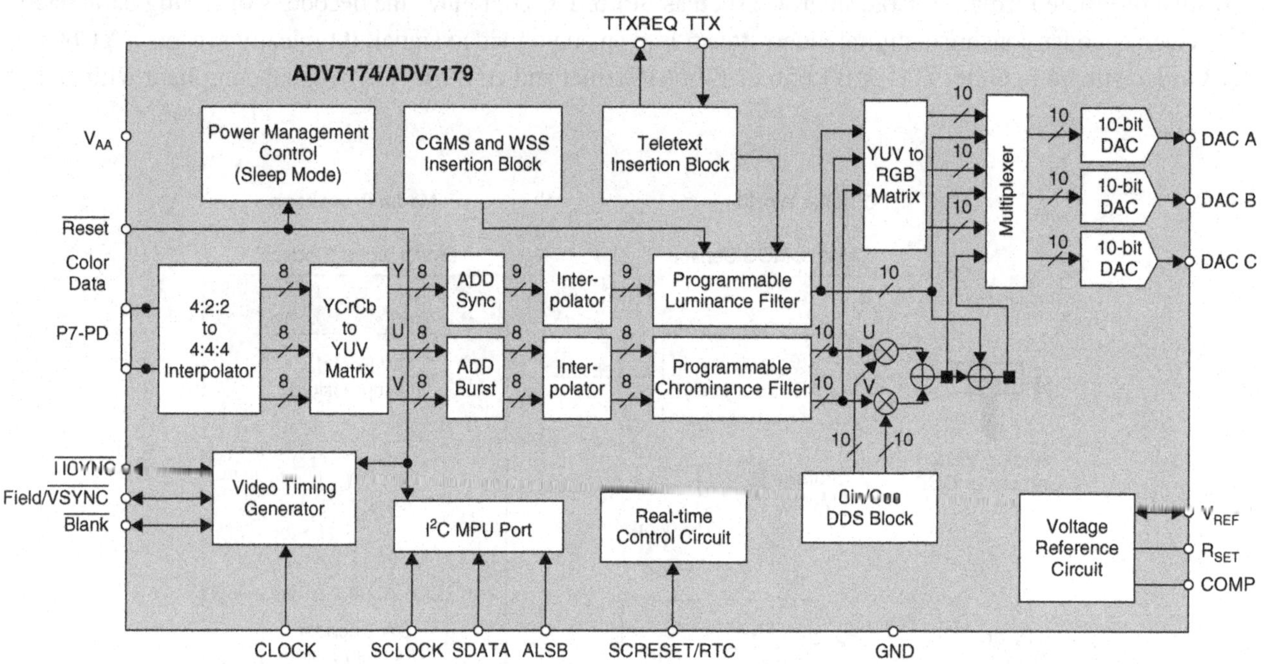

Figure 14.3: Block diagram of an ADV7179 video encoder.

several different output standards (e.g., NTSC, PAL, SECAM). A host processor controls the encoder via a serial interface like SPI or I²C, programming settings such as pixel timing, input/output formats, and luma/chroma filtering. Figure 14.3 shows a block diagram of a representative video encoder.

Advances in video coding technology and standardization along with rapid development and improvements of network infrastructures, storage capacity, and computing power are enabling an increasing number of video applications. Digitized video has played an important role in many consumer electronics applications including DVD, portable media players, HDTV, video telephony, video conferencing, Internet video streaming, and distance learning, among others.

Video coding enables the digital storage and transmission of video signals. Recent progress in digital technology has made the widespread use of compressed digital video signals practical. At the source end, the video encoder compresses the digital video for efficient storage and transmission purposes, whereas the video decoder at the destination end decompresses the received compressed video stream and sends to the display for viewing. International video coding standards such as MPEG-1/2/4 and H.261/2/3/4 are the coding engines behind the commercial success of digital video compression. They have played pivotal roles in spreading the technology by providing the power of interoperability among products developed by different manufactures, while at the same time allowing enough flexibility for creativity in optimizing and modeling the technology to fit a given application and making the cost–performance trade-offs best suited to particular applications.

For details of video signals, analog and digital video interfaces, and video signal processing, see Jack (2001). This chapter focuses on discussion of the video coding basics and the most widely used MPEG-2 and H.264 video coding standards, along with the present requirement of scalable video coding. Embedded video processing and system issues are also discussed.

14.2 Video Coding Basics

Video cameras today are overwhelmingly based on either charge-coupled device (CCD) or CMOS technology. Both of these sensor technologies convert light into electrical signals. In order to properly represent a color image, a sensor needs three color components, most commonly, red, green and blue (RGB). The RGB signals coming from a color video camera can be equivalently expressed as luminance (Y) and chrominance (UV) components. See Section 10.1 for more detail on RGB-to-YUV color conversion.

14.2.1 Digital Video

At its root, digitizing video involves both sampling and quantizing analog video signals. In the 2D context of a video frame, sampling entails dividing the image space grid-like into small regions (pixels) and assigning relative amplitude values based on the intensities of color space components in each region. Note that analog video is already sampled temporally (i.e., discrete number of frames per second). The number of pixels per row and column of the video frame defines the *frame resolution*. A few widely used video frames resolution names, and their row and column sizes ($N \times M$) are given in Table 14.1. Horizontal resolution indicates the number of pixels on each video frame line, and vertical resolution designates how many horizontal lines are displayed on the screen to create the entire video frame. For example, standard definition (SD) NTSC systems are characterized by interlaced scan, with 480 lines of active pixels, each with 720 active pixels per line (i.e., 720×480).

Table 14.1: Selected video frame resolution names and sizes

Frame Resolution Name	Row x Column Size
QCIF	176 × 144
QVGA	320 × 240
CIF	352 × 288
VGA	640 × 480
525 SD or D1	720 × 480
720p HD	1280 × 720
1080p HD	1920 × 1088
16 VGA	2560 × 1920
4k × 2k	4096 × 2048

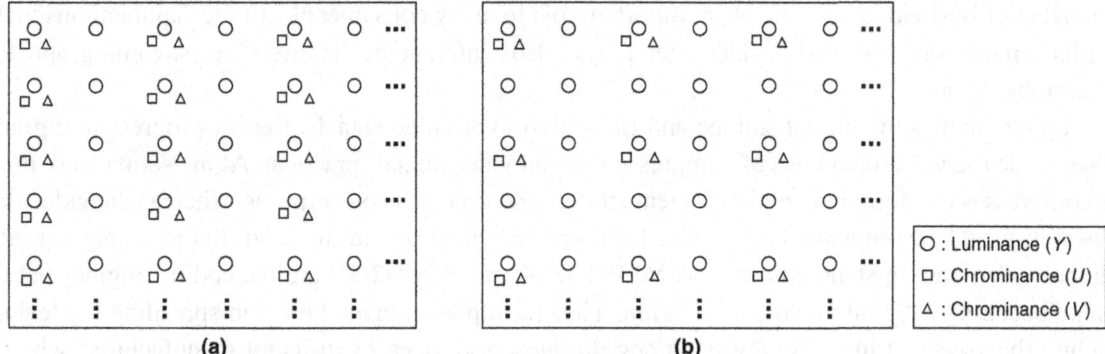

Figure 14.4: YUV format. (a) Position of luminance and chrominance samples in 4:2:2 format. (b) Position of luminance and chrominance samples in 4:2:0 format.

Pixel quantization is the process that determines discrete amplitude values assigned during the sampling process. Eight-bit video is common in consumer applications, where a value of 0 is darkest and 255 is brightest for each color component (R, G, B or Y, U, V). However, it should be noted that 10- and 12-bit quantization per color channel are rapidly entering mainstream video products, allowing extra precision that can be useful in reducing received image noise by minimizing round-off error.

The advent of digital video provided an excellent opportunity to standardize, to a large degree, the interfaces to NTSC and PAL systems. When the International Telecommunication Union (ITU) met to define recommendations for digital video standards, it focused on achieving a large degree of commonality between NTSC and PAL standards, such that the two could share the same coding formats. They defined two separate recommendations—CCIR-601 (current ITU-R BT.601) and CCIR-656 (current ITU-R BT.656). Together, the two define a structure that enables various digital video system components to interoperate, whereas BT.601 defines the parameters for digital video transfer and BT.656 defines the interface itself.

For standard definition video, CCIR-601 defines how the video component signals (YUV) can be sampled and digitized to form discrete pixels. The chrominance bandwidth may be reduced relative to the luminance without significantly affecting the picture quality. The terms YUV 4:4:4, YUV 4:2:2, and YUV 4:2:0 are often used to describe the sampling formats for digital video components. The format YUV 4:2:2 means that the chrominance is horizontally subsampled by a factor of two relative to the luminance component as shown in Figure 14.4(a), whereas the format YUV 4:2:0 means that the chrominance is both horizontally and vertically subsampled by a factor of two relative to the luminance as shown in Figure 14.4(b).

Typically, we represent either RGB or YUV components with 8 bits of data. That is, we require 24 bits to represent a single pixel's three component values in the digital domain. Video data is enormously space-consuming, and its most daunting aspect is that it just keeps coming! For example, 1 second of uncompressed 4:2:2 video NTSC video requires 27 MB of storage (or a bit rate of 216 Mbps), and a single minute requires 1.6 GB. Because raw video requires such dedicated high capacity for storage or high-bandwidth channels for transmission, the industry spent hundreds of person years in efforts to avoid transferring it in uncompressed form whenever possible. Compression algorithms have been devised that reduce bandwidth requirements for NTSC/PAL video from tens of megabytes per second to just a few hundreds of kilobytes per second, with adjustable trade-offs in video quality for bandwidth efficiency. Next, we discuss various redundancies in the video data that provide the scope for video data compression.

14.2.2 Redundancy in Video Data

At its root, a video signal is basically just a 2D array of intensity and color data that is updated at a regular frame rate, conveying the perception of motion. Video compression relies on the eye's inability to resolve high-frequency component changes, and the fact that there is a lot of redundancy within each frame and between frames. A video compression system operates by removing the redundant information from the video signal prior to transmission, and by reconstructing an approximation of the video signal from the received information at the

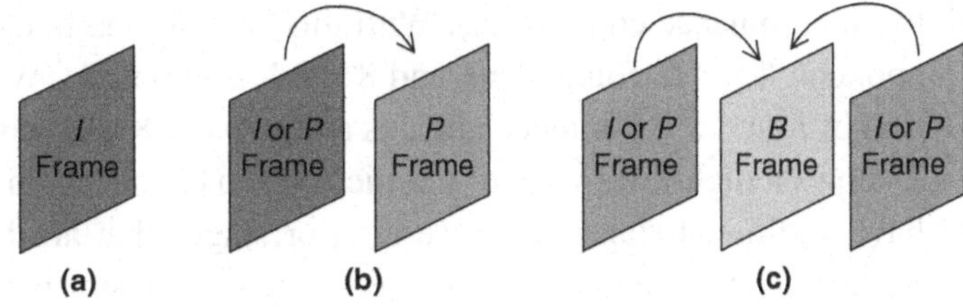

Figure 14.5: Illustration of various video frames coding. (a) *I*-frame coding. (b) *P*-frame coding. (c) *B*-frame coding.

decoder. A coder and decoder pair is referred to as a *codec*. In video signals, three distinct kinds of redundancy can be identified: *spatial-temporal redundancy, psychovisual redundancy*, and *entropy redundancy*.

Spatial-Temporal Redundancy

The video frame pixel values are not independent, but are correlated with their neighbors both within the same frame and across frames. *Spatial redundancy* is the correlation of video pixels within the same frame data, whereas *temporal redundancy* is the correlation of pixels across many video frames. To some extent, the value of a pixel is predictable, given the values of the neighboring pixels.

Decorrelation transforms (e.g., discrete cosine transforms or discrete wavelet transforms) are used to remove spatial redundancy among adjacent pixel values. This generates *intracoded frames* (or simply *I*-frames). Each of these frames is encoded using only information contained within that same frame. That is, they are coded independently of all other frames. *I*-frames are required to provide the decoder with a place to start for prediction, and they also provide a baseline for error recovery.

Interprediction (i.e., motion estimation) and motion compensation together eliminate temporal redundancy in video frames while compensating for motion by predicting pixel values in a frame from information in adjacent frames. This generates *predicted frames* (or *P*-frames) and *bidirectional predicted frames* (or *B*-frames). While the *P*-frames are coded with forward prediction from references made from previous *I*- and *P*-frames, the *B*-frames are coded with forward prediction based on the data from previous *I* or *P* references, or they may be coded with backward prediction from the most recent (in the future) *I* or *P* reference frames. The coding of video using *I*-, *P*-, and *B*-frame types is illustrated in Figure 14.5.

Psychovisual Redundancy

The human eye has a limited response to fine spatial and temporal details (i.e., the details that our eyes can resolve and the motion of objects that our eyes can track). Our eyes are less sensitive to detail near object edges or around shot changes (i.e., human eyes do not respond to all visual information with equal sensitivity). Some information is simply of less relative importance. This information is referred to as psychovisual redundancy and can be eliminated without introducing significant differences to the human eye. Consequently, we can have control of the bit rate by restricting both spatial details and temporal resolution and at the same time maintaining that the same is not visible to human observers.

Entropy Redundancy

In any nonrandom digital samples, some sample values occur more frequently than others. For example, neighboring block transform coefficients, motion information, and predictive modes do not occur entirely randomly in video frame coding. The entropy coding methods at their core functionality exploit this type of redundancy.

In the next section, we discuss various video coding modules that exploit various types of redundancies present in video frame data.

14.2.3 Video Coding

In video coding, frames are coded by dividing the frame into smaller blocks, called *macroblocks*. A macroblock contains a 16×16 area of pixels. Generally, the video format used for coding is *YUV*, and with that format a macroblock contains a section of the luminance component and spatially corresponding chrominance components. The component information for *Y*, *U*, and *V* is coded independently. As discussed, the human eye is not that sensitive to color information, therefore most video coding standards allow us to code the *YUV* 4:2:0 video format (i.e., the color components are subsampled in both horizontal and vertical directions by a factor of 2 relative to the luminance component). With this format, one macroblock coding comprises coding of the 16×16 *Y*-component, 8 × 8 *U*-component, and 8 × 8 *V*-component. With 4:2:0 representation, the macroblock comprises a total of four 8 × 8 luminance blocks and two 8 × 8 chrominance blocks as shown in Figure 14.6.

Figure 14.7 shows a high-level view of a typical video encoder. This structure is common among encoders; some might have additional stages of processing or stages that are branched off from the one shown here. Nonetheless, video encoding can be characterized by temporal and spatial encoding. In the latter, the stages that perform the discrete cosine transform (DCT), quantization, zig-zag coding, and entropy coding encompass spatial coding of the frame. As a matter of fact, these stages are similar to the ones used in JPEG image compression. We will talk about these modules a little later.

For temporal encoding, reference frames need to be created. Thus, macroblocks are reconstructed via inverse quantization and inverse DCT after the quantization stage during spatial encoding. Then, during the encoding of the next frame, the input macroblock and a search window from the reference frame are used to create motion-compensated input, otherwise known as residuals. This is done by means of motion estimation, where motion

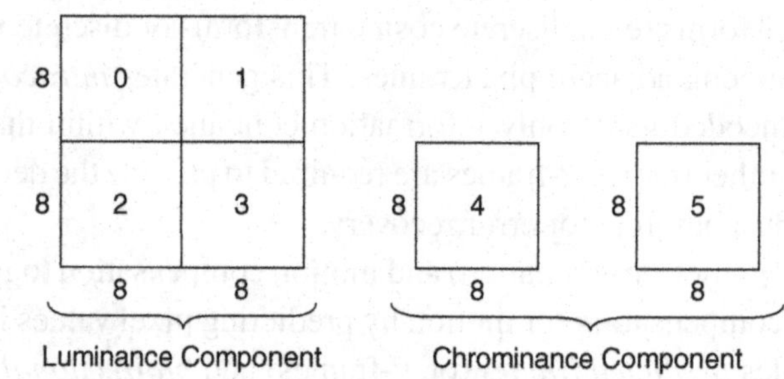

Figure 14.6: Macroblock structure in 4:2:0 representation.

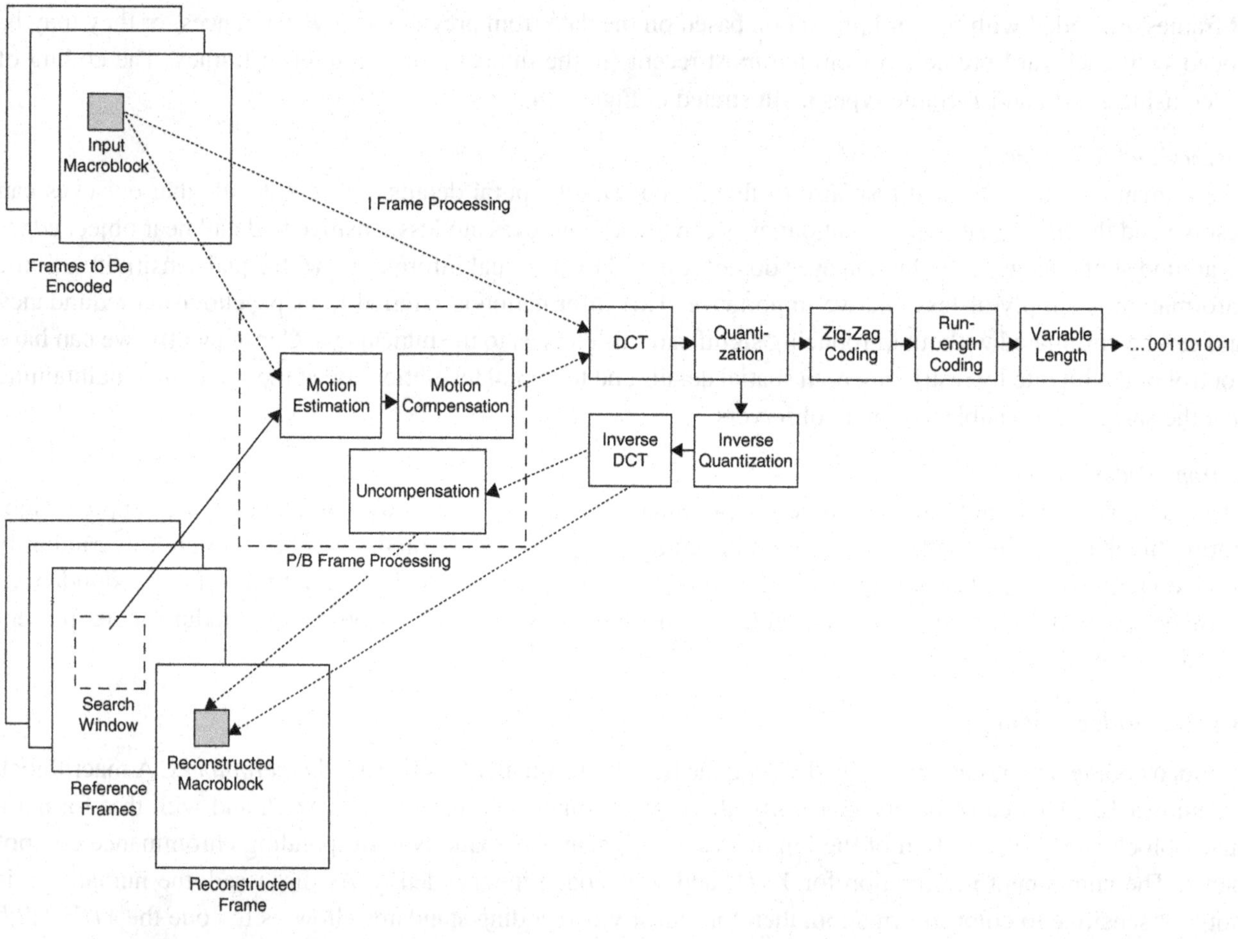

Figure 14.7: High-level general view of a typical video encoder.

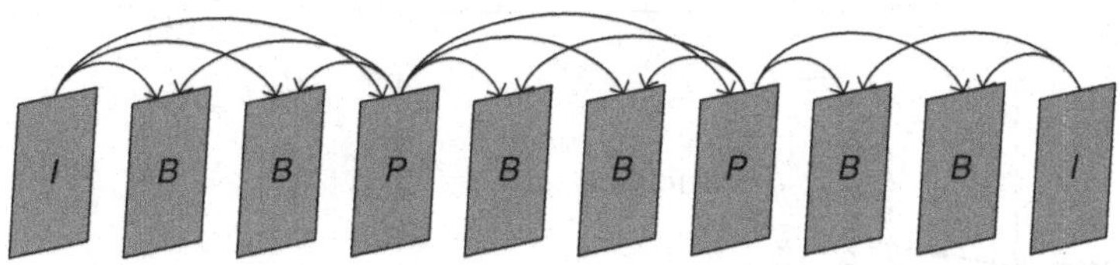

Figure 14.8: GOP (MPEG-2), and *I*-, *P*-, and *B*-frame coding.

vectors are identified, and motion compensation. In this process, the input macroblock and best-matched block from the reference is subtracted and the residuals are created.

Video encoding always starts by compressing the first frame spatially, as an intraframe (*I*-frame). This frame is coded independently, since there is no reference frame to work from. Then a typical group of picture (GOP) structure would have a run of *P*-frames and/or *B*-frames, which would be predictively encoded before encoding another *I*-frame. This is illustrated in Figure 14.8. Predictively coded frames take advantage of temporal redundancy to achieve greater compression.

Motion Estimation/Motion Compensation

At present, we are so accustomed to seeing videoclips, lectures, and so on on our computers via the Internet that we do not appreciate the technology that allows us to enjoy them in real time. But a quick estimate shows that viewing, say, a videoclip with the frame size 360×240 pixels at 30 frames per second requires, at the intermediate connection speed 768 kbps, a compression ratio of about 50:1 on average.

Image compression of video sequences (or, using an old name, "motion pictures") involves all the instruments of still-image compression as well as temporal redundancy. In brief, most of the time the differences between successive frames are small because at 30 frames per second the camera and most objects in the scene do not move.

Thus, if we find a way to estimate the motion of the object, matching certain parts of the frame with a corresponding part of a previous frame and encode only these differences, they will be small and can be encoded very efficiently. This "matching" or motion estimation is done by the encoder using various search algorithms. Because all video processing of "motion pictures" is done on a macroblock basis, we can simply search in one of the previous frames around the currently processed macroblock position and find the "best match" in a certain metric. Then in the decoder we need only the information about a "motion vector" with two components (vertical and horizontal). If it was a good match, the differences between actual pixel values and those "moved" from the stored frame are small, and most of these residual components become zero after quantization. Thus, we achieve a high compression ratio by transmitting only the information required to recover these differences at the receiver end.

In summary, one of the key components to video encoding is the temporal correlation among successive frames. If video encoding did not take advantage of this aspect, it would be nothing more than compressing individual images such as JPEG. Motion estimation is the process of finding the best temporal match between frames in a video sequence. If the match is good, most residuals would become zeros after quantization, which would result in fewer bits. Motion compensation is the process of reconstructing video frames using the received motion vectors and residual data.

The *full-search block-matching algorithm* is the most straightforward method of finding the best matched block. During the processing of a macroblock at location (a, b) of the current frame, it is overlaid on various pixels in a search window from a reference frame. Figure 14.9 shows this process. For each pixel in the search window, the macroblock is overlaid and a *prediction error* is calculated. Typically, the prediction error is stated in terms of either the *mean of absolute differences* (MAD) or the *sum of absolute differences* (SAD). The MAD calculation is just a normalized version of SAD. After calculating the prediction error for the macroblock over each pixel in the search window, the candidate with the minimum error is used. The displacement $(c\text{-}a, d\text{-}b)$ between the location of the macroblock (a, b) and the overlaid region (c, d) in memory is the *motion vector* used in future steps of frame compression.

Instead of compressing the data from a macroblock, the motion vector is used to obtain a macroblock that is the difference between the current one and a macroblock-sized region from a reference frame. If the motion

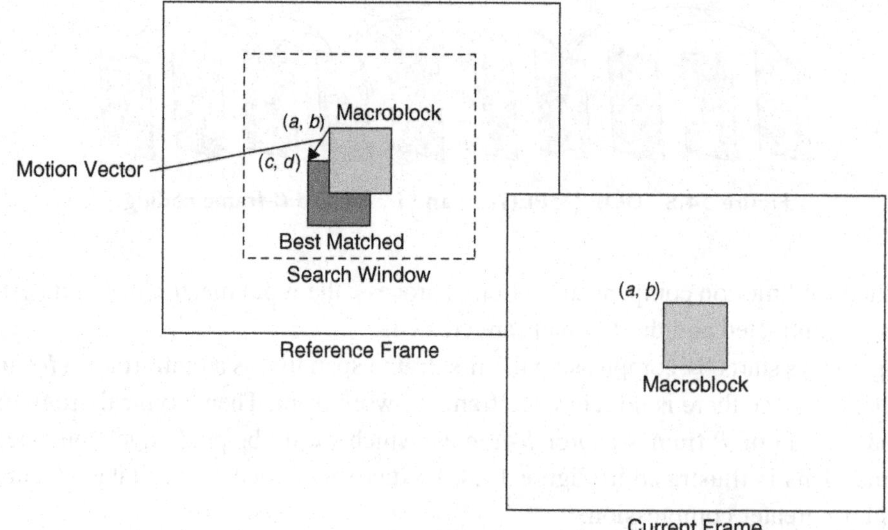

Figure 14.9: Finding a motion vector using motion estimation algorithm.

vector obtained from the motion estimation accurately captured the movement of the video sequence, then the difference between the macroblock and the overlaid reference area when quantized will result in a lot of data becoming zeros, which in turn provides greater compression.

The full-search block-matching algorithm provides the best results since it is an exhaustive search, calculating the prediction error while going over each pixel in the search window. In cost terms, this algorithm can use up more than half of the processing required to compress a single frame. Since it is so costly, researchers in academia and industry have tried to find heuristics to reduce the amount of processing needed for a solution that comes close to the full-search algorithm.

Data Movement for Motion Estimation on Embedded Processors

Typical embedded processors have a hierarchical memory structure (see Section 16.2.3) where a limited amount of fast internal memory (L1) sits near the core and the data can be accessed from L1 within a single cycle. Further down the hierarchy, the processor can access memory sizes in megabyte ranges but with a higher latency.

In order to achieve real-time processing, processing from slow, external memory (L3) would be too costly. Also, due to size limitations, entire frames cannot reside in internal memory. Therefore, a method for handling this would be to have the frames reside in external memory and bring data needed from external memory to internal memory via direct memory access (DMA), and then perform the processing in internal memory. The final results can also be exported back to external memory. This procedure can typically be pipelined to reduce the overhead from memory latencies.

In the case of video processing, macroblocks would be brought in from external memory using a DMA transfer. If the frame is going to be predictively coded, the motion estimation stage would need a corresponding search window from a reference frame that would reside in external memory. This search window would also need to be placed in internal memory via DMA.

Full-Search Motion Estimation

Even when the data is in internal memory, the full-search motion estimation algorithm absorbs most of the processing time. Consider a search range of ±8, that is, a 16×16 search window. Using a processor such as the reference embedded processor, which can perform a SAD calculation on 4 bytes in a single cycle, the SAD can ideally be calculated for a 16×16 macroblock for a single point in the search window in 64 cycles. A full search over the entire search area would take about 16,000 cycles, which is equivalent to 64 cycles per pixel. For better quality, larger search windows are used. Consider increasing the window by just 1 pixel in all directions. The resulting size of the search window will be 18×18. A bit more than 20,000 cycles would be required to process the entire search window, that is, an average 80 cycles per pixel. As seen in Figure 14.10, as the search range increases linearly, the cost increases exponentially.

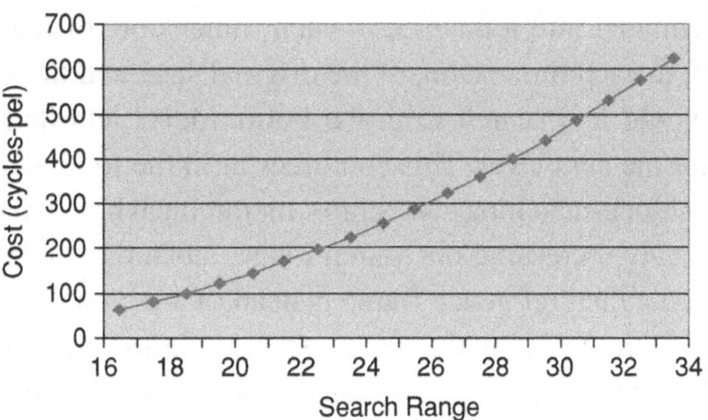

Figure 14.10: Cost in terms of cycles per pixel for full-search motion estimation as search range increases.

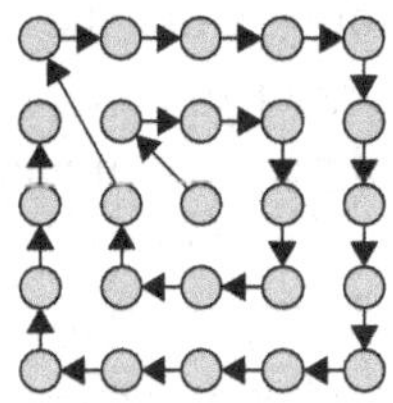

Figure 14.11: Search pattern for spiral search.

Take for example, a 700-MHz processor encoding frames sized 720 × 480 (D1), at 30 frames per second. This results in a limit of 67.5 cycles per pixel for encoding. Anything over this value would no longer qualify as real time. Yet, for a search range of ±16, the full-search motion estimation uses up almost 95% of the resources required to encode a D1-sized sequence. Obviously, a less resource-intensive algorithm is needed.

In practice, the full-search motion estimation algorithm is rarely used due to limited resources and a search range of at least ±16 required for satisfactory quality.

Alternative Methods for Motion Estimation

As seen in the calculations, full-search motion estimation is very costly. Other methods use different search patterns to limit the number of points searched in a window with comparable results. For example, a spiral or a diamond pattern starting from the center of the search window reduces the number of points searched by a significant amount.

The diamond search pattern is a diamond shape consisting of nine search points with a starting point in the middle of it. A motion estimation algorithm that uses this pattern finds the minimum block distortion for the points in the diamond. The algorithm reiterates, recentering the diamond pattern over the previously found minimum block distortion point. After finding the minimum distortion again, a smaller diamond, consisting of five search points, is used for the final search. Once the minimum distortion point is found this time, a motion vector is obtained.

The spiral search method assumes that the motion vectors of neighboring macroblocks are highly spatially correlated. Consequently, starting from the point located by the motion vector of the previous neighboring macroblock, the spiral search begins to calculate the points' minimum block distortion in the search window moving in an outward spiral fashion. Once the distortion is under a limit, the new motion vector is found. Figure 14.11 shows the spiral search pattern. The area is dependent on the search range selected for the algorithm.

Other suboptimal motion-estimation techniques include the three-step search (TSS), four-step search (FSS), and 2D logarithmic search (TDL). Like the diamond and spiral searches, these algorithms assume and take advantage of certain properties of temporal correlation among neighboring macroblocks to reduce the number of points to be searched.

Motion Estimation on Embedded Processors

For motion estimation, the search window from the reference frame is DMA'd into internal memory. So, for embedded processors, memory bandwidth is another factor that must be considered. For the previously mentioned motion estimation algorithms, the search range dictates how much bandwidth is used.

Other block-matching algorithms use a hierarchical scheme where the reference frames are filtered and decimated into scaled-down versions. For example, one algorithm might have a three-level hierarchy where the bottom level is decimated into a quarter, in each dimension, of the original size. The middle level would be decimated into half, in each dimension, of the original size, and finally the top level would be untouched.

The algorithm would first search from the bottom level and obtain a motion vector, which would lead to the search region for the next level. This continues until the top level is searched and the final motion vector is obtained. Like other block-matching algorithms, hierarchical block matching aims to reduce the number of points searched, yet effectively increasing the search range, since the intermediate motion vectors could theoretically lead to anywhere in the final reference frame instead of a confined region.

Consider a full-search algorithm that uses a search window of 48×48. For comparable results from a hierarchical block-matching algorithm, window sizes of 4×12, 10×9, and 24×20 from the bottom, middle, and top levels, respectively, can be used. For this, we can see that the bandwidth is actually less since the full search needs around 2 kB of data brought in from external memory, while the hierarchical scheme needs only 618 bytes.

It has been shown that hierarchical block matching produces better results than other algorithms such as TDL or TSS. But, this comes at a price: since the frames need to be decimated, more processing resources are needed. In addition, on embedded processors, more bandwidth is used up on both the input and output sides to bring the reference and reconstructed data in and out of internal and external memory. Finally, the encoder would also need to be carefully scheduled due to the dependency of intermediate motion vectors calculated. This means that the process is hard to be pipelined since a DMA cannot be started until the location from which to DMA'd is known.

Fine Motion Search

For even better quality, video encoders employ various techniques in addition to a basic motion-estimation algorithm. A lot of encoders find the motion vectors at half-pixel resolution where the pixels are interpolated half-way between full-pixel points. Some even go further to find the motion vectors at the quarter-pixel resolution. It is believed that capturing the motion at subpixel resolution provides greater precision for temporal coding.

Another technique is finding motion vectors for the blocks that make up the macroblock rather than the macroblock itself. For example, a 16×16-sized macroblock is composed of four 8×8 blocks, and each of the four would be associated with its own motion vector.

At the Decoder

The encoder-estimated motion vector information for P- and B-frames is conveyed to the decoder via the compressed bitstream. At the decoder, those frames are reconstructed via the motion compensation technique using the received motion vectors. We program the DMA using motion vector information to get the appropriate reference frame block residing in external memory. Depending on the motion-vector pixel resolution, we may need to interpolate the reference-frame block pixels to obtain more accurate blocks of pixels that fit the current block under reconstruction. We reconstruct the current block by adding the interpolated pixel block to the residual IDCT output. This total procedure is referred to as *motion compensation*. The cycle cost of motion compensation increases with motion-vector pixel resolution and the number of subblocks used per macroblock.

Block Transform

Block transforms such as the DCT, H.264 transform, and discrete wavelet transform exploit the spatial redundancy in video frames and transform most pixel energy into a few low-frequency coefficients. The block transform does not directly reduce the number of bits required to represent the block. In fact, the $N \times N$ DCT transform produces exactly $N \times N$ DCT coefficients, and these DCT coefficients may require more bits to represent the block transform than the original pixels. The reduction in number of bits follows from the fact that, for typical blocks of video data, the distribution of transform coefficients is nonuniform and this nonuniformity is due to spatial redundancy in the original video frames. The transform places most of the energy into a few low-frequency coefficients and many of the other coefficients are close to zero. The bit rate reduction is achieved by quantizing the near-zero coefficients and entropy coding the remaining non-zero coefficients.

Quantization

After the block transform has been performed on a small video block (4×4 or 8×8), the results are quantized in order to achieve larger gains in the compression ratio. Quantization refers the process of representing the actual coefficient values as one of a set of predetermined allowable values, so that the overall data can be encoded in fewer bits. In this process, most of the high-frequency component values of the transform output are truncated to zero and are left uncoded. Recall that the human eye is much more attuned to low-frequency information than high-frequency details. Therefore, small errors in high-frequency components after decoding are not easily noticed, and eliminating these high-frequency components entirely by quantization is often visually acceptable. As discussed in Section 11.6.1, the JPEG quantization process takes advantage of this to reduce the amount of DCT information that needs to be coded for a given 8×8 block.

Quantization is the key irreversible step in video coding. A quality scaling factor can be applied to the quantization matrix to balance video quality and amount of achievable video compression. The quantization process is straightforward once the quantization table is assembled, but the table itself can be quite complex, often with a separate quantization coefficient for each element of the transform output block. The actual process of quantization is a simple element-wise division (with rounding) between the transform output coefficient and the quantization coefficient for a given row and column.

Entropy Coding

The last stage in video sequence coding is entropy coding. In this stage, a final lossless compression is performed on the zig-zag scanned (one such zig-zag scan pattern is shown in Figure 11.50) and quantized DCT coefficients to increase the overall compression ratio. Two widely used entropy coding methods are *Huffman coding* and *arithmetic coding*. The former encodes binarized coefficients via Huffman look-up tables; therefore, Huffman coding codes a symbol with one or more bits. In contrast, arithmetic coding can represent the information with a fraction of the bits, and thus achieves 5 to 10% higher compression than Huffman coding. See Chapter 5 for more detail on entropy coding methods and respective C-simulation techniques.

Rate Control

The rate-control algorithm is responsible for generating the quantization parameter (QP) by adapting to a target transmission bit rate and output buffer fullness. Indeed, video streams are generally provided with a designated bit rate for the compressed bitstream. The bit rate varies, depending on the desired image quality, capacity of the storage/communication channel, and so on. In order to generate compressed video streams of the specified bit rate, a rate controller is implemented in practical video encoding systems. In recent video coding standards, the bit rate can be controlled through the quantization step size, which is used to quantize the DCT coefficients so that it may determine how much of spatial details are retained. When the quantization step size is very small, the bit rate is high and almost all picture details are conveyed. As the quantization step size is increased, the bit rate decreases at the cost of some quality loss. The goal of rate control is to achieve the target bit rate by adjusting the quantization step size, while minimizing quality loss. The block diagram of rate control in a typical video coding system is shown in Figure 14.12.

In any lossy coding system, there is an inherent trade-off between the rate of the transmitted data and distortion of the reconstructed signal. The purpose of rate control is to regulate the encoder to meet the bit-rate requirements imposed by the transmission or storage medium while maintaining an acceptable level of distortion. Although QP can be used to control bit rate and distortion, coding with a constant QP does not necessarily result in constant bit rate or constant perceived quality. Both of these factors depend on scene content as well. Rate-control algorithms and rate-distortion analysis are beyond the scope of this book. See Shoham and Gersho (1988), Gray (1990), and Pickering and Arnold (1994) for more detail on rate-control algorithms.

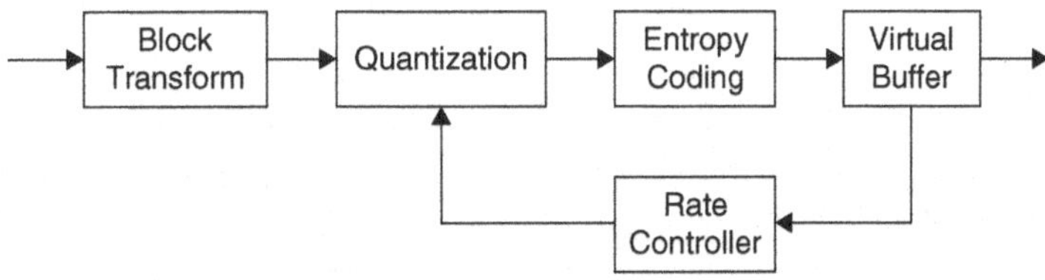

Figure 14.12: Block diagram of rate control in a typical video coding system.

Profiles and Levels

As video compression plays a very important role in video content storage, broadcasting, Internet streaming, and so on, and storage capacity and data transfer bandwidths are different for these applications; various levels of coding to support individual applications (in terms of bit rate, quality, scalability, etc.) by the same compression standard interface are very advantageous. For example, the MPEG-2 standard specifies various profiles (specify syntax or algorithm) and levels (specify parameters such as frame rate, resolution) to address different application segments. A profile is a subset of algorithmic tools and a level identifies a set of constraints on parameter values. MPEG-2 supports six profiles: simple profile (SP), main profile (MP), multiview profile (MVP), 4:2:2 profile (422P), SNR-spatial profile (SNRSP), and high profile (HP). The MPEG-2 standard supports four levels for a given profile: low (up to 352×288 resolution, 30 frames/second, 4 Mbps, etc.), main (up to 720×576 resolution, 30 frames/second, 20 Mbps, etc.), 1440 (up to 1440×1088 resolution, 60 frames/second, 80 Mbps, etc.), and high (which is intended for HDTV applications and supports up to 1920×1088 resolution, 60 frames/second, 100 Mbps, etc.). An MPEG-2 decoder that supports a particular profile and level is only required to support the corresponding subset of algorithm tools and the set of parameter constraints.

Bitstream Structure

Figure 14.13 shows the MPEG-2 bitstream format of encoded video data. This bitstream contains information about sequence layer headers, picture layer headers, slice layer headers, macroblock layer headers, motion vectors, quantization parameters, coded block pattern, and residual coefficients (both luminance and chrominance residual values). In addition, there will be synchronization information (called as sync pattern or start code) to identify the start of a slice. At the decoder, as shown in Figure 14.14, we decode the MPEG-2 bitstream starting with the decoding of sequence-layer headers, picture-layer headers, slice-layer headers, and macroblock-layer headers, followed by decoding of motion vectors, the coded block pattern, and residual coefficients. The entropy decoded transform coefficients are reconstructed (with inverse quantization) and inverse transformed to produce the prediction error. This is added to the motion-compensated prediction generated from previously decoded pictures to produce the decoded output.

Scalable Video Coding

Video coding today is used in many applications ranging from portable players, video conferencing, and Internet video streaming to standard and high-definition TV broadcasting. Diverse receivers may require the same video at different bandwidths, spatial resolutions, frame rates, computational capabilities, and so on. When we originally code the video, we do not know which client or network situation will exist in the future. To serve diversified clients

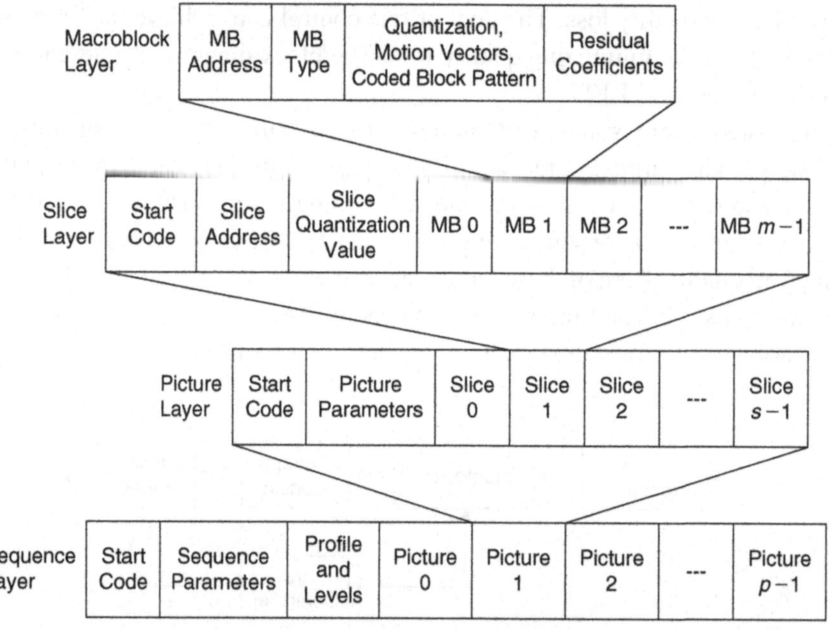

Figure 14.13: MPEG-2 video compression bitstream format.

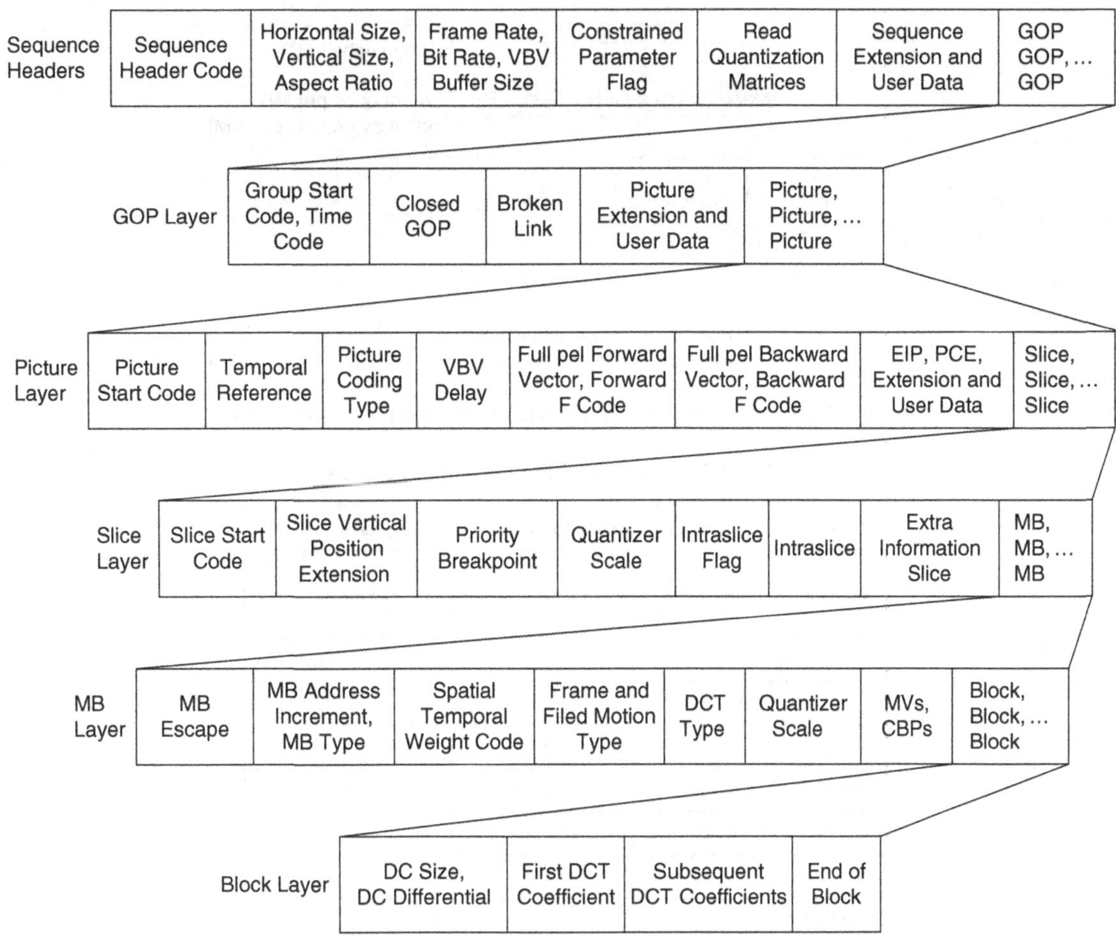

Figure 14.14: MPEG-2 video bitstream decoding steps.

over heterogeneous networks, the scalable video coding (SVC) allows on-the-fly adaptation in the spatiotemporal and quality dimensions according to network conditions and receiver capabilities. Widely used video coding standards such as MPEG-2, MPEG-4, and H.264 allow this scalability, and at the same time enable interoperability of diverse encoder and decoder products. More detail on the scalable video coding extension of the H.264/AVC standard is provided in Section 14.5.

Critical Video-Decoding Modules

Since video bitstream decoding involves entropy decoding of many headers, parameters, and residual coefficients, and computing of inverse transform, motion compensation, loop filter, and so on, proper decoder implementation on a particular processor is very important; otherwise, the video decoder consumes most of the processor MIPS and leaves much less processor time for rest of the system (which may include video post-processing, audio decoding, graphics, protocol stack, operating system, etc.). Given inefficient system design and decoder implementation, it is even possible that the video decoder cannot run in real time on an embedded processor. Sequence, picture, and slice-layer code usually contain much of the control code, and use much less processor time as they are performed once per sequence or picture. This is why most sequence and slice-layer software code will be in high-level languages. The macroblock layer is in between; it is accessed once per macroblock, and coded in high-level language or assembly language depending on the available MIPS budget.

The most critical blocks in video decoding, as highlighted in Figure 14.15, are residuals entropy decoding, zig-zag scan, inverse quantization, inverse block transform, motion compensation, and loop filter (if the standard supports the same). These blocks are critical in video decoder implementation because they are performed at the pixel level, and the way we implement them on a processor for a particular application may make or break that application on a particular processor. In addition, the computational complexity of these blocks increases with

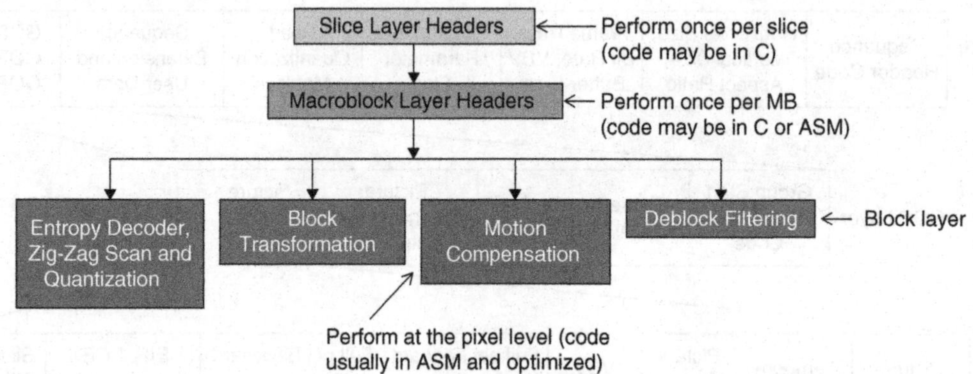

Figure 14.15: Video-decoding algorithm showing critical modules.

Table 14.2: Selected video coding standards

Video Coding Standard	Year Introduced	Originating Body
M-JPEG	1980s	ISO
H.261	1990	ITU-T
QuickTime	1990s	Apple Computer
Windows Media Video	1990s	Microsoft
MPEG-1	1993	ISO/IEC
MPEG-2, H.262	1994,1995	ISO/IEC, ITU-T
H.263, H.263+	1995–2000	ITU-T
DV	1996	IEC
RealVideo	1997	RealNetworks
MPEG-4	1998–2001	ISO/IEC
Ogg Theora	2002	Xiph Foundation
H.264	2003	ITU-T and ISO/IEC

bit rate and frame resolution. Optimization of these blocks both at the algorithm and program instruction levels is very important to minimize processing time, memory, and data-transfer bandwidth requirements. Typically, the software for these critical blocks is written in assembly language, and the code is fully optimized by utilizing all processor resources. We return to these critical modules in Sections 14.3 and 14.4 when discussing the MPEG-2 and H.264 decoder modules.

14.2.4 Video Compression Standards

Table 14.2 lists a number of popular video coding standards, as well as their originating bodies. In this section, we briefly review each.

Motion JPEG

Although not specifically encompassed by the JPEG standard, motion JPEG (M-JPEG) offered a convenient way to compress video frames before MPEG-1 formalized a method. Essentially, each video frame is individually JPEG encoded, and the resulting compressed frames are stored (and later decoded) in sequence.

A motion JPEG2000 codec also exists, which uses J2K instead of JPEG to encode individual frames. It is likely that this codec will replace M-JPEG at a rate similar to the adoption of J2K over JPEG.

H.261

This standard, developed in 1990, was the first widespread video codec. It introduced the idea of segmenting a frame into 16×16 macroblocks that are tracked between frames to determine motion compensation vectors. It is mainly targeted at video conference applications over ISDN lines (64*r* kbps, where *r* ranges from 1 to 30). Input frames are typically CIF at 30 fps, and output compressed frames occupy 64 to 128 kbps for 10-fps resolution. Although still used today, it has mostly been superseded by its successor, H.263.

MPEG-1

When MPEG-1 entered the scene in the early 1990s, it provided a way to digitally store audio and video and retrieve it at roughly VHS quality. The main focus of this codec was storage on CD-ROM media. Specifically, the primary objective was to allow storage and playback of VHS-quality video on a 650- to 750-Mbyte CD, allowing creation of a so-called video CD (VCD). The combined video/audio bitstream could fit within a 1.5 Mbps bandwidth, corresponding to the data retrieval speed from CD-ROM and digital audio tape systems at that time.

At high bit rates, it surpasses H.261 in quality (allowing over 1 Mbps for CIF input frames). Although CIF is used for some source streams, another format called SIF is perhaps more popular. It is 352 × 240 pixels per frame, which turns out to be about one-quarter of a full 720 × 480 NTSC frame. MPEG-1 was intended for compressing SIF video at 30 frames per second, a progressive scan. Compared to H.261, MPEG-1 adds bidirectional motion prediction and half-pixel motion estimation. Although MPEG-1 is still used for VCD creation, MPEG-1 pales in popularity today compared to MPEG-2.

MPEG-2

Driven by the need for scalability across various end-user markets, MPEG-2 improved on MPEG-1, with the capability to scale in an encoded bit rate from 1 Mbps up to 30 Mbps. This opened the door to high-performance applications, including DVD videos and standard- and high-definition TV. Even at the lower end of MPEG-2 bit rates, the quality of the resulting stream is superior to that of an MPEG-1 clip.

This complex standard is composed of 10 parts. The "visual" component is also called H.262. Whereas MPEG-1 focused on CDs and VHS-quality video, MPEG-2 achieved DVD-quality video with an input conforming to BT.601 (NTSC 720×480 at 30 fps), and an output in the range of 4 to 30 Mbps, depending on which performance profile is chosen. MPEG-2 supports interlaced and progressive scanning. We discuss MPEG-2 decoding modules in more detail in Section 14.3.

H.263

This codec is ubiquitous in video conferencing, outperforming H.261 at all bit rates. Input sources are usually QCIF or CIF at 30 fps, and output bit rates can be less than 28.8 kbps at 10 fps, for the same performance as H.261. Therefore, whereas H.261 needs an ISDN line, H.263 can use ordinary phone lines. H.263 is used in end markets such as video telephony and networked surveillance (including Internet-based applications).

MPEG-4

MPEG-4 starts from a baseline of H.263 and adds several improvements. Its prime focus is streaming multimedia over a network. Because the network usually has somewhat limited bandwidth, typical input sources for MPEG-4 codec are CIF resolution and lower. MPEG-4 allows diverse types of coding to be applied to different types of objects. For instance, static background textures and moving foreground shapes are treated differently to maximize the overall compression ratio. MPEG-4 uses several different performance profiles, the most popular among them being "simple" (similar to MPEG-1) and "advanced simple" (field based like MPEG-2). The simple profile is suitable for low video resolutions and low bit rates, like streaming video to cell phones. The advanced simple profile, on the other hand, is intended for higher video resolutions and higher bit rates.

DV

DV is designed expressly for consumer (and subsequently professional) video devices. Its compression scheme is similar in nature to motion JPEG and it accepts the BT.601 sampling formats for luma and chroma. It is quite popular in camcorders, and it allows several different "playability" modes that correspond to different bit rates and/or chroma subsampling schemes. DV is commonly sent over an IEEE 1394 ("FireWire") interface, and its bit-rate capability scales from the 25 Mbps commonly used for standard-definition consumer-grade devices, to beyond 100 Mbits/second for high-definition video.

QuickTime

Developed by Apple Computer, QuickTime comprises a collection of multimedia codecs and algorithms that handle digital video, audio, animation, images, and text. QuickTime 7.0 compiles with MPEG-4 and H.264.

In fact, QuickTime's file format served as the basis for the ISO-based MPEG-4 standard, partly because it provided an end-to-end solution, from video capture, editing, and storage to content playback and distribution.

RealVideo

RealVideo is a proprietary video codec developed by RealNetworks. RealVideo started as a low-bit-rate streaming format to PCs, but now it extends to the portable device market as well, for streaming over broadband and cellular infrastructures. It can be used for live streaming, as well as video-on-demand viewing of a previously downloaded file. RealNetworks bundles RealVideo with RealAudio, its proprietary audio codec, to create a RealMedia container file that can be played with the PC application RealPlayer.

Windows Media Video/VC-1

This codec is a Microsoft-developed variant on MPEG-4 (starting from WMV7). It also features Digital Rights Management (DRM) for control of how content can be viewed, copied, modified, or replayed. In an effort to standardize this proprietary codec, Microsoft submitted WMV9 to the Society of Motion Picture and Television Engineers (SMPTE) organization, and it is currently the draft standard under the name "VC-1."

Theora

Theora is an open-source, royalty-free video codec developed by the Xiph Foundation, which has also developed several open-source audio codecs (see Chapters 12 and 13 for further information about Speex [for speech] and Vorbis [for music]). Theora is based on the VP3 codec that On2 Technologies released into the public domain. It mainly competes with low-bit-rate codecs like MPEG-4 and Windows Media Video.

H.264

H.264 is also known as the MPEG-4 Part 10, H.26L, or MPEG-4 advanced video coding (AVC) standard. It actually represents a hallmark of cooperation in the form of a joint definition between the ITU-T and ISO/IEC committees. The objective of H.264 is to reduce bit rates by 50% or more for comparable video quality, relative to its predecessors. It works across a wide range of bit rates and video resolutions. H.264's dramatic bit-rate reductions come at the cost of significant implementation complexity. This complexity limits H.264 coding at high frame resolutions to work only with higher-end embedded processors, often requiring multiple processors that split the coder processing load. The H.264 decoder is discussed further in Section 14.4.

Quality, Bit Rate, and Complexity Comparison

Today many of the video compression algorithms mentioned here are competing for industry and consumer acceptance. As Figure 14.16 shows, all of these algorithms strive to provide higher-resolution video at lower bit rates than their predecessors and at comparable or better quality. But that is not all—they also extend to many more applications than the previous generation of standards by offering features like increased scalability

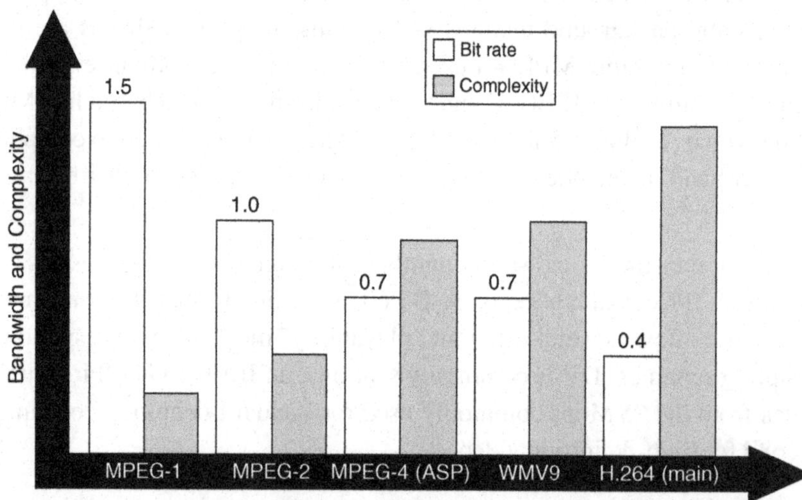

Figure 14.16: Progress in video encoding algorithms leads to lower bit rates and higher complexity for comparable video quality.

(grabbing only the subset of the encoded bitstream needed for the application), error resilience (better immunity to errors), and digital rights management capabilities (to protect content from unauthorized viewing or distribution). However, the downside of these newer algorithms is that they generally require even more processing power than their predecessors in order to achieve their remarkable results.

In the following sections, we further discuss the widely used MPEG-2, rapidly emerging H.264, and the next-generation video coding algorithm, H.264 SVC (scalable video coding).

14.3 MPEG-2 Decoder

As shown in Figure 14.13, the encoded bitstream consists of video sequence layer headers, picture layers headers, slice layer headers, macroblock layer headers, motion vectors, the coded block pattern, and residual coefficients. Figure 14.14 shows the received MPEG-2 hierarchical video bitstream with the following six layers of parameters and the coded pixel data: video sequence, group of pictures (GOP), picture layer, slice layer, macroblock parameters, and coded data block (of 8×8 pixels). After decoding all headers and parameters, the entropy-decoded transform coefficients are reconstructed (with inverse quantization) and inverse transformed to produce the prediction error. This is added to the motion-compensated prediction generated from previously decoded pictures to produce the decoded output. Providing complete details of decoding of MPEG-2 compressed video bitstream is beyond the scope of this book. See ISO/IEC (1995) and Jack (2001) for more information on MPEG-2 video bitstream decoding. Next, various layers of the MPEG-2 decoder are discussed. Later discussion focuses on the critical modules (e.g., shown in Figure 14.15) belonging to the macroblock and block layers.

14.3.1 Slice Layer and Above

A video sequence commences with a sequence header that may optionally be followed by a picture group header and then by one or more coded frames. The video sequence is the highest syntactic structure of the coded video bitstream, and in MPEG-2 it is terminated by a 32-bit *sequence_end_code*, $0 \times 000001B7$. A video sequence header commences with a *sequence_header_code* ($0 \times 000001B3$), and is followed by a series of parameters, such as frame width, height, aspect ratio, frame rate, bit rate, buffer size, quantization parameters, and so on.

A 32-bit string of $0 \times 000001B5$, referred to as *extension_start_code*, indicates the beginning of extension data beyond MPEG-1. For MPEG-2 video bitstreams, an *extension_start_code* and a sequence extension must follow each sequence header. At various points in the video sequence, a particular coded picture may be preceded by either a repeat *sequence_header( )* or a *GOP_header( )* or both. All data elements (except quantization matrices) in the *sequence_extension( )* that follow a repeat *sequence_header( )* will have the same values as in the first *sequence_extension( )*. Repeating the sequence header allows the data elements of the initial header to be repeated in order that random access into the video sequence is possible.

In MPEG-2, several extensions are used to support various levels of capability. These extensions include sequence display extension, sequence scalable extension, picture coding extension, quant matrix extension, picture display extension, picture temporal scalable extension, and picture spatial scalable extension. MPEG-2 sequence extensions are beyond the scope of this book. In addition, MPEG-2 supports both *progressive coding* (frame structured pictures) and *interlaced coding* (field-structured pictures), but discussion in this section is limited to progressive coding algorithms.

The flow chart diagram of MPEG-2-sequence layer-level bitstream parsing is shown in Figure 14.17. The layer highlighted in the gray box is the critical layer of all layers as it involves the critical video decoder modules, as shown in Figure 14.15.

A *picture_data( )* process involves decoding of one or more of the slice layers. The flow chart diagram of the MPEG-2 slice-layer-level bitstream parsing is shown in Figure 14.18. Data for each slice layer consists of a slice header followed by *macroblock_data( )*. Slice header decoding involves decoding of *slice_start_code*, optional *slice_vertical_position_extension*, optional *priority_breakpoint*, *quantizer_scale_code*, *intra_slice_ flag*, *intra_slice*, *reserved_bits*, *extra_bit_slice*, *extra_information_slice*, and *macroblock_data*. Once again, here the *macroblock_data( )* is the critical function as it involves decoding of macroblock headers, motion vectors, coded block pattern and residual coefficients.

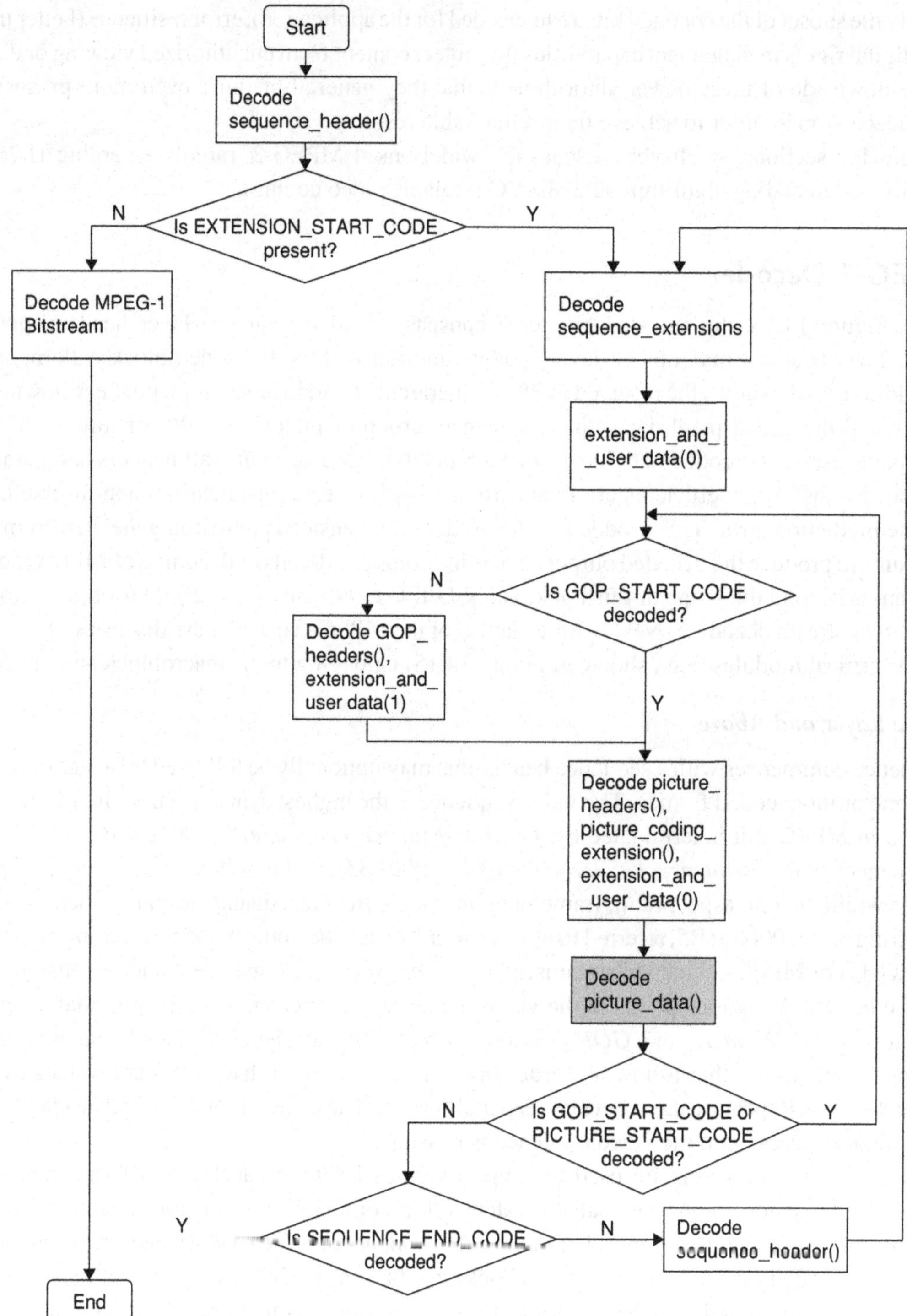

Figure 14.17: MPEG-2 sequence layer-level bitstream parsing.

14.3.2 Macroblock Layer

Data for each macroblock layer consists of a macroblock header followed by motion vectors, coded block pattern, and residual block data. The flow chart diagram of macroblock-layer bitstream parsing is shown in Figure 14.19 (see page 678). The 11-bit field 0000 0001 000, referred to as *macroblock_escape*, is used when the difference between the current macroblock address and previous macroblock address is greater than 33. A variable-length codeword, referred to as *macroblock_address_increment*, is used to update the *macroblock_address* when the difference between the current macroblock address and the previous macroblock address is less than or equal to 33. Except at the start of a slice, if the value of *macroblock_address* recovered from *macroblock_address_increment*

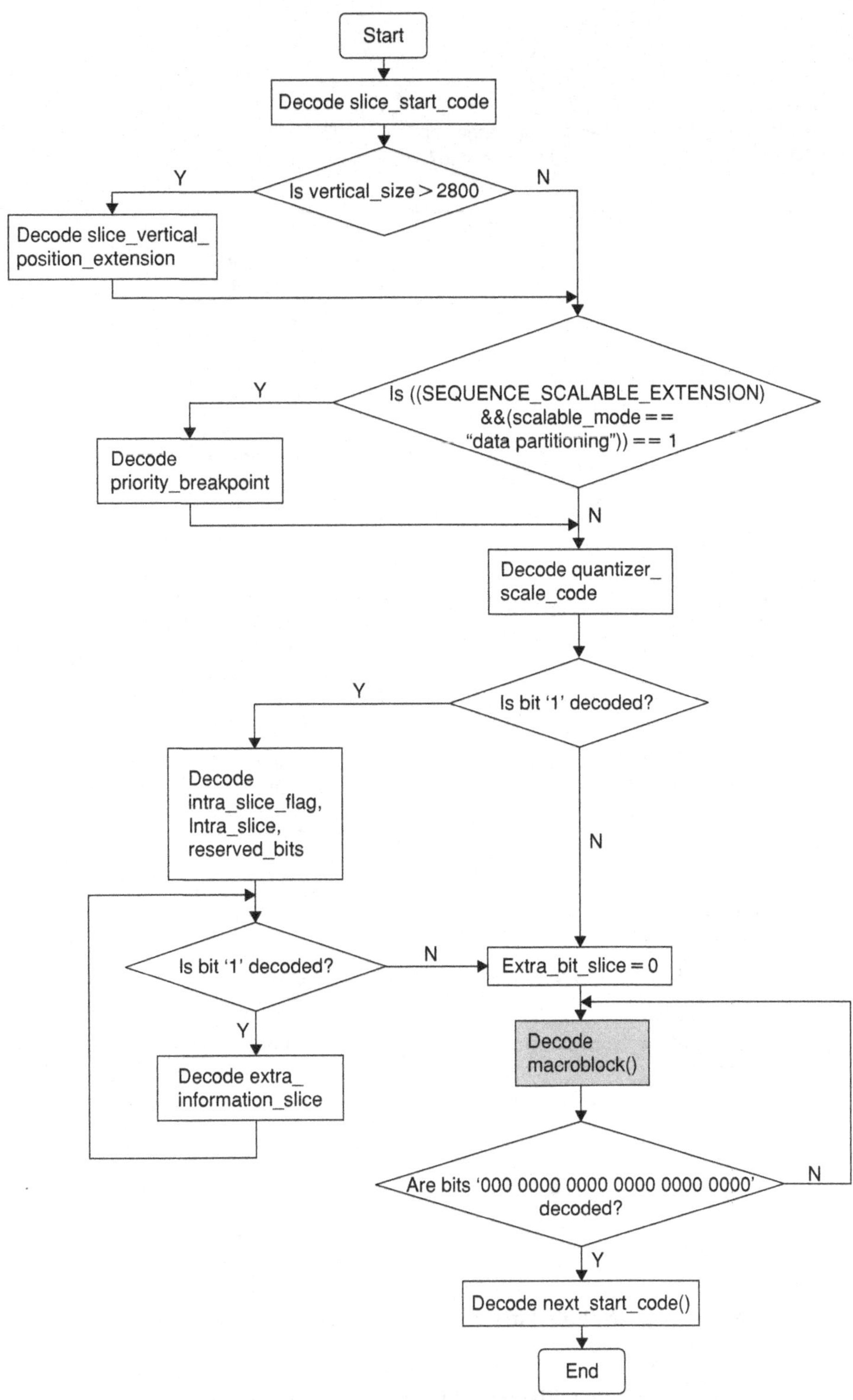

Figure 14.18: Bitstream parsing by MPEG-2 slice-layer level.

and the *macroblock_escape* codes differs from the *previous_macroblock_address* by more than 1, then some macroblocks have been skipped. A skipped macroblock is one for which no data is encoded. The skipped macroblock is constructed using the pixels of the colocated macroblock in the reference frame.

The function *macroblock_modes( )* decodes *macroblock_type*, *spatial_temporal_weight_code*, *frame_ motion_type*, *field_motion_type*, *DCT_type*, and optional *quantizer_scale_code*. The variable-length codeword, *macroblock_type*, indicates the decoding method for the macroblock content. Various parameters (e.g., *macroblock_quant*, *macroblock_intra*, *macroblock_motion_forward*) are derived from *macroblock_type*.

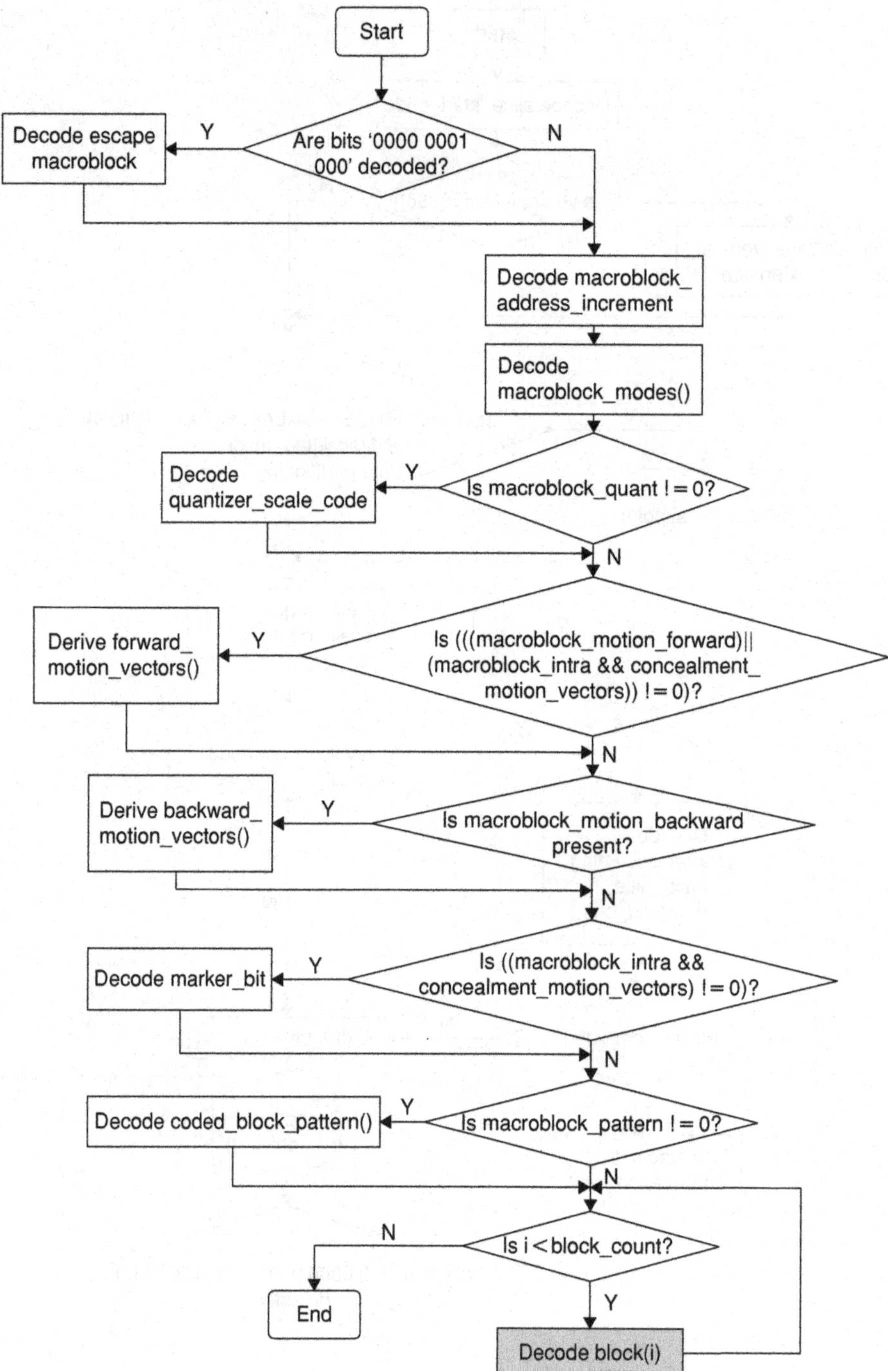

Figure 14.19: MPEG-2 macroblock layer-level bitstream parsing.

Motion vectors are coded differentially with respect to previously coded motion vectors in order to reduce the number of bits required to represent them. In order to decode the motion vectors, the decoder will maintain four motion-vector predictors denoted as MVP[i][j][k], where $i = 0$ to 1 (to hold up to two motion-vector predictors), $j = 0, 1$ (to hold forward or backward motion), and $k = 0, 1$ (to hold horizontal and vertical motion components). For each prediction, a motion vector MV[i][j][k] is derived by adding the prediction to the decoded motion difference value, *delta*. Then, a scaled motion vector, sMV[i][j][k], is derived for chrominance components. The index i also take the values 2 and 3 for derived motion vectors used with dual-prime prediction, as these motion vectors do not themselves have motion vector predictors.

The optional variable-length codeword, *coded_block_ pattern* (CBP), is used to derive the 4:2:0 CBP. The CBP indicates which blocks in the macroblock have at least one transform coefficient, and it is present only if *macroblock_pattern* = 1. The CBP is represented as $B_1B_2B_3B_4B_5B_6$, where $B_n = 1$ if at least one coefficient is in block n; otherwise, $B_n = 0$. This block numbering was shown in Figure 14.6. The most critical block in the macroblock layer is block decoding, which is highlighted with the gray box in Figure 14.19.

14.3.3 Block Layer

Data for each block layer consists of residual coefficient data. The flow chart diagram of block-layer-level bitstream parsing is shown in Figure 14.20. In this layer, we decode a block of quantized DCT coefficients from the bitstream. A block denotes an 8×8-pixel area of video data. With 4:2:0 representation, we will have six such 8×8 blocks for both luminance and chrominance decoding (as shown in Figure 14.6). The decoding complexity of the macroblock layer and all layers above it is almost independent of bit rates. However, the complexity of the block layer increases nonlinearly with the bit rate because the complexity of entropy decoding of residual data coefficients per 8×8 block increases (due to increased number of coefficients) when the bit rate increases for a given frame resolution.

As illustrated in Figure 14.15, the most critical modules of the decoder are in the macroblock and block layers. The MPEG-2 modules VLD, zig-zag scan, inverse quantization, IDCT, and motion compensation are

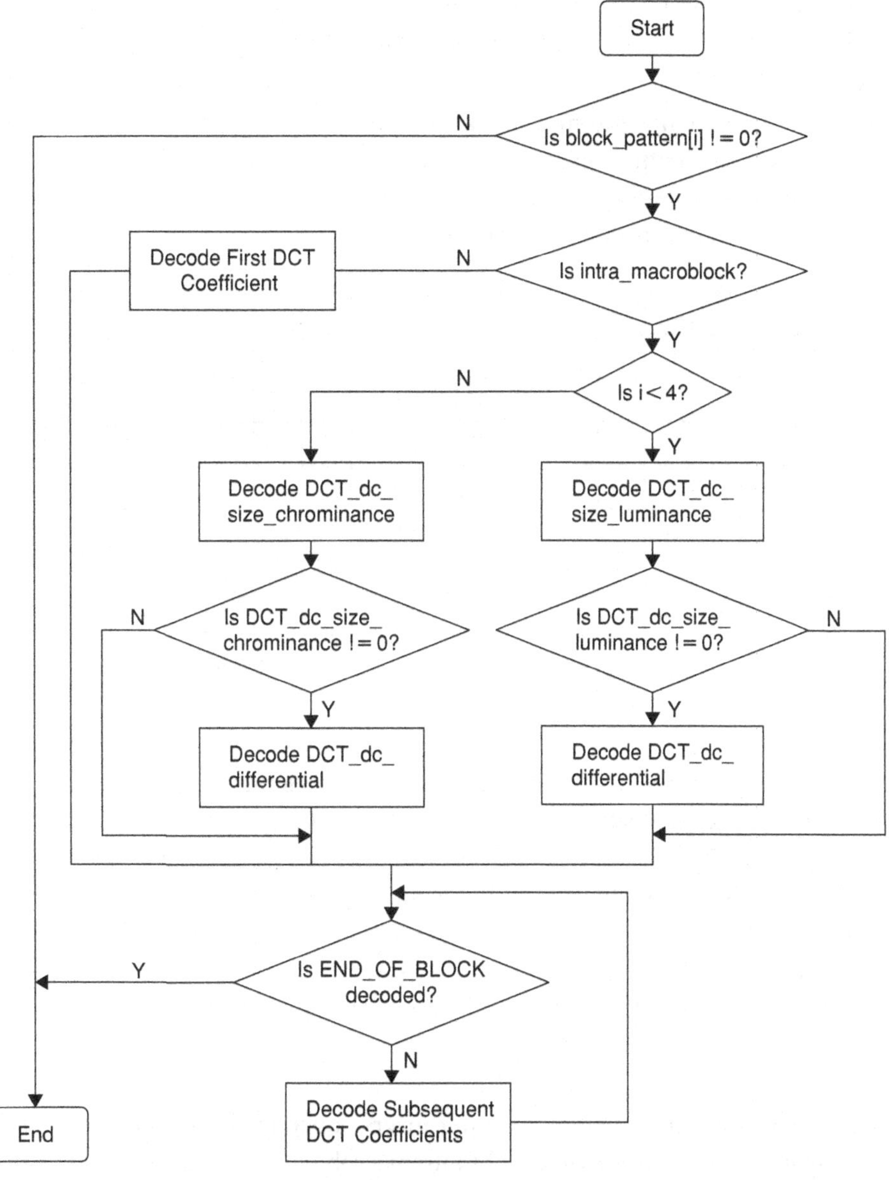

Figure 14.20: MPEG-2 block layer-level bitstream parsing.

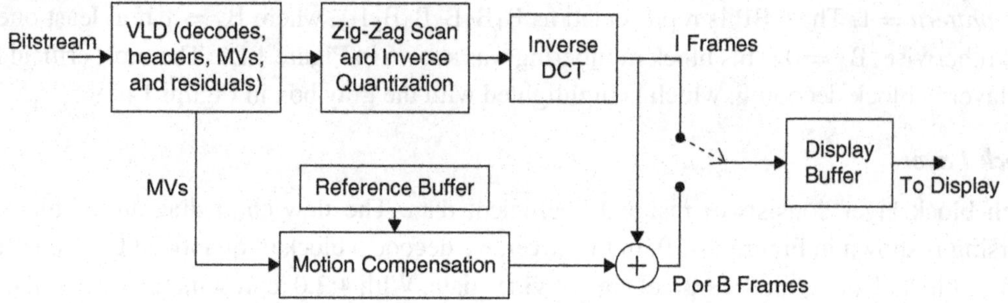

Figure 14.21: Illustration of MPEG-2 block decoding.

very critical since they are called at the pixel level. The simplified block diagram of the MPEG-2 decoder with the critical modules is shown in Figure 14.21. Next, we focus on these critical modules.

MPEG-2 VLD

The MPEG-2 standard specifies many codeword tables to encode various headers, parameters, and residual data coefficients into the bitstream using variable-length coding (VLC). At the decoder, corresponding variable-length decoding (VLD) extracts information of headers, parameters, and data coefficients from the received bitstream. Of all VLD functions, residual data coefficients decoding VLD is critical, as we needed to decode all the non-zero coefficients of an 8×8 block. See Section 5.2 for more detail on MPEG-2 VLD.

Inverse Zig-Zag Scan

The residual coefficients are rearranged from serial fashion (0 to 63) to 8×8 block fashion using inverse zig-zag scanning. The scanner places the coefficients starting at the DC position and slowly moves toward high-frequency positions according to the scan patterns given in the following table. The received bitstream contains a flag that indicates which zig-zag pattern the encoder adapted for scanning.

0	1	5	6	14	15	27	28
2	4	7	13	16	26	29	42
3	8	12	17	25	30	41	43
9	11	18	24	31	40	44	53
10	19	23	32	39	45	52	54
20	22	33	38	46	51	55	60
21	34	37	47	50	56	59	61
35	36	48	49	57	58	62	63

Zig-zag scan

0	4	6	20	22	36	38	52
1	5	7	21	23	37	39	53
2	8	19	24	34	40	50	54
3	9	18	25	35	41	51	55
10	17	26	30	42	46	56	60
11	16	27	31	43	47	57	61
12	15	28	32	44	48	58	62
13	14	29	33	45	49	59	63

Field scan

Inverse Quantization

The slice-layer parameter, *quantizer_scale_code*, specifies the scalefactor of the reconstruction level of the received DCT coefficients. The decoder uses this value until another *quantizer_scale_code* is received at the slice or macroblock layer. The 2D array of residual coefficients is inverse quantized to produce the reconstructed DCT coefficients. This process is essentially a multiplication by the quantizer step size (which is derived from the quantization matrix and a scalefactor). After the appropriate inverse quantization arithmetic, the resulting coefficients are saturated and then a mismatch control operation is performed to give the final reconstructed DCT coefficients for an 8×8 block. For complete details on inverse quantization process, see Section 7.4 in ISO/IEC (1995).

8×8 IDCT

Once the DCT coefficients are reconstructed (i.e., after inverse quantization), an 8×8 IDCT transform will be applied to obtain the spatial domain pixels (in case of intramacroblocks) or to obtain the residual data (in case of intermacroblocks). For more detail on 8×8 IDCT computation and implementation techniques, see Section 7.2.

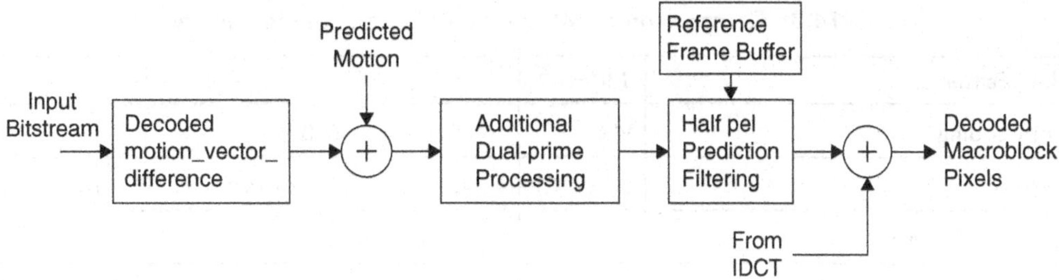

Figure 14.22: Simplified MPEG-2 motion-compensation process.

Motion Compensation

The motion compensation process forms predictions from previously decoded pictures, which are combined with the residual data coefficients from IDCT in order to recover the final decoded pixels as shown in Figure 14.22. Predictions are formed by reading prediction samples from the reference frames. A given sample is predicted by reading the corresponding sample in the reference frame offset by the motion vector. All motion vectors are specified to an accuracy of one-half sample. Thus, if a component of the motion vector is odd, the samples will be read from the midpoint between actual samples in the reference frame. These midway samples are calculated by simple linear interpolation from the actual samples. For complete details on the MPEG-2 motion compensation process, see Section 7.6 in ISO/IEC (1995).

14.3.4 MPEG-2 Decoding Complexity

The complexity of a video decoder in terms of processor MIPS and memory depends on a few parameters. For example, the computational complexity of the decoder increases with the video frame resolution (since the number of pixels to be reconstructed per frame is greater), frame rate (since the number of frames to be processed per second is greater), bit rate (since the number of coefficients per block increases with the bit rate per given resolution and frame rate), and the profile used (since algorithm complexity varies from profile to profile). All these parameters determine the complexity of video decoding. This is why most of the standards specify the coding levels for the video coder.

Next, we provide the decoding complexity in terms of cycles per pixel and the amount of L1 memory required to decode the MPEG-2 bitstream on the reference embedded processor. For D1-resolution, MPEG-2-coded video bitstream at 8 Mbps, we require a total of 35 cycles per pixel to decode it using the reference embedded processor. Cycle counts by module are given in the following:

- Parser (control code to parse bitstream at various layers): 7 cycles per pixel
- VLD (decoding all headers and residual coefficients and zig-zag scan): 10 cycles per pixel
- Quantization: 3 cycles per pixel
- IDCT: 6 cycles per pixel
- MC: 4 cycles per pixel
- Miscellaneous (DMA waits, data packing/unpacking, and others): 5 cycles per pixel

With respect to memory usage, although we require storage of one or two reference frames (occupying up to 1 MB memory with D1 frame resolution) that are used for reconstructing the current frame and the memory to hold the current frame itself (512 kB with D1 frame resolution), all of these use slow off-chip L3 memory. Typically, we will have sufficient off-chip L3 memory. The problem is that on-chip L1 memory (used to hold the program code, parameters, headers from all layers, VLD look-up tables, temporary work buffers, etc.) is costly as it occupies chip space and there is usually not much available on the chip to hold a whole video frame. For MPEG-2 decoding, we require about 48 kB of L1 memory.

14.4 H.264 Decoder

ITU-T H.264/MPEG-4 (Part 10) advanced video coding (AVC), commonly referred as H.264/AVC, is the newest entry in the series of international video coding standards. Compared with previous standards, H.264

Table 14.3: Comparison of MPEG-2 and H.264 coding features

Coding Features	MPEG-2	H.264
Entropy coding	VLC	UVLC, CAVLC, CABAC
Transform	8×8 DCT	4×4, 8×8 integer transforms, Hadamard transform
Picture-coding types	*I*, *P*, *B*	*I*, *P*, *B*, *SP*, *SI*
Intraprediction support	No	Yes
Motion estimation resolution	Half-pixel	Quarter-pixel
Number of motion vectors per macroblock	Up to 2	Up to 16
Weighted prediction	No	Yes
Multiple reference-frame support	No	Yes
Deblocking filter	No	Yes

achieves up to 50% improvement in bit-rate efficiency. It has been adapted by many application standards such as DVB-H, HD-DTV, 3G, and so on. It is currently the most powerful and state-of-the-art standard and its VLSI design technology provides balance among coding efficiency, implementation complexity, and cost. While H.264 uses the same general coding principles as previous standards, it has many new features (e.g., context-based entropy coding, intraprediction, 4×4 integer transform, quarter-pixel motion estimation, multiple reference-frame support, adaptive deblocking filter, etc.) that distinguish it from the previous standards. Table 14.3 highlights the differences between MPEG-2 and H.264 video coding standards.

H.264 supports many profiles (baseline, main, extended, high, etc.) and levels to play an important role in many industry-wide applications. The baseline profile requires less computation and system memory and is optimized for low-latency applications such as video telephony, Internet streaming, and so on. The main profile provides highest coding efficiency but at the cost of increased complexity. Broadcast and content storage applications are primarily interested in the main profile to leverage the highest possible video quality at the lowest possible bit rates. The extended profile combines the robustness of the baseline profile and greater network robustness to support video-streaming applications. The high profiles are intended for high-resolution, high-quality, high-bit-rate applications such as DVB (digital video broadcasting), BD-ROM (Blu-ray disk ROM), and so on.

As the extended and high-profile designs are based on the baseline and main profile coding techniques, here we discuss only the baseline and main profile decoder modules and respective implementation techniques.

As shown in Figure 14.23, the H.264 coded video sequence consists of a series of NAL (network abstraction layer) units, each containing an RBSP (raw-byte-sequence payload) data. The output of video encoding process consists of video-coding layer (VCL) bits that are mapped to NAL units before storage or transmission. H.264 makes a distinction between VCL data and NAL data. Bits associated with the slice layer and below are identified as VCL NAL data, and the bits associated with higher layers are identified as non-VCL NAL data. The purpose of separately specifying the VCL NAL and non-VCL NAL data is to distinguish between specific features of the video coding and of the network transport. The VCL NAL data and non-VCL NAL data can be sent together as part of a single bitstream or can be sent separately. In this book, we will focus on the VCL NAL data, which is the heart of compression capability.

As the coding of video involves coding of many types of data (e.g., parameters, supplemental information, actual video slices, end-of-sequence or stream flags), each type of data is placed in a separate RBSP unit and each of the RBSP units is transmitted in a separate NAL unit. The header of the NAL unit signals the type of RBSP unit and RBSP data makes up the rest of the NAL unit. An NAL unit specifies a generic format for use in both packet-oriented and bitstream systems. The format of NAL units for both packet-based transport and byte-stream-based systems is identical, except that each NAL unit can be preceded by a start-code prefix and extra padding bytes in the byte-stream format.

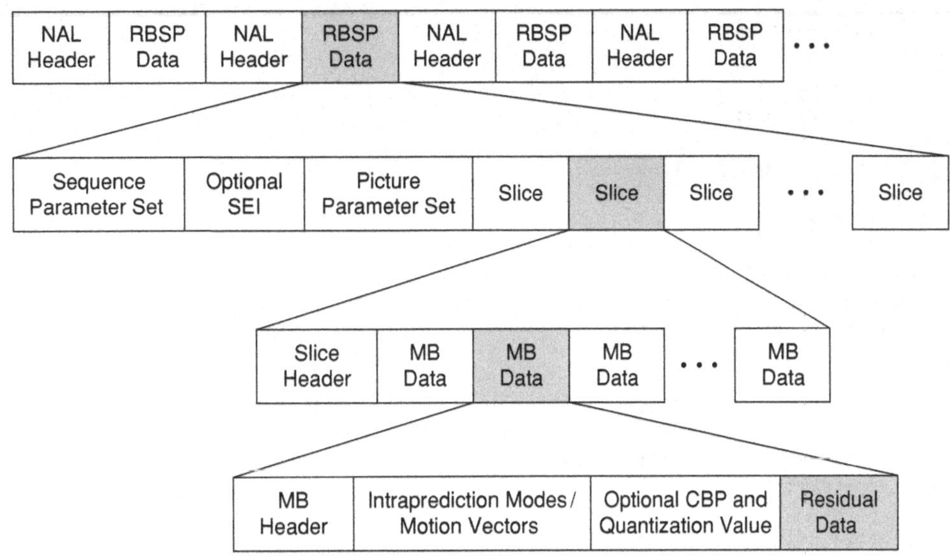

Figure 14.23: Simplified structure of H.264 bitstream format.

A pseudocode for decoding NAL unit headers is given in Pcode 14.1. Before decoding NAL headers, we search for the *start_code_prefix* to know the starting of the NAL unit in the bitstream. The simulation code for finding *start_code_prefix* is given in Pcode 14.2.

```
// ReadNalu()
found = 0;
while(!found) {
        found = SearchStartCodePrefix(buf);
        if (buf->water_mark < 512)
                 LoadData(buf,512);
        if (found) {
                 tmp = Uv(buf,8);
                 nal->forbidden_zero_bit = tmp >> 7;
                 nal->nal_ref_idc = (tmp>>5) & 0x3;
                 nal->nal_unit_type = tmp & 0x1f;
                 if ((nal->nal_unit_type == 0) || (nal->nal_unit_type > 19))
                           found = 0;
        }
 };
```

Pcode 14.1: Pseudocode for decoding NAL unit header.

The first byte of each NAL unit is a header byte (*forbidden_zero_bit*, *nal_ref_idc*, and *nal_unit_type*) that contains an indication of the type of data in the NAL unit, and the remaining bytes contain payload data of the type indicated by the header.

The pseudocode for decoding the sequence of RBSP units is given in Pcode 14.3. Depending on the NAL unit type, we decode corresponding headers, slice data, or end of sequence. In H.264, the global parameters used for coding video sequences are divided into two parameter sets: (1) sequence parameter set and (2) picture parameter set. These parameter sets contain an infrequently changing sequence and picture parameters. A sequence parameter set contains parameters applied to a complete video sequence, whereas the picture parameter set contains the parameters that are applied to a few pictures within a sequence.

The sequence parameter set includes the following: *profile_idc*, *constraint_set0/1/2/3_flags*, *reserved_zero_bits*, *level_idc*, *sequence_parameter_set_id*, *log2_max_frame_num_minus4*, *picture_order_cnt_type*, optional *log2_max_pic_order_cnt_lsb_minus4*, optional *delta_pic_order_always_zero_flag*, optional *offset_for_non_ref_pic*, optional *offset_for_top_to_bottom_field*, optional *num_ref_frames_in_pic_order_cnt_cycles*, optional *offset_for_ref_frame[i]*, *num_ref_frames*, *gaps_in_frame_num_value_allowed_flag*, *pic_width_in_mbs_minus1*, *pic_height_in_map_units_minus1*, *frame_mbs_only_flag*, optional *mb_adaptive_frame_field_flag*,

```
int SearchStartCodePrefix(InBuffer_t *buf)
{
int i;
uword value1, value2, value3;
int tmp = 1024, x = 0;
uword ref = 0xffffff00, prefix = 0x00000100;

tmp = buf->water_mark >> 2;
value1 = buf->curr_word;
for(i = 0;i < tmp-1;i++){
        value2 = buf->start_ptr[(buf->read_index++) & 0x1ff];
        if ((value1 & ref) == prefix){
                buf->read_index+ = -2;
                if (buf->read_index < 0)
                        buf->read_index = 0x1ff;
                buf->curr_word = buf->start_ptr[(buf->read_index++) & 0x1ff];
                buf->bit_pos = 24; x = 1;
                break;
        }
        value3 = value1 << 8;
        if ((value3 & ref) == prefix){
                buf->read_index--;
                if (buf->read_index < 0)
                        buf->read_index = 0x1ff;
                buf->curr_word = buf->start_ptr[(buf->read_index++) & 0x1ff];
                buf->bit_pos = 0; x = 1;
                break;
        }
        value1 = value1 << 16;
        value3 = value2 >> 16;
        value3 = value3 + value1;
        if ((value3 & ref) == prefix) {
                buf->read_index--;
                if (buf->read_index < 0)
                        buf->read_index = 0x1ff;
                buf->curr_word = buf->start_ptr[(buf->read_index++) & 0x1ff];
                buf->bit_pos = 8; x = 1;
                break;
        }
        value3 = value3 << 8;
        if ((value3 & ref) == prefix) {
                buf->read_index--;
                if (buf->read_index < 0)
                        buf->read_index = 0x1ff;
                buf->curr_word = buf->start_ptr[(buf->read_index++) & 0x1ff];
                buf->bit_pos = 16; x = 1;
                break;
        }
        value1 = value2;
 }
 return (x);
}
```

Pcode 14.2: Simulation code for finding start_code_prefix.

direct_8×8_reference_flag, *frame_cropping_flag*, optional *frame_crop_left_offset*, optional *frame_crop_right_offset*, optional *frame_crop_top_offset*, optional *frame_crop_bottom_offset*, *vui_parameters_present_flag*, and optional *vui_parameters*.

The picture parameter set includes the following: *picture_parameter_set_id*, *seq_parameter_set_id*, *entropy_coding_mode_flag*, *pic_order_present_flag*, *num_slice_groups_minus1*, *slice_group_map_type*, optional *run_length_minus1*, optional *top_left*, optional *bottom_right*, optional *slice_group_change_direction_flag*, optional *slice_group_change_rate_minus1*, optional *slice_group_id[]*, *num_ref_idx_l0_minus1*, *num_ref_idx_l1_active_minus1*, *weighted_pred_flag*, *weighted_bipred_idc*, *pic_init_qp_minus26*, *pic_init_qs_minus26*, *chroma_qp_index_offset*, *deblocking_filter_control_present_flag*, *constrained_intra_pred_flag*, and *redundant_pic_cnt_present_flag*.

```
eos_read = 0;
slice_header_read = 0;
if (buf->water_mark < 512) {
        LoadData(buf, 512);
}
while((!slice_header_read) && (!eos_read)){
        // read nal unit information
        ReadNalu(nalu);
        if (nalu->forbidden_zero_bit != 0) {
                while(nalu->forbidden_zero_bit != 0) {
                        ReadNalu(nalu);
                };
        }
        switch(nalu->nal_unit_type) {
                case 1: // coded slice of a non-IDR picture
                        SliceLayerWithoutPartitioningRbsp(pvc);
                        Break;
                case 2: //contains headers data for all MBs in the slice
                        SliceDataPartitionALayerRbsp(pvc);
                        Break;
                case 3: //contains intra coded data
                        SliceDataPartitionBLayerRbsp(pvc);
                        Break;
                case 4: //contains inter coded data
                        SliceDataPartitionCLayerRbsp(pvc);
                        Break;
                case 5: // coded slice of an IDR picture
                        ReadSliceHeaders(pvc);          // read slice headers
                        DecodeSliceData (pvc);          // decode a slice
                        slice_header_read = 1;
                        break;
                case 7: // contains sequence parameter set
                        ReadSeqParmSet(pvc);
                        break;
                case 8: // contains picture parameter set
                        ReadPicParmSet(pvc);
                        break;
                case 10:                                // end of sequence
                case 11:                                // end of stream
                        eos_read = 1;
                        break;
                default:
                        break;
        }
};
```

Pcode 14.3: Pseudocode for decoding different types of RBSP data.

The sequence and picture parameter sets can be sent well ahead of the VCL NAL units. At the decoder, one or more sequence parameter sets and picture parameter sets are decoded prior to decoding of slice headers and slice data. The sequence parameter and picture parameter sets are considered not active at the start of the operation of decoding. Each VLC NAL unit contains an identifier that refers to the content of the picture parameter set, and each picture parameter set contains an identifier that refers to the content of the relevant sequence parameter set. In other words, a decoded slice header, *pic_parameter_set_id*, activates a particular parameter set. Then the activated picture parameter set header, *seq_parameter_set_id*, in turn activates a particular sequence parameter set. The activated picture or sequence parameter set then remains active until a different picture or sequence parameter set is activated by another slice header *pic_parameter_set_id* or picture parameter set header *seq_parameter_set_id*.

H.264 uses UVLC (universal variable-length code) in decoding the sequence and picture parameter sets. UVLC codes include both fixed-length codes (Uv(n)) and exp-Golomb codes (Ue(n) and Se(n)). See Section 5.3 for more detail on UVLC decoding and implementation techniques. The simulation code for exp-Golomb codes was provided earlier in Pcodes 5.12 and 5.13.

14.4.1 Slice Layer

In H.264, a video picture is coded with one or more slices as shown in Figure 14.24 and a coded picture may be composed of different types of slices. For example, a baseline profile coded picture may contain a mixture of *I* and *P* slices, and the main profile picture may contain a mixture of *I*, *P*, and *B* slices. Each slice is a sequence of macroblocks that is processed in the order of a raster scan when not using FMO (flexible macroblock order). Each slice contains an integer number of macroblocks. The number of macroblocks per slice need not be constant. Each slice is self-contained, in the sense that, given the active sequence and picture parameter sets, its data can be decoded from the bitstream. The slice header defines the slice type. In H.264, there are five fundamental slice types: *I* slice (contains only *I* macroblocks), *P* slice (contains *P* macroblocks, and/or *I* macroblocks), *B* slice (contains *B* macroblocks and/or *I* macroblocks), *SI* slice (contains a special type of intracoded macroblocks), and *SP* slice (contains *P* and/or *I* macroblocks). The slice types *I*, *P*, and *B* are very similar to coding methods used in previous standards such as MPEG-2. The other two slice types *SI* and *SP* are newly introduced in H.264 (Karczewicz and Kurceren, 2003) and they are used with the H.264 extended profile.

The construction of *I* macroblocks uses predicted samples from previously constructed macroblocks within the same slice. The *P* macroblocks are predicted from list 0 reference pictures, whereas the *B* macroblocks are predicted from list 0 and/or list 1 reference pictures. For more detail on reference picture marking and reordering, see ISO/IEC (2003).

In H.264, an IDR (instantaneous decoder refresh) coded picture (made up of *I* slices) is used to clear the contents of the reference picture buffer. On receiving an IDR-coded picture, the decoder marks all pictures in the reference buffer as "unused for reference." After decoding of an IDR picture, all following coded pictures in decoding order can be decoded without reference to any frames decoded prior to the IDR picture. The first picture of each coded video sequence is always an IDR picture. Slice data partitioning cannot be used for IDR pictures. A "coded slice NAL unit" refers to a coded slice of a non-IDR picture NAL unit or to a coded slice of an IDR picture NAL unit.

The slice layer header, *slice_type*, directs the type of slice to be decoded. The other slice headers include *first_mb_in_slice*, *pic_parameter_set_id*, *frame_num*, and so on. The slice layer headers are decoded using UVLC (see Section 5.3). After decoding the headers, we proceed to decode the corresponding slice data. The pseudocode for decoding slice data is given in Pcode 14.4.

The slice data consists of a series of coded macroblocks and/or indication of skipped macroblocks. A skipped macroblock is one for which no data is coded other than an indication that the macroblock is to be decoded as "skipped." Both *P* and *B* slices contain the skipped macroblocks. An *end_of_slice_flag* indicates that the end of slice is reached. Depending on the *entropy_coding_mode_flag*, we use either UVLC or CABAC (context-based adaptive binary arithmetic coding) to decode the slice layer data. See Section 5.5 for more detail on decoding binary symbols with CABAC.

In H.264, the context information for CABAC is generated with the neighbor blocks information. The neighbors for current block *Q* are defined as *A* (*left*), *B* (*top*), *C* (*top right*) and *D* (*top left*) as shown in Figure 14.25. The context information is derived based on many factors (e.g., presence of neighbors *A* and *B*, their macroblock type, the corresponding parameters strength). We use this information as an offset to the context model look-up tables and obtain the context model (or the probability value) for CABAC. For example, to decode *mb_skip_flag*

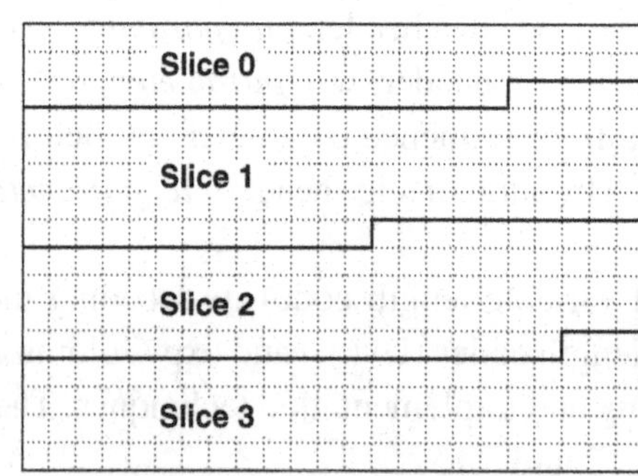

Figure 14.24: Division of picture into multiple slices.

```
void DecodeSliceData(pvc)
{
        InitSliceParameters();
        if (pvc->entropy_coding_mode_flag){
                ByteAlign();
                psh-> cabac_alignment_one_bit = BitFifo(1);
        }
        psh->CurrentMbAddr = psh->first_mb_in_slice*(1+psh->MbaffFrameFlag);
        psh->moreDataFlag = 1;      psh->prevMbSkipped = 0;
        do {
                if ((psh->slice_type != I) && (psh->slice_type != SI))
                        if(!pvc->entropy_coding_mode_flag) {
                                psh->mb_skip_run = Ue(n);
                                psh->prevMBSkipped = psh->mb_skip_run > 0 ? 1 : 0;
                                for(i = 0;i < psh->mb_skip_run;i++)
                                          psh->CurrMbAddr++;
                                psh->moreDataFlag = MoreRbspData();
                        }
                        else {
                                psh->mb_skip_flag = mb_skip_flag_cabac();
                                psh->moreDataFlag = !psh->mb_skip_flag;
                        }
                if (psh->moreDataFlag) {
                        if (psh->MbaffFrameFlag && (((psh->CurrMbAddr %2) == 0) ||
                          (((psh->CurrMbAddr % 2) == 1) && psh->prevMbSkipped)))
                          psh->mb_field_decoding_flag = mb_field_decoding_flag_cabac();
                        DecodeMacroblock();
                }
                if (!pvc->entropy_coding_mode_flag)
                        psh->moreDataFlag = MoreRbspData( );
                else {
                        if ((psh->slice_type != I) && (psh->slice_type != SI))
                                psh->prevMbSkipped = psh->mb_skip_flag;
                        if (psh->MbaffFrameFlag && ((psh->CurrMbAddr %2) == 0))
                                psh -> moreDataFlag = 1;
                        else {
                                psh->end_of_slice_flag = end_slice_flag_cabac();
                                psh->moreDataFlag = !psh->end_of_slice_flag;
                        }
                }
                psh->CurrMbAddr++;
        } while(psh->moreDataFlag);
}
```

Pcode 14.4: Pseudocode for decoding slice data.

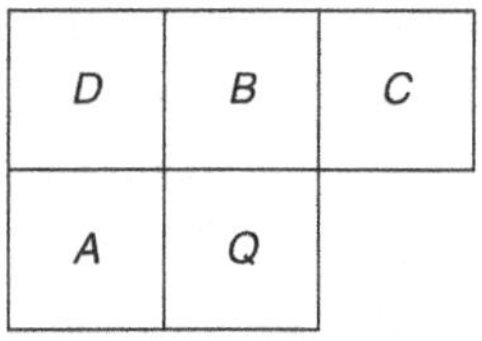

D	B	C
A	Q	

Figure 14.25: Showing neighbor blocks for current block *Q*.

using CABAC, we generate the offset for the *mb_skip_ flag* context look-up table to choose the appropriate context model as follows:

$$\text{offset} = a + b$$

where

$$a = (mb\_skip\_flag(A)! = 0)\ ?\ 0 : 1, \quad \text{and} \quad b = (mb\_skip\_flag(B)! = 0)\ ?\ 0 : 1$$

If one or both of the neighboring macroblocks (A or B) are not available (because they are outside the current slice), the corresponding values a or b is set to zero. In coding of the *mb_skip_ flag*, statistical dependencies between neighboring blocks *mb_skip_ flag* are exploited by means of the previous simple but effective context design.

The H.264 standard specifies about 460 context variables for coding various parameters and residual coefficients using CABAC. We initialize all these contexts in the slice layer using the current slice quantization parameter value. The critical part of slice decoding is decoding of macroblock data. In the next section, we discuss macroblock layer decoding.

14.4.2 Macroblock Layer

At the encoder, all luma and chroma samples of a macroblock are either spatially or temporally predicted, and the resulting prediction residual is encoded using transform coding. At the decoder, in the macroblock layer, we basically decode the macroblock type (indicates the prediction types), intraprediction modes (if *I* macroblock) or motion vectors and reference frames information (if *P* or *B* macroblocks), coded block pattern (to know the non-zero coefficient blocks), quantization offset parameters (to get quantization values from the look-up table), and residual transform data. The pseudocode for macroblock layer decoding with CABAC is given in Pcode 14.5. For more detail on the decoding process of macroblock layer headers and parameters, see Section 9.3.2 in ISO/IEC (2003).

```
void DecodeMacroblock()
{
        InitMacroblockParameters();
        pmb->mb_type = mb_type_cabac();
        if (pmb->mb_type == I_PCM)
                DecodePcmSamples();
        else {
                DecodeMbPredModes(); // for both intra and inter macroblocks
                if (pmb->MbPredType != I_16x16)
                        DecodeCodedBlcokPattern();
                else
                        DeriveCodedBlockPattern();
                if ((pmb->CodedBlockPattern > 0) || (pmb->MbPredType == I_16x16)) {
                        pmb->mb_qp_delta = mb_qp_delta_cabac();
                        DecodeResidualData();
                }
        }
}
```

Pcode 14.5: Pseudocode for decoding macroblock layer.

Macroblock Type

The macroblock layer header *mb_type* determines whether the current macroblock is coded in intra-(I) or inter-(P or B) mode. H.264 assigns the *mb_type* names (as $I\_4\times4$, $I\_16\times16$, *I_PCM*, *P_skip*, $P\_8\times8$, $B\_8\times8$, etc.) and macroblock prediction mode names (as *Intra*_4×4, *Intra*_16×16, *Pred_L*0, *Pred_L*1, *BiPred*, etc.), depending on the *mb_type* value. With I_PCM coding type, we bypass the transform decoding and prediction, and directly obtain the macroblock samples from the received bitstream. In P or B macroblocks, if the macroblock is coded in $P\_8\times8$ or $B\_8\times8$ mode, an additional *sub_mb_type* is in the bitstream that specifies the corresponding submacroblock's type. We determine the macroblock partition sizes using headers *mb_type* or *sub_mb_type*.

At the decoder, depending on the slice type, availability and *mb_type* of left (A) and up (B) neighbors (see Figure 14.25), we derive the context model look-up table offset for decoding current *mb_type* using CABAC. When the *entropy_coding_mode_flag* is zero, we use the UVLC function, Ue(n), for decoding the *mb_type* and *sub_mb_type*.

Intraprediction Modes

As discussed at the beginning of this chapter, video frames contain spatially correlated macroblocks. Macroblocks belonging to portions of picture with fewer details exhibit very high correlation. In previous standards, only transform (DCT) coding is used to exploit this spatial correlation at the 8×8 block level. In H.264, to exploit spatial correlation among pixels, intraspatial prediction is used apart from transform coding. In all slice coding types, intracoding modes *Intra*_4×4, *Intra*_16×16 together with chroma prediction are supported. The *Intra*_4×4 prediction mode is based on predicting each 4×4 luma block separately, and is well-suited for coding parts of a picture with significant details. The *Intra_16×16* prediction mode, on the other hand, performs prediction of the whole 16×16 luma block and is more suited for coding very smooth areas of picture.

At the decoder side, the prediction modes are decoded in the macroblock layer. We use most probable mode information for the context model to decode the luma intraprediction modes with CABAC. In the case of chroma prediction mode decoding, we use the left (A) and up (B) neighbors' availability and chroma prediction modes information in deriving the offset for the context model look-up table. When the *entropy_coding_mode_flag* is zero, we use functions U(1) and U(3) for decoding the luma intraprediction modes and function Ue(n) to decode the chroma intraprediction modes. The H.264 intraprediction process is further discussed in the next section.

Motion Vectors Difference and Reference Pictures

In P or B slices, temporal prediction is used in estimating the motion between pictures. The motion is estimated at the block partition (see Figure 14.26) level. The motion of the block in the horizontal and vertical directions are represented with a vector, containing horizontal displacement (x) and vertical displacement (y), as (x, y). A motion vector (x, y) is estimated for each block partition, and refers to the corresponding position of its picture signal in an already processed reference picture. Unlike in MPEG-2, where the most recent picture is used as reference picture, it is possible to refer several preceding pictures in H.264. For this purpose, an additional picture reference parameter is sent to the decoder along with the motion information. The residual error for the block resulting after the motion estimation and compensation process is transform coded.

Typically the neighbor block motion vectors are correlated and so we only send the motion vector differences (dx, dy) (between the current motion vector and the predicted vector MVP from previously calculated motion vectors) to the decoder. The method of calculating the MVP depends on availability of neighbor blocks (A, B, and C) (see Figure 14.26) and current and neighbor block partition sizes. The motion vector difference and residual error is zero in the case of skipped macroblocks.

At the decode side, we use left (A) and up (B) neighbor block availability and respective MVD information to calculate the offset for the MVD context model look-up table in decoding MVD with CABAC. We use left (A) and up (B) neighbor blocks availability and their reference frame number information to calculate the offset for the reference frame context model look-up table in decoding the current block reference frame number using CABAC. When *entropy_coding_mode_flag* is zero, we use UVLC functions Se(n) and Te(n) to decode the current block MVD and reference frame numbers.

Motion Vector Prediction

We use the motion vector predictor at the decoder to obtain the predicted vector MVP and add MVP to the MVD to retrieve actual motion vectors (x, y) information. The MVP calculation depends on neighbor block availability and partition sizes. Let A, B, and C blocks be left, up and up-right neighbors for current block Q as shown Figure 14.26(a). With different partition sizes, the choice of neighbor blocks left (A: 4 × 8), up (B: 8×8), and up-right (C: 16 × 8) for the current block (Q: 16 × 16) is shown in Figure 14.26(b). Depending on the current block Q partition size, the MVP is calculated in one of the following ways.

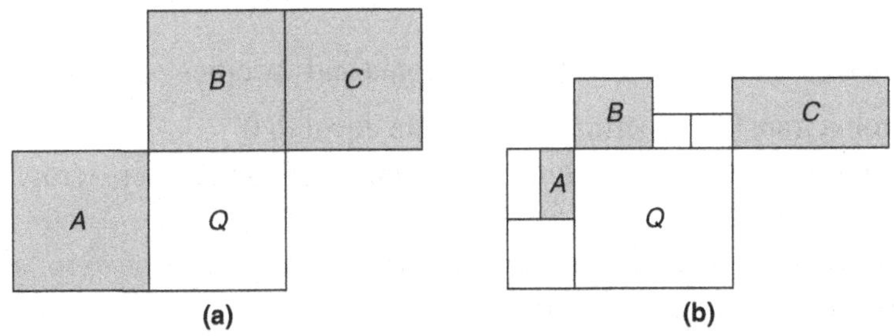

Figure 14.26: Neighboring blocks for motion vector prediction. (a) With equal partition sizes. (b) With different partition sizes.

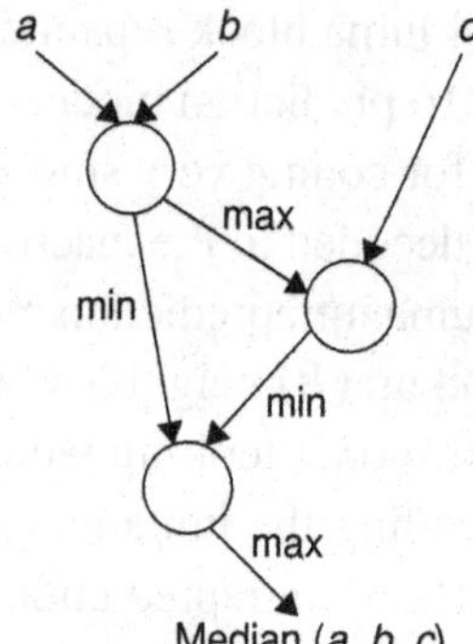

Figure 14.27: Computing median of three numbers.

If the current block Q partition size is either 16×8 or 8×16, we use directional prediction for MVP:

- For 16×8 block partitions, the MVP for the upper 16×8 partition is predicted from B, and the MVP for the lower 16×8 partition is predicted from A.
- For 8×16 block partitions, the MVP for the left 8×16 partition is predicted from A, and the MVP for the right 8×16 partition is predicted from C.

Otherwise, the MVP is the median of the motion vectors of partitions A, B, and C. Given the three values, the median can be computed with four min-max operations as shown in Figure 14.27.

For a skipped macroblock, there is no decoded MVD and a motion-compensated block is generated using MVP as the motion vector. We will discuss more about the H.264 motion compensation process in the next section.

Coded Block Pattern

The macroblock header, *coded_block_pattern*, specifies which of the six 8×8 blocks—luma and chroma—may contain non–zero-transform coefficient levels. For macroblocks with a prediction mode not equal to *Intra_16×16*, *coded_block_pattern* is in the bitstream. The *coded_block_pattern* is comprised of two parts, *CBPL* and *CBPC*, which are derived as follows:

$$CBPL = \text{coded\_block\_pattern}\ \%16,\ CBPC = \text{coded\_block\_pattern}/16$$

When *coded_block_pattern* is decoded from the bitstream, *CBPL* specifies, for each of the four 8×8 luma blocks of the macroblock, one of the following cases:

- All transform coefficient levels of the four 4×4 luma blocks in the 8×8 luma block are equal to zero
- One or more transform coefficient levels of one or more of the 4×4 luma blocks in the 8×8 luma block will be non-zero valued

When the prediction mode is *I_16×16*, the *coded_block_pattern* is derived from the decoded *mb_type*. In this case, *CBPL* specifies whether, for the luma component, non-zero AC transform coefficient levels are present. *CBPL* equal to 0 specifies that all AC transform coefficient levels in the luma component of the macroblock are equal to 0. *CBPL* equal to 15 specifies that at least one of the AC transform coefficient levels in the luma component of the macroblock is non-zero, requiring scanning of AC transform coefficient levels for all 16 of the 4×4 blocks in the 16×16 block.

CBPC contains the *coded_block_pattern* value for chroma and specifies one of the following cases:

- $CBPC = 0$, all chroma transform coefficient levels are equal to 0
- $CBPC = 1$, one or more chroma DC transform coefficient levels will be non-zero; all chroma AC transform coefficient levels are equal to 0
- $CBPC = 2$, zero or more chroma DC transform coefficient levels are non-zero; one or more chroma AC transform coefficient levels will be non-zero

At the decoder, we use left (A) and up (B) neighbor macroblock availability, *coded_block_pattern* and macroblock type in computing the offset for context model look-up table when decoding *coded_block_pattern* using CABAC. When *entropy_coding_mode_ flag* is zero, we use UVLC function Me(n) and the mapping look-up table to decode the *coded_block_ pattern*.

Quantization Parameter

A quantization parameter (*QP*) is used for determining quantization of transform coefficients in H.264. A total of 52 values of quantizer step sizes (Q_{step}) are supported by the standard, indexed by a *QP*. These values are arranged so that an increase of 1 in *QP* means an increase of Q_{step} by approximately 12% (or Q_{step} doubles in size for every increment of 6 in *QP*). By updating the Q_{step} at the macroblock level, the encoder controls the trade-off accurately between bit rate and video quality. The quantized transform coefficients of a block are generally scanned in a zig-zag fashion and transmitted using entropy coding methods.

At the decoder, to update the Q_{step} at the macroblock level, a parameter, *mb_qp_delta*, is in the bitstream when the *coded_block_ pattern* is not zero. We use previously decoded *QP* information to choose the context for decoding *mb_qp_delta* with CABAC. When *entropy_coding_mode_ flag* is zero, we use the UVLC function Se(n) to decode the *mb_qp_delta*. For more details and examples on performing fixed-point coefficient quantization in H.264, see Richardson (2003).

14.4.3 Residuals Decoding

Of all entropy decoding modules, residual decoding is the most costly module because this module works on individual data coefficients of block. For this reason, we go a little bit deeper into the residual decoding process to understand its complex functions. Residual decoding for a macroblock (with 4:2:0 sampling) involves decoding of 16 4×4 blocks luma coefficient data and eight 4×4 chroma blocks coefficient data. These 4×4 blocks are decoded in an inverse raster scan order as shown in Figure 14.28.

Residuals decoding uses either context-based adaptive variable-length coding (CAVLC) or CABAC. The CAVLC-based decoding is a bit simpler than CABAC, as CAVLC uses less complex context models. For more detail on CAVLC decoding and its implementation, see Section 5.3, which focuses on CABAC-based residual decoding.

The coded_block_pattern decoded in the macroblock layer contains the information about which 8×8 blocks (four luma 8×8 blocks and two chroma 8×8 blocks) consist of non-zero coefficients. With the *Intra_*16×16 prediction mode, the DC coefficients (i.e., 0th coefficient) of the 4×4 blocks are separately decoded, inverse zig-zag (or field, if mbaff = 1) scanned (see Figure 14.31, page 696) and passed to the Hadamard transform block, whereas with *Intra_*4×4 prediction mode, we decode all coefficients of 4×4 block in the same way. In this section, we focus on residual decoding with the *Intra_*4×4 prediction mode (i.e., no separate DC decoding and no Hadamard transformation are present).

Coded-Block-Flag Decoding

The H.264 bitstream contains flag information about the presence or absence of 27 possible types of coefficients in a macroblock. Those 27 types of coefficients are given in the Table 14.4. First, we decode the *coded_block_flag* before proceeding to decode its coefficients. If the decoded value of *coded_block_ flag* is zero then we skip the decoding of that block's coefficients. Efficient implementation of the *coded_block_flag* decoding function is very important because it must be called for every one of the 27 block types unless *coded_block_ pattern* indicates no coefficients are in that block group.

To decode each *coded_block_flag* with CABAC, we choose an appropriate context model table from the given eight context models. The offset is calculated for the chosen context model table by using the neighbor block *coded_block_ flag*. The H.264 reference software decodes and stores the *coded_block_ flag* using a C function, *read_and_store_CBP_block_bit*(). The H.264 reference software model is not written for real-time decoding;

Y

0	1	4	5
2	3	6	7
8	9	12	13
10	11	14	15

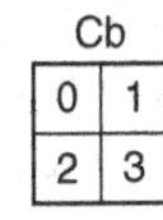

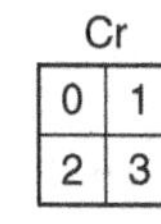

Figure 14.28: Inverse-raster-order residuals decoding for 4×4 blocks of macroblock.

Table 14.4: *coded_block_flag* index and associated coefficient type

Flag Index	Block Type
0	Luma DC
1 to 16	Sixteen 4×4 luma blocks
17	Cb DC
18	Cr DC
19 to 22	Four 4×4 Cb blocks
23 to 26	Four 4×4 Cr blocks

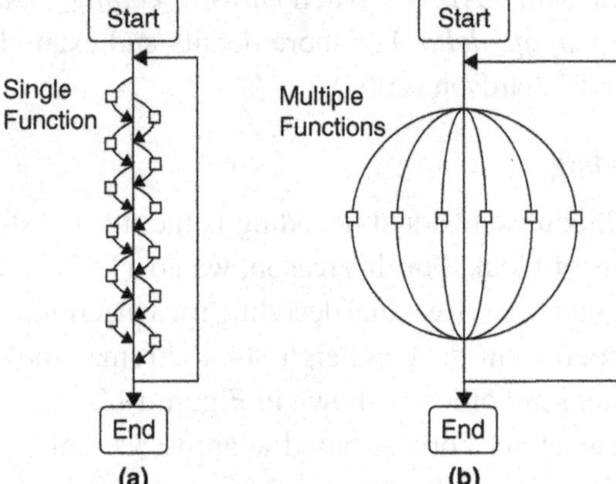

Figure 14.29: Algorithm implementation. (a) Reference software approach (chain model). (b) Optimized implementation (sphere model).

its aim is to provide general framework to decode the bitstream for all possible cases. In this particular case, for choosing appropriate context model, and to obtain the offset for the chosen context model (belonging to particular coefficient block) from the neighbor blocks *coded_block_flag* information, the reference software performs many operations such as condition checks, jumps and data extracts, and data movements. This is because the task of deriving neighbor information from many combinations (of different macroblock types, coefficient block types, block positions, context models, etc.) is performed with a single loop code as illustrated in Figure 14.29(a). A couple of thousand cycles may be needed to decode the *coded_block_flag* using the reference software model on the reference embedded processor.

For example, to store the decoded *coded_block_flag* information about 27 different coefficient blocks for future purposes (for the CABAC and loop filter), the reference software packs the flags by computing the bit-pos as follows:

```
bit-pos = (y_dc ? 0 : y_ac ? 1 + 4*j + i : u_dc ? 17 : v_dc ? 18 : u_ac ? 19 + 2*j + i : 23 + 2*j + i)
```

This C code gives the following bit position packing for the 27 block types *coded_block_flag*:

CodedBlockFlags = CBF_Cr_3|CBF_Cr2|CBF_Cr_1|CBF_Cr0|CBF_Cb3| CBF_Cb2| CBF_Cb1| CBF_Cb0| CBF_Cr_DC| CBF_Cb_DC|CBF_Y_15|CBF_Y_14|CBF_Y_11| CBF_Y_10| CBF_Y_13| CBF_Y_12| CBF_Y_9|CBF_Y_8|CBF_Y_7|CBF_Y_6|CBF_Y_3|CBF_Y_2|CBF_Y_5|CBF_Y_4|CBF_Y_1|CBF_Y_0|CBF_Y_DC

We can clearly see how many operations the reference software performs just to pack the bits in an appropriate order. We can see similar C code throughout the reference software. Thus, it is possible that an optimized H.264 C code for a particular profile and level may be 50 to 100 times faster than the reference software, because the latter is not written from a cycle optimization point of view.

Now, let us handle this and bring the cycle cost from a few thousand to 20 or less. (Note: This does not include the core CABAC symbol decoding function, to perform this we require additional 20 or more cycles. See Section 5.5 for more detail.) Instead of using a single path for decoding different blocks' *coded_block_flag*, if we handle different coefficient block types (e.g., luma DC, luma_AC_4×4, Chroma_Cb_DC) with different function codes, it is possible to derive neighbor information and to store the *coded_block_flag* information without so many condition checks and jumps. This is illustrated in Figure 14.29(b) with the sphere implementation. In this implementation, we handle different blocks with separate codes and avoid all the condition checks.

For example, if we want to decode the *coded_block_ flag* for the third 4×4 block of luma AC (i.e., with inverse raster scan index equal to 2 in Figure 14.28), we know everything about that block (i.e., its left 4×4 block neighbor is from the previous macroblock with inverse raster scan order index 7, its up neighbor's 4×4 block is from the current macroblock with inverse raster scan order index 0, its bit position for packing *coded_block_flag* is 5) without performing any condition checks and jumps. So, we use less than 20 cycles to choose the appropriate context model look-up table, to get the offset for that table from the information of *coded_block_ flag* of the neighbor blocks and to pack the decoded *coded_block_flag* information.

Once we decode the *coded_block_ flag* for the present data block, it directs us whether to proceed to decode the coefficients or to skip that data block since no residual coefficients are present and proceed to the next block. If we decode *coded_block_flag* as bit 0 for the current block, we skip that block; otherwise, we proceed to decode the coefficients by first computing the significance map of the coefficients and then the significant coefficients and their sign information.

Significance Map Decoding

The H.264 CABAC uses significance map coding instead of run-length coding to code the position of non-zero coefficients. In the decoder, the significance map is decoded before the actual coefficient values. The pseudocode for decoding the significance map is given in Pcode 14.6. The significance map decoding algorithm can be understood as follows: first, we enter into this block because the *coded_block_ flag* said that there are non-zero coefficients (but it didn't say anything about their positions and how many of these coefficients are present). The significance map algorithm assumes that there are coefficients in the current block and decodes their position by decoding conditionally two flags, *map_ flag* and *last_ flag*, in a loop (the loop count is given by the maximum number of coefficients in that block (e.g., 16 for luma DC or *Intra*_4×4, 15 for *Intra*_16×16, 4 for chroma DC, 3 for chroma AC) for each non-zero coefficient position. If the *map_flag* is decoded as bit 1, then check it for any further coefficients by decoding *last_ flag*; otherwise, it assumes there are still non-zero coefficients in the block and continues the loop by decoding *map_ flag* for the next coefficient position. One important thing here is that whatever way we optimize, there will be at least one jump in the process (except when all block coefficients are non-zero). Jumps are costly on deep-pipeline processors such as the reference embedded processor (see Appendix A on the companion website).

```
coeff_pos = -1; coeff_ctr = 0
ctx1 = &map_contexts
ctx2 = &last_contexts

loop_start:
        coeff_pos++;
        ctx2++;
        if (decode_symbol(valrng, ctx1)) {
                 ctx2--;
                 store coeff_pos;
                 coeff_ctr++;
                 if (decode_symbol(valrng,ctx2)) jump sig_map_exit;
        }
        ctx1++;
        ctx2++;
loop_end:

coeff_ctr++;
coeff_pos++;
store coeff_pos;

sig_map_exit:
```

Pcode 14.6: Pseudocode for decoding residual coefficients significance map.

In decoding the significance map, up to 15 different probability models are used for both *map_ flag* and *last_ flag*. Offset increments for the context model look-up tables depend on the scanning position, that is, map_offset($coeff[i]$) = last_offset($coeff[i]$) = i.

Decoding Significant Coefficients

Significance map decoding indicates the location of all coefficients in the array (in the inverse zig-zag scanned order). One such significance map array for *Intra*_4×4 block follows:

0	X	X	0	0	X	X	X	0	0	X	0	0	0	0	0
0	1	2	3	4	5	6	7	8	9	10	11	12	13	14	15

According to the preceding significance map, there are coefficients at positions 1, 2, 5, 6, 7, and 10. When the significance map says there is a coefficient, it means it is non-zero. It also means that the significance map itself decodes the magnitude of 1 for all non-zero coefficients. In other words, the significance map not only gives the position of non-zero coefficients but also indirectly decodes the minimum coefficient value of 1 (except for the sign). Consequently, the actual significance map array contains 1s and 0s as follows:

0	1	1	0	0	1	1	1	0	0	1	0	0	0	0	0
0	1	2	3	4	5	6	7	8	9	10	11	12	13	14	15

As given in Pcode 14.7, the significant coefficient decoding loop builds (or debinarizes) the coefficient levels if their values are greater than 1. At the beginning, we decode a *one_ flag* with the *one_contexts* probability model, and if the decoded *one_flag* value is 1, then that coefficient magnitude will be greater than 1, and we increment the coefficient value by 1 and proceed to build the coefficient value with the **unary_exp_golomb_level_decode**() function using *abs_contexts* probability models. Otherwise, we assume that the coefficient has a value of 1, and proceed to decode its sign information with the **cabac_decode_symbol_equiprob**() function.

```
c1 = 1; c2 = 0;
ctx1 = &one_contexts; ctx2 = &abs_contexts;
loop0_start: 1 to coeff_ctr
    cf = 1; a = min(c1,4);
    if (cabac_decode_symbol (valrng, ctx1[a]){
            cf+= 1;b = min(c2,4); c1 = 0;
            c2++;
            // Below code perform unary_exp_golomb_level_decode() function
            if (cabac_decode_symbol (valrng, ctx2[b]){
                    loop1_start: 1 to 12
                            if (cabac_decode_symbol (valrng, ctx2[b]));
                                    cf+=1;
                            else
                                    jump exp_golomb_eqprob_done;
                    loop1_end:
                    s = 0; k = 0; cf+= 1;
                    while(cabac_decode_symbol_eqprob (valrng)){
                            s += (1<<k);
                            k++;
                    }
                    while(k--){
                            if (cabac_decode_symbol_eqprob (calrng))
                                    s+= (1<<k);
                    }
                    cf+= s;
            }
    }
    else if (c1){
            c1++;
    }

exp_golomb_eqprob_done:
    if (cabac_decode_symbol_eqprob(valrng){
            cf = -cf;
    }
loop0_end:
```

Pcode 14.7: Pseudocode for decoding significant coefficients.

Next, we discuss, and provide an example of, the decoding of a larger coefficient value with the **unary_exp_golomb_level_decode**() or UEGk function. Assume that the coefficient value is 58. We start with a minimum coefficient value of 2 (because when the *one_ flag* is decoded as 1 we increment the coefficient value by 1). Then we decode *abs_ flag* in a loop with a max loop count of 13. We check the value of *abs_ flag* at the beginning of every iteration, and if the decoded *abs_ flag* results in zero, then we terminate the loop; otherwise, we continue it. In our example, as the coefficient value is very large, we complete all loop iterations and update the coefficient value as 15 (i.e., $2+13$). This process is equivalent to the decoding process of truncated unary code.

The rest of the magnitude 43 (i.e., $58-15$) is decoded with k-th order exponential Golomb (EGk) debinarization scheme. Exp-Golomb codes are constructed by a concatenation of a prefix and a suffix codeword. The prefix part is decoded conditionally with the expression $s+=(1<<(k++))$ with an initial $s=k=0$; the suffix part is decoded conditionally with the expression $s+=(1<<(--k))$. The prefix process is repeated as long as the decoded output of **cabac_decode_symbol_equiprob**() function is 1, and the suffix part is repeated as long as $k>0$. (Note: The suffix value is updated in a loop only if **cabac_decode_symbol_equiprob**() function outputs 1; otherwise, the loop is simply continued.) In our example, to get the magnitude of 43, the output flags of **cabac_decode_symbol_equiprob**() function are 1 1 1 1 1 0 (for the prefix part) and 0 1 1 0 0 (for the suffix part). Like in significance map decoding, there are a few unavoidable jumps in this significant coefficient decoding process.

The decoding complexity of CABAC (includes binary symbols decoding using a binary arithmetic coder and the debinarization process to construct syntax elements) is relatively very high when compared to CAVLC. At the end of this section, we provided the cycle cost of H.264 parser+cabac and parser+vlc to implement on the reference embedded processor.

14.4.4 Macroblock Reconstruction

In the previous section, we discussed decoding of macroblock parameters and residual coefficients from the received bitstream using VLC and CABAC. Once the macroblock parameters and residual data are available, we proceed to reconstruct the macroblock pixel data. The basic building blocks of the H.264 macroblock reconstruction process is shown in Figure 14.30. As previously mentioned, the modules of macroblock reconstruction are critical, and their cycle cost is 85 to 90% (which includes residual decoding) of the total video decoder. Thus, the code for these modules is written in low-level language most of the time, and highly optimized to minimize the video decoding cycle cost and to provide headroom for running remaining applications on the processor.

Like previous standards, the H.264 reconstructs the macroblocks by passing the entropy-decoded residual coefficients of 4×4 blocks (which are decoded in the inverse raster scan order as shown in Figure 14.28)

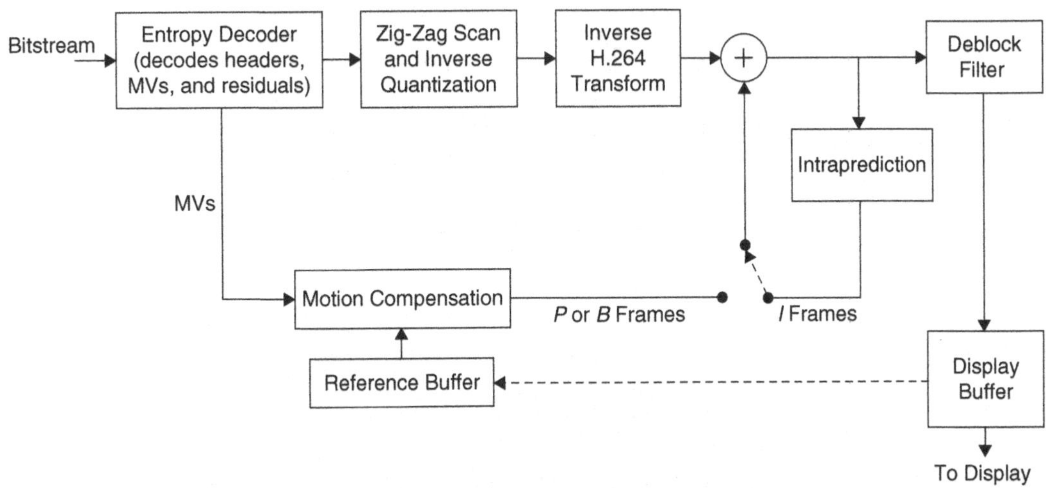

Figure 14.30: Simplified block diagram of the H.264 decoder.

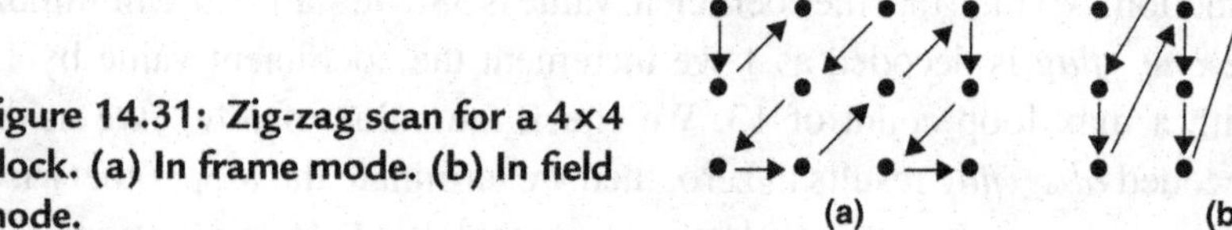

Figure 14.31: Zig-zag scan for a 4×4 block. (a) In frame mode. (b) In field mode.

through a series of block-processing modules that include zig-zag scan, inverse quantizer, inverse transform, intraprediction, or motion compensation and deblocking filter. Next, we briefly discuss these block-processing modules.

Zig-Zag Scan

In the H.264 baseline or main profile, we decode the residual coefficient array for 4×4 blocks. We map this coefficient array to the 4×4 block by using a zig-zag or field scan as shown in Figure 14.31. The zig-zag scan is used for frame macroblocks and the field scan for field macroblocks. As an example, consider an array[] containing 16 decoded residual coefficients of *Intra*_4×4 luma block:

$$\text{array}[] = \{18, 7, 4, 1, 3, 2, 1, 1, 1, 0, 1, 0, 0, 0, 0, 0\}$$

In the frame mode, this coefficient array is converted to a 4×4 block using zig-zag scan:

18	7	2	1
4	3	1	0
1	1	0	0
0	1	0	0

In the *Intra*_16×16 prediction mode, we decode 16 DC coefficients of 16 4×4 luma blocks. These DC coefficients are placed in 4×4 subblocks by scanning the subblocks in zig-zag scan or field scan order depending on the macroblock frame/field coding mode.

Inverse Quantization

Inverse quantization is performed on the zig-zag scanned block of coefficients. In this process, we basically multiply each coefficient with a quantization value obtained from the precalculated look-up table. The offset for the look-up table is derived from the *mb_qp_delta* parameter decoded in the macroblock layer. For more detail on scaling different types of residual coefficients (i.e., luma DC and AC, and chroma DC and AC), see the H.264 standard (ISO/IEC, 2003).

H.264 Inverse Transform

H.264 uses the following integer transform to transform the dequantized 4×4 AC coefficient block X to the spatial domain 4×4 block x:

$$x = \begin{bmatrix} 1 & 1 & 1 & 1/2 \\ 1 & 1/2 & -1 & -1 \\ 1 & -1/2 & -1 & 1 \\ 1 & -1 & 1 & -1/2 \end{bmatrix} ([X] \cdot [S_i]) \begin{bmatrix} 1 & 1 & 1 & 1 \\ 1 & 1/2 & -1/2 & -1 \\ 1 & -1 & -1 & 1 \\ 1/2 & -1 & 1 & -1/2 \end{bmatrix} \tag{14.1}$$

where the operation symbol $\cdot$ represents the element-wise multiplication of matrix X, with scaling matrix S_i and the elements of S_i given by

$$S_i = \begin{bmatrix} a^2 & ab & a^2 & ab \\ ab & b^2 & ab & b^2 \\ a^2 & ab & a^2 & ab \\ ab & b^2 & ab & b^2 \end{bmatrix}, \quad a = 1/2, b = \sqrt{\frac{2}{5}} \tag{14.2}$$

The scaling of X coefficients with matrix elements of S_i requires one multiplication for every coefficient, which can be absorbed into the quantization process. The rest of the transform can be carried out with integer arithmetic,

```
// horizontal
for(j = 0;j < 4;j++){
    for(i = 0;i < 4;i++)
        d[i]=X[i][j];
    e[0]=d[0]+d[2];
    e[1]=d[0]-d[2];
    e[2]=(d[1]>>1)-d[3];
    e[3]=d[1]+(d[3]>>1);
    for(i = 0;i < 2;i++){
        k = 3-i;
        w[i][j]=e[i]+e[k];
        w[k][j]=e[i]-e[k];
    }
}
// vertical
for(i = 0;i < 4;i++){
    for(j = 0;j < 4;j++)
        d[j]=w[i][j];
    e[0]=(d[0]+d[2]);
    e[1]=(d[0]-d[2]);
    e[2]=(d[1]>>1)-d[3];
    e[3]=d[1]+(d[3]>>1);
    for(j = 0;j < 2;j++){
        k = 3-j;
        x[i][j] = e[j]+e[k];
        x[i][k] = e[j]-e[k];
    }
}
```

Pcode 14.8: Pseudocode for computing H.264 4×4 integer transform.

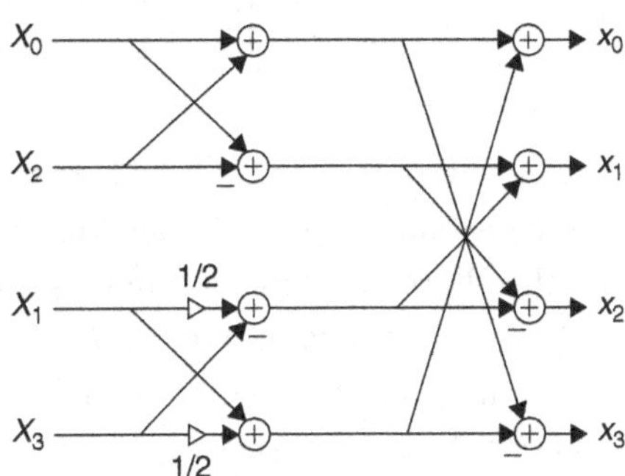

Figure 14.32: Signal-flow diagram of H.264 inverse transform.

using only additions, subtractions, and shifts as illustrated Pcode 14.8. The equivalent signal flow diagram is shown in Figure 14.32.

In the *Intra*_16 × 16 prediction mode, the 4×4 blocks' DC coefficients are separately decoded, zig-zag scanned, and inverse transformed using the Hadamard transform before performing the inverse transform of 4×4 blocks. With an *Intra*_16 × 16-coded macroblock, much of the energy is concentrated in the DC coefficients, and this extra transform helps to decorrelate the 4×4 luma DC coefficients by the encoder. At the decoder, an inverse Hadamard transform is applied as

$$y_{DC} = \begin{bmatrix} 1 & 1 & 1 & 1 \\ 1 & 1 & -1 & -1 \\ 1 & -1 & -1 & 1 \\ 1 & -1 & 1 & -1 \end{bmatrix} [Y_{DC}] \begin{bmatrix} 1 & 1 & 1 & 1 \\ 1 & 1 & -1 & -1 \\ 1 & -1 & -1 & 1 \\ 1 & -1 & 1 & -1 \end{bmatrix} \tag{14.3}$$

The preceding inverse Hadamard transform is carried out with only additions and subtractions as illustrated with the pseudocode given in Pcode 14.9. The inverse Hadamard transform output is properly scaled and inserted into respective DC positions of 4×4 blocks and each 4×4 block of coefficients is then inverse transformed using the inverse H.264 transform given in Equation (14.1).

```
// horizontal
for(j = 0;j < 4;j++){
    for(i = 0;i < 4;i++)
        d[i]=Y_dc[i][j];
    e[0]=d[0]+d[2]; e[1]=d[0]-d[2];
    e[2]=d[1]-d[3]; e[3]=d[1]+d[3];
    for(i = 0;i < 2;i++){
        k = 3-i;
        w[i][j] = e[i]+e[k]; w[k][j] = e[i]-e[k];
    }
}
// vertical
for(i = 0;i < 4;i++){
    for(j = 0;j < 4;j++)
        d[j]=w[i][j];
    e[0]=d[0]+d[2]; e[1]=d[0]-d[2];
    e[2]=d[1]-d[3]; e[3]=d[1]+d[3];
    for(j = 0;j < 2;j++){
        k = 3-j;
        y_dc[i][j] = e[j]+e[k];
        y_dc[i][k] = e[j]-e[k];
    }
}
```

Pcode 14.9: Pseudocode for inverse 4×4 Hadamard transform.

For chroma components, the inverse 2×2 Hadamard transform is applied to all 4×4 chroma block DC coefficients as

$$c_{dc} = \begin{bmatrix} 1 & 1 \\ 1 & -1 \end{bmatrix} [C_{dc}] \begin{bmatrix} 1 & 1 \\ 1 & -1 \end{bmatrix} \tag{14.4}$$

H.264 Intraprediction

In intracoded macroblocks, a predicted block is formed based on the previously decoded and reconstructed blocks, and is added to the IDCT of the residual output to reconstruct the current intracoded block. Two types of intraspatial prediction are defined in the H.264 baseline and main profiles to exploit spatial correlation among pixels in intracoded macroblocks: *4×4 luma prediction* and *full-macroblock prediction* (for 16×16 luma or corresponding chroma block size). Smooth macroblocks containing few details can be predicted more efficiently on a full macroblock basis. This kind of prediction is provided by the full macroblock (16×16) intraprediction mode, whereas the macroblocks with greater detail are predicted using 4×4 intraprediction. There are a total of nine optional prediction modes for each 4×4 luma block, four optional modes for 16×16 luma block, and four optional modes for the chroma component blocks. The encoder typically selects the prediction mode for each block that minimizes the difference between the predicted block and the block to be encoded.

In the 4×4 intraprediction mode, a 16×16 macroblock is divided into 16 4×4 blocks and each 4×4 block is predicted by the adjacent pixels of the decoded neighboring 4×4 blocks as shown in Figure 14.33. DC prediction mode and eight direction modes can be applied to a 4×4 luma block as shown in Figure 14.34. The nine 4×4-block intraprediction modes are named vertical (mode 0), horizontal (mode 1), DC (mode 2), diagonal down-left (mode 3), diagonal down-right (mode 4), vertical-right (mode 5), horizontal-down (mode 6), vertical-left (mode 7), and horizontal-up (mode 8). Different prediction modes can be selected for each of the 16 4×4 blocks in a macroblock.

Given the prediction mode, *PM*, the samples $a, b, c, \ldots, p$ of the current block Q are calculated based on the samples A to M. If any of the neighbor blocks are not available, then the participating pixels of the corresponding blocks are set to the default value as follows:

- $A = B = C = D = 128$ (if up block is not available)
- $E = F = G = H = D$ (if up-right block is not available)
- $I = J = K = L = 128$ (if left block is not available)
- $M = 128$ (if up-left block is not available)

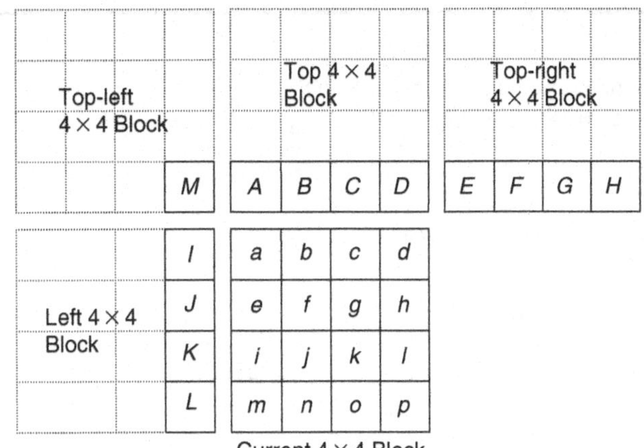

Figure 14.33: Neighboring 4x4 blocks participating in current 4x4 block intraprediction.

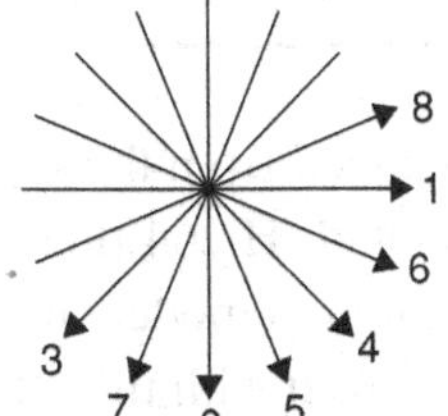

Mode 2: DC
Predicted pixel =
Mean (*A, B, C, D, I, J, K, L*)

Figure 14.34: H.264 luma 4x4 intraprediction modes.

With mode 0 (i.e., vertical), the predicted samples of 4×4 block are obtained as: $a = e = i = m = A$, $b = f = j = n = B$, $c = g = k = o = C$, and $d = h = l = p = D$. In the same way, with mode 1 (i.e., horizontal), the predicted samples of the 4×4 block are obtained as follows: $a = b = c = d = I$, $e = f = g = h = J$, $i = j = k = l = K$, and $m = n = o = p = L$. In mode 2 (i.e., DC prediction), all samples of the 4×4 block are predicted by the mean of samples A to D and I to L. For modes 3 to 8, the predicted samples are obtained from a weighted average of the samples A to M. For example, for mode 5 (i.e., vertical-right), the predicted samples of a 4×4 block are obtained with the pseudocode given in Pcode 14.10. See ISO/IEC (2003) for more detail about other 4×4 luma prediction modes.

```
a = j = (M + A + 1) >> 1;
b = k = (A + B + 1) >> 1;
c = l = (B + C + 1) >> 1;
d = (C + D + 1) >> 1;
e = n = (I + 2*M + A + 2) >> 2;
f = o = (M + 2*A + B + 2) >> 2;
g = p = (A + 2*B + C + 2) >> 2;
h = (B + 2*C + D + 2) >> 2;
i = (M + 2*I + J + 2) >> 2;
m = (I + 2*J + K + 2) >> 2;
```

Pcode 14.10: Pseudocode for predicting pixels of a current block with 4×4 luma vertical-right prediction mode.

In the 16×16 luma (i.e., full macroblock) prediction mode, only one prediction mode is used for the entire macroblock. Four different prediction modes are supported in 16×16 luma prediction: vertical (mode 0), horizontal (mode 1), DC (mode 2), and plane prediction (mode 3). Vertical, horizontal, and DC are similar to the modes of the same names for 4×4 luma prediction, whereas the plane prediction mode uses a linear function between the neighboring samples to the left and to the top in order to predict the current 16×16 block samples. The pseudocode for obtaining the samples using 16×16 luma plane prediction is given in Pcode 14.11.

The chroma samples of a macroblock are predicted using a similar prediction technique as for the luma component in 16×16 luma prediction mode, since chroma is usually smooth over large areas. The same prediction mode is always used for both chroma *Cb* and chroma *Cr* blocks. The four prediction modes are very similar to the 16×16 luma prediction modes except that the order is different. The four intrachroma predictions are; DC (mode 0), horizontal (mode 1), vertical (mode 2), and plane (mode 3).

```
Hz = 0; Vt = 0;
for(i = 1;i < 9;i++){
    Hz += i*(Up_Delay[N+7+i] - Up_Delay[N+7-i]);
    Vt += i*(Left_MB[8+i] - Left_MB[8-i]);
}
Pb=(5*Hz+32)>>6;
Pc=(5*Vt+32)>>6;
Paa=16*(Up_delay[N+15]+Left_MB[15]);
for(j = 0;j < 16;j++){
    Pcc = (j-7)*Pc;
    for(i = 0;i < 16;i++){
        Pbb = (i-7)*Pb;
        Pd = min((Paa + Pbb + Pcc + 16)>>5, 255);   // clip between 0 and 255
        d[16*j+i]=max(0,Pd);
    }
}
```

Pcode 14.11: Pseudocode for predicting samples using 16×16 luma plane prediction mode.

As discussed, the prediction mode information is decoded from the bitstream in the macroblock layer. Since the neighbor block prediction modes are highly correlated, H.264 does not encode the 4×4 luma prediction modes as it is; instead it encodes the most probable prediction mode with side information. This means that the actual 4×4 luma prediction modes at the decoder are derived with the information decoded from the bitstream. Such predictive coding is not used in encoding/decoding the full macroblock prediction modes (i.e., 16×16 luma or chroma modes) information.

H.264 Motion Compensation

The H.264 standard uses rather advanced and flexible motion estimation and motion compensation agorithms, which make this standard very efficient. It allows both *P* and *B* frames to be used as a reference frame apart from the *I*-frame, then each 8×8 subblock can have its own reference frames, and each 4×4 block of a macroblock can be assigned its own motion vector. Motion vectors can be defined with quarter-pixel accuracy, which increases the efficiency of the motion compensation. Finally, it allows weighted prediction: when samples from different frames are combined in a certain proportion with weighting coefficients, it also can improve video coding efficiency.

Assume that we have motion vectors and reference frame numbers for a certain block of data (its size and shape can be any 4×4, 4×8, 8×4, 8×16, 16×8, and 16×16 block, as shown in Figure 14.35). Because reference frames are usually stored in L3 memory and should be moved for processing into L1 memory by the DMA, we first have to find the size and position of the block of data to be moved by the DMA, and if DMA has limitations—for instance, it can work only on 16- or 32-bit addresses—then we have to perform calculations to properly organize the DMA transfer and then use some adjustments when retrieving the samples from the buffer in L1 memory where they were written by the DMA. Here we do not explore details of this mechanism, but rather describe the basic motion compensation algorithm.

If motion vectors are integer, there are no calculations—we just use the samples from the buffer where samples from the reference frame are located; it is the fine resolution of the motion vectors (one-quarter sample) that makes the algorithm computationally intensive. According to the standard, the samples at fractional (i.e., half

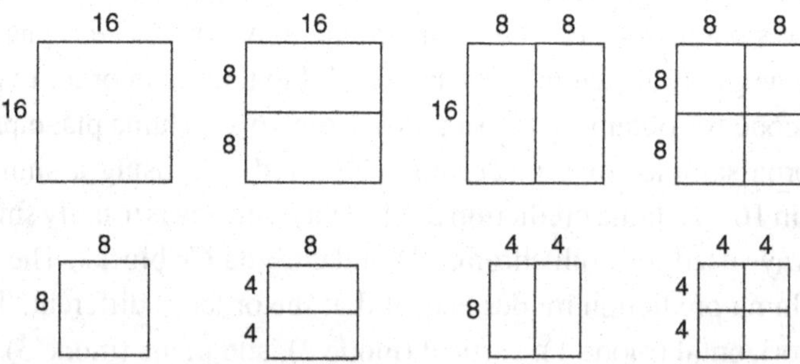

Figure 14.35: Subblock partitioning for motion compensation.

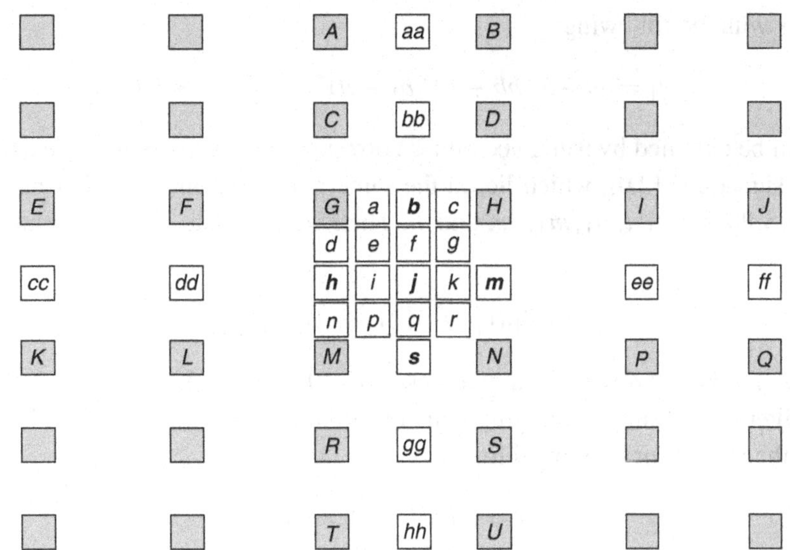

Figure 14.36: Integer samples (shaded blocks with uppercase letters) and fractional sample positions (unshaded blocks with lowercase letters for quarter sample and with bold lowercase letters for half-sample) for quarter-sample luma interpolation.

and quarter) sample positions are obtained using a 6-tap FIR filter, which closely approximates a 2D Wiener filter—an optimal low-pass filter in this situation—because a simple bilinear filter was found to be inadequate to combat aliasing introduced by the filtering process. According to the standard, in the worst case we have to perform 2D filtering of the original samples with the 6-tap filter with coefficients $(1, -5, 20, 20, -5, 1)$—this amounts to, roughly speaking, $35 = 5 * 7$ multiply-add instructions, five such instructions for every 1D filtering, and seven such computations to get the final result. The algorithm is illustrated in Figure 14.36.

It is convenient to introduce a "sample signature," which is a vector of fractional parts of horizontal and vertical components of the motion vector, x and y, and multiplied by 4 to get integer indices (i.e., the decoded motion vector is in $Q14.2$ format):

$$sig = [4 * \text{fract}(x), 4 * \text{fract}(y)].$$

First, the interpolation for half-sample positions (bold lower case letters $\boldsymbol{b, h, j, m, s}$) is defined. Sample $\boldsymbol{b}$ has signature [2,0]—it is located exactly between integer samples G and H on the horizontal line containing integer samples E, F, G, H, I, J, and is obtained by first applying our 6-tap filter to get the intermediate value

$$b_1 = E - 5 * F + 20 * G + 20 * H - 5 * I + J \tag{14.5}$$

and then rounding up, normalizing, and clipping the result between 0 and 255:

$$\boldsymbol{b} = \text{Clip}((b_1 + 16) >> 5, 0, 255) \tag{14.6}$$

Correspondingly, sample $\boldsymbol{h}$ with the signature [0,2], located between integer samples G and M on the vertical line containing integer samples A, C, G, M, R, T, is obtained in the same way from these samples:

$$h_1 = A - 5 * C + 20 * G + 20 * M - 5 * R + T \tag{14.7}$$

$$\boldsymbol{h} = \text{Clip}((h_1 + 16) >> 5, 0, 255) \tag{14.8}$$

So samples $\boldsymbol{b}$ and $\boldsymbol{h}$ are calculated with a 1D 6-tap filter.

To get sample $\boldsymbol{j}$, in which both coordinates are fractional—half-samples (signature [2,2])—we have to perform 2D filtering. First, we calculate six values corresponding to the preliminary results of 1D filtering for samples with the signatures [0,2], which lie on the same vertical line as $\boldsymbol{j}$, but have integer horizontal coordinates—namely, values aa, bb, b_1, s_1, gg, and hh. To do this, we need to apply the 6-tap filter six times (2D filtering), and then filter these values with the following:

$$j_1 = aa - 5 * bb + 20 * b_1 + 20 * s_1 - 5 * gg + hh \tag{14.9}$$

The same result can be obtained by using six values corresponding to the preliminary results of 1D filtering for samples with the signatures [2,0], which lie on the same horizontal line as j but have vertical horizontal coordinates—namely, values *cc*, *dd*, h_1, m_1, *ee*, and *ff*. Then we calculate the final result—round, normalize, and clip j_1:

$$j = \text{Clip}((j_1 + 512) >> 10, 0, 255) \tag{14.10}$$

The samples a, c, d, n, f, i, k, and q with the signatures [0,1], [0,3], [1,0], [3,0], [1,2], [2,1], [3,2], and [2,3] are obtained by bilinear filtering, or simply averaging with upward rounding of their nearest integer or half-sample–filtered neighbors on the vertical or horizontal line.

$$\begin{aligned} a &= (G + b + 1) >> 1 \\ c &= (H + b + 1) >> 1 \\ d &= (G + h + 1) >> 1 \\ n &= (M + h + 1) >> 1 \\ f &= (b + j + 1) >> 1 \\ i &= (h + j + 1) >> 1 \\ k &= (j + m + 1) >> 1 \\ q &= (j + s + 1) >> 1 \end{aligned} \tag{14.11}$$

The samples at quarter-sample positions e, g, p, and r (their signatures are [1,1], [3,1], [1,3], and [3,3]) are derived by averaging with upward rounding of the two nearest samples at half-sample positions in the diagonal direction:

$$\begin{aligned} e &= (b + h + 1) >> 1 \\ g &= (b + m + 1) >> 1 \\ p &= (h + s + 1) >> 1 \\ r &= (m + s + 1) >> 1 \end{aligned} \tag{14.12}$$

The motion compensation code should handle the algorithm related to the macroblock partition with great flexibility—there are many ways a macroblock can be partitioned from having only one motion vector for the whole macroblock and up to 16 pairs of motion vectors for every 4×4 block (see Figure 14.37). Each motion vector must be coded and transmitted, and the choice of partitions must be encoded in the compressed bitstream. With large partition sizes, we will have less motion vectors and require fewer bits for representing the motion vectors. However, the residual error will be large with a large block partition, so we need more bits to code the residual error. The opposite situation occurs when partition sizes are smaller. Typically, we use smaller partitions

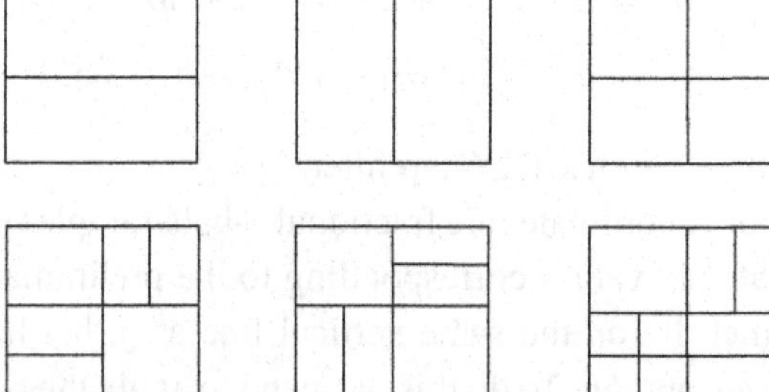

Figure 14.37: Selected possible macroblock partitions.

to accommodate fast motion of objects in the video. After the structure of the current macroblock is decoded and the total number of partitions is found, the algorithm works in the loop-over partitions.

First, DMA transfers for all partitions should be set up. This is a somewhat complicated procedure, which, for every partition, should calculate all geometry, and indicate whether samples should be copied after the DMA (if the motion vector comes close to the frame boundary or even out of the boundary, we have to copy samples on the boundary to run the filter). About 40 parameters per partition should be calculated.

After this we can start the motion compensation loop over the partitions. In the loop, we first should wait for a signal that DMA for this partition is completed, and then calculate the results of the motion compensation for one or two motion vectors, and if there were two, combine the results either by averaging with rounding up, which is default for weighted prediction, or by mixing the results with the given weights.

The main goal and challenge of this code is to use all the power of the reference processor and to work on two 16-bit samples in parallel. The complexity of the code lies not in the implementation of basic 6-tap filter operation, but in the proper organization of the pointer and data access to run the filter smoothly.

To perform 2D filters efficiently, we work on whole partitions, creating a special buffer with w intermediate results. In the worst case (j samples), the buffer size for the 4×4 partition is 9×4 so we have to run 36 1D filters, and then one more 1D filter and averaging per one motion vector. If we have two motion vectors for this block, we should calculate predicted samples with both vectors and then average them with rounding up if there is no weighing or combine them with weighing coefficients with rounding according to the standard. Thus, the worst case requires 37 basic 6-tap filtering operations per 16 samples.

To efficiently implement such an algorithm with many branches, we have to create a table with pointers to functions that will be called for different motion vectors' fractional signatures. There are 16 major cases, but to make our calculation faster, we have to create 48 functions for three possible block width values—4, 8, and 16.

Fortunately, motion vector statistics show that most of the time we have integer motion vectors, and on average, around four partitions and six motion vectors. Including all the overhead related to organizing calculations on the upper level—setting all pointers and so on—motion compensation can take an average of 15 to 20 cycles per pixel for luma samples.

In Pcodes 14.12 and 14.13, the pseudocode to perform the motion compensation filter for sample j (refer to Figure 14.36) is presented. In the same manner, a set of functions for all 16 cases can be created.

```
void get_luma_h1(short * dma_addr, short * res_addr, int dma_stride,
          int filt_height, int filt_width)
{
       int x, y;
       short * refp, h1;

       for(y = 0; y < filt_height; y++) {
            for(x = 0; x < filt_width; x++) {
                   refp = dma_addr + x;
                   h1 = 1 * (refp [0*dma_stride] + refp [5*dma_stride])
                         - 5 * (refp [1*dma_stride] + refp [4*dma_stride])
                         + 20 * (refp [2*dma_stride] + refp [3*dma_stride]);
                   res_addr[x] = h1;
            }
            dma_addr += dma_stride;
            res_addr += filt_width;
       }

}
```

Pcode 14.12: Pseudocode for computing h_1 with 6-tap filter.

Since the chroma components (Cb and Cr) of a macroblock have half the horizontal and vertical resolution (assuming 4:2:0 sampling) as that of the luma component, the same block partition with exactly half the resolution (i.e., luma 16×8 partition size corresponds to chroma 8×4 partition size) applies to chroma. The horizontal and vertical components of each motion vector are halved when applied to the chroma blocks. With this, the motion

```
void get_luma_j(short * dma_addr,        // start for DMA output buffer
     short * temp_addr,                  // store intermediate result here
     unsigned char * mb_part_addr, // store the result here
          int dma_stride,                // 10 or 12 for width 4, etc.
     int part_height,
     int part_width)
{
    int mb_part_stride = 16 - part_width;
    int filt_width = part_width + 5;
    int filt_height = part_height;
    int x, y, j1, j2;
    unsigned char j;

    get_luma_h1(dma_addr, temp_addr, dma_stride, filt_height, filt_width);

    for(y = 0; y < part_height; y++) {
         for(x = 0; x < part_width; x++) {
              j1 = 1 * (temp_addr[x] + temp_addr[x+5])
              - 5 * (temp_addr[x+1] + temp_addr[x+4])
              + 20 * (temp_addr[x+2] + temp_addr[x+3]);
              j2 = (j1+512)>>10;
              j = clip (j2,0,255);
              * mb_part_addr++ = j;
         }
         mb_part_addr += mb_part_stride;
         temp_addr += filt_width;
    }
}
```

Pcode 14.13: Pseudocode to calculate pixel *j* using multiple 6-tap filters.

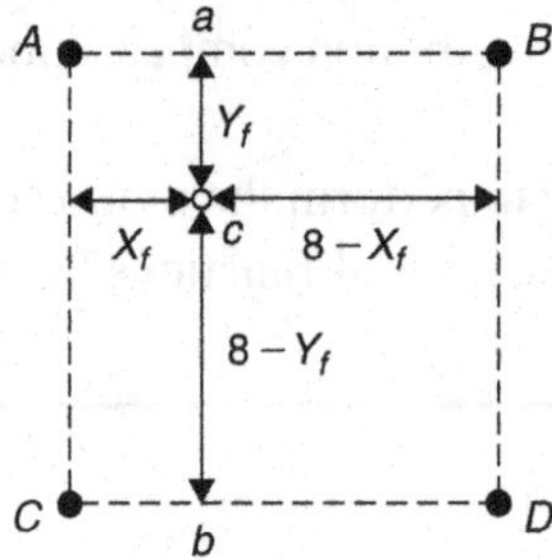

Figure 14.38: Fractional sample position dependent variables in chroma interpolation and surrounding integer position samples *A*, *B*, *C*, and *D*.

vector for chroma components has one-eighth resolution (i.e., it will be in $Q13.3$ format). Motion compensation for chroma samples is much easier—it uses bilinear 2D interpolation as shown in Figure 14.38.

Given the chroma samples A, B, C, and D at full-sample locations, the filtered chroma sample value c is obtained as follows:

$$a = A^* (8 - X_f) + B^* X_f \quad (14.13a)$$

$$b = C^* (8 - X_f) + D^* X_f \quad (14.13b)$$

$$c = (a^* (8 - Y_f) + b^* Y_f + 32) >> 6 \quad (14.13c)$$

H.264 Deblocking Filter

The need for this filter arises from the fact that blocking artifacts are inherent in the video coding because it is essentially block-based: first, the discrete cosine transform coding and decoding is performed on blocks of the size 4 * 4 or 8 * 8, and second, motion compensation is also based on blocks of the size from 4 * 4 to 16 * 16 (or the entire macroblock). In such cases, using the deblocking filter reduces the blockiness introduced in a decoded picture. The deblock filter smoothes block edges, improving the appearance of decoded video frames. An example of a decoded video frame without and with a deblocking filter is shown in Figures 14.39 and 14.40,

Figure 14.39: Decoded video before filtering with deblock filter.

Figure 14.40: Decoded video after filtering with deblock filter.

respectively. Considering the region highlighted with the dashed circle, the blockiness is clearly visible in the decoded video in the absence of deblock filter. This blockiness disappears in that region after filtering the decoded video appropriately. Recent video coding standards (e.g., MPEG-4, WMV9, H.264), specify deblock filtering for reconstructed video frames. Various standards perform deblock filtering slightly differently. In this section, we discuss the H.264 deblock filter and its complexity.

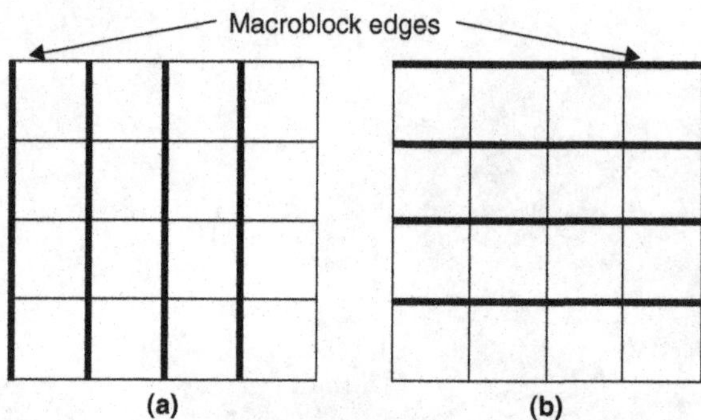

Figure 14.41: Deblock filtering on luma blocks of frame pictures.

One of the powerful features of the H.264 video coding standard is its deblocking filter, which is done not as a post-processing step but inside the coding loop. This filtered frame is used by the motion compensation modules for future frame reconstruction. Although the intracoded macroblocks are filtered using a deblock filter, intraprediction is carried out using unfiltered reconstructed macroblocks to form the prediction.

The H.264 deblock filter is rather complex because it is highly adaptive (i.e., it adjusts its strength depending on the compression mode of the macroblock, quantization parameter, motion vector, frame or field coding decision, and the pixel values) on both the edge and sample levels, so it accounts for 30 to 40% of total H.264 decoder complexity. Therefore, the code for the filter needs to be highly optimized to fit in real-time processing.

The filter operates on a macroblock-by-macroblock basis as follows: first, all four vertical edges and then all four horizontal edges are filtered in the order of increasing macroblock addresses (in a basic case, just in the raster order).

Luma filtering is illustrated in the simple case of frame pictures as shown in Figure 14.41. In the so-called adaptive frame-field mode, the filter is somewhat more complicated. In this case, each full macroblock edge filter is further subdivided into four smaller edges of the 4×4 blocks.

To filter macroblock edges, samples from neighboring macroblock have to be available—left neighbor when filtering left-most vertical edge and top neighbor when doing the upper horizontal edge. There are several parameters that control adaptive filtering. On the block edge level, for every edge between 4×4 blocks, a special parameter of boundary strength (BS) is assigned an integer value from 1 to 4 as follows:

- BS = 4 if the edge is macroblock edge and one of the macroblocks is intracoded (i.e., intraprediction is used to obtain the macroblock samples, not motion compensation)
- BS = 3 for inner edges of the intracoded macroblock
- BS = 2 if macroblock is not intracoded, and one of the blocks on either side of the edge has coded residual coefficients
- BS = 1 if the blocks motion vectors or reference frames that are used in the motion compensation are different

If none of the previous conditions is true, BS = 0 or, simply speaking, there is no filtering for this edge. The choice of filtering outcome depends on the BS and on the gradient of image samples across the boundary. Based on the value of the BS parameter, the decision is made about which filter to use: when BS = 4, the strongest 5-tap filter is used; in all other instances, less strong 4-tap filters are used.

There are two more edge-level parameters, α and β, that are tabulated functions of the quantization parameter (QP) of the macroblock (or rounded average of these parameters for two neighboring macroblocks when filtering macroblock edges) and global adaptive parameters (offsets of the QP). In brief,

$$\alpha = \alpha(Index_A), Index_A = \text{Min}(\text{Max}(0, \text{QP} + Offset_A), 51) \tag{14.14a}$$

$$\beta = \beta(Index_B), Index_B = \text{Min}(\text{Max}(0, \text{QP} + Offset_B), 51) \tag{14.14b}$$

where 51 is the maximum of QP value. They are used on the sample level where the actual filtering work is done. When QP is small, anything other than a very small gradient across the boundary is likely due to image features that should be preserved and so the thresholds α and β are low. When QP is larger, blocking distortion is likely to be more significant and α and β are higher so that more boundary samples are filtered.

The values of α and β are constant for all inner edges, but can be different for macroblock edges because an average QP of two macroblocks can be different. Finally, there is a clipping parameter tc_0, which is a tabulated function of BS and $Index_A$:

$$tc_0 = \text{tc}(Index_A, \text{BS}) \tag{14.15}$$

which also should be calculated for every block edge. Before starting the actual filtering, some work should be done that already requires some effort. Having all these parameters calculated for an edge, we start working on the sample level.

On every block edge we have to filter four lines across the edge, and every line includes up to 8 pixels participating in the filtering process, which we denote as p_0, p_1, p_2, p_3, and q_0, q_1, q_2, q_3, with the numbering starting from the edge boundary (see Figure 14.42).

First, all three filtering conditions should be satisfied to start filtering these samples:

$$\text{abs}(p_0 - q_0) < \alpha, \text{abs}(p_1 - p_0) < \beta, \text{abs}(q_1 - q_0) < \beta \tag{14.16}$$

These conditions ensure that gradients of the pixel values are limited by the adaptive (dependent on the QP) parameters α and β. For BS < 4, the filtering is defined in the following way. Two more threshold variables—$a_p = \text{abs}(p_2 - p_0)$ and $a_q = \text{abs}(q_2 - q_0)$—are used to calculate Boolean variables $b_p = a_p < \beta$ and $b_q = a_q < \beta$, and the clipping variable

$$tc_{pq} = tc_0 + b_p + b_q \tag{14.17}$$

Then the "filtering step," parameter D, is calculated:

$$D = (((q_0 - p_0) << 2) + (p_1 - q_1) + 4) >> 3 \tag{14.18}$$

D is clipped between $-tc_{pq}$ and $+tc_{pq}$

$$D = \text{clip}(D, -tc_{pq}, tc_{pq}) \tag{14.19}$$

where clipping is defined as

$$\text{clip}(D, \text{low}, \text{high}) = \min(\max(D, \text{low}), \text{high}). \tag{14.20}$$

Finally, the filtered samples p_0' and q_0', clipped between 0 and 255, are obtained as follows:

$$p_0' = \text{clip}(p_0 + D, 0, 255), q_0' = \text{clip}(q_0 - D, 0, 255) \tag{14.21}$$

To find whether we need to modify samples p_1 and q_1, we have to calculate if the conditions on the sample differences hold: $\text{abs}(p_2 - p_0) < \beta$ (or p condition), and correspondingly, $\text{abs}(q_2 - q_0) < \beta$ (or q condition). If, say, p condition is true, "filtering step" D_p is calculated as follows:

$$D_p = (p_2 + (p_0 + q_0 + 1) >> 1) - 2p_1) >> 1 \tag{14.22}$$

Then it is clipped using the original clipping variable tc_0,

$$D_p' = \text{clip}(D_p, -tc_0, tc_0) \tag{14.23}$$

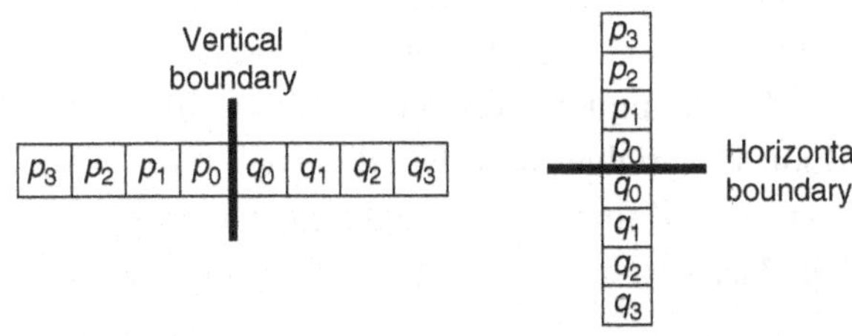

Figure 14.42: Location of pixels participating in vertical and horizontal edge filtering.

Finally, we have the result of filtering:

$$p_1' = p_1 + D_p' \tag{14.24}$$

Without clipping this can be represented after some transformations as

$$p_1' = (p_2 + ((p_0 + q_0 + 1) >> 1) >> 1 \tag{14.25}$$

which corresponds to the relatively strong low-pass impulse response, (1, 0, 0.5, 0.5)/2.

All calculations in the case of BS = 1,2,3 necessary to obtain one or two filtered samples on both sides of the edge are presented in the pseudocode given in Pcode 14.14. For clarity, Boolean variables with names starting from "*b*" are used. For BS = 4, when we filter macroblock edges of *I* macroblocks, strong filtering is done with the pseudocode given in Pcode 14.15.

```
bpq00 = abs(p0 - q0) < α, bp01 = abs(p1 - p0) < β, bq01 = abs(q1 - q0) < β;

if(bpq00 & bp01 & bq01)
{
        bp = abs(p2 - p0) < β, bq = abs(q2 - q0) < β;
        tcpq = tc0 + bp + bq;
        D = (((q0 - p0) << 2) + (p1 - q1) + 4) >> 3;
        D = clip(D, -tcpq, tcpq);
        p0' = clip(p0 + D, 0, 255),      q0' = clip(q0 - D, 0, 255);
        Dp = ((p2 + (p0 + q0 + 1) >> 1) - 2p1) >> 1;
        Dq = ((q2 + (q0 + p0 + 1) >> 1) - 2q1) >> 1;
        Dp1 = clip(Dp, -tc0, tc0), Dq1 = clip(Dq, -tc0, tc0);
        p1' = p1 + bp*Dp1,        q1' = q1 + bq*Dq1;
}
```

Pcode 14.14: Core filtering for boundary strength BS < 4.

```
bpq00 = abs(p0 - q0) < α; bp01 = abs(p1 - p0) < β; bq01 = abs(q1 - q0) < β;
if(bpq00 & bp01 & bq01) {
        bpq = abs(p0 - q0) < (α >> 2) + 2;
        bp = abs(p2 - p0) < β; bq = abs(q2 - q0) < β;
        if(bp & bpq) {
                p0' = (p2 + 2p1 + 2p0 + 2q0 + q1 + 4) >> 3;
                p1' = (p2 + p1 + p0 + q0 + 2) >> 2;
                p2' = (2p3 + 3p2 + p1 + p0 + q0 + 4) >> 3;
        }
        else
                p0' = (2p1 + p0 + q1 + 2) >> 2;
        if(bq & bpq) {
                q0' = (q2 + 2q1 + 2q0 + 2p0 + p1 + 4) >> 3;
                q1' = (q2 + q1 + q0 + p0 + 2) >> 2;
                q2' = (2q3 + 3q2 + q1 + q0 + p0 + 4) >> 3;
        }
        else
                q0' = (2q1 + q0 + p1 + 2) >> 2;
}
```

Pcode 14.15: Strong core filtering for boundary strength BS = 4.

H.264 Deblocking Filter Complexity

A quick estimate shows that to perform all these calculations, more than 40 basic instructions (add, multiply, min, and max) are needed, and the total number of cycles for a simple implementation on a generic processor is about 40. There are many possibilities for optimizing the computations, even when coding in C, but to make this filter suitable for real-time implementation is different for every DSP.

The presence of Boolean variables and the adaptive nature of the filter makes it challenging to attempt to parallelize computations even if there are enough registers to process, say, two lines in parallel, using the fact that a pixel is represented as a 16-bit value and one 32-bit register can hold two pixel values.

Hand-optimized code on the reference embedded processor makes extensive use of parallel and vector instructions (i.e., performed on two 16-bit halves of one 32-bit register independently) and some special organization of handling pointers to optimize information retrieval and storage. For BS < 4, it takes 35 cycles in the loop to filter one line across the block edge and about 40 cycles for the relatively rare case of BS $= 4$. For the entire macroblock, the computational load for only the luma samples follows: filter four lines in each of 32 vertical and horizontal edges of 16 blocks, or 128 lines, which translates to $128 * 35/256 = \sim 18$ cycles per pixel. Chroma filtering is faster and simpler; $2 * 32 = 64$ chroma lines can be filtered in ~5 cycles per pixel. But this is only "core" filtering. If we add all necessary service functions—strength calculation and DMA setup, packing the pixels into 8 bits, and conversion to 4:2:0 format, we will be close to 30 cycles per pixel if all strength values are not zero. In practice, the strength is 0 for many edges and on average, the H.264 loop filter requires about 20 cycles per pixel.

There are other issues related to the output organization in the real-time implementation of the filter when, say, macroblocks are decoded in the raster order; therefore, we should keep two "live" macroblocks, and filter with a time delay of one macroblock because we can complete processing of one macroblock only when its right neighbor is available.

For the same reason, we need to store in the history buffer up to four lines of the top neighbor pixels to filter the top horizontal edge of a macroblock as well as additional information related to the top neighbor—its type, motion vectors, reference frame, coded residuals, and so on—which is necessary to calculate the strength of the top blocks' edges. In our simple ($mbaff = 0$) case, we have to keep 140 bytes per macroblock, so the total size of the history for D1 resolution with a frame width of 45 macroblocks is 6.2 kB.

14.4.5 H.264 Decoder Complexity

We achieve better compression (for a given video quality) with H.264 coding only at the cost of encoding/decoding complexity. Implementation of H.264 coding tools is two to three times more complex when compared to earlier versions of this standard. Next, we provide H.264 bitstream decoding complexity (in terms of cycles and memory) for baseline and main profiles to decode using the reference embedded processor. As the cycles and memory requirements for video decoding depend on frame resolution and bit rate, we provide H.264 decoding complexity here for the D1 resolution video at the bit rate of 1.5 Mbps.

H.264 Baseline Profile: 45 cycles per pixel
- Parser+CAVLC+zig-zag scan: 7 cycles per pixel
- Quant+IDCT: 3 cycles per pixel
- MC/Ipred: 13 cycles per pixel
- Loop filter: 21 cycles per pixel
- Misc: 1 cycle per pixel
- L1 memory (data+program): 64 kB

H.264 Main Profile: 60 cycles per pixel
- Parser+CABAC+zig-zag scan: 21 cycles per pixel
- Quant+IDCT: 3 cycles per pixel
- MC/Ipred: 16 cycles per pixel
- Loop filter: 18 cycles per pixel
- Misc: 2 cycles per pixel
- L1 memory (data+program): 96 kB

14.5 Scalable Video Coding

Scalable video coding (SVC) is a highly attractive solution to problems posed by characteristics of modern video transmission systems. The SVC can be used for various application scenarios such as bandwidth adaptation, content adaptation, and complexity adaptation. For example, as shown in Figure 14.43, a video surveillance application transmits the recorded video to various portable devices, computer monitors, and TVs. The screen

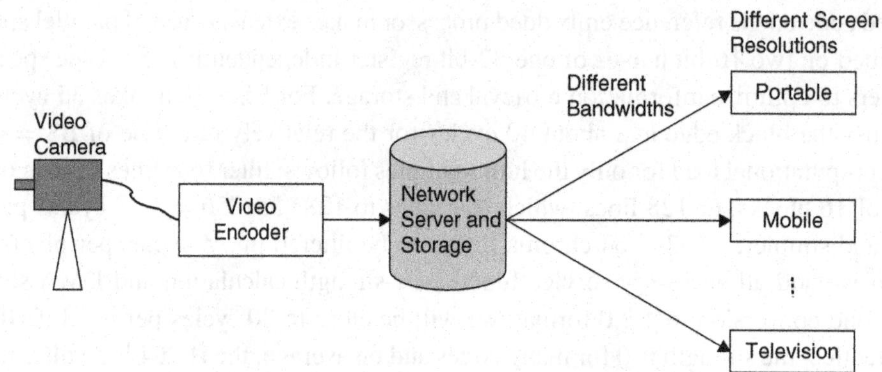

Figure 14.43: Typical video coding application.

resolutions, frame rates, processing power, and receiving bandwidths of the receiving-end devices are very different. In addition, the quality of various transmission channels and networks need not be the same. Given this application scenario, encoding and transmission of the same compressed bitstream on various channels to diverse devices is definitely not an effective solution from a user perception point of view. To serve diverse clients over heterogeneous networks, the SVC allows on-the-fly adaptation in the spatial-temporal and quality dimensions according to network conditions and receiver capabilities.

In principle, the SVC scheme supports an arbitrary number of temporal/spatial/SNR scalability layers and offers scalability at a bitstream level (in other words, SVC allows partial transmission and decoding of a bitstream). Three basic types of video scalability are temporal scalability, spatial scalability, and SNR (or quality) scalability. The SVC scheme for achieving a wide range of spatiotemporal and quality scalability can be classified as a layered video codec. At the encoder, with the scalable coding, we decompose the video into multiple layers of prioritized importance and code layers into base and enhancement bitstreams. At the decoder, progressively combine one or more bitstream layers to produce different levels of video quality. The complexity of the SVC encoding process is determined by the number of spatial, temporal, and quality (SNR) layers that are used for coding. While SVC enjoys flexible bitstream adaptation, it comes with a loss of coding efficiency.

14.5.1 Video Scalability

Spatial Scalability

Assume that we receive a low bit-rate QVGA resolution video and wish to watch the same video on cell phone and HDTV. Since the cell phone's screen resolution is in the range of QVGA to VGA, we can watch the video after proper scaling without many artifacts. However, many staircase artifacts and blurred video (due to smoothing) will be seen when we play the same video clip (with appropriate scaling) on 720p or 1080i HDTV. This is due to video scaling by the end device with a factor of 4 to 6 from a very low to very high frame resolution. The other option is to have a two-layer bitstream—base layer (low-resolution version of video) and enhancement layer (contains the coded difference between up-scaled base layer and original video)—and decoding the layered bitstream and playing the corresponding video on different resolution screens. This allows us to watch the same video clip on two different resolution screens with good perceptual quality.

With spatial scalability, we can transmit video to different screen-resolution end devices with the best possible video quality. Since video is coded at multiple spatial resolutions, the decoded samples of lower resolutions can be used to predict samples of higher resolutions in order to reduce the bit rate in coding higher-resolution frames. Many recent video coding standards support spatial-scalable coding with arbitrary resolution ratios.

Temporal Scalability

Temporal scalability is a technique that allows a single bitstream to support multiple frame rates. Motion compensation dependencies are structured so that complete video frame packets can be dropped from the bitstream. One way to achieve temporal scalability is by using B-frames. Since no I- or P-frames depend on B-frames (from the motion compensation point of view), temporal scalability can be achieved simply by discarding the B-frames without affecting the other frames.

Temporal scalability is typically supported with predetermined temporal prediction structures defined by the standard. Previous video coding standards MPEG-1, MPEG-2 video, H.263, and MPEG-4 visual all support temporal scalability to some degree. For example, in MPEG-2 video, temporal scalability is achieved by the well-known *IBBP* prediction structure. With this, three levels of temporal scalability can be achieved: one-quarter frame rate by discarding two *B*-frames and one *P*-frame, one-half frame rate by discarding two *B*-frames, and three-fourths frame rate by discarding one *B*-frame.

SNR Scalability

With SNR scalability, the bitstream provides the same spatiotemporal resolution as the complete bitstream but with a different quality. SNR scalability is achieved by refining the amplitude resolutions. For example, with two-layer SNR scalable coding, the base layer uses a coarse quantizer, and the enhancement layer applies a finer quantizer to the difference between the original DCT coefficients and the coarsely quantized base-layer coefficients. Here the base and enhancement layers are at the same spatiotemporal resolution.

Combined Scalability

With combined scalability, a bitstream can provide a wide variety of combinations of the previous basic scalability types.

14.5.2 H.264 SVC

Scalability was already available in earlier versions of video coding standards MPEG-2 video, H.263, and MPEG-4 visual in the form of scalable profiles. However, the provision of scalability in terms of picture size and reconstruction quality in these standards comes with considerable growth in decoder complexity and a significant reduction in coding efficiency. These drawbacks are addressed by the new SVC amendment of H.264/AVC standard (JVT, 2007). The original H.264/AVC specification includes the basic features necessary to enable temporal scalability. The new H.264 SVC adds scalability in terms of picture size (spatial scalability) and reconstruction quality (SNR scalability). A simplified H.264 SVC encoder architecture is shown in Figure 14.44. The SVC encodes the video into multiple spatial, temporal and SNR layers for combined scalability. The input video is spatially decimated and interpolated to support multiple spatial resolutions.

In H.264 SVC, different types of scalability are achieved using the following techniques:

- Adaptive interlayer prediction techniques, including intratexture, motion, and residue predictions, are used to exploit correlation among spatial and SNR coding layers (see Figure 14.44). For each spatial layer, prediction

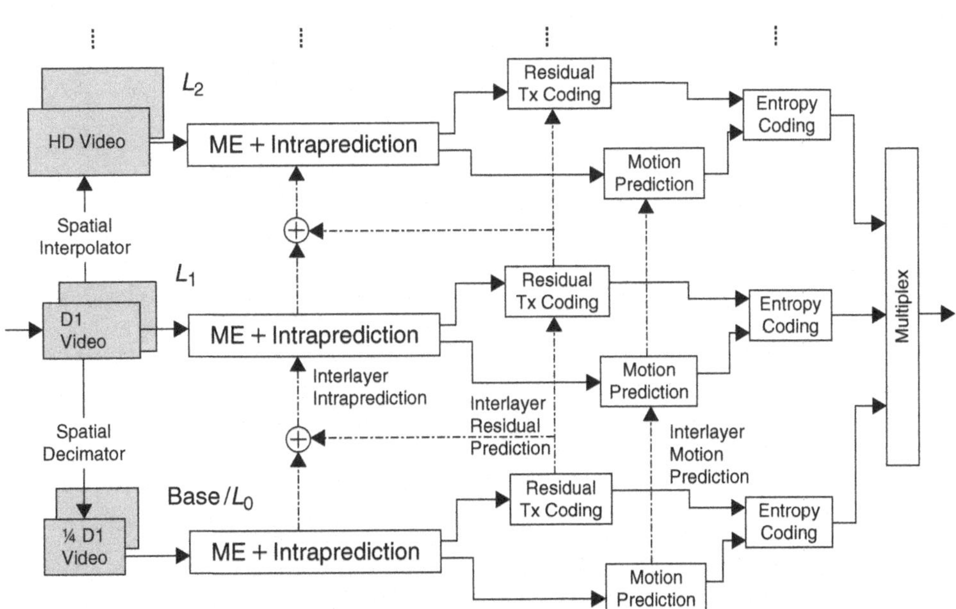

Figure 14.44: Simplified H.264 SVC encoder architecture.

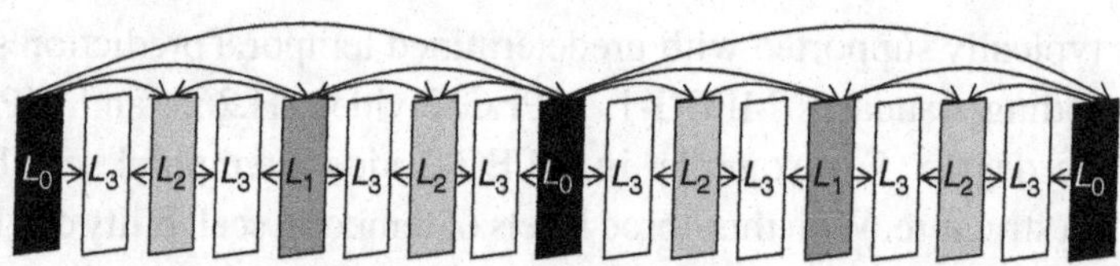

Figure 14.45: Enabling temporal scalability in H.264 AVC with hierarchical *B*-frame structure.

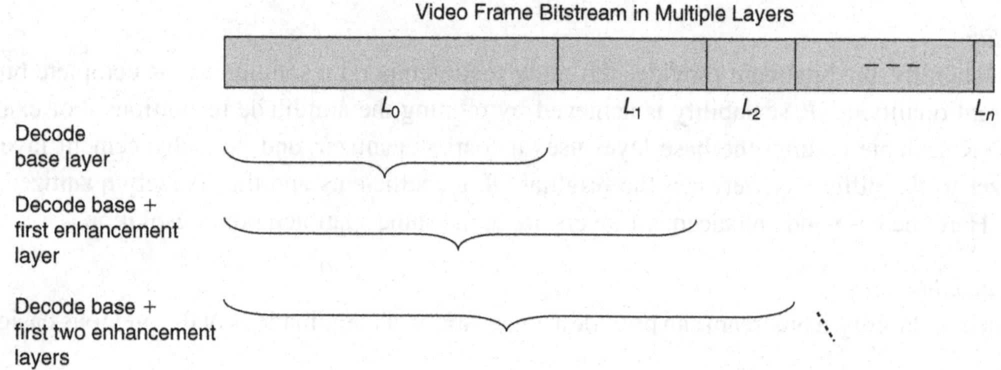

Figure 14.46: Video-frame bitstream with scalable video coding.

comes from either a spatially upsampled lower layer frame or a temporally neighboring frame at the same layer.

- A hierarchical *B*-frame structure is used to support multilevel temporal scalability as shown in Figure 14.45. The enhancement layers are typically coded as *B*-frames. Compared to MPEG-2 *IBBP* structure, the H.264 SVC hierarchical *B*-frame structure has better coding efficiency using more efficient frame-level bit allocation, especially for video sequences with fine texture and regular motion.

The bitstreams from all spatial or SNR layers are then combined to form the final SVC bitstream as shown in Figure 14.46. The number of layers in an SVC bitstream is dependent on the needs of an application. The H.264 SVC supports up to 128 layers in a bitstream. For more description of H.264 SVC, see Schwarz et al. (2007) and JVT (2007).

CHAPTER 15

Video Post-Processing

Video data is often processed after decompression to enhance it in some way before playing it on-screen. This part of video processing is known as video post-processing. The post-processing modules include video scaling, video filtering, video enhancement, alpha blending, gamma correction, and video transcoding, among others. This chapter focuses on selected video post-processing modules and respective simulation techniques.

15.1 Video Quality Measurement

In practice, the quality of processed video data is compared to reference video data. Typically, two approaches are used for comparison: objective measures such as peak-signal-to-noise-ratio (PSNR) and subjective measures such as mean opinion score (MOS). The most common objective metric is the PSNR. After processing the video data, the PSNR is computed as

$$PSNR(\text{dB}) = 20\log_{10}\frac{(2^b-1)}{\sqrt{MSE}} \tag{15.1}$$

where b denotes the number of bits used to represent the pixel. If *R_Video( )* and *P_Video( )* denote the reference video frame and processed video frame, respectively, and M and N denote the height and width of video frames, then the mean square error (MSE) is computed as

$$MSE = \frac{1}{M\times N}\sum_{j=0}^{M-1}\sum_{i=0}^{N-1}\{R\_Video(i,j) - P\_Video(i,j)\}^2 \tag{15.2}$$

In general, individuals have different perceptions of the same video sequence. Thus, there is also a need for subjective perspectives on video quality. Subjective video quality involves a group of people viewing the same video sequences and grading the quality, and an MOS is calculated.

15.2 Video Scaling

Image scaling plays a very important role when we want to work with two display systems of different resolutions (e.g., the resolution of a portable player screen is 320 × 240 whereas an HDTV screen is 1920 × 1080) and when we want to transmit image data on low-bandwidth communication channels such as the Internet. Most of the time image scaling is used to convert low-resolution images to high-resolution images or vice versa. In video applications, apart from changing the resolution, image scaling is also used for changing the aspect ratio (e.g., from 4:3 to 16:9). With the YUV video format, we must scale both luminance and chrominance components separately with the same scaling ratio, as shown in Figure 15.1. In this case, both luminance and chrominance components are scaled using the horizontal scaling (HS) ratio of 2 and vertical scaling (VS) ratio of 3/2.

The core of a video scalar is an interpolator function. The output quality of a video scalar depends on the type of interpolator function used in scaling each video component. The most commonly used interpolators are the bilinear, bicubic, spline, discrete cosine transform (DCT)-based, and Gaussian. High-end interpolators used in video scaling are nonlinear and image model based. In Section 10.7, we discussed a few interpolation

DOI: 10.1016/B978-1-85617-678-1.00015-6

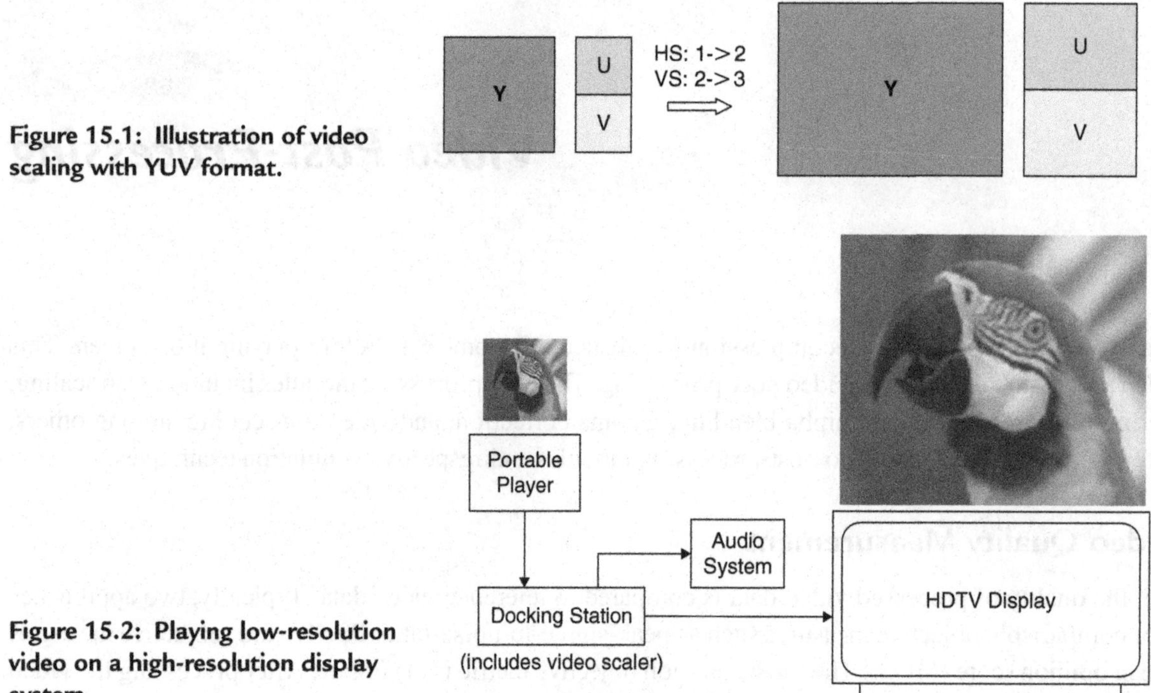

Figure 15.1: Illustration of video scaling with YUV format.

Figure 15.2: Playing low-resolution video on a high-resolution display system.

functions. Image quality was observed after using nearest-neighbor and bilinear interpolators. The nearest-neighbor technique is not used for practical applications, as its output consists of staircase artifacts. The bilinear interpolator is commonly used in many applications for scaling the chrominance component.

In this chapter, we discuss various scaling methods for scaling both luminance and chrominance components. To the human eye, scaling artifacts of chrominance components are imperceptible, whereas intensity scaling artifacts are clearly visible. Thus, different scaling algorithms are used to scale luminance and chrominance components. In Section 15.2.2, we discuss the bicubic interpolator for scaling chrominance components. For scaling luminance components, we must use high-end interpolator functions such as cubic-spline, DCT-based, nonlinear, or model-based interpolators to maintain image quality by preserving edge information and other details of small objects. Depending on the quality requirement and selected embedded processor capabilities, we choose an appropriate scaling method to scale the video frames. There are many other methods in the literature for scaling video frames; discussion of all methods is beyond the scope of this book.

15.2.1 Luminance Scaling

The human eye is very sensitive to luminance (or intensity) component variations. If we use simple interpolators to perform video scaling, the result may be unacceptable quality. For example, if we use a portable player as the video decoding engine and connect it to HDTV to watch a video, as shown in Figure 15.2, the video's quality depends entirely on the type of scalar used. One such scaled image using bilinear interpolator and using a nonlinear interpolator is shown in Figure 15.3. As shown in Figure 15.3(a), the staircase artifacts, which are not present in the original image, pop up when the luminance component of the image was upscaled using the bilinear interpolator. However, these staircase artifacts are not noticeable in the upscaled image using nonlinear interpolator as shown in Figure 15.3(b). In both cases, the chrominance components are scaled using a bilinear interpolator. Next, we discuss various interpolation techniques for scaling the luminance component of images.

Using Cubic B-Spline Interpolation

Spline interpolation is preferred over polynomial interpolation because the interpolation error can be made small even when using lower-degree splines. Many spline functions are proposed in the literature for the purpose of data point interpolation. B-splines (where B stands for basis) are the most widely used in image processing applications. A B-spline is a spline function that has minimal support with respect to a given degree,

(a)

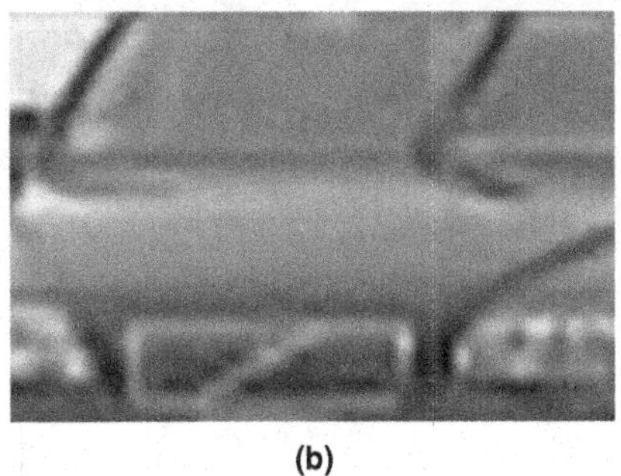
(b)

Figure 15.3: Video scaling. (a) Using bilinear interpolator. (b) Using nonlinear interpolator.

smoothness, and domain partition. Every cardinal spline (which is an actual interpolation function) of a given degree, smoothness and domain partition can be represented as a linear combination of many B-splines of the same degree and smoothness. The computation of cardinal splines involves solving many linear equations; hence, we focus on B-spline approximations for scaling images. B-splines of orders 0 and 1 coincide with the nearest-neighbor and linear interpolation functions, respectively. B-splines of order n can be constructed by a repetitive convolution of the 0-th order B-spline $h_{bs}(x)$ (i.e., nearest-neighbor or rectangle function) with itself:

$$h_{nbs}(x) = h_{bs}(x) * h_{bs}(x) * \cdots * h_{bs}(x), (n+1) \text{ times} \tag{15.3}$$

An explicit expression for n-th order B-spline generation follows:

$$h_{nbs}(x) = \frac{1}{n!} \sum_{k=0}^{n+1} C_k^{n+1} (-1)^k \left\{ \left(x + \frac{n+1}{2} - k \right)^n \right\}_+ \tag{15.4}$$

where C_k^{n+1} are the binomial coefficients, and the function $\{y\}_+$ is defined as

$$\{y\}_+ = \begin{cases} y, & \text{if } y > 0 \\ 0, & \text{otherwise} \end{cases} \tag{15.5}$$

If we substitute $n = 3$ in Equation (15.4), then we obtain the widely used cubic B-splines:

$$h_{cbs}(x) = \frac{1}{6} \left[\{(x+2)^3\}_+ - 4\{(x+1)^3\}_+ + 6\{x^3\}_+ - 4\{(x-1)^3\}_+ + \{(x-2)^3\}_+ \right] \tag{15.6}$$

If we choose two neighboring points on each side of current interpolating pixel position with variable x as the distance between the interpolation and neighboring points, then the interpolation coefficient values for neighboring points using the cubic B-spline approximation function is as follows:

$$h_{cbs}(x) = \begin{cases} \frac{1}{6} \left[|(x+2)^3| - 4|(x+1)^3| + 6|x|^3 \right], & \text{for } 0 \le |x| < 1 \\ \frac{1}{6} \left[|(x+2)^3| - 4|(x+1)^3| + 6|x|^3 - 4|(x-1)^3| \right], & \text{for } 1 \le |x| \le 2 \\ 0, & \text{otherwise} \end{cases} \tag{15.7}$$

or

$$h_{cbs}(x) = \begin{cases} (1/2)|x|^3 - |x|^2 + 2/3, & 0 \le |x| < 1 \\ -(1/6)|x|^3 + |x|^2 - 2|x| + 4/3, & 1 \le |x| \le 2 \\ 0, & \text{otherwise} \end{cases} \tag{15.8}$$

The spatial-frequency characteristics of the cubic B-spline approximation function are shown in Figure 15.4. The stopband characteristics of the cubic B-spline approximation function are far better when compared to

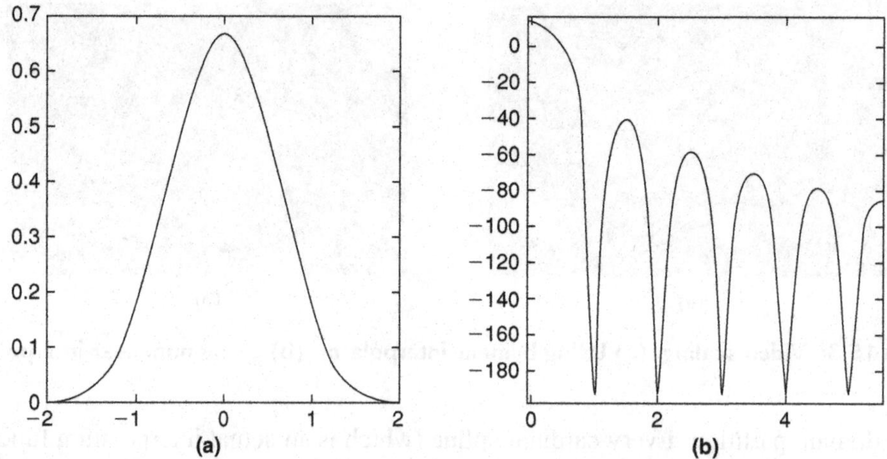

Figure 15.4: Cubic B-spline approximation characteristics. (a) Spatial domain. (b) Frequency domain.

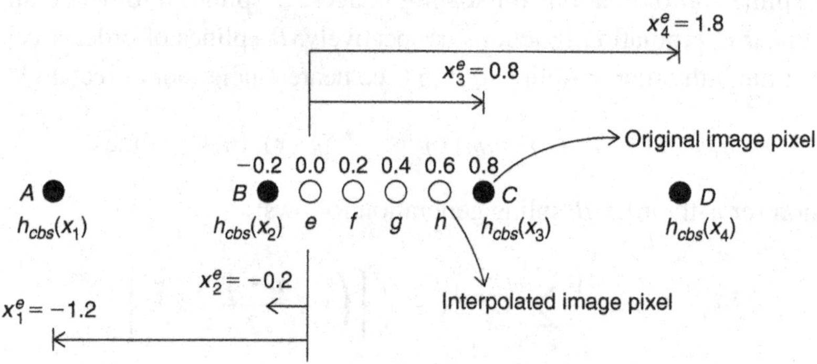

Figure 15.5: Illustration of interpolation coefficients computation.

the stopband characteristics of both nearest-neighbor interpolation and bilinear interpolation functions (see Section 10.7). Computing interpolation coefficients for given interpolating point e with four neighbor points A, B, C, and D and scaling ratio 1:5 is illustrated in Figure 15.5.

The interpolation coefficients for neighboring points A, B, C, and D to compute interpolating points e, f, g, and h are tabulated as follows:

cbs	$A: h_{cbs}(x_1)$	$B: h_{cbs}(x_2)$	$C: h_{cbs}(x_3)$	$D: h_{cbs}(x_4)$
e	0.0853	0.6307	0.2827	0.0013
f	0.0360	0.5387	0.4147	0.0107
g	0.0107	0.4147	0.5387	0.0360
h	0.0013	0.2827	0.6307	0.0853

The superior performance of cubic B-spline approximation-function interpolation compared to bilinear interpolation in scaling the parrot image by a factor of 4 can be seen in Figure 15.6. We hardly see the staircase artifacts after B-spline interpolation.

Using DCT-Based Interpolation

In scaling images at the block level, the 2D-DCT interpolator works as an optimum interpolator in the sense of generating good interpolated points using sinusoidal functions. When the scaling ratio is larger, DCT-based interpolation outperforms bilinear interpolation. It is computationally expensive to achieve arbitrary scaling ratios with DCT interpolation. However, we can always use a combination of DCT and bilinear interpolation functions to efficiently compute interpolated points for arbitrary scaling. One such DCT-based scaling scheme to scale the $n \times m$ block to the $N \times M$ block is shown in Figure 15.7. In DCT scaling, optional frequency-domain enhancement and median filtering modules are shown with dashed rectangles.

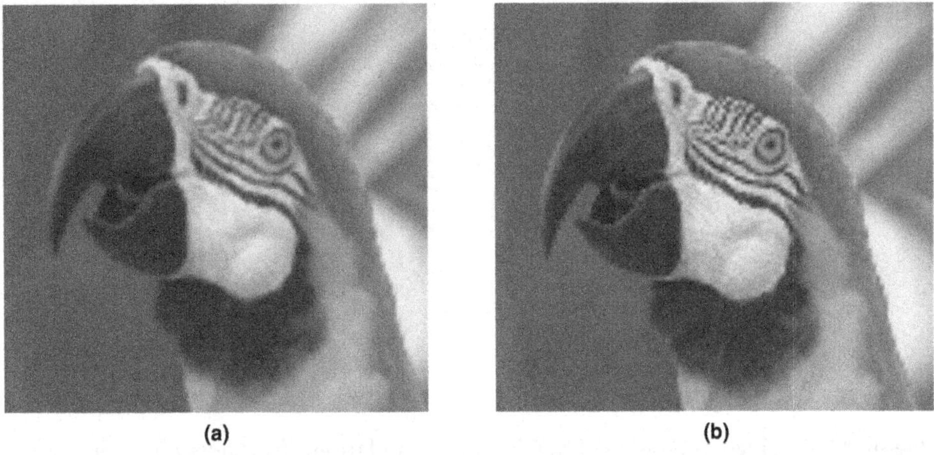

Figure 15.6: Video scaling. (a) With cubic *B*-spline approximation. (b) With bilinear interpolation.

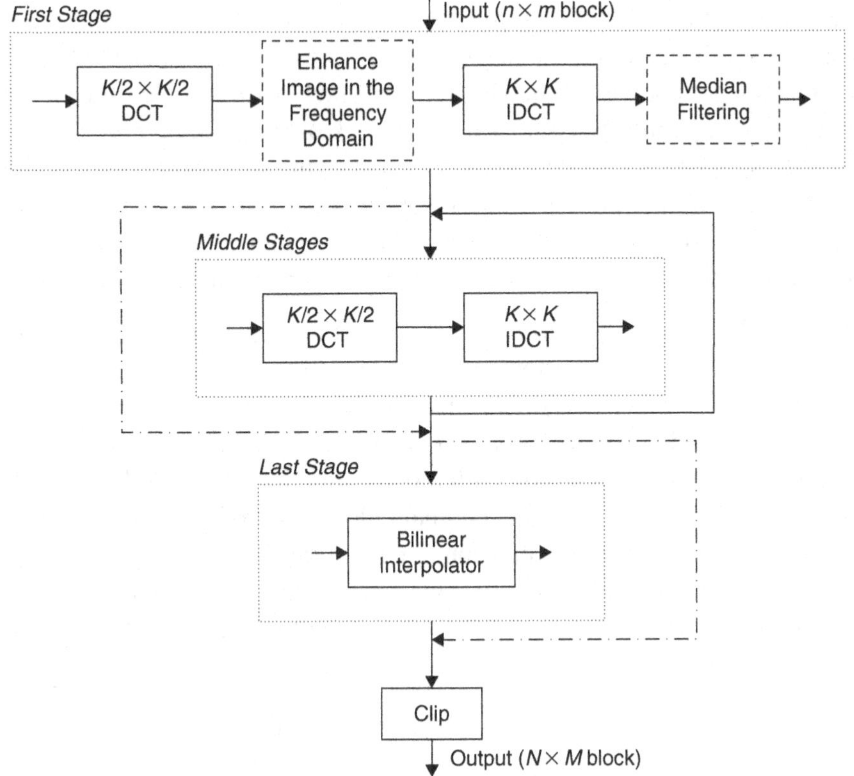

Figure 15.7: Block diagram of DCT-based video scaling.

In DCT-based video scaling, interpolation is achieved by computing the DCT and inverse DCT (IDCT) of video data blocks. Scaling happens only when DCT and IDCT sizes are different. DCT and IDCT are performed multiple times for scaling from $m \times n$ to $M \times N$. The supported scaling ratios with DCT-based interpolation are 2^k. The value of k is a positive integer for upscaling and negative for downscaling. For example, $k = 1$ doubles the image size and $k = -1$ downscales the image size by half in both directions. If we already have DCT data, then we immediately compute IDCT by choosing an appropriate IDCT matrix size for scaling the video frames. Otherwise, we first compute DCT with one of block size 4×4, 8×8, or 16×16 pixels, and then perform IDCT with a different block size to achieve appropriate scaling.

As an example, consider scaling video from QVGA (320×240) to HD (1920×1080) resolution. In this case, the horizontal scaling ratio is 6 and the vertical scaling ratio is 4.5. One way to perform this scaling is by using DCT-based scaling first to get a factor of 4 in both horizontal and vertical directions and then

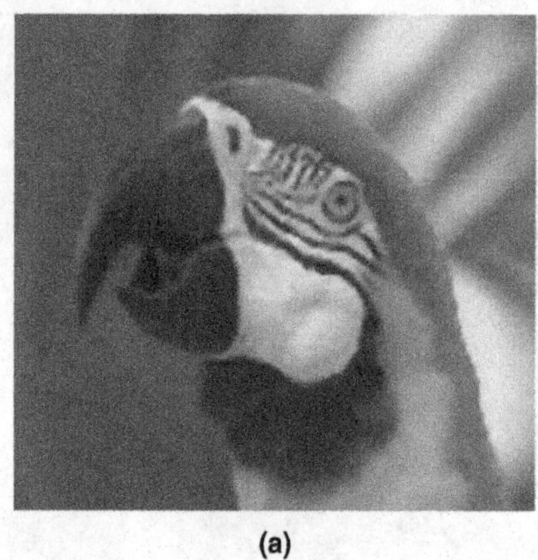

(a)

(b)

Figure 15.8: Video scaling. (a) DCT-based interpolation. (b) Bilinear interpolation.

performing horizontal scaling with factor 3/2 and vertical scaling with factor 9/8 using bilinear interpolation. To get a factor-4 scaling using the DCT-based approach, we perform scaling in two stages with factor-2 scaling as follows. We compute DCT for each 4×4 block of the original image and take the 8×8 IDCT. This scales the 4×4 of the original image to the 8×8 block—let's call this factor-2 scaled image "stage1_image." We repeat the same procedure, computing DCT for each 4×4 block of *stage1_image* and take 8×8 IDCT to form *stage2_image*. Now, *stage2_image* is a factor-4 scaled version of the original image in both the horizontal and vertical directions. Then we perform the rest of the scaling using a bilinear transform to obtain the final resolution of 1920×1080. Video scalar performance with DCT-based interpolation is shown in Figure 15.8(a), and simple bilinear interpolation in Figure 15.8(b); we can see the improved performance of DCT-based scaling.

DCT Scaling and Video Enhancement Apart from improved scaling performance, there are other advantages of DCT-based scaling. We handle transform-domain data in DCT-based scaling, and thus we can also perform filtering (i.e., smoothing or edge enhancement) of the image without much extra computational cost. Filtering with transform-domain data is achieved as follows. As the transform-domain data represents frequency components in the image, we can achieve the image filtering with modification of transform-domain data. Eliminating the high-frequency components in the 4×4 transform domain block and taking the 8×8 IDCT of the remaining coefficients results in a smooth image in the spatial domain. Similarly, boosting high-frequency components in a 4×4 block and taking its 8×8 IDCT results in edge enhancement in the spatial domain. Boosting high-frequency components can be achieved with a simple element-by-element multiplication of the 4×4 DCT block with the following 4×4 matrix elements:

$$IIF = \begin{bmatrix} 0.00 & 0.08 & 0.15 & 0.30 \\ 0.08 & 0.15 & 0.30 & 0.50 \\ 0.15 & 0.30 & 0.50 & 0.80 \\ 0.30 & 0.50 & 0.80 & 1.00 \end{bmatrix} \tag{15.9}$$

Figure 15.9 shows edge sharpening of the spatial-domain image due to high-frequency component boosting in the transform domain. The upscaled image using DCT interpolation with and without edge sharpening is shown in Figure 15.9(a) and (b), respectively.

In the same way, we smooth the image by eliminating the high-frequency content in the 4×4 transform-domain data. For example, say that we obtain $D_{4\times4}$ by taking DCT of a 4×4 pixel block and that the following are DCT coefficients of $D_{4\times4}$.

$$D_{4\times4} = \begin{bmatrix} 27.5 & 14.3 & 6.9 & 2.2 \\ 12.9 & 7.1 & 4.5 & 1.3 \\ 5.2 & 2.9 & 1.6 & 0.9 \\ 2.7 & 1.1 & 0.6 & 0.2 \end{bmatrix}, \quad D^{z}_{4\times4} = \begin{bmatrix} 27.5 & 14.3 & 6.9 & 2.2 \\ 12.9 & 7.1 & 4.5 & 0.0 \\ 5.2 & 2.9 & 0.0 & 0.0 \\ 2.7 & 0.0 & 0.0 & 0.0 \end{bmatrix}$$

(a)

(b)

Figure 15.9: Image sharpening along with scaling using DCT-based interpolation. (a) With boosting of high frequencies. (b) Without boosting of high frequencies.

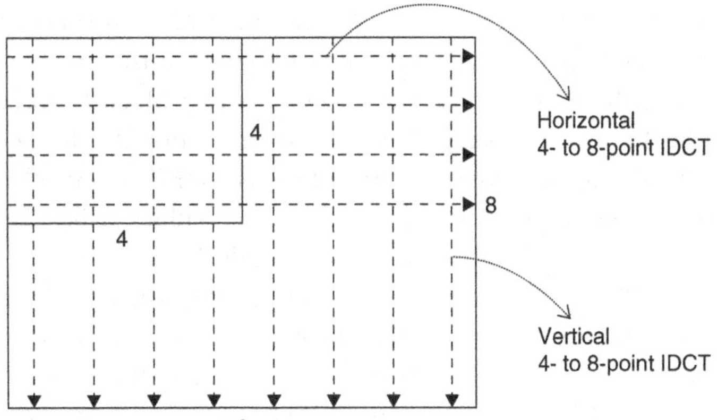

Figure 15.10: Efficient implementation of DCT-based upscaling.

Then we replace six high-frequency components in $D_{4\times4}$ with zeros and form matrix $D^z_{4\times4}$. Computing the 8×8 IDCT of $D^z_{4\times4}$ results in a filtered 8×8 block. In this way, we perform image smoothing without adding extra computations.

Efficient Implementation of DCT-Based Scaling DCT-based scaling involves the computation of DCT and IDCT. We can sometimes use bilinear interpolation along with DCT interpolation to scale the image arbitrarily. Depending on the type of scaling (i.e., up or down), DCT-based scaling can be efficiently implemented using the DCT input and output pruning techniques discussed in Section 7.2. For example, in the case of upscaling, first we compute 4×4 DCT and then 8×8 IDCT. Since we know that 50% of the inputs are not present for the 8-point IDCT, we can use the input-pruned, signal-flow diagram shown in Figure 7.11. As shown in Figure 15.10, computing four 4- to 8-point IDCTs horizontally and eight 4- to 8-point IDCTs vertically results in an 8×8 IDCT of 4×4 block data.

Image downscaling by a factor of 2 in both horizontal and vertical directions involves computing the DCT of the 8×8 spatial-domain block followed by special IDCT computation (of the 8×8 transform domain block) that outputs only 4×4 spatial-domain data. Here we have two options to efficiently implement DCT-based downscaling. In the first option, we use the output pruning technique shown in Figure 7.14 to avoid most of the computations. In the second option, we compute 4×4 IDCT directly, ignoring the high-frequency components. Now, which option is better to perform DCT-based downscaling? It depends on the number of high-frequency DCT coefficients in that particular block. If we have less high-frequency components, then performing 4×4 IDCT avoids many computations. In contrast, if we have more high-frequency components, then we must perform eight 8- to 4-point IDCTs vertically followed by four 8- to 4-point IDCTs horizontally to get better results.

Using Edge-Based Interpolation

The linear interpolator treats all image pixels in the same way during interpolation. Because of this, the scaled output image with the bilinear interpolator may not be very crisp, as its edge information and other small object details are destroyed. If we find the image edges and specifically take care of them during scaling, then the scaled image results look very sharp and crisp. In the absence of edges, the difference between bilinear output and edge-based interpolator output is negligible to the human eye. Therefore, in our scaling algorithm we apply edge-based interpolation whenever we come across edge pixels; otherwise, we use bilinear interpolation to minimize overall scaling computational complexity.

Here we discuss and simulate the edge-based interpolation algorithm presented in Raghupathy et al. (2003). Consider a block of 4×4 pixels as a working block for the edge-based interpolation algorithm. If an edge is in a block of pixels, then the difference between the pixel minimum and maximum values is very large; in the absence of an edge, the difference will be small. For example, as shown in Figure 15.11, the pixel difference in 4×4 blocks 2, 3, 4, and 5 is very large as an edge is passing through them, and the pixel difference in 4×4 blocks 1 and 6 is very small. Now, if we treat all 4×4 blocks in the same way, and scale them by the large factor using bilinear interpolation, then we see staircase artifacts along the edges. Instead, if we scale the pixel blocks 2, 3, 4, and 5 using the edge-based interpolation, scaling artifacts are minimized.

Consider 16 pixels of a 4×4 block as shown in Figure 15.12. We use the criteria of pixel difference in 4×4 blocks to loosely classify whether the current 4×4 block pixels contain an edge. If the pixel difference in the current 4×4 block is less than the threshold, then we treat it as a non-edge block and scale it with bilinear interpolation. Otherwise, we assume that the current block is an edge block, compute all pixel orientations, and scale the 4×4 block using edge-based interpolation if it has a dominant edge orientation. Sometimes we scale edge blocks using bilinear interpolation as well if dominant edge orientation is not found. In any case, we compute all interpolated points in a given 4×4 block using the same interpolation method. Two types of interpolation methods are not applied in any single 4×4 block.

The pixel difference in the 4×4 block determines whether the pixel $P(i, j)$ of a 4×4 block needs edge-oriented interpolation or bilinear interpolation for computing its neighboring pixels a, b, and c by interpolation. If we classify the current 4×4 block as edge oriented, then the orientations of all 4×4 pixels are computed and similarly oriented pixels are grouped. If any group contains more than six pixels with the same orientation, then the current pixel is strictly classified as an edge-oriented pixel and the interpolated pixels a, b, and c for

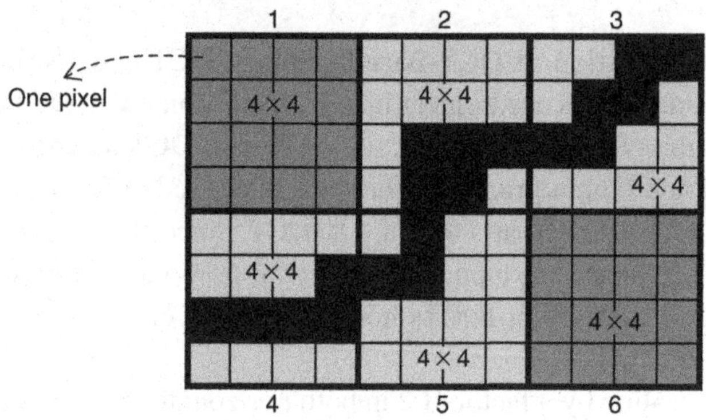

Figure 15.11: Schematic of 4 x 4 pixel blocks with edges.

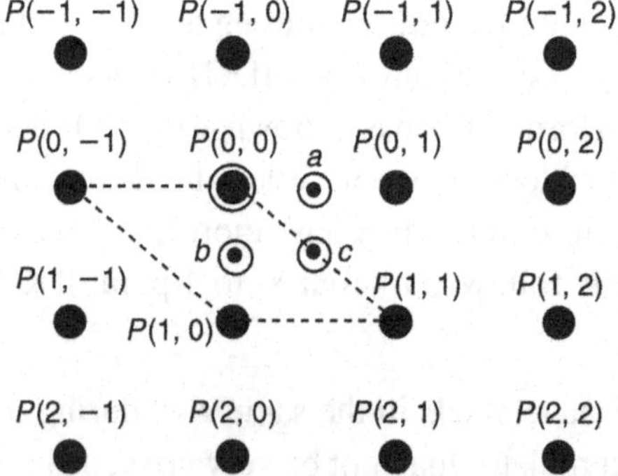

Figure 15.12: Block of 4 x 4 pixels with highlighted actual and interpolated pixels.

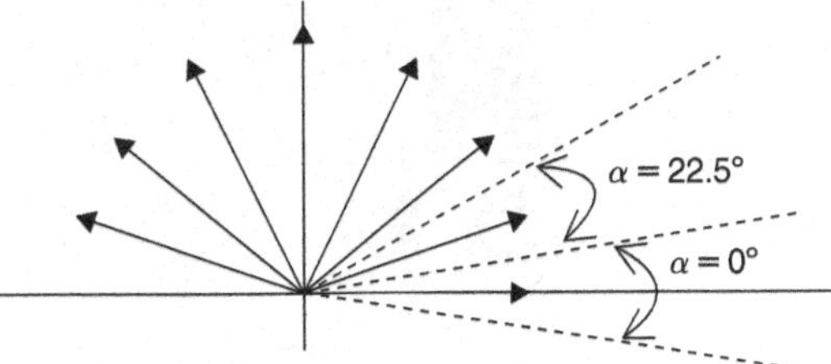

Figure 15.13: Pixel-gradient angle quantization.

the current pixel $P(i, j)$ are obtained with edge-oriented filter interpolation; otherwise, the interpolated pixels (a, b, c) are obtained with bilinear interpolation. *Note*: The edge-based interpolator discussed here is used to scale images by only a factor of 2. The filter coefficients derived are not suitable for arbitrary scaling.

Given the pixel x-gradient x_g and y-gradient y_g, we compute the pixel gradient angle θ as

$$\theta = \tan^{-1}\left(\frac{y_g}{x_g}\right) \tag{15.10}$$

We quantize the pixel gradient angle θ such that it takes any one of eight angles 0, 22.5, 45, 67.5, 90, 112.5, 135, or 157.5, as shown in Figure 15.13 using Equation (15.11).

$$\alpha = \left\lfloor \frac{\theta - 11.25}{22.5} \right\rfloor \bmod 8 \tag{15.11}$$

Based on Equation (15.11), we will have eight quantized orientations (α) in the interval [0, 180). We obtain interpolated pixels a, b, and c for one original pixel P to scale the image in both horizontal and vertical directions by a factor of 2. For each interpolated position, we will have eight types of filters to choose from depending on the orientation of current pixel gradient, and any of 16 original pixels in the 4×4 block can participate in the interpolation process.

In Raghupathy et al. (2003), a least-mean-square (LMS) algorithm is used to compute 4×4 interpolator filter weights, and with this the filter weights that are obtained will have uniform values for all pixels participating in the interpolation process for a given pixel gradient orientation.

Instead of using equal weights for all pixels participating in the interpolation, we use filter weights such that the weights of participating pixels are inversely proportional to their distances to the interpolating pixel. Also, we restrict the number of pixels participating in the interpolation process to 4, 6, or 8. For example, if the orientation of pixel gradient $P(0,0)$ is 157.5°, then for obtaining the interpolated pixel b, the chosen pixels are $P(0, -1)$, $P(0,0)$, $P(1,0)$, and $P(1,1)$, as shown in Figure 15.12, and the filter weights are given by the vector [0.1545, 0.3455, 0.3455, 0.1545]. As 4, 6, or 8 taps are used out of 16 taps, in an actual implementation we can reduce the number of computations by computing the interpolation with only non-zero filter coefficients.

The scaled images using an edge-based interpolator and bilinear interpolator are shown in Figure 15.14(a) and (b). We can clearly see the performance difference between them. As discussed, the bilinear interpolation destroys the edge information in the scaled image, whereas the edge-based interpolator preserves the edge information during the scaling process.

15.2.2 Chrominance Scaling

In scaling a YUV image, we scale the two chrominance components U and V (or Cb and Cr) using the same scaling ratio that is used for scaling the luminance component. The human eye is relatively insensitive to small artifacts arising in chrominance-component scaling. Because of this, less complex interpolation methods to scale chrominance components are acceptable. In general, bilinear or bicubic interpolation methods are widely used in scaling the chrominance component. See Section 10.7 for more detail on bilinear interpolation. In this section, we briefly discuss the bicubic interpolation function. With four neighboring points, the bicubic interpolation

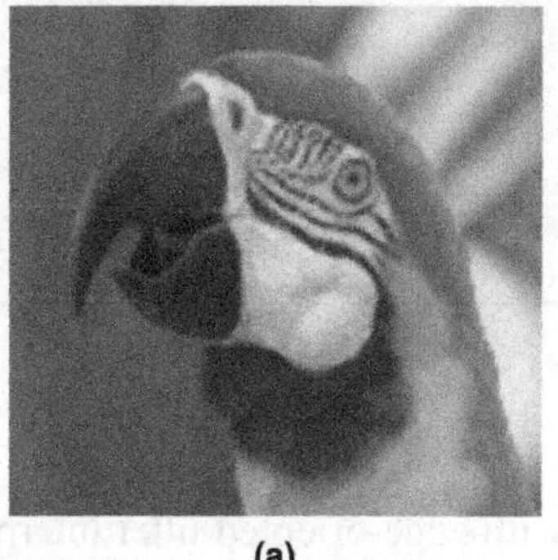

Figure 15.14: Video scaling. (a) Edge-based interpolation. (b) Bilinear interpolation.

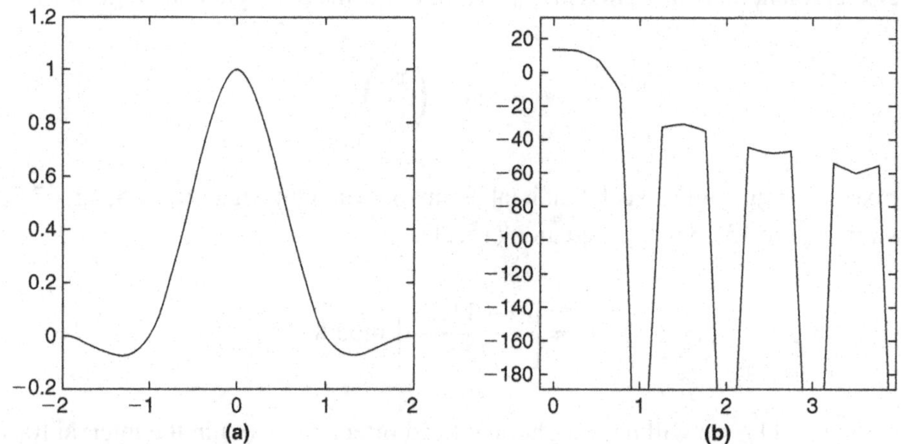

Figure 15.15: Bicubic interpolation function. (a) Spatial domain. (b) Frequency domain.

function is defined as

$$h_{cubic}(x) = \begin{cases} (3/2)|x|^3 - (5/2)|x|^2 + 1, & 0 \le |x| < 1 \\ (-1/2)|x|^3 + (5/2)|x|^2 - 4|x| + 2, & 1 \le |x| \le 2 \\ 0, & \text{otherwise} \end{cases} \tag{15.12}$$

The spatial-frequency characteristics of the bicubic interpolation function are shown in Figure 15.15; the stopband attenuation of bicubic interpolation function is better when compared to bilinear interpolation.

The interpolation coefficient computation illustrated in Figure 15.5 is also applicable for scaling chrominance components by a 1:5 scaling ratio using bicubic interpolation. The interpolation coefficients for neighboring points A, B, C, and D to compute interpolating points e, f, g, and h using bicubic interpolation follow.

cubic	$A: h_{cubic}(x_1)$	$B: h_{cubic}(x_2)$	$C: h_{cubic}(x_3)$	$D: h_{cubic}(x_4)$
e	−0.0640	0.9120	0.1680	−0.0160
f	−0.0720	0.6960	0.4240	−0.0480
g	−0.0480	0.4240	0.6960	−0.0720
h	−0.0160	0.1680	0.9120	−0.0640

Chrominance component scaling using bilinear and bicubic interpolation by a factor of 4 is shown in Figure 15.16; the figure shows that color differences are imperceptible after scaling using bilinear or bicubic methods.

15.2.3 Simulation of Interpolation Functions

In this section, the simulation code for bicubic, cubic B-spline, DCT, and edge-based interpolation methods is provided. Before calling the interpolation function, we precompute the interpolation coefficients for given

(a) (b)

Figure 15.16: Video chroma scaling. (a) Bicubic interpolation. (b) Bilinear interpolation.

scaling ratios and store them in a look-up table in fixed-point format. We simulate all interpolation functions discussed so far to scale image components by a factor of 4. To achieve factor-4 scaling, in DCT- and edge-based interpolation, scaling is performed in two steps, whereas we achieve factor-4 scaling in a single step using B-spline and bicubic interpolation. In addition, we perform block-based scaling in DCT- and edge-based interpolation methods, whereas B-spline and bicubic interpolation methods scale the images one line at a time.

We precompute the interpolation filter coefficients and store their equivalent fixed-point format values in memory. Given the scaling ratio, filter taps for B-spline and bicubic interpolation methods are obtained using Equations (15.8) and (15.12). The filter taps for DCT-based interpolation are given by DCT matrix elements. In edge-based interpolation, filter taps are obtained either by using the LMS algorithm or pixel distances.

Luminance Scaling Based on Cubic B-Splines

To scale image components by a factor of 4 using cubic B-splines, we precompute the filter taps as follows. To achieve factor-4 scaling, we must output four pixels for each input pixels as shown in Figure 15.17. The a_i, b_i, and c_i filter taps are obtained by substituting the 0.25, 0.50, and 0.75 values in Equation (15.6). The decimal and corresponding 1.15 fixed-point format for a_i, b_i, and c_i values follow:

$$a_1 = 0.0703(2303),\ a_2 = 0.6120(20054), a_3 = 0.3151(10325), a_4 = 0.0026(85)$$

$$b_1 = 0.0208(681),\ \ b_2 = 0.4792(15702), b_3 = 0.4792(15702), b_4 = 0.0208(681)$$

$$c_1 = 0.0026(85),\ \ \ c_2 = 0.3151(10325), c_3 = 0.6120(20054), c_4 = 0.0703(2303)$$

As we scale the image by a factor of 4 in both horizontal and vertical directions, we can use the same filter tap values for interpolating both directions. However, if the horizontal scaling ratio is different from the vertical

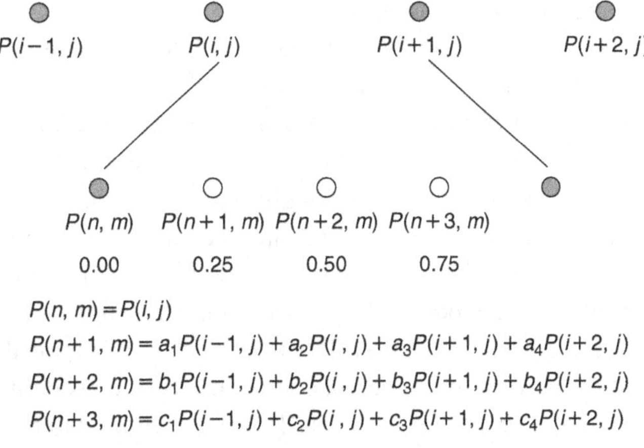

Figure 15.17: Illustration of scaling using line-based interpolation.

```
// scale luminance component from resolution mxn to MxN, m = M/4, n = N/4
for(j = 0;j < m;j++){                                   // horizontal scaling
    p = j*N; q = j*n;
    sBufY[p] = BufY[q];                                 // duplicate edge pixels
    sBufY[p+1] = BufY[q];
    sBufY[p+2] = (BufY[q]+BufY[q+1])>>1;                // linear interpolation
    sBufY[p+3] = BufY[q+1];
    for(i = 4;i < N-4;i+ = 4){                          // cubic B-spline interpolation starts
        k = i>>2;
        sBufY[p+i] = BufY[q+k];
        sBufY[p+i+1] = ((BufY[q+k-1]*a1)>>15) + ((BufY[q+k]*a2)>>15) +
                       ((BufY[q+k+1]*a3)>>15) + ((BufY[q+k+2]*a4)>>15);
        sBufY[p+i+2] = ((BufY[q+k-1]*b1)>>15) + ((BufY[q+k]*b2)>>15) +
                       ((BufY[q+k+1]*b3)>>15) + ((BufY[q+k+2]*b4)>>15);
        sBufY[p+i+3] = ((BufY[q+k-1]*c1)>>15) + ((BufY[q+k]*c2)>>15) +
                       ((BufY[q+k+1]*c3)>>15) + ((BufY[q+k+2]*c4)>>15);
    }
    sBufY[p+N-4] = BufY[q+n-1];
    sBufY[p+N-3] = BufY[q+n-1];
    sBufY[p+N-2] = BufY[q+n-1];
    sBufY[p+N-1] = BufY[q+n-1];
}
for(j = 0;j < N;j++){                                   // vertical scaling
    tBufY[j] = (unsigned char) sBufY[j];                // duplicate edge pixels
    tBufY[j+N] = (unsigned char) sBufY[j];
    tBufY[j+2*N] = (unsigned char) (sBufY[j] + sBufY[j+N])>>1;
    tBufY[j+3*N] = (unsigned char) sBufY[j+N];
    for(i = 4;i < M-4;i+=4){                            // cubic B spline interpolation starts
        k = i>>2;
        tBufY[i*N+j] = (unsigned char) sBufY[k*N+j];
        tBufY[(i+1)*N+j] = (unsigned char) ((sBufY[(k-1)*N+j]*a1)>>15) +
((sBufY[k*N+j]*a2)>>15) + ((sBufY[(k+1)*N+j]*a3)>>15) + ((sBufY[(k+2)*N+j]*a4)>>15);
                tBufY[(i+2)*N+j] = (unsigned char) ((sBufY[(k-1)*N+j]*b1)>>15) +
((sBufY[k*N+j]*b2)>>15) + ((sBufY[(k+1)*N+j]*b3)>>15) + ((sBufY[(k+2)*N+j]*b4)>>15);
                tBufY[(i+3)*N+j] = (unsigned char) ((sBufY[(k-1)*N+j]*c1)>>15) +
((sBufY[k*N+j]*c2)>>15) + ((sBufY[(k+1)*N+j]*c3)>>15) + ((sBufY[(k+2)*N+j]*c4)>>15);
    }
    tBufY[(M-4)*N+j] = (unsigned char) sBufY[(m-1)*N+j];
    tBufY[(M-3)*N+j] = (unsigned char) sBufY[(m-1)*N+j];
    tBufY[(M-2)*N+j] = (unsigned char) sBufY[(m-1)*N+j];
    tBufY[(M-1)*N+j] = (unsigned char) sBufY[(m-1)*N+j];
}
```

Pcode 15.1: Simulation code for cubic B-spline based luminance scaling.

scaling ratio, then the filter taps are different for horizontal and vertical directions; in that case we obtain the horizontal and vertical filter taps separately using Equation (15.6) to perform interpolation in both directions. The simulation code for luminance component scaling based on cubic B-splines is given in Pcode 15.1.

Luminance Scaling Based on DCT Interpolation

In DCT-based scaling, we perform DCT followed by IDCT to either upscale or downscale the video frames. To upscale the video frame, first we compute the 4×4 DCT and followed by the 8×8 IDCT. For downscaling, first we perform the 8×8 DCT followed by the 4×4 IDCT. We can efficiently perform DCT-based interpolation by using DCT input- and output-pruning techniques as discussed in Section 7.2. The fixed-point simulation code to upscale the video frame by a factor of 2 is given in Pcode 15.2.

The simulation code given in Pcode 15.2 upscales the video frames by a factor of 2. If we want to scale the video frame by a factor of 4, then we will call Pcode 15.2 two times consecutively. We can get sharpened upscaled video frames with Pcode 15.2 by performing element-by-element multiplication of the DCT data and elements of the matrix given in Equation (15.9) just before computing the 8×8 IDCT. We can also get smoothed video frames without performing any extra computations by considering a few low-frequency DCT coefficients (or ignoring a few high frequencies in the DCT data) as an input to the 8×8 IDCT.

```
a = 0x4000; b = 0x539f; c = 0x2283;                 // 1/2, sqrt(1/2)*cos(PI/8), sqrt(1/2)*cos(3*PI/8)
for(m = 0;m < M;m+=4)                               // compute 4x4 DCT
        for(n = 0;n < N;n+=4){
                for(i = 0;i < 4;i++)
                    for(j = 0;j < 4;j++)
                        blk1[4*i+j] = BufY[(m+i)*N+(n+j)];
                for(i = 0;i < 4;i++){
                    r0 = blk1[4*i+0]<<4; r1 = blk1[4*i+1]<<4;
                    r2 = blk1[4*i+2]<<4; r3 = blk1[4*i+3]<<4;
                    r4 = r0 + r3; r5 = r1 + r2;
                    r6 = (r4 + r5)>>1; r7 = (r4 - r5)>>1;
                    tmpP[4*i+0] = r6; tmpP[4*i+2] = r7;
                    r4 = r0 - r3; r5 = r1 - r2;
                    rr0 = r4 * b; rr1 = r4 * c;
                    rr2 = r5 * b; rr3 = r5 * c;
                    r6 = (rr0 + rr3 + RC) >> 15; r7 = (rr1 - rr2 + RC) >> 15;
                    tmpP[4*i+1] = r6; tmpP[4*i+3] = r7;
                }
                for(i = 0;i < 4;i++){
                    r0 = tmpP[0+i]; r1 = tmpP[4+i];
                    r2 = tmpP[8+i]; r3 = tmpP[12+i];
                    r4 = r0 + r3;   r5 = r1 + r2;
                    r6 = (r4 + r5)>>1; r7 = (r4 - r5)>>1;
                    blk1[0+i] = r6; blk1[8+i] = r7;
                    r4 = r0 - r3; r5 = r1 - r2;
                    rr0 = r4 * b; rr1 = r4 * c;
                    rr2 = r5 * b; rr3 = r5 * c;
                    r6 = (rr0 + rr3 + RC) >> 15; r7 = (rr1 - rr2 + RC) >> 15;
                    blk1[4+i] = r6; blk1[12+i] = r7;
                }
                for(i = 0;i < 4;i++)
                    for(j = 0;j < 4;j++)
                        BufX[(m+i)*N+n+j] = blk1[4*i+j];
        }

c0 = 0x5a82;                                        // (1/sqrt(2)*32768) = 23170
c1 = 0x7d8a;                                        // cos(pi/16)*32768 = 32138
c2 = 0x18f9;                                        // sin(pi/16)*32768 = 6393
c3 = 0x6a6e;                                        // cos(3*pi/16)*32768 = 27246
c4 = 0x471d;                                        // sin(3*pi/16)*32768 = 18205
c5 = 0x22a2;                                        // cos(6*pi/16)/sqrt(2)*32768 = 8867
c6 = 0x539f;                                        // sin(6*pi/16)/sqrt(2)*32768 = 21407

 for(m = 0;m < 2*M;m+=8)                            // 8x8 IDCT starts here
        for(n = 0; n < 2*N;n+=8){
                for(i = 0;i < 8;i++)
                    for(j = 0;j < 8;j++)
                        blk2[i*8+j] = 0.0;
                for(i = 0;i < 4;i++)
                    for(j = 0;j < 4;j++)
                        blk2[i*8+j] = BufX[((m>>1)+i)*N+(n>>1)+j];
                for(i = 0;i < 4;i++){
                    r0 = (blk2[8*i+0] + blk2[8*i+4]); r1 = (blk2[8*i+0] - blk2[8*i+4]);
                    rr2 = (blk2[8*i+2] * c5) >> 0; rr3 = (blk2[8*i+6] * c5) >> 0;
                    rr4 = (blk2[8*i+2] * c6) >> 0; rr5 = (blk2[8*i+6] * c6) >> 0;
                    r2 = (rr2 - rr5 + RC/2)>>14; r3 = (rr3 + rr4 + RC/2) >> 14;
                    tmp1 = (blk2[8*i+1] - blk2[8*i+7]);
                    tmp2 = (blk2[8*i+1] + blk2[8*i+7]);
                    tmp3 = (blk2[8*i+3] * c0 + RC/2) >> 14;
                    tmp4 = (blk2[8*i+5] * c0 + RC/2) >> 14;
                    r4 = tmp1 + tmp4; r6 = tmp1 - tmp4;
                    r5 = tmp2 - tmp3; r7 = tmp2 + tmp3;
                    tmp1 = r0; tmp2 = r1;
                    r0 = tmp1 + r3; r3 = tmp1 - r3;
                    r1 = tmp2 + r2; r2 = tmp2 - r2;
                    rr1 = (r5 * c1) >> 0; rr2 = (r5 * c2) >> 0;
                    rr3 = (r6 * c1) >> 0; rr4 = (r6 * c2) >> 0;

 // continued on the next page
```

```
// continuation from previous Pcode

            r5 = (rr1 - rr4 + RC) >> 15; r6 = (rr3 + rr2 + RC) >> 15;
            rr1 = (r4 * c3) >> 0; rr2 = (r4 * c4) >> 0;
            rr3 = (r7 * c3) >> 0; rr4 = (r7 * c4) >> 0;
            r4 = (rr1 - rr4 + RC) >> 15; r7 = (rr3 + rr2 + RC) >> 15;
            tmpP[8*i+0] = (r0 + r7)>>1; tmpP[8*i+7] = (r0 - r7)>>1;
            tmpP[8*i+1] = (r1 + r6)>>1; tmpP[8*i+6] = (r1 - r6)>>1;
            tmpP[8*i+2] = (r2 + r5)>>1; tmpP[8*i+5] = (r2 - r5)>>1;
            tmpP[8*i+3] = (r3 + r4)>>1; tmpP[8*i+4] = (r3 - r4)>>1;
        }

        for(i = 0;i < 8;i++){
            r0 = tmpP[8*0+i] + tmpP[8*4+i]; r1 = tmpP[8*0+i] - tmpP[8*4+i];
            rr2 = (tmpP[8*2+i] * c5) >> 0; rr3 = (tmpP[8*6+i] * c5) >>0;
            rr4 = (tmpP[8*2+i] * c6) >> 0; rr5 = (tmpP[8*6+i] * c6) >>0;
            r2 = (rr2 - rr5 + RC/2) >> 14; r3 = (rr3 + rr4 + RC/2) >>14;
            tmp1 = tmpP[8*1+i] - tmpP[8*7+i];
            tmp2 = tmpP[8*1+i] + tmpP[8*7+i];
            tmp3 = (tmpP[8*3+i] * c0 + RC/2) >> 14;
            tmp4 = (tmpP[8*5+i] * c0 + RC/2) >> 14;
            r4 = tmp1 + tmp4; r6 = tmp1 - tmp4;
            r5 = tmp2 - tmp3; r7 = tmp2 + tmp3;

            tmp1 = r0; tmp2 = r1;
            r0 = tmp1 + r3; r3 = tmp1 - r3;
            r1 = tmp2 + r2; r2 = tmp2 - r2;
            rr1 = (r5 * c1) >> 0; rr2 = (r5 * c2) >> 0;
            rr3 = (r6 * c1) >> 0; rr4 = (r6 * c2) >> 0;
            r5 = (rr1 - rr4 + RC) >> 15; r6 = (rr3 + rr2 + RC) >> 15;
            rr1 = (r4 * c3) >> 0; rr2 = (r4 * c4) >> 0;
            rr3 = (r7 * c3) >> 0; rr4 = (r7 * c4) >> 0;
            r4 = (rr1 - rr4 + RC) >> 15; r7 = (rr3 + rr2 + RC) >> 15;

            blk2[8*0+i] = (r0 + r7)>>1; blk2[8*7+i] = (r0 - r7)>>1;
            blk2[8*1+i] = (r1 + r6)>>1; blk2[8*6+i] = (r1 - r6)>>1;
            blk2[8*2+i] = (r2 + r5)>>1; blk2[8*5+i] = (r2 - r5)>>1;
            blk2[8*3+i] = (r3 + r4)>>1; blk2[8*4+i] = (r3 - r4)>>1;
        }

        for(i = 0;i < 8;i++)
            for(j = 0;j < 8;j++)
                sBufY[(m+i)*640+n+j] = blk2[i*8+j];
    }
```

Pcode 15.2: Simulation code to upscale the video frame by a factor of 2 using DCT based interpolation.

Luminance Scaling Based on Edge Interpolation

As discussed in the Section 15.2.1, there are several steps in upscaling video frames by using edge-based interpolation:

- Classification of the 4×4 block as an edge block or non-edge block
- Determining edge orientation
- Generating filter coefficients for different orientations and interpolating points (i.e., for a, b, and c)
- Performing edge-based or bilinear interpolation for current original pixel once its classification is given

The simulation code to classify the current 4×4 block as an edge block or non-edge block, determine pixel orientation in a 4×4 block, and to perform edge-based or bilinear interpolation is given in Pcode 15.3.

The fixed-point 1.15 format values of filter coefficients for edge-based interpolation are provided on the companion website. In the 2D array Tbn[3][16], coefficients Tbn[0][16], Tbn[1][16], and Tbn[2][16] are used to get the interpolated points a, b, and c, respectively.

The simulation code given in Pcode 15.3 upscales the images by a factor of 2; this Pcode is called twice consecutively to scale the image by a factor of 4. To scale from $2\times$ to $4\times$, we need not recompute all orientations for

```
for(j = 1;j < m-2;j++)                            // m: image height
 for(i = 1;i < n-2;i++) {                         // n: image width
  for(q = 0;q < 4;q++)
   for(p = 0;p < 4;p++)
    Edge[q*4+p] = BufY[(j+q-1)*n+i+p-1];          // get a 4x4 block
  x0 = 255; y0 = 0;
  for(p = 0;p < 16;p++)                           // get the minimum value of pixels in a 4x4 block
   if(x0 > Edge[p])
     x0 = Edge[p];
  for(p = 0;p < 16;p++)                           // get maximum pixel value in a 4x4 pixel block
   if(y0 < Edge[p])
     y0 = Edge[p];
  if((y0 - x0) < 25)
    orient_flag = 0;                              // classify as edge block or non-edge block
  else {
   for(q = 0;q < 4;q++)
    for(p = 0;p < 4;p++) {
     if(BufX[(j+q-1)*n+i+p-1] == 8) {
        x = BufY[(j+q)*n+(i+q)] + BufY[(j+q-1)*n+(i+q)]*2 + BufY[(j+q-
              2)*n+(i+q)] - BufY[(j+q)*n+(i+q-2)] - BufY[(j+q-1)*n+(i+q-2)]*2
              - BufY[(j+q-2)*n+(i+q-2)];   // compute pixel x-gradient
        y = BufY[(j+q)*n+(i+q)] + BufY[(j+q)*n+(i+q-1)]*2 +
             BufY[(j+q)*n+(i+q-2)] - BufY[(j+q-2)*n+(i+q)] - BufY[(j+q-
             2)*n+(i+q-1)]*2 - BufY[(j+q-2)*n+(i+q-2)]; // compute pixel y-gradient
        if (y != 0) {
         x0 = (int) -57.2958*atan(x/y);          // compute orientation
         if(x0 < 0) x0+= 180;
        }
         else
            x0 = 90;
        x0 = ((int)((x0-11.25)/22.5)+1) % 8; // quantize the orientation
        BufX[(j+q-1)*n+i+p-1] = x0;              // store quantized orientation
        Hist[x0]+=1;                             // group similar orientations
    }
    else {
      x0 = BufX[(j+q-1)*n+i+p-1];                // get previously computed present pixel orientation
      Hist[x0]+=1;
    }
   }
   x0 = 0;
   for(p = 0;p < 8;p++)
    if(Hist[p] > x0)
       x0 = Hist[p];                             // get the maximum count of similar orientations
   for(p = 0;p <8;p++)
    Hist[p] = 0;
   if(x0 > 6)                                    // if maximum count is greater than six, then classify
       orient_flag = 1;                          // the current pixel as strictly oriented
   else
       orient_flag = 0;
  }
  BufZ[j*n+i] = orient_flag;
  if(orient_flag) {                 // if the current pixel is oriented, use edge based interpolation
     x0 = BufX[j*n+i]; pTb = Tb[x0];
     tBufY[2*j*N+2*i] = BufY[j*n+i];
     x0 = 0; y0 = 0; z0 = 0;
     for(q = 0;q < 4;q++)
        for(p = 0;p < 4;p++) {
          x0 = x0 + ((pTb[0][q*4+p]*BufY[(j+q-1)*n+i+p-1])>>15);
          y0 = y0 + ((pTb[1][q*4+p]*BufY[(j+q-1)*n+i+p-1])>>15);
          z0 = z0 + ((pTb[2][q*4+p]*BufY[(j+q-1)*n+i+p-1])>>15);
        }
     tBufY[2*j*N+2*i+1] = x0; tBufY[(2*j+1)*N+2*i] = y0; tBufY[(2*j+1)*N+2*i+1] = z0;
  }
  else{                       // use bilinear interpolation if the current pixel is not oriented pixel
      tBufY[2*j*N+2*i] = BufY[j*n+i];
      tBufY[2*j*N+2*i+1] = (BufY[j*n+i] + BufY[j*n+i+1] + 1)>>1;
      tBufY[(2*j+1)*N+2*i] = (BufY[j*n+i] + BufY[(j+1)*n+i] + 1)>>1;

// continued on the next page
```

```
// continuation of previous Pcode

        tBufY[(2*j+1)*N+2*i+1] = (BufY[j*n+i] + BufY[(j+1)*n+i] + BufY[j*n+i+1] +
                                 BufY[(j+1)*n+i+1] + 2)>>2;
    }
}
```

Pcode 15.3: Simulation code for edge-based interpolation.

each pixel of the 2× image; instead, we reuse previously computed pixel orientations of the original image. In the filtering process, pixel intensity values may go out of range, so at the end each pixel is clipped between 0 and 255.

15.2.4 Chrominance Scaling Based on Bicubic Interpolation

To scale image components by a factor of 4 using bicubic interpolation, we precompute the filter taps as follows. To achieve factor-4 scaling, we must output 4 pixels for each input pixel, as shown in Figure 15.17. The a_i, b_i, and c_i filter taps are obtained by substituting values 0.25, 0.50, and 0.75 in Equation (15.12). The decimal and the corresponding 1.15 fixed-point format values for a_i, b_i, and c_i follow:

$$a_1 = -0.0703(0 \times F701),\ a_2 = 0.8672(0 \times 6F00),\ a_3 = 0.2266(0 \times 1D01),\ a_4 = -0.0234(0 \times FD02)$$
$$b_1 = -0.0625(0 \times F800),\ b_2 = 0.5625(0 \times 4800),\ b_3 = 0.5625(0 \times 4800),\ b_4 = -0.0625(0 \times F800)$$
$$c_1 = -0.0234(0 \times FD02),\ c_2 = 0.2266(0 \times 1D01),\ c_3 = 0.8672(0 \times 6F00),\ c_4 = -0.0703(0 \times F701)$$

As we scale the image by a factor of 4 in both horizontal and vertical directions, we can use the same filter-tap values for interpolating both of the directions. However, if the horizontal scaling ratio is different from the vertical scaling ratio, then the filter taps are different for the horizontal and vertical directions; in this instance, we obtain horizontal and vertical filter taps separately using Equation (15.12) to perform interpolation in both directions. The simulation code for bicubic-based chrominance component scaling is given in Pcode 15.4.

15.3 Video Processing

Apart from scaling, the other commonly used video post-processing modules are filtering, blending, and gamma correction. In Section 10.5, we discussed the median filter to filter noisy images, and the same can be used to minimize artifacts due to scaling, quantization, and so on. In this section, we discuss efficient implementation of the median filter. In addition, we briefly discuss and simulate the alpha-blending and gamma-correction modules.

15.3.1 Filtering

When we process video pixels in the digital domain, a kind of random data (noise) from many sources adds to the original pixels, such as noise from video quantization, compression, scaling, and so on. We apply a 2D filter to eliminate noisy components from video pixels. Median filters are widely used in video processing applications. In this section, we discuss efficient techniques to implement a 3 × 3 median filter.

Simulation of a 3 × 3 median filter using the bubble-sort method is given in Section 10.11.4. With a $K \times K$ median filter, we replace the center pixel of $K \times K$ (where $K = 2{*}i + 1, i = 1, 2, \ldots$) block with the median of $K \times K$-block pixels. For example, using a 3 × 3 median filter in Figure 15.18, we replace pixel p5 with the fifth pixel in the sorted (either ascending or descending) array of 3 × 3 block pixels $p1$, $p2$, $p3$, $p4$, $p5$, $p6$, $p7$, $p8$, and $p9$. Now the question is, how complex is the median filter to apply to the $L \times L$ block of pixels? For example, if $L = 16$, then the cost of the median filter with the bubble-sort method (as simulated in Pcode 10.8) is estimated as follows.

In this estimation, we are not including overhead such as data loading and storing. For finding a median pixel in a 3 × 3 block of pixels, we have to run a nested loop with two loops. Both inner and outer loops run nine times. With sorting in ascending order, we perform three operations (checking, conditional update of the minimum pixel index, and conditional update of the minimum pixel value). Assuming each operation consumes 1 cycle, the inner loop requires 27 cycles for nine iterations. Thus, to find a median for a 3 × 3 block of pixels

```
// scale chrominance component from resolution mxn to MxN, m = M/4, n = N/4
for(j = 0;j < m;j++){                                   // horizontal scaling
    p = j*N; q = j*n;
    sBufY[p] = BufY[q];                                 // duplicate edge pixels
    sBufY[p+1] = BufY[q];
    sBufY[p+2] = (BufY[q]+BufY[q+1])>>1;                // linear interpolation
    sBufY[p+3] = BufY[q+1];
    for(i = 4;i < N-4;i+=4){                            // bicubic interpolation starts
        k = i>>2;
        sBufY[p+i] = BufY[q+k];
        sBufY[p+i+1] = ((BufY[q+k-1]*a1)>>15) + ((BufY[q+k]*a2)>>15) +
                       ((BufY[q+k+1]*a3)>>15) + ((BufY[q+k+2]*a4)>>15);
        sBufY[p+i+2] = ((BufY[q+k-1]*b1)>>15) + ((BufY[q+k]*b2)>>15) +
                       ((BufY[q+k+1]*b3)>>15) + ((BufY[q+k+2]*b4)>>15);
        sBufY[p+i+3] = ((BufY[q+k-1]*c1)>>15) + ((BufY[q+k]*c2)>>15) +
                       ((BufY[q+k+1]*c3)>>15) + ((BufY[q+k+2]*c4)>>15);
    }
    sBufY[p+N-4] = BufY[q+n-1];
    sBufY[p+N-3] = BufY[q+n-1];
    sBufY[p+N-2] = BufY[q+n-1];
    sBufY[p+N-1] = BufY[q+n-1];
}
for(j = 0;j < N;j++){                                   // vertical scaling
    tBufY[j] = (unsigned char) sBufY[j];                // duplicate edge pixels
    tBufY[j+N] = (unsigned char) sBufY[j];
    tBufY[j+2*N] = (unsigned char) (sBufY[j] + sBufY[j+N])>>1;
    tBufY[j+3*N] = (unsigned char) sBufY[j+N];
    for(i = 4;i < M-4;i+=4){                            // bicubic interpolation starts
        k = i>>2;
        tBufY[i*N+j] = (unsigned char) sBufY[k*N+j];
        tBufY[(i+1)*N+j] = (unsigned char) ((sBufY[(k-1)*N+j]*a1)>>15) +
((sBufY[k*N+j]*a2)>>15) + ((sBufY[(k+1)*N+j]*a3)>>15) + ((sBufY[(k+2)*N+j]*a4)>>15);
               tBufY[(i+2)*N+j] = (unsigned char)((sBufY[(k-1)*N+j]*b1)>>15) +
((sBufY[k*N+j]*b2)>>15) + ((sBufY[(k+1)*N+j]*b3)>>15) + ((sBufY[(k+2)*N+j]*b4)>>15);
               tBufY[(i+3)*N+j] = (unsigned char)((sBufY[(k-1)*N+j]*c1)>>15) +
((sBufY[k*N+j]*c2)>>15) + ((sBufY[(k+1)*N+j]*c3)>>15) + ((sBufY[(k+2)*N+j]*c4)>>15);
   }
   tBufY[(M-4)*N+j] = (unsigned char) sBufY[(m-1)*N+j];
   tBufY[(M-3)*N+j] = (unsigned char) sBufY[(m-1)*N+j];
   tBufY[(M-2)*N+j] = (unsigned char) sBufY[(m-1)*N+j];
   tBufY[(M-1)*N+j] = (unsigned char) sBufY[(m-1)*N+j];
}
```

Pcode 15.4: Simulation code for bicubic based chrominance scaling.

p_1 p_2 p_3

p_4 p_5 p_6

p_7 p_8 p_9

Figure 15.18: Block of 3 x 3 pixels.

with the bubble-sort method, we consume about 243 (= 27 × 9) cycles. Therefore, to apply a median filter to a macroblock, we have to find 256 (= 16 × 16) medians, and the number of cycles required to find 256 medians is about 62,208 (= 256 × 243). Thus, filtering the $N \times M$ image with a median filter by the bubble-sort method is very costly in terms of cycles.

Efficient Implementation of Median Filter

In Vega-Rodriguez et al. (2002), a very efficient way of finding the 3 × 3 median by the divide-and-conquer approach is presented as in Figure 15.19. We divide the nine pixels of the 3 × 3 block into three segments and find the median pixel in three stages. The number of cycles consumed by this method to find a median for a 3 × 3 block of pixels is estimated in this section. With this method, we use a butterfly as shown at the top-right corner of Figure 15.19, and consume 2 cycles to find the minimum and maximum of 2 pixels. In the first stage, we find

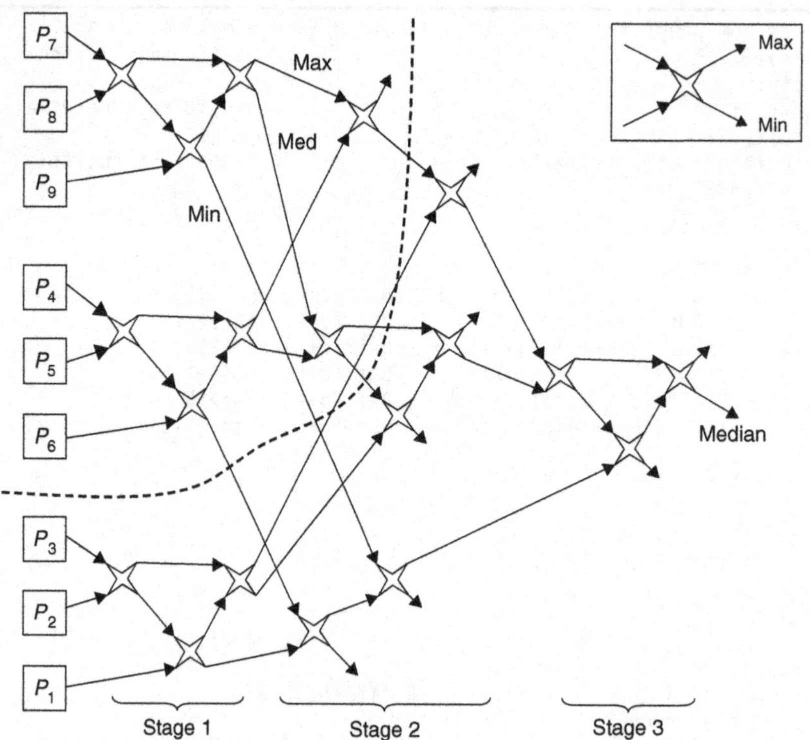

Figure 15.19: Median filter–signal-flow diagram.

the minimum, median, and maximum for 3 pixel sets by consuming 6 cycles using three butterflies for each set. The first stage consumes a total of 18 cycles.

In the second stage, we find a maximum of three minimums, a median of three medians, and a minimum of three maximums coming from the first stage. In this stage, we use a total of six butterflies and consume 8 cycles by computing only the required butterfly outputs. In the third stage, we find the median of three outputs (maximum, median, and minimum) coming from the second stage. We consume 4 cycles in the third stage. With this, we find the median for the 3×3 block of pixels by performing 30 min-max operations as shown in Figure 15.19.

On the reference embedded processor (see Appendix A on the companion website), as we have two arithmetic logic units (ALUs), we can perform two min/max operations per cycle. Therefore, only 15 cycles per pixel are required when we compute 2 pixel medians at a time. To apply a median filter for a 16×16 block of pixels with this method as shown in Figure 15.20, represented in case (1), we consume 3,840 cycles, which is about 6% of cycles when compared to cycles of the median filter with the bubble-sort method. The simulation code for this efficient 3×3 median filter method is given in Pcode 15.5.

Block-Based Median Filter Implementation

Next we discuss ways of reducing computation cycles in filtering large images. A few aspects of applying the median filter to an entire image are discussed. In general, larger images in terms of data occupy a lot of memory. Typically, we store an entire image of size 0.5 MB (for 720×480 resolution) in off-chip memory, and a small amount of image data in terms of a block of pixels (of size 256 bytes for a 16×16 block) is brought to the on-chip memory to process the image. Assuming one block of 16×16 pixels is processed at a time, we use the embedded processor DMA controller to move a block of data from off-chip memory to on-chip memory for processing the image and from on-chip memory to off-chip memory to store the processed image (see Appendix A on the companion website for more details on DMA controller usage). We filter one 16×16 block of image pixels at a time. In this approach, we will have a problem in filtering block edges as we do not have sufficient pixels to apply the median filter at the block edges. As shown in Figure 15.20, for the pixel position indicated by (2), its median is computed by using 3 pixels from the previous 16×16 block and 6 pixels from the current 16×16

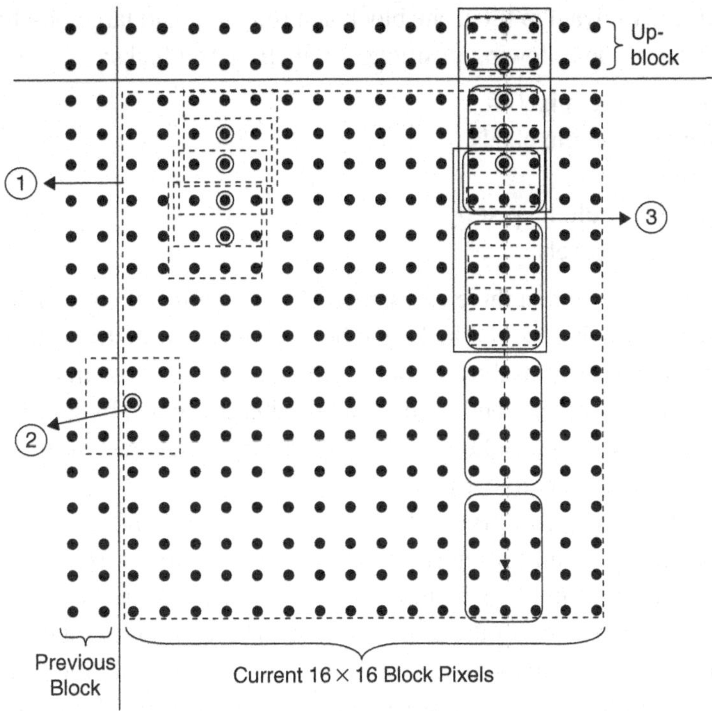

Figure 15.20: Macroblock (16 x 16 block) pixels.

```
//short Median(int j, int k)          // j: current pixel position in raster scan, k: block width, 16
// ------------------- first stage -----------------------
i = j;                      r1 = pixels[i+0];
r2 = pixels[i+1];           r3 = pixels[i+2];
tmp1 = min(r2, r3);         tmp2 = max(r2, r3);
tmp3 = min(r1, tmp1);       tmp4 = max(r1, tmp1);           // first row min, tmp3
tmp_buf[0] = tmp3;          tmp1 = min(tmp2, tmp4);         // first row med, tmp1
tmp_buf[1] = tmp1;          tmp2 = max(tmp2, tmp4);         // first row max, tmp2
tmp_buf[2] = tmp2;          i = j+k;
r1 = pixels[i+0];           r2 = pixels[i+1];
r3 = pixels[i+2];           tmp1 = min(r2, r3);
tmp2 = max(r2, r3);         tmp3 = min(r1, tmp1);           // second row min, tmp3
tmp4 = max(r1, tmp1);       tmp_buf[3] = tmp3;
tmp1 = min(tmp2, tmp4);     tmp_buf[4] = tmp1;              // second row med, tmp1
tmp2 = max(tmp2, tmp4);     tmp_buf[5] = tmp2;              // second row max, tmp2
i = j+(k<<1);               r1 = pixels[i+0];
r2 = pixels[i+1];           r3 = pixels[i+2];
tmp1 = min(r2, r3);         tmp2 = max(r2, r3);
tmp3 = min(r1, tmp1);       tmp4 = max(r1, tmp1);           // third row min, tmp3
tmp_buf[6] = tmp3;          tmp1 = min(tmp2, tmp4);         // third row med, tmp1
tmp_buf[7] = tmp1;          tmp2 = max(tmp2, tmp4);         // third row max, tmp2
tmp_buf[8] = tmp2;
// -------------------- second stage -------------------------
r1 = tmp_buf[0];            r2 = tmp_buf[3];
r3 = tmp_buf[6];            tmp1 = max(r1, r2);
tmp1 = max(tmp1, r3);       tmp_buf[9] = tmp1;
r1 = tmp_buf[1];            r2 = tmp_buf[4];
r3 = tmp_buf[7];            tmp1 = min(r2, r3);
tmp2 = max(r2, r3);         tmp4 = max(r1, tmp1);
tmp1 = min(tmp2, tmp4);     tmp_buf[10] = tmp1;
r1 = tmp_buf[2];            r2 = tmp_buf[5];
r3 = tmp_buf[8];            tmp1 = min(r1, r2);
tmp1 = min(tmp1, r3);       r1 = tmp_buf[9];
r2 = tmp_buf[10];           r3 = tmp1;
// -------------------- third stage -----------------------------
tmp1 = min(r2, r3);         tmp2 = max(r2, r3);
tmp4 = max(r1, tmp1);       tmp1 = min(tmp2, tmp4);         // median!, tmp1
```

Pcode 15.5: Simulation code for efficient 3 × 3 median filter implementation.

block. Now, if we want to filter one block at a time to avoid large on-chip memory usage, we have to find ways to filter pixels at the following positions for all 16×16 blocks:

1. Top left corner pixel
2. Left-most column pixels
3. Top row pixels
4. Right-most column pixels
5. Bottom row pixels

If we always filter the first three cases, then we automatically cover 4 and 5 for all 16×16 blocks except for the right-most column of 16×16 blocks and bottom-most row of 16×16 blocks of an image. We do not filter those edge pixels of the image as they are not much viewed. Let us assume that m and n denote image row and column indexes for 16×16 blocks, and we proceed to filter the image by filtering its 16×16 blocks in raster-scan order. We use the following procedure to always filter the first three cases and output 16×16-block of pixels. This procedure is shown in Figure 15.20, case (3).

To filter the bottom-row pixels of a 16×16 block (with index $[n, m\text{-}1]$) just above the current 16×16 block (with index $[n, m]$) and top-most–row pixels of the current 16×16 block, we maintain a delay line buffer (dl_pixels[]) to hold the two bottom-most–row pixels of the $[n, m\text{-}1]$ 16×16 block. Similarly, to filter the right-most–column pixels of the previous 16×16 block $[n\text{-}1, m]$ and left-most–column of pixels for the current 16×16 block, we maintain another buffer (lt_pixels[]) to hold the two right-most columns of pixels from the previous 16×16 block $[n\text{-}1, m]$. We load the current 16×16-block pixels from off-chip memory to the on-chip memory buffer by using the DMA. Thus, we need three types of buffers to apply the median filter for the entire image with this block-by-block approach as shown in Figure 15.21. We output a 16×16-size quantity of filtered pixels always to the DMA to send them to the processor off-chip memory.

Initialization In filtering a 16×16 block of pixels, if the row index of the current 16×16 block is zero (i.e., $m = 0$), then the buffer dl_pixels[] is initialized with zeros. If the column index of the current 16×16 block is zero (i.e., $n = 0$), then the buffer lt_pixels[] is initialized with zeros.

Filtering As shown in Figure 15.20 by case (3), in the suggested approach, we filter 4 pixels in a single iteration, and the filtering process continues column-wise. To filter one column, we go through four iterations. In this process, we will have six sets of {minimum, median, and maximum} in any iteration from six rows of three pixels each (such that the center pixel lies on the current filtering column) in the med_row_pixels[] buffer with 18 entries. Before entering the loop, we find the two sets of {minimum, median, and maximum} corresponding to the up 16×16 block bottom-most two rows (of 3 pixels each) from the dl_pixels[] buffer. Then, in the first iteration, we find four sets of {minimum, median, and maximum} corresponding to the four

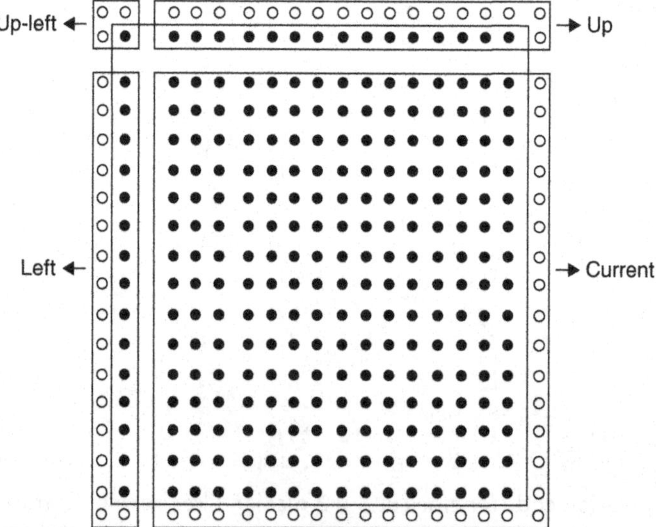

Figure 15.21: Pixel area filtered by median filter in block-by-block approach.

top-most rows from the current block of pixels. Using these six sets (four sets from the current buffer and two sets from the delay-line buffer), we find 4 median pixels. Now, we copy the two computed sets {minimum, median, and maximum} corresponding to the last two rows sets of first iteration's six row sets to the beginning of the buffer med_row_pixels[]. We compute the remaining four sets {minimum, median, and maximum} for the second iteration, again using the next four rows (of 3 pixels each). After repeating the preceding procedure four times, we find 16 median pixels for one column of the 16×16 block. The same procedure is repeated for the remaining 15 columns.

Once we complete filtering of the current 16×16 block, and before we proceed to filter the next 16×16 block, we store the right-most two columns of the current 16×16 block to the lt_pixels[] buffer and store the bottom-most two rows to dl_pixels[] for future use.

At this juncture, we estimate the cycle cost of the suggested median filter approach to filter a block of pixels. In any iteration of the loop, we reuse one-third of the first-stage outputs of the median filter from previous iterations, and we only compute two-thirds of the first stage of the median filter. In other words, in effect we compute the first stage of the median filter only once for a row, and we do not compute the first stage of the median filter multiple times as in case (1) of Figure 15.20. We ignore load/store cycles as these can be executed in parallel to compute operations. To find 16 median pixels, we compute the first stage for 18 rows (of 3 pixels each), which consumes 54 $(= 18 \times 3)$ cycles. We spend 6 cycles after the first stage of median filter to find a single median-filter output pixel. Therefore, we require 96 $(= 16 \times 6)$ cycles for computing all 16 median pixels. With this, to apply a median filter on a 16×16 block of pixels, we consume nearly 2400 $(= 16 \times (54 + 96))$ cycles, which is about 33% less when compared to implementation of case (1) in Figure 15.20. It is possible to save up to 50% of computation cycles with full reuse of intermediate outputs (refer to Figure 15.19). The intermediate outputs above the dashed line (which account for 50% of operations) in Figure 15.19 can be reused in filtering the next pixel.

The suggested method can be easily extended to multiple-ALU embedded processors, as there is no dependency between one median filter output and another median filter output. Unlike case (1) of Figure 15.20, where one median filter per iteration is outputted, in the suggested approach indicated by case (3) in Figure 15.20, we output multiple median filter outputs per iteration. So, with a four-ALU embedded processor, theoretically, we consume only $600 (= 2400/4)$ cycles per block with the preceding approach.

Implementation of Line-Based Median Filter

We can also implement the median filter row- or column-wise instead of block-wise. In the case of line-based median filtering, the pixels are filtered line by line. In row-based filtering, we bring one row of pixels from off-chip memory to on-chip memory, and filter the row just above and move the filtered row to off-chip memory. We always hold three rows of pixels—one above and one below—in buffers apart from the current row being filtered as shown in Figure 15.22. As we move the 3×3 mask horizontally, we consider 3-pixel columns as a base unit and find the median. In this case as well, intermediate results are reused to speed up the filtering process. Also, the overall overhead is less in row-based filtering, which is efficient when compared to block-based filtering in terms of cycle cost. However, we require more on-chip memory (especially with high-resolution video frames) in the case of row-based filtering to hold the full row inputs and intermediate outputs.

We use either block-based or line-based filtering depending on the context. For example, if we want to filter the scaled image, depending of the interpolation type used in scaling, we choose one of these filtering approaches.

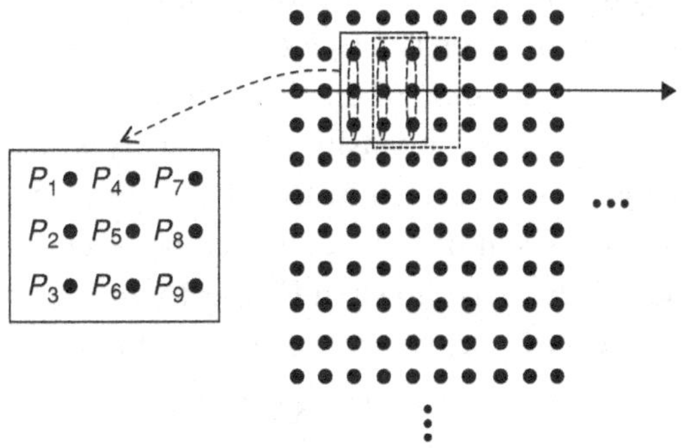

Figure 15.22: Row-wise median filtering.

If we scale the image in terms of blocks (using DCT- or edge-based interpolation), then working with block-based filtering avoids extra data transfer from L1 to L3 and L3 to L1. Similarly, line-based filtering is useful when we scale the image using line-based interpolation methods (e.g., bilinear, bicubic, and B-splines).

15.3.2 Alpha Blending

Alpha blending is a simple technique by which we can overlay two images allowing transparency of images or objects. This technique is really a form of intensity and color control, dictating what amount of information should be allowed to show through from a lower-lying image. Given two pixel values X and Y at the same location in background and foreground images, we obtain the effective pixel value Z by combining the two pixels X and Y using the following rule:

$$Z = \alpha X + (1-\alpha)Y = \alpha(\textit{background pixel}) + (1-\alpha)(\textit{foreground pixel}) \tag{15.13}$$

The parameter α in Equation (15.13) controls the amount of transparency that is allowed for lower-lying image objects. The range of parameter α is anywhere between 0.0 and 1.0. If $\alpha = 0.0$, then the objects of the background image with pixel values X are completely opaque. Similarly, if $\alpha = 1.0$, then the objects of the background image with pixel values X are completely transparent.

In practice, apart from the image pixel values, we get the α values in a separate channel called the alpha channel. For example, in 32-bit *RGBA*, 24 bits are used to specify colors R, G, and B, and the remaining 8 bits are used to specify the α value for each pixel. We compute the alpha-blend pixels using the α value before displaying the images.

The alpha-blending simulation code for a particular value of α is given in Pcode 15.6. In Pcode 15.6, a and b represent the 2.14 fixed-point format for real values of α and 1-α. Two test image pixels that require blending are stored in two buffers, BufR[] and BufY[]. Blending output will be stored in BufD[]. The alpha-blending simulation results of two grayscale test images depicting Lord Ganesh and Lord Krishna are shown in Figure 15.23. The four values of α within the allowed range—$\alpha = 0.0$, $\alpha = 0.25$, $\alpha = 0.75$, and $\alpha = 1.00$—are used in the simulation. The corresponding 2.14 fixed-point values are $a = 0{,}4096$, 12288, and 16384, and $b = 16384$, 12288, 4096, and 0.

```
for(j = 0;j < M;j++){
    p = j*N; q = (j + 1)*N;
    for(i = p;i < q;i++){
        m = (a*BufY[i]) >> 14; r = (b*BufR[i]) >> 14;            // a = alpha, b = 1-alpha
        BufD[i] = m + r;
    }
}
```

Pcode 15.6: Simulation code for alpha blending.

15.3.3 Gamma Correction

Previously, images were processed by representing each component of the image with 256 levels (or 8 bits). If we uniformly quantize the entire intensity range (i.e., 0.0 to 1.0) into 256 levels, and then process and send to the display, then the display output of the processed image need not be as good as the raw image. This is due to two factors: (1) improper intensity quantization, and (2) the gamma factor associated with display systems. The proper way for achieving intensity quantization is discussed later. The gamma factor of the display system does not affect all colors in the same way at the time of display. Displaying an image without gamma correction is likely to cause problems, because the eye is more sensitive to intensity variations at the dark end of the luminance scale. The nonlinear effect of the gamma factor is illustrated in Figure 15.24. For display, we choose the input shown in Figure 15.24(a) with intensities uniformly quantized between 0 and 255. The display system output scales the intensities in a nonlinear fashion as shown in Figure 15.24(b).

Display systems have an intensity-to-voltage response curve, which is a power function, as follows:

$$I = KV^{\gamma} \tag{15.14}$$

Figure 15.23: Alpha blending for various alpha values. (a) Lord Ganesh with 100% pixel intensity completely transparent using $\alpha = 0$. (b) Lord Ganesh with 75% pixel intensity and Lord Krishna with 25% pixel intensity using $\alpha = 0.25$. (c) Lord Ganesh with 25% pixel intensity and Lord Krishna with 75% pixel intensity using $\alpha = 0.75$. (d) Lord Krishna with 100% pixel intensity and Lord Ganesh is completely opaque with $\alpha = 1.00$.

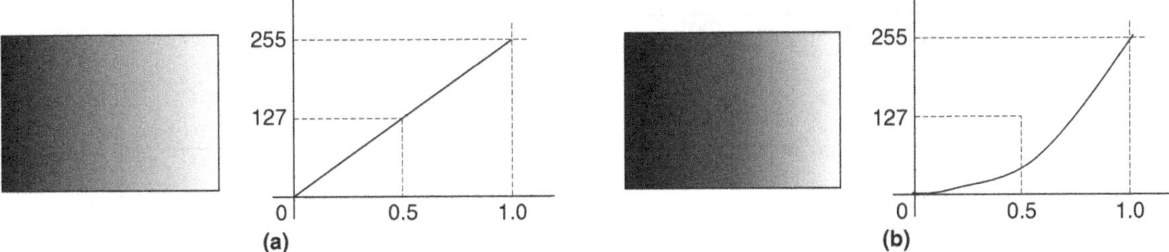

Figure 15.24: Illustration of display system gamma effect. (a) Input intensity pixels. (b) Displayed intensity pixels.

The value of gamma (i.e., exponent value) is in the range 2.2 to 2.5 for nearly all display systems. To transform an intensity value into a voltage to drive the display system, it is necessary to perform gamma correction before displaying, using a power function with an exponent that is the inverse of the gamma value:

$$V = (I/K)^{1/\gamma} \tag{15.15}$$

Gamma correction, then, is the process of precompensating for the nonlinear intensity-voltage function of the display system in order to obtain correct intensity reproduction. Gamma correction is important for good picture quality on the display screen. The values of constant K and factor γ in Equations (15.14) and (15.15) depend on the particular display system used in our applications.

Suppose that we want to display 256 different intensities in the range 0.0 to 1.0. Which 256 intensity levels should we use for the display? If we use the uniformly quantized intensities as shown in Figure 15.24(a), then we ignore an important characteristic of the human eye. That is, the eye is sensitive to ratios of intensity levels rather than to absolute values of intensity. For example, our eye sees a big difference in brightness if we change the intensity from 0.20 to 0.25 when compared to 0.70 to 0.75. To see the same effect of brightness, we should change from 0.70 to 0.875 instead of 0.75. This is because 0.20/0.25 = 0.8 = 0.70/0.875, results in the same intensity ratio. Therefore, the intensity levels should be spaced nonlinearly rather than linearly to achieve equal steps in brightness. In general, we determine the initial intensity value I_0 for a given display system, and then obtain the 256 different intensity levels as

$$I_n = r^n I_0 \text{ for } 0 \le n \le 255 \tag{15.16}$$

where $r = (1/I_0)^{1/255}$. Then we determine the pixel value V_n needed to create I_n by using Equations (15.15) and (15.16) as follows:

$$V_n = \lfloor (I_n/K)^{1/\gamma} \rfloor \tag{15.17}$$

Figures 15.25 and 15.26 illustrate the importance of gamma correction. The test image for gamma correction is shown in Figure 15.26(a), and the corresponding pixel-to-intensity map is shown in Figure 15.25(a) with a solid

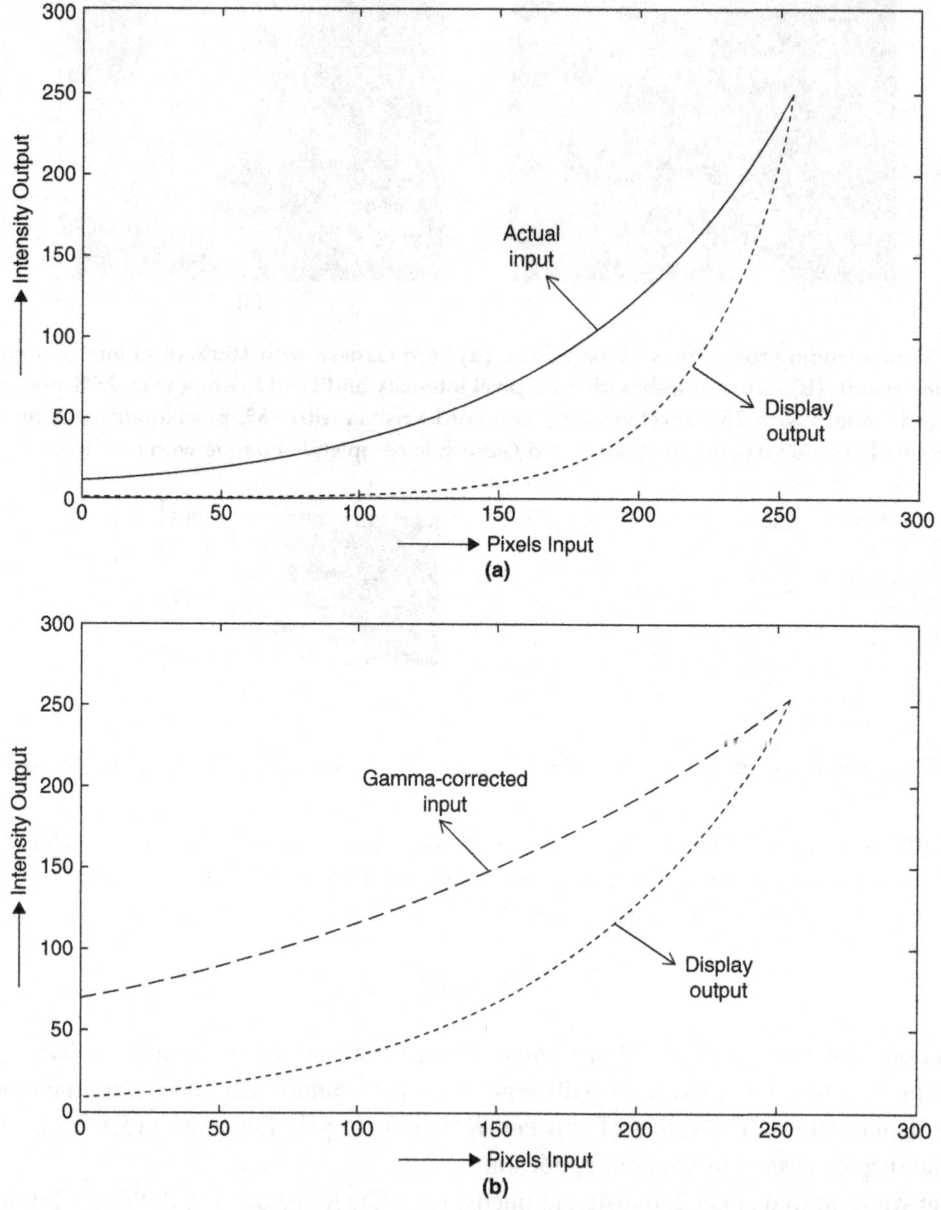

Figure 15.25: Pixel to intensity map. (a) Without gamma correction. (b) With gamma correction.

(a) (b) (c) (d)

Figure 15.26: Gamma correction with $\gamma = 2.5$. (a) Original input image. (b) Display output (simulated) image without gamma correction. (c) Gamma-corrected input image. (d) Display output (simulated) image with gamma correction.

line. The pixel-to-intensity map of the display system for the uncorrected input image is shown in Figure 15.25(a) with a dashed line and the corresponding display output (simulated) image is shown in Figure 15.26(b). A gamma-corrected pixel-to-intensity map is shown in Figure 15.25(b) with a dashed line and the corresponding image is shown in Figure 15.26(c). Finally, the pixel-to-intensity map of display output with gamma corrected input is shown in Figure 15.25(b) with dotted line and the corresponding image is shown in Figure 15.26(d).

Next, we simulate the gamma correction process. We assume that the pixel values (i.e., I_n/K) are obtained with proper nonlinear quantization and are available in buffer BufY[]. We can implement Equation (15.17) for gamma correction efficiently by using the look-up table GmC[]. In this approach, we precompute the look-up table values for various gammas. The look-up table consists of pixel values that are obtained by raising the values between 0 and 255 to the power γ. An example look-up table for $\gamma = 2.5$ is given on the companion website. The simulation code for the look-up table-based gamma correction is given in Pcode 15.7.

```
for(j = 0;j < M;j++){
    p = j*N;q = (j + 1)*N;
    for(i = p;i < q; i++){
        y0 = BufY[i];
        x0 = GmC[y0];
        BufR[i] = x0;
    }
}
```

Pcode 15.7: Simulation code for look-up table-based Gamma correction.

15.4 Video Transcoding

Video transcoding is the process of converting a video from one format to another format. A format is defined by characteristics such as bit rate, temporal resolution, spatial resolution, frame format, and coding standard

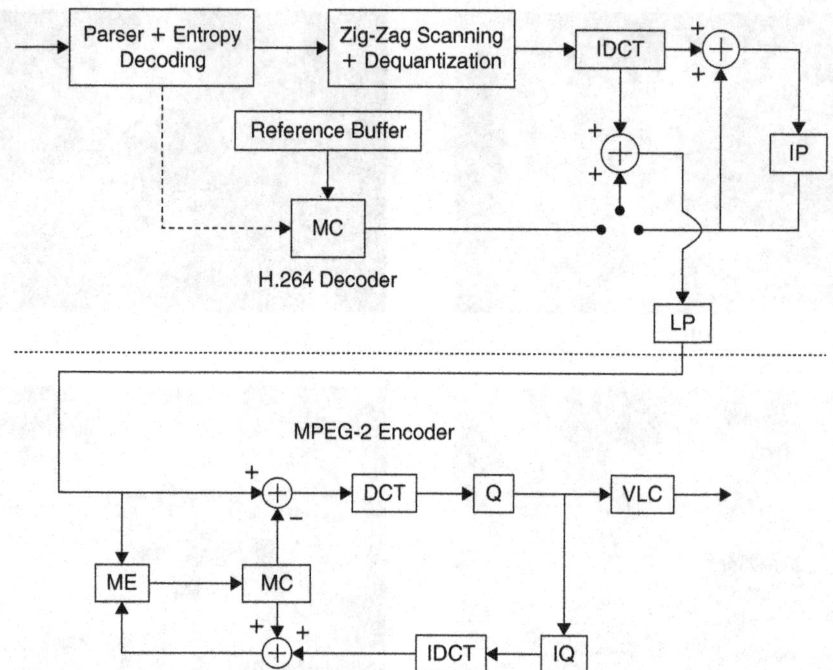

Figure 15.27: H.264 to MPEG-2 reference video transcoder.

format. Video transcoding, due to high demand for a wide range of networked video applications, has become an important research topic in recent years. In Vetro et al. (2003), many approaches are suggested to efficiently perform video transcoding. In the straightforward method (SFM), we completely decode the given compressed video and then fully re-encode it to get the target video format. This approach is computationally very expensive, and sometimes the best quality may not be achieved with this approach. An example of MPEG-2 decoding of an H.264 encoded bitstream is shown in Figure 15.27. This situation can occur when we have MPEG-2 supporting player at the customer end and we encode the video data using H.264 encoder to reduce the memory requirement for video storage or to minimize video transmission bandwidth. In this case we should have MPEG-2 encoded video by the time customer wants to play the video. For this we require a transcoder that decodes H.264-encoded video and encodes it as MPEG-2 video.

As seen in Figure 15.27, the complexity of the SFM transcoder is the sum of the complexity of H.264 decoder and the complexity of MPEG-2 encoder. In practice, we do not implement the transcoder in the way that SFM describes transcoding. We take many shortcuts and reuse a lot of information to reduce overall complexity and memory requirements, and to improve video quality. For example, the decoder part of transcoding provides details such as motion information, transform domain coefficients, and so on, and we may reuse this information as it is or derive the information from already decoded information instead of recomputing everything. The cost of motion estimation in the video encoder is about 40 to 60% of the encoder cost, and we can avoid motion estimation if we can reuse already available information in the decoding process.

In the literature, by considering the SFM as the reference, the performance of various new transcoding methods is discussed. Computational complexity of various transcoding approaches is discussed, and complexity reduction of 10% (with good video quality) to 50% (with average video quality) with respect to SFM is reported. Because video transcoding involves many parameters, the transcoding complexity depends on a particular application. If we just want to increase the frame rate with the same coding format, then the transcoder may not have many modules or parameters to take care of and the complexity of transcoding will also be relatively low.

In this section, we consider two transcoding applications and discuss various methods to reduce overall transcoder complexity. The first transcoding application converts the DV (digital video) to MPEG-2 video to play the DV on DVD players, and the second converts MPEG-2 to H.264 video.

15.4.1 DV to MPEG-2 Transcoding

As shown in Figure 15.28, the DV decoder of the DV-MPEG-2 transcoder consists of variable-length decoding, inverse quantization, and inverse DCT, and it has no motion compensation nodules (i.e., DV handles only intraframes). On the other hand, MPEG-2 is based on the hybrid DCT motion-compensated scheme. Motion compensation and DCT effectively remove temporal and spatial redundancies in the video.

Because both coding methods utilize DCT, transcoding in the DCT domain can minimize computational complexity. The following steps are used for transcoding video from DV to MPEG-2:

1. Get DV 8×8 block or 4×8 block symbols from the bitstream using the DV VLD table.
2. Get DV 8×8 or 4×8 DCT domain data values by dequantizing the symbols in (1).
3. If 4×8 DCT data blocks are present, then convert them directly to 8×8 DCT data blocks using Equation (15.18).

$$X_{8\times8} = A_{8\times8}\begin{bmatrix} D1_{4\times8} \\ D2_{4\times8} \end{bmatrix} \tag{15.18}$$

   where $A_{8\times8}$ is a conversion matrix (Kim et al., 2001) to convert two 4×8 DCT matrices to one 8×8 DCT matrix.
4. Convert DV chroma-color format (4:1:1) to MPEG-2 chroma-color format (4:2:0), and also convert DV macroblock (MB) luma space (8×32 pixels) to MPEG-2 MB luma space (16×16), as shown in Figure 15.29.
5. If the current frame is intraframe coding, then go to step 7.
6. Interframe coding:
   (a) Decide intra/inter-MB mode, depending on DCT block variance
   (b) Motion search
      (i) Method 1: Three-step search
         - With 2×2 IDCT (coarse)
         - With MB-integer pixel
         - MB half-pixel (fine)
      (ii) Method 2: Five/four step search
         - With 4 subblock (i.e., four 8×8 blocks) DC values
         - With 2×2 IDCT data

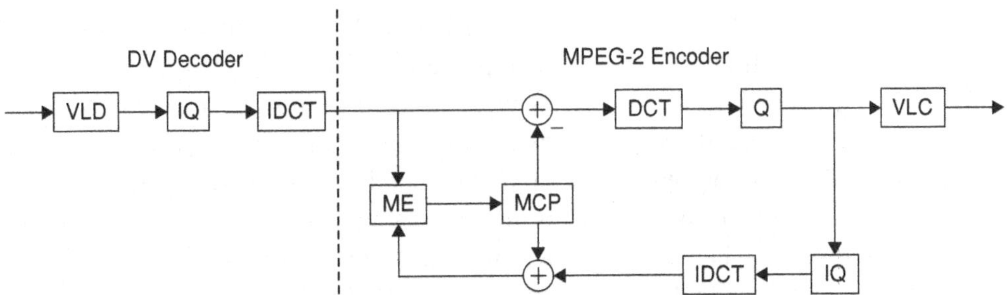

Figure 15.28: DV to MPEG-2 using SFM approach.

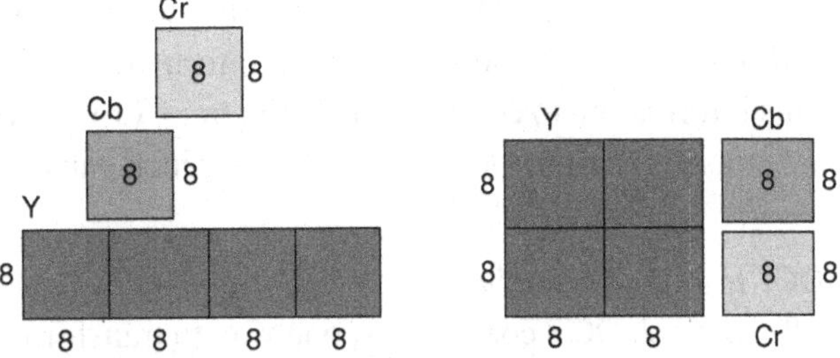

Figure 15.29: DV 4:1:1 to MPEG-2 4:2:0 conversion.

- With 4 × 4 IDCT data
- With 8 × 8 IDCT-data or MB-integer pixel
- With half-pixel
  - Without overlap
  - With overlap

7. MPEG-2 quantization parameter calculation:
   (a) Compute as the multiplication of virtual buffer fullness by macroblock subblock least variance, σ^2_{sub}

$$\sigma^2_{sub} = \sum_{n=1}^{64}(x^2(n) - (\bar{x})^2) \tag{15.19}$$

   (b)

$$Q_{mpeg} = 31^{*}d/r \text{ where } d = S - \alpha C \text{ and } \alpha \neq 1 \tag{15.20}$$

   $r =$ 2*DV(bits/frame)
   $C =$ cumulative bit count of DV bitstream
   $S =$ cumulative bit count for resulting MPEG-2 output bitstream

8. Apply quantization to DCT coefficients.
9. Encode quantized symbols with MPEG-2 VLC tables.

15.4.2 MPEG-2 to H.264 Transcoding

Both MPEG-2 and H.264 video coding standards use block-based hybrid algorithms that employ transform coding of the motion-compensated prediction error. While motion compensation exploits temporal redundancies, the DCT transform exploits spatial redundancies. Although the basic principle is the same in both algorithms, H.264 achieves the same quality of video with the half-bit rate when compared to MPEG-2 video coding. However, this bit-rate savings of H.264 is at the cost of more computational complexity. The reason for the huge complexity of H.264 is that its modules are enhanced a lot relative to MPEG-2. In addition, the H.264 coding standard includes two extra modules—intraprediction and loop filter—that do not exist in MPEG-2 coding.

MPEG-2 is well established and deployed in many applications, whereas H.264 is more recent, with better compression qualities and penetrating all applications wherever MPEG-2 is used. However, establishing the infrastructure to replace MPEG-2 with H.264 takes many years. So, transcoding is a quick fix to enjoy the better qualities of H.264 before its establishment. The reference architecture (SFM) for transcoding MPEG-2 to H.264 is shown in Figure 15.30.

The MPEG-2 standard consists of VLD, 8 × 8, 8 × 16, or 16 × 16 block partitions, and 8 × 8 DCT and simple interpolation with one reference frame for motion compensation, whereas H.264 uses UVLC, CAVLC, and CABAC algorithms for entropy coding, 4 × 4 or 8 × 8 integer transforms for transforming the pixels, uses 4 × 4, 4 × 8, 8 × 4, 8 × 8, 8 × 16, 16 × 8, and 16 × 16 block partitions for motion compensation, six-tap interpolator function up to one-fourth pixel motion search, multiple reference-frame support, intraprediction for I-frames, a complex loop filter, and more. Given these many differences between the MPEG-2 and H.264 modules, accomplishing efficient transcoding between MPEG-2 and H.264 and obtaining all H.264 enhancements is not simple. We discuss a few simple methods for transcoding from MPEG-2 to H.264; of course, the approaches discussed here may not guarantee the best performance of H.264.

Our discussion is limited to MPEG-2-to-H.264 baseline profile transcoding as other H.264 profiles are relatively complex for transcoding. Given MPEG-2 encoded video data, we focus on the following parameters for transcoding from MPEG-2 to H.264: MPEG-2 frame information to determine frame type for H.264 frames, 8 × 8 DCT coefficients information to compute the H264 transform coefficients and to decide the intraprediction modes, and MPEG-2 motion vector information to decide block partitions and to simplify the motion search for H.264 encoding.

Mapping MPEG-2 DCT to H.264 Transform

Given the MPEG-2 8 × 8 block DCT coefficients, one way to transform 8 × 8 MPEG-2 transform coefficients to four 4 × 4 H.264 transform (HT) coefficients is by first computing the IDCT followed by applying four H.264

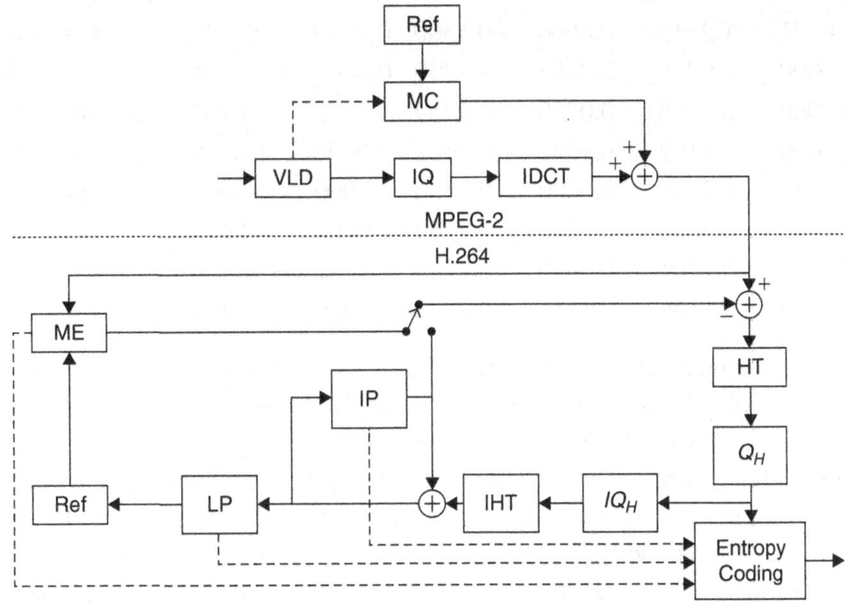

Figure 15.30: Reference architecture for MPEG-2 to H.264 transcoding.

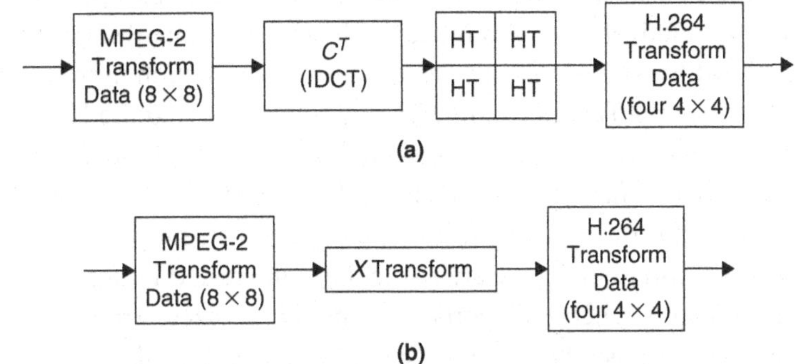

Figure 15.31: Transcoding MPEG-2 to H.264 transform data.

transforms as shown in Figure 15.31(a). The other way is to directly transform the 8 × 8 DCT to H.264 transform coefficients using the X-transform as shown in Figure 15.31(b). One such X-transform is given in Quian et al. (2006).

The values of matrix elements used for the transformations in Figure 15.31 follow:

$$C^T = \begin{bmatrix} 0.3536 & 0.3536 & 0.3536 & 0.3536 & 0.3536 & 0.3536 & 0.3536 & 0.3536 \\ 0.4904 & 0.4157 & 0.2778 & 0.0975 & -0.0975 & -0.2778 & -0.4157 & -0.4904 \\ 0.4619 & 0.1913 & -0.1913 & -0.4619 & -0.4619 & -0.1913 & 0.1913 & 0.4619 \\ 0.4157 & -0.0975 & -0.4904 & -0.2778 & 0.2778 & 0.4904 & 0.0975 & -0.4157 \\ 0.3536 & -0.3536 & -0.3536 & 0.3536 & 0.3536 & -0.3536 & -0.3536 & 0.3536 \\ 0.2778 & -0.4904 & 0.0975 & 0.4157 & -0.4157 & -0.0975 & 0.4904 & -0.2778 \\ 0.1913 & -0.4619 & 0.4619 & -0.1913 & -0.1913 & 0.4619 & -0.4619 & 0.1913 \\ 0.0975 & -0.2778 & 0.4157 & -0.4904 & 0.4904 & -0.4157 & 0.2778 & -0.0975 \end{bmatrix}$$

$$HT = \begin{bmatrix} 1 & 1 & 1 & 1 \\ 2 & 1 & -1 & -2 \\ 1 & -1 & -1 & 1 \\ 1 & -2 & 2 & -1 \end{bmatrix}$$

$$X = \begin{bmatrix} 1.4142 & 1.2815 & 0.0000 & -0.4500 & 0.0000 & 0.3007 & 0.0000 & -0.2549 \\ 0.0000 & -0.9236 & 2.2304 & 1.7799 & 0.0000 & -0.8638 & -0.1585 & 0.4824 \\ 0.0000 & -0.1056 & 0.0000 & 0.7259 & 1.4142 & 1.0864 & 0.0000 & -0.5308 \\ 0.0000 & 0.1169 & 0.1585 & -0.0922 & 0.0000 & 1.0379 & 2.2304 & 1.9750 \\ 1.4142 & -1.2815 & 0.0000 & 0.4500 & 0.0000 & -0.3007 & 0.0000 & 0.2549 \\ 0.0000 & 0.9236 & -2.2304 & 1.7799 & 0.0000 & 0.8638 & 0.1585 & 0.4824 \\ 0.0000 & 0.1506 & 0.0000 & -0.7259 & 1.4142 & -1.0864 & 0.0000 & 0.5308 \\ 0.0000 & 0.1169 & -0.1585 & -0.0922 & 0.0000 & 1.0379 & -2.2304 & 1.9750 \end{bmatrix}$$

As elements of the preceding matrices are symmetric either in the horizontal or vertical direction, we can further reduce the number of multiplications required to perform matrix multiplication. With the X-transform method, we have 30% fewer operations when compared to the IDCT-HT transform method.

Both MPEG-2 and H.264 support I (intrapredictive), P (interpredictive), and B (bidirectional predictive) frame types. Whatever information we have on frame type in the MPEG-2 bitstream can be directly used in the transcoding of MPEG-2-to-H.264 coding format. After knowing the frame type, we continue to transcode bits for that frame type. Next, we briefly discuss transcoding techniques for intraframe (I) and inter (P or B) frames.

Intraframe Transcoding

In video coding, intraframe coding deals with video-frame spatial redundancy, and we do not have the costly motion-estimation block in this case. However, we have an intraprediction module in H.264 intraframes coding, which is also a relatively complex module. The H.264 standard supports many intraprediction modes. Compared with H.264, MPEG-2 has only the DC differential prediction used in intra-MB, but lets the AC coefficients be coded independently. Thus, the intra-MB mode decision is required in MPEG-2-to-H.264 transcoding. The H.264 intraprediction requires two parameters—prediction size and prediction mode—for performing intraprediction. Making decisions on these two parameters following the H.264 reference software is a costly process. To quickly determine prediction size and mode, many techniques are proposed in the literature (Shengfa et al., 2006). As we are in the transform domain, we are particularly interested in decision-making techniques based on transform-domain coefficients. H.264 supports two prediction sizes, 16×16 and 4×4. Typically, the prediction size 16×16 is used for macroblocks with fewer details, and the 4×4 prediction size is used if the macroblock has high spatial activity. If the image block is smooth without many details, then the DCT of that block results in fewer coefficients; if the block has more information, then the DCT of that block contains many coefficients. Thus, we decide which prediction size to choose depending on the number of DCT coefficients present for a given quantization level as follows:

```
if (Coeff_Count_Q > Threshold)
        Pred_Size = 4x4
else
        Pred_Size = 16x16
```

In Wang et al. (2006) and Kalva et al. (2005), fast decision making on intraprediction modes is proposed using transformed domain coefficients. Depending on the presence of transform coefficients and the nature of DC and AC coefficients in the current and neighboring blocks, we can make a decision on prediction modes for the current block. These algorithms significantly reduce computations toward making decisions on intraprediction modes, while maintaining a similar PSNR as reference architectures.

Interframe Transcoding

Interframes compress video data by removing temporal redundancies in video frames. Both MPEG-2 and H.264 use block-motion estimation/compensation-based interframe coding. The only difference between MPEG-2 and H.264 is that the size of the block partitions, the number of reference frames, and the interpolation functions used in block motion estimation/compensation are different. The MPEG-2 standard supports 16×16, 8×16, or 16×8 block partitions, whereas H.264 supports all block partitions (with multiples of 4) from 4×4 to 16×16. Depending on the motion of objects in the current block, we choose one of the block partition sizes and search for that size blocks in the reference frame buffer to match it with the actual block, and then transmit the matched

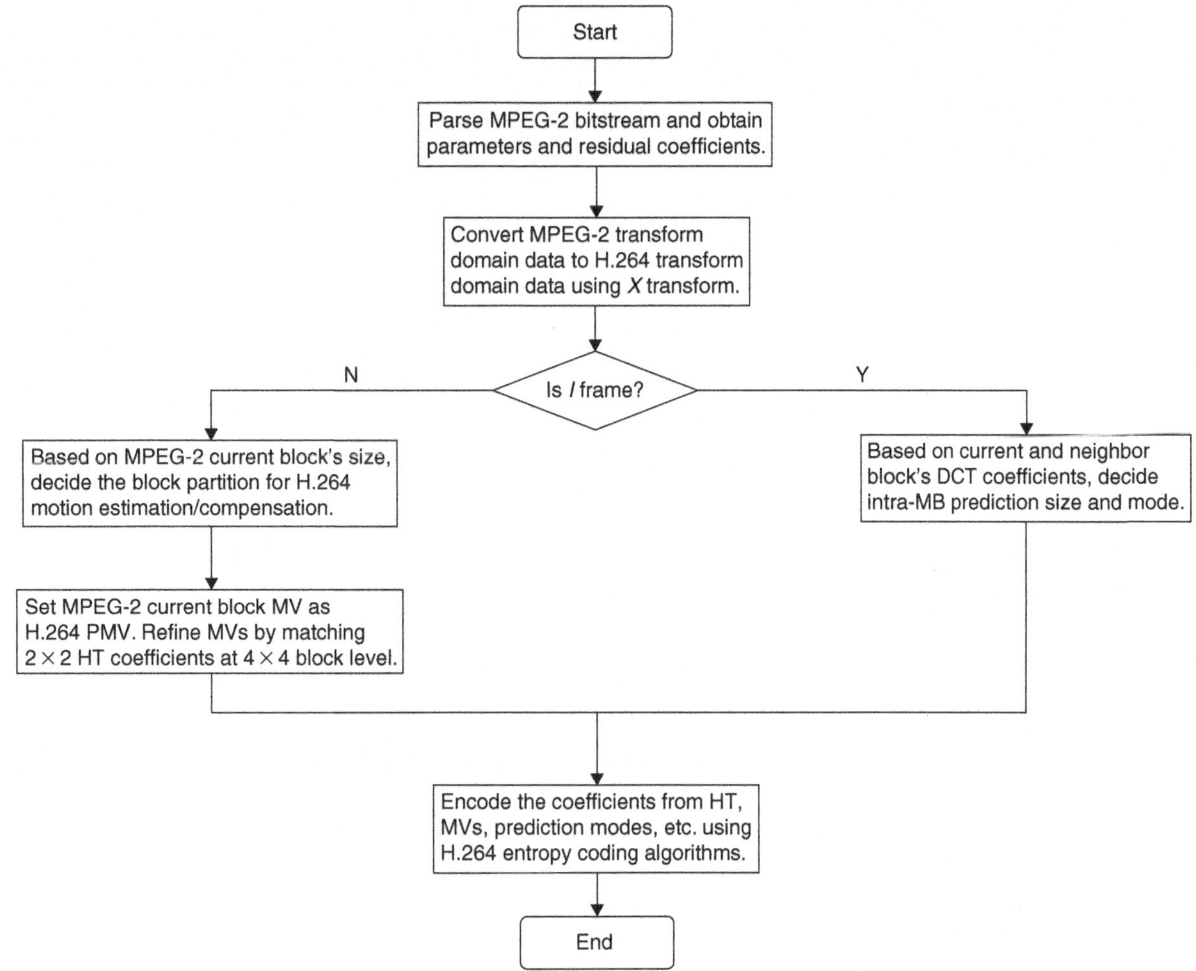

Figure 15.32: Flow chart diagram of MPEG-2 to H.264 transcoding.

location (i.e., motion information), and the difference between the actual block and matched block (i.e., residual). Typically, we have more temporal redundancies among video frames with slow-motion objects, and we find less temporal redundancy in the video with fast-motion objects. We use bigger block partitions with slow-motion video interframe coding, and smaller block partitions with fast-motion video interframe coding to have good PSNR after decompressing video.

After decoding the block partition size and its motion information from the MPEG-2 bitstream, we can use this information to get block partition size and motion information for the H.264 encoder in transcoding of MPEG-2 coding format to H.264 coding format. Without using this MPEG-2 block partition size and motion information, performing full-motion estimation for generating H.264 compressed bitstream, as shown in Figure 15.30, is very costly in terms of cycles. The Kim et al. (2005) approach of reusing the MPEG-2 block-partition size and motion information for transcoding from MPEG-2 to H.264 is suggested. Using this method, we choose block partitions for H.264 as 16×16, 16×8, or 8×16 when MPEG-2 block partition is 16×16 and choose partitions 4×4, 4×8, 8×4, or 8×8 when MPEG-2 block partition is either 16×8 or 8×16, assuming that the current block contains fast-motion objects. Also, we use MPEG-2 motion vector information as H.264 motion-vector prediction (MVP) value, and from there we search for finer-motion estimation using H.264 transform-domain coefficients. Figure 15.32 shows the flow chart diagram of MPEG-2 to H.264 transcoding.

Index

DOI: 10.1016/B978-1-85617-678-1.00024-7

D

J

K

L

M

N

O

S

T

U

V

W

Printed in the United States
By Bookmasters